Marketing Management

Canadian Tenth Edition

Philip Kotler

Northwestern University

Peggy H. Cunningham

Queen's University

Ronald E. Turner

Queen's University

Prentice
Hall

Toronto

Canadian Cataloguing in Publication Data

Kotler, Philip
   Marketing management

Canadian 10th ed.
Includes index.
ISBN 0-13-014429-0

1. Marketing — Management. I. Turner, Ronald E., 1931-
II. Cunningham, Margaret H.   III. Title.

HF5415.13.K68 2001   658.8'02   C99-932942-1

ISBN 0-13-014429-0

Vice President, Editorial Director: Michael Young
Acquisitions Editor: Mike Ryan
Marketing Manager: James Buchanan
Developmental Editor: Madhu Ranadive
Production Editor: Marisa D'Andrea
Copy Editor: Dianne Broad
Production Coordinator: Janette Lush
Page Layout: Debbie Kumpf
Photo Research: Alene McNeill
Creative Director: Mary Opper
Interior Design: Sarah Battersby
Cover Design: Sarah Battersby
Cover Image: Stuart Westmorland/First Light

1 2 3 4 5   05 04 03 02 01

Printed and bound in Canada

This book is dedicated to my wife and best friend, Nancy, with love.

PK

This book is dedicated to my wife Caroline with love.

RT

This book is dedicated to my two best friends, my husband Paul and my daughter Krista.

PC

ACKNOWLEDGEMENTS

I wish to thank the following colleagues at other universities who reviewed this edition:

Lanita S. Carter, Memorial University of Newfoundland
Shannon Goodspeed, Mount Royal College
Robert Jershy, St. Clair College
Judith Madill, Carleton University
Paul R. Messinger, University of Alberta
Alan R. Miciak, University of Calgary
John Milne, York University
Roy Morley, University of Toronto
Edward Pascal, University of Ottawa
Donald N. Thompson, York University

This book is truly a team effort rather than the product of any single person's work. I therefore wish to thank Dianne Broad, Jeannine Ciliotta, Lesley Mann and the entire Pearson team for their hard work, efficiency, and good humour. My colleagues at Queen's have also greatly influenced my thinking on current and important trends in marketing. My overriding debt continues to be my ever-patient husband who provides me with the love, time, support and inspiration needed to prepare this edition. I also wish to thank my daughter, a business student, who reads and critiques my work with a user's vigilant eye.

Peggy H. Cunningham

ABOUT THE AUTHORS

Philip Kotler, one of the world's leading authorities on marketing, is the S.C. Johnson & Son Distinguished Professor of International Marketing at the Kellogg Graduate School of Management, Northwestern University. He received his master's degree at the University of Chicago and his Ph.D Degree at M.I.T, both in economics. He did postdoctoral work in mathematics at Harvard University and behavioural science at the University of Chicago.

Dr. Kotler is the author of *Principles of Marketing: An Introduction*. His *Strategic Marketing for Nonprofit Organizations*, now in its fifth edition, is the best seller in that specialized area. Dr. Kotler's other books include *Marketing Models; The New Competition; Marketing Professional Services; Strategic Marketing for Educational Institutions; Marketing for Health Care Organizations; Marketing Congregations; High Visibility; Social Marketing; Marketing Places; The Marketing of Nations; Marketing for Hospitality and Tourism; Standing Room Only—Strategies for Marketing the Performing Arts; Museum Strategy and Marketing;* and *Kotler on Marketing*.

In addition, he has published over 100 articles in leading journals, including *Harvard Business Review, Sloan Management Review, Business Horizons, California Management Review, Journal of Marketing, Journal of Marketing Research, Management Science, Journal of Business Strategy,* and *Futurist*. He is the only three-time winner of the coveted Alpha Kappa Psi award for the best annual article published in the *Journal of Marketing*.

Professor Kotler was the first recipient of the American Marketing Association's (AMA) Distinguished Marketing Educator Award (1985). The European Association of Marketing Consultants and Sales Trainers awarded him their prize for Marketing Excellence. He was chosen as the Leader in Marketing Thought by the Academic Members of the AMA in a 1975 survey. He also received the 1978 Paul Converse Award of the AMA, honouring his original contribution to marketing. In 1995, the Sales and Marketing Executives International (SMEI) named him Marketer of the Year. He has received honorary doctoral degrees from Stockholm University, University of Zurich, Athens University of Economics and Business, DePaul University, Cracow School of Business and Economics, Groupe H.E.C. in Paris, and University of Economics and Business Administration in Vienna. Professor Kotler has been a consultant to many major U.S. and foreign companies, including IBM, General Electric, AT&T, Honeywell, Bank of America, Merck, SAS Airlines, Michelin, and others in the areas of marketing strategy and planning, marketing organization and international marketing.

He has been Chairman of the College of Marketing of the Institute of Management Sciences, a Director of the American Marketing Association, a Trustee of the Marketing Science Institute, a Director of the MAC Group, a former member of the Yankelovich Advisory Board, and a member of the Copernicus Advisory Board. He is a Member of the Board of Governors of the School of the Art Institute of Chicago and a Member of the Advisory Board of the Drucker Foundation. He has travelled extensively throughout Europe, Asia and South America, advising and lecturing to many companies about global marketing opportunities.

Peggy H. Cunningham (Ph.D., Texas A&M University, College Station), one of Canada's leading educators, is an associate professor of marketing at Queen's University's School of Business in Kingston, Ontario, Canada where she has worked for the past 10 years. She teaches a course she developed on marketing ethics to fourth-year undergraduate business students, as well as marketing strategy courses in the B.Comm. and M.Sc./Ph.D. programs. She has also taught courses in the MBA for Science and Technology program, the MBA program, and on a number of executive programs. She has received a number of teaching awards including the Frank Knox Award for Teaching Excellence, one of the most prestigious awards given at Queen's for undergraduate teaching. She was a marketing practitioner before com-  ing to Queen's and has considerable international experience having worked and/or taught in Germany, China, the UK, and the US.

Dr. Cunningham's research interests centre on two related themes: marketing ethics and marketing partnerships (international strategic alliances and partnerships between for-profit and not-for-profit organizations). While these may seem like totally divergent areas of study, they are linked by their focus on the concepts of trust, integrity, and commitment, which are the core elements to both ethical behaviour and successful partnership behaviour. Her most recent work examines the ethical challenges of marketing on the World Wide Web. Her work is published in a number of journals including the *Journal of the Academy of Marketing Science, Social Marketing and Fundraising, Journal of International Marketing, the Festival Management & Event Tourism Journal, The Philanthropist,* and *Journal of Marketing Education.* She is also the author of the Canadian edition of *Principles of Marketing* (co-authored with Philip Kotler and Gary Armstrong). This text is the top-selling marketing textbook in Canada and has been widely praised by both educators and practitioners for its focus on ethical marketing practices and its innovative and comprehensive coverage of marketing in Canada.

Ron Turner is Professor Emeritus at Queen's University where he has taught marketing-related courses for the past 25 years. His academic background includes a BASc in engineering from the University of Toronto, an MBA from McMaster University, and an MSc and PhD in management from Northwestern University. Dr. Turner was a member of the faculties of the University of Chicago and Carnegie-Mellon University before joining Queen's. He has served in several marketing and sales management positions in the industry, and as a consultant to numerous corporations and government departments. He has been active in organizing and participating in conferences of the AMA, ASAC, and other academic associations. In more than 50 research publications, Dr. Turner has pursued research interests across a broad range of the challenges facing marketing managers. He has taught at the undergraduate, masters, doctoral, and executive levels. His interest in the practice of marketing in other societies has resulted in visiting professorships in China, India, the Philippines, New Zealand, Mexico, and several European countries.

BRIEF CONTENTS

CONTENTS

MARKETING
INSIGHT

Sara Lee Corp.:
From Manufacturer to
Nimble Marketer   70

MARKETING
MEMO

Checklist for Performing
Strengths/Weaknesses
Analysis   82

MARKETING FOR THE
21st CENTURY

The Strategic Alliance
Boom   85

CBC

MARKETING
MEMO

Secondary Sources
of Data Online   112

MARKETING FOR THE
21st CENTURY

Companies Turn to Data
Warehousing and Data
Mining: Exercise Care 113

MARKETING
INSIGHT

Marketing Researchers
Challenge Conventional
Wisdom   121

MARKETING
MEMO

Breaking Through the
Mature-Product
Syndrome   310

MARKETING FOR THE
21st CENTURY

Monsanto Co.: From
Old Line Chemicals to
Cutting-Edge "Life
Sciences"   314

MARKETING
INSIGHT

Mr. Failure's Lessons for
Sweet Success   324

MARKETING
INSIGHT

The Wisdom of Cross-
Functional Teams   328

MARKETING
MEMO

Ten Ways to Great
New-Product Ideas   330

MARKETING FOR THE
21st CENTURY

The Story of Netscape's
Navigator   340

MARKETING FOR THE
21st CENTURY

The Ins and Outs of
Global E-commerce   362

MARKETING
MEMO

Marketing Your Web Site
World-Wide and
Worldly Wise   366

CBC 🔵

PREFACE

When the first edition of *Marketing Management* was written in 1967, marketing was a far simpler subject. Consumer marketing largely operated on mass marketing principles, and business marketing primarily concerned itself with how to build the best sales force. The retail landscape was populated with major department stores, regional supermarket food chains, and a very large number of mom-and-pop stores.

In those days, marketers faced a number of tough decisions. They had to determine product features and quality, establish accompanying services, set the price, determine the distribution channels, decide how much to spend on marketing, and decide how to divide their resources among advertising, sales force, and other promotion tools.

Today's marketers, of course, face the same tough decisions. But today's marketplace is enormously more complex. Domestic markets, at one time safe from foreign invaders, are now the happy hunting grounds of giant global corporations as well as global niche specialists. Major strides in technology have considerably shortened time and distance: New products are launched at an astonishing pace and are available worldwide in a short time. Communications media are proliferating. New distribution channels and formats keep appearing. Competitors are everywhere—and hungry.

In the midst of these changes, busy consumers are changing their ways. To save time, they are shopping with catalogues, the telephone, and the computer. Today consumers can search the Internet to find the best price for a car. They can handle most of their banking needs over the phone or by computer. They can buy insurance and carry out financial transactions without working with an agent or broker. Consumers don't even need to visit the supermarket: Using Peapod, Streamline, or Netgrocer, they can place orders over the Internet and have the groceries delivered to their homes. Nor do they need to buy newspapers or magazines to get their news; they can download the latest editions of *Maclean's*, the *Globe and Mail*, or the *National Post*.

The changes for business buyers are also profound. Using the Internet, purchasing agents can search for the best vendors and values. General Electric has created the Trading Process Network (TPN) where GE, along with other subscribers to GE's service, can request quotes, negotiate terms, and place orders with global suppliers. Purchasing agents can go on-line to www.Dell.ca and order specific computers with customized features.

These new shopping capabilities signify a brand new world of proliferating opportunities and proliferating threats. Silicon Valleys are proliferating in both Ottawa and Montreal and they are only one symbol of a Brave New World characterized by digitalization, robotization, telecommuting, artificial intelligence, virtual reality, and other technological advances. At the same time, what is a magnificent opportunity for millions of consumers and businesses is a major and sometimes deadly threat to others. Banks will have to close branches; travel agencies and brokerage firms will need to reduce staffs; automobile manufacturers will reduce the number of auto dealerships; and many bookstores, music stores, and video stores will close their doors. Technological advances are a double-edged sword: They create opportunities and they destroy opportunities.

This new world is also characterized by an amazingly rich information environment. Consumers will be able to access objective information on competing brands, including costs, prices, features, and quality, without relying on individual manufacturers or retailers. In many cases, they will be able to specify the customized features they want. They will even be able to specify the prices they are willing to pay, and wait for the most eager sellers to respond. The result is a dramatic shift of economic power from sellers to buyers.

Savvy companies are recognizing the inevitability of customer value migration: Customers will continuously shift toward suppliers who can deliver greater value. As buyers adopt new shopping routines, companies that have heavy investments in the older ways of providing value have only two courses of action. They can pursue maintenance marketing, an effort to convince customers that they still offer the most value, or they can pursue transformational marketing, an effort to reorganize to deliver greater value.

Savvy companies recognize that a major revolution is taking place in markets and marketing. More companies today are striving for leadership in specific markets instead of accepting second-rate positions in mass markets. Companies are emphasizing retaining customers rather than simply acquiring new ones. Companies are expanding their offerings mix in a bid for customer share, not just market share. Companies are identifying their more profitable customers and giving them extraordinary service. Companies are basing their decisions on customer lifetime value rather than on immediate profit maximization.

Every company's set of beliefs and practices is undergoing challenge and change:

1. From engineers designing products alone to involving marketing and other functions as well as customers in product development.

2. From pricing the product by an arbitrary markup over cost to pricing on the basis of delivered or perceived customer value.

3. From communicating and promoting offerings mainly through persuasion-based advertising and salespeople to using a much broader set of communication vehicles and platforms.

4. From relying mainly on one channel of distribution to building a mix of channels for reaching customers.

5. From running the company as a separate entity to building a superior value delivery network with suppliers and distributors as committed partners.

Yet even companies that undertake these changes need marketing vision and marketing know-how to succeed. Many managers think of marketing as a company department whose job is to analyze the market, discern opportunities, formulate marketing strategies, develop specific strategies and tactics, propose a budget, and establish a set of controls. But there is more to marketing: Marketing must also push the rest of the company to be customer-oriented and market-driven. Marketing must convince everyone in the company and in its larger network to create and deliver superior customer value.

Marketing is more than a company department: It is an orderly and insightful process for thinking about and planning for markets. The process is applicable to more than just goods and services. Anything can be marketed—ideas, events, organizations, places, personalities. The process begins with researching the relevant marketplace to understand its dynamics and to identify opportunities to meet existing or latent needs. It involves segmenting the market and selecting those segments that the company can satisfy in a superior way. It involves formulating a broad strategy and refining it into a detailed marketing mix and action plan. It involves carrying out the plan, evaluating the results, and making further improvements.

THE CANADIAN TENTH EDITION

The beginning of a new century is an exciting and challenging time to launch a new edition. It provides the opportunity to select the best of past theory and practice and to introduce the new marketing ideas, tools, and practices that companies will need to operate successfully in the 21st century. Profiles of Canadian marketing excellence have been written to capture and exemplify these concepts. Hundreds of minicase examples have been added to illustrate what leading companies are doing to meet the challenges of the new environment. Throughout the book, we show how the World Wide Web and e-commerce are dramatically altering the marketing landscape.

At the same time, this enhanced edition continues to build on the fundamental strengths of past editions:

1. **A Managerial Orientation.** This book focuses on the major decisions marketing managers and top management face in their efforts to harmonize the organization's objectives, capabilities, and resources with marketplace needs and opportunities.

2. **An Analytical Approach.** This book presents a framework for analyzing recurrent problems in marketing management. Cases and examples illustrate effective marketing principles, strategies, and practices.

3. **A Basic Disciplines Perspective.** This book draws on the rich findings of various scientific disciplines—economics, behavioural science, management theory, and mathematics—for fundamental concepts and tools.

4. **Universal Applications.** This book applies marketing thinking to the complete spectrum of marketing: products and services, consumer and business markets, profit and nonprofit organizations, domestic and foreign companies, small and large firms, manufacturing and intermediary businesses, and low- and high-tech industries.

5. **Comprehensive and Balanced Coverage.** This book covers all the topics an informed marketing manager needs to understand: the major issues in strategic, tactical, and administrative marketing.

FEATURES OF THE CANADIAN TENTH EDITION

This edition has been both streamlined and expanded. It is still the same book, but every word has been scrutinized and much has been condensed to bring the essentials and the classic examples into sharper focus.

"The same but different": streamlining

■ FEWER CHAPTERS: The tenth edition has been streamlined from 24 chapters to 22 by combining topics that fit naturally together. Chapter 8 now covers all the aspects of dealing with the competition, including the material on market strategies for leaders, challengers, nichers, and followers. Chapter 10 now covers differentiating and positioning the market offering over the product life cycle.

■ ORGANIZATION: The book is still organized in five parts, but in a different configuration: Part I, "Understanding Marketing Management," includes chapters on the societal, managerial, and strategic underpinnings of marketing theory and practice. Part II, "Analyzing Marketing Opportunities," presents concepts and tools for analyzing markets and marketing environments to find opportunities. Part III, "Developing Marketing Strategies," focuses on positioning, new market offerings, and global strategies. Part IV, "Shaping the Market Offering," deals with developing and managing brands and product lines, services, and pricing strategies and programs. Part V, "Managing and Delivering Marketing Programs," deals with the tactical and administrative side of marketing; the logistics of marketing channels; retailing and wholesaling; integrated marketing communications; advertising, promotion, and public relations; the salesforce; direct and on-line marketing; and managing the total marketing effort.

■ BOXED MATERIAL: The book still contains three series of boxes: Marketing Insight boxes highlight current research work and findings in marketing management. Marketing Memo boxes present tips and suggestions for marketing managers at all stages of the marketing management process. Marketing for the Twenty-First Century boxes focus on technological advances and e-commerce. Boxes in both the Insight and the Memo series have been revised and updated, and new topics have been added; all Twenty-First Century boxes are entirely new.

New features, expanded coverage

Streamlining and condensing have also made room for expansion and for new features:

■ *New End-of-Chapter Exercises*. The Applications section includes several new types of extremely practical exercises to challenge students:

- *Concept Checks* review important material developed in the chapter.

- *Marketing and Advertising* exercises focus on real companies and include the ads; they give the student practice in analyzing the marketing objectives advertising is intended to realize.

- *Focus on Technology* exercises help the student learn to deal with advances in technology, again using real organizations and real Internet Web sites.

- *Marketing for the 21st Century* exercises again focus on real companies with real Web sites to give the student the opportunity to analyze trends and changing marketing opportunities.

- *You're the Marketer* asks students to make a formal marketing plan using the hypothetical example of the Sonic Company from chapter 3; it is linked to the Marketing Plan Pro software.

■ Revised and expanded Direct and On-line Marketing Chapter covers all the new marketing and information channels and explains their impact on marketing management strategies and tactics. It includes revised and expanded coverage of electronic business: e-commerce, the on-line consumer, the advantages/disadvantages of on-line marketing, methods of conducting on-line marketing, and the promise and challenges of on-line marketing.

■ Minicase and In-text Examples have been replaced, updated, and added to focus on e-commerce companies, uses of the Internet, and service businesses, as well as classic cases. Profiles in Canadian Marketing Excellence and new minicases include Chapters.ca, Sony Music Canada's New Media Group, Big Rock Brewery, Saturn Canada, Canadian Tourism Commission, Rogers Cantel Mobile Communications Inc., GAP Adventures Inc., The Mutual Group, the Calgary Stampeders, Ch!ckaboom, Grouse Mountain Resorts, and SNC Lavalin Group. Inc. Classic minicases such as Canadian Pacific Hotels, Ben & Jerry's, Absolut vodka, and Kodak have been retained.

- New and updated *Marketing Insight boxes* include such topics as "Scholars and Dollars: Marketing and Selling Comes to University"; "Sara Lee: From Manufacturer to Nimble Marketer"; "Mr. Failure's Lessons for Sweet Success: Robert McGrath's New Product Showcase and Learning Centre"; and "The Rise of Corporate Branding."

- New and updated *Marketing Memo* boxes focus on such topics as "Tapping into the Net Generation," "Internet Ethics for Kids," and "Commandments of Discounting."

- New *advertisements* plus screen captures showing Web pages from real companies illustrate topics discussed in boxes or presented in minicases in that chapter.

- The 21st Century theme appears throughout the book:

  - A new *Marketing for the 21st Century* box focuses on looking forward and on trends that will mark the twenty-first century. Topics include "Monsanto: From Old Line Chemicals to Cutting-Edge Life Sciences," describing how companies are reinventing themselves, and Internet topics such as "The Business-to-Business Cyberbuying Bazaar" and "Developing Products on Internet Time: The Story of Netscape's Navigator."

  - Key chapters—such as chapters 1, 3, and 21—contain twenty-first century sections focused on the future.

THE TEACHING AND LEARNING PACKAGE

This edition of *Marketing Management* includes a number of ancillaries designed to make the marketing management course an exciting, dynamic, interactive experience.

- A comprehensive, extensively revised *Instructor's Resource Manual* and *CBC Video Guide* include chapter/summary overviews, key teaching objectives, teaching suggestions and questions based on the chapter opening Profiles in Marketing vignettes, answers to all end-of-chapter Applications exercises, supplementary resource suggestions, exercises, and transparency lecture notes. Detailed lecture outlines integrate video material and transparency notes. The *CBC Video Guide* includes teaching notes and suggested answers to the CBC video questions.

- *The Test Item File* contains more than 2000 multiple-choice, true-false, and essay questions. Each question is rated by level of difficulty and includes a text page reference. In electronic format, it is available in Windows in *Prentice Hall Test Manager*; it is also available in print.

- All-new *full colour presentations* are available in electronic form on PowerPoint 7.0 for Windows 97.

- Broadcast television and marketing education have joined forces to create the most exciting and valuable video series ever produced for business education, the CBC/Prentice Hall Video Library. This supplement features five segments from the prestigious CBC business program *Venture*. Full cases focusing on these videos are included at the end of each Part of the text.

■ ON LOCATION! videos hold students' attention by linking video to all the major conceptual elements of the text. Each clip weaves facilities, advertisements, product shots, text illustrations, and interviews with marketing managers and customers. With ON LOCATION! you can take your class on these marketing field trips without leaving the classroom: Airline, DHL, DuPont, Got Milk, House of Blues, Intel, Kodak, Levi's, NASCAR, Nike, Nivea, Sputnik, Starbucks, The Forum, Shops, WNBA, and Yahoo!

■ The *New York Festivals International Advertising Awards* recognize the best advertising from around the world. Each year a distinguished panel of judges reviews nearly 10 000 campaign entries from more than 50 countries and awards gold, silver, and bronze medals. Prentice Hall is the exclusive educational distributor of the gold medal winners in the television and cinema category: three videocassettes with nearly 200 of these award-winning spots are available upon adoption of this book.

■ *Marketing Plan Pro.* This highly rated software is totally interactive, featuring 10 sample marketing plans, excellent help, customizable charts, and professional-looking colour printouts. The plan wizards enable you to easily customize your marketing plan to fit your marketing needs. Then follow the clearly outlined steps—define, plan, budget, forecast, track, and measure—from strategy to implementation. Click to print, and your text, spreadsheet, and charts come together to create a powerful marketing plan.

■ *PhotoWars CD-ROM.* PhotoWars is a brand-new simulation by Mohan Sawhney (Northwestern University) and Raj Malhotra, together with Power-Sim and Arthur Andersen. It provides a software-based learning environment to help users improve their skills for navigating in high-change digital markets. PhotoWars is designed to be an "action learning" exercise whereby students will learn concepts, and apply what they learn, based upon the Digistrat management framework. The PhotoWars environment allows repeated plays and provides instant feedback by employing powerful system dynamics models based on a PowerSim simulation software engine. This allows managers to learn by doing, and to learn by failing safely. Observing and experimenting with such interactions allows the user to grasp the model's structure. Available at a nominal cost, packaged with the millennium edition, PhotoWars can be assigned outside of class or incorporated into two to three class sessions.

Marketing in the Twenty-First Century

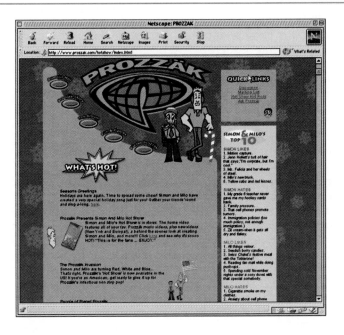

PROFILE:

Canadian Marketing Excellence

"*The future isn't ahead of us. It has already happened.*" Philip Kotler's quotation could easily be the hallmark of Sony Music Canada's New Media Group. The team recently asked themselves, "How do you get restless Web site visitors to stick around and interact with your brand?" Their solution was a novel one. Create a "virtual band"—Prozzäk, based on the Philosopher Kings (a real band). Create a myth and an on-line game designed to take players inside the music world and have them interact with your brand. The team invented the tale of Simon and Milo, members of a Canadian dance pop group called Prozzäk. Simon is looking for love and the player can help him find it.

The site has been a hit with both visitors and analysts. It won the award for the best band site at the recent South X Southwest Music Festival in Austin, Texas. But the site has done more than just win awards.

Having virtual characters has given Sony lots of marketing flexibility. It has helped attract and involve the target market tweens and teens, and it has resulted in repeated requests for airplay of the Prozzäk song "Sucks to Be You" on MuchMusic. Internet games have been around for some time, but this is the first time they have been used as a marketing tool. Since the Net is about fun and entertainment, Sony believes that the games are much more effective than using banner advertising in building and retaining site traffic.

Source: Raju Mudhar, "Play Power," *Marketing,* May 24, 1999, pp. 19–20.

In this chapter we examine the following questions:

- What are the tasks of marketing?

- What are the major concepts and tools of marketing?

- What orientations do companies exhibit in the marketplace?

- How are companies and marketers responding to the new challenges?

Prozzäk
www.prozzak.com

Said Charles Dickens in *A Tale of Two Cities,* written over 100 years ago: "It was the best of times, it was the worst of times." Though he was writing about the tumultuous era of the French Revolution, Dickens' words are as apt as ever. Today there are many blessings: vast improvements in modern medicine, extremely high productivity because of mechanization and automation, the promise of computers and the Internet, the rapid growth of global trade, and the end of the Cold War. Humankind today has the capacity to end hunger in the world and to cure many epidemic diseases. But alongside these blessings intractable problems persist: poverty, religious and ethnic conflict, environmental degradation, political dictatorships, corruption, human rights violations, and the dangers of terrorism and weapons of mass destruction.

In the business world, leaders who must plot the future of their companies are challenged to find a path that makes sense. Change is occurring at an accelerating rate; today is not like yesterday, and tomorrow will be different from today. Continuing today's strategy is risky; so is turning to a new strategy.

There are certainties that must be heeded. First, global forces will continue to affect everyone's business and personal lives. Manufacturing will move to more economically favourable locations or protectionist measures will stop these moves but raise costs for everyone. Second, technology will continue to advance and amaze us. The cloning of the sheep Dolly was only the beginning of the biogenetic revolution. The Human Genome Project—an effort to map every gene containing human DNA, with a central database residing at Toronto's Hospital for Sick Children—promises to usher in new medical cures. The Digital Revolution is releasing smart chips to make smart homes, smart cars, and even smart clothes. Third, there is a continuous push toward deregulation of the economic sector. More people, in more countries, are convinced that markets work better under relatively free conditions where buyers can decide what and where to buy and companies are free to decide what to make and sell. Competitive economies produce more wealth than highly regulated or planned economies. Many countries are privatizing state-owned companies to unleash the benefits of competition.

These three developments—globalization, technological advances, and deregulation—spell endless opportunities. As American novelist John Gardner observed many years ago, "Behind every problem is a brilliantly disguised opportunity."

But what is marketing and what does it have to do with these issues? Marketing deals with identifying and meeting human and social needs. One of the shortest definitions of marketing is "meeting needs profitably." The marketer may be Procter & Gamble (P&G), which notices that people want odour-free fabrics and invents Febreze; or CarMax, which realizes that people want more certainty when they buy a used automobile and invents a new system for selling used cars; or the Canadian Tourism

Human Genome Project
www.orn.govTechResources.
Human Genome/home.html

Car Max
www.carmax.com

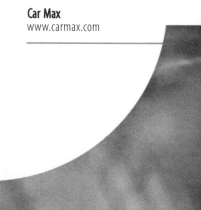

Commission, which notes that people want destination vacations and all-inclusive pricing, and so forms partnerships with private firms such as Air Canada to deliver vacation packages. But what each of these organizations illustrates is a drive to turn a private or social need into a profitable business opportunity.

M ARKETING TASKS

Harley-Davidson
www.harley-davidson.com

A recent book, *Radical Marketing*, praises companies such as Harley-Davidson, Virgin Atlantic Airways, and Boston Beer for succeeding by breaking all the rules of marketing.[1] These companies, instead of commissioning expensive marketing research, spending huge sums on mass advertising, and operating large marketing departments, stretched their limited resources, lived close to their customers, and created more satisfying solutions to their customers' needs. They formed buyers' clubs, used creative public relations, and focused on delivering high product quality and winning long-term customer loyalty. It seems that not all marketing must follow in the footsteps of traditional marketing exemplars like P&G.

In fact, we can distinguish three stages through which marketing practice might pass:

Big Rock Brewery
www.bigrockbeer.com

1. *Entrepreneurial marketing*: Most companies are started by individuals who live by their wits. They visualize an opportunity and knock on every door to gain attention. Big Rock Brewery of Calgary, for example, was the inspiration of one man, Ed McNally, who began the brewery in 1984. He founded his business on one guiding principle: "the marketplace will take notice of a superior product backed by superior service." His credo, "to create a masterpiece no compromise may be tolerated," manifests this doctrine. His unpasturized beers broke the mould when it came to the rules of beer marketing. Ed, for example, didn't want just labels for his new beers, he wanted art so he commissioned a local Calgary artist, Dirk Van Wyk, to create them. Many small pubs couldn't afford traditional refrigerated draught beer systems so Alastair Smart, a member of Ed's sales staff, invented a new, less expensive system that helped Big Rock's products penetrate the market.

2. *Formulated marketing*: As small companies achieve success, they inevitably move toward more formulated marketing. Seeing other firms leverage the power of sporting events, Big Rock took advantage of the Calgary 1988 Winter Olympics to widen the market for its products. It developed a new beer, Cold Cock Winter Porter, to celebrate the Games and it created an event, the *Alelympics*, to draw attention to its products.

3. *Intrepreneurial marketing*. Many large companies get stuck in formulated marketing, poring over the latest Nielsen numbers, scanning market research reports, trying to fine-tune dealer relations and advertising messages. These companies lack the creativity and passion of marketers in the first or entrepreneurial stage.[2] Their brand and product managers need to get out of the office, start living with their customers, and visualize new ways to add value to their customers' lives.

The bottom line is that effective marketing can take many forms. There will be a constant tension between the formulated side of marketing and the creative side. It is easier to learn the formulated side of marketing, which will occupy most of our attention in this book. But we will also see how real creativity and passion operate in many companies and can be used by today's and tomorrow's managers.

THE SCOPE OF MARKETING

Marketing is typically seen as the task of creating, promoting, and delivering goods and services to consumers and businesses. In fact, marketing people are involved in marketing 10 types of entities: *goods, services, experiences, events, persons, places, properties, organizations, information,* and *ideas*.

Goods

In developing nations, physical goods, particularly food, commodities, clothing, and housing, are the mainstay of the economy. However, in advanced economies, the production and marketing of goods may represent only a small portion of the country's economic efforts. For example, despite Canada's history as a resource-based economy, today primary industries (agriculture, fishing, forestry, and mining, petroleum) constitute only six percent of the gross domestic product.[3]

Services

As economies advance, a growing proportion of their activities are focused on the production of services. The North American economy today consists of a 70:30 services/goods mix. Services include the work of airlines, banks, consultants, hotels, insurance companies, car rental firms, barbers and beauticians, maintenance and repair people, as well as professionals working within or for companies, such as accountants, lawyers, engineers, doctors, and software programmers. Many *market offerings* consist of a variable mix of goods and services. At the pure service end would be a psychiatrist listening to a patient or a string quartet performing Mozart; in the middle level would be a fast-food establishment where the customer consumes both a good and a service; and at a pure product end are offerings dominated by physical products like table salt or steel.

Experiences

By orchestrating several services and goods, one can create, stage, and market experiences. Walt Disney World's Magic Kingdom is an experience, one of visiting a fairy kingdom, a pirate ship, or a haunted house. So are skiing at Whistler or visiting the Toronto Zoo. There are markets for different experiences, such as spending a week at a baseball camp playing with some retired all-time baseball greats, or paying to climb Mount Everest.[4]

Events

Marketers promote time-based events, such as the Olympics, company anniversaries, major trade shows, sports events, and artistic performances. There is a whole profession of meetings planners who work out the details of an event and stage it to come off perfectly.

Persons

Celebrity marketing has become a major business. Years ago, someone seeking fame would hire a press agent to plant stories in newspapers and magazines. Today every major film star has an agent, a personal manager, and ties to a public relations agency. Artists, musicians, CEOs, physicians, high-profile lawyers and financiers, and other professionals are drawing help from celebrity marketers.[5] Management consultant Tom Peters, himself a master at self-branding, has advised each person to become a "brand."

Places

Places—cities, provinces, regions, and whole nations—compete actively to attract tourists, factories, company headquarters, and new residents.[6] Stratford, Ontario had one asset, its association (through its name and situation on the Avon River) with the birthplace in England of William Shakespeare. This became the basis for an annual Shakespeare festival that put Stratford on the tourist map. Ireland has performed as an outstanding place marketer, having attracted over 500 companies to locate their plants in Ireland. It operates the Irish Development Board, Irish Tourist Board, and Irish Export Board, responsible for inward investment, tourists, and exports, respectively. Place marketers include economic development specialists, real estate agents, commercial banks, local business associations, and advertising and public relations agencies.

Properties

Properties are intangible rights of ownership of either real property (real estate) or financial property (stocks, bonds). When properties are bought and sold, this occasions a marketing effort. Real estate agents work for property owners or seekers to sell or buy residential or commercial real estate. Investment companies and banks are involved in marketing securities to both institutional and individual investors.

Organizations

Organizations actively work to build a strong, favourable image in the mind of their publics. We see *corporate identity ads* by companies seeking more public recognition. Philips, the Dutch electronics company, puts out ads with the tag line, "Let's Make Things Better." The Body Shop and the Royal Bank gain attention by promoting social causes. Other companies owe their visibility to a dramatic leader, such as Virgin Atlantic Airways' Richard Branson or Hollinger's Conrad Black. Universities, museums, and performing arts organizations all lay plans to boost their public image and compete more successfully for audiences and funds.

Information

Information can be produced and marketed as a product. This is essentially what schools and universities produce and distribute at a price to parents, students, and communities. Encyclopedias and most non-fiction books market information. Magazines such as *Road and Track* and *Byte* supply considerable information about the car and computer worlds, respectively. We buy CDs and visit the Internet for information. The production, packaging, and distribution of information is one of society's major industries.[7]

Ideas

Every market offering includes a basic idea at its core. Charley Revson of Revlon observed: "In the factory, we make cosmetics; in the store, we sell hope." The buyer of a drill is really buying a "hole." Products and services are platforms for delivering some idea or benefit. Marketers search hard for the core need they are trying to satisfy. A synagogue, church, or mosque, for example, must decide whether to market itself as a place of worship or a community centre; the design of the place of worship will be different depending on the choice.

Royal Bank
www.royalbank.ca

GRASS CLIPPINGS ARE
90% WATER.
PLEASE LEAVE THEM ON YOUR LAWN.

Put away the hose – grasscycle instead. Grass clippings aren't accepted for yard waste collection. Leave them on the lawn or use them for garden mulch. Valuable nutrients like potassium, phosphorus and nitrogen will be

returned to the soil, and that helps develop a healthy root system.
Most importantly, grasscycling provides your lawn with moisture, which means you water less. That should make your yard work 90% easier.

🏙 **TORONTO**
GRASSCYCLING. IT GROWS ON YOU.

Composting Helpline 392-4686 • Lawn Improvement Line 397-LAWN • www.city.toronto.on.ca/compost

Grasscycling is an idea the City of Toronto is trying to market.

Marketer Frequently Asked Questions (FAQs)

- How can we identify and choose the right market segment(s) to serve?
- How can we differentiate our offering from competitive offerings?
- How should we respond to customers who press us for a lower price?
- How can we compete against lower-cost, lower-price competitors from here and abroad?
- How far can we go in customizing our offering for each customer?
- What are the major ways in which we can grow our business?
- How can we build stronger brands?
- How can we reduce the cost of customer acquisition?
- How can we keep our customers loyal for a longer period?
- How can we tell which customers are more important?
- How can we measure the payback from advertising, sales promotion, and public relations?
- How can we improve sales-force productivity?
- How can we establish multiple channels and yet manage channel conflict?
- How can we get the other company departments to be more customer-oriented?

A BROADENED VIEW OF MARKETING TASKS

Marketers are skilled in stimulating demand for a company's products. But this is too limited a view of the tasks marketers perform. Just as production and logistics professionals are responsible for *supply management,* marketers are responsible for *demand management.* Marketing managers seek to influence the *level, timing,* and *composition* of demand to meet the organization's objectives. Table 1-1 distinguishes eight states of demand and the corresponding tasks facing marketing managers.

DECISIONS MARKETERS MAKE

Marketing managers face a host of decisions, from major ones such as what product features to design into a new product, how many salespeople to hire, or how much to spend on advertising, to minor decisions such as the exact wording or colour for some new packaging. The Marketing Memo "Marketer Frequently Asked Questions" lists many of the questions marketing managers ask that this book hopes to answer.

These questions vary in importance in different marketplaces. Consider the following four markets: consumer, business, global, and nonprofit.

Consumer Markets

Companies selling mass consumer goods and services such as soft drinks, toothpaste, television sets, and air travel spend a great deal of time trying to establish a superior brand image. This requires getting a clear sense of their target customers and what need(s) their product will meet, and then communicating brand positioning forcefully and creatively. Much of a brand's strength depends on developing a superior product and packaging and backing it with continuous advertising and reliable service. The sales force plays a role in obtaining and maintaining trade distribution, but this has less to do with establishing the brand image. Consumer marketers decide on the features, quality level, distribution coverage, and promotion expenditures that will help their brand achieve a number-one or -two position in their target market.

Business Markets

Companies selling business goods and services face well-trained and well-informed professional buyers who are skilled in evaluating competitive offerings. Business buyers buy goods for their utility in enabling them to make or resell a product to others. Business buyers purchase products to make profits. Business marketers must demonstrate how their products will help business customers achieve their profit goals. Advertising plays a role, but a stronger role is played by the sales force, price, and the company's reputation for reliability and quality.

Global Markets

Companies selling their goods and services in the global marketplace face additional decisions and challenges. They must decide which countries to enter; how to enter each country (as an exporter, licensor, joint venture partner, contract manufacturer, or solo manufacturer); how to adapt their product and service features to each country; how to price their product in different countries in a narrow enough band to avoid creating a grey market for their goods; and how to adapt their communications to fit the cultural practices of each country. These decisions must be made in the face of a different legal system; different styles of negotiation; different requirements for buying, owning, and disposing of property; a currency that might fluctuate in value; conditions of corruption or political favouritism; and so on.

Non-profit and Governmental Markets

Companies selling their goods to nonprofit organizations such as places of worship, universities, charitable organizations, or government agencies must exert extra care when making pricing decisions. Non-profits may have limited budgets. Lower prices affect the features and quality that the seller can build into the offering. Government agencies may also have strict rules about using the lowest-priced bidder. Marketers also have to decide whether the cost of navigating departmental bureaucracies and filling out extensive forms will result in the benefit of increased sales.

1. Negative demand	A market is in a state of negative demand if a major part of the market dislikes the product and may even pay a price to avoid it—vaccinations, dental work, vasectomies, and gallbladder operations, for instance. Employers have a negative demand for ex-convicts and alcoholics as employees. The marketing task is to analyze why the market dislikes the product and whether a marketing program consisting of product redesign, lower prices, and more positive promotion can change beliefs and attitudes.
2. No demand	Target consumers may be unaware of or uninterested in the product. Farmers may not be interested in a new farming method, and university students may not be interested in foreign-language courses. The marketing task is to find ways to connect the benefits of the product with the person's natural needs and interests.
3. Latent demand	Many consumers may share a strong need that cannot be satisfied by any existing product. There is a strong latent demand for a cure for cancer and environmentally friendly, fuel-efficient cars. The marketing task is to measure the size of the potential market and develop goods and services to satisfy the demand.
4. Declining demand	Every organization, sooner or later, faces declining demand for one or more of its products. Places of worship have seen membership decline; Canada Post has seen demand for stamps for personal correspondence fall. The marketer must analyze the causes of the decline and determine whether demand can be restimulated by new target markets, by changing product features, or by more effective communication. The marketing task is to reverse declining demand through creative remarketing.
5. Irregular demand	Many organizations face demand that varies on a seasonal, daily, or even hourly basis, causing problems of idle or overworked capacity. Much mass-transit equipment is idle during off-peak hours and insufficient during peak travel hours. Museums are undervisited on weekdays and overcrowded on weekends. The marketing task, called synchromarketing, is to find ways to alter the pattern of demand through flexible pricing, promotion, and other incentives.
6. Full demand	Organizations face full demand when they are pleased with their volume of business. The marketing task is to maintain the current level of demand in the face of changing consumer preferences and increasing competition. The organization must maintain or improve its quality and continually measure consumer satisfaction.
7. Overfull demand	Some organizations face a demand level that is higher than they can or want to handle. Banff National Park is terribly overcrowded in the summertime. The marketing task, called demarketing, requires finding ways to reduce demand temporarily or permanently. General demarketing seeks to discourage overall demand and consists of such steps as raising prices and reducing promotion and service. Selective demarketing consists of trying to reduce demand from those parts of the market that are less profitable or less in need of the product.
8. Unwholesome demand	Unwholesome products will attract organized efforts to discourage their consumption. Campaigns have been conducted against cigarettes, alcohol, hard drugs, unprotected sex, X-rated movies, and large families. The marketing task is to get people who like something to give it up, using such tools as fear messages, price hikes, and reduced availability.

Source: See Philip Kotler, "The Major Tasks of Marketing Management," *Journal of Marketing*, October 1973, pp. 42-49; and Philip Kotler and Sidney J. Levy, "Demarketing, Yes, Demarketing," *Harvard Business Review*, November-December 1971, pp. 74-80.

Banff National Park
www.banffnationalpark.com

Marketing boasts a rich array of concepts and tools. We will start by defining marketing, then describe its major concepts and tools.

DEFINING MARKETING

Of the numerous definitions offered for marketing, we can distinguish between a social and a managerial definition. A social definition shows the role marketing plays in society. One marketer said that marketing's role is to "deliver a higher standard of living." A social definition that serves our purpose follows:

■ *Marketing* is a societal process by which individuals and groups obtain what they need and want through creating, offering, and exchanging products and services of value with others.

For a managerial definition, marketing has often been described as "the art of selling products." But people are surprised when they hear that the most important part of marketing is not selling! Selling is only the tip of the marketing iceberg. Peter Drucker, a leading management theorist, puts it this way:

There will always, one can assume, be need for some selling. But the aim of marketing is to make selling superfluous. The aim of marketing is to know and understand the customer so well that the product or service fits him [her] and sells itself. Ideally, marketing should result in a customer who is ready to buy. All that should be needed then is to make the product or service available. . . .[8]

When Sony designed its Walkman, when Nintendo designed a superior video game, and when Toyota introduced its Lexus automobile, these manufacturers were swamped with orders because they had designed the "right" product based on careful marketing homework.

The American Marketing Association (whose membership comprises marketing professionals from both Canada and the United States), offers the following definition:

■ *Marketing (management)* is the process of planning and executing the conception, pricing, promotion, and distribution of ideas, goods and services to create exchanges that satisfy individual and organizational goals.[9]

Coping with exchange processes calls for a considerable amount of work and skill. Marketing management takes place when at least one party to a potential exchange thinks about the means of achieving desired responses from other parties. We see marketing management as the art and science of choosing target markets and getting, keeping, and growing customers through creating, delivering, and communicating superior customer value.

CORE MARKETING CONCEPTS

Marketing can be further understood by defining several of its core concepts.

Target Markets and Segmentation

A marketer can rarely satisfy everyone in a market. Not everyone likes the same soft drink, hotel room, restaurant, automobile, university, and movie. Therefore, marketers start with *market segmentation*. They identify and profile distinct groups of buyers who might prefer or require varying products and marketing mixes. Market segments can be identified by examining demographic, psychographic, and behavioural differences among buyers. The firm then decides which segments present the greatest opportunity—those whose needs the firm can meet in a superior fashion.

For each chosen target market, the firm develops a *market offering*. The offering is *positioned* in the minds of the target buyers as delivering some central benefit(s). For example, Volvo develops its cars for the target market of buyers for whom automobile safety is a major concern. Volvo therefore positions its car as the safest a customer can buy.

American Marketing Association
www.ama.org

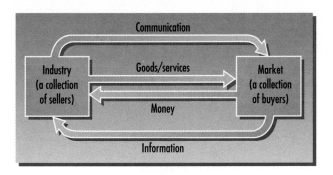

FIGURE 1.1

A Simple Marketing System

Traditionally, a "market" was a physical place where buyers and sellers gathered to exchange goods. Economists now describe a market as a collection of buyers and sellers who transact over a particular product or product class (the housing market, grain market). But marketers view the sellers as constituting the *industry* and the buyers as constituting the *market*. Figure 1-1 shows the relationship between the industry and the market. Sellers and buyers are connected by four flows. The sellers send goods and services and communications (ads, direct mail) to the market; in return they receive money and information (attitudes, sales data). The inner loop shows an exchange of money for goods and services; the outer loop shows an exchange of information.

Businesspeople often use the term "markets" to cover various groupings of customers. They discuss need markets (the diet-seeking market); product markets (the shoe market); demographic markets (the youth market); and geographic markets (the French market). Or they extend the concept to cover other markets, such as voter markets, labour markets, and donor markets.

Modern economies abound in markets. Five basic markets and their connecting flows are shown in Figure 1-2. Manufacturers go to *resource markets* (raw-material markets, labour markets, money markets), buy resources, turn resources into goods and services, and then sell finished products to intermediaries, who sell them to consumers. Consumers sell their labour and receive money with which they pay for goods and services. The government collects tax revenues to buy goods from resource, manufacturer, and intermediary markets, and uses these goods and services to provide public services. Each nation's economy and the global economy consist of complex interacting sets of markets linked through exchange processes.

Today we can distinguish between a *marketplace* and *marketspace*. The marketplace is physical, as when one goes shopping in a store; marketspace is digital, as when one goes shopping on the Internet. Many observers believe that an increasing amount of purchasing will shift from the marketplace to marketspace.[10] See the Marketing for the 21st Century box, "E-Commerce: The Kitty Hawk Era."

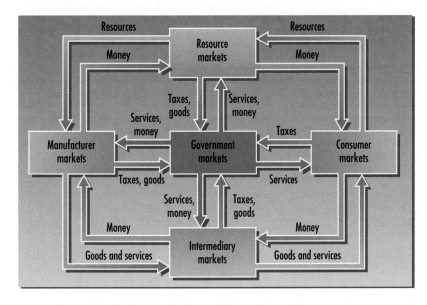

FIGURE 1.2

Structure of Flows in a Modern Exchange Economy

E-COMMERCE: The Kitty Hawk Era

In 1997, the entire sales volume of e-commerce—business transactions conducted online—amounted to a mere $3 billion. That's just a few days of business for a megastore chain like Wal-Mart and a tiny percentage of the entire economy.

Given the seemingly poor performance of e-commerce, why are investors so bullish on Internet stocks? For instance, investors are willing to pay considerably more for Amazon.com shares than they are to pay for its brick-and-mortar cousin, Barnes & Noble, even though Amazon has consistently lost money.

Investors are betting that cyberspace will be the business model of the future. As Amazon.com CEO Jeff Bezos says, "It's the Kitty Hawk era of electronic commerce," comparing the adoption of Internet technology to the early days of the airplane. Slowly but surely, consumers are leaving malls to shop on-line, often in their pajamas at 11:00 p.m. Forrester Research estimates that on-line-commerce will boom to $490 billion by the year 2000, a 233 percent increase over 1997 sales. A 1999 survey by the Vancouver offices of The Angus Reid Group and Deloitte & Touche shows that Canadians are rapidly taking to Internet shopping. Its results suggest that Canadian electronic shoppers spent $1.1 to $1.3 billion on e-commerce transactions. Anyone who doubts the potential power of the e-commerce juggernaut hasn't grasped the advantages for both consumers and businesses:

- **Convenience**: Cyberstores never close their doors. In a recent survey of active web shoppers, Forrester Research rated convenience the primary reason for shopping on-line. Seattle's recreational equipment company, REI, generates 30 percent of its orders from 10 p.m. to 7 a.m. without the expense of keeping a store open or hiring customer service representatives. The lure of convenience has also created opportunities for start-ups like on-line grocers who want to reach today's harried consumers.

- **Savings**: Businesses such as Dell Computer Corp. and General Electric are using the Internet to link directly to suppliers, factories, distributors, and customers. They are wringing waste out of the system and passing on savings to customers. On-line retailers such as Chapters.ca reap the advantage of a negative operating cycle: Chapters receives cash from credit card companies just a day after customers place an order. Then it can hold onto the money for 46 days until it pays its suppliers, the book distributors, and

publishers. Customers stand to benefit most of all, since they can scour the Web to search for the lowest price. There are even sites such as Compare.Net, which offers a free on-line buyer's guide that allows users to compare features of 10 000 products.

- **Selection**: The world's the limit for the Web. Unrestrained by physical boundaries, cyberstores can offer an almost unlimited selection. GardenCrazy Ltd. of Saint-Timothé, Que. claims to be "the most complete garden centre on-line". Go to the CDNow and Virtual Vineyards sites and then compare the selection with the offerings of HMV or the local liquor store. Collapsed geographic boundaries also open up markets all over the world and make upstarts indistinguishable from established companies.

- **Personalization**: With the computer's ability to slice and dice information captured on the Web, businesses can personalize their sales pitches and even their products. CNN's Web site enables individuals to create personal profiles of their news interests and updates them every 15 minutes. Dell gives its corporate customers customized Web pages, otherwise known as premier pages, to purchase Dell computers. Shell Oil Company's site keeps purchasing managers up-to-date on product and pricing changes.

- **Information**. While it's true that the human interface is missing, the Web makes up for it tenfold with the amount of information available. Good sites provide more information in more useful forms than even the most solicitous sales clerk. Etoys, for example, offers parents toy recommendations from consumer and educational groups. CDNow offers record reviews and previews of selected tracks. And information flows two ways. Every time a consumer purchases an item from a Web site, the company has access to valuable market research information.

All the advantages of e-commerce don't come without a price, however. Those most threatened by the e-commerce upheaval will be intermediaries such as travel agents, stockbrokers, insurance salespeople, car dealers, and even traditional retailers. All companies fear the leverage gained by consumers who can demand ever-lower prices. Finally, businesses are rapidly learning that it isn't enough to tack the suffix "dot com" or "dot ca" onto the company name. Businesses need to reorganize and redefine themselves in order to succeed online.

Based on: "E-Commerce," *The Globe and Mail Special Interest Report*, March 30, 1999, pp. C1, C15. Angus Reid Press Release *http://www.angusreid.com/pressrel/pr990526_1.html*. Robert D. Hof, "The Click Here Economy," *Business Week*, June 22, 1998, pp. 122-128. Michael Krantz, "Click Till You Drop," *Time*, July 20, 1998, pp. 34-39. Tina Kelley, "Internet Shopping: A Mixed Bag," *New York Times*, July 30, 1998, G, 1:2. Cynthia Mayer, "Does Amazon = 2 Barnes & Nobles?: Market Values May Not Be so Crazy," *New York Times*, July 19, 1998, p. 4. Rajiv Chandrasekaran, More Shoppers Are Buying Online," *The Washington Post*, December 24, 1997, C01. Edward R. Berryman, "Viewpoint: Web Commerce: Be Prepared," *New York Times*, October 12, 1997, p. 3. 14:4. Joel Kotkin, "The Mother of All Malls," *Forbes*, April 6, 1998, pp. 60-65.

Mohan Sawhney has proposed the concept of a *metamarket,* to describe a cluster of complementary products and services that are closely related in the minds of consumers, but are spread across a diverse set of industries. The automobile metamarket consists of automobile manufacturers, new car and used car dealers, financing companies, insurance companies, mechanics, spare parts dealers, service shops, auto magazines, classified auto ads in newspapers, and auto sites on the Internet. In planning or buying a car, a buyer will come into contact with many parts of this metamarket. This has created an opportunity for *metamediaries* to assist buyers to move seamlessly through these groups, despite their separation in physical space. One example is Edmund's, a web site where a car buyer can find the stated prices of different automobiles and easily click to other sites to search for the lowest price dealer, financing, car accessories, and used cars at bargain prices. Metamediaries can also serve other metamarkets such as the home ownership market, the parenting and baby care market, and the wedding market.[11]

Marketers and Prospects

A *marketer* is someone seeking a response (attention, a purchase, a vote, a donation) from another party, called the *prospect.* If two parties are seeking to sell something to each other, we call them both marketers.

Needs, Wants, and Demands

The marketer must try to understand the target market's needs, wants, and demands. Needs describe basic human requirements. People need food, air, water, clothing and shelter to survive. People also have strong needs for recreation, education, and entertainment. These needs become wants when they are directed to specific objects that might satisfy the need. A Canadian *needs* food but *wants* a hamburger, French fries, and a soft drink. A person in Mauritius *needs* food but *wants* a mango, rice, lentils, and beans. Wants are shaped by one's society.

Demands are wants for specific products backed by an ability to pay. Many people want a Mercedes; only a few are able and willing to buy one. Companies must measure not only how many people want their product, but also how many would actually be *willing and able* to buy it.

These distinctions shed light on the frequent criticism that "marketers create needs" or "marketers get people to buy things they don't want." Marketers do not create needs: needs pre-exist marketers. Marketers, along with other societal influences, influence wants. Marketers might promote the idea that a Mercedes would satisfy a person's need for social status. They do not, however, create the need for social status.

Product or Offering

People satisfy their needs and wants with products. A *product* is any offering that can satisfy a need or want. We mentioned earlier the major types of basic offerings: goods, services, experiences, events, persons, places, properties, organizations, information, and ideas.

A brand is an offering from a known source. A brand name such as McDonald's carries many associations in the minds of people: hamburgers, fun, children, fast food, Ronald McDonald, playgrounds, Golden Arches. These associations make up the brand image. All companies strive to build brand strength—that is, a strong, favourable brand image.

Value and Satisfaction

The product or offering will be successful if it delivers value and satisfaction to the target buyer. The buyer chooses between different offerings on the basis of which is perceived to deliver the most value. We define value as a ratio between what the customer *gets* and what he *gives.* The customer gets *benefits* and assumes *costs.* The benefits include functional benefits and emotional benefits. The costs include monetary costs, time costs, energy costs, and psychic costs. Thus value is given by:

$$\text{Value} = \frac{\text{Benefits}}{\text{Costs}} = \frac{\text{Functional benefits} + \text{emotional benefits}}{\text{Monetary costs} + \text{time costs} + \text{energy costs} + \text{psychic costs}}$$

The marketer can increase the value of the customer offering in several ways:

Raise benefits

Reduce costs

Raise benefits and reduce costs

Raise benefits by more than the rise in costs

Lower benefits by less than the reduction in costs

The customer who is choosing between two value offerings, V_1 and V_2, will examine the ratio V_1 / V_2. She will favour V_1 if the ratio is larger than one; she will favour V_2 if the ratio is smaller than one; and she will be indifferent if the ratio equals one.

Exchange and Transactions

Exchange is only one of four ways in which a person can obtain a product. The person can self-produce the product or service, as when a person hunts, fishes, or gathers fruit. The person can use force to get a product, as in a holdup or robbery. The person can beg, as happens when a homeless person asks for food. Or the person can offer a product, service, or money in exchange for something the person desires.

Exchange, which is the core concept of marketing, involves obtaining a desired product from someone by offering something in return. For exchange potential to exist, five conditions must be satisfied:

1. There are at least two parties.

2. Each party has something that might be of value to the other party.

3. Each party is capable of communication and delivery.

4. Each party is free to accept or reject the exchange offer.

5. Each party believes it is appropriate or desirable to deal with the other party.

Whether exchange actually takes place depends on whether the two parties can agree on terms that will leave them both better off (or at least not worse off) than before. Exchange is a value-creating process because it normally leaves both parties better off.

Exchange is a process rather than an event. Two parties are engaged in exchange if they are *negotiating*—trying to arrive at mutually agreeable terms. When an agreement is reached, we say that a transaction takes place. A *transaction* is a trade of values between two or more parties: A gives X to B and receives Y in return. Smith sells Jones a television set and Jones pays $400 to Smith. This is a classic *monetary transaction*. But transactions do not require money as one of the traded values. A *barter transaction* involves trading goods or services for other goods or services, as when lawyer Jones writes a will for physician Smith in return for a medical examination.

A transaction involves several dimensions: at least two things of value, agreed-upon conditions, a time of agreement, and a place of agreement. Usually a legal system exists to support and enforce compliance on the part of the transactors. Without a law of contracts, people would approach transactions with some distrust, and everyone would lose.

A transaction differs from a transfer. In a *transfer*, A gives X to B but does not receive anything tangible in return. Gifts, subsidies, and charitable contributions are all transfers. Transfer behaviour can also be understood through the concept of exchange. Typically, the transferor expects to receive something in exchange for his or her gift—for example, gratitude or seeing changed behaviour in the recipient. Professional fundraisers provide benefits to donors, such as thank-you notes, donor magazines, and invitations to events. Marketers have broadened the concept of marketing to include the study of transfer behaviour as well as transaction behaviour.

In the most generic sense, marketers seek to elicit a *behavioural response* from another party. A business firm wants a purchase, a political candidate wants a vote, a mosque wants an active member, and a social-action group wants the passionate adoption of some cause. Marketing consists of actions undertaken to elicit desired responses from a target audience.

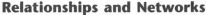

FIGURE 1.3

Two-Party Exchange Map Showing Want Lists of Both Parties

Construction Co. Want List
1. High-quality, durable equipment
2. Fair price
3. On-time delivery of equipment
4. Good financing terms
5. Good parts and service

Caterpillar (marketer) → Construction Co. (prospect)

Caterpillar Want List
1. Good price for equipment
2. On-time payment
3. Good word of mouth

Caterpillar
www.caterpillar.com

To effect successful exchanges, marketers analyze what each party expects from the transaction. Simple exchange situations can be mapped by showing the two actors and the wants and offerings flowing between them. Suppose Caterpillar, the world's largest manufacturer of earth-moving equipment, researches the benefits that a typical construction company wants when it buys earth-moving equipment. These benefits, listed at the top of the exchange map in Figure 1-3, include high-quality equipment, a fair price, on-time delivery, good financing terms, and good parts and service. The items on this *want list* are not equally important and may vary from buyer to buyer. One of Caterpillar's tasks is to discover the relative importance of these different wants to the buyer.

Caterpillar also has a want list. It wants a good price for the equipment, on-time payment, and good word of mouth. If there is a sufficient match or overlap in the want lists, a basis for a transaction exists. Caterpillar's task is to formulate an offer that motivates the construction company to buy Caterpillar equipment. The construction company might in turn make a counteroffer. This process of negotiation leads to mutually acceptable terms or a decision not to transact.

Relationships and Networks

Transaction marketing is part of a larger idea called relationship marketing. *Relationship marketing* has the aim of building long-term mutually satisfying relations with key parties—customers, suppliers, distributors—in order to earn and retain their long-term preference and business.[12] Marketers accomplish this by promising and delivering high-quality products and services at fair prices to the other parties over time. Relationship marketing builds strong economic, technical, and social ties among the parties. It cuts down on transaction costs and time. In the most successful cases, transactions move from being negotiated each time to being a matter of routine.

The ultimate outcome of relationship marketing is the building of a unique company asset called a *marketing network*. A marketing network consists of the company and its supporting *stakeholders* (customers, employees, suppliers, distributors, retailers, ad agencies, university scientists, and others) with whom it has built mutually beneficial business relationships. Increasingly, competition is not between companies but rather between marketing networks, with the prize going to the company that has built the better network. The operating principle is simple: Build an effective network of relationships with key stakeholders, and profits will follow.[13]

Marketing Channels

To reach a target market, the marketer uses three kinds of marketing channels.

The marketer uses *communication channels* to deliver and receive messages from target buyers. They include newspapers, magazines, radio, television, mail, telephone, billboards, posters, flyers, CDs, audiotapes, and the Internet. Beyond these, communications are conveyed by employees' facial expressions and clothing, the look of retail stores, and many other media. Marketers are increasingly adding *dialogue channels* (e-mail, toll-free numbers) to counterbalance the more normal *monologue channels* (such as ads).

The marketer uses *distribution channels* to display or deliver the physical product and/or service(s) to the buyer or user. There are physical distribution channels and service distribution channels. They include warehouses, transportation vehicles, and various *trade channels* such as distributors, wholesalers, and retailers.

The marketer also uses *selling channels* to effect transactions with potential buyers. Selling channels include the distributors and retailers but also banks and insurance companies that facilitate transactions. Marketers clearly face a design problem in choosing the best mix of communication, distribution, and selling channels for their offerings.

Supply chain

While marketing channels connect the marketer to the target buyers, the supply chain describes a longer channel stretching from raw materials to components to final products that are carried to final buyers. The supply chain for women's purses proceeds from hides, tanning operations, cutting operations, and manufacturing to the marketing channels that bring products to customers. Each company captures only a certain percentage of the total value generated by the supply chain. When a company acquires competitors or moves upstream or downstream, its aim is to capture a higher percentage of supply chain value.

Competition

Competition includes all the actual and potential rival offerings and substitutes that a buyer might consider.

Suppose a company like Dofasco is hoping to sell steel to a car manufacturer. Algoma, Dofasco, and Stelco are all large, integrated steel mills and thus are close rivals. Together they produce three-fifths of the country's steel. Clearly Dofasco would be thinking too narrowly of competition if it thought only of other integrated steel companies. Canada also has 10 smaller mills that use electric arc furnaces to produce specialized items such as carbon steel plant, bar and rod products, and specialty steels. However, since 90 percent of Canada's steel exports go to the United States, Dofasco

FIGURE 1.4

Dofasco Radar Screen

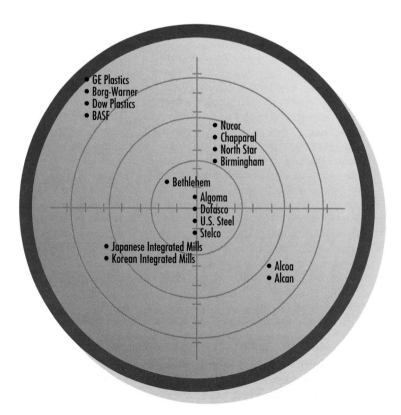

cannot ignore its American rivals in this increasingly integrated market. Rivalry is further increased by the fact that automobile manufacturers are replacing steel with other materials like plastic, aluminum, magnesium, and carbon fibre. In fact, Dofasco is more likely to be hurt in the long run by substitutes than by its immediate rivals. Thus, it may have to closely watch the moves of Alcan, the aluminum manufacturer that has been investing in research to develop component and parts that will lighten the cars' weight.

Alcan
www.alcan.com

We can broaden the picture further by distinguishing four levels of competition, based on degree of product substitutability:

1. *Brand competition:* A company sees its competitors as other companies offering a similar product and services to the same customers at similar prices. Volkswagen might see its major competitors as Toyota, Honda, Renault, and other manufacturers of medium-price automobiles. It would not see itself as competing with Mercedes or with Hyundai.

2. *Industry competition:* A company sees its competitors as all companies making the same product or class of products. Volkswagen would see itself as competing against all other automobile manufacturers.

3. *Form competition:* A company sees its competitors as all companies manufacturing products that supply the same service. Volkswagen would see itself competing against not only other automobile manufacturers, but also against manufacturers of motorcycles, bicycles, and trucks.

4. *Generic competition:* A company sees its competitors as all companies that compete for the same consumer dollars. Volkswagen would see itself competing with companies that sell major consumer durables, foreign vacations, and new homes.

Marketing Environment

Competition represents only one force in the environment in which the marketer operates. The marketing environment consists of the *task environment* and the *broad environment.*

The task environment includes the immediate actors involved in producing, distributing, and promoting the offering. The main actors are the company, suppliers, distributors, dealers, and the target customers. Included in the supplier group are material suppliers and service suppliers such as marketing research agencies, advertising agencies, banking and insurance companies, transportation and telecommunications companies. Included with distributors and dealers are agents, brokers, manufacturer representatives, and others who facilitate finding and selling to customers.

The broad environment consists of six components: *demographic environment, economic environment, natural environment, technological environment, political-legal environment,* and *social/cultural environment.* These environments contain forces that can have a major impact on the actors in the task environment. Market actors must pay close attention to the trends and developments in these environments and make timely adjustments to their marketing strategies.

Marketing Mix

Marketers use numerous tools to elicit desired responses from their target markets. These tools constitute a *marketing mix:*[14]

■ *Marketing mix* is the set of marketing tools the firm uses to pursue its marketing objectives in the target market.

E. Jerome McCarthy classified these tools into four broad groups that he called the Four Ps of marketing: Product, Price, Place, and Promotion.[15] The particular marketing variables under each *P* are shown in Figure 1-5. Marketing-mix decisions must be made for influencing the trade channels as well as the final consumers. Figure 1-6 shows the company preparing an *offer mix* of products, services, and prices, and utilizing a *promotion mix* of sales promotion, advertising, sales force, public relations, direct mail, and telemarketing to reach the trade channels and the target customers.

The Four P Components of the
Marketing Mix

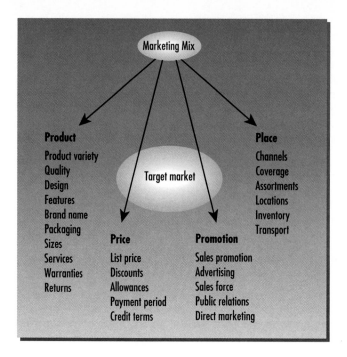

Typically, the firm can change its price, sales force size, and advertising expenditures in the short run. It can develop new products and modify its distribution channels only in the long run. Thus the firm typically makes fewer period-to-period marketing-mix changes in the short run than the number of marketing-mix decision variables might suggest.

Note that the 4Ps represent the sellers' view of the marketing tools available for influencing buyers. From a buyer's point of view, each marketing tool is designed to deliver a customer benefit. Robert Lauterborn suggested that the sellers' 4Ps correspond to the customers' 4Cs.[16]

F I G U R E 1.6

Marketing-Mix Strategy

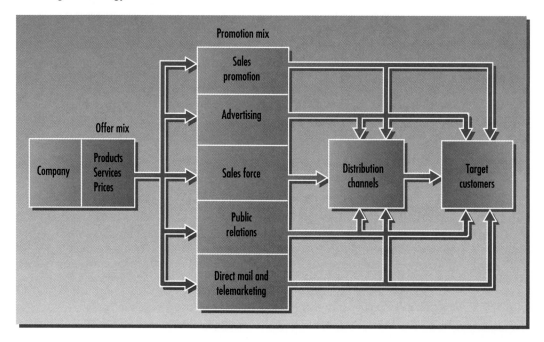

Four Ps	Four Cs
Product	Customer solution
Price	Customer cost
Place	Convenience
Promotion	Communication

Winning companies will be those who can meet customer needs economically and conveniently and with effective communication.

COMPANY ORIENTATIONS TOWARD THE MARKETPLACE

We have defined marketing management as the conscious effort to achieve desired exchange outcomes with target markets. But what philosophy should guide a company's marketing efforts? What relative weights should be given to the interests of the organization, the customers, and society? Very often these interests conflict.

■ **Dexter.** One of Dexter Corporation's most popular products was a profitable grade of paper that prevented tea bags from disintegrating in hot water. Unfortunately, the materials used to produce the paper accounted for 98 percent of Dexter's annual hazardous wastes. So while Dexter's product was extremely popular with customers, it was obviously detrimental to the environment. Dexter assigned an employee task force representing the company's environmental, legal, R&D, and marketing departments to solve the problem. The task force succeeded, and the company increased its market share and virtually eliminated hazardous waste in the process.[17]

Dexter Corporation
www.dexter.com

Clearly, marketing activities should be carried out under a well-thought-out philosophy of efficient, effective, and socially responsible marketing. However, there are five competing concepts under which organizations conduct marketing activities: the production concept, product concept, selling concept, marketing concept, and societal marketing concept. Before describing the concepts, it must be noted that many marketing textbooks use these headings to describe the evolution and history of marketing. Nothing could be further from the truth! In fact, renowned marketing historian, Stanley Hollander asked, "Why is it so difficult to kill this infamous, misleading, warped, stupid, moronic, hateful doctrine?"[18]

PRODUCTION CONCEPT

The production concept is one of the oldest concepts in business.

■ The *production concept* holds that consumers will prefer products that are widely available and inexpensive.

Managers of production-oriented businesses concentrate on achieving high production efficiency, low costs, and mass distribution. They assume that consumers are primarily interested in product availability and low prices. This orientation makes sense in developing countries, where consumers are more interested in obtaining the product than in its features. It is also used when a company wants to expand the market.

Texas Instruments
www.ti.com

■ **Texas Instruments.** Texas Instruments is one of the leading North American exponents of the "get-out-production, cut-the-price" philosophy that Henry Ford pioneered in the early 1900s to expand the automobile market. Texas Instruments puts all of its efforts in building production volume and upgrading technology in order to bring down costs. It uses its lower costs to cut prices further and expand the market size. It strives to achieve the dominant position in its target markets. This orientation has also been a key strategy of many Japanese companies.

Some service organizations also operate on the production concept. Many medical and dental practices are organized on assembly-line principles, as are some government agencies (such as unemployment offices and licence bureaus). While this management orientation can handle many cases per hour, it is open to charges of impersonal and poor-quality service.

PRODUCT CONCEPT

Other businesses are guided by the product concept.

■ The *product concept* holds that consumers will favour those products that offer the most quality, performance, or innovative features.

Managers in these organizations focus on making superior products and improving them over time. They assume that buyers admire well-made products and can appraise quality and performance. However, these managers are sometimes caught up in a love affair with their product and do not realize what the market needs. Management might commit the "better-mousetrap" fallacy, believing that a better mousetrap will lead people to beat a path to its door. Such was the case when WebTV debuted during Christmas 1996 to disappointing results.

WebTV Networks
www.webtv.net

■ **Web TV.** It seemed like a couch potato's dream: a TV with a set-top box that allows you to surf the Web and watch TV. Yet, despite a $50 million promotional blitz by WebTV and partners Sony and Philips Electronics, only 50 000 subscribers signed up. Nothing was wrong with the product itself, which displayed Internet information on a standard TV set; it's just that the original owner of WebTV (now owned by Microsoft) didn't know the market. The problem was the wrong marketing message. Couch potatoes want to be better entertained while computer users want to surf the Web and gather information. The World Wide Web had trouble competing with TV. To people conditioned by the tube, the Web is slow, static, and arcane, at least when compared with *Star Trek* or *Baywatch* reruns. A revamped campaign now emphasizes entertainment over education.[19]

Product-oriented companies often design their products with little or no customer input. They trust that their engineers can design exceptional products. Very often they will not even examine competitors' products. A General Motors executive said years ago: "How can the public know what kind of car they want until they see what is available?" GM's designers and engineers would design the new car. Then manufacturing would make it. The finance department would price it. Finally, marketing and sales would try to sell it. No wonder the car required such a hard sell! GM today asks customers what they value in a car and includes marketing people in the very beginning stages of design.

The product concept can lead to *marketing myopia*.[20] Railway management thought that travellers wanted trains rather than transportation and overlooked the growing competition from airlines, buses, trucks, and automobiles. Canada Post assumed people wanted efficient mail services when people really wanted efficient communication. Such organizations assume that they are offering the public the right product and then wonder why their sales slip. These organizations too often are looking into a mirror when they should be looking out of the window.

Canada Post
www.canadapost.ca

SELLING CONCEPT

The selling concept is another common business orientation.

■ The *selling concept* holds that consumers and businesses, if left alone, will ordinarily not buy enough of the organization's products. The organization must therefore undertake an aggressive selling and promotion effort.

This concept assumes that consumers typically show buying inertia or resistance and must be coaxed into buying. It also assumes that the company has a whole battery of effective selling and promotion tools to stimulate more buying.

The selling concept is practised most aggressively with unsought goods—that is, goods that buyers normally do not think of buying, such as insurance, encyclopedias, and burial plots. These industries have perfected various sales techniques to locate prospects and use a hard-sell approach when outlining their product's benefits.

The selling concept is also practised in the nonprofit area by fundraisers, university admissions offices, and political parties. A political party vigorously "sells" its candidate to voters. The candidate moves through voting precincts from early morning to late evening, shaking hands, kissing babies, meeting donors, and making speeches. Countless dollars are spent on radio and television advertising, posters, and mailings. The candidate's flaws are concealed from the public because the aim is to make the sale, not worry about postpurchase satisfaction. After the election, the new official continues to take a sales-oriented view. There is little research into what the public wants and a lot of selling to get the public to accept policies the politician or party wants.[21]

Most firms practise the selling concept when they have overcapacity. *Their aim is to sell what they make rather than make what the market wants.* In modern industrial economies, productive capacity has been built up to a point where most markets are buyer markets (the buyers are dominant) and sellers must scramble for customers. Prospects are bombarded with TV commercials, newspaper ads, direct mail, and sales calls. At every turn, someone is trying to sell something. As a result, the public often identifies marketing with hard selling and advertising.

But marketing based on hard selling carries high risks. It assumes that customers who are coaxed into buying a product will like it; and if they don't, that they won't bad-mouth it or complain to consumer organizations and will forget their disappointment and buy it again. These are indefensible assumptions. One study showed that dissatisfied customers may bad-mouth the product to 10 or more acquaintances. Bad news travels fast.[22]

MARKETING CONCEPT

The marketing concept is a business philosophy that challenges the three business orientations we just discussed.[23]

■ The **marketing concept** holds that the key to achieving its organizational goals consists of the company being more effective than competitors in creating, delivering, and communicating customer value to its chosen target markets.

The marketing concept has been expressed in many colourful ways:

"Meeting needs profitably."

"Find wants and fill them."

"Love the customer, not the product."

"Have it your way." (Burger King)

"You're the boss." (United Airlines)

"Putting people first." (British Airways)

"People Helping People...one customer at a time." (Royal Bank Financial Group)

Theodore Levitt of Harvard drew a perceptive contrast between the selling and marketing concepts:

Selling focuses on the needs of the seller; marketing on the needs of the buyer. Selling is preoccupied with the seller's need to convert his product into cash; marketing with the idea of satisfying the needs of the customer by means of the product and the whole cluster of things associated with creating, delivering and finally consuming it. [24]

The marketing concept rests on four pillars: *target market, customer needs, integrated marketing,* and *profitability*. They are illustrated in Figure 1-7, where they are contrasted with a selling orientation. The selling concept takes an inside-out perspective. It starts

FIGURE 1.7

The Selling and Marketing Concepts Contrasted

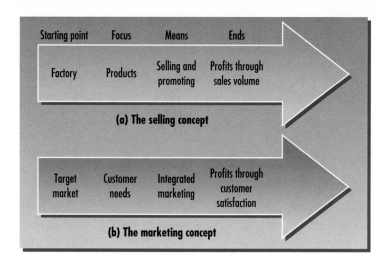

Starting point	Focus	Means	Ends
Factory	Products	Selling and promoting	Profits through sales volume

(a) The selling concept

Target market	Customer needs	Integrated marketing	Profits through customer satisfaction

(b) The marketing concept

with the factory, focuses on existing products, and calls for heavy selling and promoting to produce profitable sales. The marketing concept takes an outside-in perspective. It starts with a well-defined market, focuses on customer needs, co-ordinates all the activities that will affect customers, and produces profits by satisfying customers. See the Marketing Insight box "Scholars and Dollars: Marketing and Selling Comes to University."

Target Market

Companies do best when they choose their target market(s) carefully and prepare tailored marketing programs.

- **Estée Lauder.** After the U.S. 1990 census focused marketers' attention on minority groups' increasing buying power, the cosmetic giant Estée Lauder targeted people of African origin with special product lines designed for darker skin tones. In the fall of 1992, Estée Lauder's subsidiary, Prescriptives, launched an "All Skins" line offering 115 different foundation shades. The senior executive of creative marketing at Prescriptives credits All Skins for a 45 percent increase in sales since the new line was launched.

CUSTOMER NEEDS

A company can define its target market but fail to correctly understand customers' needs. Consider the following example:

When a major chemical company invented a marble-like substance and tried to persuade bathtub manufacturers to use the material, they failed to account for two important facts: the price of their bathtubs was four times that of regular bathtubs, exceeding even the price of real marble or onyx tubs, and the bathtubs were so heavy that homeowners would have to reinforce their floors to install them.

Understanding customer needs and wants is not always simple. Some customers have needs of which they are not fully conscious. Or they cannot articulate these needs. Or they use words that require some interpretation. What does it mean when the customer asks for an "inexpensive" car, a "powerful" lawn mower, a "fast" lathe, an "attractive" bathing suit, or a "peaceful" hotel?

Consider the customer who says he wants an "inexpensive" car. The marketer must probe further. We can distinguish among five types of needs:

1. *Stated needs* (the customer wants an inexpensive car)

2. *Real needs* (the customer wants a car whose operating cost, not its initial price, is low)

Scholars and Dollars: Marketing and Selling Comes to University

Higher education today is facing myriad challenges that are forcing institutions to make changes in the way they do business. Many community colleges and universities in both Canada and the United States are dogged by government budget cuts, calls for accountability, competition for private funding, and heavy media scrutiny.

From 1990 to 1995, Canadian government support for universities fell. Whereas government support covered 80 percent of universities' operating budgets in 1990, today it supports less than 70 percent. Tuition fees have had to rise as part of universities' response to this situation. However, growing dependence on tuition fees is increasingly problematic since universities and colleges have seen their full-time and part-time enrollments fall during the early 1990s. Educational institutions have had to rethink their strategies for pursuing students. They have also had to rethink the types of students they want to pursue. More and more universities are developing or running executive education programs and these programs have brought universities into head-to-head competition with a group of rivals unknown to them previously. Some are responding to these challenges with an all-out marketing blitz designed to redefine their images. Other, once-staid and ivy-covered institutions, are turning to the marketing techniques of big business to lure more students and donations from the private sector.

■ **Segmentation and Branding**: According to a study of 1200 institutions conducted by the University of Pennsylvania's Institute for Research in Higher Education, universities and colleges are sorting themselves into identifiable market segments. "Name-brand" schools, such as Western, Harvard, McGill, Yale, and Princeton, offer comprehensive programs and provide small classes and well-paid faculty but charge students high tuition fees. A second group offers convenience and user friendliness to appeal to students who want quick, less expensive degrees to advance their careers. For example, while an Executive MBA degree costs $13 000 a year at St. Mary's, students pay $52 000 for the same degree program at Queen's or Western. A third group offers highly specialized programs aimed at niche markets. The University of Calgary, for instance, has built its reputation as a school with a entrepreneurial focus; Dalhousie University offers an MBA program that focuses on the financial services sector; Mount Saint Vincent University in Halifax has a women's focus in all of its programs; Queen's School of Business has a one-year MBA program aimed at students with undergraduate degrees in science and technology. Montreal's École des Hautes Études Commerciales (HEC), Canada's largest business school, prides itself on being the only business school originally established by the private sector.

■ **Sales Pitches**: These days it isn't enough to turn out course catalogues with titles like "Chaucer and His Times," or "Introduction to Evolutionary Biology," or "Twentieth-Century Fiction." Instead, catalogues list snappy course titles like "Great Hits of Medieval Literature," "Dinosaurs, Mass Extinctions, and Other Headlines from the History of Life," and "Really Fantastic Fiction." Some educators view course titles such as these as the natural result of a system that pressures professors to market themselves and their courses. And the professorial marketing isn't over when the course catalogue is published; many professors are also pressured to become "entertainers" in the classroom.

■ **Advertising Campaigns**: Traditional university marketing efforts could hardly have been called marketing, as we understand it. "Registration begins on Monday," or "Take this

Effective Communication for Business and Professional Women

presented by the Centre for Women in Business Mount Saint Vincent University with Professor Judith Scrimger, Department of Public Relations

In a single day you will learn to:
• apply the components of effective communication
• use non-verbal communication to your advantage
• create power through language
• chair an effective meeting
• enhance your professional image
To register and for more information call

(902) 457-6449

Turbo Days
Powerful professional development for women

April 21, 1999
8:30 am - 4:30 pm
Mount Saint Vincent University, Halifax
$129.00 per person plus HST – Lunch Included

course and get a good job," were some typical "marketing" messages. Contrast that with the all-out marketing blitzes conducted by universities vying for executive students in both Europe and North America. Executive MBA programs, such as those offered by the Rotterdam School of Management at Erasmus University, Netherlands, the Richard Ivey School of Business at the University of Western Ontario, or the School of Business at Queen's University compete for the best students using newspaper advertising, advertorials in magazines such as *Canadian Business,* direct marketing and sales presentations, one-to-one recruiting meetings, videos, glossy brochures, and promises of international trips to round out their programs.

■ **New Channels of Distribution:** Universities no longer have to restrict their enrollment to the number of students they can fit into their physical classrooms. "Distance education" is becoming a new competitive buzzword. Universities as diverse as Athabasca University in Alberta and Heriot-Watt University in Edinburgh, Scotland are offering interactive programs through video-conferencing facilities. Since 1995, the Executive Education Network has beamed courses by satellite from major U.S. universities, such as Harvard and the University of California, directly into Canadian corporations such as the Royal Bank.

- **Merchandising:** The commercialization of universities isn't just an American phenomenon. In the U.K. at Oxford Ltd., projected sales of official merchandise exceeded £4 million in 1997. By licensing and franchising its redesigned and trademarked "brand logo" to commercial third parties, prestigious Oxford University watched income from merchandising double in the past three years. Interestingly, the merchandising is an international venture; Oxford Ltd. sells 75 percent of its merchandise in Southeast Asia and Japan, where teens snap up branded apparel.

- **Quality and Accountability Initiatives:** Faced with sharp cuts in university appropriations, the University of Florida at Gainesville has remodelled itself after a corporation. Defying traditional academic notions, all departments now vie openly for resources. Departments that meet quality and productivity criteria win shares of $3 million (US) in discretionary funding. Such measures are hardly popular with faculty, many of whom are not used to justifying their use of funds.

- **Sponsorship:** Universities and community colleges have begun to realize that fewer corporations are willing to make "no-strings-attached" donations. Some institutions, therefore, are responding by offering sponsorship opportunities to private-sector firms. York University's Atkinson College, for example, viewed this as a cost-effective way to support its move to put degree courses on the Internet. For a fee, companies can put their logos on written course material as well as showing it on-line. Seeking corporate sponsorship has not been without controversy, however. Many educators believe that there are ethical issues with exposing captive student audiences to corporate messages. Others believe that having a corporate name attached to educational materials will be negatively perceived by the public.

These steps are a mixture of the selling and marketing concepts. Marketing occurs when the university really studies what students need and want and prepares new and improved programs and services. It is only selling if the university or community college just advertises.

Sources: Based on: Jill Borra, "Universities Jockey for New Students," *Financial Post*, November 29, 1997, pp. E1-2, E5. Keith H. Hammonds, "The New U: A Tough Market Is Reshaping Colleges," *Business Week*, December 22, 1997, pp. 96-102. "University Launches Image Campaign," *Marketing News*, March 3, 1997, p. 36. Randy Ray, "How Small Business Schools Go Up Against Heavy Hitters," *Globe and Mail Report on Executive Education*, August 19, 1997, p. C4. Oliver Swanton, "Higher Education: Pocahontas, Eat Your Heart Out. You've Read the Course Books, Now Buy the T-shirt: Oliver Swanton Reports on the Universities Turning to Disney-style Merchandising," *The Guardian*, February 25, 1997, EDUCATION, vi: 1. William H. Honan, "The Dry Yields to the Droll," *New York Times*, July 3, 1996, B, 7:1. Erica Zlomislic, "Sponsorship: York May Get Sponsored Courses," *Strategy: The Canadian Marketing Report*, February 17, 1997, p. 1.

3. *Unstated needs* (the customer expects good service from the dealer)

4. *Delight needs* (the customer would like the dealer to include a gift of a road atlas)

5. *Secret needs* (the customer wants to be seen by friends as a savvy consumer)

Responding only to the stated need may shortchange the customer. A woman enters a hardware store and asks for a sealant to seal glass window panes. This customer is stating a *solution*, not a need. The salesperson might suggest that tape would provide a better solution. The customer may appreciate that the salesperson met her need, not her stated solution.

A distinction needs to be drawn between *responsive marketing, anticipative marketing* and *creative marketing*. A responsive marketer finds a stated need and fills it. An anticipative marketer looks ahead into what needs customers may have in the near future. A creative marketer discovers and produces solutions customers did not ask for but to which they enthusiastically respond. Hamel and Prahalad believe that companies must go beyond just asking consumers what they want. They note that customers are notoriously lacking in foresight and ask how many of us were demanding cellular telephones, fax machines, 24-hour discount brokerage accounts, compact disc players, cars with on-board navigation systems, hand-held global satellite positioning receivers, automated teller machines, or the Home Shopping Network 10 years ago?[25]

Sony exemplifies a creative marketer because it has introduced many successful new products that customers never asked for or even thought were possible: Walkmans, VCRs, videocameras, CDs, and so on. Sony goes beyond customer-led marketing; it is a *market-driving* firm, not just a market-driven firm. Akio Morita, its founder, proclaimed that he doesn't serve markets; he creates markets.[26]

Why is it supremely important to satisfy target customers? Because a company's sales each period come from two groups: new customers and repeat customers. One estimate is that attracting a new customer can cost five times as much as pleasing an existing one.[27] And it might cost 16 times as much to bring the new customer to the same level of profitability as the lost customer. *Customer retention* is thus more important than *customer attraction*.

Integrated Marketing

When all the company's departments work together to serve the customer's interests, the result is *integrated marketing*. Unfortunately, not all employees are trained and motivated to work for the customer. An engineer once complained that the salespeople are "always protecting the customer and not thinking of the company's interest"! He went on to blast customers for "asking for too much." The following example highlights the coordination problem:

> *The marketing vice-president of a major European airline wants to increase the airline's traffic share. His strategy is to build up customer satisfaction through providing better food, cleaner cabins, better-trained cabin crews, and lower fares. Yet he has no authority in these matters. The catering department chooses food that keeps down food costs; the maintenance department uses cleaning services that keep down cleaning costs; the human resources department hires people without regard to whether they are naturally friendly; the finance department sets the fares. Since these departments generally take a cost or production point of view, he is stymied in creating an integrated marketing mix.*

Integrated marketing takes place on two levels. First, the various marketing functions—sales force, advertising, customer service, product management, marketing research—must work together. Too often the sales force thinks product managers set prices or sale quotas "too high"; or the advertising director and a brand manager cannot agree on an advertising campaign. All these marketing functions must be coordinated from the customer's point of view.

Second, marketing must be embraced by the other departments; they must also "think customer." According to David Packard of Hewlett Packard: "Marketing is far too important to be left only to the marketing department!" Marketing is not a department so much as a company-wide orientation. Xerox goes so far as to include in every job description an explanation of how that job affects the customer. Xerox factory managers know that visits to the factory can help sell a potential customer if the factory is clean and efficient. Xerox accountants know that customer attitudes are affected by Xerox's billing accuracy and promptness in returning calls.

Xerox Canada
www.xerox.ca

To foster teamwork among all departments, the company carries out internal marketing as well as external marketing. *External marketing* is marketing directed at people outside the company. *Internal marketing* is the task of hiring, training, and motivating able employees who want to serve customers well. In fact, internal marketing must precede external marketing. It makes no sense to promise excellent service before the company's staff is ready to provide it.

Managers who believe the customer is the company's only true "profit centre" consider the traditional organization chart in Figure 1-8(a)—a pyramid with the president at the top, management in the middle, and front-line people at the bottom—obsolete. Master marketing companies invert the chart, as shown in Figure 1-8(b). At the top are the customers; next in importance are the front-line people who meet, serve, and satisfy the customers; under them are the middle managers, whose job is to support the frontline people so they can serve the customers well; and at the base is top management, whose job is to hire and support good middle managers. We have added customers along the sides of Figure 1-8(b) to indicate that all the company's managers must be personally involved in knowing, meeting, and serving customers.

Profitability

The ultimate purpose of the marketing concept is to help organizations achieve their objectives. In the case of private firms, the major objective is profit; in the case of nonprofit and public organizations, it is surviving and attracting enough funds to

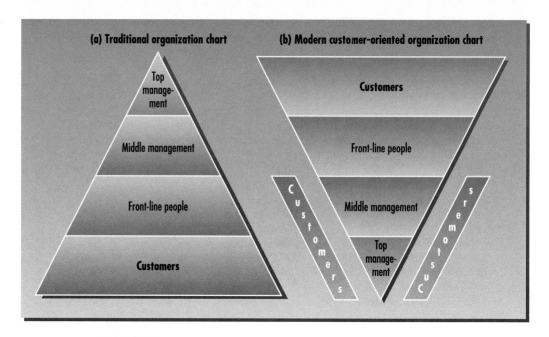

(a) Traditional organization chart

- Top management
- Middle management
- Front-line people
- Customers

(b) Modern customer-oriented organization chart

- Customers
- Front-line people
- Middle management
- Top management

Customers

Customers

F I G U R E 1.8

Traditional Organization Chart versus Modern Customer-Oriented Company Organization Chart

perform useful work. Private firms should not aim for profits as such but to achieve profits as a consequence of creating superior customer value. A company makes money by satisfying customer needs better than its competitors. Consider Frank Perdue's philosophy:

■ **Perdue Chicken Farms**   Perdue Farms is a $2.25-billion chicken business whose margins are substantially above the industry average and whose market shares in its major markets reach 50 percent. And the product is chicken—a commodity if there ever was one! Yet its colourful founder, Frank Perdue, does not believe that "a chicken is a chicken is a chicken," nor do his customers. The company has always aimed to produce tender-tasting chickens for which discriminating customers will pay a price premium. Perdue controls the breeding operation to produce a quality bird with distinct characteristics. Its chickens are raised on a chemical-free and steroid-free diet. Recent advertising campaigns emphasize the values of freshness and quality that the company has promoted through the years. "After three generations, the Perdues know more about breeding chickens than chickens do," says one of the ads."[28]

How many companies actually practice the marketing concept? Unfortunately, too few. Only a handful of companies stand out as master marketers: Air Canada, Procter & Gamble, Disney, Bombardier, Nordstrom, Wal-Mart, Milliken, McDonald's, Marriott Hotels, and several Japanese (Sony, Toyota, Canon) and European companies (IKEA, Club Med, Bang & Olufsen, Electrolux, Nokia, ABB, Lego). These companies focus on the customer and are organized to respond effectively to changing customer needs. They all have well-staffed marketing departments, and all their other departments—manufacturing, finance, research and development, personnel, and purchasing—also accept the concept that the customer rules.

Most companies do not embrace the marketing concept until driven to it by circumstances. Various developments may compel them to take the marketing concept to heart:

- *Sales decline:* When sales fall, companies panic and look for answers. Today, newspapers are experiencing declining circulation as more people rely on radio, TV, and the Internet for their news. Some publishers now realize that they know little about why people read newspapers. Publishers, like those at the *National Post*, are commissioning consumer research and attempting to redesign newspapers to be contemporary, relevant, and interesting to readers. They are also starting Web pages.

- *Slow growth:* Slow sales growth leads some companies to search for new markets. They realize they need marketing skill to identify and select new opportunities. Wanting new sources of revenue, Dow Chemical entered consumer markets and invested heavily to acquire consumer marketing expertise to perform well in these markets.

- *Changing buying patterns:* Many companies operate in markets characterized by rapidly changing customer wants. These companies need more marketing know-how if they are to track buyers' changing values.

- *Increasing competition:* Complacent companies may suddenly be attacked by powerful competitors. Bell Canada was a regulated, marketing-naive telephone company until the 1970s, when the government began allowing other companies to sell telecommunications equipment. Bell plunged into the marketing waters and hired the best marketers it could find to help it compete. Companies in deregulated industries all find it necessary to build up marketing expertise.[29]

- *Increasing marketing expenditures:* Companies may find their expenditures for advertising, sales promotion, marketing research, and customer service are expensive and ineffective. Management then decides it is time to undertake an audit to improve its marketing.[30]

In the course of converting to a marketing orientation, a company faces three hurdles: organized resistance, slow learning, and fast forgetting.

Some company departments (often manufacturing, finance, and R&D) believe that a stronger marketing function threatens their power in the organization. The nature of the threat is illustrated in Figure 1-9(a) through (e). Initially, the marketing function is viewed as one of several equally important functions in a check-and-balance relationship. Lack of demand leads marketers to argue that their function is more important. A few enthusiasts go further and say marketing is the major function of the enterprise, for without customers there would be no company. Enlightened marketers clarify the issue by putting the customer rather than marketing at the centre of the company. They argue for a customer orientation in which all functions work together to respond to, serve, and satisfy the customer. Some marketers say that marketing still needs to command a central position if customers' needs are to be correctly interpreted and efficiently satisfied. See the Marketing Memo "Reasons to Embrace the Marketing Concept."

Resistance is especially strong in industries where marketing is being introduced for the first time—for instance, in law offices, universities, deregulated industries, and government agencies. But in spite of resistance, many companies manage to introduce some marketing thinking into their organization. The company president establishes a marketing department; marketing talent is hired; key managers attend marketing seminars; the marketing budget is substantially increased; marketing planning and control systems are introduced. Even with these steps, however, learning comes slowly.

And even after marketing has been installed, management must fight a tendency to forget basic principles, especially in the wake of success. For example, many North American companies entered European markets in the 1950s and 1960s expecting to achieve outstanding success with their sophisticated products and marketing capabilities. A number of them failed because they forgot the basic marketing maxim: *Know your target market and how to satisfy it.* North American companies introduced their current products and advertising programs instead of adapting them. General Mills introduced its Betty Crocker cake mixes in Britain only to withdraw them a short time later—angel food cake and devil's food cake sounded too exotic for British consumers. And many Britons felt that the perfect-looking cakes pictured on the packages must be too hard to make.

(a) Marketing as an equal function

(b) Marketing as a more important function

(c) Marketing as the major function

(d) The customer as the controlling function

(e) The customer as the controlling function and marketing as the integrative function

FIGURE 1.9

Evolving Views of Marketing's Role in the Company

Reasons to Embrace the Marketing Concept

The marketer's argument for embracing the marketing concept is simple:

1. The company's assets have little value without the existence of customers.

2. The key company task is therefore to attract and retain customers.

3. Customers are attracted through competitively superior offerings and retained through satisfaction.

4. Marketing's task is to develop a superior offering and deliver customer satisfaction.

5. Customer satisfaction is affected by the performance of the other departments.

6. Marketing needs to influence these other departments to cooperate in delivering customer satisfaction.

Companies face a particularly difficult task in adapting ad slogans to international markets. Perdue's slogan—"It takes a tough man to make a tender chicken"—was rendered into Spanish as "It takes a sexually excited man to make a chick affectionate." And, even when the language is the same, words carry different meanings: Electrolux's British ad line for its vacuum cleaners—"Nothing sucks like an Electrolux"—would certainly not lure customers in North America![31]

THE SOCIETAL MARKETING CONCEPT

Some have questioned whether the marketing concept is an appropriate philosophy in an age of environmental deterioration, resource shortages, explosive population growth, world hunger and poverty, and neglected social services. Are companies that do an excellent job of satisfying consumer wants necessarily acting in the best long-run interests of consumers and society? The marketing concept sidesteps the potential conflicts among consumer wants, consumer interests, and long-run societal welfare.

Consider the following criticism:

> *The fast-food hamburger industry offers tasty but unhealthful food. The hamburgers have a high fat content, and the restaurants promote fries and pies, two products high in starch and fat. The products are wrapped in convenient packaging, which leads to much waste. In satisfying consumer wants, these restaurants may be hurting consumer health and causing environmental problems.*

Situations like this one call for a new term that enlarges the marketing concept. Among those suggested are "humanistic marketing" and "ecological marketing." We propose calling it the societal marketing concept.

■ The ***societal marketing concept*** holds that the organization's task is to determine the needs, wants, and interests of target markets and to deliver the desired satisfactions more effectively and efficiently than competitors in a way that preserves or enhances the consumer's and the society's well-being.

The societal marketing concept calls upon marketers to build social and ethical considerations into their marketing practices. They must balance and juggle the often conflicting criteria of company profits, consumer want satisfaction, and public interest. Yet a number of companies have achieved notable sales and profit gains by adopting and practising the societal marketing concept. Two pioneers of the societal marketing concept are Loblaw Companies and The Body Shop. But, as recent events show, even they encounter difficulties.

Loblaw Cos.
www.loblaw.com

■ **Loblaw.** Pat Carson is the vice-president of environmental affairs for Toronto-based Loblaw Cos. As part of this role, he spearheaded the company's green-product development program in the 1980s. The products were endorsed by the firm's high-profile pitchman, Dave Nichol. The initiatives brought a storm of attention from competitors, consumers, environmentalists, and the media. Some sang Loblaw's praises; others damned the firm for its flagrant commercialism of legitimate environmental concerns. But where are green products today? They only account for 0.3 percent of Loblaw sales. Don Watt of the Watt Group, who helped Loblaw develop the initial green line, explains,—"Everybody has forgotten about green products." Pat Carson confesses that the firm made some mistakes (like "biodegradable plastic garbage bags that didn't biodegrade"), but argues that it also brought out a lot of good products—such as the recycled paper products—that still occupy store shelves today. Moreover, Loblaw was instrumental in increasing environmental awareness among both its suppliers and its consumers. Today, Loblaw and other firms that mimicked its stance have taken on a subtler form of green positioning, says Carson. "They've incorporated environmental practices into the core of their operations: recycling programs, reduced-waste and clean-water programs." Carson views Loblaw as taking a holistic view of what it means to be green today. It has a broader meaning, he believes. It is not just products but almost any action that demonstrates a company is socially responsible.[32]

■ **The Body Shop.** In 1976, Anita Roddick opened The Body Shop in Brighton, England, as a tiny storefront selling beauty products out of urine sample bottles. Today The Body Shop boasts over 1600 branches in 47 countries. It opened its first outlets in Canada in 1980. The company created a market for natural-ingredient cosmetics packaged in simple recyclable containers. Today, its success is being mimicked by competitors such as Bath & Body Works, Aveda, and Origins. From its inception, the company has focused on social issues as well as business demands. Its campaigns against human rights abuses, animal testing of cosmetics, and stereotypes of beauty perpetuated by the rest of the cosmetic industry have brought it both criticism and praise. Even efforts like its "Community Trade" program, an effort aimed at developing sustainable trading relationships with communities in need around the world has drawn heated debate. Declining store sales in the early 1990s jolted The Body Shop into some new management and marketing moves. Outspoken Anita Roddick stepped down as CEO, though she is still actively involved in crafting the social agenda. The company has revamped its stores, winning the prestigious Retail Week Store Design of the Year award. Its dynamic new product development division has been responsible for a host of new product winners—everything from a line of nail colours to hair mascara. It has added catalogues to its merchandising initiatives and it has started advertising—a tactic shunned in its early years. Its efforts are paying off, however. Its worldwide sales jumped five percent in 1996-97 alone.

Body Shop Canada
www.thebodyshop.ca

Other companies practise a form of the societal marketing concept called cause-related marketing. Pringle and Thompson define this as "activity by which a company with an image, product, or service to market builds a relationship or partnership with a 'cause' or a number of 'causes', for mutual benefit."[33] They see it as affording an opportunity for companies to enhance their corporate reputation, raise brand awareness, increase customer loyalty, build sales, and increase press coverage. They believe that customers will increasingly look for demonstrations of good corporate citizenship. Smart companies will respond by adding "higher-order" image attributes rather than simply rational and emotional benefits. Some critics, however, complain that cause-related marketing might make consumers feel they have fulfilled their philanthropic duties by buying a product instead of donating directly to chosen causes.

HOW BUSINESS AND MARKETING ARE CHANGING

We can say with some confidence that "the marketplace isn't what it used to be." It is changing radically as a result of major societal forces such as technological advances, globalization, and deregulation. These major forces have created new behaviours and challenges:

Customers increasingly expect higher quality and service and some customization. They perceive fewer real product differences and show less brand loyalty. They can obtain extensive product information from the Internet and other sources, enabling them to shop more intelligently. They are showing greater price sensitivity in their search for value.

Brand manufacturers are facing intense competition from domestic and foreign brands, which is resulting in rising promotion costs and shrinking profit margins. They are being further buffeted by powerful retailers who command limited shelf space and are putting out their own store brands in competition with national brands.

Store-based retailers are suffering from an oversaturation of retailing. Small retailers are succumbing to the growing power of giant retailers and "category killers." Store-based retailers are facing growing competition from catalogue houses; direct mail firms; newspaper, magazine, and TV direct-to-customer ads; home shopping TV; and the Internet. As a result, they are experiencing shrinking margins. In response, entrepreneurial retailers, like Chapters and Indigo, are building entertainment into stores with coffee bars, lectures, demonstrations, and performances. They are marketing an "experience" rather than a product assortment.

COMPANY RESPONSES AND ADJUSTMENTS

Companies are doing a lot of soul-searching, and many highly respected companies are changing in a number of ways. Here are some current trends:

- **Re-engineering.** From focusing on functional departments to reorganizing into multidiscipline teams, each managing a key business process.
- **Outsourcing.** From making everything inside the company to buying more goods and services from outside if they can be obtained better and more cheaply. A few companies are moving toward outsourcing everything, making them *virtual companies* owning very few assets and therefore earning extraordinary rates of return.
- **E-Commerce.** From attracting customers to stores and having salespeople call on offices to making virtually all products available on the Internet. Consumers can access pictures of products, read the specs, shop among online vendors for the best prices and terms, and click to order and pay. Business-to-business purchasing is growing fast on the Net. Purchasing agents can use bookmarked websites to shop for routine items. Personal selling can increasingly be conducted electronically, with buyer and seller seeing each other on their computer screens in real time.
- **Benchmarking.** From relying on self-improvement to studying "world-class performers" and adopting "best practices."
- **Alliances.** From trying to win alone to forming networks of partner firms.
- **Partner-suppliers.** From using many suppliers to using fewer but more reliable suppliers who work closely in a "partnership" relationship with the company.
- **Market-centred.** From organizing by products to organizing by market segment.
- **Global and local.** From being local to being both global and local.
- **Decentralized.** From being managed from the top to encouraging more initiative and "intrepreneurship" at the local level.

MARKETER RESPONSES AND ADJUSTMENTS

Marketers too are rethinking their philosophies, concepts, and tools. Here are the major marketing themes as the millennium approaches:

- **Relationship marketing.** From focusing on transactions to building long-term, profitable customer relationships. Companies focus on their most profitable customers, products, and channels.
- **Customer lifetime value.** From making a profit on each sale to making profits by managing customer lifetime value. Some companies offer to deliver a constantly needed product on a regular basis at a lower price per unit because they will enjoy the customer's business for a longer period.
- **Customer share.** From a focus on gaining market share to a focus on building customer share. Companies build customer share by offering a larger variety of goods to their existing customers. They train their employees in cross-selling and up-selling.
- **Target marketing.** From selling to everyone to trying to be the best firm serving well-defined target markets. Target marketing is being facilitated by the proliferation of special interest magazines, TV channels, and Internet newsgroups.
- **Individualization.** From selling the same offer in the same way to everyone in the target market to individualizing and customizing messages and offerings. Customers will be able to design their own product features on the company's web page.

- **Customer database.** From collecting sales data to building a rich *data warehouse* of information about individual customers' purchases, preferences, demographics, and profitability. Companies can "data-mine" their proprietary databases to detect different customer need clusters and make differentiated offerings to each cluster.

- **Integrated marketing communications.** From heavy reliance on one communication tool such as advertising or salesforce to blending several tools to deliver a consistent brand image to customers at every brand contact.

- **Channels as partners.** From thinking of intermediaries as customers to treating them as partners in delivering value to final customers.

- **Every employee a marketer.** From thinking that marketing is done only by marketing, sales, and customer support personnel to recognizing that every employee must be customer-focused.

- **Model-based decision making.** From making decisions on intuition or slim data to basing decisions on models and facts on how the marketplace works.

These major themes will be examined throughout *Marketing Management* to help marketers and companies sail safely through the rough but promising waters ahead. Successful companies will be those who can keep their marketing changing as fast as their marketplace—and marketspace.

SUMMARY

1. Businesses today face three major challenges and opportunities: globalization, advances in technology, and deregulation.

2. Marketing is typically seen as the task of creating, promoting, and delivering goods and services to consumers and businesses. Effective marketing can take many forms: it can be entrepreneurial, formulated, and intrepreneurial. And marketers are involved in marketing many types of entities: goods, services, experiences, events, persons, places, properties, organizations, information, ideas.

3. Marketers are skilled at managing demand: they seek to influence the level, timing, and composition of demand. To do this, they face a host of decisions, from major ones such as what features a new product should have to minor ones such as the colour of packaging. They also operate in four different marketplaces: consumer, business, global, and nonprofit.

4. For each chosen target market, a firm develops a market offering that is positioned in the minds of buyers as delivering some central benefits.

Marketers must try to understand the target market's needs, wants, and demands: A product or offering will be successful if it delivers value and satisfaction to the target buyer. The term "markets" covers various groupings of customers. Today there are both physical marketplaces and digital marketspaces, as well as mega-markets.

5. Exchange involves obtaining a desired product from someone by offering something in return. A transaction is a trade of values between two or more parties: it involves at least two things of value, agreed-upon conditions, a time of agreement, and a place of agreement. In the most generic sense, marketers seek to elicit a behavioural response from another party: a purchase, a vote, active membership, adoption of a cause.

6. Relationship marketing has the aim of building long-term mutually satisfying relations with key parties—customers, suppliers, distributors—in order to earn and retain their long-term preference and business. The ultimate outcome of relationship marketing is the building of a unique company asset called a marketing network.

7. Marketers reach their markets through various channels—communication, distribution, trade, selling. Marketers operate in several environments, one of which includes the competition, all the actual and potential rival offerings and substitutes a buyer might consider. The set of tools marketers use to elicit the desired responses from their target markets is called the marketing mix.

8. There are five competing concepts under which organizations can choose to conduct their business: the production concept, the product concept, the selling/sales concept, the marketing concept, and the societal marketing concept. The first three concepts are of limited in scope. The *marketing concept* holds that the key to achieving organizational goals consists of determining the needs and wants of target markets and delivering the desired satisfactions more effectively and efficiently than competitors. It starts with a well-defined market, focuses on customer needs, coordinates all the activities that will affect customers, and produces profits by satisfying customers.

9. In recent years, some have questioned whether the marketing concept is an appropriate philosophy in a world faced with major demographic and environmental challenges. The societal marketing concept holds that the organization's task is to determine the needs, wants, and interests of target markets and to deliver the desired satisfactions more effectively and efficiently than competitors in a way that preserves or enhances the consumer's and the society's well-being. The concept calls upon marketers to balance three considerations: company profits, consumer want satisfaction, and public interest.

APPLICATIONS

CHAPTER CONCEPTS

1. Relationship marketing is one of the hottest trends in marketing today, and you will find this concept integrated throughout this book. Experts have defined the term in many ways—but—the bottom line is always "getting to know your customers (clients, publics, etc.) better so you can meet their wants and needs better."

   Keep a record of the next four transactions in which you participate, and classify each one as very satisfying, satisfying, adequate, dissatisfying, or very dissatisfying. For those experiences that you found dissatisfying, what could the company or salesperson have done better? For those that you find satisfying, what specific factors led to your satisfaction?

2. Describe the marketing mixes used by each of the organizations listed below. For information, check general business publications such as *Canadian Business*, specialized publications such as *Marketing, Advertising Age,* and *Restaurant News*, and each company's website. Specifically, what is each company or organization's approach to product, price, place, and promotion?
   a. Outward Bound
   b. Canon Copiers
   c. Intrawest
   d. Newbridge Networks

3. Russell Stover, a manufacturer of moderately priced chocolates sold in drug stores and discount chains, is looking to improve its market share. How might Russell Stover team with Hallmark to accomplish its goals? What benefits would Russell Stover receive? What benefits would Hallmark receive? If the two companies were to enter into an alliance, how might they develop advertisements that promote both their products?

1. The Air Canada ad in Figure 1 stresses the time-saving aspect of its flights between the United States and Canada as well as the frequent-flyer mileage benefits. How do these two elements affect the ratio of benefits to cost in the value equation? Other than advertising lower ticket prices, how else can Air Canada use its advertising to affect the value perceived by customers? Suggest at least two specific value-enhancing approaches Air Canada might take.

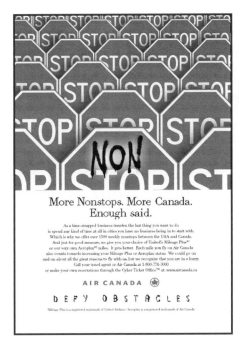

Figure 1

Figure 2

2. As shown in Figure 2, the marketing network of Dow Chemical Company consists of a wide range of stakeholders, including customers, employees, suppliers, distributors, and volunteers and beneficiaries of nonprofit organizations such as Habitat for Humanity. Why would Dow advertise its support of Habitat for Humanity? What effect does the company expect this ad to have on its relationships with stakeholders? How can Dow build on strong stakeholder relationships to compete more effectively in the construction industry?

FOCUS ON TECHNOLOGY

Sophisticated information technology systems are helping master marketers such as the Toronto Dominion Bank make accurate, complete, up-to-date customer data available to the front-line employees who work with customers on a daily basis. Today, Toronto Dominion is much more than a bank. It is also a giant discount brokerage firm offering a wide range of investment and financial services options. When someone visits a Toronto Dominion branch or calls the company, employees can immediately bring up that customer's online records and talk knowledgeably about investments and services suited to that customer's individual situation. Account representatives at TD show customers how to open accounts, locate financial research, place trades, and track market trends on its website.

Browse the TD Investment Services website (http://www.tdbank.ca/tdbank/investctr). How does this website confirm TD's focus on the customer? How does this site compare to that of its American rivals like Charles Schwab, the San Francisco discount brokerage giant (http://www.schwab.com). Look at the on-line demonstration of Schwab's capabilities. Why is employee access to complete and current customer records especially important in the brokerage business? What other parts of the Toronto Dominion Bank must be properly coordinated to ensure integrated marketing for customer satisfaction?

MARKETING FOR THE 21ST CENTURY

E-commerce is growing exponentially because of its convenience, savings, selection, personalization, and information. Over one-half of the Canadian population is connected to the Internet, and over one-quarter surf the Web each week. Still, figuring out exactly how to reach the right cybercustomers can be challenging for even the largest marketers.

IAB Canada forecasts that Internet advertising spending will leap to $56.9 million in 1999. This figure is down from their earlier estimate on on-line ad spending because the cost of banner ads is dropping. In 1998, DoubleClick Canada reported that advertisers paid $45 per 1000 impressions (CPM); in 1999, rates have fallen to $30–$35 (CPM).

Kraft Foods, Kellogg, and other companies are learning to use targeted banner advertising to reach the customer segments most likely to be interested in their products. In the United States, these companies boosted online sales significantly by placing banner ads on Peapod, an Internet-based grocery shopping service. In Canada, some firms, such as IBM, Microsoft, and AT&T, are placing banner ads on the government's

Chapters' award-winning web site attracts a lot of banner advertising.

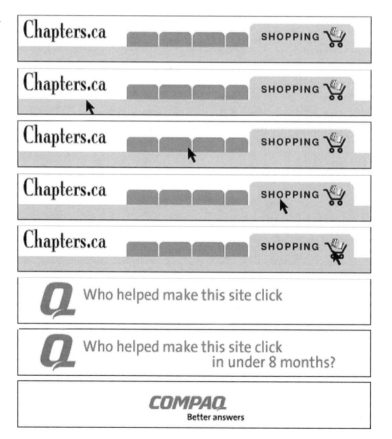

National Graduate Register website (http://www.ngr.schoolnet.ca) in the hopes of better targeting new university graduates. Untargeted ad banners, by comparison, are inexpensive but draw less customer response.

While some analysts believe banner ads are ineffective, other research suggests that they are as effective as television advertising. A research study jointly undertaken by America Online and Ipsos-ASI reported that 40 percent of the participants in the study viewing a banner ad remembered it, compared to 41 percent who viewed a 30-second television ad.

Visit a site that features banner advertising. For example, try http://www.ca.yahoo.com or http://www.chapters.ca (see the photo of the banner ad on page 32). As you search the site and use different items from the site menus, or search the site using your own key words, note the banner ads that appear. Are they linked to the areas you searched? Are these advertisements effective? What types of products could potentially benefit from advertising on the site you have chosen? What kind of information would these marketers want from the site owner?[34]

Building Customer Satisfaction and Retention

0-60 in 8.2 seconds. Who says nice folks always finish last?

Apparently, those gentle engineers at Saturn also have an aggressive side too. Just look what they've done with the new, larger L-Series. First, a techie description of the LS2: 3.0-litre, DOHC 182-horsepower V6 engine. Electronically controlled four-speed automatic transmission. Four-wheel disc brakes, and sport-tuned suspension. The layman's description: a blast to drive. Of course, it still comes with Saturn innovations like rust and dent resistant polymer panels, steel modified spaceframe, no hassle no haggle buying experience, and 30 day money-back guarantee. Saturn LS sedans start at $20,075 and the LS2 model shown at $26,940. (MSRPs exclude licence, taxes, and registration.) Your nearest Saturn Retailer has the keys for a test drive. (Just promise not to bring that lead foot.) A DIFFERENT KIND of COMPANY. A DIFFERENT KIND of CAR.

PROFILE:

Canadian Marketing Excellence

Saturn. Chuck Novak, brand manager for Saturn Canada, lives and breathes relationship marketing. The excitement in his voice when he talks about the upcoming launch of a new Saturn model or the loyalty programs he has helped to build lets you know immediately that he loves working for a "different kind of company." He also knows that "it is no longer enough to satisfy customers. You must delight them!"

In the late 1980s, Saturn changed the whole buyer-seller relationship with a "new deal" for car buyers. There would be a non-negotiable price and none of the traditional haggling. With careful salesforce selection and training, the normal pitfalls of commission selling can be avoided, Saturn believes. Once a sale is made, the new owner is introduced to everyone at the Saturn retail facility so that he or she knows the head of the service department as well as the person who answers the dealership phone. New Saturn owners don't just show up and drive their car off the lot. The owner gets into their new vehicle in a special delivery module attached to the showroom. Everyone at the Saturn dealership surrounds the new owner for a commemorative photo. Only then do the glass doors open up. The last thing the new owner sees in the rear-view mirror is everyone smiling and waving as he or she drives away.

Saturn was among the first automobile manufacturers to realize that the relationship with the customer must be strong right through the period of ownership. Chuck Novak talks about "moments of truth"—that satisfaction that must be created each and every time the customer comes in contact with Saturn or one of its brand messages. People must be totally comfortable with all elements of Saturn. Because of this, Saturn has one of the most extensive training programs for its car retailers. Saturn salespeople don't push cars; they act as consultants that fit the car to the customers' needs. If they don't think a Saturn is right for the buyer, they tell them so. They don't rush people through the buying process since Saturn wants people to be satisfied. They know it takes four to five visits for a customer to make a decision. Once a purchase is made, Saturn offers a 30-day, total-satisfaction, no-questions-asked guarantee. Saturn pays special attention to current owners. For example, they were allowed to preview the new model even before the national advertising campaign was launched.

Another means whereby Saturn maintains relationships is through its now-famous Drive-In Reunions. These have been powerful, as Saturn's president notes: "Saturn is more than a car. . . . It's a whole new way of doing things, of working with our customers and with one another." Saturn has proven this is more than just hollow rhetoric. Beginning in 1994, Saturn invited Canadian owners and their families to attend drive-in movies to see *Apollo 13*. Thirty-nine thousand people responded to the invitation. Although the event was highly successful, Chuck Novak asked himself, "How does this reflect our commitment to Saturn communities." This question led to Saturn's playground-building program. Because many Saturn owners are families with young children, Saturn's efforts focus on things that enhance children's quality of life. The first program consisted of the car-maker bringing together its staff and the community of Saturn owners to voluntarily build over 50 playgrounds in towns across Canada. When Saturn dedicated the new playground built on the grounds of the Metro Toronto Zoo, 6700 owners and their families participated. Saturn has learned to plan such events for the same time every year since owners often plan their vacations around Saturn activities. It makes people feel part of the Saturn family. "I can't remember my dentist inviting me over," quips Novak. But playgrounds aren't the only things needed by communities. Saturn retailers are the eyes and ears of the company and when a community need arises, Chuck hears about it and tries to respond. For example, Saturn planted

- What are customer value and satisfaction, and how do leading companies produce and deliver them?

- What makes a high-performance business?

- How can companies both retain and attract customers?

- How can companies improve customer profitability?

- How can companies practise total quality management?

trees in areas hard hit by the 1997 ice storm. In North Bay, they provided funds for a new heart-monitoring unit.

Have Saturn's efforts paid off? Just ask Chuck. He can't help but smile when he reads Saturn's loyalty scores. Repurchase rates of Saturn vehicles rival those of Honda Civic and the Toyota Corolla. Not bad for a car introduced into Canada less than 10 years ago!

Source: Chuck Novak, Brand Manager, Saturn Canada provided much of the information for this highlight in an interview with Peggy Cunningham on July 21, 1999. David Bosworth, "GM Attracts Site Seers," *Strategy: The Canadian Marketing Report*, June 22, 1998, p. D1; Sinclair Steward, "Putting the Customer First," *Strategy: The Canadian Marketing Report*, November 9, 1998, p. 21.

Today's companies are facing their toughest competition ever. We argue in Chapter 1 that companies can outperform the competition if they can move from a product and sales philosophy to a marketing philosophy. In this chapter, we spell out in detail how companies can go about winning customers and outperforming competitors. The answer lies in doing a better job of meeting and satisfying customer needs. Only customer-centred companies are adept at building customers, not just products. They are skilled in market engineering, not just product engineering.

Too many companies think that it is the marketing/sales department's job to procure customers. If they cannot, the company draws the conclusion that its marketing people aren't very good. But, in fact, marketing is only one factor in attracting and keeping customers. The best marketing department in the world cannot sell products that are poorly made or services that are poorly conceived and fail to meet anyone's need. The marketing department can be effective only in companies whose various departments and employees have designed and implemented a competitively superior customer value-delivery system.

Take McDonald's. Every day an average of 38 million people visit its 23 500 restaurants in 109 countries. People do not swarm to McDonald's outlets solely because they love the hamburgers. Some other restaurants make better-tasting hamburgers. People are flocking to a system, not a hamburger. Throughout the world, this fine-tuned system delivers a high standard of what McDonald's calls QSCV—quality, service, cleanliness, and value. McDonald's is effective to the extent that it works with its suppliers, franchise owners, employees, and others to deliver exceptionally high value to its customers.[1]

This chapter describes and illustrates the philosophy of the customer-focused firm and value marketing.[2]

McDonald's Restaurants of Canada
www.mcdonalds.com

DEFINING CUSTOMER VALUE AND SATISFACTION

Over 35 years ago, Peter Drucker observed that a company's first task is "to create customers." But today's customers face a vast array of product and brand choices, prices, and suppliers. How do customers make their choices?

We believe that customers estimate which offer will deliver the most value. Customers are value-maximizers within the bounds of search costs and limited knowledge, mobility, and income. They form an expectation of value and act on it. Whether or not the offer lives up to the value expectation affects both satisfaction and repurchase probability.

CUSTOMER VALUE

Our premise is that customers will buy from the firm that they perceive offers the highest customer delivered value (Figure 2-1):

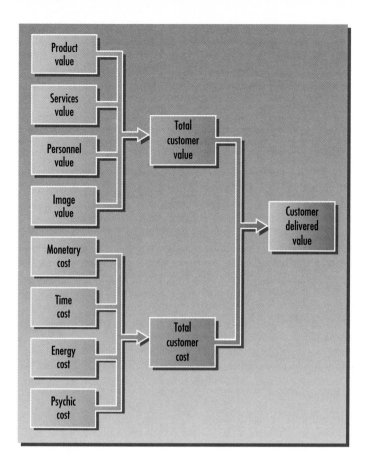

FIGURE 2.1

Determinants of Customer Delivered Value

■ *Customer delivered value* is the difference between total customer value and total customer cost. *Total customer value* is the bundle of benefits customers expect from a given product or service. *Total customer cost* is the bundle of costs customers expect to incur in evaluating, obtaining, using, and disposing of the product or service.

An example will help here. Suppose the buyer for a large construction company wants to buy a tractor. She will buy it from Caterpillar or Komatsu. The competing salespeople carefully describe their respective offers to the buyer. The buyer has a particular application in mind: She wants to use the tractor in residential construction work. She would like the tractor to deliver certain levels of reliability, durability, performance, and resale value. She evaluates the two tractors and decides that Caterpillar has a higher product value based on these criteria. She also perceives differences in the accompanying services—delivery, training, and maintenance—and decides that Caterpillar provides better service. She also perceives Caterpillar's personnel to be more knowledgeable and responsive. Finally, she places higher value on Caterpillar's corporate image. She adds all the values from these four sources—*product, services, personnel*, and *image*—and perceives Caterpillar as offering more total customer value.

Does she buy the Caterpillar tractor? Not necessarily. She also examines her total cost of transacting with Caterpillar versus Komatsu. The total cost consists of more than the monetary cost. As Adam Smith observed over two centuries ago, "The real price of anything is the toil and trouble of acquiring it." In addition to *monetary cost*, total customer cost includes the buyer's *time, energy,* and *psychic costs*. The buyer evaluates these costs along with the monetary cost to form a picture of total customer cost. After calculating the costs, the buyer considers whether Caterpillar's total customer cost is too high in relation to the total customer value Caterpillar delivers. If it is, the buyer might choose the Komatsu tractor. The buyer will buy from whoever offers the highest delivered value.

Now let's use this theory of buyer decision making to help Caterpillar succeed in selling its tractor to this buyer. Caterpillar can improve its offer in three ways. First, it can increase total customer value by improving product, services, personnel, and/or image benefits. Second, it can reduce the buyer's non-monetary costs by lessening the time, energy, and psychic costs. Third, it can reduce its product's monetary cost to the buyer.

Suppose Caterpillar concludes that the buyer sees Caterpillar's offer as worth $20 000. Further, suppose Caterpillar's cost of producing the tractor is $14 000. This means that Caterpillar's offer potentially generates $6000 over the company's cost ($20 000 minus $14 000).

Caterpillar needs to charge a price between $14 000 and $20 000. If it charges less than $14 000, it won't cover its costs. If it charges more than $20 000, it will price itself out of the market. The price Caterpillar charges will determine how much value will be delivered to the buyer and how much will flow to Caterpillar. For example, if Caterpillar charges $19 000, it is granting $1000 of customer delivered value and keeping $5000 for itself. The lower Caterpillar sets its price, the higher is the delivered value and, therefore, the higher is the customer's incentive to purchase.

Given that Caterpillar wants to win the sale, it must offer more delivered value than Komatsu does. Delivered value can be measured as a difference or a ratio. If total customer value is $20 000 and total customer cost is $16 000, then the delivered value is $4000 (measured as a difference) or 1.25 (measured as a ratio). Ratios that are used to compare offers are often called *value/price ratios*.[3]

Some marketers might argue that the process we've described is too rational. They cite examples where buyers did not choose the offer with the highest delivered value. Suppose the customer chose the Komatsu tractor. How can we explain this choice? Here are three possibilities:

1. The buyer might be under orders to buy at the lowest price. The buyer is prevented from making a choice based on delivered value. The Caterpillar salesperson's task is to convince the buyer's manager that buying on price alone will result in lower long-term profits.

2. The buyer will retire before the company realizes that the Komatsu tractor is more expensive to operate than the Caterpillar tractor. The buyer will look good in the short run; she is maximizing personal benefit. The salesperson's task is to convince other people in the customer company that Caterpillar's offer delivers greater long-term value.

3. The buyer enjoys a long-term friendship with the Komatsu salesperson. In this case, Caterpillar's salesperson needs to show the buyer that the Komatsu tractor will draw complaints from the tractor operators when they discover its high fuel cost and need for frequent repairs.

The point of these examples is clear: Buyers operate under various constraints and occasionally make choices that give more weight to their personal benefit than to the company's benefit. However, delivered-value maximization is a useful framework that applies to many situations and yields rich insights. Here are its implications: First, the seller must assess the total customer value and total customer cost associated with each competitor's offer to know how his or her own offer rates in the buyer's mind. Second, the seller who is at a delivered-value disadvantage has two alternatives. She can try to increase total customer value or decrease total customer cost. The former calls for strengthening or augmenting the offer's product, services, personnel, and/or image benefits. The latter calls for reducing the buyer's costs by reducing the price, simplifying the ordering and delivery process, or absorbing some buyer risk by offering a warranty.

CUSTOMER SATISFACTION

Whether the buyer is satisfied after purchase depends on the offer's performance in relation to the buyer's expectations. In general:

- **Satisfaction** is a person's feelings of pleasure or disappointment resulting from comparing a product's perceived performance (or outcome) in relation to his or her expectations.

As this definition makes clear, satisfaction is a function of *perceived performance* and *expectations*. If the performance falls short of expectations, the customer is dissatisfied. If the performance matches the expectations, the customer is satisfied. If the performance exceeds expectations, the customer is highly satisfied or delighted.

Many companies are aiming for high satisfaction because customers who are just satisfied still find it easy to switch when a better offer comes along. Those who are highly satisfied are much less ready to switch. High satisfaction or delight creates an emotional bond with the brand, not just a rational preference. The result is high customer loyalty. Xerox's senior management believes that a very satisfied or delighted customer is worth 10 times as much to the company as a satisfied customer. A very satisfied customer is likely to stay with Xerox many more years and buy more than a satisfied customer.

How do buyers form their expectations? They form as the result of past buying experience, friends' and associates' advice, and marketers' and competitors' information and promises. If marketers raise expectations too high, the buyer is likely to be disappointed. For example, Holiday Inn ran a campaign a few years ago called "No Surprises." But hotel guests still encountered a host of problems and Holiday Inn had to withdraw the campaign. However, if the company sets expectations too low, it won't attract enough buyers (although it will satisfy those who do buy).

Some of today's most successful companies are raising expectations and delivering performances to match. These companies are aiming for *TCS—total customer satisfaction*. Xerox, for example, guarantees "total satisfaction" and will replace at its expense any dissatisfied customer's equipment within a period of three years after purchase. Cigna advertises: "We'll never be 100% satisfied until you are, too." And one of Honda's ads says: "One reason our customers are so satisfied is that we aren't." Nissan invites potential Infiniti buyers to drop in for a "guest drive" (not a "test drive"), since the Japanese word for customer is "honoured guest."

Look at what one company does to ensure high satisfaction:

Lexus Canada
www.lexus.ca

- **Lexus Canada.** The Lexus Canada advertisement that appears on page 40 recounts a tale of how Lexus delighted one of its customers by going to great lengths to get a car key to a driver who had lost his key while fishing on Lake Kenogami, located north of Regina. Superior quality products accompanied by extraordinary service have been Lexus' hallmarks from its inception. The Lexus idea was born in Japan in 1984. From day one the development team focused on understanding customers and building a car to meet their needs. Since North America is the largest market for luxury vehicles, a team was sent to North America in May 1985, to get to know the customers and understand how they perceive style. It was also important for the team to absorb the environment since the Lexus designers held the premise that physical surroundings—street width, buildings, even foliage—affect how a car looks. By August 1985, the first of 450 prototype test cars was ready. Heavily disguised, the prototypes were tested on the world's most demanding roads. They went to Germany to "fly" the Autobahn and to Sweden and Canada in the winters of '87 and '88 to perfect the new traction control and antilock braking systems. They also teamed up with tire companies until they mastered snow and ice. One automobile industry writer noted, "Manufacturers are from Mars, dealers are from Venus," to stress the fact that dealers and manufacturers have different priorities that often lead to adverse relationships. Not so with Lexus. While the first model was under development, North American dealer networks were woven. Lexus was as meticulous about choosing dealers as it was about making cars. Dealers were thoroughly trained so that they lived and breathed Lexus' vision and knew every aspect of the cars and every aspect of the market. On October 3, 1990, in Quebec City, Lexus was officially launched in Canada. Today, owners call Lexus the ultimate ownership experience. Lexus

We'd like to take this opportunity to discuss our level of service.

On the road to superior customer service, you'll find Lake Kenogami.

It was here, during a fishing trip, that a Lexus owner lost the key to his ES 300.

For the owner, it meant paddling to a remote village to call his Lexus dealer by radio telephone.

For the dealer, it meant not only cutting a new key, but, having missed the once-a-week flight from Regina, chartering a plane for its delivery.

Suffice it to say, the Lexus owner was more than a little impressed with his dealer. But not nearly so much as when he discovered the cost for this service: No charge.

As in any fish tale, there will be a disbelieving few who would deem this story as pure fiction. To those, we offer some hard facts: in many Customer Service Satisfaction Surveys, Lexus dealers have been rated so highly as to become the standard for the industry.

Backing this up (along with every automobile we make) is one of the best warranties in the industry. It has a minimum of fine print and absolutely no deductibles.

It also includes our comprehensive Roadside Assistance Protection

program, 24 hours a day, 365 days a year. Which could prove beneficial next time you're up around Lake Kenogami.

If you'd like to hear more about our service or have your own story to tell, call or visit us at our website. 1-800-26-LEXUS • www.lexuscanada.com

The 1999 RX 300. Starting from $46,460.

The Relentless Pursuit Of Perfection. LEXUS

Lexus goes to great lengths to ensure customer satisfaction.

works constantly to maintain relationships with its customers and relies heavily on database marketing to glean insights about its customers.[4]

A customer's decision to be loyal or to defect is the sum of many small encounters with the company. Consulting firm Forum Corp. says that in order for all these small encounters to add up to customer loyalty, companies need to create a "branded customer experience." Here's how Canadian Pacific Hotels, a chain with 69 properties and 29,000 rooms, did just that:

Canadian Pacific Hotels
www.cphotels.ca

■ **Canadian Pacific Hotels.** Canadian Pacific Hotels has sought to put its brand on every aspect of its relationships with customers. First, the company targeted individual business travellers. They asked these customers what they wanted, and it wasn't simply a frequent-guest club but recognition of their individual quirks and preferences. So CP Hotels offered these customers a contract: "Join our frequent-guest club and tell us what you want," even such details as whether you want a hypoallergenic pillow on your bed to whether you want *The Globe and Mail* at your door or Mountain Dew in the mini-bar. Keeping the contract with customers was no simple task. Previously oriented toward a group culture, CP Hotels had to undergo a sea change. Also, small enhancements such as offering free local phone calls or gift-shop discounts required new investment in technology. Yet, all the details eventually added up to something much greater. In 1997, CP Hotels' share of Canada's business travel jumped 15 percent, though the market as a whole increased just three percent. A full quarter of CP Hotel Club members stopped frequenting other hotels altogether.[5]

The key to generating high customer loyalty is to deliver high customer value. According to Michael Lanning, in his *Delivering Profitable Value,* a company must develop a competitively superior *value proposition* and a superior *value delivery system.* A company's value proposition is much more than its positioning on a single attribute; it is a statement about the *resulting experience* customers will have from the offering and their relationship with the supplier. The brand must represent a promise about the total resulting experience that customers can expect. Whether the promise is kept

part one
Understanding Marketing Management

40

depends upon the company's ability to manage its value delivery system. The value delivery system includes all the communications and channel experiences the customer will have on the way to obtaining the offering.

A similar theme is emphasized by Simon Knox and Stan Maklan in their *Competing on Value*. They see companies committing a *value gap* by failing to align *brand value* and *customer value*. Brand marketers try to distinguish their brand from others by a *slogan* ("washes whiter"), or a *unique selling proposition* ("Hallmark: When you care enough to give the very best.") or by *augmenting* the basic offering with added services ("our hotel will provide a computer upon request"). But they are less successful in delivering customer value, primarily because their marketing people focus on brand development. Whether customers will actually receive the promised value proposition will depend upon the marketer's ability to influence various core processes of the organization, including the supply partnerships, network coordination, business planning, asset management, and company reputation. Knox and Maklan want company marketers to spend as much time influencing the company's core processes as designing the brand profile.[6]

In addition to tracking customer expectations, perceived company performance, customer satisfaction, and delivered value, companies need to monitor their competitors' performance in these areas. For example, a company was pleased to find that 80 percent of its customers said they were satisfied. Then the CEO found out that its leading competitor attained a 90 percent customer satisfaction score. He was further dismayed when he learned that this competitor was aiming to reach a 95 percent satisfaction score. Table 2-1 describes four methods companies use to track customer satisfaction.

For customer-centred companies, customer satisfaction is both a goal and a marketing tool. Companies that achieve high customer satisfaction ratings ensure that their target market knows it. The Honda Accord has received the number-one rating in customer satisfaction from J.D. Powers for several years, and Honda's advertising of this fact has helped sell more Accords. Dell Computer's meteoric growth in the personal computer industry can be partly attributed to achieving and advertising its number-one rank in customer satisfaction. For more information on how Dell computer Corp. gets closer to customers, see he Marketing Insight box entitled "Customer Configured: How Dell Computer Corp. Clicks with Customers."

Dell Computer
www.dell.com

Although the customer-centred firm seeks to create high customer satisfaction, its main goal is not to maximize customer satisfaction. If the company increases customer satisfaction by lowering its price or increasing its services, the result may be lower profits. The company might be able to increase its profitability by means other than increased satisfaction (for example, by improving manufacturing processes or investing more in R&D). Also, the company has many stakeholders, including employees, dealers, suppliers, and stockholders. Spending more to increase customer satisfaction might divert funds from increasing the satisfaction of other "partners." Ultimately, the company must operate on the philosophy that it is trying to deliver a high level of customer satisfaction while at the same time delivering acceptable levels of satisfaction to the other stakeholders within the constraints of its total resources.

When customers rate their satisfaction with an element of the company's performance—say, delivery—the company needs to recognize that customers vary in how they define good delivery. It could mean early delivery, on-time delivery, order completeness, and so on. Yet if the company had to spell out every element in detail, customers would face a huge questionnaire. The company must also realize that two customers can report being "highly satisfied" for different reasons. One may be easily satisfied most of the time and the other might be hard to please but was pleased on this occasion.

Companies should also note that managers and salespeople can manipulate customer satisfaction ratings. They can be especially nice to customers just before the survey. They can also try to exclude unhappy customers from the survey. Another danger is that if customers know the company will go out of its way to please customers, some may express high dissatisfaction (even if satisfied) in order to receive more concessions.

Some companies navigate all these pitfalls to reach their customer value and satisfaction goals. We call these companies high-performance businesses.

TABLE	2.1

Tools for Tracking and Measuring Customer Satisfaction

Complaint and suggestion systems	A customer-centred organization makes it easy for its customers to deliver suggestions and complaints. Many restaurants and hotels provide forms for guests to report likes and dislikes. Some customer-centred companies—P&G, General Electric, Whirlpool—establish hotlines with toll-free 800 telephone numbers. Companies are also adding Web pages and e-mail to facilitate two-way communication. These information flows provide companies with many good ideas and enable them to act quickly to resolve problems.
Customer satisfaction surveys	Studies show that while customers are dissatisfied with one out of every four purchases, less than five percent of dissatisfied customers will complain. Most customers will buy less or switch suppliers. Complaint levels are thus not a good measure of customer satisfaction. Responsive companies measure customer satisfaction directly by conducting periodic surveys. They send questionnaires or make telephone calls to a random sample of recent customers. They also solicit buyers' views on their competitors' performances. While collecting customer satisfaction data, it is also useful to ask additional questions to measure *repurchase intention*; this will normally be high if the customer's satisfaction is high. It is also useful to measure the likelihood or willingness to recommend the company and brand to others. A high positive *word-of-mouth score* indicates that the company is producing high customer satisfaction.
Ghost shopping	Companies can hire persons to pose as potential buyers to report on strong and weak points experienced in buying the company's and competitors' products. These *ghost shoppers* can even test whether the company's sales personnel handle various situations well. Thus, a ghost shopper can complain about a restaurant's food to test how the restaurant handles this complaint. Not only should companies hire ghost shoppers, but managers themselves should leave their offices from time to time, enter company and competitor sales situations where they are unknown, and experience firsthand the treatment they receive as "customers." A variant of this is for managers to phone their own company with questions and complaints to see how the calls are handled.
Lost customer analysis	Companies should contact customers who have stopped buying or who have switched to another supplier to learn why this happened. When IBM loses a customer, it mounts a thorough effort to learn where it failed. Not only is it important to conduct *exit interviews* when customers first stop buying, but it is also necessary to monitor the *customer loss rate*. If it is increasing, this clearly indicates that the company is failing to satisfy customers. For customer-centred companies, customer satisfaction is both a goal and a marketing tool. Companies that achieve high customer satisfaction ratings ensure that their target market knows it. The Honda Accord has received the number-one rating in customer satisfaction from J. D. Powers for several years, and Honda's advertising of this fact has helped sell more Accords. Dell Computer's meteoric growth in the personal computer industry can be partly attributed to achieving and advertising its number-one rank in customer satisfaction. For more information on how Dell Computer Corp. gets closer to customers, see the Marketing Insight box entitled "Customer Configured: How Dell Computer Corp. Clicks with Customers."

THE NATURE OF HIGH-PERFORMANCE BUSINESSES

The consulting firm of Arthur D. Little proposed a model of the characteristics of a *high-performance business*. It pointed to the four factors shown in Figure 2-2 as keys to success: stakeholders, processes, resources, and organization.[7]

Customer Configured: How Dell Computer Corporation Clicks with Customers

"Think Customer" says a huge sign in the lobby of Dell Computer Corporation's many office buildings. The reminder almost seems redundant since that's what Dell Computer Corp. has come to symbolize since its humble beginnings in Michael Dell's dorm room in 1983. Rather than let the computer resellers mediate the relationship between company and customer, Dell began with a radically different business model for a high-tech company: sell computers directly to customers and offer them direct technical support. "We have a tremendously clear business model," says Michael Dell, the 33-year-old founder. "There's no confusion about what the value proposition is, what the company offers, and why it's great for customers. That's a very simple thing, but it has tremendous power and appeal." And, it garners tremendous profits for the company. In 1998, Dell's revenues were U.S.$18.5 billion, and the company is growing at the rate of 52 percent a year. It recently passed IBM to become the nation's second-largest seller of business computers and is quickly gaining on Compaq.

Dell is running rings around competitors because the direct-to-customer business model allows the company to be extremely responsive. By clicking on the Dell Canada Web site, customers can order a computer built to their individual specifications. Since Dell's computers are built-to-order, it can slash inventories and keep costs so low it can price products 10 to 15 percent less than rivals can. Dell now takes delivery of components just minutes before they are needed. At its factory, a Dell PC can be built, have the software installed, be tested and packed in eight hours, down from 10 hours previously. Speed is only one part of the Dell equation. Service is the other. The company has created a service capability based on "the Dell vision, which states that a customer "must have a quality experience and must be pleased, not just satisfied."

In fact, it was through veering away from its successful business model that the company discovered the importance of customer service. In 1993, the company began trying to sell to retailers, mainly because everyone else was. Customers were disgruntled because the Wal-Marts of the world didn't offer the same type of customer service. Dell ultimately abandoned the retail channel; most important, Michael Dell decided that "there would be more things we'd have to do besides build a PC." Dell decided his company had two kinds of customers: corporate and consumer. While the consumer would buy mainly because of price, the corporate buyer needed a carefully developed relationship. Like most successful companies, Dell put the most resources into building relationships with its most profitable customers.

Corporate customers comprise 90 percent of Dell's business, and the company manages its corporate accounts with a top-notch sales team. Dell now also installs custom software and keeps track of business customers' inventory for them. Its efforts have lured many huge corporate customers from the competition, including Ernst & Young, which began buying occasional PCs from Dell in 1992. Now the accounting firm buys servers from Compaq, multimedia laptops from IBM, and nearly all of its desktop machines and regular laptops from Dell—17 000 systems last year.

Dell was one of the first firms to realize the power of the Internet for forging customer relationships. One of the first companies to make a profit through on-line sales, Dell now has a growing portion of its business online. The Net has quickly become an obvious extension of Dell's direct-to-customer business model. Through the use of Premier Pages, customized customer Web pages at the Dell site, Dell is creating a 24-hour order-entry system. Big customers, such as Shell Oil or Boeing, which buy 1000 PCs a week, can click on the site to see all kinds of information about their preferences and needs. The site can be accessed worldwide by any company subsidiary and—here's the beauty of it—employees, and not just purchasing agents, can use the Premier Page to purchase computers according to an automated policy. "It's the ultimate network," Michael Dell says, "and a fabulous way for us to interact with our customers."

Sources: Based on: Michele Marchetti, "Dell Computer," *Sales & Marketing Management*, October 1997, pp. 50-53. Evan Ramstad, "Dell Fights PC Wars by Emphasizing Customer Service-focus Wins Big Clients and Gives IBM and Compaq a Run for Their Money," *Wall Street Journal*, August 15, 1997, B4. Robert D. Hof, "The Click Here Economy," *Business Week*, June 22, 1998, pp. 122-128. Saroja Girishankar, "Dell's Site Has Business in Crosshairs," *Internetweek*, April 13, 1998, p. 1. Anonymous, "The InternetWeek Interview "Michael Dell, Chairman and CEO, Dell Computer," *Internetweek*, April 13, 1998, p.8.

FIGURE 2.2

The High Performance Business

Source: P. Ranganath Nayak, Erica Drazen, and George Kastner, "The High-Performance Business: Accelerating Performance Improvement," *Prism*, First Quarter 1992, p. 6. Reprinted by permission of Arthur D. Little, Inc.

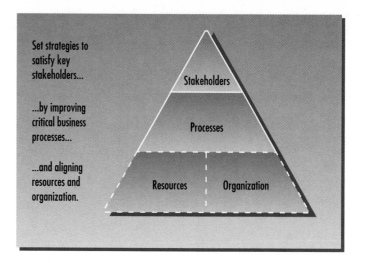

Set strategies to satisfy key stakeholders...

...by improving critical business processes...

...and aligning resources and organization.

STAKEHOLDERS

As its first stop on the road to high performance, the business must define its stakeholders and their needs. Traditionally, most businesses paid most attention to their stockholders. Today's businesses are increasingly recognizing that unless they nourish other *stakeholders*—customers, employees, suppliers, distributors—the business may never earn sufficient profits for the stockholders.

A business must strive to satisfy the minimum (threshold) expectations of each stakeholder group. At the same time, the company can aim to deliver satisfaction levels above the minimum for different stakeholders. For example, the company might aim to delight its customers, perform well for its employees, and deliver a threshold level of satisfaction to its suppliers. In setting these levels, the company must be careful not to violate the various stakeholder groups' sense of fairness about the relative treatment they are receiving.[8]

There is a dynamic relationship connecting the stakeholder groups. A smart company creates a high level of employee satisfaction. This in turn leads to higher effort, which leads to higher-quality products and services, which creates higher customer satisfaction. High satisfaction leads to more repeat business, which leads to higher growth and profits, which leads to high stockholder satisfaction, which leads to more investment, and so on. This is the virtuous circle that spells profits and growth.

PROCESSES

A company can reach its satisfaction-related goals only by managing and linking *work processes*. Company work is traditionally carried on in departments. But departmental organization poses some problems. Departments typically operate to maximize their own objectives, which are not necessarily the company's objectives. Work slows down and plans are altered as they pass from department to department.

High-performance companies are increasingly focusing on the need to manage core business processes such as new-product development, customer attraction and retention, and order fulfilment. They are *re-engineering* the work flows and building *cross-functional teams* responsible for each process.[9] For example, at Xerox a Customer Operations Group links sales, shipping, installation, service, and billing so that these activities flow smoothly into one another. Winning companies will be those that achieve excellent capabilities in managing core business processes through cross-functional teams. A McKinsey & Company study reported: "High-performing companies emphasize a set of skills notably different from their less successful counterparts. They value cross-functional skills, while other companies pride themselves on their functional strengths. High performers boast, "We've got the best project managers in the world." Low performers say, "We've got the best circuit designers."[10] AT&T, Polaroid, and

Motorola are just some of the companies that have reorganized their workers into cross-functional teams. But cross-functional teams have become common in nonprofits and government organizations as well. For example:

■ **Canadian Tourism Commission:** The Commission was created in 1995 by the Canadian federal government as a replacement for the Federal Department of Tourism. One of its main objectives was to build a greater sense of partnership between government and the private sector to better promote Canada as a tourist destination. Today, the Commission is a unique public/private-sector partnership that is industry led and market driven. From its first day of operation, the Commission faced a daunting task. For some time, Canada had been experiencing a "travel deficit." In the early 1990s, Canadians were spending $8.2 billion more dollars on travel outside the country than foreign travellers were spending on visits to Canada. Part of the Commission's mandate was to reverse this flow. The partners formed teams to undertake a number of initiatives such as one in which 12 partners joined together in an effort to entice travellers from the U.K. to visit Canada during the off season. Partners included Via Rail, Canadian Pacific Hotels, two British travel wholesalers (Thomas Cook Travel and All Canada), and eight provincial tourism boards. The Commission doesn't only partner with tourist operators. In a campaign called "Rediscover Canada," the Commission partnered with the Ford Motor Company of Canada to develop TV spots that featured tourist destinations from across the country. Not only did the ads feature Canada's beauty spots, but they also featured two Ford vehicles recommended as the means of seeing these destinations: the Ford Escort and Ford Windstar. Ford supplemented the TV ads with messages on the back of its product brochures that urged customers to call a toll-free number to receive more information about Canadian travel. The Commission's efforts have met with considerable success and the travel deficit has finally begun to shrink.[11]

Canadian Tourism Commission
www.canadatourism.com

Ford Motor Company
www.ford.ca

R ESOURCES

To carry out processes, a company needs *resources*—labour power, materials, machines, information, energy, and so on. Resources can be owned, leased, or rented. Traditionally, companies owned and controlled most of the resources that entered their business. But this situation is changing. Companies are finding that some resources under their control are not performing as well as those that they could obtain from outside the company. Many companies today have decided to *outsource* less-critical resources if they can be obtained at better quality and/or lower cost from outside the organization. Frequently outsourced resources include cleaning services, lawn care, and auto fleet management.

Competitive advantage also accrues to companies that possess *distinctive capabilities*. Whereas core competencies tend to refer to areas of special technical and production expertise, capabilities tend to describe excellence in broader business processes. For example, Wal-Mart has a distinctive capability in product replenishment based on several core competencies including information system design and logistics. Professor George Day sees market-driven organizations as excelling in three distinctive capabilities, namely *market sensing, customer linking,* and *channel bonding*.[12]

ORGANIZATION AND ORGANIZATIONAL CULTURE

A company's *organization* consists of its structures, policies, and corporate culture, all of which can become dysfunctional in a rapidly changing business environment. While structures and policies can be changed (with difficulty), the company's culture is very hard to change. Yet changing a corporate culture is often the key to implementing a new strategy successfully.

What exactly is a *corporate culture*? Most businesspeople would be hard-pressed to find words to describe this elusive concept, which some define as "the shared experiences, stories, beliefs, and norms that characterize an organization." Yet, walk into any company and the first thing that strikes you is the corporate culture—the way people are dressed, how they talk to one another, the way they greet customers.

Sometimes corporate culture develops organically and is transmitted directly from the CEO's personality and habits to the company employees. Such is the case with computer giant Microsoft, which began as an entrepreneurial upstart. Even as it has grown to a $14 billion company, Microsoft hasn't lost the hard-driving culture perpetuated by founder Bill Gates. In fact, most people believe that Microsoft's ultra-competitive culture is the biggest key to its success and to its much-criticized dominance in the computing industry.[13]

- **Microsoft.** Don't let the relaxed, strictly casual dress code fool you. Micro-softies, as Microsoft employees refer to themselves, are fuelled with a take-no-prisoners competitive drive that mirrors Gates' own persona. A recruiting pitch developed by Gates himself reads, "Microsoft people are part brainiacs, part free-spirited individualists, and 100% passionate about technology." Rivals refer to them as "microserfs" in reference to their seemingly slavish dedication to the company. Like Gates, who founded the company as a teenager, Microsofties are young; nearly a third are 29 or younger, with an average age of 34. Their casual anything-goes dress code also stems from Gates, who used to fall asleep on the floor of his garage after an all-night code-writing session and get up to work in his rumpled clothing the next morning. While you wouldn't know it to look at the T-shirt-and-Tevas-clad employees, many of them are rolling in money, and part of their competitive zeal is due to the need to sustain a share price that trades in multiples over 35, two times that of Standard and Poor's 500. Insiders own 38 percent of the company, and there are more millionaires on staff than in any other firm on earth.

What happens when entrepreneurial companies grow and need to create a tighter structure? What happens when companies with clashing cultures enter a joint venture or merger, such as when Germany's Daimler merged with Chrysler in 1998? To survive its brushes with bankruptcy, Chrysler became the most nimble and lean player in Detroit. In contrast, Daimler has a bureaucratic and ponderous culture. The jury is out on this megamerger, but if history is any guide, clashing cultures will be the biggest challenge for DaimlerChrysler. In a 1992 study by Coopers & Lybrand of 100 companies with failed or troubled mergers, 855 of executives polled said that differences in management style and practices were the major problem. This was certainly the case in the merger between Novell and WordPerfect Corp.[14]:

- **Novell and WordPerfect.** When Novell acquired WordPerfect Corp. in 1994, WordPerfect owned a little over half the market for word-processing software and Novell was well established in software products and competing intensely with Microsoft. Everything about the deal seemed perfect, yet the two companies had diametrically opposing views about basics such as customer service. Before it was acquired, WordPerfect was famous for its outstanding customer helpline, so WordPerfect's people deeply resented service cutbacks by Novell. The two companies also could not agree about how decisions were to be made and who would be involved in the process. Even lower-level Word-Perfect employees were used to a fair degree of autonomy and had been involved in the decision-making process before. However, Novell's people were used to a bureaucratic hierarchy and a formal decision-making process. When arguments broke out among Novell and WordPerfect managers, the merged company's focus shifted to internal strife when it should have been concentrating on the monster just outside the door who was waiting to eat the company for lunch: Microsoft. In an interesting epilogue to the WordPerfect-Novell marriage, WordPerfect once again improved its position in the market within a year of being acquired from Novell by Canada's Corel Corp., which had a more sympathetic culture.

The question of what accounts for the long-lasting success high-performance companies was recently addressed in a six-year study called *Built to Last* by Collins and

Corel Corp.
www.corel.ca

Porras.[15] The Stanford researchers identified two companies in each of 18 industries, one that they called a "visionary company" and one that they referred to as a "comparison company." The visionary companies were acknowledged as the industry leaders and widely admired; they set ambitious goals, communicated them to their employees, and embraced a high purpose beyond making money. They also outperformed the comparison companies by a wide margin. The visionary companies included General Electric, Hewlett Packard, and Boeing; the corresponding comparison companies were Westinghouse, Texas Instruments, and McDonnell Douglas.

The authors found three commonalities among the 18 market leaders. First, the visionary companies each held a distinctive set of values from which they didn't deviate. Thus IBM has held to the principles of respect for the individual, customer satisfaction, and continuous quality improvement throughout its history.[16] And Johnson & Johnson holds to the principle that its first responsibility is to its customers, its second to its employees, its third to its community, and its fourth to its stockholders. The second commonality is that visionary companies express their purpose in enlightened terms. Xerox wants to improve "office productivity" and Monsanto wants to "help end hunger in the world." According to Collins and Porras, a company's core purpose should not be confused with specific business goals or strategies and should not be simply a description of a company's product line. See the Marketing Memo entitled "Why Do You Exist and What Do You Stand For?" for two exercises recommended by Collins and Porras for uncovering two crucial elements of corporate vision: core purpose (a company's reason for being) and core values.

The third commonality is that visionary companies have developed a vision of their future and act to implement it. IBM is now working to establish leadership as a "network-centric" company, and not simply as the leading computer manufacturer.

Successful companies may need to adopt a new view of how to craft their strategy. The traditional view is that senior management hammers out the strategy and hands it down. Gary Hamel offers the contrasting view that imaginative ideas on strategy exist in many places within a company.[17] Senior management should identify and encourage fresh ideas from three groups that tend to be underrepresented in strategy making: employees with youthful perspectives; employees who are far removed from company headquarters; and employees who are new to the industry. Each group is capable of challenging company orthodoxy and stimulating new ideas.

Strategy must be prepared with respect to identifying and selecting among different views of the future. The Royal Dutch/Shell Group has pioneered *scenario analysis*. A scenario analysis consists of developing plausible representations of a firm's possible future that make different assumptions about forces driving the market and include different uncertainties. Managers need to think through each scenario with the question: "What will we do if it happens?" They need to adopt one scenario as the most probable and watch for signposts as time goes by that might confirm or disconfirm that scenario.[18]

High-performance companies are set up to deliver customer value and satisfaction. Let's see how this is done.

DELIVERING CUSTOMER VALUE AND SATISFACTION

Given the importance of customer value and satisfaction, what does it take to produce and deliver them? To answer this question, we need to discuss the concepts of a value chain and value-delivery systems.

VALUE CHAIN

Michael Porter of Harvard proposed the *value chain* as a tool for identifying ways to create more customer value (Figure 2-3).[19] Every firm is a collection of activities that are performed to design, produce, market, deliver, and support its product. The value chain identifies nine strategically relevant activities that create value and cost in a

FIGURE 2.3

The Generic Value Chain

Source: Reprinted with the permission of The Free Press, an imprint of Simon & Schuster from *Competitive Advantage. Creating and Sustaining Superior Performance* by Michael E. Porter. Copyright © 1985 by Michael E. Porter.

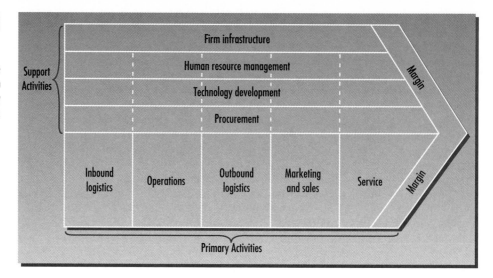

specific business. These nine value-creating activities consist of five primary activities and four support activities.

The primary activities represent the sequence of bringing materials into the business (inbound logistics), converting them into final products (operations), shipping out final products (outbound logistics), marketing them (marketing and sales), and servicing them (service). The support activities—procurement, technology development, human resource management, and firm infrastructure—are handled in certain specialized departments, but not only there. For example, other departments may do some procurement and hiring of people. The firm's infrastructure covers the costs of general management, planning, finance, accounting, legal, and government affairs that are borne by all the primary and support activities.

The firm's task is to examine its costs and performance in each value-creating activity and to look for ways to improve it. The firm should estimate its competitors' costs and performances as *benchmarks* against which to compare its own costs and performances. To the extent that it can perform certain activities better than its competitors, it can achieve a competitive advantage.

The firm's success depends not only on how well each department performs its work but also on how well the various departmental activities are coordinated. Too often, company departments act to maximize their interests rather than the company's and customers' interests. A credit department may take a long time to check a prospective customer's credit so as not to incur bad debts. Meanwhile, the customer waits and the salesperson is frustrated. A traffic department chooses to ship the goods by rail to save money and again the customer waits. Each department has erected walls that slow down the delivery of quality customer service.

The solution to this problem is to place more emphasis on the smooth management of *core business processes*. Many companies are *re-engineering* their businesses, creating cross-disciplinary teams to manage core processes.[20] The core business processes include:

■ *New-product realization:* All the activities involved in researching, developing, and launching new high-quality products quickly and within budget.

■ *Inventory management*: All the activities involved in developing and managing the inventory levels of raw materials, semifinished materials, and finished goods so that adequate supplies are available and the costs of overstocks are low.

■ *Customer acquisition and retention.* All the activities involved in finding and retaining customers and growing their business.

■ *Order-to-remittance*: All the activities involved in receiving and approving orders, shipping the goods on time, and collecting payment.

- *Customer service*: All the activities involved in making it easy for customers to reach the right parties within the company and receive quick and satisfactory service, answers, and resolutions of problems.

Strong companies develop superior capabilities in managing these core processes. For example, one of Wal-Mart's great strengths is its efficiency in moving goods from suppliers to individual stores. As Wal-Mart stores sell their goods, sales information flows via computer not only to Wal-Mart's headquarters but also to Wal-Mart's suppliers, which ship replacement merchandise to the stores almost at the rate it moves off the shelf.[21]

VALUE-DELIVERY NETWORK

To be successful the firm also needs to look for competitive advantages beyond its own operations, into the value chains of its suppliers, distributors, and customers. Many companies today have partnered with specific suppliers (also called a *supply chain*) and distributors to create a superior *value-delivery network*. For example:

- **Bailey Controls.** This firm treats some of its suppliers as if they were departments within Bailey. The company recently plugged two of its suppliers directly into its inventory-management system. Every week Bailey electronically sends Montreal-based Future Electronics its latest forecasts of the materials it will need for the next six months so that Future can stock up. Whenever a bin of parts falls below a designated level, a Bailey employee passes a laser scanner over the bin's bar code, instantly alerting Future to send the parts immediately. Although arrangements like this shift inventory costs to the suppliers, the suppliers expect those costs to be more than offset by the gain in volume. It's a win-win partnership.

Future Electronics
www.future.ca

- **Rogers Cantel Mobile Communications Inc.** Rogers Cantel, Canada's largest wireless company with 1.74 million subscribers, recently teamed up with Amway Corp. and its 100 000 door-to-door sales representatives. While unorthodox, this new channel of distribution is part of an effort to increase sales of its wireless telephones. This new channel will allow Cantel to offer its customers another level of convenience and more opportunities to acquire its telephones. Cantel's strategy is to offer its products wherever a customer chooses to shop. The door-to-door selling effort will augment Cantel's retail stores and Internet marketing programs. The deal will also benefit Amway. Instead of just selling soap, the pyramid firm is providing its sales representatives with a wider array of products to promote to its clients.[22]

Rogers Cantel
www.rogers.ca

Another excellent example of a value-delivery network is the one that connects Levi Strauss, the famous maker of blue jeans, with its suppliers and distributors (Figure 2-4). One of Levi's major retailers is Sears Canada. Overnight, thanks to electronic

---

FIGURE 2.4

Levi Strauss's Value-Delivery Network

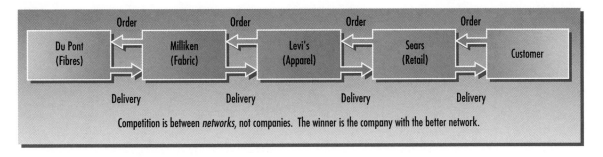

Competition is between *networks*, not companies. The winner is the company with the better network.

Sears Canada
www.sears.ca

data interchange (EDI), Levi's learns the sizes and styles of its blue jeans sold through Sears and other major outlets. Levi's then electronically orders more fabric for next-day delivery from the Milliken Company, its fabric supplier. Milliken, in turn, relays an order for more fibre to Du Pont, its fibre supplier. In this way, the partners in the supply chain use the most current sales information to manufacture what is selling, rather than to manufacture for a forecast that may be at variance with current demand. In this *quick response system*, the goods are pulled by demand rather than pushed by supply. Levi's performance against another jeans maker—say, Wrangler—depends on the quality of Levi's *marketing network* versus Wrangler's marketing network. Companies no longer compete—marketing networks do.

ATTRACTING AND RETAINING CUSTOMERS

In addition to improving their relations with their partners in the supply chain, many companies are intent on developing stronger bonds and loyalty with their ultimate customers. In the past, many companies took their customers for granted. Their customers may not have had many alternative sources of supply, or all suppliers were equally deficient in service, or the market was growing so fast that the company did not worry about satisfying its customers. Clearly, things have changed.

Today's customers are harder to please. They are smarter, more price conscious, more demanding, less forgiving, and approached by more competitors with equal or better offers. The challenge, according to Jeffrey Gitomer, is not to produce satisfied customers; several competitors can do this. The challenge is to produce loyal customers.[23]

ATTRACTING CUSTOMERS

Companies seeking to grow their profits and sales have to spend considerable time and resources searching for new customers. Figure 2-5 shows the main steps in the *customer-development process. Customer acquisition* requires substantial skills in *lead generation, lead qualification,* and *account conversion.* To generate leads, the company develops ads and places them in media that will reach new prospects; it sends direct mail and makes phone calls to possible new prospects; its salespeople participate in trade shows where they might find new leads; and so on. All this activity produces a list of *suspects*—everyone who might conceivably buy the product or service. The company looks hard at the suspects to determine who are the most likely *prospects*—the people who have a strong potential interest in the product and the ability to pay for it. *Disqualified prospects* are those people or firms the company rejects because they have poor credit or would be unprofitable. The company hopes to convert many of its *qualified prospects* into first-time customers, and to then convert those satisfied first-time customers into *repeat customers*. Both first-time and repeat customers may continue

FIGURE 2.5

The Customer-Development Process

Source: See Jill Griffin, *Customer Loyalty: How to Earn It, How to Keep It* (New York: Lexington Books, 1995), p. 36. Also see Murray Raphel and Neil Raphel, *Up the Loyalty Ladder: Turning Sometime Customers into Full-Time Advocates of Your Business* (New York: HarperBusiness, 1995).

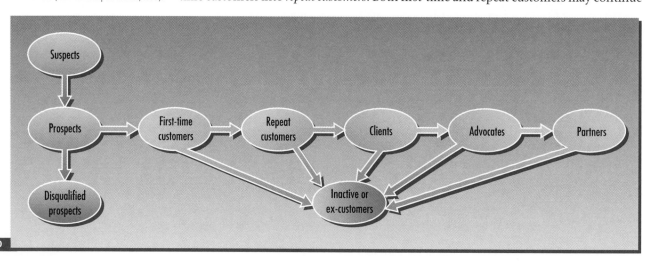

to buy from competitors as well. The company then acts to convert repeat customers into *clients*—people whom the company treats very specially and knowledgeably. The next challenge is to turn clients into *members,* by starting a membership program that offers joining customers a whole set of benefits. Hopefully then, the members will turn into *advocates*, customers who enthusiastically recommend the company and its products and services to others. The ultimate challenge is to turn advocates into *partners,* where the customer and the company work actively together.

Some customers will inevitably become inactive or drop out, for reasons of bankruptcy, moves to other locations, dissatisfaction, and so on. Here the company's challenge is to reactivate dissatisfied customers through *customer win-back strategies*. It is often easier to reattract ex-customers because the company knows their names and histories than to find new ones.

COMPUTING THE COST OF LOST CUSTOMERS

It is not enough to be skilful in attracting new customers; the company must keep them. Too many companies suffer from high customer *churn*—namely, they gain new customers only to lose many of them. It is like constantly adding water to a leaking pot. Today's companies must pay closer attention to their *customer defection rate* (the rate at which they lose customers). Cellular carriers, for example, lose 25 percent of their subscribers each year at a cost estimated at $3 to $6 billion. There are four steps in trying to reduce the defection rate.

First, the company must define and measure its retention rate. For a magazine, the renewal rate is a good measure of retention. For a university, it could be the first-to second-year retention rate, or the class graduation rate.

Second, the company must distinguish the causes of customer attrition and identify those that can be managed better. (See the Marketing Memo, "Asking Questions When Customers Leave.") The Forum Corporation analyzed the customers lost by 14 major companies for reasons other than leaving the region or going out of business: 15 percent switched because they found a better product; another 15 percent found a cheaper product; and 70 percent left because of poor or little attention from the supplier. Not much can be done about customers who leave the region or go out of business, but much can be done about customers who leave because of poor service, shoddy products, or high prices. The company needs to examine the percentages of customers who defect for different reasons.[24]

Third, the company needs to estimate how much profit it loses when it loses customers. In the case of an individual customer, the lost profit is equal to the customer's *lifetime value*—that is, the present value of the profit stream that the company would have realized if the customer had not defected prematurely. For a group of lost customers, one major transportation carrier estimated its lost profit as follows:

- The company had 64 000 accounts.
- The company lost five percent of its accounts this year due to poor service: This was a loss of 3200 accounts (.05 x 64 000).
- The average lost account represented a $40 000 loss in revenue. Therefore, the company lost $128 000 000 in revenue (3200 x $40 000).
- The company's profit margin is 10 percent. Therefore, the company lost $12 800 000 (.10 x $128 000 000) this year. Since the customers left prematurely, the company's actual loss over time is much greater.

Fourth, the company needs to determine how much it would cost to reduce the defection rate. As long as the cost is less than the lost profit, the company should spend that amount to reduce the defection rate.

Finally, nothing beats plain old listening to customers. Some companies have created an ongoing mechanism that keeps senior managers permanently plugged into frontline customer feedback. MBNA, the credit card giant, asks every executive to listen in on telephone conversations in the customer service area or customer recovery units. Deere & Company, which makes John Deere tractors and which has a superb record of customer loyalty—nearly 98 percent annual retention in some product areas—uses retired employees to interview defectors and customers.[25]

L.L. Bean Inc.
www.llbean.com

THE NEED FOR CUSTOMER RETENTION

Unfortunately, most marketing theory and practice centre on the art of attracting new customers rather than on retaining existing ones. The emphasis traditionally has been on making sales rather than building relationships; on preselling and selling rather than caring for the customer afterward.

Some companies, however, have always cared passionately about customer loyalty and retention.[26] The key to customer retention is customer satisfaction. A highly satisfied customer:

- Stays loyal longer
- Buys more as the company introduces new products and upgrades existing products
- Talks favourably about the company and its products
- Pays less attention to competing brands and advertising and is less sensitive to price
- Offers product/service ideas to the company
- Costs less to serve than new customers because transactions are routinized

Thus a company would be wise to measure customer satisfaction regularly. The company could phone recent buyers and inquire how many are very satisfied, satisfied, indifferent, dissatisfied, and very dissatisfied. It might lose as many as 80 percent of the very dissatisfied customers, maybe about 40 percent of the dissatisfied customers, about 20 percent of the indifferent customers; and maybe 10 percent of the satisfied customers. But it may lose only one or two percent of its very satisfied customers. The moral: try to exceed customer expectations, not merely meet them.

Some companies think they are getting a sense of customer satisfaction by tallying customer complaints. But 95 percent of dissatisfied customers don't complain; many just stop buying.[27] The best thing a company can do is to make it easy for the customer to complain. Suggestion forms and company toll-free numbers and e-mail addresses serve this purpose. The 3M company hopes that customers will call them with suggestions, inquiries, and complaints. 3M claims that over two-thirds of its product-improvement ideas come from listening to customer complaints.

Listening is not enough, however. The company must respond quickly and constructively to the complaints:

> *Of the customers who register a complaint, between 54 and 70 percent will do business again with the organization if their complaint is resolved. The figure goes up to a staggering 95 percent if the customer feels that the complaint was resolved quickly. Customers who have complained to an organization and had their complaints satisfactorily resolved tell an average of five people about the treatment they received.*[28]

Because loyal customers account for a substantial amount of company profits, a company should not risk losing a customer by ignoring a grievance or quarrelling over a small amount. IBM requires every salesperson to write a full report on each lost customer and all the steps taken to restore satisfaction. Winning back lost customers is an important marketing activity, and often costs less than attracting first-time customers.

One company long recognized for its emphasis on customer satisfaction is L.L. Bean, Inc., which runs a mail-order catalogue business in clothing and equipment for rugged living. L.L. Bean has carefully blended its external and internal marketing programs. To its customers, it offers the following:[29]

100% Guarantee

All of our products are guaranteed to give 100% satisfaction in every way. Return anything purchased from us at any time if it proves otherwise. We will replace it, refund your purchase price or credit your credit card, as you wish. We do not want you to have anything from L.L. Bean that is not completely satisfactory.

To motivate its employees to serve the customers well, it displays the following poster prominently around its offices:[30]

> *What Is a Customer?*
>
> A Customer is the most important person ever in this office . . . in person or by mail.
>
> A Customer is not dependent on us . . . we are dependent on him.
>
> A Customer is not an interruption of our work . . . he is the purpose of it. We are not doing a favor by serving him . . . he is doing us a favor by giving us the opportunity to do so.
>
> A Customer is not someone to argue or match wits with. Nobody ever won an argument with a Customer.
>
> A Customer is a person who brings us his wants. It is our job to handle them profitably to him and to ourselves.

Today, more and more companies are recognizing the importance of satisfying and retaining current customers. Here are some interesting facts bearing on customer retention:[31]

- Acquiring new customers can cost five times more than the costs involved in satisfying and retaining current customers. It requires a great deal of effort to induce satisfied customers to switch away from their current suppliers.

- The average company loses 10 percent of its customers each year.

- A five percent reduction in the customer defection rate can increase profits by 25 percent to 85 percent, depending on the industry.

- The customer profit rate tends to increase over the life of the retained customer.

- We can work out an example to support the case for emphasizing customer retention. Suppose a company analyzes its new customer acquisition cost:

Cost of an average sales call (including salary, commission, benefits, and expenses)	$300
Average number of sales calls to convert an average prospect into a customer	×4
Cost of attracting a new customer	$1,200

This is an underestimate because we are omitting the cost of advertising and promotion, plus the fact that only a fraction of all pursued prospects end up being converted into customers.

Now suppose the company estimates average customer lifetime value as follows:

Annual customer revenue	$5,000
Average number of loyal years	×2
Company profit margin	×.10
Customer lifetime value	$1,000

This company is spending more to attract new customers than they are worth. Unless the company can sign up customers with fewer sales calls, spend less per sales call, stimulate higher new-customer annual spending, retain customers longer, or sell them higher-profit products, the company is headed for bankruptcy.

There are two ways to strengthen customer retention. One is to erect high switching barriers. Customers are less inclined to switch to another supplier when this would involve high capital costs, high search costs, or the loss of loyal-customer discounts. The better approach is to deliver high customer satisfaction. This makes it harder for competitors to overcome switching barriers by simply offering lower prices or switching inducements. The task of creating strong customer loyalty is called *relationship marketing*. Relationship marketing embraces all those steps that companies undertake to better know and serve their valued customers.

RELATIONSHIP MARKETING: THE KEY

Canadian marketing consultant Ian Gordon defines relationship marketing as "the ongoing process of identifying and *creating new* value with individual customers and then *sharing the benefits* from this over a lifetime of association. It involves the understanding, focusing and management of ongoing collaboration between suppliers and selected customers for mutual value creation and sharing through interdependence and organizational alignment." Etobicoke, Ontario-based Bayer, for example, works with employers to help them assess how they are spending their health-care dollars and finds ways to save them money. Its Care Program involves more than just selling pills. The program shows employees how to better manage their health.[32] Key facets of relationship marketing are:

- Creating new value that is shared with customers
- Seeing customers as more than purchasers—customers define the values they want and their suppliers work to provide and deliver those values

Air Canada
www.aircanada.ca

In 1998, Air Canada embarked on a global brand repositioning strategy that reflects its move towards one-to-one relationship marketing. The effort began with a Customer Relationship Management survey that sought responses from more than 15 000 business customers on what they wanted and expected from the airline. The data helped Air Canada better segment its market. It helped them realize that there was a group of people who literally fly almost all the time. It helped them understand that this group didn't want to be treated like everybody else and that they had unique needs. Air Canada designed a new program, Super Elite, to meet these frequent travellers' specific needs. The airline works to treat these lucrative passengers like royalty and offers them such important benefits as guaranteed reservations, free seat upgrades, dedicated agents who serve Super Elite clients only on a 24-hour-a-day basis, and international toll-free telephone assistance.[33]

To understand how relationship marketing differs from traditional approaches, consider five different levels of investment in selling and customer-relationship building:

- *Basic selling*: The salesperson simply sells the product.
- *Reactive selling*: The salesperson sells the product and encourages the customer to call if he or she has questions, comments, or complaints.
- *Accountable selling*: The salesperson phones the customer a short time after the sale to check whether the product is meeting expectations. The salesperson also asks the customer for any product or service improvement suggestions and any specific disappointments. This information helps the company continuously improve its performance.
- *Proactive marketing*: The company salesperson contacts the customer from time to time with suggestions about improved product uses or helpful new products. (Kraft's sales reps used to limit their customer efforts to devising promotions in supermarkets; now they are more proactive, offering research and tips for improving a store's profits.)
- *Partnership marketing*: The company works continuously with the customer to discover ways to effect customer savings or help the customer perform better. (General Electric has stationed some of its engineers full time at the head offices of its major customers to help them improve their productivity.)

Many companies practise only basic selling when their markets contain many customers and their unit profit margins are small. At the other extreme, in markets with few customers and high profit margins, most sellers will move toward partnership marketing. Westinghouse Canada works closely with Ontario Hydro in developing appropriate electrical switchgears that fully satisfy Hydro's requirements. As Figure 2-6 shows, the likely level of relationship marketing depends on the number of customers and the profit margin level.

The best relationship marketing going on today is driven by technology. GE Plastics couldn't target its newsletter so effectively to customers if it weren't for advances in database software. Dell, discussed earlier, couldn't customize computer ordering for its global corporate customers without advances in Web technology. Companies are using e-mail, Web sites, call centres, databases, and database software to foster continuous contact between company and customer. Here's how CIBC used one of its Web sites to build stronger customer relationships:

FIGURE 2.6

Levels of Relationship Marketing

	HIGH MARGIN	MEDIUM MARGIN	LOW MARGIN
Many customers/ distributors	Accountable	Reactive	Basic or reactive
Medium number of customers/ distributors	Proactive	Accountable	Reactive
Few customers/ distributors	Partnership	Proactive	Accountable

CIBC World Markets
www.schoolfp.cibc.com

■ **CIBC World Markets** markets a range of financial products, including derivatives, to corporations, financial institutions, and institutional investors. The objective of their Web site is not to "sell" these complex financial products, but to meet their customers' needs for ongoing education. The site functions as a 24-hour-a-day on-line tutor. Site users can access articles, research papers, and surveys that track how other corporations are using derivatives. They can price various options by using interactive calculators. The site not only helps investors learn about complex financial products, but it also helps CIBC learn about these customers and potential customers. Registration data, e-mail correspondence, and the software CIBC uses to monitor site traffic has helped them understand their customers better.[34]

Integrate the telephone—long a medium for developing customer relationships—with Web technology, and you have an extremely powerful means of attracting and retaining customers. See the Marketing for the 21st Century box entitled "From Telephone to Teleweb: How the New Call Centres Keep Customers Coming."

What specific marketing tools can a company use to develop stronger customer bonding and satisfaction? Service marketing specialists Berry and Parasuraman have distinguished three value-building approaches:[35] adding financial benefits, adding social benefits, and adding structural ties.

Adding Financial Benefits

Two financial benefits that companies can offer are frequency marketing programs and club marketing programs. Frequency marketing programs (FMPs) are designed to provide rewards to customers who buy frequently and/or in substantial amounts. Frequency marketing is an acknowledgment of the fact that 20 percent of a company's customers might account for 80 percent of their business.

American Airlines was one of the first companies to pioneer a frequency marketing program when it decided to offer free mileage credit to its customers in the early 1980s. Hotels next adopted FMPs, with Marriott taking the lead with its Honoured Guest Program. Shortly thereafter, car rental firms sponsored FMPs. Then credit card companies began to offer points based on their cards' usage level. Sears offers rebates to its Discover cardholders on charges made on the card. Today, even discount retailers, like Zellers, offer members "club cards" that provide members with additional benefits.

Typically, the first company to introduce an FMP gains the most benefit, especially if competitors are slow to respond. After competitors respond, FMPs can become a financial burden to all the offering companies.

Many companies have created affinity groups, or clubs, among their customers to bond them closer to the company. Club membership can be open to everyone who purchases a product or service, such as a frequent flyers or frequent diners club, or it can be limited, requiring a small fee. While open clubs are good for building a database or snagging customers from competitors, limited-membership clubs are more powerful long-term loyalty builders. Fees and membership conditions prevent those

FROM TELEPHONE TO TELEWEB: HOW THE NEW CALL CENTRES KEEP CUSTOMERS COMING

Whenever cigar enthusiast Cara Biden has called Famous Smoke Shops in search of the highly coveted Short Stories cigars, they've been out of stock. Yet, this hasn't stopped Biden from being a loyal customer at Famous and calling another half dozen times.

Every time Biden phones Famous, a system known as an ACD (automatic call distributor) immediately kicks in to answer the call and route it to the appropriate contact person. While not many people like receiving an automated response when they dial a company, Biden was impressed with how fast the ACD funnelled her to a customer service rep, and she also enjoyed chatting with the highly knowledgeable representative about alternatives to the tough-to-find cigars. Not only was the rep knowledgeable, but he was also knowledgeable about Biden since her sales history and previous queries popped up on his computer screen.

Companies like Famous Smoke Shop view the automated call centre as a potent technological tool for making the most out of each and every customer interaction. Not just a bank of phones, the call centre is a high-tech telemarketing operation that enables companies to target the most profitable customers, increase repeat customer purchases, keep customers from defecting, lure customers from the competition, and more. In fact, the term "call centre" might be a misnomer. Call centres are "really more like contact centres," states Carter Lusher, vice-president of the Gartner Group, an information-technology and research firm, "accommodating customers accessing companies via phone, fax, the Web, e-mail, even interactive video kiosk."

Whether a call centre is in-bound (receiving calls) or out-bound (a telemarketing centre), the idea is to make customers' interactions with companies seamless and uniform, no matter which form of communication they choose. In fact, the latest technology lets a customer browse a World Wide Web site on a PC at the same time as a customer service agent browses the same site. They can talk over a separate telephone line or an Internet connection to compare products or discuss how they work. Supreet Manachada, CIO at technology company, Logistix, Inc., says, "We're growing like crazy, and it's definitely because customers are coming to us through this technology." Logistix is testing Web Agent software from Aspect Telecommunications, Inc.

Web Agent synchronizes Web screens viewed by the agent and customer as they talk, and even lets either party draw circles around words or pictures for both to see. This may not seem like a big deal, but it helps customers if an agent can explain a complex technological device, such as a router, while they view a diagram on a screen. Another thing Logistix is pleased about is the technology's ability to turn the call centre into a central point of customer contact.

Forrester Research, Inc. has dubbed the Web-to-call centre relationship "teleweb." "The endgame," says David Cooperstein, a Forrester analyst, "is to let the customer choose how they want to contact you and to make sure any choice results in consistent interface, so that if a customer calls, the agent knows about the e-mail he just sent." While teleweb applications will be booming, those most likely to reap their benefits are companies selling complicated, high-tech products, such as Logistix. People like Cara Biden will probably continue to inquire after cigars, or other low-tech products, over the phone.

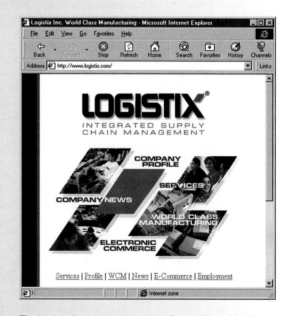

The Logistix home page: Logistix sells complicated high-tech products using teleweb applications that allow customers and sales reps to connect directly in order to make buying products and solving problems quick, direct, and easy.

Sources: Based on Alessandra Bianchi, "Lines of Fire," *Inc. Tech,* 1998, pp. 36-48; Matt Hamblen, "Call Centers and Web Sites Cozy Up," *Computerworld,* March 2, 1998, p. 1; and John F. Yarbrough, "Dialing for Dollars," *Sales & Marketing Management,* January 1997, pp. 60-67.

with only a fleeting interest in a company's products from joining. Limited customer clubs attract and keep the small percentage of a company's customers who are responsible for the largest portion of business. Some clubs started in Europe have been spectacularly successful.

- **Telepizza S.A.** Spain's Telepizza S.A. was able to eclipse multinational Pizza Hut in Spain through the skilful use of marketing to children via a magic club. So far Telepizza boasts the largest membership club in Spain, with three million children enrolled. The magic club offers children small prizes, usually simple magic tricks, with every order. Telepizza now has nearly 500 restaurants in Spain, where its market share is 65 percent compared to less than 20 percent for Pizza Hut.[36]

- **Swatch.** Swatch afficionados buy nine of the company's quirky watches every year, so Swiss watchmaker, Swatch, uses its club to cater to collectors. Club members can buy exclusives, such as the "Garden Turf" watch, a clear watch with an Astroturf band. Club members also receive a newsletter, the *World Journal*, a magazine filled with Swatch-centric news from the four corners of the globe. Swatch counts on enthusiastic word-of-mouth from club members as a boost to business. "Our members are like walking billboards," says the manager of Swatch's club, Trish O'Callaghan. "They love, live, and breathe our product. They are ambassadors for Swatch."

Swatch
www.swatch.com

- **Harley-Davidson.** The world-famous motorcycle company sponsors the Harley Owners Group (HOG), which now numbers 360 000 members. A first-time buyer of a Harley-Davidson motorcycle receives a free one-year membership. HOG benefits include a magazine (*Hog Tales*), a touring handbook, emergency road service, a specially designed insurance program, theft reward service, discount hotel rates, and a Fly & Ride program, enabling members to rent Harleys while on vacation.

Adding Social Benefits

Here company personnel work on increasing their social bonds with customers by individualizing and personalizing customer relationships. Table 2-2 contrasts a socially sensitive approach with a socially insensitive approach to customers. In essence,

Good Things	Bad Things
Initiate positive phone calls	Make only callbacks
Make recommendations	Make justifications
Candor in language	Accommodative language
Use phone	Use correspondence
Show appreciation	Wait for misunderstandings
Make service suggestions	Wait for service requests
Use "we" problem-solving language	Use "owe-us" legal language
Get to problems	Only respond to problems
Use jargon or shorthand	Use long-winded communications
Personality problems aired	Personality problems hidden
Talk of "our future together"	Talk about making good on the past
Routinize responses	Fire drill and emergency responsiveness
Accept responsibility	Shift blame
Plan the future	Rehash the past

TABLE 2.2

Social Actions Affecting Buyer-Seller Relationships

Source: Theodore Levitt, *The Marketing Imagination* (New York: Free Press, 1983), p. 119. Reprinted by permission of the *Harvard Business Review.* An exhibit from Theodore Levitt, "After the Sale Is Over," *Harvard Business Review* (September–October 1983, p. 119). Copyright ©1983 by the President and Fellows of Harvard College.

thoughtful companies turn their customers into clients. Donnelly, Berry, and Thompson draw this distinction:

> *Customers may be nameless to the institution; clients cannot be nameless. Customers are served as part of the mass or as part of larger segments; clients are served on an individual basis . . . Customers are served by anyone who happens to be available; clients are served by the professional assigned to them.*[37]

Some companies take steps to bring their customers together to meet and enjoy each other. Companies such as Harley Davidson, Porsche, Saturn, and Apple Computers are said to be engaged in building *brand communities*.

Adding Structural Ties

The company may supply customers with special equipment or computer linkages that help customers manage their orders, payroll, inventory, and so on. A good example is McKesson Corporation, a leading pharmaceutical wholesaler, which invested millions of dollars in EDI capabilities to help independent pharmacies manage inventory, order-entry processes, and shelf space. Another example is Milliken, which provides proprietary software programs, marketing research, sales training, and sales leads to loyal customers.

 USTOMER PROFITABILITY: THE ULTIMATE TEST

Ultimately, marketing is the art of attracting and keeping profitable customers. According to James V. Putten of American Express, the best customers outspend others by ratios of 16 to 1 in retailing, 13 to 1 in the restaurant business, 12 to 1 in the airline business, and 5 to 1 in the hotel/motel industry.[38] Carl Sewell, who runs one of the best-managed auto dealerships in the world, estimates that a typical auto buyer represents a potential lifetime value of over $300 000 in car purchases and services.[39]

Yet every company loses money on some of its customers. The well-known *20/80 rule* says that the top 20 percent of the customers may generate as much as 80 percent of the company's profits. Sherden suggested amending the rule to read 20/80/30, to reflect the idea that the top 20 percent of customers generate 80 percent of the company's profits, half of which is lost serving the bottom 30 percent of unprofitable customers."[40] The implication is that a company could improve its profits by "firing" its worst customers. However, there are two other alternatives: raise the prices or lower the costs of serving those customers.

Furthermore, it isn't necessarily the company's largest customers who are yielding the most profit. The largest customers demand considerable service and receive the deepest discounts. The smallest customers pay full price and receive minimal service, but the costs of transacting with small customers reduce their profitability. The midsize customers receive good service and pay nearly full price and are often the most profitable. This fact helps explain why many large firms that formerly targeted only large customers are now invading the middle market. Major air express carriers, for instance, are finding that it doesn't pay to ignore the small and mid-size international shippers. Programs geared toward smaller customers are as simple as a network of drop boxes, which allow for substantial discounts over letters and packages picked up at the shipper's place of business. In addition to putting more drop boxes in place, United Parcel Service (UPS) conducts a series of seminars to instruct exporters in the finer points of shipping overseas.[41]

A company should not pursue and satisfy all customers. For example, if customers of Courtyard (Marriott Hotels' less expensive chain of motels) start asking for Marriott-level business services, Courtyard will say "no." Granting these requests would only confuse the Marriott and Courtyard systems. Lanning and Phillips make this point well:

> *Some organizations try to do anything and everything customers suggest . . . Yet, while customers often make many good suggestions, they also suggest many courses*

of action that are unactionable or unprofitable. Randomly following these suggestions is fundamentally different from market-focus—making a disciplined choice of which customers to serve and which specific combination of benefits and price to deliver to them (and which to deny them).[42]

What makes a customer profitable? We define a profitable customer as follows:

- A profitable customer is a person, household, company, or organization that over time yields a revenue stream that exceeds by an acceptable amount the company's cost stream of attracting, selling, and servicing that customer.

Note that the emphasis is on the lifetime stream of revenue and cost, not on the profit from a particular transaction. Here are two illustrations of customer lifetime value:

- **Taco Bell.** When tacos cost less than a dollar each, you wouldn't think Taco Bell would fret over lost customers. However, executives at Taco Bell have determined that a repeat customer is worth as much as $11 000. By sharing such estimates of customer lifetime value, Taco Bell's managers help employees understand the value of keeping customers satisfied.[43]

- **Tom Peters.** The noted author of several books on managerial excellence, Tom Peters runs a business that spends $1500 a month on Federal Express service. He spends this amount 12 months a year and expects to remain in business for another 10 years. Therefore, he expects to spend $180 000 on future Federal Express service. If Federal Express makes a 10 percent profit margin, his lifetime business will contribute $18 000 to Federal Express profits. All this is at risk if he starts getting poor service from Federal Express or if a competitor offers better service.

Although many companies measure customer satisfaction, most companies fail to measure individual customer profitability. Banks claim that this is a difficult task because a customer uses different banking services and the transactions are logged in different departments. However, banks that have succeeded in linking customer transactions have been appalled by the number of unprofitable customers in their customer base. Some banks report losing money on over 45 percent of their customers. It is not surprising that banks are increasingly charging fees for various services that they formerly supplied free.

A useful type of profitability analysis is shown in Figure 2-7.[44] Customers are arrayed along the columns and products along the rows. Each cell contains a symbol for the profitability of selling that product to that customer. Customer 1 is very profitable;

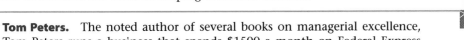

	Customers			
	C_1	C_2	C_3	
P_1	+	+	+	Highly profitable product
P_2	+			Profitable product
P_3		−	−	Losing product
P_4	+		−	Mixed-bag product
	High-profit customer	Mixed-bag customer	Losing customer	

(Products)

FIGURE 2.7

Customer–Product Profitability Analysis

he buys three profit-making products (P1, P2, and P4). Customer 2 yields a picture of mixed profitability; he buys one profitable product and one unprofitable product. Customer 3 is a losing customer because he buys one profitable product and two unprofitable products. What can the company do about Customers 2 and 3? It has two options: (1) It can raise the price of its less profitable products or eliminate them, or (2) it can try to sell its profit-making products to the unprofitable customers. Unprofitable customers who defect should not concern the company. In fact, the company would benefit by encouraging these customers to switch to competitors.

Ultimately, the company's profitability depends on three elements: value creation, internal operations, and competitive advantage. Profit will be higher, the higher the company's value-creation ability, the more efficient its internal operations, and the greater its competitive advantage. Companies must not only be able to create high absolute value but also high value relative to competitors at a sufficiently low cost. *Competitive advantage* is a company's ability to perform in one or more ways that competitors cannot or will not match. Hopefully, the competitive advantage is seen as a *customer advantage*. If the customer doesn't care about the company's competitive advantage, then it is not a customer advantage.

Companies strive to build sustainable and meaningful customer advantages. Those that succeed deliver high customer value and satisfaction, which leads to high repeat purchases and therefore high company profitability. One of the major values that customers expect from vendors is high product and service quality, a subject to which we now turn.

 # IMPLEMENTING TOTAL QUALITY MANAGEMENT

Today's executives view the task of improving product and service quality as their top priority. The successes of many Japanese companies are due to the exceptional quality of their products. Most customers will no longer accept or tolerate average quality. If companies want to stay in the race, let alone be profitable, they have no choice but to adopt total quality management (TQM).

■ Total quality management (TQM) is an organization-wide approach to continuously improving the quality of all the organization's processes, products, and services.

According to G.E.'s Chairman, John F. Welch, Jr.: "Quality is our best assurance of customer allegiance, our strongest defence against foreign competition, and the only path to sustained growth and earnings."[45]

The drive to produce goods that are superior in world markets has led some countries—and groups of countries—to recognize or award prizes to companies that exemplify the best quality practices.

■ *Japan*. In 1951, Japan became the first country to award a national quality prize, the Deming Prize (named after W. Edwards Deming, the American statistician who taught the importance and methodology of quality improvement to postwar Japan). Deming's work formed the basis of many TQM practices.

■ *United States*. In the mid-1980s, the United States established the Malcolm Baldrige National Quality Award in honour of the late Secretary of Commerce. The Baldrige award criteria consist of seven measures, each carrying a certain number of award points: customer focus and satisfaction (with the most points), quality and operational results, management of process quality, human resource development and management, strategic quality planning, information and analysis, and senior executive leadership. Xerox, Motorola, Federal Express, IBM, Texas Instruments, the Cadillac division of General Motors, and Ritz-Carlton hotels are some past winners. One of the latest quality awards went to Custom Research, a highly regarded marketing research firm in Minneapolis.

- *Europe and Canada.* The European Quality Award was established in 1993 by the European Foundation for Quality Management and the European Organization for Quality. It is awarded to companies that have achieved high grades on certain criteria: leadership, people management, policy and strategy, resources, processes, people satisfaction, customer satisfaction, impact on society, and business results. The award is an offshoot of a program of standards developed and administered by the Geneva-based International Standards Organization (ISO). Today, these standards have become an exacting set of international quality standards. The Standards Council of Canada is this country's representative of the ISO. Canadian entrepreneur K.C. Irving recently established the K.C. Irving Quality Award to recognize Canadian firms that have leveraged quality programs to their advantage.

Standards Council of Canada
www.scc.ca

The first series was the *ISO 9000* standards that are now generally accepted principles for documenting quality. ISO 9000 provides a framework for showing customers how quality-oriented business around the world test products, train employees, keep records, and fix defects. Earning the ISO 9000 certification involves a quality audit every six months from a registered ISO assessor. The program has been expanded to include environmental standards—the ISO 14000 standards.[46]

There is an intimate connection among product and service quality, customer satisfaction, and company profitability. Higher levels of quality result in higher levels of customer satisfaction while supporting higher prices and (often) lower costs. Therefore, *quality improvement programs (QIPs)* normally increase profitability. The well-known PIMS studies (Profit Impact of Market Strategy) show a high correlation between relative product quality and company profitability.[47]

But what exactly is quality? Various experts have defined it as "fitness for use," "conformance to requirements," "freedom from variation," and so on.[48] We will use the American Society for Quality Control's definition, which has been adopted worldwide:[49]

- *Quality* is the totality of features and characteristics of a product or service that bear on its ability to satisfy stated or implied needs.

This is clearly a customer-centred definition. We can say that the seller has delivered quality whenever the seller's product or service meets or exceeds the customers' expectations. A company that satisfies most of its customers' needs most of the time is called a *quality company*.

It is important to distinguish between conformance quality and performance quality (or grade). A Mercedes provides higher *performance quality* than a Hyundai: The Mercedes rides smoother, goes faster, lasts longer, and so on. Yet both a Mercedes and a Hyundai can be said to deliver the same *conformance quality* if all the units deliver their respective promised quality.

Total quality is the key to value creation and customer satisfaction. Total quality is everyone's job, just as marketing is everyone's job. This idea was expressed well by Daniel Beckham:

> Marketers who don't learn the language of quality improvement, manufacturing, and operations, will become as obsolete as buggy whips. The days of functional marketing are gone. We can no longer afford to think of ourselves as market researchers, advertising people, direct marketers, strategists—we have to think of ourselves as customer satisfiers—customer advocates focused on whole processes.[50]

Marketing managers have two responsibilities in a quality-centred company. First, they must participate in formulating strategies and policies designed to help the company win through total quality excellence. Second, they must deliver marketing quality alongside production quality. Each marketing activity—marketing research, sales training, advertising, customer service, and so on—must be performed to high standards.

Marketers play several roles in helping their company define and deliver high-quality goods and services to target customers. First, they bear the major responsibility for correctly identifying customers' needs and requirements. Second, they must communicate customer expectations correctly to product designers. Third, they must ensure that customers' orders are filled correctly and on time. Fourth, they must check that customers have received proper instructions, training, and technical assistance in the use of the product. Fifth, they must stay in touch with customers after the sale to ensure that they are satisfied and remain satisfied. Sixth, they must gather customer ideas for product and service improvements and convey them to the appropriate company departments. When marketers do all this, they are making substantial contributions to total quality management and customer satisfaction.

One implication of TQM is that marketing people must spend time and effort not only to improve *external marketing* but also to improve *internal marketing*. The marketer must complain like the customer complains when the product or the service is not right. Marketing must be the customer's watchdog or guardian, and must constantly hold up the standard of "giving the customer the best solution."

SUMMARY

1. Customers are value-maximizers. They form an expectation of value and act on it. Buyers will buy from the firm that they perceive to offer the highest *customer delivered value*, defined as the difference between total customer value and total customer cost. This means that sellers must assess the total customer value and total customer cost associated with each competitor's offer to know how their own offer stacks up. Sellers who are at a delivered-value disadvantage can either try to increase total customer value or decrease total customer cost. The former calls for strengthening or augmenting the offer's product, services, personnel, and/or image benefits. The latter calls for reducing the buyer's costs. The seller can reduce the price, simplify the ordering and delivery process, or absorb some buyer risk by offering a warranty.

2. A buyer's satisfaction is a function of the product's perceived performance and the buyer's expectations. Recognizing that high satisfaction leads to high customer loyalty, many companies today are aiming for TCS—total customer satisfaction. For such companies, customer satisfaction is both a goal and a marketing tool.

3. Strong companies develop superior capabilities in managing core business processes such as new-product realization, inventory management, customer acquisition and retention, order-to-remittance, and customer service. Managing these core processes effectively means creating a *marketing network* in which the company works closely with all parties in the production and distribution chain, from suppliers of raw materials to retail distributors. Companies no longer compete—marketing networks do.

4. Losing profitable customers can dramatically affect a firm's profits. The cost of attracting a new customer is estimated to be five times the cost of keeping a current customer happy. The key to retaining customers is relationship marketing. To keep customers happy, marketers can add financial or social benefits to products, and/or create structural ties between itself and its customers.

5. *Quality* is the totality of features and characteristics of a product or service that bear on its ability to satisfy stated or implied needs. Today's companies have no choice but to implement total quality management programs if they are to remain solvent and profitable. Total quality is the key to value creation and customer satisfaction.

6. Marketing managers have two responsibilities in a quality-centred company. First, they must participate in formulating strategies and policies designed to help the company win through total quality excellence. Second, they must deliver marketing quality alongside production quality. Each marketing activity—marketing research, sales training, advertising, customer service, and so on—must be performed to high standards. In all of these activities, marketers must work closely with the company's other departments.

CHAPTER CONCEPTS

1. Zeithaml, Parasuraman, and Berry identified five dimensions of quality service. They are: (1) reliability—the ability to provide dependably and accurately what was promised, (2) assurance—the knowledge and courtesy of employees, and the ability to convey trust and confidence, (3) tangibles—the physical facilities and equipment and the professional appearance of personnel, (4) empathy—the degree of caring and individual attention provided to customers, and (5) responsiveness— the willingness to help customers and provide prompt service. Describe how Canadian Airlines might deliver each of these dimensions to its customers. Is the company better at delivering some of these dimensions than others?

2. A subcommittee of the Board of Directors of Hampton Inns has made a bold proposal that customers be given a guarantee of "complete satisfaction or your night's stay is free." Employees will be permitted to make good on this guarantee without the approval of managers. But although the proposed guarantee would show great confidence in the hotels' quality and would give Hampton Inns a competitive advantage, most managers oppose the plan. Why would they not want to guarantee customer satisfaction? What are possible customer reactions to such a guarantee? What controls can be introduced to reduce customer abuse?

MARKETING AND ADVERTISING

1. Toyota, like many automotive manufacturers, emphasizes excellent product quality and high customer satisfaction. But what exactly is quality—and how does a marketer prove that its quality satisfies the stated or implied needs of its customers? The Toyota ad in Figure 2 shows one approach. What element of quality is the ad stressing, and how does this element satisfy customer needs? Is the ad focusing on performance or conformance quality? What are the implications for customers? For Toyota's marketing strategy?

Figure 1

Figure 2

2. Roadway Express wants to be the trucking firm of choice for companies that choose to outsource their shipping function, as this ad indicates. What is Roadway's core competence? Why would Rawlings, the customer featured in the ad, prefer to outsource to Roadway rather than handle its own shipments? Of the three distinctive capabilities identified by George Day, which does Roadway appear to be emphasizing in this ad? Why would that capability be valued by customers?

FOCUS ON TECHNOLOGY

How can a company use its Web site for cost-effective customer-relationship building? Fuji Film, the giant Japanese maker of photographic equipment and supplies, maintains an extensive Internet presence for consumers and business customers. Generally, the profit margins in consumer products are too small to allow for expensive outreach beyond basic marketing. Yet Kodak, Fuji's arch-rival, has an interesting relationship-building idea: it invites consumers to become members of its Web site. Members receive Kodak information via e-mail and are able to upload their own photo images for inclusion in electronic postcards. Visit the Web sites of Kodak and Fuji Film and examine how each reaches out to consumers. What can Fuji learn from Kodak's membership approach? How can Fuji use its Web site to stay in touch with consumers on a regular basis? As your instructor directs, prepare an oral or written presentation of your ideas, explaining how your approach would help Fuji strengthen relationships with individual consumers.

MARKETING FOR THE 21ST CENTURY

As noted earlier, Logistix, is testing Web Agent software from Aspect Telecommunications that allows an employee and a customer to simultaneously view the same web screen while they are having a telephone conversation. Web Agent is only one of the products Aspect offers for teleweb applications. Visit Aspect's Web site and locate its integrated call centre solutions. Try an online demo of one of the featured products or read the detailed description of Web Agent. How does this Aspect product deliver value to Logistix and other marketers that purchase it for use with a customer contact system? What value does it add for the business customer who contacts Logistix through its call centre? How can Logistix use this product to build relationships with its business customers? What relationship-building obstacles do you think Logistix might encounter early in the next millennium, and how should the company respond?

Winning Markets: Market-Oriented Strategic Planning

PROFILE:

Canadian Marketing Excellence

It is more important to do what is strategically right than what is immediately profitable. Bruce Poon Tip, president and founder of GAP Adventures Inc. (GAP = the Great Adventure People), is someone who understands this maxim. After taking some business courses and realizing that the traditional corporate world wasn't for him, Poon Tip founded GAP in 1991 after he had taken two trips to Thailand. On the first, he went on an expensive five-star bus trip; on the second, he travelled for $10 per day and found a country rich in local culture instead of one full of Yuppies and beautiful hotels. "I realized I'd been ripped off the first time," says Poon Tip. Believing that others would also want to escape mass tours and get to know foreign landscapes, people, and cultures intimately, Bruce founded GAP. Today, GAP earns $10.3 million in revenues and is among the world's top 10 adventure firms. GAP offers trips to over 100 countries such as camel safaris in India and treks through Peruvian rainforests for small groups. His company was recently listed in sixth position in *Profit* magazine's list of the 100 fastest-growing businesses in Canada, and Bruce himself has made *The Globe and Mail's Report on Business'* list of Canada's Top 40 under 40. What advice does Bruce give to people planning their business strategy? "Realize your dreams and goals on your own terms with integrity," carefully manage meagre resources, and act in a socially responsible fashion—sustainable tourism is a significant part of GAP's mission.

Sources: Aaron Lam, "Success Story: Bruce Poon Tip," *Business $ense*, Vol 1 (1), Spring 1999, pp. 23-25; "Canada's Top 40 Under 40," *Globe and Mail's Report on Business*, May 1999, pp. 51-52.

In this chapter, we examine the following questions:

- How is strategic planning carried out at the corporate and division levels?

- How is planning carried out at the business unit level?

- What are the major steps in the marketing process?

- How is planning carried out at the product level?

- What does a marketing plan include?

In Chapters 1 and 2, we asked the question: How do companies compete in a global marketplace? One part of the answer is a commitment to creating and retaining satisfied customers. We can now add a second part: Successful companies know how to adapt to a continuously changing marketplace. They practise the art of market-oriented strategic planning.

- **Market-oriented strategic planning** is the managerial process of developing and maintaining a viable fit between the organization's objectives, skills, and resources and its changing market opportunities. The aim of strategic planning is to shape and reshape the company's businesses and products so that they yield target profits and growth.

The concepts and tools that underlie strategic planning emerged in the 1970s as a result of a succession of shock waves that hit North America—the energy crisis, double-digit inflation, economic stagnation, Japanese competitive victories, deregulation of key industries. No longer could North American companies rely on simple growth projections to plan production, sales, and profits. Today, the main goal of strategic planning is to help a company select and organize its businesses in a way that will keep the company healthy even when unexpected events adversely affect any of its specific businesses or product lines.

Strategic planning calls for action in three key areas: The first is managing a company's businesses as an investment portfolio. The second key area involves assessing each business' strength by considering the market's growth rate and the company's position and fit in that market rather than using current sales or profits as a guide. The third key area is *strategy*. For each of its businesses, the company must develop a game plan for achieving its long-run objectives. Each company must determine what makes the most sense in the light of its industry position, objectives, opportunities, skills, and resources.

Marketing plays a critical role in the strategic-planning process. According to a strategic-planning manager at General Electric:

> . . . *the marketing manager is the most significant functional contributor to the strategic-planning process, with leadership roles in defining the business mission; analysis of*

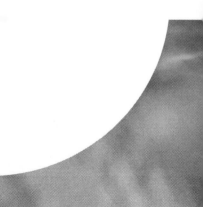

the environmental, competitive, and business situations; developing objectives, goals, and strategies; and defining product, market, distribution, and quality plans to implement the business strategies. This involvement extends to the development of programs and operating plans that are fully linked with the strategic plan.[1]

To understand marketing management, we must understand strategic planning. And to understand strategic planning, we need to recognize that most large companies consist of four organizational levels: the corporate level, division level, business level, and product level. To illustrate each level of strategic planning, we will turn to Noranda Inc.'s 1998 Annual Report. Corporate headquarters is responsible for designing a *corporate strategic plan* to guide the whole enterprise; it makes decisions on the amount of resources to allocate to each division, as well as which businesses to start or eliminate. Each division establishes a *division plan* covering the allocation of funds to each business unit within the division. Each business unit develops a *business unit strategic plan* to carry that business unit into a profitable future. Finally, each product level (product line, brand) within a business unit develops a *marketing plan* for achieving its objectives in its product market.

The marketing plan operates at two levels. The *strategic marketing plan* lays out the broad marketing objectives and strategy based on an analysis of the current market situation and opportunities. The *tactical marketing plan* outlines specific marketing tactics, including advertising, merchandising, pricing, channels, and service.

The marketing plan is the central instrument for directing and coordinating the marketing effort. In today's organizations the marketing department does not set the marketing plan by itself. Rather, plans are developed by teams, with inputs and signoffs from every important function. These plans are then implemented at the appropriate levels of the organization. Results are monitored, and corrective action is taken when necessary. The complete planning, implementation, and control cycle is shown in Figure 3-1.

Noranda Inc.
www.noranda.ca

CORPORATE AND DIVISION STRATEGIC PLANNING

By preparing statements of mission, policy, strategy, and goals, headquarters establishes the framework within which the divisions and business units prepare their plans. Some corporations give a lot of freedom to their business units to set their own sales and profit goals and strategies. Others set goals for their business units but let them develop their own strategies. Still others set the goals and get heavily involved in the individual business unit strategies.[2]

All corporate headquarters undertake three planning activities:

- Defining the corporate mission
- Assigning resources to each SBU
- Planning new businesses

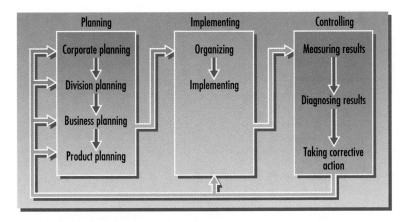

FIGURE 3.1

The Strategic-Planning, Implementation, and Control Process

DEFINING THE CORPORATE MISSION

An organization exists to accomplish something: to make cars, lend money, provide a night's lodging, and so on. Its specific mission or purpose is usually clear when the business starts. Over time the mission may lose its relevance because of changed market conditions or become unclear as the corporation adds new products and markets to its portfolio.

When management senses that the organization is drifting from its mission, it must renew its search for purpose. According to Peter Drucker, it is time to ask some fundamental questions.[3] *What is our business? Who is the customer? How does the customer define value? What will our business be? What should our business be?* These simple-sounding questions are among the most difficult the company will ever have to answer. Successful companies continuously raise these questions and answer them thoughtfully and thoroughly.

One reason firms must carefully think about what markets, what products, and what customers they hope to serve is that these decisions have a significant impact on the ethical decisions and dilemmas a firm will face. If a firm decides to send its sales teams to some international markets, for example, it will face the issues of gift giving and bribery. If the firm decides to market certain types of products such as lawn chemicals, it will face decisions about environmental safety, impact on human and animal health, and product liability. Since certain market segments are more capable of understanding marketing information than are others, special care must be used when targeting vulnerable segments like children, the elderly, or physically challenged individuals. Robin and Reidenbach stress that these decisions must be considered during the strategic planning process. They developed a framework to guide strategic planners through this process. The framework illustrates that managers developing the firm's mission statement must also consider the firm's ethical profile since this guides the development of its marketing objectives. They must also identify publics affected by the firm's strategy, develop actionable ethical core values, and disseminate these through the organization.[4]

Organizations develop mission statements to share with managers, employees, and (in many cases) customers. Eric Gilboord, a Toronto-based marketing consultant, says, "A good mission statement should tell your story in less than 30 seconds. Everyone connected with your business should know it, understand it, believe in it and tell it to others in exactly the same way."[5] A well-worked-out mission statement provides employees with a shared sense of purpose, direction, and opportunity. The statement guides geographically dispersed employees to work independently and yet collectively toward realizing the organization's goals. Mission statements are at their best when they are guided by a vision—an almost "impossible dream" that provides a direction for the company for the next 10 to 20 years. Sony's former president, Akio Morita, wanted everyone to have access to "personal portable sound," so his company created the Walkman and portable CD player. Fred Smith wanted to deliver mail anywhere in the United States before 10:30 a.m. the next day, so he created Federal Express.

Here are three examples of mission statements:

Canarie Inc.
www.canarie.ca

Service Master
www.svm.com

Canarie Inc.   An industry-led, not-for-profit corporation established in 1993, the mission of Canarie (The Canadian Network for the Advancement of Research, Industry and Education) Inc. is to facilitate the development of critical aspects of the communications infrastructure in Canada; stimulate next-generation products, applications, and services; and communicate the benefits of an information-based society. Canarie will thereby contribute to Canadian competitiveness, to wealth and job creation, and to quality of life.

ServiceMaster is committed to keeping your homes clean, functional, and pest free; your lawns healthy and attractive; and your hospitals, children's schools, and businesses running smoothly and efficiently. The philosophy of a company is at the core of its business. It defines the way customers are served and people are treated. It is the foundation upon which all else is built. The ServiceMaster philosophy is expressed in four objectives. The first two objectives are end goals. The second two are means goals. Our company objectives are: To honour God in all we do; To help people develop; To pursue excellence; To grow profitably.[6]

Nortel Networks – The Future of Networking: Nortel Networks delivers the combined expertise and proven leadership in telephony and IP-based data, wireline and wireless networking to bring all your communications together over a single network. As the first and only company of its kind in the world, our experience is unmatched by anyone else in building and supporting Unified Networks—global, scalable, high-capacity public and private network built on the innovation, IP technology, and application-focus driving the Internet.[7]

Nortel Networks
www.nortelnetworks.com

Good mission statements have three major characteristics. First, they focus on a limited number of goals. The statement, "We want to produce the highest-quality products, offer the most service, achieve the widest distribution, and sell at the lowest prices" claims too much. Second, mission statements stress the major policies and values that the company wants to honour. *Policies* define how the company will deal with stakeholders, employees, customers, suppliers, distributors, and other important groups. Policies narrow the range of individual discretion so that employees act consistently on important issues. Third, they define the major *competitive scopes* within which the company will operate:

- *Industry scope*: The range of industries in which a company will operate. Some companies will operate in only one industry; some only in a set of related industries; some only in industrial goods, consumer goods, or services; and some in any industry. For example, Du Pont prefers to operate in the industrial market, while Dow is willing to operate in the industrial and consumer markets. 3M will get into almost any industry where it can make money.

- *Products and applications scope*: The range of products and applications that a company will supply. Thus, Dofasco, whose slogan is, "We're a company focused on developing solutions in steel," rose to prominence by supplying on the more profitable types of steel products, and competed effectively with the industry leader, Stelco, which produced a much broader line.

- *Competence scope*: The range of technological and other core competencies that a company will master and leverage. Japan's NEC has built its core competencies in computing, communications, and components. These competencies support its production of laptop computers, television receivers, and hand-held telephones.

- *Market-segment scope*: The type of market or customers a company will serve. Some companies will serve only the upscale market. For example, Porsche makes only expensive cars and licenses its name for high-quality sunglasses and other accessories. Gerber serves primarily the baby market.

- *Vertical scope*: The number of channel levels from raw material to final product and distribution in which a company will participate. At one extreme are companies with a large vertical scope like Noranda Inc. Noranda operates 15 mines, 18 metallurgical plants and 11 fabricating facilities worldwide, employing more than 18 000 people at operations and offices in 20 countries.[8] At the other extreme are corporations with low or no vertical integration. These "hollow corporations" or "pure marketing companies" consist of a person with a phone, fax, computer, and desk who contracts out for every service including design, manufacture, marketing, and physical distribution.[9]

- *Geographical scope*: The range of regions, countries, or country groups in which a company will operate. At one extreme are companies that operate in a specific city or state. At the other extreme are multinationals like Unilever and Caterpillar, which operate in almost every country.

Mission statements should not be revised every few years in response to every new turn in the economy. However, a company must redefine its mission if that mission

SARA LEE CORP.: FROM MANUFACTURER TO NIMBLE MARKETER

What do Hanes underwear, Coach leather bags, Kiwi Shoe Polish, Ball Park hot dogs, and Wonder Bra have in common? They're all brands manufactured and sold by Sara Lee Corp., a company most people associate with frozen cheesecake. The Sara Lee brand accounts for a paltry 25 percent of the company's $29 billion revenues, and it is the brand on which its namesake company has spent the least time, money, and focus. Yet, on September 29, 1997, Sara Lee Corp. stunned the business world by announcing an abrupt shift in strategy and focus; it would outsource its manufacturing operations and concentrate on both building the Sara Lee brand and marketing its other name brands. Outsourcing will allow Sara Lee to lower its cost structure to make its brands price-competitive and release more funds for marketing.

Sara Lee's strategic change represents a nod to the future. Companies are increasingly focusing on their core competencies and leaving the dirty, less glamorous manufacturing operations to lower-cost manufacturers located overseas. Coca-Cola Co. and Nike, for instance, are global brands that own little but sell much. "It's passé for us to be as vertically integrated as we were," says John Bryan, in his twenty-third year of being Sara Lee's CEO. The company even coined its own word for the new strategy: "de-verticalize." Those most surprised by Sara Lee's move are those in the heavily "verticalized" home-textiles industry, in which Sara Lee, with Hanes and other brands, earns a third of its revenues. The home-textiles industry is dominated by the giant mills. They are state-of-the-art, highly efficient, and extremely automated manufacturing operations. Yet, according to Sara Lee, they are edging toward obsolescence.

With its many different products, Sara Lee will certainly have a harder time transforming itself into a nimble marketer than a company with only one brand to sell. Also, most of Sara Lee's brands are ones that are not noted for style and panache. It's a largely unexciting business mix in what are mainly mature industries. Still, the company plans to generate $64 billion by adopting the three-year policy to build its core brands through marketing and outsourcing. Ad spending on the Sara Lee brand alone will rise to $33 million, and the company will move the brand from the freezer to the meat case and bakery sections of the supermarket. It is also targeting consumers who have less time to prepare food than they used to or who don't sit down to eat with a family. New products include smaller cheesecake portions that don't have to be defrosted.

Many applaud the company's decision to slice up the cheesecake rather than sell it off. It's hard work to maintain strong brands over the long haul. The key will be in how Sara Lee manages its marketing efforts. The company, at least, has great name recognition among consumers. It remains to be seen whether the new strategy will enable it to live up to its name.

Sources: Based on: "Sara Lee to Build Brand Through Outstanding Marketing," *Discount Store News*, October 20, 1997, p. A4. Rance Crain, "Sara Lee Uses Smart Alternative to Selling Some Valuable Brands," *Advertising Age*, September 22, 1997, p. 25. David Leonhardt, "Sara Lee: Playing with the Recipe," *Business Week*, April 27, 1998, p. 114. Warren Shoulberg, "Que Sara," *Home Textiles Today*, September 29, 1997, p. 70.

has lost credibility or no longer defines an optimal course for the company.[10] Kodak has redefined itself from a film company to an image company so that it could add digital imaging. IBM has redefined itself from a hardware and software manufacturer to a "builder of networks." Sara Lee is redefining itself by outsourcing manufacturing and becoming a marketer of brands. See the Marketing Insight, "Sara Lee Corp.: From Manufacturer to Nimble Marketer."

ESTABLISHING STRATEGIC BUSINESS UNITS

Most companies operate several businesses. They often define their businesses in terms of products: They are in the "auto business" or the "slide-rule business." But Levitt argued that market definitions of a business are superior to product definitions.[11] A business must be viewed as a customer-satisfying process, not a goods-producing process. Products are transient, but basic needs and customer groups endure forever. A horse-carriage company will go out of business soon after the automobile is invented, unless it switches to making cars. Levitt encouraged companies to redefine their business in terms of needs, not products. Table 3-1 gives several examples of companies that moved from a product to a market definition of their business.

A business can be defined in terms of three dimensions: *customer groups, customer needs,* and *technology.*[12] Consider, for example, a small company that defines its business as designing incandescent lighting systems for television studios. Its customer group is television studios; the customer need is lighting; and the technology is

TABLE 3.1

Company	Product Definition	Market Definition
Canadian National Railroad	We run a railroad.	We are a people-and-goods mover.
Xerox	We make copying equipment.	We help improve office productivity.
Imperial Oil	We sell gasoline.	We supply energy.
Columbia Pictures	We make movies.	We market entertainment.
Encyclopaedia Britannica	We sell encyclopedias.	We distribute information.
Carrier	We make air conditioners and furnaces.	We provide climate control in the home.

Product-Oriented versus Market-Oriented Definitions of a Business

incandescent lighting. The company might want to expand into additional businesses. For example, it could make lighting for other customer groups, such as homes, factories, and offices. Or it could supply other services needed by television studios, such as heating, ventilation, or air conditioning. Or it could design other lighting technologies for television studios, such as infrared or ultraviolet lighting.

Large companies normally manage quite different businesses, each requiring its own strategy. General Electric classified its businesses into 49 *strategic business units* (SBUs). An SBU has three characteristics:

1. It is a single business or collection of related businesses that can be planned separately from the rest of the company.

2. It has its own set of competitors.

3. It has a manager who is responsible for strategic planning and profit performance and who controls most of the factors affecting profit.

ASSIGNING RESOURCES TO EACH SBU

The purpose of identifying the company's strategic business units is to develop separate strategies and assign appropriate funding. Senior management knows that its portfolio of businesses usually includes a number of "yesterday's has-beens" as well as "tomorrow's breadwinners." But it cannot rely just on impressions; it needs analytical tools for classifying its businesses by profit potential. Two of the best-known business portfolio evaluation models are the Boston Consulting Group model and the General Electric model.[13]

Boston Consulting Group Approach

The Boston Consulting Group (BCG), a leading management consulting firm, developed and popularized the *growth-share matrix* shown in Figure 3-2. The eight circles represent the current sizes and positions of eight business units in a hypothetical company. The dollar-volume size of each business is proportional to the circle's area. Thus, the two largest businesses are 5 and 6. The location of each business unit indicates its market growth rate and relative market share.

The *market growth rate* on the vertical axis indicates the annual growth rate of the market in which the business operates. In Figure 3-2, it ranges from 0 to 20 percent. A market growth rate above 10 percent is considered high. *Relative market share*, which is measured on the horizontal axis, refers to the SBU's market share relative to that of its largest competitor in the segment. It serves as a measure of the company's strength in the relevant market segment. A relative market share of 0.1 means that the company's sales volume is only 10 percent of the leader's sales volume; a relative share of 10 means that the company's SBU is the leader and has 10 times the sales of the next-strongest competitor in that market. Relative market share is divided into high and low share, using 1.0 as the dividing line. Relative market share is drawn in log scale, so that equal distances represent the same percentage increase.

FIGURE 3.2

The Boston Consulting Group's Growth-Share Matrix

Source: Reprinted from *Long Range Planning*, February 1977, p. 12, copyright ©1977 with kind permission from Elsevier Science Ltd. The Boulevard, Langford Lane, Kidlington OX5 1GB, UK.

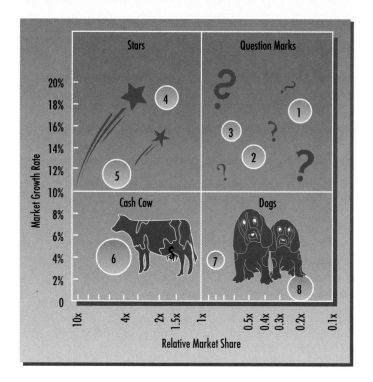

The growth-share matrix is divided into four cells, each indicating a different type of business:

1. *Question marks*: Question marks are businesses that operate in high-growth markets but have low relative market shares. Most businesses start off as question marks as the company tries to enter a high-growth market in which there is already a market leader. A question mark requires a lot of cash because the company has to spend money on plant, equipment, and personnel to keep up with the fast-growing market, and because it wants to overtake the leader. The term "question mark" is appropriate because the company must think hard about whether to keep pouring money into this business. The company in Figure 3-2 operates three question-mark businesses, and this may be too many. The company might be better off investing more cash in one or two of these businesses.

2. *Stars*: If the question-mark business is successful, it becomes a star. A star is the market leader in a high-growth market. A star does not necessarily produce a positive cash flow for the company. The company must spend substantial funds to keep up with the high market growth and fight off competitors' attacks. In Figure 3-2, the company has two stars. The company would justifiably be concerned if it had no stars.

3. *Cash cows*: When a market's annual growth rate falls to less than 10 percent, the star becomes a cash cow if it still has the largest relative market share. A cash cow produces a lot of cash for the company. The company does not have to finance capacity expansion because the market's growth rate has slowed down. And since the business is the market leader, it enjoys economies of scale and higher profit margins. The company uses its cash-cow businesses to pay its bills and support its other businesses. The company in Figure 3-2 has only one cash cow and is therefore highly vulnerable. If this cash cow starts losing relative market share, the company will have to pump money back into it to maintain market leadership. If it does not, the cash cow may devolve into a dog.

4. *Dogs*: Dogs are businesses that have weak market shares in low-growth markets. They typically generate low profits or losses. The company in Figure 3-2 holds two dogs, and this may be two too many. The company should consider whether it is holding on to these businesses for good reasons (such as an expected turnaround in the market growth rate or a new chance at market leadership) or for sentimental reasons.

After plotting its various businesses in the growth-share matrix, a company must determine whether its portfolio is healthy. An unbalanced portfolio would have too many dogs or question marks and/or too few stars and cash cows.

The company's next task is to determine what objective, strategy, and budget to assign to each SBU. Four strategies can be pursued:

1. *Build*: Here the objective is to increase market share, even forgoing short-term earnings to achieve this objective if necessary. Building is appropriate for question marks whose market shares must grow if they are to become stars.

2. *Hold*: Here the objective is to preserve market share. This strategy is appropriate for strong cash cows if they are to continue yielding a large positive cash flow.

3. *Harvest*: Here the objective is to increase short-term cash flow regardless of long-term effect. Harvesting involves a decision to withdraw from a business by implementing a program of continuous cost retrenchment. The company plans to cash in on its "crop," to "milk its business." Harvesting generally involves eliminating R&D expenditures, not replacing the physical plant as it wears out, not replacing salespeople, reducing advertising expenditures, and so on. The hope is to reduce costs at a faster rate than any potential drop in sales, thus resulting in an increase in positive cash flow. This strategy is appropriate for weak cash cows whose future is dim and from which more cash flow is needed. Harvesting can also be used with question marks and dogs. The company carrying out a harvesting strategy faces prickly social and ethical questions over how much information to share with various stakeholders.

4. *Divest*: Here the objective is to sell or liquidate the business because resources can be better used elsewhere. This strategy is appropriate for dogs and question marks that are acting as a drag on the company's profits.

Companies must decide whether harvesting or divestment is a better strategy for a weak business. Harvesting reduces the business' future value and therefore the price at which it could later be sold. An early decision to divest, in contrast, is likely to produce fairly good bids if the business is in relatively good shape and of more value to another firm.

As time passes, SBUs change their position in the growth-share matrix. Successful SBUs have a life cycle. They start as question marks, become stars, then cash cows, and finally dogs. For this reason, companies should examine not only their businesses' current positions in the growth-share matrix (as in a snapshot) but also their moving positions (as in a motion picture). Each business should be reviewed as to where it was in past years and where it will probably move in future years. If a given SBU's expected trajectory is not satisfactory, the corporation should ask its manager to propose a new strategy and the likely resulting trajectory.

The worst mistake a company could make would be to require all its SBUs to aim for the same growth rate or return level. The very point of SBU analysis is that each business has a different potential and requires its own objective. Other mistakes include: leaving cash cows with too little in retained funds (in which case they grow weak) or leaving them with too much in retained funds (in which case the company fails to invest enough in new businesses with growth potential); making major investments in dogs in hopes of turning them around but failing each time; and maintaining too many question marks and underinvesting in each. Question marks should either receive enough support to achieve segment dominance or be dropped.

The General Electric Model

An SBU's appropriate objective cannot be determined solely by its position in the growth-share matrix. If additional factors are considered, the growth-share matrix can

FIGURE 3.3

**Market Attractiveness–
Competitive–Position Portfolio
Classification and Strategies**

Source: Reprinted by permission from pages 202 and 204 of *Analysis for Strategic Marketing Decisions* by George S. Day. Copyright © 1986 by West Publishing Company.
All rights reserved. Reprinted by permission of South-Western College Publishing, a division of International Thompson Publishing, Inc., Cincinnati, OH, 45227.

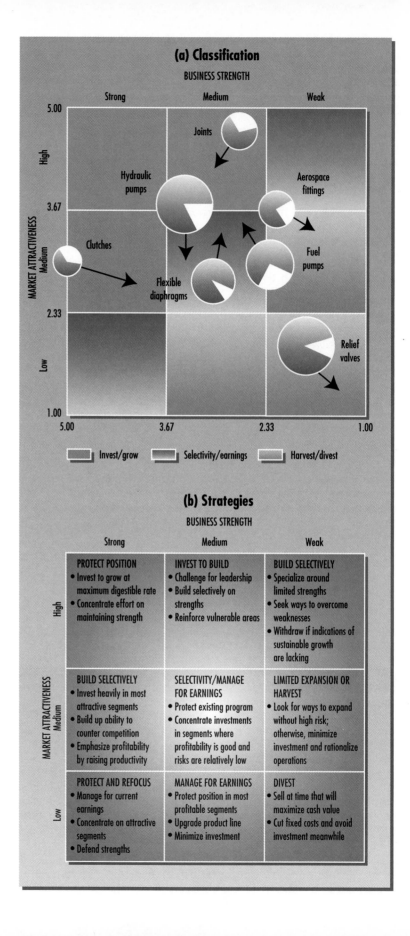

be seen as a special case of a multifactor portfolio matrix that General Electric (GE) pioneered. This model is shown in Figure 3-3(a), where one company's seven businesses are plotted. This time the size of each circle represents the size of the relevant market rather than the size of the company's business. The shaded part of the circle represents that business' market share. Thus, the company's clutch business operates in a moderate-size market and enjoys approximately a 30 percent market share.

Each business is rated in terms of two major dimensions: market attractiveness and business strength (Figure 3-3[b]). These two factors make excellent marketing sense for rating a business. Companies are successful to the extent that they enter attractive markets and possess the required business strengths to succeed in those markets. If one of these factors is missing, the business will not produce outstanding results. Neither a strong company operating in an unattractive market nor a weak company operating in an attractive market will do very well.

To measure these two dimensions, strategic planners must identify the factors underlying each dimension and find a way to measure them and combine them into an index. Table 3-2 lists two possible sets of factors making up the two dimensions for the hydraulic-pumps business in Figure 3-3. (Each company must decide on its own list of factors.) For the hydraulic pumps business, market attractiveness varies with the market's size, annual market growth rate, historical profit margins, and so on. And business strength varies with the company's market share, share growth, product quality, and so on. Note that the two BCG factors—market growth rate and market share—are subsumed under the two major variables of the GE model. The GE model leads strategic planners to look at more factors in evaluating an actual or potential business than the BCG model does.

How does the company arrive at the data in Table 3-2 and the circles in Figure 3-3(a)? Management rates each factor from 1 (very unattractive) to 5 (very attractive). The hydraulic-pumps business is rated 4 on overall market size, indicating that the market size is pretty large (a 5 would be very large). Clearly, evaluating these factors requires data and assessment from marketing and other company personnel. The ratings are then multiplied by weights reflecting the factors' relative importance to arrive at the values, which are summed for each dimension. The hydraulic-pumps business scored a 3.70 on market attractiveness and a 3.40 on business strength, out of a maximum possible score of 5.00 for each. The analyst places a point representing this business in the multifactor matrix in Figure 3-3(a) and draws a circle around it whose size is proportional to the size of the relevant market. The company's market share of approximately 14 percent is shaded in. Clearly, the hydraulic-pumps business is in a fairly attractive part of the matrix.

In fact, the GE matrix is divided into nine cells, which in turn fall into three zones (Figure 3-3[b]). The three cells in the upper-left corner indicate strong SBUs in which the company should invest/grow. The diagonal cells stretching from the lower left to the upper right indicate SBUs that are medium in overall attractiveness. The company should pursue selectivity and manage for earnings in these SBUs. The three cells in the lower-right corner indicate SBUs that are low in overall attractiveness: The company should give serious thought to harvesting/divesting these companies. For example, the relief-valves business represents an SBU with a small market share in a fair-size market that is not very attractive and in which the company has a weak competitive position: It is a fit candidate for harvest/divest.[14]

Management should also forecast each SBU's expected position in the next three to five years given current strategy. Making this determination involves analyzing where each product is in its product life cycle as well as expected competitor strategies, new technologies, economic events, and so on. The results are indicated by the length and direction of the arrows in Figure 3-3(a). For example, the hydraulic-pumps business is expected to decline slightly in market attractiveness, and the clutches business is expected to decline strongly in the company's business strength.

The company's objective is not always to build sales in each SBU. Rather, the objective might be to maintain the existing demand with fewer marketing dollars or to take cash out of the business and allow demand to fall. Thus, the task of marketing management is to manage demand or revenue to the target level negotiated with the corporate management. Marketing contributes to assessing each SBU's sales and profit

TABLE	3.2

Factors Underlying Market Attractiveness and Competitive Position in GE Multifactor Portfolio Model: Hydraulic-Pumps Market

		Weight	Rating = (1–5)	Value
Market Attractiveness	Overall market size	0.20	4	0.80
	Annual market growth rate	0.20	5	1.00
	Historical profit margin	0.15	4	0.60
	Competitive intensity	0.15	2	0.30
	Technological requirements	0.15	4	0.60
	Inflationary vulnerability	0.05	3	0.15
	Energy requirements	0.05	2	0.10
	Environmental impact	0.05	3	0.15
	Social-political-legal	Must be acceptable		
		1.00		3.70

		Weight	Rating = (1–5)	Value
Business Strength	Market share	0.10	4	0.40
	Share growth	0.15	2	0.30
	Product quality	0.10	4	0.40
	Brand reputation	0.10	5	0.50
	Distribution network	0.05	4	0.20
	Promotional effectiveness	0.05	3	0.15
	Productive capacity	0.05	3	0.15
	Productive efficiency	0.05	2	0.10
	Unit costs	0.15	3	0.45
	Material supplies	0.05	5	0.25
	R&D performance	0.10	3	0.30
	Managerial personnel	0.05	4	0.20
		1.00		3.40

Source: Adapted from La Rue T. Hosmer, *Strategic Management* (Upper Saddle River, NJ: Prentice Hall, 1982), p. 310.

potential, but once the SBU's objectives and budget are set, marketing's job is to carry out the plan efficiently and profitably.

Critique of Portfolio Models

In addition to the BCG and GE models, other portfolio models have been developed and used, particularly the Arthur D. Little model and the Shell directional-policy model.[15] Portfolio models have had a number of benefits. They have helped managers think more strategically, understand the economics of their businesses better, improve the quality of their plans, improve communication between business and corporate management, identify information gaps and important issues, eliminate weaker businesses, and strengthen their investment in more promising businesses.

However, portfolio models must be used cautiously. They may lead the company to place too much emphasis on market-share growth and entry into high-growth businesses or to neglect its current businesses. The models' results are sensitive to the ratings and weights and can be manipulated to produce a desired location in the matrix. Furthermore, since these models use an averaging process, two or more businesses may end up in the same cell position but differ greatly in their underlying ratings and weights. Many businesses will end up in the middle of the matrix as a result of compromises in ratings, and this makes it hard to know what the appropriate strategy should be. Finally, the models fail to delineate the synergies between two or more businesses, which means that making decisions for one business at a time might be risky. There is a danger of terminating a losing business unit that actually provides an essential core competence needed by several other business units. Overall, though, portfolio models have improved managers' analytical and strategic capabilities and permitted them to make better decisions than they could with mere impressions.[16]

PLANNING NEW BUSINESSES, DOWNSIZING OLDER BUSINESSES

The company's plans for its existing businesses allow it to project total sales and profits. Often, projected sales and profit are less than what corporate management wants them to be. If there is a strategic-planning gap between future desired sales and projected sales, corporate management will have to develop or acquire new businesses to fill it.

Figure 3-4 illustrates this strategic-planning gap for a major manufacturer of audiocassette tapes called Musicale (name disguised). The lowest curve projects the expected sales over the next five years from the company's current business portfolio. The highest curve describes the corporation's desired sales over the next five years. Evidently the company wants to grow much faster than its current businesses will permit. How can it fill the strategic-planning gap?

Three options are available. The first is to identify opportunities to achieve further growth within the company's current businesses (intensive growth opportunities). The second is to identify opportunities to build or acquire businesses that are related to the company's current businesses (integrative growth opportunities). The third is to identify opportunities to add attractive businesses that are unrelated to the company's current businesses (diversification growth opportunities).

Intensive Growth

Corporate management's first course of action should be a review of whether any opportunities exist for improving its existing businesses' performance. Ansoff has proposed a useful framework for detecting new intensive growth opportunities called a product/market expansion grid (Figure 3-5).[17] The company first considers whether it could gain more market share with its current products in their current markets (market-penetration strategy). Next it considers whether it can find or develop new markets for its current products (market-development strategy). Then it considers whether it can develop new products of potential interest to its current markets (product-development strategy). Later it will also review opportunities to develop new products for new markets—diversification strategy. How might Musicale use these three major intensive growth strategies to increase its sales?

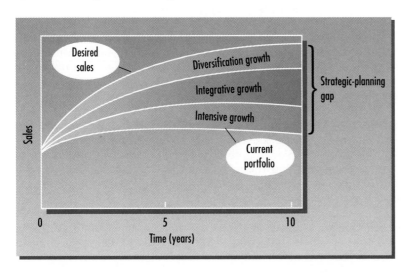

FIGURE 3.4

The Strategic-Planning Gap

FIGURE 3.5

Three Intensive Growth Strategies: Ansoff's Product–Market Expansion Grid

Source: Adapted from Igor Ansoff, "Strategies for Diversification," *Harvard Business Review,* September–October 1957, p. 114.

There are three major approaches to increasing current products' market share in their current market. Musicale could try to encourage its current customers to buy more cassettes per period. This could work if its customers purchase cassettes infrequently and could be shown the benefits of using more cassettes for music recording or dictation. Or Musicale could try to attract competitors' customers. This could work if Musicale noticed major weaknesses in competitors' product or marketing programs. Finally, Musicale could try to convince non-users of cassettes to start using them. This could work if there are still many people who do not own cassette recorders.

How can management look for new markets whose needs might be met by its current products? First, Musicale might try to identify potential user groups in the current sales areas whose interest in cassettes the company might stimulate. If Musicale has been selling cassette tapes only to consumer markets, it might pursue office and factory markets. Second, Musicale might seek additional distribution channels in its present locations. If it has been selling its tape only through stereo-equipment dealers, it might add mass-merchandising channels. Third, the company might consider selling in new locations in its home country or abroad. Thus, if Musicale sold only in the eastern part of the United States, it could consider entering eastern and western Canada or Europe. Management should also consider new-product possibilities. Musicale could develop new cassette-tape features, such as a longer-playing tape and a tape that buzzes at the end of its play. It could develop different quality levels, such as a higher-quality tape for fine-music listeners and a lower-quality tape for the mass market. Or it could research an alternative technology to cassette tape such as compact discs and digital audiotape.

By examining these three intensive growth strategies, management may discover several ways to grow. Still, that growth may not be enough. In that case, management must also examine integrative growth opportunities.

Integrative Growth

Often a business' sales and profits can be increased through backward, forward, or horizontal integration within its industry. Musicale might acquire one or more of its suppliers (such as plastic-material producers) to gain more control or generate more profit (*backward integration*). Or Musicale might acquire some wholesalers or retailers, especially if they are highly profitable (*forward integration*). Finally, Musicale might acquire one or more competitors, provided that the government does not bar this move (*horizontal integration*). These new sources may still not deliver the desired sales volume, however. In that case, the company must consider diversification.

Diversification Growth

Diversification growth makes sense when good opportunities can be found outside the present businesses. A good opportunity is one in which the industry is highly attractive and the company has the mix of business strengths to be successful. Three types of diversification are possible. The company could seek new products that have technological and/or marketing synergies with existing product lines, even though the new products themselves may appeal to a different group of customers (*concentric diversification strategy*). Musicale might start a computer-tape manufacturing operation because it knows how to manufacture audiocassette tape. Second, the company might search for new products that could appeal to its current customers even though the new products are technologically unrelated to its current product line (*horizontal diversification strategy*). Musicale might produce cassette-holding trays, even though producing them requires a different manufacturing process. Finally, the company might seek new businesses that have no relationship to the company's current technology, products, or markets (*conglomerate diversification strategy*). Musicale might want to consider such new businesses as making application software or personal organizers.

Downsizing Older Businesses

Companies must not only develop new businesses but also carefully prune, harvest, or divest tired old businesses in order to release needed resources and reduce costs. Weak businesses require a disproportionate amount of managerial attention. Managers should focus on a company's growth opportunities, not fritter away energy and resources trying to salvage hemorrhaging businesses.

B USINESS STRATEGIC PLANNING

The business unit strategic-planning process consists of the eight steps shown in Figure 3-6. We examine each step in the sections that follow.

BUSINESS MISSION

Each business unit needs to define its specific mission within the broader company mission. Thus, a television studio-lighting-equipment company might define its mission as: "The company aims to target major television studios and become their vendor of choice for lighting technologies that represent the most advanced and reliable studio lighting arrangements." Notice that this mission does not attempt to win business from smaller television studios, win business by being lowest in price, or venture into non-lighting products.

SWOT ANALYSIS

The overall evaluation of a company's strengths, weaknesses, opportunities, and threats is called SWOT analysis.

External Environment Analysis (Opportunity and Threat Analysis)

In general, a business unit must think constantly about what it takes to win in its chosen markets and then it has to monitor key macroenvironment forces

FIGURE 3.6

The Business Strategic-Planning Process

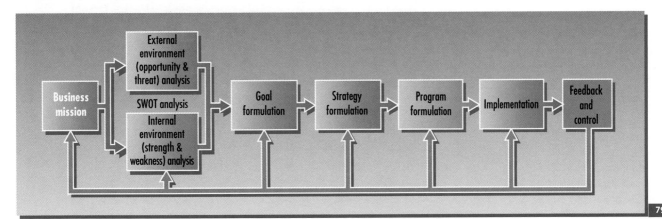

(demographic/economic, technological, political/legal, and social/cultural) and significant microenvironment actors (customers, competitors, distributors, suppliers) that affect its ability to achieve its objectives and earn profits. The business unit should set up a marketing intelligence system to track trends and important developments. For each trend or development, management needs to identify the associated opportunities and threats.

A major purpose of environmental scanning is to discern new marketing opportunities.

■ A *marketing opportunity* is an area of buyer need in which a company can perform profitably.

Opportunities can be classified according to their *attractiveness* and their *success probability*. The company's success probability depends on whether its business strengths not only match the key success requirements for operating in the target market but also exceed those of its competitors. Mere competence does not constitute a competitive advantage. The best-performing company will be the one that can generate the greatest customer value and sustain it over time.

In the opportunity matrix in Figure 3-7(a), the best marketing opportunities facing the TV-lighting-equipment company are listed in the upper-left cell (#1); management should pursue these opportunities. The opportunities in the lower-right cell (#4) are too minor to consider. The opportunities in the upper-right cell (#2) and lower-left cell (#3) should be monitored in the event that any improve in their attractiveness and success probability.

Some developments in the external environment represent threats.

■ An *environmental threat* is a challenge posed by an unfavourable trend or development that would lead, in the absence of defensive marketing action, to deterioration in sales or profit.

Threats should be classified according to *seriousness* and *probability of occurrence*. Figure 3-7(b) illustrates the threats matrix facing the TV-lighting-equipment company.

FIGURE 3.7

Opportunity and Threat Matrixes

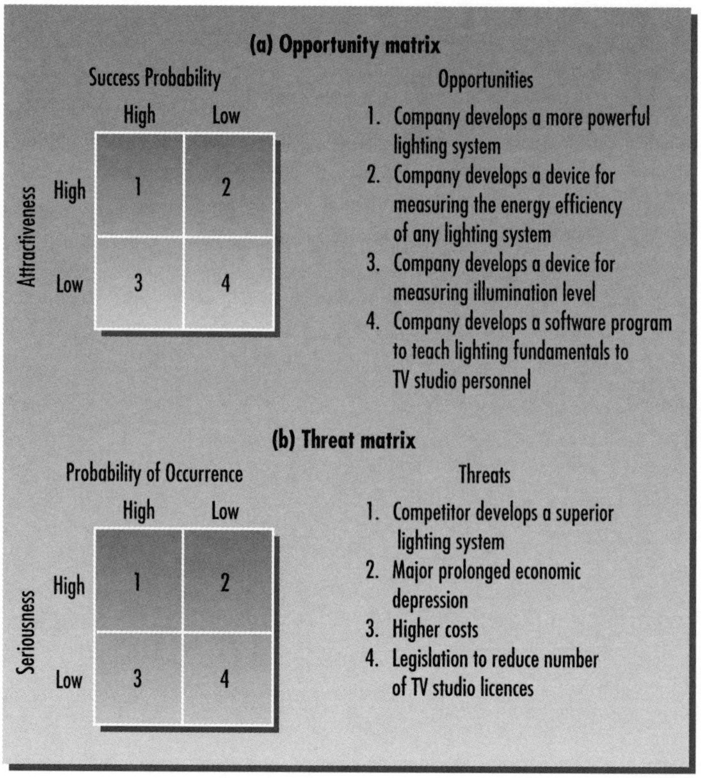

(a) Opportunity matrix

Success Probability — High, Low
Attractiveness — High: 1, 2; Low: 3, 4

Opportunities
1. Company develops a more powerful lighting system
2. Company develops a device for measuring the energy efficiency of any lighting system
3. Company develops a device for measuring illumination level
4. Company develops a software program to teach lighting fundamentals to TV studio personnel

(b) Threat matrix

Probability of Occurrence — High, Low
Seriousness — High: 1, 2; Low: 3, 4

Threats
1. Competitor develops a superior lighting system
2. Major prolonged economic depression
3. Higher costs
4. Legislation to reduce number of TV studio licences

The threats in the upper-left cell are major threats, since they can seriously hurt the company and have a high probability of occurrence. To deal with these threats, the company needs to prepare contingency plans that spell out changes the company can make before or during the threat. The threats in the lower-right cell are very minor and can be ignored. The threats in the upper-right and lower-left cells do not require contingency planning but need to be carefully monitored in the event that they grow more serious.

Once management has identified the major threats and opportunities facing a specific business unit, it can characterize that business' overall attractiveness. Four outcomes are possible:

An *ideal business* is high in major opportunities and low in major threats.

A *speculative business* is high in both major opportunities and threats.

A *mature business* is low in major opportunities and low in threats.

A *troubled business* is low in opportunities and high in threats.

INTERNAL ENVIRONMENT ANALYSIS (STRENGTHS/ WEAKNESSES ANALYSIS)

It is one thing to discern attractive opportunities, another to have the competencies to succeed in these opportunities. Each business needs to evaluate its internal strengths and weaknesses periodically. It can do so by using a form like the one shown in the Marketing Memo entitled "Checklist for Performing Strengths/Weaknesses Analysis." Management—or an outside consultant—reviews marketing, financial, manufacturing, and organizational competencies and rates each factor as a major strength, minor strength, neutral factor, minor weakness, or major weakness.

Clearly, the business does not have to correct all its weaknesses, nor should it gloat about all its strengths. The big question is whether the business should limit itself to those opportunities where it possesses the required strengths or should consider better opportunities where it might have to acquire or develop certain strengths. For example, managers at Texas Instruments (TI) split between those who want TI to stick to industrial electronics (where it has clear strength) and those who want the company to continue introducing consumer electronic products (where it lacks some required marketing strengths).

Sometimes a business does poorly not because its departments lack the required strengths but because they do not work together as a team. In one major electronics company the engineers look down on the salespeople as "engineers who couldn't make it" and the salespeople look down on the service people as "salespeople who couldn't make it." It is therefore critically important to assess interdepartmental working relationships as part of the internal environmental audit. Honeywell does exactly this:

Honeywell. Every year, Honeywell asks each department to rate its own strengths and weaknesses and those of the other departments with which it interacts. The notion is that each department is a "supplier" to some departments and a "customer" of other departments. Thus, if Honeywell engineers frequently underestimate the cost and completion time of new products, their "internal customers" (manufacturing, finance, and sales) will be hurt. Once each department's weaknesses are identified, work can be undertaken to correct them.

Honeywell Ltd.
www.honeywell.ca

George Stalk, a leading BCG consultant, suggests that winning companies are those that have achieved superior in-company capabilities, not just core competences.[18] Every company must manage some basic processes, such as new-product development, sales generation, and order fulfilment. Each process creates value and requires interdepartmental teamwork. Although each department may possess specific core competencies, the challenge is to develop superior competitive capability in managing the company's key processes. Stalk calls this capabilities-based competition.

Checklist for Performing Strengths/Weaknesses Analysis

	PERFORMANCE					IMPORTANCE		
	MAJOR STRENGTH	MINOR STRENGTH	NEUTRAL	MINOR WEAK-NESS	MAJOR WEAK-NESS	HIGH	MEDIUM	LOW
MARKETING								
1. Company reputation	___	___	___	___	___	___	___	___
2. Market share	___	___	___	___	___	___	___	___
3. Product quality	___	___	___	___	___	___	___	___
4. Service quality	___	___	___	___	___	___	___	___
5. Pricing effectiveness	___	___	___	___	___	___	___	___
6. Distribution effectiveness	___	___	___	___	___	___	___	___
7. Promotion effectiveness	___	___	___	___	___	___	___	___
8. Sales force effectiveness	___	___	___	___	___	___	___	___
9. Innovation effectiveness	___	___	___	___	___	___	___	___
10. Geographical coverage	___	___	___	___	___	___	___	___
FINANCE								
11. Cost/availability of capital	___	___	___	___	___	___	___	___
12. Cash flow	___	___	___	___	___	___	___	___
13. Financial stability	___	___	___	___	___	___	___	___
MANUFACTURING								
14. Facilities	___	___	___	___	___	___	___	___
15. Economies of scale	___	___	___	___	___	___	___	___
16. Capacity	___	___	___	___	___	___	___	___
17. Able dedicated workforce	___	___	___	___	___	___	___	___
18. Ability to produce on time	___	___	___	___	___	___	___	___
19. Technical manufacturing skill	___	___	___	___	___	___	___	___
ORGANIZATION								
20. Visionary capable leadership	___	___	___	___	___	___	___	___
21. Dedicated employees	___	___	___	___	___	___	___	___
22. Entrepreneurial orientation	___	___	___	___	___	___	___	___
23. Flexible/responsive	___	___	___	___	___	___	___	___

GOAL FORMULATION

Once the company has performed a SWOT analysis, it can proceed to develop specific goals for the planning period. This stage of the process is called goal formulation. Managers use the term goals to describe objectives that are specific with respect to magnitude and time. Turning objectives into measurable goals facilitates management planning, implementation, and control.

Very few businesses pursue only one objective. Most business units pursue a mix of objectives including profitability, sales growth, market-share improvement, risk containment, innovativeness, and reputation. The business unit sets these objectives and then manages by objectives (MBO). For an MBO system to work, the unit's various objectives must meet four criteria:

- First, objectives must be arranged hierarchically, from the most to the least important. For example, the business unit's key objective for the period may be to increase the rate of return on investment. This can be accomplished by increasing the profit level and/or reducing the amount of invested capital. Profit itself can be increased by increasing revenue and/or reducing expenses. Revenue can be increased in turn by increasing market share and/or prices. By proceeding this way, the business can move from broad objectives to specific objectives for specific departments and individuals.

- Second, objectives should be stated quantitatively whenever possible. The objective "increase the return on investment (ROI)" is better stated as the goal "increase ROI to 15 percent within two years."

- Third, goals should be realistic. They should arise from an analysis of the business unit's opportunities and strengths, not from wishful thinking.

- Finally, the company's objectives must be consistent. It is not possible to maximize both sales and profits simultaneously.

Other important trade-offs include short-term profit versus long-term growth, deep penetration of existing markets versus developing new markets, profit goals versus nonprofit goals, and high growth versus low risk. Each choice in this set of goal trade-offs calls for a different marketing strategy.

STRATEGY FORMULATION

Goals indicate what a business unit wants to achieve; *strategy* is a game plan for getting there. Every business must tailor a strategy for achieving its goals, consisting of a *marketing strategy* and a compatible *technology strategy* and *sourcing strategy*. Although many types of marketing strategies are available, Michael Porter has condensed them into three generic types that provide a good starting point for strategic thinking: overall cost leadership, differentiation, or focus.[19]

- *Overall cost leadership*. Here the business works hard to achieve the lowest production and distribution costs so that it can price lower than its competitors and win a large market share. Firms pursuing this strategy must be good at engineering, purchasing, manufacturing, and physical distribution. They need less skill in marketing. Texas Instruments is a leading practitioner of this strategy. The problem with this strategy is that other firms will usually emerge with still lower costs and hurt the firm that rested its whole future on being low cost.

- *Differentiation*. Here the business concentrates on achieving superior performance in an important customer benefit area valued by a large part of the market. It can strive to be the service leader, the quality leader, the style leader, the technology leader, and so on, but it is not possible to be all of these things. The firm cultivates those strengths that will contribute to the intended differentiation. Thus the firm seeking quality leadership must use the best components, put them together expertly, inspect them carefully, and effectively communicate its quality. Intel, for instance, has established itself as a technology leader, coming out with new microprocessors at breakneck speed.

- *Focus*. Here the business focuses on one or more narrow market segments. The firm gets to know these segments intimately and pursues either cost leadership or differentiation within the target segment. Airwalk shoes came to fame by focusing on the very narrow extreme-sports segment.

According to Porter, those firms pursuing the same strategy directed to the same target market constitute a *strategic group*. The firm that carries off that strategy best will make the most profits. Firms that do not pursue a clear strategy—"middle-of-the-roaders"—do the worst. International Harvester fell upon hard times because it did not stand out in its industry as lowest in cost, highest in perceived value, or best in serving some market segment. Middle-of-the-roaders try to be good on all strategic dimensions, but since strategic dimensions require different and often inconsistent ways of organizing the firm, these firms end up being not particularly excellent at anything.

In a recent article entitled "What is Strategy?" Porter drew a distinction between *operational effectiveness* and *strategy*.[20] Many companies believe that they can establish a long-lasting competitive advantage by performing similar activities better than their competitors. But today, competitors can rapidly copy the operational effective company using benchmarking and other tools, thus diminishing the advantage of operational effectiveness. In contrast, Porter defines strategy "as the creation of a unique and valuable position involving a different set of activities." A company that is strategically positioned "performs different activities from rivals or performs similar activities in different ways." He cites such companies as Ikea and Southwest Airlines as having distinctive strategies consisting of many different but consistent and synergistic activities that would be hard for competitors to imitate as a whole.

STRATEGIC ALLIANCES

Companies are also discovering that they need strategic partners if they hope to be effective. Even giant companies—AT&T, IBM, Philips, Siemens—often cannot achieve leadership, either nationally or globally, without forming *strategic alliances* with domestic and/or multinational companies that complement or leverage their capabilities and resources. The Star Alliance, for example, brings together Air Canada, Lufthansa, United Airlines, SAS, Thai Airways, Varig, Air New Zealand, and Ansett Australia in a huge global partnership that allows travellers to make nearly seamless connections to about 700 destinations.

New technology is requiring global standards, and to meet them you need global alliances. For instance, two of the world's largest credit-card issuers will forget rivalries and join forces to develop a worldwide standard for 'smart cards.' American Express Co. and Visa International became shareholders in a company called Proton World International together with two electronic payment network operators, Banskys SA of Belgium and Interplay of the Netherlands, and transport ticketing and telecommunications group, ERG Ltd. of Australia. The Proton World partners said they would welcome MasterCard and other interested parties in this venture to develop smart-card technology and create worldwide standards for smart-card payments. The Proton venture "is part of a trend toward realizing that the global alliance is the way to go," said Gerry Hopkinson, head of corporate affairs at Mondex, another smart-card technology company.[21]

Just doing business in another country may require the firm to license its product, form a joint venture with a local firm, or buy from local suppliers to meet "domestic-content" requirements. As a result, many firms are rapidly developing global strategic networks. And victory is going to those who build the better global network. For more details, see the Marketing in the 21st Century box "The Strategic Alliance Boom."

THE STRATEGIC ALLIANCE BOOM

In the new global environment, with greater competition from more and more products and choices, alliances are not just a planning option but a strategic necessity. As Jim Kelly, CEO of UPS, which has a number of global alliances, puts it, "The old adage 'If you can't beat 'em, join 'em,' is being replaced by 'Join 'em and you can't be beat." In fact, new technology companies in software, biotechnology, or telecommunications are now usually "born global." HDM, a computer mapping company, had a joint venture in Japan and development groups in Canada and Russia within two years of its formation. "Virtually everything we do is partnerships," says Tom Parmeter, president of Protein Polymer Technologies, Inc., a biomaterials manufacturer in San Diego. Alliances are crucial because Protein Polymer can't build markets on its own.

Strategic alliances are booming across the entire spectrum of industries and services and for a wide variety of purposes. According to Booz Allen & Hamilton, the number of North American firms with partners in Europe, Asia, and Latin America is growing at a rate of 25 percent annually. Why the boom? Here are several strategic reasons companies enter into alliances:

- Fill gaps in current market and technology
- Turn excess manufacturing capacity into profits
- Reduce risk and entry costs into new markets
- Accelerate product introductions
- Achieve economies of scale
- Overcome legal and trade barriers
- Extend the scope of existing operations
- Cut exit costs when divesting operations

Despite the many good reasons for pursuing alliances, a high percentage end in failure. A study by McKinskey revealed that roughly one-third of 49 alliances failed to live up to the partners' expectations. But such painful lessons are teaching companies how to craft a winning alliance. Three keys seem to be:

1. *Strategic fit.* Before even considering an alliance, companies need to assess their own core competencies. Then they need to find a partner that will complement them in business lines, geographic positions, or competencies. A good example of strategic fit is AT&T and Sovintel, a Russian telephone company. The two joined forces to offer high-speed ISDN services for digitized voice, data, and video communication between the two countries. By joining together, the two telecommunications companies can offer new services for more business customers than either could do alone.

2. *A focus on the long term.* Rather than joining forces to save a few dollars, strategic partners should focus more on gains that can be harvested for years to come. Corning, the $5-billion-a-year glass and ceramics maker, is renowned for making partnerships. It has derived half of its products from joint ventures and even defines itself as a "network of organizations." That network includes German and Korean electronics giants, Siemens and Samsung, and Mexico's biggest glassmaker, Vitro.

3. *Flexibility. Alliances can last only if they're flexible.* One example of a flexible partnership is Merck's alliance with AB Astra of Sweden. Merck started out simply with U.S. rights to its partner's new drugs. For the next phase, Merck set up a new corporation to handle the partnership's $500-million-a-year business and sold half the equity to Astra.

Sources: Julie Cohen Mason, "Strategic Alliances: Partnering for Success," *Management Review,* May 1993, pp. 10–15; Stratford Sherman, "Are Strategic Alliances Working?" *Fortune,* September 21, 1992, pp. 77–78; Edwin Whenmouth, "Rivals Become Partners: Japan Seeks Links with U.S. and European Firms," *Industry Week,* February 1, 1993, pp. 11–12, 14; John Naisbitt, *The Global Paradox* (New York: William Morrow, 1994), pp. 18–21; Rosabeth Moss Kantner, "The Power of Partnering," *Sales & Marketing Management,* June 1997, pp. 26–28; Jim Kelly, "All Together, Now," *Chief Executive,* November 1997, pp. 60-63; Roberta Maynard, "Striking the Right Match," *Nation's Business,* May 1996, p. 18.

Many strategic alliances take the form of *marketing alliances*. These fall into four major categories.[22]

1. *Product and/or service alliances.* One company licenses another to produce its product, or two companies jointly market their complementary products or a new product. For instance, Seagram Co. Ltd. allied its Universal Music Division with Germany's BMG Entertainment to sell music over the Internet. When announcing the alliance, Edgar Bronfman Jr. stressed, "In order to reach consumers in a meaningful way, one needs scale, scope, depth and richness…our partnership…will provide an unmatched breadth of music programming and content, generating tremendous exposure for our artists."[23]

2. *Promotional alliances*. One company agrees to carry a promotion for another company's product or service. For example, Chapters Inc. signed a partnership agreement with Alta Vista Canada, an Internet search engine. Not only will Chapters' banner advertisements appear prominently on the site, but users of the Alta Vista site will also be automatically directed to Chapters when they search for books.[24]

3. *Logistics alliances*. One company offers logistical services for another company's product. For example, Abbott Laboratories warehouses and delivers all of 3M's medical and surgical products to hospitals across North America.

4. *Pricing collaborations*. One or more companies join in a special pricing collaboration. It is common for hotel and rental car companies to offer mutual price discounts.

Companies need to give creative thought to finding partners who might complement their strengths and offset their weaknesses. Well-managed alliances allow companies to obtain a greater sales impact at less cost. To keep their strategic alliances thriving, corporations have begun to develop organizational structures to support them and have come to view the ability to form and manage partnerships as core skills in and of themselves. Disney and Hewlett-Packard, for example, have alliance executives. Lotus and Xerox, whose early alliances were handled with business development departments, have set up alliance groups. Smaller companies can designate a core group in charge of partnerships, even if it's not formal, to manage and monitor alliances.[25]

PROGRAM FORMULATION

Once the business unit has developed its principal strategies, it must work out detailed supporting programs. Thus if the business has decided to attain technological leadership, it must plan programs to strengthen its R&D department, gather technological intelligence, develop leading-edge products, train the technical sales force, and develop ads to communicate its technological leadership.

Once the programs are tentatively formulated, the marketing people must evaluate their costs. Questions arise: Is participating in a particular trade show worth it? Will a specific sales contest pay for itself? Will hiring another salesperson contribute to the bottom line? *Activity-based cost* (ABC) accounting should be applied to each marketing activity to determine whether the activity is likely to produce sufficient results to justify the cost.[26]

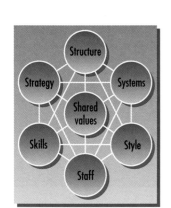

F I G U R E 3.8

McKinsey 7-S Framework

Source: McKinsey 7-S Framework from *In Search of Excellence: Lessons from America's Best Run Companies*, by Thomas J. Peters and Robert H. Waterman Jr. Copyright © 1982 by Thomas J. Peters and Robert H. Waterman, Jr. Reprinted by permission of HarperCollins, Publishers, Inc.

IMPLEMENTATION

A clear strategy and well-thought-out supporting program may be useless if the firm fails to implement them carefully. Indeed, strategy is only one of seven elements, according to the McKinsey Consulting Firm, that the best-managed companies exhibit.[27] The McKinsey 7-S framework for business success is shown in Figure 3-8. The first three elements—strategy, structure, and systems—are considered the "hardware" of success. The next four—style, staff, skills, and shared values—are the "software."

The first "soft" element, *style*, means that company employees share a common way of thinking and behaving. Thus Tim Horton's employees smile at the customer, and IBM employees are very professional in their customer dealings. The second, *skills*, means that the employees have the skills needed to carry out the company's strategy. The third, *staffing*, means that the company has hired able people, trained them well, and assigned them to the right jobs. The fourth, *shared values*, means that the employees share the same guiding values. When these soft elements are present, companies are usually more successful at strategy implementation.[28]

FEEDBACK AND CONTROL

As it implements its strategy, the firm needs to track the results and monitor new developments in the internal and external environment. Some environments are fairly stable from year to year. Other environments evolve slowly in a fairly predictable way. Still other environments change rapidly in major and unpredictable ways. Nonetheless, the company can count on one thing: The marketplace will change. And when it does, the company will need to review and revise its implementation, programs, strategies, or even objectives. Consider what happened at computer-services giant Electronic Data Systems Corp. (EDS):

EDS
www.eds.com

Andersen Consulting
www.andersenconsulting.com

EDS, Computer Sciences Corp., and Andersen Consulting. For years EDS saw its base business—outsourcing—grow by 25 percent annually. But in 1993 that percentage dropped to a mere seven percent. EDS's primary business had been managing the data-processing operations of clients such as Continental Airlines and General Motors. But technological developments have led to a shift from mainframes to new platforms, including networks of personal computers. There was thus less demand for EDS' core talent: providing lots of software engineers and technicians to write programs and keep these programs running in giant data centres. Customers now want computer-services companies to act as management consultants to help re-engineer key business processes. Computer Sciences Corp. and Andersen Consulting have already established themselves in this area, and EDS is undergoing a rocky transition as it attempts to respond to the changed environment. To counter loss of market share, EDS cut costs, expanded efforts in client-server setups, hired more consultants for re-engineering, and developed alliances with telecommunications partners.[29]

A company's strategic fit with the environment will inevitably erode because the market environment almost always changes faster than the company's 7-Ss. Thus it is possible for a company to remain efficient while it loses effectiveness. Peter Drucker pointed out that it is more important to "do the right thing" (effectiveness) than "to do things right" (efficiency). The most successful companies excel at both.

Once an organization fails to respond to a changed environment, it becomes increasingly hard to restore its lost position. This has happened to the once-unassailable Motorola since it failed to respond to the new digital technology and kept rolling out analogue phones. Also consider what happened to Lotus Development Corp. Its Lotus 1-2-3 software was once the world's leading software program, but Lotus didn't keep pace as the PC evolved, allowing Microsoft's Excel to grab the market. Now its market share in desktop software has slipped so low that analysts don't even bother to track it.

Organizations, especially large ones, are subject to inertia. They are set up as efficient machines, and it is difficult to change one part without adjusting everything else. Yet organizations can be changed through leadership, preferably in advance of a crisis but certainly in the midst of one. The key to organizational health is the organization's willingness to examine the changing environment and to adopt appropriate new goals and behaviours. High-performance organizations continuously monitor the environment and attempt through flexible strategic planning to maintain a viable fit with the evolving environment.

THE MARKETING PROCESS

Planning at the corporate, division, and business levels is an integral part of the marketing process. To fully understand that process, we must first look at how a company defines its business.

The task of any business is to deliver value to the market at a profit. There are at least two views of the *value-delivery process*.[30] The traditional view is that the firm makes something and then sells it (Figure 3-9[a]). For example, Thomas Edison invents the phonograph and then hires people to make and sell it. In this view, marketing takes place in the second half of the value-delivery process. The traditional view assumes that the company knows what to make and that the market will buy enough units to produce profits for the company.

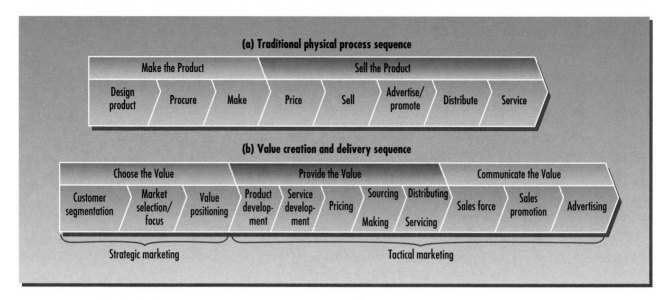

(a) Traditional physical process sequence

Make the Product			Sell the Product				
Design product	Procure	Make	Price	Sell	Advertise/ promote	Distribute	Service

(b) Value creation and delivery sequence

Choose the Value			Provide the Value					Communicate the Value		
Customer segmentation	Market selection/ focus	Value positioning	Product develop-ment	Service develop-ment	Pricing	Sourcing / Making	Distributing / Servicing	Sales force	Sales promotion	Advertising

Strategic marketing ← Choose the Value | Tactical marketing ← Provide the Value / Communicate the Value

FIGURE 3.9

Two Views of the Value-Delivery Process

Source: Michael J. Lanning and Edward G. Michaels, "A Business Is a Value Delivery System," McKinsey staff paper no. 41, June 1988. © McKinsey & Co., Inc.

Companies that subscribe to this traditional view have the best chance of succeeding in economies marked by goods shortages where consumers are not fussy about quality, features, or style. But the traditional view of the business process will not work in more competitive economies where people face abundant choices. The "mass market" is actually splintering into numerous micromarkets, each with its own wants, perceptions, preferences, and buying criteria. The smart competitor therefore must design the offer for well-defined target markets.

THE VALUE-DELIVERY SEQUENCE

This belief is at the core of the new view of business processes, which places marketing at the beginning of the planning process. Instead of emphasizing making and selling, companies see themselves as part of a value creation and delivery sequence (Figure 3-9[b]). This sequence consists of three parts.

The first phase, *choosing the value,* represents the "homework" that marketing must do before any product exists. The marketing staff must segment the market, select the appropriate market target, and develop the offer's value positioning. The formula *"segmentation, targeting, positioning (STP)"* is the essence of strategic marketing.

Once the business unit has chosen the value, it is ready to *provide the value.* The tangible product's specifications and services must be detailed, a target price must be established, and the product must be made and distributed. Developing specific product features, prices, and distribution occur at this stage and are part of *tactical marketing.*

The task in the third phase is *communicating the value.* Here further tactical marketing occurs in utilizing the sales force, sales promotion, advertising, and other promotional tools to inform the market about the product. As Figure 3-9(b) shows, the marketing process begins before there is a product and continues while it is being developed and after it becomes available. The Japanese have further developed this view by promulgating the following concepts:

- *Zero customer feedback time:* Customer feedback should be continuously collected after purchase to learn how to improve the product and its marketing.

- *Zero product-improvement time*: The company should evaluate all the customers' and employees' improvement ideas and introduce the most valued and feasible improvements as soon as possible.

- *Zero purchasing time*: The company should receive the required parts and supplies continuously through just-in-time arrangements with suppliers. By lowering its inventories, the company can reduce its costs.

- *Zero setup time*: The company should be able to manufacture any of its products as soon as they are ordered, without facing high setup time or costs.
- *Zero defects*: The products should be of high quality and free of flaws.

STEPS IN THE PLANNING PROCESS

To carry out their responsibilities, marketing managers—whether at the corporate, division, business, or product level—follow a marketing process. Working within the plans set by the levels above them, product managers come up with a marketing plan for individual products, lines, or brands.

- The **marketing process** consists of analyzing marketing opportunities; researching and selecting target markets; designing marketing strategies; planning marketing programs; and organizing, implementing, and controlling the marketing effort.

    We will illustrate each step here in connection with the following situation:

    Zeus, Inc. (name disguised), operates in several industries, including chemicals, cameras, and film. The company is organized into SBUs. Corporate management is considering what to do with its Atlas camera division. At present, Atlas produces a range of 35-mm cameras. The market for standard cameras is intensely competitive. On a growth-share matrix, this business is becoming a weak cash cow. Zeus' corporate management wants Atlas' marketing group to produce a strong turnaround plan. Marketing management has to come up with a convincing marketing plan, sell corporate management on the plan, and then implement and control it.

The sections that follow apply to marketing planning at all levels of the organization. Later in this chapter, we will examine the components of a specific marketing plan developed to support a product line.

Analyzing Market Opportunities

The first task facing Atlas is to identify its potential long-run opportunities given its market experience and core competencies. Atlas can, of course, develop standard film cameras with better features. It can also consider designing a line of digital cameras and/or video cameras. Or Atlas can use its core competency in optics to design a line of binoculars and telescopes.

To evaluate its competing opportunities, Atlas needs to operate a reliable marketing research and information system (Chapter 4). Marketing research is an indispensable marketing tool for assessing buyer wants and behaviour and assessing market size. The marketing people can research secondary sources; run focus groups; and conduct telephone, mail, and personal surveys. By analyzing the collected data, Atlas will gain a better picture of the size of each market opportunity.

Marketing research gathers significant information about the marketing environment (Chapter 5). Atlas' *microenvironment* consists of all the players who affect the company's ability to produce and sell cameras—suppliers, marketing intermediaries, customers, competitors. Atlas' *macroenvironment* consists of demographic, economic, physical, technological, political/legal, and social/cultural forces that affect its sales and profits. An important part of gathering environmental information includes measuring market potential and forecasting future demand.

Atlas needs to understand *consumer markets* (Chapter 6). It needs to know: How many households plan to buy cameras? Who buys and why do they buy? What are they looking for in the way of features and prices? Where do they shop? What are their images of different brands? Atlas also sells cameras to *business markets*, including large corporations, professional firms, retailers, and government agencies (Chapter 7). Purchasing agents or buying committees make the decisions. Atlas needs to gain a full understanding of how organizational buyers buy. Atlas needs a sales force that is well trained in presenting product benefits. Atlas must also pay close attention to competitors (Chapter 8), anticipating its competitors' moves and knowing how to react quickly and decisively. It may want to initiate some surprise moves, in which case it needs to anticipate how its competitors will respond.

Once Atlas has analyzed its market opportunities, it is ready to select target markets. Modern marketing practice calls for dividing the market into major market segments, evaluating each segment, and targeting those market segments that the company can best serve (Chapter 9).

Developing Marketing Strategies

Suppose Atlas decides to focus on the consumer market and develop a *differentiating and positioning* strategy (Chapter 10). Should Atlas position its cameras as the "Cadillac" brand, offering a superior camera at a premium price with excellent service and strong advertising? Should it build a simple low-price camera aimed at more price-conscious consumers? Or should it develop a medium-quality, medium-price camera? Once Atlas decides on its product positioning, it must initiate new-product development, testing, and launching (Chapter 11). Different decision tools and controls are needed at different stages of the new-product development process.

After launch, the product's strategy will need modification at the different stages in the product life cycle: introduction, growth, maturity, and decline (Chapter 10). Furthermore, strategy choice will depend on whether the firm is a market leader, challenger, follower, or nicher (Chapter 8). Finally, strategy will have to take into account changing global opportunities and challenges (Chapter 12).

Planning Marketing Programs

To transform marketing strategy into marketing programs, marketing managers must make basic decisions on marketing expenditures, marketing mix, and marketing allocation. First, Atlas must decide what level of marketing expenditures will achieve its marketing objectives. Companies typically establish their marketing budget at a percentage of the sales goal. A particular company may spend more than the normal percentage ratio in the hope of achieving a higher market share.

Second, the company has to decide how to divide the total marketing budget among the various tools in the marketing mix. Marketing mix is one of the key concepts in modern marketing theory.

- *Marketing mix* is the set of marketing tools that the firm uses to pursue its marketing objectives in the target market.

There are literally dozens of marketing-mix tools. McCarthy popularized a four-factor classification of these tools called the *four Ps*: product, price, place (i.e., distribution), and promotion.[31] The particular marketing variables under each *P* are shown in Figure 1-5. Marketing-mix decisions must be made for both distribution channels and final consumers. Figure 1-6 shows the company preparing an *offering mix* of products, services, and prices, and utilizing a *promotion mix* of sales promotion, advertising, sales force, public relations, direct mail, telemarketing, and Internet to reach the distribution channels and the target customers.

Not all marketing-mix variables can be adjusted in the short run. Typically, the firm can change its price, sales force size, and advertising expenditures in the short run. It can develop new products and modify its distribution channels only in the long run. Thus the firm typically makes fewer period-to-period marketing-mix changes in the short run than the number of marketing-mix variables might suggest.

Finally, marketers must decide on the allocation of the marketing budget to the various products, channels, promotion media, and sales areas. How many dollars should support Atlas' two or three camera lines? Direct versus distributor sales? Direct-mail advertising versus trade-magazine advertising? East Coast markets versus West Coast markets? To make these allocations, marketing managers use *sales-response functions* that show how sales would be affected by the amount of money spent in each application.

The most basic marketing-mix tool is *product*—the firm's tangible offering to the market, which includes the product quality, design, features, branding, and packaging (Chapter 13). As part of its product offering, Atlas may provide various services, such as leasing, delivery, repair, and training (Chapter 14). Such support services can provide a competitive advantage in the globally competitive marketplace.

A critical marketing-mix tool is *price* (Chapter 15). Atlas has to decide on whole-sale and retail prices, discounts, allowances, and credit terms. Its price should be commensurate with the offer's perceived value. Otherwise, buyers will turn to competitors' products.

Place includes the various activities the company undertakes to make the product accessible and available to target customers (Chapters 16 and 17). Atlas must identify, recruit, and link various marketing facilitators to supply its products and services efficiently to the target market. It must understand the various types of retailers, whole-salers, and physical-distribution firms and how they make their decisions.

Promotion includes all the activities the company undertakes to communicate and promote its products to the target market (Chapters 18-21). Atlas has to hire, train, and motivate salespeople. It has to set up communication and promotion programs consisting of advertising, sales promotion, public relations, and direct and online marketing.

Note that the 4Ps represent the sellers' view of the marketing tools available for influencing buyers. From a buyer's point of view, each marketing tool is designed to deliver a customer benefit. Robert Lauterborn suggested that the sellers' 4Ps correspond to the customers 4Cs[32]: customer needs and wants; cost to the customer; convenience; and communication. Winning companies will be those that can meet customer needs economically and conveniently and with effective communication.

Managing the Marketing Effort

The final step in the marketing process is organizing the marketing resources and then implementing and controlling the marketing plan. The company must build a marketing organization that is capable of *implementing* the marketing plan (Chapter 22). In a small company, one person might carry out all the marketing tasks. Large companies such as Atlas will have several marketing specialists: salespeople, sales managers, marketing researchers, advertising personnel, product and brand managers, market-segment managers, and customer-service personnel.

Marketing departments are typically headed by a marketing vice-president who performs three tasks. The first is to coordinate the work of all of the marketing personnel. The second task is to work closely with the other functional vice-presidents. The third task is selecting, training, directing, motivating, and evaluating personnel.

Because of surprises and disappointments as marketing plans are implemented, the company needs feedback and control. There are three types of marketing control:

1. *Annual-plan control* is the task of ensuring that the company is achieving its current sales, profits, and other goals. First, management must state well-defined goals for each month or quarter. Second, management must measure its performance in the marketplace. Third, management must determine the underlying causes of any serious performance gaps. Fourth, management must choose corrective actions to close gaps between goals and performance.

2. *Profitability control* is the task of measuring the actual profitability of products, customer groups, trade channels, and order sizes. This is not a simple task. A company's accounting system is seldom designed to report the real profitability of different marketing entities and activities. *Marketing profitability analysis* measures the profitability of different marketing activities. *Marketing efficiency studies* try to determine how various marketing activities could be carried out more efficiently.

3. *Strategic control* is the task of evaluating whether the company's marketing strategy is appropriate to market conditions. Because of rapid changes in the marketing environment, each company needs to periodically reassess its marketing effectiveness through a control instrument known as the *marketing audit*.

Figure 3-10 presents a grand summary of the marketing process and the forces shaping the company's marketing strategy.

FIGURE 3.10

**Factors Influencing Company
Marketing Strategy**

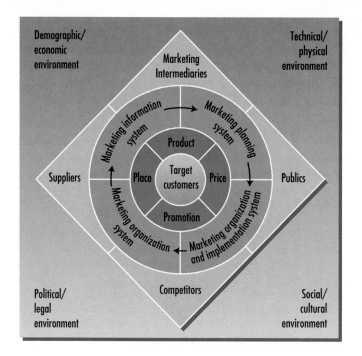

 PRODUCT PLANNING: THE NATURE AND
CONTENTS OF A MARKETING PLAN

Each product level (product line, brand) must develop a *marketing plan* for achieving its goals. The marketing plan is one of the most important outputs of the marketing process. But what does a marketing plan look like? What does it contain? Marketing plans have several sections, such as those listed in Table 3-3.

CONTENTS OF THE MARKETING PLAN

■ *Executive Summary and Table of Contents*. The marketing plan should open with a brief summary of the plan's main goals and recommendations. The executive summary permits senior management to grasp the plan's major thrust. A table of contents should follow the executive summary.

TABLE 3.3

Contents of a Marketing Plan

I. Executive summary and table of contents	Presents a brief overview of the proposed plan.
II. Current marketing situation	Presents relevant background data on sales, costs, profits, the market, competitors, distribution, and the macroenvironment.
III. Opportunity and issue analysis	Identifies the main opportunities/threats, strengths/weaknesses, and issues facing the product line.
IV. Objectives	Defines the plan's financial and marketing goals in terms of sales volume, market share, and profit.
V. Marketing strategy	Presents the broad marketing approach that will be used to achieve the plan's objectives.
VI. Action programs	Presents the special marketing programs designed to achieve the business objectives.
VII. Projected profit-and-loss statement	Forecasts the plan's expected financial outcomes.
VIII. Controls	Indicates how the plan will be monitored.

- *Current Marketing Situation*. This section presents relevant background data on the market, product, competition, distribution, and macroenvironment. The data are drawn from a product fact book maintained by the product manager.

- *Opportunity and Issue Analysis*. After summarizing the current marketing situation, the product manager proceeds to identify the major opportunities/threats, strengths/weaknesses, and issues facing the product line.

- *Objectives*. Once the product manager has summarized the issues, he or she must decide on the plan's financial and marketing objectives.

- *Marketing Strategy*. The product manager now outlines the broad marketing strategy or "game plan" that he or she will use to accomplish the plan's objectives. The marketing strategy is often presented in list form. In developing the strategy, the product manager needs to talk with the purchasing and manufacturing people to ensure that they are able to buy enough material and produce enough units to meet the needed sales volume levels. He or she also need to talk to the sales manager to obtain the planned sales force support, and to the financial officer to make sure enough advertising and promotion funds will be available.

- *Action Programs*. The marketing plan must specify the broad marketing programs designed to achieve the business objectives. Each marketing strategy element must now be elaborated to answer these questions: What will be done? When will it be done? Who will do it? How much will it cost?

- *Projected Profit and Loss Statement*. Action plans allow the product manager to build a supporting budget. On the revenue side, this budget shows the forecasted sales volume in units and the average price. On the expense side, it shows the cost of production, physical distribution, and marketing, broken down into finer categories. The difference between revenues and sales is projected profit. Once approved, the budget is the basis for developing plans and schedules for material procurement, production scheduling, employee recruitment, and marketing operations.

- *Controls*. The last section of the marketing plan outlines the controls for monitoring the plan. Typically the goals and budget are spelled out for each month or quarter. Senior management can review the results each period. Some control sections include contingency plans. A contingency plan outlines the steps management would take in response to specific adverse developments, such as price wars or strikes.

SONIC'S SHELF STEREOS: AN EXAMPLE

Jane Melody is the product manager of Sonic's line of shelf stereo systems. Each system consists of an AM-FM tuner/amplifier, CD player, tape deck, and separate speakers. Sonic offers several different models that sell in the $150 to $400 range. Sonic's main goal is to increase its market share and profitability in the shelf-stereo-system market. As product manager, Jane Melody must prepare a marketing plan to improve the line's performance.

The 2000 Sonic marketing plan seeks to generate a significant increase in company sales and profits over the preceding year. The profit target is $1.8 million. The sales-revenue target is $18 million, which represents a planned nine percent sales gain over last year. This increase is seen as attainable through improved pricing, advertising, and distribution. The required marketing budget will be $2 290 000, a 14 percent increase over last year. . . . [More details would follow.]

Market Situation

Here data are presented on the target market. The size and growth of the market (in units and/or dollars) are shown for several past years and by market and geographical segments. Data on customer needs, perceptions, and buying-behaviour trends are also presented.

The shelf stereo market accounts for approximately $400 million, or 20 percent of the home stereo market. Sales are expected to be stable over the next few years. The primary buyers are middle-income consumers, ages 20 to 40, who want to listen to good music but do not want to invest in expensive stereo component equipment. They want to buy a complete system produced by a name they can trust. They want a system with good sound and whose looks fit the decor primarily of family rooms.

Product Situation

Here the sales, prices, contribution margins, and net profits are shown for several past years, usually in table form.

Row 1, in Table 3-4, shows the total industry sales in units growing at five percent annually until 1999, when demand declined slightly. Row 2 shows Sonic's market share hovering around three percent, although it reached four percent in 1998. Row 3 shows the average price for Sonic's stereos rising about 10 percent per year except the last year, when it rose four percent. Row 4 shows variable costs—materials, labour, energy—rising each year. Row 5 shows that the gross contribution margin per unit—the difference between price (row 3) and unit variable cost (row 4)—rose the first few years and remained at $100 in the latest year. Rows 6 and 7 show sales volume in units and dollars, and row 8 shows the total gross contribution margin, which rose until the latest year, when it fell. Row 9 shows that overhead remained constant during 1996 and 1997 and increased to a high level during 1998 and 1999, owing to an increase in manufacturing capacity. Row 10 shows net contribution margin—that is, gross contribution margin less overhead. Rows 11, 12, and 13 show marketing expenditures on advertising and promotion, sales force and distribution, and marketing research. Finally, row 14 shows net operating profit after marketing expenses. The picture is one of increasing profits until 1999, when they fell to about one-third of the 1998 level. Clearly Sonic needs to find a strategy for 2000 that will restore healthy growth in sales and profits to the product line.

TABLE 3.4

Historical Product Data

Variable	Rows	1996	1997	1998	1999
1. Industry sales in units		2 000 000	2 100 000	2 205 000	2 200 000
2. Company market share		0.03	0.03	0.04	0.03
3. Average price per unit $		200	220	240	250
4. Variable cost per unit $		120	125	140	150
5. Gross contribution margin per unit ($)	(3 − 4)	80	95	100	100
6. Sales volume in units	(12)	60 000	63 000	88 200	66 000
7. Sales revenue ($)	(36)	12 000 000	13 860 000	21 168 000	16 500 000
8. Gross contribution margin ($)	(56)	4 800 000	5 985 000	8 820 000	6 6 00 000
9. Overhead ($)		2 000 000	2 000 000	3 500 000	3 500 000
10. Net contribution margin ($)	(8 − 9)	2 800 000	3 985 000	5 320 000	3 100 000
11. Advertising and promotion ($)		800 000	1 000 000	1 000 000	900 000
12. Sales force and distribution ($)		700 000	1 000 000	1 100 000	1 000 000
13. Marketing research ($)		100 000	120 000	150 000	100 000
14. Net operating profit ($)	(10 − 11 − 12 − 13)	1 200 000	1 865 000	3 070 000	1 100 000

Competitive Situation

Here the major competitors are identified and described in terms of size, goals, market share, product quality, marketing strategies, and other characteristics that are needed to understand their intentions and behaviour.

Sonic's major competitors in the shelf-stereo-system market are Aiwa, Panasonic, Sony, and Philips. Each competitor has a specific strategy and niche in the market. Aiwa, for example, offers four models covering the whole price range, sells primarily in department stores and discount stores, and is a heavy advertising spender. It plans to dominate the market through product proliferation and price discounting. . . . [Similar descriptions are prepared for the other competitors.]

Distribution Situation

This section presents data on the size and importance of each distribution channel. Shelf stereo sets are sold through department stores, radio/TV stores, appliance stores, discount stores, furniture stores, music stores, audio specialty stores, and mail order. Sonic sells 37 percent of its sets through appliance stores, 23 percent through radio/TV stores, 10 percent through furniture stores, 3 percent through department stores, and the remainder through other channels. Sonic dominates in channels that are declining in importance, while it is a weak competitor in the faster-growing channels, such as discount stores. Sonic gives about a 30 percent margin to its dealers, which is similar to what other competitors give.

Macroenvironment Situation

This section describes broad macroenvironment trends—demographic, economic, technological, political/legal, social/cultural—that bear on the product line's future.

About 70 percent of U.S. households now have stereo equipment. Consumers are spending more time watching television and videos than listening to music. They are spending more of their discretionary income on computers, exercise equipment, and travel, leaving less to spend on stereos. The only bright spots are home theatres and speakers in every room. As the market approaches saturation, effort must be turned to convincing consumers to upgrade their equipment.

Opportunities/Threats Analysis

Here the product manager identifies the main opportunities and threats facing the business. The main opportunities facing Sonic's line are as follows:

■ Consumers are showing increased interest in more compact stereo systems.

■ Two national department store chains are willing to carry the Sonic line if we will give them extra advertising support.

■ A major mass-merchandise chain is willing to carry the Sonic line if we will offer a deeper discount.

The main threats facing Sonic's line are as follows:

■ An increasing number of consumers are buying their sets in mass-merchandise and discount stores, in which Sonic has weak representation.

■ Some competitors have introduced smaller speakers with excellent sound quality, and consumers are favouring these smaller speakers.

■ The federal government may pass a more stringent product-safety law, which would entail product redesign work.

Strengths/Weaknesses Analysis

The product manager needs to identify product strengths and weaknesses. Sonic's main strengths are as follows:

■ Sonic's name has excellent brand awareness and a high-quality image.

■ Dealers who sell the Sonic line are knowledgeable and well trained in selling.

■ Sonic has an excellent service network, and consumers know they will get quick repair service.

The main weaknesses of Sonic's line are as follows:

- Sonic's sound quality is not demonstrably better than that of competing sets. Sound quality can make a big difference in brand choice.
- Sonic is budgeting only five percent of its sales revenue for advertising and promotion, while some major competitors are spending twice that level.
- Sonic's line is not clearly positioned compared with Panasonic ("low price") and Sony ("innovation"). Sonic needs a unique selling proposition. The current advertising campaign is not particularly creative or exciting.
- Sonic's brand is priced higher than other brands, but this higher price is not supported by a real perceived difference in quality. The pricing strategy should be re-evaluated.

Issues Analysis

In this section of the marketing plan, the product manager uses the strengths/weaknesses analysis to define the main issues that the plan must address. Sonic must consider the following basic issues:

- Should Sonic stay in the stereo-equipment business? Can it compete effectively? Or should it divest this product line?
- If Sonic stays in the business, should it continue with its present products, distribution channels, and price and promotion policies?
- Should Sonic switch to high-growth channels (such as discount stores)? Can it do this and yet retain the loyalty of its current channel partners?
- Should Sonic increase its advertising and promotion expenditures to match competitors' expenditures?
- Should Sonic pour money into R&D to develop advanced features, sound, and styling?

Financial Objectives

Sonic's management wants each business unit to deliver a good financial performance. The product manager sets the following financial objectives:

- Earn an annual rate of return on investment over the next five years of 15 percent after taxes.
- Produce net profits of $1 800 000 in 2000.
- Produce a cash flow of $2 000 000 in 2000.

Marketing Objectives

The financial objectives must be converted into marketing objectives. For example, if the company wants to earn $1 800 000 profit and its target profit margin is 10 percent on sales, then it must set a goal of $18 million in sales revenue. If the company sets an average price of $260, it must sell 69 230 units. If it expects total industry sales to reach 2.3 million units, it must gain three percent of the market share to achieve its goals. To maintain this market share, the company will have to set certain goals for consumer awareness, distribution coverage, and so on. Thus the marketing objectives might read:

- Achieve total sales revenue of $18 000 000 in 2000, which represents a nine percent increase from last year. Therefore, achieve a unit sales volume of 69 230, which represents an expected market share of three percent.
- Expand consumer awareness of the Sonic brand from 15 to 30 percent over the planning period.
- Expand the number of dealers by 10 percent.
- Aim for an average price of $260.

Marketing Strategy

Here is Sonic's game plan:

Target market:	Upscale households, with particular emphasis on female buyers.
Positioning:	The best-sounding and most reliable shelf stereo system.
Product line:	Add one lower-priced model and two higher-priced models.
Price:	Price somewhat above competitive brands.
Distribution outlets:	Heavy in radio/TV stores and electronic appliance stores; increased efforts to penetrate discount stores.
Sales force:	Expand by 10 percent and introduce a national account-management system.
Service:	Widely available and quick service.
Advertising:	Develop a new advertising campaign that supports the positioning strategy; emphasize higher-priced units in the ads; increase the advertising budget by 20 percent.
Sales promotion:	Increase the sales-promotion budget by 15 percent to develop a point-of-purchase display and to participate to a greater extent in dealer trade shows.
Research and development:	Increase expenditures by 25 percent to develop better styling.
Marketing research:	Increase expenditures by 10 percent to improve knowledge of consumer-choice process and to monitor competitor moves.

Action Programs

Here is how Sonic will carry out its marketing strategy:

- February. Sonic will advertise in the newspapers that a free Barbra Streisand CD will be given to everyone buying a Sonic stereo system this month. Ann Morris, consumer promotion director, will handle this project at a planned cost of $5000.

- April. Sonic will participate in the Consumer Electronics Trade Show in Toronto. Robert Jones, dealer promotion director, will make the arrangements. The expected cost is $14 000.

- August. A sales contest will be conducted, which will award three Hawaiian vacations to the three dealers producing the greatest percentage increase in Sonic sales. The contest will be handled by Mary Tyler at a planned cost of $13 000.

- September. A newspaper advertisement will announce that consumers who attend a Sonic store demonstration in the second week of September will have their names entered in a sweepstakes. Ten lucky winners will receive free Sonics. Ann Morris will handle this project at a planned cost of $6000.

MARKETING PLANNING FOR THE 21st CENTURY

Business plans are becoming more customer- and competitor-oriented and better reasoned and more realistic than they were in the past. The plans draw more inputs from all the functions and are team-developed. Marketing executives increasingly see themselves as professional managers first, and specialists second. Planning is becoming a continuous process to respond to rapidly changing market conditions. The trends we've discussed so far are in full force in the world of marketing!

At the same time, marketing planning procedures and content vary considerably among companies. The plan is variously called a "business plan," a "marketing plan," and sometimes a "battle plan." Most marketing plans cover one year. The plans vary in length from under 5 pages to over 50 pages. Some companies take their plans very seriously, while others view them as only a rough guide to action. The most frequently cited shortcomings of current marketing plans, according to marketing executives, are lack of realism, insufficient competitive analysis, and a short-run focus.

SUMMARY

1. Market-oriented strategic planning is the managerial process of developing and maintaining a viable fit between the organization's objectives, skills, and resources and its changing market opportunities. The aim of strategic planning is to shape and reshape the company's businesses and products so that they yield target profits and growth. Strategic planning takes place at four levels: corporate, division, business unit, and product.

2. Corporate headquarters is responsible for setting into motion the strategic planning process. The corporate strategy establishes the framework within which the division and business units prepare their strategic plans. Setting a corporate strategy entails four activities: Defining the corporate mission, establishing strategic business units (SBUs), assigning resources to each SBU based on its market attractiveness and business strength, and planning new businesses.

3. Strategic planning for individual businesses entails the following activities: defining the business mission, analyzing external opportunities and threats, analyzing internal strengths and weaknesses, formulating goals, formulating strategy, formulating supporting programs, implementing the programs, and gathering feedback and exercising control.

4. The marketing process consists of four steps: analyzing market opportunities; developing marketing strategies; planning marketing programs; and organizing, implementing, and controlling the marketing effort.

5. Each product level within a business unit must develop a marketing plan for achieving its goals. The marketing plan is one of the most important outputs of the marketing process, and it should contain the following elements: an executive summary and table of contents; an overview of the current marketing situation; an analysis of the opportunities and issues facing the product; a summary of the plan's financial and marketing objectives; an overview of the marketing strategy to be used to achieve the plan's objectives; a description of the action programs to be implemented to achieve the plan's objectives; a projected profit-and-loss statement; and a summary of the controls to be used in monitoring the plan's progress.

APPLICATIONS

CHAPTER CONCEPTS

1. What competitive advantages have each of the following companies achieved in the marketplace? How has each company's marketing strategy communicated these competitive advantages to the marketplace?

   a. Wal-Mart

   b. Snap-on-Tools

   c. Pfizer Canada

   d. The Toronto-Dominion Bank

   e. Kodak

2. As a member of a management consulting group, you have been retained by a business-to-business office equipment manufacturer. The company's product line consists of the five strategic business units (SBUs) shown in the table below. Use the Boston Consulting Group portfolio analysis (as illustrated in Figure 3-2) to determine each SBU's relative market share and whether the company as a whole is healthy. Describe the nature of the BCG Market Growth/Market Share matrix to top management and make recommendations as to future strategies.

STRATEGIC BUSINESS UNIT (SBU)	DOLLAR SALES (IN MILLIONS)	NUMBER OF COMPETITORS	DOLLAR SALES OF THE TOP 3 (IN MILLIONS)	MARKET GROWTH RATE
A	0.5	8	0.7, 0.7, 0.5	15%
B	1.6	22	1.6, 1.6, 1.0	18
C	1.8	14	1.8, 1.2, 1.0	7
D	3.2	5	3.2, 0.8, 0.7	4
E	0.5	10	2.5, 1.8, 1.7	4

3. You are the executive director of your local United Way. Describe the factors influencing your organization's marketing strategy, using Figure 3-10 as an outline. Who are the stakeholders and the players? How are your decisions affected by the environment in which you operate?

4. For years the Canadian airline industry has been plagued with stiff competition. Air Canada recently acquired Canadian Airlines. Perform a SWOT analysis for Air Canada and make recommendations to management of the airline based on your analysis.

5. "With more than 80 percent of the market already in its grasp, Campbell Soup Co. really doesn't need to increase its share of the $1.8 billion of condensed soup sold annually in food stores. What the company does need is to make folks hungrier for soup." What intensive growth strategy is being pursued here, and how might the company accomplish its objective?

MARKETING AND ADVERTISING

1. The Kelly Services ad shown in Figure 1 names the company's seven main strategic business units. Kelly Temporary Services is the oldest of the firm's SBUs. Overall, the company's 750 000 employees work on temporary assignments for more than 200 000 customers, mainly businesses. Do the newer SBUs represent concentric diversification, horizontal diversification, or conglomerate diversification? Explain your answer. How might Kelly Temporary Services define its business mission? What opportunities and threats would this SBU be likely to confront in the North American market for temporary services?

2. United Parcel Service delivers packages and documents to customers in more than 200 countries every day, as this ad indicates. Overall, the company's global volume of three billion yearly deliveries rings up over $33 billion in annual revenues. Is UPS pursuing a cost leadership strategy, differentiation strategy, or focus strategy? How do you know? Based on this ad, how important are systems to the successful implementation of UPS's strategy? Why would customers care about the systems support that UPS provides? What are the implications for UPS's marketing strategy?

Figure 1   Figure 2

FOCUS ON TECHNOLOGY

Marketers can use geographic information systems (GIS) to support analysis and planning of the geographic scope of their competitive scope. A GIS is a computerized system designed to present data about an area in map form. This system enables marketers to select and analyze all kinds of data and then view the results on the screen. For example, a regional gasoline marketer might decide where to expand its geographic scope after viewing population, economic, and vehicle ownership data overlaid on a map showing main highways and streets in selected areas.

To see some of the companies and products available in Canada, go to the Canadian Geomatics site at http://www.giac.ca/site/index.ctm.

To see a GIS in action, visit the Montana State Library Natural Resource Information System Web site (URL: http://www.nris.mt.gov/gis/mtmaps.html) and go to the Montana Maps Interactive section. There you will be able to view state maps that display population density, land use, legislative districts, and other data. If you were a farm equipment marketer trying to decide whether to expand into Montana, what data would you want to obtain from a GIS and why? Could you use a GIS to make decisions about other competitive scopes within which your firm will operate? Explain.

MARKETING FOR THE 21ST CENTURY

AT&T has forged alliances with a number of major companies in the telecommunications industry. Visit AT&T's Web site (http://www.att.com) and look for information about its international strategic alliances with British Telecom (BT) and other companies. Then use your favourite search engine to find recent news stories about BT and about other AT&T strategic alliances. Of the eight strategic reasons why companies enter into alliances, which seem to apply to AT&T's alliances? Why? How is the alliance between AT&T and BT a strategic fit? Why would BT agree to this alliance? Do you expect the alliance between AT&T and BT to change in any way during the first years of the new millennium? Why and how?

Every marketing plan must include the company's mission and objectives. These guide the implementation of specific strategies and programs during the period covered by the plan. The plan must also indicate the competitive scope of the business.

As Jane Melody's assistant at Sonic, you are responsible for drafting the mission statement, reviewing the objectives, and recommending the competitive scope. The marketing objectives have already been developed, as shown in this chapter. Using your knowledge of marketing, Sonic's data, and library or Internet resources, answer the following questions:

- What should Sonic's mission be?

- Are the proposed marketing objectives reasonable, given the industry's output? Visit the Trade Data On-line Web site (http://www.strategis.ic.gc.ca/sc_mrkti/tdst/eng-doc/hsearch.html#sic and search for industry sales trends and information using the radio and television SIC code (3340). You can also search the site of the U.S. Census (http://www.census.gov/epcd/www/sic.html) and check under SIC 3651 or the equivalent NAICS code for industry statistics.

- What non-financial objectives should Sonic set? How will these help Sonic fulfil its mission?

- How would you define the major competitive scopes within which Sonic will operate?

- As your instructor directs, enter the mission statement and all objectives in a written marketing plan or type them into the Mission and Objectives section of the Marketing Plan Pro software. Also enter information on the competitive scopes in the executive summary of the marketing plan.

A Marketing Revolution? Relationship Marketing

Relationship marketing is the buzzword of the day. A recent survey by *The Economist* magazine revealed that over 70 percent of companies are in the midst of realigning their marketing efforts to be more relationship driven in an attempt to gain a competitive edge by getting closer to their customers, employees, and distribution channel members. Some marketers, like Canada's Ian Gordon, even go so far as to say that traditional marketing has been killed by relationship marketing.

Both businesses and academics extol the merits of relationship marketing. Consultants, like high-tech specialist Regis McKenna stress that customers are demanding that firms be more responsive to customer needs. Firms view relationship marketing as a means of gaining a better understanding of customers, avoiding being lost in seas of advertising, reducing costs, and improving revenues. Many see it as a move from trying to sell to everyone to selling just to you. When practised well, relationship marketing helps firms know customers so well that they can give each customer the unique value he or she wants. Many firms view relationships as the main asset of their enterprises and thus they focus all their efforts toward building these associations. But meaningful relationships can only start when both the firm and its customers see that it is in their mutual interest to get together for the long term. More value must be created by the partnership than can be created by the firm or the buyer acting independently.

Firms have been highly inventive in how they try and form relationships with their best customers. Harry Rosen, for example, throws elaborate parties for his best customers. The Royal Bank—which is seen as Canada's best relationship marketing organization—carries on a back-and-forth dialogue with its clients. Using its database of 8.6 million names, the Royal Bank works to find clues about life-cycle stage and buying patterns of potential customers. For example, it can track customers of home-buying age who have an apartment number in their address. The Royal Bank sends a mailing to these people asking when they hope to buy home. For all those who respond, the Royal Bank offers favourable mortgage rates. All recipients receive a follow-up phone call.

While relationship marketing has its merits, it also has its limitations. When a group of Harvard researchers asked consumers about their so-called corporate partners, they did not hear words of praise. Instead they got words of damnation as consumers described the confusion, stressful, insensitive, and manipulative marketplace in which they felt trapped and victimized. In other words, the researchers noted that relationship marketing is a powerful tool in theory but troubled in practice.

Firms must realize that customers may not be willing participants in firms' relationship building efforts. Firms may be asking consumers to have so many relationships that the term itself seems trivial and meaningless. For example, in a recent article in *The Retail Monitor*, a newsletter published by Coopers & Lybrand, it was reported that about 70 active loyalty programs are currently operating in Canada. Instead of offering consumers something uniquely valuable, firms invade customers privacy without returning benefits. So when you are next asked to cozy up with a firm, ask yourself how the association will benefit you.

Questions

1. Figure 2.6, on page 51, illustrates the different levels of relationship marketing. Use this matrix to classify the various relationship marketing efforts shown in the case.

2. How can the Web be used to develop relationships with consumers? Why is it so important to integrate a firm's web marketing efforts with the rest of its programs?

3. Describe one firm that has succeeded in forming a relationship with you. Describe a situation in which another firm tried to form a relationship, but failed. What factors differentiated the two efforts?

Sources: Based on "Relationship Marketing," *Venture* 684 (April 7, 1998); Susan Fournier, Susan Dobscha, and David Glen Mick, "Preventing the Premature Death of Relationship Marketing," *Harvard Business Review*, January-February 1998, reprint # 98106. Ian Gordon, "Opinion: Healthy Relationship Requires Work: Author Replaces Four Ps of Marketing with 11 Cs of Relationship Marketing," *Strategy: The Canadian Marketing Report*, March 2, 1998, p. DR8. "Carlson Marketing Group: Building Clients' Businesses One Relationship at a Time," Special Supplement, *Strategy: The Canadian Marketing Report*, March 1, 1999, p. SA4. Barbara Smith, "Special Report: Database Marketing: Associations Help Decipher Relationship Marketing," , *Strategy: The Canadian Marketing Report*, January 22, 1996, p. 31.

Gathering Information and Measuring Market Demand

CHAPTER

4

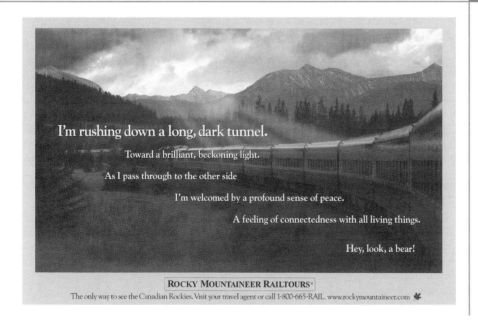

I'm rushing down a long, dark tunnel.

Toward a brilliant, beckoning light.

As I pass through to the other side

I'm welcomed by a profound sense of peace.

A feeling of connectedness with all living things.

Hey, look, a bear!

ROCKY MOUNTAINEER RAILTOURS®

The only way to see the Canadian Rockies. Visit your travel agent or call 1-800-665-RAIL. www.rockymountaineer.com

PROFILE:

Canadian Marketing Excellence

P hilip Kotler notes that marketing is becoming more of a battle based on information than one based on sales power. However, the type of information to gather information and the methods used to gather it are not always straightforward decisions. More and more companies are turning to observational methods, called ethnographic studies. Market Insights, a research firm located in St. John's, Newfoundland is a pioneer in this field. In a recent study on consumers' milk-buying habits, the research firm compared the results of what they observed consumers doing in stores and what consumers said they do when asked about their purchase behaviour in interviews. While consumers claimed to be brand loyal, observation revealed this was not the case. Consumers also told interviewers that expiry date was an important buying criterion, but again observation revealed that few consumers bothered to check this information.

On the other side of the country, ethnographic research conducted by Vancouver ad agency Bryant Fulton & Shee helped Rocky Mountaineer Railtours develop a new ad campaign that increased its bookings by 23 percent. After riding the trains and observing passengers, researchers discovered that even though the price of a two-day trip was $2000, people just didn't realize how high quality the experience would be. It didn't take the researchers long to realize that people were head over heels in love with the service. People didn't sit, they stood—gazing open-mouthed out the windows. At the end of the trip, people often embraced train staff and even exchanged phone numbers with them. So how did these observations help the agency understand its advertising task? Simple: they led to the insight that the agency had to create ads that raised people's expectations not just about the wonders of the Rockies, but also about the train service itself. Using catchy phrases like, "No one ever wrote a folk song about a minivan," the agency developed a campaign that included the beautiful ad you see below.

Source: Chris Daniels, "Real-Life Research," *Marketing*, May 17, 1999, pp. 15-16.

In this chapter we examine the following questions:

■ What are the components of a modern marketing information system?

■ What constitutes good marketing research?

■ How can marketing decision support systems help marketing managers make better decisions?

■ How can demand be more accurately measured and forecasted?

The marketing environment is changing at an accelerating rate. Given the following changes, the need for real-time market information is greater than at any time in the past:

From local to national to global marketing: As companies expand their geographical market coverage, their managers need more information more quickly.

From buyer needs to buyer wants: As incomes improve, buyers become more selective in their choice of goods. To predict buyers' response to different features, styles, and other attributes, sellers must turn to marketing research.

From price to nonprice competition: As sellers increase their use of branding, product differentiation, advertising, and sales promotion, they require information on these marketing tools' effectiveness.

From uninformed buyers to highly informed consumers: With a click of a mouse, consumers can now download information that compares product quality and the prices of hundreds of products or services. As a minimum, marketers must be as informed about competitive offerings as the buyers are.

Fortunately, the exploding information requirements have given rise to impressive new information technologies: laptop computers, palm pilots, cellular phones, scanners, videoconferencing, videodisc players, CD-ROM drives, and the Internet.[1] Some firms have developed marketing information systems that provide company management with rapid and incredible detail about buyer wants, preferences, and behaviour. For example, the Coca-Cola Company knows that we put 3.2 ice cubes in a glass, see 69 of its commercials every year, and prefer cans to pop out of vending machines at a temperature of 35 degrees. Kimberly Clark, which makes Kleenex, has calculated that the average person blows his or her nose 256 times a year. Hoover learned that we spend about 35 minutes each week vacuuming, sucking up about four kilograms of dust each year and using six bags to do so.[2] Marketers also have extensive information about consumption patterns in other countries. On a per-capita basis within Western Europe, for example, the Swiss consume the most chocolate, the Greeks eat the most cheese, the Irish drink the most tea, and the Austrians smoke the most cigarettes.[3]

Nevertheless, many business firms lack information sophistication. Many lack a marketing research department. Others have departments that limit work to routine forecasting, sales analysis, and occasional surveys. In addition, many managers complain about not knowing where critical information is located in the company; getting too much information that they can't use and too little that they really need; getting important information too late; and doubting the information's accuracy.

THE COMPONENTS OF A MODERN MARKETING INFORMATION SYSTEM

Every firm must organize a rich flow of information to its marketing managers. Competitive companies study their managers' information needs and design marketing information systems (MIS) to meet these needs.

■   A *marketing information system* (MIS) consists of people, equipment, and procedures to gather, sort, analyze, evaluate, and distribute needed, timely, and accurate information to marketing decision makers.

To carry out their analysis, planning, implementation, and control responsibilities, marketing managers need information about developments in the marketing environment. The role of the MIS is to assess the manager's information needs, develop the needed information, and distribute that information in a timely fashion. The information is developed through internal company records, marketing intelligence activities, marketing research, and marketing decision support analysis.

INTERNAL RECORDS SYSTEM

Marketing managers rely on internal reports on orders, sales, prices, costs, inventory levels, receivables, payables, and so on. By analyzing this information, they can spot important opportunities and problems.

THE ORDER-TO-PAYMENT CYCLE

The heart of the internal records system is the *order-to-payment cycle*. Sales representatives, dealers, and customers dispatch orders to the firm. The sales department prepares invoices and transmits copies to various departments. Out-of-stock items are back ordered. Shipped items are accompanied by shipping and billing documents that are sent to various departments.

Today's companies need to perform these steps quickly and accurately. Customers favour those firms that can promise timely delivery. Customers and sales representatives fax or e-mail their orders. Computerized warehouses fulfil these orders quickly. The billing department sends out invoices as quickly as possible. An increasing number of companies are using *electronic data interchange (EDI)* to improve the speed, accuracy, and efficiency of the order-to-payment cycle. Retail giant Wal-Mart tracks the stock levels of its products and its computers send automatic replenishment orders to its vendor.[4]

SALES INFORMATION SYSTEMS

Marketing managers need up-to-the-minute reports on current sales. Armed with laptop computers, sales reps can access information about prospects and customers and provide immediate feedback and sales reports. Firms like SalesCTRL that market a sales automation software package can help a firm's salespeople in Regina know what Customer Service in Montreal told customers in Moncton this morning. Sales managers can monitor everything in their territories and get current sales forecasts any time."

Sales Force Automation (SFA) software has come a long way already. Earlier versions mainly helped managers track sales and marketing results or acted as glorified datebooks.

Recent editions have put even more knowledge at marketers' fingertips. Software packages, such as those produced by the MEI Group, a Montreal-based software company, allows firms to integrate the efforts of their salesforces, helps users manage their client lists, contacts, price lists, order forms and product information while providing them with electronic access to their company's corporate information systems. Pivotal Software, a Vancouver-based software company, stresses that it isn't even accurate to call these systems salesforce automation systems. Sharka Stuyt, director of marketing at Pivotal calls the more advanced systems *customer interaction software*. These systems integrate sales, marketing and customer service all into one. In fact, they are systems for the entire company, so that anyone in the organization who interacts with the customer, can access the same knowledge base.[5] Here are two companies that are using computer technology to design fast and comprehensive sales reporting and customer integration systems:

Clarica
www.clarica.com

- **The Mutual Group of Waterloo, Ontario.** The Mutual Group, now renamed Clarica, has been a leader in embracing technology to aid its sales agents. Agents have been equipped with laptops since 1990. Today, agent's computers are loaded with client management information systems that can be updated daily over the phone lines. The system helps agents work more efficiently and enhances customer service. It allows agents to complete 90 percent of the applications for insurance electronically and enables the company to deliver policies to clients the day after they apply.[6]

- **Alliance Health Care.** Formerly called Baxter, Alliance supplies hospital purchasing departments with computers so that the hospitals can electronically transmit orders directly to Alliance. The timely arrival of orders enables Alliance to cut inventories, improve customer service, and obtain better terms from suppliers for higher volumes. Alliance has achieved a great advantage over competitors, and its market share has soared.

The company's marketing information system should represent a cross between what managers think they need, what managers really need, and what is economically feasible. An *internal MIS committee* can be established to interview a cross-section of marketing managers to discover their information needs. Some useful questions are:

1. What decisions do you regularly make?
2. What information do you need to make these decisions?
3. What information do you regularly get?
4. What special studies do you periodically request?
5. What information would you want that you are not getting now?
6. What information would you want daily? Weekly? Monthly? Yearly?
7. What magazines and trade reports would you like to see on a regular basis?
8. What topics would you like to be kept informed of?
9. What data analysis programs would you want?
10. What are the four most helpful improvements that could be made in the present marketing information system?

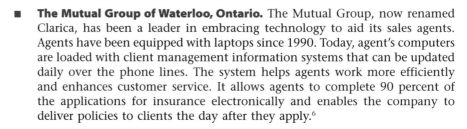

MARKETING INTELLIGENCE SYSTEM

While the internal records system supplies *results data*, the marketing intelligence system supplies *happenings data*.

- A *marketing intelligence system* is a set of procedures and sources used by managers to obtain everyday information about developments in the marketing environment.

Marketing managers collect marketing intelligence by reading books, newspapers, and trade publications; talking to customers, suppliers, and distributors; and meeting with other company managers. A company can take several steps to improve the quality of its marketing intelligence.

First, the firm can train and motivate the sales force to spot and report new developments. Sales representatives are the company's "eyes and ears"; they are positioned to pick up information missed by other means. Yet they are very busy and often fail to pass on significant information. The company must "sell" its sales force on their importance as intelligence gatherers. Sales reps should know which types of information to send to which managers. For instance, the Prentice Hall sales reps who sell this textbook let their editors know what is going on in each discipline, who is doing exciting research, and who plans to write cutting-edge textbooks.

Second, the company can motivate distributors, retailers, and other intermediaries to pass along important intelligence. Many companies hire outside specialists to gather marketing intelligence. Retailers often send "mystery shoppers" to their stores to assess how employees treat customers. For example, Dallas-based Neiman Marcus employs the firm, Feedback Plus, at its 26 stores.[7] Mystery shoppers are also a good way to investigate questionable practices by dealers such as "bait and switch" ploys.[8]

Third, companies can learn about competitors by hiring a competitive intelligence gathering professional or by training its own personnel in the art of competitive intelligence gathering. Competitive intelligence is the continuous process of legally and ethically monitoring the competitive environment so that senior managers can make informed decisions. With the development of global markets and information-based economies, the need for competitive intelligence has been exploding. In response to this demand, more and more courses and seminars in competitive intelligence gathering are being offered by universities (e.g., York University's Schulich School of Business), the Society of Competitive Intelligence Professionals, and by consulting firms such as Ottawa-based Business Intelligence and Security.[9] Tactics used in gathering competitive intelligence include purchasing competitors' products; surfing competitors' web sites; attending open houses and trade shows; reading competitors' published reports; attending stockholders' meetings; talking to employees, dealers, distributors, suppliers, and freight agents; collecting competitors' ads; and reading business periodicals such as *Canadian Business, The Economist, The Wall Street Journal, The Financial Post*, and trade association papers. Good competitive intelligence is worth its weight in gold. For example, NutraSweet Co. estimated that the intelligence it gathered on its rivals 10 years ago has been worth about $50 million a year.[10]

Society of Competitive Intelligence Professionals
http://www.scip.org

Fourth, the company can set up a *customer advisory panel* made up of representative customers, or the company's largest customers, or its most outspoken or sophisticated customers. Hitachi Data Systems, for example, holds a three-day meeting with its customer panel of 20 members every nine months. They discuss service issues, new technologies, and customers' strategic requirements. The process enables the company to gain valuable information about customer needs. Panel members feel more bonded to a company that listens closely to their comments.[11]

Fifth, the company can purchase information from outside suppliers such as the A.C. Nielsen Company and Information Resources, Inc. (see Table 4-1, part D). These research firms gather store and consumer-panel data at a much lower cost than the company could do on its own.

Sixth, some companies have established a *marketing information centre* to collect and circulate marketing intelligence. The staff scans the Internet and major publications, abstract relevant news, and disseminate a news bulletin to marketing managers. They collect and file relevant information and assist managers in evaluating new information.

MARKETING RESEARCH SYSTEM

Marketing managers often commission formal marketing studies of specific problems and opportunities. They may request a market survey, a product-preference test, a sales forecast by region, or an advertising evaluation. We define marketing research as follows:

TABLE 4.1

Secondary Data Sources

A. Internal Sources

Company profit-loss statements, balance sheets, sales figures, sales-call reports, invoices, inventory records, and prior research reports.

B. Government Publications

- *Statistics Canada Catalogue and Current Publication Index*
- *Canadian Socioeconomic Information Management System (CANSIM)*
- *Industry Canada World Wide Web site at www.strategis.ic.gc.ca.*
- *Provincial governments' publications, municipal records, including city directories*
- *Chambers of Commerce and Boards of Trade publications*
- Other government publications include *the Annual Survey of Manufacturers; Business Statistics; Census of Manufacturers; Census of Population; Census of Retail Trade, Wholesale Trade, and Selected Service Industries; Census of Transportation; Monthly Labour Review; Survey of Current Business; and Vital Statistics Report.*

C. Periodicals and Books

- *Business Periodicals Index, Canadian Trade Index, Fraser's Canadian Trade Directory, A Bibliography of Canadian Bibliographies, Canadian Rates and Data, Canadian Statistical Review, Standard and Poor's Industry Surveys, Moody's Manuals, Encyclopedia of Associations*
- Marketing journals include *the Journal of Marketing, Journal of Marketing Research, Journal of International Marketing, Journal of Consumer Research, Journal of the Academy of Marketing Science, Journal of the Administrative Sciences Association of Canada.*
- Useful trade magazines include *Strategy: The Canadian Marketing Report, Marketing Magazine, Advertising Age, Chain Store Age, Canadian Grocer, Sales and Marketing Management, and Stores.*
- Useful general business magazines include *Globe and Mail's Report on Business Magazine, Financial Post Magazine, Canadian Business, Profit, Business Week, Fortune, Forbes, The Economist, Inc., and Harvard Business Review.*

D. Commercial Data

- *Nielsen Company:* data on products and brands sold through retail outlets (Retail Index Services), supermarket scanner data (Scantrack), data on television audiences (Media Research Services), magazine circulation data (Neodata Services, Inc.), and others.
- *Financial Post Survey of Markets*
- *Information Resources, Inc.:* supermarket scanner data (InfoScan) and data on the impact of supermarket promotions (PromotioScan).
- *SAMI/Burke:* reports on warehouse withdrawals to food stores in selected market areas (SAMI reports) and supermarket scanner data (Samscam).
- *Simmons Market Research Bureau* (MRB Group): annual reports covering television markets, sporting goods, and proprietary drugs, with demographic data by sex, income, age, and brand preferences (selective markets and media reaching them).
- Other commercial research houses selling data to subscribers include the Audit Bureau of Circulation; Arbitron, Audits and Surveys; Dun and Bradstreet; National Family Opinion; Standard Rate & Data Service; and Starch.

- *Marketing research* is the systematic design, collection, analysis, and reporting of data and findings relevant to a specific marketing situation facing the company.

SUPPLIERS OF MARKETING RESEARCH

A company can obtain marketing research in a number of ways. Most large companies have their own marketing research departments.[12]

- **Procter & Gamble.** P&G assigns marketing researchers to each product operating division to conduct research for existing brands. There are two separate in-house research groups, one in charge of overall company advertising research and the other in charge of market testing. Each group's staff consists of marketing research managers, supporting specialists (survey designers, statisticians, behavioural scientists), and in-house field representatives to conduct and supervise interviewing. Each year, Procter & Gamble calls or visits over one million people in connection with about 1000 research projects.

- **Hewlett-Packard.** At HP, marketing research is handled by the Market Research & Information Center (MRIC), located at HP headquarters. The MRIC is a shared resource for all HP divisions worldwide and is divided into three groups. The Market Information Center provides background information on industries, markets, and competitors using syndicated and other information services. Decision Support Teams provide research consulting services. Regional Satellites in specific locales worldwide support regional HP initiatives.[13]

Proctor & Gamble
www.pg.com

Hewlett-Packard
www.hp.com

Small companies can hire the services of a marketing research firm or conduct research in creative and affordable ways, such as:

- *Engaging students or professors to design and carry out projects:* As part of their marketing course work, students are often required to conduct "real-world" research projects. One Boston University MBA project, designed to help American Express develop a campaign geared toward young professionals, led to a very successful advertising program. The cost: $15 000. Many universities, like Queen's University, have small business consulting groups staffed by highly motivated business students that conduct projects for reasonable fees.

- *Using the Internet:* A company can collect considerable information at very little cost by examining competitors' Web sites, monitoring chat rooms, and accessing published data.

- *Checking out rivals:* Many companies routinely visit their competitors. You can frequently see managers from Loeb's grocery stores walking the aisles of Loblaws. Sam Walton, founder of Wal-Mart, was famous for visiting retailers no matter where he travelled around the world.

Companies normally budget marketing research at one to two percent of company sales. A large percentage is spent buying the services of outside firms. Marketing research firms fall into three categories:

- *Syndicated-service research firms*: These firms gather consumer and trade information, which they sell for a fee. Examples: A.C. Nielsen, SAMI/Burke.

- *Custom marketing research firms*: These firms are hired to carry out specific projects. They design the study and present a report on the findings.

- *Specialty-line marketing research firms*: These firms provide specialized research services. The best example is the field-service firm, which sells field interviewing services to other firms.

Marketing researchers have steadily expanded their activities and techniques over the years.

THE MARKETING RESEARCH PROCESS

Effective marketing research involves the five steps shown in Figure 4-1. We will illustrate these steps with the following situation:

VIA Rail Canada is concerned about finding ways to improve its participation in the intercity passenger market in the Windsor-Quebec corridor. VIA management recognized that many travellers preferred other means of travel, including the automobile,

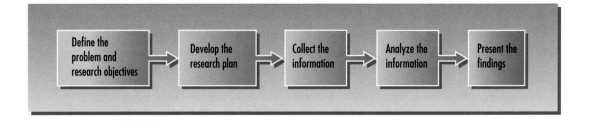

The Marketing Research Process

airplane, and bus. Although travel by rail had declined substantially since the 1950s, a minority of Canadian travellers still preferred to take the train. Knowing that the quality of the service provided influenced travellers' choices, management wanted to determine the most appropriate services to offer, in order to expand its business beyond the base of loyal travellers. The marketing researcher was directed to propose a research design that would obtain the needed information.

Step 1: Define the Problem and Research Objectives.

An old adage says, "A problem well defined is half solved." There is a danger of defining the problem too broadly or too narrowly. A marketing manager who tells the marketing researcher, "Find out everything you can about rail travellers' needs," will get a lot of unnecessary information. Similarly, a marketing manager who says, "Find out what additional services the passengers on our Toronto-Montreal trains would like," is taking too narrow a view of the problem. Many potential users of new VIA services would not be users of the present services.

Further reflection about the problem brought the realization that people take trips for various reasons. Some travel on business, some for recreation, and others travel to visit friends and relatives. It seemed plausible that the services that people would like to receive might depend on the purpose of the trip. This line of thought suggested that the research purpose should be to discover why people travel, and what needs the different kinds of travellers would like to satisfy.

After discussing that overall purpose, the marketing manager and the marketing researcher agreed to define the research problem as follows: "Why do people travel, and what needs do the different kinds of travellers want to satisfy?" They then agreed that the research objectives should be to answer the following specific questions:

1. What are the main reasons why people aged 18 years or more take intercity trips in the Windsor-Quebec corridor?

2. What are the characteristics of the people who travel for each purpose?

3. What are the perceived travel service characteristics that differentiate the train from the automobile, the airplane, and the bus?

4. Which of these service characteristics should management try to provide with VIA's service?

Not all research projects can be this specific in their objectives. Some research is *exploratory*—its goal is to gather preliminary data to shed light on the real nature of the problem and to suggest possible solutions or new ideas. Some research is *descriptive*—it seeks to ascertain certain magnitudes, such as how many people would pay a premium fare for VIA club-car service. Some research is *causal*—its purpose is to test a cause-and-effect relationship. For example, would a 20 percent reduction of the club-car premium lead to an increase of at least 20 percent in club-car patronage?

Step 2: Developing the Research Plan.

The second stage of marketing research calls for developing the most efficient plan for gathering the needed information. The marketing manager needs to know the cost of the research plan before approving it. Suppose the marketing manager estimates that introducing the club-car service without doing any marketing research would yield a long-term profit of $50 000. The manager believes that doing the research would lead to an improved promotional plan and a long-term profit of $90 000. In this case, the manager should be willing to spend up to $40 000 on this research. If the research cost estimate is more than $40 000, it is not worth doing.[14] Designing a research plan calls for decisions on *the data sources, research approaches, research instruments, sampling plan,* and *contact methods.*

Data Sources.   The research plan can call for gathering secondary data, primary data, or both. *Secondary data* are data that were collected for another purpose and already exist somewhere. *Primary data* are data gathered for a specific purpose or for a specific research project.

Researchers usually start their investigation by examining secondary data to see whether their problem can be partly or wholly solved without collecting costly primary data. (Table 4-1 shows the rich variety of secondary-data sources available in Canada.)[15] Secondary data provide a starting point for research and offer the advantages of low cost and ready availability.

The Internet, or more particularly, the World Wide Web, is now the greatest repository of information the world has seen. In an incredibly short span of time, the Web has become a key tool for sales and marketing professionals to access competitive information or conduct demographic, industry, or customer research. See the Marketing Memo entitled "Secondary Sources of Data Online" for a mini-directory of sites where you can conduct free or at least inexpensive market research.

When the data needed by the researcher do not exist, or are dated, inaccurate, incomplete, or unreliable, the researcher will have to collect primary data. Most marketing research projects involve some primary-data collection. The normal procedure is to interview some people individually and/or in groups to get a preliminary sense of how people feel about the topic in question and then develop a formal research instrument, debug it, and carry it into the field.

When stored and used properly, the data collected in the field can form the backbone of later marketing campaigns. Direct marketers such as record clubs, credit-card companies, and catalogue houses have long been wise to the power of database marketing.

- A **customer** or **prospect database** is an organized collection of comprehensive data about individual customers, prospects, or suspects that is current, accessible, and actionable for marketing purposes such as lead generation, lead qualification, sale of a product or service, or maintenance of customer relationships.

Some techniques that are becoming increasingly popular are data warehousing and data mining—but they are not without risks. See the Marketing for the 21st Century box, "Companies turn to Data Warehousing and Data Mining: Exercise Care."

Research Approaches.   Primary data can be collected in five ways: observation, focus groups, surveys, behavioural data, and experiments.

- *Observational research:* Fresh data can be gathered by observing the relevant actors and settings. The VIA Rail researchers might meander around airports, bus terminals, and travel agencies to hear how travellers talk about the different carriers. The researchers can also travel by bus and by air to observe the quality of service and hear the reactions of their competitors' customers. This exploratory research might yield some useful hypotheses about how travellers choose their carriers.

- *Focus-group research:* A *focus group* is a gathering of six to ten people who are invited to spend a few hours with a skilled moderator to discuss a product, service, organization, or other marketing entity (Figure 4-2). The moderator

MARKETING *memo*

Secondary Sources of Data Online

The number of online government and business information sources is truly overwhelming. Here is a sample of several that should prove useful when conducting online market research and many offer information for free or a reasonable fee. Note that because the Web is changing at such a rapid rate, the addresses may change.

Associations

- American Marketing Association—http://www.ama.org/hmpage.htm
- CommerceNet—industry association for Internet commerce—http://www.commerce.net
- Canadian Advanced Technology Association—is a collective of Canada's leading technology companies. Site features a range of business tools—http://www.cata.ca
- Canadian Direct Marketing Association– site allows you to find out more about direct marketing. Membership comprises over 650 corporate members—http://www.cdma.org.
- Gale's Encyclopedia of Associations—http://www.gale.com—Business Information
- Retail Council of Canada – voice of retailing in Canada. Site contains information about membership as well as on-line retailing resources—http://www.retailcouncil.org.

Business Information

- Canadian Corporate News – full-text database of news releases from over 1000 Canadian companies – http//www.cdn-news.com
- Conference Board of Canada—information on a wide range of business topics as well as research on tourism within Canada—*http://www.conferenceboard.ca*
- A Business Compass (ABC)—selectively describes and links to key business sites on the Web—*http://www.abcompass.com*
- A Business Researcher's Interests—provides links to business directories, media sites, marketing-related resources, and much more—*http://www.brint.com*
- Bloomberg Personal—timely news and financial services—*http://www.bloomberg.com*
- C/Net—journalistic coverage of high technology, computers, and the Internet—*http://www.cnet.com*
- Company Link—free basic directory data, press releases, stock prices and SEC data on 45 000 U.S. firms and more information available to subscribers—*http://www.companylink.com*
- EDGAR—public company financial filings—*http://www.sec.gov/edgarhp.htm*
- Hoover's—directory of company information—*http://www.hoovers.com*
- U.S. National Trade Data Bank—free access to over 18 000 market research reports analyzing trends and competition in scores of industries and for hundreds of products—*http://www.stat-usa.gov*
- Public Register's Annual Report Service—allows searches of 3200 public companies by company name or industry and offers annual reports via e-mail—*http://www.prars.com/index.html*
- Quote.Com—access to a wide range of business wires, companies directories and stock quotes—*http://www.quote.com*

Government Information

- Statistics Canada—http://www.statcan.ca
- Canada Business Service Centres—information about federal and provincial programs and regulations—http://www.info.ic.gc.ca/cbsc/english
- Strategis (Industry Canada)—information on a wide range of topics with respect to the economic development of Canada—http://www.strategi.ic.gc.ca/engdoc/main.html
- U.S. Census Bureau—http://www.census.gov
- Trade/Exporting/business: Stat-USA—http://www.stat-usa.gov
- US Business Advisor—http://www.business.gov

International Information

- Asia Pacific Foundation of Canada – non-profit organization whose purpose is to make Canadian business more successful in the Asia-Pacific region – http://www.apfnet.org
- BorderNet—a Canada-U.S. affiliation of business groups whose purpose is to improve trade, tourism and investment in the border region – http://www.bordernet.org
- OECD – international perspective on international economic development. Site features information on their reports as well as a lending library and on-line bookstore – http://www.oecd.org.
- World Bank – international lending organization – http://worldbank.org/html/welcome.html
- CIA World Factbook—a comprehensive statistical and demographic directory covering 264 countries around the world—*http://www.odic.gov/cia/publications*
- I-Trade—a free and fee-based information services for firms wishing to do business internationally—*http://www.i-trade.com*
- The United Nations—*http://www.un.org*

Sources: Based on information from Andrew T. Stull and Don Cassel, *Surfing for Success in Business and Economics: A Student's Guide to the Internet,* 2nd Canadian ed. (Scarborough: Prentice Hall Canada, 1999); Jim Carroll and Rick Broadhead, *1998 Canadian Internet Directory & Research Guide* (Scarborough: Prentice Hall Canada, 1998); Robert I. Berkman, *Find It Fast: How to Uncover Expert Information on Any Subject in Print or Online* (New York: HarperCollins, 1997); Christine Galea, "Surf City: The Best Places for Business on the Web," *Sales & Marketing Management,* January 1997, pp. 69–73; David Curle, "Out-of-the-Way Sources of Market Research on the Web," Online, January–February 1998, pp. 63–68. See also Jan Davis Tudor, "Brewing Up: A Web Approach to Industry Research," *Online,* July–August 1996, p. 12.

Companies Turn to Data Warehousing and Data Mining: Exercise Care

Companies are using data mining, a set of methods that extracts patterns from large masses of data organized in what is called a *data warehouse.* Jonathan Calof of the University of Ottawa notes that unlike other analysis techniques, where researchers use data to help support preconceived notions about what drives behaviour, data mining helps you uncover unexpected relationships. Banks and credit card companies, telephone companies, catalogue marketers, and many other companies have a great deal of information about their customers, including not only their addresses, but also their transactions and enhanced data on age, family size, income, and other demographic information. By carefully mining this data, a company could benefit in several ways:

■ Knowing which customers may be ready for a product upgrade offer

■ Knowing which customers might buy other products of the company

■ Knowing which customers would make the best prospects for a special offer

■ Knowing which customers have the most lifetime value and giving them more attention and perks

■ Knowing which customers might tend to exit and taking steps to prevent this

Some observers believe that a proprietary database can provide a company with a significant competitive advantage. No wonder at a secret location in Phoenix, security guards watch over American Express' 500 billion bytes of data on how its customers have used the company's 35 million green, gold, and platinum charge cards. Amex uses the database to include precisely targeted offers in its monthly mailing of millions of customer bills.

Here are some examples of the uses of database marketing:

■ MCI Communications Corp., the long-distance carrier, sifts through one trillion bytes of customer phoning data to craft new discount calling plans for different types of customers.

■ The NBA's Orlando Magic used an IBM's data mining developed specifically for them called Advanced Scout to analyze game statistics to detect patterns.

■ Marriott's Vacation Club International has managed to reduce its volume of mail and yet increase its response rate by developing a model showing which customers in its database are most likely to respond to specific vacation offerings.

■ Tesco, the British supermarket chain, notifies different groups, such as wine buyers or cheese buyers, when there will be a special sale of wine or cheese.

■ Land's End can tell which of its two million customers should receive special mailings of specific clothing items that would fit their wardrobe needs.

■ Toronto's Loyalty Marketing Group, best known for its Air Miles program, combines data from its extensive data bank with that from Statistics Canada to help its clients build models of consumer demand and select store locations.

These benefits don't come without heavy cost, not only in collecting the original customer data but also in maintaining it and mining it. But when it works, it yields more than it costs. A 1996 study by DWI estimated that the average return on investment for a data warehouse over the course of three years is more than 400 percent. The data have to be in good condition, and the discovered relationships must be valid. Mistakes are always possible: British Columbia Telecom wanted to invite 100 of its best customers to a Vancouver Grizzlies basketball game and selected customers who were heavy 900-number users. The invitations were already at the printer when the marketing staff discovered that heavy 900-number users included sex-line enthusiasts. They quickly added other criteria to mine for a new list of guests.

Sources: Greg Crone, "There's Gold in That There Data," *Financial Post,* December 3, 1998, p. C13. Peter R. Peacock, "Data Mining in Marketing: Part 1," *Marketing Management,* Winter 1998, pp. 9-18, and "Data Mining in Marketing: Part 2," *Marketing Management,* Spring 1998, pp. 15-25; Ginger Conlon, "What the !@#!*?!! is a Data Warehouse? *Sales & Marketing Management,* April 1997, pp. 41-48; Skip Press, "Fool's Gold? As Companies Rush to Mine Data, They May Dig Up Real Gems—or False Trends," *Sales & Marketing Management,* date TK, pp. 58, 60, 62. [MCI] John Verity, "A Trillion-Byte Weapon," *Business Week,* July 31, 1995, pp. 80-81.

needs to be objective, knowledgeable on the issue, and versed in group dynamics and consumer behaviour. The participants are normally paid a small sum for attending the focus group. The meeting is typically held in pleasant surroundings (a home, for example), and refreshments are served.

In the VIA Rail research, the moderator might start with a broad question, such as "How do you feel about intercity travel in Canada?" Questions then move to how people regard the different methods of travel and the various services that they would

FIGURE 4.2

Focus Group Research

like. The moderator encourages free and easy discussion, hoping that the group dynamics will reveal deep feelings and thoughts. At the same time, the moderator "focuses" the discussion. The discussion, recorded through note taking or on audio-tape or videotape, is subsequently studied to understand consumer beliefs, attitudes, and behaviour.

■ Focus-group research is a useful exploratory step to take before designing a large-scale survey. Consumer-goods companies have been using focus groups for many years, and an increasing number of public and nonprofit organizations are also discovering the value of focus groups. However, researchers must avoid generalizing the reported feelings of the focus-group participants to the whole market, since the sample size is too small and the sample is not drawn randomly.[16]

With the development of the World Wide Web, many companies are now conducting online focus groups:[17]

> *Janice Gjersten of WPStudio, an online entertainment company, found that on-line focus-group respondents could be much more honest than those in her traditional in-person focus groups. Gjersten contacted Cyber Dialogue, and they provided focus-group respondents drawn from their 10 000-person database. The focus group was held in a chat room that Gjersten "looked in on" from her office computer. Gjersten could interrupt the moderator at any time with flash e-mails unseen by the respondents. While the online focus group lacked voice and body cues, Gjersten says she will never conduct a traditional focus group again. Not only were respondents more honest, but the cost for the online group was one-third that of a traditional focus group and a full report came to her in one day, compared to four weeks.*

■ *Survey research:* While observation and focus groups are best suited for exploratory research, surveys are best suited for descriptive research. Companies undertake surveys to learn about people's knowledge, beliefs, preferences, satisfaction, and so on, and to measure these magnitudes in the general population. Thus VIA Rail researchers might want to survey travellers to determine the levels of awareness, interest, and preference for rail travel, their satisfaction with the travel experience, and the services provided. We will say more about survey research when we discuss research instruments, sampling plans, and contact methods in the next few pages.

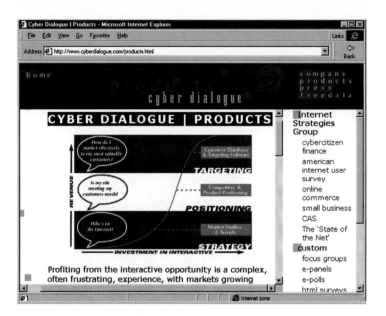

Cyber Dialogue's Products home page gives some idea of the range of on-line services the company provides.

- *Behavioural data.* Customers leave traces of their purchasing behaviour in store scanning data, catalogue purchase records, and customer databases. Much can be learned by analyzing this data. Customers' actual purchases reflect *revealed preferences* and often are more reliable than statements they offer to market researchers. People often report preferences for popular brands, and yet the data show them actually buying other brands. For example, grocery shopping data show that high-income people do not necessarily buy the more expensive brands, contrary to what they might state in interviews; and many low-income people buy some expensive brands. Clearly VIA can learn many useful things about its passengers by analyzing ticket purchase records.

- *Ethnography.* Some research involves observing a small number of research subjects who are chosen with great care. Researchers, often from the fields of anthropology and psychology, study people in their homes and workplaces unobtrusively as they go about their normal lives. Often referred to as the "fly-on-the-wall" technique, *ethnography* can provide firms with insights about product and service needs.

Intel, for example, watched people struggling to use their new electronic organizers and heard them venting their frustration. The research has helped them design better, more user-friendly products such as the "couch-pad" for users of WebTV and Team Station Video Phone, which was derived from information gathered by observing teenagers in their bedrooms. McDonald's researchers analyzed 6000 hours of videotape of customer transactions. They discovered that their restaurants weren't as customer friendly as they had thought. VIA might learn a lot, for example, by having researchers travel with patrons and watch how they buy tickets, what they do during the trip, who they talk to, how they handle their luggage, what they do when faced with a delay, and whether they travel alone or in groups.[18]

- *Experimental research.* The most scientifically valid research is *experimental research.* The purpose of experimental research is to capture cause-and-effect relationships by eliminating competing explanations of the observed findings. To the extent that the design and execution of the experiment eliminate alternative hypotheses that might explain the results, the research and marketing managers can have confidence in the conclusions. It calls for selecting matched groups of subjects, subjecting them to different treatments, controlling extraneous variables, and checking whether observed response differences are statistically significant. To the extent that extraneous factors

TABLE 4.2

Types of Questions

A. Closed-end Questions

Name	Description	Example
Dichotomous	A question with two possible answers.	In arranging this trip, did you personally phone VIA? Yes No
Multiple choice	A question with three or more answers.	With whom are you travelling on this trip? ☐ No one ☐ Spouse ☐ Spouse and children ☐ Children only ☐ Business associates/friends/relatives ☐ An organized tour group
Likert scale	A statement with which the respondent shows the amount of agreement/ disagreement.	VIA Rail generally gives better service than the airlines. Strongly disagree (1__) Disagree (2__) Neither agree nor disagree (3__) Agree (4__) Strongly agree (5__)
Semantic differential	A scale connecting two bipolar words. The respondent selects the point that represents his or her opinion.	VIA Rail Large _ _ _ _ _ _ _ Small Experienced_ _ _ _ _ _ _Inexperienced Modern _ _ _ _ _ _ _Old-fashioned
Importance scale	A scale that rates the importance of some attribute.	Train food service to me is Extremely important (1___) Very important (2___) Some what important (3___) Not very important (4___) Not at all important (5___)
Rating scale	A scale that rates some attribute from "poor" to "excellent."	VIA food service is Excellent (1___) Very Good (2___) Good (3___) Fair (4___) Poor (5___)
Intention-to-buy or use scale	A scale that describes the respondent's intention to buy.	If a telephone were available at my seat, I would Definitely use (1___) Probably use (2___) Not sure (3___) Probably not use (4___) Definitely not use (5___)

(continued)

are eliminated or controlled, the observed effects can be related to the variations in the treatments. For example, VIA Rail might set up a special rail-car where travellers can watch movies for a nominal surcharge. The amount of the surcharge could be varied over time, and the numbers of travellers paying the various amounts would be recorded. This would permit the researchers to determine the effect of the level of the surcharge on the amount of revenue generated by the movie service. To the extent that the design and execution of the experiment eliminate alternative hypotheses that might explain the results, such as the types of movies shown, the research and marketing managers can have confidence in the conclusions.

Research Instruments. Marketing researchers have a choice of two main research instruments in collecting primary data: questionnaires and mechanical devices.

■ *Questionnaires:* A questionnaire consists of a set of questions presented to respondents for their answers. Because of its flexibility, the questionnaire is by far the most common instrument used to collect primary data. Questionnaires

TABLE 4.2 *(continued)*

Types of Questions

B. Open-end Questions

Name	Description	Example
Completely unstructured	A question that respondents can answer in an almost unlimited number of ways.	What is your opinion of VIA Rail?
Word association	Words are presented, one at a time, and respondents mention the first word that comes to mind.	What is the first word that comes to your mind when you hear the following? Business Travel _____ VIA Rail _____ Travel _____
Sentence completion	An incomplete sentence is presented and respondents complete the sentence.	When I choose a mode of transportation,, the most important consideration for me is _____
Story completion	An incomplete story is presented, and respondents are asked to complete it.	"I used VIA a few days ago. I noticed that the exterior and interior of the train had very bright colours. This aroused in me the following thoughts and feelings. . . . Now complete the story."
Picture	A picture of two characters is presented, with one making a statement. Respondents are asked to identify with the other and fill in the empty balloon.	
Thematic Apperception Test (TAT)	A picture is presented and respondents are asked to make up a story about what they think is happening or may happen in the picture.	

need to be carefully developed, tested, and debugged before they are administered on a large scale.

In preparing a questionnaire, the professional marketing researcher carefully chooses the questions and their form, wording, and sequence. The form of the question asked can influence the response. Marketing researchers distinguish between open-end and closed-end questions. *Closed-end questions* pre-specify all the possible answers, and respondents make a choice among them. *Open-end questions* allow respondents to answer in their own words. Closed-end questions provide answers that are easier to interpret and tabulate. Open-end questions often reveal more because they do not constrain respondents' answers. Open-end questions are especially useful in the exploratory stage of research, where the researcher is looking for insight into how people think rather than in measuring how many people think a certain way. Table 4-2 provides examples of both types of questions.

Finally, the questionnaire designer should exercise care in the wording and sequencing of questions. The questionnaire should use simple, direct, unbiased wording and should be pretested with a sample of respondents before it is used. The lead question should attempt to create interest. Difficult or personal questions should be asked toward the end of the questionnaire so that respondents do not become defensive early. Finally, the questions should flow in a logical order.

■ *Mechanical instruments:* Mechanical devices are used less frequently in marketing research. Galvanometers measure the subject's interest or emotions aroused by exposure to a specific ad or picture. The tachistoscope flashes an ad to a subject with an exposure interval that may range from less than one hundredth of a second to several seconds. After each exposure, the respondent describes everything he or she recalls. Eye cameras study respondents' eye movements to see where their eyes land first, how long they linger on a given item, and so on. The audiometer is attached to television sets in participating homes to record when the set is on and to which channel it is tuned.[19]

Sampling Plan. After deciding on the research approach and instruments, the marketing researcher must design a sampling plan. This plan calls for three decisions:

1. *Sampling unit: Who is to be surveyed?* The marketing researcher must define the target population that will be sampled. In the VIA Rail survey, should the sampling unit be business travellers, vacation travellers, or both? Should travellers under age 21 be interviewed? Should both husbands and wives be interviewed? Once the sampling unit is determined, a sampling frame must be developed so that everyone in the target population has an equal chance of being sampled.

2. *Sample size: How many people should be surveyed?* Large samples give more reliable results than small samples. However, it is not necessary to sample the entire target population or even a substantial portion to achieve reliable results. Samples of less than one percent of a population can often provide good reliability, given a credible sampling procedure.

3. *Sampling procedure: How should the respondents be chosen?* To obtain a representative sample, a probability sample of the population should be drawn. *Probability sampling* allows the calculation of confidence limits for sampling error. Thus one could conclude after the sample is taken that "the interval five to seven trips per year has 95 chances in 100 of containing the true number of trips taken annually by travellers in the Toronto-Montreal corridor." Three types of probability sampling are described in Table 4-3, section A. When the cost or time involved in probability sampling is too high, marketing researchers will take nonprobability samples. Table 4-3, section B describes three types of *nonprobability sampling*. Some marketing researchers feel that nonprobability samples are very useful in many circumstances, even though they do not allow sampling error to be measured.

TABLE 4.3		
Probability and Nonprobability Samples	**A. Probability Sample**	
	Simple random sample	Every member of the population has an equal chance of selection.
	Stratified random sample	The population is divided into mutually exclusive groups (such as age groups), and random samples are drawn from each group.
	Cluster (area) sample	The population is divided into mutually exclusive groups (such as city blocks), and the researcher draws a sample of the groups to interview.
	B. Nonprobability Sample	
	Convenience sample	The researcher selects the most accessible population members.
	Judgment sample	The researcher selects population members who are good prospects for accurate information.
	Quota sample	The researcher finds and interviews a prescribed number of people in each of several categories.

Contact Methods.   Once the sampling plan has been determined, the marketing researcher must decide how the subject should be contacted: mail, telephone, online, or personal interviews.

The *mail questionnaire* is the best way to reach people who would not give personal interviews or whose responses might be biased or distorted by the interviewers. Mail questionnaires require simple and clearly worded questions. Unfortunately the response rate is usually low and/or slow. *Telephone interviewing* is the best method for gathering information quickly; the interviewer is also able to clarify questions if respondents do not understand them. The response rate is typically higher than in the case of mailed questionnaires. The main drawback is that the interviews must be short and not too personal. Telephone interviewing is becoming more difficult because of answering machines and people becoming suspicious of telemarketing.

Personal interviewing is the most versatile method. The interviewer can ask more questions and record additional observations about the respondent, such as dress and body language. Personal interviewing is the most expensive method and requires more administrative planning and supervision than the other two. It is also subject to interviewer bias or distortion. Personal interviewing takes two forms. In *arranged interviews*, respondents are contacted for an appointment. Often a small payment or incentive is offered. *Intercept interviews* involve stopping people at a shopping mall or busy street corner and requesting an interview. Intercept interviews have the drawback of being nonprobability samples, and the interviews must not require too much time.

There is increased use of online interviewing. A company can include a questionnaire at its Web page and offer an incentive to answer the questionnaire. Or it can place a banner on some frequently visited site inviting people to answer some questions and possibly win a prize. Or the company can enter a target chat room and seek volunteers for a survey. In collecting data online, however, the company must recognize the data's limitations. The company cannot assume that the data are representative of a target population, since the respondents are self-selected. People in the target market who do not use the Internet or who don't want to answer a questionnaire can bias the results. Still the information can be useful for exploratory research in suggesting hypotheses that might be investigated in a more scientific subsequent survey.

Many companies are now using automated telephone surveys to solicit market research information. MetroHealth Systems used to have a dismal return rate of 50 percent on its paper patient satisfaction surveys. Then the company teamed up with Sprint Healthcare systems to deliver an interactive phone survey. Under the pilot project, patients who left the hospital received a phone card with a toll-free number. When they dialled, a recording asked them several questions about their hospital experience. Results that once took months to sort now came back in a few days, and more patients completed the survey.[20]

And how do you provide incentives for customers to answer your automated survey? One popular approach is to use prepaid phone cards as an incentive. A survey is programmed into an interactive call system that not only administers the survey but also sorts the results virtually any way the client wants them. Then the client distributes the calling cards to its selected market segment. When the call users place their free calls, a voice prompt asks them if they would like to gain additional minutes by taking a short survey. NBC, Coca-Cola, and Bell Canada are some of the companies that have used prepaid phone cards to survey their customers.[21]

Step 3: Collect the Information.

The data collection phase of marketing research is generally the most expensive and the most prone to error. In the case of surveys, four major problems arise. Some respondents will not be at home and must be recontacted or replaced. Other respondents will refuse to cooperate. Still others will give biased or dishonest answers. Finally, some interviewers will be biased or dishonest.

Yet data collection methods are rapidly improving thanks to computers and telecommunications. Some research firms interview from a centralized location. Professional interviewers sit in booths and draw telephone numbers at random. When the phone is answered, the interviewer reads a set of questions from a monitor and types the respondents' answers into a computer. This procedure eliminates editing and coding, reduces errors, saves time, and produces all the required statistics. Other research firms have set up interactive terminals in shopping centres. Persons willing to be interviewed sit at a terminal, read the questions from the monitor and type in their answers. Most respondents enjoy this form of "robot" interviewing.[22]

Several recent technical advances have permitted marketers to research the sales impact of ads and sales promotion. Information Resources, Inc. recruits a panel of supermarkets equipped with scanners and electronic cash registers. Scanners read the universal product code on each product purchased, recording the brand, size, and price for inventory and ordering purposes. Meanwhile, the firm has recruited a panel of these stores' customers who have agreed to charge their purchases with a special Shopper's Hotline ID card that holds information about household characteristics, lifestyle, and income. These same customers have also agreed to let their television-viewing habits be monitored by a black box. All consumer panelists receive their programs through cable television, and Information Resources controls the advertising messages being sent to their houses. The firm can then capture through store purchases which ads led to more purchasing and by which customers.[23]

Step 4: Analyze the Information.

The next-to-last step in the marketing research process is to extract findings from the collected data. The researcher tabulates the data and develops frequency distributions. Averages and measures of dispersion are computed for the major variables. The researcher will also apply some advanced statistical techniques and decision models in the hope of discovering additional findings. (Techniques and models are described later in this chapter.)

Step 5: Present the Findings.

As the last step, the researcher presents the findings to the relevant parties. The researcher should present major findings that are relevant to the major marketing decisions facing management. Suppose that the main results obtained from VIA Rail's experimental use of a special rail car where travellers can watch movies were:

1. About 10 passengers out of an average trainload of 200 watched a movie at a price of eight dollars. When the price was five dollars, 40 passengers watched a movie. Thus, the lower price generated more revenue ($200) than the higher price ($80).

2. Suppose further that the results of VIA's survey indicated that offering the movie service would add five passengers to the average train, bringing in additional ticket revenues of $60 per passenger or $300 in total.

3. Based on the above findings, if the extra cost of offering the movie service were less than $500 per train (i.e. $200 + $300), it would be profitable for VIA to offer the service. The findings should be checked for the usual sources of survey error (such as sampling error from drawing a sample that may be unrepresentative of the target population). But it seems clear that the marketing research has helped VIA's management to make a better decision than would have resulted from "seat-of-the-pants" decision making.

OVERCOMING BARRIERS TO THE USE OF MARKETING RESEARCH

In spite of the rapid growth of marketing research, many companies still fail to use it sufficiently or correctly, for several reasons:

- *A narrow conception of marketing research.* Many managers see marketing research as a fact-finding operation. They expect the researcher to design a questionnaire, choose a sample, conduct interviews, and report results, often without a careful definition of the problem or of the decision alternatives facing management. When fact finding fails to be useful, management's idea of the limited usefulness of marketing research is reinforced.

Information Resources Inc.
www.infores.com

TABLE	4.4

The Seven Characteristics of Good Marketing Research

Scientific Method.	Effective marketing research uses the principles of the scientific method: careful observation, formulation of hypotheses, prediction, and testing.
Research Creativity.	At its best, marketing research develops innovative ways to solve a problem: a clothing company catering to teenagers gave several young men video cameras, then used the videos for focus groups held in restaurants and other places that teens frequent.
Multiple Methods.	Good marketing researchers shy away from overreliance on any one method. They also recognize the value of using two or three methods to increase confidence in the results.
Interdependence of Models and Data.	Good marketing researchers recognize that data are interpreted from underlying models that guide the type of information sought.
Value and Cost of Information	Good marketing researchers show concern for estimating the value of information against its cost. Costs are typically easy to determine, but the value of research is harder to quantify. It depends on the reliability and validity of the findings and management's willingness to accept and act on those findings.
Healthy Skepticism.	Good marketing researchers show a healthy skepticism toward glib assumptions made by managers about how a market works. They are alert to the problems caused by "marketing myths."
Ethical Marketing.	Good marketing research benefits both the sponsoring company and its customers. The misuse of marketing research can harm or annoy consumers. Increasing consumer resentment at what they regard as an invasion of their privacy or a sales pitch has become a major problem for the research industry.

MARKETING INSIGHT

Marketing Researchers Challenge Conventional Marketing Wisdom

Kevin Clancy and Robert Shulman charge that too many companies build their marketing plans on "marketing myths." Webster's dictionary defines a myth as "an ill-founded belief held uncritically, especially by an interested group." Clancy and Shulman list the following myths that have led marketing managers down the wrong path:

1. A brand's best prospects are the heavy buyers in the category. Although most companies pursue heavy buyers, these people may not be the best target of marketing efforts. Many heavy users are highly committed to specific competitors, and those who are not are often willing to switch products when a competitor offers them a better deal.

2. *The more appealing a new product is, the more likely it will be a success.* This philosophy can lead the company to give away too much to the customer and result in lower profitability.

3. *The effectiveness of advertising is revealed by how memorable and persuasive it is.* Actually, the best ads, when measured by recall and persuasion scores, are not necessarily the most effective ads. A much better predictor of an ad's effectiveness is the buyer's attitude toward the advertising—specifically, whether the buyer feels he or she received useful information and whether the buyer liked the advertising.

4. *A company is wise to spend the major portion of its research budget on focus groups and qualitative research.* Focus groups and qualitative research are useful but the major part of the research budget should be spent on quantitative research and surveys.

Some marketers will undoubtedly present counterexamples where these "myths" have actually yielded positive results. Nevertheless, the authors deserve credit for forcing marketers to rethink some of their basic assumptions.

Source: Kevin J. Clancy and Robert S. Shulman, *The Marketing Revolution: A Radical Manifesto for Dominating the Marketplace* (New York: HarperBusiness, 1991).

- *Uneven calibre of marketing researchers.* Some managers view marketing research as little more than a clerical activity and reward it as such. Less competent marketing researchers are hired, and their weak training and deficient creativity lead to unimpressive results. The disappointing results reinforce management's prejudice against marketing research. Management continues to pay low salaries to its market researchers, thus perpetuating the basic problem.

- *Late and occasionally erroneous findings by marketing research.* Managers want quick results that are accurate and conclusive. But good marketing research takes time and money. Managers are disappointed when marketing research costs too much or takes too much time. They also point to well-known cases where the marketing research predicted the wrong result, as when Coca-Cola introduced the New Coke.

- *Personality and presentational differences.* Differences between the styles of line managers and marketing researchers often get in the way of productive relationships. To a manager who wants concreteness, simplicity, and certainty, a marketing researcher's report may seem abstract, complicated, and tentative. Yet in the more progressive companies, marketing researchers are increasingly being included as members of the product management team, and their influence on marketing strategy is growing.

MARKETING DECISION SUPPORT SYSTEM

A growing number of organizations are using a marketing decision support system to help their marketing managers make better decisions. Little defines an MDSS as follows:

- A *marketing decision support system (MDSS)* is a coordinated collection of data, systems, tools, and techniques with supporting software and hardware by which an organization gathers and interprets relevant information from business and environment and turns it into a basis for marketing action.[24]

Table 4-5 describes the major statistical tools, models, and optimization routines that comprise a modern MDSS. Lilien and Rangaswamy recently published *Marketing Engineering: Computer-Assisted Marketing Analysis and Planning*, which provides a package of widely used modelling software tools.[25]

Marketing News, April 13, 1998, lists over 100 current marketing and sales software programs that assist in designing marketing research studies, segmenting markets, setting prices and advertising budgets, analyzing media, planning sales force activity, and so on. Here are examples of decision models that have been used by marketing managers:

BRANDAID: A flexible marketing-mix model focused on consumer packaged goods whose elements are a manufacturer, competitors, retailers, consumers, and the general environment. The model contains submodels for advertising, pricing, and competition. The model is calibrated with a creative blending of judgment, historical analysis, tracking, field experimentation, and adaptive control.[26]

CALLPLAN: A model to help salespeople determine the number of calls to make per period to each prospect and current client. The model takes into account travel time as well as selling time. The model was tested at United Airlines with an experimental group that managed to increase its sales over a matched control group by eight percentage points.[27]

DETAILER: A model to help salespeople determine which customers to call on and which products to represent on each call. This model was largely developed for pharmaceutical detail people calling on physicians where they could represent no more than three products on a call. In two applications, the model yielded strong profit improvements.[28]

	TABLE	4.5

Statistical Tools

1. *Multiple regression.* A statistical technique for estimating a "best fitting" equation showing how the value of a dependent variable varies with changing values in a number of independent variables. *Example*: A company can estimate how unit sales are influenced by changes in the level of company advertising expenditures, sales force size, and price.

2. *Discriminant analysis.* A statistical technique for classifying an object or persons into two or more categories. *Example*: A large retail chain store can determine the variables that discriminate between successful and unsuccessful store locations.[a]

3. *Factor analysis.* A statistical technique used to determine the few underlying dimensions of a larger set of intercorrelated variables. *Example*: A broadcast network can reduce a large set of TV programs down to a small set of basic program types.[b]

4. *Cluster analysis.* A statistical technique for separating objects into a specified number of mutually exclusive groups such that the groups are relatively homogeneous. *Example*: A marketing researcher might want to classify a miscellaneous set of cities into four groups of similar cities.

5. *Conjoint analysis.* A statistical technique whereby respondents' ranked preferences for different offers are decomposed to determine the person's inferred utility function for each attribute and the relative importance of each attribute. *Example:* An airline can determine the total utility delivered by different combinations of passenger services.

6. *Multidimensional scaling.* A variety of techniques for producing perceptual maps of competitive products or brands. Objects are represented as points in a multidimensional space of attributes where their distance from each other is a measure of dissimilarity. *Example*: A computer manufacturer wants to see where his brand is positioned in relation to competitive brands.

Models

1. *Markov-process model.* This model shows the probability of moving from a current state to any future state. *Example*: A branded packaged-goods manufacturer can determine the period-to-period switching and staying rates for her brand and, if the probabilities are stable, the brand's ultimate brand share.

2. *Queuing model.* This model shows the waiting times and queue lengths that can be expected in any system, given the arrival and service times and the number of service channels. *Example*: A supermarket can use the model to predict queue lengths at different times of the day given the number of service channels and service speed.

3. *New-product pretest models.* This model involves estimating functional relations between buyer states of awareness, trial, and repurchase based on consumer preferences and actions in a pretest situation of the marketing offer and campaign. Among the well-known models are ASSESSOR, COMP, DEMON, NEWS and SPRINTER.[c]

4. *Sales-response models.* This is a set of models that estimate functional relations between one or more marketing variables—such as sales force size, advertising expenditure, sales-promotion expenditure, etc.—and the resulting demand level.

Optimization Routines

1. *Differential calculus.* This technique allows finding the maximum or minimum value along a well-behaved function.

2. *Mathematical programming.* This technique allows finding the values that would optimize some objective function that is subject to a set of constraints.

3. *Statistical decision theory.* This technique allows determining the course of action that produces the maximum expected value.

4. *Game theory.* This technique allows determining the course of action that will minimize the decision maker's maximum loss in the face of the uncertain behaviour of one or more competitors.

5. *Heuristics.* This involves using a set of rules of thumb that shorten the time or work required to find a reasonably good solution in a complex system.

Quantitative Tools Used in Marketing Decision Support Systems

---

[a] S. Sands, "Store Site Selection by Discriminant Analysis," *Journal of the Market Research Society*, 1981, pp. 40-51.
[b] V. R. Rao, "Taxonomy of Television Programs Based on Viewing Behavior," *Journal of Marketing Research*, August 1975, pp. 355-58.
[c] See Kevin J. Clancy, Robert Shulman, and Marianne Wolf, *Simulated Test Marketing* (New York: Lexington Books, 1994).

GEOLINE: A model for designing sales and service territories that satisfies three principles: the territories equalize sales workloads; each territory consists of adjacent areas; and the territories are compact. Several successful applications were reported.[29]

MEDIAC: A model to help an advertiser buy media for a year. The media planning model includes market segment delineation, sales potential estimation, diminishing marginal returns, forgetting, timing issues, and competitor media schedules.[30]

Some models now claim to duplicate the way expert marketers normally make their decisions. Some recent expert system models include:

PROMOTER evaluates sales promotions by determining baseline sales (what sales would have been without promotion) and measuring the increase over baseline associated with the promotion.[31]

ADCAD recommends the type of ad (humorous, slice of life, and so on) to use given the marketing.[32]

COVERSTORY examines a mass of syndicated sales data and writes an English-language memo reporting the highlights.[33] The first decade of the 21st century will undoubtedly usher in further software programs and decision models.

AN OVERVIEW OF FORECASTING AND DEMAND MEASUREMENT

One major reason for undertaking marketing research is to identify market opportunities. Once the research is complete, the company must measure and forecast the size, growth, and profit potential of each market opportunity. Sales forecasts are used by finance to raise the needed cash for investment and operations; by the manufacturing department to establish capacity and output levels; by purchasing to acquire the right amount of supplies; and by human resources to hire the needed number of workers. Marketing is responsible for preparing the sales forecasts. If its forecast is far off the mark, the company will be saddled with excess inventory or have inadequate inventory.

Sales forecasts are based on estimates of demand. Managers need to define what they mean by market demand.

MEASURES OF MARKET DEMAND

Companies can prepare as many as 90 different types of demand estimates (see Figure 4-3). Demand can be measured for six different *product levels*, five different *space levels*, and three different *time levels*.

Each demand measure serves a specific purpose. A company might forecast short-run demand for a particular product for the purpose of ordering raw materials, planning production, and borrowing cash. It might forecast regional demand for its major product line to decide whether to set up regional distribution.

WHICH MARKET TO MEASURE?

Marketers talk about potential markets, available markets, served markets, and penetrated markets. Let us start with the definition of market:

■ A *market* is the set of all actual and potential buyers of a market offer.

The size of a market hinges on the number of buyers who might exist for a particular market offer. The *potential market* is the set of consumers who profess a sufficient level of interest in a market offer.

Consumer interest is not enough to define a market. Potential consumers must have enough income and must have access to the product offer. The *available market* is the set of consumers who have interest, income, and access to a particular offer.

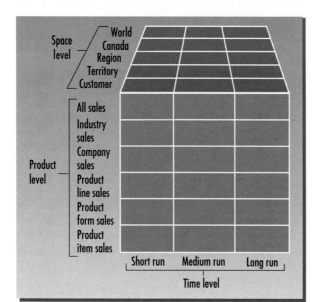

For some market offers, the company or government may restrict sales to certain groups. For example, a particular province might ban motorcycle sales to anyone under 21 years of age. The eligible adults constitute the *qualified available market*—the set of consumers who have interest, income, access, and qualifications for the particular market offer.

A company can go after the whole available market or concentrate on certain segments. The *target market* (also called the *served market*) is the part of the qualified available market the company decides to pursue. The company, for example, might decide to concentrate its marketing and distribution effort on the East Coast.

The company will end up selling to a certain number of buyers in its target market. The *penetrated market* is the set of consumers who are buying the company's product.

These market definitions are a useful tool for market planning. If the company is not satisfied with its current sales, it can take a number of actions. It can try to attract a larger percentage of buyers from its target market. It can lower the qualifications of potential buyers. It can expand its available market by opening distribution elsewhere or lowering its price. Ultimately, the company can try to expand the potential market by advertising the product to less interested consumers. Ultimately, the company can try to expand the potential market by advertising the product to less interested consumers or ones not previously targeted.

Some organizations have been successful at repositioning themselves so that they can aim at new markets. Consider the following cases:

■ **Royal Roads.** Royal Roads was founded in 1940 as a university specializing in the training of military cadets and officers. In 1995, it suddenly faced a major challenge. The government cut its funding and decided to train military cadets at its other facilities. Rather than closing its doors, the university repositioned itself as an elite school targeting mid-career professionals who cannot afford to take a year or more off work to round out their education. Royal Roads developed a modular system of course delivery to overcome this problem. Under this model, on-campus courses are combined with Internet learning. Royal Roads has attracted over 750 full-time students, but it still faces significant challenges since it needs almost 2000 students to be self-supporting.[34]

Royal Roads
www.royalroads.ca

■ **Corel Corp.** Corel began as a firm specializing in software for graphic artists and illustrators and it was lauded for its leading-edge programs in this field. Then, with the acquisition of WordPerfect, Corel aimed beyond its niche market and had the audacity to take on Microsoft and challenge its leadership in the office suite market. This time, however, David did not beat Goliath. Corel is about to transform itself once again, but is going the route of related diversification this time. It has recently acquired GraphicCorp. as part of its move towards a focus on Internet graphic arts.[35]

A VOCABULARY FOR DEMAND MEASUREMENT

The major concepts in demand measurement are *market demand* and *company demand*. Within each, we distinguish among a demand function, a sales forecast, and a potential.

Market Demand

As we've seen, the marketer's first step in evaluating marketing opportunities is to estimate total market demand.

■ *Market demand* for a product is the total volume that would be bought by a defined customer group in a defined geographical area in a defined time period in a defined marketing environment under a defined marketing program.

Market demand is not a fixed number but rather a function of the stated conditions. For this reason, it can be called the *market demand function*. The dependence of total market demand on underlying conditions is illustrated in Figure 4-4(a). The horizontal axis shows different possible levels of industry marketing expenditure in a given time period. The vertical axis shows the resulting demand level. The curve represents the estimated market demand associated with varying levels of industry marketing expenditure. Some base sales (called the *market minimum* labelled Q_1 in the figure) would take place without any demand-stimulating expenditures. Higher levels of industry marketing expenditures would yield higher levels of demand, first at an increasing rate, then at a decreasing rate. Marketing expenditures beyond a certain level would not stimulate much further demand, thus suggesting an upper limit to market demand called the *market potential* (labelled Q_2 in the figure).

The distance between the market minimum and the market potential shows the overall *marketing sensitivity of demand*. We can think of two extreme types of markets: the expansible and the nonexpansible. An *expansible* market, such as the market for racquetball playing, is very much affected in its total size by the level of industry marketing expenditures. In terms of Figure 4-4(a), the distance between Q_1 and Q_2 is relatively large. A *nonexpansible* market—for example, the market for opera—is not

FIGURE 4.4

Market Demand Functions

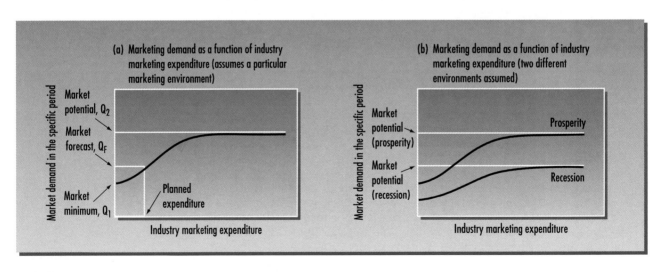

(a) Marketing demand as a function of industry marketing expenditure (assumes a particular marketing environment)

Market demand in the specific period

Market potential, Q_2

Market forecast, Q_F

Market minimum, Q_1

Planned expenditure

Industry marketing expenditure

(b) Marketing demand as a function of industry marketing expenditure (two different environments assumed)

Market demand in the specific period

Market potential (prosperity)

Market potential (recession)

Prosperity

Recession

Industry marketing expenditure

much affected by the level of marketing expenditures; the distance between Q_1 and Q_2 is relatively small. Organizations selling in a nonexpansible market must accept the market's size (the level of *primary demand* for the product class) and direct their efforts to winning a larger market share for their product (the level of *selective demand* for the company's product).

It is important to emphasize that the market demand function is *not* a picture of market demand over time. Rather, the curve shows alternative current forecasts of market demand associated with alternative possible levels of industry marketing effort in the current period.

Market Forecast

Only one level of industry marketing expenditure will actually occur. The market demand corresponding to this level is called the *market forecast*.

Market Potential

The market forecast shows expected market demand, not maximum market demand. For the latter, we have to visualize the level of market demand resulting from a "very high" level of industry marketing expenditure, where further increases in marketing effort would have little effect in stimulating further demand.

- **Market potential** is the limit approached by market demand as industry marketing expenditures approach infinity, for a given marketing environment.

The phrase "for a given market environment" is crucial. Consider the market potential for automobiles in a period of recession versus a period of prosperity. The market potential is higher during prosperity. The dependence of market potential on the environment is illustrated in Figure 4-4(b). Market analysts distinguish between the position of the market demand function and movement along it. Companies cannot do anything about the position of the market demand function, which is determined by the marketing environment. However, companies influence their particular location on the function when they decide how much to spend on marketing.

Company Demand

We are now ready to define company demand.

- **Company demand** is the company's estimated share of market demand at alternative levels of company marketing effort in a given time period.

The company's share of market demand depends on how its products, services, prices, communications, and so on are perceived relative to the competitors'. If other things are equal, the company's market share would depend on the size and effectiveness of its market expenditures relative to competitors. Marketing model builders have developed *sales-response functions* to measure how a company's sales are affected by its marketing expenditure level, marketing mix, and marketing effectiveness.[36]

Company Sales Forecast

Once marketers have estimated company demand, their next task is to choose a level of marketing effort. The chosen level will produce an expected level of sales.

- The **company sales forecast** is the expected level of company sales based on a chosen marketing plan and an assumed marketing environment.

The company sales forecast is represented graphically with company sales on the vertical axis and company marketing effort on the horizontal axis, as in Figure 4-4.

Too often the sequential relationship between the company forecast and the company marketing plan is confused. One frequently hears that the company should develop its marketing plan on the basis of its sales forecast. This forecast-to-plan sequence is valid if "forecast" means an estimate of national economic activity or if company demand is nonexpansible. The sequence is not valid, however, where market demand is expansible or where "forecast" means an estimate of company sales. The company sales forecast does not establish a basis for deciding what to spend on marketing. On the contrary, the sales forecast is the *result* of an assumed marketing expenditure plan.

Two other concepts are worth mentioning in relation to the company sales forecast.

- A *sales quota* is the sales goal set for a product line, company division, or sales representative. It is primarily a managerial device for defining and stimulating sales effort.

Management sets sales quotas on the basis of the company sales forecast and the psychology of stimulating its achievement. Generally, sales quotas are set slightly higher than estimated sales to stretch the sales force's effort.

- A *sales budget* is a conservative estimate of the expected volume of sales and is used primarily for making current purchasing, production, and cash-flow decisions.

The sales budget considers the sales forecast and the need to avoid excessive risk. Sales budgets are generally set slightly lower than the sales forecast.

Company Sales Potential

Company sales potential is the sales limit approached by company demand as company marketing effort increases relative to competitors. The absolute limit of company demand is, of course, the market potential. The two would be equal if the company achieved 100 percent of the market. In most cases, company sales potential is less than market potential, even when company marketing expenditures increase considerably relative to competitors'. The reason is that each competitor has a hard core of loyal buyers who are not very responsive to other companies' efforts to woo them.

ESTIMATING CURRENT DEMAND

We are now ready to examine practical methods for estimating current market demand. Marketing executives want to estimate total market potential, area market potential, and total industry sales and market shares.

Total Market Potential

Total market potential is the maximum amount of sales that might be available to all the firms in an industry during a given period under a given level of industry marketing effort and given environmental conditions. A common way to estimate total market potential is as follows: estimate the potential number of buyers times the average quantity purchased by a buyer times the price.

If 100 million people buy books each year, and the average book buyer buys three books a year, and the average price of a book is $10, then the total market potential for books is $3 billion (= 100,000,000 x 3 x $10). The most difficult component to estimate is the number of buyers in the specific product/market. One can always start with the total population in Canada, say 31 million people. The next step is to eliminate groups that obviously would not buy the product. Let us assume that illiterate people and children under age 12 do not buy books, and they constitute 20 percent of the population. This means that only 80 percent of the population, or approximately 24.8 million people, would be in the *suspect pool*. We might do further research and find that people of low income and low education do not read books, and they constitute over 30 percent of the suspect pool. Eliminating them, we arrive at a *prospect pool* of approximately 17.3 million book buyers. We would use this number of potential buyers to calculate total market potential.

A variation on this method is the *chain-ratio method*. It involves multiplying a base number by several adjusting percentages. Suppose a brewery is interested in estimating the market potential for a new light beer. An estimate can be made by the following calculation:[37]

> *Demand for the new light beer = Population × personal discretionary income per capita × average percentage of discretionary income spent on food × average percentage of amount spent on food that is spent on beverages × average percentage of amount spent on beverages that is spent on alcoholic beverages × average percentage of amount spent on alcoholic beverages that is spent on beer × expected percentage of amount spent on beer that will be spent on light beer.*

Area Market Potential

Companies face the problem of selecting the best territories and allocating their marketing budget optimally among these territories. Therefore they need to estimate the market potential of different cities, provinces, and nations. Two major methods of assessing area market potential are available: the market-buildup method, which is used primarily by business marketers, and the multiple-factor index method, which is used primarily by consumer marketers.

Market-Buildup Method. The *market-buildup method* calls for identifying all the potential buyers in each market and estimating their potential purchases. This method produces accurate results if we have a list of all potential buyers *and* a good estimate of what each will buy. Unfortunately, this information is not always easy to gather. An efficient method of estimating area market potentials makes use of the new North American Industry Classification System (NAICS), which was developed by the statistical agencies of Canada, Mexico, and the United States to provide statistics that are comparable across the three countries. Previously, Canada and the United States had used the Standard Industrial Classification coding system, but this caused considerable problems since different codes were used by the two countries. Thus, NAICS was developed to provide a consistent framework for the collection, analysis, and dissemination of industrial statistics used by government policy analysts, academics and researchers, the business community, and the public. NAICS classifies 350 new industries. It is composed of 20 broad economic sectors. These include sectors for construction, retail trade, information and cultural industries, manufacturing, and finance and insurance. Industries are identified by a six-digit code rather than the four-digit codes used under the SIC system. The last digit changes depending on the country. An on-line publication about the new system can be obtained at the Statistics Canada Web site. Using the sector and industry codes, people can determine the economic activity in that industry and estimate the sales that will result. This information may not be sufficient to develop a good forecast, however.

Statistics Canada
www.statcan.ca/english/subjects/
Standard/

Additional information about each market, such as the extent of market saturation, the number of competitors, the market growth rate, and the average age of existing equipment will also be needed. Companies also have to identify the best-prospect companies. In the old days, sales reps called on companies door to door; this was called *bird-dogging* or *smokestacking*. Cold calls are far too costly today. The company should get a list of companies from *Dun's Market Identifiers*, which lists 27 key facts for over nine million business locations in Canada and the United States. The firm must then qualify them by direct mail or telemarketing to identify the best prospects.

Multiple-Factor Index Method. Like business marketers, consumer companies also have to estimate area market potentials. But the customers of consumer companies are too numerous to be listed. Thus the method most commonly used in consumer markets is a straightforward index method. A drug manufacturer, for example, might assume that the market potential for drugs is directly related to population size. A drug manufacturer, for example, might assume that the market potential for drugs is directly related to population size. If the province of British Columbia has 10.79 percent of the Canadian population, the company might assume that British Columbia will be a market for 10.79 percent of total drugs sold.

A single factor, however, is rarely a complete indicator of sales opportunity. Regional drug sales are also influenced by per-capita income and the number of physicians per 10 000 people. Thus it makes sense to develop a *multiple-factor index* with each factor assigned a specific weight. Consider the following buying-power index:

$$B_I = 0.5y_I + {}_{0.3}3r_I + 0.2p_i \qquad (4\text{-}3)$$

where:

B_I = *percentage of total national buying power found in area i*

y_I = *percentage of national effective buying income originating in area i*

r_I = *percentage of national retail sales in area i*

p_I = *percentage of national population of ages 18 and over per household located in area i*

The numbers are the weights attached to each variable. For example, suppose British Columbia has 12.04 percent of the Canadian disposable personal income, 11.71 percent of Canadian retail sales, and 10.79 percent of the Canadian population. The buying-power index for British Columbia would be

$$0.5 (12.04) + 0.3 (11.71) + 0.2 (10.79) = 11.69$$

Thus 11.69 percent of the nation's drug sales might be expected to take place in British Columbia.

The weights used in the buying-power index are somewhat arbitrary. Other weights can be assigned if appropriate. Furthermore, a manufacturer would want to adjust the market potential for additional factors, such as competitors' presence in that market, local promotional costs, seasonal factors, and local market idiosyncrasies.

Many companies compute other area indexes as a guide to allocating marketing resources. Suppose the drug company is reviewing the six cities listed in Table 4-6. The first two columns show each city's percentage of national brand and category sales in these six cities. Column 3 shows the *brand development index (BDI)*, which is the index of brand sales to category sales. Montreal, for example, has a BDI of 114 because the brand is relatively more developed than the category in Montreal. Toronto has a BDI of 65, which means that the brand in Toronto is relatively underdeveloped. Normally, the lower the BDI, the higher the market opportunity, in that there is room to grow the brand. However, other marketers would argue the opposite, that marketing funds should go into the brand's strongest markets—where it might be easy to capture more brand share. Clearly, other factors must be considered.[38]

After the company decides on the city-by-city allocation of its budget, it can refine each city allocation down to enumeration areas or postal codes. Enumeration areas are the neighbourhoods that make up political constituencies, and typically contain fewer than 1000 people. Postal codes are assigned by Canada Post to areas that can vary from large office buildings to rural post offices, but these areas are generally smaller than enumeration areas.

Census-based data on population size, median family income, and other characteristics are available for both enumeration areas and postal codes. Marketers have found these data extremely useful for identifying high-potential retail areas within large cities or for buying mailing lists to use in direct-mail campaigns.

Industry Sales and Market Shares

Besides estimating total potential and area potential, a company needs to know the actual industry sales taking place in its market. This means identifying its competitors and estimating their sales.

TABLE 4.6

Calculating the Brand Development Index (BDI)

Territory	(1) Percent of Brand Sales	(2) Percent of Category Sales	BDI (1 ÷ 2) × 100
Montreal	3.09	2.71	114
Toronto	6.74	10.41	65
Vancouver	3.49	3.85	91
Calgary	97	.81	120
Ottawa	1.13	.81	140
Halifax	3.12	3.00	104

The industry's trade association will often collect and publish total industry sales, although it usually does not list individual company sales separately. Using this information, each company can evaluate its performance against the whole industry. Suppose a company's sales are increasing five percent a year, and industry sales are increasing 10 percent. This company is actually losing its relative standing in the industry.

Another way to estimate sales is to buy reports from a marketing research firm that audits total sales and brand sales. For example, A.C. Nielsen Company audits retail sales in various product categories in supermarkets and drug stores and sells this information to interested companies. These audits can give a company valuable information about its total product-category sales as well as brand sales. It can compare its performance to the total industry and/or any particular competitor to determine whether it is gaining or losing share.

Business-goods marketers typically have a harder time estimating industry sales and market shares than consumer-goods manufacturers. Business marketers have no Nielsens to rely on. Distributors typically will not supply information about how much of competitors' products they are selling. Business-goods marketers therefore operate with less knowledge of their market-share results.

ESTIMATING FUTURE DEMAND

We are now ready to examine methods of estimating future demand. Very few products or services lend themselves to easy forecasting. For example, the Royal Canadian Mint significantly underestimated demand when it launched the new $2 coin. No one could have foreseen the way Canadians decided to hoard the new coins instead of keeping them in circulation.[39] Those that do generally involve a product whose absolute level or trend is fairly constant and where competition is nonexistent (public utilities) or stable (pure oligopolies). In most markets, total demand and company demand are not stable. Good forecasting becomes a key factor in company success. The more unstable the demand, the more critical is forecast accuracy, and the more elaborate is forecasting procedure.

Companies commonly use a three-stage procedure to prepare a sales forecast. They prepare a macroeconomic forecast first, followed by an industry forecast, followed by a company sales forecast. The macroeconomic forecast calls for projecting inflation, unemployment, interest rates, consumer spending, business investment, government expenditures, net exports, and other variables. The end result is a forecast of gross national product, which is then used, along with other environmental indicators, to forecast industry sales. The company derives its sales forecast by assuming that it will win a certain market share.

How do firms develop their forecasts? Firms may do it internally or buy forecasts from outside sources such as:

- *Marketing research firms*, which develop a forecast by interviewing customers, distributors, and other knowledgeable parties.

- *Specialized forecasting firms*, which produce long-range forecasts of particular macroenvironmental components, such as population, natural resources, and technology. Some examples are Data Resources and the Economist Intelligence Unit.

- *Futurist research firms*, which produce speculative scenarios. Some examples are the Hudson Institute, the Futures Group, and the Institute for the Future.

All forecasts are built on one of three information bases: what people say, what people do, or what people have done. The first basis—what people say—involves surveying the opinions of buyers or those close to them, such as salespeople or outside experts. It encompasses three methods: surveys of buyer's intentions, composites of sales-force opinions, and expert opinion. Building a forecast on what people do involves another method, putting the product into a test market to measure buyer response. The final basis—what people have done—involves analyzing records of past buying behaviour or using time-series analysis or statistical demand analysis.

Survey of Buyers' Intentions

Forecasting is the art of anticipating what buyers are likely to do under a given set of conditions. Because buyer behaviour is so important, buyers should be surveyed.

With respect to major consumer durables (for example, major appliances), several research organizations conduct periodic surveys of consumer buying intentions. These organizations ask questions such as the following:

Do you intend to buy an automobile within the next six months?					
0.00	0.20	0.40	0.60	0.80	1.00
No chance	Slight possibility	Fair possibility	Good possibility	High probability	Certain

This is called a *purchase probability scale*. The various surveys also inquire into consumers' present and future personal finances and their expectations about the economy. The various bits of information are then combined into a consumer sentiment measure or a consumer confidence measure. For example, an Index of Consumer Confidence is computer each quarter by the Conference Board of Canada. It is based on survey responses by consumers regarding their present and expected finances, their attitudes towards the job market, and whether now is an appropriate time to make a major purchase. Consumer durable-goods producers subscribe to these indexes in the hope of anticipating major shifts in consumer-buying intentions so that they can adjust their production and marketing plans accordingly.

Some surveys measuring purchase probability are geared toward getting feedback on specific new products before they are released in the marketplace:

AcuPOLL
www.acupoll.com

- **AcuPOLL.** AcuPOLL is one of North America's biggest screeners of new products. In 1997 it sifted through more than 25 000 new items, choosing 400 of the most innovative to test on 100 representative primary grocery-store shoppers. The consumers see a photo and brief description and are asked (a) whether they would buy the product and (b) whether they think it is new and different. Products deemed both unique and "buys" are dubbed "pure gold." Products that are just unique but not desired by consumers are dubbed "fool's gold." AcuPOLL's pure gold list in 1997 included "Hair-off Mittens" to easily remove hair from women's legs, Uncle Ben's Calcium Plus rice, and Shout Wipes stain-treater towelettes. Fool's gold products included Juiced OJ (PLUS) Caffeine, a potent cocktail of caffeine-laced orange juice, Lumident ChewBrush, a toothbrush that can be chewed like gum, and Back to Basics, a "microbrewed" beer shampoo that starts with malted barley so you can put a "head" on your head.[40]

For business buying, various agencies carry out buyer-intention surveys regarding plant, equipment, and materials. This is done for large corporations by Industry Canada. At the other extreme, the Canadian Federation of Independent Business polls 55 000 small businesses from time to time on a variety of issues. Buyer-intention surveys are particularly useful in estimating demand for industrial products, consumer durables, product purchases where advanced planning is required, and new products. The value of a buyer-intention survey increases to the extent that the cost of reaching buyers is small, the buyers are few, they have clear intentions, they implement their intentions, and they willingly disclose their intentions.

Composite of Sales Force Opinions

Where buyer interviewing is impractical, the company may ask its sales representatives to estimate their future sales. Each sales representative estimates how much each current and prospective customer will buy of each of the company's products.

Few companies use their sales force's estimates without making some adjustments. Sales representatives might be pessimistic or optimistic, or they might go from one extreme to another because of a recent setback or success. Furthermore, they are often unaware of larger economic developments and do not know how their company's marketing plans will influence future sales in their territory. They might deliberately underestimate demand so that the company will set a low sales quota. Or they might lack the time to prepare careful estimates, or might not consider the effort worthwhile.

To encourage better estimating, the company could supply certain aids or incentives to the sales force. For example, sales reps might receive a record of their past forecasts compared with their actual sales and also a description of company assumptions on the business outlook, competitor behaviour, and marketing plans.

Involving the sales force in forecasting brings a number of benefits. Sales reps might have better insight into developing trends than any other single group. After participating in the forecasting process, sales reps might have greater confidence in their sales quotas and more incentive to achieve them.[41] Also, a "grassroots" forecasting procedure provides very detailed estimates broken down by product, territory, customer, and sales reps.

Expert Opinion

Companies can also obtain forecasts from experts, including dealers, distributors, suppliers, marketing consultants, and trade associations. Large appliance companies survey dealers periodically for their forecasts of short-term demand, as do car companies. Dealer estimates are subject to the same strengths and weaknesses as sales force estimates. Many companies buy economic and industry forecasts from well-known economic-forecasting firms. These specialists are able to prepare better economic forecasts than the company because they have more data available and more forecasting expertise.

Occasionally companies will invite a group of experts to prepare a forecast. The experts exchange views and produce a group estimate (*group-discussion methods*). Or the experts supply their estimates individually, and an analyst combines them into a single estimate (*pooling of individual estimates*). Alternatively, the experts supply individual estimates and assumptions that are reviewed by the company, then revised. Further rounds of estimating and refining follow (*Delphi method*).[42]

Past-Sales Analysis

Sales forecasts can be developed on the basis of past sales. *Time-series analysis* consists of breaking down past time series into four components (trend, cycle, seasonal, and erratic), and projecting these components into the future. *Exponential smoothing* consists of projecting the next period's sales by combining an average of past sales and the most recent sales, giving more weight to the latter. *Statistical demand analysis* consists of measuring the impact level of each of a set of causal factors (e.g., income, marketing expenditures, price) on the sales level. Finally, *econometric analysis* consists of building sets of equations that describe a system and proceeding to statistically fit the parameters.

Market-Test Method

Where buyers do not plan their purchases carefully or experts are not available or reliable, a direct market test is desirable. A direct market test is especially desirable in forecasting new-product sales or established product sales in a new distribution channel or territory. (We discuss market testing in detail in Chapter 11.)

SUMMARY

1. Three developments make the need for marketing information greater now than at any time in the past: the rise of global marketing, the new emphasis on buyers' wants, and the trend toward nonprice competition.

2. To carry out their analysis, planning, implementation, and control responsibilities, marketing managers need a *marketing information system (MIS)*. The MIS's role is to assess the managers' information needs, develop the needed information, and distribute the information in a timely manner.

3. An MIS has four components: (1) An internal records system, which includes information on the order-to-payment cycle and sales reporting systems; (2) A marketing intelligence system, a set of procedures and sources used by managers to obtain everyday information about pertinent developments in the marketing environment; (3) A marketing research system that allows for the systematic design, collection, analysis, and reporting of data and findings relevant to a specific marketing situation; and (4) A computerized marketing decision support system that helps managers interpret relevant data and information and turn it into a basis for marketing action.

4. Companies can conduct their own marketing research or hire other companies to do it for them. Good marketing research is characterized by the scientific method, creativity, multiple research methods, accurate model building, cost/benefit analysis, healthy skepticism, and an ethical focus.

5. The process consists of defining the problem and research objective, developing the research plan, collecting the information, analyzing the information, and presenting the findings to management. In conducting research, firms must decide whether to collect their own data or use data that already exist. They must also decide which research approach (observational, focus-group, survey, experimental) and which research instrument (questionnaire or mechanical instruments) to use. In addition, they must decide on a sampling plan and contact methods.

6. One major reason for undertaking marketing research is to discover market opportunities. Once the research is complete, the company must carefully evaluate its opportunities and decide which markets to enter. Once in the market, it must prepare sales forecasts based on estimates of demand.

7. There are two types of demand: market demand and company demand. To estimate current demand, companies attempt to determine total market potential, area market potential, industry sales, and market share. To estimate future demand, companies survey buyers' intentions, solicit their sales force's input, gather expert opinions, and/or engage in market testing. Mathematical models, advanced statistical techniques, and computerized data-collection procedures are essential to all types of demand and sales forecasting.

APPLICATIONS

CHAPTER CONCEPTS

1. Each of the following questions appears on a paper questionnaire that respondents fill out and return to a research firm. Rephrase and/or reformat each question so that the respondent is more likely to provide the research firm with the information it needs.

    a. Which brand do you like best?

    b. Can you tell me how many children you have, whether they are girls or boys, and how old they are?

    c. How much say do you have regarding the charities that your place of worship contributes to?

    d. With what frequency have you experienced this phenomenon of late?

    e. Are auto manufacturers making satisfactory progress in controlling auto emissions?

2. Levi Strauss is interested in developing a new line of dress suits that would appeal to young, independent, professional men who usually shop in specialty stores. The marketing team has determined that the men who buy Levi's jeans fall into five categories:

- *Utilitarian jeans customer*: the Levi loyalist who wears jeans for work and play

- *Trendy casual*: high-fashion customers who come to life at night

- *Price shopper*: buys on the basis of price at department stores and discount stores

- *Mainstream traditionalist*: over 45 years old and shops in a department store accompanied by his wife

- *Classic independent*: independent buyer, shops alone in specialty stores, and wants clothes that make him "look right" (the target in this case)

The marketing team's task is to determine (1) whether the Levi name should be used on the new product, and (2) whether this product could be successfully marketed through Levi's current channels of distribution. How could the team "get the ball rolling" in terms of answering these questions and generating a plan for conducting more intensive research into the preferences of the "classic independent" segment? What kinds of formal market research should the company conduct to help it make a decision whether to pursue this segment? If it does go after classic independents, what challenges might Levi's face?

3. Suggest creative ways to help companies research the following issues:

a. Why contributions to a local charity fall below rates in other communities across Canada.

b. A magazine distribution house wants to know how many people read a specific magazine in doctors' offices.

c. A producer of men's hair grooming products wants to know at least four ways it can find and interview the men who use its products.

4. A children's toy manufacturer is developing its sales forecast for next year. The company's forecaster has estimated sales for six different environment/strategy combinations (See Table 1).

TABLE 1 Demand States and Marketing Tasks		High Marketing Budget	Medium Marketing Budget	Low Marketing Budget
	Recession	15	12	10
	Normal	20	16	14

The forecaster believes that there is an 0.20 probability of recession and an 0.80 probability of normal times. He also believes the probabilities of a high, medium, and low company market budget are 0.30, 0.50, and 0.20, respectively. How might he arrive at a single-point sales forecast? What assumptions are being made?

1. Marriott has boosted annual revenues over $18 billion by working to identify and satisfy the differing needs and preferences of travellers. The Marriott ad shown in Figure 1 is targeted toward health-conscious business travellers. What internal data sources can the company use to identify opportunities such as this? To identify problems with a particular part of the service offering such as the health club or pool? How would a marketing intelligence system help Marriott compete against Hilton and other rivals who target the business travel market? If you were designing Marriott's marketing intelligence system, what would you include? Why?

2. Bayer Aspirin, the product featured in this ad, is locked in competitive battle with Tylenol, Advil, and a wide range of other painkillers. In planning next year's marketing programs, the company wants to estimate future demand. Would a survey of buyers' intentions be appropriate for this product? Why or why not? Would you suggest using past-sales analysis or a direct market test? Explain your answers. What effect would the unexpected introduction of a new pain-killing drug from a rival firm—supported by a high-profile, multi-million dollar campaign—be likely to have on Bayer's forecast of future demand?

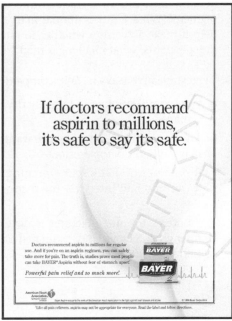

Figure 1

Figure 2

FOCUS ON TECHNOLOGY

Every year since 1994, the Georgia Institute of Technology has conducted two World Wide Web user surveys. The purpose is to find out who is using the Web, what technology is being used, the problems users are encountering, how much individuals and companies are spending online, and how they are using online financial services. The results are available to all, which means that companies can download the latest results (as well as earlier results) and apply the findings to their own marketing efforts.

To learn more, point your Web browser to Georgia Tech's WWW Survey site. Read the general background section and look through the latest survey results. What limitations should companies bear in mind when using these survey results? Why aren't there publicly available surveys of this type available in Canada? What kind of sample does this survey represent, and why should marketers care? How could a company such as Air Canada apply the results of this survey in its efforts to sell more airline tickets on the Web?

Georgia Institute of Technology
http://www.cc.gatech.edu/gvu/
user_surveys/

MARKETING FOR THE 21ST CENTURY

At the turn of the millennium, one of marketing's hottest techniques is data mining, which involves extracting patterns from large masses of data (data warehouses and data marts) using sophisticated computerized analyses. Data mining helps marketers better target their marketing activities for improved efficiency and effectiveness. However, data mining can sometimes lead companies to dig up false trends rather than real gems. This is why marketers must ask the right business questions, take steps to ensure the quality and validity of the data in the data warehouse, and step back to analyze their findings before they implement a program based on data mining.

Prudential
http://www.prudential.com

Prudential is one of many companies using data mining to target its marketing outreach. Through data mining, the firm has saved money and improved response by more narrowly targeting the mailing lists for specific product offers. Visit Prudential's Web site and select one type of product, such as life insurance or mutual funds. Identify two ways that data mining could be applied to market your chosen product. What kinds of objectives would you set for using data mining in this situation? What potential problems or dangers do you see in using data mining in this situation? Looking ahead to the new millennium, what additional marketing applications can you foresee for Prudential's use of data mining?

YOU'RE THE MARKETER: SONIC MARKETING PLAN

Marketing information systems, marketing intelligence systems, and marketing research systems are used to gather and analyze data for various parts of the marketing plan. These systems can help marketers examine changes and trends in markets, competition, product usage, and distribution channels, among other areas. They can also turn up evidence of important opportunities and threats that must be addressed.

You are continuing as Jane Melody's assistant at Sonic. Using Table 3-3 in Chapter 3, answer the following questions about how you can use MIS and marketing research to support the development and implementation of Sonic's marketing plan:

■ For which sections will you need secondary data? Primary data? Both? Why do you need the information for each section?

■ Where can you find suitable secondary data? Identify two non-Internet sources and two Internet sources, describe what you plan to draw from each source, and indicate how you will use the data in your marketing planning.

- What surveys, focus groups, observation, behavioural data, and/or experiments will Sonic need to support its marketing strategy, including product management, pricing, distribution, and marketing communication? Be specific about the questions or issues that Sonic should be able to resolve using market research.
- As your instructor directs, enter information about Sonic's use of marketing data and research in the appropriate sections of a written marketing plan or in the corresponding sections of the Marketing Plan Pro software.

Scanning the Marketing Environment

998 GREY CUP CHAMPIONS
1999 MEDIA GUIDE

PROFILE:

Canadian Marketing Excellence

"What do you do to get 'bums into seats?'" asks Ron Rooke, vice president of marketing and communications for the Calgary Stampeders. Gone are the days when the Canadian Football League and clubs like the Stampeders had a corner on fan support. With the emergence of inexpensive home entertainment in the 1980s, the fan base started to dwindle. Few seemed to take notice or to recognize the fact that the image of football had also changed. Rather than being viewed as great family entertainment, people perceived stadiums to be full of beer-swilling louts. Things went from bad to worse with the arrival of even more competition. Hockey and baseball teams eroded more and more of the traditional fan base. New marketing plays had to be found.

The Stampeders' first move was an end-run towards repositioning football as an affordable family activity. Season ticket prices were slashed from more than $350 to $100. Touchdown—sales climbed from 9300 to 18 000. Next, a blitz to change football from just another sport to genuine entertainment. From the parking lot to the stands, fans are regaled with the antics of clowns, contests, giveaways, bands, and a carnival-like atmosphere that rivals that of the Stampede. Kids get special treatment—everything from face painting to a Kids Club. Special ladies-only seminars, called "It's a Snap!," are offered to convert this non-traditional market into fans. Is Rooke's theory working? You just have to look at all those "bums in seats!"

Source: Holly Quan, "Bums Into Seats," *Marketing*, October 19, 1998, pp. 12-13.

Successful companies take an outside-inside view of their business. They recognize that the marketing environment is constantly spinning new opportunities and threats and understand the importance of continuously monitoring and adapting to that environment. One company that has continually reinvented one of its brands to keep up with changing facets of the marketing environment is Mattel with its Barbie doll:[1]

- **Mattel.** Lordy, lordy, Barbie's forty…and Mattel, the world's leading toy maker, fears her age is starting to show. Shipments of the brand fell 14 percent in 1998. Not a small concern when Barbie accounts for 40 to 50 percent of Mattel's profits. Until recently, Mattel's genius has been in keeping its Barbie doll both timeless and trendy. For years, Barbie has changed as much as children changed. To appeal to a more diverse audience, Mattel began producing African-American Barbie in 1968—the time of the civil rights movement—and then it introduced Hispanic, Asian, and Puerto Rican Barbie dolls as part of its "dolls of the world" collection. Industry analysts estimate that two Barbie dolls are sold every second and that the average North American girl owns eight versions of Barbie. Every year since 1993, sales have exceeded $1.5 billion. But today, Mattel and Barbie are facing new threats and opportunities as the toy industry rapidly evolves. Children now favour computer games and new toys, such as Beanie Babies, from small, upstart firms. Direct marketing and catalogue sales are making in-roads against firms that sell through traditional retail channels. In response, Mattel bought Pleasant Co, another doll company, but one with direct marketing experience so that it could gain expertise in this area. However, the question remains as to whether Mattel can dress up and renew profits in the face of these new challenges.

Many companies fail to see change as opportunity. They ignore or resist changes until it is too late. Their strategies, structures, systems, and organizational culture grow increasingly obsolete and dysfunctional. Corporations as mighty as General Motors and IBM have passed through difficult times because they ignored macroenvironmental changes too long.

The major responsibility for identifying significant marketplace changes falls to the company's marketers. More than any other group in the company, they must be the trend trackers and opportunity seekers. Although every manager in an organization

In this and the next four chapters, we examine the firm's *external environment*—the macro-environment—forces that affect it, its consumer markets, its business markets, and its competitors. In this chapter, we focus on two questions:

- What are the key methods for tracking and identifying opportunities in the macroenvironment?

- What are the key demographic, economic, natural, technological, political, and cultural developments?

Mattel
www.mattell.com

needs to observe the outside environment, marketers have two advantages: They have disciplined methods—marketing intelligence and marketing research—for collecting information about the marketing environment. They also spend more time with customers and more time watching competitors.

ANALYZING NEEDS AND TRENDS IN THE MACROENVIRONMENT

Successful companies recognize and respond profitably to unmet needs and trends. Companies could make a fortune if they could solve any of these problems: a cure for cancer, chemical cures for mental diseases, desalinization of seawater, nonfattening tasty nutritious food, practical electric cars, and affordable housing.

Enterprising individuals and companies manage to create new solutions to unmet needs. Club Mediterranee emerged to meet the needs of single people for exotic vacations; the Walkman and CD Man were created for active people who wanted to listen to music; Nautilus was created for men and women who wanted to tone their bodies; and Federal Express was created to meet the need for next-day mail delivery. Many opportunities are found by identifying *trends*.

■ A *trend* is a direction or sequence of events that have some momentum and durability.

One major trend is the increasing participation of women in the work force, which has spawned the child day-care business, increased consumption of microwavable foods, office-oriented women's clothing, and other business opportunities.

■ **General Mills Canada Inc.** As consumers become more time pressed, food manufacturers are churning out products whose main attribute is convenience. General Mills has responded to this trend by reinventing instant mashed potatoes marketed under its Betty Crocker line. With new flavours such as butter and herb, roasted garlic and homestyle, and a $8-million launch budget, General Mills hopes to win over sceptical Canadian consumers. While instant potatoes are very popular in the United States, they only account for approximately 25 percent of the market in Canada. General Mills thinks the Canada market is hungry for their new improved products.[2]

General Mills Canada
www.generalmills.com

We need to draw distinctions among fads, trends, and megatrends. Unlike a trend, a *fad* is "unpredictable, short-lived, and without social, economic, and political significance."[3] A company can cash in on a fad such as Tamagotchi pets, but this is more a matter of luck and good timing than anything else.

Trends are more predictable and durable. A trend reveals the shape of the future. According to futurist Faith Popcorn, a trend has longevity, is observable across several market areas and consumer activities, and is consistent with other significant indicators occurring or emerging at the same time.[4] (See the Marketing Insight titled "Faith Popcorn Points to Ten Trends in the Economy.")

John Kettle, the Canadian futurist who has provided predictions to many influential organizations including IBM, United Nations, Shell, and Statistics Canada, and who regularly writes a column in *The Globe and Mail*, thinks eight major trends will affect Canada today and in the future.

1. *The gradual engulfing of the Western, industrialized nations by the developing and newly industrializing nations.* The world's agenda will increasingly be set by East Asia and Islam.

2. *Americanization of world culture.* Canada is the most advanced victim of American culture. Within two generations, the two cultures will be indistinguishable, in fact or in practice.

3. *Sovereignty.* The growth of increasingly large economic alliances such as NAFTA and the European Common market have led to counter movements

Faith Popcorn Points to 16 Trends in the Economy

Famous trend-watcher Faith Popcorn runs BrainReserve, a marketing consulting firm that monitors cultural trends and advises companies like AT&T, Black & Decker, Hoffman-LaRoche, Nissan, Rubbermaid, and many more. Popcorn and her associates have identified 16 major cultural trends affecting the North American economy. How many of these trends have you noticed in your own life?

1. **Anchoring**. The tendency to use ancient practices as anchors or support for modern lifestyles. This trend explains the widespread popularity of aromatherapy, meditation, yoga, and Eastern religions.

2. **Being Alive.** The desire to lead longer and more enjoyable lives. Vegetarianism, low-tech medicine, meditation, and other life extenders and enhancers are part of this trend. Marketers can capitalize on the trend by designing healthier products and services.

3. **Cashing Out.** The desire for a simpler, less hectic lifestyle, as when an executive suddenly quits a high-profile career, escapes the hassles of big-city life, and turns up in P.E.I. running a bed-and-breakfast. The trend is marked by a nostalgic return to small-town values.

4. **Clanning.** The growing need to join up with and belong to groups in order to confront a more chaotic world. Marketers are responding with products, services, and programs that help make consumers feel a part of something, for example, Harley-Davidson's Harley Owners Group (HOG).

5. **Cocooning.** The impulse to stay inside when the going outside gets too tough and scary. People are turning their homes into nests: redecorating, watching TV and rental movies, ordering from catalogues, and using answering machines to filter out the outside world. Socialized cocoons gather inside for conversation or a "salon." Wandering cocoons are people who hole up in their cars with take-out foods and their car phones.

6. **Down-aging.** The tendency for older people to act and feel younger than their age. They spend more on youthful clothes and hair colouring, and they engage in more playful behaviour, such as buying adult toys, attending adult camps, or signing up for adventure vacations.

7. **Egonomics.** The wish to individualize oneself through possessions and experience. Egonomics gives marketers an opportunity to succeed by offering customized goods, services, and experiences.

8. **Fantasy Adventure.** The need to find emotional escapes to offset daily routines. People following this trend seek safari vacations or eat exotic foods. For marketers, this is an opportunity to create fantasy products and services. The trend will certainly feed the growth of virtual reality throughout the first decade of the new millennium.

9. **Female Think.** The recognition that men and women act and think differently. A strong indicator of female think is the popularity of books such as *Men Are From Mars, Women Are From Venus*. Because relationships are powerful motivators for women, for example, Saturn Car Company has created strong relationships with its customers, many of whom are women.

towards independence in other spheres of people's lives such as culture and politics. Quebec is a manifestation of this trend.

4. *Aging Population.* As the birth rate falls and people live longer, the proportion of young people within the population is falling. While one-third of Canada's population was under 20 in 1975, this group represents less than one-quarter of the population today and will fall to one-fifth of the population by 2025.

5. *Slowing economy.* Since Canada is already affluent, economic increases will come at a slower pace. Per-capita gross domestic product increased at over three percent in the 1960s, 2.5 percent in the 1970, 1.5 percent in the 1980s, and 0.5 percent in the 1990s. Higher rates of growth are unlikely in the future. Higher unemployment (or lower rates of participation in the labour force) and shorter work hours will result from this trend. Already 20 percent of Canada's workers put in less than 30 hours a week.

6. *Rise of the service economy.* With the migration of manufacturing to third-world countries, Canada is increasingly becoming a service economy. The ratio of service-producing to goods-producing workers is currently three to one. By 2025, this ratio will be five to one.

(continued)

10. **Icon Toppling.** The idea that "if it's big, it's bad." Small business marketers are benefiting from this trend. For example, beers from microbreweries, like Creamore Cream Ale, are eroding the share of the mega-brewers, Labatt and Molson.

11. **Mancipation.** The emancipation of men from stereotypical male roles. Men are no longer required to be macho, distant, and strong. This trend is revealed in ads featuring men as nurturing dads and concerned husbands.

12. **99 Lives.** The attempt to relieve time pressures by doing many things at once. People become adept at "multitasking," doing many tasks at once, such as talking on a portable phone while surfing the Net. Marketers can cash in on the 99 Lives trend by creating cluster marketing enterprises—all-in-one service stops.

13. **Pleasure Revenge.** The proud and public pursuit of pleasure as a rebellion against self-control and deprivation. Fed up with the health kick of the early 1990s, people are consuming more red meat, fats, and sugars and turning away from health food alternatives.

14. **S.O.S. (Save Our Society).** The desire to make society more socially responsible with respect to education, ethics, and the environment. The best response for marketers is to urge their own companies to practise more socially responsible marketing.

15. **Small Indulgences.** A penchant to indulge in small-scale splurges to obtain an occasional emotional lift. A consumer might eat healthy all week, and then splurge on a litre of superpremium Häagen-Dazs ice cream on the weekend, or might brown bag it for lunch but buy an expensive Second Cup latte and pastries for breakfast.

16. **The Vigilante Consumer.** Intolerance for shoddy products and poor service. Vigilante consumers want companies to be more aware and responsive, so they act up, boycott, write letters, and buy "green products."

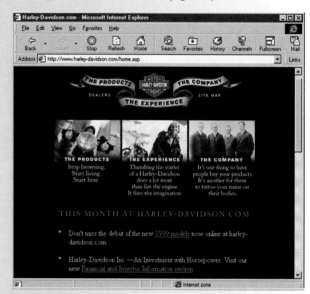

The Harley-Davidson home page makes Harley owners part of a family.

Source: This summary is adapted from various pages of Faith Popcorn's *The Popcorn Report* (New York: HarperBusiness, 1992). Also see the additional trends in Faith Popcorn and Lys Marigold, Clicking (New York: HarperCollins, 1996).

7. *The information economy.* About one-third of Canada's economic product is in the form of information. Information production includes the creation, gathering, processing, and distribution of information, but not the manufacture of information technology such as computers or telephones. Information services include banking, insurance, communications, Internet services, publishing, education, entertainment, advertising, data processing, religious organizations, and almost all activities of government.

8. *Household services.* Historically food expenditures accounted for the largest portion of household budgets; today it is services. They account for more than half of household spending. Such spending includes cable TV, housemaid services, health clubs, lawyers, and dog-walking services.[5]

John Naisbitt, another futurist, prefers to talk about *megatrends*, which are "large social, economic, political and technological changes [that] are slow to form, and once in place, they influence us for some time—between seven and ten years, or longer."[6] Among the megatrends Naisbitt identified are a booming global economy, a renaissance in the arts, the emergence of free-market socialism, global lifestyles, privatization of the welfare state, the decade of women in leadership, a religious revival, and the triumph of the individual.

Trends merit marketers' close attention. A new product or marketing program is likely to be more successful if it is in line with strong trends rather than opposed to them. But detecting a new market opportunity does not guarantee its success, even if it is technically feasible. For example, today it is possible to offer a customized daily newspaper that will appear on a computer screen and cover only items subscribers are interested in. But there may not be a sufficient number of people interested in such a product or willing to pay the required price. This is why market research is necessary to determine an opportunity's profit potential.

IDENTIFYING AND RESPONDING TO THE MAJOR MACROENVIRONMENT FORCES

Companies and their suppliers, marketing intermediaries, customers, competitors, and publics all operate in a macroenvironment of forces and trends that shape opportunities and pose threats. While many marketers think of these forces as "noncontrollables," others recognize that marketing has the power to shape trends and must take responsibility for its actions. In the economic arena, companies and consumers are increasingly affected by global forces. These include:

- The substantial speedup of international transportation, communication, and financial transactions, leading to the rapid growth of world trade and investment, especially tri-polar trade (North America, Western Europe, Far East).
- The rising economic power of several Asian countries in world markets.
- The rise of trade blocs such as the European Union and the NAFTA signatories.
- The severe debt problems of a number of countries, along with the increasing fragility of the international financial system.
- The increasing use of barter and countertrade to support international transactions.
- The move toward market economies in formerly socialist countries along with rapid privatization of publicly owned companies.
- The rapid dissemination of global lifestyles.
- The gradual opening of major new markets, namely China, India, Eastern Europe, and Arab countries.
- The increasing tendency of multinationals to transcend their locational and national characteristics and become transnational firms.
- The increasing number of cross-border corporate strategic alliances—for example, MCI and British Telecom, and Texas Instruments and Hitachi.
- The increasing ethnic and religious conflicts in certain countries and regions.
- The growth of global brands in autos, food, clothing, electronics, and so on.

- **Colgate-Palmolive**, for example, test-marketed Total, its antibacterial plaque-fighting toothpaste, in six countries: the Philippines, Australia, Colombia, Greece, Portugal, and the United Kingdom. The team in charge of the global launch was a veritable corporate United Nations of operations, logistics, and marketing strategists. Their efforts paid off handsomely: Total was soon a $225-million brand worldwide, selling in 75 countries, with virtually identical packaging, positioning, and advertising [Figure 5-1].[7]

Within the rapidly changing global picture, the firm must monitor six major forces: demographic, economic, natural, technological, political/legal, and social/cultural. Although these forces will be described separately, marketers must pay attention to their causal interactions, since these set the stage for new opportunities as well as threats. For example, explosive population growth (demographic) leads to more resource depletion and pollution (natural environment), which leads consumers to call for more laws (political/legal). The imposed restrictions stimulate new technological solutions and products (technology), which if they are affordable (economic forces) may actually change attitudes and behaviour (social/cultural).

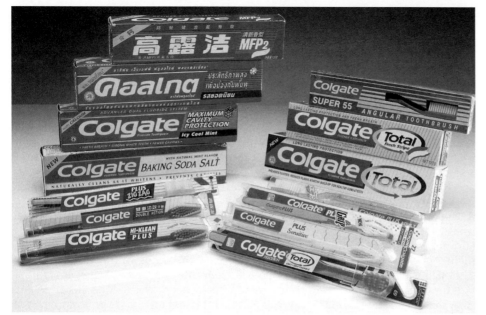

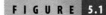

FIGURE 5.1

Colgate-Palmolive's Total Global Branding Strategy

Colgate-Palmolive has had global success with its Colgate line of tooth-care products. The products and their packaging design do not vary from country to country; the only thing that changes is the language on the packages.

DEMOGRAPHIC ENVIRONMENT

The first macroenvironmental force that marketers monitor is population because people make up markets. Marketers are keenly interested in the size and growth rate of population in different cities, regions, and nations; age distribution and ethnic mix; educational levels; household patterns; and regional characteristics and movements.

Worldwide Population Growth.

The world population is showing "explosive" growth. It totalled 5.4 billion in 1991 and is growing at 1.7 percent per year. At this rate, the world's population will reach 6.2 billion by the year 2000.[8]

The world population explosion has been a source of major concern, for two reasons. The first is the fact that certain resources needed to support this much human life (fuel, foods, and so forth) are limited and may run out at some point. First published in 1972, *The Limits to Growth,* called for the worldwide marketing of family planning in the face of evidence that unchecked population growth and consumption would result in insufficient food supply, depletion of key minerals, overcrowding, pollution, and deterioration in the quality of life.[9]

The second cause for concern is that population growth is highest in countries and communities that can least afford it. The highest growth rates are in Africa, Central and South America. Whereas Africa accounted for only 8 percent of the world's population in 1900, it will comprise 13 percent by the millennium. Growth rates have stabilized in the Asian-Pacific countries. These countries account for 61 percent of the world's population. Overall, the less developed regions of the world currently account for 76 percent of the world population and are growing at 2 percent per year compared to 0.6 percent in the more developed countries. Europe, which once accounted for 25 percent of the population, is now home to only 12 percent. In some developing countries, feeding, clothing, educating, and providing a decent standard of living for children is nearly impossible.[10]

The explosive world population growth has major implications for business. A growing population does not mean growing markets unless these markets have sufficient purchasing power. Nonetheless, companies that carefully analyze their markets can find major opportunities. For example, to curb its skyrocketing population, the Chinese government has passed regulations limiting families to one child per family for urban dwellers, two for rural residents. Toy marketers, in particular, are paying attention to one consequence of these regulations: these children are spoiled and fussed over as never before. Known in China as "little emperors," Chinese children are being showered with everything from candy to computers as a result of what's known as the "six-pocket syndrome." As many as six adults—parents, grandparents, great-grandparents, and aunts and uncles—may be indulging the whims of each child. This trend has encouraged such companies as Japan's Bandai Co. (famous for its Mighty Morphin' Power Rangers), Denmark's Lego Group, and Mattel to enter the Chinese market.[11]

Population Age Mix

National populations vary in their age mix. At one extreme is Mexico, a country with a very young population and rapid population growth. At the other extreme is Japan, a country with one of the world's oldest populations. Milk, diapers, school supplies, and toys would be important products in Mexico. Japan's population would consume many more products valued by the elderly.

A population can be subdivided into six age groups: preschool, school-age children, teens, young adults age 25–40; middle-aged adults age 40–65; and older adults age 65 and up. For marketers, the most populous age groups shape the marketing environment. "Baby boomers" have had a great influence on trends within North America. Although there was a baby boom in both Canada and the United States, it is important for Canadian marketers to realize that our baby boom was unique. It started later than the American version (1947 versus 1946) and lasted for a more prolonged period. (The American boom ended in 1964; the Canadian boom continued until 1966). While the American baby boom resulted in 3.5 children per family, the Canadian boom produced four children. Furthermore, the baby boom was not a worldwide phenomenon. No developed countries, other than Australia and New Zealand, experienced the same expansion in the birth rate. In Europe, there was no baby boom, and in Japan, the birth rate declined during the baby boom years, explaining why these countries have a higher proportion of older people in their societies. The median age of the Canadian population is now 35; 35-year-olds are at the trailing end of the baby boom. Baby boomers are fixated on their youth, not their age, and ads geared to them tend to capitalize on nostalgia for their past, such as those for the newly redesigned Volkswagen Beetle or the Mercedes Benz ad featuring the rock music of Janis Joplin.[12] The age groups that will experience the most rapid growth in Canada in the coming decades will be older adults and teenagers. Not good news for products aimed at other market segments. Here's what one organization did to respond to population age shifts:

Chatelaine
www.chatelaine.com

■ **Chatelaine.** "How do you stay healthy if you don't add new readers to the franchise?" An important question if you are Donna Clark, the new editor of Chatelaine, Canada's most-read women's magazine. The magazine had traditionally been aimed at the baby-boom generation, but with the aging of this group, Clark found that she had few readers in the 20–30 age group. A $2 million makeover of the venerable magazine was undertaken. Care had to be used, however. Clark regarded her task as "growth of readership, not replacement." She certainly didn't want to alienate her traditional audience in the process. The new Chatelaine is glossier and more sophisticated. Not only has it drawn new readers, but it has also lured in new advertisers—not simply more cosmetics and packaged goods firms, but also telecommunications and entertainment firms who, like the revamped magazine, have a younger target audience.[13]

Boomers grew up with television advertising, so they are an easier market to reach than the 4.5 million born between 1967 and 1976, dubbed Generation X (and also the Shadow Generation, Twentysomethings, and Baby Busters). Gen-Xers are typically cynical about hard-sell marketing pitches that promise more than they can deliver. Ads created to woo this market often puzzle older people, since they often don't seem to "sell" at all[14]:

■ **Diesel Jeans.** Diesel jeans ads revolve around a celebration of the bizarre, and they playfully poke fun at mainstream situations. Called "Reasons for Living," the ads reverse our code of ethics with images like one of humans serving a roasted girl to pigs sitting at a dining table laden with exotic foods.[15]

Finally, both baby boomers and Gen-Xers will be passing the torch to the latest demographic group, the Baby Boomlet, born between 1977 and 1994. Now numbering 7.2 million, this group is almost equal in size to baby boomers. One distinguishing characteristic of this age group is their utter fluency and comfort with computer and Internet technology. Douglas Tapscott, author of *Growing Up Digital: The Rise of the Net Generation*, has christened them Net-Gens for this reason. He says: "To them, digital technology is no more intimidating than a VCR or a toaster." See the Marketing Memo entitled "Tapping into the Net Generation."[16]

But do marketers have to create separate ads for each generation? J. Walker Smith, co-author of *Rocking the Ages: The Yankelovich Report on Generational Marketing*, says that marketers do have to be careful about turning off one generation each time they craft a message that appeals effectively to another. "I think the idea is to try to be broadly inclusive and at the same time offer each generation something specifically designed for it. Tommy Hilfiger has big brand logos on his clothes for teenagers and little pocket polo logos on his shirts for baby boomers. It's a brand that has a more inclusive than exclusive strategy."[17]

A Cultural Mosaic

Countries also vary in ethnic and racial makeup. At one extreme is Japan, where almost everyone is Japanese; at the other are Canada and the United States, where people come from virtually all nations. The 1996 census revealed that there are 3.2 million Canadians, or 11 percent of the population, who identify themselves as members of non-white racial groups. Cultural diversity is particularly noteworthy in Canada's larger cities. Toronto is the city with the highest concentration of racial minority groups with 40 percent, or one out of three residents, coming from non-white backgrounds. Racial diversity in Canada's cities is expected to continue to increase as an average of 245 000 immigrants come to Canada each year. Most come from Asia, the Caribbean, the Middle East, Latin America, and the Indo-Pakistani region.[18]

Canadian government policy has been to maintain the essential differences in this "cultural mosaic." The United States was originally called a "melting pot" but now people call the United States a "salad bowl" to denote its distinct elements. The U.S. population is 73 percent white. African-Americans constitute another 13 percent, and Latinos another 10 percent. Most cultural minorities have a local, or possibly a regional, significance for marketers. Product designers, marketers, and retailers especially should be aware of specific wants and buying habits of such groups. Many of their needs are unmet. Asian consumers, for example, often complain that off-the-rack clothing found in most Canadian stores does not fit them well and that the colours are all wrong for Asian complexions. Until recently, many black women have had to mix their own cosmetic shades to obtain the right tones. Many African-Canadians complain that they can't find furniture that meets their ergonomic needs. And even more serious are the concerns of Asian-Canadians who often find that they experience side-effects when they take the recommended dosages of over-the-counter drugs. Some firms are starting to listen to these voices.[19] Revlon Canada is marketing products for black Canadians. Nielsen Dairies have launched Soy Delight, a product that is an alternative to milk for lactose-intolerant Asians. Nike, a global sponsor of the 1998 World Cup soccer tournament, wanted to promote its affiliation in Canada. To accomplish its aim, it turned toward the Italian and Portuguese communities of Toronto since it believed that these people were the most passionate devotees of the sport in Canada in Nike's view. As Jeff Spreit, Nike Canada's advertising manager, noted, "We ended up delivering a very relevant message to a very passionate consumer." Nike's advertising consisted mainly of billboards, but it also distributed posters of the board ads. Nike knew it had reached its target when it handed out over 5000 posters to teenage fans on a single night.

The French-Canadian minority deserves special attention because of its large size and its dispersion through several provinces. Comprising 83 percent of Quebec households and 23 percent of Canadian households, this minority cannot be ignored by

Growing Up Digital
www.growingupdigital.com

national marketers. Canada is officially a bicultural country, and Canadian marketers must be sensitive to cultural differences. French-Canadians have traditionally emphasized family, home, and Church. But in recent decades, a growing secularism has weakened these ties in favour of materialism and nationalism, and more recently, in favour of political separatism. The question of whether French-Canadian consumers are becoming more like other Canadians is debatable. But most marketers would agree that existing differences make it hazardous to employ a uniform promotional strategy across Canada. Differences in lifestyle, attitudes, and product usage make separate copy strategy and media decisions essential.

Yet marketers must be careful not to overgeneralize about ethnic groups. Within each ethnic group are consumers who are as different from each other as they are from Canadians of European background. Bobby Siu, president of Inforworth Consulting, an agency specializing in ethnic markets, emphasizes that "each Asian ethnic group has its own identity, values and lifestyle; yet they share common experiences as Asians in Canada. Asian Canadians are not homogeneous. The identities and values of Filipinos, Sri Lankans, Chinese, and Koreans are different.[20]

Educational Groups

The population in any society falls into five educational groups: illiterates, high school dropouts, high school degrees, university and college degrees, and professional or graduate degrees. In Japan, 99 percent of the population is literate. Even though 36 percent of the U.S. population has a college degree, another 10 to 15 percent of the population may be functionally illiterate. In Canada, only 2.5 percent of people aged 15 or older falls within this category. Almost 19 percent of Canada's population in the age group 25 to 44 has a university degree. These people represent the market for quality books, magazines, and travel.

Household Patterns

The "traditional household" consists of a husband, wife, and children (and sometimes grandparents). Yet, in North America today, many households are "diverse" or "nontraditional," and include single live-alones, adult live-togethers of one or both sexes, single-parent families, childless married couples, and empty nesters. There is a growing trend in Canada toward non-marital cohabitation. People who live in the Northwest Territories and the Yukon have the highest rates of co-habitation, 33 percent and 27 percent respectively, according to a study undertaken by University of Victoria researcher, Zheng Wu. Quebec has the next highest rate at almost 25 percent. The study also found that people who live together before marriage also are more likely to get divorced.[21] Marketers must increasingly consider the needs of nontraditional households, since they are now growing more rapidly than traditional households. For example, people in the SSWD group (single, separated, widowed, divorced) need smaller apartments; inexpensive and smaller appliances, furniture, and furnishings; and food packaged in smaller sizes.

The gay market, in particular, is a lucrative one. A 1997 Simmons Market Research study of readers of the National Gay Newspaper Guild's 12 publications found that, compared to the average person, respondents are 11.7 times more likely to be in professional jobs, almost twice as likely to own a vacation home, eight times more likely to own a computer notebook, and twice as likely to own individual stocks.[22] Insurance companies and financial services companies are now waking up to the needs and potential of not only the gay market, but also the nontraditional household market as a whole:

- **American Express Financial Advisors, Inc.** American Express Financial Advisors, Inc., launched print ads that depict same-sex couples planning their financial futures. The ads ran in *Out* and *The Advocate*, the two highest-circulation national gay publications. The company's director of segment marketing, Margaret Vergeyle, said: "We're targeting gay audiences with targeted ads and promotions that are relevant to them and say that we understand their specific needs. Often, gay couples are very concerned about issues like [pension] benefits and estate planning, since same-sex marriages often are not recognized under the law."[23]

Geographical Shifts in Population

This is a period of great migratory movements between and within countries. Since the collapse of Soviet Eastern Europe, nationalities are reasserting themselves and forming independent countries. The new countries are making certain ethnic groups unwelcome (such as Russians in Latvia or Muslims in Serbia), and many of these groups are migrating to safer areas.

Population movement also occurs as people migrate from one region of the country to another. About 12 in 1000 Canadians had itchy feet in 1998 and swapped provinces. Alberta and Ontario were the top two choices when it came to interprovincial moves. While these provinces gain from population shifts, Newfoundland lost almost 40 of every 1000 residents during the same period. Population movement also occurs as people migrate from rural to urban areas, and then to suburban areas. This movement has been occurring for more than half a century. Today, 57 percent of people born in Canada live in urban areas. Cities such as Montreal, Toronto, and Vancouver are characterized by a faster pace of living, higher incomes, and a greater variety of goods, services, and cultural offerings than can be found in Canada's small towns and rural areas. Canada's cities are ethnically diverse and attract 93 percent of new immigrants. But many people classed as urban dwellers actually live in the suburbs. Canada's fastest-growing town, Blainville, Quebec, is a town that typifies the movement to suburban dwelling. It draws families with its low property taxes and spacious parks. Its residents earn approximately $1500 more than the national average. Suburban dwellers are the source of much of the demand for garden furniture, home workshop equipment, gardening tools, and barbecues. Recognizing the importance of a convenient location, retailers have brought their stores out to suburban shopping malls.[24]

Some people are countering this trend towards urbanization and are moving out to the "country" or to small towns away from apartment living and the hectic pace found in many cities. Kelowna, B.C. and its subdivision, Central Okanagan, is Canada's second fastest-growing town. It has been the destination of choice for West Coasters fleeing Victoria and Vancouver. Location makes a difference in goods and service preferences. Businesses with potential to cash in on the rural rebound might be those that cater to the growing SOHO (small office/home office) segment. For instance, makers of RTA (ready-to-assemble) furniture might find a strong consumer base among all the cashed-out former city residents setting up offices in small towns or telecommuting from there to larger companies.

Shift from a Mass Market to Micromarkets

The effect of all these changes is fragmentation of the mass market into numerous *micromarkets* differentiated by age, sex, ethnic background, education, geography, lifestyle, and other characteristics. Each group has strong preferences and is reached through increasingly targeted communication and distribution channels. Companies are abandoning the "shotgun approach" that aimed at a mythical "average" consumer and are increasingly designing their products and marketing programs for specific micromarkets.

Demographic trends are highly reliable for the short and intermediate run. There is little excuse for a company's being suddenly surprised by demographic developments. The Singer Company should have known for years that its sewing-machine business would be hurt by smaller families and more working women, yet it was slow in responding. In contrast, think of the rewards marketers reap when they focus on a demographic development. For example, Statistics Canada data reveal that households headed by people aged 55 to 64 spend more on clothing but less on eating out than households headed by people under age 25. Population age shifts have also affected spending patterns on other goods and services. Gambling has exploded. Spending on games of chance grew by 56 percent over the 10-year period from 1986 to 1996. Nearly five million Canadians gambled in the past three months. While people aged 18 to 34 are more likely to gamble, they comprise only 15 percent of the market. Gambling is most popular among those aged 35 to 49 (28 percent of the market) living in Manitoba and Saskatchewan. Casinos and video lottery terminals are the most popular gambling venues. Such information can help marketers of gambling pinpoint their offerings.[25]

ECONOMIC ENVIRONMENT

Markets require purchasing power as well as people. The available purchasing power in an economy depends on current income, prices, savings, debt, and credit availability. Marketers must pay close attention to major trends in income and consumer-spending patterns.

Income Distribution

Nations vary greatly in level and distribution of income and industrial structure. There are four types of industrial structures:

1. *Subsistence economies:* In a subsistence economy, the vast majority of people engage in simple agriculture, consume most of their output, and barter the rest for simple goods and services. These economies offer few opportunities for marketers.

2. *Raw-material-exporting economies:* These economies are rich in one or more natural resources but poor in other respects. Much of their revenue comes from exporting these resources. Examples are Zaire (copper) and Saudi Arabia (oil). These countries are good markets for extractive equipment, tools and supplies, materials-handling equipment, and trucks. Depending on the number of foreign residents and wealthy native rulers and landholders, they are also a market for western-style commodities and luxury goods.

3. *Industrializing economies:* In an industrializing economy, manufacturing begins to account for 10 to 20 percent of gross domestic product. Examples include India, Egypt, and the Philippines. As manufacturing increases, the country relies more on imports of raw materials, steel, and heavy machinery and less on imports of finished textiles, paper products, and processed foods. Industrialization creates a new rich class and a small but growing middle class, both demanding new types of goods.

4. *Industrial economies:* Industrial economies are major exporters of manufactured goods and investment funds. They buy manufactured goods from each other and also export them to other types of economies in exchange for raw materials and semifinished goods. The large and varied manufacturing activities of these nations and their sizable middle class make them rich markets for all types of goods.

Marketers often distinguish countries with five different income-distribution patterns: (1) very low incomes, (2) mostly low incomes, (3) very low, very high incomes, (4) low, medium, high incomes, and (5) mostly medium incomes. Consider the market for Lamborghinis, an automobile costing more than $225 000. The market would be very small in countries with type 1 or 2 income patterns. One of the largest single markets for Lamborghinis turns out to be Portugal (income pattern 3)—one of the poorer countries in Western Europe, but one with enough wealthy families to afford expensive cars.

Many Canadians have the impression that Americans are financially better off. However, Statistics Canada data reveal this impression is accurate only for the richest quintile of the population. In the top income bracket, family disposable income is $77 000 in the U.S. compared to $72 250 in Canada. In the other four categories, however, Canadian families are better off than their American counterparts. For example, middle-income Canadian families actually have more spending power than their U.S. counterparts. In 1995, the median Canadian family after-tax income disposable income was $30 200 compared to $29 500 for an America family (both figures are expressed in Canadian dollars). Moreover, there is greater polarization of income between the rich and the poor in the United States than there is in Canada. The gap between rich and poor shrunk in Canada between 1974 and 1995. Thus, while there is a distinct two-tier U.S. market, with affluent people buying expensive goods from upscale retailers and working-class people spending more carefully, shopping at discount stores, and factory outlet malls, this layering of the market hasn't occurred to the same degree in Canada.[26]

The Gap Online Store is one tool the firm uses to help it reach micro markets.

Savings, Debt, and Credit Availability

Consumer expenditures are affected by consumer savings, debt, and credit availability. The Japanese, for example, save about 13.1 percent of their income. The result has been that Japanese banks were able to loan money to Japanese companies at a much lower interest rate than North American banks could offer to companies. Figures for 1998 suggest that Canadian and U.S. consumers have negative savings rates (i.e., expenditures exceed after-tax earnings). In Canada, the 1998 savings rate was –0.7 percent while in the United States it was –0.2 percent. Although savings rates in both countries have traditionally been low, this is the first time they have dipped into negative numbers. The figures suggest that people are supporting their spending by liquidating their investments or savings, or they are turning to credit.[27] While credit is readily available, interest rates, especially on credit cards, are high. Marketers must pay careful attention to major changes in incomes, cost of living, interest rates, savings, and borrowing patterns because they can have a high impact on business, especially for companies whose products have high income and price sensitivity.

NATURAL ENVIRONMENT

The deterioration of the natural environment is a major global concern. In many world cities, air and water pollution have reached dangerous levels. There is great concern about certain chemicals creating a hole in the ozone layer and producing a "greenhouse effect" that will lead to dangerous warming of the earth. In Western Europe, "green" parties have vigorously pressed for public action to reduce industrial pollution. In North America, several thought leaders have documented ecological deterioration, while watchdog groups such as the Sierra Club, Canadian Wildlife Federation, and Friends of the Earth carried these concerns into political and social action.

New legislation passed as a result has hit certain industries very hard. Steel companies and public utilities have had to invest billions of dollars in pollution-control equipment and more environmentally friendly fuels. The auto industry has had to introduce expensive emission controls in cars. The soap industry has had to increase its products' biodegradability.

Marketers need to be aware of the threats and opportunities associated with four trends in the natural environment: the shortage of raw materials, the increased cost of energy, increased levels of pollution, and the changing role of governments.

Canadian Wildlife Federation
www.cwf-fcf.org

Shortage of Raw Materials

The earth's raw materials consist of the infinite, the finite renewable, and the finite nonrenewable. Infinite resources, such as air and water, pose no immediate problem, although some groups recognize a long-run danger. Environmental groups have lobbied for a ban on certain propellants used in aerosol cans because of the potential damage they can cause to the ozone layer. Water shortages and pollution are already major problems in some parts of the world.

Finite *renewable* resources, such as forests and food, must be used wisely. Forestry companies are required to reforest timberlands in order to protect the soil and to ensure sufficient wood to meet future demand. Because the amount of arable land is fixed and urban areas are constantly encroaching on farmland, food supply can also be a major problem. Finite *nonrenewable* resources—oil, coal, platinum, zinc, silver—will pose a serious problem as the point of depletion approaches. Firms making products that require these increasingly scarce minerals face substantial cost increases. They may not find it easy to pass these cost increases on to customers. Firms engaged in research and development have an excellent opportunity to develop substitute materials.

Increased Energy Costs

One finite nonrenewable resource, oil, has created serious problems for the world economy. Oil prices shot up from US$2.23 a barrel in 1970 to US$34.00 a barrel in 1982, creating a frantic search for alternative energy forms. Coal became popular again, and companies searched for practical means to harness solar, nuclear, wind, and other forms of energy. In the solar energy field alone, hundreds of firms introduced first-generation products to harness solar energy for heating homes and other uses. Other firms searched for ways to make a practical electric automobile, with a potential prize of billions for the winner.

The development of alternative sources of energy and more efficient ways to use energy and the weakening of the oil cartel led to a subsequent decline in oil prices. Lower prices had an adverse effect on the oil-exploration industry but considerably improved the income of oil-using industries and consumers. In the meantime, the search continues for alternative sources of energy.

Increased Pollution Levels

Some industrial activity will inevitably damage the natural environment. Consider the dangerous mercury levels in fish in Northern Quebec, the quantity of DDT and other chemical pollutants in the soil and food supply, and the littering of the environment with bottles, plastics, and other packaging materials.

Business Council on National Issues
www.bcni.com

Results of a recent survey conducted in 24 countries on five continents found that Canadians are second on the list in terms of their concern about the environment. New Zealand tops the ranking. In fact, Canadians said protecting the environment was more important than promoting economic growth. Some people, such as Tom D'Aquino, president of the Business Council on National Issues, says this is a false trade-off. "Good environmental practice is consistent with good economic practice."[28] Part of this concern is reflected in research that has shown that about 42 percent of consumers are willing to pay higher prices for "green" products. This willingness creates a large market for pollution-control solutions, such as scrubbers, recycling centres, and landfill systems. It leads to a search for alternative ways to produce and package goods. Smart companies are initiating environment-friendly moves to show their concern. 3M runs a Pollution Prevention Pays program that has led to a substantial reduction in pollution and costs. Dow built a new ethylene plant in Alberta that uses 40 percent less energy and releases 97 percent less wastewater. AT&T uses a special software package to choose the least harmful materials, cut hazardous waste, reduce energy use, and improve product recycling in its operations. McDonald's and Burger King eliminated their polystyrene cartons and now use smaller, recyclable paper wrappings and paper napkins.[29]

New concerns over the toxic nature of dry cleaning solvents has opened up opportunities for a new breed of "green cleaners," though these new businesses face an uphill battle. See the Marketing for the 21st Century box entitled "A New Guard of Green Cleaners Vies for Concerned Customers."

21ST CENTURY

A New Guard of Green Cleaners Vies for Concerned Customers

You need to get your business suit cleaned for a sales conference in Vancouver and your flight leaves in 24 hours. Are you going to go to the dry cleaner on the corner, which uses environmentally damaging, possibly carcinogenic chemicals? Or are you going to go across town and use a "wet cleaner," who will get your clothes clean without damaging you or the environment (and make them smell a lot less toxic, too)? If you're like most consumers, you'll choose convenience and the quick fix over concerns about health and environment.

Perchloroethylene, or "perc," the solvent used by the majority of dry cleaners, was labelled a probable human carcinogen by the EPA. More conclusive reports on its damaging effects are expected soon. Yet when it comes to products that enhance their own or their clothing's appearance, consumers are notably indifferent to environmental concerns. In a 1996 survey of 30 dry cleaners, Dan Kovacks asked customers what they would do if they learned dry cleaning posed a threat to their well-being. Unable to think up alternatives, most said they would just get

clothes dry-cleaned less frequently. Yet a new guard of new environmentally friendly dry cleaners is willing to bet that consumers will choose green over toxic if green alternatives are readily available. There are already 6000 North American dry cleaning stores using alternative cleaning materials. About 95 percent of those use odourless petroleum-based solvents that actually get rid of stains that seemed impervious to perc. A much smaller group of stores are "wet cleaners," going back to soap-and-water basics. All the alternatives, with names such as Cleaner-by-Nature, Eco-Mat, and Greener Cleaner, are price-competitive with their toxic counterparts. Cleaner-by-Nature, which opened up smack between two traditional dry cleaners, broke even only six months after opening.

While dry cleaners are the quintessential small business, the green cleaning trend could open up opportunities for giant multinational corporations. Exxon Corp. has come up with a new petroleum solvent. Procter & Gamble has introduced a perc-free alternative for home use, Dryel, which allows people to do their dry cleaning at home. Yet, as a testimony to the resistance faced by companies in this burgeoning product category, Procter & Gamble advertises Dryel's convenience, not its green advantage.

Sources: Jacquelyn Ottman, "Innovative marketers give new products the green light," *Marketing News,* March 30, 1998, p. 10. Shelly Reese, "Dressed to Kill," *American Demographics,* May 1998, pp. 22-25. Stacy Kravetz, "Dry Cleaners' New Wrinkle: Going Green," *Wall Street Journal,* June 3, 1998, B1.

Changing Role of Governments

Governments vary in their concern and efforts to promote a clean environment. For example, the German government is vigorous in its pursuit of environmental quality, partly because of the strong green movement in Germany and partly because of the ecological devastation in the former East Germany. Many poor nations are doing little about pollution, largely because they lack funds or the political will. It is in the richer nations' interest to help the poorer nations control their pollution, but even the richer nations today lack the necessary funds. The major hopes are that companies around the world will accept more social responsibility and that less expensive devices will be invented to control and reduce pollution.

TECHNOLOGICAL ENVIRONMENT

One of the most dramatic forces shaping people's lives is technology. Technology has released such wonders as penicillin, open-heart surgery, and Viagra. It has released such horrors as the hydrogen bomb, nerve gas, and the submachine gun. It has also released such mixed blessings as the automobile and video games.

Every new technology is a force for "creative destruction." Transistors hurt the vacuum-tube industry, xerography hurt the carbon-paper business, autos hurt the railways, and television hurt the newspapers. Instead of moving into the new technologies, many old industries fought or ignored them, and their businesses declined.

The economy's growth rate is affected by how many major new technologies are discovered. Unfortunately, technological discoveries do not arise evenly through time—the railway industry created a lot of investment, and then investment petered out until the auto industry emerged. Later, radio created a lot of investment, which then petered out until television appeared. In the time between major innovations, the economy can stagnate. In the meantime, minor innovations fill the gap: freeze-dried coffee, pizza pops, combination shampoo and conditioner, and the like. Minor innovations involve less risk, but critics argue that today too much research effort is going into producing minor improvements rather than major breakthroughs.

New technology creates major long-run consequences that are not always fore-seeable. The contraceptive pill, for example, led to smaller families, more working women, and larger discretionary incomes—resulting in higher expenditures on vacation travel, durable goods, and luxury items.

A recent Statistics Canada study revealed that more than 70 percent of successful new companies are high-tech in that they innovate, use advanced technologies, employ skilled workers, or emphasize training. They operate in all sectors of the economy, including publishing and farm services, not just in those industries those usually thought of as high-tech such as biotechnology and information technology.[30] The marketer should monitor the following trends in technology: the pace of change, the opportunities for innovation, varying R&D budgets, and increased regulation.

Accelerating Pace of Technological Change

Many of today's common products were not available 40 years ago – your parents didn't have personal computers, digital wristwatches, video recorders, or fax machines. More ideas are being worked on; the time lag between new ideas and their successful implementation is decreasing rapidly; and the time between introduction and peak production is shortening considerably. Ninety percent of all the scientists who ever lived are alive today, and technology feeds upon itself.

The advent of personal computers and fax machines has made it possible for people to *telecommute*—that is, work at home instead of travelling to offices that may be 30 or more minutes away. Some hope that this trend will reduce auto pollution, bring the family closer together, and create more home-centred entertainment and activity. It will also have substantial impact on shopping behaviour and marketing performance.

Unlimited Opportunities for Innovation

Scientists today are working on a startling range of new technologies that will revolutionize products and production processes. Some of the most exciting work is being done in biotechnology, solid-state electronics, robotics, and materials sciences.[31] Researchers are working on AIDS cures, happiness pills, painkillers, totally safe contraceptives, and nonfattening foods. They are designing robots for firefighting, underwater exploration, and home nursing. In addition, scientists also work on fantasy products, such as small flying cars, three-dimensional television, and space colonies. The challenge in each case is not only technical but also commercial—to develop affordable versions of these products.

Companies are already harnessing the power of *virtual reality (VR)*, the combination of technologies that allows users to experience three-dimensional, computer-generated environments through sound, sight, and touch (Figure 5-2). Virtual reality has already been applied to gathering consumer reactions to new automobile designs, kitchen layouts, exterior home designs, and other potential offerings.

Varying R&D Budgets

The United States leads the world in annual R&D expenditures ($74 billion), but nearly 60 percent of these funds are still earmarked for defence. Japan has increased its R&D expenditures much faster than the United States and is spending it mostly on non-defence-related research in physics, biophysics, and computer science. In comparison, Canada's R&D spending is low. In the recently published OECD Innovation Index, which is compiled based on information about a country's patent filings, people employed in R&D, and government and private R&D spending, Canada was ranked in ninth place. It held sixth place in the mid-eighties. A partial explanation of Canada's lower spending on R&D is that many of its corporations, 31.5 percent, are foreign owned and, thus, R&D is done elsewhere.[32]

Rather than innovating, many companies are content to put their money into copying competitors' products and making minor feature and style improvements.

Even basic-research companies such as Du Pont, Bell Laboratories, and Pfizer are proceeding cautiously. Much of the research is defensive rather than offensive. And, increasingly, research directed toward major breakthroughs is being conducted by consortiums of companies rather than by single companies.

Increased Regulation of Technological Change

As products become more complex, the public needs to be assured of their safety. Consequently, government agencies' powers to investigate and ban potentially unsafe products have been expanded. Marketers must be aware of these regulations when proposing, developing, and launching new products.

POLITICAL/LEGAL ENVIRONMENT

Marketing decisions are strongly affected by developments in the political and legal environment. This environment is composed of laws, government agencies, and pressure groups that influence and limit various organizations and individuals. Sometimes these laws also create new opportunities for business. For example, mandatory recycling laws have given the recycling industry a major boost and spurred the creation of dozens of new companies that make new products from recycled materials.

Legislation Regulating Business

Business legislation has three main purposes: to protect companies from unfair competition, to protect consumers from unfair business practices, and to protect the interests of society from unbridled business behaviour. A major purpose of business legislation and/or enforcement is to charge businesses with the social costs created by their products or production processes. Legislation affecting business has steadily increased over the years. The European Commission has been active in establishing a new framework of laws covering competitive behaviour, product standards, product liability, and commercial transactions for the 15 member nations of the European Union. Ex-Soviet nations are rapidly passing laws to promote and regulate an open market economy. Canada has a complex web of regulatory agencies that oversee the safety of products and technologies while fostering a competitive business arena. For example, Agriculture Canada regulates the safety of food products. Health Canada has both food safety and product safety divisions (see Health Canada's Product Safety Bureau Web site). Environment Canada focuses on pollution prevention. The Department of Transport governs road and vehicle safety. The Hazardous Products Act was developed to control high-risk products. The Competition Act covers such topics as mergers (Section 33), pricing (Sections 34 and 38), and advertising (Section 37). Canadian business is also subject to provincial regulations and may come up against rulings by Canada's marketing boards. Regulations outlined in the North American Free Trade Agreement also must be respected. It is no wonder that most Canadian firms have large legal departments to help marketers stay within the law! Several countries

FIGURE 5.2

Virtual Reality Applications in Marketing

Virtual reality technology lets users interact with computer-generated worlds through sight, sound, and touch. A handset and some sort of handheld input device are necessary for many current VR applications. (left) CyberSim's VR program allows prospective home buyers to simulate their future homes and move around inside as if they were actually living in the as-yet-unbuilt house. (right) Another VR program allows prospective car buyers to simulate driving around town in the car of their choice.

Health Canada's Product Safety Bureau
http://www.hc-sc.gc.ca

have gone even further in passing strong consumer-protection legislation. Norway bans several forms of sales promotion—trading stamps, contests, premiums—as inappropriate or "unfair" instruments for promoting products. Thailand requires food processors selling national brands to market low-price brands also so that low-income consumers can find economy brands. In India, food companies need special approval to launch brands that duplicate what already exists on the market, such as another cola drink or brand of rice. A central concern about business legislation is: At what point do the costs of regulation exceed the benefits? The laws are not always administered fairly; regulators and enforcers may be lax or overzealous. Although each new law may have a legitimate rationale, it may have the unintended effect of sapping initiative and retarding economic growth.

Marketers must have a good working knowledge of the major laws protecting competition, consumers, and society. Companies generally establish legal review procedures and promulgate ethical standards to guide their marketing managers. As more and more business takes place in cyberspace, marketers must establish new parameters for doing business ethically. While America Online has been hugely successful and is the country's most popular online service provider, it has lost millions of dollars due to consumer complaints regarding unethical marketing tactics:

- **America Online, Inc.** In 1998, America Online, Inc. agreed to pay a U.S.$2.6 million penalty and revamp some of its business practices to settle deceptive-marketing complaints. The case arose because AOL failed to clearly notify consumers that the "50 free hours" in its online service's much-touted trial memberships must be used within a one-month period and that users would incur subscription fees after the first month.[33]

Growth of Special-Interest Groups

The number and power of special-interest groups have increased over the past three decades. *Political-action committees* (PACs) lobby government officials and pressure business executives to pay more attention to consumer rights, women's rights, senior citizen rights, minority rights, and gay rights. Many companies have established public-affairs departments to deal with these groups and issues.

An important force affecting business is the *consumerist movement*—an organized movement of citizens and government to strengthen the rights and powers of buyers in relation to sellers. Consumerists have advocated and won the right to know the true interest cost of a loan, the true cost per standard unit of competing brands (unit pricing), the basic ingredients in a product, the nutritional quality of food, the freshness of products, and the true benefits of a product. In response to consumerism, several companies have established consumer-affairs departments to help formulate policies and respond to consumer complaints. Whirlpool Corporation is just one of the companies that have installed toll-free phone numbers for consumers. Whirlpool even expanded the coverage of its product warranties and rewrote them in plain English.

Clearly, new laws and growing numbers of pressure groups have put more restraints on marketers. Marketers have to clear their plans with the company's legal, public-relations, public-affairs, and consumer-affairs departments. Insurance companies directly or indirectly affect the design of smoke detectors; scientific groups affect the design of spray products by condemning aerosols. In essence, many private marketing transactions have moved into the public domain.

SOCIAL/CULTURAL ENVIRONMENT

Society shapes our beliefs, values, and norms. People absorb, almost subconsciously, a world view that defines their relationship to themselves, to others, to nature, and to the universe.

- *Views of themselves.* People vary in the relative emphasis they place on self-gratification. The 1960s and 1970s were characterized by "pleasure seekers," people who sought fun, change, and escape. Others sought "self-realization." People bought products, brands, and services as a means of self-expression. They bought dream cars and dream vacations. They spent more time in health activities (jogging, tennis), in introspection, and in arts and crafts. Today, in contrast, people are adopting more conservative behaviours and ambitions. They have witnessed harder times and cannot rely on continuous employment and rising real income. They are more cautious in their spending pattern and more value-driven in their purchases.

- *Views of others.* Some observers have pointed to a countermovement from a "me society" to a "we society." People are concerned about the homeless, about crime and victims, and other social problems. They would like to live in a more humane society. At the same time, people are seeking out their "own kind" and avoiding strangers. People hunger for serious and long-lasting relationships with a few significant others. These trends portend a growing market for social-support products and services that promote direct relations between human beings, such as health clubs, cruises, and religious activity. They also suggest a growing market for "social surrogates," things that allow people who are alone to feel that they are not, such as television, home video games, and chat rooms on the Internet.

- *Views of organizations.* People vary in their attitudes toward corporations, government agencies, trade unions, and other organizations. Most people are willing to work for these organizations, although they may be critical of particular ones. But there has been an overall decline in organizational loyalty. The massive wave of company downsizings has bred cynicism and distrust. Many people today see work not as a source of satisfaction but as a required chore to earn money to enjoy their nonwork hours.

    This outlook has several marketing implications. Companies need to find new ways to win back consumer and employee confidence. They need to make sure they are good corporate citizens. They need to make sure their consumer messages are honest. More companies are turning to social audits and public relations to improve their image with their publics.

- *Views of society.* People vary in their attitudes toward their society. Some defend it (preservers), some run it (makers), some take what they can from it (takers), some want to change it (changers), some are looking for something deeper (seekers), and some want to leave it (escapers).[34] Often consumption patterns reflect social attitude. Makers tend to be high achievers who eat, dress, and live well. Changers usually live more frugally, driving smaller cars, and wearing simpler clothes. Escapers and seekers are a major market for movies, music, wind surfing, and camping.

- *Views of nature.* People vary in their attitude toward nature. Some feel subjugated by it, others feel harmony with it, and still others seek mastery over it. A long-term trend has been growing mastery over nature through technology. More recently, however, people have awakened to nature's fragility and finite resources. They recognize that nature can be destroyed by human activities.

    Love of nature is leading to more camping, hiking, boating, and fishing. Business has responded with hiking boots, tenting equipment, and other gear. Tour operators are packaging more tours to wilderness areas. Marketing communicators are using more scenic backgrounds in advertising. Food producers have found growing markets for "natural" products, such as natural cereal, natural ice cream, and health foods.

- *Views of the universe.* People vary in their beliefs about the origin of the universe and their place in it. Although religious conviction and practice have been waning through the years, some of the religious impulse has been redirected into an interest in Eastern religions, mysticism, the occult, and the human-potential movement. As people lose their religious orientation, they seek self-fulfilment and immediate gratification.

Here are some other cultural characteristics of interest to marketers:

High Persistence of Core Cultural Values

The people living in a particular society hold many *core beliefs* and values that tend to persist. As futurist John Kettle pointed out earlier in this chapter, research has shown that Canadians and Americans, especially those who live along the border between the two countries, hold many values in common. Both believe in freedom, equality, and striving for happiness, mature love, self-respect, and true friendship. Canadians rank inner harmony, mature love, and true friendship higher than do Americans who count the search for wisdom and a sense of accomplishment among the highest of their values. When Canadians relate their values to the realm of social policy, they strive for self-reliance and fiscal responsibility but also have compassion for others. Values are often translated into actions, and those sometimes quirky behaviours that Canadians are known for, such as standing well back from the ATM even when the lines are long, not violating the non-smoking policy in public places, or avoiding littering by politely mentioning to someone, "Pardon me, you dropped this."[35]

Mothers Against Drunk Driving
www.madd.org

Core beliefs and values are passed on from parents to children and are reinforced by major social institutions—schools, places of worship, business, and government. *Secondary beliefs* and values are more open to change. Believing in the institution of marriage is a core belief; believing that people ought to get married early is a secondary belief. Thus family-planning marketers could make some headway arguing that people should get married later rather than that they should not get married at all. Marketers have some chance of changing secondary values but little chance of changing core values. For instance, the nonprofit organization Mothers Against Drunk Drivers (MADD) does not try to stop the sale of alcohol, but it does promote the idea of appointing a designated driver who will not drink that evening. The group also lobbies to raise the legal drinking age.

Existence of Subcultures

Each society contains *subcultures*, groups with shared values emerging from their special life experiences or circumstances. Native Canadians, teenagers, and Hell's Angels all represent subcultures whose members share common beliefs, preferences, and behaviours. To the extent that subcultural groups exhibit different wants and consumption behaviour, marketers can choose particular subcultures as target markets.

Marketers sometimes reap unexpected rewards in targeting subcultures. For instance, marketers have always loved teens because they're society's trendsetters in fashion, music, entertainment, ideas, and attitudes. And marketers also know that if they attract someone as a teen, there's a good chance they'll keep her as a customer in the years ahead. Frito-Lay, which draws 15 percent of its sales from teens, says it has seen a rise in chip-snacking by grown-ups. "We think it's because we brought them in as teenagers," says a Frito-Lay marketing director.[36]

Shifts of Secondary Cultural Values Through Time

Although core values are fairly persistent, cultural swings do occur. The advent in the 1960s of hippies, the Beatles, Elvis Presley, and other cultural phenomena had a major impact on young people's hairstyles, clothing, sexual norms, and life goals. Today's young people are influenced by new heroes and fads: Sarah McLachlan, Michael Jordan, and inline skating.

Marketers have a keen interest in spotting cultural shifts that might bring new marketing opportunities or threats. Several firms offer social/cultural forecasts. The *Yankelovich Monitor* interviews 2500 people each year and tracks 35 social trends, such as "anti-bigness," "mysticism," "living for today," "away from possessions," and "sensuousness." It describes the percentage of the population who share the attitude as well as the percentage who do not. For example, the percentage of people who value physical fitness and well-being has risen steadily over the years, especially in the under-thirty group, the young women and upscale group, and people living in the West. Marketers of health foods and exercise equipment cater to this trend with appropriate products and communications. For example, in 1995, Taco Bell unveiled a new lower-fat "Border Lights" menu.[37]

1. Successful companies realize that the marketing environment presents a never-ending series of opportunities and threats. The major responsibility for identifying significant changes in the macroenvironment falls to a company's marketers. More than any other group in the company, marketing managers must be the trend trackers and opportunity seekers.

2. Many opportunities are found by identifying *trends* (directions or sequences of events that have some momentum and durability) and *megatrends* (large social, economic, political, and technological changes that are slow to form, and once in place have long-lasting influence).

3. Within the rapidly changing global picture, marketers must monitor six major environmental forces: demographic, economic, natural, technological, political/legal, and social/cultural.

4. In the *demographic* environment, marketers must be aware of worldwide population growth; changing mixes of age, ethnic composition, and educational levels; the rise of nontraditional families; large geographic shifts in population; and the move to micromarketing and away from mass marketing.

5. In the *economic* arena, they need to focus on income distribution and levels of savings, debt, and credit availability.

6. In the *natural* environment, they need to be aware of raw-materials shortages, increased energy costs and pollution levels, and the changing role of governments in environmental protection.

7. In the *technological* arena, they should take account of the accelerating pace of technological change, opportunities for innovation, varying R&D budgets, and the increased governmental regulation brought about by technological change.

8. In the *political/legal* environment, they must work within the many laws regulating business practices and with various special-interest groups.

9. In the *social/cultural* arena, they must understand people's views of themselves, others, organizations, society, nature, and the universe. They must market products that correspond to society's core and secondary values; and address the needs of different subcultures within a society.

APPLICATIONS

CHAPTER CONCEPTS

1. One of the changes in the demographic environment is the increasing proportion of older adults, who comprise many markets for certain products. Discuss how this demographic trend could affect the product features and/ or distribution arrangements of the following:
   a. Minute Maid orange juice
   b. Mail-order businesses
   c. Health Canada.

2. You are a product manager at Minolta. Your boss has just received a copy of *The Popcorn Report* (see the Marketing Insight box in this chapter for a review of Faith Popcorn's work). Although her background is in engineering, she has always been interested in the sensory appeal of product features and this book has aroused her curiosity about this phenomenon. Prepare a report summarizing the potential impact of each of Popcorn's 10 trends on Minolta's product (cameras). Specifically, how will each trend affect product development, features, and marketing?

3. Molson's Canadian, Calvin Klein, McDonald's, Coca-Cola, and Roots are examples of brands that have become cultural symbols for Canadians. List some brand names and products that are cultural symbols for the following countries: (a) Japan (b) Germany (c) Russia (d) France (e) Italy (f) Ireland (g) Colombia (h) Mexico (i) England (j) Switzerland (k) the Middle Eastern nations, and (l) Australia.

MARKETING AND ADVERTISING

1. The ad in Figure 1, from Stockholm-based Ericsson, uses a baby to capture the attention of businesspeople who make buying decisions or influence the buying of telecommunications equipment and technologies. Which of John Naisbett's mega-trends or John Kettle's predictions about the future are represented in this ad? Support your answers. What does this ad imply about Ericsson's response to the technological environment?

Figure 1   Figure 2

2. Most ads include a picture of the product being promoted, but not the Energizer ad shown here. What demographic segment does this ad appear to be targeting? How do you know? What attitudes are reflected in this ad? How would other segments be likely to respond to it? If you were Energizer, what magazines would you choose to run these ads? Explain your choices.

FOCUS ON TECHNOLOGY

The accelerating pace of technological change is leading to marketing opportunities based on new needs and lifestyles. Consider the trend toward increased telecommuting—people working at home instead of commuting to business offices some distance away. Every year, more employees and entrepreneurs opt to work from home, creating higher demand for personal computers, printers, fax machines, telephone services, Internet access, and related goods and services.

Increased sales of home office equipment and communication services are not the only consequences of this technological change. Now that more people are working from home, their lifestyles are changing, creating both opportunities and threats. For example, people who no longer drive long distances to work may buy new cars less often and use less gasoline. On the other hand, their expenditures on household meals and casual clothing will increase. Identify two more marketing opportunities and threats that result from the trend toward more telecommuting. Telecommuters are not listed in any central directory, so how can companies locate and market to this growing segment?

At the start of the new millennium, environmental concerns are driving marketing in new directions. Consider trends in the dry cleaning industry. Thousands of green cleaners are opening their doors all over North America, shunning possibly toxic substances like percloroethylene in favour of more environmentally safe methods. Manufacturers such as Procter & Gamble and Exxon are also jumping on the green bandwagon, developing safer cleaning formulas for use at home and in commercial cleaning establishments.

Center for Neighbourhood Technology
http://www.cnt.org

What are the marketing implications of this trend? Get some ideas from the links on the Web site of the non-profit Center for Neighbourhood Technology, which promotes economic and community development through ecological improvement. Look under "sustainable manufacturing" to find the "wet cleaning" section. Going beyond cleaning fluids and equipment, identify two additional opportunities for new products related to green cleaning. If consumers are mainly motivated by convenience, should marketing for these new products stress environmental safety? Looking ahead to the early part of the millennium, how might increased competition from environmentally sound products affect the marketing strategy for these new products? For traditional dry cleaning outlets?

YOU'RE THE MARKETER: SONIC MARKETING PLAN

Every firm must examine its macroenvironment to understand the key developments that shape opportunities and pose threats. This environmental scanning uncovers emerging trends and changes that can potentially affect the needs of customers, the competition, and the firm's markets.

Statistics Canada
http://www.statcan.ca

U.S. Census
http://www.census.gov

Jane Melody asks you to scan Sonic's external environment for signs of change that indicate opportunities and threats for shelf stereo systems. Review Sonic's current situation and then, using library or Internet resources (or both), locate information to answer the following questions about Sonic's macroenvironment:

- What demographic changes are likely to affect Sonic's target market, buyers 20-40? For example, check Statistics Canada data and/or U.S. Census data to see information about age projections in North America.

UHF Magazine
http://www.uhfmag.com

- What technological changes can potentially affect product development and buyer acceptance of current product? Look at the Web site of UHF Magazine for news about stereo technologies such as DVD; check industry sources for more technological trends.

- What economic trends might influence the product line's future?

Trade Data On-line
http://www.strategis.ic.gc.ca/sc_
mrkti/tdst/engdoc/hsearch.html#sic

- What political/legal issues might affect Sonic and its competitors? Search the Trade Data On-line for any relevant federal legislation on import/export opportunities, using key word searches such as "import + stereo" and "export + stereo." Also use search engines to find any new regulations that affect competitors' import/export activities.

- Once you have completed your environmental scan, analyze the results and their implications for Sonic's marketing efforts. As your instructor directs, summarize your findings and conclusions in a written marketing plan or type them into the Marketing Situation section of the Marketing Plan Pro software.

Analyzing Consumer Markets and Buyer Behaviour

ch!ckaboom
y o r k d a l e

PROFILE:

Canadian
Marketing
Excellence

//"*The most important thing is to forecast where customers are moving, and to be in front of them."* Anyone trying to market to Canada's tween market should sleep with the above slogan under their pillow. And one has to suspect that Nancy Dennis, founder of Toronto's Ch!ckaboom, does just that. The retailer specializes in serving girls aged 5 to 13 and provides them with a venue where they can drop in, meet friends, fiddle with accessories, and shop to their heart's content without having to deal with snobby salespeople breathing down their necks. The upper end of the "tween" market, the 9- to 14-year-old offspring of the baby-boom generation, is 2.5 million strong. They are grabbing marketers' attention not just because of the size of this "echo-boom" market but also because of its spending power. It is estimated that young girls alone have in excess of $700 million in disposable income. And they are twice as likely as boys the same age to spend it on clothes. Wired and media savvy, marketers are rushing to build brand loyalty among this group or create new brands they might regard as "cool." Firms as disparate as YTV, Schneider Corporation, and Bank of Montreal are scrambling to keep pace with them. An open audience for branded products, lovers of brand icons like Coke and Nike, new products are being developed just for them—GT Global Mutual Funds for kids, Pillsbury's Pizza Pops, portable milkshakes called Milk Mania, L'Oreal Kids Shampoo and Conditioner, and Bonne Bell Lip Smakers.

Ch!ckaboom has some major competition, the likes of Le Chateau Junior Girl, GUESS?, and La Senza Girls line. What has Ch!ckaboom done that has made it stand out from this growing crowd? "The best practice in retail is to respect my customer," says Nancy Dennis. She knows that the "tween girl" wants to have fun just as much as she wants to find the "in" clothes in her size. Thus the stores offer events such as Spice Girl Days, birthday clubs, and Valentine's Day and Halloween parties. An advocate of relationship marketing, Ch!ckaboom leverages its database to keep in contact with its diminutive customers. Ch!ckaboom hopes to expand across the country. You can bet there are many "tweens" hoping it does just that.

Sources: Mikala Folb, "Totally Girl," *Marketing*, January 4/11, 1999, pp. 10-12; Shawna Steinberg, "Have Allowance, Will Transform Economy," *Canadian Business*, March 13, 1998, pp. 59-71.

This chapter examines two questions:

- How do the buyer's characteristics—cultural, social, personal, and psychological—influence buying behaviour?

- How does the buyer make purchasing decisions?

The aim of marketing is to meet and satisfy target customers' needs and wants. The field of consumer behaviour studies how individuals, groups, and organizations select, buy, use, and dispose of goods, services, ideas, or experiences to satisfy their needs and desires.

Understanding consumer behaviour and "knowing customers" are never simple. Customers may say one thing but do another. They may not be in touch with their deeper motivations. They may respond to influences that change their mind at the last minute. Small companies, like Israeli-based start-up Sky is the Ltd., as well as huge corporations, stand to profit from understanding how and why their customers buy:

- **Bible Bread.** Seemingly casual observance of unknowing customers provided Peter Shamir with pertinent feedback on the best venues for consumers to purchase his company's wafer-thin cracker, Bible Bread. After spending six months quietly stalking consumers at supermarkets, delis, and gourmet stores, Shamir, of Sky is the Ltd., noticed that the average consumer took about 10 seconds to find the cracker he or she wanted. Because of this tiny window of time, Shamir realized that Bible Bread would easily be overlooked in cracker aisles of big markets. With their more limited selection, gourmet, health food, and kosher stores were a better match. Now the Israeli-based start-up's crackers are available in gourmet and specialty stores across North America.[1]

Not understanding your customer's motivations, needs, and preferences can hurt. Consider what happened when Kodak introduced its Advanta camera—a costly bust.

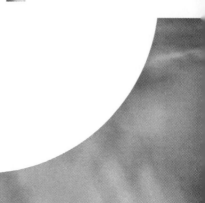

The company had proudly touted it as a high-tech product, but the marketplace was dominated by middle-aged baby boomers. In mid-life, the bells and whistles of new technology generally begin to lose their appeal, and simplicity begins to edge out complexity in consumer preferences.

Studying customers provides clues for developing new products, product features, prices, channels, messages, and other marketing-mix elements. This chapter explores individual consumers' buying dynamics; the next chapter explores the buying dynamics of business buyers.

A MODEL OF CONSUMER BEHAVIOUR

The starting point for understanding buyer behaviour is the stimulus-response model shown in Figure 6-1. Marketing and environmental stimuli enter the buyer's consciousness. The buyer's characteristics and decision process lead to certain purchase decisions. The marketer's task is to understand what happens in the buyer's consciousness between the arrival of outside stimuli and the buyer's purchase decisions.

THE MAJOR FACTORS INFLUENCING BUYING BEHAVIOUR

A consumer's buying behaviour is influenced by cultural, social, personal, and psychological factors. Cultural factors exert the broadest and deepest influence.

CULTURAL FACTORS

Culture, subculture, and social class are particularly important in buying behaviour.

Culture

Culture is the most fundamental determinant of a person's wants and behaviour. The growing child acquires a set of values, perceptions, preferences, and behaviours through his or her family and other key institutions. A child growing up in Canada is exposed to the following values: respect for diversity, respect for basic human rights and individual freedoms (e.g., freedom of speech, freedom of religion, the right to be equal before and under the law), love of the outdoors and nature, achievement and success, activity, efficiency and practicality, progress, material comfort, external comfort, humanitarianism, and youthfulness.[2] The culturally based, shared understanding of certain symbols can provide marketers with powerful communication tools. Savvy marketers are creating associations with such Canadian icons as the Canadian flag, Canadian wildlife, and the Mounties to help tie their products to the sense of pride that many Canadians take in their country and its products. While companies such as Roots have long followed this practice, others are getting on the bandwagon. Kraft Canada launched its Maple Crunch Shreddies by creating such an association between its product and the imagery of the Canadian flag. Zellers brought attention

FIGURE **6.1**

Model of Buyer Behaviour

part two
Analyzing
Marketing
Opportunities

164

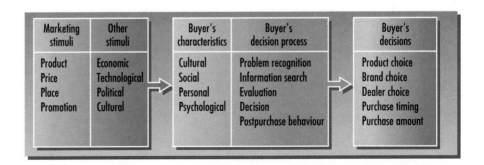

Marketing stimuli	Other stimuli	Buyer's characteristics	Buyer's decision process	Buyer's decisions
Product	Economic	Cultural	Problem recognition	Product choice
Price	Technological	Social	Information search	Brand choice
Place	Political	Personal	Evaluation	Dealer choice
Promotion	Cultural	Psychological	Decision	Purchase timing
			Postpurchase behaviour	Purchase amount

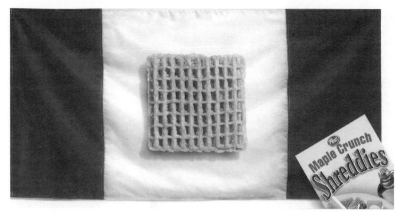
Use of Canadian icons helps firms achieve strong brand identity.

to its new Martha Stewart line using billboards featuring Martha and a Mountie. Marketers mustn't use such national symbols in an insensitive way, however. When Bell Canada ran its Dieppe television spot that told the story of a teenager visiting the beaches where his grandfather fought, some viewers found the ad offensive and argued that it exploited Canadian heroism merely to sell a product.[3]

Subculture

Each culture consists of smaller subcultures that provide more specific identification and socialization for their members. Subcultures include nationalities, religions, racial groups, and geographic regions. Many subcultures make up important market segments, and marketers often design products and marketing programs tailored to their needs. (See the Marketing Insight titled "Marketing to Three Segments: French-Canadian, Mature, and Tween.") Others are using their distinct differences to market themselves. For example, some native bands are exploiting the growing international demand for experience vacations. Tourists, especially those from Germany and France, want to learn about and take part in native culture. Grouse Mountain Resorts in North Vancouver formed an alliance with members from the Sechelt Band, including Coast Salist artist Richard Krentz, and the Squamish Nation to launch the *hiwus* feasthouse. This venue will allow some 20 000 visitors a year to become familiar with native

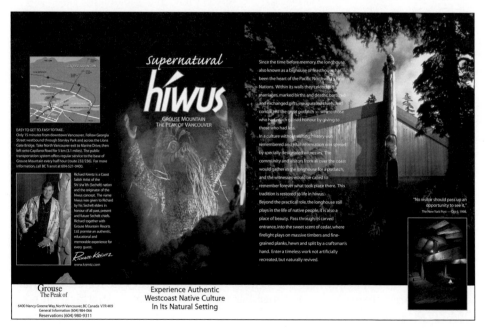

Native bands are using their distinct differences to market themselves internationally.

Marketing to Three Segments: French-Canadian, Mature, and Tween

When subcultures grow large and affluent enough, companies often design special marketing programs to serve them. Here are examples from three important subculture groups.

French-Canadian Consumers

Canadians whose mother tongue is French number 6.2 million or 23 percent of the population. They constitute 83 percent of the population in Quebec, 34 percent in New Brunswick, and lesser percentages in Ontario and Manitoba. Marketers who would appeal to these consumers need to do more than communicate in French. Research has revealed differences in the activities, interests, opinions, and consumption habits of French-Canadian versus English-Canadian consumers. French-Canadian women are more family oriented and fashion conscious. Research conducted by S.C. Johnson revealed that even attitudes towards cleaning vary between English Canada and French Canada. While English-Canadians just want to get the job done and see cleaning as a necessary evil, people in Quebec get a sense of pride and accomplishment after they clean. Using these and insights about a distinctly Quebec custom—July 1, Moving Day—Quebecers tend to move from one apartment to another on July 1 because leases traditionally expire in Quebec on June 30–S.C. Johnson designed a highly successful campaign for its cleaning products.

Such differences are partly derived from culture; their Latin roots may make French-Canadians more emotional and impulsive. Demographic and socioeconomic differences also exist; education and income are both lower in Quebec than in Ontario. The legal environment is also different for marketers in Quebec; besides strict language laws, there are stronger restrictions on advertising to children, for example. To be successful in French Canada, marketers must develop appeals that take these differences into account. For example, while many marketers are using national symbols to appeal to their customers, Quebec politics makes this unwise.

Mature Consumers

Mature consumers—"those aged 65 years or more"—are becoming a very attractive market. These "seniors" constituted 12 percent of the Canadian population in 1995, and because of its rapid growth, the segment is expected to make up 23 percent of the total by the year 2041. Seventy-eight percent of the group are married couples. They love to travel. One-third of all new cars are bought by seniors. This market loves *big* comfortable cars that are easy to get into and out of with lots of luggage space. They have considerably more disposable income than the under-35 age segments, in fact, it is reported that they account for 55 percent of all the discretionary dollars spent in Canada. Sixty-four percent own their homes. In the last 15 years, seniors' incomes have risen faster than those of people under the age of 65.

The segment is not homogeneous, but consists of a number of sub-segments labelled the active "go-gos," the frail "go-slows," and the nursing-dependent "no-gos." A new Statistics Canada publication, *A Portrait of Seniors in Canada*, is designed to help people understanding this evolving group of Canadians. Older consumers, for example, think of themselves as years younger and resent the sedentary image. They maintain an active lifestyle—travelling, shopping, and eating out. Effective marketing to this segment must avoid old-age stereotyping and recognize its true potential. Mature consumers tend to be buyers of large cars, clothes, and jewellery, and have positive attitudes toward fitness and nutrition. Many are indulgent grandparents who lavish expensive toys and designer clothing on their grandchildren.

Tweens

Gone are the days when marketers could assume that the youth market was a homogeneous mass. Smart practitioners realize that it comprises many diverse segments. One of the hottest niche markets within the youth market category is the "tween" market. Over two million strong in Canada, these media-savvy young people are between the ages of 7 to 12 years old. They spend a whopping $1.5 billion annually. "Kids rule" is their motto and they enjoy being the "big kids" that little kids look up to. They are big on contests and collecting. Watching TV is their most frequent leisure activity and they love wacky animation and humour (the Bart Simpson type). While they love such products as candy "snot" packaged in a plastic nose, they find close-ups of couples kissing totally gross. Their favourite purchases

culture. There are challenges with marketing cutlures, however. Those operators specializing in aboriginal tourism must strike a balance between offering visitors educational cultural experiences while also perserving the integrity of the cultures. They must draw distinctions between those aspects of culture that can be shared and those that are so spiritual and sacred that they are not for sale.[4]

Social Class

Virtually all human societies exhibit social stratification. Stratification sometimes takes the form of a caste system where the members of different castes are reared for certain roles and cannot change their caste membership. More frequently, stratification takes the form of social classes.

(continued)

are food, entertainment, and clothing. Marketers who want to tap this market constantly update their research—this is a fickle market. YTV, for example, conducts an annual survey of the lifestyles, attitudes, and beliefs of tweens. They found that they are more techno-savvy, more self-reliant, have more disposable income, and are more aware of current events that their counterparts were in the survey just three years ago. They realize they must do well in school, and, in fact, 81 percent say getting good grades is "cool." Special publications, such as *Bang,* distributed free throughout Canadian schools, are aimed specifically at this market. *Sports Illustrated for Kids* notes that tweens make up the majority of its audience. Tweens look through each issue an average of seven times, and they are more likely to read all the copy. Moreover, they are 76 percent more likely than adult readers to recall advertisements.

Some marketers are dividing this market up even further and are targeting young girls since they begin shopping earlier and buy a wider range of products than do boys the same age. Television shows aimed at this audience such as *Ready or Not, Clueless,* and *Sabrina the Teenage Witch* are effective vehicles for reaching this audience. Advertisers are warned that girls in this segment have an "extremely low threshold for stupidity" and have no time for advertisers that talk down to them. Instead, low key ads such as the recent Gap campaign, with its simple white background and creative use of music, are cited as effective examples. Tweens are influenced by such icons as the Spice Girls. Since this group is very fashion conscious, La Senza launched La Senza Girl and Le Chateau offers Junior Girl lines specifically designed to appeal to this market, knowing that female tweens want to dress to look older and more independent than they actually are.

While adults may shudder, images, such as as the one above, make for breakthrough advertising for the tween market.

Sources: See Jarrett Churchill, "Tweens Have More Money" YTV Study," *Strategy: The Canadian Marketing Report,* November 24, 1997, p. 15; Wendy Cuthbert, "Special Report: Youth Marketing: Thank Heaven for Little Girls," *Strategy: The Canadian Marketing Report,* July 6, 1998, p. 21; Lynne DeCew, "Special Report: Youth Marketing: Tailor Message to Reach Subgroups: Kids, Tweens, Teens All Require Different Marketing Approaches, Says Expert," ," *Strategy: The Canadian Marketing Report,* July 8, 1996, p. 19; Leanne Delap, "Tween Trail is Paved with Gold," *The Kingston Whig Standard,* April 19, 1999, p. 27; Helena Katz, "Johnson Sharpens its Quebec Strategy," *Marketing,* October 12, 1998, p. 3; Shawna Steinberg, "Only in English Canada, You Say?," *Marketing,* November 12, 1998, p. 10; Sinclair Stewart, "Youth Culture Targets Teens with a Bang," *Strategy: The Canadian Marketing Report,* January 4, 1999, p. 24; John Straiton, "Marketing to Seniors: How to Sell Me a Car," *Marketing,* April 24/31, 1998, p. 22; *A Portrait of Seniors in Canada* (http:www.statcan.ca/english/ads/89-519-XPE/index.htm); *Canada Yearbook 1986,* pp. 2-5; "Chasing the Over-50 Market," *Marketing,* April 4, 1985, p. 25.

■   *Social classes* are relatively homogeneous and enduring divisions in a society, which are hierarchically ordered and whose members share similar values, interests, and behaviour.

Social classes do not reflect income alone, but also other indicators such as occupation, education, and area of residence. Social classes differ in dress, speech patterns, recreational preferences, and many other characteristics. Table 6-1 describes the seven social classes identified by social scientists.

Social classes have several characteristics. First, those within each social class tend to behave more alike than persons from two different social classes. Second, persons are perceived as occupying inferior or superior positions according to social class.

1. Upper Uppers (less than 1%)	The social elite who live on inherited wealth. They give large sums to charity, run the debutante balls, maintain more than one home, send their children to the finest schools. They are a market for jewellery, antiques, homes, and vacations. They often buy and dress conservatively. While small as a group, they serve as a reference group to the extent that their consumption decisions are imitated by the other social classes.
2. Lower Uppers (about 2%)	Persons who have earned high income or wealth through exceptional ability in the professions or business. They usually come from the middle class. They tend to be active in social and civic affairs and seek to buy the symbols of status for themselves and their children. They include the nouveau riche, whose pattern of conspicuous consumption is designed to impress those below them. The ambition of lower uppers is to be accepted in the upper-upper stratum.
3. Upper Middles (12%)	Possess neither family status nor unusual wealth. They are primarily concerned with "career." They have attained positions as professionals, independent businesspersons, and corporate managers. They believe in education and want their children to develop professional or administrative skills. Members of this class like to deal in ideas and are highly civic minded. They are home-oriented and are the quality market for good homes, clothes, furniture, and appliances.
4. Middle Class (32%)	Average-pay white- and blue-collar workers who live on "the right side of town." Often, they buy products that are popular to keep up with trends. Twenty-five percent own imported cars, and most are concerned with fashion. The middle class believes in spending more money on "worthwhile experiences" for their children and aiming them toward a university education.
5. Working Class (38%)	Average-pay blue-collar workers and those who lead a working-class lifestyle, whatever their income, school background, or job. The working class depends heavily on relatives for economic and emotional support, for tips on job opportunities, for advice, and for assistance. A working-class vacation means staying in town, and "going away" means to a lake or resort no more than two hours away. The working class tends to maintain sharp sex-role divisions and stereotyping.
6. Upper Lowers (9%)	Upper lowers are working, although their living standard is just above poverty. They perform unskilled work and are very poorly paid. Often, upper lowers are educationally deficient..
7. Lower Lowers (7%)	Lower lowers are on welfare, visibly poverty stricken, and usually out of work. Some are not interested in finding a permanent job and most are dependent on public aid or charity for income.

Sources: Richard P. Coleman, "The Continuing Significance of Social Class to Marketing." *Journal of Consumer Research*, December 1983, pp. 265–80; and Richard P. Coleman and Lee P. Rainwater, *Social Standing in America: New Dimension of Class* (New York: Basic Books, 1978).

Third, social class is indicated by a cluster of variables—for example, occupation, income, wealth, education, and value orientation—rather than by any single variable. Fourth, individuals can move from one social class to another—up and down—during their lifetime. The extent of this mobility varies according to the rigidity of social stratification in a given society.

Social classes show distinct product and brand preferences in many areas, including clothing, home furnishings, leisure activities, and automobiles. Some marketers focus their efforts on one social class. Thus the Auberge du Pommier restaurant located in northern Toronto focuses on upper-class customers, while McDonald's caters to middle-class families. Social classes differ in media preferences, with upper-class consumers preferring magazines and books and lower-class consumers preferring television. Even within a media category such as TV, upper-class consumers prefer news and drama, and lower-class consumers prefer soap operas and sports programs. There are also language differences among the social classes. The advertiser must compose copy and dialogue that ring true to the targeted social class.

SOCIAL FACTORS

In addition to cultural factors, a consumer's behaviour is influenced by such social factors as reference groups, family, and social roles and statuses.

Reference Groups

■ A person's *reference groups* consist of all the groups that have a direct (face-to-face) or indirect influence on the person's attitudes or behaviour. Groups having a direct influence on a person are called *membership groups.*

Some membership groups are primary groups, such as family, friends, neighbours, and co-workers, with whom the person interacts fairly continuously and informally. People also belong to secondary groups, such as religious, professional, and trade-union groups, which tend to be more formal and require less continuous interaction.

People are significantly influenced by their reference groups in at least three ways. Reference groups expose an individual to new behaviours and lifestyles. They influence attitudes and self-concept. And they create pressures for conformity that may affect actual product and brand choices.

People are also influenced by groups to which they do not belong. *Aspirational groups* are those the person hopes to join; *dissociative groups* are those whose values or behaviour an individual rejects.

Marketers try to identify target customers' reference groups. However, the level of reference-group influence varies among products and brands. Reference groups appear to strongly influence both product and brand choice only in the case of automobiles and colour televisions; mainly brand choice in such items as furniture and clothing; and mainly product choice in such items as beer and cigarettes.

Manufacturers of products and brands where group influence is strong must determine how to reach and influence the opinion leaders in these reference groups. An *opinion leader* is the person in informal product-related communications who offers advice or information about a specific product or product category, such as which of several brands is best or how a particular product may be used.[5] Opinion leaders are found in all strata of society, and a person can be an opinion leader in certain product areas and an opinion follower in other areas. Marketers try to reach opinion leaders by identifying demographic and psychographic characteristics associated with opinion leadership, identifying the media read by opinion leaders, and directing messages at the opinion leaders. The hottest trends in teenage music, language, and fashion start in Canada's major cities, then quickly spread to more mainstream youth in the suburbs. Clothing companies that hope to appeal to the fickle and fashion-conscious youth market are making a concerted effort to monitor urban opinion leaders' style and behaviour:

■ **Levi Strauss & Company.** Levi-Strauss has been squeezed by the competition as teens and youth flock to designer labels and more "cool" brands. To revitalize sales for its Silver Tab line of clothing, the company's ad agency, TBWA Chiat/Day, sent out employees to build a network of contacts familiar with the urban scene, including club-hoppers, stylists, photographers, and disc jockeys. The agency kept a scrapbook of people and looks and separated them into "tribes" defined by the music they like, including repetitive synthetic music known as electronica, hip-hop and rap, and retro soul music. Its illustrated ads appealing to hip-hop and rap culture featured the statement "It's bangin' son," which means "cool," and teenagers clad in Silver Tab clothing—baggy pants, hip huggers, tiny tops—and wearing accessories such as nose-rings, beepers, and chunky gold jewellery.[6]

Family

The family is the most important consumer-buying organization in society, and it has been researched extensively.[7] Family members constitute the most influential primary reference group. We can distinguish between two families in the buyer's life. The *family of orientation* consists of one's parents and siblings. From parents a person acquires an orientation toward religion, politics, and economics and a sense of personal ambition, self-worth, and love.[8] Even if the buyer no longer interacts very much with his or her parents, their influence on the buyer's behaviour can be significant. In countries where parents live with their grown children, their influence can be substantial. A more direct influence on everyday buying behaviour is one's *family of procreation*—namely, one's spouse and children.

Marketers are interested in the roles and relative influence of the husband, wife, and children in the purchase of a large variety of products and services. These roles vary widely in different countries and social classes. Vietnamese Canadians, for example, are more likely to adhere to the traditional model in which the man makes the decisions for any large purchase. Similarly, successful ads for Korean-Canadians will usually feature a man in his thirties or forties unless the ad is for a specifically female product, such as jewellery.[9]

In North America, husband-wife involvement has traditionally varied widely by product category. The wife has traditionally acted as the family's main purchasing agent, especially for food, sundries, and staple-clothing items while men were targetted as the audience for electronics, stereo equipments, sports gear, power tools, and cars. However, these traditional roles are changing. In 1978 only 10 percent of males were classified as primary shoppers; in 1998 the figure has risen to 17 percent. *Canadian Grocer Magazine* estimates that 25 to 30 percent of men do the grocery shopping for their household. Some males are forced into the role of shopper by demographic and lifestyle changes such as late marriage and high divorce rates, but most assume the role as a result of being part of a time-pressed, two-income household. family.[10]

Marketers need to determine which member normally has the greater influence in choosing various products. Often it is a matter of who has more power, time, or expertise. In certain product categories, women purchasers have been ignored. Business guru Tom Peters cites women as the number-one business marketing opportunity, and says:

> *The market research is clear: Women make or greatly influence most purchasing decisions. Homes. . . . Medical care. Cars. Vacations. And hammers and nails in the huge DIY (do-it-yourself) industry: One (rare) female DIY-chain exec remarked to me about her male colleagues' amazement that 60% of their customers were women. . . . Women are where the real bucks are. Now close to 8 million women own enterprises, up from about 400,000 in 1970. They employ about 18.5 million of us . . . 40% more than old Forbes 500 industrials. About 22% of working wives outearn their hubbies, and women constitute about half the population of those with $500,000 or more in net worth.*[11]

This is already happening in the car business:

■ **Cadillac.** Women now make up 34 percent of the luxury-car market, and auto-makers are paying attention. Male car designers at Cadillac are going about their work with paper clips on their fingers to simulate what it feels like to operate buttons, knobs, and other interior features with longer fingernails. The Cadillac Catera features an air-conditioned glove box to preserve such items as lipstick and film. Under the hood, yellow markings highlight where fluid fills go.[12]

Another shift in buying patterns is an increase in the amount of dollars spent and influence wielded by children.[13] This is now an era where children are not only seen and heard, but are also catered to as never before. The numbers show it. Children aged 4 to 12 spent an estimated $36 billion—three times the value of the ready-to-eat cereal market. Kids' power over their own money is precisely what induced Ty, Inc., to introduce Beanie Babies, the fabulously successful line of about 100 different small stuffed creatures. Beanie Babies sell for about $9, just the right amount for a kid's weekly allowance. The indirect influence on parental spending by children aged 2 to 14 accounted for $450 billion of household purchases in 1997. Indirect influence means that parents know the brands and product choices and preferences of their children without hints or outright requests. Direct influence describes children's hints, requests, and demands—"I want to go to McDonald's." Direct influence peaked around $280 billion in 1997. Nontraditional marketers are now figuring out that the fastest route to Mom and Dad's wallets may be through Junior.

■ **General Motors.** In the May 1997 issue of *Sports Illustrated for Kids*, a magazine targeted to 8- to14-year-olds, the inside cover featured a brightly coloured two-page spread advertising the Chevy Venture minivan. This was GM's first attempt to woo what they call "backseat consumers." The Venture's brand manager sent the minivan into malls and showed previews of Disney's *Hercules* on a VCR inside it. These days, kids often play a tie-breaking role in deciding what car to buy.[14]

General Motors
www.gm.com

While GM showed off its minivan in a mall, today companies are more likely to show off their products to children—and solicit marketing information from them—over the Internet. This practice has consumer groups and parents up in arms. Some four million kids under the age of 17 went online in 1996, and the number is skyrocketing. Marketers have jumped online with them, often offering freebies to kids in exchange for personal information (solicited without parental consent). Many have come under fire for this practice and for not clearly differentiating ads from games or entertainment. The Direct Marketing Association is taking a strong stand on marketing to children on the Internet. For their guidelines, see the Marketing Memo entitled "What Every Marketer Needs to Know: Internet Ethics for Targeting Kids." One company that uses ethical tactics to market to children is also one of the most popular sites for children, Disney Online:

■ **Disney Online.** Disney considers itself a leader in educating parents and children to the benefits of the Internet, as well as its risks. And with good reason. Disney clearly states its online policies with a link on its home page and on the home pages of its other sites, including Disney's Daily Blast, a proprietary subscription-based Internet service geared to children aged 3 to 12. Disney's online practices include alerting parents through e-mail when a child has submitted personal information to a Web site, whether it be to enter a contest, cast a vote, or register at a site. While many sites and advertisers used "cookies," tiny bits of data a Web site puts on a user's computer to enhance their visit, Disney does not use cookies for promotional or marketing purposes and does not share them with third parties.[15]

Disney Online
www.disney.com

Roles and Statuses

A person participates in many groups—family, clubs, organizations. The person's position in each group can be defined in terms of role and status. A *role* consists of the activities that a person is expected to perform. Each role carries a *status*. A Supreme Court justice has more status than a sales manager, and a sales manager has more status than an office clerk. People choose products that communicate their role and status in society. Thus company presidents often drive Mercedes and wear expensive suits and expensive jewellery. Marketers are aware of the *status symbol* potential of products and brands.

PERSONAL FACTORS

A buyer's decisions are also influenced by personal characteristics. These include the buyer's age and stage in the life cycle, occupation, economic circumstances, lifestyle, and personality and self-concept.

Age and Stage in the Life Cycle

People buy different goods and services over a lifetime. They eat baby food in the early years, most foods in the growing and mature years, and special diets in the later years. Taste in clothes, furniture, and recreation is also age related.

Consumption is shaped by the *family life cycle*. Nine stages of the family life cycle are listed in Table 6-2, along with the financial situation and typical product interests of each group. Marketers often choose life-cycle groups as their target market. But target households are not always family based: there are also single households, gay households, and cohabitor households.

Some recent work has identified *psychological life-cycle stages*. Adults experience certain "passages" or "transformations" as they go through life.[16] Marketers pay close attention to changing life circumstances—divorce, widowhood, remarriage—and their effect on consumption behaviour.

Occupation and Economic Circumstances

Occupation also influences a person's consumption pattern. A blue-collar worker will buy work clothes, work shoes, and lunchboxes. A company president will buy expensive business attire, air travel, country-club membership, and a large sailboat. Marketers try to identify the occupational groups that have above-average interest in their products and services. A company can even specialize its products for certain occupational groups: computer software companies design different products for brand managers, engineers, lawyers, and physicians.

Product choice is greatly affected by economic circumstances: spendable income (level, stability, and time pattern), savings and assets (including the percentage that is liquid), debts, borrowing power, and attitude toward spending versus saving. Marketers of income-sensitive goods pay constant attention to trends in personal income, savings, and interest rates. If economic indicators point to a recession, marketers can take steps to redesign, reposition, and reprice their products so they continue to offer value to target customers.

Lifestyle

People from the same subculture, social class, and occupation may lead quite different lifestyles.

- A *lifestyle* is the person's pattern of living in the world as expressed in activities, interests, and opinions. Lifestyle portrays the "whole person" interacting with his or her environment.

Marketers search for relationships between their products and lifestyle groups. For example, a computer manufacturer might find that most computer buyers are achievement oriented. The marketer may then aim the brand more clearly at the achiever lifestyle.

Psychographics is the science of measuring and categorizing consumer lifestyles. One of the most popular classifications based on psychographic measurements is the VALS 2 framework. SRI International's Values and Lifestyles (VALS) framework has been the only commercially available psychographic segmentation system to gain widespread acceptance. The VALS 2 system is continually updated to better serve the business world. VALS 2 classifies adults into eight groups based on psychological attributes. The segmentation system is based on responses to a questionnaire featuring five demographics and 42 attitudinal questions as well as questions about use of online services and Web sites.[17]

The VALS 2 questionnaire asks them to agree or disagree with statements such as "I like my life to be pretty much the same from week to week," "I often crave excitement," and "I would rather make something than buy it."

TABLE 6.2

Stage in Family Life Cycle
Buying or Behavioural Pattern

1. Bachelor stage: young, single, not living at home.	Few financial burdens. Fashion opinion leaders. Recreation oriented. Buy: basic home equipment, furniture, cars, equipment for the mating game; vacations.
2. Newly married couples: Young, no children.	Highest purchase rate and highest average purchase of durables: cars, appliances, furniture, vacations.
3. Full nest I: youngest child under six.	Home purchasing at peak. Liquid assets low. Interested in new products, advertised products. Buy: washers, dryers, TV, baby food, chest rubs and cough medicines, vitamins, dolls, wagons, sleds, skates.
4. Full nest II: youngest child six or over.	Financial position better. Less influenced by advertising. Buy larger-size packages, multiple-unit deals. Buy: many foods, cleaning materials, bicycles, music lessons, pianos.
5. Full nest III: older married couples with dependent children.	Financial position still better. Some children get jobs. Hard to influence with advertising. High average purchase of durables: new, more tasteful furniture, auto travel, unnecessary appliances, boats, dental services, magazines.
6. Empty nest I: older married couples, no children living with them, head of household in labour force.	Home ownership at peak. Most satisfied with financial position and money saved. Interested in travel, recreation, self-education. Make gifts and contributions. Not interested in new products. Buy: vacations, luxuries, home improvements.
7. Empty nest II: older married. No children living at home, head of household retired.	Drastic cut in income. Keep home. Buy: medical appliances, medical-care products.
8. Solitary survivor, in labour force.	Income still good but likely to sell home.
9. Solitary survivor, retired.	Same medical and product needs as other retired group; drastic cut in income. Special need for attention, affection, and security.

Sources: William D. Wells and George Gubar, "Life-Cycle Concepts in Marketing Research," *Journal of Marketing Research*, November 1966, p. 362. Also see Patrick E. Murphy and William A. Staples, "A Modernized Family Life Cycle," *Journal of Consumer Research*, June 1979, pp. 12–22; and Frederick W. Derrick and Alane E. Linfield, "The Family Life Cycle: An Alternative Approach," *Journal of Consumer Research*, September 1980, pp. 214–17.

The major tendencies of the four groups with greater resources are:

■ **Actualizers**: Successful, sophisticated, active, "take-charge" people. Purchases often reflect cultivated tastes for relatively upscale, niche-oriented products .

■ **Fulfilleds**: Mature, satisfied, comfortable, reflective. Favour durability, functionality, and value in products.

■ **Achievers**: Successful, career- and work-oriented. Favour established, prestige products that demonstrate success to their peers.

■ **Experiencers**: Young, vital, enthusiastic, impulsive, and rebellious. Spend a comparatively high proportion of their income on clothing, fast food, music, movies, and video.

The major tendencies of the four groups with fewer resources are:

■ **Believers**: Conservative, conventional, and traditional. Favour familiar products and established brands.

■ **Strivers:** Uncertain, insecure, approval-seeking, resource constrained. Favour stylish products that emulate the purchases of those with greater material wealth.

■ **Makers:** Practical, self-sufficient, traditional, family oriented. Favour only products with a practical or functional purpose such as tools, utility vehicles, fishing equipment.

Are You a Mouse Potato or a Techno-Striver? New Research Focuses on What Makes Technology Buyers Click

Traditional market research may tell you who is buying a computer for the household. It may even tell you the kind of lifestyle she or he has. However, it won't tell you who in the household is using the computer and why. It won't tell you that the wife is using the PC to take a distance-learning course, that the son is using it to download computer games from various Web sites, that the daughter is using it to log onto about a dozen chat groups, or that the husband, a confirmed technophobe, only logs on once in a blue moon to get stock quotes. A marketer who sends a promo to the husband for the newest online gizmo will surely miss the mark.

Marketers of technology products can get a read on the buying habits of technology buyers and users with several new market research tools. These new frameworks seek to segment consumers based on technology types. Two of the most prominent technology research tools under development are Forrester Research Inc.'s "Technographics," which segments consumers according to motivation, desire, and ability to invest in technology (see Table), and SRI Consulting's iVALS, which focuses on the attitudes, preferences, and behaviour of online service and Internet users. Forrester Research developed the former by hiring NPD, a polling and research firm, to survey 131 000 consumers. The Technographics scheme segregates people into nine categories shown in the accompanying table:

SRI's iVALS also divides consumers into 10 segments, but the focus is on Internet use. Some of the segments are:

Wizards—the most skilled and active Internet users for whom mastery of technology figures prominently in their identities.

Immigrants—recent arrivals to cyberspace usually familiar with only very specific parts of the Net and drawn online because they have to be for work or school.

Socialites—users who are strongly oriented toward social aspects of the Internet and who are prominent participants in online discussions. They are iVALS' youngest segment, mostly under 30 years of age.

Both Technographics and iVALS reinforce the idea of a dual-tier society, but one based on knowledge, not income. For instance, people who are more computer savvy are perfect targets for an electronic banking product that allows them to pay bills, switch money between accounts, and check balances on the computer. Those who are not computer literate will still write cheques by hand, send payments through "snail mail," and stand in line for a bank teller. Yet the new market research tools reveal many shades in the spectrum between "the knows" and "the know nots." For instance, Delta Airlines wants to use Technographics to better target online ticket sales. It is creating marketing campaigns for time-strapped "Fast Forwards" and "New Age Nurturers," and it will eliminate those who are technology pessimists from its solicitations. "Traditional market research gives you a picture of the universe," says Paula Lai, manager of Delta's marketing research. "But what good is that picture, she went on to say, if it doesn't tell you who will book tickets online?

Sources: Based on: Andy Hines, "Do You Know Your Technology Type?" *The Futurist,* Sep/Oct 1997, pp. 10-11. Rebecca Piirto Heath, "The Frontiers of Psychographics," *American Demographics*, July 1996, pp. 38-43. Information on iVALS segments from http://www.future.sri.com (August 1998). Paul C. Judge, "Are Tech Buyers Different?" *Business Week*, January 26, 1998, pp. 64-65, 68.

■ **Strugglers**: Elderly, resigned, passive, concerned, resource constrained. Cautious consumers who are loyal to favourite brands.

If you want to find out which VALS 2 type you are, or find out about the VALS 2 segments in general, go to SRI's Web site (http://www.future.sri.com). You can complete the VALS 2 and other lifestyle questionnaires and get results back in real time.

While psychographics continues to be a valid and valued methodology for many marketers, it may become less valid in the information economy. Social scientists are realizing that old tools for predicting consumer behaviour don't always work when it comes to use of the Internet or online services and purchases of technology products. See the Marketing for the 21st Century box entitled "Are You a Mouse Potato or a Techno-Striver? New Research Focuses on What Makes Technology Buyers Click."

Lifestyle segmentation schemes are by no means universal. McCann-Erickson London, for example, identified the following British lifestyles: Avant-Gardians (interested in change), Pontificators (traditionalists, very British), Chameleons (follow the crowd), and Sleepwalkers (contented underachievers). In 1992 the advertising agency D'Arcy, Masius, Benton & Bowles published *The Russian Consumer: A New Perspective and a*

(continued)

How Tech Customers Stack Up

▭ MORE AFFLUENT   ▭ LESS AFFLUENT

	CAREER	FAMILY	ENTERTAINMENT
OPTIMISTS	**FAST FORWARDS** These consumers are the biggest spenders, and they're early adopters of new technology for home, office, and personal use.	**NEW AGE NURTURERS** Also big spenders, but focused on technology for home uses, such as a family PC.	**MOUSE POTATOES** They like the on-line world for entertainment and are willing to spend for the latest in technotainment.
OPTIMISTS	**TECHNO-STRIVERS** Use technology from cell phones and pagers to on-line services primarily to gain a career edge.	**DIGITAL HOPEFULS** Families with a limited budget but still interested in new technology. Good candidates for under-$1,000 PC.	**GADGET-GRABBERS** They also favor on-line entertainment but have less cash to spend on it.
PESSIMISTS	**HAND-SHAKERS** Older consumers—typically managers—who don't touch their computers at work. They leave that to younger assistants.	**TRADITIONALISTS** Willing to use technology but slow to upgrade. Not convinced upgrades and other add-ons are worth paying for.	**MEDIA JUNKIES** Seek entertainment and can't find much of it on-line. Prefer TV and other older media.

SIDELINED CITIZENS (not interested in technology)

Source: Paul C. Judge, "Are Tech Buyers Different," *Business Week,* January 26, 1998, p. 65; Data Forrester Research Inc.

Marketing Approach, which revealed five categories of Russian consumers: "Kuptsi" (merchants), "Cossacks," "Students," "Business Executives," and "Russian Souls." Cossacks are characterized as ambitious, independent, and status seeking, while Russian Souls are passive, fearful of choices, and hopeful. Cossacks would drive a BMW, smoke Dunhill cigarettes, and drink Remy Martin, Russian Souls would drive a Lada, smoke Marlboros, and drink Smirnoff.[18]

Personality and Self-Concept

Each person has a distinct personality that influences buying behaviour.

■ By *personality*, we mean distinguishing psychological characteristics that lead to relatively consistent and enduring responses to environment.

Personality is usually described in terms of such traits as self-confidence, dominance, autonomy, deference, sociability, defensiveness, and adaptability.[19] Personality can be a useful variable in analyzing consumer behaviour, provided that personality types can be classified accurately and that strong correlations exist between certain personality types and product or brand choices. For example, a computer company might discover that many prospects show high self-confidence, dominance, and autonomy. This suggests designing computer advertisements to appeal to these traits.

Related to personality is *self-concept* (or self-image). Marketers try to develop brand images that match the target market's self-image. It is possible that a person's *actual self-concept* (how she views herself) differs from her *ideal self-concept* (how she would like to view herself) and from her *others-self-concept* (how she thinks others see her). Which self will she try to satisfy in making a purchase? Because it is difficult to answer this question, self-concept theory has had a mixed record of success in predicting consumer responses to brand images.[20]

PSYCHOLOGICAL FACTORS

A person's buying choices are influenced by four major psychological factors—motivation, perception, learning, and beliefs and attitudes.

Motivation

A person has many needs at any given time. Some needs are *biogenic*; they arise from physiological states of tension such as hunger, thirst, or discomfort. Other needs are *psychogenic*; they arise from psychological states of tension such as the need for recognition, esteem, or belonging. A need becomes a motive when it is aroused to a sufficient level of intensity. A *motive* is a need that is sufficiently pressing to drive the person to act.

Psychologists have developed theories of human motivation. Three of the best known—the theories of Sigmund Freud, Abraham Maslow, and Frederick Herzberg—carry quite different implications for consumer analysis and marketing strategy.

Freud's Theory. Sigmund Freud assumed that the psychological forces shaping people's behaviour are largely unconscious, and that a person cannot fully understand his or her own motivations. A technique called *laddering* can be used to trace a person's motivations from the stated instrumental ones to the more terminal ones. Then the marketer can decide at what level to develop the message and appeal.[21]

When a person examines specific brands, he or she will react not only to their stated capabilities but also to other, less conscious cues. Shape, size, weight, material, colour, and brand name can all trigger certain associations and emotions.

Motivation researchers often collect "in-depth interviews" with a few dozen consumers to uncover deeper motives triggered by a product. They use various "projective techniques" such as *word association, sentence completion, picture interpretation*, and *role playing*. Their research has produced interesting and occasionally bizarre hypotheses: consumers resist prunes because prunes are wrinkled looking and remind people of old age, men smoke cigars as an adult version of thumb sucking, and women prefer vegetable shortening to animal fats because the latter arouse a sense of guilt over killing animals.

More recent research holds that each product is capable of arousing a unique set of motives in consumers. For example, whisky can attract someone who seeks social relaxation, status, or fun. Therefore, different whisky brands have specialized in one of these three different appeals. Jan Callebaut calls this approach "motivational positioning."[22]

Maslow's Theory. Abraham Maslow sought to explain why people are driven by particular needs at particular times.[23] Why does one person spend considerable time and energy on personal safety and another on pursuing the high opinion of others? Maslow's answer is that human needs are arranged in a hierarchy, from the most pressing to the least pressing. In their order of importance, they are physiological needs, safety needs, social needs, esteem needs, and self-actualization needs (Figure 6-2). People will try to satisfy their most important needs first. When a person succeeds in satisfying an important need, that need will cease being a current motivator, and the person will try to satisfy the next-most-important need. For example, a starving man (need 1) will not take an interest in the latest happenings in the art world (need 5), nor in how he is viewed by others (need 3 or 4), nor even in whether he is breathing clean air (need 2). But when he has enough food and water, the next-most-important need will become salient.

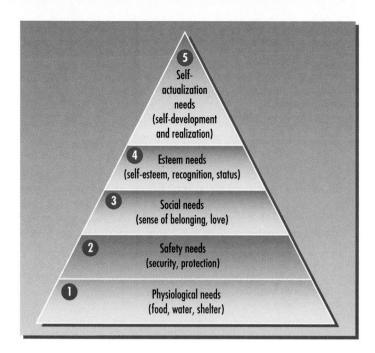

FIGURE 6.2

Maslow's Hierarchy of Needs

Maslow's theory helps marketers understand how various products fit into the plans, goals, and lives of consumers.

Herzberg's Theory. Frederick Herzberg developed a *two-factor theory* that distinguishes dissatisfiers (factors that cause dissatisfaction) and satisfiers (factor that cause satisfaction).[24] The absence of dissatisfiers is not enough; satisfiers must be actively present to motivate a purchase. For example, a computer that does not come with a warranty would be a dissatisfier. Yet the presence of a product warranty would not act as a satisfier or motivator of a purchase, since it is not a source of intrinsic satisfaction with the computer. Ease of use would be a satisfier.

Herzberg's theory has two implications. First, sellers should do their best to avoid dissatisfiers (for example, a poor training manual or a poor service policy). While these things will not sell a product, they might easily unsell it. Second, the manufacturer should identify the major satisfiers or motivators of purchase in the market and then supply them. These satisfiers will make the major difference as to which brand the customer buys.

Perception

A motivated person is ready to act. How the motivated person actually acts is influenced by his or her perception of the situation.

■ *Perception* is the process by which an individual selects, organizes, and interprets information inputs to create a meaningful picture of the world.[25]

Perception depends not only on the physical stimuli but also on the stimuli's relation to the surrounding field and on conditions within the individual.

The key word in the definition of perception is "individual." One person might perceive a fast-talking salesperson as aggressive and insincere; another, as intelligent and helpful. People can emerge with different perceptions of the same object because of three perceptual processes: selective attention, selective distortion, and selective retention.

Selective Attention. People are exposed to a tremendous amount of daily stimuli: the average person may be exposed to over 1500 ads a day. Because a person cannot possibly attend to all of these, most stimuli will be screened out—a process called *selective attention.* Selective attention means that marketers have to work hard to attract consumers' notice. The real challenge is to explain which stimuli people will notice. Here are some findings:

- *People are more likely to notice stimuli that relate to a current need.* A person who is motivated to buy a computer will notice computer ads; he or she will probably not notice stereo-equipment ads.

- *People are more likely to notice stimuli that they anticipate.* You are more likely to notice computers than radios in a computer store because you do not expect the store to carry radios.

- *People are more likely to notice stimuli whose deviations are large in relation to the normal size of the stimuli.* You are more likely to notice an ad offering $100 off the list price of a computer than one offering $5 off.

Selective Distortion. Even noticed stimuli do not always come across in the way the senders intended. *Selective distortion* is the tendency to twist information into personal meanings and interpret information in a way that will fit our preconceptions. Unfortunately, there is not much that marketers can do about selective distortion.

Selective Retention. People will forget much that they learn, but will tend to retain information that supports their attitudes and beliefs. Because of *selective retention*, we are likely to remember good points mentioned about a product we like and forget good points mentioned about competing products. Selective retention explains why marketers use drama and repetition in sending messages to their target market.

Learning

When people act, they learn.

- *Learning* involves changes in an individual's behaviour arising from experience.

Most human behaviour is learned. Learning theorists believe that learning is produced through the interplay of drives, stimuli, cues, responses, and reinforcement.

A *drive* is a strong internal stimulus impelling action. *Cues* are minor stimuli that determine when, where, and how a person responds.

Suppose you buy an IBM computer. If your experience is rewarding, your response to computers and IBM will be positively reinforced. Later on, when you want to buy a printer, you may assume that since IBM makes good computers, IBM also makes good printers. In other words, you *generalize* your response to similar stimuli. A counter-tendency to generalization is *discrimination*. Discrimination means that the person has learned to recognize differences in sets of similar stimuli and can adjust responses accordingly.

Learning theory teaches marketers that they can build up demand for a product by associating it with strong drives, using motivating cues, and providing positive reinforcement. A new company can enter the market by appealing to the same drives that competitors use and providing similar cue configurations because buyers are more likely to transfer loyalty to similar brands (generalization). Or the company might design its brand to appeal to a different set of drives and offer strong cue inducements to switch (discrimination).

Beliefs and Attitudes

Through doing and learning, people acquire beliefs and attitudes. These in turn influence buying behaviour.

- A *belief* is a descriptive thought that a person holds about something.

Beliefs may be based on knowledge, opinion, or faith. They may or may not carry an emotional charge. Of course, manufacturers are very interested in the beliefs people carry in their heads about their products and services. These beliefs make up product and brand images, and people act on their images. If some beliefs are wrong and inhibit purchase, the manufacturer will want to launch a campaign to correct these beliefs.[26]

Particularly important to global marketers is the fact that buyers often hold distinct beliefs about brands or products based on their country of origin. Several country-of-origin studies have found the following:

part two
Analyzing
Marketing
Opportunities

- The impact of country of origin varies with the type of product. Consumers would want to know where a car was made but not where the lubricating oil came from.

- Certain countries enjoy a reputation for certain goods: Japan for automobiles and consumer electronics; the United States for high-tech innovations, soft drinks, toys, cigarettes, and jeans; Canada for high-quality grain, beef, telecommunications, and aerospace products, and France for wine, perfume, and luxury goods.

- Sometimes the country-of-origin perception can extend beyond certain products and encompass an entire country's products. In a recent study, Chinese consumers in Hong Kong perceived American products as prestigious, Japanese products as innovative, and Chinese products as cheap.[27]

- The more favourable a country's image, the more prominently the "Made in . . . " label should be displayed in promoting the brand.

- Attitudes toward country of origin can change over time. Japan had a poor quality image before World War II.

A company has several options when its products are competitively priced but their place of origin turns off consumers. The company can consider co-production with a foreign company that has a better name: South Korea could make a fine leather jacket that it sends to Italy for finishing. Or the company can adopt a strategy to achieve world-class quality in the local industry, as is the case with Belgian chocolates, Polish ham, and Colombian coffee. This is what South African wineries are attempting to do.

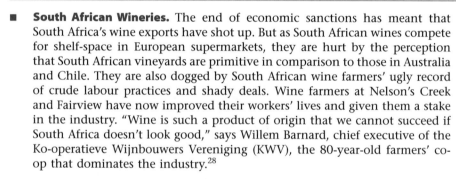

- **South African Wineries.** The end of economic sanctions has meant that South Africa's wine exports have shot up. But as South African wines compete for shelf-space in European supermarkets, they are hurt by the perception that South African vineyards are primitive in comparison to those in Australia and Chile. They are also dogged by South African wine farmers' ugly record of crude labour practices and shady deals. Wine farmers at Nelson's Creek and Fairview have now improved their workers' lives and given them a stake in the industry. "Wine is such a product of origin that we cannot succeed if South Africa doesn't look good," says Willem Barnard, chief executive of the Ko-operatieve Wijnbouwers Vereniging (KWV), the 80-year-old farmers' co-op that dominates the industry.[28]

Finally, the company can hire a well-known celebrity to endorse the product. Nike has had a great deal of success using basketball star Michael Jordan to promote its footware in Europe.[29]

Just as important as beliefs are attitudes.

- An *attitude* is a person's enduring favourable or unfavourable evaluations, emotional feelings, and action tendencies toward some object or idea.[30]

People have attitudes toward almost everything: religion, politics, clothes, music, food. Attitudes put them into a frame of mind of liking or disliking an object, moving toward or away from it. Attitudes lead people to behave in a fairly consistent way toward similar objects. People do not have to interpret and react to every object in a fresh way. Because attitudes economize on energy and thought, they are very difficult to change. A person's attitudes settle into a consistent pattern: to change a single attitude may require major adjustments in other attitudes.

Thus a company would be well advised to fit its product into existing attitudes rather than to try to change people's attitudes. Of course, there are exceptions where the cost of trying to change attitudes might pay off. The dairy industry has found that even a bland, white commodity like milk can benefit from creative and diverse marketing.[31]

- **Quebec Milk Producers.** This group went against conventional wisdom that suggested showing food in poor-quality newspaper ads just wasn't a good idea. Because of the poor quality of newspaper photo reproduction, food shots tend to lose their appeal. The campaign was targeted at adults over age 30 who no longer drink milk on a regular basis. Instead of promoting the health benefits of milk (people already knew milk was good for them), the ad creators played upon the consumer's nostalgia and the emotional connection to milk. Ads reminded the audience that milk was part of their life when they were growing up. The soft-focus black and white ads were simple and featured headlines such as "The mother of all beverages", "What your inner child is thirsting for," and "Remember, you used to cry for it." While the sales impact is still unknown, the creator of the campaign notes, "This is the first time in 25 years of working in advertising that I've gotten so many calls and letters from people saying they love our campaign."

Dairy Farmers of Ontario
www.milk.org

■   **Dairy Farmers of Ontario.** The now famous mooing milk cartons and the cow spotted clothing are the hallmarks of this now-famous campaign, which is part of the larger "Drink Milk. Love Life" marketing effort. The five-year-old effort is targeted at teens, a critical market for dairy farmers, since they want teens to get in the habit of drinking milk now so they will continue this consumption as they get older. In addition to the mooing cartons, the program features the MoOOolpaplooze Dance Party for high schools.

Never goes to waist.

milk

Stay healthy. Get in shape. Drink at least two glasses of milk a day.

THE BUYING DECISION PROCESS

Marketers must go beyond the various influences on buyers and develop an understanding of how consumers actually make their buying decisions. Specifically, marketers must identify who makes the buying decision, the types of buying decisions, and the steps in the buying process.

BUYING ROLES

It is easy to identify the buyer for many products. In North America, men normally choose their shaving equipment and women choose their hair products. But even here marketers must be careful in making their targeting decisions, because buying roles change. ICI, the giant British chemical company, discovered to its surprise that women made 60 percent of the decisions on the brand of household paint; ICI therefore decided to advertise its DeLux brand to women.

We can distinguish five roles people might play in a buying decision:

- *Initiator:* A person who first suggests the idea of buying the product or service
- *Influencer:* A person whose view or advice influences the decision
- *Decider:* A person who decides on any component of a buying decision: whether to buy, what to buy, how to buy, or where to buy
- *Buyer:* The person who makes the actual purchase
- *User:* A person who consumes or uses the product or service

BUYING BEHAVIOUR

Consumer decision making varies with the type of buying decision. The decisions to buy toothpaste, a tennis racket, a personal computer, and a new car are all very different. Complex and expensive purchases are likely to involve more buyer deliberation and more participants. Assael distinguished four types of consumer buying behaviour based on the degree of buyer involvement and the degree of differences among brands[32] (Table 6-3).

Complex Buying Behaviour

Complex buying behaviour involves a three-step process. First, the buyer develops beliefs about the product. Second, he or she develops attitudes about the product. Third, he or she makes a thoughtful choice. Consumers engage in complex buying behaviour when they are highly involved in a purchase and aware of significant differences among brands. This is usually the case when the product is expensive, bought infrequently, risky, and highly self-expressive. Typically the consumer does not know much about the product category. For example, a person buying a personal computer may not know what attributes to look for. Many product features carry no meaning unless the buyer has done some research.

The marketer of a high-involvement product must understand consumers' information-gathering and evaluation behaviour. The marketer needs to develop strategies that assist the buyer in learning about the product's attributes and their relative importance, and that call attention to the high standing of the company's brand on the more important attributes. The marketer needs to differentiate the brand's features, use print media to describe the brand's benefits, and motivate store sales personnel and the buyer's acquaintances to influence the final brand choice.

Dissonance-Reducing Buyer Behaviour

Sometimes the consumer is highly involved in a purchase but sees little difference in brands. The high involvement is based on the fact that the purchase is expensive, infrequent, and risky. In this case, the buyer will shop around to learn what is available but will buy fairly quickly, perhaps responding primarily to a good price or to purchase convenience. For example, carpet buying is a high-involvement decision because carpeting is expensive and self-expressive, yet the buyer may consider most carpet brands in a given price range to be the same.

	High Involvement	Low Involvement
Significant Differences between Brands	Complex buying behaviour	Variety-seeking buying behaviour
Few Differences between Brands	Dissonance-reducing buying behaviour	Habitual buying behaviour

TABLE 6.3

Four Types of Buying Behaviour

Source: Modified from Henry Assael, *Consumer Behavior and Marketing Action* (Boston: Kent Publishing Co., 1987), p. 87. Copyright © 1987 by Wadsworth, Inc. Printed by permission of Kent Publishing Co., a division of Wadsworth, Inc.

After the purchase, the consumer might experience dissonance that stems from noticing certain disquieting features or hearing favourable things about other brands. The consumer will be alert to information that supports his or her decision. In this example, the consumer first acted, then acquired new beliefs, then ended up with a set of attitudes. Marketing communications should supply beliefs and evaluations that help the consumer feel good about his or her brand choice.

Habitual Buying Behaviour

Many products are bought under conditions of low involvement and the absence of significant brand differences. Consider salt. Consumers have little involvement in this product category. They go to the store and reach for the brand. If they keep reaching for the same brand, it is out of habit, not strong brand loyalty. There is good evidence that consumers have low involvement with most low-cost, frequently purchased products.

With these products, consumer behaviour does not pass through the normal belief/attitude/behaviour sequence. Consumers do not search extensively for information, evaluate characteristics, and make a decision on which brand to buy. Instead, they are passive recipients of information in television or print ads. Ad repetition creates *brand familiarity* rather than *brand conviction*. After purchase, they may not even evaluate the choice because they are not highly involved with the product. For low-involvement products the buying process begins with brand beliefs formed by passive learning and is followed by purchase behaviour, which may be followed by evaluation.

Marketers of such products find it effective to use price and sales promotions to stimulate product trial. Television advertising is more effective than print because it is a low-involvement medium that is suitable for passive learning.[33] Marketers use four techniques to try to convert a low-involvement product into one of higher involvement. First, they can link the product to some involving issue, as when Crest toothpaste is linked to avoiding cavities. Second, they can link the product to some involving personal situation—for instance, by advertising a coffee brand early in the morning when the consumer wants to shake off sleepiness. Third, they might design advertising to trigger strong emotions related to personal values or ego defence. Fourth, they might add an important feature (for example, fortifying orange juice with calcium). These strategies at best raise consumer involvement from a low to a moderate level; they do not propel the consumer into highly involved buying behaviour.

Variety-Seeking Buying Behaviour

Some buying situations are characterized by low involvement but significant brand differences. Here consumers often do a lot of brand switching. Think about cookies. The consumer has some beliefs about cookies, chooses a brand of cookies without much evaluation, and evaluates the product during consumption. Next time, the consumer may reach for another brand out of a wish for a different taste. Brand switching occurs for the sake of variety rather than dissatisfaction.

The market leader and the minor brands in this product category have different marketing strategies. The market leader will try to encourage habitual buying behaviour by dominating the shelf space, avoiding out-of-stock conditions, and sponsoring frequent reminder advertising. Challenger firms will encourage variety seeking by offering lower prices, deals, coupons, free samples, and advertising that presents reasons for trying something new.

THE STAGES OF THE BUYING DECISION PROCESS

Smart companies research the buying decision process involved in their product category. They ask consumers when they first became acquainted with the product category and brands, what their brand beliefs are, how involved they are with the product, how they make their brand choices, and how satisfied they are after purchase.

How can marketers learn about the stages in the buying process for their product? They can think about how they themselves would act (*introspective method*). They can interview a small number of recent purchasers, asking them to recall the events leading to their purchase (*retrospective method*). They can locate consumers who plan to buy the product and ask them to think out loud about going through the buying process (*prospective method*). Or they can ask consumers to describe the ideal way to buy the product (*prescriptive method*). Each method yields a picture of the steps in the consumer buying process.

Figure 6-3 shows a "stage model" of the typical buying process. The consumer passes through five stages: problem recognition, information search, evaluation of alternatives, purchase decision, and postpurchase behaviour. Clearly the buying process starts long before the actual purchase and has consequences long afterwards.[34]

The model in Figure 6-3 implies that consumers pass sequentially through all five stages in buying a product. But this is not the case: Consumers may skip or reverse some stages. A woman buying her regular brand of toothpaste goes directly from the need for toothpaste to the purchase decision, skipping information search and evaluation. However, we will use the model in Figure 6-3 because it captures the full range of considerations that arise when a consumer faces a highly involving new purchase.[35]

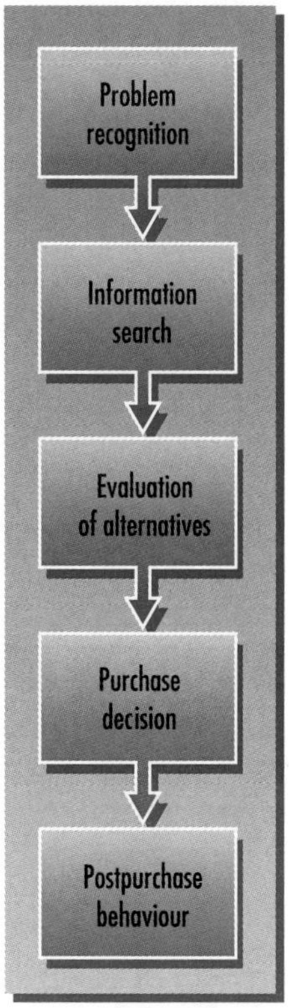

PROBLEM RECOGNITION

The buying process starts when the buyer recognizes a problem or need. The need can be triggered by internal or external stimuli. In the former case, one of the person's normal needs—hunger, thirst, sex—rises to a threshold level and becomes a drive. In the latter case, a need is aroused by an external stimulus. A person passes a bakery and sees freshly baked bread that stimulates her hunger; she admires a neighbour's new car; or she watches a television ad for a Hawaiian vacation.

Marketers need to identify the circumstances that trigger a particular need. By gathering information from a number of consumers, marketers can identify the most frequent stimuli that spark an interest in a product category. They can then develop marketing strategies that trigger consumer interest.

INFORMATION SEARCH

An aroused consumer will be inclined to search for more information. We can distinguish between two levels of arousal. The milder search state is called *heightened attention*. At this level a person simply becomes more receptive to information about a product.

At the next level, the person may enter *active information search:* looking for reading material, phoning friends, and visiting stores to learn about the product. Of key interest to the marketer are the major information sources to which the consumer will turn and the relative influence each will have on the subsequent purchase decision. Consumer information sources fall into four groups:

■ *Personal sources:* Family, friends, neighbours, acquaintances
■ *Commercial sources:* Advertising, salespersons, dealers, packaging, displays
■ *Public sources:* Mass media, consumer-rating organizations
■ *Experiential sources:* Handling, examining, using the product

The relative amount and influence of these information sources vary with the product category and the buyer's characteristics. Generally speaking, the consumer receives the most information about a product from commercial sources—that is, marketer-dominated sources. But the most effective information comes from personal sources. Each information source performs a different function in influencing the buying decision. Commercial information normally performs an informing function, and personal sources perform a legitimizing and/or evaluation function. For example, physicians often learn of new drugs from commercial sources but turn to other doctors for evaluative information.

FIGURE 6.3

Five-Stage Model of the Consumer Buying Process

FIGURE 6.4

Successive Sets Involved in Consumer Decision Making

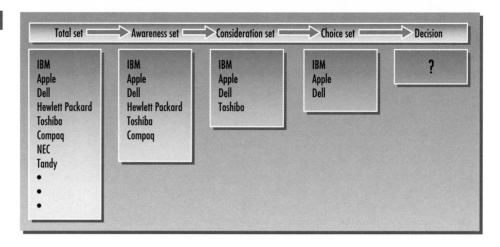

Through gathering information, the consumer learns about competing brands and their features. The first box in Figure 6-4 shows the *total set* of brands available to the consumer. The individual consumer will come to know only a subset of these brands (*awareness set*). Some brands will meet initial buying criteria (*consideration set*). As the person gathers more information, only a few will remain as strong contenders (*choice set*). The brands in the choice set might all be acceptable. The person makes a final choice from this set.[36]

Figure 6-4 makes it clear that a company must strategize to get its brand into the prospect's awareness set, consideration set, and choice set. The company must also identify the other brands in the consumer's choice set so that it can plan competitive appeals. In addition, the company should identify the consumer's information sources and evaluate their relative importance. Consumers should be asked how they first heard about the brand, what information came in later, and the relative importance of the different information sources. The answers will help the company prepare effective communications for the target market.

EVALUATION OF ALTERNATIVES

How does the consumer process competitive brand information and make a final value judgment? There is no single evaluation process used by all consumers or by one consumer in all buying situations. There are several decision evaluation processes, the most current models of which see the process as cognitively oriented. That is, they see the consumer as forming judgments largely on a conscious and rational basis.

Some basic concepts will help us understand consumer evaluation processes: First, the consumer is trying to satisfy a *need*. Second, the consumer is looking for certain *benefits* from the product solution. Third, the consumer sees each product as a *bundle of attributes* with varying abilities of delivering the benefits sought to satisfy this need. The attributes of interest to buyers vary by product:

- *Cameras*: Picture sharpness, camera speeds, camera size, price
- *Hotels*: Location, cleanliness, atmosphere, price
- *Mouthwash*: Colour, effectiveness, germ-killing capacity, price, taste/flavour
- *Tires*: Safety, tread life, ride quality, price

Consumers vary as to which product attributes they see as most relevant and the importance they attach to each attribute. They will pay the most attention to attributes that deliver the sought benefits. The market for a product can often be segmented according to attributes that are salient to different consumer groups.

The consumer develops a set of *brand beliefs* about where each brand stands on each attribute. The set of beliefs about a brand make up the *brand image*. The consumer's brand image will vary with his or her experiences as filtered by the effects of selective perception, selective distortion, and selective retention.

The consumer arrives at attitudes (judgments, preferences) toward the various brands through an attribute evaluation procedure.[37] Suppose that a consumer, Linda Brown, has narrowed her choice set to four computers (A, B, C, D). Assume that she is interested in four attributes: memory capacity, graphics capability, size and weight, and price. Table 6-4 shows her beliefs about how each brand rates on the four attributes. If one computer dominated the others on all the criteria, we could predict that Linda would choose it. But her choice set consists of brands that vary in their appeal. If Linda wants the best memory capacity, she should buy A; if she wants the best graphics capability, she should buy B; and so on.

Most buyers consider several attributes in their purchase decision. If we knew the weights that Linda Brown attaches to the four attributes, we could more reliably predict her computer choice. Suppose Linda assigned 40 percent of the importance to the computer's memory capacity, 30 percent to its graphics capability, 20 percent to its software availability, and 10 percent to its price. To find Linda's perceived value for each computer, we multiply her weights by her beliefs about each computer's attributes. This computation leads to the following perceived values:

Computer A = 0.4(10) + 0.3(8) + 0.2(6) + 0.1(4) = 8.0

Computer B = 0.4(8) + 0.3(9) + 0.2(8) + 0.1(3) = 7.8

Computer C = 0.4(6) + 0.3(8) + 0.2(10) + 0.1(5) = 7.3

Computer D = 0.4(4) + 0.3(3) + 0.2(7) + 0.1(8) = 4.7

We would predict that Linda will favour computer A, which (at 8.0) has the highest perceived value.[38]

Suppose most computer buyers form their preferences the same way. Knowing this, a computer manufacturer can do a number of things to influence buyer decisions. The marketer of computer C, for example, could apply the following strategies to stimulate greater interest in brand C:

- *Redesign the computer:* This technique is called real repositioning.
- *Alter beliefs about the brand:* Attempting to alter beliefs about the brand is called psychological repositioning.
- *Alter beliefs about competitors' brands:* This strategy, called competitive depositioning, makes sense when buyers mistakenly believe a competitor's brand has more quality than it actually has.
- *Alter the importance weights:* The marketer could try to persuade buyers to attach more importance to the attributes in which the brand excels.
- *Call attention to neglected attributes:* The marketer could draw the buyer's attention to neglected attributes, such as styling or processing speed.
- *Shift the buyer's ideals:* The marketer could try to persuade buyers to change their ideal levels for one or more attributes.[39]

TABLE 6.4

A Consumer's Brand Beliefs about Computers

Computer	Attribute			
	Memory Capacity	Graphics Capability	Size and Weight	Price
A	10	8	6	4
B	8	9	8	3
C	6	8	10	5
D	4	3	7	8

Note: Each attribute is rated from 0 to 10, where 10 represents the highest level on that attribute. Price, however, is indexed in a reverse manner, with a 10 representing the lowest price, since a consumer prefers a low price to a high price.

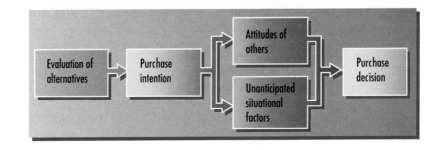

PURCHASE DECISION

In the evaluation stage, the consumer forms preferences among the brands in the choice set. The consumer may also form an intention to buy the most preferred brand. However, two factors can intervene between the purchase intention and the purchase decision (Figure 6-5).[40]

The first factor is the *attitudes of others*. The extent to which another person's attitude reduces one's preferred alternative depends on two things: (1) the intensity of the other person's negative attitude toward the consumer's preferred alternative and (2) the consumer's motivation to comply with the other person's wishes.[41] The more intense the other person's negativism and the closer the other person is to the consumer, the more the consumer will adjust his or her purchase intention. The converse is also true: A buyer's preference for a brand will increase if someone whom he or she respects favours the same brand strongly. The influence of others becomes complex when several people close to the buyer hold contradictory opinions and the buyer would like to please them all.

The second factor is *unanticipated situational factors* that may erupt to change the purchase intention. A consumer might lose his or her job, some other purchase might become more urgent, or a store salesperson may turn him or her off. Preferences and even purchase intentions are not completely reliable predictors of purchase behaviour.

A consumer's decision to modify, postpone, or avoid a purchase decision is heavily influenced by *perceived risk*.[42] The amount of perceived risk varies with the amount of money at stake, the amount of attribute uncertainty, and the amount of consumer self-confidence. Consumers develop routines for reducing risk, such as decision avoidance, information gathering from friends, and preference for national brand names and warranties. Marketers must understand the factors that provoke a feeling of risk in consumers and provide information and support to reduce the perceived risk.

In executing a purchase intention, the consumer may make up to five purchase subdecisions: a *brand decision* (brand A), *vendor decision* (dealer 2), *quantity decision* (one computer), *timing decision* (weekend), and *payment-method decision* (credit card). Purchases of everyday products involve fewer decisions and less deliberation. For example, in buying sugar, a consumer gives little thought to the vendor or payment method.

POSTPURCHASE BEHAVIOUR

After purchasing the product, the consumer will experience some level of satisfaction or dissatisfaction. The marketer's job does not end when the product is bought. Marketers must monitor postpurchase satisfaction, postpurchase actions, and postpurchase product uses.

Postpurchase Satisfaction

What determines whether the buyer will be highly satisfied, somewhat satisfied, or dissatisfied with a purchase? The buyer's satisfaction is a function of the closeness between the buyer's expectations and the product's perceived performance.[43] If performance falls short of expectations, the customer is *disappointed*; if it meets expectations, the customer is *satisfied*; if it exceeds expectations, the customer is *delighted*. These feelings make a difference in whether the customer buys the product again and talks favourably or unfavourably about the product to others.

Consumers form their expectations on the basis of messages received from sellers, friends, and other information sources. The larger the gap between expectations and performance, the greater the consumer's dissatisfaction. Here the consumer's coping style comes into play. Some consumers magnify the gap when the product is not perfect, and they are highly dissatisfied. Other consumers minimize the gap and are less dissatisfied.[44]

The importance of postpurchase satisfaction suggests that product claims must truthfully represent the product's likely performance. Some sellers might even understate performance levels so that consumers experience higher-than-expected satisfaction with the product.

Postpurchase Actions

The consumer's satisfaction or dissatisfaction with the product will influence subsequent behaviour. If the consumer is satisfied, he or she will exhibit a higher probability of purchasing the product again. For example, data on automobile brand choice show a high correlation between being highly satisfied with the last brand bought and intention to rebuy the brand. One survey showed that 75 percent of Toyota buyers were highly satisfied and about 75 percent intended to buy a Toyota again; 35 percent of Chevrolet buyers were highly satisfied and about 35 percent intended to buy a Chevrolet again. The satisfied customer will also tend to say good things about the brand to others. Marketers say: "Our best advertisement is a satisfied customer."[45]

Dissatisfied consumers may abandon or return the product. They may seek information that confirms its high value. They may take public action by complaining to the company, going to a lawyer, or complaining to other groups (such as business, private, or government agencies). Private actions include making a decision to stop buying the product (*exit option*) or warning friends (*voice option*).[46] In all these cases, the seller has done a poor job of satisfying the customer.[47]

Postpurchase communications to buyers have been shown to result in fewer product returns and order cancellations.[48] Computer companies, for example, can send a letter to new computer owners congratulating them on having selected a fine computer. They can place ads showing satisfied brand owners. They can solicit customer suggestions for improvements and list the location of available services. They can write instruction booklets that are intelligible. They can send owners a magazine containing articles describing new computer applications. In addition, they can provide good channels for speedy redress of customer grievances.

Postpurchase Use and Disposal

Marketers should also monitor how buyers use and dispose of the product (Figure 6-6). If consumers store the product in a closet, the product is probably not very satisfying,

Toyota Canada
www.toyota.ca

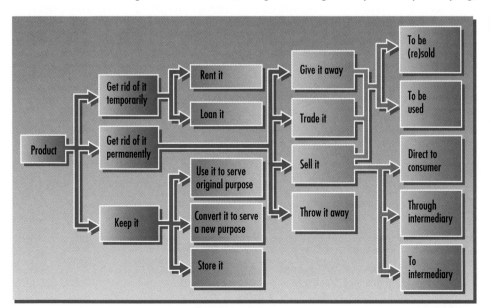

FIGURE 6.6

How Customers Use or Dispose of Products

Source: From Jacob Jacoby, Carol K. Berning, and Thomas F. Dietvorst, "What about Disposition?" *Journal of Marketing,* July 1977, p. 23. Reprinted with permission of the American Marketing Association.

chapter 6
Analyzing Consumer
Markets and Buyer
Behaviour

and word-of-mouth will not be strong. If they sell or trade the product, new-product sales will be depressed. Consumers may also find new uses for the product. For years Avon's customers have been spreading the word that Skin-So-Soft bath oil and moisturizer is a terrific insect repellent.[49]

If consumers throw the product away, the marketer needs to know how they dispose of it, especially if it can hurt the environment (as in the case with beverage containers and disposable diapers). Increased public awareness of recycling and ecological concerns as well as consumer complaints about having to throw away beautiful bottles led French perfume maker Rochas to think about introducing a new refillable fragrance line.

SUMMARY

1. Before developing their marketing plans, marketers need to study consumer markets and consumer behaviour. In analyzing consumer markets, firms need to research who constitutes the market (occupants), what the market buys (objects), why the market buys (objectives), who participates in the buying (organizations), how the market buys (operations), when the market buys (occasions), and where the market buys (outlets).

2. Consumer behaviour is influenced by four factors: cultural (culture, subculture, and social class), social (reference groups, family, and social roles and statuses), personal (age, stage in the life cycle, occupation, economic circumstances, lifestyle, personality, and self-concept), and psychological (motivation, perception, learning, beliefs, and attitudes). Research into all these factors can provide clues as to how to reach and serve consumers more effectively.

3. To understand how consumers actually make their buying decisions, marketers must identify who makes and has input into the buying decision; people can be initiators, influencers, deciders, buyers, or users, and different marketing campaigns might be targeted to each type of person. Marketers must also examine buyers' levels of involvement and the number of brands available to determine whether consumers are engaging in complex buying behaviour, dissonance-reducing buying behaviour, habitual buying behaviour, or variety-seeking buying behaviour.

4. The typical buying process consists of the following sequence of events: problem recognition, information search, evaluation of alternatives, purchase decision, and postpurchase behaviour. The marketers's job is to understand the buyer's behaviour at each stage and what influences are operating. The attitudes of others, unanticipated situational factors, and perceived risk may all affect the decision to buy, as will consumers' levels of postpurchase satisfaction and postpurchase actions on the part of the company. Satisfied customers will continue to purchase; dissatisfied customers will stop purchasing the product and are likely to spread the word among their friends. For this reaon, companies must work to ensure customer satisfaction at all levels of the buying process.

APPLICATIONS

CHAPTER CONCEPTS

1. Use the appropriate components of the model of buyer behaviour in the chapter (Figure 6-1) to explain the following consumer behaviours:

   a. Bird's nest soup (which is made from dried bird spittle) is not generally viewed as a delicacy in North America, but honey (which is regurgitated nectar) is highly esteemed.

b. Some consumers shop in a broad variety of stores while other stick to a few known stores.

c. Some products are purchased after extensive searching, while others are bought at a moment's notice.

d. Two people are exposed to the same ad—one notices and processes the ad, while the other is unaware of its existence.

2. How could a marketing manager for each of the following organizations use Maslow's needs hierarchy to develop marketing strategy?

   a. Canadian Cancer Society

   b. Revlon cosmetics

   c. Canada Life Assurance Company

   d. Girl Guides

   e. Gap jeans

3. Which of the following products are susceptible to the most post-purchase dissonance by consumers? Why? How might retailers reducing post-purchase dissonance for those products?

   a. Jaguar

   b. Tide detergent

   c. Sony CD player

   d. Encyclopaedia Britannica

   e. Head and Shoulders shampoo

4. Select a low-involvement brand name product (e.g., Windsor salt, Heinz Ketchup) that is frequently purchased by consumers and assume that your company is its competitive challenger. What actions can you recommend to convince consumers to switch to your brand? What counteractions would you recommend to the original company to persuade its customers not to switch brands?

MARKETING AND ADVERTISING

1. Business travellers have specific needs to be addressed through buying behaviour, as this Sheraton Four Points Hotels ad indicates. What personal and psychological factors in the buying process have been incorporated into this ad? In terms of the

Figure 1

buying decision for hotel accommodations during a business trip, which role or roles are being addressed by this ad? Which stage of the consumer buying process is this ad most likely geared toward? Why?

FOCUS ON TECHNOLOGY

Cookies—tiny bits of data about online activities that are stored on a user's computer—are controversial. Online marketers like cookies because they reveal what consumers are buying, which sites they are visiting, and other personal details. Based on cookie data, CDnow and Indigo Books are two of a growing number of marketers that can create personalized Web pages geared to individual consumers' preferences and purchasing patterns.

Indigo Books
http://www.indigo.ca

Many companies post their Internet privacy policies so consumers can see how cookie data are collected and used. Still, privacy advocates worry about allowing marketers access to personal information. Consumers who use Internet browsers by Netscape and Microsoft can block cookies, but the default setting for these programs allows cookies. As a result, consumers may not even know that cookies are being stored on their computers. If you headed the marketing department at online book-seller, Indigo Books, what would you say in your privacy policy? How would you expect this policy to influence consumer attitudes and behaviour?

MARKETING FOR THE 21ST CENTURY

Psychographic research has gone digital. Marketers getting ready for the new millennium can use psychographic research tools such as SRI Consulting's iVALS and Forrester Research's Technographics to segment consumers based on technology types. The iVALS approach, for example, groups consumers into 10 segments: Wizards, Pioneers, Upstreamers, Socialites, Workers, Surfers, Mainstreamers, Sociables, Seekers, and Immigrants.

SRI Consulting
http://future.sri.com/vals/surveynew.
html

iVALS
http://future.sri.com/ vals/ivals.segs.
html

To see how iVALS operates, visit SRI Consulting's Web site and take the latest survey, which includes questions about new media. Also examine the section on iVALS types. Why would marketers want to use this type of psychographic segmentation? Which marketers (or products) would benefit most from the application of iVALS segmentation? Why?

YOU'RE THE MARKETER:
SONIC MARKETING PLAN

Every marketer has to study consumer markets and behaviour prior to developing its marketing plan. This enables marketers to understand who constitutes the market, what and why the market buys, who participates in the buying, and how, when, and where the market buys.

You are responsible for researching and analyzing the market for Sonic's shelf stereos. Look again at the company's current situation, then answer these questions about the market and buyer behaviour (noting the need for additional research where necessary):

■ What cultural, social, personal, and psychological factors have the most influence on buyers of shelf stereos? What research tools would help you better understand the effect on buyer attitudes and behaviour?

■ Which specific factors should Sonic's marketing plan focus on?

■ What buying roles and buying behaviours relate to shelf stereo products?

- What kind of marketing activities should Sonic plan to coincide with each stage of the consumer buying process?

- After you have analyzed your markets and consumer behaviour, consider the implications for Sonic's marketing efforts. As your instructor directs, summarize your findings and conclusions in a written marketing plan or type them into the Marketing Situation, SWOT/Issue Analysis, and Target Markets/Positioning sections of the Marketing Plan Pro software.

Analyzing Business Markets and Business Buying Behaviour

PROFILE:

Canadian Marketing Excellence

In 1997, STS Systems Ltd. of Pointe-Claire, Quebec was given a special citation for its product and marketing excellence in the *Canadian Business* "Entrepreneur of the Year" award. STS is a firm that epitomizes the axiom: Marketing thinking is shifting from trying to maximize company profit from each transaction to maximizing the mutual profit from each relationship. STS is an exemplar of a firm that has marketing excellence, product and service quality, relationship marketing, marketing technology-based products, marketing with technology, and a global perspective.

STS Systems Ltd. supplies software products that help retailers track warehouse inventory, clothing prices, store performance, and customers. STS Systems has more than 300 retail clients, some large, some small, including such well-known names as Ralph Lauren and Tommy Hilfiger. In fact, more than 85 percent of its revenues come from its U.S. sales. The firm is poised on the brink of global expansion and has just opened new offices in the U.K.

What is the secret of STS' success? Simply the ability to understand its customers' needs and challenges. STS finds total solutions to customers' problems, providing comprehensive training and implementation support for its software solutions, all with 24-hour service. The firm also publishes two magazines, *The Retailer* and *Response,* that help retailers stay abreast of industry trends.

STS believes it will continue to lead the industry because it invests in its customers' future through ongoing R&D. As the firm notes, "While serving current customers on legacy and other systems, [our 120 development specialists] are also working on the next generation of products, leveraging the speed, accessibility and flexibility of the Internet to create better products for retailers.

To learn more about STS Systems, visit their Web page at: *http://www.stssystems.com/.*

Sources: "Fashion Police," *Canadian Business,* December 26, 1998, p. 65, *http://www.stssystems.com/.*

In this chapter, we examine the following questions:

- What is the business market, and how does it differ from the consumer market?

- What buying situations do organizational buyers face?

- Who participates in the business buying process?

- What are the major influences on organizational buyers?

- How do business buyers make their decisions?

- How do institutions and government agencies do their buying?

STS Systems
www.stssystems.com

Business organizations do not only sell. They also buy vast quantities of raw materials, manufactured components, plant and equipment, supplies, and business services. There are over 14 million buying organizations in North America alone. Sellers need to understand these organizations' needs, resources, policies, and buying procedures.

WHAT IS ORGANIZATIONAL BUYING?

Webster and Wind define organizational buying as follows:

- *Organizational buying* is the decision-making process by which formal organizations establish the need for purchased products and services and identify, evaluate, and choose among alternative brands and suppliers.[1]

Although no two companies buy in the same way, the seller hopes to identify clusters of business firms that buy in similar ways to permit marketing strategy targeting.

THE BUSINESS MARKET VERSUS THE CONSUMER MARKET

The *business market* consists of all the organizations that acquire goods and services used in the production of other products or services that are sold, rented, or supplied to others. The major industries comprising the business market are agriculture, forestry, and fisheries; mining; manufacturing; construction; transportation; communication; public utilities; banking, finance, and insurance; distribution; and services.

More dollars and items are involved in sales to business buyers than to consumers. Consider the process of producing and selling a simple pair of shoes. Hide dealers must

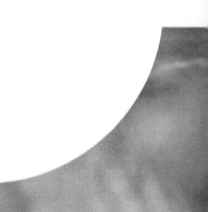

sell hides to tanners, who sell leather to shoe manufacturers, who sell shoes to whole-salers, who sell shoes to retailers, who finally sell them to consumers. Each party in the supply chain also must buy many other goods and services.

Business markets have several characteristics that contrast sharply with consumer markets.

- *Fewer buyers.* The business marketer normally deals with far fewer buyers than the consumer marketer does: Goodyear Tire Company's fate depends on getting an order from one of the big three automakers.

- *Larger buyers.* A few large buyers do most of the purchasing in such industries as aircraft engines and defence weapons.

- *Close supplier-customer relationship.* Because of the smaller customer base and the importance and power of the larger customers, suppliers are frequently expected to customize their offerings to individual business customer needs. Sometimes the buyers require the sellers to change their practices and performance. In recent years, relationships between customers and suppliers have been changing from down-right adversarial to close and chummy.

- **Motoman Inc. and Stillwater Technologies.** Motoman Inc., a leading sup-plier of industry robotic systems, and Stillwater Technologies, a contract tool-ing and machinery company and a key supplier to Motoman, are tightly integrated. Not only do they occupy office and manufacturing space in the same facility, but also their telephone and computer systems are linked, and they share a common lobby, conference room, and employee cafeteria. Philip V. Morrison, chairman and CEO of Motoman, says it's like "a joint venture without the paperwork." Short delivery distances are just one benefit of the unusual partnership. Also key is the fact that employees of both companies have ready access to each other and can share ideas on improving quality and reducing costs. This close relationship has also opened the door to new opportunities. Both companies had been doing work for Honda Motor Co. and Honda suggested that the two work together on systems projects. The symbiotic relationship makes the two bigger than they are individually.[2]

- *Geographically concentrated buyers.* More than half of Canadian business buyers are concentrated in eight metropolitan areas between Windsor and Quebec. Industries such as petroleum, rubber, and steel show an even greater geographical concen-tration. Most agricultural output comes from relatively few provinces. This geographical concentration of producers helps to reduce selling costs. At the same time, business marketers need to monitor regional shifts of certain industries, as when labour-intensive companies migrate to lower-wage provinces and towns.

- *Derived demand.* The demand for business goods is ultimately derived from the de-mand for consumer goods. For this reason, the business marketer must closely monitor the buying patterns of ultimate consumers. For instance, automakers are driving the boom in demand for steel-bar products. Much of that demand is derived from consumers' continued love affair with minivans, SUVs, and other light trucks, which consume far more steel than cars. Demand also depends on the needs of busi-ness customers. Compaq's profits fell in the first quarter of 1999 as the result of two forces: falling PC prices and fewer computers being purchased by corporations.[3]

- *Inelastic demand.* The total demand for many business goods and services is in-elastic—that is, not much affected by price changes. Shoe manufacturers are not going to buy much more leather if the price of leather falls. Nor are they going to buy much less leather if the price rises unless they can find satisfactory substitutes. Demand is especially inelastic in the short run because producers cannot make quick changes in production methods. Demand is also inelastic for business goods that represent a small percentage of the item's total cost.

- *Fluctuating demand.* The demand for business goods and services tends to be more volatile than the demand for consumer goods and services. A given percentage increase in consumer demand can lead to a much larger percentage increase in the

Motoman Inc.
www.motoman.com

demand for plant and equipment necessary to produce the additional output. Economists refer to this as the *acceleration effect*. Sometimes a rise of only 10 percent in consumer demand can cause as much as a 200 percent rise in business demand for products in the next period; a 10 percent fall in consumer demand may cause a complete collapse in business demand.

■ *Professional purchasing*. Business goods are purchased by trained purchasing agents, who must follow the organization's purchasing policies, constraints, and requirements. Many of the buying instruments—for example, requests for quotations, proposals, and purchase contracts—are not typically found in consumer buying.

Professional buyers spend their professional lives learning how to buy better. Many belong to the Purchasing Management Association of Canada (PMAC), which seeks to improve professional buyers' effectiveness and status. This means that business marketers have to provide greater technical data about their product and its advantages over competitors' products. Business marketers now put their products, prices, and other information on the Internet. Purchasing agents and brokers are able to access more information, more easily, than ever before. For example:[4]

Purchasing Management Association of Canada
www.pmac.ca

Cisco Systems
www.cisco.com

■ **Cisco Systems Inc.** Since mid-1996 Cisco Systems Inc. has moved 57 percent of its sales in routers, switches, and other gear, onto the Web. Its goal for 1999 is 80 percent. When Cisco first offered routers and switches over its new business-to-business Web site, Cisco Connection Online, customers quickly saw the advantage of seeing prices and configuring products electronically. They simply click onto a program called Configuration Agent, which walks them through the dozen major components that go into a router. If they choose the wrong combination of circuit boards, the program posts an error message and guides them to an acceptable choice. Once the right item is selected, its current price pops up automatically. At Sprint, a major customer of Cisco, it used to take 60 days from the signing of a contract to complete a networking project. Now, thanks partly to the efficiency of ordering Cisco equipment online, it takes 35 to 45 days.

Canadian Tourism Exchange
www.ctc-ctx.com

■ **The Canadian Tourism Commission's** new Web site, called the Canadian Tourism Exchange, allows companies from across the country to find up-to-date information about each other's offerings and make connections to others operating in Canada's tourism industry. The site also allows firms to access reports, statistics and industry news in addition to opportunities to advertise and promote themselves. The Exchange expects to have 10 000 registered members by the end of 2000, but hope to see the numbers rise to over 40 000. As Doug Fyfe, president and CEO of the Commission, notes, "Today, more and more Canadians in tourism are turning to the Internet to overcome the communications difficulties that many in the industry face due to Canada's geographical vastness."

■ *Several buying influences*. More people typically influence business buying decisions. Buying committees consisting of technical experts and even senior management are common in the purchase of major goods. Business marketers must send well-trained sales representatives and often sales teams to deal with the well-trained buyers. Personal selling usually serves as the main marketing tool. For example, Phelps Dodge (a metal supplier) pursues an "account management approach" in its attempt to reach the key people who influence their customers' buying decisions.[5]

■ **Cutler-Hammer.** Cutler-Hammer is a leader in the team-selling concept. Cutler-Hammer supplies circuit breakers, motor starters, and other electrical equipment to heavy industrial manufacturers such as Ford Motor. In response to the growing complexity and proliferation of its products, C-H developed "pods" of salespeople focused on a particular geographical region, industry, or market concentration. Each individual brought a degree of expertise about a product or service that the other members of the team could take to the

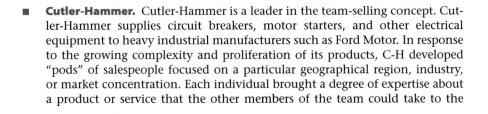

customer. Now the salespeople could leverage the knowledge of co-workers to sell to increasingly sophisticated buying teams instead of working in isolation.[6]

- *Multiple sales calls:* Because more people are involved in the selling process, it takes multiple sales calls to win most business orders, and the sales cycle can take years. A study by McGraw-Hill showed that it takes 4 to 4.5 calls to close an average industrial sale. In the case of capital equipment sales for large projects, it may take multiple attempts to fund a project, and the sales cycle, between quoting a job and delivering the product, is often measured in years.[7]

  Business marketers also need to remember that women and minorities now account for a significant share of decision makers. A study by Penton publishing shows that women and minorities now account for 43 percent of all managers, engineers, and purchasing agents, up from 35 percent in 1987.[8]

- *Direct purchasing.* Business buyers often buy directly from manufacturers rather than through intermediaries, especially items that are technically complex and/or expensive (such as mainframes or aircraft).

- *Reciprocity.* Business buyers often select suppliers who also buy from them. An example would be a paper manufacturer that buys chemicals from a chemical company that buys a considerable amount of its paper.

- *Leasing.* Many industrial buyers lease heavy equipment like machinery and trucks instead of buying it. The lessee gains a number of advantages: conserving capital, getting the latest products, receiving better service, and gaining some tax advantages. The lessor often ends up with a larger net income and the chance to sell to customers who could not afford outright purchase.

BUYING SITUATIONS

The business buyer faces many decisions in making a purchase. The number of decisions depends on the type of buying situation. Robinson and others distinguish three types of buying situations: the straight rebuy, modified rebuy, and new task.[9]

- *Straight rebuy.* The *straight rebuy* is a buying situation in which the purchasing department reorders on a routine basis (e.g., office supplies, bulk chemicals). The buyer chooses from suppliers on an "approved list." These suppliers make an effort to maintain product and service quality. They often propose automatic reordering systems so that the purchasing agent will save reordering time. The "out-suppliers" attempt to offer something new or to exploit dissatisfaction with a current supplier. Out-suppliers try to get a small order and then enlarge their purchase share over time.

- *Modified rebuy.* The *modified rebuy* is a situation in which the buyer wants to modify product specifications, prices, delivery requirements, or other terms. The modified rebuy usually involves additional decision participants on both sides. The in-suppliers become nervous and must to protect the account. The out-suppliers see an opportunity to propose a better offer to gain some business.

- *New task.* The *new task* is a buying situation in which a purchaser buys a product or service for the first time (e.g., office building, new security system). The greater the cost and/or risk, the larger the number of decision participants and the greater their information gathering—and therefore the longer the time to decision completion.[10]

  New-task buying passes through several stages: awareness, interest, evaluation, trial, and adoption.[11] Communication tools' effectiveness varies at each stage. Mass media are most important during the initial awareness stage; salespeople have their greatest impact at the interest stage; and technical sources are the most important during the evaluation stage.

  The business buyer makes the fewest decisions in the straight-rebuy situation and the most in the new-task situation. In the new-task situation, the buyer must determine product specifications, price limits, delivery terms and times, service terms, payment terms, order quantities, acceptable suppliers, and the selected supplier. Different decision participants influence each decision, and the order varies in which these decisions are made. The new-task situation is the marketer's greatest opportunity and challenge. The marketer tries to reach as many key buying influencers as possible and provide helpful information and assistance. Because of the complicated selling involved in the new task, many companies use a *missionary sales force* consisting of their best salespeople.

SYSTEMS BUYING AND SELLING

Many business buyers prefer to buy a total solution to their problem from one seller. Called *systems buying*, this practice originated with government purchases of major weapons and communication systems. The government would solicit bids from prime contractors, who would assemble the package or system. The contractor who was awarded the contract would be responsible for bidding out and assembling the system's subcomponents from second-tier contractors. The prime contractor would thus provide a "turnkey solution," so called because the buyer simply had to turn one key to get the job done.

Sellers have increasingly recognized that buyers like to purchase in this way and many have adopted systems selling as a marketing tool. Systems selling can take different forms. For example, many autoparts manufacturers now sell whole systems, such as the seating system, the braking system, or the door system. A variant on systems selling is systems contracting, where a single supply source provides the buyer with his or her entire requirement of MRO (maintenance, repair, operating) supplies. The customer benefits from reduced costs because the seller maintains the inventory. Savings also result from reduced time spent on supplier selection and from price protection over the term of the contract. The seller benefits from lower operating costs because of a steady demand and reduced paperwork. Consider the following example:

■ **SNC Lavalin Group Inc.** Systems selling is a key marketing strategy in bidding to build large-scale industrial and infrastructure projects, such as airports, highways, dams, steel factories, irrigation systems, sanitation systems, pipelines, utilities, and even new towns. Project engineering firms must compete on price, quality, reliability, and other attributes to win contracts. Ontario's first privatized highway, #407, for example, was built by a consortium of engineering firms including the giant Spanish construction firm, Grupo Ferrovial SA, Canada's largest engineering construction firm, SNC Lavalin Group Inc. of Montreal, and a subsidiary of Caisse de depot du Quebec. The consortium used a systems selling approach called *Build/Own/Operate (BOT)*. They raised the financing for the project, they built it, and now they operate the toll highway. Canadian engineering firms have been highly successful in winning similar projects overseas including the recently constructed airport in Budapest, harbours in Malaysia, and irrigation and power projects in Indonesia.[12]

SNC Lavalin Group Inc.
www.snc-lavalin.com

PARTICIPANTS IN THE BUSINESS BUYING PROCESS

Who does the buying of the trillions of dollars' worth of goods and services needed by business organizations? Purchasing agents are influential in straight-rebuy and modified-rebuy situations, while other department personnel are more influential in new-buy situations. Engineering personnel usually have major influence in selecting product components, and purchasing agents dominate in selecting suppliers.[13]

THE BUYING CENTRE

Webster and Wind call the decision-making unit of a buying organization the *buying centre*. The buying centre is composed of "all those individuals and groups who participate in the purchasing decision-making process, who share some common goals and the risks arising from the decisions."[14] The buying centre includes all members of the organization who play any of seven roles in the purchase decision process.[15]

- *Initiators.* Those who request that something be purchased. They may be users or others in the organization.
- *Users.* Those who will use the product or service. In many cases, the users initiate the buying proposal and help define the product requirements.
- *Influencers.* People who influence the buying decision. They often help define specifications and also provide information for evaluating alternatives. Technical personnel are particularly important influencers.
- *Deciders.* People who decide on product requirements and/or on suppliers.
- *Approvers.* People who authorize the proposed actions of deciders or buyers.
- *Buyers.* People who have formal authority to select the supplier and arrange the purchase terms. Buyers may help shape product specifications, but they play their major role in selecting vendors and negotiating. In more complex purchases, the buyers might include high-level managers participating in the negotiations.
- *Gatekeepers.* People who have the power to prevent sellers or information from reaching members of the buying centre. For example, purchasing agents, receptionists, and telephone operators may prevent salespersons from contacting users or deciders.

The average number of people involved in a buying decision ranges from about three (for services and items used in day-to-day operations) to almost five (for such high-ticket purchases as construction work and machinery). There is also a trend toward team-based buying; another survey found that 87 percent of the purchasing executives at Fortune 1000 companies expect teams of people from different departments and functions to be making buying decisions in the year 2000.[16]

To target their efforts properly, business marketers have to figure out: Who are the major decision participants? What decisions do they influence? What is their level of influence? What evaluation criteria do they use? Consider the following example: A company sells nonwoven disposable surgical gowns to hospitals. The hospital personnel who participate in this buying decision include the vice-president of purchasing, the operating-room administrator, and the surgeons. The vice-president of purchasing analyzes whether the hospital should buy disposable gowns or reusable gowns. If the findings favour disposable gowns, then the operating-room administrator compares various competitors' products and prices and makes a choice. This administrator considers absorbency, antiseptic quality, design, and cost, and normally buys the brand that meets the functional requirements at the lowest cost. Surgeons influence the decision retroactively by reporting their satisfaction with the particular brand.

When a buying centre includes many participants, the business marketer will not have the time or resources to reach all of them. Small sellers concentrate on reaching the *key buying influencers.* Larger sellers go for *multilevel in-depth selling* to reach as many participants as possible. Their salespeople virtually "live" with their high-volume customers. Companies will have to rely more heavily on their communications program to reach hidden buying influences and keep their current customers sold.[17]

Business marketers must periodically review their assumptions about different buying centre participants. For years, Kodak sold X-ray film to hospital lab technicians. Kodak did not notice that the decision was increasingly being made by professional administrators. As sales declined, Kodak hurriedly revised its market target strategy.

MAJOR INFLUENCES

Business buyers respond to many influences when they make their decisions. When supplier offerings are similar, business buyers can satisfy the purchasing requirements with any supplier, and they place more weight on the personal treatment they receive. Where supplier offerings differ substantially, business buyers are more accountable for their choices and pay more attention to economic factors.

Kodak Canada
www.kodak.ca

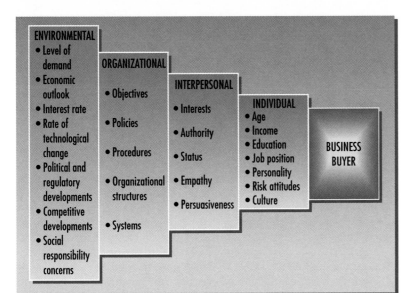

FIGURE 7.1

Major Influences on Business
Buying Behaviour

Business buyers respond to four main influences: environmental, organizational, interpersonal, and individual (Figure 7-1).[18]

Environmental Factors

Business buyers pay close attention to current and expected economic factors, such as the level of production, investment, consumer spending, and the interest rate. In a recession, business buyers reduce their investment in plant, equipment, and inventories. Business marketers can do little to stimulate total demand in this environment. They can only fight harder to increase or maintain their share of demand.

Companies that fear a shortage of key materials are willing to buy and hold large inventories. They will sign long-term contracts with suppliers to ensure a steady flow of materials. Du Pont, Ford, Chrysler, and several other major companies regard long-term *supply planning* as a major responsibility of their purchasing managers.

Business buyers actively monitor technological, political/regulatory, and competitive developments. For example, environmental concerns cause changes in business buyer behaviour and have created opportunities to launch new businesses.

■ **Shred-Tech.** The Cambridge, Ontario firm was born when its owner found a way to turn used computers into valuable resources. It dumps them into a scrap recycling system that separates valuable metals that make up the many computer components. Although there are other recyclers around, most of the industry has concentrated on recycling low-value products such as glass or plastic. Shred-Tech extracts have value materials—gold, silver, platinum—from computers and peripheral devices. While there is a huge supply of used computers, many organizations, such as the military, were reluctant to recycle them because of the sensitive information that they might contain. However, Shred-Tech allayed such concerns since its technology destroys the hard drive that contains any confidential information. The firm won the 1998 *Financial Post's* Gold Award for Environmental Technology for its breakthrough.[19]

Shred-Tech
www.shred-tech.com

Organizational Factors

Every organization has specific purchasing objectives, policies, procedures, organizational structures, and systems. Business marketers need to be aware of the following organizational trends in the purchasing area:

Purchasing-Department Upgrading. Purchasing departments in the past occupied a low position in the management hierarchy, in spite of managing often more than

half of the company's costs. The typical firm spends about 60 percent of its net sales on purchased goods and services. However, recent competitive pressures have led many companies to upgrade their purchasing departments and elevate their administrators to vice-presidential status. Today's purchasing departments are staffed with MBAs who aspire to be CEOs—like Thomas Stallkamp, Chrysler's former executive vice president of procurement and supply, who cut costs and streamlined the auto maker's manufacturing processes. For his efforts, Stallkamp was promoted to president of the company.[20] These new, more strategically oriented purchasing departments have been changed from old-fashioned "purchasing departments" with an emphasis on buying at the lowest cost to "procurement departments" with a mission to seek the best value from fewer and better suppliers. Some multinationals have even elevated them into "strategic supply departments" with responsibility for global sourcing and partnering. At Caterpillar, purchasing, inventory control, production scheduling, and traffic have been combined into one department.

The upgrading of purchasing means that business marketers must correspondingly upgrade their sales personnel to match the higher calibre of the business buyers.

Cross-functional Roles. In a recent *Purchasing* magazine survey, most purchasing professionals described their job as less clerical, more strategic, technical, team-oriented, and involving more responsibility than ever before. "Purchasing is doing more cross-functional work than it did in the past," says David Duprey, a buyer for Anaren Microwave Inc., a producer of microwave-signal processing devices for satellite and wireless communication and defence electronics. Sixty-one percent of buyers surveyed said the buying group was more involved in new product design and development than it was five years ago. And more than half of the buyers participate in cross-functional teams, with suppliers well represented.[21]

Centralized Purchasing. In multidivisional companies, most purchasing is carried out by separate divisions because of their differing needs. Some companies, however, have started to recentralize their purchasing. Headquarters identifies materials purchased by several divisions and buys them centrally, thereby gaining more purchasing clout. The individual divisions can buy from another source if they can get a better deal, but in general centralized purchasing produces substantial savings. For the business marketer, this development means dealing with fewer and higher-level buyers. The company will use a national account sales group to deal with large corporate buyers.

Decentralized Purchasing of Small-Ticket Items. At the same time, companies are decentralizing some purchasing operations by empowering employees to purchase small-ticket items such as special binders, coffee makers, or Christmas trees. This has come about through the availability of corporate purchasing cards issued by credit card organizations. Companies distribute the cards to forepersons, clerks, and administrative assistants; the cards incorporate codes that set credit limits and restrict where they can be used. National Semiconductor's purchasing chief has noted that the cards have cut processing costs from $45 per order to a few cents. The additional benefit is that buyers and suppliers now spend less time on paperwork, so purchasing departments have more time for building partnerships.[22]

Internet Purchasing. By the millennium, business-to-business buying on "the Web" may amount to over $200 billion per year. The move to Internet purchasing has far-reaching implications for suppliers and will, no doubt, change the shape of purchasing for years to come. See the Marketing for the 21st Century box, "The Business-to-Business Cyberbuying Bazaar."

Long-Term Contracts. Business buyers are increasingly initiating or accepting long-term contracts with reliable suppliers. For example, General Motors wants to buy from fewer suppliers, who are willing to locate close to its plants and produce high-quality components. In addition, business marketers are supplying electronic data-interchange (EDI) systems to their customers. The customer can enter orders directly on the computer, and the orders are automatically transmitted to the supplier. Many hospitals order directly in this way, and so do many bookstores.

Purchasing-Performance Evaluation and Buyers' Professional Development. Many companies have set up incentive systems to reward purchasing managers for good buying performance, in much the same way that sales personnel receive bonuses

The Business-to-Business Cyberbuying Bazaar

With all the buzz about Amazon, Chapters, Virtual Vineyards, CD-Now, and other consumer online shopping venues, it's easy to lose sight of one of the most significant trends in electronic commerce: the tremendous growth of business-to-business cyber-transactions. In fact, business-to-business commerce over the Internet accounted for 78 percent of the dollar value of cyber-transactions in 1998, says Forrester Research Inc. In addition to companies posting their own Web pages on the Internet, they are establishing intranets for company members to communicate with one another, and extranets that link a company's communications and data with its regular suppliers and distributors.

So far, most of the products businesses are buying through extranet technology are MRO materials—maintenance, repair, and operations. For instance, many provincial and municipal governments purchase everything from chickens to condoms over the Internet. National Semiconductor has automated almost all of the company's 3500 monthly requisitions to buy materials ranging from the sterile booties worn in its fabrication plants to state-of-the-art software. The actual dollar amount spent on these types of MRO materials pales in comparison to the amount spent for items such as airplane parts, computer systems, and steel tubing. Yet, MRO materials make up 80 percent of business purchases and the transaction costs for order processing are high, which means there is a huge incentive to streamline the process on the Web. General Electric, one of the world's biggest purchasers, not only plans to buy all of its general operating supplies online by the year 2000, but also plans to purchase all of its industrial supplies that way. Now that General Electric Information Services (GEIS) has opened up its buying site to other companies, the company is well on its way to creating a vast electronic clearinghouse. Hundreds of thousands of firms will exchange trillions of dollars of industrial inputs—with GEIS running the show, of course.

Here, then, are just a few of the implications—both positive and negative—of business-to-business cyberpurchasing. The online business-buying juggernaut promises to:

- **Shave transaction costs** for both buyers and suppliers. A Web-powered purchasing program eliminates the paper chase associated with traditional requisition and ordering procedures. At National Semiconductor, the $110 to $375 cost of processing each paper-based requisition has been cut to just $4.50 per electronic order.

- **Reduce time between order and delivery.** Time savings are particularly dramatic for companies with many overseas suppliers. Adaptec Inc., a leading supplier of computer storage, used an extranet to tie all of its Taiwanese chip suppliers together in a kind of virtual *keiretsu*. Now messages from Adaptec flow in seconds from its headquarters to its

Asian partners, and Adaptec has reduced the time between the order and delivery of its chips from as long as 16 weeks to just 55 days—the same turnaround time for companies that build their own chips.

- **Consolidate purchasing systems.** One key motivation for GE's massive move to online purchasing has been a desire to get rid of redundancy. "We have too many purchasing systems to count," said Randy Rowe, manager of GE's corporate initiatives group. "We're looking to enable each division to manage their purchasing on extranets with financial data funnelling to a centralized platform."

- **Cut jobs** for millions of clerks and order processors. Of course, all these savings and efficiencies don't come without a price. National Semiconductor reduced its purchasing staff by more than half when it took its purchasing activities online. On the other hand, for many purchasing professionals, going online means reducing drudgery and paperwork and spending more time managing inventory and working creatively with suppliers.

- **Forge more intimate relationships** between partners and buyers. Robert Mondavi Corp. puts satellite images of its vineyards out over the extranet so that its independent growers can identify potential vineyard problems and improve the grapes Mondavi purchases from them.

- **Erode supplier-buyer loyalty.** Yet, just as the Web makes it possible for suppliers and customers to share business data and even collaborate on product design, it also has the capacity to erode decades-old customer-supplier relationships. Many firms are beginning to use the Web to search for better suppliers. Japan Airlines (JAL) has used the Internet to post orders for in-flight materials such as plastic cups. On its Web site it posts drawings and specifications in order to get business from any firm that comes across its site, rather than the usual Japanese suppliers.

- **Disintermediation**. Instead of using distributors and lengthy channels of distribution, many firms are beginning to sell their products and services directly to customers. Most of the world's major airlines, for example, have cut out travel agents and now sell tickets on-line to business and vacation travellers. The Organization for Economic Co-operation and Development (OECD) estimates that the total amount of customer expenditures carried out via e-commerce without the benefit of the services of intermediaries exceeds $2.85 trillion.

- **Level the playing field** between large and small suppliers. Today, 60 percent of Canada's small businesses are using the Internet to reduce buying costs and reach a wider range
(continued)

(continued)

of customers. For example, Image Control, a Toronto retailer that sells and recycles toner cartridges for fax machines, printers, and copiers saw its business double in the three-year period following the launch of its Web site. Today it ships products to customers in 10 countries. By using the Internet's technology to establish secure, standing information links between companies, extranets have helped firms do business with smaller suppliers. Currently most large manufacturers use electronic data interchange (EDI) to order supplies, because it provides a secure means of coding and exchanging standardized business forms. However, EDI is an expensive proprietary system; it can cost as much as $50 000 to add a single trading partner to an EDI network, compared to $1000 for a company to join GE's Trading Process Network. Moving business-to-business commerce onto the Web also levels the playing field between local and foreign suppliers since purchasers can source materials from suppliers all over the globe for no additional transaction cost.

■ **Create potential security disasters.** More than 80 percent of companies say security is the leading barrier to expanding electronic links with customers and partners. While E-mail and home banking transactions can be protected through basic encryption, the secure environment that businesses need to carry out lots of confidential interactions still doesn't exist. Protecting the database compiled by tracking Web-site visits is another key consideration. Molson discovered this lesson the hard way. It lost its entire database profiling people visiting its Web site after a server failure. Yet, the good news is that security is of such high priority that companies are spending millions of research dollars on it. Companies are creating their own defensive strategies for keeping hackers at bay. Cisco Systems, Inc., for example, specifies the types of routers, firewalls, and security

@wonder

www.nationalgeographic.com is an IBM e-business.
National Geographic covers the world. IBM Web technology brings it all home to you.

IBM

IBM Canada stresses its expertise in creating secure systems for its e-commerce customers.

procedures to safeguard extranet connections with its partners. The company goes further by sending its own security engineers to examine a partner's defences and holds the partner liable for any security breach that originates from its computer.

Sources: Dawn Walton, "Small Business Clicking on Electronic Commerce," *Globe and Mail*, May 5, 1999, p. B10. Organization for Economic Co-operation and Development, *The Economic and Social Impact of Electronic Commerce: Preliminary Findings and Research Agenda*, Paris: OECD, 1999, pp. 64-65. Robert Yoegel, "The Evolution of B-to-B Selling on the 'Net," *Target Marketing*, August 1998, p. 34. Andy Reinhardt in San Mateo, "Extranets: Log on, Link up, Save Big," *Business Week*, June 22, 1998, p. 134. Anonymous, "To Byte the Hand that Feeds," *The Economist*, January 17, 1998, pp. 61-62. John Evan Frook, "Buying Behemoth— By Shifting $5B in Spending to Extranets, GE Could Ignite a Development Frenzy," *Internetweek*, August 17, 1998, p. 1. John Jesitus, "Procuring an Edge," *Industry Week*, June 23, 1997, pp. 56-62.

for good selling performance. These systems are leading purchasing managers to increase their pressure on sellers for the best terms.

Lean Production. Many manufacturers have moved toward a new way of manufacturing called lean production, which enables them to produce a greater variety of high-quality products at lower cost, in less time, using less labour. Among the elements of this new system are just-in-time (JIT) production, stricter quality control, frequent and reliable delivery from suppliers, suppliers locating closer to major customers, computerized purchasing systems, stable production schedules made available to suppliers, and single sourcing with early supplier involvement.

The linchpin of lean production, just-in-time (JIT) inventory, has dramatically changed the way companies purchase products. Just-in-time was a method pioneered by Japanese companies in which the goal is zero inventory with 100 percent quality. JIT brings together all materials and parts needed at each stage of production at the precise time that they are required. JIT has now given way to JIT II and a further streamlining of the purchasing process. See the Marketing Insight box, "Just-In-Time II (JIT II): The Next Level of Customer-Supplier Partnerships."

Just-In-Time II (JIT II): The Next Level of Customer-Supplier Partnerships

The Bose Corp. has won numerous awards for the streamlined design of its minuscule, but powerful, stereo systems. However, the company is equally revered for having streamlined the world of purchasing and materials planning with a home-grown process called Just-In-Time II.

In 1987, Lance Dixon, the company's director of purchasing and logistics, came up with a startling idea. Why not remove the salesperson, buyer, and planner from the typical relationship Bose had with suppliers? In striving to answer this question, Dixon created JIT II, a refinement of the JIT inventory system. Rather than concentrating on reducing inventory, as JIT does, JIT II's focus is on reducing the costs and time involved in day-to-day transactions with suppliers.

The central concept of JIT II is that the supplier, at his or her own expense, places one or more full-time employees at its customer's site. These "inplants," as Dixon calls them, work full time at the customer's location and take the place of the customer's buyer and materials planner and of the supplier's sales representative. Three relationships have been streamlined into one. According to Dixon, "You no longer have information being handed off from a material planner to a buyer, who then hands it off to a salesperson, who eventually hands it off back to the plant. Three or four of those transactions are now occurring within the mind of one individual with the authority to act. It's seamless."

In addition to saving time, the use of inplants also adds value. For instance, Bose found that its inplanted suppliers provided welcome expertise in the creation of audio equipment. At the same time, Bose employees profit from the stimulus of imaginative suggestions for improved product design and engineering. Intrigued by the obvious benefits of JIT II, many other companies have since implemented it. Eventually, Lance Dixon left his job in purchasing and logistics at Bose to head up a non-profit JIT II Educational Research Center.

Among the companies now using JIT II to streamline purchasing and materials planning are IBM, JLG Industries, Intel's New Mexico Plant, S.C. Johnson Wax, and Motorola Automotive Electronics. Purchasing management at Intel's Rio Rancho, New Mexico plant has changed dramatically. Cross-functional and cross-site teams called commodity teams (CT) and equipment support teams (EST) now manage the suppliers, including international suppliers. Buyers and engineers are on the same team, usually led by a purchasing manager.

Of course, for the process to go smoothly, customers need to choose the right suppliers, and they must hire the right person from the supplier's company. John Stewart, corporate director of purchasing at JLG Industries Inc., chose suppliers that were relatively important and to whom JLG was an important customer. For efficiency, it also targeted suppliers with whom it had a high number of transactions, with the idea that JIT II could whittle the transaction time down once the supplier was on site. JLG's Stewart also advises companies to ask the right questions of potential in-plant hires to spotlight problem-solving ability. For instance, JLG asks how they would address shortage situations and how they would seek new applications for their product line. Of course, the key ingredient that greases the wheels of JIT II is "trust." Says Christ Labonte, materials manager for G&F Industries, Bose's first inplant supplier, "It's a fresh, nontraditional agreement based on trust. After people get comfortable in their partnering, they start turning up rocks they wouldn't have turned up and revealing causes that were sacred cows."

Sources: Robert Hiebeler, Thomas B. Kelly, and Charles Ketteman, *Best Practices; Building Your Business with Customer-Focused Solutions,* (New York: Arthur Anderson/Simon & Schuster, 1998) pp. 94-96. Anonymous, "Professional Profile: Intel," *Purchasing,* February 13, 1997, p. 33. Lance Dixon, "JLG Industries Offers JIT II Advice," *Purchasing,* January 15, 1998, p. 39.

Interpersonal Factors

Buying centres usually include several participants with differing interests, authority, status, empathy, and persuasiveness. The business marketer is not likely to know what kind of group dynamics occurs during the buying decision process, although whatever information he or she can discover about the personalities and interpersonal factors would be useful.

Individual Factors

Each buyer carries personal motivations, perceptions, and preferences, as influenced by the buyer's age, income, education, job position, personality, attitudes toward risk, and culture. Buyers definitely exhibit different buying styles. There are "keep-it-simple" buyers, "own-expert" buyers, "want-the-best" buyers, and "want-everything-done" buyers. Some younger, highly educated buyers are computer experts who conduct rigorous analyses of competitive proposals before choosing a supplier. Other buyers are "toughies" from the old school and pit the competing sellers against one another.

Cultural Factors

Buying factors vary from one country to another. Here are some rules of social and business etiquette that marketers should understand when doing business in other countries:[23]

France
: If you don't speak French, apologize for your lack of knowledge. The French are quite proud of their language and believe that everyone should be able to speak it.

Germany
: Germans are sticklers for titles. Try to introduce people using their full, correct title, no matter how long it is. Also, Germans shake hands at both the beginning and the end of business meetings.

Japan
: Most Japanese businesspeople know what will be discussed at a meeting, how everyone feels about it, and how it will affect their business before they even get there. The purpose of a meeting is to reach consensus. A flexible agenda is necessary so that discussions flow more freely. Foreigners should not try to adhere religiously to a set agenda.

Korea
: While doing business with Koreans, North Americans need to be sensitive to Korea's historical relationship with Japan, which made a virtual colony of the Korean peninsula. Koreans do not like foreigners to assume that their culture is the same as Japan's. However, Koreans do have great respect for Japanese business acumen, and like the Japanese, they still observe Confucian ethics based on respect for authority and the primacy of the group over the individual.

Latin America
: Although individual Latin American countries may vary in terms of business protocol, there are some commonalities. In Latin America, it's *de rigueur* to make initial face-to-face contact through an outside liaison who knows the customer's company well. The liaison, or *enchufe*, introduces the salespeople or business representatives to key players.

THE PURCHASING/PROCUREMENT PROCESS

Business buyers buy goods and services to make money, to reduce operating costs, or to satisfy a social or legal obligation. A steel company will add another furnace if it sees a chance to make more money. It will computerize its accounting system to reduce the costs of doing business. It will add pollution-control equipment to meet legal requirements.

In principle, business buyers seek to obtain the highest benefit package (economic, technical, service, and social) in relation to a market offering's costs. A business buyer's *incentive to purchase* will be greater, the greater the ratio of perceived benefits to costs—that is, the greater the perceived value. The marketer's task is to set an offering that delivers superior customer value to the target buyers.

We can distinguish between three company purchasing orientations—buying, procurement, and supply management.[24] *Buying* means executing discrete transactions with suppliers where the relationships are usually arm's length and at times adversarial. The buyer's focus is short-term and heavily tactical. The buyer is rewarded for ability to obtain the lowest price from suppliers for the given level of quality and availability. Buyers operate on the assumption that the "value pie" is fixed and they must bargain hard to achieve the largest share of the pie. Buyers use two tactics: *commoditization*, where they imply that the product is a commodity and only care about price; and *multisourcing,* where they use several sources and make them compete for share of the company's purchases. To reduce risk, these buyers follow established procedures and rely on proven vendors.

Many firms have moved to a *procurement orientation* where they simultaneously seek quality improvements and cost reductions. Rather than forcing lower supplier prices to achieve cost reductions, procurement-oriented buyers develop more collaborative relationships with a smaller number of suppliers and seek savings through better management of acquisition, conversion, and disposal costs. They work closely with their suppliers in *early supplier involvement programs* on materials handling, inventory levels, just-in-time management, and even product co-design. Procurement buyers focus their efforts on negotiating long-term contracts with major suppliers to ensure the timely flow of materials. Their goal is to establish win-win relationships with suppliers and to share any savings equitably. Within the firm, the procurement people work closely with the manufacturing group on *materials requirement planning* (MRP) to ensure that supplies arrive on time.

A *supply management orientation* involves a further broadening of purchasing's role where purchasing is less of a department and more of a strategic value-adding operation. The firm focuses on how to improve the whole value chain from raw materials to end users. Here's how one company is trying to optimize every link on the value chain:

Pioneer HiBred International Inc
www.pioneer.com

- ■ **Pioneer HiBred.** Pioneer HiBred is a major supplier of corn seed and other agricultural commodities. Its patented hybrid seeds yield 10 percent more corn than its major competitors' seeds and earn a price premium. Still, Pioneer recognizes that seeds account for only .21 cents of the farm operator's value chain. To gain more, Pioneer can explore three alternatives. (1) They can win through producing a more disease-resistant seed and charging more since this would reduce farmers' need for chemicals. (2) They can win through bundling fertilizers and chemicals in addition to seeds, but this might require certain competencies and scale they don't presently have. (3) They can win through providing value-added services, such as information. Pioneer HiBred can equip its representatives with notebook computers to provide farmers with customized information and reports. The rep can plug in the hybrid that the farmer is using along with information about his pricing, acreage, and yield characteristics. This information helps the farmer decide among alternative farming methods. As a result of an investment Pioneer made in this two-way information flow, Pioneer HiBred's share of the North American corn market has grown from 35 percent during the mid-1980s to its current level of 44 percent.[25]

It operates as a *lean enterprise* responding to demand pull rather than demand push. The supply managers determine which supplies to source internally and which to outsource. They work with a smaller group of suppliers who participate more actively in product design as well as in cost-saving programs.

STAGES IN THE PROCESS

Here we will describe the stages found in the normal buying process. Robinson et al. have identified eight stages of the industrial buying process and called them *buyphases*.[26]

These stages are shown in Table 7-1. This model is called the *buygrid* framework. The eight steps for the typical new-task buying situation are as follows.

		Buyclasses		
		New Task	Modified Rebuy	Straight Rebuy
BUYPHASES	1. Problem recognition	Yes	Maybe	No
	2. General need description	Yes	Maybe	No
	3. Product specification	Yes	Yes	Yes
	4. Supplier search	Yes	Maybe	No
	5. Proposal solicitation	Yes	Maybe	No
	6. Supplier selection	Yes	Maybe	No
	7. Order-routine specification	Yes	Maybe	No
	8. Performance review	Yes	Yes	Yes

Source: Adapted from Patrick J. Robinson, Charles W. Faris, and Yoram Wind, *Industrial Buying and Creative Marketing* (Boston: Allyn & Bacon, 1967), p. 14.

TABLE 7.1

Buygrid Framework: Major Stages (Buyphases) of the Industrial Buying Process in Relation to Major Buying Situations (Buyclasses)

Problem Recognition

The buying process begins when someone in the company recognizes a problem or need that can be met by acquiring a good or service. The recognition can be triggered by internal or external stimuli. Internally, the most common events leading to problem recognition are the following:

- The company decides to develop a new product and needs new equipment and materials.
- A machine breaks down and requires new parts.
- Purchased material turns out to be unsatisfactory, and the company searches for another supplier.
- A purchasing manager senses an opportunity to obtain lower prices or better quality.

Externally, the buyer may get new ideas at a trade show, see an ad, or receive a call from a sales representative who offers a better product or a lower price. Business marketers can stimulate problem recognition by direct mail, telemarketing, and calling on prospects.

General Need Description

Now the buyer determines the needed item's general characteristics and required quantity. For standard items, this is not a very involved process. For complex items, the buyer will work with others—engineers, users, and so on—to define the needed characteristics. These may include reliability, durability, price, or other attributes. Business marketers can assist buyers by describing how their products would meet the buyer's needs.

Product Specification

The buying organization now develops the item's technical specifications. Often, the company will assign a product-value-analysis (PVA) engineering team to the project.

- *Product value analysis* is an approach to cost reduction in which components are carefully studied to determine if they can be redesigned or standardized or made by cheaper methods of production.

The PVA team will examine the high-cost components in a given product—usually 20 percent of the parts account for 80 percent of the costs of manufacturing it. The team will also identify overdesigned product components that last longer than the product itself, then decide on the optimal product characteristics. Tightly written specifications will allow the buyer to refuse components that are too expensive or that fail to meet the specified standards.

Suppliers, too, can use product-value analysis as a tool for positioning themselves to win an account. By getting in early and influencing buyer specifications, the supplier increases its chances of being chosen.

Supplier Search

The buyer now tries to identify the most appropriate suppliers. The buyer can examine trade directories, do a computer search, phone other companies for recommendations, watch trade advertisements, and attend trade shows. However, these days the most likely place to look is on the Internet. For suppliers, this means that the playing field is levelled. Smaller suppliers have the same advantages as larger ones and are listed in the same online catalogues for a nominal fee.

WIZ-net
www.wiznet.ca

- **Worldwide Internet Solutions Network Inc.** Worldwide Internet Solutions Network Inc., better known as WIZ-net, is building a "virtual product catalogue library" that is global in coverage. At last report, in 1998, its database included full catalogues from more than 72 000 manufacturers, distributors, and industrial service providers with more than eight million product specifications. For purchasing managers, who routinely receive a half-metre-high stack of mail each day, much of it catalogues, this kind of one-stop shopping will be an incredible time saver (and price saver, since it allows easier comparison shopping). When asked by a management consultant, "Do a search for 10-cm platinum ball valves available from a Michigan source," WIZ-net found six Michigan sources for buying the exact product in about 15 seconds. More than just electric Yellow Pages, such as the Thomas Register or Industry.net, WIZ-net includes all specifications for the products right in the system and offers secure e-mail to communicate directly with vendors to ask for request for bids or to place an order. So far over 10 000 product specs are added to WIZ-net per week, and its database includes catalogues from Germany, Taiwan, the Czech Republic, and other countries.[27]

The supplier's task is to get listed in major online catalogues or services, develop a strong advertising and promotion program, and build a good reputation in the marketplace. Suppliers who lack the required production capacity or suffer from a poor reputation will be rejected. Those who qualify may be visited by the buyer's agents, who will examine the suppliers' manufacturing facilities and meet their personnel. After evaluating each company, the buyer will end up with a short list of qualified suppliers.

Proposal Solicitation

The buyer will now invite qualified suppliers to submit proposals. Where the item is complex or expensive, the buyer will require a detailed written proposal from each qualified supplier. After evaluating the proposals, the buyer will invite a few suppliers to make formal presentations.

Business marketers must thus be skilled in researching, writing, and presenting proposals. Their written proposals should be marketing documents, not just technical documents. Their oral presentations should inspire confidence, positioning their company's capabilities and resources so that they stand out from the competition.

Consider the hurdles that Xerox set up in qualifying suppliers:

- **Xerox.** Xerox qualifies only suppliers who meet the ISO 9000 quality standards (see Chapter 2). But to win the company's top award—certification status—a supplier must first complete the Xerox Multinational Supplier Quality Survey. The survey requires the supplier to issue a quality assurance manual, to adhere to continuous improvement principles, and to demonstrate effective systems implementation. Once a supplier has been qualified, it must participate in Xerox's Continuos Supplier Involvement process, in which the two companies work together to create specifications for quality, cost, delivery times, and process capability. The final step toward certification requires a supplier to undergo additional rigorous quality training and an evaluation based on the same criteria as the Malcolm Baldrige National Quality Award. Not surprisingly, only 176 suppliers worldwide have achieved the 95 percent rating required for certification as a Xerox supplier.[28]

Xerox Canada
www.xerox.ca

Supplier Selection

Before selecting a supplier, the buying centre will specify desired supplier attributes and indicate their relative importance. It will then rate suppliers on these attributes and identify the most attractive suppliers. Buying centres often use a supplier-evaluation model such as the one shown in Table 7-2.

TABLE 7.2

Attributes	Importance Weights	Poor (1)	Fair (2)	Good (3)	Excellent (4)
Price	.30				X
Supplier reputation	.20			X	
Product reliability	.30				X
Service reliability	.10		X		
Supplier flexibility	.10			X	

Rating Scale

Total score: .30(4) + .20(3) + .30(4) + .10(2) + .10(3) = 3.5

An Example of Vendor Analysis

Methods of Assessing Customer Value

1. *Internal engineering assessment:* Company's engineers use laboratory tests to estimate the product's performance characteristics. If the performance is 1.5 times better than the closest competitor's performance, the company feels that it can charge up to 1.5 times more. Weakness: ignores the fact that in different applications, the product will have different economic value.

2. *Field value-in-use assessment:* Customers are interviewed about cost elements associated with using the new product offering compared to an incumbent product. Customers assign money values to these cost elements. An example would be pricing a Caterpillar tractor against a competitor. Caterpillar tractors have less downtime, quicker repair time, more used value, etc. The task is to assess how much each element is worth to the buyer.

3. *Focus-group value assessment:* Customers in a focus group are asked what value they would put on potential market offerings.

4. *Direct survey questions:* Customers are asked to place a direct dollar value on one or more changes in the market offering.

(continued)

In practice, business buyers use a variety of methods to assess supplier value. Business marketers need to do a better job of understanding how business buyers arrive at their valuations. Three researchers who conducted a study of the main methods business marketers use to assess customer value found eight different customer value assessment methods. Companies tended to use the simpler methods although the more sophisticated ones promise to produce a more accurate picture of customer perceived value. (See the Marketing Memo on "Methods of Assessing Customer Value").

The choice and importance of different attributes varies with the type of buying situation.[29] Delivery reliability, price, and supplier reputation are highly important for *routine-order products*. For *procedural-problem products*, such as a copying machine, the three most important attributes are technical service, supplier flexibility, and product reliability. For *political-problem products* that stir rivalries in the organization (such as the choice of a computer system), the most important attributes are price, supplier reputation, product reliability, service reliability, and supplier flexibility.

The buying centre may attempt to negotiate with its preferred suppliers for better prices and terms before making the final selection. Despite moves toward strategic sourcing, partnering, and participation in cross-functional teams, buyers still spend a large chunk of their time haggling with suppliers on price. In 1998, 92 percent of buyers responding to a *Purchasing* magazine survey cited negotiating price as one of their top responsibilities. Nearly as many respondents said price remains a key criterion they use to select suppliers.[30] Marketers can counter the request for a lower price in a number of ways. They may be able to show evidence that the "life-cycle cost" of using its product is lower than that of competitors' products. They can also cite the value of the services the buyer now receives, especially where those services are superior to those offered by competitors. Here's an example of how two suppliers are using value-added services to gain a competitive edge:

- **Hewlett-Packard.** Hewlett-Packard's marketing division has developed a concept called "trusted advisor." The marketers felt that if H-P were to gain market share, it needed to move beyond selling systems to selling itself as an advisor and had to work hard to offer customers specific solutions to unique problems. What H-P has discovered since implementing the concept is that some companies want a partner and others simply want a product that works. While H-P will sell laser printers on the basis of operational excellence, it must assume an advisory role when it sells a network computer system, a more complex product. While there is no direct measure of the impact to the bottom line of cultivating the trusted-advisor approach, H-P estimates that the new way of selling has contributed to 60 percent growth of the high-end computer business at Hewlett-Packard. The company has increased its consulting business and is working on enterprise-wide projects through a series of partnerships with systems integrators and software companies.[31]

Even service companies can add value by offering an extra personal touch:

Advanced Travel Management
www.advtravel.com

- **Advanced Travel Management.** Extra service with a personal touch has helped a corporate travel agency, Advanced Travel Management (ATM), recruit a roster of high-profile, demanding clients—including NatWest Markets and DDB Needham Worldwide Inc.—who booked a combined $150 million in gross air sales in 1997. ATM encourages its agents to confirm hotel reservations, check weather reports to foresee cancelled flights, and ask if travellers need driving instructions generated from mapping software or the Internet. ATM also has developed written city guides with information on local restaurants, sporting events, hospitals, and even dentists. If a hotel that ATM has booked forgets to give a client a wake-up call and the client complains, ATM takes action. Partners Michael Share or Frank Kogen call both the hotel and the person in charge of travel at the customer's company to see if they can somehow make the client happy, and they send flowers to the client. Without spending money on an organized sales and marketing effort, this small boutique-style agency is stealing business from the likes of industry leader American Express Travel Related Services Company, Inc.[32]

As part of the buyer selection process, buying centres must decide how many suppliers to use. In the past, many companies preferred a large supplier base to ensure adequate supplies and to obtain price concessions. These companies would insist on annual negotiations for contract renewal and would often shift the amount of business they gave to each supplier from year to year. The company would normally place most of the year's order with a prime supplier, and the rest with secondary suppliers. The prime supplier would make an effort to protect its position, while the secondary suppliers would try to expand their share. Out-suppliers would try to get their foot in the door by offering an especially low price.

Increasingly, however, companies are reducing the number of suppliers. Companies such as Ford, Motorola, and Allied Signal have cut the number of suppliers anywhere from 20 to 80 percent. These companies want their chosen suppliers to be responsible for a larger component system. They want their chosen suppliers to achieve continuous quality and performance improvement while at the same time lowering the supply price each year by a given percentage. These companies expect their suppliers to work closely with them during product development and they value their suggestions.

There is even a trend toward single sourcing, using one supplier. Some newspapers, for example, get all their paper from Canada's Quebecor Inc., the newsprint, media, and printing giant. Companies that use multiple sources often cite the threat of a labour strike as the biggest deterrent to single sourcing. Another reason companies may be reluctant to use a single source is the tendency to become complacent. These companies fear that they will become too comfortable in the relationship and lose their competitive edge. Some shrewd value-added marketers have identified ways to counter this fear:

■ **GC Electronics.** GC Electronics has a "one source lowest price guarantee program," which plays up the reduced transaction and purchasing costs of using them as a single source. However, if, after being with the program for a while, distributors think they could have gotten a better deal elsewhere, GC offers them a six percent rebate if they have the quotes to substantiate their claims.[33]

Order-Routine Specification

After selecting the suppliers, the buyer negotiates the final order, listing the technical specifications, the quantity needed, the expected time of delivery, return policies, warranties, and so on. In the case of maintenance, repair, and operating items, buyers are moving toward blanket contracts rather than periodic purchase orders. A *blanket contract* establishes a long-term relationship in which the supplier promises to resupply the buyer as needed at agreed-upon prices over a specified period of time. Because the stock is held by the seller, blanket contracts are sometimes called *stockless purchase plans*. The buyer's computer automatically sends an order to the seller when stock is needed.

Blanket contracting leads to more single-source buying and ordering of more items from that single source. This system locks suppliers in tighter with the buyer and makes it difficult for out-suppliers to break in unless the buyer becomes dissatisfied with the in-supplier's prices, quality, or service.

Performance Review

The buyer periodically reviews the performance of the chosen supplier(s). Three methods are commonly used. The buyer may contact the end users and ask for their evaluations. Or the buyer may rate the supplier on several criteria using a weighted score method. Or the buyer might aggregate the cost of poor supplier performance to come up with adjusted costs of purchase, including price. The performance review may lead the buyer to continue, modify, or end the relationship with the supplier. The supplier should monitor the same variables that are monitored by the product's buyers and end users.

We have described the buying stages involved in a new-task buying situation. In modified-rebuy or straight-rebuy situations, some of these stages would be compressed or bypassed. For example, in a straight-rebuy situation, the buyer normally has a

5. *Conjoint Analysis:* Customers are asked to rank their preference for alternative market offerings or concepts. Statistical analysis is used to estimate the implicit value placed on each attribute making up the offering.

6. *Benchmarks:* Customers are shown a "benchmark" offering and then a new market offering. They are asked how much more they would pay for the new offering. They can also be asked how much less they would pay if certain features were removed from the benchmark offering.

7. *Compositional Approach:* Customers are asked to attach a monetary value to each of three alternative levels of a given attribute. This is repeated for other attributes. The values are then added together for any offer configuration.

8. *Importance Ratings:* Customers are asked to rate the importance of different attributes. They are also asked to rate the supplier firms with respect to their performance on these attributes. The company can then estimate the relative value of each competitor's offer.

Source: James C. Anderson, Dipak C. Jain, and Pradeep K. Chintagunta, "A Customer Value Assessment in Business Markets: A State-of-Practice Study," *Journal of Business-to-Business Marketing,* vol.1(1), 1993, pp. 3-29.

FIGURE 7.2

Organizational Buying Behaviour in Japan: Packaging-Machine Purchase Process

Source: "Japanese Firms Use Unique Buying Behavior," *The Japan Economic Journal*, December 23, 1980, p. 29. Reprinted by permission.

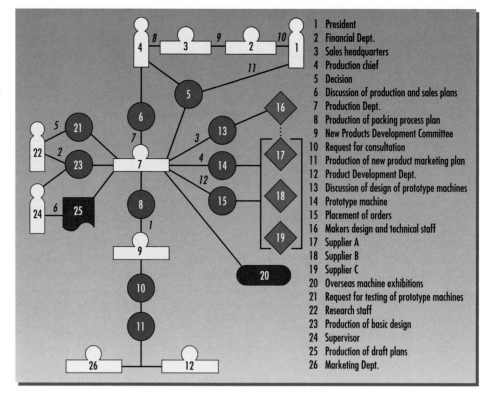

1 President
2 Financial Dept.
3 Sales headquarters
4 Production chief
5 Decision
6 Discussion of production and sales plans
7 Production Dept.
8 Production of packing process plan
9 New Products Development Committee
10 Request for consultation
11 Production of new product marketing plan
12 Product Development Dept.
13 Discussion of design of prototype machines
14 Prototype machine
15 Placement of orders
16 Makers design and technical staff
17 Supplier A
18 Supplier B
19 Supplier C
20 Overseas machine exhibitions
21 Request for testing of prototype machines
22 Research staff
23 Production of basic design
24 Supervisor
25 Production of draft plans
26 Marketing Dept.

favourite supplier or a ranked list of suppliers. Thus the supplier search and proposal solicitation stages would be skipped.

Buyflow Maps. The eight-stage buyphase model describes the major steps in the business buying process. Tracing out a *buyflow map* can provide many clues to the business marketer. A buyflow map for the purchase of a packaging machine in Japan is shown in Figure 7-2. The numbers within the icons are defined at the right. The italicized numbers between icons show the flow of events. Over 20 people in the purchasing company were involved, including the production manager and staff, new-product committee, company laboratory, marketing department, and the department for market development. The entire decision-making process took 121 days.

INSTITUTIONAL AND GOVERNMENT MARKETS

Our discussion has concentrated largely on the buying behaviour of profit-seeking companies. Much of what we said also applies to the buying practices of institutional and government organizations. However, we want to highlight certain special features found in these markets.

The *institutional market* consists of schools, hospitals, nursing homes, prisons, and other institutions that must provide goods and services to people in their care. Many of these organizations are characterized by low budgets and captive clienteles. For example, hospitals must decide what quality of food to buy for the patients. The buying objective here is not profit, since the food is provided to the patients as part of the total service package. Nor is cost minimization the sole objective because poor food will cause patients to complain and hurt the hospital's reputation. The hospital purchasing agent has to search for institutional-food vendors whose quality meets or exceeds a certain minimum standard and whose prices are low. In fact, many food vendors set up a separate division to sell to institutional buyers because of these buyers' special needs and characteristics. Thus Heinz will produce, package, and price its ketchup differently to meet the different requirements of hospitals, universities, and prisons.

Being a supplier of choice for the nation's schools or hospitals means big business.

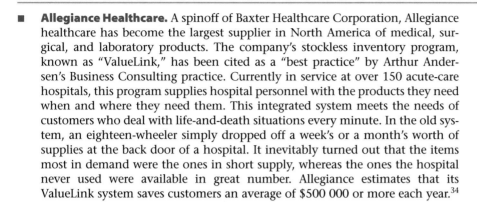

■ **Allegiance Healthcare.** A spinoff of Baxter Healthcare Corporation, Allegiance healthcare has become the largest supplier in North America of medical, surgical, and laboratory products. The company's stockless inventory program, known as "ValueLink," has been cited as a "best practice" by Arthur Andersen's Business Consulting practice. Currently in service at over 150 acute-care hospitals, this program supplies hospital personnel with the products they need when and where they need them. This integrated system meets the needs of customers who deal with life-and-death situations every minute. In the old system, an eighteen-wheeler simply dropped off a week's or a month's worth of supplies at the back door of a hospital. It inevitably turned out that the items most in demand were the ones in short supply, whereas the ones the hospital never used were available in great number. Allegiance estimates that its ValueLink system saves customers an average of \$500 000 or more each year.[34]

In most countries, government organizations are a major buyer of goods and services. Government organizations typically require suppliers to submit bids, and normally they award the contract to the lowest bidder. In some cases, the government unit will make allowance for the supplier's superior quality or reputation for completing contracts on time. Governments will also buy on a negotiated contract basis, primarily in the case of complex projects involving major R&D costs and risks, and in cases where there is little competition.

Government organizations tend to favour domestic suppliers over foreign suppliers. A major complaint of multinationals operating in Europe was that each country showed favouritism toward its nationals in spite of superior offers that were available from foreign firms. The European Economic Commission is removing this bias.

Because their spending decisions are subject to public review, government organizations require considerable paperwork from suppliers, who often complain about excessive paperwork, bureaucracy, regulations, decision-making delays, and frequent shifts in procurement personnel. However, the effort is often worth it. Governments are often countries' largest purchasers. The Internet is making the government procurement process more transparent. Public Works and Government Services Canada, the country's main purchasing branch, has an extensive Web site that outlines its mission, procedures, and principles for fair purchasing. Provincial governments also have purchasing arms. The Government of British Columbia, for example, provides information for potential suppliers and information about the tendering process on its web site. Many Canadian firms also seek to do business with the U.S. government, which buys goods and services valued at \$300 billion. That makes Uncle Sam the largest customer in the world.

Public Works and Government Services Canada http://w3.pwgsc.gc.ca

Government of British Columbi http://www.pc.gov.bc.ca/

The government purchases billions of dollars' worth of technology each year, but government decision makers often think that technology vendors haven't done their homework. One common mistake is assuming product applications are obvious to government officials. In addition, vendors don't pay enough attention to cost justification, which is a major activity for government procurement professionals. Companies gunning to be government contractors need to help government agencies see the bottom-line impact of products.

Many companies that sell to the government have not manifested a marketing orientation—for a number of reasons. The government's procurement policies have traditionally emphasized price, leading the suppliers to invest considerable effort in bringing down costs. Where product characteristics are carefully specified, product differentiation is not a marketing factor. Nor are advertising and personal selling of much consequence in winning bids.

Several companies, however, have established separate government marketing departments. Gateway 2000 is one example:

■ **Gateway 2000 Inc.** Gateway markets particular products specifically to the government. The Destination PC is an example. The Destination, which is

aimed at the K-12 education market, combines a big-screen TV with a PC that includes a wireless keyboard and remote. Salespeople who call on education departments discuss the product in terms of case studies, rather than megahertz rates and technical specifications. At the end of 1996, Gateway's government sales were an estimated 41 percent of its $230 million total for that year.[35]

Companies such as Gateway anticipate government needs and projects, participate in the product specification phase, gather competitive intelligence, prepare bids carefully, and produce strong communications to describe and enhance their companies' reputations.

SUMMARY

1. Organizational buying is the decision-making process by which formal organizations establish the need for purchased products and services, then identify, evaluate, and choose among alternative brands and suppliers. The business market consists of all the organizations that acquire goods and services used in the production of other products or services that are sold, rented, or supplied to others.

2. Compared to consumer markets, business markets generally have fewer and larger buyers, a closer customer-supplier relationship, and more geographically concentrated buyers. Demand in the business market is derived from demand in the consumer market and fluctuates with the business cycle. Nonetheless, the total demand for many business goods and services is quite price-inelastic. Business marketers need to be aware of the role of professional purchasers and their influencers, as well as the importance of direct purchasing, reciprocity, and leasing.

3. The buying centre is the decision-making unit of a buying organization. It consists of initiators, users, influencers, deciders, approvers, buyers, and gatekeepers. To sell to each of these parties, marketers must be aware of environmental, organizational, interpersonal, and individual factors. Environmental factors include the level of demand for the product, the economic outlook, interest rate, rate of technological change, political and regulatory developments, competitive developments, and social responsibility concerns. At the organizational level, marketers must be aware of their clients' objectives, policies, procedures, organizational structures, and systems, as well as trends toward purchasing-department upgrading, centralized purchasing in multidivisional companies, decentralized purchasing of small-ticket items, Internet purchasing, long-term contracts, and increasing incentives for purchasing agents. At the interpersonal level, the buying centre includes participants with different interests, authority, status, empathy, and persuasiveness. An individual's approach to the buying process is affected by his or her age, income, education, job position, personality, attitudes toward risk, and culture.

4. The buying process consists of eight stages called *buyphases*: (1) problem recognition, (2) general need description, (3) product specification, (4) supplier search, (5) proposal solicitation, (6) supplier selection, (7) order-routine specification, and (8) performance review. As business buyers become more sophisticated, business-to-business marketers must upgrade their marketing capabilities.

5. The *institutional market* consists of schools, hospitals, nursing homes, prisons, and other institutions that must provide goods and services to people in their care. Institutional buyers are now becoming more concerned with profit or cost minimization. Though attempts to computerize operations are ongoing, buyers for government organizations tend to require a great deal of paperwork from their vendors and tend to favour open bidding and domestic companies. Suppliers must be prepared to adapt their offers to the special needs and procedures found in institutional and government markets.

CHAPTER CONCEPTS

1. A professional purchasing agent's decision process is more elaborate when greater risk is involved. How would a purchasing agent be likely to behave in each of the following buying situations? For each situation, how likely is the buyer to get other people in the organization involved? Which situation is likely to take the most time for the buyer to reach a decision? Which situation is a new task, which is a modified rebuy, and which is a straight rebuy?

a. The agent needs to purchase a custom-designed machine to manufacture steering columns for vehicles.

b. The agent is purchasing brake systems from a regular supplier. The buyer has bought brake systems from this supplier before.

c. The agent is purchasing improved and updated motherboards for PCs from a recognized and well-respected supplier. However, this supplier did not supply the current motherboards.

2. The market for prescription drugs is unique in many ways. Prescription drug makers must convince a third party—a physician—to "sell" their product to the ultimate consumer, the patient. In other words, the decider in this business-to-business transaction is the physician, and drug manufacturers' promotional efforts have traditionally been directed toward this member of the buying centre. Today drug firms are appealing directly to buyers and encouraging them to ask their doctors about specific drugs. Furthermore, drug firms increasingly have to influence committees in hospitals and provincial regulators since these groups may determine which drugs physicians can prescribe. Using the outline in Figure 7-1, analyze the four major influences (environmental, organizational, interpersonal, and individual) that affect the sales efforts of a pharmaceutical manufacturer like Pfizer.

3. You are the leader of a sales team for an industrial seller of rubber hoses. Next week you are scheduled to meet with the buying team for Saturn. You have observed the following buyer behaviour on the part of members on this buying team. Prepare a sales strategy for dealing with each member of Saturn's buying team.

Dan Beavens	Bill Smith	Cathy Jones	Phil Hazard
critical	pushy	supportive	enthusiastic
picky	tough	respectful	egotistical
serious	dominating	dependable	ambitious
orderly	efficient	agreeable	excitable
exacting	decisive	conferring	dramatic
persistent	practical	pliable	undisciplined

MARKETING AND ADVERTISING

1. Business people have a wealth of choices when it comes to hiring consultants and getting financial support. The Export Development Corporation hopes to encourage Canadian businesspeople to think of them first when it comes to getting support for their global ventures. Where should the EDC place an ad like this? What other methods might it use convince potential clients of the value of using its services?

2. This Aramark ad targets businesses and organizations of all sizes. Is the information in this ad geared toward a straight rebuy, a modified rebuy, or a new task? How do you know? Would buyers, approvers, or initiators be most likely to respond to this

Figure 1   Figure 2

ad? Why? How does the ad relate to problem recognition and supplier selection in the business purchasing process? What kind of performance review might a business buyer apply to its purchasing of Aramark's services?

FOCUS ON TECHNOLOGY

Technology is changing the way government organizations buy goods and services. For example, cities like Montreal, Vancouver, Edmonton, and Toronto buy all kinds of products, such as computers and flooring. Increasingly, municipalities announce the city's needs and requests for proposals on a special page on its Web site (for example, even small towns like Kingston, Ontario have begun posting their information on-line. These sites often explain the city's purchasing process and offers standard documents for downloading by suppliers.

Determine if your municipality has a Web site (you can use the AltaVista search engine using your municipality name). Search the site to see if there is a page that describes its purchasing needs and tendering procedures. If your city/town has a site, review it and consider: What does the city require of its suppliers. How does this technology benefit the city? How does it benefit suppliers who want to provide goods and services to the city? What other information about the city's purchasing process might a supplier want to see on these pages? Do you think more government organizations and suppliers will be using this technology in the future? Why? If your town/city does not have this information on-line, find out what procedures it uses to ask for bids, to conduct supplier reviews and to carry out purchasing. In either case, what would a supplier of cleaning services (or service/product of your choice) have to do to be considered as a supplier by your municipality?

MARKETING FOR THE 21ST CENTURY

The "cyberbuying bazaar" is busier than ever before as more businesses go online in search of MRO (maintenance, repair, and operations) materials. Business-to-business electronic commerce can streamline the purchasing process for MRO items, saving time and money for both parties.

General Electric Information Services (GEIS) is a leader in helping businesses use the Internet to buy from and sell to other businesses. Visit the Electronic Marketplaces page on the GEIS Web site, where you will see various products for business-to-business buying and selling. Then click on the link to TPN Register Buyer Services, a service specifically designed for MRO items. Why would a business buyer want to access information about suppliers using the Thomas Register Classification System? Why is reducing cycle time important for MRO items? Why would a supplier want to participate in this service? What potential disadvantages can you see for suppliers?

Electronic Marketplaces
http://www.geis.com/html/emindx.
html

YOU'RE THE MARKETER: SONIC MARKETING PLAN

Like consumer marketers, business-to-business marketers need to understand their markets and the behaviour of members of the buying centre in order to develop appropriate marketing plans.

At Sonic, you have decided to investigate the business market for the company's shelf stereo systems, such as small restaurants and stores that want to play music for their customers. Given Sonic's current situation and your knowledge of business marketing, answer the following questions (noting the need for additional research where necessary):

- In addition to restaurants and stores, what other types of businesses might want to buy a shelf stereo system?

- How can you find out the overall size of business markets such as small restaurants? (Hint: Check the Industry Canada Web site and do a keyword search or try the AltaVista site. If you are interested in the U.S. as well as Canada, try the U.S. Census Web site listing of businesses by SIC—eating places are SIC 5812, for example.

- What specific needs could Sonic's product address for these businesses?

- What type of purchase would a Sonic system represent for these businesses? Who would participate in and influence this type of purchase? What are the implications for your marketing strategy?

- Think about the opportunities, threats, and issues represented by the business markets you have researched. Then, as your instructor directs, summarize your findings and conclusions in a written marketing plan or type them into the Marketing Situation, SWOT/Issue Analysis, and Target Markets/Positioning sections of the Marketing Plan Pro software.

Industry Canada Web
http://www.strategis.ic.gc.ca

U.S. Census Web
http://www.census.gov/epcd/cbp/
view/us94.txt

Dealing with the Competition

PROFILE:

Canadian
Marketing
Excellence

P oor firms ignore their competitors; average firms copy their competitors; winning firms lead their
competitors. *One of Canada's most admired companies, Montreal-based Bombardier, is certainly one of
those firms that lead the pack. Its focus on leadership is captured in its mission statement:*

Bombardier's mission is to be the leader in all the markets in which it operates. This objective will be
achieved through excellence in the fields of aerospace, rail transportation equipment, recreational products, and financial services and services related to its products and core businesses.

Its aerospace group is the largest of these, generating $6444.1 million in revenue in 1999. It has domi-
nated the regional jet market with its 50- and 70-seat aircraft and has orders on its books from airlines
around the world. Not bad considering the division was only founded in 1986 when Bombardier purchased

Canadair. Bombardier has posted annual rates of return in excess of 20 percent throughout the 1990s. It employs 22 000 people in Canada and it operates on five continents.

Authors Coley, Baghai, and White cited Bombardier in their new book *Alchemy of Growth* as among the world's 30 greatest growth companies. Bombardier, the authors say, exemplifies "three horizons" of growth: (1) maintain and expand the company's core line of business, (2) invest in R&D in emerging ventures, and (3) explore ideas that have an equal chance of either success of failure.

However, Bombardier's success doesn't mean that it flies in nothing but clear skies. It has encountered severe turbulence in recent years in the form of intense competition from its Brazilian rival Embraer. The bitter feud began in 1996. In just two years, Bombardier went from having almost a monopoly position, to having just over half the market. The market decline began when Embraer began selling its regional jets $3 million cheaper than Bombardier. Moreover, Embraer offered would-be purchasers financing deals that cut another $4.5 million off the price. How was Embraer able to do this? With export subsidies provided by the Brazilian government under its Pro-ex program that radically reduces the aerospace manufacturer's cost of borrowing money.

Not being a firm to run from a fight, Bombardier enlisted the help of the Canadian government and took the dispute to the World Trade Commission. Embraer and the Brazilian government countered these claims with accusations of their own about Canadian subsidies. In March 1999 the Commission ruled that the Brazilian program was illegal. But both firms are claiming victory. Bombardier hopes for increased sales since Embraer must revoke the subsidy on all undelivered jets. Embraer crows that since the Technology Partnerships Canada program was also ruled anti-competitive, the playing field is levelled once again. Is the "dog-fight" over? Hardly, says one Canadian analyst. "The stakes are too important for Canada, Brazil—and for the United States and Europe for that matter—to leave their aerospace companies by the wayside." It is suspected that both firms and their respective governments will find new ways to continue the battle for the skies.

Sources: Kim Hanson, "Bombardier Names as Exemplar of Growth," *Financial Post*, April 20, 1999, p. C6. Konrad Yakabuski and Heather Scoffield, "Canada, Brazil Claim Victory over Decision," *Globe and Mail*, August 3, 1999, B1, B4. "Embraer Sales, Profit Soaring," *Globe and Mail*, April 6, 1999, p. B11. "Bombardier May Come Up a Winner at Other's Expense," *Globe and Mail*, March 11, 1999, p. A8. Heather Scoffield, "Bombardier-Embraer Dogfight Heats Up," *Globe and Mail*, February 19, 1999, pp. B1, B6. Heather Scoffield, "Bombardier Faces WTO Today," *Globe and Mail*, August 2, 1999, pp. B1, B3. Konrad, Yakabuski, "Bombardier Soars on Jet Orders, But Turbulence May Loom Ahead," *Globe and Mail*, February 22, 1999, pp. B1, B5. Bombardier Web site (http://www.bombardier.com).

Companies need to know five things about the competition:

- Who are our primary competitors?
- How to ascertain their strategies, objectives, strengths, and weaknesses, and reaction patterns
- How to design a competitive intelligence system
- Whether to position as market leader, challenger, follower, or nicher
- How to balance a customer vs. competitor orientation

In the two previous chapters we examined the dynamics of consumer and business markets. This chapter examines the role competition plays and how companies position themselves relative to competitors.

**Five Forces Determining
Segment Structural
Attractiveness**

Source: Reprinted with the permission of the
Free Press, an imprint of Simon & Schuster, from
*Competitive Advantage: Creating and Sustaining
Superior Performance*, by Michael E. Porter.
Copyright © 1985 by Michael E. Porter.

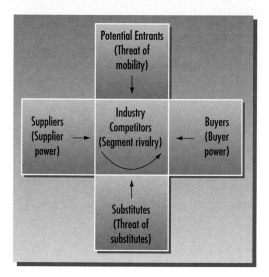

Michael Porter identified five forces that determine the intrinsic long-run profit
attractiveness of a market or market segment: industry competitors, potential entrants,
substitutes, buyers, and suppliers. His model is shown in Figure 8-1. The threats these
forces pose are as follows:

1. *Threat of intense segment rivalry.* A segment is unattractive if it already contains
   numerous, strong, or aggressive competitors. It is even more unattractive if
   the segment is stable or declining, if plant capacity additions are done in large
   increments, if fixed costs are high, if exit barriers are high, or if competitors
   have high stakes in staying in the segment. These conditions will lead to
   frequent price wars, advertising battles, and new-product introductions and
   will make it expensive to compete.

2. *Threat of new entrants.* A segment's attractiveness varies with the height of its
   entry and exit barriers.[1] The most attractive segment is one in which entry
   barriers are high and exit barriers are low (Figure 8-2). Few new firms can
   enter the industry, and poor-performing firms can easily exit. When both
   entry and exit barriers are high, profit potential is high, but firms face more
   risk because poorer-performing firms stay in and fight it out. When entry and
   exit barriers are both low, firms easily enter and leave the industry, and the
   returns are stable and low. The worst case is when entry barriers are low and
   exit barriers are high: Here firms enter during good times but find it hard to
   leave during bad times. The result is chronic overcapacity and depressed
   earnings for all.

3. *Threat of substitute products.* A segment is unattractive when there are actual or
   potential substitutes for the product. Substitutes place a limit on prices and
   on the profits that a segment can earn. The company must monitor the price

Barriers and Profitability

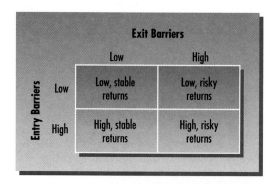

trends in the substitutes closely. If technology advances or competition increases in these substitute industries, prices and profits in the segment are likely to fall.

4. *Threat of buyers' growing bargaining power.* A segment is unattractive if the buyers possess strong or growing bargaining power. Buyers will try to force prices down, demand more quality or services, and set competitors against each other, all at the expense of seller profitability. Buyers' bargaining power grows when they become more concentrated or organized, when the product represents a significant fraction of the buyers' costs, when the product is undifferentiated, when the buyers' switching costs are low, when buyers are price sensitive because of low profits, or when buyers can integrate upstream. To protect themselves, sellers might select buyers who have the least power to negotiate or switch suppliers. A better defence consists of developing superior offers that strong buyers cannot refuse.

5. *Threat of suppliers' growing bargaining power.* A segment is unattractive if the company's suppliers are able to raise prices or reduce quantity supplied. Suppliers tend to be powerful when they are concentrated or organized, when there are few substitutes, when the supplied product is an important input, when the costs of switching suppliers are high, and when the suppliers can integrate downstream. The best defences are to build win-win relations with suppliers or use multiple supply sources.

Today, competition is not only rife but growing more intense every year. Many North American, European, and Japanese companies are setting up production in lower-cost countries and bringing cheaper goods to market.

These developments explain the current talk about "marketing warfare," and "competitive intelligence systems."[2] Because markets have become so competitive, understanding customers is no longer enough. Companies must start paying keen attention to their competitors. Successful companies design and operate systems for gathering continuous intelligence about competitors.[3]

IDENTIFYING COMPETITORS

It would seem a simple task for a company to identify its competitors. Coca-Cola knows that Pepsi-Cola is its major competitor, and Sony knows that Matsushita is a major competitor.[4] But the range of a company's actual and potential competitors is actually much broader. A company is more likely to be hurt by emerging competitors or new technologies than by current competitors.

In recent years, many businesses have failed to look to the Internet for their most formidable competitors. For instance, it was only four years ago that Barnes and Noble, Chapters, and Indigo bookstore chains were competing to see who could build the most megastores where book browsers could sink into comfortable couches and sip cappuccino. However, while these massive bookstore chains were deciding which products to stock in their cafes, Jeffrey Bezos was building an online empire called Amazon.com. Bezos' innovative new cyberstore had the advantage of offering an almost unlimited selection of books without the expense of stocking inventory. Now both Chapters and Indigo are playing catch-up in building their own on-line stores and will no doubt survive and thrive. Yet, "competitor myopia"—a focus on current competitors rather than latent ones—has rendered some businesses extinct:[5]

Encyclopedia Britannica
www.britannica.com

■ **Encyclopedia Britannica.** In 1996, 230-year-old Encyclopedia Britannica dismissed its entire home sales force after the arrival of the Internet at $12.00 a month made the idea of owning a $2000 32-volume set of books less appealing to parents. Computer-savvy kids can get their information online and from a CD-ROM, such as Microsoft's Encarta, an encyclopedia on a CD-ROM that was introduced and sold for only $75. What really smarts is that Encyclopedia Britannica had the opportunity to partner with Microsoft in providing content for Encarta, but stubbornly resisted.

Displaced But Not Discouraged: What Happens When E-Commerce Edges Out the Intermediary

Bayridge Travel in Kingston, Ontario typifies the kind of business most threatened by the advent of online selling over the Internet. In addition to having seen airline commissions drop, Bayridge Travel discovered that it must now compete against giant online travel supersites, like Expedia or Travelocity, that allow consumers to surf the Web for rock-bottom ticket prices. It is estimated that 25 percent of all Web sites, or over 100 000 sites, are related to travel. In face of this competition, Canadian travel agencies are disappearing at record rates. In 1990, there were approximately 5000 agencies across the country. By 1995, according to the Canadian Tourism Commission, the numbers had fallen to 4000. In 1997 Web surfers booked over $1350 million in travel reservations. While that's still less than one percent of the total travel market, Jupiter Communications predicts that total online travel sales will increase to $18 billion by 2002. And, as travel agents have established Web sites to reduce their own costs and expand their markets, airlines quickly reduced the commission for online sales by agencies, cutting the travel agent's revenue even further. What's more, airline Web sites are beginning to sell seats not only on their own airline but also on competitors'. Through United Airline's Web site, visitors can reserve and purchase tickets on more than 500 other airlines.

The Web is forcing change on a huge swath of businesses—mainly small businesses, at that. By facilitating direct contact between buyers and sellers, the Internet is displacing the travel agents, insurance brokers, car dealers, real estate brokers, and stockbrokers and headhunters who have traditionally been the intermediaries. There's even a fancy 17-letter word to describe the phenomenon: *disintermediation*—the demise of the intermediary. And here's a short list of some online pioneers that have helped bring it about.

www.expedia.com www.travelocity.com www.previewtravel.com	Not only offer no-hassle ways to purchase airline tickets but also have links to restaurants, hotels and local sights and sounds.
www.carpoint.com www.autodepot.ca www.edmunds.com	Provide services ranging from pricing reports and test-drive reviews to leasing options and links to financing sights.
www.owners.com http://townsearch.com/realty www.bchomesforsale.com	Real estate information is available on a wide range of sites. For example, there are "multiple listing services" available on-line for most Canadian cities. Many people use these sites to do their initial house search.
www.lifequote.com	300 surfers visit the site each month to request life insurance quotes, and 17 percent end up becoming paying customers. Most large Canadian insurance companies and brokers now offer on-line information (do a search using Yahoo.ca)
www.monster.com www.careerclick.com www.Globecareers.com www.canadacareers.com www.employment.yahoo.com	There are a number of Canadian and North American career sites. The Monster Board lists more than 50 000 jobs from over 4500 companies. Both the Globe and Mail and Southam Publishing offer on-line career listings.

What can traditional intermediaries do when facing competition from these digital sites? Businesses most threatened by the Internet use strategies that fall into a continuum. At one end are those who wholeheartedly embrace the Internet, snipping their non-cyber roots. Others are wholeheartedly rejecting the new Internet business model. Judy McLoughlin, owner of a children's bookstore, Reading in the Park, says, "I won't want to buy or sell a book I cannot touch." McLoughlin tries to gain an edge through attentiveness to customers. Most businesses fall somewhere in between. Firms, like Bayridge Travel, are becoming market nichers going after specialty markets. Rather than facing

Other publishing businesses feel similarly threatened by the encroachment of the Internet upon their territory. Web sites that offer jobs, real estate listings, and automobiles online threaten newspapers, which derive a huge portion of their revenue from classified employment, real estate, and automobile ads. And when you can get news content online for free, why should you buy a newspaper? The businesses with the most to fear from Internet technology are the world's intermediaries. See how these businesses are faring against their new, unexpected competitors in the Marketing for the Twenty-First Century box entitled, "Displaced But Not Discouraged: What Happens When E-Commerce Edges Out the Intermediary."

(continued)

increasingly low margins on airfares booked by business travellers, Bayridge Travel has decided to concentrate on vacation travellers, particularly those people taking cruise holidays. There are still high margins to be made in this segment. People in this market were often less sophisticated travellers who relied more on travel agents for advice.

Others, such as brokerage Charles Schwab, are using the Web to provide customers with a wealth of information and options while providing the value-added personalized services:

■ **Charles Schwab** Charles Schwab, the North America's largest discount stock broker, jumped onto the Internet to face a horde of price-cutting e-commerce competitors who had been there first—including E*trade and Ameritrade. Not only did Schwab face cheaper competitors, but it also had to cannibalize its own accounts. Yet, the gamble paid off because the volume of trades grew tremendously. Also, instead of simply becoming a no-frills Internet trading operation like competitors, Schwab has plied customers with a wealth of financial and company information and kept its role as an investment advisor helping customers research and manage their accounts. Schwab is even teaching courses in Web trading at some of its 270 branches.

The truth is that most people need some handholding from real persons, especially when purchasing such complex or costly products and services as cars, life insurance, or a three-week vacation that includes stops in the Galapagos Islands and Tierra del Fuego. A 1999 survey of Canadians conducted by Ernst and Young reported that 97 percent of those polled said they were still uncomfortable with sending credit card information over the Net. Another 53 percent want to see the product before they purchase. Thus, while the Internet has created a raft of new competitors for traditional intermediaries, it

has also opened up a great opportunity. While deluging consumers with more information, the Internet leaves it up to the human intermediary to lead consumers through the maze. An additional problem for Canadian consumers is the scarcity of Canadian sites. While a 1999 Angus Reid survey suggested that 90 percent of Canadian Internet users consciously sought domestic sites, only 38 percent were successful in their search and purchased from a domestic site.

Visit our Web site for the other 7,056 jobs.

globecareers.com
YOUR BEST OPPORTUNITY

New services, like The Globe and Mail career site, put pressure on traditional suppliers like placement firms.

Sources: Angus Reid and Deloitte & Touche, "Shoppers Turning to Cyberspace," *Globe and Mail Special Interest Report, E-Commerce,* March 30, 1999, pp. C1, C15. Anonymous, "Internet Taking Big Toll on Travel Agencies," *Globe and Mail Special Interest Report, E-Commerce,* March 30, 1999, p. C5. "Canadians Not Sold on E-Commerce," *CBC News Online,* March 31, 1999. Marcia Stepanek, "Rebirth of the Salesman," *Business Week,* June 22, 1998, p. 146. Evan I. Schwartz, "How Middlemen Can Come Out on Top," *Business Week,* February 9, 1998, pp. ENT4-ENT7. Bernard Warner, "Prepare for Takeoff," *Brandweek,* January 19, 1998, pp. 38-40. Ira Lewis, Janjaap Semeijn, and Alexander Talalayevsky, "The impact of Information Technology on Travel Agents," *Transportation Journal,* summer 1998, pp. 20-25. Mary J. Cronin, "The Travel Agents' Dilemma," *Fortune,* May 11, 1998, pp. 163-164. John Hughes, "Auto Dealers See Future in Internet," Marketing News, March 2, 1998, p. 13. Saroja Girishankar, "Virtual Markets Create New Roles for Distributors," *Internetweek,* April 6, 1998, p. S10. Laurie J. Flynn, "Eating Your Young," *Context,* Summer 1998, pp. 45-51.

We can examine competition by considering various levels (brand, industry, form, generic) or by looking at competition from an industry and a marketing point of view.

INDUSTRY CONCEPT OF COMPETITION

What exactly is an industry?

■ An *industry* is a group of firms that offer a product or class of products that are close substitutes for each other.

Industries are classified according to number of sellers, degree of product differentiation, presence or absence of entry and exit barriers, cost structure, degree of vertical integration, and degree of globalization.

Number of Sellers and Degree of Differentiation

The starting point for describing an industry is to specify the number of sellers and whether the product is homogeneous or highly differentiated. These characteristics give rise to four industry structure types:

- *Pure monopoly.* Only one firm provides a certain product or service in a certain country or area (Canadian Postal Service, a provincial electricity company). An unregulated monopolist might charge a high price, do little or no advertising, and offer minimal service. If partial substitutes are available and there is some danger of competition, the monopolist might invest in more service and technology. A regulated monopolist is required to charge a lower price and provide more service as a matter of public interest.

- *Oligopoly.* A small number of (usually) large firms produce products that range from highly differentiated to standardized. *Pure oligopoly* consists of a few companies producing essentially the same commodity (oil, steel). Such companies would find it hard to charge anything more than the going price. If competitors match on services, the only way to gain a competitive advantage is through lower costs. *Differentiated oligopoly* consists of a few companies producing products (autos, cameras) partially differentiated along lines of quality, features, styling, or services. Each competitor may seek leadership in one of these major attributes, attract the customers favouring that attribute, and charge a price premium for that attribute.

- *Monopolistic competition.* Many competitors are able to differentiate their offers in whole or part (restaurants, beauty shops). Competitors focus on market segments where they can meet customer needs in a superior way and command a price premium.

- *Pure competition.* Many competitors offer the same product and service (stock market, commodity market). Since there is no basis for differentiation, competitors' prices will be the same. No competitor will advertise unless advertising can create psychological differentiation (cigarettes, beer), in which case it would be more proper to describe the industry as monopolistically competitive.

An industry's competitive structure can change over time:

- **Palm Pilot.** When Palm Computing (now owned by 3Com) innovated the Palm Pilot, a hand-held computer and organizer with no keyboard, only a stylus, it started as a monopolist and rolled out over one million units in 18 months. There was simply no other product like it on the market. Soon, however, a few other companies, such as Casio and Everex, entered the market, turning it into an oligopoly. As even more competitors offer their version of the Palm Pilot, the industry will take on a monopolistically competitive structure. When demand growth slows, however, one can expect some competitors to exit, returning it to an oligopoly dominated by Palm Pilot and a few key competitors.

Entry, Mobility, Exit Barriers

Industries differ greatly in ease of entry. It is easy to open a new restaurant but difficult to enter the aircraft industry. Major *entry barriers* include high capital requirements; economies of scale; patents and licensing requirements; scarce locations, raw materials, or distributors; and reputation requirements. Even after a firm enters an industry, it might face *mobility barriers* when it tries to enter more attractive market segments.

- **Corel Corp.** Corel, the Canadian software company that forged its reputation through its CorelDRAW program, found it wasn't easy to move from this niche into the broader office-suite market. Corel acquired Word Perfect and tried to establish it as the office standard. However, it came up against software giant, Microsoft. Despite claims that Corel was the David who could

Palm Pilot
www.palmpilot.com

beat this modern-day Goliath, Corel wasn't able to get widespread adoption among original equipment manufacturers (OEMs) and couldn't get the widespread distribution or corporate acceptance that its larger rival had achieved.

Firms often face *exit barriers*,[6] such as legal or moral obligations to customers, creditors, and employees; government restrictions; low asset salvage value due to overspecialization or obsolescence; lack of alternative opportunities; high vertical integration; and emotional barriers. Many firms stay in an industry as long as they cover their variable costs and some or all of their fixed costs. Their continued presence, however, dampens profits for everyone.

Even if some firms do not want to exit the industry, they might decrease their size. Companies can try to reduce shrinkage barriers to help ailing competitors get smaller gracefully.[7]

Cost Structures

Each industry has a certain cost burden that shapes much of its strategic conduct. For example, steel making involves heavy manufacturing and raw-material costs; toy manufacturing involves heavy distribution and marketing costs. Firms will strategize to reduce these costs. The steel company with the most modern (i.e., most cost-efficient) plant will have a great advantage over other steel companies.

Degree of Vertical Integration

Companies find it advantageous to integrate backward and/or forward (*vertical integration*). Major oil producers carry on exploration, drilling, refining, chemical manufacturing, and service-station operations. Vertical integration often lowers costs and the company gains a larger share of the value-added stream. In addition, vertically integrated firms can manipulate prices and costs in different parts of the value chain to earn profits where taxes are lowest. Vertical integration can create certain disadvantages, such as high costs in certain parts of the value chain and a certain lack of flexibility.

Degree of Globalization

Some industries are highly local (such as lawn care); others are global (such as oil, aircraft engines, cameras). Companies in global industries need to compete on a global basis if they are to achieve economies of scale and keep up with the latest advances in technology.[8] Consider, for example, how U.S. forklift manufacturers lost their market leadership:

■ **The Forklift Industry.** Five companies formerly dominated the U.S. forklift market—Clark Equipment, Caterpillar, Allis Chalmers, Hyster, and Yale. By 1992, debt-burdened Clark had sold its assets and Caterpillar had become a minor partner in a venture with Mitsubishi. Only Hyster held on to its market share. By speeding up product development, concentrating on low-end models, and moving some production to job-hungry Ireland, Hyster was able to compete against Nissan, Toyota, and Komatsu. Hyster also filed an antidumping suit against Japanese models, and won the case.

MARKET CONCEPT OF COMPETITION

In addition to the industry approach, we can identify competitors using the market approach: competitors are companies that satisfy the same customer need. For example, a customer who buys a word processing package really wants "writing ability"—a need that can be satisfied by pencils, pens, typewriters, and so on. The market concept of competition opens up a broader set of actual and potential competitors.

ANALYZING COMPETITORS

Once a company identifies its primary competitors, it must ascertain their characteristics, specifically their strategies, objectives, strengths and weaknesses, and reaction patterns.

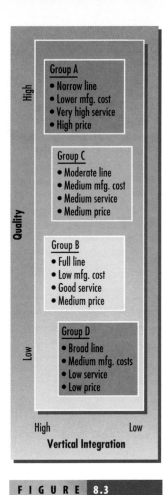

FIGURE 8.3

Strategic Groups in the Major Appliance Industry

STRATEGIES

A group of firms following the same strategy in a given target market is called a *strategic group*.[9] Suppose a company wants to enter the major appliance industry. What is its strategic group? It develops the chart shown in Figure 8-3 and discovers four strategic groups based on product quality and level of vertical integration. Group A has one competitor (Maytag), group B has three (General Electric, Whirlpool, and Sears), group C has four, and group D has of two. Important insights emerge from this exercise. First, the height of the entry barriers differs for each group. Second, if the company successfully enters a group, the members of that group become its key competitors.

A company must continuously monitor its competitors' strategies. Resourceful competitors revise their strategy through time. When U.S. automakers just about caught up in quality, Japanese automakers shifted to sensory qualities. A Ford engineer explained: "It's the turn-signal lever that doesn't wobble . . . the speed of the power window up and down . . . the feel of a climate-control knob . . . this is the next nuance of customer competition."[10]

OBJECTIVES

Once a company has identified its main competitors and their strategies, it must ask: What is each competitor seeking in the marketplace? What drives each competitor's behaviour? One useful initial assumption is that competitors strive to maximize profits. However, companies differ in the weights they put on short-term versus long-term profits. Most North American firms operate on a short-run profit-maximization model, largely because their current performance is judged by stockholders who might lose confidence, sell their stock, and cause the company's cost of capital to rise. Japanese firms operate largely on a market-share-maximization model. They receive many of their funds from banks at a lower interest rate, and in the past have been satisfied with earning lower profits. An alternative assumption is that each competitor pursues some mix of objectives: current profitability, market share growth, cash flow, technological leadership, service leadership. Knowing how a competitor weighs each objective will help the company anticipate its reactions.

Many factors shape a competitor's objectives, including size, history, current management, and financial situation. If the competitor is a division of a larger company, it is important to know whether the parent company is running it for growth or milking it.[11]

Finally, a company must monitor its competitors' expansion plans. Figure 8-4 shows a product/market battlefield map for the personal computer industry. Dell, which is a strong force in selling personal computers to individual users, is also pursuing commercial and industrial buyers and selling servers. Other incumbents may therefore want to set up mobility barriers to Dell's expansion.

FIGURE 8.4

A Competitor's Expansion Plans

	Individual Users	Commercial and Industrial	Educational
Personal Computers	Dell →		
Hardware Accessories			
Software			

STRENGTHS AND WEAKNESSES

Whether competitors can carry out their strategies and reach their goals depends on their resources and capabilities. A company needs to gather information on each competitor's strengths and weaknesses. According to the Arthur D. Little consulting firm, a firm will occupy one of six competitive positions in the target market:[12]

- *Dominant:* This firm controls the behaviour of other competitors and has a wide choice of strategic options.

- *Strong:* This firm can take independent action without endangering its long-term position and can maintain its long-term position regardless of competitors' actions.

- *Favourable:* This firm has an exploitable strength and a more-than-average opportunity to improve its position.

- *Tenable:* This firm is performing at a sufficiently satisfactory level to warrant continuing in business, but it exists at the sufferance of the dominant company and has a less-than-average opportunity to improve its position.

- *Weak:* This firm has unsatisfactory performance but an opportunity exists for improvement. The firm must change or else exit.

- *Nonviable:* This firm has unsatisfactory performance and no opportunity for improvement.

This assessment helped one company decide whom to attack in the programmable-controls market:

> The company faced three entrenched competitors: Allen Bradley, Texas Instruments, and Gould. Its research showed that Allen Bradley had an excellent reputation for technological leadership; Texas Instruments had low costs and engaged in bloody battles for market share; and Gould did a good job but not a distinguished job. The company concluded that its best target was Gould.

Table 8-1 shows the results of a company survey that asked customers to rate its three competitors, A, B, and C, on five attributes. Competitor A turns out to be well known and respected for producing high-quality products sold by a good sales force. Competitor A is poor at providing product availability and technical assistance. Competitor B is good across the board and excellent in product availability and sales force. Competitor C rates poor to fair on most attributes. This information suggests that the company could attack competitor A on product availability and technical assistance and competitor C on almost anything, but should not attack competitor B, which has no glaring weaknesses.

In general, a company should monitor three variables when analyzing each of its competitors:

- *Share of market:* The competitor's share of the target market.

- *Share of mind:* The percentage of customers who named the competitor in responding to the statement, "Name the first company that comes to mind in this industry."

- *Share of heart:* The percentage of customers who named the competitor in responding to the statement, "Name the company from whom you would prefer to buy the product."

There is an interesting relationship among these three measures. Table 8-2 shows the numbers for these three measures for the three competitors listed in Table 8-1.

	Customer Awareness	Product Quality	Product Availability	Technical Assistance	Selling Staff
Competitor A	E	E	P	P	G
Competitor B	G	G	E	G	E
Competitor C	F	P	G	F	F

Note: E = excellent, G = good, F = fair, P = poor.

TABLE 8.1

Customer's Ratings of Competitors on Key Success Factors

TABLE 8.2

Market Share, Mind Share, and
Heart Share

	MARKET SHARE			MIND SHARE			HEART SHARE		
	1997	**1998**	**1999**	**1997**	**1998**	**1999**	**1997**	**1998**	**1999**
Competitor A	50%	47%	44%	60%	58%	54%	45%	42%	39%
Competitor B	30	34	37	30	31	35	44	47	53
Competitor C	20	19	19	10	11	11	11	11	8

Competitor A enjoys the highest market share, but is slipping. A partial explanation may lie in the fact that its mind share and heart share are also slipping, probably because it is not providing good product availability and technical assistance. Competitor B is steadily gaining market share, probably due to strategies that are increasing its mind share and heart share. Competitor C seems to be stuck at a low level of market share, mind share, and heart share, probably because of its poor product and marketing attributes. We could generalize as follows: *Companies that make steady gains in mind share and heart share will inevitably make gains in market share and profitability.*

To improve market share, many companies have begun *benchmarking* their most successful competitors. The technique and its benefits are described in the Marketing Insight box "How Benchmarking Helps Improve Competitive Performance."

In searching for weaknesses, we should identify any assumptions competitors hold that are no longer valid. Some companies believe they produce the best quality in the industry when they do not. Many companies mistakenly subscribe to conventional wisdom like "Customers prefer full-line companies," "The sales force is the only important marketing tool," and "Customers value service more than price." If we know that a competitor is operating on such a wrong assumption, we can take advantage of it.

REACTION PATTERNS

Each competitor has a certain philosophy of doing business, a certain internal culture, and certain guiding beliefs. Most competitors fall into one of four categories:

1. *The laid-back competitor.* A competitor that does not react quickly or strongly to a rival's move. Air Canada and Canadian Airlines did little more than shrug when West Jet entered the market. Today, however, West Jet has become such a force that Air Canada is considering a merger with the discount airline. Reasons for slow response vary. Laid-back competitors may feel their customers are loyal; they may be milking the business; they may be slow in noticing the move; they may lack the funds to react. Rivals must try to assess the reasons for the behaviour.

2. *The selective competitor.* A competitor that reacts only to certain types of attacks. It might respond to price cuts, but not to advertising expenditure increases. Shell and Imperial Oil are selective competitors, responding only to price cuts but not to promotions. Knowing what a key competitor reacts to gives its rivals a clue as to the most feasible lines of attack.

3. *The tiger competitor.* A competitor that reacts swiftly and strongly to any assault. P&G does not let a new detergent come easily into the market. Lever Brothers found this out during its first foray into the "ultra" detergent market. Ultras are more concentrated detergents that come in smaller bottles. Retailers like them because they take up less shelf space, yet when Lever introduced its Ultra versions of Wisk and Surf, it couldn't get shelf space for long. P&G vastly outspent Lever to support its own brands.

4. *The stochastic competitor.* A competitor that does not exhibit a predictable reaction pattern. There is no way of predicting the competitor's action on the basis of its economic situation, history, or anything else. Many small businesses are stochastic competitors, competing on miscellaneous fronts when they can afford it.

How Benchmarking Helps Improve Competitive Performance

Benchmarking is the art of learning from companies that perform certain tasks better than other companies. There can be as much as a tenfold difference in the quality, speed, and cost performance of a world-class company versus an average company. Xerox has used benchmarking to reduce lead time. Kodak has used it to gain machine reliability. The list could go on and on.

The aim is to copy or improve upon "best practices." Some companies benchmark only the best companies in their industry. Halifax Direct, a leading British telemarketing company, has benchmarking partnerships with key companies in its industry: Abbey National, Barclaycalls, and Great Universal Stores. Others benchmark the "best practices" in the world and search for "best of breed." According to one Motorola executive, "The further away from our industry we reach for comparisons, the happier we are. We are seeking competitive superiority, after all, not just competitive parity."

Robert C. Camp, Xerox's benchmarking expert, flew to Freeport, Maine to visit L. L. Bean to find out how Bean's warehouse workers managed to "pick and pack" items three times as fast as Xerox workers. On later occasions, Xerox benchmarked American Express for its billing expertise and Cummins Engine for its production scheduling expertise. And in an unlikely pairing, Marriott Hotels improved its guest check-in procedures by benchmarking hospital emergency-room patient-administration processes.

Benchmarking involves seven steps: (1) determine which functions to benchmark; (2) identify the key performance variables to measure; (3) identify the best-in-class companies; (4) measure performance of best-in-class companies; (5) measure the company's performance; (6) specify programs and actions to close the gap; and (7) implement and monitor results. Yet, beyond these seven steps, it's helpful to have a "benchmarking" frame of mind at all times— a willingness to find best practices at companies that may not even be in the running. Tom Stemberg, CEO and chairman of office-supply superstore Staples, warns, "You must never have the hubris to take competition for granted because that can come back and hurt you." Stemberg tells a story about Wal-Mart founder Sam Walton: "He [Walton] went into a store in Tennessee, and the place was god-awful. The produce smelled, and it was just a disaster. And his associates were kidding each other and saying, 'I wonder what Sam is going to say now.' And Sam looked at the back of the store and saw this cigarette rack and said, 'You know, that's the finest cigarette merchandising I've seen in a year.' We try to have the same discipline."

One must be prepared to mount a resourceful and committed search for best practice partners. But how can a company identify "best-practice" companies?

A good starting point is asking customers, suppliers, and distributors whom they rate as doing the best job. In addition, major consulting firms have built voluminous files of best practices. Andersen Consulting has spent six years and invested $30 million to create a Global Best Practices Database to uncover breakthrough thinking at world-class companies. Some of the findings are condensed in the Andersen book, *Best Practices: Building Your Business with Customer Focused Solutions,* and data can also be accessed at the Andersen Web site (www.arthurandersen.com/bestpractices).

To keep costs under control, a company should focus on benchmarking those critical tasks that deeply affect customer satisfaction and company cost and where substantially better performance is known to exist.

Sources: Robert C. Camp, *Benchmarking: The Search for Industry-Best Practices that Lead to Superior Performance* (White Plains, NY: Quality Resources, 1989); Michael J. Spendolini, *The Benchmarking Book* (New York: AMACOM, 1992); Jeremy Main, "How to Steal the Best Ideas Around," *Fortune,* October 19, 1992; A. Steven Walleck, et al., "Benchmarking World Class Performance," *McKinsey Quarterly,* No. 1, 1990, pp. 3-24; Otis Port, "Beg, Borrow—and Benchmark," *Business Week,* November 30, 1992, pp. 74-75; and Stanley Brown, "Don't Innovate—Imitate!" *Sales & Marketing Management,* January 1995, pp. 24-25. Tom Stemberg, "Spies Like Us," *Inc.,* August 1998, pp. 45-49. See also: http://www.benchmarking.org/. Michael Hope, "Contrast and compare," *Marketing,* August 28, 1997, pp. 11-13. Robert Hiebeler, Thomas B. Kelly, and Charles Ketteman, *Best Practices; Building Your Business with Customer-Focused Solutions,* (New York: Arthur Anderson/Simon & Schuster, 1998).

Some industries are marked by relative accord among the competitors, and others by constant fighting. Bruce Henderson thinks that much depends on the industry's "competitive equilibrium." Here are his observations:[13]

1. *If competitors are nearly identical and make their living in the same way, then their competitive equilibrium is unstable.* Perpetual conflict characterizes industries where competitive differentiation is hard to maintain, such as steel or newsprint. The competitive equilibrium will be upset if any firm lowers its price to relieve overcapacity. Price wars frequently break out in these industries.

2. *If a single major factor is the critical factor, then the competitive equilibrium is unstable.* This is the case in industries where cost-differentiation opportunities exist through economies of scale, advanced technology, or experience. Any company that achieves a cost breakthrough can cut its price and win market share at the expense of other firms, which can defend their market shares only at great cost. Price wars frequently break out in these industries as a result of cost breakthroughs.

3. *If multiple factors may be critical factors, then it is possible for each competitor to have some advantage and be differentially attractive to some customers. The more factors that may provide an advantage, the more competitors who can co-exist. Competitors all have their competitive segment, defined by the preference for the factor trade-offs that they offer.* Multiple factors exist in industries that can differentiate quality, service, convenience, and so on. If customers place different values on these factors, then many firms can co-exist through specialization.

4. *The fewer the number of critical competitive variables, the fewer the number of competitors.* If only one factor is critical, then no more than two or three competitors are likely to co-exist.

   A ratio of 2 to 1 in market share between any two competitors seems to be the equilibrium point at which it is neither practical nor advantageous for either competitor to increase or decrease share. At this level, the costs of extra promotion or distribution would outweigh the gains in market share.

D ESIGNING THE COMPETITIVE INTELLIGENCE SYSTEM

FOUR MAIN STEPS

There are four main steps in designing a competitive intelligence system: setting up the system, collecting the data, evaluating and analyzing the data, and disseminating information and responding to queries.

Setting Up the System

The first step calls for identifying vital types of competitive information, identifying the best sources of this information, and assigning a person who will manage the system and its services. In smaller companies that cannot afford to set up a formal competitive intelligence office, specific executives should be assigned to watch specific competitors. A manager who used to work for a competitor would closely follow that competitor and serve as the in-house expert on that competitor. Any manager who needs to know about a specific competitor would contact the corresponding in-house expert.[14]

Collecting the Data

The data are collected on a continuous basis from the field (sales force, channels, suppliers, market research firms, trade associations), from people who do business with competitors, from observing competitors, and from published data. In addition, a vast store of data on both domestic and overseas companies is available via CD-ROM and online services.

The Internet is creating a vast new arsenal of capabilities for those skilled at gathering intelligence on competitors' moves. Now companies place volumes of information on their Web sites, providing details to attract customers, partners, suppliers, or franchisees, and that same information is available to competitors at the click of a mouse. Press releases that never made it into the press are achieved on Web sites, so you can keep abreast of competitors' new products and organizational changes. Help-wanted ads posted on the Web quickly let you know of competitors' expansion priorities. Here's a sample of what can be found:

- **Allied Signal.** Allied Signal's Web site provides revenue goals and reveals the company's production-defect rate along with its plans to improve it.

- **Mail Boxes Etc.** Mail Boxes Etc., a chain of mailing services, provides data on its average franchise, including square footage, number of employees, operating hours, and more—all valuable insights for a competitor.

It's not only company-sponsored Web sites that hold the richest competitor-intelligence booty. One can also glean valuable nuggets of information from trade association Web sites. When he was controller of Stone Container's specialty-packaging division, Gary Owen visited a trade association Web site and noticed that a rival had won an award for a new process using ultraviolet resistant lacquers. The site revealed the machines' configuration and run rate, which Stone's engineers used to determine how to replicate the process.[15]

Although most information-gathering techniques are legal, some involve questionable ethics. Companies have been known to advertise and hold interviews for jobs that don't exist in order to pump competitors' employees for information. Although it is illegal for a company to photograph a competitor's plant from the air, aerial photos are often on file with government geological survey services. Some companies even buy their competitors' garbage. Once it has left the competitor's premises, refuse is legally considered abandoned property.[16] Companies need to develop ways of acquiring information about competitors without violating legal or ethical standards. See the Marketing Memo, "Outsmarting the Competition with Guerrilla Marketing Research."

Evaluating and Analyzing the Data
The data are checked for validity and reliability, interpreted, and organized.

Disseminating Information and Responding
Key information is sent to relevant decision makers, and managers' inquiries are answered. With a well-designed system, company managers receive timely information about competitors via phone calls, bulletins, newsletters, and reports. Managers can also contact the market intelligence department when they need help interpreting a competitor's sudden move, when they need to know a competitor's weaknesses and strengths, or when they want to discuss a competitor's likely response to a contemplated company move.

SELECTING COMPETITORS TO ATTACK AND AVOID

With good competitive intelligence, managers will find it easier to formulate their competitive strategies.

Customer Value Analysis
Very often, managers conduct a *customer value analysis* to reveal the company's strengths and weaknesses relative to various competitors. The major steps in such an analysis are:

1. *Identify the major attributes that customers value.* Customers are asked what attributes and performance levels they look for in choosing a product and vendors.

2. *Assess the quantitative importance of the different attributes.* Customers are asked to rate the importance of the different attributes. If the customers diverge too much in their ratings, they should be clustered into different customer segments.

3. *Assess the company's and competitors' performances on the different customer values against their rated importance.* Customers describe where they see the company's and competitors' performances on each attribute.

4. *Examine how customers in a specific segment rate the company's performance against a specific major competitor on an attribute-by-attribute basis.* If the company's offer exceeds the competitor's offer on all important attributes, the company can charge a higher price (thereby earning higher profits), or it can charge the same price and gain more market share.

5. *Monitor customer values over time.* The company must periodically redo its studies of customer values and competitors' standings as the economy, technology, and features change.

affect your firm's competitive position? For instance, when a pulp and paper company hires a marketing director with significant experience in Eastern Europe, the company could be looking toward that market.

4. *Be aware of licensing agreements.* These provide useful information about where, how, and when a company can sell a new product.

5. Monitor the formation of business contracts and alliances.

6. Find out about new business practices that are saving your competitors money. What does it mean if a competing insurance company has bought thousands of laptops and portable printers? Very likely, that its claims adjusters soon will be writing estimates and generating cheques on the spot, saving time and overhead.

7. Follow changes in pricing. For instance, when luxury items become cheap enough for the mass market, they supplant some of the more expensive equipment, as when camcorders supplanted home movie cameras in the late 1980s.

8. Be aware of social changes and changes in consumer tastes and preferences that could alter the business environment. Consumers are fickle. During the past 15 years, jogging has given way to aerobics, and now walking is the preferred leisure activity. By anticipating changing fads, some shoe companies were able to introduce new types of athletic shoes.

Source: Ruth Winett, "Guerrilla Marketing Research Outsmarts the Competition," *Marketing News*, January 2, 1995, p. 33. "Fizzy Aqua-blue Powder Pays Off for Enterprising Dental Technician," *The Whig-Standard*, July 20, 1991, p. 19.

Classes of Competitors

After the company has conducted its customer value analysis, it can focus its attack on one of the following classes of competitors: strong versus weak competitors, close versus distant competitors, and "good" versus "bad" competitors.

Strong versus Weak. Most companies aim their shots at weak competitors, because this requires fewer resources per share point gained. But in attacking weak competitors, the firm will achieve little in the way of improved capabilities. The firm should also compete with strong competitors to keep up with the best. Even strong competitors have some weaknesses, and the firm may prove to be a worthy opponent.

Close versus Distant. Most companies compete with competitors who resemble them the most. Chevrolet competes with Ford, not with Jaguar. At the same time, the company should avoid trying to destroy the closest competitor. Porter cites two examples of counterproductive "victories":

> *Bausch and Lomb in the late 1970s moved aggressively against other soft contact lens manufacturers with great success. However, this led each weak competitor to sell out to larger firms, such as Revlon, Johnson & Johnson, and Schering-Plough, with the result that Bausch and Lomb now faced much larger competitors.*

> *A specialty rubber manufacturer attacked another specialty rubber manufacturer and gained share. This led the specialty divisions of large tire companies to move quickly into specialty rubber markets, using them as a dumping ground for excess capacity.[17]*

"Good" versus "Bad." Every industry contains "good" and "bad" competitors.[18] A company should support its good competitors and attack its bad competitors. Good competitors play by the industry's rules; they make realistic assumptions about the industry's growth potential; they set prices in reasonable relation to costs; they favour a healthy industry; they limit themselves to a portion or segment of the industry; they motivate others to lower costs or improve differentiation; and they accept the general level of their share and profits. Bad competitors try to buy share rather than earn it; they take large risks; they invest in overcapacity; and they upset industrial equilibrium.

IBM Canada
www.ibm.ca

- ■ **IBM and Cray.** IBM finds Cray Research to be a good competitor because it plays by the rules, sticks to its segment (high-end super computers), and does not attack IBM's core markets; but IBM finds Fujitsu a bad competitor because it attacks IBM in its core markets with subsidized prices and little differentiation.

DESIGNING COMPETITIVE STRATEGIES

We can gain further insight by classifying firms by the role they play in the target market: leader, challenger, follower, or nicher. Suppose a market is occupied by the firms shown in Figure 8-5. Forty percent of the market is in the hands of a *market leader*. Another 30 percent is in the hands of a *market challenger*. Another 20 percent is in the hands of a *market follower*, a firm that is willing to maintain its market share and not rock the boat. The remaining 10 percent is in the hands of *market nichers*, firms that serve small market segments not being served by larger firms.

MARKET-LEADER STRATEGIES

Many industries contain one firm that is the acknowledged market leader. This firm has the largest market share in the relevant product market. It usually leads the other firms in price changes, new-product introductions, distribution coverage, and promotional intensity. Some of the best-known market leaders are Kodak (photography), Microsoft (computer software), Bombardier (transportation), Xerox (copying), Procter & Gamble (consumer packaged goods), Caterpillar (earth-moving equipment), Coca-Cola (soft drinks), McDonald's (fast food), and Gillette (razor blades).

Unless a dominant firm enjoys a legal monopoly, its life is not altogether easy. It must maintain constant vigilance. A product innovation may come along and hurt the leader (Nokia's and Ericsson's digital cell phones taking over from Motorola's analogue models). The leader might spend conservatively while a challenger spends liberally. The leader might misjudge its competition and find itself left behind (as Zellers and The Bay when they underestimated Wal-Mart). The dominant firm might look old-fashioned against new and peppier rivals (Levi's ceding ground to more stylish megabrands like Tommy Hilfiger, Calvin Klein, and The Gap, as well as fresh names like Paris Blues, Mudd, and JNCO). The dominant firm's costs might rise excessively and hurt its profits.

Remaining number one calls for action on three fronts. First, the firm must find ways to expand total market demand. Second, the firm must protect its current market share through good defensive and offensive actions. Third, the firm can try to increase its market share further, even if market size remains constant.

FIGURE 8.5

Hypothetical Market Structure

Expanding the Total Market

The dominant firm normally gains the most when the total market expands. If North Americans increase their picture taking, Kodak stands to gain the most because it sells over 80 percent of the film. If Kodak can convince more people to buy cameras and take pictures, or to take pictures on other occasions besides holidays, or to take more pictures on each occasion, Kodak will benefit considerably. In general, the market leader should look for new users, new uses, and more usage of its products.

New Users. Every product class has the potential of attracting buyers who are unaware of the product or who are resisting it because of price or lack of certain features. A company can search for new users among three groups: those who might use it but do not (*market-penetration strategy*), those who have never used it (*new-market segment strategy*), or those who live elsewhere (*geographical-expansion strategy*).

- **Johnson & Johnson.** Johnson & Johnson accomplished one of the great marketing successes of recent years by developing a new class of users for its baby shampoo. The company became concerned about future sales growth when the birth rate slowed down. Their marketers noticed that other family members occasionally used the baby shampoo. Management decided to develop an advertising campaign aimed at adults. In a short time, Johnson & Johnson baby shampoo became a leading brand in the total shampoo market.

Johnson & Johnson
www.jnj.com

New Uses. Markets can be expanded through discovering and promoting new uses for the product. In many cases, customers deserve credit for discovering new uses. For example, when Procter & Gamble first test-marketed its fabric freshener product, Febreze, it first advertised the product as a way of ridding household fabrics of pet odours and the smell of cigarette smoke. The product failed to achieve substantial sales numbers until P&G discovered that a group of devoted users were using it for all kinds of odour problems. Upon launching globally, P&G encourages users to identify new uses for the product and this versatility has been responsible for the product's success.

More Usage. A third market-expansion strategy is to convince people to use more product per use occasion. Shampoo manufacturers convince consumers to use more shampoo by printing the directions "lather, rinse, and repeat" on every bottle when no one really knows if there's any benefit to washing one's hair twice![19] Or consider what Michelin did:

- **Michelin Tire Company.** Michelin wanted to encourage French car owners to drive their cars more kilometres per year—thus leading to more tire replacement. It conceived the idea of rating French restaurants on a three-star system. Michelin promoted the names of many of the best restaurants in the South of France, leading Parisians to take weekend drives to Provence and the Riviera. Michelin also published guidebooks with maps and lists of sights along the way to encourage additional driving.

HUNG UP TRYING TO GET ODOURS OUT OF FABRICS? **THE SOLUTION IS HERE.**

Don't wait until you get to the end of your rope. Febreze safely cleans away odours from so many of your favorite fabrics. For good. And it doesn't just cover one smell with another. Febreze actually cleans the odours away. No wonder you can find it in the laundry aisle.

Cleans bad smells out of fabrics. For good.

Trade mark owned by Procter & Gamble Inc.

P&G created a market for fabric deodorizers with Febreeze. Competitors were quick to enter. Now P&G must defend its share.

Companies have long used a strategy to get people to replace products. Called "planned obsolescence," it is the idea of spurring repeat sales by making goods that break down or wear out. Ever wonder why no one has yet marketed a lightbulb that never burns out or a battery that never wears down? Now manufacturers have taken this concept further by making products that actually "tell" consumers when they are breaking down or wearing out. Gillette's new Mach3 shaving system is a prime example.

■ **Gillette.** Each Gillette Mach3 Cartridge features a blue stripe that slowly fades with repeated use. After about a dozen shaves, it fades away completely, signalling the user to move on to the next cartridge or in Gillette's more subtle wording, this "alerts men that they're not getting the optimal Mach3 shaving experience," regardless of whether the blade really needs replacing. As Gillette executive Robert King said bluntly, "I wish we could get men to change the cartridge every four days. The more they change it, the more we sell."

Defending Market Share

While trying to expand total market size, the dominant firm must continuously defend its current business against rival attacks. The leader is like a large elephant being attacked by a swarm of bees. Coca-Cola must constantly guard against Pepsi-Cola; Gillette against Bic; Hertz against Avis; Bell must defend its market share from the inroads of the likes of Sprint, Cantel, and AT&T, while Air Canada wards off the efforts of Canadian and West Jet.[20] Sometimes the competitor is domestic; sometimes it is foreign:

■ **Kodak and Fuji.** For more than 100 years, Eastman Kodak has been known for its easy-to-use cameras, high-quality film, and solid profits. During the past decade, however, Kodak's sales have flattened and its profits have declined. Kodak seemed to be outpaced by more innovative competitors like Fuji. The Fuji Photo Film Company moved in on Kodak's bread-and-butter colour film business when it entered the North American market offering high-quality, regular and high-speed colour films at prices 10 percent lower than Kodak's. Kodak fought back, fiercely matching Fuji's lower prices and unleashing a series of product improvements. It outspent Fuji by 20 to 1 on advertising and promotion, resulting in a successful defence of its 80 percent market share. But Kodak took the battle a step further: It set up a separate subsidiary—Kodak Japan—tripled its Japanese staff, increased its Japanese promotion and publicity, added distribution, and invested in a new research facility. Kodak gained several benefits from its stepped-up attack on Japan. First, the Japanese film and photo paper market is second only to that of the United States so Kodak improved its sales opportunities. Second, since much of today's new photographic technology originates in Japan, its joint venture there will help

Kodak better understand Japanese manufacturing and obtain new product insights. Finally, Kodak reaps one more important benefit: If Fuji must devote heavy resources to defending its home turf, it will have fewer resources to use against Kodak in North America.

What can the market leader do to defend its terrain? Twenty centuries ago, in a treatise called *The Art of War*, the famed Chinese military strategist Sun Tsu told his warriors: "One does not rely on the enemy not attacking, but relies on the fact that he himself is unassailable." The most constructive response is *continuous innovation*. The leader heads the industry in developing new product and customer services, distribution effectiveness, and cost cutting. It keeps increasing its competitive strength and value to customers. The leader applies the military principle of the offensive: *The commander exercises initiative, sets the pace, and exploits enemy weaknesses*. The best defence is a good offence.

■ **International Gaming Technology.** International Gaming Technology, a company that manufactures slot machines and video poker machines for casinos around the world, has achieved the daunting feat of maintaining 75 percent market share in a mature market with a limited number of new customers. Unlike the people who use its products, the company doesn't rely on luck. IGT has formed partnerships with both casino operators and competitive gaming manufacturers to develop innovative new equipment to replace the old. IGT spends aggressively on R&D, allocating $45 million annually to create new games. Dedication to service is also a company mantra. "We know months, years, in advance what our customers want," says Robert Shay, a sales director for IGT. That's because it involves casino operators throughout the sales process, from initial product development to final placement on the casino floor.[21]

Even when it does not launch offensives, the market leader must not leave any major flanks exposed. It must keep its costs down, its prices must be consonant with the value the customers see in the brand, and it must strive to retain its current customers. Here's a dramatic example of what happens when customer defection from a leading company and its competitors becomes the norm:

■ **Churn in the Wireless Phone Industry.** Churn is jargon for customer turnover and according to analysts, it has become endemic in the wireless cellular-phone industry. Churn is a major problem due to the high costs of signing up customers—in the range of $600/customer that includes marketing costs, overhead, and handsets. Canada's four major cellular companies may lose up to one-quarter of their customers every year. BCE Mobile Communications Inc. and Clearnet Communications have the lowest defection rates. While the cellular industry isn't alone in its struggle to achieve customer loyalty, churn is a self-inflicted problem in this industry. All the players have encouraged turnover with their tactics of price cutting, enrolment incentives, and no-term contracts while they have done little to differentiate their services or add customer value. This is starting to change. Clearnet and its Mike service are focusing on business users and are trying to distinguish themselves by concentrating on network and service improvements.[22]

The market leader must consider carefully which terrains are important to defend even at a loss and which can be surrendered.[23] The aim of defensive strategy is to reduce the probability of attack, divert attacks to less threatening areas, and lessen their intensity. Any attack is likely to hurt profits. But the defender's speed of response can make an important difference in the profit consequences. Researchers are currently exploring the most appropriate forms of response to price and their attacks. A dominant firm can use the six defence strategies summarized in Figure 8-6 and described in the following paragraphs.[24]

Position Defence. The basic defence is to build an impregnable fortification around one's territory. Coca-Cola today, in spite of selling nearly half the soft drinks of the world, has acquired fruit-drink companies and diversified into desalinization

FIGURE 8.6

Defence Strategies

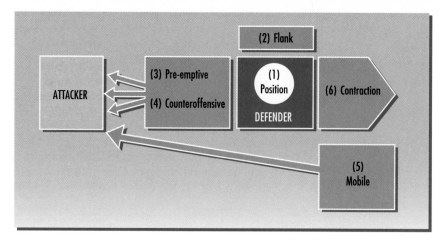

equipment and plastics. While defence is important, leaders under attack would be foolish to put all their resources into building fortifications only around their current product.

Flanking Defence. The market leader should also erect outposts to protect a weak front or possibly serve as an invasion base for counterattack. Here is a good example of a flanking defence:

Starbucks Coffee Co.
www.starbucks.com

- **Starbucks Coffee Co.** Starbucks was the company that first made people lust for café latte and spend $3 for a cup of coffee. Yet, in doing so the company spawned a host of competitors and now it sees its own sales growth slowing. To stay ahead of mounting competition, ranging from giants like Tim Horton's Donuts and The Second Cup, to smaller independent operators, Starbucks is using a number of flanking defences. For one thing, it is feverishly trying to push out innovative new, non-coffee-related products, such as its combo of tea and juice, Tiazzi. It is also selling its premium beans in supermarkets and is getting into the restaurant business in an attempt to stretch Starbucks' business further into the evening, since 85 percent of business is completed by 3 p.m. in the company's retail stores.[25]

Pre-emptive Defence. A more aggressive manoeuvre is to attack *before* the enemy starts its offence. A company can launch a pre-emptive defence in several ways. It can wage guerrilla action across the market—hitting one competitor here, another there—and keep everyone off balance. Or it can try to achieve a grand market envelopment, as Seiko has done with 2300 watch models distributed worldwide. It can begin sustained price attacks, as Texas Instruments often did. Or it can send out market signals to dissuade competitors from attacking.[26] A major pharmaceutical firm might leak news that it may cut its drug price to discourage a competitor from entering the market.

Market leaders with strong resources may even choose to entice opponents into costly attacks:

- **Heinz & Hunt's.** Heinz let Hunt's carry out its massive attack in the ketchup market without much counteroffensive. Hunt's attacked Heinz with two new flavours of ketchup; it lowered its price to 70 percent of Heinz's price; it offered heavy trade allowances to retailers; it raised its advertising budget to over twice the level of Heinz's. Hunt's was willing to lose money during the attack. The strategy failed and the Heinz brand continued to enjoy consumer preference. Hunt's finally gave up. Clearly, Heinz showed great confidence in the ultimate superiority of its brand.

Counteroffensive Defence. Most market leaders, when attacked, will respond with a counterattack. The leader cannot remain passive in the face of a competitor's price cut, promotion blitz, product improvement, or sales-territory invasion. In a counteroffensive, the leader can meet the attacker frontally, or hit his flank, or launch a pincer movement.

An effective counterattack is to invade the attacker's main territory so that it will have to pull back some troops to defend the territory. See the earlier example of what Kodak did when it attached Fuji home markets. Another common form of counteroffensive defence is the exercise of economic or political clout to deter the attacker. The leader may try to crush a competitor by subsidizing lower prices for the vulnerable product with revenue from its more profitable products. Or the leader may prematurely announce that a product upgrade will be available to prevent customers from buying the competitor's product. Or the leader may lobby legislators to take political action that would inhibit or cripple the competition.

Mobile Defence. In mobile defence, the leader stretches its domain over new territories that can serve as future centres for defence and offence. It spreads through market broadening and market diversification.

Market broadening involves the company in shifting its focus from the current product to the underlying generic need. The company gets involved in R&D across the whole range of technology associated with that need. Thus "petroleum" companies sought to recast themselves into "energy" companies. Implicitly, this change demanded that they dip their research fingers into the oil, coal, nuclear, hydroelectric, and chemical industries.

Such a strategy should not be carried too far, lest it fault two fundamental military principles—the *principle of the objective* (pursue a clearly defined, decisive, and attainable objective) and the *principle of mass* (concentrate your efforts at a point of enemy weakness). Reasonable broadening, however, makes sense.

■ **Wal-Mart.** Wal-Mart's supercentres already stock groceries, so the giant chain didn't consider it too much of a leap to broaden into the grocery business. In 1998, Wal-Mart Stores Inc. announced plans for three experimental grocery stores. The 40 000-square-metre "Neighbourhood Markets" will leverage the company's distribution and buying strengths. Wal-Mart hopes the new markets will be able to beat grocery stores with lower everyday prices while offering more conveniences than its supercentres. Supermarket industry executives are quaking in their boots. Already the move has pressured giants like Safeway to cut costs and boost service.[27]

Wal-Mart
www.wal-mart.com

Market diversification into unrelated industries is the other alternative. When tobacco companies like Reynolds and Philip Morris acknowledged the growing curbs on cigarette smoking, they were not content with position defence or even with looking for substitutes for the cigarette. Instead they moved quickly into new industries, such as beer, liquor, soft drinks, and frozen foods.

Contraction Defence. Large companies sometimes recognize that they can no longer defend all of their territory. The best course of action then appears to be *planned contraction* (also called *strategic withdrawal*). Planned contraction means giving up weaker territories and reassigning resources to stronger territories. It is a move to consolidate competitive strength in the market and concentrate mass at pivotal positions. Seagrams, Molsons, Heinz, General Mills, Del Monte, and General Electric are among companies that have significantly pruned their product lines in recent years.

Expanding Market Share

Market leaders can improve their profitability by increasing their market share. In many markets, one share point is worth tens of millions of dollars. A one-share-point gain in coffee is worth $75 million and in soft drinks, $180 million! No wonder normal competition has turned into marketing warfare.

A study by the Strategic Planning Institute (called Profit Impact of Market Strategy or PIMS) found that a company's profitability, measured by pre-tax return on investment (ROI), rises with its *relative market share* of its served market,[28] as shown in Figure 8-7(a).[29] The average ROI for businesses with under 10% market share was about 11 percent. A difference of 10 percentage points in market share is accompanied by a difference of about five points in pre-tax ROI. The PIMS study shows that businesses with market shares above 40 percent earn an average ROI of 30 percent, or three times that of those with shares under 10 percent.[30] These findings led many companies to

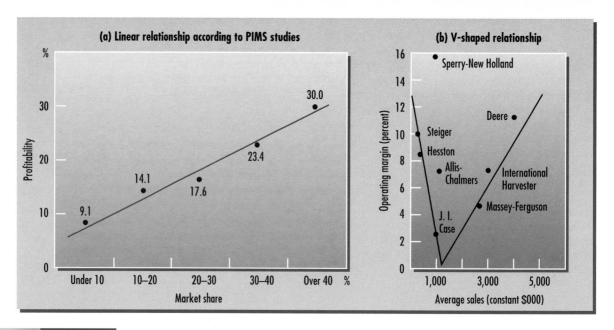

(a) Linear relationship according to PIMS studies

Profitability (%): values shown at data points: 9.1, 14.1, 17.6, 23.4, 30.0

Market share (%): Under 10, 10–20, 20–30, 30–40, Over 40

(b) V-shaped relationship

Operating margin (percent) vs. Average sales (constant $000): 1,000, 3,000, 5,000

Companies: Sperry-New Holland, Deere, Steiger, Hesston, Allis-Chalmers, International Harvester, J. I. Case, Massey-Ferguson

F I G U R E   8.7

Relationship Between Market Share and Profitability

Figure (a) from Strategic Planning Institute (The PIMS Program), 1030 Massachusetts Avenue, Cambridge, MA 02138.

pursue market-share expansion and leadership as their objective. General Electric decided it must be number one or two in each market or else get out. GE divested its computer business and its air-conditioning business because it could not achieve leadership in these industries.

Some critics have attacked the PIMS findings as either weak or spurious. Hamermesh cited many profitable companies with low market shares.[31] Woo and Cooper identified 40 low-share businesses that enjoyed pretax ROIs of 20 percent or more; these businesses tended to have high relative product quality, medium-to-low prices, narrow product lines, and low total costs.[32] Most of these companies produced industrial components or supplies.

Some industry studies have yielded a **V**-shaped relationship between market share and profitability.[33] Figure 8-7(b) shows a **V**-curve for agricultural-equipment firms. The industry leader, Deere & Company, earns a high return. However, two small specialty firms, Hesston and Steiger, also earn high returns. J.I. Case and Massey-Ferguson are trapped in the valley, and International Harvester commands substantial market share but earns lower returns. Thus such industries have one or a few highly profitable large firms, several profitable small and more-focused firms, and several medium-sized firms with poorer profit performance.

How can the two graphs in Figure 8-7 be reconciled? The PIMS findings argue that profitability increases as a business gains share relative to its competitors in its *served (target) market*. The **V**-shaped curve ignores market segments and looks at profitability relative to size in the *total market*. Mercedes earns high profit because it is a high-share company in its served market of luxury cars even though it is a low-share company in the total auto market. And it has achieved this high share in its served market because it does many things right, such as producing high relative product quality.

However, gaining increased market share in the served market will not automatically improve profitability. Much depends on a company's strategy for gaining increased market share.

■ **McDonald's.** Since 1987, McDonald's share of fast-food sales in North America has slipped almost two percentage points. The drop has come even as the company has increased its number of restaurants by 50 percent, far outpacing the industry's expansion rate. Ill-fated product innovations are what sent McDonald's share sliding, at first. Customers weren't thrilled about the fast-food chain's pizza and veggie burger offerings. Then the company tried to expand its way out of crisis. By building thousands of new restaurants, however, McDonald's stole customers and profits from its existing franchises. Relations between McDonald's and its operators worsened. The company is still trying to come up with ways to shore up its sagging market share.[34]

Because the cost of buying higher market share may far exceed its revenue value, a company should consider three factors before pursuing increased market share:

■ The first factor is the possibility of provoking antitrust action. Jealous competitors are likely to cry "monopoly" if a dominant firm makes further inroads. This rise in risk would cut down the attractiveness of pushing market-share gains too far. This is what has happened to software monopolist Microsoft.

Microsoft
www.microsoft.com

■ **Microsoft.** In 1997, Microsoft's $5.1 billion in net income accounted for 41 percent of the profits of the 10 largest publicly traded software companies. Its reach extends beyond the PC into everything from computerized toys and TV set-top boxes to selling cars and airline tickets over the Internet. In its zeal to become a leader not just in operating systems but on the Internet, the company bundled its Internet Explorer browser into its Windows software. This move sparked an antitrust suit by the government, much to the delight of Microsoft's rivals. After all, Web-browsing innovator Netscape has seen its market share plummet as it tries to sell what Microsoft gives away for free.[35]

■ The second factor is economic cost. Figure 8-8 shows that profitability might fall with further market-share gains after some level. In the illustration, the firm's *optimal market share* is 50 percent. The cost of gaining further market share might exceed the value. A company that has, say, 60 percent of the market must recognize that the "holdout" customers may dislike the company, be loyal to competitive suppliers, have unique needs, or prefer dealing with smaller suppliers. The cost of legal work, public relations, and lobbying rises with market share. Pushing for higher market share is less justified when there are few scale or experience economies, unattractive market segments exist, buyers want multiple sources of supply, and exit barriers are high. Some market leaders have even increased profitability by selectively decreasing market share in weaker areas.[36]

■ The third factor is that companies might pursue the wrong marketing-mix strategy in their bid for higher market share and therefore fail to increase profits. Companies that win more market share by cutting price are buying, not earning, a larger share, and their profits may be lower.

Buzzell and Wiersema found that share-gaining companies typically outperform competitors in three areas: new-product activity, relative product quality, and marketing expenditures.[37] Specifically: share-gaining companies typically develop and add more new products to their lines. Companies that increase product quality relative to competitors enjoy greater share gains. Companies that increase marketing expenditures faster than the rate of market growth typically achieve share gains. Increases in sales-force expenditures are effective in producing share gains for both industrial and consumer markets. Increased advertising expenditures produce share gains mainly for consumer-goods companies. Increased sales-promotion expenditures are effective in producing share gains for all kinds of companies. Companies that cut prices more

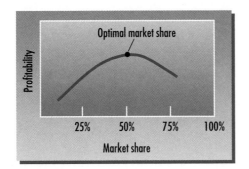

The Concept of Optimal Market Share

deeply than competitors do not achieve significant market-share gains. Presumably, enough rivals meet the price cuts, and others offer other values to buyers, so that buyers do not switch to the price cutter.

 C ASE STUDY: PROCTER & GAMBLE

Market leaders who stay on top have learned the art of expanding the total market, defending their current territory, and increasing market share profitably. Here we look at Procter & Gamble, which has shown a remarkable ability to protect their market shares against able challengers.

Procter & Gamble (P&G) is one of the most skilled marketers of consumer packaged goods. It markets the leading brand in 19 of the 39 categories in which it competes. Its average market share is close to 25 percent. Its market leadership rests on several principles:

- *Customer knowledge:* P&G studies its customers—both final consumers and the trade—through continuous marketing research and intelligence gathering. It prints its toll-free 800 number on every product.

- *Long-term outlook:* P&G takes the time to carefully analyze each opportunity and prepare the best product, then commits itself for the long run to make this product a success. It struggled with Pringles potato chips for almost a decade before achieving market success.

- *Product Innovation:* P&G is an active product innovator, devoting $1.8 billion (3.4 percent of sales) to research and development, an impressively high amount for a packaged goods company. It holds more than 2500 active patents protecting 250 proprietary technologies. Part of its innovation process is developing brands that offer new consumer benefits. P&G spent 10 years researching and developing the first effective anticavity toothpaste, Crest. Its most recent innovation is fat-substitute olestra, marketed as Olean. Since its approval by the FDA, salty snacks made with olestra—such as Frito-Lay's WOW! fat-free chips—are turning into one of the decade's most successful new food-product introductions.[38]

- *Quality strategy:* P&G designs products of above-average quality and continuously improves them. When P&G announces "new and improved," it means it.

- *Line-extension strategy:* P&G produces its brands in several sizes and forms. This strategy gains more shelf space and prevents competitors from moving in to satisfy unmet market needs.

- *Brand-extension strategy:* P&G often uses its strong brand names to launch new products. The Ivory brand has been extended from a soap to include liquid soap, a dishwashing detergent, and a shampoo. Launching a new product under a strong existing brand name gives the new brand instant recognition and credibility with much less advertising outlay.

- *Multibrand strategy:* P&G markets several brands in the same product category. It produces eight brands of hand soap and six shampoo brands. Each brand meets a different consumer want and competes against specific competitors' brands. Each brand manager competes for company resources. More recently, P&G has begun to reduce its vast array of products, sizes, flavours, and varieties to bring down costs.[39]

- *Heavy advertising and media pioneer:* P&G is North America's second-largest consumer-packaged-goods advertiser, spending over $4.5 billion on advertising a year. A pioneer in using the power of television to create strong consumer awareness and preference, P&G is now taking a leading role in building its brand on the Web. In 1998, P&G hosted a high-powered industry "summit" meeting that brought together some 400 top executives from Internet and consumer marketing companies. The goal: figuring out how to best sell products over the Internet.[40]

- *Aggressive sales force:* In 1998, P&G's sales force was named one of the top 25 sales forces by *Sales & Marketing Management* magazine. A key to P&G's success is the close ties its sales force forms with retailers, notably Wal-Mart. The 150-person team that serves the retail giant works closely with Wal-Mart to improve both the products that go to the stores and the process by which they get there.

- *Effective sales promotion:* P&G's sales-promotion department counsels its brand managers on the most effective promotions to achieve particular objectives. The department develops an expert sense of these deals' effectiveness under varying circumstances. At the same time, P&G tries to minimize the use of sales promotion and move towards "everyday low prices."

- *Competitive toughness:* P&G carries a big stick when it comes to aggressors. P&G is willing to spend large sums of money to outpromote new competitive brands and prevent them from gaining a market foothold.

- *Manufacturing efficiency and cost cutting:* P&G's reputation as a great marketing company is matched by its excellence as a manufacturing company. P&G spends large sums developing and improving production operations to keep its costs among the lowest in the industry. And P&G has recently begun slashing its costs even further, allowing it to reduce the premium prices at which some of its goods sell.

- *Brand-management system:* P&G originated the brand-management system, in which one executive is responsible for each brand. The system has been copied by many competitors but frequently without P&G's success. Recently P&G modified its general management structure so that each brand category is now run by a *category manager* with volume and profit responsibility. While this new organization does not replace the brand-management system, it helps to sharpen strategic focus on key consumer needs and competition in the category.

Thus P&G's market leadership is not based on doing one thing well, but on the successful orchestration of myriad factors that contribute to market leadership.

MARKET-CHALLENGER STRATEGIES

Firms that occupy second, third, and lower ranks in an industry are often called runner-up, or trailing, firms. Some, such as Colgate, Ford, Avis, and Pepsi-Cola, are quite large in their own right. These firms can adopt one of two postures. They can attack the leader and other competitors in an aggressive bid for further market share (market challengers). Or they can play ball and not "rock the boat" (market followers).

There are many cases of market challengers that gained ground or even overtook the leader. Toyota today produces more cars than General Motors, and British Airways flies more international passengers than the former leader, Pan Am, did in its heyday as an international carrier. These challengers set high aspirations and leveraged their smaller resources while the market leaders ran their businesses as usual.

Dolan found that competitive rivalry and price cutting are most intense in industries with high fixed costs, high inventory costs, and stagnant primary demand, such as steel, auto, paper, and chemicals.[41] We will now examine the competitive attack strategies available to market challengers.

Defining the Strategic Objective and Opponent(s)

A market challenger must first define its strategic objective. Most aim to increase market share. The challenger must decide whom to attack:

- *It can attack the market leader.* This is a high-risk but potentially high-payoff strategy and makes good sense if the leader is not serving the market well. Corel tried this tactic when it entered the office software market taking on Microsoft. When this tactic failed, it tried an alternative strategy, which is to out-innovate the leader across the whole segment. Corel first tried innovations using Java script. Next it tried developing its own line of computers. Neither initiative has met with significant success. Other firms have been able to beat the leader at their own game. Canon grabbed a large chunk of Xerox's market when it introduced desk copiers.

- *It can attack firms of its own size that are not doing the job and are underfinanced.* These firms have aging products, are charging excessive prices, or are not satisfying customers in other ways.

- *It can attack small local and regional firms.* Several major beer companies grew to their present size by gobbling up smaller firms, or "guppies."

If the attacking company goes after the market leader, its objective might be to wrest a certain share. Bic is under no illusion that it can topple Gillette in the razor market—it is simply seeking a larger share. If the attacking company goes after a small local company, its objective might be to drive that company out of existence.

Choosing a General Attack Strategy

Given clear opponents and objectives, what attack options are available? We can distinguish among five attack strategies shown in Figure 8-9: frontal, flank, encirclement, bypass, and guerrilla attack.

In a pure frontal attack, the attacker matches its opponent's product, advertising, price, and distribution. The *principle of force* says that *the side with the greater manpower (resources) will win.* This rule is modified if the defender enjoys a terrain advantage (such as holding a mountaintop). The military dogma is that for a frontal attack to succeed against a well-entrenched opponent or one controlling the high ground, the attacking forces must have at least a 3:1 advantage in combat firepower. The runner-up razor-blade manufacturer in Brazil attacked Gillette, the market leader. The attacker was asked if it offers the consumer a better razor blade. "No," was the reply. "A lower price?" "No." "A better package?" "No." "A clever advertising campaign?" "No." "Better allowances to the trade?" "No." "Then how do you expect to take share away from Gillette?" "Sheer determination" was the reply. Needless to say, the offensive failed.

A modified frontal attack, such as cutting price vis-à-vis the opponent's, can work if the market leader does not retaliate and if the competitor convinces the market that its product is equal to the leader's. Helene Curtis is a master at convincing the market that its brands—such as Suave and Finesse—are equal in quality but a better value than higher-priced brands.

An opponent's army is strongest where it expects to be attacked; it is necessarily less secure in its flanks and rear. Its weak spots are, therefore, natural targets. The major principle of offensive warfare is *concentration of strength against weakness.* The challenger

FIGURE 8.9

Attack Strategies

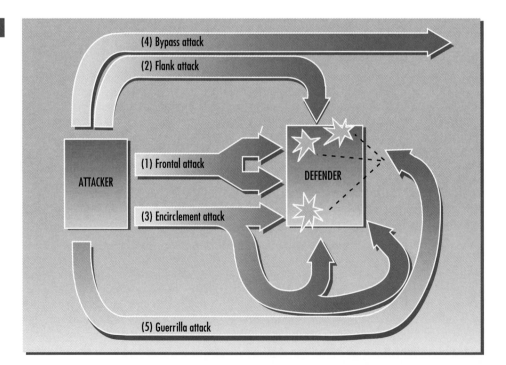

may attack the strong side to tie up the defender's troops but launch the real attack at the side or rear.

A flank attack can be directed along two strategic dimensions—geographical and segmental. In a geographical attack, the challenger spots areas where the opponent is underperforming. For example, some of IBM's rivals, such as Honeywell, chose to set up strong sales branches in medium- and smaller-size cities that were relatively neglected by IBM. The other flanking strategy is to serve uncovered market needs, as Japanese auto makers did when they developed more fuel-efficient cars, and as Molson's did when it introduced light beer.

A flanking strategy is another name for identifying shifts in market segments that are causing gaps to develop, then rushing in to fill the gaps and develop them into strong segments. Flanking is in the best tradition of modern marketing, which holds that the purpose of marketing is to discover needs and satisfy them. Flank attacks make excellent marketing sense and are particularly attractive to a challenger with fewer resources than its opponent. Flank attacks are much more likely to be successful than frontal attacks.

The encirclement manoeuvre is an attempt to capture a wide slice of the enemy's territory through a "blitz." It involves launching a grand offensive on several fronts. Encirclement makes sense when the challenger commands superior resources and believes a swift encirclement will break the opponent's will.

- **Sun Microsystems Inc.** In making a stand against archrival Microsoft, whose software is ubiquitous, Sun Microsystems is licensing its Java software for all sorts of consumer devices. As consumer-electronic products go digital, Java is jumping into a wide range of gadgets. Delphi Automotive Systems, the electronics supplier owned by General Motors, plans to offer carmakers a Java-based system to outfit autos with features like voice-activated E-mail. Motorola expects to use Java in everything from pagers and cell phones to chips that run Java in appliances like toasters. Sun Microsystems Chief Executive Scott G. McNealy is the driving force behind the flurry of licensing deals. His aim: to make Java the *lingua franca* for every imaginable digital device.[42]

Sun Microsystems
www.sun.com

The most indirect assault strategy is the bypass. It means bypassing the enemy and attacking easier markets to broaden one's resource base. This strategy offers three lines of approach: diversifying into unrelated products, diversifying into new geographical markets, and leapfrogging into new technologies to supplant existing products. While Pepsi-Cola and Coca-Cola often go head to head, the bypass attack is also part of their competitive battle plan. Here's how Pepsi used a bypass strategy against Coke:

- **Coca-Cola Co.** In the summer of 1998, many people wondered why Pepsi Cola paid $3.3 billion for juice giant Tropicana. Unlike soft drinks, juice is a product that is subject to commodity markets, bad weather, and crop failures, and delivering such a perishable product is tough. Yet, as the world's largest juice company, Tropicana arms Pepsi—thwarted in its core soft-drink market—with a powerful new weapon in the war against Coca-Cola Co. In the $3-billion market for orange juice, Tropicana's 42 percent share blows away Coke-owned Minute-Maid, which has only 24 percent of the market. The purchase gave Pepsi at least one way to beat Coke.[43]

Technological leapfrogging is a bypass strategy practised in high-tech industries. The challenger patiently researches and develops the next technology and launches an attack, shifting the battleground to its territory, where it has an advantage. Nintendo's successful attack in the video-game market was precisely about wresting market share by introducing a superior technology and redefining the "competitive space." Now Sega/Genesis is doing the same with more advanced technology, as are the creators of virtual-reality-based entertainment. The giant Netherlands financial services giant, ING Groep NV, has been aggressively using technology to take market share away from Canada's traditional financial institutions. With consumers being increasingly

Guerrilla marketer WestJet has used market segmentation, low prices, and humorous ads to establish itself as a player in the highly competitive Canadian airline industry.

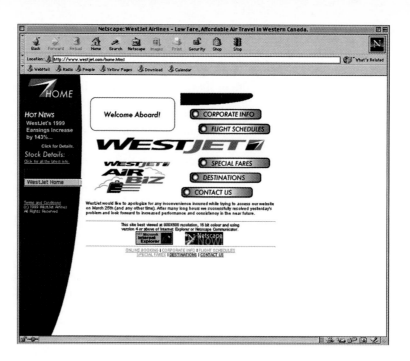

WestJet Airlines
www.westjet.com

willing to bank and buy insurance on-line, the firm has made considerable inroads into the Canadian marketplace.[44] Guerrilla warfare consists of waging small, intermittent attacks to harass and demoralize the opponent and eventually secure permanent footholds. The guerrilla challenger uses both conventional and unconventional means of attack. These include selective price cuts, intense promotional blitzes, and occasional legal actions. Here is an example of a very successful guerrilla strategy:

■ **WestJet Airlines.** Calgary-based WestJet has done what other giant airlines thought impossible. Despite the fact that it began in February 1996 with only three planes and 220 employees, it has grown steadily and has caused ticket prices to plunge by as much as 70 percent in every market it has entered. Moreover, it has been a consistently profitable, low-cost airline that doesn't have a mountain of debt. Rather than attacking its major competitors head on, and relying on business travellers to ensure profitability, WestJet has specialized in serving what it calls "VFR" customers (people visiting friends and relatives) in Western Canada. Its humorous ads drew attention to the new firm and its remarkable prices. WestJet's guerrilla marketing strategy has been so successful it may be copied by its larger rival, Canadian. The airline is considering offering lower-priced no-frills service on some of its routes.[45]

Normally, guerrilla warfare is practised by a smaller firm against a larger one. The smaller firm launches a barrage of short promotional and price attacks in random corners of the larger opponent's market in a manner calculated to gradually weaken the opponent's market power. Military dogma holds that a continual stream of minor attacks usually creates more cumulative impact, disorganization, and confusion in the enemy than a few major attacks. The guerrilla attacker chooses to attack small, isolated, weakly defended markets rather than major stronghold markets.

A guerrilla campaign can be expensive, although admittedly less expensive than a frontal, encirclement, or flank attack. Guerrilla war is more a preparation for war than a war itself. Ultimately it must be backed by a stronger attack if the challenger hopes to beat the opponent. See the Marketing Memo, "The Spoils of War."

Choosing a Specific Attack Strategy

The challenger must go beyond the five broad strategies and develop more specific strategies:

- *Price-discount:* The challenger can offer a comparable product at a lower price. This is the strategy of discount retailers. Three conditions must be fulfilled. First, the challenger must convince buyers that its product and service are comparable to the leader's. Second, buyers must be price-sensitive. Third, the market leader must refuse to cut its price in spite of the competitor's attack.

- *Cheaper goods:* The challenger can offer an average- or low-quality product at a much lower price. Little Debbie snack cakes are lower in quality than Drake's but sell at less than half the price. Firms that establish themselves through this strategy, however, can be attacked by firms whose prices are even lower.

- *Prestige goods:* A market challenger can launch a higher-quality product and charge a higher price than the leader. Mercedes gained on Cadillac in the North American market by offering a car of higher quality at a higher price.

- *Product proliferation:* The challenger can attack the leader by launching a larger product variety, thus giving buyers more choice. Baskin-Robbins achieved its growth in the ice-cream business by promoting more flavours—31—than its larger competitors.

- *Product-innovation:* The challenger can pursue product innovation. 3M typically enters new markets by introducing a product improvement or breakthrough.

- *Improved services:* The challenger can offer new or better services to customers. Avis's famous attack on Hertz, "We're only second. We try harder," was based on promising and delivering cleaner cars and faster service than Hertz.

- *Distribution innovation:* A challenger might develop a new channel of distribution. Avon became a major cosmetics company by perfecting door-to-door selling instead of battling other cosmetic firms in conventional stores.

- *Manufacturing cost reduction:* The challenger might achieve lower manufacturing costs than its competitors through more efficient purchasing, lower labour costs, and/or more modern production equipment.

- *Intensive advertising promotion:* Some challengers attack the leader by increasing expenditures on advertising and promotion. Miller Beer outspent Budweiser in its attempt to increase its market share. Substantial promotional spending, however, is usually not a sensible strategy unless the challenger's product or advertising message is superior.

A challenger rarely improves its market share by relying on only one strategy. Its success depends on combining several strategies to improve its position over time.

MARKET-FOLLOWER STRATEGIES

Some years ago, Theodore Levitt wrote an article titled "Innovative Imitation," in which he argued that a strategy of *product imitation* might be as profitable as a strategy of *product innovation*.[46] The innovator bears the expense of developing the new product, getting it into distribution, and informing and educating the market. The reward for all this work and risk is normally market leadership. However, another firm can come along and copy or improve on the new product. Although it probably will not overtake the leader, the follower can achieve high profits because it did not bear any of the innovation expense.

Many companies prefer to follow rather than challenge the market leader. Patterns of "conscious parallelism" are common in capital-intensive homogeneous-product industries, such as steel, fertilizers, and chemicals. The opportunities for product differentiation and image differentiation are low; service quality is often comparable; and price sensitivity runs high. Price wars can erupt at any time. The mood in these industries is against short-run grabs for market share because that strategy only provokes retaliation. Most firms decide against stealing each other's customers. Instead, they present similar offers to buyers, usually by copying the leader. Market shares show a high stability.

This is not to say that market followers lack strategies. A market follower must know how to hold current customers and win a fair share of new customers. Each follower tries to bring distinctive advantages to its target market—location, services, financing. And because the follower is often a major target of attack by challengers, it must keep its manufacturing costs low and its product quality and services high. It must also enter new markets as they open up. The follower must define a growth path, but one that does not invite competitive retaliation. Three broad strategies can be distinguished:

- *Counterfeiter:* The counterfeiter duplicates the leader's product and package and sells it on the black market or through disreputable dealers. Music-record firms, Apple Computer, and Rolex have been plagued with the counterfeiter problem, especially in the Far East.

- *Cloner:* The cloner emulates the leader's products, name, and packaging, with slight variations. Store brands of soup have packaging that highly resembles Campbell's, and there are numerous clones of the world's top perfume and brand-name clothing products.

- *Imitator:* The imitator copies some things from the leader but maintains differentiation in terms of packaging, advertising, pricing, and so on. The leader doesn't mind the imitator as long as the imitator doesn't attack the leader aggressively.

- *Adapter:* The adapter takes the leader's products and adapts or improves them. The adapter may choose to sell to different markets. But often the adapter grows into the future challenger, as many Japanese firms have done after adapting and improving products developed elsewhere.

- **S&S Cycle.** S&S Cycle is the biggest supplier of complete engines and major motor parts to more than 15 companies that build several thousand Harley-like cruiser bikes each year. These clonemakers charge as much as $30 000 for their customized creations. S&S has built its name by improving on Harley's handiwork. Its customers are often would-be Harley buyers frustrated by long waiting lines at the dealers. Other customers simply want the incredibly powerful S&S engines. S&S stays abreast of its evolving market by ordering a new Harley bike every year and taking apart the engine to see what it can improve upon.[47]

What does a follower earn? Normally, less than the leader. For example, a study of food processing companies showed the largest firm averaging a 16 percent return on investment; the number-two firm, 6 percent; the number-three firm, -1 percent, and number-four firm, -6 percent. In this case, only the top two firms have profits. No wonder Jack Welch, CEO of GE, told his business units that each must reach the number-one or -two position in their market or else! Followership is often not a rewarding path.

MARKET-NICHER STRATEGIES

An alternative to being a follower in a large market is to be a leader in a small market, or niche. Smaller firms normally avoid competing with larger firms by targeting small markets of little or no interest to the larger firms. Here are two examples:

- **Logitech International.** Logitech has become a $450-million global success story by making every variation of computer mouse imaginable. Producing a mouse every 1.6 seconds, the company turns out mice for left- and right-handed people, cordless mice that use radio waves, mice shaped like real mice for children, and 3-D mice that let the user appear to move behind screen objects. Breeding only computer mice has been so successful that Logitech dominates the world market, with Microsoft as its runner-up.[48]

- **ATI Technologies Inc.** By focusing on graphics chips and boards (components of PCs and laptops) and providing high levels of customer service, Kwok Yuen Ho, president and CEO of the firm, built his fledgling firm into a $1.1-billion enterprise. Such market focus combined with strong customer relationships helped the firm win the 1998 *Canadian Business* Entrepreneur of the Year award. Ho explains his formula for success as one of opening "our mind and our ears and listen to our customers [so that they] meet the customers' requirements and make sure that [they] have the right product...Once customers come, I don't let them go."[49]

Yet cultivating a niche is only one facet of these companies' success. Ultimate success in market niching can be attributed to an ability to pick a fight carefully, keep costs down by developing and producing products in-house, innovate constantly and acquire smaller rivals to help stretch and expand the product offerings.

Increasingly, even large firms are setting up business units, or companies, to serve niches. Here are some examples of large, profitable companies that have pursued niching strategies:

- **The Beer Industry.** Microbrewers' specialty beers—such as Banks beer from the Hart Brewing Co. Ltd. of Ottawa or Hemp Cream Ale from B.C.'s Bowen Island Brewing Company—are the only markets showing any growth potential in the late 1990s. Today, they account for approximately five percent of the country's beer sales. Growth in this segment has prompted Canada's two mega-brewers—Labatt and Molson—to launch their own specialty beers. Labatt launched Kokanee, a beer positioned to reflect a B.C. attitude and lifestyle. Molson was even more targeted in their efforts. They recently developed a new amber lager called Toronto's Own.

Thus firms with low shares of the total market can be highly profitable through smart niching. Clifford and Cavanagh identified over two dozen highly successful midsize companies and studied their success factors.[50] They found that virtually all these companies were nichers. A. T. Cross niched itself in the high-price writing instruments market with its famous gold writing instruments. Such companies tend to offer high value, charge a premium price, achieve lower manufacturing costs, and shape a strong corporate culture and vision.

- **Alberto Culver Co.** Alberto Culver Co. is a classic example of a midsize company that has used market nicher strategies to grow earnings by 36 percent to $128 million on sales of $2.66 billion in 1997. CEO Howard Bernick explains the Alberto Culver philosophy this way: "We know who we are and, perhaps more importantly, we know who we are not. We know that if we try to out-Procter Procter, we will fall flat on our face." Instead, the company known mainly for its Alberto VO5 hair products focused its marketing muscle on acquiring a stable of small niche brands, including such non-beauty items as flavour enhancers Molly McButter and Mrs. Dash and static-cling fighter Static Guard.[51]

In a study of hundreds of business units, the Strategic Planning Institute found that the return on investment averaged 27 percent in smaller markets, but only 11 percent in larger markets.[52] Why is niching so profitable? The main reason is that the market nicher ends up knowing the target customers so well that it meets their needs better than other firms that are selling to this niche casually. As a result, the nicher can charge a substantial price over costs. The nicher achieves high margin, while the mass marketer achieves high volume. Nichers have three tasks: creating niches, expanding niches, and protecting niches.

Niching carries a major risk in that the market niche might dry up or be attacked. The company is then stuck with highly specialized resources that may not have high-value alternative uses. The key idea in nichemanship is specialization. The following specialist roles are open to nichers:

- *End-user specialist:* The firm specializes in serving one type of end-use customer. For example, a *value-added resellers (VAR)* customizes the computer hardware and software for specific customer segments and earns a price premium in the process.[53]
- *Vertical-level specialist:* The firm specializes at some vertical level of the production-distribution value chain. A copper firm may concentrate on producing raw copper, copper components, or finished copper products.

- *Customer-size specialist:* The firm concentrates on selling to either small, medium-size, or large customers. Many nichers specialize in serving small customers who are neglected by the majors.

- *Specific-customer specialist:* The firm limits its selling to one or a few customers. Many firms sell their entire output to a single company, such as Sears or General Motors.

- *Geographic specialist:* The firm sells only in a certain locality, region, or area of the world.

- *Product or product-line specialist:* The firm carries or produces only one product line or product. A firm may produce only lenses for microscopes. A retailer may carry only ties.

- *Product-feature specialist:* The firm specializes in producing a certain type of product or product feature. Rent-a-Wreck, for example, is a car-rental agency that rents only "beat-up" cars.

- *Job-shop specialist:* The firm customizes its products for individual customers.

- *Quality/price specialist:* The firm operates at the low or high quality ends of the market. Hewlett-Packard specializes in the high-quality, high-price end of the hand-calculator market.

- *Service specialist:* The firm offers one or more services not available from other firms. An example would be a bank that takes loan requests over the phone and hand-delivers the money to the customer.

- *Channel specialist:* The firm specializes in serving only one channel of distribution. For example, a soft-drink company decides to make a very large-size soft drink available only at gas stations.

Because niches can weaken, the firm must continually create new niches. The firm should "stick to its niching" but not necessarily to its niche. That is why *multiple niching* is preferable to *single niching*. By developing strength in two or more niches, the company increases its chances of survival.

Firms entering a market should aim at a niche initially rather than the whole market. See the Marketing Insight titled "Strategies for Entering Markets Held by Incumbent Firms."

BALANCING CUSTOMER AND COMPETITOR ORIENTATIONS

We have stressed the importance of a company's positioning itself competitively as a market leader, challenger, follower, or nicher. Yet a company must not spend all its time focusing on competitors. We can distinguish between two types of companies: competitor-centred and customer-centred. A *competitor-centred company* sets its course as follows:

Situation
- Competitor W is going all out to crush us in Winnipeg.
- Competitor X is improving its distribution coverage in Montreal and hurting our sales.
- Competitor Y has cut its price in Halifax, and we lost three share points.
- Competitor Z has introduced a new service feature in Regina, and we are losing sales.

Reactions
- We will withdraw from the Winnipeg market because we cannot afford to fight this battle.
- We will increase our advertising expenditure in Montreal.
- We will meet competitor Y's price cut in Halifax.
- We will increase our sales-promotion budget in Regina.

Strategies for Entering Markets Held by Incumbent Firms

What marketing strategies can companies use to enter a market held by incumbent firms? Biggadike examined the strategies of 40 invading firms. He found that 10 firms entered at a lower price, nine matched the incumbents' prices, and 21 entered at a higher price. Of these, 28 claimed superior quality, five matched incumbents' quality, and seven reported inferior product quality. Most entrants offered a specialist product line and served a narrower market segment. Less than 20 percent managed to innovate a new channel of distribution. Over half the entrants offered a higher level of customer service. Over half the entrants spent less than incumbents on sales force, advertising, and promotion. The winning marketing mix was: (1) higher prices and higher quality, (2) narrower product line, (3) narrower market segment, (4) similar distribution channels, (5) superior service, and (6) lower expenditure on sales force, advertising, and promotion.

Carpenter and Nakamoto examined strategies for launching a new product into a market dominated by one brand, such as Jell-O or Federal Express. (These brands, which include many market pioneers, are particularly difficult to attack because many are the standard against which others are judged.) They identified four strategies that have good profit potential in this situation:

1. *Differentiation*—positioning away from the dominant brand with a comparable or premium price and heavy advertising spending to establish the new brand as a credible alternative. Example: Honda's motorcycle challenges Harley Davidson.

2. *Challenger*—positioning close to the dominant brand with heavy advertising spending and comparable or premium price to challenge the dominant brand as the category standard. Examples: Pepsi competing against Coke.

3. *Niche*—positioning away from the dominant brand with a high price and a low advertising budget to exploit a profitable niche. Example: Kingston's White Mountain All-Natural Ice Cream competing against its nationally branded rivals.

4. *Premium*—positioning near the dominant brand with little advertising spending but a premium price to move "up market" relative to the dominant brand. Examples: Godiva chocolate competing against Cadbury brands.

Schnaars examined the strategies of successful invading firms that entered occupied markets and eventually took leadership. He detailed more than 30 cases in which the imitator displaced the innovator, including:

Product	Innovator	Imitator
Word processing software	Word Star	WordPerfect
Spreadsheet software	Unicalc	later Word
Credit cards	Diners' Club	Visa and MasterCard
Ball-point pens	Reynolds	Parker
CAT scanners	EMI	General Electric
Hand calculators	Bowmar	Texas Instruments
Food processors	Cuisinart	Black & Decker

The imitators captured the market by offering lower prices, selling an improved product, or using superior market power and resources.

Sources: See Ralph Biggadike, *Entering New Markets: Strategies and Performance* (Cambridge, MA: Marketing Science Institute, 1977), pp. 12–20; Gregory S. Carpenter and Kent Nakamoto, "Competitive Strategies for Late Entry into a Market with a Dominant Brand," *Management Science*, October 1990, pp. 1268–78; Gregory S. Carpenter and Kent Nakamoto, "Competitive Late Mover Strategies," working paper, Northwestern University, 1993; and Steven P. Schnaars, *Managing Imitation Strategies: How Later Entrants Seize Markets from Pioneers* (New York: Free Press, 1994).

This kind of planning has some pluses and minuses. On the positive side, the company develops a fighter orientation. It trains its marketers to be on constant alert, to watch for weaknesses in its competitors' and its own position. On the negative side, the company is too reactive. Rather than formulating and executing a consistent customer-oriented strategy, it determines its moves based on its competitors' moves. It does not move toward its own goals. It does not know where it will end up, since so much depends on what its competitors do.

A *customer-centred company* focuses more on customer developments in formulating its strategies. It would pay attention to the following:

Situation

- The total market is growing at four percent annually.
- The quality-sensitive segment is growing at eight percent annually.
- The deal-prone customer segment is also growing fast, but these customers do not stay with any supplier very long.
- A growing number of customers have expressed an interest in a 24-hour hotline, which no one in the industry offers.

Reactions

- We will focus more effort on reaching and satisfying the quality segment of the market. We will buy better components, improve quality control, and shift our advertising theme to quality.

- We will avoid cutting prices and making deals because we do not want the kind of customer that buys this way.

- We will install a 24-hour hotline if it looks promising.

Clearly, the customer-centred company is in a better position to identify new opportunities and set a strategy course that promises to deliver long-run profits. By monitoring customer needs, it can decide which customer groups and emerging needs are the most important to serve, given its resources and objectives.

In practice, companies must carefully monitor both customers and competitors.

SUMMARY

1. To prepare an effective marketing strategy, a company must study its competitors as well as its actual and potential customers. Companies need to identify competitors' strategies, objectives, strengths, weaknesses, and reaction patterns. They also need to know how to design an effective competitive intelligence system—which competitors to attack and which to avoid.

2. A company's closest competitors are those seeking to satisfy the same customers and needs and making similar offers. A company should also pay attention to latent competitors, who may offer new or other ways to satisfy the same needs. The company should identify competitors by using both industry and market-based analyses.

3. Competitive intelligence needs to be collected, interpreted, and disseminated continuously. Managers should be able to receive timely information about competitors. With good competitive intelligence, managers can more easily formulate their strategies.

4. Managers need to conduct a customer value analysis to reveal the company's strengths and weaknesses relative to competitors. The aim of this analysis is to determine the benefits that customers want and how they perceive the relative value of competitors' offers.

5. A market leader has the largest market share in the relevant product market. To remain dominant, the leader looks for ways to expand total market demand, attempts to protect its current market share, and perhaps tries to increase its market share.

6. A market challenger attacks the market leader and other competitors in an aggressive bid for more market share. Challengers can choose from five types of general attack: frontal, flank, encirclement, bypass, guerrilla, or any combination of these. Challengers must also choose specific strategies: discount prices, produce cheaper goods, produce prestige goods, produce a wide variety of goods, innovate in products or distribution, improve services, reduce manufacturing costs, or engage in intensive advertising.

7. A market follower is a runner-up firm that is willing to maintain its market share and not rock the boat. A follower can play the role of counterfeiter, cloner, imitator, or adapter.

8. A market nicher serves small market segments not being served by larger firms. The key to nichemanship is specialization. Nichers can select one or more of the following areas: end user, vertical level, customer size, specific customer, geographic, product or product line, product feature, job shop, quality/price, service, or channel. Multiple niching is generally preferable to single niching.

9. As important as a competitive orientation is in today's global markets, companies should not overdo the emphasis on competitors. Companies should manage a good balance of consumer and competitor monitoring.

CHAPTER CONCEPTS

1. You are part of a product-management team for a Lever Brothers laundry detergent line. Your group's objective is to challenge P&G's laundry detergent line and to become the market leader, but you are not sure how you should proceed. Discuss the pros and cons of each of the following strategies in this market: (a) frontal attack, (b) flank attack, (c) encirclement attack, (d) bypass attack, and (e) guerrilla attack.

2. In the medical field, there is a battle between old and new technologies. Traditionally, a surgeon would make large incisions in patients, but in endoscopic surgery the doctor makes a tiny cut and inserts a slender, tubular instrument called a trochar into the body to perform the surgery. The United States Surgical Corporation (USSC) began marketing endoscopic surgery equipment in the late 1980s, followed by Ethicon Endo-Surgery, a Johnson & Johnson company, in the early 1990s. The following table summarizes the customer-value research conducted by J&J into traditional vs. endoscopic surgery.

    Assuming that the surgeons charge the same amount for both kinds of surgery, which form of surgery is better—traditional or endoscopic? How can J&J's Ethicon Endo-Surgery business gain a competitive advantage over USSC—which already has the first-to-market advantage?

3. Listed below are several company strengths revealed during an internal audit of an office-supply retailer that competes with Office Depot.

    a. Innovative product features

    b. Broad distribution

    c. Lower costs and prices

    d. Broad product line

    e. Strong technical service

How could each of these business strengths be translated into customer benefits that would give this retailer a competitive advantage over Office Depot?

Quality Attributes	(1) Performance Endo Method	(2) Performance Traditional Method	(3) Ratio[a]	(4) Relative Weight	(5) Weight Times Ratio
At-home recovery	1–2 weeks	6–8 weeks	3.0	40	120
Hospital stay	1–2 days	3–7 days	2.0	30	60
Operation time	1/2–1 hour	1–2 hours	2.0	15	30
Complication rate	5%	10%	1.5	10	15
Postoperative scar	0.5–1 inch	3–5 inches	1.4	05	07
		Sum of quality weights:		100	
		Market-perceived quality score:			232
		Market-perceived quality ratio:			2.32

[a]In this example the ratios are not calculated directly from performance measures shown in columns 1 and 2. They are based on performance scores from 1 to 10 that are linked to the performance data shown.

TABLE 1

Quality profile: Gallbladder operations: Endoscopic versus traditional surgery

1. Canada Post uses advertising to show a number of different types of organizations the benefits of reaching customers through direct marketing. Figure 1 is a Canada Post ad. The headline reads, "Get the Power to Go Direct with This Free Offer." The text of the ad claims, "Whether you're a consumer, business-to-business, social services or fundraising marketer, The Complete Direct Marketer will provide you with a powerful knowledge base to expand your marketing activities. You'll be learning from the accumulated experiece of some of the most successful direct marketers in the industry. Load up on the information you need to take your company to new levels of marketing success. Call 1-888-280-3101. Quantities are limited." Is the direct marketing industry structure a pure monopoly, an oligopoly, monopolistic competition, or pure competition? Support your answer. Analyze the direct marketing industry by using the information on pages 218–219 and Figure 8.1. Is this an attractive or unattractive industry? Why do you think Canada Post is offering this free offer to prospective customers?

Figure 1

Levi Strauss
http://www.levi.com/originalspin/

Levi Strauss is using mass-customization manufacturing technology to bring customer-size specialization to a new level in an innovative market-nicher strategy for its jeans. The program, titled Levi's Original Spin, allows customers to order jeans specially manufactured to their personal specifications. Levi's salespeople take just three body measurements, and customers get to choose the colour, fabric, leg opening, fly type, and model cut. These specifications are electronically transmitted to the Levi's factory, where the automated equipment manufactures custom-fit jeans in two to three weeks.

Visit the Original Spin pages on Levi's Web site to read about this program. How does this program help Levi's compete more effectively against Wrangler and Lee, two traditional competitors in the jeans market? Is Levi's aiming for high margin or high volume with this niche strategy? How do you know?

part two
Analyzing
Marketing
Opportunities

Disintermediation via the Internet is changing the competitive playing field in many industries, from tangible goods such as cars (exemplified by Auto Depot) to intangible services such as insurance (exemplified by ING Direct). Taking a closer look at disintermediation in the travel industry, consider the competition that a local travel agency faces from airline Web sites such as American Airlines and travel Web sites such as Microsoft's Expedia.

Visit the either the Canadian Airlines or Air Canada Web site to see what is offered, including special fares, flight schedules and pricing, frequent flyer programs, information about airport access, and so on. Next, visit the Expedia Web site to sample its offerings, including booking air travel, rental cars, and hotel rooms, finding information about travel destinations, maps, and more. How are these sites similar, and how are they different? What do these sites offer that traditional travel agencies do not? What do traditional travel agencies offer that these sites do not? What are the implications for the traditional agencies that compete with these online sites?

Canadian Airlines
http://www.cdair.ca

Air Canada
http://www.aircanada.ca

Expedia
http://www.expedia.com

YOU'RE THE MARKETER:
SONIC MARKETING PLAN

Competitive strategy comes into play in two areas of the marketing plan. First, in assessing the current marketing situation, companies must examine their competitors' strengths and weaknesses and competitors' reaction patterns. Second, they must use competitive intelligence to shape their overall competitive strategy, which is supported by the marketing mix.

As Jane Melody's assistant, you are analyzing Sonic's competitive situation and preparing its competitive strategy for shelf stereo systems. Review Sonic's current situation and the research you have already collected for your marketing plan. Then, assuming that Sonic is not the market leader, answer the following questions about competitive strategy (noting the need for competitive intelligence where necessary):

- What is the strategic group for Sonic?

- Which firm is the market leader, and what are its objectives, strengths, and weaknesses? (What additional competitive intelligence is needed?)

- As a market challenger, what competitive strategy would be most effective for Sonic?

- Given this competitive strategy, how would you define Sonic's strategic objective and attack strategy?

- Think carefully about how Sonic's competitive strategy will affect its marketing mix. Then, as your instructor directs, summarize your findings and conclusions in a written marketing plan or type them into the Marketing Situation and Marketing Strategy sections of the Marketing Plan Pro software.

Identifying Market Segments and Selecting Target Markets

CHAPTER 9

PROFILE:

Canadian Marketing Excellence

D on't buy market share. Figure out how to earn it. Not an easy task if you are trying to influence modern farmers. Farming is no longer the simple venture that the song "Old Macdonald Had a Farm" would suggest. It is a high-tech business requiring business savvy and huge investments. Companies targeting this market, like DuPont Canada, use sophisticated database-marketing techniques. A recent campaign for its herbicide, Refine Extra® Toss-n-Go®, won the firm and its agency, OgilvyOne Worldwide, the 1998 RSVP Award for Best Direct Mail.

The nature of the family farm today means you need a hybrid of business-to-business and business-to-consumer marketing. Using traditional segmentation strategies isn't possible either. While it might seem logical to segment the market based on geographic variables, agri-marketers, like DuPont, realize that this isn't very effective since you can have a small operator living right next to a major agricultural corporation. "There's much more market fragmentation than in, say, a suburb of Toronto, where you can extrapolate that everyone in that suburb has a family income in excess of $100 000." Firms rely instead on proprietary databases to help them target their products.

Two key insights helped DuPont develop such a successful campaign: offer the recipient added value, and keep the message straightforward. Each of the targeted farmers received a brief letter and a sample of the product packaging. No glossy four-colour brochures accompanied the mailing. The reasoning: "In business-to-business, we have always found plainer is better. It doesn't look so promotional." If recipients agreed to test the herbicide, they would receive a gift, a multi-tool, which was pictured in the offer. This value-added approach turned out to be widely successful. DuPont Canada had hoped to receive 500 calls—it received 2500 instead!

Sources: Norma Ramage, "How DuPont Topped Its Goal by 500%," Marketing, February 15, 1999, p.11. Norma Ramage, "Selling to Jaded Farmers," Marketing, February 15, 1999, p.11.

This chapter will answer the following questions:

■ How can a company identify the segments that make up a market?

■ What criteria can a company use to choose the most attractive target markets?

As Maria Chapin noted, "There isn't any one Canada, any average Canadian, any average place, any type." A company cannot serve all customers in a broad market such as computers or soft drinks. The customers are too numerous and diverse in their buying requirements. The company needs to identify the market segments that it can serve more effectively. Here we will examine levels of segmentation, patterns of segmentation, market-segmentation procedure, bases for segmenting consumer and business markets, and requirements for effective segmentation.

Many companies are embracing *target marketing*. Here sellers distinguish the major market segments, target one or more of those segments, and develop products and marketing programs tailored to each. Instead of using a "shotgun" approach that scatters their marketing effort, they concentrate on the buyers that they have the greatest chance of satisfying (a "rifle" approach).

Target marketing requires marketers to take three major steps:

1. Identify and profile distinct groups of buyers who might require separate products and/or marketing mixes (market segmentation).

2. Select one or more market segments to enter (market targeting).

3. Establish and communicate the products' key distinctive benefits in the market (market positioning).

This chapter will focus on the first two steps. The next chapter will discuss market positioning.

LEVELS AND PATTERNS OF MARKET SEGMENTATION

We begin by examining the various levels and patterns of market segmentation.

LEVELS OF MARKET SEGMENTATION

Market segmentation is an effort to increase a company's precision marketing. The starting point of any segmentation discussion is *mass marketing*. In mass marketing, the seller engages in the mass production, mass distribution, and mass promotion of one product for all buyers. Henry Ford epitomized this marketing strategy when he offered the Model T Ford "in any colour as long as it is black." Coca Cola also practised mass marketing when it sold only one kind of Coke in a 6.5-ounce bottle.

The argument for mass marketing is that it creates the largest potential market, which leads to the lowest costs, which in turn can lead to lower prices or higher margins. It is the philosophy that has driven many *global* programs in which products and marketing programs are standardized for worldwide markets. However, many critics point to the increasing splintering of the market, which makes mass marketing more difficult. According to Regis McKenna:

> [Consumers] ...have more ways to shop: at giant malls, specialty shops, and superstores; through mail-order catalogues, home shopping networks, and virtual stores on the Internet. And they are bombarded with messages pitched through a growing number of channels: broadcast and narrow-cast television, radio, on-line computer networks, the Internet, telephone services such as fax and telemarketing, and niche magazines and other print media.[1]

The proliferation of advertising media and distribution channels is making it difficult to practise "one-size-fits-all" marketing. Some claim that mass marketing is dying. Not surprisingly, many companies are turning to micromarketing at one of four levels: segments, niches, local areas, and individuals.

Segment Marketing

A *market segment* consists of a large identifiable group within a market differing in wants, purchasing power, geographical location, buying attitudes, or buying habits. For example, an auto company may identify four broad segments: car buyers who are primarily seeking basic transportation, or high performance, or luxury, or safety.

Segmentation is an approach midway between mass marketing and individual marketing. Each segment's buyers are assumed to be quite similar in wants and needs, yet no two buyers are really alike. Anderson and Narus urge marketers to present *flexible market offerings* instead of a standard offering to all members within a segment.[2] A flexible market offering consists of two parts: a *naked solution* consisting of product and service elements that all segment members value—and *options* that some segment members value. Each option carries an additional charge. For example, Via Rail offers all economy passengers a seat, but it charges extra for food, soft drinks, and alcoholic beverages for those passengers wanting them. Siemens sells metal-clad boxes whose price includes free delivery and a warranty but also offers installation, tests, and communication peripherals as extra-cost options.

Segment marketing offers several benefits over mass marketing. The company can create a more fine-tuned product/service offer and price it appropriately for the target audience. The choice of distribution channels and communications channels becomes much easier. And the company may face fewer competitors in the particular segment.

Niche Marketing

A *niche* is a more narrowly defined group, typically a small market whose needs are not well served. Marketers usually identify niches by dividing a segment into subsegments or by defining a group seeking a distinctive mix of benefits. For example, the Royal Bank recently teamed up with SFNB Securities First Network Bank of Atlanta to offer McGill University's 165 000 alumni living in both Canada and the United States a cross-border McGill University Visa card that has benefits such as worldwide cash access, convenience cheques, and purchase security insurance.[3]

While segments are fairly large and normally attract several competitors, niches are fairly small and normally attract only one or two. Larger companies, such as IBM, lose pieces of their market to nichers: Dalgic and Leeuw labelled this confrontation "guerrillas against gorillas."[4]

The prevalence of niche—and even "microniche"—marketing can be seen in the media. Witness the proliferation of new magazines (in 1998 there were 1000 first-edition magazines launched) targeting specific niches, divided and subdivided along lines of ethnicity, gender, and/or sexual orientation: *B1G2* (meaning "black first, gay second") is a New York-based lifestyle magazine. In July 1999, the Canadian Nurses Association of Ottawa launched a new on-line journal targeting the francophone nursing community. Canadian publisher Brunico, specializes in trade publications targeted at niche markets around the world. It publishes *Strategy: The Canadian Marketing Report* aimed at marketing professionals, *Kidscreen* for people working in the children's media industry, and *Realscreen* for documentary film makers.

Brunico
www.brunico.com

Niche marketers presumably understand their customers' needs so well that customers willingly pay a premium. Ferrari gets a high price for its cars because loyal buyers feel no other automobile comes close to offering the product-service-membership benefit bundle that Ferrari does.

An attractive niche is characterized as follows: The customers in the niche have a distinct set of needs; they will pay a premium to the firm that best satisfies their needs; the niche is not likely to attract other competitors; the nicher gains certain economies through specialization; and the niche has size, profit, and growth potential.

Both small and large companies can practise niche marketing. Some larger companies have therefore turned to niche marketing, which has required more decentralization and some changes in the way they do business. Johnson & Johnson, for example, consists of 170 affiliates (business units), many of which pursue niche markets.

- ■ **Ramada Franchises Enterprises** offers lodgings in a variety of niches: Ramada Limited for economy travellers; Ramada Inn for those seeking a mid-priced full-service hotel; Ramada Plaza, a new offering in the upper-mid-price niche; Ramada Hotels offering three-star service; and Ramada Renaissance hotels, offering four-star service.

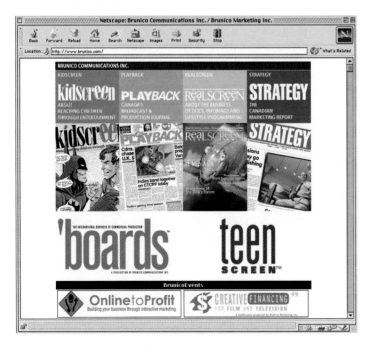

Brunico, a trade magazine publisher, has carved out several successful global niche markets.

Linneman and Stanton claim that there are riches in niches and believe that companies will have to niche or risk being niched.[5] Blattberg and Deighton claim that "niches too small to be served profitably today will become viable as marketing efficiency improves."[6] The low cost of setting up shop in the Internet is a key factor making it more profitable to serve even seemingly minuscule niches. Small businesses, in particular, are realizing riches from serving small niches on the World Wide Web. Fifteen percent of the commercial Web sites with fewer than 10 employees take in more than $150 000 and two percent even rang up more than $1 million. The recipe for Internet niching success: choose a hard-to-find product that customers don't need to see and touch. These three "Webpreneurs" followed this recipe with astonishing results:[7]

- **Ostrichesonline.com.** While Internet giants like music retailer CDnow and bookseller Amazon.com have yet to even realize a profit, Steve Warrington is earning a six-figure income selling ostriches, and every product derived from them, online (www.ostrichesonline.com). Launched for next to nothing on the Web, Warrington's business generated $6 million in sales in 1998. Visitors to the site can buy ostrich meat, feathers, leather jackets, videos, eggshells, and skin-care products derived from ostrich body oil.

- **ESeeds.com.** Vancouver's Mala Gunadasa-Rohling discovered that she could turn her interest in gardening into a business. Not only does she design and maintain the web sites for about 40 garden clubs, but she also found a response from Canadian gardeners who hunger for information geared to their specific climates. She specializes in seeds coming from Canadian suppliers. Although her sales have been small to date, Gunadasa-Rohling is now receiving orders from Europe and the United States as well as Canada.

- **Gaia-ultimate.com.** Devotees of Ultimate, a game best described as football with frisbees, were often out of luck if they didn't live in the Vancouver or Ottawa area, the only two markets with Gaia Sports Stores. Today, they can now find their gear on-line at the company's well-designed, user-friendly web site.

In many markets today, niches are the norm. See the Marketing Insight titled "Hidden Champions: German Mid-size Companies Grow Prosperous through Niching."

Local Marketing

Target marketing is leading to marketing programs being tailored to the needs and wants of local customer groups (trading areas, neighbourhoods, even individual stores). Kraft helps supermarket chains identify the cheese assortment and shelf positioning that will optimize cheese sales in low-, middle-, and high-income stores, and in different ethnic neighbourhoods.

Those favouring localizing a company's marketing view national advertising as wasteful because it fails to address local needs. Those against local marketing argue that it drives up manufacturing and marketing costs by reducing economies of scale. Logistical problems become magnified when companies try to meet varying local requirements. And a brand's overall image might be diluted if the product and message differ in different localities.

Individual Marketing

The ultimate level of segmentation leads to "segments of one," "customized marketing," or "one-to-one marketing."[8] For centuries, consumers were served as individuals: The tailor made the suit and the cobbler designed shoes for the individual. Much business-to-business marketing today is customized, in that a manufacturer will customize the offer, logistics, communications, and financial terms for each major account. New technologies—computers, databases, robotic production, e-mail, and fax—permit companies to return to customized marketing, or what is called "mass customization."[9] *Mass customization* is the ability to prepare on a mass basis individually designed products and communications to meet each customer's requirements.

Hidden Champions: German Mid-size Companies Grow Prosperous Through Niching

The German economy has over 300 000 small and mid-size companies (known as the *Mittelstand*) which collectively account for two-thirds of Germany's gross national product and employ four out of every five workers. Although these companies have fewer than 500 employees, many enjoy greater than 50 percent market shares in well-defined global niches. Hermann Simon dubbed these global niche leaders *Hidden Champions* and defines them as businesses that are number one or two in the world market or number one in the European market, earning less than $1 billion in annual sales, and having generally low public visibility. Here are some examples:

- Tetra Food has 80 percent of the world tropical fish market.

- Hohner has 85 percent of the world harmonica market.

- Becher has 50 percent of the world's very large umbrella market.

- Steiner Optical has 80 percent of the world's military field glasses market.

These hidden champions tend to be found in stable markets, are typically family owned or closely held, and long-lived. Their success can be explained as follows:

- They are very dedicated to their customers and offer superior performance, responsive service, and punctual delivery (rather than low price) as well as customer intimacy.

- Their top management stays in direct and regular contact with top customers.

- They emphasize continuous innovation directed at benefiting customers.

Hidden champions are found in many other countries besides Germany. They all share the characteristic of combining high product focus with geographic diversity and establishing the leading reputation in the targeted niche.

Source: Hermann Simon, *Hidden Champions* (Boston: Harvard Business School Press, 1996).

- **Andersen Windows.** Andersen Windows, a $1.5-billion manufacturer of windows for the home-building industry, turned to mass customization after additions to its product line led to fat and unwieldy catalogues and a bewildering array of choices for homeowners and contractors. In a six-year period, the number of products had tripled. To create order—or, rather, customized orders—in the chaos, Andersen developed an interactive computer version of the catalogues for distributors and retailers that is linked directly to the factory. With the system, now in 650 showrooms, salespeople can help customers customize each window, check the design for structural soundness, and generate a price quote. From there Andersen went on to develop a "batch of one" manufacturing process in which everything was made to order, thus reducing its finished parts inventory (a major cost to the company).[10]

For more detailed information on how mass customization is being used in consumer and business-to-business marketing, and its prospects for the future, see the Marketing for the 21st Century box "A Segment of One: Mass Customization Comes of Age."

According to Arnold Ostle, chief designer for Mazda, "Customers will want to express their individuality with the products they buy."[11] The opportunities offered by these technologies promise to turn marketing from "a broadcast medium to a dialogue medium," where the customer participates actively in the design of the product and offer.

Today customers are taking more individual initiative in determining what and how to buy. They log onto the Internet; look up information and evaluations of product/service offers; dialog with suppliers, users, and product critics; and make up their own minds about the best offer.

Marketers will still influence the process but in new ways. They will need to set up toll-free phone numbers and e-mail addresses to enable buyers to reach them with questions, suggestions, and complaints. They will involve customers more in the product-specification process. They will sponsor an Internet home page that provides full information about the company's products, guarantees, and locations.

A Segment of One: Mass Customization Comes of Age

Imagine walking into a booth that bathes your body in patterns of white light and, in a matter of seconds, determines your exact three-dimensional structure. The digitized measurement data are then collected on a credit card, which you use to order customized clothing. No, this isn't how the crew of the Starship Enterprise order their clothing, but how you will be able to buy clothing in the not-so-distant future. A consortium of over 100 apparel companies, including Levi's, has banded together to develop body-scanning technology in the hope of making mass customization commonplace.

While body-scanning technology and smart cards carrying customer measurements are still in development, a number of companies are using existing technologies to customize their products to the individual. We all know about Dell and its customer-configured computers, but here's a host of non-techie companies in the forefront of the have-it-your-way economy:

■ **Mattel.** Starting in 1998, girls were able to log onto barbie.com and design their own Barbie Pal. They choose the doll's skin tone, eye colour, hairdo and hair colour, clothes, accessories, and name. They even fill out a questionnaire detailing their doll's likes and dislikes. When Barbie's Pal arrives in the mail, girls find the doll's name on the packaging along with a computer-generated paragraph about her personality.

■ **Custom Foot.** This five-store chain takes 13 different measurements of women's feet and sends the results electronically to Italy. There shoes are custom-made to take into account individual bumps, bulges, and bunions.

■ **Levi's.** Levi's has made measure-to-fit women's jeans under the Personal Pair banner since 1994. It is now launching an expanded version called Original Spin, which will offer even more style options and feature men's jeans as well. Today, a fully stocked Levi's store carries 130 ready-to-wear pairs of jeans for a given waist and inseam. With Personal Pair the number jumped to 430, and with Original Spin it will jump to 750.

■ **CDuctive.** New York's hip, Tribeca-based CDuctive lets customers cut their own CDs online. If a customer likes acid jazz, he can click on the category, see 30 titles and sample a 45-second snatch of each. With a few keystrokes he can then order a $21 CD with all the tunes he has selected.

■ **Bell Mobility,** the Toronto-based subsidiary of BCE Mobile Communications Inc., recently launched Digital DATA to Go, a service that provides customers access to a suite of personal productivity applications including on-line banking, e-mail, and web browsing. Its PCS Mobile Browser allows users to access live Internet data directly on their telephone handset.

Just as mass production was the organizing principle of the last century, mass customization is becoming the organizing principle for the 21st century. Two trends are converging to make this so. One is the predominance of the customer and the importance of true customer service. Consumers are not only demanding quality products, but also products that meet their individual needs. Marketing expert Regis McKenna says, "Choice has become a higher value than brand." Yet, it would be prohibitively expensive, if not downright impossible, to offer customers so many choices if it weren't for another trend: the

PATTERNS OF MARKET SEGMENTATION

Market segments can be built up in many ways. One way is to identify *preference segments*. Suppose ice-cream buyers are asked how much they value sweetness and creaminess as two product attributes. Three different patterns can emerge.

■ *Homogeneous preferences:* Figure 9-1(a) shows a market where all the consumers have roughly the same preference. The market shows no natural segments. We would predict that existing brands would be similar and cluster around the middle of the scale in both sweetness and creaminess.

■ *Diffused preferences:* At the other extreme, consumer preferences may be scattered throughout the space (Figure 9-1[b]), indicating that consumers vary greatly in their preferences. The first brand to enter the market is likely to position in the centre to appeal to the most people. A brand in the centre minimizes the sum of total consumer dissatisfaction. A second competitor could locate next to the first brand and fight for market share. Or it could locate in a corner to attract a customer group that was not satisfied with the centre brand. If several brands are in the market, they are likely to position throughout the space and show real differences to match consumer-preference differences.

(continued)

emergence of new technologies. Computer-controlled factory equipment and industrial robots can now quickly readjust assembly lines. Bar-code scanners make it possible to track parts and products. Data warehouses can store trillions of bytes of customer information. Most important of all, the Internet ties it all together and makes it easy for a company to interact with customers, learn about their preferences, and respond. Joseph Pine, author of *Mass Customization*, says, "Anything you can digitize, you can customize."

Consumer-goods marketers aren't the only ones riding these trends. Business-to-business marketers are also finding that they can provide customers with tailor-made goods and services as cheaply as, and in the same amount of time as, it used to take to make standardized ones. Particularly for small companies, mass customization provides a way to stand out against larger competitors:

ChemStation. This $37 million company offers its industrial customers—ranging from car washes to the military—individually concocted soap formulas. What cleans a car won't work to clean an airplane or equipment in a mineshaft. Salespeople visit customer sites to gather information about customers' cleaning needs. All the information from the company's chemical lab and the field sits in a central customized database called Tank Management System (TMS). TMS is linked directly to both the lab and the company's 40 plants, where computer-run machines mix each customer's special formula.

Ross/Flex. Ross Controls, a manufacturer of pneumatic valves, landed a $375 million client, Danly-Komatsu, by offering them a customized-valve system under its Ross/Flex program. Using CAD/CAM technology, Ross was able to ship a prototype to Danly-Komatsu's engineers in only two days. Because the system was a custom fit, the engineers were able to install it in their presses in less than half the time it would have taken to assemble and load up standard parts.

For both consumer marketers and business marketers, relationship marketing is an important ingredient of mass customization programs. Unlike mass production, which eliminates the need for human interaction, mass customization has made relationships with customers more important than ever. For instance, Ross Controls limits the number of clients for which it provides customized valve systems because there is so much upfront collaboration necessary. At ChemStation, 95 percent of clients never leave because teaching another company their cleansing needs is not worth the effort. For consumer marketers, the relationship typically begins after the sale is made. When Levi's sells off-the-shelf jeans, the customer walks out of the store, perhaps never to return. When Levi's sells its made-to-order jeans, the company not only captures consumer data in digitized form, but also becomes the customer's "jeans advisor." Mattel is building a database of information from all the children who purchase Barbie's Pal, so they can start a one-to-one relationship with each child, and determine future sales possibilities.

Sources: Erick Schonfeld, "The Customized, Digitized, Have-It-Your-Way Economy," " *Fortune*, September 28, 1998, pp. 115-124. "Bell Mobility Offers Data To Go," *Ad News On-Line Daily*, May 19, 1999, p. 2. Bruce Fox, "Levi's Personal Pair prognosis positive," *Chain Store Age*, March 1996, p. 35. Jim Barlow, "Individualizing Mass Production," Houston Chronicle, April 13, 1997, p. E, 1:1. Sarah Schafer, *Inc.*, November 18, 1997, pp. 56-64. Marc Ballon, "Sale of Modern Music Keyed to Customization," *Inc.*, May 1998, pp. 23, 25. Anne Eisenberg, "If the Shoe Fits, Click it," *New York Times*, August 13, 1998, p. 1.

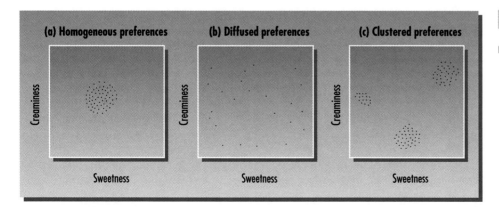

(a) Homogeneous preferences **(b) Diffused preferences** **(c) Clustered preferences**

Creaminess / Sweetness

FIGURE 9.1

Basic Market-Preference Patterns

- *Clustered preferences:* The market might reveal distinct preference clusters, called *natural market segments* (Figure 9-1[c]). The first firm in this market has three options. It might position in the centre, hoping to appeal to all groups. It might position in the largest market segment (*concentrated marketing*). It might develop several brands, each positioned in a different segment. If the first firm developed only one brand, competitors would enter and introduce brands in the other segments.

MARKET-SEGMENTATION PROCEDURE

Here is a three-step procedure for identifying market segments: survey, analysis, and profiling.

Step One: Survey Stage
The researcher conducts exploratory interviews and focus groups to gain insight into consumer motivations, attitudes, and behaviour. Then the researcher prepares a questionnaire and collects data on attributes and their importance ratings; brand awareness and brand ratings; product-usage patterns; attitudes toward the product category; and demographics, geographics, psychographics, and mediagraphics of the respondents.

Step Two: Analysis Stage
The researcher applies *factor analysis* to the data to remove highly correlated variables, then applies *cluster analysis* to create a specified number of maximally different segments.

Step Three: Profiling Stage
Each cluster is profiled in terms of its distinguishing attitudes, behaviour, demographics, psychographics, and media patterns. Each segment is given a name based on its dominant characteristic. In a study of the leisure market, Andreasen and Belk found six segments:[12] passive homebody, active sports enthusiast, inner-directed self-sufficient, culture patron, active homebody, and socially active. They found that performing arts organizations could sell the most tickets by targeting culture patrons and socially active people.

Market segmentation must be redone periodically because market segments change. At one time the personal computer industry segmented its products purely on speed and power, thus appealing to two broad swathes, high-end users and low-end users, but missing out on the prosperous middle. Later PC marketers recognized an emerging "SoHo" market, named for "small office and home office." Mail-order companies like Dell and Gateway appealed to this market's requirement for high performance coupled with low price and user friendliness. Shortly thereafter PC makers began to see SoHo as comprised of smaller segments. "Small-office needs might be very different from home-office needs," says one Dell executive.[13]

One way to discover new segments is to investigate the hierarchy of attributes that consumers examine in choosing a brand. This process is called *market partitioning*. Years ago, most car buyers first decided on the manufacturer and then on one of its car divisions (*brand-dominant hierarchy*). A buyer might favour General Motors cars and, within this set, Pontiac. Today, many buyers decide first on the nation from which they want to buy a car (*nation-dominant hierarchy*). Buyers may first decide they want to buy a Japanese car, then Toyota, and then the Corolla model of Toyota. Companies must monitor potential shifts in the consumers' hierarchy of attributes and adjust to changing priorities.

The hierarchy of attributes can reveal customer segments. Buyers who first decide on price are price dominant; those who first decide on the type of car (e.g., sports, passenger, station wagon) are type dominant; those who first decide on the car brand are brand dominant; and so on. One can identify those who are type/price/brand dominant, in that order, as making up a segment; those who are quality/service/type dominant as making up another segment. Each segment may have distinct demographics, psychographics, and mediagraphics.[14]

SEGMENTING CONSUMER AND BUSINESS MARKETS

BASES FOR SEGMENTING CONSUMER MARKETS

Two broad groups of variables are used to segment consumer markets. Some researchers try to form segments by looking at *consumer characteristics*: geographic, demographic, and psychographic. Then they examine whether these customer segments exhibit different needs or product responses. For example, they might examine the differing attitudes of "professionals," "blue collars," and other groups toward, say, "safety" as a car benefit.

Other researchers try to form segments by looking at *consumer responses* to benefits sought, use occasions, or brands. Once the segments are formed, the researcher sees whether different characteristics are associated with each consumer-response segment. For example, the researcher might examine whether people who want "quality" versus "low price" in buying an automobile differ in their geographic, demographic, and psychographic makeup.

The major segmentation variables—geographics, demographics, psychographics, and behavioural segmentation—are summarized in Table 9-1.

Geographic Segmentation

Geographic segmentation calls for dividing the market into different geographical units such as nations, provinces, regions, counties, cities, or neighbourhoods. The company can operate in one or a few geographic areas or operate in all but pay attention to local variations. For example, Hilton Hotels customizes rooms and lobbies according to the location of its hotels. *Your Office* magazine, published by the Canadian Office Products Association, recently launched a French-language version called *Votre Bureau* to better reach Quebec home businesses. Another company recognizing the unique demands of the Quebec market is Hallmark Canada. Its new line of cards, called *Homage au Quebec*, feature a series of paintings designed to capture the essence of Quebec have been produced exclusively to target French-Canadian consumers. More and more regional marketing means marketing right down to a specific postal code:[15]

- **Blockbuster Entertainment.** Blockbuster has invested in complex databases to track the video preferences of its 85 million members and buys additional demographic data from outside companies. It then stocks each of its stores accordingly. Vancouver stores may carry more videos portraying gay relationships, reflecting the city's large gay population. Maritime stores are big on family pictures and dramas. Blockbuster can even measure the difference between patterns of East and West Montreal.

Blockbuster Entertainment
www.blockbuster.com

Demographic Segmentation

In *demographic segmentation*, the market is divided into groups on the basis of variables such as age, family size, family life cycle, gender, income, occupation, education, religion, race, generation, nationality, social class. Demographic variables are the most popular bases for distinguishing customer groups. One reason is that consumer wants, preferences, and usage rates are often associated with demographic variables. Another is that demographic variables are easier to measure. Even when the target market is described in nondemographic terms (say, a personality type), the link back to demographic characteristics is needed in order to estimate the size of the target market and the media that should be used to reach it efficiently.

Here is how certain demographic variables have been used to segment markets.

Age and Life-Cycle Stage. Consumer wants and abilities change with age and their life-cycle stage. In the summer of 1999, Zellers introduced its Special Delivery Baby Catalogue that was distributed to new mothers in hospitals across Canada. Zellers worked with *Today's Parent* magazine so that the catalogue not only offered products, but also included tips to help new parents deal with their busy schedules. Broad age-

TABLE 9.1

Geographic

Region	Atlantic Provinces, Central Canada, Western Provinces, Northern Territories
City or Metro size	Under 4999; 5000-19 999; 20 000-49 999; 50 000-99 999; 100 000-249 999; 250 000-499 999; 500 000-999 999; 1 000 000-3 999 999; 4 000 000 or over
Density	Urban, suburban, rural
Climate	Far north, near north, southern, maritime

Demographic

Age	Under 6, 6-11, 12-19, 20-34, 35-49, 50-64, 65+
Family size	1-2, 3-4, 5+
Family life cycle	Young, single; young, married, no children; young, married, youngest child under 6; young, married, youngest child 6 or over; older, married, with children; older, married, no children under 18; older, single; other
Gender	Male, female
Income	Under $9999; $10 000-$14 999; $15 000-$19 999; $20 000-$29 999; $30 000-$49 999; $50 000-$99 999; $100 000 and over
Occupation	Professional and technical; managers, officials, and proprietors; clerical, sales; craftspeople; forepersons; operatives; farmers; retired; students; homemakers; unemployed
Education	Grade school or less; some high school; high school graduate; community college graduate; some university, university graduate; post-graduate degree
Religion	Catholic, Protestant, Jewish, Muslim, Hindu, other
Ethnicity	English, French, First Nations, Inuit, Italian, German, Asian, Middle Eastern, African
Generation	Baby Boomers, Generation X
Nationality	North American, South American, British, French, German, Italian, Japanese
Social class	Lower lowers, upper lowers, working class, middle class, upper middles, lower uppers, upper uppers

Psychographic

Lifestyle	Straights, gay/lesbian, longhairs
Personality	Compulsive, gregarious, authoritarian, ambitious

Behavioural

Occasions	Regular occasion, special occasion
Benefits	Quality, service, economy, speed
User status	Nonuser, ex-user, potential user, first-time user, regular user
Usage rate	Light user, medium user, heavy user
Loyalty status	None, medium, strong, absolute
Readiness stage	Unaware, aware, informed, interested, desirous, intending to buy
Attitude toward product	Enthusiastic, positive, indifferent, negative, hostile

based categories may not be sufficient to target products.[16] Gerber realized this and began expanding beyond its traditional baby foods line. Its new "Graduates" line is geared for the one— to three-year-old.[17] Sega, the computer-games giant, has a similar goal of retaining the loyalty of its main market segment. Sega is launching a range of merchandise for adults, including clothes, sports equipment, and watches, under its Sega Sports brand. Sega's core market lies in the 10 to 18 age range. Says a Sega licensing executive, "They sit in their bedrooms playing games for hours, then they turn 18 and discover girls . . . and the computer gets locked away." Clothing and other products are a way of taking the brand to a more mature market.[18]

Photo companies are now applying age and life-cycle segmentation to the film market. With film sales down, makers are working hard to exploit promising niche markets: moms, kids, and older people:

■ **Eastman Kodak.** Kodak has begun selling camera sets to kids. These single-use cameras are packaged with an envelope to mail the film back to Kodak for developing. The goal is to make kids independent; they needn't pester mom for a lift to the mall to get their film processed, a factor inhibiting picture taking among kids. Mom also won't see photos of late-night pranks at a slumber party, Kodak insinuates in its advertising to children. To further play up kids' independence, Kodak calls the campaign "Big Shots." On the other end of the demographic spectrum, Kodak trains its own retirees to hold photography workshops for other retirees. Since 1992, Kodak's Ambassador program has been sending retirees on safaris in Kenya, hikes in national parks, and cruises to Nassau and Disney World. The tour organizer or cruise line pays for the Kodak travellers, who earn their keep by providing daily photo demonstrations, games, and activities to teach tour members or passengers to take pictures.[19]

Nevertheless, age and life cycle can be tricky variables. For example, the Ford Motor Company designed its Mustang automobile to appeal to young people who wanted an inexpensive sporty car. But Ford found that the car was being purchased by all age groups. It then realized that its target market was not the chronologically young but the psychologically young.

The Neugartens' research indicates that age stereotypes need to be guarded against:

> Age has become a poor predictor of the timing of life events, as well as a poor predictor of a person's health, work status, family status, and therefore, also, of a person's interests, preoccupations, and needs. We have multiple images of persons of the same age: there is the 70-year-old in a wheelchair and the 70-year-old on the tennis court. Likewise, there are 35-year-olds sending children off to college and 35-year-olds furnishing the nursery for newborns, producing in turn, first-time grand-parenthood for persons who range in age from 35 to 75.[20]

Gender. Gender segmentation has long been applied in clothing, hairstyling, cosmetics, and magazines. Occasionally other marketers notice an opportunity for gender segmentation.

■ **iVillage.com.** iVillage.com, a Web site devoted to women, reaped the benefits of gender segmentation after initially going to a broader market. iVillage.com began with little more than the premise of "Internet for the rest of us," and a focus on baby boomers. Offerings geared for women were the ones that really took off, like Parent Soup where parents (mainly moms) exchange advice and tips. So iVillage soon evolved into the leading women's online community. Its home page entreats visitors to "Join our community of smart, compassionate, real women." While the company has yet to turn a profit, its popularity has helped it raise $100 million in venture capital financing.[21]

The automobile industry is beginning to recognize gender segmentation. With more women car owners, some manufacturers are designing certain features to appeal to women, although stopping short of advertising the cars as women's cars.

Income. Income segmentation is a long-standing practice in such product and service categories as automobiles, boats, clothing, cosmetics, and travel. However, income does not always predict the best customers for a given product. Blue-collar workers were among the first purchasers of colour television sets; it was cheaper for them to buy these sets than to go to movies and restaurants. The most economical cars are not bought by the really poor, but rather by those who think of themselves as poor relative to their status aspirations. Medium-price and expensive cars tend to be purchased by the overprivileged segments of each social class. While many charities focus on targeting the rich, a recent Statistics Canada poll revealed that people who earn less than $20 000 per year donate a higher portion of their income (1.48 percent) than do families with incomes in excess of $80 000. Richer families only donate 0.43 percent.[22]

Generation. Many researchers are now turning to generation segmentation. Each generation is profoundly influenced by the times in which it grows up—the music, movies, politics, and events of that period. Some marketers target Baby Boomers (those born between 1947 and 1966) using communications and symbols that appeal to the optimism of that generation. Even the venerable Canadian National Exhibition is using generation segmentation: CNE's Boomers Building is described as "..a sprawling fun house for members of a certain generation."[23] Other marketers are targeting Generation X (those born between 1967 and 1984), aware that the members of this generation grew up distrustful of society, politicians, and slick advertising and merchandising. Generation Xers are more sophisticated in evaluating products. Many are turned off by advertising that has too much hype or takes itself too seriously. But creative advertising targeted to this group can be powerful as Volkswagen recently discovered. Its recent ad that showed a twenty-something couple driving down a New Orleans street who suddenly realize that everything outside their car windows is synchronized to the beat of their windshield wipers and music helped the firm increase its sales of the Jetta from a mere 50 000 units to over 260 000.[24]

Meredith and Schewe have proposed a more focused concept of generation segmentation that they call cohort segmentation.[25] Cohorts are groups of people who share experiences of major external events that have deeply affected their attitudes and preferences. There is a cohort group that experienced the Great Depression, another that experienced World War II, another that experienced the Vietnam War, and so on. Members of a cohort group feel a bonding with each other for having shared the same major experiences. Marketers often advertise to a cohort group by using the icons and images prominent in their experience. For example, in the summer of 1999, Harvey's used retro advertising relating to the classic rock festival, Woodstock, to reach people who were teenagers in the 1960s.[26]

Social Class. Social class has a strong influence on preference in cars, clothing, home furnishings, leisure activities, reading habits, and retailers. Many companies design products and/or services for specific social classes.

The tastes of social classes can change with the years. The 1980s were about greed and ostentation for the upper classes, but the 1990s were more about values and self-fulfilment. Affluent tastes now run more towards the utilitarian, a Range Rover or Lincoln Navigator rather than a Mercedes.[27]

Volkswagen was "in tune" with its Gen-X audience with this award-winning ad.

Psychographic Segmentation

In *psychographic segmentation*, buyers are divided into different groups on the basis of lifestyle and/or personality and values. People within the same demographic group can exhibit very different psychographic profiles.

Lifestyle. People exhibit many more lifestyles than are suggested by the seven social classes. The goods they consume express their lifestyles. For example, people who make pampered pets an integral part of their lifestyles represent a huge market for an unbelievable range of products. For the cyberspace shopper there is CoolPet Stuff.com. They purchase everything from Christmas stockings for their cats and dogs to pet luggage for the travelling canine, terry-cloth bathrobes for the lie-about cat, genuine Napa Valley wine barrel dog houses, or CDs featuring cat hymns.[28] Other lifestyle marketers include:

CoolPet Stuff.com
www.coolpetstuff.com

- **Yves Vegetarian Cuisine.** Vancouver entrepreneur Yves Potvin is betting that the mainstream market in both Canada and the United States is finally ready for a wider variety of vegetarian products. Posting growth rates of over 40 percent per year for the last 14 years, Potvin isn't often wrong. Meat alternatives are a $1-billion North American market. He is basing his strategy on the belief that the lifestyles of today's older, health-conscious, time-pressed consumers will lead to greater demand for healthy, convenient, comforting fast food that looks like familiar meat-based products. His product line includes fat-free products like Veggie Bacon, Veggie Pizza Pepperoni, and Veggie Ground Round—sound tasty?[29]

Companies making cosmetics, alcoholic beverages, and furniture are always seeking opportunities in lifestyle segmentation. But lifestyle segmentation does not always work. Nestlé introduced a special brand of decaffeinated coffee for "late nighters," and it failed.

Personality. Marketers have used personality variables to segment markets. They endow their products with *brand personalities* that correspond to consumer personalities. When focus-group research showed David Kincaid, vice-president of marketing for Labatt Breweries, that Blue was viewed by young male consumers as the beer my father drinks, he went about changing the brand's personality. Research suggested that he focus on the characteristic of "spontaneity." Labatt's highly successful "Out of the Blue" advertising campaign was the result of this insight.

Values. Some marketers segment by core values, the belief systems that underlie consumer attitudes and behaviours. Core values go much deeper than behaviour or attitude, and determine, at a basic level, people's choices and desires over the long term. Marketers that segment by values believe that by appealing to people's inner selves it is possible to influence their outer selves—their purchase behaviour. Marketing research firm Roper Reports Worldwide Global Consumer Survey has developed a values segmentation scheme for global markets, see the Marketing Memo entitled "Tapping into Core Values Around the Globe."

Behavioural Segmentation

In *behavioural segmentation*, buyers are divided into groups on the basis of their knowledge of, attitude toward, use of, or response to a product. Many marketers believe that behavioural variables—occasions, benefits, user status, usage rate, loyalty status, buyer-readiness stage, and attitude—are the best starting points for constructing market segments.

Occasions. Buyers can be distinguished according to the occasions they develop a need, purchase a product, or use a product. For example, air travel is triggered by occasions related to business, vacation, or family. An airline can specialize in serving people for whom one of these occasions dominates. Air Transat has become highly successful by focusing solely on those groups of people who fly for vacation.

Occasion segmentation can help firms expand product usage. For example, orange juice is usually consumed at breakfast. An orange-juice company can try to promote drinking orange juice on other occasions—lunch, dinner, midday. Certain holidays—Mother's Day and Father's Day, for example—were established partly to increase the sale of candy and flowers. The Curtis Candy Company promoted the trick-or-treat custom at Halloween, with every home ready to dispense candy to eager little callers knocking at their doors.

A company can consider critical life events to see whether they are accompanied by certain needs. This kind of analysis has led to service providers such as marriage, employment, and bereavement counsellors.

Benefits. Buyers can be classified according to the benefits they seek. One study of travellers uncovered three benefit segments: those who travel to be with their family, those who travel for adventure or educational purposes, and people who enjoy the "gambling" and "fun" aspects of travel.[30]

Haley reported a successful benefit segmentation of the toothpaste market (Table 9-2). He found four benefit segments: economy, medicinal, cosmetic, and taste. Each benefit-seeking group had particular demographic, behavioural, and psychographic characteristics. For example, decay-prevention seekers had large families, were heavy toothpaste users, and were conservative. Each segment favoured certain brands. A toothpaste company can use these findings to focus its brand better and to launch new brands.

User Status. Markets can be segmented into nonusers, ex-users, potential users, first-time users, and regular users of a product. Canada's new blood service cannot rely only on regular donors to supply blood. They must recruit new first-time donors and contact ex-donors, and each will require a different marketing strategy. The company's market position will also influence its focus. Market-share leaders will focus on attracting potential users, while smaller firms will attract current users away from the market leader.

Usage Rate. Markets can be segmented into light, medium, and heavy product users. Heavy users are often a small percentage of the market but account for a high percentage of total consumption. Marketers usually prefer to attract one heavy user rather than several light users, and they vary their promotional efforts accordingly.

■ **Repp's Big & Tall Stores.** A catalogue and retail outfit with 200 stores throughout North America, Repp's slices customers into 12 segments according to response rates, average sales, and the like. Some get six to eight mailings a year, some three to five, some only one to three. Repp tries to steer low-volume catalogue shoppers into nearby stores they may not even know exist. Infrequent store shoppers might be offered an extra incentive, such as 15 percent off, for a particular weekend. Repp gets a six percent response rate to its segmented mailings, far superior to the typical huge non-segmented mailing of 750 000 pieces that might only get a .5 percent response rate.[31]

Figure 9-2 shows usage rates for some popular consumer products. For example, 41 percent of the sampled households buy beer. But heavy users accounted for 87 percent of the beer consumed—almost seven times as much as the light users. Thus, most beer companies target heavy beer drinkers, using appeals such as Molson's "I Am Canadian." Heavy beer drinkers have the following profile: working class; age 25 to 50; heavy viewers of television, particularly sports programs. These profiles can assist marketers in developing price, message, and media strategies.

TABLE 9.2				
Benefit Segmentation of the Toothpaste Market				

Benefit Segments	Demographics	Behaviouristics	Psychographics	Favoured Brands
Economy (low price)	Men	Heavy users	High autonomy, value oriented	Brands on sale
Medicinal (decay prevention)	Large families	Heavy users	Hypochondriac, conservative	Crest
Cosmetic (bright teeth)	Teens, young adults	Smokers	High sociability, active	Maclean's, Ultra Brite
Taste (good tasting)	Children	Spearmint lovers	High self-involvement, hedonistic	Colgate, Aim

Source: Adapted from Russell J. Haley, "Benefit Segmentation: A Decision Oriented Research Tool," *Journal of Marketing*, July 1963, pp. 30–35.

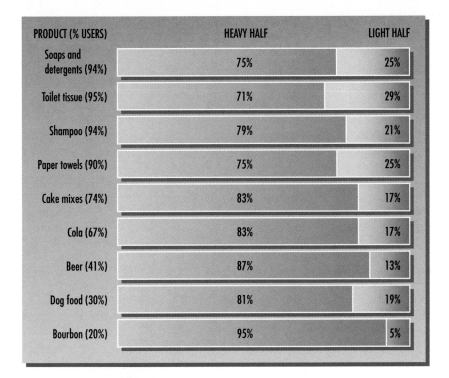

PRODUCT (% USERS)	HEAVY HALF	LIGHT HALF
Soaps and detergents (94%)	75%	25%
Toilet tissue (95%)	71%	29%
Shampoo (94%)	79%	21%
Paper towels (90%)	75%	25%
Cake mixes (74%)	83%	17%
Cola (67%)	83%	17%
Beer (41%)	87%	13%
Dog food (30%)	81%	19%
Bourbon (20%)	95%	5%

FIGURE 9.2

Heavy and Light Users of Common Consumer Products

Source: See Victor J. Cook and William Mindak, "A Search for Constants: The 'Heavy User' Revisited," *Journal of Consumer Marketing*, Spring 1984, p. 80.

Social marketing agencies face a heavy-user dilemma. A family-planning agency would normally target poor families who have many children, but these families are usually the most resistant to birth control messages. MADD (Mothers Against Drunk Drivers) targets those who abuse alcohol, but these drivers are the most resistant to safe-driving appeals. The agencies must decide whether to go after a few highly resistant heavy offenders or many less-resistant light offenders.

Loyal Status. Consumers have varying degrees of loyalty to specific brands, stores, and other entities. Buyers can be divided into four groups according to brand loyalty status:

- *Hard-core loyals:* Consumers who buy one brand all the time.
- *Split loyals:* Consumers who are loyal to two or three brands.
- *Shifting loyals:* Consumers who shift from one brand to another
- *Switchers:* Consumers who show no loyalty to any brand.[32]

Each market consists of different numbers of the four types of buyers. A *brand-loyal market* is one with a high percentage of hardcore brand-loyal buyers. The toothpaste market and the beer market are fairly high brand-loyal markets. Companies selling in a brand-loyal market have a hard time gaining more market share, and companies that enter such a market have a hard time getting in.

A company can learn a great deal by analyzing the degrees of brand loyalty: By studying its hardcore loyals, the company can identify its products' strengths. By studying its split loyals, the company can identify which brands are most competitive with its own. By looking at customers who are shifting away from its brand, the company can learn about its marketing weaknesses and attempt to correct them.

(continued)

- *Altruists:* This group is 18 percent of adults, with a slightly higher percentage of females. Altruists are interested in social issues and the welfare of society. With a median age of 44, this group is older. More Altruists live in Latin America and Russia than other countries.

- *Intimates:* Comprising 15 percent of the world's population, Intimates value close personal relationships and family above all else. They are almost as likely to be men as women. One in four Europeans and Americans qualify compared with just seven percent of developing Asia.

- *Fun Seekers:* Although found in disproportionate numbers in developed Asia, this group accounts for 12 percent of the global population. Not surprisingly, Fun Seekers are the youngest group, with a male-female ration of 54 to 46.

- *Creatives:* This group is the smallest at 10 percent worldwide. Their hallmark trait is a strong interest in education, knowledge, and technology. Creatives are more common in Latin America and Western Europe. Along with Intimates, this group has the most balanced gender mix.

Roper's research shows that people in different segments generally pursue different activities, buy different products, and use different media. Knowing which segments dominate in a country helps with marketing efforts and enables advertisers to tailor their message to those parts of the population most likely to buy.

Source: Adapted from Tom Miller, "Global Segments from 'Strivers' to 'Creatives,'" *Marketing News*, July 20, 1998, p. 11.

One caution: what appear to be brand-loyal purchase patterns may reflect habit, indifference, a low price, a high switching cost, or the nonavailability of other brands. Thus a company must carefully interpret what is behind the observed purchase patterns.

Buyer-Readiness Stage. A market consists of people in different stages of readiness to buy a product. Some are unaware of the product, some are aware, some are informed, some are interested, some desire the product, and some intend to buy. The relative numbers make a big difference in designing the marketing program.

Suppose a health agency wants to encourage women to take an annual Pap test to detect possible cervical cancer. At the beginning, most women may be unaware of the Pap test. The marketing effort should go into high-awareness-building advertising using a simple message. Later, to move more women into desiring the test, the advertising should dramatize the benefits of the Pap test and the risks of not taking it. A special offer of a free health examination might be made to motivate women into actually signing up for the test.

Attitude. Five attitude groups can be found in a market: enthusiastic, positive, indifferent, negative, and hostile. Door-to-door workers in a political campaign use the voter's attitude to determine how much time to spend with that voter. They thank enthusiastic voters and remind them to vote; they reinforce those who are positively disposed; they try to win the votes of indifferent voters; they spend no time trying to change the attitudes of negative and hostile voters. To the extent that attitudes are correlated with demographic descriptors, the political party can more efficiently locate the best prospects.

Multi-Attribute Segmentation (Geoclustering)

Marketers no longer talk about the average consumer, or even limit their analysis to only a few market segments. Rather, they are increasingly crossing several variables in an effort to identify smaller, better-defined target groups. Thus a bank may not only identify a group of wealthy retired adults, but also within that group distinguish several segments depending on current income, assets, and savings and risk preferences.

Claritas International
www.claritas.com

One of the most promising developments in multi-attribute segmentation is called *geoclustering*. Geoclustering yields richer descriptions of consumers and neighbourhoods than traditional demographics. Claritas Inc. has developed a geoclustering approach called PRIZM (Potential Rating Index by Zip Markets) that classifies over 500 000 U.S. residential neighbourhoods into 62 distinct lifestyle groupings called PRIZM Clusters.[33] The groupings take into consideration 39 factors in five broad categories: (1) education and affluence, (2) family life cycle, (3) urbanization, (4) race and ethnicity, and (5) mobility. The neighbourhoods are broken down by ZIP code, ZIP + 4, or census tract and block group. The clusters have descriptive titles such as *Blue Blood Estates, Winner's Circle, Hometown Retired, Latino America, Shotguns and Pickups*, and *Back Country Folks*. The inhabitants in a cluster tend to lead similar lives, drive similar cars, have similar jobs, and read similar magazines.[34]

Marketers can use PRIZM to answer such questions as these: Which clusters (neighbourhoods or ZIP codes) contain our most valuable customers? How deeply have we already penetrated these segments? Which markets, performance sites, and promotional media provide us with the best opportunities for growth? Spiegel, a direct marketer, uses geoclustering information to search for where to mail their catalogues. In marketing its Suave shampoo, Helene Curtis, now part of Unilever, used PRIZM to identify neighbourhoods with high concentrations of young working women. These women responded best to advertising messages that Suave is inexpensive, yet will make their hair "look like a million."

Geoclustering's importance as a segmentation tool is growing. It captures the increasing diversity of the American population and marketing to microsegments has become accessible to even small organizations as database costs decline, PCs proliferate, software becomes easier to use, data integration increases, and the Internet grows.[35]

Targeting Multiple Segments

Very often, companies start marketing to one segment, then expand to others. Consider the experiences of one small technology company:

- **Paging Network Inc.** "PageNet" is a small developer of paging systems and competes with Southwestern Bell and other Bell companies. It sets its prices about 20 percent below its competitors'. PageNet used several segmentation strategies to compete.

   1. PageNet initially used geographic segmentation and aimed at areas in Ohio and Texas. In both areas, local competitors were vulnerable to PageNet's aggressive pricing.

   2. PageNet then proceeded to develop a profile of users for paging services. It targeted salespeople, messengers, and service people. PageNet used lifestyle segmentation to target additional consumer groups, such as parents who leave their baby with a sitter and elderly people living alone whose families wanted them to have a pager.

   3. PageNet then decided to distribute its pagers through Kmart, Wal-Mart, and Home Depot. It gave very attractive discounts in return for the right to keep the revenue from the monthly service charges on any pagers sold.

   4. PageNet is the first to offer voice mail on the pager.[36]

Many shoppers cannot be neatly pigeonholed into one segment. Many consumers are cross-shoppers. Consider the "cross-dresser" who buys an expensive Harry Rosen suit but shops at Wal-Mart for underwear. Or the "cross-eater" who eats a Healthy Choice frozen dinner followed by White Mountain ice cream for dessert. It is dangerous to interpret segment membership by observing one purchase. Segmentation ignores the whole customer profile, which becomes clear only with individual customer profiling.

BASES FOR SEGMENTING BUSINESS MARKETS

Business markets can be segmented with some variables employed in consumer market segmentation, such as geography, benefits sought, and usage rate. Yet business marketers can also use several other variables. Bonoma and Shapiro proposed segmenting the business market with the variables shown in Table 9-3. The demographic variables are the most important, followed by the operating variables—down to the personal characteristics of the buyer.

The table lists major questions that business marketers should ask in determining which segments and customers to serve. A rubber-tire company should first decide which industries it wants to serve. It can sell tires to manufacturers of automobiles, trucks, farm tractors, fork-lift trucks, or aircraft.

Within a chosen target industry, a company can further segment by company size. The company might set up separate operations for selling to large and small customers. Consider how Dell is organized:

- **Dell Computer Corporation.** Dell is divided into Dell Direct, which sells to two segments: consumers and small businesses. Then there is Dells' relationship group, which manages the company's corporate accounts. Three key segments are included under this umbrella, the enterprise group (Fortune 500 companies), large corporate accounts (multinational companies in what would be the Fortune 501 to 2000 range), and preferred accounts (medium businesses with 200 to 2000 employees). This is Dell's fastest-growing division, and it serves such customers as Rollerblade and the Associated Press. Actually a large chunk of Dell's preferred accounts would be considered small businesses by many companies.[37]

Dell Computers
www.dell.com

Small businesses, in particular, have become a Holy Grail for business marketers. In North America small businesses are now responsible for 50 percent of the gross national product and this segment is growing at 11 percent annually, three percentage points higher than the growth of large companies. IBM is one company that is pursuing this segment with almost religious zeal:

TABLE	9.3

Major Segmentation Variables for Business Markets

Demographic

1. *Industry:* Which industries should we serve?
2. *Company size:* What size companies should we serve?
3. *Location:* What geographical areas should we serve?

Operating Variables

4. *Technology:* What customer technologies should we focus on?
5. *User or nonuser status:* Should we serve heavy users, medium users, light users, or nonusers?
6. *Customer capabilities:* Should we serve customers needing many or few services?

Purchasing Approaches

7. *Purchasing-function organization:* Should we serve companies with highly centralized or decentralized purchasing organizations?
8. *Power structure:* Should we serve companies that are engineering dominated, financially dominated, and so on?
9. *Nature of existing relationships:* Should we serve companies with which we have strong relationships or simply go after the most desirable companies?
10. *General purchase policies:* Should we serve companies that prefer leasing? Service contracts? Systems purchases? Sealed bidding?
11. *Purchasing criteria:* Should we serve companies that are seeking quality? Service? Price?

Situational Factors

12. *Urgency:* Should we serve companies that need quick and sudden delivery or service?
13. *Specific application:* Should we focus on certain applications of our product rather than all applications?
14. *Size of order:* Should we focus on large or small orders?

Personal Characteristics

15. *Buyer–seller similarity:* Should we serve companies whose people and values are similar to ours?
16. *Attitudes toward risk:* Should we serve risk-taking or risk-avoiding customers?
17. *Loyalty:* Should we serve companies that show high loyalty to their suppliers?

Source: Adapted from Thomas V. Bonoma and Benson P. Shapiro, *Segmenting the Industrial Market* (Lexington, MA: Lexington Books, 1983).

■ **IBM.** The $117 billion technology company has already proved that it can market successfully to fellow corporate giants like General Motors and Citibank. Now it's trying to prove that it's nimble enough to market to the millions of enterprises with 1000 or fewer employees. In addition to devoting field salespeople exclusively to small and medium-size businesses (SMBs), the company is putting greater emphasis on telesales and service, a radical break from tradition. Small businesses have typically felt ignored by IBM. Within the small business segment, IBM is targeting minority-owned businesses. Small business owners are more likely to be women, people from various ethnic groups, gay, or lesbian than white males. IBM has even hired executives responsible for targeting each segment.[38]

Service businesses are approaching small-business customers as well. Publishers of business magazines like on-line magazine Canadaone.ca, or *Profit* specialize in issues affecting small Canadian businesses. Although Canada's large banks have been accused of ignoring the needs of small business, this is also starting to change. For example, if you use the Yahoo search engine and its directory of small business information, a banner ad for the Royal Bank pops up. The Business Development Bank of Canada advertises its Montreal headquarters and 80 branches as Canada's small business bank. Canada Post offers assistance to small business people. Even telecommunications giants like Bell and AT&T Canada are focusing more on small business. Governments are also realizing the power of small business to fuel the economy. To foster small business growth, the B.C. government has developed on-line workshops where small business people download free information on business planning, marketing, and financing their enterprises.

B.C. Government
sb.gov.bc.ca/smallbusiness/workshop/

part two
Analyzing
Marketing
Opportunities

Within a given target industry and customer size, the company can segment by purchase criteria. For example, government laboratories, in buying scientific equipment, need low prices and service contracts; university laboratories need equipment that requires little service; and industrial laboratories need equipment that is highly reliable and accurate.

Business marketers generally identify segments through a sequential segmentation process. Consider an aluminum company:

> The aluminum company first undertook macrosegmentation consisting of three steps. It looked at which end-use market to serve: automobile, residential, or beverage containers. Choosing the residential market, it needed to determine the most attractive product application: semifinished material, building components, or aluminum mobile homes. Deciding to focus on building components, it considered the best customer size and chose large customers. The second stage consisted of microsegmentation. The company distinguished among customers buying on price, service, or quality. Because the aluminum company had a high-service profile, it decided to concentrate on the service-motivated segment of the market.

Business buyers seek different benefit bundles based on their stage in the purchase decision process:[39]

1. *First-time prospects:* Customers who have not yet purchased want to buy from a vendor who understands their business, who explains things well, and whom they can trust.

2. *Novices:* Customers who are starting their purchasing relationship want easy-to-read manuals, hotlines, a high level of training, and knowledgeable sales reps.

3. *Sophisticates:* Established customers want speed in maintenance and repair, product customization, and high technical support.

These segments may also have different channel preferences. First-time prospects would prefer to deal with a company salesperson instead of a catalogue/direct-mail channel, since the latter provides too little information. Sophisticates, on the other hand, may want to conduct more of their buying over electronic channels.

Rangan, Moriarty, and Swartz studied a mature commodity market, steel strapping, and found four business segments:[40]

1. *Programmed buyers:* Buyers who view the product as not very important to their operation. They buy it as a routine purchase item, usually paying full price and receiving below-average service. Clearly this is a highly profitable segment for the vendor.

2. *Relationship buyers:* Buyers who regard the product as moderately important and are knowledgeable about competitive offerings. They get a small discount and a modest amount of service and prefer the vendor as long as the price is not far out of line. They are the second most profitable group.

3. *Transaction buyers:* Buyers who see the product as very important to their operations. They are price- and service-sensitive. They receive about a 10 percent discount and above-average service. They are knowledgeable about competitive offerings and are ready to switch for a better price, even at the sacrifice of some service.

4. *Bargain hunters:* Buyers who see the product as very important and demand the deepest discount and the highest service. They know the alternative suppliers, bargain hard, and are ready to switch at the slightest dissatisfaction. The company needs these buyers for volume purposes, but they are not very profitable.

This segmentation scheme can help a company in a mature commodity industry do a better job of figuring out where to apply price and service increases and decreases, since each segment would react differently.[41]

EFFECTIVE SEGMENTATION

Not all segmentations are useful. For example, table salt buyers could be divided into blond and brunette customers, but hair colour is not relevant to the purchase of salt. Furthermore, if all salt buyers buy the same amount of salt each month, believe all salt is the same, and would pay only one price for salt, this market would be minimally segmentable from a marketing point of view.

To be useful, market segments must be:

- *Measurable.* The size, purchasing power, and characteristics of the segments can be measured.

- *Substantial:* The segments are large and profitable enough to serve. A segment should be the largest possible homogeneous group worth going after with a tailored marketing program. It would not pay, for example, for an automobile manufacturer to develop cars for people who are shorter than one metre.

- *Accessible.* The segments can be effectively reached and served.

- *Differentiable.* The segments are conceptually distinguishable and respond differently to different marketing-mix elements and programs. If married and unmarried women respond similarly to a sale on perfume, they do not constitute separate segments.

- *Actionable.* Effective programs can be formulated for attracting and serving the segments.

 MARKET TARGETING

Once the firm has identified its market-segment opportunities, it has to decide how many and which ones to target.

EVALUATING THE MARKET SEGMENTS

In evaluating different market segments, the firm must consider two factors: the segment's overall attractiveness and the company's objectives and resources. First, the firm must ask whether a potential segment has the characteristics that make it generally attractive, such as size, growth, profitability, scale economies, and low risk. Second, the firm must consider whether investing in the segment makes sense given the firm's objectives and resources. Some attractive segments could be dismissed because they do not mesh with the company's long-run objectives, or the segment should be dismissed if the company lacks one or more necessary competencies to offer superior value.

SELECTING THE MARKET SEGMENTS

Having evaluated different segments, the company can consider five patterns of target market selection shown in Figure 9-3.

Single-Segment Concentration
The company may select a single segment. Volkswagen concentrates on the small-car market and Porsche on the sports-car market. Through concentrated marketing, the firm gains a strong knowledge of the segment's needs and achieves a strong market position. Furthermore, the firm enjoys operating economies through specializing its production, distribution, and promotion. If it captures segment leadership, the firm can earn a high return on its investment. It has to retain its focus, however. Consider the case of Birks:

- **Birks.** Despite the fact that Birks' little blue boxes were an icon in the Canadian marketplace, the 120-year old, family run chain teetered on the brink of bankruptcy in 1992. Long known for its fine jewellery, the firm went on

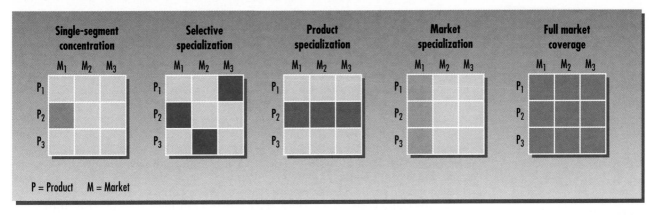

an acquisition spree in the 1980s in an attempt to be everything to everybody. Explaining its near-death experience, CEO Thomas Andruskevich declared, "The Birks of the past traded a rifle for a shotgun, and, in doing so, lost its sharpshooter focus. Today, we've traded that shotgun for a laser. We're zeroing in on a few key strategies." These include a focus on high-end merchandise, store makeovers, a private shopping service for corporate clients, and an on-line presence.[42]

However, concentrated marketing involves higher than normal risks. A particular market segment can turn sour. Another recession might again threaten Birks. Or a competitor may invade the segment. For these reasons, many companies prefer to operate in more than one segment.

Selective Specialization

Here the firm selects a number of segments, each objectively attractive and appropriate. There may be little or no synergy among the segments, but each segment promises to be a money maker. This multisegment coverage strategy has the advantage of diversifying the firm's risk.

Consider a radio broadcaster that wants to appeal to people with different tastes and interests. CBC Radio, for example, not only has regional programming that features coverage of news and events of interest to people fom a specific area, but also has stations that feaure programming in Canada's two oficial languages, and two different stations—one that features news and special events and the other that highlights classical music.

Product Specialization

Here the firm specializes in making a certain product that it sells to several segments. An example would be a microscope manufacturer that sells microscopes to university laboratories, government laboratories, and commercial laboratories. The firm makes different microscopes for different customer groups, but does not manufacture other instruments that laboratories might use. Through a product specialization strategy, the firm builds a strong reputation in the specific product area. The downside risk is that the product may be supplanted by an entirely new technology.

Market Specialization

Here the firm concentrates on serving many needs of a particular customer group. An example would be a firm that sells an assortment of products only to university laboratories, including microscopes, oscilloscopes, Bunsen burners, and chemical flasks. The firm gains a strong reputation in serving this customer group and becomes a channel for further products that the customer group could use. The downside risk is that the customer group may have its budgets cut.

Full Market Coverage

Here a firm attempts to serve all customer groups with all the products they might need. Only very large firms can undertake a full market coverage strategy. Examples

FIGURE 9.3

Five Patterns of Target Market Selection

Source: Adapted from Derek F. Abell, *Defining the Business: The Starting Point of Strategic Planning* (Upper Saddle River, NJ: Prentice Hall, 1980), ch. 8, pp. 192–96.

include IBM (computer market), General Motors (vehicle market), and Coca-Cola (drink market).

Large firms can cover a whole market in two broad ways: through undifferentiated marketing or differentiated marketing.

In *undifferentiated marketing*, the firm ignores market-segment differences and goes after the whole market with one market offer. It focuses on a basic buyer need rather than on differences among buyers. It designs a product and a marketing program that will appeal to the broadest number of buyers. It relies on mass distribution and mass advertising. It aims to endow the product with a superior image in people's minds. Undifferentiated marketing is "the marketing counterpart to standardization and mass production in manufacturing."[43] The narrow product line keeps down costs of research and development, production, inventory, transportation, marketing research, advertising, and product management. The undifferentiated advertising program keeps down advertising costs. Presumably, the company can turn its lower costs into lower prices to win the price-sensitive segment of the market.

In *differentiated marketing*, the firm operates in several market segments and designs different programs for each segment. General Motors does this when it says that it produces a car for every "purse, purpose, and personality." IBM offers many hardware and software packages for different segments in the computer market. Differentiated marketing typically creates more total sales than undifferentiated marketing. However, it also increases the costs of doing business. The following costs are likely to be higher:

- *Product modification costs:* Modifying a product to meet different market segment requirements usually involves some R&D, engineering, and/or special tooling costs.

- *Manufacturing costs:* It is usually more expensive to produce 10 units of 10 different products than 100 units of one product. The longer the production setup time and the smaller the sales volume of each product, the more expensive the product becomes. However, if each model is sold in sufficiently large volume, the higher costs of setup time may be quite small per unit.

- *Administrative costs:* The company has to develop separate marketing plans for each market segment. This requires extra marketing research, forecasting, sales analysis, promotion, planning, and channel management.

- *Inventory costs:* It is more costly to manage inventories containing many products.

- *Promotion costs:* The company has to reach different market segments with different promotion programs. The result is increased promotion-planning costs and media costs.

Since differentiated marketing leads to both higher sales and higher costs, nothing general can be said regarding this strategy's profitability. Companies should be cautious about oversegmenting their market. If this happens, they may want to turn to countersegmentation to broaden the customer base. Johnson & Johnson, for example, broadened its target market for its baby shampoo to include adults. And Smith Kline Beecham launched its Aquafresh toothpaste to attract simultaneously three benefit segments: those seeking fresh breath, whiter teeth, and cavity protection.

ADDITIONAL CONSIDERATIONS

Four other considerations must be taken into account in evaluating and selecting segments: ethical choice of market targets, segment interrelationships and supersegments, segment-by-segment invasion plans, and intersegment cooperation.

Ethical Choice of Market Targets

Market targeting sometimes generates public controversy.[44] The public is concerned when marketers take unfair advantage of vulnerable groups (such as children) or disadvantaged groups (such as the learning disabled), or promote potentially harmful products. The cereal industry has been heavily criticized for marketing efforts directed toward children. Critics worry that high-powered appeals presented through the mouths of lovable animated characters will overwhelm children's defences and lead them to eat too much sugared cereal or poorly balanced breakfasts. Toy marketers have been similarly criticized. McDonald's and other chains have drawn criticism for pitching their high-fat, salt-laden fare to low-income urban residents. To improve marketing aimed at children, the Canadian Marketing Association amended its code of ethics in 1999. It clearly defined children as those persons under the age of 13 and added guidelines to help marketers understand the need for greater privacy protection for children. If marketers seek to gather information from a child, they need positive consent from a parent or guardian before collecting information. When thinking about segmentation and target marketing, both the intended and unintended targets have to be considered. For example, both of Canada's large breweries have been accused of targeting underage drinkers with their high alcohol brews like "ice" beer. If marketers ignore equity issues, other concerns appear. A number of firms have been criticized for imposing a "gender tax" on women who often pay more for services like clothing alterations, dry cleaning, and haircuts. Research has also shown that women pay more in situations where price is negotiated, like car buying.[45]

Not all attempts to target children, minorities, or other special segments draw criticism. Colgate-Palmolive's Colgate Junior toothpaste has special features designed to get children to brush longer and more often. Golden Ribbon Playthings has developed a highly acclaimed and very successful black character doll named "Huggy Bean" to connect minority consumers with their African heritage. Thus, in market targeting, the issue is not *who* is targeted but rather *how* and for *what*. Socially responsible marketing calls for targeting that serves not only the company's interests, but also the interests of those targeted.[46]

Colgate-Palmolive
www.colgate.com

Segment Interrelationships and Supersegments

In selecting more than one segment to serve, the company should pay close attention to segment interrelationships on the cost, performance, and technology side. A company carrying a fixed cost (sales force, store outlets) can add products to absorb and share some costs. The sales force will sell additional products, and a fast-food outlet will offer additional menu items. Economies of scope can be just as important as economies of scale.

Companies should try to operate in supersegments rather than in isolated segments. A *supersegment* is a set of segments sharing some exploitable similarity. For example, many symphony orchestras target people who have broad cultural interests, rather than only those who regularly attend concerts.

Segment-by-Segment Invasion Plans

A company would be wise to enter one segment at a time without revealing its total invasion plans. The competitors must not know to what segment(s) the firm will move

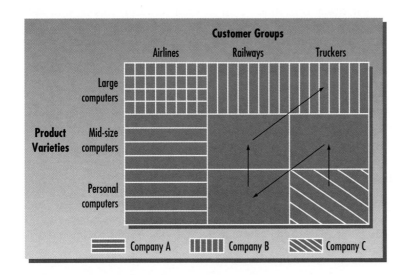

next. Segment-by-segment invasion plans are illustrated in Figure 9-4. Three firms, A, B, and C, have specialized in adapting computer systems to the needs of airlines, railways, and trucking companies. Company A meets all the computer needs of airlines. Company B sells large computer systems to all three transportation sectors. Company sells personal computers to trucking companies.

Where should company C move next? The arrows have been added to the chart to show the planned sequence of segment invasions. Company C will next offer midsize computers to trucking companies. Then, to allay company B's concern about losing some large computer business with trucking companies, C's next move will be to sell personal computers to railways. Later, C will offer midsize computers to railways. Finally, it may launch a full-scale attack on company B's large computer position in trucking companies. Of course, C's hidden planned moves are provisional in that much depends on the competitors' planned segment moves and responses.

Unfortunately, too many companies fail to develop a long-term invasion plan. Pepsi-Cola is an exception. In its attack on Coca-Cola, Pepsi first attacked Coca-Cola in the grocery market, then in the vending-machine market, then in the fast-food market, and so on. Japanese firms also plot their invasion sequence. They first gain a foothold in a market, then enter new segments with products. Toyota began by introducing small cars (e.g., Tercel, Corolla), then expanded into mid-size cars (Camry, Cressida), and finally into luxury cars (Lexus).

A company's invasion plans can be thwarted when it confronts blocked markets. The invader must then figure out a way to break in. The problem of entering *blocked markets* calls for a megamarketing approach.

■ *Megamarketing* is the strategic coordination of economic, psychological, political, and public-relations skills to gain the cooperation of a number of parties in order to enter and/or operate in a given market.

Pepsi used megamarketing to enter the Indian market:

Pepsi Co.
www.pepsi.com

■ **PepsiCo.** After Coca-Cola left India, Pepsi laid plans to enter this huge market. Pepsi worked with an Indian business group to gain government approval for its entry over the objections of domestic soft-drink companies and anti-multinational legislators. Pepsi offered to help India export some agricultural products in a volume that would more than cover the cost of importing soft-drink concentrate. Pepsi also promised to reach into rural areas to help in their economic development. Pepsi further offered to transfer food-processing, packaging, and water-treatment technology to India. Pepsi bundled a set of benefits that won the support of various interest groups in India. Instead of relying on the normal four Ps for entering a market, Pepsi added two additional Ps, namely Politics and Public Opinion.

Once in, a multinational must be on its best behaviour. This calls for well-thought-out *civic positioning*. Olivetti, for example, enters new markets by building housing for workers, generously supporting local arts and charities, and hiring and training indigenous managers.[47]

Intersegment Cooperation
The best way to manage segments is to appoint segment managers with sufficient authority and responsibility for building their segment's business. At the same time, segment managers should not be so segment-focused as to resist cooperation with other company personnel. Consider the following example:

■ **Baxter.** Baxter operates several divisions selling different products and services to hospitals. Each division sends out its own invoices. Some hospitals complain about receiving as many as seven different invoices from Baxter each month. Baxter's marketers finally convinced the separate divisions to send the invoices to Baxter's headquarters so that Baxter could send only one invoice a month to its customers.

1. To choose its markets and serve them well, companies must target their markets. Target marketing involves three activities: market segmentation, market targeting, and market positioning.

2. Companies are increasingly turning to micromarketing at four levels: segments, niches, local areas, and individuals. *Market segments* are large identifiable groups within a market. A *niche* is a more narrowly defined group. At the local level, marketers are customizing their campaigns for trading areas, neighbourhoods, and even individual stores. At the individual level, companies are practising both individual and mass customization. The future is likely to see more *self-marketing*, a form of individual marketing in which individual consumers take more responsibility for determining which products and brands to buy.

3. There are two bases for segmenting consumer markets: consumer characteristics and consumer responses. The major segmentation variables for consumer markets are geographic, demographic, psychographic, and behavioural. These variables can be used singly or in combination. Business marketers use all these variables as well, along with operating variables, purchasing approaches, and situational factors. To be useful, market segments must be measurable, substantial, accessible, differentiable, and actionable.

4. Once a firm has identified its market-segment opportunities, it must evaluate the various segments and decide how many and which ones to target. In evaluating segments, it must look at the segment's attractiveness indicators and the company's objectives and resources. In choosing which segments to target, the company can choose to focus on a single segment, several segments, a specific product, a specific market, or the full market. If it decides to serve the full market, it must choose between differentiated and undifferentiated marketing.

5. Marketers must choose target markets in a socially responsible manner. Marketers must also monitor segment interrelationships, seeking out economies of scope and the potential for marketing to supersegments. Marketers should develop segment-by-segment invasion plans. Finally, market segment managers should be prepared to cooperate in the interest of overall company performance.

A P P L I C A T I O N S

CHAPTER CONCEPTS

1. The Nestlé Company is considering introducing either a hot or a cold coffee product in Thailand. Market research has revealed the following information about Thai society and culture: People in the traffic-congested urban areas of Thailand tend to experience high levels of stress. Temperatures in the country are often above 80 degrees. Given this information, should Nestlé use traditional advertising to promote the coffee's taste, aroma, and stimulative properties, or should it choose other factors?

2. Suggest a useful way to segment the markets for the following products:
   (a) high-speed laser printers
   (b) colour print film
   (c) household coffee
   (d) automobile tires

3. For each of the following product categories, choose a specific product. Name (1) the brand, (2) the size, (3) the manufacturer, and (4) the product's market segment/positioning strategy. In each case, why do you think the manufacturer chose

to target this particular segment? How is each product's segmentation strategy obvious from its packaging or promotion?

(a) dry breakfast cereal

(b) facial tissue

(c) bar soap

(d) toothpaste

(e) dry dog food

(f) compact desktop photocopier

MARKETING AND ADVERTISING

1. As the ad in Figure 1 shows, Olympus has developed an extremely tiny 35 mm zoom camera. Is the company engaging in mass marketing, segment marketing, local marketing, niche marketing, or individual marketing? Support your answer. Based on this ad, which demographic, psychographic, and behavioural variables do you think Olympus is using to segment its consumer markets?

Figure 1   Figure 2

2. Praxair supplies atmospheric, process, and specialty gases for a variety of industrial applications. The ad in Figure 2, which appeared in a national business magazine, describes how Praxair's carbon-dioxide products help businesses in the food industry eliminate beetles and other bugs without the use of dangerous pesticides. Which of the major segmentation variables do you think Praxair is using on its business markets? Be as specific as possible. What personal characteristics might be particularly important in Praxair's business markets? Why?

FOCUS ON TECHNOLOGY

Companies that use outbound telemarketing (company reps calling customers and prospects) or inbound telemarketing (company reps answering calls from customers and prospects) can now apply Claritas' PRIZM geoclustering technology to their telemarketing activities. Outbound telemarketers can use TelePRIZM, as this specialized technology is called, to target the customers and prospects most likely to purchase their goods and services. Inbound telemarketers can use TelePRIZM to analyze the profile of consumers who call the company to see whether any changes are needed to the offerings and advertising.

Find out more by reading about TelePRIZM on the Claritas Web site. What type of companies would find TelePRIZM most useful for their inbound calls? Select one company and suggest how it might apply this technology to calls received from current customers. What benefits can you see for callers who contact this company?

TelePRIZM
www.claritas.com/telepriz.htm

MARKETING FOR THE 21ST CENTURY

Mass customization is helping high-tech and non-tech companies alike to build consumer relationships one at a time through individual marketing. This level of segmentation will be increasingly important to marketers in the new millennium. Dell, for example, is a leader in mass customization.

Visit Dell's home page) and look at the way it segments its market. Also visit the store information page to see how Dell's mass customization process works.

Why does Dell highlight the various segments so prominently? Why does it offer a 30-day money-back guarantee? If Dell is aggressively pursing online commerce, why does it include a toll-free phone number on its home page? What competitive challenges do you think Dell will face in continuing its individual marketing strategy into the new millennium?

Dell
www.dell.ca

Dell's mass customization process
www.commerce.us.dell.com/
storeinfo/howto.htm

YOU'RE THE MARKETER: SONIC MARKETING PLAN

Defining a target marketing strategy through market segmentation is a critical aspect of any marketing plan. The goal is to identify and describe distinct market segments, target specific segments, and then pinpoint the differentiating benefits to be stressed.

In your role as Jane Melody's assistant, you are responsible for market segmentation, target marketing, and positioning for Sonic's shelf stereo products. Review the data you previously gathered about the company's marketing situation, your analysis of SWOT and critical issues, and market needs and requirements. Then answer the following questions about market segments, target markets, and positioning:

- Which variables should Sonic use to segment its consumer markets? (For example, in addition to age, does Sonic want to focus on consumers in specific areas? Consumers who have specific attitudes toward music? Consumers in particular stages of the family life cycle?)

- If Sonic is pursuing business customers, which variables should be used to segment business markets? (For example, should Sonic segment the business market by industry and company size? By specific product application?)

- How can Sonic evaluate the attractiveness of each identified segment? Should Sonic market to one segment or more than one segment? (For example, is each segment accessible? Is it substantial? How does each segment fit with Sonic's objectives and resources?)

- What differentiates Sonic's shelf stereos from competing products? How can Sonic use differentiation to develop and communicate a powerful positioning strategy? (For example, does the product have competitively superior performance or reliability? Which point(s) of differentiation would be the most compelling as the basis of Sonic's promotional strategy?)

Next, consider how your answers to these questions will affect Sonic's marketing efforts. Then, as your instructor directs, summarize your findings and conclusions in a written marketing plan or type them into the Target Markets/Positioning section of the Marketing Plan Pro software.

A WAR FOR CORPORATE CUSTOMERS

As a result of deregulation, a revolution has overtaken the telephone industry. Competition is rampant. While this is great news for buyers who have seen prices fall while services and technology improve, it isn't such a happy situation for companies that used to have a monopoly. Bell Canada, in particular, is under attack.

For years, Bell enjoyed its insulated Ontario and Quebec marketplace. It became one of Canada's biggest and wealthiest provincial phone companies—largely as a result of the fact that 75 percent of corporate headquarters are located in Ontario and Quebec. Corporate clients are the big money makers for telecommunications firms. But the situation isn't as rosy today for Bell as it was just a few years ago. Its market is now under attack. Firms such as Calgary's MetroNet have laid fibre-optic cable across the country and are now set to bid for customers in Bell's backyard. MetroNet isn't the only firm being attracted to this rich territory. BC Tel, AT&T Canada, Sprint Canada, Telus, and Quebec cable firms Videotron and Cogeco are all entering the fray.

Many corporations have responded by switching away from Bell. Some, like University Avenue Funds, found that they could lower their costs from $45 per line to $30 per line for local service. Moreover, the new competitors are often able to provide this service faster than Bell.

Bell Canada isn't about to roll over and play dead. It is in the fight of its lifetime to retain market share. Not only is it putting renewed emphasis on its direct sales force, but it is also working to reduce prices to a more competitive level while striving to offer the best technology to its clients. It has been experimenting and innovating. For example, Bell created a new technology that allows its corporate clients to add a human touch to online customer interactions. Called Advantage Web Live Voice, the technology allows a firm's Internet users to initiate a live conversation with a call-centre operator by simply clicking on an icon. Businesses like Charles Schwab Canada adopted the service to help win in its own business. The Internet telephony allows Schwab's on-line customers to link directly to a company representative. The software's synchronized browsing feature allows the customer and service representative to review the same documents simultaneously online.

Bell has had other successes. For example, the Canadian Imperial Bank of Commerce recently signed with the new Bell since it was so impressed with Bell's vision of how it could convert the bank's legacy systems into the systems it needs to operate in today's on-line environment. And it is the on-line environment that is driving much of the change in the telecommunications industry. While the voice market is only growing at a rate of three percent per year, the data market is increasing at a rate of over 30 percent per year.

Questions

1. Describe the changes in the macroenvironment that have affected the telephone industry.

2. Bell believes that size has its advantages in the strategic battle for corporate customers. What does it see as its keys to future success? How is it countering the competition it has found in its own backyard?

3. Many of the new firms are competing on price. How can Bell work to counter increasing price sensitivity in the marketplace?

Sources: Based on "The Treasure Chest," *Venture* 706 (December 1, 1998); "Technology File," Strategy: *The Canadian Marketing Report*, September 27, 1999, p. 6.

Positioning the Market Offering Through the Product Life Cycle

CHAPTER

10

PROFILE:

Canadian Marketing Excellence

P hilip Kotler's dictate, "Don't watch the product life cycle: watch the market life cycle," could well be Air Canada's motto. A study of Air Canada's history illustrates just how many times a company may have to reinvent itself. Although Air Canada is one of two major national airlines operating in the country today, having a national Canadian airline was once viewed as an impractical dream. One government minister even went so far as to say, "I do not think that Canada will ever have need of an air service." Undaunted by such opposition, Trans-Canada Airlines, the forerunner of Air Canada, was founded as a Crown corporation in 1937. Its first commercial route linked Vancouver with Seattle, Washington. In its first months of operation, it served a whopping 144 passengers. Flights across Canada were soon introduced, but it wasn't until after the war that international service became a reality. It was then that the airline recognized the need to have a name that required no translation. Trans-Canada Airlines thus became Air Canada in 1965 when it also unveiled its distinctive maple-leaf brand logo.

Throughout the 1960s and 1970s, Air Canada upgraded its fleet and ushered in a host of new services and special prices for families, youth, and seniors. In the 1980s, the airline severed its government roots and became a private company. It launched its first loyalty program, Aeroplan, in 1988. The early 1990s were spent making the airline more efficient so that it could better meet the challenges brought about by the 1995 Open Skies agreement between Canada and the United States.

In 1998 Air Canada celebrated its sixtieth anniversary. It has grown from its initial staff of 71 people to a firm with over 24 000 employees. It has annual revenues of $3.5 billion. It logs 1200 flights a day and serves 120 destinations in Canada, the United States, the Caribbean, the Middle East, and Asia. To extend its services, Air Canada joined with five partners to form the Star Alliance, which is the world's first multi-airline coalition. The alliance enables Air Canada to fly passengers seamlessly around the globe.

With the formation of the Star Alliance and Air Canada's move into the global marketplace, new communication challenges faced the firm. How, it wondered, could it develop a global identity and a brand recognized worldwide? After considerable brainstorming by its 11 communication suppliers, a common vision to reposition the airline was developed. Instead of talking about better seats or better schedules, the new integrated communication strategy focused on Air Canada's culture and its desire to make passengers feel like valued individuals. Its brand vision says it all: "I am not a seat number, I am a person." This vision informs everything that Air Canada does and says. It promised customers that when they meet an Air Canada employee, whether a baggage handler or a ticket agent, they will feel different than they would with any other airline. The goal of every employee is to understand what customers want from the airline and to exceed their expectations with new products and new services. An example of this new philosophy is evident in the food that the airline now offers its passengers. They can now choose from 17 different menus. Today, Air Canada's efforts have received wide acclaim and it has received a number of international awards for its passenger service including the 1998 Air Transport World Magazine Award.

Sources: Air Canada Web Site: *http://aircanada.ca/about-us/*, De Wolf, Mark, "Air Canada Dream Team Scores," *Strategy: The Canadian Marketing Report*, 16 February 1998, p. 1. Pratt, Laura, "Retrospective: Air Canada: Flying High for 60 Years," *Strategy: The Canadian Marketing Report*, 16 February 1998, p. 30-35. "Delicious, Nutritious Airline Food? Get Used to It," *The Globe and Mail*, April 21, 1999, p. C4.

This chapter addresses the following questions:

- What are the major differentiating attributes available to firms?

- How can the firm choose and communicate an effective positioning in the market?

- What marketing strategies are appropriate at each stage of the product life cycle?

- What marketing strategies are appropriate at each stage of the market's evolution?

As the Air Canada example shows, companies are constantly trying to differentiate their market offering from competitors'. They dream up new services and guarantees, special rewards for loyal users, new conveniences, and enjoyments. When they succeed, competitors may copy their market offering. As a result, most competitive advantages last only a short time. Companies therefore need to constantly think up new value-adding features and benefits to win the attention and interest of choice-rich, price-prone consumers.

Companies normally reformulate their marketing strategy several times during a product's life. Economic conditions change, competitors launch new assaults, and the product passes through new stages of buyer interest and requirements. Consequently, a company must plan strategies appropriate to each stage in the product's life cycle. The company hopes to extend the product's life and profitability, keeping in mind that the product will not last forever. This chapter explores specific ways a company can effectively differentiate and position its offering to achieve competitive advantage throughout a product's or an offering's life cycle.

 OW TO DIFFERENTIATE

Sony is a good example of a company that constantly comes up with new benefits. As soon as Sony develops a new product, it assembles three teams that view the new product as if it were a competitor's. The first team thinks of minor improvements, the second team thinks of major improvements, and the third team thinks of ways to make the product obsolete.

A major chemical company held a brainstorming session and came up with a dozen ways to create extra value for its customers. These included: helping reduce process costs by improving yield and reducing waste; helping reduce inventory by consignments, just-in-time delivery, and reduced cycle time; helping reduce administrative costs by simplified billing and electronic data interchange; improving safety for customer's employees; and reducing price to the customer by substituting components and reducing supplier costs. For more examples of diversification, see the Marketing Insight box, "Airlines Show They Aren't Commodities as They Jockey for Position."

Crego and Schiffrin have proposed that customer-centred organizations should study what customers value and then prepare an offering that *exceeds* their expectations.[1] They see this as a three-step process:

1. *Defining the customer value model.* The company first lists all the product and service factors that might influence the target customers' perception of value.

2. *Building the customer value hierarchy.* The company now assigns each factor to one of four groups: basic, expected, desired, and unanticipated. Consider the set of factors at a fine restaurant:
   - *Basic*: The food is edible and delivered in a timely fashion. (If this is all the restaurant does right, the customer would normally not be satisfied.)
   - *Expected*: There is good china and tableware, a linen tablecloth and napkin, flowers, discreet service, and well-prepared food. (These factors make the offering acceptable, but not exceptional.)
   - *Desired*: The restaurant is pleasant and quiet, and the food is especially good and interesting.
   - *Unanticipated*: The restaurant serves a complimentary sorbet between the courses and places candy on the table after the last course is served.

3. *Deciding on the customer value package.* Now the company chooses that combination of tangible and intangible items, experiences, and outcomes designed to outperform competitors and win the customers' delight and loyalty.

Airlines Show They Aren't Commodities as They Jockey for Position

It used to be that air travel was regarded as a commodity. However, deregulation and the 1995 Open Skies agreement have led to an era of fierce competition and have opened the way for some upstart "Davids" to differentiate themselves and steal passengers from airline "Goliaths." Here are two airlines that have been particularly successful at distinguishing themselves.

Virgin Atlantic. Founded in 1983, many analysts predicted that this classy, iconoclastic airline would be another doomed transatlantic startup. Yet, in its 15-year history, Virgin has shaken the industry. Rather than competing solely on price, Virgin offers entertainment and creature comforts. The airline was the first to offer seatback videos, and it provides onboard manicures, massages, and magicians—and not just for first-class passengers. "We didn't want to get into the transportation industry. We're still in the entertainment industry—at 25 000 feet," says Richard Branson, chairman and CEO of the Virgin Group, which owns a host of companies from Virgin Cola to Virgin Megastores. The Virgin brand is closely identified with Branson's flashy, daredevil personality, and this, too, is a point of differentiation for the airline.

Branson's publicity stunts, such as trying to circumnavigate the globe in a hot-air balloon, give the airline a certain cachet. Virgin Atlantic earned $193 million on sales of $2.1 billion in 1998.

WestJet. Calgary's WestJet used Southwes Airlines as a model to emulate when first developing its business plan. Founded in 1995, it stuck to one key point of differentiation—low-cost fares. Its no-debt, equity-financing model, and its use of technology such as its efficient on-line booking program has helped WestJet keep its costs low. Until recently, it has focused on serving markets in Western Canada, but after the Canadian-Air Canada merger, it started eyeing markets in the east. Fasten your seatbelts—the airline wars may not be over yet!

Canada's WestJet used Southwest Airlines as a model to emulate. It's also worth noting that advances in technology will make it possible for airlines to add yet another level of competition through *hightech differentiation*. For instance, Japan Airlines offers video games. Singapore Airlines makes inseat laptop computer power supply available. Soon other carriers will offer casino gambling. The only problem is that whatever really works can be copied … at a cost, raising the cost to all passengers.

Sources: Chris Woodyard, "Southwest Airlines Makes Flying Fun: The Dallas-based Carrier's Policy Is to Hire Hams and Let Their Personalities Shine Through," *USA Today,* September 22, 1998, p, E, 4. Chad Kaydo, "Riding High," *Sales & Marketing Management,* July 1998, pp. 64-69. Daniel Pedersen, "Cookies and Champagne," *Newsweek,* April 27, 1998, p. 60. Julia Flynn, "Then Came Branson," *Business Week,* October 26, 1998, pp. 116-120. WestJet Web site: http://www.westjet.com.

 DIFFERENTIATION TOOLS

A company must try to differentiate its offering.

■ **Differentiation** is the act of designing a set of meaningful differences to distinguish the company's offering from competitors' offerings.

The number of differentiation opportunities varies with the type of industry. The Boston Consulting Group has distinguished four types of industries based on the number of available competitive advantages and their size (Figure 10-1):

1. *Volume industry.* One in which companies can gain only a few, but rather large, competitive advantages. In the construction-equipment industry, a company can strive for the low-cost position or the highly differentiated position and win big on either basis. Profitability is correlated with company size and market share.

2. *Stalemated industry.* One in which there are few potential competitive advantages and each is small. In the steel industry, it is hard to differentiate the product or decrease manufacturing cost. Companies can try to hire better salespeople, entertain more lavishly, and the like, but these are small advantages. Profitability is unrelated to company market share.

3. *Fragmented industry.* One in which companies face many opportunities for differentiation, but each opportunity for competitive advantage is small. A restaurant can differentiate in many ways but end up not gaining a large market share. Both small and large restaurants can be profitable or unprofitable.

4. *Specialized industry.* One in which companies face many differentiation opportunities, and each differentiation can have a high payoff. Among companies making specialized machinery for selected market segments, some small companies can be as profitable as some large companies.

Milind Lele observed that companies differ in their potential "manoeuvrability" along five dimensions: target market, product, place (channels), promotion, and price. The company's freedom of manoeuvre is affected by the industry structure and the firm's position in the industry. For each potential manoeuvre, the company needs to estimate the return. Those manoeuvres that promise the highest return define the company's strategic leverage. Companies in a stalemated industry have very little manoeuvrability and strategic leverage, and those in specialized industries enjoy great manoeuvrability and strategic leverage.

Here we will examine how a company can differentiate its market offering along five dimensions: product, services, personnel, channel, or image (Table 10-1).

PRODUCT DIFFERENTIATION

Physical products vary in their potential for differentiation. At one extreme we find products that allow little variation: chicken, steel, aspirin. Yet even here, some differentiation is possible. Frank Perdue claims that his chickens are more tender—and he gets a 10 percent price premium. P&G makes several brands of laundry detergent, each with a separate brand identity. At the other extreme are products capable of high differentiation, such as automobiles, commercial buildings, and furniture. Here the seller faces an abundance of design parameters, including form, features, performance, conformance, durability, reliability, repairability, style, and design.[2]

Form

Many products can be differentiated in *form*, the size, shape, or physical structure of a product. Consider the many possible forms taken by products such as aspirin. Although aspirin is essentially a commodity, it can be differentiated by dosage size, shape, coating, action time, and so on.

Features

Most products can be offered with varying *features*, characteristics that supplement the product's basic function. Being the first to introduce valued new features is one of the most effective ways to compete.

Structure of Flows in a Modern Exchange Economy

Product	Services	Personnel	Channel	Image
Form	Ordering ease	Competence	Coverage	Symbols
Features	Delivery	Courtesy	Expertise	Media
Performance	Installation	Credibility	Performance	Atmosphere
Conformance	Customer training	Reliability		Events
Durability	Customer consulting	Responsiveness		
Reliability	Maintenance and repair	Communication		
Repairability	Miscellaneous			
Style				
Design				

TABLE 10.1

Differentiation Variables

chapter 10
Positioning the Market
Offering Through the
Product Life Cycle

285

How can a company identify and select appropriate new features? The company can ask recent buyers: How do you like the product? Are there any features that could be added that would improve your satisfaction? How much would you pay for each? How do you feel about the features other customers have suggested?

The next task is to decide which features are worth adding. For each potential feature, the company should calculate customer value versus company cost. Suppose an auto manufacturer is considering the three possible improvements shown in Table 10-2. Rear-window defrosting would cost the company $100 per car to add at the factory level. The average customer said this feature was worth $200. The company could therefore generate $2 of incremental customer satisfaction for every $1 increase in company cost. Looking at the other two features, it appears that automatic transmission would create the most customer value per dollar of company cost. The company would also need to consider how many people want each feature, how long it would take to introduce each feature, and whether competitors could easily copy the feature.

Companies must also think in terms of feature bundles or packages. Japanese car companies often manufacture cars at three "trim levels." This lowers manufacturing and inventory costs. Each company must decide whether to offer feature customization at a higher cost or a few standard packages at a lower cost.

Performance Quality

Most products are established at one of four performance levels: low, average, high, or superior. *Performance quality* refers to the level at which the product's primary characteristics operate. The important question here is: Does offering higher product performance produce higher profitability? The Strategic Planning Institute studied the impact of higher relative product quality and found a significantly positive correlation between relative product quality and return on investment (ROI). High-quality business units earned more because their premium quality allowed them to charge a premium price; they benefited from more repeat purchasing, consumer loyalty, and positive word of mouth; and their costs of delivering more quality were not much higher than for business units producing low quality.

Quality's link to profitability does not mean that the firm should design the highest performance level possible. There are diminishing returns to ever-increasing performance. The manufacturer must design a performance level appropriate to the target market and competitors' performance levels.

A company must also manage performance quality through time. Three strategies are available. The first, where the manufacturer continuously improves the product, often produces the highest return and market share. The second strategy is to maintain product quality at a given level. Many companies leave their quality unaltered after its initial formulation unless glaring faults or opportunities occur. The third strategy is to reduce product quality through time. Some companies cut quality to offset rising costs; others reduce quality deliberately in order to increase current profits. This isn't something that Purdy's chocolates will ever consider, however.

■ **RC Purdy Chocolates Ltd.** Since 1907, one thing has remained a constant throughout Purdy's history—a commitment to quality and tradition." We take pride in using only the finest quality, purest, freshest ingredients—just as Mr. Purdy did all those years ago" says Charles Flavelle, Chairman of Purdy's. The quality of Purdy's products is what first attracted Flavelle to the business in

TABLE	10.2

Measuring Customer Effectiveness Value

Feature	Company Cost (a)	Customer Value (b)	Customer Value ÷ Customer Cost (c = b ÷ a)
Rear-window defrosting	$ 100	$ 200	2
Cruise control	600	600	1
Automatic transmission	800	2,400	3

1963. Today, using only the finest ingredients means chocolate from Belgium, ginger from Australia, cashews from India, and dairy products delivered fresh daily from farmers in British Columbia's Fraser Valley. Purdy's is the largest chocolate retailer in Western Canada, with 44 stores in British Columbia and Alberta. Don't mourn if you don't live in the West! Purdy's wonderful chocolate is now available on-line.[3]

RC Purdy's Chocolates Ltd.
www.purdys.com

Conformance Quality

Buyers expect products to have a high *conformance quality*, which is the degree to which all the produced units are identical and meet the promised target specifications. Suppose a Porsche 944 is designed to accelerate to 100 kilometres an hour within 10 seconds. If every Porsche 944 coming off the assembly line does this, the model is said to have high conformance quality. The problem with low conformance quality is that the product will disappoint some buyers.

Durability

Durability, a measure of the product's expected operating life under natural and/or stressful conditions, is a valued attribute for certain products. Buyers will generally pay more for vehicles and kitchen appliances that have a long-lasting reputation. However, this rule is subject to some qualifications. The extra price must not be excessive. Furthermore, the product must not be subject to rapid technological obsolescence, as is the case with personal computers and videocameras.

Reliability

Buyers normally will pay a premium for more reliable products. *Reliability* is a measure of the probability that a product will not malfunction or fail within a specified time period. Maytag, which manufactures major home appliances, has an outstanding reputation for creating reliable appliances. And when Matsushita acquired Motorola's Quasar division, which manufactured television receivers, Matsushita reduced the defect rate from 141 to 6 per 100 sets.

Repairability

Buyers prefer products that are easy to repair. *Repairability* is a measure of the ease of fixing a product when it malfunctions or fails. An automobile made with standard parts that are easily replaced has high repairability. Ideal repairability would exist if users could fix the product themselves with little cost or time. Some products include a diagnostic feature that allows servicepeople to correct a problem over the telephone or advise the user how to correct it. Before GE sends a repairperson to fix a home appliance, it tries to solve the problem over the phone. It succeeds in over 50 percent of the cases, saving the customer money. Many computer hardware and software companies offer technical support to their customers over the phone, or by fax or e-mail. Consider the steps taken by Cisco.

■ **Cisco Systems, Inc.** Cisco, a major manufacturer of Internet components, is now selling over 40 percent of its products over the Internet. Its customers often need answers to questions about its equipment and Cisco needs a large staff for its telephone support system. To handle the problem, Cisco puts together a Knowledge Base of Frequently Asked Questions (FAQs) on the Internet. Cisco eliminated 50 000 phone calls a month that had cost $200 a phone call, and is now saving $10 million a month. Each new call and solution goes to a tech writer who adds the solution to FAQ, thus reducing the number of future phone calls.

Cisco Systems
www.cisco.com

Style

Style describes the product's look and feel to the buyer. Buyers are normally willing to pay a premium for products that are attractively styled. Car buyers pay a premium for Jaguars because of their extraordinary look. Aesthetics have played a key role in such brands as Absolut vodka, Starbucks coffee, Apple computers, Montblanc pens, Godiva chocolate, and Harley Davidson motorcycles.[4]

Too many products are yawn-producing rather than eye-catching. Style has the advantage of creating distinctiveness that is difficult to copy. On the negative side, strong style does not always mean high performance. A car like Jaguar may look sensational, but in the past, Jaguars spent a lot of time in the repair shop.

We must include packaging as a styling weapon, especially in food products, cosmetics, toiletries, and small consumer appliances. The package is the buyer's first encounter with the product and is capable of turning the buyer on or off. For Arizona Iced Tea, packaging is definitely a turn-on.[5]

■ **Arizona Iced Tea.** Arizona Iced Tea marketer Ferolito, Vultaggio & Sons has gained success by taking a rather straightforward drink—tea—and putting it into unusual bottles with elaborate designs. The widemouthed, longnecked bottles have been trendsetters in the new age beverage industry, and customers often buy the tea just for the bottle. Because consumers are known to hang on to their empties or convert them into lamps and other household objects, the company is coming out with limited-edition bottles. In 1998, for instance, it brought out a limited quality of Lemon Tea bottles in four designs by pop artist Peter Max. Ferolito, Vultaggio & Sons even destroyed the printing cylinders to ensure that the labels can't be reproduced in the future.

Design: The Integrating Force

As competition intensifies, design offers a potent way to differentiate and position a company's products and services.[6] Harvard professor Robert Hayes summed it up best when he said, "Fifteen years ago, companies competed on price. Today, it's quality. Tomorrow, it's design." In increasingly fast-paced markets, price and technology are not enough. Design is the factor that will often give a company its competitive edge. *Design* is the totality of features that affect how a product looks and functions in terms of customer requirements. Design is particularly important in making and marketing durable equipment, apparel, retail services, and packaged goods. All the qualities we've discussed are design parameters. The designer must determine how much to invest in form, feature development, performance, conformance, reliability, repairability, and style. To the company, a well-designed product is one that is easy to manufacture and distribute. To the customer, a well-designed product is one that is pleasant to look at and easy to open, install, use, repair, and dispose of. The designer must take all these factors into account.

Apple Computers proved the value of the form-follows-function maxim with its recent iMac launch.

Apple Computers
www.apple.com

■ **Apple Computers.** Who said that computers have to be beige and boxy? Apple's newest computer, the iMac, is anything but. The computers are configured to applications such as games faster than IBM-based machines, but they cost about half as much. The iMac features a sleek, curvy monitor and hard drive, all in one unit, in translucent strawberry, blueberry, grape, tangerine, or lime casings. There's no clunky tower or desktop hard drive to clutter up your office area. There's also no floppy drive, simply because Apple believes that the floppy is on the verge of extinction; more and more software is being distributed via CD or the Internet. With its one-button Internet access, this machine is designed specifically for cruising the Internet (that's what the "i" in "iMac" stands for). Only one month after the iMac hit the stores in January 1999, it was the number-two bestselling computer. More than 15 percent of iMac buyers are first-time PC owners and an additional 12 percent are converts from Intel models. They are turning up in design shops and advertising agencies where looking cool is as important as efficiency. The space-age design combined with the availability of specialized medical software also drove Orangeville, Ontario's Family Medical centre to purchase 28 iMacs. The computers have been so popular that Apple Canada Inc.'s supply has been "severely constrained" and many retailers have had to post "sold out" signs on their shelves instead of stocking them with the eye-catching computers.[7]

Some companies confuse design with styling and think that design is a matter of enclosing an average product in a stylish casing. Or they think that reliability is something

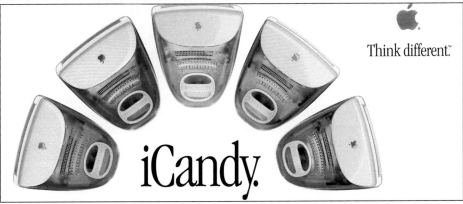

to catch during inspections rather than designing it into the manufacturing process. They may think of designers as artists who pay insufficient attention to cost or who produce designs that are too radical for the market to accept.

Certain countries are winning on design: Italian design in apparel and furniture; Scandinavian design for functionality, aesthetics, and environmental consciousness; German design for austerity and robustness. Braun, a German division of Gillette, has elevated design to a high art in its electric shavers, coffee makers, hair dryers, and food processors. The company's design department enjoys equal status with engineering and manufacturing. The Danish firm Bang & Olufsen has received many kudos for the design of its stereo, TV equipment, and telephones.

The Design Innovation Group in Great Britain surveyed 221 product, engineering, industrial, and graphic-design projects supported by government subsidies. The study found that 90 percent of the projects made a profit with an average payback period of 15 months from product launch. The average design project cost about $100 000 and produced an average sales increase of 41 percent.

SERVICES DIFFERENTIATION

When the physical product cannot easily be differentiated, the key to competitive success may lie in adding valued services and improving their quality. The main service differentiators are ordering ease, delivery, installation, customer training, customer consulting, and maintenance and repair.

Ordering Ease
Ordering ease refers to how easy it is for the customer to place an order with the company. In some cities, like Toronto, consumers can order their groceries on-line. Professors can order case and teaching materials on-line using the Ivey Business School's web page. Baxter Healthcare has eased the ordering process by supplying hospitals with computer terminals through which they send orders directly to Baxter. Banks are moving away from bricks and mortar as a result of their strategies of improving access to banking services. Banks today provide such a range of electronic services—

everything from smart cards to home-banking software—that the Canadian Banking Association estimates that 85 percent of daily bank transactions are done electronically via automatic teller machines, debit cards, and telephone and Internet connections.[8]

Delivery

Delivery refers to how well the product or service is delivered to the customer. It includes speed, accuracy, and care attending the delivery process. Deluxe Check Printers, Inc., has built an impressive reputation for shipping out its cheques one day after receiving an order—without being late once in 18 years. Levi Strauss, Benetton, and The Limited have adopted computerized "quick response systems" that link the information systems of their suppliers, manufacturing plants, distribution centres, and retailing outlets. Chapter's knew that many Canadians were buying books on-line from the American giant, Amazon.com. However, Chapters also knew that Canadians were frustrated at the time it took to receive their orders and the cost of shipping those orders. Thus, when they developed Chapters.com, they promising Canadians free or low-cost shipping, same-day delivery in the Toronto area, or two-day delivery in the rest of Canada. These benefits have helped the firm build a lot of repeat business. Buyers will often choose a supplier with a better reputation for on-time delivery.[9]

Installation

Installation refers to the work done to make a product operational in its planned location. Buyers of heavy equipment expect good installation service. Differentiating at this point in the consumption chain is particularly important for companies with complex products. Ease of installation becomes a true selling point especially when the target market is technology novices who are notoriously intolerant of on-screen messages such as "Disk Error 23."

■ **Compaq Computer.** Compaq, with its Presario line, was among the first to use installation as a source of differentiation. Instead of providing an instruction book filled with unintelligible terminology, Compaq offers customers a poster that clearly illustrates the 10 installation steps. The company uses colour-coded cords, cables, and outlets to further simplify installation, and has rigged up computers with a cheerful video and audio presentation that leads new users through setup and registration.[10]

Customer Training

Customer training refers to training the customer's employees to use the vendor's equipment properly and efficiently. General Electric not only sells and installs expensive X-ray equipment in hospitals but also gives extensive training to users of this equipment. McDonald's requires its new franchisees to attend Hamburger University in Oakbrook, Illinois, for two weeks to learn how to manage their franchise properly.

Customer Consulting

Customer consulting refers to data, information systems, and advising services that the seller offers to buyers. One of the best providers of value-adding consulting service is Milliken & Company:

■ **Milliken & Company.** Milliken sells shop towels to industrial launderers, who rent them to factories. These towels are physically similar to competitors' towels. Yet Milliken charges a higher price for its towels and enjoys the leading market share. How can it charge more? The answer is that Milliken adds to its product through continuous service enhancements for laundry customers. Milliken trains its customers' salespeople, supplies prospect leads and sales-promotional material, supplies online computer-order-entry and route-optimization systems, carries on marketing research for customers, sponsors quality-improvement workshops, and sends its salespeople to work with customers. Laundries are more than willing to buy Milliken towels and pay a price premium because the extra services improve their profitability.[11]

Compaq Computer
www.compaq.com

Consumer consulting isn't limited to for-profit operations.

■ **Heart and Stroke Foundation of Canada.** As the population ages, many people have growing health concerns. The Heart and Stroke Foundation of Canada helps to address heart health issues using its web site. The site contains information about healthy eating programs for children and adults, provides resources for stroke victims and their families, outlines the latest research, and allows consumers to test their knowledge of issues related to heart health.

The Heart and Stroke Foundation
of Canada
www.hsf.ca/main_e.htm

Maintenance and Repair
Maintenance and repair describes the service program for helping customers keep purchased products in good working order. Consider Tandem's remote repair capabilities.

■ **Tandem Computers.** Tandem makes computers with parallel central-processing units for applications in which downtime is a major problem. To keep customers' computers running, Tandem tries to repair their products before customers are even aware that such service is needed. Tandem staff members can spot a malfunctioning component through remote diagnostics and send the appropriate part and instructions to the customer by express mail. They then walk the customer through the repair process over the phone. Not only has this technique eliminated costly downtime for customers, but for Tandem it has also eliminated the need for a costly onsite service force.[12]

Miscellaneous Services
Companies can find other ways to differentiate customer services. They can offer an improved product warranty or maintenance contract. They can establish rewards for certain behaviours. For example, to encourage customers to use interactive touch-screen kiosks, mallgoers receive daily discount retail coupons, prizes awarded randomly each week, and a calendar of events after they become kiosk members. To qualify for membership they fill out a short application that asks simple demographic and psychographic questions. Customers view this as a value-added service while mall retailers receive valuable marketing information about their customers.[13] MacMillan and McGrath say companies have opportunities to differentiate at every stage of the

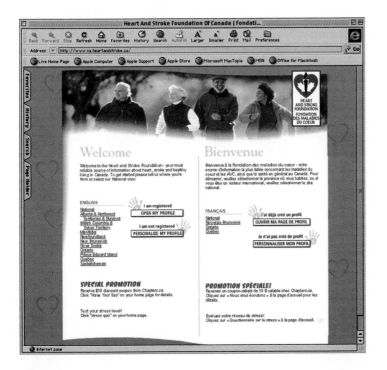

The Heart and Stroke Foundation offers a broad range of information services through its web site.

consumption chain. They point out that companies can even differentiate at the point when their product is no longer in use. Canon, for example, has developed a system that allows customers to return spent printer cartridges at Canon's expense.[14]

PERSONNEL DIFFERENTIATION

Companies can gain a strong competitive advantage through having better-trained people. Singapore Airlines enjoys an excellent reputation in large part because of its flight attendants. The McDonald's people are courteous, the IBM people are professional, and the Disney people are upbeat. The sales forces of such companies as Bombardier, General Electric, Cisco, Frito-Lay, The Investors Group, and Pfizer enjoy an excellent reputation.[15] Better-trained personnel exhibit six characteristics: *Competence:* They possess the required skill and knowledge; *courtesy:* They are friendly, respectful, and considerate; *credibility:* They are trustworthy; *reliability:* They perform the service consistently and accurately; *responsiveness:* They respond quickly to customers' requests and problems; and *communication:* They make an effort to understand the customer and communicate clearly.[16]

In an age when competitors can knock off products or services in an instant, some savvy companies are marketing their employees' unique know-how:

The Orvis Company
www.orvis.com

- **The Orvis Company.** Founded in 1856, The Orvis Company is a mail-order and retail supplier of "country" clothing, gifts, and sporting gear that competes with the likes of L.L. Bean and Eddie Bauer. Yet Orvis differentiates itself by selling its long history of fly-fishing expertise. Orvis fly-fishing schools make a tough sport accessible to novices. The schools, not coincidentally, are usually located near Orvis retail outlets. Orvis had sales of less than $1.5 million in 1968, when it opened its first fly-fishing school. Now the company boasts sales of $525 million. While actual fly-fishing products account for only a small portion of overall sales, catalogue manager and VP Tom Rosenbauer says, "Without our fly-fishing heritage, we'd be just another rag vendor."[17]

CHANNEL DIFFERENTIATION

Companies can achieve competitive advantage through the way they design their distribution channels' coverage, expertise, and performance. Caterpillar's success in the construction-equipment industry is based partly on superior channel development. Its dealers are found in more locations than competitors' dealers, and they are typically better trained and perform more reliably. Dell in computers and Avon in cosmetics distinguish themselves by developing and managing direct marketing channels of high quality. Iams Pet Food provides an instructive case on how going against tradition, in selecting channels, can pay off.

- **Iams Pet Food.** Back in 1946, when Paul Iams founded the company, pet food was cheap, not too nutritious, and sold exclusively in supermarkets and the occasional feed store. Iams ignored the traditional channels and went to regional veterinarians, breeders, and pet stores. When current owner Clay Mathile joined the company in the early 1970s, he took this marketing channel strategy national. From 1982 to 1996, Iams' annual sales have soared from $24 million to $750 million.[18]

IMAGE DIFFERENTIATION

Buyers respond differently to company and brand images. The primary way to account for Marlboro's extraordinary worldwide market share (around 30 percent) is that Marlboro's "macho cowboy" image has struck a responsive chord with much of the cigarette-smoking public. Wine and liquor companies also work hard to develop distinctive images for their brands. For example, while Tequila was once regarded as the drink of choice for the lower classes, the industry has been successful in revolutionizing its image to the extent that now it is regarded as the trendiest drink among stylish Mexicans. Moreover, the effect is moving north. In the period 1996-98, Canadian consumption rose 27 percent.[19]

Identity and image need to be distinguished. *Identity* comprises the ways that a company aims to identify or position its product. *Image* is the way the public perceives the company or its products. The T. Eaton Company, for example, has recently attempted to change its identity and has begun talking about itself as a youth-oriented company.[20] Many consumers, however, still retain the image of the company as a conservative retailer who appeals to the "Mom" set.

Image is affected by many factors beyond the company's control. The fact that image can have a life of its own is exemplified by Nike's problems in maintaining its appeal to the fickle youth market.

■ **Nike and Airwalk.** Nike succeeded in convincing millions of young consumers that a shoe is not simply a shoe; it's an attitude. The company was so successful in its strategy that the Nike swoosh is one of the most recognizable symbols in the world. Yet the popularity of Nike—its transformation from hip to mainstream—turns off important core consumers, the 12- to 24-year-olds. Other brands with more alternative images, such as Airwalk, which started off as a technical skateboarder and snowboarder shoe, have gained share. Kids liked the extreme sports image associated with the shoe, which Airwalk promotes in its offbeat advertising.[21]

Nike
www.nike.com

An effective image does three things. First, it establishes the product's character and value proposition. Second, it conveys this character in a distinctive way so as not to confuse it with competitors'. Third, it delivers emotional power beyond a mental image. For the image to work, it must be conveyed through every available communication vehicle and brand contact. If "IBM means service," this message must be expressed in symbols, written and audiovisual media, atmosphere, and employee behaviour.

Symbols
Images can be amplified by strong symbols. The company can choose a symbol such as the beaver (Roots), apple (Apple Computer), or doughboy (Pillsbury). A brand can be built around a famous person, as with new perfumes—Passion (Elizabeth Taylor) and Uninhibited (Cher). Companies may choose a colour identifier such as blue green, (TD Bank), blue (IBM), yellow (Kodak), or red (Campbell soup), or a specific piece of sound/music. Figure 10-2 reproduces logos of some of North America's most admired companies.

Media
The chosen image must be worked into advertisements that convey a story, a mood, a claim—something distinctive. It should appear in annual reports, brochures, catalogues, the company stationery, and business cards.

Atmosphere
The physical space occupied by the company is another powerful image generator. Hyatt Regency hotels developed a distinctive image through its atrium lobbies. A bank that wants to convey the image of a safe bank must communicate this through the right building design, interior design, layout, colours, materials, and furnishings.

Events
A company can build an identity through the type of event it sponsors. Perrier, the bottled water company, came into prominence by laying out exercise tracks and sponsoring health sports events. Becel margarine developed a position as a heart-healthy product by working with the Heart and Stroke Foundation of Canada on such events as the "Ride for Life." ReMax increases its visibility among people buying larger, family homes when it sponsors the Children's Miracle Network's telethon that aids Canada's children's hospitals.

An excellent example of a product that has used multiple image-building techniques to etch its image on the public mind is the Swatch watch from Switzerland.

FIGURE 10.2

Logos of some of North America's most admired companies.

BOMBARDIER
AEROSPACE

BOMBARDIER

N⊘RTEL
NETWORKS

- **Swatch.** Nicholas G. Hayek, Swatch's founder, launched Swatch watches in 1983 by hanging a 150-metre-long sign from the tallest bank in Frankfurt. Within a few weeks, every German in the target market of young, active, and trendy people knew Swatch—the analogue watch with the colourful plastic bands. Swatch also differentiated itself by using many different watch faces and bands that celebrate famous artists, sports, events, and anniversaries. Over 200 million of the $60 to $150 Swatch watches have been sold in more than 30 countries. Swatch's limited edition watches have become collectors' items. Swatch operates some of its own retail stores. On the famous Via Monte Napoleone in Milan, Swatch attracts more visitors than any other store on the street. Swatch continues to innovate and keep people buzzing about its state-of-the-art products. Alongside the standard plastic watches there are new developments such as the Irony (a metal Swatch), a lightpowered Swatch Solar, and a melodious alarm clock called the Swatch Musicall. Swatch clearly has written the marketing book on how to build a cult following by applying superior styling, merchandising, and promotion.[22]

DEVELOPING AND COMMUNICATING A POSITIONING STRATEGY

All products can be differentiated to some extent.[23] But not all brand differences are meaningful or worthwhile. A difference is worth establishing to the extent that it satisfies the following criteria:

- *Important:* The difference delivers a highly valued benefit to a sufficient number of buyers.
- *Distinctive:* The difference is delivered in a distinctive way.
- *Superior:* The difference is superior to other ways of obtaining the benefit.
- *Pre-emptive:* The difference cannot be easily copied by competitors.
- *Affordable:* The buyer can afford to pay for the difference.
- *Profitable:* The company will find it profitable to introduce the difference.

Many companies have introduced differentiations that failed on one or more of these tests. The Westin Stamford hotel in Singapore advertises that it is the world's tallest hotel. But a hotel's height is not important to many tourists. Polaroid's Polarvision, while distinctive and pre-emptive, was inferior to another way of capturing motion—namely, videocameras. When the Turner Broadcasting System installed TV monitors to beam Cable News Network (CNN) to bored shoppers in store checkout lines, it didn't pass the "superior" test. Customers weren't looking for a new source of entertainment in supermarkets, and Turner took a $24 million tax write-down.

Company and Product	Target Customers	Benefits	Price	Value Proposition
Perdue (chicken)	Quality-conscious consumers of chicken	Tenderness	10% premium	More tender golden chicken at a moderate premium price
Volvo (station wagon)	Safety-conscious "upscale" families	Durability and safety	20% premium	The safest, most durable wagon in which your family can ride
Domino's (pizza)	Convenience-minded pizza lovers	Delivery speed and good quality	15% premium	A good hot pizza, delivered to your door within 30 minutes of ordering, at a moderate price

Yet Carpenter, Glazer, and Nakamoto posit that brands can sometimes successfully differentiate on irrelevant attributes.[24] Procter & Gamble differentiates its Folger's instant coffee by its "flaked coffee crystals" created through a "unique patented process." In reality, the coffee particle's shape is irrelevant because the crystal immediately dissolves in the hot water. Alberto Culver's Alberto Natural Silk shampoo is advertised with the slogan "We put silk in a bottle." However, a company spokesperson conceded that silk doesn't really do anything for hair.

Each firm needs to develop a distinctive positioning for its market offering.

■ *Positioning* is the act of designing the company's offering and image to deliver a distinctive benefit(s) to target customers.

The end result of positioning is the successful creation of a market-focused value proposition, a cogent reason why the target market should buy the product. Table 10-3 shows how three companies—Perdue, Volvo, and Domino's—defined their value proposition given their target customers, benefits, and prices.

POSITIONING ACCORDING TO RIES AND TROUT

The word "positioning" was popularized by two advertising executives, Al Ries and Jack Trout. They see positioning as a creative exercise done with an existing product:

> Positioning starts with a product. A piece of merchandise, a service, a company, an institution, or even a person. . . . But positioning is not what you do to a product. Positioning is what you do to the mind of the prospect. That is, you position the product in the mind of the prospect.

Toronto-based Indian Motorcycle certainly understands the importance of positioning:

■ **Indian Motorcycle Co.** People watching the efforts of Murray Smith, president of Indian Motorcycle Co. of Toronto, may shake their heads and wonder what vintage motorcycles, restaurants, and clothing have in common. Smith is bringing the Indian brand back to life. Founded in 1901, Indian Motorcycle specialized in the heavy bikes that grew to become the standard machine of the military and police forces. However, bad management led to its demise after World War II. Today, Smith not only plans to produce the bikes, but is also working to position Indian as a lifestyle brand so that it speaks with one voice to potential buyers. As the millennium approaches, Indian believes that people long for simpler times and old-fashioned values. Using mostly billboards, Indian is hoping to cash in on the "retro" and "nostalgia" craze. The billboards are minimalist in design and feature colour photos of the chrome-laden bikes with simple captions like "The last one was made in '53. We've

Indian Motorcycle Co.
www.indianmotorcycle.com

Indian
MOTORCYCLE CAFÉ & LOUNGE
355 KING STREET WEST

had a long time to think about refinements." Indian is leveraging the brand to clothing featuring stylized logos of the motorcycle. It is also opening motorcycle "shrine" restaurants that will help build the image and maintain customer contact while supporting the lifestyle campaign.[25]

Ries and Trout argue that well-known products generally hold a distinctive position in consumers' minds. Hertz is thought of as the world's largest auto-rental agency, Coca-Cola as the world's largest soft-drink company, and Porsche as one of the world's best sports cars. These brands own these positions and it would be hard for a competitor to claim them. A competitor has three strategic alternatives.

The first is to strengthen its own current position in the consumer's mind. Avis acknowledged its second position in rental cars business and claimed: "We're number two. We try harder." And 7-Up capitalized on not being a cola drink by advertising itself as the Uncola. The second strategy is to grab an unoccupied position. Three Musketeers chocolate bar advertised itself as having 45 percent less fat than other chocolate bars. The third strategy is to deposition or reposition the competition. Most North American buyers of dinnerware thought that Lenox and Royal Doulton china both come from England. Royal Doulton depositioned Lenox china by showing that it is made in New Jersey. Molson tried to undermine Labatt's Kokanee beer by advertising that it was actually brewed in London, Ontario.

Ries and Trout argue that, in an overadvertised society, the mind often knows brands in the form of *product ladders*, such as Coke/Pepsi/President's Choice or Hertz/Avis/National. The top firm is remembered best. For example, when asked "Who was the first person to successfully fly alone across the Atlantic Ocean?" we answer "Charles Lindbergh." When asked, "Who was the second person to do it?" we draw a blank. This is why companies fight for the number-one position. The "largest firm" position can be held by only one brand. The second brand should invent and lead in a new category. Thus 7-Up is the number-one Uncola, Porsche is the number-one small sports car, and Dial is the number-one deodorant soap. The marketer should identify an important attribute or benefit that a brand can convincingly own.

A fourth strategy is the exclusive-club strategy. For example, a company can promote the idea that it is one of the Big Three. The Big Three idea was invented by the third-largest U.S. auto firm, Chrysler. (The market leader never invents this concept.) The implication is that those in the club are the "best."

Ries and Trout essentially deal with communication strategies for positioning or repositioning a brand in the consumer's mind. Yet they acknowledge positioning requires that every tangible aspect of product, price, place, and promotion must support the chosen positioning strategy.[26]

HOW MANY DIFFERENCES TO PROMOTE?

Each company must decide how many differences (e.g., benefits, features) to promote to its target customers. Many marketers advocate promoting only one central benefit. Rosser Reeves said a company should develop a *unique selling proposition (USP)* for each brand and stick to it.[27] Crest toothpaste consistently promotes its anticavity protection, and Mercedes promotes its great engineering. Ries and Trout favour one consistent positioning message.[28] Each brand should select an attribute and tout itself as "number one" on that attribute.

Number-one positionings include "best quality," "best service," "lowest price," "best value," "safest," "fastest," "most customized," "most convenient," and "most advanced technology." If a company hammers away at one of these positionings and delivers on it, it will probably be best known and recalled for this strength. Canadian Tire has consistently positioned itself as the most complete auto-parts and service store.

Not everyone agrees that single-benefit positioning is always best. *Double-benefit positioning* may be necessary if two or more firms claim to be best on the same attribute. Steelcase, Inc., a leading office-furniture-systems company, claims two benefits: best on-time delivery and best installation support. Volvo positions its automobiles as "safest" and "most durable."

There are even cases of successful triple-benefit positioning. Smith Kline Beecham promotes its Aquafresh toothpaste as offering three benefits: anticavity protection, better breath, and whiter teeth. The challenge is to convince consumers that the brand delivers all three. Smith Kline's solution was to create a toothpaste that squeezes out of the tube in three colours, thus visually confirming the three benefits. In doing this, Beecham "countersegmented"; that is, it attracted three segments instead of one.

As companies increase the number of claims for their brand, they risk disbelief and a loss of clear positioning. In general, a company must avoid four major positioning errors:

1. *Underpositioning:* Some companies discover that buyers have only a vague idea of the brand. The brand is just seen as another entry in a crowded marketplace. When Pepsi introduced its clear Crystal Pepsi in 1993, customers were distinctly unimpressed. They didn't see "clarity" as an important benefit in a soft drink.

2. *Overpositioning:* Buyers may have too narrow an image of the brand. This was the problem Febreze faced when it was first introduced. Consumers believed it was only for people who smoked or owned pets—they didn't see it as a versatile fabric freshener.

3. *Confused positioning:* Buyers might have a confused image of the brand resulting from the company's making too many claims or changing the brand's positioning too frequently. This was the case with Stephen Jobs' sleek and powerful NeXT desktop computer, which was positioned first for students, then for engineers and then for business people, all unsuccessfully.

4. *Doubtful positioning:* Buyers may find it hard to believe the brand claims in view of the product's features, price, or manufacturer. When GM's Cadillac division introduced the Cimarron, it positioned the car as a luxury competitor with BMW, Mercedes, and Audi. While the car featured leather seats, a luggage rack, lots of chrome, and a Cadillac logo stamped on the chassis,

customers saw the car as merely a dolled-up version of Chevy's Cavalier and Oldsmobile's Firenza. While the car was positioned as "more for more," the customers saw it as "less for more."

Solving the positioning problem enables the company to solve the marketing-mix problem. Seizing the "high-quality position" requires the firm to produce high-quality products, charge a high price, distribute through high-class dealers, and advertise in high-quality magazines.

How do companies select their positioning? As an example of product positioning using perceptual mapping, consider a brewery that is attempting to develop an advertising program for one of its beer brands. To do this successfully, management must understand how the target market segments perceive its brand relative to the major competing brands. The basis for these comparisons is a set of attributes, of which it is assumed that at least some are relevant to the brands, the consumers, and the beer-drinking occasions.

To reposition a brand through advertising, it is necessary to alter consumers' perceptions or preferences or both. The advertising that accomplishes this in a cost-effective manner must be believable. This means that the beer-drinking occasion and the people portrayed in the advertisement must not seem incompatible with the brand. Even the media vehicle that is used should seem appropriate.

Darmon has proposed a method for portraying all of these elements of the repositioning challenge. Figure 10-3 shows his joint space for one segment of the Quebec beer-drinking market represented by a sample of English-speaking MBA students. This

FIGURE 10.3

Perceptual Map

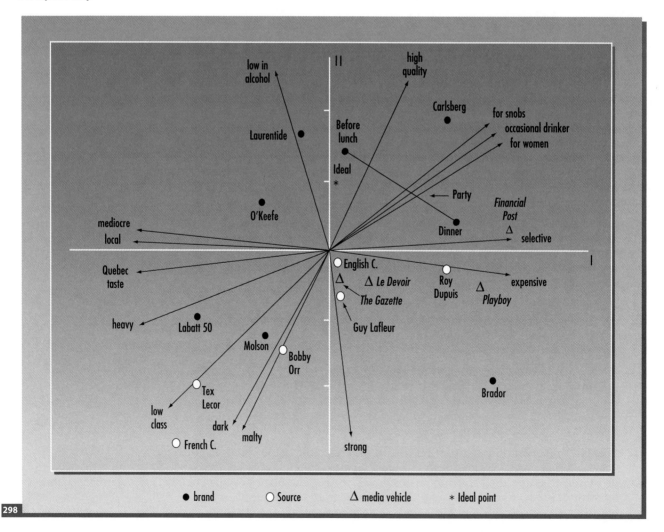

was derived from a series of judgments elicited from the students, using Johnson's multiple discriminant analysis technique.[29]

The positions of the six brands of beer are shown in Figure 10-3 beside their respective boxes. The various attributes are represented by the arrows pointing out from the origin. The relative amount of an attribute possessed by a brand can be estimated by projecting a perpendicular line from it to the appropriate arrow. Thus, Brador is perceived as being stronger than Molson or Labatt.

Molson
www.molson.com

Labatt
www.labatt.com

Also shown in the figure are several potential spokespersons (Guy Lafleur, Bobby Orr, Frank Sinatra, and Tex Lecor), and several potential print media vehicles (*The Gazette, Le Devoir, Playboy,* and *The Financial Post*). The relative positions in the figure suggest, for example, that if the management of Brador wanted to position it as an expensive beer, it would be appropriate to employ Frank Sinatra as a spokesperson and buy advertising space in Playboy.

But it seems unlikely that this would be an appropriate strategy, given consumers' preferences. These are implied by the location of the "ideal" brand, which would be less expensive and less strong than Brador is perceived to be. To reposition Brador in the "ideal" direction, it would be more appropriate to employ Guy Lafleur as a spokesperson and buy advertising in *The Gazette.*

Before adopting any advertising program, it is advisable to perform similar analyses for other significant market segments. Indeed, Darmon's analysis of the French-speaking segment produced a mapping that was similar but not identical.

In general a company can adopt the following different types of positioning strategies:[30]

- *Attribute positioning:* A company positions itself on an attribute, such as size or number of years in existence. For example, Molson management might position its brand as dark and malty.

- *Benefit positioning:* The product is positioned as the leader in a certain benefit. Thus, Laurentide's advertising might claim that its brand has low alcohol content.

- *Use/application positioning:* Positioning the product as best for some use or application. A related claim that Laurentide might make it that it is the best beer to drink before lunch, especially for business entertainers who want to keep a clear head.

- *User positioning:* Positioning the product as best for some user group. Carlsberg might be positioned as the beer for women.

- *Competitor positioning:* The product claims to be better in some way than a named competitor. For example, Labatt 50 might vie with O'Keefe for the "Quebec taste" positioning.

- *Quality/price positioning:* The product is positioned as offering the best value. Thus, Carlsberg is seen as having the highest quality, but since it is not seen as the most expensive, it might be positioned as offering the best value.

WHICH DIFFERENCES TO PROMOTE?

Suppose a company has identified four alternative positioning platforms: technology, cost, quality, and service (Table 10-4). It has one major competitor. Both companies stand at 8 on technology (1 = low score, 10 = high score), which means they both have good technology. The competitor has a better standing on cost (8 instead of 6). The company offers higher quality than its competitors (8 compared to 6). Finally, both companies provide below-average service.

It would seem that the company should go after cost or service to improve its market appeal. However, other considerations arise. The first is how target customers feel about improvements in each of these attributes. Column 4 indicates that improvements in cost and service would be of high importance to customers. But can the company afford to make the improvements in cost and service, and how fast can it provide them? Column 5 shows that improving service would have high affordability and speed. But would the competitor be able to match the improved service? Column 6 shows that the competitor's ability to improve service is low. Based on this information, Column 7 shows the appropriate actions to take with respect to each attribute.

(1)	(2)	(3)	(4)	(5)	(6)	(7)
					Competitor's	
			Importance		Ability to	
			of Improving	Affordability	Improve	
Competitive	Company	Competitor	Standing	and Speed	Standing	Recommended
Advantage	Standing	Standing	(H-M-L)*	(H-M-L)	(H-M-L)	Action
Technology	8	8	L	L	M	Hold
Cost	6	8	H	M	M	Monitor
Quality	8	6	L	L	H	Monitor
Service	4	3	H	H	L	Invest

*H = high; M = medium; L = low

TABLE 10.4

Method for Competitive-Advantage Selection

The one that makes the most sense is for the company to improve its service and promote this improvement. This was the conclusion Monsanto reached in one of its chemical markets. Monsanto hired additional technical service people. When they were trained and ready, Monsanto promoted itself as the "technical service leader."

COMMUNICATING THE COMPANY'S POSITIONING

Once the company has developed a clear positioning strategy, it must communicate that positioning effectively. Suppose a company chooses the "best-in-quality" strategy. Quality is communicated by choosing those physical signs and cues that people normally use to judge quality. Here are some examples:

> A lawn-mower manufacturer claims its lawn mower is "powerful" and uses a noisy motor because buyers think noisy lawn mowers are more powerful.

> A car manufacturer makes cars with good-slamming doors because many buyers slam the doors in the showroom to test how well the car is built.

> Ritz Carlton Hotels signal high quality by training employees to answer calls within three rings, to answer with a genuine "smile" in their voices, and to be extremely knowledgeable about all hotel information.

Quality is also communicated through other marketing elements. A high price usually signals a premium-quality product to buyers. The product's quality image is also affected by packaging, distribution, advertising, and promotion. Here are some cases where a brand's quality image was hurt:

- A well-known frozen-food brand lost its prestige image by being on sale too often.
- A premium beer's image was hurt when it switched from bottles to cans.
- A highly regarded television receiver lost its quality image when mass-merchandise outlets began to carry it.

A manufacturer's reputation also contributes to the perception of quality. Certain companies are sticklers for quality; consumers expect Nestlé and IBM products to be well made. Smart companies communicate their quality to buyers and guarantee customer satisfaction or "your money back."

PRODUCT LIFE CYCLE MARKETING STRATEGIES

A company's differentiating and positioning strategy must change as the product, market, and competitors change over time. Here we will describe the concept of the product life cycle and the changes that are normally made as the product passes through each state of the life cycle.

THE CONCEPT OF THE PRODUCT LIFE CYCLE

To say that a product has a life cycle is to assert four things:

1. Products have a limited life.

2. Product sales pass through distinct stages, each posing different challenges, opportunities, and problems to the seller.

3. Profits rise and fall at different stages of the product life cycle.

4. Products require different marketing, financial, manufacturing, purchasing, and human resource strategies in each stage of their life cycle.

Most product life cycle curves are portrayed as bell-shaped. (Figure 10-4). This curve is typically divided into four stages: introduction, growth, maturity, and decline.[31]

1. *Introduction:* A period of slow sales growth as the product is introduced in the market. Profits are nonexistent in this stage because of the heavy expenses incurred with product introduction.

2. *Growth:* A period of rapid market acceptance and substantial profit improvement.

3. *Maturity:* A period of a slowdown in sales growth because the product has achieved acceptance by most potential buyers. Profits stabilize or decline because of increased competition.

4. *Decline:* The period when sales show a downward drift and profits erode.

The PLC concept can be used to analyze a product category (liquor), a product form (white liquor), a product (vodka), or a brand (Smirnoff).

■ *Product categories* have the longest life cycles. Many product categories stay in the mature stage indefinitely and grow only at the population growth rate. Some major product categories—typewriters, movie cameras—seem to have entered the decline stage of the PLC. Some others—cellular telephones, palm pilots, on-line banking—are clearly in the growth stage.

■ *Product forms* follow the standard PLC more faithfully. Large, mainframe computers passed through the stages of introduction, growth, maturity, and decline; their successors—desktop computers—passed through these same stages.

■ *Products* follow either the standard PLC or one of several variant shapes.

■ *Branded products* can have a short or long PLC. Although many new brands die an early death, some brand names—such as Ivory, Jell-O, Hershey's—have a very long PLC and are used to name and launch new products. Hershey's has successfully introduced Hershey's Hugs, Hershey's Kisses with Almonds, and Hershey's Cookies & Mint candy bar. Hershey believes it can keep its strong brand name going forever.

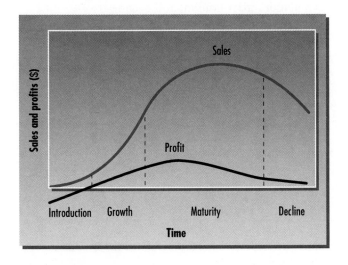

FIGURE 10.4

Sales and Profit Life Cycles

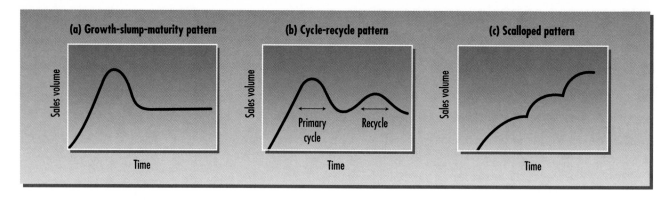

| (a) Growth-slump-maturity pattern | (b) Cycle-recycle pattern | (c) Scalloped pattern |

**Common Product Life-Cycle
Patterns**

Other Shapes of the Product Life Cycle

Not all products exhibit a bell-shaped PLC. Researchers have identified from six to seventeen different PLC patterns.[32] Three common alternate patterns are shown in Figure 10-5. Figure 10-5(a) shows a *growth-slump-maturity pattern*, often characteristic of small kitchen appliances. Some years ago, the sales of electric knives grew rapidly when the product was first introduced and then fell to a "petrified" level. The petrified level is sustained by late adopters buying the product for the first time and early adopters replacing the product.

The *cycle-recycle pattern* in Figure 10-5(b) often describes the sales of new drugs. The pharmaceutical company aggressively promotes its new drug, and this produces the first cycle. Later, sales start declining and the company gives the drug another promotion push, which produces a second cycle (usually of smaller magnitude and duration).[33]

Another common pattern is the *scalloped PLC* in Figure 10-5(c). Here sales pass through a succession of life cycles based on the discovery of new-product characteristics, uses, or users. Nylon's sales, for example, show a scalloped pattern because of the many new uses—parachutes, hosiery, shirts, carpeting, boat sails, automobile tires—that continue to be discovered over time.[34]

Style, Fashion, and Fad Life Cycles

Three special categories of product life cycles should be distinguished—styles, fashions, and fads (Figure 10-6). A *style* is a basic and distinctive mode of expression appearing in a field of human endeavour. Styles appear in homes (colonial, ranch, Georgian); clothing (formal, casual, goth); and art (realistic, surrealistic, abstract). A style can last for generations, going in and out of vogue. A *fashion* is a currently accepted or popular style in a given field. Fashions pass through four stages:[35] distinctiveness, emulation, mass fashion, and decline.

**Style, Fashion, and Fad Life
Cycles**

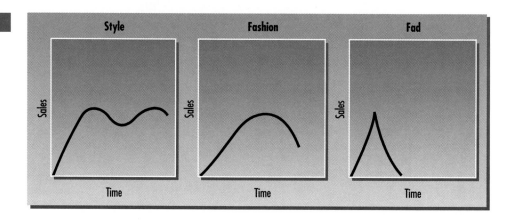

| Style | Fashion | Fad |

The length of a fashion cycle is hard to predict. Wasson believes that fashions end because they represent a purchase compromise, and consumers start looking for missing attributes.[36] For example, as automobiles become smaller, they become less comfortable, and then a growing number of buyers start wanting larger cars. Furthermore, too many consumers adopt the fashion, thus turning others away. Reynolds suggests that the length of a particular fashion cycle depends on the extent to which the fashion meets a genuine need, is consistent with other trends in the society, satisfies societal norms and values, and does not exceed technological limits as it develops.[37]

Fads are fashions that come quickly into public view, are adopted with great zeal, peak early, and decline very fast. Their acceptance cycle is short, and they tend to attract only a limited following of those who are searching for excitement or want to distinguish themselves from others. They often have a novel or capricious aspect, such as body piercing and tattooing. Fads do not survive because they do not normally satisfy a strong need.

The marketing winners are those who recognize fads early and leverage them into products with staying power. Here is the success story of a company that managed to extend a fad's life span:

- **Trivial Pursuit.** Since its Canadian inventors introduced their creation at the International Toy Fair in 1982, Trivial Pursuit has sold 65 million copies in 18 languages in 32 countries, and it remains the bestselling adult game. Parker Brothers has maintained the product's popularity by making a new game with updated questions every year. It also keeps creating offshoots—travel packs, a children's version, Trivial Pursuit Genus IV, an interactive CD-ROM from Virgin Entertainment Interactive. The game also has its own Web site, which received 100 000 visitors in its initial two-month test period. And if you're having trouble making dinner conversation on a date—no problem: NTN Entertainment Network has put Trivial Pursuit in about 3000 restaurants.[38]

Trivial Pursuit
www.trivialpursuit.com/

MARKETING STRATEGIES: INTRODUCTION STAGE

Because it takes time to roll out a new product and fill dealer pipelines, sales growth tends to be slow at this stage. Buzzell identified several causes for the slow growth: delays in the expansion of production capacity; technical problems ("working out the bugs"); delays in obtaining adequate distribution through retail outlets; and customer reluctance to change established behaviours.[39] Sales of expensive new products such as high-definition TV are retarded by additional factors such as product complexity and fewer buyers.

Profits are negative or low in the introduction stage because of low sales and heavy distribution and promotion expenses. Much money is needed to attract distributors. Promotional expenditures are at their highest ratio to sales because of the need to (1) inform potential consumers, (2) induce product trial, and (3) secure distribution in retail outlets. Firms focus their selling on those buyers who are the readiest to buy, usually higher-income groups. Prices tend to be high because costs are high due to relatively low output rates, technological problems in production, and high required margins to support the heavy promotional expenditures. Consider the challenges faced by this Quebec-based company:

- **Biscuits Leclerc ltée.** It takes confidence to take on the market leader, but this is exactly what *Biscuits Leclerc ltée* of Saint-Augustin-de-Desmaures, Québec has done. After two years of research to uncover the closely guarded secret of making cornflakes and over $23 million in investments, the firm hopes to challenge Kellogg Co., and generate $50 million in sales over the next two to three years. Using the brand names *Sweet Mornings* and *P'tits Bonjours* along with packaging featuring popular Looney Tunes characters like Bugs Bunny and the Tasmanian Devil, the firm hopes to beat Kellogg at its own game. The new cereals will be priced at the same level as Kellogg's products and the launch will be accompanied by a national advertising campaign. The firm is

Biscuits Leclerc ltée
www.leclerc.ca

also banking on the fact that its large sales force will provide superior service to Canadian supermarkets and convince them to carry the brand. "It's going to be a real fight—a marketing battle with coupons and premiums—a real war on the shelf," says the marketing director of Biscuits Leclerc ltée.[40]

In launching a new product, marketing management can set a high or a low level for each marketing variable (price, promotion, distribution, product quality). Considering only price and promotion, management can pursue one of four strategies.

1. *Rapid skimming:* launching the new product at a high price and a high promotion level. This strategy makes sense when a large part of the potential market is unaware of the product; those who become aware of the product are eager to have it and can pay the asking price; and the firm faces potential competition and wants to build brand preference.

2. *Slow skimming:* launching the new product at a high price and low promotion. This strategy makes sense when the market is limited in size; most of the market is aware of the product; buyers are willing to pay a high price; and potential competition is not imminent.

3. *Rapid penetration:* launching the product at a low price and spending heavily on promotion. This strategy makes sense when the market is large, the market is unaware of the product, most buyers are price sensitive, there is strong potential competition, and the unit manufacturing costs fall with the company's scale of production and accumulated manufacturing experience.

4. *Slow penetration:* launching the new product at a low price and low level of promotion. This strategy makes sense when the market is large, is highly aware of the product, is price sensitive, and there is some potential competition.

We discuss skimming and penetration strategies in more detail in Chapter 17.

The Pioneer Advantage

Companies that plan to introduce a new product must decide when to enter the market. To be first can be highly rewarding, but risky and expensive. To come in later makes sense if the firm can bring superior technology, quality, or brand strength.

Speeding up innovation time is essential in an age of shortening product life cycles. Competitors in many industries learn about new technologies and new market opportunities at about the same time. Those companies that first reach practical solutions will enjoy "first-mover" advantages in the market. Being early rather than late pays off. One study found that products that came out six months late but on budget earned an average of 33 percent less profit in their first five years; products that came out on time but 50 percent over budget cut their profits by only four percent.

Most studies indicate that the market pioneer gains the most advantage. Such pioneering companies as Amazon.com, Campbell's, Coca-Cola, Eastman Kodak, Hallmark, and Xerox developed sustained market dominance. Robinson and Fornell studied a broad range of mature consumer and industrial-goods businesses, and found that market pioneers generally enjoy a substantially higher market share than do early followers and late entrants:[41] Urban's study also found a pioneer advantage: It appears that the second entrant obtained only 71 percent of the pioneer's market share, and the third entrant obtained only 58 percent.[42] Carpenter and Nakamoto found that 19 out of 25 companies who were market leaders in 1923 were still the market leaders in 1983, 60 years later.[43]

What are the sources of the pioneer's advantage? Research has shown that consumers often prefer pioneering brands.[44] Early users will favour the pioneer's brand if they try it and it satisfies them. The pioneer's brand also establishes the attributes the product class should possess. The pioneer's brand normally aims at the middle of the market and so captures more users. There are also producer advantages: economies of scale, technological leadership, ownership of scarce assets, and other barriers to entry.

However, the pioneer advantage is not inevitable. One only has to reflect on the fate of Bowmar (hand calculators), Reynolds (ballpoint pens), and Osborne (portable computers), market pioneers who were overtaken by later entrants. Schnaars studied 28 industries where the imitators surpassed the innovators.[45] He found several weaknesses among the failing pioneers, including new products that were too crude, improperly positioned, or appeared before there was strong demand; product development costs that exhausted the innovator's resources; a lack of resources to compete against entering larger firms; and managerial incompetence or unhealthy complacency. Successful imitators thrived by offering lower prices, improving the product more continuously, or using brute market power to overtake the pioneer.

Golder and Tellis raise further doubts about the pioneer advantage.[46] They distinguish between an *inventor* (first to develop patents in a new-product category), *product pioneer* (first to develop a working model), and a *market pioneer* (first to sell in the new-product category). They also include nonsurviving pioneers in their sample. They conclude that while pioneers may still have an advantage, it is less pronounced than claimed. A larger number of market pioneers fail than has been reported and a larger number of early market leaders (though not pioneers) succeed, especially if they enter decisively and commit substantial resources. Examples of later entrants overtaking market pioneers are IBM over Sperry in mainframe computers, Matsushita over Sony in VCRs, Texas Instruments over Bowmar in hand calculators, and GE over EMI in CAT scan equipment. Under the right circumstances, the late entrant can overcome the pioneer advantage. Yet an alert pioneer, according to Robertson and Gatignon, can pursue various strategies to prevent later entrants from wresting away leadership.[47]

The pioneer should visualize the various product markets it could initially enter, knowing that it cannot enter all of them at once. Suppose market-segmentation analysis reveals the product market segments shown in Figure 10-7. The pioneer should analyze the profit potential of each product market singly and in combination and decide on a market expansion path. Thus the pioneer in Figure 10-7 plans first to enter product market P_1M_1, then move the product into a second market (P_1M_2), then surprise competition by developing a second product for the second market (P_2M_2), then take the second product back into the first market (P_2M_1), and then launch a third product for the first market (P_3M_1). If this game plan works, the pioneer firm will own a good part of the first two segments and serve them with two or three products.

The Competitive Cycle

The pioneer knows that competition will eventually enter and cause prices and its market share to fall. When will this happen? What should the pioneer do at each stage? Frey describes five stages of the *competitive cycle* that the pioneer must anticipate (Figure 10-8).[48]

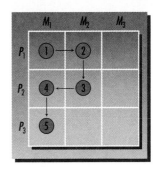

FIGURE 10.7

Long-Range Product Market Expansion Strategy
(P_i = product *i*; M_j = Market *j*)

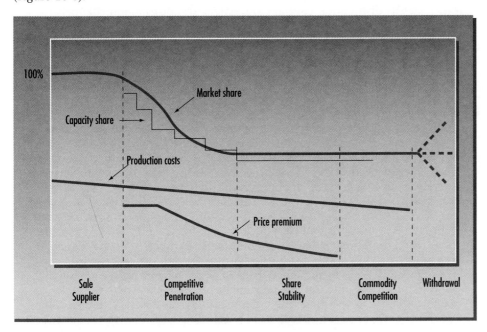

FIGURE 10.8

Stages of the Competitive Cycle

Source: John B. Frey, "Pricing Over the Competitive Cycle," speech at the 1982 Marketing Conference. © 1982, The Conference Board, New York.

- Initially the pioneer is the *sole supplier*, with 100 percent of production capacity and sales. *Competitive penetration* starts when a new competitor has built production capacity and begins commercial sales. The leader's share of production capacity and share of sales falls. As more competitors enter the market and charge a lower price, the perceived relative value of the leader's offer declines, forcing a reduction in the leader's price premium.

- Capacity tends to be overbuilt during rapid growth. When a cyclical slowdown occurs, industry overcapacity drives down margins to lower levels. New competitors decide not to enter, and existing competitors try to solidify their positions. This leads to *share stability*.

- Stability is followed by *commodity competition*. The product is viewed as a commodity, buyers no longer pay a price premium, and the suppliers earn only an average rate of return. At this point, *withdrawal* begins. The pioneer might decide to build share further as other firms withdraw.

MARKETING STRATEGIES: GROWTH STAGE

The growth stage is marked by a rapid climb in sales. Early adopters like the product, and additional consumers start buying it. New competitors enter, attracted by the opportunities. They introduce new product features and expand distribution.

Prices remain where they are or fall slightly, depending on how fast demand increases. Companies maintain their promotional expenditures at the same or at a slightly increased level to meet competition and to continue to educate the market. Sales rise much faster than promotional expenditures, causing a welcome decline in the promotion-sales ratio.

Profits increase during this stage as promotion costs are spread over a larger volume and unit manufacturing costs fall faster than price declines owing to the producer learning effect. Firms must watch for a change from an accelerating to a decelerating rate of growth in order to prepare new strategies.

During this stage, the firm uses several strategies to sustain rapid market growth as long as possible:

- It improves product quality and adds new product features and improved styling.

- It adds new models and flanker products (i.e., products of different sizes, flavours, and so forth that protect the main product).

- It enters new market segments.

- It increases its distribution coverage and enters new distribution channels.

- It shifts from product-awareness advertising to product-preference advertising.

- It lowers prices to attract the next layer of price-sensitive buyers.

These market-expansion strategies strengthen the firm's competitive position. Consider the case of Yahoo!.[49]

- **Yahoo!** From its founding in 1994 by Web-surfing grad students, Yahoo is now the number-one place to be on the Web. More than just a search engine, Yahoo offers a full-blown package of information and services—from real estate and finance to news, shopping, and personalized content. In 1998 the company's stock soared to US$200 a share, but just as Yahoo has experienced a meteoric rise, the competition has gone from just stiff to downright scary. Existing portals such as Infoseek have been beefed up with cash and TV networks are making inroads into cyberspace. Microsoft, Netscape, American Online Inc. and General Electric Co./NBC are all poised for combat. Yahoo's strategy: growth, growth and more growth. Yahoo is promising to go where no portal has gone before—to telephones, pagers, handheld organizers, and the like. The company is also furiously licensing the Yahoo name to build brand identity, and it's using push technology to tailor information and deliver Web material to the desktop. Yahoo also plans to get more into e-commerce by launching an online billing and buying service, and it already has a relationship with Visa International.

The firm in the growth stage faces a trade-off between high market share and high current profit. By spending money on product improvement, promotion, and distribution, it can capture a dominant position. It forgoes maximum current profit in the hope of making even greater profits in the next stage.

MARKETING STRATEGIES: MATURITY STAGE

At some point, the rate of sales growth will slow, and the product will enter a stage of relative maturity. This stage normally lasts longer than the previous stages, and poses formidable challenges to marketing management. *Most products are in the maturity stage of the life cycle, and most marketing managers cope with the problem of marketing the mature product.*

The maturity stage divides into three phases: growth, stable, and decaying maturity. In the first phase, the sales growth rate starts to decline. There are no new distribution channels to fill. In the second phase, sales flatten on a per-capita basis because of market saturation. Most potential consumers have tried the product, and future sales are governed by population growth and replacement demand. In the third phase, *decaying maturity*, the absolute level of sales starts to decline, and customers begin switching to other products and substitutes.

The sales slowdown creates overcapacity in the industry, which leads to intensified competition. Competitors scramble to find niches. They engage in frequent markdowns. They increase advertising and trade and consumer promotion. They increase R&D budgets to develop product improvements and line extensions. They make deals to supply private brands. A shakeout begins, and weaker competitors withdraw. The industry eventually consists of well-entrenched competitors whose basic drive is to gain or maintain market share.

Dominating the industry are a few giant firms—perhaps a quality leader, a service leader, and a cost leader—that serve the whole market and make their profits mainly through high volume and lower costs. Surrounding these dominant firms are a multitude of market nichers, including market specialists, product specialists, and customizing firms. The issue facing a firm in a mature market is whether to struggle to become one of the "big three" and achieve profits through high volume and low cost or to pursue a niching strategy and achieve profits through a high margin.

In the maturity stage, some companies abandon weaker products and concentrate on more profitable products and on new products. Yet they may be ignoring the high potential many mature markets and old products still have. Many industries widely thought to be mature—autos, motorcycles, television, watches, cameras—were proved otherwise by the Japanese, who found ways to offer new values to customers. Seemingly moribund brands like Jell-O, Ovaltine, and Arm & Hammer baking soda have achieved major sales revivals several times, through the exercise of marketing imagination.[50] The resurgence in Hush Puppies' popularity in the footwear category is a case study in reviving old, nearly forgotten brands.

■ **Hush Puppies.** Once the ruler of the casual footwear industry, the Hush Puppies brand slid into irrelevance in the 1980s. It took a bit of luck, plus some savvy marketing moves, to bring the brand back from oblivion. In 1994, New York fashion designer John Barrett took some Hush Puppies classic styles and dyed them in colours—purple, green, and orange—to match his runway shows. Soon after, a menswear trade publication ran a headline saying that Hush Puppies were back. Now, here's where the company did some smart marketing: It brought out new Hush Puppies in updated hues such as powder blue, lime green, and electric orange and limited distribution to six of the most avant-garde shoe stores in the country. Wolverine also jacked the price up to $105 from $60, and showered free shoes on Hollywood celebrities. Once the shoes had garnered enough buzz, the company made them more widely available by distributing them to better department stores. Hush Puppies sales went from 30 000 pairs in 1994 to more than 1.7 million pairs just two years later. Profits soared to 300 percent that same year.[51]

Market Modification

The company might try to expand the market for its mature brand by working with the two factors that make up sales volume:

$$\text{Volume} = \text{number of brand users} \times \text{usage rate per user}$$

The company can try to expand the number of brand users in three ways:

1. *Convert nonusers:* The key to the growth of air freight service is the constant search for new users to whom air carriers can demonstrate the benefits of using air freight rather than ground transportation.

2. *Enter new market segments:* RC Purdy Chocolates of Vancouver has dabbled in the Asian market, but with 1999 being the Year of the Rabbit, a natural for a chocolate-producing company, Purdy's hopes to increase its sales beyond Taiwan into mainland China. On the home front, the 92-year-old company isn't contemplating expanding its retail outlets beyond the 44 shops it currently has in British Columbia and Alberta. Instead, it will try selling its premium chocolate over the Internet. This could spell trouble for the waistlines of Canadians across the country![52]

3. *Win competitors' customers:* Pepsi-Cola is constantly tempting Coca-Cola users to switch.

Volume can also be increased by convincing current brand users to increase their usage of the brand. Here are three strategies: (1) The company can try to get customers to use the product more frequently: Orange-juice marketers try to get people to drink orange juice at occasions other than breakfast time. (2) The company can try to interest users in using more of the product on each occasion: A shampoo manufacturer might indicate that the shampoo is more effective with two applications than one. (3) The company can try to discover new product uses and convince people to use the product in more varied ways: Food manufacturers list several recipes on their packages to broaden consumers' uses of the product.[53]

Product Modification

Managers also try to stimulate sales by modifying the product's characteristics through quality improvement, feature improvement, or style improvement.

Quality improvement aims at increasing the product's functional performance—its durability, reliability, speed, taste. A manufacturer can often overtake its competition by launching a "new and improved" product. Grocery manufacturers call this a "plus launch" and promote a new additive or advertise something as "stronger," "bigger," or "better." This strategy is effective to the extent that the quality is improved, buyers accept the claim of improved quality, and a sufficient number of buyers will pay for higher quality. There is nothing like a powerful new competitor to provide the incentive to make quality improvements. Many Canada's newspapers, the Montreal *Gazette*, Toronto's *Globe and Mail* and *Toronto Star,* Halifax's *Chronicle-Herald*, and Vancouver's *Sun* all worked to improve their quality in an attempt to increase readership and build loyalty in the face of the launch of Conrad's Black's *National Post*. The papers made content and design changes. New columnists were hired. They invested millions in upgrading colour printing. They gave their papers facelifts in the form of new page designs. The battles aren't just being fought over readers, however, but also over advertising dollars. The *Toronto Star*, for example, worked frantically to improve its track record in servicing advertisers using a campaign that portrayed the paper as the "Friendlier Giant." The improvement has been much needed since many media agencies found the paper to be inflexible and unresponsive.[54]

Feature improvement aims at adding new features (for example, size, weight, materials, additives, accessories) that expand the product's versatility, safety, or convenience. For instance, you wouldn't think one could do much to change a sliced pickle, but Vlasic R&D people worked for years to modify its core product:

- **Vlasic Foods International.** Pickle consumption has been declining about two percent a year since the 1980s, but following successful new-product introductions, sales generally get a prolonged boost, Vlasic began its quest for a blockbuster pickle in the mid-1990s after focus groups revealed that people hate it when pickle slices slither out the sides of hamburgers and sandwiches. At first the company decided to slice its average pickles horizontally into strips and marketed them as "Sandwich Stackers." The only problem was that the strips usually contained the soft seedy part of the cucumber, not the crunchy part. The company then embarked on "Project Frisbee," an effort to create a giant pickle chip. In 1998, after years of research and development, Vlasic created a cucumber 10 times larger than the traditional pickle cucumber. The pickle slice, or "chip," is large enough to cover the entire surface of a hamburger and is stacked a dozen high in jars.[55]

This strategy has several advantages. New features build the company's image as an innovator and win the loyalty of market segments that value these features. They provide an opportunity for free publicity and they generate sales force and distributor enthusiasm. The chief disadvantage is that feature improvements are easily imitated; unless there is a permanent gain from being first, the feature improvement might not pay off in the long run.[56]

A strategy of *style improvement* aims at increasing the product's aesthetic appeal. The periodic introduction of new car models amounts to style competition rather than quality or feature competition. In the case of packaged-food and household products, companies introduce colour and texture variations and restyle the package. A style strategy might give the product a unique market identity. Yet style competition has problems. First, it is difficult to predict whether people—and which people—will like a new style. Second, a style change usually requires discontinuing the old style, and the company risks losing customers.

Marketing-Mix Modification

Product managers might also try to stimulate sales by modifying other marketing-mix elements. They should ask the following questions:

- *Prices:* Would a price cut attract new buyers? If so, should the list price be lowered, or should prices be lowered through price specials, volume or early-purchase discounts, freight cost absorption, or easier credit terms? Or would it be better to raise the price to signal higher quality?

- *Distribution:* Can the company obtain more product support and display in existing outlets? Can more outlets be penetrated? Can the company introduce the product into new distribution channels? When Goodyear decided to sell its tires via Wal-Mart, Sears, and Discount Tire, it boosted market share from 14 to 16 percent in the first year.[57]

- *Advertising:* Should advertising expenditures be increased? Should the message or copy be changed? Should the media mix be changed? Should the timing, frequency, or size of ads be changed?

- *Sales promotion:* Should the company step up sales promotion—trade deals, cents-off coupons, rebates, warranties, gifts, and contests?

- *Personal selling:* Should the number or quality of salespeople be increased? Should the basis for sales force specialization be changed? Should sales territories be revised? Should sales force incentives be revised? Can sales-call planning be improved?

- *Services:* Can the company speed up delivery? Can it extend more technical assistance to customers? Can it extend more credit?

Marketers often debate which tools are most effective in the mature stage. For example, would the company gain more by increasing its advertising or its sales-promotion budget? Sales promotion has more impact at this stage because consumers have reached an equilibrium in their buying habits and preferences, and psychological persuasion (advertising) is not as effective as financial persuasion (sales-promotion deals). Many consumer-packaged-goods companies now spend over 60 percent of their total promotion budget on sales promotion to support mature products. Other marketers argue that brands should be managed as capital assets and supported by advertising. Advertising expenditures should be treated as a capital investment, not a current expense. Brand managers, however, use sales promotion because its effects are quicker and more visible to their superiors. But excessive sales-promotion activity can hurt the brand's image and long-run profit performance.

A major problem with marketing-mix modifications, especially price reductions and additional services, is that they are easily imitated. The firm may not gain as much as expected, and all firms might experience profit erosion as they step up their marketing attacks on each other. See the Marketing Memo titled "Breaking Through the Mature-Product Syndrome."

MARKETING STRATEGIES: THE DECLINE STAGE

The sales of most product forms and brands eventually decline. The decline might be slow, as in the case of oatmeal; or rapid, as in the case of the Edsel automobile. Sales may plunge to zero, or they may petrify at a low level.

Sales decline for a number of reasons, including technological advances, shifts in consumer tastes, and increased domestic and foreign competition. All lead to overcapacity, increased price cutting, and profit erosion.

As sales and profits decline, some firms withdraw from the market. Those remaining may reduce the number of products they offer. They may withdraw from smaller market segments and weaker trade channels, and they may cut their promotion budget and reduce their prices further.

Unfortunately, most companies have not developed a well-thought-out policy for handling their aging products. Sentiment often plays a role:

> Putting products to death—or letting them die—is a drab business, and often engenders much of the sadness of a final parting with old and tried friends. The portable, six-sided pretzel was the first product The Company ever made. Our line will no longer be our line without it.[58]

Logic may also play a role. Management believes that product sales will improve when the economy improves, or when the marketing strategy is revised, or when the product is improved. Or the weak product may be retained because of its alleged contribution to the sales of the company's other products. Or its revenue may cover out-of-pocket costs, even if it is not turning a profit.

Unless strong reasons for retention exist, carrying a weak product is very costly to the firm. The cost is not just the amount of uncovered overhead and profit: there are many hidden costs. Weak products often consume a disproportionate amount of management's time, require frequent price and inventory adjustments, generally involve short production runs in spite of expensive setup times, require both advertising and sales force attention that might be better used to make the healthy products more profitable, and can cause customer misgivings and cast a shadow on the company's image. The biggest cost might well lie in the future. Failing to eliminate weak products delays the aggressive search for replacement products. The weak products create a lopsided product mix, long on yesterday's breadwinners and short on tomorrow's.

In handling its aging products, a company faces a number of tasks and decisions. The first task is to establish a system for identifying weak products. Many companies appoint a product-review committee with representatives from marketing, R&D, manufacturing, and finance, which develops a system for identifying weak products. The controller's office supplies data for each product showing trends in market size, market share, prices, costs, and profits. A computer program then analyzes this information. The managers responsible for dubious products fill out rating forms showing where they think sales and profits will go, with and without any changes in marketing strategy. The product-review committee makes a recommendation for each dubious product—leave it alone, modify its marketing strategy, or drop it.[59]

Some firms will abandon declining markets earlier than others. Much depends on the presence and height of exit barriers in the industry.[60] The lower the exit barriers, the easier it is for firms to leave the industry, and the more tempting it is for the remaining firms to remain and attract the withdrawing firms' customers.

In a study of company strategies in declining industries, Harrigan identified five decline strategies available to the firm:

1. Increasing the firm's investment (to dominate the market or strengthen its competitive position)

2. Maintaining the firm's investment level until the uncertainties about the industry are resolved

3. Decreasing the firm's investment level selectively, by dropping unprofitable customer groups, while simultaneously strengthening the firm's investment in lucrative niches

4. Harvesting ("milking") the firm's investment to recover cash quickly

5. Divesting the business quickly by disposing of its assets as advantageously as possible.[61]

The appropriate decline strategy depends on the industry's relative attractiveness and the company's competitive strength in that industry. A company that is in an unattractive industry but possesses competitive strength should consider shrinking selectively. A company that is in an attractive industry and has competitive strength should consider strengthening its investment. Procter & Gamble on a number of occasions has taken disappointing brands that were in strong markets and restaged them.

■ **Procter & Gamble.** P&G launched a "not oily" hand cream called Wondra that was packaged in an inverted bottle so the cream would flow out from the bottom. Although initial sales were high, repeat purchases were disappointing. Consumers complained that the bottom got sticky and that "not oily" suggested it wouldn't work well. P&G carried out two restagings: First, it reintroduced Wondra in an upright bottle, and later reformulated the ingredients so they would work better. Sales then picked up.

P&G prefers restaging to abandoning brand names. P&G spokespersons like to claim that there is no such thing as a product life cycle, and they point to Ivory, Camay, and many other "dowager" brands that are still thriving.

If the company were choosing between harvesting and divesting, its strategies would be quite different. *Harvesting* calls for gradually reducing a product or business's costs while trying to maintain its sales. The first costs to cut are R&D costs and plant and equipment investment. The company might also reduce product quality, salesforce size, marginal services, and advertising expenditures. It would try to cut these costs without letting customers, competitors, and employees know what's happening. If customers knew, they would switch suppliers; if competitors knew, they would tell customers; if employees knew, they would seek new jobs elsewhere. Harvesting is an ethically ambivalent strategy, and it is also difficult to execute. Yet many mature products warrant this strategy. Harvesting can substantially increase the company's current cash flow.[62] If the firm had decided instead to divest the business, it would have first looked for a buyer. It would have tried to increase the business's attractiveness.

When a company decides to drop a product, it faces further decisions. If the product has strong distribution and residual goodwill, the company can probably sell it to another firm.

■ **Coleco, Hasbro, and Cabbage Patch Kids.** In the mid-1980s, Cabbage Patch dolls caught the nation's fancy and enjoyed three years as the nation's best-selling toys. Sales in 1984 and 1985 exceeded half a billion dollars before the dolls lost popularity and nearly vanished. In 1989, Coleco Industries decided to sell the production and marketing rights to Hasbro Industries. Hasbro advertised the doll heavily and increased shipments to big toy stores, and managed to revive sales.[63]

If the company can't find any buyers, it must decide whether to liquidate the brand quickly or slowly. It must also decide on how much inventory and service to maintain for past customers.

(continued)

7. *Increase amount used on each use occasion:* Can more Kool-Aid be put in each package at a higher price?

8. *Close existing product and price gaps:* Should new sizes of Kool-Aid be introduced?

9. *Create new product-line elements:* Should Kool-Aid introduce new flavours?

10. *Expand distribution coverage:* Can Kool-Aid distribution coverage be expanded to Europe and the Far East?

11. *Expand distribution intensity:* Can the percentage of convenience stores in Quebec that carry Kool-Aid be increased from 70 to 90 percent?

12. *Expand distribution exposure:* Can offers to the trade win more shelf space for Kool-Aid?

13. *Penetrate substitutes' positions:* Can consumers be convinced that Kool-Aid is better than other soft drinks?

14. *Penetrate direct competitors' position(s):* Can consumers of other brands be convinced to switch to Kool-Aid?

15. *Defend firm's present position:* Can Kool-Aid satisfy the current users more so that they remain loyal?

Source: John A. Weber, *Identifying and Solving Marketing Problems with Gap Analysis* (Notre Dame, IN, PO Box 77: Strategic Business Systems, 1986).

Hasbro Toys
www.hasbro.com

THE PRODUCT LIFE-CYCLE CONCEPT: CRITIQUE

The PLC concept is best used to interpret product and market dynamics. As a planning tool, the PLC concept helps managers characterize the main marketing challenges in each stage of a product's life and develop major alternative marketing strategies. As a control tool, the PLC concept helps the company measure product performance against similar products launched in the past. The PLC concept is less useful as a forecasting tool because sales histories exhibit diverse patterns, and the stages vary in duration.

PLC theory has its share of critics. They claim that life-cycle patterns are too variable in their shape and duration. PLCs lack what living organisms have—namely, a fixed sequence of stages and a fixed length of each stage. Critics also charge that marketers can seldom tell what stage the product is in. A product may appear to be mature when actually it has only reached a temporary plateau prior to another upsurge. They charge that the PLC pattern is the result of marketing strategies rather than an inevitable course that sales must follow:

> *Suppose a brand is acceptable to consumers but has a few bad years because of other factors—for instance, poor advertising, delisting by a major chain, or entry of a "me-too" competitive product backed by massive sampling. Instead of thinking in terms of corrective measures, management begins to feel that its brand has entered a declining stage. It therefore withdraws funds from the promotion budget to finance R&D on new items. The next year the brand does even worse, panic increases. . . . Clearly, the PLC is a dependent variable which is determined by marketing actions; it is not an independent variable to which companies should adapt their marketing programs.*[64]

Table 10-5 summarizes the characteristics, marketing objectives, and marketing strategies of the four stages of the PLC.

 M ARKET EVOLUTION

Because the PLC focuses on what is happening to a particular product or brand rather than on what is happening to the overall market, it yields a product-oriented picture rather than a market-oriented picture. Firms need to visualize a market's evolutionary path as it is affected by new needs, competitors, technology, channels, and other developments.

In the course of a company, product's or brand's existence, its positioning must change to keep pace with market developments. The Marketing for the Twenty-First Century Box "Monsanto Co.: From Old Line Chemicals to Cutting Edge 'Life Sciences,'" presents a company that rapidly repositioned and some of the challenges it faces.

STAGES IN MARKET EVOLUTION

Like products, markets evolve through four stages: emergence, growth, maturity, and decline.

Emergence

Before a market materializes, it exists as a latent market: some people who share a similar need or want for something that does not yet exist. For example, for centuries people have wanted a means of calculation more rapid than can be provided by a paper and pencil. This need was imperfectly satisfied through abacuses, slide rules, and large adding machines. Suppose an entrepreneur recognizes this need and imagines a technological solution in the form of a small, hand-held electronic calculator. She now must determine the product attributes, including physical size and number of mathematical functions. Because she is market oriented, she interviews potential buyers. She finds that target customers vary greatly in their preferences. Some want a four-function calculator (adding, subtracting, multiplying, and dividing) and others

	Introduction	Growth	Maturity	Decline
Characteristics				
Sales	Low sales	Rapidly rising sales	Peak sales	Declining sales
Costs	High cost per customer	Average cost per customer	Low cost per customer	Low cost per customer
Profits	Negative	Rising profits	High profits	Declining profits
Customers	Innovators	Early adopters	Middle majority	Laggards
Competitors	Few	Growing number	Stable number beginning to decline	Declining number
Marketing Objectives				
	Create product awareness and trial	Maximize market share	Maximize profit while defending market share	Reduce expenditure and milk the brand
Strategies				
Product	Offer a basic product	Offer product extensions, service, warranty	Diversify brands and items	Phase out weak models
Price	Charge cost-plus	Price to penetrate market	Price to match or best competitors'	Cut price
Distribution	Build selective distribution	Build intensive distribution	Build more intensive distribution	Go selective: phase out unprofitable outlets
Advertising	Build product awareness among early adopters and dealers	Build awareness and interest in the mass market	Stress brand differences and benefits	Reduce to level needed to retain hard-core loyals
Sales Promotion	Use heavy sales promotion to entice trial	Reduce to take advantage of heavy consumer consumer demand	Increase to encourage brand switching	Reduce to minimal level

TABLE 10.5

Sources: Chester R. Wasson, *Dynamic Competitive Strategy and Product Life Cycles* (Austin, TX: Austin Press, 1978); John A. Weber, "Planning Corporate Growth with Inverted Product Life Cycles," *Long Range Planning,* October 1976, pp. 12–29; and Peter Doyle, "The Realities of the Product Life Cycle," *Quarterly Review of Marketing,* Summer 1976.

Summary of Product Life-Cycle Characteristics, Objectives, and Strategies

want more functions (calculating percentages, square roots, logs). Some want a small hand calculator and others want a large one. This type of market, in which buyer preferences scatter evenly, is called a *diffused-preference market.*

The entrepreneur's problem is to design an optimal product for this market. She has three options:

1. The new product can be designed to meet the preferences of one of the corners of the market (a *single-niche strategy*).

2. Two or more products can be simultaneously launched to capture two or more parts of the market (a *multiple-niche strategy*).

3. The new product can be designed for the middle of the market (a *mass-market strategy*).

Monsanto Co.: From Old Line Chemicals to Cutting-Edge "Life Sciences"

In less than a decade, St. Louis-based Monsanto Co. has shed its identity as a dull plastic and fibres business and repositioned itself as a cutting-edge biotech firm with a concentration on food and nutrition. In 1996 CEO Robert Shapiro spun off Monsanto's $3-billion chemicals business, the old core of the company, to shareholders. What is left now is a $2-billion drug division, a $1.2-billion food ingredients division, and, dearest to Shapiro's vision for the company, a $3-billion maker of agricultural products such as genetically engineered potatoes.

The $6 billion collection of companies is positioned to cash in on the biotech revolution. World population is growing by 800 million per decade and is expected to double, to 11 billion, by 2100. Shapiro believes that biotech is the key to feeding the world's rising population and to raising world nutrition standards. He claims that genetically superior crops of corn, wheat, tomatoes and soybeans will yield larger harvests, and biotech improvements in the food supply will help prevent illness and boost human productivity. In Shapiro's view: the next two decades will witness a biotechnology and genetic engineering revolution that will blend the pharmaceutical, agricultural, and food and nutrition businesses into a single life-science industry. Shapiro has spent millions amassing biotechnology patents by swallowing smaller companies and cutting deals with agribusiness firms.

Wall Street is certainly excited about Monsanto's repositioning and the firm's stock prices have continued to rise. However, the company must confront suspicious consumers and irate environmentalists. In Britain and France genetically modified (GM) crops have been banned or are having trouble getting approval for commercial use. In Canada, there has been an outcry about Monsanto's Bovine Growth Hormone. Web sites bearing such names as "Cremate Monsanto" (see http:home.ica.net/~fresch/ndp/monsant2.htm#TOP) have proliferated. Canadians from Prince Edward Island to British Columbia worry about the long-term effects of plants genetically altered to resist herbicides. Monsanto has been aggressive in combating such negative tactics. It has developed a series of full-page ads with tag lines such as "We believe food should be grown with less pesticides," "More biotechnology plants mean less industrial ones," and "Worrying about starving future generations won't feed them. Biotechnology will." Each Monsanto ad carried the phone number or Web address of a group opposed to genetic modification, such as Greenpeace or Friends of the Earth, and encouraged readers to hear all sides of the argument before making up their minds. It has developed its own web site, called Farmcentral, aimed at Canada's farmers (http://www.farmcentral.com/monsanto/home.htm). Not only is Monsanto positioning itself as the pioneer of the biotechnology revolution, but it is also casting itself as the leader of public discourse on this controversial and exciting new field.

Sources: Robert Lenzner and Bruce Upbin, "Monsanto v. Malthus," *Forbes*, March 10, 1997, pp. 58-64. Maria Margaronis, "Greenwashed," *The Nation*, October 19, 1998, p. 10. Merrill Goozner, "Giant Poised to Enter a New Era Firm Plans to be at Vanguard of a Revolution in Biotechnology," *Chicago Tribune*, June 2, 1998, p. 1. See also: Forest L. Reinhardt, "Environmental Product Differentiation: Implications for Corporate Strategy," *California Management Review*, Summer 1998, pp. 43-70.

For small firms, a single-niche market strategy makes the most sense. A small firm does not have the resources for capturing and holding the mass market. See how a small Canadian venture paddled its way to success:

Tieken Kayaks
www.tieken.com

■ **Tieken Kayaks.** Over the last 30 years, this small company, nestled in the centre of the Thousand Islands district of Ontario, has built an international reputation for kayak design. Although it started out as a small Nova Scotia manufacturer, mushrooming demand by North America's three million kayaking enthusiasts soon outstripped Tieken's ability to supply the market. A partnership with a North Carolina boatbuilder saved the day and enabled the firm to stretch its limited resources and exploit the opportunity.[65]

A large firm might go after the mass market by designing a product that is medium in size and number of functions. A product in the centre minimizes the sum of the distances of existing preferences from the actual product, thereby minimizing total dissatisfaction. Assume that the pioneer firm is large and designs its product for the mass market. On launching the product, the *emergence stage* begins.

Growth

If sales of the new product are good, new firms will enter the market, ushering in a *market growth stage*. An interesting question is: Where will a second firm enter the market, assuming that the first firm established itself in the centre? The second firm has three options:

1. It can position its brand in one of the corners (single-niche strategy).

2. It can position its brand next to the first competitor (mass-market strategy).

3. It can launch two or more products in different unoccupied corners (multiple-niche strategy).

If the second firm is small, it is likely to avoid head-on competition with the pioneer and to launch its brand in one of the market corners. If the second firm is large, it might launch its brand in the centre against the pioneer. The two firms can easily end up sharing the mass market almost equally. Or a large second firm can implement a multiniche strategy.

■ **Procter & Gamble.** P&G occasionally will enter a market containing a large, entrenched competitor. Instead of launching a me-too product or single-segment product, it introduces a succession of products aimed at different segments. Each entry creates a loyal following and takes some business away from the major competitor. Soon the major competitor is surrounded, its revenue is weakened, and it is too late to launch new brands in outlying segments. P&G, in a moment of triumph, then launches a brand against the major segment.

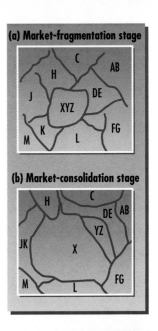

FIGURE 10.9

Market-Fragmentation and Market-Consolidation Strategies

Maturity

Eventually, the competitors cover and serve all the major market segments and the market enters the *maturity stage*. In fact, they go further and invade each other's segments, reducing everyone's profits in the process. As market growth slows down, the market splits into finer segments and high *market fragmentation* occurs. This situation is illustrated in Figure 10-9(a), where the letters represent different companies supplying various segments. Note that two segments are unserved because they are too small to yield a profit.

Mature markets swing between fragmentation and consolidation. The fragmentation is brought about by competition, and the consolidation is brought about by innovation. For example, market consolidation took place in the toothpaste market when P&G introduced Crest, which effectively retarded dental decay. Suddenly toothpaste brands that claimed whitening power, cleaning power, sex appeal, taste, or mouthwash effectiveness were pushed into the corners because consumers primarily wanted dental-protection. Crest won a lion's share of the market, as shown by the X territory in Figure 10-9(b). But P&G became complacent and Colgate's Total managed to steal a major share of the market. Other companies will copy a successful brand, and the market will eventually splinter again.

Decline

Eventually, demand for the present products will begin to decrease, and the market will enter the *decline stage*. Either society's total need level declines or a new technology replaces the old. Thus an entrepreneur might invent a mouth-rinse liquid that is superior to toothpaste. In this case, the old technology will eventually disappear and a new life cycle will emerge.

DYNAMICS OF ATTRIBUTE COMPETITION

Competition produces a continuous round of new product attributes. If a new attribute succeeds, several competitors soon offer it. To the extent that most airlines serve in-flight meals, meals are no longer a basis for air-carrier choice. *Customer expectations are progressive.* This fact underlines the strategic importance of maintaining the lead in introducing new attributes. Each new attribute, if successful, creates a competitive advantage for the firm, leading to temporarily higher-than-average market share and profits. The market leader must learn to routinize the innovation process.

Can a firm look ahead and anticipate the succession of attributes that are likely to win favour and be technologically feasible? How can the firm discover new attributes? There are four approaches.

■ The first approach employs a *customer-survey process*. The company asks consumers what benefits they would like added to the product and their desire level for each. The firm also examines the cost of developing each new attribute and likely competitive responses.

■ The second approach uses an *intuitive process*. Entrepreneurs get hunches and undertake product development without much marketing research. Natural selection determines winners and losers. If a manufacturer has intuited an attribute that the market wants, that manufacturer is considered smart or lucky.

■ A third approach says that new attributes emerge through a *dialectical process*. Innovators should not march with the crowd but rather in the opposite direction. Thus blue jeans, starting out as an inexpensive clothing article, over time became fashionable and more expensive. This unidirectional movement, however, contains the seeds of its own destruction. Eventually the price falls again or some manufacturer introduces another cheap material for pants.

■ A fourth approach holds that new attributes emerge through a *needs-hierarchy process* (see Maslow's theory in Chapter 6). We would predict that the first automobiles would provide basic transportation and be designed for safety. Later, automobiles would start appealing to social acceptance and status needs. Still later, automobiles would be designed to help people "fulfil" themselves. The innovator's task is to assess when the market is ready to satisfy a higher-order need.

The actual unfolding of new attributes in a market is more complex than simple theories suggest.[66] We should not underestimate the role of technology and societal processes in introducing new attributes. For example, the strong consumer interest in portable computers remained unmet until miniaturization technology was sufficiently developed. Developments such as inflation, shortages, environmentalism, consumerism, and new lifestyles lead consumers to reevaluate product attributes. Inflation increases the desire for a smaller car, and a desire for car safety increases the desire for a heavier car. The innovator must use marketing research to gauge the demand potency of different attributes in order to determine the company's best move.

SUMMARY

1. In a competitive industry, the key to competitive advantage is product differentiation. A market offering can be differentiated along five dimensions: product (form, features, performance quality, conformance quality, durability, reliability, repairability, style, design), services (order ease, delivery, installation, customer training, customer consulting, maintenance and repair, miscellaneous services), personnel, channel, or image (symbols, written and audiovisual media, atmosphere, and events). A difference is worth establishing to the extent that it is important, distinctive, superior, communicable, pre-emptive, affordable, and profitable.

2. Many marketers advocate promoting only one product benefit, thus creating a unique selling proposition as they position their product. People tend to remember "number one." Double-benefit position and triple-benefit positioning can also be successful, but must be used carefully.

3. Because economic conditions change and competitive activity varies, companies normally find it necessary to reformulate their marketing strategy several times during a product's life cycle. Technologies, product forms, and brands also exhibit life cycles with distinct stages. The general sequence of stages in any life cycle is introduction, growth, maturity, and decline. Most products today are in the maturity stage.

4. Although many products exhibit a bell-shaped product life cycle (PLC), there are many other patterns, including the growth-slump-maturity pattern, cycle-recycle pattern, and scalloped pattern. The PLCs of styles, fashions, and fads can be erratic; the key to success in these areas lies in creating products with staying power.

5. Each stage of the PLC calls for different marketing strategies. The *introduction* stage is marked by slow growth and minimal profits as the product is pushed into distribution. The company must decide among strategies of rapid skimming, slow skimming, rapid penetration, or slow penetration. It must also decide when to enter the market. If successful, the product enters a *growth* stage marked by rapid sales growth and increasing profits. The company attempts to improve the product, enter new market segments and distribution channels, and reduce its prices slightly. There follows a *maturity* stage in which sales growth slows and profits stabilize. The company seeks innovative strategies to renew sales growth, including market, product, and marketing-mix modification. Finally, the product enters a *decline* stage. The company's task is to identify the truly weak products; develop for each one a strategy of continuation, focusing, or milking; and finally phase out weak products in a way that minimizes the hardship to company profits, employees, and customers.

6. Like products, markets evolve through four stages: emergence, growth, maturity, and decline. A new market emerges when a new product is created to serve the needs of a latent market. Competitors enter the market, leading to market growth. Growth eventually slows down and the market enters maturity; in this stage the market undergoes increasing fragmentation until some firms introduces a powerful new attribute that consolidates the market into fewer and larger segments. This stage does not last, because competitors copy the new attributes.

7. Companies must try to anticipate new attributes that the market wants. Profits go to those who introduce new and valued benefits early. Successful marketing comes through creatively visualizing the market's evolutionary potential.

APPLICATIONS

CHAPTER CONCEPTS

1. Define the following concepts and describe their relationship to each other:
   a. image
   b. differentiation
   c. value proposition
   d. positioning strategy

2. Analyze the following perceptual map and decide how you would reposition Lever 2000 bar soap based on competitive positioning. This map profiles the bar and hand soap industry. (Data created for demonstration purposes only.) How does your brand awareness compare to that of the competition? What positioning error might your brand be suffering from?

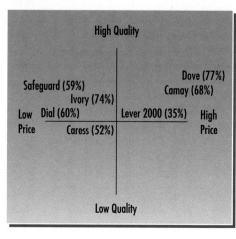

3. Examine the data in Table 1, which summarizes selected results from a fabric softener usage monitoring study. The study was commissioned by a fabric-softener manufacturer whose product is in the mature stage of the product life cycle. What product and promotional suggestions would you make to this manufacturer? What type of brand extension might be warranted?

TABLE 1

Selected Results from Fabric Softener Usage Monitoring Study Demand States and Marketing Tasks

	June 1997	February 1999
Percentage of respondents who were:		
Fabric softener users[a]	60.0%	60.0%
Nonusers	40.0	40.0
Homemakers aware that fabric softeners allegedly harm the environment:		
Fabric softener users	55.0%	74.0%
Nonusers	66.0	70.0
Fabric softener users claiming to:[b]		
Use less fabric softener per load	18.0%	24.0%
Soften fewer loads	16.0	14.0
Total (unduplicated)	26.0	27.0
Reasons nonusers never used or stopped using softener:		
Environmental reasons	42.0%	48.0%
Softness dissatisfaction	26.0	13.0
Effects on skin	29.0	23.0
Drying on clothesline	20.0	29.0

[a]Fabric softener users had used the product at least once in the previous three months before the interview; nonusers had not.

[b]Seventy-two percent of the users who used less softener or softened fewer loads claimed to be doing so for environmental reasons.

Source: Adapted from Harvard Case Study 9-592-016.

MARKETING AND ADVERTISING

1. As the ad in Figure 1 on page 319 explains, Experian offers access to a large database of businesses for business-to-business marketers that reach out to prospects via direct mail. How does Experian differentiate its product relative to competing databases? Why do you think these differences are important? Explain Experian's value proposition in a single sentence, similar to the value proposition statements in Table 10-3.

2. This ad encourages consumers to seek out clothing made of pure Merino wool. What unique selling proposition is this ad promoting? Which of the nine product differentiation variables is being communicated in this ad? Why is this differentiation variable important to the target market? How does the ad use image to support the promoted differentiation?

FOCUS ON TECHNOLOGY

Being first in the industry to offer a valuable new feature is one of the most effective ways for a company to compete—especially in high-tech industries such as computers, software, and consumer electronics, where the continual introduction of improved and innovative products is a fact of life. Identifying and selecting appropriate new features for these products is an art as much as a science, because customers often cannot articulate a need (or even recognize it) until they have been exposed to the new features. For example, the Apple iMac computer offers one-button access to the Internet, a feature that Web-surfers might not have requested but very much appreciate.

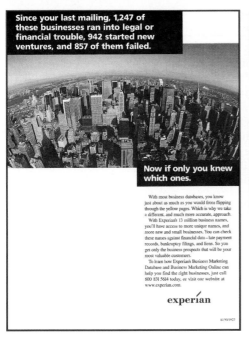

Figure 1

Figure 2

Select a high-tech product (such as a personal digital assistant, a mobile phone, or a DVD player) and use the Internet, ads, and other methods to research at least two features offered by a number of manufacturers. Also research a unique product feature offered by only one of the manufacturers. Why would customers value each of these features? How does the unique product feature help that company compete more effectively? Should the other competitors copy this unique feature? How long do you think it will take for this feature to become more commonplace (or even standard) on similar products throughout the industry? Be prepared to support your answers.

MARKETING FOR THE 21ST CENTURY

Over time, it is important to change the positioning of a company, product, or brand to keep pace with market developments. As discussed earlier, Monsanto has successfully made this transition. Founded in 1901, Monsanto steadily added products and divisions in plastics, chemicals, and related areas. Starting in 1985, however, the company began buying and selling products and divisions as it changed its positioning for the new millennium. By 1997, Monsanto had spun off its final chemical division, completing the evolution to a cutting-edge company specializing in life sciences products.

To learn more about Monsanto's past, present, and future, visit its Web site. Browse the sections about Monsanto, its products and the product pipeline, and the media centre. In terms of the product life cycle, how does Monsanto's new positioning offer more opportunity for growth? How do the newer products (including those in the pipeline) support the company's new positioning?

To understand some of the concerns about Monsanto, do a search using the Alta-Vista Canada search engine. If you were a defender of Monsanto, how would you react to some of these sites? If you were a Monsanto critique, how could you leverage support for your position?

Monsanto
www.monsanto.com

AltaVista Canada
www.altavistacanada.com

In the course of developing a marketing strategy, marketers must select and communicate an effective positioning to differentiate their offerings. They also have to plan appropriate marketing strategies for each stage of the product life cycle and the market's evolution.

As before, you are working with Jane Melody on Sonic's marketing plan for shelf stereo systems. Review the company's situation and your work on previous sections of the marketing plan. Then answer these questions about positioning and marketing strategies for the stage(s) in the product life cycle that relate to Sonic's products (noting the need for further research where necessary):

- *Which of the differentiation variables related to product, services, personnel, channels, and image are best suited to Sonic's situation, strategy, and goals? Include the rationale for your selection.*

- *In developing your positioning, identify the benefits most valued by your target customers. Will you stress single-benefit or double-benefit positioning? In a sentence, what is the value proposition for your product?*

- *In which stage of the product life cycle would you place Sonic's shelf stereo systems? What does this mean for Sonic's immediate marketing objectives and for its future product development/management plans?*

- Knowing the stage of Sonic's products in the life cycle, what are the implications for its marketing mix, its product management strategy, service strategy, and R&D strategy?

Once you have answered these questions and considered the effects on Sonic's marketing efforts, either summarize your findings and conclusions in a written marketing plan or type them into the Target Markets/Positioning, Marketing Strategy, and Product Development/Management sections of the Marketing Plan Pro software.

Developing New Market Offerings

PROFILE:

Canadian Marketing Excellence

*W*ho should ultimately design the product? The customer, of course. Perhaps no Canadian marketer understands this phrase better than Steve "Sal" Debus. The secret of his success? Designing new products and selling them to people just like himself.

Twenty-nine-year-old Debus is the founder of Toronto-based Modrobes Saldebus Lounge Clothing Inc. His line of comfortable, easy-care, casual clothing has been a hit with young people. With the unique insight that only an end-consumer could have, Sal came up with the idea for his first product while he was still a student at Brock University. His class assignment: to create a product that people needed. After wracking his brain for ideas, Sal finally had an inspiration about what he and other students needed – exam pants! "I had the idea to design these pants for student life," he says. "You could eat, sleep, drink, party, get up the next day and go to class in them and still look good." Although his professor wasn't overly impressed and he only received 75 percent on the assignment, Sal couldn't drop the idea. After graduation, he pitched it to his new boss, a manufacturer of specialty sports clothing. Again, he met with resistance. So, in 1996, Sal quit his job and started his own company. With little money for distribution, he went from campus to campus selling Exam Pants off folding tables. Nonetheless, his sales pitch grabbed a lot of attention. He promised prospective buyers that if his pants weren't the most comfortable piece of clothing they had ever owned, he would refund their money. Who could resist such an offer? As the cash started to flow in, he moved to selling at trade shows and events such as concerts. Today, he can leave the selling to someone else. His pants are available in over 350 stores, including Athletes World, across the country. He also has his own retail outlet in Toronto, and he recently signed a contract to clothe Molson's Extreme Team. Creative new products, consumer insight, advertising that is carefully crafted and designed to speak to people like himself, and a will to make things happen have certainly proved to be a model of success for Modrobes.

Source: Astrid Van Den Broek, "Targeting Yourself," *Marketing*, August 2, 1999, p. 9. Philip Kotler, opening quotation.

This chapter examines the following questions:

- What challenges does a company face in developing new products?

- What organizational structures are used to manage new-product development?

- What are the main stages in developing new products, and how can they be managed better?

- What factors affect the rate of diffusion and consumer adoption of newly launched products?

Once a company has carefully segmented the market, chosen its target customers, identified their needs, and determined its market positioning, it is better able to develop new products. Marketers play a key role in the new-product process, by identifying and evaluating new-product ideas and working with R&D and others in every stage of development.

Every company must develop new products. New-product development shapes the company's future. Replacement products must be created to maintain or build sales. Customers want new products, and competitors will do their best to supply them. Each year over 16 000 new products (including line extensions and new brands) are introduced into groceries and drugstores.

A company can add new products through acquisition or development. The acquisition route can take three forms. The company can buy other companies, it can acquire patents from other companies, or it can buy a licence or franchise from another company. The development route can take two forms. The company can develop new products in its own laboratories. Or it can contract with independent researchers or new-product-development firms to develop specific new products.

The consulting firm Booz, Allen, and Hamilton has identified six categories of new products:[1]

1. *New-to-the-world products:* New products that create an entirely new market.

2. *New product lines:* New products that allow a company to enter an established market for the first time.

3. *Additions to existing product lines:* New products that supplement a company's established product lines (package sizes, flavours, and so on).

4. *Improvements and revisions of existing products:* New products that provide improved performance or greater perceived value and replace existing products.

5. *Repositionings:* Existing products that are targeted to new markets or market segments.

6. *Cost reductions:* New products that provide similar performance at lower cost.

Less than 10 percent of all new products are truly innovative and new to the world. These products involve the greatest cost and risk because they are new to both the company and the marketplace. Most new-product activity is devoted to improving existing products. At Sony, over 80 percent of new-product activity is undertaken to modify and improve existing Sony products.

CHALLENGES IN NEW-PRODUCT DEVELOPMENT

Companies that fail to develop new products are putting themselves at great risk. Their existing products are vulnerable to changing customer needs and tastes, new technologies, shortened product life cycles, and increased domestic and foreign competition.

At the same time, new-product development is risky. Texas Instruments lost $990 million before withdrawing from the home computer business, RCA lost $750 million on its videodisc players, Federal Express lost $510 million on its Zap mail, and the infamous birth of Greyhound Air was named the worst new product launch of the year by *Canadian Business* magazine. If you had listened to Bank of Montreal President, Jeff Chisholm, in 1996, you would have believed that mbanx would have one million customers by 2001. However, with only a year to go to reach this goal, mbanx has only 160 000 clients and is considered a major flop by industry analysts. [2]

mbanx
www.mbanx.com

New products continue to fail at a disturbing rate. In 1997, a record 25 261 new packaged-goods products were launched, and that doesn't even include products you won't find at your local supermarket, like techno-gizmos and software programs. But equally stunning is the number that fail: Tom Vierhile, general manager of Market Intelligence Service Ltd., a new-product reporting and retrieval firm, estimates that 80 percent of recently launched products aren't around today.[3] When you consider that it costs $30 million to $75 million to launch a new product, you wonder why people continue to innovate at all. Yet product failures can serve one useful purpose: Inventors, entrepreneurs, and new-product team leaders can learn valuable lessons about what *not* to do. With this credo in mind, marketing consultant Robert McMath has collected about 80 000 consumer products, most of them abject flops. See the Marketing Insight box, "Mr. Failure's Lessons for Sweet Success: Robert McMath's New Product Showcase and Learning Center," for some insights on product failure.

Why do new products fail?

■ A high-level executive pushes a favourite idea through in spite of negative market research findings.

■ The idea is good, but the market size is overestimated.

■ The product is not well designed.

■ The product is incorrectly positioned in the market, not advertised effectively, or overpriced.

■ Development costs are higher than expected.

■ Competitors fight back harder than expected.

Toronto-based new product consultant Thomas Keane says lack of research or the wrong kind of research is the cause of many new product failures. Even when research is done, it is often done too early and the market changes and evolves before the product is actually launched.[4]

Mr. Failure's Lessons for Sweet Success: Robert McMath's New Product Showcase and Learning Center

Strolling the aisles at Robert McMath's New Product Showcase and Learning Center of Ithaca, New York, is like being in some nightmare version of a supermarket. There's Gerber food for adults—pureed sweet-and-sour pork and chicken Madeira—microwaveable ice-cream sundaes, parsnip chips, aerosol mustard, Ben-Gay aspirin, and Miller Clear Beer. How about Richard Simmons' Dijon Vinaigrette Salad Spray, garlic cake in a jar, and Farrah shampoo? Most of the 80 000 products on display were flops. Behind each of them are squandered dollars and hopes, but the genial curator of this Smithsonian of consumerism, a former marketer for Colgate-Palmolive, believes that even—and perhaps, especially—failure has valuable lessons to teach.

The New Product Showcase and Learning Center is a place where product developers pay hundreds of dollars an hour to visit and learn from others' mistakes. McMath's unusual showcase represents $4 billion in product investment. From it he has distilled dozens of lessons for an industry that, by its own admission, has a very short memory. For those who can't make the trip to the Center or pay a steep consulting fee, McMath has now put his unique insights into a book, *What Were They Thinking?* Here are a few of the marketing lessons McMath espouses:

■ The value of a brand is its good name, which it earns over time. People become loyal to it. They trust it to deliver a consistent set of attributes. Don't squander this trust by attaching your good name to something totally out of character. When you hear Ben-Gay aspirin, don't you immediately think of the way that Ben-Gay cream sears your skin? Can you imagine swallowing it? Louis Sherry No Sugar Added Gorgonzola Cheese dressing was everything that Louis Sherry, known for its rich candies and ice cream, shouldn't be: sugarless, cheese, and salad dressing. Cracker Jack cereal, Smucker's premium ketchup, and Fruit of the Loom laundry detergent were other misbegotten attempts to stretch a good name.

■ Me-too marketing is the number-one killer of new products. Most such attempts fail. The ones that succeed usually require resources and persistence beyond the capabilities of most marketers. Pepsi-Cola led a very precarious existence for decades before establishing itself as the major competitor to Coca-Cola. More to the point, though, is that Pepsi is one of the few survivors among dozens of other brands that have challenged Coke for more than a century. Ever hear of Toca-Cola? Coco-Cola? Yum-Yum Cola? French Wine of Cola? How about King-Cola, "the royal drink"? More recently, Afri Cola failed to attract African-American pop drinkers, and Cajun Cola pretty well flopped in the land of gumbo. All things being equal, an established product has a distinct advantage over any new product that is not radically different from it.

■ Don't be fooled by the success of the Complete Dummy's Guide to ... line of books. People usually don't buy products that remind them of their shortcomings. Gillette's For Oily Hair Only shampoo flopped because people did not want to confess that they had greasy hair. People will use products that discreetly say "for oily hair" or "for sensitive skin" in small print on containers that are otherwise identical to the regular product. But they do not want to be hit over the head with reminders that they are overweight, have bad breath, sweat too much, or are elderly. Nor do they wish to advertise their faults and foibles to other people by carrying such products in their grocery carts.

■ Some products are radically different from the products, services, or experiences that consumers normally purchase. Too radically different. They fail because consumers don't relate to them. You can tell that some innovative products are doomed as soon as you hear their names: Toaster Eggs. Cucumber Antiperspirant spray. Health-Sea Sea Sausage. Other innovative ideas have been victims of a brand's past success. For example, Nabisco's Oreo Little Fudgies, a confectionery product with a chocolate coating meant to compete with candy, sounds like a natural. But for many years Nabisco has encouraged people to pull apart Oreo cookies and lick out the filling. It's very messy to open an Oreo with a chocolate coating, however; so Oreo Little Fudgies struck a discordant note with consumers.

Sources: Paul Lukas, "The Ghastliest Product Launches," *Fortune*, March 16, 1996, p. 44; Jan Alexander, "Failure Inc." *Worldbusiness*, May–June 1996, p. 46; Ted Anthony, "Where's Farrah Shampoo? Next to the Salsa Ketchup," *Marketing News*, May 6, 1996, p. 13; bulleted points are adapted from Robert M. McMath and Thom Forbes, *What Were They Thinking? Marketing Lessons I've Learned from Over 80,000 New-Product Innovations and Idiocies* (New York: Times Business, 1998), pp. 22–24, 28, 30–31, and 129–30.

Several other factors hinder new-product development:

■ *Shortage of important ideas in certain areas:* There may be few ways left to improve some basic products (such as steel, detergents).

■ *Fragmented markets:* Keen competition is leading to market fragmentation. Companies must aim their new products at smaller market segments, and this can mean lower sales and profits for each product.

- *Social and governmental constraints:* New products have to satisfy consumer safety and environmental concerns. Government requirements slow down innovation in drugs, toys, and some other industries.

- *Costliness of the development process:* A company typically has to generate many ideas to find just one worthy of development. Furthermore, the company often faces high R&D, manufacturing, and marketing costs.

- *Capital shortages:* Some companies with good ideas cannot raise the funds needed to research and launch them.

- *Faster required development time:* Companies that cannot develop new products quickly will be at a disadvantage. Companies must learn how to compress development time by using computer-aided design and manufacturing techniques, strategic partners, early concept tests, and advanced marketing planning. Alert companies use *concurrent new-product development*, in which cross-functional teams collaborate to push new products through development and to market. Concurrent product development resembles a rugby match rather than a relay race, with team members passing the new product back and forth as they head toward the goal. The Allen-Bradley Corporation (a maker of industrial controls) was able to develop a new electrical control device in just two years, as opposed to six years under its old system.

- *Shorter product life cycles:* When a new product is successful, rivals are quick to copy it. Sony used to enjoy a three-year-lead on its new products. Now Matsushita will copy the product within six months, leaving hardly enough time for Sony to recoup its investment.

Given these challenges, what can a company do to develop successful new products? Cooper and Kleinschmidt found that the number-one success factor is a unique, superior product. Products with a high product advantage succeed 98 percent of the time, compared to products with a moderate advantage (58 percent success) or minimal advantage (18 percent success). This was the secret of success for two young product designers who won Queen's University's 1999 National Entrepreneurship competition. The winning idea came from two students from Brock University, Jamie Lauzon and Rich VanderWal. It was one for which they had a particular passion. Both paraplegics, the two designed a sleek wheelchair that was not only within their budgets but would also allow them to participate in sports like tennis and skiing. Another success factor is a well-defined product concept prior to development. The company carefully defines and assesses the target market, product requirements, and benefits before proceeding. Other success factors are technological and marketing synergy, quality of execution in all stages, and market attractiveness.[5]

Madique and Zirger, in a study of successful product launches in the electronics industry, found eight factors accounting for new-product success. New-product success is greater the deeper the company's understanding of customer needs, the higher the performance-to-cost ratio, the earlier the product is introduced ahead of competition, the greater the expected contribution margin, the more spent on announcing and launching the product, the greater the top management support, and the greater the cross-functional teamwork.[6]

New-product development is most effective when there is teamwork among R&D, engineering, manufacturing, purchasing, marketing, and finance. The product idea must be researched from a marketing point of view, and a specific cross-functional team must guide the project throughout its development. Studies of Japanese companies show that their new-product successes are due in large part to cross-functional teamwork.

EFFECTIVE ORGANIZATIONAL ARRANGEMENTS

Top management is ultimately accountable for the success of new products. New-product development requires senior management to define business domains, product categories, and specific criteria. For example, the Gould Corporation established the following acceptance criteria:

- The product can be introduced within five years.
- The product has a market potential of at least $75 million and a 15 percent growth rate.
- The product would provide at least 30 percent return on sales and 40 percent on investment.
- The product would achieve technical or market leadership.

CALCULATING THE COST

Senior management must decide how much to budget for new-product development. R&D outcomes are so uncertain that it is difficult to use normal investment criteria. Some companies solve this problem by financing as many projects as possible, hoping to achieve a few winners. Other companies set their budget by applying a conventional percentage of sales figures or by spending what the competition spends. Still other companies decide how many successful new products they need and work backward to estimate the required investment.

The North American company best known for its commitment to new-product research and development is the 3M Company:

3M
www.mmm.com

- **3M**, whose Canadian headquarters are found in London, Ontario, has a culture of innovation and improvisation that was evident at its very beginnings: In 1906 the directors were faced with a failed mining operation, but they ended up making sandpaper out of the grit and wastage. Today 3M makes more than 60 000 products, including sandpaper, adhesives, computer diskettes, contact lenses, and Post-it notes. Each year 3M launches scores of new products. This $22.5-billion company's immodest goal is to have each of its divisions generate at least 30 percent of sales from products less than four years on the market. While many products are developed in its own labs, 3M also uses strategic alliances to leverage and market new product offerings. For example, in 1998, 3M's Canadian pharmaceutical division formed an alliance with Hoechst Marion Roussel to co-promote a line of asthma products being developed and manufactured by 3M. In another venture, it partnered with Hydro Quebec to develop new battery technology aimed at the emerging electric vehicle market.[7]

3M in Canada and throughout the world is known for its culture of innovation.

- 3M encourages everyone, not just engineers, to become "product champions." The company's 15 percent rule allows all employees to spend up to 15 percent of their time working on projects of personal interest. Products such as Post-it notes, masking tape, and 3M's microreplication technology grew from 15 percent-rule activities.

- Each promising new idea is assigned to a multidisciplinary venture team headed by an "executive champion."

- 3M expects some failures and learns from them. Its slogan is "You have to kiss a lot of frogs to find a prince."

- 3M hands out its Golden Step awards each year to the venture teams whose new product earned more than $2 million in U.S. sales or $4 million in worldwide sales within three years of its commercial introduction.

Table 11.1 shows how a company might calculate the cost of new-product development. The new-products manager at a large consumer packaged-goods company reviewed the results of 64 new-product ideas. Only one in four ideas, or 16, passed the screening stage. It cost $1000 to review each idea at this stage. Half of these ideas, or eight, survived the concept-testing stage, at a cost of $20 000 each. Half of these, or four, survived the product-development stage, at a cost of $200 000 each. Half of these, or two, did well in the test market, at a cost of $500 000 each. When these two ideas were launched, at a cost of $5 million each, only one was highly successful. Thus the one successful idea had cost the company $5 721 000 to develop. In the process, 63 other ideas fell by the wayside. The total cost for developing one successful new product was $13 984 400. Unless the company can improve the pass ratios and reduce the costs at each stage, it will have to budget nearly $14 million for each successful new idea it hopes to find. If top management wants four successful new products in the next few years, it will have to budget at least $56 million ($4 \times 14$ million) for new-product development.

ORGANIZING NEW-PRODUCT DEVELOPMENT

Companies handle the organizational aspect of new-product development in several ways.[8] The most common are:

- *Product managers:* Many companies assign responsibility for new-product ideas to product managers. In practice, this system has several faults. Product managers are so busy managing existing lines that they give little thought to new products other than line extensions. They also lack the specific skills and knowledge needed to develop and critique new products.

- *New-product managers:* Kraft and Johnson & Johnson have new-product managers who report to category managers. This position professionalizes the new-product function. However, like product managers, new-product managers tend to think in terms of modifications and line extensions limited to their product market.

- *New-product committees:* Many companies have a high-level management committee charged with reviewing and approving proposals.

TABLE 11.1

Stage	Number of Ideas	Pass Ratio	Cost per Product Idea	Total Cost
1. Idea screening	64	1:4	$ 1 000	$ 64 000
2. Concept testing	16	1:2	20 000	320 000
3. Product development	8	1:2	200 000	1 600 000
4. Test marketing	4	1:2	500 000	2 000 000
5. National launch	2	1:2	5 000 000	10 000 000
			$5 721 000	$13 984 000

Estimated Cost of Finding One Successful New Product (Starting with 64 New Ideas)

New-Product Development Not Just for Engineers: The Wisdom of Cross-Functional Teams

In his best-selling book, *The Soul of a New Machine*, Tracy Kidder described how a group of engineers in a tightly knit team developed a revolutionary new computer for Data General. These engineers were part of a long tradition in product development, in which engineers and scientists worked in isolation, not only from the outsiders but also from other company departments, to develop original products. Although relegating new-product development solely to engineers or scientists often reaped brilliant results, it also produced crushing inefficiencies and marketing myopia—engineers driven to create a "better mousetrap" when potential customers didn't really need or want a better mousetrap.

The venerable tradition of engineers working in isolation finally burst apart in the late 1980s and early 1990s with the implementation of cross-functional new-product teams. Under pressure to shrink design cycles, leverage new techniques, and lower product-development costs, manufacturers are transforming product design from a solitary activity handled by engineering to a dynamic process involving the input of multiple company functions and key suppliers, too. In a survey of *Design News and Purchasing* magazine readers, 80 percent of respondents reported that their companies use cross-functional teams to develop new products.

Chrysler, now the most profitable automaker in the world, is a pioneer in the use of these new-product teams. In the late 1980s, Chrysler began pairing car designers with cohorts in purchasing. The result: A whole layer of bureaucracy has been cut from the product-development process. Since instituting cross-functional design teams, Chrysler has slashed new-vehicle development cycles by over 40 percent and reduced costs dramatically. For instance, in the late 1980s, development lead times for domestic automakers often spanned five years. Today,

Chrysler typically gets new cars or trucks from concept to market in three years or less. Another important benefit of adding key people from other functions is the creation of more knowledge. Harley-Davidson pairs engineering, purchasing, manufacturing, marketing, and suppliers for the conceptual stage of design. For complex components, such as brake systems, it has tapped suppliers to lead development. "Instead of hiring this expertise in-house, we're relying on the competence that already exists within our supply base," says Leroy Zimdars, Harley-Davidson's director of development purchasing.

For all the benefits that come from the cross-functional design team process, no one should be lulled into thinking that forming a team and working on one is easy. Don H. Lester, a manager of operations for a Hoechst division, knows this first-hand. Lester has over 10 years of experience as a new-product venture team leader, and he's developed the following criteria for staffing new-product venture teams:

- *Desired team leadership style and level of expertise*: The more complex the new-product concept, the greater the expertise that is desirable.

- *Team member skills and expertise*: Hoechst staffs its new venture teams with people with skills and expertise in chemistry, engineering, market research, financial analysis, and manufacturing. A different company would choose different functions to be represented.

- *Level of interest in the particular new-product concept*: Is there interest or, even better, a high level of ownership and commitment (a "concept champion")?

- *Potential for personal reward*: "What's in it for me?" What motivates individuals to want to participate in this effort?

- *Diversity of team members, in the broadest sense*: This includes race, gender, nationality, breadth of experience, depth of expertise, and personality. The greater the diversity, the greater the range of viewpoints and the team's decision-making potential.

Sources: Don H. Lester, "Critical Success Factors for New Product Development," *Research Technology Management*, January–February 1998, pp. 36–43; Tim Minahan, "Harley-Davidson Revs Up Development Process," *Design News*, May 18, 1998, pp. S18–S23; Tim Minahan, "Platform Teams Pair with Suppliers to Drive Chrysler to Better Designs," *Purchasing*, May 7, 1998, pp. 44S3–44S7; Design Teams Bring Radical Change in Product Development," *Design News*, May 18, 1998, p. S2; see also Gary S. Lynn, "New Product Team Learning: Developing and Profiting from Your Knowledge Capital," *California Management Review*, Summer 1998, pp. 74–93.

- *New-product departments*: Large companies often establish a department headed by a manager who has substantial authority and access to top management. The department's major responsibilities include generating and screening new ideas, working with the R&D department, and carrying out field testing and commercialization.

- *New-product venture teams:* 3M, Dow, Westinghouse, and General Mills often assign new-product development work to venture teams. A *venture team* is a group brought together from various operating departments and charged with developing a specific product or business. They are "intrapreneurs" relieved of their other duties and given a budget, a time frame, and a "skunkworks" setting. *Skunkworks* are informal workplaces, sometimes garages, where intrapreneurial teams attempt to develop new products. See the Marketing Insight box, "New-Product Development

Not Just for Engineers: The Wisdom of Cross-Functional Teams," for more information on how companies benefit from cross-functional teamwork when developing new products.

The most sophisticated tool for managing the innovation process is the *stage-gate system* used by 3M and a number of other companies.[9] The innovation process is divided into several stages. At the end of each stage is a gate or checkpoint. The project leader, working with a cross-functional team, must bring a set of known deliverables to each gate before the project can pass to the next stage. To move from the business plan stage into product development requires a convincing market research study of consumer needs and interest, a competitive analysis, and a technical appraisal. Senior managers review the criteria at each gate to judge whether the project deserves to move to the next stage. The gatekeepers make one of four decisions: go, kill, hold, or recycle.

Stage-gate systems put strong discipline into the innovation process, making its steps visible to all involved and clarifying the project leader's and team's responsibilities at each point. Some of the companies that rely on the stage-gate process are Mobil, 3M, Hewlett-Packard, and Seattle-based Fluke, a pioneer in handheld electronic instruments. Lego, the Danish toy maker, replaces about one-third of its product line every year with new products. Since the late 1980s, Lego has been relying on a stage-gate new-product process to ensure that everything comes together for rapid product launches.[10]

We will now look at the marketing challenges arising at each of the eight stages of the development process: idea generation, idea screening, concept development and testing, marketing strategy development, business analysis, product development, market testing, and commercialization. A preview of the various steps and decisions in the process is presented in Figure 11.1.

FIGURE 11.1

The New-Product-Development Decision Process

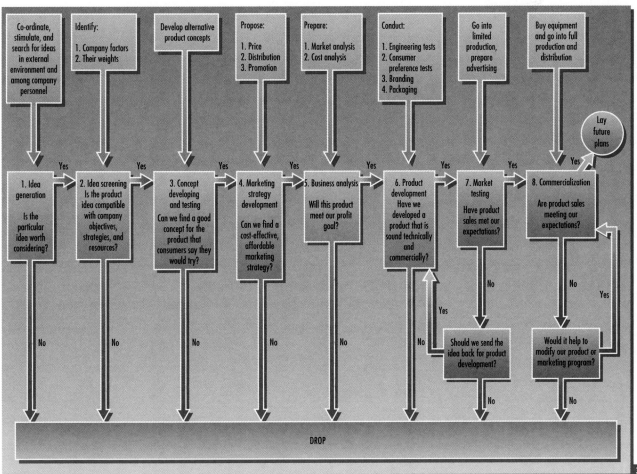

329

M ANAGING THE DEVELOPMENT PROCESS: IDEAS

IDEA GENERATION

The new-product development process starts with the search for ideas. Top managers should define the product and market scope and the new product's objectives. They should state how much effort should be devoted to developing breakthrough products, modifying existing products, and copying competitors' products. New-product ideas can come from many sources: customers, scientists, competitors, employees, channel members, and top management.

The marketing concept holds that *customer needs and wants* are the logical place to start the search for ideas. Hippel has shown that the highest percentage of ideas for new industrial products originate with customers.[11] Technical companies can learn a great deal by studying their *lead users,* those customers who make the most advanced use of the company's products and who recognize the need for improvements before other customers do. Many of the best ideas come from asking customers to describe their problems with current products. For instance, in an attempt to grab a foothold in steel-wool soap pads, a niche dominated by SOS and Brillo, 3M arranged eight focus groups with consumers around the country. 3M asked what problems consumers found with traditional soap pads, and found the most frequent complaint was that the pads scratched expensive cookware. This finding produced the idea for the Scotch-Brite Never Scratch soap pad. Sales of the new soap pad have now exceeded 3M's expectations by 25 percent.[12]

Successful companies have established a company culture that encourages every employee to seek new ways of improving production, products, and services. Toyota claims its employees submit two million ideas annually (about 35 suggestions per employee), over 85 percent of which are implemented. Kodak and other firms give monetary, holiday, or recognition awards to employees who submit the best ideas.

Companies can also find good ideas by researching their *competitors' products and services*. They can learn from distributors, suppliers, and sales representatives. They can find out what customers like and dislike in their competitors' products. They can buy their competitors' products, take them apart, and build better ones. Company *sales representatives* and *intermediaries* are a particularly good source of ideas. These groups have firsthand exposure to customers and are often the first to learn about competitive developments. An increasing number of companies train and reward sales representatives, distributors, and dealers for finding new ideas.

Top management can be another major source of ideas. Some company leaders, such as Edwin H. Land, former CEO of Polaroid, took personal responsibility for technological innovation in their companies. On the other hand, Lewis Platt, CEO of Hewlett-Packard, believes senior management's role is to create an environment that encourages business managers to take risks and create new growth opportunities. Under Platt's leadership, HP has been structured as a collection of highly autonomous entrepreneurial businesses.

New-product ideas can come from other sources as well, including inventors, patent attorneys, university and commercial laboratories, industrial consultants, advertising agencies, marketing research firms, and industrial publications. But although ideas can flow from many sources, their chances of receiving serious attention often depend on someone in the organization taking the role of *product champion*. The product idea is not likely to receive serious consideration unless it has a strong advocate. See the Marketing Memo "Ten Ways to Great New-Product Ideas."

IDEA SCREENING

Any company can attract good ideas by organizing itself properly. The company should motivate its employees to submit their ideas to an *idea manager* whose name and phone number are widely circulated. Ideas should be written down and reviewed each week by an *idea committee*, which sorts them into three groups: promising ideas, marginal ideas, and rejects. Each promising idea is researched by a committee member, who reports back to the committee. The surviving promising ideas then move into a full-scale screening process. The company should reward employees submitting the best ideas.

In screening ideas, the company must avoid two types of errors. A *DROP-error* occurs when the company dismisses an otherwise good idea. It is extremely easy to find fault with other people's ideas (Figure 11.2). Some companies shudder when they look back at ideas they dismissed: Xerox saw the novel promise of Chester Carlson's copying machine, but IBM and Eastman Kodak did not. IBM thought the market for personal computers was minuscule. RCA saw the opportunity of radio; the Victor Talking Machine Company did not. Leon's understood the unique market-development possibilities of instalment buying; Eaton's did not. Sears dismissed the importance of discounting; Wal-Mart and Costco did not.[13] If a company makes too many DROP-errors, its standards are too conservative.

A *GO-error* occurs when the company permits a poor idea to move into development and commercialization. We can distinguish three types of product failures. An *absolute product failure* loses money; its sales do not cover variable costs. A *partial product failure* loses money, but its sales cover all its variable costs and some of its fixed costs. A *relative product failure* yields a profit that is less than the company's target rate of return.

The purpose of screening is to drop poor ideas as early as possible. The rationale is that product-development costs rise substantially with each successive development stage. Most companies require new-product ideas to be described on a standard form that can be reviewed by a new-product committee. The description states the product idea, the target market, and the competition, and roughly estimates market size, product price, development time and costs, manufacturing costs, and rate of return.

The executive committee then reviews each idea against a set of criteria. Does the product meet a need? Would it offer superior value? Can it be distinctively advertised? Does the company have the necessary know-how and capital? Will the new product deliver the expected sales volume, sales growth, and profit? The surviving ideas can be rated using a weighted-index method like that in Table 11.2. The first column lists factors required for successful product launches, and the second column assigns importance weights. The third column scores the product idea on a scale from 0 to 1.0, with 1.0 the highest score. The final step multiplies each factor's importance by the product score to obtain an overall rating. In this example, the product idea scores .69, which places it in the "good idea" level. The purpose of this basic rating device is to promote systematic product-idea evaluation and discussion. It is not supposed to make the decision for management.

As the new-product idea moves through development, the company will constantly need to revise its estimate of the product's overall probability of success, using the following formula:

Overall probability of success	=	Probability of technical completion	×	Probability of commercialization given technical completion	×	Probability of economic success given commercialization

For example, if the three probabilities are estimated as .50, .65, and .74, respectively, the company would conclude that the overall probability of success is .24. The company then must judge whether this probability is high enough to warrant continued development.

MANAGING THE DEVELOPMENT PROCESS: CONCEPT TO STRATEGY

CONCEPT DEVELOPMENT AND TESTING

Attractive ideas must be refined into testable product concepts. A *product idea* is a possible product the company might offer to the market. A *product concept* is an elaborated version of the idea expressed in meaningful consumer terms.

FIGURE 11.2

Forces Fighting New Ideas

Source: With permisson of Jerold Panas, Young & Partners, Inc.

TABLE 11.2

Product-Idea Rating Device

Product Success Requirements	Relative Weight (a)	Product Score (b)	Product Rating (c = a × b)
Unique or superior product	.40	.8	.32
High performance-to-cost ratio	.30	.6	.18
High marketing dollar support	.20	.7	.14
Lack of strong competition	.10	.5	.05
Total	1.00		.69*

*Rating scale: .00–.30 poor; .31–.60 fair; .61–.80 good. Minimum acceptance rate: .61

Concept Development

We will illustrate concept development with the following situation: A large food processing company gets the idea of producing a powder to add to milk to increase its nutritional value and taste. This is a product idea. But consumers do not buy product ideas; they buy product concepts.

A product idea can be turned into several concepts. The first question is: Who will use this product? The powder can be aimed at infants, children, teenagers, young or middle-aged adults, or older adults. Second, what primary benefit should this product provide? Taste, nutrition, refreshment, energy? Third, when will people consume this drink? Breakfast, midmorning, lunch, mid-afternoon, dinner, late evening? By answering these questions, a company can form several concepts:

(a) Product-positioning map (breakfast market)

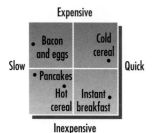

- *Concept 1:* An instant breakfast drink for adults who want a quick nutritious breakfast without preparing a breakfast.
- *Concept 2:* A tasty snack drink for children to drink as a midday refreshment.
- *Concept 3:* A health supplement for older adults to drink in the late evening before they go to bed.

Each concept represents a *category concept* that defines the product's competition. An instant breakfast drink would compete against bacon and eggs, breakfast cereals, coffee and pastry, and other breakfast alternatives. A tasty snack drink would compete against soft drinks, fruit juices, and other thirst quenchers. Suppose the instant-breakfast-drink concept looks best. The next task is to show where this powdered product would stand in relation to other breakfast products. Figure 11.3(a) uses the two dimensions of cost and preparation time to create a *product-positioning map* for the breakfast drink. An instant breakfast drink offers low cost and quick preparation. Its nearest competitor is cold cereal; its most distant competitor is bacon and eggs. These contrasts can be utilized in communicating and promoting the concept to the market.

(b) Brand-positioning map (instant breakfast market)

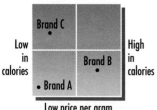

Next, the product concept has to be turned into a *brand concept.* Figure 11.3(b) is a *brand-positioning map* showing the current positions of three existing brands of instant breakfast drinks. The company needs to decide how much to charge and how calorific to make its drink. The new brand would be distinctive in the medium-price, medium-calorie market or in the high-price, high-calorie market. The company would not want to position it next to an existing brand, where it would have to fight for market share.

FIGURE 11.3

Product and Brand Positioning

Concept Testing

Concept testing involves presenting the product concept to appropriate target consumers and getting their reactions. The concepts can be presented symbolically or physically. However, the more the tested concepts resemble the final product or experience, the more dependable concept testing is. In the past, creating physical prototypes was costly and time-consuming, but computer-aided design and manufacturing programs have changed that. Today firms can design alternative physical products (for example, small appliances or toys) on a computer, and then produce plastic models of each. Potential consumers can view the plastic models and give their reactions.[14]

Companies are also using virtual reality to test product concepts. Virtual-reality programs use computers and sensory devices (such as gloves or goggles) to simulate reality. Gadd International has developed a research tool called Simul-Shop, a CD-ROM virtual-reality approach that re-creates shopping situations in which researchers can test consumer reactions to factors such as product positioning, store layouts, and package designs. Suppose a cereal marketer wants to test reactions to a new package design and store shelf positioning. Using Simul-Shop on a standard desktop PC, test shoppers begin their shopping spree with a screen showing the outside of a grocery store. They click to enter the virtual store and are guided to the appropriate store section. Once there, they can scan the shelf, pick up various cereal packages, rotate them, study the labels—even look around to see what is on the shelf behind them. A Gadd's research director explains: "Once users move toward the item we want to test, [they] can look at different packaging, shelf layouts, and package colours. Depending on the activity, we can even ask users why they did what they did."[15]

Many companies today use *customer-driven engineering* to design new products. Customer-driven engineering attaches high importance to incorporating customer preferences in the final design. Here's how one company uses the World Wide Web to enhance its customer-driven engineering:

■ **National Semiconductor**. National Semiconductor has used "applets"—simple multimedia applications written in Java—and parametric search technologies to make its entire product database available on the Web. With the means to track customer searches, National Semiconductor can determine the performance metrics that are most important to them. Sometimes, says the company's Web services manager, it's more important to know when a customer didn't find a product than when he or she did. That information helps National Semiconductor shrink the time needed to identify market niches and to develop new products. It's basically high-quality market research—for free.[16]

National Semiconductor
www.national.com

Concept testing entails presenting consumers with an elaborated version of the concept. Here is the elaboration of Concept 1 in our breakfast-drink example:

Our product is a powdered mixture that is added to milk to make an instant breakfast that gives the person all the needed nutrition along with good taste and high convenience. The product would be offered in three flavours (chocolate, vanilla, and strawberry) and would come in individual packets, six to a box, at $2.49 a box.

After receiving this information, consumers respond to the following questions:

Question	Product Dimension Measured
1. Are the benefits clear to you and believable?	*Communicability* and *believability*. If the scores are low, the concept must be refined or revised.
2. Do you see this product solving a problem or filling a need for you?	*Need level.* The stronger the need, the higher the expected consumer interest.
3. Do other products currently meet this need and satisfy you?	*Gap level.* The greater the gap, the higher the expected consumer interest. The need level can be multiplied by the gap level to produce a *need-gap score.* A high need-gap score means that the consumer sees the product as filling a strong need that is not satisfied by available alternatives.
4. Is the price reasonable in relation to the value?	*Perceived value.* The higher the perceived value, the higher the expected consumer interest.
5. Would you (definitely, probably, probably not, definitely not) buy the product?	*Purchase intention.* This would be high for consumers who answered the previous three questions positively.
6. Who would use this product, and when and how often will the product be used?	*User targets, purchase occasions,* and *purchasing frequency.*

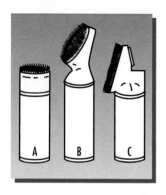

FIGURE 11.4

Samples for Conjoint Analysis

Respondents' answers indicate whether the concept has a broad and strong consumer appeal, what products this new product competes against, and which consumers are the best targets. The need-gap levels and purchase-intention levels can be checked against norms for the product category to see whether the concept appears to be a winner, a long shot, or a loser. One food manufacturer rejects any concept that draws a definitely-would-buy score of less than 40 percent.

Conjoint Analysis

Consumer preferences for alternative product concepts can be measured through *conjoint analysis*, a method for deriving the utility values that consumers attach to varying levels of a product's attributes. Respondents are shown different hypothetical offers formed by combining varying levels of the attributes, then asked to rank the various offers. Management can identify the most appealing offer and the estimated market share and profit the company might realize.

Green and Wind have illustrated this approach in connection with developing a new spot-removing carpet-cleaning agent for home use.[17] Suppose the new-product marketer is considering five design elements:

- Three package designs (A, B, C—see Figure 11.4)
- Three brand names (K2R, Glory, Bissell)
- Three prices ($3.99, $4.59, $4.99)
- A possible Good Housekeeping seal (yes, no)
- A possible money-back guarantee (yes, no)

Although the researcher can form 108 possible product concepts (3x3x3x2x2), it would be too much to ask consumers to rank 108 concepts. A sample of, say, 18 contrasting product concepts can be chosen, and consumers would rank them from the most preferred to the least preferred.

The marketer now uses a statistical program to derive the consumer's utility functions for each of the five attributes (Figure 11.5). Utility ranges between zero and one; the higher the utility, the stronger the consumer's preference for that level of the attribute. Looking at packaging, we see that package B is the most favoured, followed by C and then A (A hardly has any utility). The preferred names are Bissell, K2R, and Glory, in that order. The consumer's utility varies inversely with price. A Good Housekeeping seal is preferred, but it does not add that much utility and may not be worth the effort to obtain it. A money-back guarantee is strongly preferred. Putting these results together, we can see that the consumer's most desired offer would be package design B, with the brand name Bissell, selling at the price of $3.99, with a Good Housekeeping seal and a money-back guarantee.

We can also determine the relative importance of each attribute to this consumer—the difference between the highest and lowest utility level for that attribute. The greater the difference, the more important the attribute. Clearly, this consumer sees price and package design as the most important attributes followed by money-back guarantee, brand name, and last, a Good Housekeeping seal.

When preference data are collected from a sufficient sample of target consumers, the data can be used to estimate the market share any specific offer is likely to achieve, given any assumptions about competitive response. The company, however, may not launch the market offer that promises to gain the greatest market share because of cost considerations. The most customer-appealing offer is not always the most profitable offer to make.

Under some conditions, researchers will collect the data not with a full-profile description of each offer but by presenting two factors at a time. For example, respondents may be shown a table with three price levels and three package types and asked which of the nine combinations they would like most, followed by which one they would prefer next, and so on. They would then be shown a further table consisting of trade-offs between two other variables. The trade-off approach may be easier to use when there are many variables and possible offers. However, it is less realistic in that respondents are focusing on only two variables at a time.

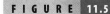

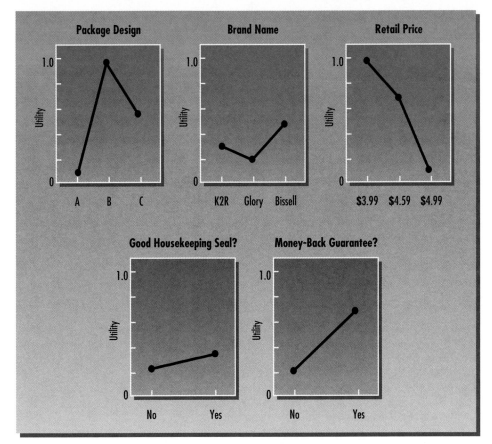

FIGURE 11.5

Utility Functions Based on Conjoint Analysis

Conjoint analysis has become one of the most popular concept development and testing tools. Marriott designed its Courtyard hotel concept with the benefit of conjoint analysis. Other applications have included airline travel services, ethical drug design, and credit-card features.

MARKETING-STRATEGY DEVELOPMENT

After testing, the new-product manager must develop a preliminary marketing-strategy plan for introducing the new product into the market. The plan consists of three parts. The first part describes the target market's size, structure, and behaviour; the planned product positioning; and the sales, market share, and profit goals sought in the first few years:

> *The target market for the instant breakfast drink is families with children who are receptive to a new, convenient, nutritious, and inexpensive form of breakfast. The company's brand will be positioned at the higher-price, higher-quality end of the instant-breakfast-drink category. The company will aim initially to sell 500 000 cases or 10 percent of the market, with a loss in the first year not exceeding $1.3 million. The second year will aim for 700 000 cases or 14 percent of the market, with a planned profit of $2.2 million.*

The second part outlines the planned price, distribution strategy, and marketing budget for the first year:

> *The product will be offered in chocolate, vanilla, and strawberry in individual packets of six to a box at a retail price of $2.49 a box. There will be 48 boxes per case, and the case price to distributors will be $24. For the first two months, dealers will be offered one case free for every four cases bought, plus cooperative-advertising allowances. Free samples will be distributed door to door. Coupons for $0.20 off will*

appear in newspapers. The total sales-promotional budget will be $2.9 million. An advertising budget of $6 million will be split 50:50 between national and local. Two-thirds will go into television and one-third into newspapers. Advertising copy will emphasize the benefit concepts of nutrition and convenience. The advertising-execution concept will revolve around a small boy who drinks instant breakfast and grows strong. During the first year, $100 000 will be spent on marketing research to buy store audits and consumer-panel information to monitor market reaction and buying rates.

The third part of the marketing-strategy plan describes the long-run sales and profit goals and marketing-mix strategy over time:

The company intends to win a 25 percent market share and realize an after-tax return on investment of 12 percent. To achieve this return, product quality will start high and be improved over time through technical research. Price will initially be set at a high level and lowered gradually to expand the market and meet competition. The total promotion budget will be boosted each year about 20 percent, with the initial advertising–sales promotion split of 65:35 evolving eventually to 50:50. Marketing research will be reduced to $60 000 per year after the first year.

BUSINESS ANALYSIS

After management develops the product concept and marketing strategy, it can evaluate the proposal's business attractiveness. Management needs to prepare sales, cost, and profit projections to determine whether they satisfy company objectives. If they do, the product concept can move to the product-development stage. As new information comes in, the business analysis will undergo revision and expansion.

Estimating Total Sales

Management needs to estimate whether sales will be high enough to yield a satisfactory profit. Total estimated sales are the sum of estimated first-time sales, replacement sales, and repeat sales. Sales-estimation methods depend on whether the product is a one-time purchase (such as an engagement ring or retirement home), an infrequently purchased product, or a frequently purchased product. For one-time purchased products, sales rise at the beginning, peak, and later approach zero as the number of potential buyers is exhausted (Figure 11.6[a]). If new buyers keep entering the market, the curve will not go down to zero.

Infrequently purchased products—such as automobiles, toasters, and industrial equipment—exhibit replacement cycles dictated by physical wearing out or by obsolescence associated with changing styles, features, and performance. Sales forecasting for this product category calls for estimating first-time sales and replacement sales separately (Figure 11.6[b]).

Frequently purchased products, such as consumer and industrial nondurables, have product life-cycle sales resembling Figure 11.6(c). The number of first-time buyers

FIGURE 11.6

Product Life-Cycle Sales for Three Types of Products

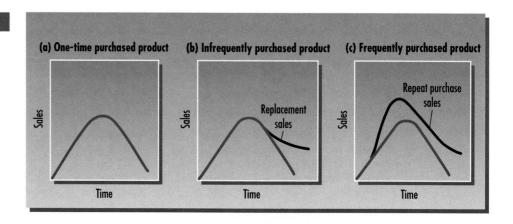

initially increases and then decreases as fewer buyers are left (assuming a fixed population). Repeat purchases occur soon, providing that the product satisfies some buyers. The sales curve eventually falls to a plateau representing a level of steady repeat-purchase volume; by this time, the product is no longer a new product.

In estimating a new product's sales, the manager's first task is to estimate first-time purchases of the new product in each period. A variety of techniques are available. To estimate replacement sales, management must research the product's *survival-age distribution*—that is, the number of units that fail in year one, two, three, and so on. The low end of the distribution indicates when the first replacement sales will occur. The actual timing of replacement will be influenced by a variety of factors. Because replacement sales are difficult to estimate before the product is in use, some manufacturers base the decision to launch a new product solely on the estimate of first-time sales.

For a frequently purchased new product, the seller has to estimate repeat sales as well as first-time sales. A high rate of repeat purchasing means that customers are satisfied; sales are likely to stay high even after all first-time purchases take place. The seller should note the percentage of repeat purchases that take place in each repeat-purchase class: those who rebuy once, twice, three times, and so on. Some products and brands are bought a few times and dropped.[18]

Estimating Costs and Profits

After preparing the sales forecast, management should estimate expected costs and profits. Costs are estimated by the R&D, manufacturing, marketing, and finance departments. Table 11.3 illustrates a five-year projection of sales, costs, and profits for the instant breakfast drink.

Row 1 shows the projected sales revenue over the five-year period. The company expects to sell $11 889 000 (approximately 500 000 cases at $24 per case) in the first year. Behind this sales projection is a set of assumptions about the rate of market growth, the company's market share, and the factory-realized price.

Row 2 shows the cost of goods sold, which hovers around 33 percent of sales revenue. This cost is found by estimating the average cost of labour, ingredients, and packaging per case.

Row 3 shows the expected gross margin, which is the difference between sales revenue and cost of goods sold.

Row 4 shows anticipated development costs of $3.5 million, including product-development cost, marketing research costs, and manufacturing-development costs.

Row 5 shows the estimated marketing costs over the five-year period to cover advertising, sales promotion, and marketing research and an amount allocated for sales force coverage and marketing administration.

Row 6 shows the allocated overhead to this new product to cover its share of the cost of executive salaries, heat, light, and so on.

Row 7, the gross contribution, is found by subtracting the preceding three costs from the gross margin.

Row 8, supplementary contribution, lists any change in income from other company products caused by the introduction of the new product. It has two components. Dragalong income is additional income on other company products resulting from adding this product to the line. Cannibalized income is the reduced income on other company products resulting from adding this product to the line.[19] Table 11.3 assumes no supplementary contributions.

Row 9 shows the net contribution, which in this case is the same as the gross contribution.

Row 10 shows the discounted contribution—that is, the present value of each future contribution discounted at 15 percent per annum. For example, the company will not receive $4 716 000 until the fifth year. This amount is worth only $2 346 000 today if the company can earn 15 percent on its money through other investments.[20]

Finally, *row 11* shows the cumulative discounted cash flow, which is the cumulation of the annual contributions in row 10. Two things are of central interest. The first is the maximum investment exposure, which is the highest loss that the project can create. We see that the company will be in a maximum loss position of $4 613 000

	Year 0	Year 1	Year 2	Year 3	Year 4	Year 5
1. Sales revenue	$0	$11,889	$15,381	$19,654	$28,253	$32,491
2. Cost of goods sold	0	3,981	5,150	6,581	9,461	10,880
3. Gross margin	0	7,908	10,231	13,073	18,792	21,611
4. Development costs	−3,500	0	0	0	0	0
5. Marketing costs	0	8,000	6,460	8,255	11,866	13,646
6. Allocated overhead	0	1,189	1,538	1,965	2,825	3,249
7. Gross contribution	−3,500	−1,281	2,233	2,853	4,101	4,716
8. Supplementary contribution	0	0	0	0	0	0
9. Net contribution	−3,500	−1,281	2,233	2,853	4,101	4,716
10. Discounted contribution (15%)	−3,500	−1,113	1,691	1,877	2,343	2,346
11. Cumulative discounted cash flow	−3,500	−4,613	−2,922	−1,045	1,298	3,644

TABLE 11.3

Projected Five-Year Cash-Flow Statement (in thousands of dollars)

in year 1. The second is the payback period, which is the time when the company recovers all of its investment including the built-in return of 15 percent. The payback period here is approximately three and a half years. Management therefore has to decide whether to risk a maximum investment loss of $4.6 million and a possible payback period of 3.5 years.

Companies use other financial measures to evaluate the merit of a new-product proposal. The simplest is *break-even analysis*, in which management estimates how many units of the product the company would have to sell to break even with the given price and cost structure. If management believes sales could easily reach the break-even number, it is likely to move the project into product development.

The most complex method of estimating profit is *risk analysis*. Here three estimates (optimistic, pessimistic, and most likely) are obtained for each uncertain variable affecting profitability under an assumed marketing environment and marketing strategy for the planning period. The computer simulates possible outcomes and computes a rate-of-return probability distribution showing the range of possible rates of returns and their probabilities.[21]

MANAGING THE DEVELOPMENT PROCESS: DEVELOPMENT TO COMMERCIALIZATION

PRODUCT DEVELOPMENT

If the product concept passes the business test, it moves to R&D or engineering to be developed into a physical product. Up until now it has existed only as a word description, a drawing, or a prototype. This step involves a large jump in investment that dwarfs the costs incurred in the earlier stages. At this stage the company will determine whether the product idea can be translated into a technically and commercially feasible product. If it cannot, the accumulated project cost will be lost except for any useful information gained in the process.

The job of translating target customer requirements into a working prototype is helped by a set of methods known as *quality function deployment* (QFD). The methodology takes the list of desired *customer attributes* (CAs) generated by market research and turns them into a list of *engineering attributes* (EAs) that the engineers can use. For example, customers of a proposed truck may want a certain acceleration rate (CA). Engineers can turn this into the required horsepower and other engineering equivalents (EAs). The methodology permits measuring the trade-offs and costs of providing the customer requirements. A major contribution of QFD is that it improves communication between marketers, engineers, and the manufacturing people.[22]

The R&D department will develop one or more physical versions of the product concept. Its goal is to find a prototype that consumers see as embodying the key attributes described in the product-concept statement, that performs safely under normal use and conditions, and that can be produced within the budgeted manufacturing costs.

Developing and manufacturing a successful prototype can take days, weeks, months, or even years. Designing a new commercial aircraft takes several years of development work, yet sophisticated virtual reality technology is speeding the process. By designing and testing product designs through simulation, for example, companies achieve the flexibility to respond to new information and to resolve uncertainties by quickly exploring alternatives.

■ **Boeing.** At Boeing, the all-digital development of the 777 aircraft made use of a computer-generated "human" who would climb inside the three-dimensional design on-screen to show how difficult maintenance access would be for a live mechanic. Such computer modelling allowed engineers to identify design errors that otherwise would have remained undiscovered until a person began to work on a physical prototype. By avoiding the time and cost associated with building physical prototypes at several stages, Boeing's development process has acquired the flexibility to evaluate a wider range of design options than previously thought possible.[23]

Boeing
www.boeing.com

Even developing a new taste formula can take time. Maxwell House discovered that consumers wanted coffee that was "bold, vigorous, and deep tasting." Its laboratory technicians spent over four months working with various coffee blends and flavours to formulate a corresponding taste that turned out to be too expensive to produce. The company cost-reduced the blend to meet the target manufacturing cost. The change compromised the taste, and the new brand did not sell well in the market.

With the rise of the World Wide Web, there is a need for more rapid prototyping and more flexible development processes. Michael Schrage, research associate at MIT's media lab, has correctly predicted: "Effective prototyping may be the most valuable 'core competence' an innovative organization can hope to have."[24] This has certainly been true for software companies such as Microsoft, Netscape, and the hundreds of Silicon Valley start-ups. Although Schrage says that specification-driven companies require that every "i" be dotted and "t" be crossed before anything can be shown to the next level of management, prototype-driven companies—such as Yahoo!, Microsoft, and Netscape—cherish quick-and-dirty tests and experiments. See the Marketing for the 21st Century box, "Developing Products on Internet Time: The Story of Netscape's Navigator."

Lab scientists must not only design the product's functional characteristics but also communicate its psychological aspects through physical cues. How will consumers react to different colours, sizes, and weights? In the case of a mouthwash, a yellow colour supports an "antiseptic" claim (Listerine), a red colour supports a "refreshing" claim (Lavoris), and a green or blue colour supports a "cool" claim (Scope). Marketers need to supply lab people with information on what attributes consumers seek and how consumers judge whether these attributes are present.

When the prototypes are ready, they must be put through rigorous *functional tests* and *customer tests*. *Alpha testing* is the name given to testing the product within the firm to see how it performs in different applications. After refining the prototype further, the company moves to *beta testing*. It enlists a set of customers to use the prototype and give feedback on their experiences. Beta testing is most useful when the potential customers are heterogeneous, the potential applications are not fully known, several decision makers are involved in purchasing the product, and opinion leadership from early adopters is sought.[25] Here are some of the functional tests that products go through before they enter the marketplace:

■ **Shaw Industries.** At Shaw Industries, temps are paid to pace up and down five long rows of sample carpets for up to eight hours a day, logging an average of 22 kilometres each. One regular reads three mysteries a week while pacing and shed 20 kilograms in two years. Shaw Industries counts walkers' steps and figures that 20 000 steps equal several years of average wear.

Developing Products on Internet Time: The Story of Netscape's Navigator

Traditional product development processes are highly structured. A future product is designed, developed, transferred to production, and rolled out to the market in clearly articulated, sequential phases. In contrast, flexible product development delays until as late as possible any commitment to a final design configuration. The concept development phase and the implementation phase—the translation of concept into reality—thus overlap instead of following each other sequentially. By accepting the need for and reducing the cost of changes, companies are able to respond to new information that arises during the course of a product's development.

When technology, product features, and competitive conditions are predictable or evolve slowly, a traditional development process works well. But in turbulent business environments, a sequential approach is more than inefficient; it risks creating an obsolete product—one that fails to address customer needs and to make use of the latest technologies. [Netscape faced just such a turbulent environment when it developed the second generation of its Navigator Web browser.] Industry giant Microsoft, which had already developed its own flexible product-development process, was readying a product to compete with Navigator.

Netscape introduced Navigator 2.0 to the market in January 1996 and immediately thereafter began to develop the next version of the Web browser, Navigator 3.0, which was to be released in August of the same year. The Netscape development group—which included staff from engineering, marketing, and customer support—produced the first prototype quickly. By February 14, just six weeks into the project, it had put a beta 0 version of the program up on the company's internal project Web site for testing by the development staff. Although many of the intended functions were not yet available, the prototype captured enough of the essence of the new product to generate meaningful feedback from members of the development group. On February 22, less than two weeks later, the team posted an updated version, Beta 1, again for internal development staff only. In early March, with major bugs in the product worked out, the first public release, Beta 2, appeared on Netscape's Internet Web site. Additional public releases followed thereafter every few weeks until the official release date in August, with gradual refinements appearing in each beta iteration.

The sequence of beta versions was extremely useful to Netscape because it enabled the development team to react both to feedback from users and to changes in the marketplace while the team was still working on the Web browser's design. Beta users by and large are more sophisticated than Netscape's broader customer base and therefore are a valuable source of information.... the team also paid careful attention to competing products. Netscape continually monitored the latest beta versions of Microsoft's competing product, Explorer, to compare features and format.

To facilitate the integration of the vast amounts of information generated during the project, Netscape set up a project Web site on its Intranet. The site contained the product's development schedule and specifications, each of which was updated as target dates changed or new features were added. In addition, it contained bulletin boards through which team members could monitor the evolution of various parts of the design, noting the completion of specific features and logging problems in the existing version. Once the Navigator moved to public beta testing, these Intranet features became especially valuable because an increasing amount of information then had to be received, classified, and processed....

Source: Adapted from Marco Iansiti and Alan MacCormack, "Developing Products on Internet Time," *Harvard Business Review*, September–October 1997, pp. 108–17.

■ **Apple Computer.** Apple Computer assumes the worst for its PowerBook customers and submits the computers to a battery of indignities: It drenches the computers in Pepsi and other sodas, smears them with mayonnaise, and bakes them in ovens at temperatures of 140 degrees or more to simulate conditions in a car trunk.

■ **Gillette.** At Gillette, 200 volunteers from various departments come to work unshaven each day, troop to the second floor of the company's manufacturing and research plant, and enter small booths with a sink and mirror. There they take instructions from technicians on the other side of a small window as to which razor, shaving cream, or aftershave to use, and then they fill out questionnaires. "We bleed so you'll get a good shave at home," says one Gillette employee.[26]

Companies that position products on the basis of their durability even incorporate functional product testing into their advertising:

- **Corelle Dinnerware.** High durability was the focus of some unusual advertising for Corning's Consumer Products Division's Corelle dinnerware. On five city buses in Phoenix, out-of-home media network TDI constructed a special Plexiglas cage, one metre long by 25 centimetres high, that housed a Corelle plate. Within the cage, the plate was free to roll back and forth as the bus accelerated, decelerated, and took turns.[27]

Consumer testing can take a variety of forms, from bringing consumers into a laboratory to giving them samples to use in their homes. In-home placement tests are common with products ranging from ice-cream flavours to new appliances. When DuPont developed its new synthetic carpeting, it installed free carpeting in several homes in exchange for the homeowners' willingness to report their likes and dislikes about the carpeting.

When testing cutting-edge products such as electric cars, marketers must be as creative as the product designers and engineers: Rügen, a small island in the Baltic Sea, has become the testing ground for the cars of the future. Fifty-eight residents of the former East German island have gone from driving decrepit gas-guzzling cars to sleek new electric models manufactured by BMW, Daimler Chrysler, and Audi. The Rügen tests have made the auto manufacturers aware of several problems: Rügen drivers have found that trips of any length must be carefully mapped out because of the batteries' limited life. Recharging the batteries can consume anywhere from a half hour to an entire evening.[28]

Consumer preferences can be measured in several ways. Suppose a consumer is shown three items—A, B, and C, such as three cameras, three insurance plans, or three advertisements.

- The *simple-rank-order* method asks the consumer to rank the three items in order of preference. The consumer might respond with A.B.C. Although this method has the advantage of simplicity, it does not reveal how intensely the consumer feels about each item nor whether the consumer likes any item very much. It is also difficult to use this method when there are many objects to be ranked.

- The *paired-comparison* method calls for presenting pairs of items and asking the consumer which one is preferred in each pair. Thus the consumer could be presented with the pairs AB, AC, and BC and say that she prefers A to B, A to C, and B to C. Then we could conclude that A.B.C. People find it easy to state their preference between two items, and this method allows the consumer to focus on the two items, noting their differences and similarities.

- The *monadic-rating* method asks the consumer to rate liking of each product on a scale. Suppose a seven-point scale is used, where 1 signifies intense dislike, 4 indifference, and 7 intense like. Suppose the consumer returns the following ratings: A56, B55, C53. We can derive the individual's preference order (i.e., A.B.C) and even know the qualitative levels of the person's preference for each and the rough distance between preferences.

MARKET TESTING

After management is satisfied with functional and psychological performance, the product is ready to be dressed up with a brand name and packaging, and put to a market test. The new product is introduced into an authentic setting to learn how large the market is and how consumers and dealers react to handling, using, and repurchasing the product.

Not all companies undertake market testing. A company officer at Revlon, Inc., stated: "In our field—primarily higher-priced cosmetics not geared for mass distribution—it would be unnecessary for us to market test. When we develop a new product, say an improved liquid makeup, we know it's going to sell because we're familiar with the field. And we've got 1500 demonstrators in department stores to promote it."

Most companies, however, know that market testing can yield valuable information about buyers, dealers, marketing program effectiveness, and market potential. The main issues are: How much market testing should be done, and what kind(s)?

The amount of market testing is influenced by the investment cost and risk on the one hand, and the time pressure and research cost on the other. High investment–high risk products, where the chance of failure is high, must be market tested; the cost of the market tests will be an insignificant percentage of the total project cost. High-risk products—those that create new-product categories (first instant breakfast drink) or have novel features (first fluoride toothpaste)—warrant more market testing than modified products (another toothpaste brand). But the amount of market testing may be severely reduced if the company is under great time pressure because the season is just starting or because competitors are about to launch their brands. The company may therefore prefer to face the risk of a product failure to the risk of losing distribution or market penetration on a highly successful product. Consider the case of Olestra.

Health Canada
www.hc-sc.gc.ca

Olestra. Procter & Gamble spent two years market testing its new no-calorie fat substitute, Olestra. While the U.S. Food and Drug Administration (FDA) approved the new product in 1996, it still hasn't been approved by the Food Directorate of Health Canada's Health Protection Branch despite almost a decade in the review process. P&G has submitted over 150 000 pages of data to Health Canada—enough paper to fill a tractor trailer—and has invested more than $300 million developing and testing the product over a 30-year period. After the product was introduced in the United States, a very small percentage (estimated at two percent) of consumers experienced stomach problems and the indelicately named side effect, "anal leakage." The company made a slight change in the formula, but even after test marketing has proved that these side effects do not occur, the FDA requires that every package containing food made with Olestra bear a label that reads: "This product contains Olestra. Olestra may cause abdominal cramping and loose stools. Olestra inhibits the absorption of some vitamins and other nutrients...."[29]

Next we describe consumer-goods market testing and business-goods testing.

Consumer-Goods Market Testing

In testing consumer products, the company seeks to estimate four variables: trial, first repeat, adoption, and purchase frequency. The company hopes to find all these variables at high levels. In some cases, it will find many consumers trying the product but few rebuying it. Or it might find high permanent adoption but low purchase frequency (as with gourmet frozen foods).

Here we describe the major methods of consumer-goods market testing, from the least to the most costly.

Sales-Wave Research. In *sales-wave research*, consumers who initially try the product at no cost are reoffered the product, or a competitor's product, at slightly reduced prices. They might be reoffered the product as many as three to five times (sales waves), with the company noting how many customers selected that company's product again and their reported level of satisfaction. Sales-wave research can also include exposing consumers to one or more advertising concepts to see the impact of that advertising on repeat purchase.

Sales-wave research can be implemented quickly, conducted with a fair amount of security, and carried out without final packaging and advertising. However, sales-wave research does not indicate the trial rates that would be achieved with different sales-promotion incentives, because the consumers are preselected to try the product. Nor does it indicate the brand's power to gain distribution and favourable shelf position.

Simulated Test Marketing. *Simulated test marketing* calls for finding 30 to 40 qualified shoppers and questioning them about brand familiarity and preferences in a specific product category. These people are then invited to a brief screening of both well-known and new commercials or print ads. One ad advertises the new product, but it is not singled out for attention. Consumers receive a small amount of money and are invited into a store where they may buy any items. The company notes how many consumers buy the new brand and competing brands. This provides a measure of the ad's relative effectiveness against competing ads in stimulating trial. Consumers are asked the reasons for their purchases or nonpurchases. Those who did not buy the new brand are given a free sample. Some weeks later, they are reinterviewed by phone to determine product attitudes, usage, satisfaction, and repurchase intention and are offered an opportunity to repurchase any products.

This method has several advantages. It gives fairly accurate results on advertising effectiveness and trial rates (and repeat rates if extended) in a much shorter time and at a fraction of the cost of using real test markets. Pretests often take only three months and may cost $375 000.[30] The results are incorporated into new-product forecasting models to project ultimate sales levels. Marketing research firms report surprisingly accurate predictions of sales levels of products that are subsequently launched in the market.[31]

Controlled Test Marketing. In this method, a research firm manages a panel of stores that will carry new products for a fee. The company with the new product specifies the number of stores and geographic locations it wants to test. The research firm delivers the product to the participating stores and controls shelf position; number of facings, displays, and point-of-purchase promotions; and pricing. Sales results can be measured through electronic scanners at the checkout. The company can also evaluate the impact of local advertising and promotions during the test.

Controlled test marketing allows the company to test the impact of in-store factors and limited advertising on buying behaviour. A sample of consumers can be interviewed later to give their impressions of the product. The company does not have to use its own sales force, give trade allowances, or "buy" distribution. However, controlled test marketing provides no information on how to sell the trade on carrying the new product. This technique also exposes the product and its features to competitors' scrutiny.

Test Markets. The ultimate way to test a new consumer product is to put it into full-blown test markets. The company chooses a few representative cities, and the sales force tries to sell the trade on carrying the product and giving it good shelf exposure. The company puts on a full advertising and promotion campaign in these markets similar to the one that it would use in national marketing. A full-scale test can cost over $1 million, depending on the number of test cities, the test duration, and the amount of data the company wants to collect.

Management faces several questions:

1. *How many test cities?* Most tests use between two and six cities. The greater the maximum possible loss, the greater the number of contending marketing strategies, the greater the regional differences, and the greater the chance of test-market interference by competitors, the greater the number of cities that should be used.

2. *Which cities?* Each company must develop test-city selection criteria. One company looks for test cities that have diversified industry, good media coverage, cooperative chain stores, average competitive activity, and no evidence of being overtested.

3. *Length of test?* Market tests last anywhere from a few months to a year. The longer the product's average repurchase period, the longer the test period necessary to observe repeat-purchase rates. This period should be reduced if competitors are rushing to the market.

4. *What information?* Warehouse shipment data will show gross inventory buying but will not indicate weekly sales at the retail level. *Store audits* will show retail sales and competitors' market shares but will not reveal buyer characteristics. *Consumer panels* will indicate which people are buying which brands and their loyalty and switching rates. *Buyer surveys* will yield in-depth information about consumer attitudes, usage, and satisfaction.

5. *What action to take?* If the test markets show high trial and repurchase rates, the product should be launched nationally. If the test markets show a high

trial rate and a low repurchase rate, customers are not satisfied and the product should be redesigned or dropped. If the test markets show a low trial rate and a high repurchase rate, the product is satisfying but more people must try it. This means increasing advertising and sales promotion. If trial and repurchase rates are both low, the product should be abandoned.

Test marketing permits testing the impact of alternative marketing plans. Colgate-Palmolive used a different marketing mix in each of four cities to market a new soap product: (1) an average amount of advertising coupled with free samples distributed door to door, (2) heavy advertising plus samples, (3) an average amount of advertising linked with mailed redeemable coupons, and (4) an average amount of advertising with no special introductory offer. The third alternative generated the best profit level, although not the highest sales level.

In spite of the benefits of test marketing, many companies question its value today. In a fast-changing marketplace, companies are eager to get to market first. Test marketing slows them down and reveals their plans to competitors. Procter & Gamble began testing a ready-to-spread Duncan Hines frosting. General Mills took note and rushed out its own Betty Crocker brand, which now dominates the category. Furthermore, aggressive competitors increasingly take steps to spoil the test markets. When Pepsi tested its Mountain Dew sport drink, Gatorade counterattacked furiously with coupons and ads.[32]

Many companies today are skipping test marketing and relying on faster and more economical market-testing methods. General Mills now prefers to launch new products in perhaps 25 percent of the country, an area too large for rivals to disrupt. Managers review retail scanner data, which tell them within days how the product is doing and what corrective fine-tuning to do. Colgate-Palmolive often launches a new product in a set of small "lead countries" and keeps rolling it out if it proves successful.

Nonetheless, managers should consider all the angles before deciding to dispense with test marketing. In this case, not testing a formula modification before the product launch had disastrous—and soggy—results:

- **Nabisco Foods Company.** Nabisco hit a marketing home run with its Teddy Grahams, teddy-bear-shaped graham crackers in several different flavours. So, the company decided to extend Teddy Grahams into a new area. It introduced chocolate, cinnamon, and honey versions of Breakfast Bears Graham Cereal. When the product came out, however, consumers didn't like the taste enough, so the product developers went back to the kitchen and modified the formula, but didn't test it. The result was a disaster. Although the cereal may have tasted better, it no longer stayed crunchy in milk, as the advertising on the box promised. Instead, it left a gooey mess of graham mush on the bottom of cereal bowls. Supermarket managers soon refused to restock the cereal, and Nabisco executives decided it was too late to reformulate the product again. So a promising new product was killed through haste to get it to market.[33]

Business-Goods Market Testing

Business goods can also benefit from market testing. Expensive industrial goods and new technologies will normally undergo *alpha testing* (within the company) and *beta testing* (with outside customers). During beta testing, the vendor's technical people observe how test customers use the product, a practice that often exposes unanticipated problems of safety and servicing and alerts the vendor to customer training and servicing requirements. The vendor can also observe how much value the equipment adds to the customer's operation as a clue to subsequent pricing. The vendor will ask the test customers to express their purchase intention and other reactions after the test.

The test customers benefit in several ways: They can influence product design, gain experience with the new product ahead of competitors, receive a price break in return for cooperation, and enhance their reputation as technological pioneers. Vendors must carefully interpret the beta test results because only a small number of test customers are used, they are not randomly drawn, and the tests are somewhat customized to each site. Another risk is that test customers who are unimpressed with the product may leak unfavourable reports about it.

A second common test method for business goods is to introduce the new product at trade shows. Trade shows draw a large number of buyers, who view many new products in a few concentrated days. The vendor can observe how much interest buyers show in the new product, how they react to various features and terms, and how many express purchase intentions or place orders. Canadian executives are increasingly understanding the value of displaying their goods at International Trade Shows. The Ottawa-based Association for the Export of Canadian Books, for example, estimates that book exports have increased by 300 percent in the two years after the Association encouraged aggressive trade-show participation. Even attending domestic shows can be beneficial. While a major objective may be meeting prospective clients face-to-face, retail exhibitors from over 10 countries who attended the Asia Show held recently at the Canadian Exhibition Grounds in Toronto found that it helped them forge links with potential distributors and associates that helped them develop worldwide networks.[34] The disadvantage of trade shows is that they reveal the product to competitors; therefore, the vendor should be ready to launch the product soon after the trade show.

New industrial products can be tested in distributor and dealer display rooms, where they may stand next to the manufacturer's other products and possibly competitors' products. This method yields preference and pricing information in the product's normal selling atmosphere. The disadvantages are that the customers might want to place early orders that cannot be filled, and those customers who come in might not represent the target market.

Industrial manufacturers come close to using full test marketing when they give a limited supply of the product to the sales force to sell in a limited number of areas that receive promotion support and printed catalogue sheets. In this way, management can make a more informed decision about commercializing the product.

COMMERCIALIZATION

If the company goes ahead with commercialization, it will face its largest costs to date. The company will have to contract for manufacture or build or rent a full-scale manufacturing facility. Plant size will be a critical decision. The company can build a smaller plant than called for by the sales forecast, to be on the safe side. That is what Quaker Oats did when it launched its 100 Percent Natural breakfast cereal. The demand so exceeded the company's sales forecast that for about a year it could not supply enough product to the stores. Although Quaker Oats was gratified with the response, the low forecast cost it a considerable amount of profit.

Another major cost is marketing. To introduce a major new consumer packaged good into the national market, the company may have to spend $30 million to $120 million in advertising and promotion in the first year. In the introduction of new food products, marketing expenditures typically represent 57 percent of sales during the first year. While the much-touted budget film, the *Blair Witch Project* cost only $45 000 to produce, over $40 million was spent to promote it.[35] In the movie business, it's not unusual for the cost of marketing a movie to eclipse the cost of making it, particularly for what Hollywood calls "tentpole" films, those big summer blockbusters that can carry the rest of the studio's projects on the strength of their revenues. In the decade between 1987 and 1997, the average cost of making a movie went from $30 million to $80 million, but marketing costs zoomed from $10.5 million to $33 million.

When (Timing)

In commercializing a new product, market-entry timing is critical. Suppose a company has almost completed the development work on its new product and learns that a competitor is nearing the end of its development work. The company faces three choices:

1. *First entry:* The first firm entering a market usually enjoys the "first mover advantages" of locking up key distributors and customers and gaining reputational leadership. But, if the product is rushed to market before it is thoroughly debugged, the product can acquire a flawed image.

2. *Parallel entry:* The firm might time its entry to coincide with the competitor's entry. The market may pay more attention when two companies are advertising the new product.

3. *Late entry:* The firm might delay its launch until after the competitor has entered. The competitor will have borne the cost of educating the market. The competitor's product may reveal faults the late entrant can avoid. The company can also learn the size of the market.

The timing decision involves additional considerations. If a new product replaces an older product, the company might delay the introduction until the old product's stock is drawn down. If the product is highly seasonal, it might be delayed until the right season arrives.[36]

Where (Geographic Strategy)

The company must decide whether to launch the new product in a single locality, a region, several regions, the national market, or the international market. Most will develop a planned market rollout over time. For instance, U.S.-based Kera Vision is using Vancouver as the Canadian test market for a branded medical device, Intacs, a product designed to correct mild cases of myopia. Tom Loarie, president and CEO, says Vancouver was selected because its citizens are generally accepting of new and unconventional products. "Vancouver is a lot like California," he says. "The people there are not bound by orthodoxy."[37] Company size is an important factor here. Small companies will select an attractive city and put on a blitz campaign. They will enter other cities one at a time. Large companies will introduce their product into a whole region and then move to the next region. Companies with national distribution networks, such as auto companies, will launch their new models in the national market.

Most companies design new products to sell primarily in the domestic market. If the product does well, the company considers exporting to neighbouring countries or the world market, redesigning if necessary. Cooper and Kleinschmidt, in their study of industrial products, found that domestic products designed solely for the domestic market tend to show a high failure rate, low market share, and low growth. In contrast, products designed for the world market—or at least to include neighbouring countries—achieve significantly more profits, both at home and abroad. Yet only 17 percent of the products in Cooper and Kleinschmidt's study were designed with an international orientation.[38] The implication is that companies should adopt an international focus in designing and developing new products.

In choosing rollout markets, the candidate markets can be listed as rows, and rollout attractiveness criteria can be listed as columns. The major rating criteria are market potential, company's local reputation, cost of filling the pipeline, cost of communication media, influence of area on other areas, and competitive penetration.

The presence of strong competitors will influence rollout strategy. Suppose McDonald's wants to launch a new chain of fast-food pizza parlours. Pizza Hut, a formidable competitor, is strongly entrenched on the East Coast. Another pizza chain is entrenched on the West Coast but is weak. The Prairies is the battleground between two other chains. Central Canada is open, but Shakey's is planning to move in. McDonald's faces a complex decision in choosing a geographic rollout strategy.

With the World Wide Web connecting far-flung parts of the globe, competition is more likely to cross national borders. Companies are increasingly rolling out new products simultaneously across the globe, rather than nationally or even regionally. However, masterminding a global launch provides challenges. Autodesk, the world's leading supplier of PC design software and multimedia tools, has three million customers in more than 150 countries. Carol Bartz, chairman and CEO, says that the biggest obstacle to a global launch success is getting all the different marketers to agree with the positioning: "Then the issue is speed—getting the materials out fast enough.

We get them to agree on the look (using one image), and then it's a matter of putting a local spin on it. It requires an immense amount of concentration."[39] Coordinating an international launch also requires very deep pockets, as was the case with the launch of Iridium's "world phone."

■ **Iridium Inc.** It's a phone the size of a brick with an antenna as thick as a stout breadstick. It costs $4500, but this satellite-linked phone allows users to communicate from anywhere on earth. Iridium faced countless challenges in marketing this unwieldy, expensive device to a diverse, globe-trotting market. Brazil expected to presell 46 000 Iridium phones because of the country's creaky phone system. Iridium Mideast wanted the phone in hunting-supply shops, because it was the perfect toy for desert falconry. An executive from Iridium India planned exclusive parties for rich businesspeople who might want the new status symbol. Eventually, the company relied on APL, a division of Interpublic Group, to craft a single campaign for what is, arguably, the most intensive effort ever to build a global brand overnight. The $210 million campaign is running in 45 countries. Direct-mail materials are being translated into 13 languages. Television ads are scheduled on 17 different airlines. Iridium booths, where travellers will be able to handle the phones in person, are being set up in executive lounges in airports around the world. Finally, in what is surely the ultimate symbol of a global launch, APL hired laser specialists to beam the company's Big Dipper logo onto the clouds.[40]

Iridium Inc.
www.iridium.com

To Whom (Target-Market Prospects)

Within the rollout markets, the company must target its initial distribution and promotion to the best prospect groups. Presumably, the company has already profiled the prime prospects, who would ideally have the following characteristics: They would be early adopters, heavy users, and opinion leaders, and they could be reached at a low cost.[41] Few groups have all these characteristics. The company should rate the various prospect groups on these characteristics and target the best prospect group. The aim is to generate strong sales as soon as possible to motivate the sales force and attract further prospects.

Many companies are surprised to learn who really buys their product and why. Microwave ovens began to enjoy explosive growth only after microwave-oven popcorn was developed. Households dramatically increased their purchase of computers when the CD-ROM multimedia feature was introduced.

How (Introductory Market Strategy)

The company must develop an action plan for introducing the new product into the rollout markets. With its debut in 1998, the competitively priced iMac represented Apple Computer's re-entry into the computer PC business after a hiatus of 14 years. The company staged a massive marketing blitz to launch the new machine.

- **Apple Computer Inc.** Apple's launch of the iMac, the sleek, egg-shaped computer with one-touch Internet access, was dramatic. For starters, the iMac was a closely guarded secret until May 6, 1998, when Jobs literally unveiled the machine to awe-struck reporters. The buzz continued to mount, on-line and off, until the machine went on sale in August. On the weekend of August 14, computer retailers prepared Midnight Madness sales featuring seven-metre-high inflatable iMacs flying above the stores. Radio stations across the country began an iMac countdown, topped off with iMac giveaways. Jobs personally signed five "golden" tickets and placed them in the boxes of five iMacs, with the winner receiving a free iMac each year for the next five years. Apple augmented these efforts with a $100 million ad campaign, its biggest ever, to promote iMac through TV, print, radio, and billboards. The campaign featured images of the iMac alongside slogans such as "Mental Floss" and "I think, therefore iMac."[42]

To coordinate the many activities involved in launching a new product, management can use network-planning techniques such as critical path scheduling. *Critical path scheduling (CPS)* calls for developing a master chart showing the simultaneous and sequential activities that must take place to launch the product. By estimating how much time each activity takes, the planners estimate completion time for the entire project. Any delay in any activity on the critical path will cause the project to be delayed. If the launch must be completed earlier, the planner searches for ways to reduce time along the critical path.[43]

Apple on-line: The media blitz to launch this eye-catching new product seems to have paid off.

THE CONSUMER-ADOPTION PROCESS

How do potential customers learn about new products, try them, and adopt or reject them? (*Adoption* is an individual's decision to become a regular user of a product.) *The consumer-adoption process* is later followed by the *consumer-loyalty process*, which is the concern of the established producer.

Years ago, new-product marketers used a *mass-market approach* in launching products. They would distribute a product everywhere and advertise it to everyone on the assumption that most people are potential buyers. This approach had two main drawbacks: It called for heavy marketing expenditures, and it involved many wasted exposures to people who are not potential consumers. These drawbacks led to a second approach, *heavy-user target marketing*, where the product is initially aimed at heavy users.

This approach makes sense, provided that heavy users are identifiable and are early adopters. But even within the heavy-user group, consumers differ in interest in new products and brands; many heavy users are loyal to existing brands. Many new-product marketers now aim at consumers who are early adopters. According to *early-adopter theory*:

- Persons within a target market differ in the amount of elapsed time between their exposure to a new product and their trying it.
- Early adopters share some traits that differentiate them from late adopters.
- Efficient media exist for reaching early adopters.
- Early adopters tend to be opinion leaders and helpful in "advertising" the new product to other potential buyers.

The theory of innovation diffusion and consumer adoption helps marketers identify early adopters.

STAGES IN THE ADOPTION PROCESS

An *innovation* refers to any good, service, or idea that is *perceived* by someone as new. The idea may have a long history, but it is an innovation to the person who sees it as new. Innovations take time to spread through the social system. Rogers defines the *innovation diffusion process* as "the spread of a new idea from its source of invention or creation to its ultimate users or adopters."[44] The consumer-adoption process focuses on the mental process through which an individual passes from first hearing about an innovation to final adoption.

Adopters of new products have been observed to move through five stages:

1. *Awareness:* The consumer becomes aware of the innovation but lacks information about it.

2. *Interest:* The consumer is stimulated to seek information about the innovation.

3. *Evaluation:* The consumer considers whether to try the innovation.

4. *Trial:* The consumer tries the innovation to improve his or her estimate of its value.

5. *Adoption:* The consumer decides to make full and regular use of the innovation.

The new-product marketer should facilitate consumer movement through these stages. A portable electric-dishwasher manufacturer might discover that many consumers are stuck in the interest stage; they do not buy because of their uncertainty and the large investment cost. But these same consumers would be willing to use an electric dishwasher on a trial basis for a small monthly fee. The manufacturer should consider offering a trial-use plan with an option to buy. Developers of most general-interest interactive CD-ROM titles found that consumers were stuck in the interest or trial stage and moved less rapidly to adoption.

- **CD-ROMs.** In the early 1990s, there seemed to be room in the CD-ROM industry for everyone. Multimedia developers were producing action games and educational software and moving into a hodgepodge of interactive products that ranged from hypertext novels to multimedia music anthologies. Today, few of these titles are selling well or even on the market. One of the main causes of the poor sales is the ascendance of the Web. Most CD-ROMs, particularly reference titles, found a more cost-effective home on the Web, a medium that also enables them to keep up-to-date and link to a community of users. CD-ROMs also faced hundreds of competitors in an extremely fragmented entertainment market. Another problem was the glut of titles with serious quality problems. Although consumers were willing to tolerate lower quality, they were not patient with technical glitches. When Disney was beset by massive store returns of its defective Lion King CD-ROM, the *New York Times* promptly claimed that CD-ROMs were dead.[45]

FACTORS INFLUENCING THE ADOPTION PROCESS

Marketers recognize the following characteristics of the adoption process: differences in individual readiness to try new products; the effect of personal influence; differing rates of adoption; and differences in organizations' readiness to try new products.

People Differ in Readiness to Try New Products

Rogers defines a person's innovativeness as "the degree to which an individual is relatively earlier in adopting new ideas than the other members of his social system." In each product area, there are consumption pioneers and early adopters. Some people are the first to adopt new clothing fashions or new appliances; some doctors are the first to prescribe new medicines; and some farmers are the first to adopt new farming methods. Other individuals adopt new products much later. People can be classified into the adopter categories shown in Figure 11.7. After a slow start, an increasing number of people adopt the innovation, the number reaches a peak, and then it diminishes as fewer nonadopters remain.

Rogers sees the five adopter groups as differing in their value orientations. Innovators are venturesome; they are willing to try new ideas. Early adopters are guided by respect; they are opinion leaders in their community and adopt new ideas early but carefully. The early majority are deliberate; they adopt new ideas before the average person, although they rarely are leaders. The late majority are skeptical; they adopt an innovation only after a majority of people have tried it. Finally, laggards are tradition bound; they are suspicious of change, mix with other tradition-bound people, and adopt the innovation only when it takes on a measure of tradition itself.

FIGURE 11.7

Adopter Categorization on the Basis of Relative Time of Adoption of Innovations

Source: Redrawn from Everett M. Rogers, *Diffusion of Innovations* (New York: Free Press, 1983).

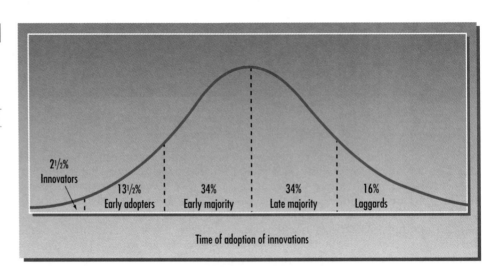

2½% Innovators

13½% Early adopters

34% Early majority

34% Late majority

16% Laggards

Time of adoption of innovations

This classification suggests that an innovating firm should research the demographic, psychographic, and media characteristics of innovators and early adopters and direct communications specifically to them. For example, innovative farmers are likely to be better educated and more efficient. Innovative homemakers are more gregarious and usually higher in social status. Certain communities have a high share of early adopters. According to Rogers, earlier adopters tend to be younger in age, have higher social status, and a more favourable financial position. They utilize a greater number of more cosmopolitan information sources than do later adopters.[46]

Personal Influence Plays a Large Role

Personal influence is the effect one person has on another's attitude or purchase probability. Although personal influence is an important factor, its significance is greater in some situations and for some individuals than for others. Personal influence is more important in the evaluation stage of the adoption process than in the other stages. It has more influence on late adopters than early adopters. It also is more important in risky situations.

Characteristics of the Innovation Affect Rate of Adoption

Some products catch on immediately (e.g., in-line skates), whereas others take a long time to gain acceptance (e.g., diesel-engine autos). Five characteristics influence the rate of adoption of an innovation. We will consider them in relation to the adoption of personal computers for home use.

The first is *relative advantage*—the degree to which the innovation appears superior to existing products. The greater the perceived relative advantage of using a personal computer, say, in preparing income taxes and keeping financial records, the more quickly personal computers will be adopted.

The second is *compatibility*—the degree to which the innovation matches the values and experiences of the individuals. Personal computers, for example, are highly compatible with upper-middle-class lifestyles.

Third is *complexity*—the degree to which the innovation is relatively difficult to understand or use. Personal computers are complex and will therefore take longer to penetrate into home use.

Fourth is *divisibility*—the degree to which the innovation can be tried on a limited basis. The availability of rentals of personal computers with an option to buy increases their rate of adoption.

Fifth is *communicability*—the degree to which the beneficial results of use are observable or describable to others. The fact that personal computers lend themselves to demonstration and description helps them diffuse faster in the social system. Dairyworld Foods of Burnaby, B.C. certainly understands the importance of superior communication programs to support its new products. It was named by *Marketing* magazine as one of the top marketers of 1999 for its innovative product development and insightful advertising and positioning. For example, when it launched its new product, Take Milk 2 Go, regular and flavoured milk in resealable rounded plastic bottles that fit into car cup-holders, its sales hit double digits. The launch was supported by a $12-million campaign titled, "Your fresh ideas dairy" that increased brand awareness by over 30 percent.[47]

Other characteristics that influence the rate of adoption are cost, risk and uncertainty, scientific credibility, and social approval. The new-product marketer must research all these factors and give the key ones maximum attention in designing the new-product and marketing program.[48]

Organizations Also Vary in Readiness to Adopt Innovations

The creator of a new teaching method would want to identify innovative schools. The producer of a new piece of medical equipment would want to identify innovative hospitals. Adoption is associated with variables in the organization's environment (community progressiveness, community income), the organization itself (size, profits, pressure to change), and the administrators (education level, age, sophistication). Other forces come into play when trying to get a product adopted into organizations that receive the bulk of their funding from the government, such as public schools.

A controversial or innovative product can be squelched by negative public opinion. This was certainly the case with Christopher Whittle's Channel One, a television station for secondary schools, that was killed because of resistance by teachers and parents.[49]

SUMMARY

1. Once a company has segmented the market, chosen its target customer groups, identified their needs, and determined its desired market positioning, it is ready to develop and launch appropriate new products. Marketing should actively participate with other departments in every stage of new-product development.

2. Successful new-product development requires the company to establish an effective organization for managing the development process. Companies can choose to use product managers, new-product managers, new-product committees, new-product departments, or new-product venture teams.

3. Eight stages are involved in the new-product development process: idea generation, screening, concept development and testing, marketing strategy development, business analysis, product development, market testing, and commercialization. The purpose of each stage is to determine whether the idea should be dropped or moved to the next stage.

4. The consumer-adoption process is the process by which customers learn about new products, try them, and adopt or reject them. Today many marketers are targeting heavy users and early adopters of new products, because both groups can be reached by specific media and tend to be opinion leaders. The consumer-adoption process is influenced by many factors beyond the marketer's control, including consumers' and organizations' willingness to try new products, personal influences, and the characteristics of the new product or innovation.

APPLICATIONS

CHAPTER CONCEPTS

1. To generate really good new-product ideas you need inspiration, perspiration, and good techniques. Some companies struggle with trying to develop new-product ideas because they place more emphasis on inspiration and perspiration than they do on technique. Attribute listing, Alex Osborn's powerful creative tool, can activate the creative juices in just about everyone. Identify a product or service that you are familiar with and list its attributes. Then modify each attribute in search of an improved product. The following form will be useful in your deliberations. If you are having trouble getting started, consider a famous example of attribute alteration and expansion: that of Oreo cookies. From the simple, black-and-white

---

Attribute Listing Worksheet

Attributes	Magnify	Minify	Substitute	Adapt	Rearrange	Reverse	Combine	New Uses	Replace

Oreo, Nabisco has developed double-stuff Oreos, chocolate-covered Oreos, giant-size Oreos, mini-size Oreos, low-fat Oreos, lower-calorie Oreos, different packaging and package sizes, Oreo cookie ice cream, Oreo cookie ice cream cones, Oreo granola bars, Oreo cereal, and Oreo snack treats.

2. Prepare a list of questions that management should answer prior to developing a new product or service. Organize the questions according to the following categories: (a) market opportunity, (b) competition, (c) production, (d) patentable features, (e) distribution (for products) or delivery (for services), and (f) finance. Then answer each question for a new-product idea you have. Would the development and testing of a new service differ from those of a new product?

3. Before beginning an in-home-use test of Odor-Eater socks, each consumer participant selected the Odor-Eaters sock style he or she preferred. At the end of the test, the participants summarized how likely they would be to purchase Odor-Eaters in the future. These data are reported in Table 1. What conclusions can you draw from these data? What type of sock is most popular with consumers? Assuming that the consumer testers are representative of the market, how price sensitive is this market? Should the company package Odor-Eaters one to the box (columns 6 and 7), or would multiple packs (columns 8 and 9) be preferable?

MARKETING AND ADVERTISING

1. Orville Redenbacher markets a number of popcorn products for consumers. The firm recently introduced Double Feature microwave popcorn, shown in the ad in Figure 1 on page 354. How could this idea have been described as a product concept during the product-development process? Suggest an appropriate concept statement. What forms of consumer testing would be appropriate for this popcorn product? Why? Would you have used controlled test marketing or test markets to gauge consumer reaction prior to launching this product? Explain your answer.

FOCUS ON TECHNOLOGY

During the new-product-development process, marketers can use conjoint analysis to analyze offers, identify the most appealing, and learn how customers see the relative importance of each attribute. Because the most appealing offer is not necessarily the most profitable, marketers must also estimate the potential market share

TABLE 1

Likelihood of Purchasing Odor-Eaters

	(1)	(2)	(3)	(4)	(5)	(6)	(7)	(8)	(9)
			Type of Sock			**Package Size and Price**			
	Total Respon-dents	24-inch Tube Sock	18-inch Tube Sock	Athletic Sock	Crew Sock	1 pair at $1.79–$1.99	1 pair at $1.99–$2.49	3 pairs at $4.99–$5.99	3 pairs at $5.49–$6.49
Respondent base*	(185)	(60)	(22)	(34)	(69)	(53)	(42)	(42)	(48)
Definitely would buy	38%	43%	45%	42%	29%	42%	45%	31%	33%
Probably would buy	44	47	27	35	51	38	40	48	50
Might or might not buy	14	7	23	15	16	13	20	19	13
Probably would not buy	3	3	5	6	1	4	5	—	4
Definitely would not buy	2	—	—	3	3	4	—	2	—

*Based on four-week consumer home-use test.
Source: CU Market Research.

Figure 1

and profits to be gained from the top alternatives. Because of the complexity of this technique, marketers use sophisticated software to score the results.

For a hands-on demonstration of how conjoint analysis looks from the respondents' perspective, point your Web browser to SurveySite (www.surveysite.com/), the home page of an on-line market research firm. Click on "demos" to locate the conjoint analysis sample. After you have completed this sample, click on the Conjoint Analysis Tutorial. Based on this sample conjoint analysis, what attributes are being tested? Why would the automaker want to test these attributes? Which of the product concepts do you think would prove most appealing to those being surveyed? Why?

MARKETING FOR THE 21ST CENTURY

At the start of the new millennium, turbulent business environments and extreme competitive pressures are everyday phenomena for companies with a presence on the Web. To stay ahead of the curve, these marketers are taking the new-product-development process two steps at a time, overlapping concept development and implementation as they continue to gather information on the fly.

To see new-product development on the fast track, look at Microsoft, which has a special place on its Web site (www.microsoft.com) for program previews (translation: beta versions of soon-to-be-released software). Months before its Office 2000 software was introduced, the company offered preview versions for the bargain price of $19.95. A disclaimer noted the beta version "is not at the level of performance and compatibility of the final, generally available, product offering.... The entire risk of the use or results of the use of this software remains with the user, and Microsoft Corporation makes no warranties, either express or implied." Why would users want to participate in this beta testing—and pay for the privilege? What does Microsoft stand to gain? How early in the development process should Microsoft start beta testing?

YOU'RE THE MARKETER:
SONIC MARKETING PLAN

Product strategy is based on the choices companies make as they segment their markets, identify target audiences and research their needs, and create an appropriate market positioning. With this foundation, marketers are ready to plan for new-product development and management.

Now you are considering Sonic's new-product-development options. Look back at the company's situational analysis and the parts of the marketing plan you have developed so far. Then answer these questions (noting the need for additional research where necessary):

■ *What kinds of new products would help Sonic achieve its goals and compete more effectively in the marketplace—while meeting the needs of its targeted segments? Be specific.*

■ *Working alone or with other students, generate four or five ideas for new products, and indicate how you can screen these ideas.*

■ *Develop the most promising idea into a product concept and indicate how you plan to test this concept. What dimensions must be tested?*

■ Assuming that this idea has tested well, develop a marketing strategy for the introduction of the new product. Include a description of the target market; your positioning for the product; the estimated sales, profit, and market-share goals for the first two years; your price strategy; your channel strategy; and the marketing budget you will set for this new product introduction.

As your instructor directs, summarize your product-development and management ideas in a written marketing plan or type them into the Product Development/Management section of the Marketing Plan Pro software. Be sure to include long-range estimates of sales, profits, and budget requirements for each new product you plan to introduce.

Designing Global Market Offerings

PROFILE:

Canadian Marketing Excellence

*Y*our company does not belong in markets where it can't be the best. Philip Kotler's dictate could well be the slogan governing the 10 firms that were awarded the 1998 Canada Export Awards. Who were some of the winners? They came from locations across Canada and ranged from high-tech firms like CrossKeys Systems Corporation of Kanata, Ontario, and A.L.I. Technologies of Richmond, B.C., to a manufacturer of above-ground swimming pools, a mature product produced by Vogue Pool Products of LaSalle, Quebec. Six criteria distinguished the winning firms:

- The ability to look beyond their domestic market and compete globally
- The willingness to invest in research and innovation
- A strong sense of community
- A dedicated workforce
- An appetite for risk; and
- A commitment to excellence.

CrossKeys Systems, for example, invested $6.2 million in 1997 alone so that it could expand its product portfolio by 12 percent. As CEO John Selwyn notes, "Our investment in product R&D has been critical to export success. . .In dealing with foreign, multi-billion-dollar telecommunications companies, we have to demonstrate a strong commitment to researching and developing innovative products that not only satisfy our customers' current needs but anticipate their future needs." Furthermore, to provide service to its scattered customer base, CrossKeys has devoted part of its Web site to customer service so that customers can access information 24 hours a day.

Another key is a firm's ability to cultivate relationships and understand the unique needs and challenges of channel members and end customers. Forming quality relationships with dealers and distributors in key markets has been the key to Vogue Pool's success. More-over, the firm quickly realized that even though it was selling virtually the same products around the world, it needed very different distribution strategies to meet the needs of cus-tomers in various countries. For example, in Canada, 90 percent of pools are sold through specialized pool retailers who offer their customers installation service. In Europe, however, just the opposite is true; 90 percent of people buying pools do their own installation. Rather than forming relationships with a large distributor that will standardize distribution across the continent, Vogue believes local distributors are the key to success. Gilles Lebuis, Vice President of Marketing, notes, "A distributor in France will know his market much better…than someone from Switzerland. . . . " This thinking has helped the firm sell over $11 million worth of pool kits through major do-it-yourself chains in France, whereas in Belgium, Switzerland, Germany and Austria, it uses pool distributors.

Quickly realizing that buying a pool kit is one thing, but installing it creates its own problems, Vogue Pools also worked to develop an innovative pool design that simplifies the installation process. The company has adopted an IKEA approach to pools. Customers must still dig a hole, but they can use a single tool to assemble their pool—avoiding the need to use a confusing array of nuts and bolts. Given these insights, it is no wonder that today over 70 percent of Vogue Pool's sales are made in foreign markets.

Sources: Adam Pletsch, "Vogue Pool Products Dives into Europe," Maclean Hunter Publishing Limited, 1999, *http://www.plant.ca/Content/1999/990118/pla01189904.html*. CrossKey's Web site, "About CrossKeys," *http://www. crosskeys.com*. "Celebrating Excellence in Exporting," Information Supplement, Canadian Business Magazine, February 12, 1999.

In this chapter, we will examine the following questions:

- What factors should a company review before deciding to go abroad?

- How can companies evaluate and select specific foreign markets to enter?

- To what extent must the company adapt its products and marketing program to each foreign country?

- How should the company manage and organize its international activities?

Crosskeys Systems
www.crosskeys.com

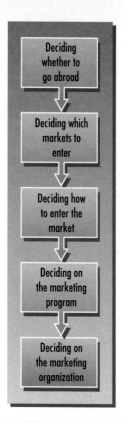

FIGURE 12.1

Major Decisions in International Marketing

The world is rapidly shrinking with the advent of faster communication, transportation, and financial flows. Products developed in one country— Gucci purses, Mont Blanc pens, McDonald's hamburgers, Japanese sushi, Chanel suits, German BMWs— are finding enthusiastic acceptance in other countries. A German businessman may wear an Armani suit to meet an English friend at a Japanese restaurant who later returns home to drink Canadian ice wine and watch *Friends* on TV.

Since 1969, the number of multinational corporations in the world's 14 richest countries has more than tripled, from 7000 to 24 000. In fact, these companies today control one-third of all private-sector assets and enjoy worldwide sales of $9 trillion. Canada is very trade dependent. One job out of every three in Canada depends on our ability to trade abroad. International trade now accounts for 40 percent of our GDP. This compares to the fact that trade only accounts for 25 percent of GDP in the United States. In 1998, export sales expanded by 5.5 percent, with Canadian businesses exporting a record $362 billion in goods and services. Manufactured and processed goods now account for 74 percent of the value to Canadian exports, services account for 12 percent, and raw materials, once the mainstay of Canada's overseas trade, now only make up 14 percent of our export trade.[1]

True, many companies have conducted international marketing for decades. Nestlé, Shell, Bayer, Nortel, and Toshiba are familiar to consumers around the world. But global competition is intensifying: Domestic companies that never thought about foreign competitors suddenly find these competitors in their backyards. Newspapers report on Japanese victories over North American producers in consumer electronics, motorcycles, copying machines, cameras, and watches; the gains of Japanese, German, Swedish, and Korean car imports in the North American market; and the loss of textile and shoe markets to Third World imports. Many companies that are thought to be North American firms are really foreign firms: Bantam Books, Baskin-Robbins Ice Cream, Firestone Tires, Dr. Pepper soft drinks, and Pillsbury cake mixes.

Although some North American businesses may want to eliminate foreign competition through protective legislation, the better way to compete is to continuously improve products at home and expand into foreign markets. Ironically, although companies need to enter and compete in foreign markets, the risks are high: shifting borders, unstable governments, foreign-exchange problems, corruption, and technological pirating.[2] But we argue that companies selling in global industries have no choice but to internationalize their operations. To do this, they must make a series of decisions (see Figure 12.1).

- A *global industry* is an industry in which the strategic positions of competitors in major geographic or national markets are fundamentally affected by their overall global positions.[3] A *global firm* is a firm that operates in more than one country and captures R&D, production, logistical, marketing, and financial advantages in its costs and reputation that are not available to purely domestic competitors.

Global firms plan, operate, and coordinate their activities on a worldwide basis. Ford's "world truck" has a European-made cab and a North American–built chassis, is assembled in Brazil, and is imported into North America for sale. Otis Elevator gets its door systems from France, small geared parts from Spain, electronics from Germany, and special motor drives from Japan, and uses the United States for systems integration. A company need not be large to sell globally. Small and medium-size firms can practise global niche marketing. Even a sports league can be global:

- **The NBA.** When the NBA season is over, basketball's big stars don't head to Florida for rest and recreation. No, Shaquille O'Neal is off to South Korea, Karl Malone to Hong Kong, Allen Iverson to Chile. Deployed by the NBA and global sponsors Coca-Cola, Reebok, and McDonald's, these well-paid travelling salesmen hawk soft drinks, running shoes, burgers, and basketball to legions of young fans. Boys in China wear Bulls gear because they all want to be like Michael Jordan. The NBA, which has 105 global staff members, has emerged as the first truly global sports league. NBA games are televised everywhere, global sponsors have signed up, and the league and its partners have sold nearly $750 million of NBA-licensed basketballs, backboards, T-shirts, and caps outside the United States.[4]

DECIDING WHETHER TO GO ABROAD

Most companies would prefer to remain domestic if their domestic market were large enough. Managers would not need to learn other languages and laws, deal with volatile currencies, face political and legal uncertainties, or redesign their products to suit different customer needs and expectations. Business would be easier and safer.

Yet several factors are drawing more and more companies into the international arena:

- Global firms offering better products or lower prices can attack the company's domestic market. The company might want to counterattack these competitors in their home markets.
- The company discovers that some foreign markets present higher profit opportunities than the domestic market.
- The company needs a larger customer base to achieve economies of scale.
- The company wants to reduce its dependence on any one market.
- The company's customers are going abroad and require international servicing.

Before making a decision to go abroad, the company must weigh several risks:

- The company might not understand foreign customer preferences and fail to offer a competitively attractive product. Table 12.1 lists some famous blunders in this regard.
- The company might not understand the foreign country's business culture or know how to deal effectively with foreign nationals. Table 12.2 lists some of the many challenges.
- The company might underestimate foreign regulations and incur unexpected costs.
- The company might realize that it lacks managers with international experience.
- The foreign country might change its commercial laws, devalue its currency, or undergo a political revolution and expropriate foreign property.

Because of the competing advantages and risks, companies often do not act until some event thrusts them into the international arena. Someone—a domestic exporter, a foreign importer, a foreign government—solicits the company to sell abroad. Or the company is saddled with overcapacity and must find additional markets for its goods.

TABLE 12.1

Blunders in International Marketing

Hallmark cards failed when they were introduced in France. The French dislike syrupy sentiment and prefer writing their own cards.

Philips began to earn a profit in Japan only after it had reduced the size of its coffeemakers to fit into smaller Japanese kitchens and its shavers to fit smaller Japanese hands.

Coca-Cola had to withdraw its two-liter bottle in Spain after discovering that few Spaniards owned refrigerators with large enough compartments to accommodate it.

General Foods' Tang initially failed in France because it was positioned as a substitute for orange juice at breakfast. The French drink little orange juice and almost none at breakfast.

Kellogg's Pop-Tarts failed in Britain because the percentage of British homes with toasters was significantly lower than in the United States, and the product was too sweet for British tastes.

P&G's Crest toothpaste initially failed in Mexico when it used the U.S. campaign. Mexicans did not care as much for the decay-prevention benefit, nor did scientifically oriented advertising appeal to them.

General Foods squandered millions trying to introduce packaged cake mixes to Japanese consumers. The company failed to note that only 3 percent of Japanese homes were equipped with ovens. Then they promoted the idea of baking cakes in Japanese rice cookers, overlooking the fact that the Japanese use their rice cookers throughout the day to keep rice warm and ready.

S. C. Johnson's wax floor polish initially failed in Japan. The wax made the floors too slippery, and Johnson had overlooked the fact that Japanese do not wear shoes in their homes.

TABLE 12.2

Challenges in International Marketing

1. *Huge foreign indebtedness:*	Many countries have accumulated huge foreign debts on which it is difficult to pay even the interest. Among these countries are Indonesia, Mexico, and Russia.
2. *Unstable governments:*	High indebtedness, high inflation, and high unemployment in several countries have resulted in unstable governments that expose foreign firms to the risks of expropriation, nationalization, and limits on profit repatriation. Many companies buy political-risk-assessment reports such as Business International's (BI) Country Assessment Service, BERI, or Frost & Sullivan's World Political Risk Forecasts.
3. *Foreign-exchange problems:*	High indebtedness and economic and political instability decrease the value of a country's currency. Foreign firms want payment in hard currency with profit-repatriation rights, but these options are not available in many markets.
4. *Foreign-government entry requirements and bureaucracy:*	Governments place many regulations on foreign firms. For example, they might require joint ventures with the majority share going to the domestic partner, a high number of nationals to be hired, transfer of technology know-how, and limits on profit repatriation.
5. *Tariffs and other trade barriers:*	Governments often impose high tariffs to protect their industries. They also resort to invisible trade barriers such as slowing down important approvals and inspections, and requiring costly product adjustments.
6. *Corruption:*	Officials award business to the highest briber rather than the lowest bidder. U.S. managers are prohibited by the Foreign Corrupt Practices Act of 1977 from paying bribes, but competitors from other countries operate under no such limitation. The OECD group of leading industrial countries recently agreed that bribery of foreign officials by companies should become a criminal offense.
7. *Technological pirating:*	A company locating its plant abroad worries about foreign managers learning how to make its product and breaking away to compete openly or clandestinely. This has happened in such diverse areas as machinery, electronics, chemicals, and pharmaceuticals.
8. *High cost of product and communication adaptation:*	A company going abroad must study each foreign market carefully, become sensitive to its economics, laws, politics, and culture, and adapt its products and communications to each market's tastes.
9. *Shifting borders:*	National borders are fundamental to marketing because they dominate and shape economic behavior within the country's borders. Changing boundaries may mean moving targets for marketers.

DECIDING WHICH MARKETS TO ENTER

In deciding to go abroad, the company needs to define its international marketing objectives and policies. What proportion of foreign to total sales will it seek? Most companies start small when they venture abroad. Some plan to stay small. Others have bigger plans, believing that their foreign business will eventually be equal to, or even more important than, their domestic business. "Going abroad" on the Internet poses special challenges; see the Marketing for the 21st Century box, "www.The-WorldIsYourOyster.com: The Ins and Outs of Global E-Commerce."

The company must decide whether to market in a few countries or many countries and determine how fast to expand. Consider Tyco:

■ **Tyco Toys Inc.** When Tyco Toys Inc. began expanding into Europe in 1990, a slew of acquisitions and best-sellers at home had propelled the company to fourth place among U.S. toy makers, from twenty-second place only four years before. Yet non-U.S. sales still accounted for only 13 percent of total sales, and the company's rivals had significant overseas sales. Tyco wanted to close the gap quickly and better serve global-minded retailers such as Toys "R" Us. The initial plan was to open one European subsidiary a year, with each expected to turn a profit 12 months later. But the company then speeded up the pace by starting subsidiaries in Italy, Spain, Germany, and Belgium all in one year. Tyco also bought Universal Matchbox Group Ltd., a major Hong Kong producer of die-cast toy vehicles. Tyco's unusually rapid push abroad, coupled with a domestic sales slump, soon strained the ranks of its senior executives, who knew little about running a far-flung empire. In its 1995 annual report, the company reported its third consecutive year of net losses, mainly from Europe. To cut its losses, Tyco ended up liquidating the Italian subsidiary, merging operations in three other countries, and dismissing one-third of its European staff.[5]

In contrast, consider Amway's experience:

■ **Amway**. Known for its neighbour-to-neighbour direct-selling networks, consumer-product company Amway expanded into Australia in 1971, a country far away from but similar to the North American market. In the 1980s, Amway expanded into 10 more countries, and the pace increased rapidly from then on. By 1997, Amway had evolved into a multinational juggernaut with a sales force of 2.5 million hauling in $10.2 billion on doorsteps from Hungary to Malaysia to Brazil. Today, Amway sells products in 43 countries. Its goal: to have overseas markets account for 80 percent of its sales during the next decade. This is not an unrealistic or overly ambitious goal considering that Amway already gains 70 percent of its sales revenue from foreign markets.[6]

Amway
www.amway.com

Generally speaking, it makes sense to operate in fewer countries with a deeper commitment and penetration in each. Ayal and Zif have argued that a company should enter fewer countries when

■ Market entry and market control costs are high.
■ Product and communication adaptation costs are high.
■ Population and income size and growth are high in the initial countries chosen.
■ Dominant foreign firms can establish high barriers to entry.[7]

The company must also decide on the types of countries to consider. Attractiveness is influenced by the product, geography, income and population, political climate, and other factors. The seller might have a predilection for certain countries or regions. Kenichi Ohmae recommends that companies concentrate on selling in the "triad markets"— the United States, Western Europe, and the Far East—because these markets account for a large percent of all international trade.[8]

Although Ohmae's position makes short-run sense, it can spell disaster for the world economy in the long run. The unmet needs of the developing world represent huge potential markets for food, clothing, shelter, consumer electronics, appliances, and other goods. Many market leaders are now rushing into Eastern Europe, China, Vietnam, and Cuba where there are many unmet needs to satisfy.

Regional economic integration—trading agreements between blocs of countries—has intensified in recent years. This development means that companies are more likely to enter entire regions overseas rather than do business with one nation at a time.

www.TheWorldIsYourOyster.com: The Ins and Outs of Global E-commerce

Just a few years ago, Cardiac Science was itching to break into foreign markets, but it didn't know where to start. The company knew there was an overseas market for its medical devices and products, but figuring out how to get to that market is a challenge for small companies. Fast forward to today: Fully 85 percent of Cardiac's revenue is international. A growing number of Cardiac Science's overseas customers are simply finding the company's defibrillators and heart monitors by clicking on www.cardiacscience.com.

Companies small and large are taking advantage of cyberspace's vanishing national boundaries. Major marketers doing global e-commerce range from automakers (General Motors) to direct-mail companies (Mountain Equipment Co-op, L.L. Bean, and Lands' End) to running-shoe giants (Nike and Reebok) to Internet superstars like Amazon.com, which purchased three European companies to build its European book and video sales. Small firms, like Toronto's Image Control, have doubled their business since going on-line. The firm sells and recycles toner cartridges for fax machines, printers, and copiers. In 1998, it shipped products in 39 U.S. states and nine countries without spending a cent on foreign advertising.

For some, marketing has been a hit-or-miss affair. They put up content in English for the North American market, and if any international users stumble across it and end up buying something, great. Hyperspace Cowgirls, a three-year-old, New York City–based developer of children's software, has several European deals in the works even though it has no marketing effort overseas. "We don't advertise overseas at all," says Susan Shaw, president of the company, whose web address is www.hygirls.com. "People just find you."

Other marketers have made a strategic decision to become part of the global cyberbazaar. They're using the Web and on-line services to reach new customers outside their home countries, to support existing customers who live abroad, to source from international suppliers, and to build global brand awareness. Some of these companies adapt their Web sites to provide country-specific content and services to their best potential international markets, ideally in the local language. Reebok has launched a multilingual European Web site— available in English, French, German, Spanish, and Italian—in an attempt to increase brand awareness in its individual markets. The site, located at www.europe.reebok.com, is aimed at sports and fitness enthusiasts and includes local events in each market. Because of the expected global e-commerce boom, some enterprising companies are making Internet transactions between different countries much easier and effective. For instance, in 1998 Digital Equipment Corporation and Globalink began offering automated e-mail and Web translation.

Yet, before companies have their Web pages automatically translated, they need to find the countries or regions with the largest potential on-line populations. Right now Europe and Japan are prime targets. Europe had lagged about four years behind North America, but it's catching up quickly: On-line subscribers are expected to grow from 7 percent of Europe's population in 1998 to 13 percent in 2001. Several factors promise to quicken that pace. Once telephone deregulation takes hold in Europe, Internet usage will certainly surge. Europeans may also move faster because they don't have to retrofit systems or go

(continued)

REGIONAL FREE TRADE ZONES

Certain countries have formed free trade zones or economic communities—groups of nations organized to work toward common goals in the regulation of international trade. One such community is the European Union (EU). Formed in 1957, the European Union set out to create a single European market by reducing barriers to the free flow of products, services, finances, and labour among member countries and developing policies on trade with non-member nations. Today, the European Union is using a common currency, the euro monetary system. In 1998, 11 participating countries locked their exchange rates together, as a first step in a multiyear plan for a common currency (Britain, Denmark, and Sweden are the holdouts, so far). The euro coins and bills that will eventually replace member countries' currencies will not be in circulation until 2002, and businesses and private citizens will not be required to switch before then. While some analysts predict that the new euro will rival the U.S. dollar as the standard for international trade, others say it won't pose much of a threat because it is a currency without a track record.

through a pioneer phase. Europe and Canada are slightly ahead of the United States when it comes to secure transactions. Visa, in fact, has chosen the EC for its largest pilot program to test security. Also, as European businesses invest some $125 billion to prepare computers for the euro, they are simultaneously putting their businesses on-line. A 150-year-old Italian winemaker, Casa Garcia, now uses the Internet to replace annual communications traffic of 35 000 faxes and letters between its offices, warehouses, and agents. With the Web, it is extending its network to 60 countries.

Despite encouraging e-commerce developments in Europe and Asia, Internet marketers sometimes overstate global opportunities. Although Hong Kong alone had more than 90 Internet service providers, less developed countries in Central and South America or Africa have fewer or none at all, forcing users to make international calls to go on-line. Because the backbone for the Internet originates in the United States, response times overseas can be dismal. Even with acceptable phone lines and PC penetration, high connection costs sharply restrict Internet use. In Europe, Internet subscriptions typically run $110 a month, triple the North American rates that allow unlimited Internet access on free local lines.

In addition, the global marketer may run up against governmental or cultural restrictions. In Germany, a vendor can't accept payment via credit card until two weeks after an order has been sent. You also can't display a swastika on a computer screen. So, if Amazon.com has a book on Nazi Germany with a swastika on the cover, is it legally responsible for breaking German law? The issue of who pays sales taxes and duties on global e-commerce is murkier still.

Finally, businesses need to realize that the Web does not offer complete solutions for transacting global business—and probably never will. Most companies will never cut a final deal via e-mail. People will still need to see and feel products at international trade shows. The Web will not surmount customs red tape or local regulations regarding import or export of certain goods. The Web also can't guarantee that goods will arrive in perfect condition.

What the Web can do is make foreign customers aware of one's business. The Web has certainly done that for upscale retailer and cataloguer The Sharper Image, which now gets a full 25 percent of its on-line business from overseas customers. The company is thrilled about its global prospects but admits it is still overwhelmed by the logistical challenges of serving overseas markets, such as language and currency issues.

Sources: Dawn Walton, "Small Business Clicking on Electronic Commerce," *Globe and Mail*, May 5, 1999, p. B10. Alice LaPlante, "Global Boundaries.com," *Computerworld*, October 6, 1997, pp. G6–G9; Roberta Maynard, "Trade Links via the Internet," *Nation's Business*, December 1997, pp. 51–53; Michelle V. Rafter, "Multilingual Sites Give Companies Access to Global Revenue Sources," *Chicago Tribune*, May 11, 1998, Business Section, p. 9; Marla Dickerson, "Small Business Strategies; Technology; Foreign Concept; All Those Inflated Expectations Aside, Many Firms Are Finding the Internet Invaluable in Pursuing International Trade," *Los Angeles Times*, October 14, 1998, pp. C2, C10; Stephen Baker, Finally, Europeans Are Storming the Net," *Business Week*, May 11, 1998, p. 48; Eric J. Adams, "Ready, SET, Go!" *World Trade*, April 1997, pp. 34–35; "Reebok Targets Its New Web Site at Euro Markets," *Marketing*, October 1, 1998, p. 16; Peter Krasilovsky, "A Whole New World," *Marketing Tools* supplement, *American Demographics*, May 1996, pp. 22–25; Richard N. Miller, "The Year Ahead," *Direct Marketing*, January 1997, pp. 42–44; Jack Gee, "Parlez-Vous Inter-Net?" *Industry Week*, April 21, 1997, pp. 78–79.

Today, the European Union represents one of the world's single largest markets. Its 15 member countries contain more than 370 million consumers and account for 20 percent of the world's exports. As more European nations seek admission to the EU in the twenty-first century, it could contain as many as 450 million people in 28 countries.

European unification offers tremendous trade opportunities. The GDP of the trade block is $9.5 trillion compared to $11.7 trillion for the U.S. and $6.3 trillion for Japan. Canada's merchandise exports to Europe grew by 3.8 percent in 1998 largely due to the depreciation of the Canadian dollar relative to European currencies. While the EU can present opportunities, it also poses threats. As a result of increased unification, European companies will grow bigger and more competitive. Witness the competition in the consulting engineering business, for example. European firms compete with those from Canada for lucrative contracts in former Eastern bloc countries and Asian markets. Canadian banks attempted to merge so that they could better compete with their European and other global rivals. Perhaps an even bigger concern, however, is that lower barriers inside Europe will only create thicker outside walls. Some observers envision a "fortress Europe" that heaps favours on firms from EU countries but hinders outsiders by imposing obstacles such as stiffer import quotas, local content requirements, and other non-tariff (non-tax) barriers.

Also, companies that plan to create "pan-European" marketing campaigns directed to a unified Europe should proceed with caution. Even if the European Union truly does manage to standardize its general trade regulations, creating an economic community will not create a homogenous market. Companies marketing in Europe face 14 different languages, 2000 years of historical and cultural differences, and a daunting mass of local rules. Consider the experience of the acclaimed Leo Burnett ad agency when it took on the goal of creating a single European campaign for United Distillers' Johnnie Walker account:

- **Johnnie Walker.** It was only after many painful tests and revisions that the final ad rolled out and achieved success. In an ad with the headline "The Water of Life," a man attends the running of the bulls in Pamplona and, after narrowly escaping being trampled, celebrates with a glass of Johnnie Walker Red Label. In many countries, the Pamplona setting raised hackles because people said, "The Spanish don't know anything about whiskey." The ad was a total failure in Germany because to Germans it seemed simply reckless. "Also," said Jenny Vaughn, worldwide brand director for Johnnie Walker, "because of the German animal rights campaigners, you can't show a goldfish in a goldfish bowl on German television, so a bull run was just not on."[9]

The most successful pan-European ads are those that are highly visual and symbolic. These ads focus on the product and consumer and are aimed at one of the two audiences that market researchers really agree are turning into Euroconsumers—the young and the rich. One such ad is for TAG Heuer watches in which a swimmer races a shark, a hurdler leaps over an oversized razor blade, and a relay runner grabs a dynamite baton, all mind games that athletes everywhere use to rev up their performance.

The United States and Canada phased out trade barriers in 1989. The U.S.-Canada trading relationship is the largest in the world, with over $550 billion in two-way trade taking place each year. Since the advent of the U.S.-Canada Free Trade Agreement on January 1, 1989, trade between the two countries has more than doubled. In January 1994, the North American Free Trade Agreement (NAFTA) established a free trade zone among the United States, Mexico, and Canada. The agreement created a single market of 360 million people who produce and consume $10 trillion worth of goods and services. As it is implemented over a 15-year period, NAFTA will eliminate all trade barriers and investment restrictions among the three countries. In 1998 alone, Canada's export trade with the United States grew by 8.5 percent, with Canada's export sales reaching a record $265 billion. Primary U.S. markets for Canadian goods are automotive products, industrial materials and equipment, computer equipment, energy, paper, and primary metals.

Other free trade areas are forming in Latin America and South America. For example, MERCOSUL now links Brazil, Colombia, and Mexico. Chile and Mexico have formed a successful free trade zone. MERCOSUL not only represents a huge marketing opportunity with its 220 million consumers; its entire Pacific Coast also beckons towards Asia. Thus, the region stands to become an important low-cost platform for world export. Venezuela, Colombia, and Mexico—the "Group of Three"—are also negotiating a free trade area. It is likely that NAFTA will eventually merge with this and other arrangements to form an all-Americas free trade zone.

Firms from European nations have often been more successful in tapping this market's enormous potential than have North American firms. When Latin and South American countries instituted market reforms and privatized public utilities, European companies rushed in to grab up lucrative contracts for rebuilding Latin America's infrastructure. Spain's Telefonica de Espana has spent $7.5 billion buying phone companies in Brazil, Chile, Peru, and Argentina. European companies have moved rapidly into the private sector. In Brazil, seven of the ten largest private companies are European owned, compared to two controlled by Americans. Among the notable European companies operating in Latin America are automotive giants Volkswagen and Fiat, the French supermarket chain Carrefours, and the Anglo-Dutch personal care products group Gessy-Lever.

The European dominance of Latin American trade may be slipping. Canada's exports to the region grew by 20 percent in 1998 and are expected to grow another 12 percent in 1999. The one South American country in which Canada has been particularly successful is Chile. The two countries recently instituted a free trade agreement that paves the way for increased trade between the two countries. Canada's investment in Chile currently totals $2.4 billion and the Export Development Corporation forecasts that this could double in the near future. Trade between the two countries is over $700 million. Canada's main exports to Chile include grain, machinery, minerals, and paper, while Canada imports Chilean fruits, copper, wine, and seafood.[10]

Eighteen Pacific Rim countries, including the NAFTA member states, Japan, and China, have been discussing the possible creation of a pan-Pacific free trade area under the auspices of the Asian Pacific Economic Cooperation forum (APEC). There are also active attempts at regional economic integration in the Caribbean, Southeast Asia, and parts of Africa.

Yet, however much nations and regions integrate their trading policies and standards, each nation still has unique features that must be understood. A nation's readiness for different products and services and its attractiveness as a market to foreign firms depend on its economic, political–legal, and cultural environments.

EVALUATING POTENTIAL MARKETS

Suppose a company has assembled a list of potential markets to enter. How does it choose among them? Many companies prefer to sell to neighbouring countries because they understand these countries better, and they can control their costs better. At other times, *psychic proximity* determines choices. Many Canadian firms prefer to sell in England or Australia—rather than in larger markets such as Germany and France—because they feel more comfortable with the language, laws, and culture. It is not surprising that the United States is Canada's largest market, or that Swedish companies first sold to their Scandinavian neighbours. As growing numbers of Canadian companies expand abroad, many are deciding the best place to start is next door, in the United States. Despite its size and apparent similarities, it is not an easy market to crack as many retailers have recently discovered.

Future Shop
www.futureshop.com

■ **Future Shop Ltd.** The Vancouver-based electronics retailer closed its 23 U.S. outlets that had generated 19 percent of its sales in 1999. The decision marked years of struggle to make it south of the border. Retailing electronic products is a tough business on either side of the border. Margins are razor-thin and rapid advances in technology make inventory obsolescence a looming threat. Future Shop just couldn't make inroads against the likes of Best Buy Inc. and Circuit City. Rather than continuing to fight a losing battle, Future Shop has decided to expand its Canadian business and open an Internet operation so that it can take advantage of borderless retailing.

When Canadian retailers attack U.S. markets, they often find the competition more intense and change is more rapid than they expected. Moreover, U.S. retailers often have the advantage of larger size and name recognition over their Canadian rivals. Until recently only 20 percent of retailers entering the U.S. market succeeded. Mark's Work Wearhouse, Second Cup Ltd., Canadian Tire, and People's Jewellers have all tested the U.S. waters, only to withdraw in defeat. Today, however, the success rate has risen to 50 percent. Retailers such as Harry Rosen, Club Monaco, and Jean Coutu have led the charge. The more successful entrants have tended to be smaller, specialized retailers that aim at niche markets where they don't have to challenge U.S. competitors head on.[11]

In general, a company prefers to enter countries (1) that rank high on market attractiveness, (2) that are low in market risk, and (3) in which the company possesses a competitive advantage. Here's how Bechtel Corporation, the construction giant, goes about evaluating overseas markets.

■ **Bechtel Corporation.** Before Bechtel ventures into new markets, the company starts with a detailed strategic market analysis. It looks at its markets over the next five to ten years and tries to determine where it should be in four or five years' time. A management team looks at the big picture and does a cost–benefit analysis that factors in the position of competitors, infrastructure, regulatory and trade barriers, and the tax situation (both corporate and individual). Ideally, the new market would be a country with an untapped need for its products or services; a quality, skilled labour pool capable of manufacturing the product; and a welcoming environment (governmental and physical).

Are there countries that meet Bechtel's requirements? Each has its pluses and minuses. For instance, although Singapore has an educated, English-speaking labour force, basks in political stability, and encourages foreign investment, it has a small population. Although many countries in central Europe possess an eager, hungry-to-learn labour pool, their infrastructures create difficulties. The team evaluating a new market must determine whether the company could earn enough on its investment to cover the risk factors or other negatives.[12]

DECIDING HOW TO ENTER THE MARKET

Once a company decides to target a particular country, it has to determine the best mode of entry. Its broad choices are *indirect exporting, direct exporting, licensing, joint ventures,* and *direct investment.* These five market-entry strategies are shown in Figure 12.2. Each succeeding strategy involves more commitment, risk, control, and profit potential.

INDIRECT EXPORT

The normal way to get involved in a foreign market is through export. *Occasional exporting* is a passive level of involvement in which the company exports from time to time, either on its own initiative or in response to unsolicited orders from abroad. *Active exporting* takes place when the company makes a commitment to expand its exports to a particular market. In either case, the company produces its goods in the home country and might or might not adapt them to the foreign market.

Companies typically start with *indirect exporting*—that is, they work through independent intermediaries to export their product. There are four types of intermediaries: *Domestic-based export merchants* buy the manufacturer's products and then sell them abroad. *Domestic-based export agents* seek and negotiate foreign purchases and are paid a commission. Included in this group are trading companies. *Cooperative organizations* carry on exporting activities on behalf of several producers and are partly under their administrative control. They are often used by producers of primary products such as fruits or nuts. *Export-management companies* agree to manage a company's export activities for a fee. Indirect export has two advantages. First, it involves less investment. The firm does not have to develop an export department, an overseas sales force, or a set of foreign contacts. Second, it involves less risk. Because international-marketing intermediaries bring know-how and services to the relationship, the seller will normally make fewer mistakes.

DIRECT EXPORT

Companies eventually may decide to handle their own exports. The investment and risk are somewhat greater, but so is the potential return. Nelson Homes of Lloydminster, Alberta, has been extremely successful in selling "whole houses" directly into the Japanese market. It loads the prefabricated, numbered pieces into two containers and ships them to Japanese developers. University Games of Burlingame, California, has blossomed into a $75-million-per-year international company through careful entry into overseas ventures.

■ **University Games.** Bob Moog, president and founder of University Games, says that his company's international sales strategy relies heavily on third-party distributors and has a fair degree of flexibility. "We identify the foreign markets we want to penetrate," says Moog, "and then form a business venture with a local distributor that will give us a large degree of control. In Australia, we expect to run a print of 5000 board games. These we will manufacture in the United States. If we reach a run of 25 000 games, however, we would then establish a sub-contracting venture with a local manufacturer in Australia or New Zealand to print the games."[13]

A company can carry on direct exporting in several ways:

■ *Domestic-based export department or division:* Might evolve into a self-contained export department operating as a profit centre.

■ *Overseas sales branch or subsidiary:* The sales branch handles sales and distribution and might handle warehousing and promotion as well. It often serves as a display and customer service centre.

■ *Travelling export sales representatives:* Home-based sales representatives are sent abroad to find business.

■ *Foreign-based distributors or agents:* These distributors and agents might be given exclusive rights to represent the company in that country or only limited rights.

Whether companies decide to export indirectly or directly, many companies use exporting as a way to "test the waters" before building a plant and manufacturing a product overseas. This strategy worked well for IPSCO, Inc. In the early 1980s, this Saskatchewan-based steel producer exported its steel pipe and flat steel to the United States from Canada—despite significant transportation costs. Once the company realized there was a significant U.S. demand for its products, it decided to set up shop there.[14]

One of the best ways to initiate or extend export activities is by exhibiting at an overseas trade show. A Canadian software firm might show its product at an international software expo in Hong Kong. With the World Wide Web, it may not even be necessary to attend trade shows to show one's wares to overseas buyers and distributors. Electronic communication via the Internet is extending the reach of companies, particularly small ones, to worldwide markets. The Internet has become an effective means of everything from gaining free exporting information and guidelines, conducting market research, and offering customers several time zones away a secure process for ordering and paying for products. See Table 12.3 for five sources of free on-line exporting help. Then check the Marketing Memo "Making Your Web Site Worldwide and Worldly Wise" for tips on Web sites that attract, rather than frustrate, overseas customers.

LICENSING

Licensing is a simple way to become involved in international marketing. The licensor licenses a foreign company to use a manufacturing process, trademark, patent, trade secret, or other item of value for a fee or royalty. The licensor gains entry at little risk; the licensee gains production expertise or a well-known product or brand name. E-Trade Group, the Palo Alto, California, on-line broker-dealer, has entered into

(continued)

even with every transaction in the home currency of the visitor. Finally, for apparel companies, don't forget to include size conversion tables so overseas customers can figure out sizes.

■ Avoid alphanumeric fields in forms, and make address fields internationally meaningful: It sounds like a tiny detail, but people do get annoyed when registration or order forms refuse to recognize punctuation such as accents. Also, address fields should accommodate international postal codes. Most countries don't have a postal counterpart to a state, so don't require every visitor to the site to specify one.

■ Provide enough information about your company, and make contact information prominent: The portion of a Web site that provides company information is typically one of the most frequently visited areas. Providing as much detail as possible about your company's strengths is a good way to establish credibility, which is particularly critical for a small business that is unknown overseas. Also, don't bury contact information——names, telephone numbers, or fax numbers——deep within the site. Make it as clear and visible as possible.

■ Don't leave site development to the technicians: Involve your marketing people so you can ensure that your site is consistent with the image you want to project. You may even want to have your Web site vetted by an overseas rep or supplier to make sure it appeals to the foreign market you wish to reach.

Sources: Eric J. Adams, "Electronic Commerce Goes Global," *World Trade,* April 1998, pp. 90–92; Roberta Maynard, "Creating an Export-Friendly Site," *Nation's Business,* December 1997, p. 51; J. D. Mosely-Matchett, "Remember, It's the World Wide Web," *Marketing News,* January 20, 1997, p. 16.

TABLE	12.3

Going On-line for Exporting Help

Finding free information about trade and exporting has never been easier. Here are some places to start your search:

■ For answers to the most frequently asked questions about trade in general and for market information on regions and countries, you can call Team Canada Inc. at 1-888-811-1119 or visit their Web site http://exportsource.gc.ca. You can also try www.ita.doc.gov (the U.S. Department of Commerce's International Trade Administration).

■ For information about obtaining working capital, direct loans, financing guarantees, and export insurance: www.edcinfo.com (the Export Development Corporation, the organization that tailors its services to meet the needs of small Canadian exporters. It helped 3500 small and medium sized exporters do business in over 130 markets last year).

■ For notices about international business opportunities and worldwide tender calls, you can visit the Department of Foreign Affairs and International Trade's CanadExport Online: www.dfait-maeci.gc.ca/english/news/newsletr/canex.

■ To access market research reports that focus on specific sectors or specific countries, the Department of Foreign Affairs and International Trade's InfoExport site can be easily accessed (http://www.infoexport.gc.ca/section2).

■ To get information about thousands of trade shows and conferences around the world: www.tscentral.com (Trade Show Central, a Wellesley, Massachusetts, company).

Also, check with your province's export-promotion office to learn if it has on-line resources and allows businesses to link to its site. For example, you can access Ontario's site at www.ontario-canada.com/export.

Sources: "CanadExport," Department of Foreign Affairs and International Trade, Vol 17, (9), May 17, 1999, "Going On-line for Exporting Help," Nation's Business, December 1997, p. 52.

a licensing agreement with Jerusalem Global Ltd., an Israeli investment banking operation. E-Trade's agreement with the Israeli firm is part of a strategy to form licensing agreements and international joint ventures in an effort to bring its brand of no-frills investing to people abroad. E-Trade has already created E-Trade Australia and has announced plans to form E-Trade Germany and E-Trade Central Europe.[15]

Licensing has some potential disadvantages. The licensor has less control over the licensee than if it had set up its own production and sales facilities. Furthermore, if the licensee is very successful, the firm has given up profits; and if and when the contract ends, the company might find that it has created a competitor. To avoid this, the licensor usually supplies some proprietary ingredients or components needed in the product (as Coca-Cola does). But the best strategy is for the licensor to lead in innovation so that the licensee will continue to depend on the licensor.

There are several variations on a licensing arrangement. Companies such as Hyatt and Marriott sell *management contracts* to owners of foreign hotels to manage these businesses for a fee. The management firm may even be given the option to purchase some share in the managed company within a stated period.

Another variation is *contract manufacturing*, in which the firm hires local manufacturers to produce the product. When Sears opened department stores in Mexico and Spain, it found qualified local manufacturers to produce many of its products. Contract manufacturing has the drawback of giving the company less control over the manufacturing process and the loss of potential profits on manufacturing. However, it offers a chance to start faster, with less risk and with the opportunity to form a partnership or buy out the local manufacturer later.

Finally, a company can enter a foreign market through *franchising*, which is a more complete form of licensing. The franchiser offers a complete brand concept and operating system. In return, the franchisee invests in and pays certain fees to the franchiser. McDonald's, KFC, and Avis have entered scores of countries by franchising their retail concepts.

Along with McDonald's, Kentucky Fried Chicken (KFC) was one of the first fast-food franchises to break into the semi-closed market of Japan.

■ **KFC Corporation.** Although the initial reception in Japan was great, KFC still had a number of obstacles to overcome. The Japanese were uncomfortable with the idea of fast food and franchising. They saw fast food as artificial, made by mechanical means, and unhealthy. KFC's ad agency in Japan, Mc-Cann-Erickson Japan, knew that it had to build trust in the KFC brand and flew to Kentucky to do it. There it filmed the most authentic version of Colonel Sanders' beginnings possible. To show the philosophy of KFC—the southern hospitality, old American tradition, and authentic home cooking—the agency first created the quintessential southern mother. With "My Old Kentucky Home" by Stephen Foster playing in the background, the commercial showed Colonel Sanders' mother making and feeding her grandchildren KFC chicken made with 11 secret spices. It conjured up scenes of good home cookin' from the deep American South delivered straight to the Japanese people. In the end, the Japanese people could not get enough of this special American chicken made with 11 spices. The campaign was hugely successful, and in less than eight years KFC expanded its presence from 400 locations to more than 1000. Many Japanese now know "My Old Kentucky Home" by heart.[16]

KFC Corporation
www.kfc.com

JOINT VENTURES

Foreign investors may join with local investors to create a joint venture company in which they share ownership and control. For instance:[17]

■ Coca-Cola and Nestlé joined forces to develop the international market for "ready to drink" tea and coffee, which currently sell in significant amounts only in Japan.

chapter 12
Designing
Global Market
Offerings

- Procter & Gamble formed a joint venture with its Italian arch-rival Fater to cover babies' bottoms in the United Kingdom and Italy.

- Whirlpool took a 53 percent stake in the Dutch electronics group Philips's white-goods business to leapfrog into the European market.

- TD Bank's Financial Group joined New York-based Waterhouse to become the world's second-largest discount broker. The venture is focusing on targeting new customers in the U.S., Germany, France, and Asia, whereas in Canada the focus will be on customer retention.

Forming a joint venture may be necessary or desirable for economic or political reasons. The foreign firm might lack the financial, physical, or managerial resources to undertake the venture alone. Or the foreign government might require joint ownership as a condition for entry. Even corporate giants need joint ventures to crack the toughest markets. When it wanted to enter China's ice-cream market, Unilever joined forces with Sumstar, a state-owned Chinese investment company. The venture's general manager says Sumstar's help with the formidable Chinese bureaucracy was crucial in getting a high-tech ice-cream plant up and running in just 12 months.[18]

Joint ownership has certain drawbacks. The partners might disagree over investment, marketing, or other policies. One partner might want to reinvest earnings for growth, and the other partner might want to declare more dividends. The failure of the joint venture between AT&T and Olivetti was due to the companies' inability to agree on strategy. Furthermore, joint ownership can prevent a multinational company from carrying out specific manufacturing and marketing policies on a worldwide basis.

DIRECT INVESTMENT

The ultimate form of foreign involvement is direct ownership of foreign-based assembly or manufacturing facilities. The foreign company can buy part or full interest in a local company or build its own facilities. If the foreign market appears large enough, foreign production facilities offer distinct advantages. First, the firm secures cost economies in the form of cheaper labour or raw materials, foreign-government investment incentives, and freight savings. Second, the firm strengthens its image in the host country because it creates jobs. Third, the firm develops a deeper relationship with government, customers, local suppliers, and distributors, enabling it to adapt its products better to the local environment. Fourth, the firm retains full control over its investment and therefore can develop manufacturing and marketing policies that serve its long-term international objectives. Fifth, the firm assures itself access to the market in case the host country starts insisting that locally purchased goods have domestic content. Here is how one firm uses local relationships to advantage in its overseas plants.

- **CPC Internationale.** CPC, manufacturer of such well-known food brands as Hellmann's Mayonnaise and the Knorr's line of soups, prefers full-scale overseas manufacturing to either foreign product assembly or exporting. So far, the company manufactures in 62 of the 110 countries in which it markets its products. CPC uses local personnel and managers almost exclusively when operating overseas, particularly people who understand the markets and who can compete effectively within them. CPC also hands off marketing to local managers, figuring that they know their own markets and how to compete there better than the folks back at their headquarters do.[19]

The main disadvantage of direct investment is that the firm exposes a large investment to risks such as blocked or devalued currencies, worsening markets, or expropriation. The firm will find it expensive to reduce or close down its operations, because the host country might require substantial severance pay to the employees.

THE INTERNATIONALIZATION PROCESS

Most countries lament that too few of their companies participate in foreign trade. This keeps the country from earning sufficient foreign exchange to pay for needed imports. Many governments sponsor aggressive export-promotion programs to get their companies to export. These programs require a deep understanding of how companies become internationalized.

Johanson and Wiedersheim-Paul have studied the *internationalization process* among Swedish companies.[20] They see firms moving through four stages:

1. No regular export activities

2. Export via independent representatives (agents)

3. Establishment of one or more sales subsidiaries

4. Establishment of production facilities abroad

The first task is to get companies to move from stage 1 to stage 2. This move is helped by studying how firms make their first export decisions.[21] Most firms work with an independent agent and enter a nearby or similar country. A company then engages further agents to enter additional countries. Later, it establishes an export department to manage its agent relationships. Still later, the company replaces its agents with its own sales subsidiaries in its larger export markets. This increases the company's investment and risk but also its earning potential. To manage these subsidiaries, the company replaces the export department with an international department. If certain markets continue to be large and stable, or if the host country insists on local production, the company takes the next step of locating production facilities in those markets, representing a still larger commitment and still larger potential earnings. By this time, the company is operating as a multinational company and engaged in optimizing its global sourcing, financing, manufacturing, and marketing.

DECIDING ON THE MARKETING PROGRAM

International companies must decide how much to adapt their marketing strategy to local conditions. At one extreme are companies that use a globally *standardized marketing mix* worldwide. Standardization of the product, advertising, and distribution channels promises the lowest costs. At the other extreme is an *adapted marketing mix*, where the producer adjusts the marketing-mix elements to each target market. The Marketing Insight box, "Global Standardization or Adaptation?" discusses the main issues.

Between the two extremes, many possibilities exist. Here we will examine potential adaptations that firms might make to their product, promotion, price, and distribution as they enter foreign markets.

PRODUCT

Keegan has distinguished five adaptation strategies of product and promotion to a foreign market (Figure 12.3).[22]

Straight extension means introducing the product in the foreign market without any change. Top management instructs its salespeople: "Find customers for the product as it is." However, the company should first determine whether foreign consumers

	Product		
	Do Not Change Product	Adapt Product	Develop New Product
Do Not Change Promotion	Straight extension	Product adaptation	Product invention
Adapt Promotion	Communication adaptation	Dual adaptation	

FIGURE 12.3

Five International Product and Promotion Strategies

GLOBAL STANDARDIZATION OR ADAPTATION?

The marketing concept holds that consumer needs vary and that marketing programs will be more effective when they are tailored to each target group. This also applies to foreign markets where economic, political, and cultural conditions vary widely.

Yet in 1983, in a groundbreaking article in the *Harvard Business Review*, Harvard Professor Theodore Levitt challenged this view and supplied the intellectual rationale for global standardization:

> The world is becoming a common marketplace in which people—no matter where they live—desire the same products and lifestyles. Global companies must forget the idiosyncratic differences between countries and cultures and instead concentrate on satisfying universal drives.

Levitt wrote that new communication and transportation technologies are creating a more homogeneous world market. His words have proved prophetic. The development of the World Wide Web, the rapid spread of cable and satellite TV around the world, and the creation of telecommunications networks linking previously remote places have all brought Levitt's predictions closer to fruition. For instance, the disproportionately American programming beamed into homes in the developing world has sparked a convergence of consumer appetites, particularly among youth. A "global MTV generation" is what Joseph Quinlan, senior economist at Dean, Witter Reynolds, calls these emerging consumers. Says Quinlan, "They prefer Coke to tea, Nikes to sandals, and Chicken McNuggets to rice, credit cards to cash." Fashion trends are moving almost instantly, propelled by TV and Internet chat groups. Buzz on new movies and TV shows can be accessed anywhere in the world at the ain't.it.cool Web site (www.ain't.it.cool.com). The convergence of needs and wants has created global markets for standardized products, particularly among the young middle class.

According to Levitt, traditional multinational corporations don't focus on the convergence of tastes in the global market but on the differences between specific markets. They produce a proliferation of highly adapted products. The result is less efficiency and higher prices to consumers.

In contrast, Levitt favours global corporations that try to sell the same product the same way to all consumers. They focus on similarities across world markets and "sensibly force suitably standardized products and services on the entire globe." These global marketers achieve substantial economies through standardization of production, distribution, marketing, and management. They translate their efficiency into greater value for consumers by offering high quality and more reliable products at lower prices. Coca-Cola, McDonald's, Marlboro, Nike, the NBA, and Gillette are among the companies that have successfully marketed global products. Consider Gillette:

> Some 1.2 billion people use at least one Gillette product daily, according to the company's latest estimates. Gillette razors—the product from which the company derives 50 percent of its $2.4 billion operating profit—have captured 91 percent of the market in Latin America and 69 percent in India. Gillette enjoys huge economies of scale by selling a few types of razor blades in every single market. Currently, the company faces challenges when trying to sell its higher-priced high-tech razors, such as Sensor and

(continued)

use that product. Deodorant usage among men ranges from 80 percent in North America to 55 percent in Sweden to 28 percent in Italy to 8 percent in the Philippines. In interviewing women in one country about how often they used a deodorant, a typical response was "I use it when I go dancing once a year": hardly grounds for introducing the product.

Straight extension has been successful with cameras, consumer electronics, and many machine tools. In other cases, it has been a disaster. General Foods introduced its standard powdered Jell-O in the British market only to find that British consumers prefer the solid wafer or cake form. Campbell Soup lost an estimated $45 million in introducing its condensed soups in England; consumers saw expensive small-sized cans and did not realize that water needed to be added. Straight extension is tempting because it involves no additional R&D expense, manufacturing retooling, or promotional modification. But it can be costly in the long run.

Product adaptation involves altering the product to meet local conditions or preferences. There are several levels of adaptation. A company can produce a *regional version* of its product, such as a Western European version. Finnish cellular-phone superstar Nokia customized its 6100 series phone for every major market. Developers built in rudimentary voice recognition for Asia, where keyboards are a problem and raised the ring volume so the phone could be heard on crowded Asian streets. Or it can produce a *country version*. In Japan, Mister Donut's coffee cup is smaller and lighter

(continued)

the newly unveiled Mach3, in countries that underwent currency devaluation. Still, Gillette has no plans to give up its global focus.

Impressed with the potential savings from global standardization, many companies have tried to launch their version of a world product. Toyota had built its Corolla on a world platform, and Ford is currently creating a world car, the Focus. Yet, most products require some adaptation. Toyota's Corolla will exhibit some differences in styling. McDonald's uses chili sauce instead of ketchup on its hamburgers in Mexico. Coca-Cola is sweeter or less carbonated in certain countries. Procter & Gamble knows that Asian shoppers shy away from the family-size packages so popular with Americans. Most of the shampoo P&G sells in the Far East is in single-use sachets.

Whereas companies are justified in seeking standardization to save some costs, local competitors are always ready to offer more of what customers in each country want. Even MTV, which provided the label for the "global MTV generation" with its largely global programming, has retrenched along more local lines:

Pummelled by dozens of local music channels in Europe, such as Germany's Viva, Holland's The Music Factory, and Scandinavia's ZTV, MTV Europe has had to drop its pan-European programming, which featured a large amount of American and British pop along with local European favourites. In its place, the division created regional channels broadcast by four separate MTV stations: MTV UK, and Northern, Central, and Southern Europe. Each of the four channels shows programs tailored to music tastes of its local market, along with more traditional pan-European pop selections and, of course, a healthy serving of Beavis and Butthead.

Rather than assuming that its domestic product can be introduced as is in another country, the company should review the following adaptation elements and determine which would add more revenue than cost:

- Product features
- Colors
- Advertising themes
- Brand name
- Materials
- Advertising media
- Labeling
- Prices
- Advertising execution
- Packaging
- Sales promotion

One study showed that companies made one or more marketing-mix adaptations in 80 percent of their foreign products and that the average number of adapted elements was four. Some host countries require adaptations, whether or not the company wants to make them. The French do not allow children to be used in ads; the Germans ban the use of the word best to describe a product.

So perhaps Levitt's globalization dictum should be rephrased. Global marketing, yes.

Global standardization, not necessarily.

Sources: Theodore Levitt, "The Globalization of Markets," *Harvard Business Review*, May–June 1983, pp. 92–102; Bernard Wysocki Jr., "The Global Mall: In Developing Nations, Many Youths Splurge, Mainly on U.S. Goods," *Wall Street Journal*, June 26, 1997, p. A1; "What Makes a Company Great?" *Fortune*, October 26, 1998, pp. 218–26; Lawrence Donegan, "Heavy Job Rotation MTV Europe Sacks 80 Employees in the Name of 'Regionalisation.' Is This the End for Europop as We Know It, Asks Lawrence Donegan," *The Guardian*, November 21, 1997, p. 19; David M. Szymanski, Sundar G. Bharadwaj, and P. Rajan Varadarajan, "Standardization versus Adaptation of International Marketing Strategy: An Empirical Investigation," *Journal of Marketing*, October 1993, pp. 1-17.

---

to fit the hand of the average Japanese consumer; even the doughnuts are a little smaller. Kraft blends different coffees for the British (who drink their coffee with milk), the French (who drink their coffee black), and Latin Americans (who want a chicory taste). A company can produce a *city version* of its product—for instance, a beer to meet Munich tastes or Tokyo tastes. Finally, a company can produce different *retailer versions* of its product, such as one coffee brew for the Migros chain store and another for the Cooperative chain store, both in Switzerland.

Although products are frequently adapted to local tastes, in some instances they must be adapted to local superstitions or beliefs, too. The concept of *feng shui* is a good example:

- **Hyatt Hotels.** A practice widely followed in China, Hong Kong, and Singapore, *feng shui* means "wind and water." Practitioners of *feng shui*, or geomancers, will recommend the most favourable conditions for any venture, particularly the placement of office buildings and the arrangement of desks, doors, and other items within. To have good *feng shui*, a building should face the water and be flanked by mountains. It also should not block the view of the mountain spirits. The Hyatt hotel in Singapore was designed without *feng shui*, and, as a result, had to be redesigned to boost business. Originally the front desk was parallel to the doors and road, and this was thought to lead

Hyatt Hotels
www.hyatt.com

to wealth flowing out. Furthermore, the doors were facing northwest, which easily let undesirable spirits in. The geomancer recommended design alterations so that wealth could be retained and undesirable spirits kept out.[23]

Product invention consists of creating something new. It can take two forms. *Backward invention* is reintroducing earlier product forms that are well adapted to a foreign country's needs. The National Cash Register Company reintroduced its crank-operated cash register at half the price of a modern cash register and sold substantial numbers in Latin America and Africa. (This illustrates a good understanding of the international product life cycle, where countries stand at different stages of readiness to adopt a particular product.) *Forward invention* is creating a new product to meet a need in another country. There is an enormous need in less developed countries for low-cost, high-protein foods. Companies such as Quaker Oats, Swift, and Monsanto are researching these countries' nutrition needs, formulating new foods, and developing advertising campaigns to gain product trial and acceptance. Toyota produces vehicles, such as the Soluna in Thailand and the Toyota Utility Vehicle in Indonesia, the Philippines, and Taiwan, which were specifically designed with the help of local employees to suit the tastes of these markets.[24] In globalization's latest twist, American companies are not only inventing new products for overseas markets but also lifting products and ideas from their international operations and bringing them home. As an example, Häagen-Dazs had developed a flavour for sale solely in Argentina called *dulce de leche*, named for the caramelized milk that is one of the most popular flavours in Argentina. Just one year later, the company rolled out *dulce de leche* in supermarkets from Boston to Los Angeles to Paris. The co-opted flavour now does $1 million a month in the United States and is particularly popular in Miami, where it sells twice as fast as any other flavour.[25] Product invention is a costly strategy, but the payoffs can be great, particularly if you can parlay a product innovation overseas into a new hit at home.

A growing part of international trade is taking place in services. The world market for services is growing at double the rate of world merchandise trade. Large firms in accounting, advertising, banking, communications, construction, insurance, law, management consulting, and retailing are pursuing global expansion. Arthur Andersen, American Express, Citicorp, Club Med, Hilton, SNC-Lavalin, and Thomas Cook are known worldwide. Faced with slowing growth in their home markets, many retailers are trying to make similar inroads. Wal-Mart is using cash flow from its North American business to fuel the growth of its $13.5 billion international division. In November 1997, Wal-Mart acquired German retailer Wertkauf, adding 21 hypermarkets with annual sales of $2.1 billion. Just two months earlier, the retailer had purchased its Mexican joint-venture partner, CIFRA, making it the largest retailer in Mexico. Wal-Mart has also opened outlets in Argentina, Indonesia, and China. As of 1998, Wal-Mart employed 105 000 international sales associates in 602 international retail units.[26] Brick-and-mortar retailers are not the only ones expanding overseas. Cyberretailer Amazon.com has purchased three European companies—two in Britain, one in Germany—to build European book and video sales.

At the same time, many countries have erected entry barriers or regulations. Brazil requires all accountants to possess a professional degree from a Brazilian university. Many Western European countries want to limit the number of U.S. television programs and films shown in their countries. Many U.S. states bar foreign bank branches. The General Agreement of Tariffs and Trade (GATT) is pressing for more free trade in international services, but the progress is slow.

Retailers, who sell books, videos, or CD-ROMs, and entertainment companies have also had to contend with a culture of censorship in certain countries, such as China and Singapore. Consider the case of Borders Books and Music.

■ **Borders Books and Music.** Borders expanded into Singapore in late 1997. Despite the Asian currency crisis and the worst retail sales slump in Singapore's history, the store was a huge success. Many of its 140 000-odd titles had never been offered before in Singapore. Local bookstores were too small and none had ever tried to stock the range of titles common in most bookstores in the

West. Yet, Borders had to fall in line with Singapore's culture of self-censorship. Borders censors its offerings internally and in concert with the Committee on Undesirable Publications (CUP). Borders must submit potentially "hot" titles to CUP for approval. Inspectors have objected to the Marquis de Sade and William Burroughs' *Naked Lunch*. Yet Borders has managed to push the envelope a little. It has five shelves of books in its sex and fertility section, and it has even managed to get approval to stock academic studies on homosexuality, not available elsewhere in the country.[27]

Borders
www.borders.com

Clearly, ethics or ideals that are upheld in the home country may be challenged when firms do business in other countries.

PROMOTION

Companies can run the same advertising and promotion campaigns used in the home market or change them for each local market, a process called *communication adaptation*. If it adapts both the product and the communication, the company engages in *dual adaptation*.

Consider the message. The company can change its message at four different levels. The company can use one message everywhere, varying only the language, name, and colours. Exxon used "Put a tiger in your tank" with minor variations and gained international recognition. Colours might be changed to avoid taboos in some countries. Purple is associated with death in Burma and some Latin American nations; white is a mourning colour in India; and green is associated with disease in Malaysia. Even names and headlines may have to be modified. When Clairol introduced the "Mist Stick," a curling iron, into Germany, it found that *mist* is slang for manure. Few Germans wanted to purchase a "manure stick." The Dairy Association brought its "Got Milk?" advertising campaign to Mexico only to find that the Spanish translation read, "Are you lactating?" When Coors put its slogan "turn it loose," into Spanish, it was read by some as "suffer from diarrhoea." In Spain, Chevrolet's *Nova* translated as "it doesn't go." A laundry soap ad claiming to wash "really dirty parts" was translated in French-speaking Quebec to read "a soap for washing private parts."[28]

The second possibility is to use the same theme globally but adapt the copy to each local market. For example, a Camay soap commercial showed a beautiful woman bathing. In Venezuela, a man was seen in the bathroom; in Italy and France, only a man's hand was seen; and in Japan, the man waited outside. Danish beer company, Carlsberg, goes so far as to adapt copy not to countries but to individual cities and even neighbourhoods within those cities. The 151-year-old Danish beer is available in more than 140 countries around the world, but because of the competitiveness and maturity of the U.S. market, it has to take a local tack in its approach to win new customers who aren't familiar with the brand. All advertisements feature the same single image of the Carlsberg bottle, along with a humorous message about the specific city. For example, in Manhattan, one headline on an ad reads: "Went all night without hearing car alarm. Celebrate special occasions with Carlsberg."[29]

The third approach consists of developing a global pool of ads, from which each country selects the most appropriate one. Coca-Cola and Goodyear use this approach. Finally, some companies allow their country managers to create country-specific ads—within guidelines, of course. Kraft uses different ads for Cheez Whiz in different countries, given that household penetration is 95 percent in Puerto Rico, where the cheese is put on everything; 65 percent in Canada, where it is spread on morning breakfast toast; and 35 percent in the United States, where it is considered a junk food.

The use of media also requires international adaptation because media availability varies from country to country. Norway, Belgium, and France do not allow cigarettes and alcohol to be advertised on TV. Austria and Italy regulate TV advertising to children. Saudi Arabia does not want advertisers to use women in ads. India taxes advertising. Magazines vary in availability and effectiveness; they play a major role in Italy and a minor one in Austria. Newspapers have a national reach in the United Kingdom, but the advertiser can buy only local newspaper coverage in Spain.

Marketers must also adapt sales-promotion techniques to different markets. Greece prohibits coupons, and France prohibits games of chance and limits premiums and gifts to 5 percent of product value. People in Europe and Japan tend to make inquiries via mail rather than phone—which may have ramifications for direct-mail and other sales-promotion campaigns. The result of these varying preferences and restrictions is that international companies generally assign sales promotion as a responsibility of local management.

PRICE

Multinationals face several pricing problems when selling abroad. They must deal with price escalation, transfer prices, dumping charges, and grey markets.

When companies sell their goods abroad, they face a *price escalation* problem. A Gucci handbag may sell for $120 in Italy and $240 in Canada. Why? Gucci has to add the cost of transportation, tariffs, importer margin, wholesaler margin, and retailer margin to its factory price. Depending on these added costs, as well as the currency-fluctuation risk, the product might have to sell for two to five times as much in another country to make the same profit for the manufacturer. Because the cost escalation varies from country to country, the question is how to set the prices in different countries. Companies have three choices:

1. *Setting a uniform price everywhere:* Coca-Cola might want to charge 60 cents for Coke everywhere in the world. But then Coca-Cola would earn quite different profit rates in different countries because of varying escalation costs. Also, this strategy would result in the price being too high in poor countries and not high enough in rich countries.

2. *Setting a market-based price in each country:* Here Coca-Cola would charge what each country could afford. But this strategy ignores differences in the actual cost from country to country. Also, it could lead to a situation in which intermediaries in low-price countries reship their Coca-Cola to high-price countries.

3. *Setting a cost-based price in each country:* Here Coca-Cola would use a standard markup of its costs everywhere. But this strategy might price Coca-Cola out of the market in countries where its costs are high.

Another problem arises when a company sets a *transfer price* (i.e., the price that it charges to another unit in the company) for goods that it ships to its foreign subsidiaries. Consider the following:

- **Hoffman-LaRoche.** Some years ago, the Swiss pharmaceutical company Hoffman-LaRoche charged its Italian subsidiary only $22 a kilo for Librium so that it could report high profits in Italy, where corporate taxes were lower. It charged its British subsidiary more than $100 per kilo for the same Librium so that it could make high profits at home instead of in Britain, where corporate taxes were high. The British Monopoly Commission sued Hoffman-LaRoche for back taxes and won.

If the company charges too high a price to a subsidiary, it may end up paying higher tariff duties, although it may pay lower income taxes in the foreign country. If the company charges too low a price to its subsidiary, it can be charged with *dumping*. Dumping occurs when a company charges either less than its costs or less than it charges in its home market, in order to enter or win a market. Zenith accused Japanese television manufacturers of dumping their TV sets on the U.S. market. Revenue Canada maintains a Web site to assist Canadian producers in preparing a properly documented complaint if they suspect a rival of dumping products or using unfair subsidies. When customs services find evidence of dumping, they can levy a dumping tariff on the guilty company. Various governments are watching for abuses and often force companies to charge the *arm's-length price*—that is, the price charged by other competitors for the same or a similar product.

Revenue Canada
www.rc.gc.ca/sima/

Many multinationals are plagued by the grey-market problem. A *grey market* occurs when the same product sells at different prices geographically. Dealers in the low-price country find ways to sell some of their products in higher-price countries, thus earning more. For example:

- **Minolta.** Because of lower transportation costs and tariffs, Minolta sold its cameras to dealers in Hong Kong for a lower price than it sold the same cameras to dealers in Germany. The Hong Kong dealers worked on smaller margins than the German retailers, who preferred high markups to high volume. Minolta's cameras ended up selling at retail for $174 in Hong Kong and $270 in Germany. Some Hong Kong wholesalers noticed this price difference and shipped Minolta cameras to German dealers for less than they were paying the German distributor. The German distributors couldn't sell their stock and complained to Minolta.

Very often a company finds some enterprising distributors buying more than they can sell in their own country and reshipping goods to another country to take advantage of price differences. Multinationals try to prevent grey markets by policing the distributors, by raising their prices to lower-cost distributors, or by altering the product characteristics or service warranties for different countries.

In the European Union, the grey market may disappear altogether with the transition to a single currency unit. The adoption of the single currency by 11 countries will certainly reduce the amount of price differentiation. In 1998, a bottle of Gatorade, for instance, cost 3.5 European currency units (ECU) in Germany but only about 0.9 in Spain. Once consumers recognize price differentiation by country, companies will be forced to harmonize prices throughout the countries that have adopted the single currency. Companies and marketers that offer the most innovative, specialized, or necessary products or services will be least affected by price transparency. For instance, Mail Boxes, Etc., which has 350 stores in Europe, believes that customers who need to send faxes won't refuse to do so because it costs more in Paris than in Italy.[30]

The Internet will also reduce price differentiation between countries. When companies sell their wares over the Internet, price will become transparent as customers can easily find out how much products sell for in different countries. Take an on-line training course, for instance. Whereas the price of a classroom-delivered day of training can vary significantly from the United States to France to Thailand, the price of an on-line-delivered day of training would have to be similar.[31]

Another global pricing challenge that has arisen in recent years is that countries with overcapacity, cheap currencies, and the need to export aggressively have pushed prices down and devalued their currencies. For multinational firms this poses challenges: sluggish demand and reluctance to pay higher prices make selling in these emerging markets difficult. Instead of lowering prices, and taking a loss, some multinationals have found more lucrative and creative means of coping:[32]

- **General Electric Company.** Rather than driving for larger market share, GE's power systems unit focused on winning a larger percentage of each customer's expenditures. The unit asked its top 100 customers what services were most critical to them and how GE could provide or improve them. The answers prompted the company to cut its response time for replacing old or damaged parts from twelve weeks to six. It began advising customers on the nuances of doing business in the diverse environments of Europe and Asia and began providing the maintenance staff that customers needed for occasional equipment upgrades. By adding value and helping customers reduce their costs and become more efficient, GE was able to avoid a move to commodity pricing and was actually able to generate bigger margins.

- **Praxair Inc.** For Praxair, a supplier of industrial gases, the name of the game was decreasing costs faster than pricing falls. The Praxair purchasing team became every bit as important as sales and marketing. Praxair formed global procurement teams that use information technology to coordinate scattered local operations on purchases of telecom equipment and services, freight fuel, and computer and office supplies. The goal is to buy more from fewer suppliers to get the best possible volume pricing. Although bottom-line results aren't in yet, one of five such global teams aims to reduce its network of suppliers from 1200 to 300.

PLACE (DISTRIBUTION CHANNELS)

Too many manufacturers think their job is done once the product leaves the factory. They should pay attention to how the product moves within the foreign country. They should take a whole-channel view of the problem of distributing products to final users. Figure 12.4 shows the three major links between seller and ultimate user. In the first link, *seller's international marketing headquarters*, the export department or international division makes decisions on channels and other marketing-mix elements. The second link, *channels between nations*, gets the products to the borders of the foreign nation. The decisions made in this link include the types of intermediaries (agents, trading companies) that will be used, the type of transportation (air, sea), and the financing and risk arrangements. The third link, *channels within foreign nations*, gets the products from their entry point to final buyers and users.

Within-country distribution channels vary considerably among countries. To sell soap in Japan, Procter & Gamble has to work through one of the most complicated distribution systems in the world. It must sell to a general wholesaler, who sells to a product wholesaler, who sells to a product-specialty wholesaler, who sells to a regional wholesaler, who sells to a local wholesaler, who finally sells to retailers. All these distribution levels can mean that the consumer's price ends up double or triple the importer's price. If P&G takes the soap to tropical Africa, the company might sell to an import wholesaler, who sells to several jobbers, who sell to petty traders (mostly women) working in local markets.

Another difference lies in the size and character of retail units abroad. Large-scale retail chains dominate the Canadian and U.S. scene, but much foreign retailing is in the hands of small independent retailers. In India, millions of retailers operate tiny shops or sell in open markets. Their markups are high, but the real price is brought down through haggling. Incomes are low, and people must shop daily for small amounts and are limited to whatever quantity can be carried home on foot or on a bicycle. Most homes lack storage and refrigeration space to keep food fresh. Packaging costs are kept low in order to keep prices low. In India, cigarettes are often bought singly. Breaking bulk remains an important function of intermediaries and helps perpetuate the long channels of distribution, which are a major obstacle to the expansion of large-scale retailing in developing countries.

DECIDING ON THE MARKETING ORGANIZATION

Companies manage their international marketing activities in three ways: through export departments, international divisions, or a global organization.

FIGURE 12.4

Whole-Channel Concept for International Marketing

part three
Developing
Marketing
Strategies

378

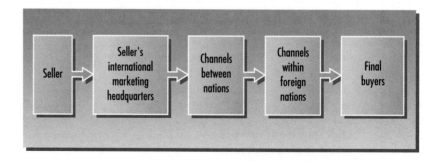

| Seller | Seller's international marketing headquarters | Channels between nations | Channels within foreign nations | Final buyers |

EXPORT DEPARTMENT

A firm normally gets into international marketing by simply shipping out its goods. If its international sales expand, the company organizes an export department consisting of a sales manager and a few assistants. As sales increase further, the export department is expanded to include various marketing services so that the company can pursue business more aggressively. If the firm moves into joint ventures or direct investment, the export department will no longer be adequate to manage international operations.

INTERNATIONAL DIVISION

Many companies become involved in several international markets and ventures. Sooner or later they will create international divisions to handle all their international activity. The international division is headed by a division president, who sets goals and budgets and is responsible for the company's international growth.

The international division's corporate staff consists of functional specialists who provide services to various operating units. Operating units can be organized in several ways. First, they can be *geographical organizations*. Reporting to the international-division president might be regional vice presidents for North America, Latin America, Europe, Africa, the Middle East, and the Far East. Reporting to the regional vice presidents are country managers who are responsible for a sales force, sales branches, distributors, and licensees in the respective countries. Or the operating units may be *world product groups*, each with an international vice president responsible for worldwide sales of each product group. The vice presidents may draw on corporate-staff area specialists for expertise on different geographical areas. Finally, operating units may be *international subsidiaries*, each headed by a president. The various subsidiary presidents report to the president of the international division.

Many multinationals shift between types of organization:

- ■ **IBM.** Part of IBM's massive reorganization strategy has been to put 235 000 employees into 14 customer-focused groups such as oil and gas, entertainment, and financial services. This way a big customer will be able to cut one deal with a central sales office to have IBM computers installed worldwide. Under the old system, a corporate customer with operations in 20 countries had to contract, in effect, with 20 little Big Blues, each with its own pricing structure and service standards.[33]

GLOBAL ORGANIZATION

Several firms have become truly global organizations. Their top corporate management and staff plan worldwide manufacturing facilities, marketing policies, financial flows, and logistical systems. The global operating units report directly to the chief executive or executive committee, not to the head of an international division. Executives are trained in worldwide operations, not just domestic or international. Management is recruited from many countries; components and supplies are purchased where they can be obtained at the least cost; and investments are made where the anticipated returns are greatest.

These companies face several organizational complexities. For example, when pricing a company's mainframe computers to a large banking system in Germany, how much influence should be wielded by the headquarters product manager, by the company's market manager for the banking sector, and by the company's German country manager? Bartlett and Ghoshal have proposed circumstances under which different approaches work best. In their *Managing Across Borders*, they describe forces that favour "global integration" (e.g., capital-intensive production, homogeneous demand) versus "national responsiveness" (e.g., local standards and barriers, strong local preferences). They distinguish three organizational strategies:[34]

1. A *global strategy* treats the world as a single market. This strategy is warranted when the forces for global integration are strong and the forces for national

responsiveness are weak. This is true of the consumer electronics market, for example, where most buyers will accept a fairly standardized pocket radio, CD player, or TV. Matsushita has performed better than GE and Philips in the consumer electronics market because Matsushita operates in a more globally coordinated and standardized way.

2. A *multinational strategy* treats the world as a portfolio of national opportunities. This strategy is warranted when the forces favouring national responsiveness are strong and the forces favouring global integration are weak. This is the situation in the branded packaged-goods business (food products, cleaning products). Bartlett and Ghoshal cite Unilever as a better performer than Kao and P&G because Unilever grants more decision-making autonomy to its local branches.

3. A *"glocal" strategy* standardizes certain core elements and localizes other elements. This strategy makes sense for an industry (such as telecommunications) where each nation requires some adaptation of its equipment but the providing company can also standardize some of the core components. Bartlett and Ghoshal cite Ericsson as balancing these considerations better than NEC (too globally oriented) and ITT (too locally oriented).

One of the most successful "glocal" companies is ABB, formed by a merger between the Swedish company ASEA and the Swiss company Brown Boveri.[35]

ABB
www.abb.com

■ **ABB.** ABB's products include power transformers, electrical installations, instrumentation, auto components, air-conditioning equipment, and railroad equipment. With annual revenues of $46.5 billion and 219 000 employees, ABB is headed by Goeran Lindahl. The company's motto is "ABB is a global company local everywhere." It established English—or "broken English," as Lindahl says—as the company's official language (all ABB managers must be conversant in English), and all financial results must be reported in dollars. ABB aims to reconcile three contradictions: to be global and local; to be big and small; and to be radically decentralized with centralized reporting and control. ABB has only 170 staff people at headquarters (with about 19 nationalities among them), compared to the 3000 who populate Siemens headquarters. The company's many product lines are organized into eight business segments, 65 business areas, 1300 companies, and 5000 profit centres, with the average employee belonging to a profit centre of around 50 employees. Managers are regularly rotated among countries and mixed-nationality teams are encouraged. Depending on the type of business, some are treated as super-local businesses with lots of autonomy and others as global businesses with major central control.

SUMMARY

1. Companies cannot simply stay domestic and expect to maintain their markets. Despite the many challenges in the international arena (shifting borders, unstable governments, foreign-exchange problems, corruption, and technological pirating), companies selling in global industries need to internationalize their operations.

2. In deciding to go abroad, a company needs to define its international marketing objectives and policies. The company must determine whether to market in a few countries or many countries. Then it must decide on which types of countries to consider. In general, the candidate countries should be rated on three criteria: market attractiveness, risk, and competitive advantage.

3. Once a company decides on a particular country, it must determine the best mode of entry. Its broad choices are indirect exporting, direct exporting, licensing, joint ventures, and direct investment. Each succeeding strategy involves more commit-

ment, risk, control, and profit potential. Companies generally begin with indirect exporting, then proceed through later stages as they gain more experience in the international arena.

4. In deciding on the marketing program, a company must decide how much to adapt its marketing mix (product, promotion, price, and place) to local conditions. At the two ends of the spectrum are standardized and adapted marketing mixes, with many steps in between. At the product level, firms can pursue a strategy of straight extension, product adaptation, or product invention. At the promotion level, firms may choose communication adaptation or dual adaptation. At the price level, firms may encounter price escalation and grey markets, and it may be very difficult to set standard prices. At the distribution level, firms need to take a whole-channel view of the challenge of distributing its products to the final users. In creating all elements of the marketing mix, firms must be aware of the cultural, social, political, technological, environmental, and legal limitations they face in other countries.

5. Depending on the level of international involvement, companies manage their international marketing activity in three ways: through export departments, international divisions, or a global organization. Most firms start with an export department and graduate to an international division. A few become global companies in which the top management plans and organizes on a global basis.

APPLICATIONS

CHAPTER CONCEPTS

1. Because of shrinking domestic markets due to competition, a moderate-size company in the salad-dressing industry is trying to decide "whether to go abroad." What are some questions concerning political, religious, and cultural factors that the company should ask itself before it decides to engage in international business? Choose a country and answer the questions in Figure 12.1, then decide whether to market salad dressing in that country.

2. Select one of the following countries or regions and prepare a brief (two- to five-page) report on its marketing institutions and practices. Also discuss the challenges that face domestic marketers within those countries, as well as the challenges faced by Canadian and U.S. marketers who want to do business there.

   a. Mexico   **d.** People's Republic of China

   b. the European Union   **e.** Japan

   c. Ukraine   **f.** South Africa

3. A Canadian heavy-equipment manufacturer operating in Western Europe has been using Canadians as salespeople. The company feels that it could reduce its costs by hiring and training nationals as salespeople. What are the advantages and disadvantages to using Americans versus nationals for selling abroad?

MARKETING AND ADVERTISING

Oracle ran the ad shown on page 382 in the business sections of Canadian newspapers. Do you think that this is an ad used only to advertise in Canada, is it a "glocalized" ad, or is it a standard one that the company uses to communicate its benefits worldwide? What are the advantages of using a standardized advertising format? What are the advantages of customizing advertising from one country to the next? Can a firm "glocalize" its advertising by combining the two approaches?

Figure 1

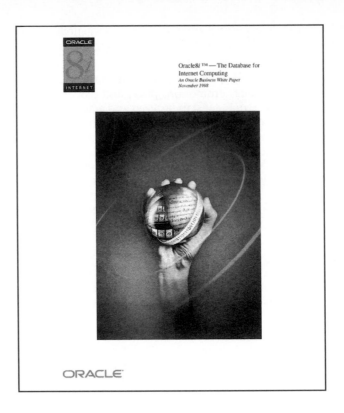

Revenue Canada
www.rc.gc

U.S. Customs Service
www.customs.ustreas.gov

FOCUS ON TECHNOLOGY

Details, details—the exporter's day is filled with details, including a blizzard of government paperwork. Now technology is helping exporters cut through the federal paper chase. Canada is developing an automated Customs and Information service. Exporters from across the country can call a toll-free number (1-800-461-9999; press 1 for English, then press 2 for business information.) They can also access customs information on the Revenue Canada Web site. There are plans to make access to customs information interactive through the use of Interactive television. Similarly, the U.S. Customs Service, U.S. Department of Commerce, and other federal agencies have jointly developed the Automated Export System (AES), an electronic version of the multiple forms that exporters used to have to complete by hand for several government agencies. With AES, exporters input data only once, using the Electronic Data Interchange (EDI) format, then transmit the form to the U.S. Customs Service. This system streamlines the exporting process, saving time and improving the accuracy of the data collected.

Visit Revenue Canada's site and the U.S. Customs Service Web site (www.customs.ustreas.gov—on the opening page, click on the Importing/Exporting button and then follow the path of automated systems and AES.) Which site is easier to use? Why do you think the U.S. government developed AES? Who benefits from expediting the paperwork associated with exporting? If you were an importer or exporter, what suggestions would you make to Revenue Canada that would help them improve their site to serve you better? Explain your answers.

MARKETING FOR THE 21ST CENTURY

Marketers participating in global e-commerce need to speak the languages of their target customers. Two good examples are the Web sites of Reebok (www.reebok.com/) and Nestlé (www.nestle.com/html/network.html). The Reebok home page is a gateway for specialized Web sites designed for consumers in Europe, France, Germany, Italy, Spain, the United Kingdom, Hong Kong, and Korea. The Nestlé site links to company sites for Taiwan, Australia, Brazil, Chile, New Zealand, Switzerland, Spain, Germany, France, Japan, Sweden, Greece, and the United Kingdom.

Point your Web browser to either the Reebok or the Nestlé Web site, then follow two of the links to company sites in other languages. What visual differences and similarities do you notice between the sites in other languages? Which of the sites (if any) allow on-line purchases? How do the sites encourage consumers to contact the company? Why are local contact points (phone, mail, address) important for local customers?

YOU'RE THE MARKETER: SONIC MARKETING PLAN

Global marketing offers a way for companies of all sizes to grow by expanding their customer base beyond the domestic market. However, the complexities of global marketing demand careful planning and proper execution.

As Jane Melody's assistant, you are researching the global market for Sonic's shelf stereo systems. Review the company's current situation and the research you have already gathered for your marketing plan. Then answer these questions about Sonic's global marketing strategy (noting the need for additional research where necessary):

- *If Sonic wants to start marketing its products in other countries, should it use exporting, licensing, joint ventures, or direct investment? Why?*

- *What international markets seem most promising for Sonic? For data about international trade and marketing in specific countries, visit the Trade Compass Web site (www.trade-compass.com). Also check the links on the Web site of the University of Michigan Center for International Business Education and Research (ciber.bus.msu.edu/busres.htm).*

- *Is global standardization or adaptation most appropriate for Sonic? To answer, you will have to research electronics standards in your chosen market(s) as well as consumer behaviour and competitive products. How can you collect such data?*

- *What marketing-mix strategy and tactics are most appropriate for Sonic to use in other countries?*

After you have examined potential global markets and marketing-mix strategies and tactics, summarize your ideas in a written marketing plan or type them into the appropriate sections of the Marketing Plan Pro software, including Markets, SWOT and Issue Analysis, and Marketing Strategy.

EUROPE BOUND

Companies from Vancouver, Ottawa, and Montreal are changing focus. Whereas only recently Asia was seen as the "land of opportunity," today more and more Canadian firms are looking to expand their operations into Europe. The journey isn't an easy one, however, and many wonder whether Europe can fulfill expectations as the new place to grow.

Europe represents a market of almost 300 million people. The 1990s have seen a renaissance trade between the European Union (EU) and Canada. The EU is Canada's second most important trading partner after the United States. Since 1985, EU exports to Canada have increased in value by 210 percent. While much of Europe's exports are in the form of services, led by tourism and business services, Canada's exports to the EU show an increasing share for value-added products such as manufactured and high-technology goods. The United Kingdom, Germany, Belgium, France, Italy, and the Netherlands are the major targets of Canadian exporters. The United Kingdom itself accounts for more than one-quarter of Canada's exports to the EU. In fact, the United Kingdom is Canada's third-largest market for exports. Only the United States and Japan represent larger export markets.

High-technology firms, such as Newbridge Networks, based in Ottawa, have long nurtured operations in Europe. Today they are seeing the rewards of their efforts, and sales in Europe are surging. In fact, over 25 percent of the firm's revenue growth is accounted for by its European sales. Newbridge has over 40 sales offices in Europe and its position is stronger in this market than it is in North America.

Another firm, Montreal's Unican, one of the largest lock-and-key companies in the world, has also experienced great success in the European marketplace. It has seen its sales soar from $8 million to $130 million. Increasing sales have resulted from the firm's willingness to change its products to meet sophisticated European design standards. Acquisitions have been another key to its growth. Unican has followed a strategy of acquiring its competitors. It buys up small companies in Europe that weren't prepared for global competition.

Despite these success stories, however, Canadian firms shouldn't enter the EU blindly. Many firms didn't understand the rigours of marketing here and have entered only to retreat in abject failure.

Questions

1. Why have Canadian firms developed a renewed interest in Europe?
2. Why is the EU a particularly attractive market for Canadian high-technology firms?
3. Why is competing in Europe more difficult than some firms expect it to be?
4. In an era of rapid change and global competition, what do Canadian firms have to think about and plan for?

Sources: Based on "Europebound," *Venture* 709 (January 19, 1999); The Canadian Trade Commissioner Service Web site (http://www.infoexport.gc.ca).

Managing Product Lines and Brands

CHAPTER

13

PROFILE:

Canadian Marketing Excellence

For years, Habitant has been a Canadian soup favourite. The soup is about to have its sixtieth birthday, but instead of celebrating, Campbells, owner of the venerable brand, must face a grim reality. Although Habitant has the largest share of the growing ready-to-eat canned soup market, its share declined by two percent in the last year alone. The solution…a little cosmetic surgery to revitalize the brand and its packaging.

Tomas Pigeon Design, the agency that helped Campbells with this project believes a well-executed brand design alone can dramatically revitalize a product and drive a business forward. Diane Teer, Campbell's Vice President of Marketing in charge of the project, agrees. "I think marketers often underestimate the power of packaging," she says.

Repositioning a brand is never an easy task, however. Painstaking care must be paid to every minute detail of the brand's image. Habitant presented a complex challenge because of its French/English duality. Habitant's roots go back to 1929 in Quebec, yet, despite its ancestry, Quebec is not the single largest market. Thus, the new design had to respect the product's bi-cultural character.

Each element of the brand symbol and package contribute to the way the product speaks to consumers and, thus, no change is made lightly. For example, when updating Habitant, the first task was to pump up the power of the yellow colour used on the soup's can without making it a look-alike for store brands. Next, hours were spent in photographic studios selecting picture-worthy pieces of ham and white peas that would be the focal point of new labels. Every detail was agonized over—everything from the right bowl in which to present the soup to the design of the home that had traditionally appeared on the label. Images also had to upgrade the brand's appetite appeal. Since care had to be taken not to alienate loyal users while at the same time attracting a new audience, nine full-colour presentations of the new concept came before the brand managers. Each was carefully screened to find just the right one that was both bold and clear, yet representative of the brand's positioning. "Wholesome goodness" was the watchword of the project since the brand character is that of a warm, caring, uncomplicated, and traditionally Canadian individual. Designers created electronic versions of store shelves so the marketers could see how the redesigned products would look next to its competitors. Today, the new design is ready. Now for the real test: will consumers respond and take the soup home to warm their hearts on cold winter days?

Sources: Astrid Van den Broek, "Souped-up Design," *Marketing*, October 26, 1998, pp. 14-16. James Fitzgerald, "Thomas Pigeon Design," "Unleashing the Power of Brands Through Design," *Strategy: The Canadian Marketing Report*, November 9, 1998, p. D8.

A&E's award-winning television show, *Biography,* is another organization that offers lessons in excellent product and brand management.

- **Arts & Entertainment Network.** A&E is steadily building Biography, its nightly look at historical figures, into its trademark masterbrand, one that is crossing a spectrum of media from home video and the Internet to kids' books, calendars, and CDs. Now in its eleventh season, the cable series has profiled over 500 people. Executives at A&E are practising product line extension into new formats. Home videos were the obvious first extension. Sold through direct response, through catalogues, on-line, and in dedicated space at some 500 Barnes & Noble bookstores, documentaries on Jesus, Jackie Onassis, and Santa Claus are the leading sellers. A Biography Web site, born in 1996, has grown to include 22 000 personalities; its traffic now surpasses that of A&E's own site with two million views a month. Then, in a flurry of activity, the company launched Biography books and a Biography line of CDs featuring musicians who have been profiled on the show. In its original

Arts and Entertainment Network
www.AandE.com

In this chapter we will address the following questions about products:

- What are the characteristics of products?

- How can a company build and manage its product mix and product lines?

- How can a company make better brand decisions?

- How can packaging and labelling be used as marketing tools?

medium, Biography will eventually be extended into a series of made-for-TV movies for prime time. All of the new products have only enhanced the core product, which is the nightly show. Its ratings continue to jump; in 1997 Biography showed a 17 percent increase in ratings from the previous year.

A&E's success story underscores the importance of the first and most important element of the marketing mix: the product. All the advertising and promotion in the world won't make consumers turn on a television show if they find it boring, irritating, or irrelevant.[1]

Product is a key element in the *market offering*. Marketing-mix planning begins with formulating an offering to meet target customers' needs or wants. The customer will judge the offering by three basic elements: product features and quality, services mix and quality, and price appropriateness (Figure 13.1). In this chapter, we examine product; in the next chapter, services; and in the following chapter, prices. All three elements must be meshed into a competitively attractive offering.

FIGURE 13.1

Components of the Market Offering

THE PRODUCT AND THE PRODUCT MIX

■ A *product* is anything that can be offered to a market to satisfy a want or need.

Products that are marketed include physical goods, services, experiences, events, persons, places, properties, organizations, information, and ideas.

PRODUCT LEVELS

In planning its market offering, the marketer needs to think through five levels of the product (Figure 13.2).[2] Each level adds more customer value, and the five constitute a *customer value hierarchy*. The most fundamental level is the *core benefit*: the fundamental service or benefit that the customer is really buying. A hotel guest is buying "rest and sleep." The purchaser of a drill is buying "holes." Marketers must see themselves as benefit providers.

At the second level, the marketer must turn the core benefit into a *basic product*. Thus a hotel room includes a bed, bathroom, towels, desk, dresser, and closet.

At the third level, the marketer prepares an *expected product*, a set of attributes and conditions buyers normally expect when they purchase this product. Hotel guests expect a clean bed, fresh towels, working lamps, and a relative degree of quiet. Because most hotels can meet this minimum expectation, the traveller normally will settle for whichever hotel is most convenient or least expensive.

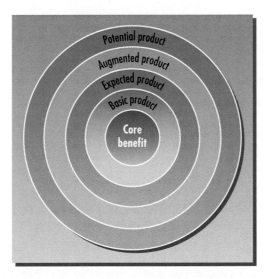

FIGURE 13.2

Five Product Levels

At the fourth level, the marketer prepares an *augmented product* that exceeds customer expectations. A hotel can include a remote-control television set, fresh flowers, rapid check-in, express checkout, and fine dining and room service. Elmer Wheeler once observed, "Don't sell the steak—sell the sizzle."

Today's competition essentially takes place at the product-augmentation level. (In less developed countries, competition takes place mostly at the expected product level.) Product augmentation leads the marketer to look at the user's total *consumption system:* the way the user performs the tasks of getting, using, fixing, and disposing of the product.[3] According to Levitt:

> *The new competition is not between what companies produce in their factories, but between what they add to their factory output in the form of packaging, services, advertising, customer advice, financing, delivery arrangements, warehousing, and other things that people value.*[4]

Some things should be noted about product-augmentation strategy. First, each augmentation adds cost. The marketer has to ask whether customers will pay enough to cover the extra cost. Second, augmented benefits soon become expected benefits. Today's hotel guests expect a remote-control television set and other amenities. This means that competitors will have to search for still other features and benefits. Third, as companies raise the price of their augmented product, some competitors can offer a "stripped-down" version at a much lower price. Thus alongside the growth of fine hotels like Four Seasons and Ritz Carlton we see the emergence of lower-cost hotels and motels (Motel Six, Comfort Inn) catering to clients who simply want the basic product.

At the fifth level stands the *potential product*, which encompasses all the possible augmentations and transformations the product might undergo in the future. Here is where companies search for new ways to satisfy customers and distinguish their offer. All-suite hotels where the guest occupies a set of rooms represent an innovative transformation of the traditional hotel product.

Successful companies add benefits to their offering that not only *satisfy* customers but also surprise and *delight* them. Delighting is a matter of exceeding expectations. Thus the hotel guest finds candy on the pillow or a bowl of fruit or a video recorder with optional videotapes. Ritz-Carlton hotels, for example, remember individual guests' preferences and prepare rooms with these preferences in mind.

PRODUCT HIERARCHY

Each product is related to certain other products. The product hierarchy stretches from basic needs to particular items that satisfy those needs. We can identify seven levels of the product hierarchy (here for life insurance):

1. *Need family:* The core need that underlies the existence of a product family. Example: security.

2. *Product family:* All the product classes that can satisfy a core need with reasonable effectiveness. Example: savings and income.

3. *Product class:* A group of products within the product family recognized as having a certain functional coherence. Example: financial instruments.

4. *Product line:* A group of products within a product class that are closely related because they perform a similar function, are sold to the same customer groups, are marketed through the same channels, or fall within given price ranges. Example: life insurance.

5. *Product type:* A group of items within a product line that share one of several possible forms of the product. Example: term life.

6. *Brand:* The name, associated with one or more items in the product line, that is used to identify the source or character of the item(s). Example: Prudential.

7. *Item* (also called *stockkeeping unit* or *product variant*): A distinct unit within a brand or product line distinguishable by size, price, appearance, or some other attribute. Example: Prudential renewable term life insurance.

Two other terms are frequently used with respect to the product hierarchy. A *product system* is a group of diverse but related items that function in a compatible manner. The Nikon Company sells a basic 35-mm camera along with an extensive set of lenses, filters, and other options that constitute a product system. A *product mix* (or product assortment) is the set of all products and items that a particular seller offers for sale to buyers.

PRODUCT CLASSIFICATIONS

Marketers have traditionally classified products on the basis of characteristics: durability, tangibility, and use (consumer or industrial). Each product type has an appropriate marketing-mix strategy.[5]

Durability and Tangibility
Products can be classified into three groups, according to durability and tangibility:

1. *Non-durable goods:* Non-durable goods are tangible goods normally consumed in one or a few uses: beer and soap. Because these goods are consumed quickly and purchased frequently, the appropriate strategy is to make them available in many locations, charge only a small markup, and advertise heavily to induce trial and build preference.

2. *Durable goods:* Durable goods are tangible goods that normally survive many uses: refrigerators, machine tools, and clothing. Durable products normally require more personal selling and service, command a higher margin, and require more seller guarantees.

3. *Services:* Services are intangible, inseparable, variable, and perishable products. As a result, they normally require more quality control, supplier credibility, and adaptability. Examples include haircuts and repairs.

Consumer-Goods Classification
The vast array of goods consumers buy can be classified on the basis of shopping habits. We can distinguish among convenience, shopping, specialty, and unsought goods.

- *Convenience goods* are goods that the customer usually purchases frequently, immediately, and with a minimum of effort. Examples include tobacco products, soaps, and newspapers.

  Convenience goods can be further divided. *Staples* are goods consumers purchase on a regular basis. A buyer might routinely purchase Heinz ketchup, Crest toothpaste, and Ritz crackers. *Impulse goods* are purchased without any planning or search effort. Chocolate bars and magazines are placed next to checkout counters because shoppers may not have thought of buying them until they spot them. *Emergency goods* are purchased when a need is urgent—umbrellas during a rainstorm, boots, and shovels during the first winter snowstorm. Manufacturers of emergency goods will place them in many outlets to capture the sale when the customer needs them.

- *Shopping goods* are goods that the customer, in the process of selection and purchase, characteristically compares on such bases as suitability, quality, price, and style. Examples include CDs, computers, furniture, clothing, used cars, and major appliances.

  Shopping goods can be further divided. *Homogeneous shopping goods* are similar in quality but different enough in price to justify shopping comparisons. *Heterogeneous shopping goods* differ in product features and services that may be more important than price. The seller of heterogeneous shopping goods carries a wide assortment to satisfy individual tastes and must have well-trained salespeople to inform and advise customers.

- *Specialty goods* are goods with unique characteristics or brand identification for which a sufficient number of buyers is willing to make a special purchasing effort. Examples include cars, stereo components, photographic equipment, and men's suits.

A Mercedes is a specialty good because interested buyers will travel far to buy one. Specialty goods do not involve making comparisons; buyers invest time only to reach dealers carrying the wanted products. Dealers do not need convenient locations; however, they must let prospective buyers know their locations.

■ *Unsought goods* are goods the consumer does not know about or does not normally think of buying. Smoke detectors are unsought goods until the consumer is made aware of them through advertising. The classic examples of known but unsought goods are life insurance, cemetery plots, gravestones, and encyclopedias.

Unsought goods require advertising and personal-selling support.

INDUSTRIAL-GOODS CLASSIFICATION

Industrial goods can be classified in terms of how they enter the production process and their relative costliness. We can distinguish three groups of industrial goods: materials and parts, capital items, and supplies and business services.

■ *Materials and parts* are goods that enter the manufacturer's product completely. They fall into two classes: raw materials and manufactured materials and parts.

Raw materials fall into two major classes: *farm products* (e.g., wheat, cotton, livestock, fruits, and vegetables) and *natural products* (e.g., fish, lumber, crude petroleum, iron ore). Farm products are supplied by many producers, who turn them over to marketing intermediaries, who provide assembly, grading, storage, transportation, and selling services. Their perishable and seasonal nature gives rise to special marketing practices. Their commodity character results in relatively little advertising and promotional activity, with some exceptions. At times, commodity groups will launch campaigns to promote their product—potatoes, prunes, milk. Some producers brand their product—Sunkist oranges, BC Hot House.

Natural products are limited in supply. They usually have great bulk and low unit value and must be moved from producer to user. Fewer and larger producers often market them directly to industrial users. Because the users depend on these materials, long-term supply contracts are common. The homogeneity of natural materials limits the amount of demand-creation activity. Price and delivery reliability are the major factors influencing the selection of suppliers.

Manufactured materials and parts fall into two categories: component materials (iron, yarn, cement, wires) and component parts (small motors, tires, castings). *Component materials* are usually fabricated further—pig iron is made into steel, and yarn is woven into cloth. The standardized nature of component materials usually means that price and supplier reliability are key purchase factors. *Component parts* enter the finished product with no further change in form, as when small motors are put into vacuum cleaners, and tires are put on automobiles. Most manufactured materials and parts are sold directly to industrial users, with orders often placed a year or more in advance. Price and service are major marketing considerations, and branding and advertising tend to be less important.

■ *Capital items* are long-lasting goods that facilitate developing or managing the finished product. They include two groups: installations and equipment.

Installations consist of buildings (factories, offices) and equipment (generators, drill presses, mainframe computers, elevators). Installations are major purchases. They are usually bought directly from the producer, with the typical sale preceded by a long negotiation period. The producer's sales force includes technical personnel. Producers have to be willing to design to specification and to supply postsale services. Advertising is much less important than personal selling.

Equipment comprises portable factory equipment and tools (hand tools, lift trucks) and office equipment (personal computers, desks). These types of equipment do not become part of a finished product. They have a shorter life than installations but a longer life than operating supplies. Although some equipment manufacturers sell direct, more often they use intermediaries, because the market is geographically dispersed, the buyers are numerous, and the orders are small. Quality, features, price, and service are major considerations. The sales force tends to be more important than advertising, although the latter can be used effectively.

■ *Supplies and business services* are short-lasting goods and services that facilitate developing or managing the finished product.

Supplies are of two kinds: *operating supplies* (lubricants, coal, writing paper, pencils) and *maintenance and repair items* (paint, nails, brooms). Supplies are the equivalent of convenience goods; they are usually purchased with minimum effort on a straight rebuy basis. They are normally marketed through intermediaries because of their low unit value and the great number and geographic dispersion of customers. Price and service are important considerations, because suppliers are standardized and brand preference is not high.

Business services include *maintenance and repair services* (window cleaning, typewriter repair) and *business advisory services* (legal, management consulting, advertising). Maintenance and repair services are usually supplied under contract by small producers or are available from the manufacturers of the original equipment. Business advisory services are usually purchased on the basis of the supplier's reputation and staff.

PRODUCT MIX

■ A *product mix* (also called *product assortment*) is the set of all products and items that a particular seller offers for sale.

Kodak's product mix consists of two strong product lines: information products and image products. NEC's (Japan) product mix consists of communication products and computer products. Michelin has three product lines: tires, maps, and restaurant-rating services.

A company's product mix has a certain width, length, depth, and consistency. These concepts are illustrated in Table 13.1 for selected Procter & Gamble consumer products.

■ The *width* of a product mix refers to how many different product lines the company carries. Table 13.1 shows a product-mix width of five lines. (In fact, P&G produces many additional lines.)

■ The *length* of a product mix refers to the total number of items in the mix. In Table 13.1, it is 25. We can also talk about the average length of a line. This is obtained by dividing the total length (here 25) by the number of lines (here 5), or an average product length of 5.

T A B L E 13.1

Product-Mix Width and Product-Line Length for Procter & Gamble Products (Including Dates of Introduction)

			Product-Mix Width		
	Detergents	**Toothpaste**	**Bar Soap**	**Disposable Diapers**	**Paper Tissue**
	Ivory Snow 1930	Gleem 1952	Ivory 1879	Pampers 1961	Charmin 1928
	Dreft 1933	Crest 1955	Kirk's 1885	Luvs 1976	Puffs 1960
	Tide 1946		Lava 1893		Banner 1982
PRODUCT-	Cheer 1950		Camay 1926		Summit 1100's 1992
LINE	Oxydol 1954		Zest 1952		
LENGTH	Dash 1954		Safeguard 1963		
	Bold 1965		Coast 1974		
	Gain 1966		Oil of Olay 1993		
	Era 1972				

- The *depth* of a product mix refers to how many variants are offered of each product in the line. If Crest comes in three sizes and two formulations (regular and mint), Crest has a depth of six. The average depth of P&G's product mix can be calculated by averaging the number of variants within the brand groups.

- The *consistency* of the product mix refers to how closely related the various product lines are in end use, production requirements, distribution channels, or some other way. P&G's product lines are consistent insofar as they are consumer goods that go through the same distribution channels. The lines are less consistent insofar as they perform different functions for the buyers.

These four product-mix dimensions permit the company to expand its business in four ways. It can add new product lines, thus widening its product mix. It can lengthen each product line. It can add more product variants to each product and deepen its product mix. Finally, a company can pursue more product-line consistency.

PRODUCT-LINE DECISIONS

A product mix consists of various product lines. In General Electric's Consumer Appliance Division, there are product-line managers for refrigerators, stoves, and washing machines. At Queen's University, there are separate academic deans for the Faculty of Applied Science, Faculty of Arts and Science, Faculty of Education, Faculty of Health Sciences, Faculty of Law, School of Business, and School of Physical and Health Sciences.

In offering a product line, companies normally develop a *basic platform and modules* that can be added to meet different customer requirements. Car manufacturers build their cars around a basic platform. Home builders show a model home around which additional features can be added. This modularized approach enables the company to offer variety while lowering its production costs.

PRODUCT-LINE ANALYSIS

Product-line managers need to know the sales and profits of each item in their line in order to determine which items to build, maintain, harvest, or divest. They also need to understand each product line's market profile.

Sales and Profits

Figure 13.3 shows a sales and profit report for a five-item product line. The first item accounts for 50 percent of total sales and 30 percent of total profits. The first two items account for 80 percent of total sales and 60 percent of total profits. If these two items were suddenly hurt by a competitor, the line's sales and profitability could collapse. A high concentration of sales in a few items means line vulnerability. These

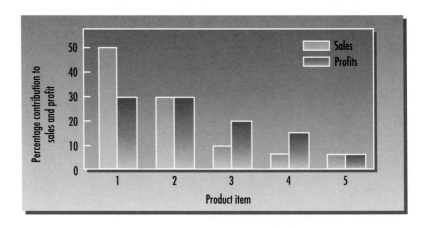

items must be carefully monitored and protected. At the other end, the last item delivers only five percent of the product line's sales and profits. The product-line manager may consider dropping this item unless it has strong growth potential.

Market Profile

The product-line manager must review how the line is positioned against competitors' lines. Consider paper company X with a paper board product line.[6] Two paper board attributes are weight and finish quality. Paper weight is usually offered at standard levels of 90, 120, 150, and 180 weight. Finish quality is offered at low, medium, and high levels. Figure 13.4 shows the location of the various product-line items of company X and four competitors, A, B, C, and D. Competitor A sells two product items in the extra-high weight class ranging from medium to low finish quality. Competitor B sells four items that vary in weight and finish quality. Competitor C sells three items in which the greater the weight, the greater the finish quality. Competitor D sells three items, all lightweight but varying in finish quality. Company X offers three items that vary in weight and finish quality.

The product map is useful for designing product-line marketing strategy. It shows which competitors' items are competing against company X's items. For example, company X's low-weight, medium-quality paper competes against competitor D's and B's papers. But its high-weight, medium-quality paper has no direct competitor. The map also reveals possible locations for new items. No manufacturer offers a high-weight, low-quality paper. If company X estimates a strong unmet demand and can produce and price this paper at low cost, it could consider adding this item to its line.

Another benefit of product mapping is that it identifies market segments. Figure 13.4 shows the types of paper, by weight and quality, preferred by the general printing industry, the point-of-purchase display industry, and the office-supply industry. The map shows that company X is well positioned to serve the needs of the general printing industry but is less effective in serving the other two industries.

After performing a product-line analysis, the product-line manager has to consider decisions on product-line length, line modernization, line featuring, and line pruning.

PRODUCT-LINE LENGTH

Product-line managers are concerned with length. A product line is too short if profits can be increased by adding items; the line is too long if profits can be increased by dropping items.

Company objectives influence product-line length. Companies seeking high market share and market growth will carry longer lines. Companies that emphasize high profitability will carry shorter lines consisting of carefully chosen items.

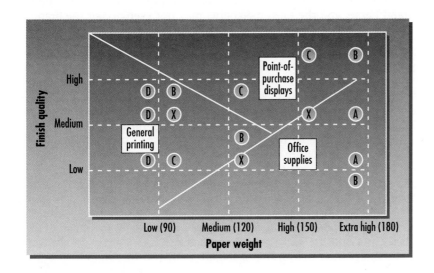

FIGURE 13.4

Product Map for a Paper-Product Line

Source: Industrial Product Policy: Managing the Existing Product Line by Benson P. Shapiro. Cambridge, MA: Marketing Science Institute Report No. 77-110.

Product lines tend to lengthen over time. Excess manufacturing capacity puts pressure on the product-line manager to develop new items. The sales force and distributors also pressure the company for a more complete product line to satisfy their customers. But as items are added, several costs rise: design and engineering costs, inventory-carrying costs, manufacturing-changeover costs, order-processing costs, transportation costs, and new-item promotional costs. Eventually someone calls a halt: Top management may stop development because of insufficient funds or manufacturing capacity. The controller may call for a study of the line's money-losing items. A pattern of product-line growth followed by massive pruning may repeat itself many times.

A company lengthens its product line in two ways: by line stretching and line filling.

Line Stretching

Every company's product line covers a certain part of the total possible range. For example, BMW automobiles are located in the upper price range of the automobile market. *Line stretching* occurs when a company lengthens its product line beyond its current range. The company can stretch its line downmarket, upmarket, or both ways.

Downmarket Stretch. A company positioned in the middle market may want to introduce a lower price line for any of three reasons:

1. The company may notice strong growth opportunities in the downmarket as mass retailers such as Wal-Mart, Best Buy, and others attract a growing number of shoppers who want value-priced goods.

2. The company may wish to tie up lower-end competitors who might otherwise try to move upmarket. If the company has been attacked by a low-end competitor, it often decides to counterattack by entering the low end of the market.

3. The company may find that the middle market is stagnating or declining.

A company faces a number of naming choices in deciding to move downmarket. Sony, for example, faced three choices:

1. Use the name Sony on all of its offerings. (Sony did this.)

2. Introduce the lower price offerings using a sub-brand name, such as Sony Value Line. Other companies have done this, such as Gillette with Gillette Good News and Air Canada with Air Ontario. The risks are that the Sony name loses some of its quality image and that some Sony buyers might switch to the lower price offerings.

3. Introduce the lower price offerings under a different name, without mentioning Sony. But Sony would have to spend a lot of money to build up the new brand name, and the mass merchants may not even accept the brand when it lacks the Sony name.

Moving downmarket carries risks. Kodak introduced Kodak Funtime film to counter lower-priced brands. But it didn't price Kodak Funtime low enough to match the lower-priced film. It also found some of its regular customers buying Funtime, thereby cannibalizing its core brand. So it withdrew Funtime. On the other hand, Mercedes successfully introduced its C-Class cars at $45 000 without injuring its ability to sell other Mercedes cars for $150 000 and up. John Deere introduced a lower price line of lawn tractors called Sabre from John Deere while still selling its more expensive tractors under the John Deere name.

Upmarket Stretch. Companies may wish to enter the high end of the market for more growth, higher margins, or simply to position themselves as full-line manufacturers. Many markets have spawned surprising upscale segments such as Starbucks in coffee, Häagen-Dazs in ice cream, and Evian in bottled water. The leading Japanese auto companies have each introduced an upscale automobile: Toyota launched Lexus; Nissan launched Infinity; and Honda launched Acura. Note that they invented entirely new names rather than using or including their own names.

Other companies have included their own name in moving upmarket. Loblaw introduced its President's Choice line. Gallo introduced Ernest and Julio Gallo Varietals and priced these wines more than twice as high as their regular wines. General Electric introduced the GE Profile brand for its large appliance offerings in the upscale market.[7]

Two-Way Stretch. Companies serving the middle market might decide to stretch their line in both directions. Texas Instruments (TI) introduced its first calculators in the medium-price–medium-quality end of the market. Gradually, it added calculators at the lower end, taking market share away from Bowmar and in the higher end to compete with Hewlett-Packard. This two-way stretch won TI early market leadership in the hand-calculator market.

The Marriott Hotel group also has performed a two-way stretch of its hotel product line (Figure 13.5). Alongside its medium-price hotels, it added the Marriott Marquis line to serve the upper end of the market, the Courtyard line to serve a lower end of the market, and Fairfield Inns to serve the economy end of the market. Each branded hotel line is aimed at a different target market. The major risk with this strategy is that some travellers will trade down after finding the lower-price hotels in the Marriott chain have pretty much everything they want. But it is still better for Marriott to capture customers who move downward than to lose them to competitors.

Line Filling

A product line can also be lengthened by adding more items within the present range. There are several motives for *line filling*: reaching for incremental profits, trying to satisfy dealers who complain about lost sales because of missing items in the line, trying to utilize excess capacity, trying to be the leading full-line company, and trying to plug holes to keep out competitors.

Line filling is overdone if it results in self-cannibalization and customer confusion. The company needs to differentiate each item in the consumer's mind. Each item should possess a *just-noticeable difference*. According to Weber's law, customers are more attuned to relative than to absolute difference.[8] They will perceive the difference between boards 2 and 3 metres long and boards 20 and 30 metres long but not between boards 29 and 30 metres long. The company should make sure that new-product items have a noticeable difference. The company should also check that the proposed item meets a market need and is not being added simply to satisfy an internal need.

LINE MODERNIZATION

Product lines need to be modernized. A company's machine tools might have a 1950s look and lose out to newer-styled competitors' lines. The issue is whether to overhaul the line piecemeal or all at once. A piecemeal approach allows the company to see

E&J Gallo Winery
www.gallo.com

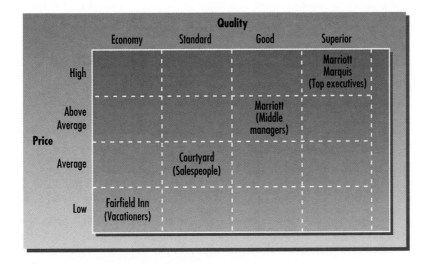

FIGURE 13.5

Two-Way Product-Line Stretch: Marriott Hotels

how customers and dealers take to the new style. It is also less draining on the company's cash flow. But it allows competitors to see changes and to start redesigning their own lines.

In rapidly changing product markets, modernization is carried on continuously. Companies plan improvements to encourage *customer migration* to higher-valued, higher-priced items. Microprocessor companies such as Intel and Motorola, and software companies such as Microsoft and Lotus, continually introduce more advanced versions of their products. A major issue is timing improvements so they do not appear too early (damaging sales of the current line) or too late (after competition has established a strong reputation for more advanced equipment).

LINE FEATURING AND LINE PRUNING

The product-line manager typically selects one or a few items in the line to feature. Sears will announce a special low-price washing machine to attract customers. At other times, managers will feature a high-end item to lend prestige to the product line. Stetson promotes a man's hat selling for $225. Few men buy it, but it acts as a "crown jewel" to enhance the line's image.

Sometimes a company finds one end of its line selling well and the other end selling poorly. The company may try to boost demand for the slower sellers, especially if they are produced in a factory that is idled by lack of demand. This situation faced Honeywell when its medium-size computers were not selling as well as its large computers. But it could be counterargued that the company should promote items that sell well rather than try to prop up weak items.

Product-line managers must periodically review the line for pruning. The product line can include deadwood that is depressing profits. The weak items can be identified through sales and cost analysis. A chemical company cut down its line from 217 to the 93 products with the largest volume, the largest contribution to profits, and the greatest long-term potential.

Another occasion for pruning is when the company is short of production capacity. Companies typically shorten their product lines in periods of tight demand and lengthen their lines in periods of slow demand.

 B RAND DECISIONS

Branding is a major issue in both product and corporate strategy. While some companies only focus on the unique brands they associate with individual products or services, others build corporate brands that they link to all their product lines. While product brands typically appear only on packages and in advertising, corporate brands appear on a wide range of company communications ranging from billing statements, to annual reports, to Internet sites. Findings from *The Financial Post*'s third annual survey of branding practices revealed that 68 percent of respondents rated corporate branding as either important or very important to the organization's success, up from 45 percent two years ago. Furthermore, 86 percent expect the issue to become more important to their future success. The power of brands isn't restricted to domestic markets. Japanese and South Korean companies, for example, spent liberally to build up brand names such as Sony, Toyota, Goldstar, and Samsung, which have increased their world marketing power.[9]

WHAT IS A BRAND?

Perhaps the most distinctive skill of professional marketers is their ability to create, maintain, protect, and enhance brands. Marketers say that "branding is the art and cornerstone of marketing." The American Marketing Association defines a brand as follows:

■ A ***brand*** is a name, term, sign, symbol, or design, or a combination of them, intended to identify the goods or services of one seller or group of sellers and to differentiate them from those of competitors.

In essence, a brand identifies the seller or maker. It can be a name, trademark, logo, or other symbol. Under trademark law, the seller is granted exclusive rights to the use of the brand name in perpetuity. Brands differ from other assets such as patents and copyrights, which have expiration dates.

A brand is essentially a seller's promise to deliver a specific set of features, benefits, and services consistently to the buyers. The best brands convey a warranty of quality. But a brand is an even more complex symbol.[10] It can convey up to six levels of meaning:

1. *Attributes:* A brand brings to mind certain attributes. Mercedes suggests expensive, well-built, well-engineered, durable, high-prestige automobiles.

2. *Benefits:* Attributes must be translated into functional and emotional benefits. The attribute "durable" could translate into the functional benefit "I won't have to buy another car for several years." The attribute "expensive" translates into the emotional benefit "The car makes me feel important and admired."

3. *Values:* The brand also says something about the producer's values. Mercedes stands for high performance, safety, and prestige.

4. *Culture:* The brand may represent a certain culture. The Mercedes represents German culture: organized, efficient, high quality.

5. *Personality:* The brand can project a certain personality. Mercedes may suggest a no-nonsense boss (person), a reigning lion (animal), or an austere palace (object).

6. *User:* The brand suggests the kind of consumer who buys or uses the product. We would expect to see a 55-year-old top executive behind the wheel of a Mercedes, not a 20-year-old mail carrier.

If a company treats a brand only as a name, it misses the point. The branding challenge is to develop a deep set of positive associations for the brand. Marketers must decide at which level(s) to anchor the brand's identity. One mistake would be to promote only attributes. First, the buyer is not as interested in attributes as in benefits. Second, competitors can easily copy attributes. Third, the current attributes may become less desirable later.

Promoting the brand only on one benefit can also be risky. Eaton's discovered this the hard way. Seeing that it was going out of fashion with the buying public, it moved away from its department-store roots and tried to associate its brand with high-end fashion aimed at the youth market. Explaining the company's failure, an expert in insolvency noted, "It had the brand Eaton's but not the merchandise to go with the brand image."[11]

The most enduring meanings of a brand are its values, culture, and personality. They define the brand's essence. The Mercedes stands for high technology, performance, and success. Mercedes must project this in its brand strategy. Mercedes must resist marketing an inexpensive car bearing the name; doing so would dilute the value and personality Mercedes has built up over the years.

BRAND EQUITY

Brands vary in the amount of power and value they have in the marketplace. At one extreme are brands that are not known by most buyers. Then there are brands for which buyers have a fairly high degree of *brand awareness*. Beyond this are brands with a high degree of *brand acceptability*. Then there are brands that enjoy a high degree of *brand preference*. Finally there are brands that command a high degree of *brand loyalty*. Tony O'Reilly, former CEO of H. J. Heinz, proposed this test of brand loyalty: "My acid test. . . is whether [the customer], intending to buy Heinz tomato ketchup in a store, finding it to be out of stock, will walk out of the store to buy it elsewhere."

Few customers are as brand-loyal as O'Reilly hopes Heinz's customers will be. Aaker distinguished five levels of customer attitude toward his or her brand, from lowest to highest:

1. Customer will change brands, especially for price reasons. No brand loyalty.

2. Customer is satisfied. No reason to change the brand.

3. Customer is satisfied and would incur costs by changing brand.

4. Customer values the brand and sees it as a friend.

5. Customer is devoted to the brand.

Brand equity is highly related to how many customers are in classes 3, 4, or 5. It is also related, according to Aaker, to the degree of brand-name recognition, perceived brand quality, strong mental and emotional associations, and other assets such as patents, trademarks, and channel relationships.[12]

Certain companies base their growth on acquiring and building rich *brand portfolios*. Grand Metropolitan acquired various Pillsbury brands, Green Giant vegetables, Häagen-Dazs ice cream, and Burger King. Nestlé acquired Rowntree (U.K.), Carnation (U.S.), Stouffer (U.S.), Buitoni-Perugina (Italy), and Perrier (France), making it the world's largest food company. Nestlé paid $4.5 billion to buy Rowntree, five times its book value. Companies do not normally list brand equity on their balance sheets because of the arbitrariness of the estimate. But clearly brand equity relates to the price premium the brand commands times the extra volume it moves over an average brand. Rex McCafferty, a Toronto-based brand valuation expert, calls brands an identifiable intangible that, as legal entities, are more like a patent than company goodwill.[13]

The world's 10 most valuable brands in 1997 were (in rank order): Coca-Cola, Marlboro, IBM, McDonald's, Disney, Sony, Kodak, Intel, Gillette, and Budweiser. Coca-Cola's brand equity was $72 billion, Marlboro's $70 billion, and IBM's $36 billion.[14]

High brand equity provides a number of competitive advantages:

■ The company will enjoy reduced marketing costs because of consumer brand awareness and loyalty.

■ The company will have more trade leverage in bargaining with distributors and retailers because customers expect them to carry the brand.

■ The company can charge a higher price than its competitors because the brand has higher perceived quality.

■ The company can more easily launch extensions because the brand name carries high credibility.

■ The brand offers the company some defence against price competition.

A brand name needs to be carefully managed so that its equity doesn't depreciate. This requires maintaining or improving brand awareness, perceived quality and functionality, and positive associations. These tasks require continuous R&D investment, skilful advertising, and excellent trade and consumer service. Canada Dry and Colgate-Palmolive have appointed "brand equity managers" to guard the brand's image, associations, and quality and prevent short-term tactical actions by overzealous brand managers from hurting the brand. That's why some companies put their branding in the hands of an entirely different company that can focus only on brand management and nothing else. Henry Silverman of Cendant Corporation has made a business of managing—not owning—brands.

■ **Cendant Corporation.** Cendant's Henry Silverman has gone as far as anyone in arguing that brand is everything and in showing how a brand can even be split away from the operational aspect of the business. Cendant owns and manages brands that range from budget-conscious motels (Days Inn and Super 8) to faded icons (Howard Johnson and Ramada) to powerful real estate franchises (Century 21 and Coldwell Banker) to Avis, the rental car company. The brands are all he owns. While other companies own and operate the messy, real-world parts of the business, Silverman spends his time and energy distilling, refurbishing, extending, linking, and leveraging brand names. For instance, he was able to change the brand image of Century 21. Old TV ads emphasized the company's vast real estate network, but Silverman's research showed that home buyers didn't care how *big* Century 21 was; they cared about building good relationships with the company's real estate agents. Silverman launched a new campaign focusing on those more personal attributes, and Century 21's annual fees have doubled.[15]

P&G believes that well-managed brands are not subject to a brand life cycle. Many brand leaders of 70 years ago are still today's brand leaders: Kodak, Wrigley's, Gillette, Coca-Cola, Heinz, and Campbell Soup.

Some analysts see brands as outlasting a company's specific products and facilities. They see brands as the company's major enduring asset. Yet every powerful brand really represents a set of loyal customers. Therefore, the fundamental asset underlying brand equity is *customer equity*. This suggests that the proper focus of marketing planning is that of extending *loyal customer lifetime value*, with brand management serving as a major marketing tool.

Unfortunately, many companies have mismanaged their greatest asset—their brands. In the quest for ever-increasing profits, it's easy for a brand to lose its focus. This is what befell Snapple Beverage Corporation almost as soon as Quaker Oats bought it in 1994. Quaker didn't understand Snapple's mass-market appeal. It changed the ad campaign, dropped its famous brand icon—the Snapple Lady—and revamped the unique distribution system. The results were immediate: Snapple lost money and market share. Unable to revive the floundering brand, Quaker sold the company in 1997.[16]

A recent study of companies in a wide range of industries revealed that only 43 percent of companies measured brand equity. While 72 percent of companies were confident enough in their brand equity to project that it would last two years with no financial support, over two-thirds of the respondents had no formal long-term brand strategy.[17] Also, while we normally think of brand equity as something accruing to the products of manufacturers, service companies also prize it. Canadian Airlines, for example, went to great lengths in 1998 to refresh its brand. The firm believed that its image had become dowdy and didn't adequately promote the airline's domestic services, so it changed its name and uniforms and adopted a retro look for its new brand symbol. It revived the Canada goose logo that had graced its planes throughout the period from 1927 to 1968. The stylized goose logo was originally selected because "it represented nationality, strength of wing, regularity, and organized flight.[18]

BRANDING CHALLENGES

Branding poses several challenges to the marketer. The key decisions are shown in Figure 13.6 and discussed in the following sections.

FIGURE 13.6

An Overview of Branding Decisions

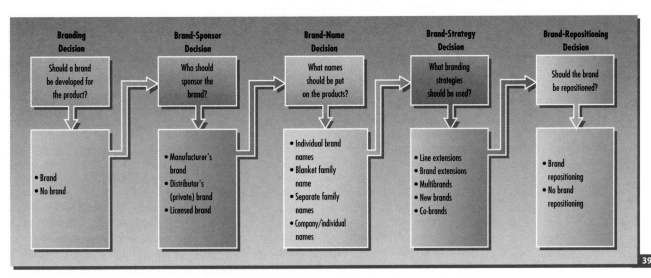

Branding Decision: To Brand or Not to Brand?

The first decision is whether the company should develop a brand name for its product. In the past, most products went unbranded. Producers and intermediaries sold their goods out of barrels, bins, and cases, without any supplier identification. Buyers depended on the seller's integrity. The earliest signs of branding were the medieval guilds' efforts to require craftspeople to put trademarks on their products to protect themselves and consumers against inferior quality. In the fine arts, too, branding began with artists signing their works.

Today, branding is such a strong force that hardly anything goes unbranded. Salt is packaged in distinctive manufacturers' containers, oranges are stamped with growers' names, nuts and bolts are packaged in cellophane with a distributor's label, and automobile components—spark plugs, tires, filters—bear separate brand names from the automakers. Fresh food products—such as chicken, turkey, and salmon—are increasingly being sold under strongly advertised brand names.

In some cases, there has been a return to "no branding" of certain staple consumer goods and pharmaceuticals. Carrefours, the originator of the French hypermarket, introduced a line of "no brands" or generics in its stores in the early 1970s. *Generics* are unbranded, plainly packaged, less expensive versions of common products such as spaghetti, paper towels, and canned peaches. They offer standard or lower quality at a price that may be as much as 20 percent to 40 percent lower than nationally advertised brands and 10 percent to 20 percent lower than retailer private-label brands. The lower price is made possible by lower-quality ingredients, lower-cost labelling and packaging, and minimal advertising.

National brands have fought generics in a number of ways. Ralston-Purina increased its quality and targeted pet owners who identified strongly with their pets and cared most about quality. Procter & Gamble introduced its Banner paper products, a line offering lower quality than its higher lines but greater quality than generics and at a competitive price. Other companies simply have cut their prices to compete with generics.[19]

Why do sellers brand their products when doing so clearly involves costs? Branding gives the seller several advantages:

- The brand name makes it easier for the seller to process orders and track down problems.
- The seller's brand name and trademark provide legal protection of unique product features.
- Branding gives the seller the opportunity to attract a loyal and profitable set of customers. Brand loyalty gives sellers some protection from competition.
- Branding helps the seller segment markets. Instead of P&G's selling a simple detergent, it can offer eight detergent brands, each formulated differently and aimed at specific benefit-seeking segments.
- Strong brands help build the corporate image, making it easier to launch new brands and gain acceptance by distributors and consumers.

Distributors and retailers want brand names because brands make the product easier to handle, hold production to certain quality standards, strengthen buyer preferences, and make it easier to identify suppliers. Consumers want brand names to help them identify quality differences and shop more efficiently.

Brand-Sponsor Decision

A manufacturer has several options with respect to brand sponsorship. The product may be launched as a *manufacturer brand* (sometimes called a national brand), a *distributor brand* (also called reseller, store, house, or private brand), or a *licensed brand name*. Another alternative is for the manufacturer to produce some output under its own name and some under reseller labels. Kellogg, John Deere & Company, and IBM sell virtually all of their output under their own brand names. Hart Schaffner & Marx sells some of its manufactured clothes under licensed names such as Christian Dior and Pierre Cardin. Whirlpool produces both under its own name and under distributors' names (Sears Kenmore appliances).

Although manufacturers' brands dominate, large retailers and wholesalers have been developing their own brands by contracting production from willing manufacturers. Sears has created several names—Diehard batteries, Craftsman tools, Kenmore appliances—that command brand preference and even brand loyalty. Retailers such as The Limited, Benetton, The Body Shop, Gap, and Marks & Spencer carry mostly own-brand merchandise.

Store brands, or private-label brands as they are sometimes called, are especially prevalent on the aisles of grocery stores. IGA, for example, stocks 1400 products under three different private labels. While U.S. supermarkets average 19.7 percent in private-brand sales, Canadian consumers snap up store brands to the extent that they comprise almost 30 percent of their grocery purchases. The Canada/U.S. discrepancy is at least partially explained by the absence of U.S. premium private-label brands, such as President's Choice and Our Compliments.

■ **Loblaw.** Since 1984, when its President's Choice line of foods made its debut, it's been difficult to say "private label" without Loblaw and President's Choice coming instantly to mind. Toronto-based Loblaw's supermarket chain has demonstrated the power of store brands. A finely tuned strategy involving its trademarked President's Choice and "no name" labels has helped differentiate its stores and build the retailer into a powerhouse in Canada and the United States. Some of Loblaw's own store groups have over 40 percent private-label products. By bringing out private labels in new product areas—such as frozen Jambalaya, frozen bread pudding, and frozen hors d'oeuvres—Loblaw stores can reduce units of expensive national and secondary brands but still increase variety. Its store brands have become so successful that Loblaw is licensing them to non-competitive retailers in other countries, thus turning a local store brand into—believe it or not—a global brand. Today, 17 supermarket chains representing 1700 stores carry President's Choice.[20]

In Britain, Sainsbury, the country's largest food chain, sells 50 percent store-label goods. The success of store brands in the grocery trade has inspired other retailers to launch their own lines. For example, in 1999 Zellers launched 200 new items under its Truly label, while Shoppers Drug Mart took on high-end cosmetic manufacturers with its new line of cosmetics called Quo. Zellers' Truly branded products are priced 20 percent lower than similar quality national brands and Zellers is betting that this price incentive will generate $200 million in annual sales for the line. National brands will still remain important, however, even with retailers featuring their own house brands. Some experts believe private brands will never make up more than 50 percent of a store's sales because (1) consumers prefer certain national brands, and (2) many product categories are not feasible or attractive on a private-brand basis.[21]

Why do intermediaries bother to sponsor their own brands? They have to hunt down qualified suppliers who can deliver consistent quality, order large quantities and tie up their capital in inventories, and spend money promoting a private label. Nevertheless, private brands offer two advantages. First, they are more profitable. Intermediaries search for manufacturers with excess capacity who will produce the private label at a low cost. Other costs, such as research and development, advertising, sales promotion, and physical distribution are also much lower. This means that the private brander can charge a lower price and yet make a higher profit margin. Second, retailers develop exclusive store brands to differentiate themselves from competitors. Many consumers don't distinguish between national and store brands.

In the confrontation between manufacturers' and private brands, retailers have many advantages and increasing market power. Because shelf space is scarce, many supermarkets now charge a *slotting fee* for accepting a new brand to cover the cost of listing and stocking it. Safeway, the giant supermarket chain, required a payment of $37 000 from a small pizza-roll manufacturer to stock its product. Retailers also charge for special display space and in-store advertising space. They typically give more prominent display to their own brands and ensure that they are well stocked. Retailers are now building better quality in their store brands.

Manufacturers of national brands are frustrated by the growing power of retailer brands. Kevin Price put it well: "A decade ago, the retailer was a chihuahua nipping at the manufacturer's heels—a nuisance, yes, but only a minor irritant; you fed it and it went away. Today it's a pit bull and it wants to rip your arms and legs off. You'd like to see it roll over, but you're too busy defending yourself to even try."[22] Some marketing commentators predict that private brands will eventually knock out all but the strongest manufacturers' brands.

In years past, consumers viewed the brands in a category arranged in a *brand ladder*, with their favourite brand at the top and remaining brands in descending order of preference. There are now signs that this ladder is being replaced with a consumer perception of *brand parity*—that many brands are equivalent.[23] Instead of a strongly preferred brand, consumers buy from a set of acceptable brands, choosing whichever is on sale that day. As Joel D. Weiner, a former Kraft executive, said: "People don't think the world will come to a screeching halt if they use Tide instead of Cheer." A study by DDB Needham Worldwide reported that the percentage of packaged-goods consumers saying that they bought only well-known brands fell from 77 percent to 62 percent between 1975 and 1990. A Grey Advertising Inc. study reported that 66 percent of consumers said they were trading down to lower-priced brands, particularly store brands.

The growing power of store brands is not the only factor weakening national brands. Consumers are more price sensitive. They are noting more quality equivalence as competing manufacturers and national retailers copy and duplicate the qualities of the best brands. The continuous barrage of coupons and price specials has trained a generation of shoppers to buy on price. The fact that companies have reduced advertising to 30 percent of their total promotion budget has weakened their brand equity. The endless stream of brand extensions and line extensions has blurred brand identity and led to a confusing amount of product proliferation. Of course, one of the newest factors that is not necessarily weakening national brands but changing the entire branding landscape is the Internet. While some "born digital" companies, like Netscape and America Online, have used the Internet to gain brand recognition seemingly overnight, other companies have poured millions of dollars into on-line advertising with no significant effect on brand awareness. See the Marketing for the 21st Century box, "The Elusive Goal of Branding on the World Wide Web."

Manufacturers have reacted by spending substantial amounts of money on consumer-directed advertising and promotion to maintain strong brand preference. Their price has to be somewhat higher to cover the higher promotion cost. At the same time, mass distributors pressure manufacturers to put more promotional money into trade allowances and deals if they want adequate shelf space. Once manufacturers start giving in, they have less to spend on advertising and consumer promotion, and their brand leadership starts spiralling down. This is the national brand manufacturers' dilemma.

To maintain their power vis-à-vis the trade, leading brand marketers need to invest in heavy and continuous R&D to bring out new brands, line extensions, features, and quality improvements. They must sustain a strong "pull" advertising program to maintain high consumer brand recognition and preference. They must find ways to "partner" with major mass distributors in a joint search for logistical economies and competitive strategies that produce savings.

But what if a company is small or just starting out and can't pump millions into expensive advertising campaigns? Technology companies in particular have been adept at achieving levels of brand recognition through less conventional marketing approaches. Here is an example:[24]

- ■ **Sun Microsystems Inc.** Sun has built the visibility of Java, its flagship software program, within the corporate community almost entirely through conducting a public-relations war. It has aimed its guerrilla PR largely at the company's nemesis, Microsoft. For example, after Microsoft developed a technology that competed with Sun's "Java Beans," Sun learned when and where Microsoft planned to introduce it. The day before Microsoft's announcement, Sun mailed bags of coffee beans to reporters with a note saying "Why is Microsoft so jittery?" and inviting them to attend a Sun training seminar on Java Beans at a hotel next to where Microsoft was holding a developers' conference and

Kraft
www.kraft.com

making its announcement. Sun says the tactic was a hit: It attracted over 250 people and planted seeds of doubt in reporters' minds about the Microsoft technology. "Think of it as a military operation," said John Loiacono, Sun's vice president of brand marketing.

For more tips on building brand awareness without resorting to advertising, see the Marketing Memo "Rx for Brand Awareness: Nine Brand Strengtheners."

BRAND-NAME DECISION

Manufacturers and service companies that brand their products must choose which brand names to use. Four strategies are available:

1. *Individual names:* This policy is followed by General Mills (Bisquick, Gold Medal, Betty Crocker, Nature Valley). A major advantage of an individual-names strategy is that the company does not tie its reputation to the product's. If the product fails or appears to have low quality, the company's name or image is not hurt. A manufacturer of good-quality watches, such as Seiko, can introduce a lower-quality line of watches (called Pulsar) without diluting the Seiko name. The strategy permits the firm to search for the best name for each new product.

2. *Blanket family names:* This policy is followed by Heinz and General Electric. A blanket family name also has advantages. Development cost is less because there is no need for "name" research or heavy advertising expenditures to create brand-name recognition. Furthermore, sales of the new product are likely to be strong if the manufacturer's name is good. Campbell's introduces new soups under its brand name with extreme simplicity and achieves instant recognition.

3. *Separate family names for all products:* This policy is followed by Sears (Kenmore for appliances, Craftsman for tools, and Homart for major home installations). Where a company produces quite different products, it is not desirable to use one blanket family name. Swift and Company developed separate family names for its hams (Premium) and fertilizers (Vigoro). When Mead Johnson developed a diet supplement for gaining weight, it created a new family name, Nutriment, to avoid confusion with its weight-reducing products, Metrecal. Companies often invent different family names for different quality lines within the same product class. Thus A&P food stores sold a first-grade, second-grade, and third-grade set of brands—Ann Page, Sultana, and Iona, respectively.

4. *Company trade name combined with individual product names:* This policy is followed by Kellogg (Kellogg's Rice Krispies, Kellogg's Raisin Bran, and Kellogg's Corn Flakes). Some manufacturers tie their company name to an individual brand name for each product. The company name legitimizes, and the individual name individualizes, the new product.

Once a company decides on its brand-name strategy, it faces the task of choosing a specific brand name. The company could choose the name of a person (Honda, Estée Lauder), location (American Airlines, Kentucky Fried Chicken), quality (Safeway, Duracell), lifestyle (Weight Watchers, Healthy Choice), or an artificial name (Exxon, Kodak). Among the desirable qualities for a brand name are the following:[25]

- *It should suggest something about the product's benefits:* Examples: Clearnet, Beauty-rest, Craftsman, Accutron.

- *It should suggest product qualities such as action or colour:* Examples: Fido, Sunkist, Spic and Span, Firebird.

- *It should be easy to pronounce, recognize, and remember:* Short names help. Examples: Bell, Tide, Crest, Puffs.

- *It should be distinctive:* Examples: Esso, Cognos, Mustang, Kodak.

THE ELUSIVE GOAL OF BRANDING ON THE WORLD WIDE WEB

Ever had a day when you couldn't get a TV commercial out of your head? Or, were ad jingles stuck in your cranium, like "I'd like to buy the world a Coke," or "I'm just mad about saffron." If you're like most people, you sop up a certain amount of TV advertising. Now, try to remember the last ad you saw while surfing the Web. Drawing a blank? That's not surprising. The ineffectiveness of the Web as a brand-building tool is one of the most pressing issues facing marketers today.

The issue of building brands through Web advertising has so confounded marketers that Procter & Gamble held a summit on the topic in the summer of 1998. Over 400 executives converged at P&G headquarters in Cincinnati, from Internet companies such as America Online and agency.com to packaged-goods giants like Unilever and Kraft. Their goal: to harness the interactivity of the Internet to build and maintain brands. Here are some of the challenges marketers confront.

- The one-to-one nature of the Web does not build mass brand awareness: On the World Wide Web, it's as if millions of private conversations are going on. So, how do you establish the universal meanings, like "Coke is it," that are at the heart of brand recognition and brand value? It's not the same as when millions of people watch the Superbowl and see the same 30-second Budweiser spot at the same time. That's why tactics that have worked on TV have failed on the Web. Bell Atlantic developed an on-line soap opera that revolved around yuppie newlyweds Troy and Linda. Although the site won raves from critics and had lots of fans, Bell Atlantic's research showed it did nothing to boost the brand. Meyer Berlow, America Online's head of sales, expresses the issue this way: "[the] basic method of advertising ... has been breaking and entering. I jump in front of you, amuse you a little, give you a piece of information I hope will change your behaviour, but that's a brain-dead model.

It worked when there were only three channels and the bathroom. Now the consumer has a million choices."

- The format of Internet advertising has so far been ineffective: P&G and others countered Berlow by saying that the same breaking and entering model could be effective if bandwidth increased to allow high-fidelity sound and full motion video. P&G has been pushing to get Internet publishers to allow larger, more complex types of ads. So far, ads on the Internet are all too ignorable. The two most common are banner ads and interstitials. Banner ads are those tiny rectangular ads on which you can click for more information. In a discouraging Jupiter Communications survey, 21 percent of Internet users polled said they never clicked on banner ads and another 51 percent said they clicked only rarely. Interstitial ads, which flash in the browser window before the site is loaded, have proved annoying to most consumers.

- In the digital world consumers are in control: Even if advertisers put larger, richer ads on the Web, they would likely face a consumer backlash. Those who have grown up with the Web, the kids Don Tapscott christened "the Net Gen," are skeptical of ads in general and resentful of ads on the Web in particular. More important, digital developments allow Web surfers to choose products solely on real value and not just intangibles, like brand associations. Already compare.net offers a free on-line buyer's guide that allows users to compare features on more than 10 000 products. Soon digital personal assistants, called soft bots, knowbots, or just "bots," will know all your preferences. These tireless workers will surf the Internet looking for information you've requested—finding the perfect chocolate-chip cookie or the most appropriate laptop computer for your needs. This development is sure to weaken brands further.

It's therefore not surprising that some of the biggest superstars of e-commerce still conduct most of their branding

(continued)

- *It should not carry poor meanings in other countries and languages:* Example: *Nova* is a poor name for a car to be sold in Spanish-speaking countries; it means "doesn't go."

Normally, companies choose brand names by generating a list of possible names, debating their merits, eliminating all but a few, testing them with target consumers, and making a final choice. Today many companies hire a marketing research firm to develop and test names. These companies use human brainstorming sessions and vast computer databases, catalogued by association, sounds, and other qualities. Name-research procedures include *association tests* (What images come to mind?), *learning tests* (How easily is the name pronounced?), *memory tests* (How well is the name remembered?), and *preference tests* (Which names are preferred?). Of course, the firm must also conduct searches through other databases to make sure the chosen name hasn't already been registered. The whole process, however, isn't cheap. One of the

(continued)

efforts off-line. Cisco spends ad money for full-page ads in the *Wall Street Journal* rather than on Web banners; Dell was the fifth-largest spender in tech trade magazines in 1997 and broke a $100-million-plus branding campaign almost entirely on TV. Although Dell hopes to conduct 50 percent of all transactions on-line, it contends that that kind of volume won't come from Web advertising.

At the same time, the almost overnight success of Netscape Communications, Amazon.com and Yahoo! say that a brand can grow and secure customer loyalty on the Web. How? Companies that have powerful brand awareness on the Web all have sites that help consumers do something—whether it's configuring a computer system on-line at Dell.com or offering a host of options for customizing services at Yahoo.com. Marketers who are set on building their brands in the on-line world have to offer consumers an on-line experience or service. "Experiences—not advertising induced perceptions—will drive brand attitudes," says Forrester Research Inc.'s Jim Nail. The latest theory of how to do that involves something called "rational branding." The idea is to wed the emotional pitch of traditional brand marketing with a real service offered only on-line. Television ads for Saturn still offer the same old-fashioned humorous appeal. But now they point viewers to the company's Web site, which offers lots of help and very little hype. The site helps serious car buyers select a model, calculate payments, and find a dealer on-line.

Yet rational branding is not a panacea. There is not much potential in using the Internet as a commerce vehicle when you're selling soap or shampoo. These companies don't have products that lend themselves to exciting Web-based experiences and services. Still, the packaged-goods powerhouses are hardly throwing in the towel. P&G, for instance, has put most of its small on-line marketing budget behind brands like Always panty liners, Tampax tampons, and Pampers diapers, which have

narrow target audiences with more personal subject matter. The company has turned Pampers.com into the Pampers Parenting Institute, addressing various issues of concern to new or expectant parents. Unilever has struck a deal with on-line supermarket Netgrocer to use pop-up ads to promote its products as people shop on-line, much as the company works with supermarket chains to create in-store promotions. One thing consumers can be sure of is that there will be more, not less, advertising and brand building on the Web as e-commerce develops.

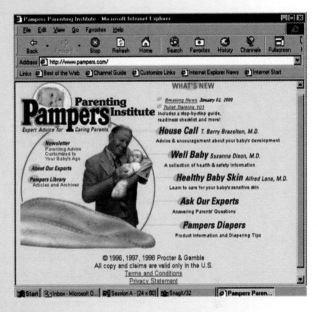

The Pampers Parenting Institute home page.

Sources: Jeffrey O'Brien, "Web Advertising and the Branding Mission," *Upside*, September 1998, pp. 90–94; Don Tapscott, "Net Culture Reshapes Brand Opportunities," *Advertising Age*, November 10, 1997; Saul Hansell, "Selling Soap Without the Soap Operas, Mass Marketers Seek Ways to Build Brands on the Web," *New York Times*, August 24, 1998, p. D1; Ellen Neuborne, "Branding on the Net," *Business Week*, November 9, 1998, pp. 76–86.

best-known specialists in the "name game" is Namelab Inc., which says its jobs run about $90 000 on average. Namelab is responsible for such brand names as Acura and Compaq.[26]

Many firms strive to build a unique brand name that eventually will become intimately identified with the product category. Examples are Frigidaire, Kleenex, Kitty Litter, Levis, Jell-O, Popsicle, Scotch Tape, Xerox, Rollerblade, and Fiberglas. In 1994 Federal Express officially shortened its marketing identity to FedEx, a term that has become a synonym for "to ship overnight." Yet identifying a brand name with a product category may threaten the company's exclusive rights to that name. Cellophane and shredded wheat are now in the public domain and available for any manufacturer to use.

Given the rapid growth of the global marketplace, companies should choose brand names that work globally. These names should be meaningful and pronounceable in other languages. One thing Compaq liked about the name Presario for its line of home computers is that it conjures up similar meanings in various Latin-influenced languages. In French, Spanish, Latin, or Portuguese, Presario has the same, or similar, association that it does in English. It makes one immediately think of an "Impresario," the magical master of the whirl and fantasy of a stage production. Companies also should not choose names owned by someone in another country. For example, Anheuser-Busch cannot use the name "Budweiser" in Germany.

BRAND-STRATEGY DECISION

A company has five choices when it comes to brand strategy. The company can introduce *line extensions* (existing brand name extended to new sizes or flavours in the existing product category), *brand extensions* (brand names extended to new-product categories), *multibrands* (new brand names introduced in the same product category), *new brands* (new brand name for a new category product), and *cobrands* (brands bearing two or more well-known brand names).

Line Extensions. Line extensions consist of introducing additional items in the same product category under the same brand name, such as new flavours, forms, colours, added ingredients, and package sizes. For example, Zeller's has extended its Martha Stewart Everyday lines of household goods after Canadian consumers literally had the products flying off the shelves. It now offers over 1700 products in bed, bath, and kitchen goods.[27]

Many companies are now introducing *branded variants*, which are specific brand lines supplied to specific retailers or distribution channels. They result from the pressure retailers put on manufacturers to enable the retailers to provide distinctive offerings. A camera company may supply its low-end cameras to mass merchandisers while limiting its higher-priced items to specialty camera shops. Or Valentino may design and supply different lines of its suits and jackets to different department stores.[28]

Line extension involves risks and has provoked heated debate among marketing professionals.[29] On the downside, extensions may lead to the brand name losing its specific meaning; Ries and Trout call this the "line-extension trap."[30] When a person asked for a Coke in the past, she received a 6.5-ounce bottle. Today the seller will have to ask: New, Classic, or Cherry Coke? Regular or diet? Caffeine or caffeine-free? Bottle or can? Sometimes the original brand identity is so strong that its line extensions serve only to confuse and don't sell enough to cover development and promotion costs. A-1 poultry sauce flopped because people identify A-1 with beef, and Clorox detergent was doomed because Clorox means "bleach" and people don't want their clothes to come out colourless. Consider the following misfire:

- **Nabisco.** Even when a new line extension sells well, its sales may come at the expense of other items in the line. Although Fig Newton's cousins Cranberry Newtons, Blueberry Newtons, and Apple Newtons are all doing well for Nabisco, the original Fig Newton brand now seems like just another flavour. A line extension works best when it takes sales away from competing brands, not when it deflates or cannibalizes the company's other items.

However, line extensions can and often do have a positive side. They have a much higher chance of survival than brand-new products. Some marketing executives defend line extensions as the best way to build a business. Kimberly-Clark's Kleenex unit has had great success with line extensions. "We try to get facial tissue in every room of the home," says one Kimberly-Clark executive. "If it is there, it will get used." This philosophy led to 20 varieties of Kleenex facial tissues, including lotion-impregnated tissues, boxes with nursery-rhyme drawings for children's rooms, and a "man-sized" box with tissues 60 percent larger than regular Kleenex.

Line extensions are also fuelled by fierce competition in the marketplace, calling for matching competitors' new offerings. Nabisco has had such success with its Snackwell Fat-Free cookies that every competitor has had to extend its product line in defence. One study, by Reddy, Holak, and Bhat, examined what makes a line extension succeed or fail. Data on 75 line extensions of 34 cigarette brands over a 20-year period yielded these findings: Line extensions of strong brands, symbolic brands, brands given strong advertising and promotion support, and those entering earlier into a project subcategory are more successful. The size of the company and its marketing competence also play a role.[31]

Brand Extensions. A company may use its existing brand name to launch new products in other categories. Honda uses its company name to cover such different products as automobiles, motorcycles, snowblowers, lawn mowers, marine engines, and snowmobiles. This allows Honda to advertise that it can fit "six Hondas in a two-car garage." Gap stores now feature its name on soap, lotion, shampoo, conditioner, shower gel, bath salts, and perfume spray. A new trend in corporate brand building is that corporations are licensing their names to manufacturers of a wide range of products—from bedding to shoes. See the Marketing Insight box, "From Harley-Davidson Armchairs to Coca-Cola Fishing Lures: The Rise of Corporate Branding," for a closer look at the new trend in corporate image branding.

Brand-extension strategy offers many of the same advantages as line extensions. Sony puts its name on most of its new electronic products and instantly establishes the new product's high quality. Like line extension, brand extension also involves risks. The new product might disappoint buyers and damage their respect for the company's other products. The brand name may be inappropriate to the new product—consider buying Standard Oil ketchup, Drano milk, or Boeing cologne. The brand name may lose its special positioning in the consumer's mind through overextension. *Brand dilution* occurs when consumers no longer associate a brand with a specific product or highly similar products. Competitors benefit from brand dilution. A brand is stronger the more narrow its focus. Richard Branson, the flamboyant CEO and founder of London-based Virgin Group, is ambitiously putting the Virgin name on a host of diverse products. Yet naysayers think he is diluting the Virgin brand:

- **Virgin Group.** Known originally for its music stores and now primarily for its airline, the Virgin Group spans three continents and includes planes, trains, financial services, music stores, cinemas, and cola. Yet, with the name attached to dozens of unrelated ventures, marketing experts and financial analysts warn that Branson risks diluting the brand's strength. For Branson, brand extension strengthens the company's image as a brash upstart. Branson prefers to enter industries in which customers have few choices—as when he pits his Virgin Cola against industry giants Pepsi and Coca-Cola. "We have a strategy of using the credibility of our brand to challenge the dominant players in a range of industries where we believe the consumer is not getting value for money," says Branson. Yet, if Branson can't turn a profit on the company's Virgin Cola or improve the service on its rail line, as promised, the Virgin name will inevitably be tarnished.[32]

Virgin Group
www.virgin.com

Companies that are tempted to transfer their brand name must research how well the brand's associations fit the new product. The best result would occur when the brand name builds the sales of both the new product and the existing product. An acceptable result would be one in which the new product sells well without affecting the sales of the existing product. The worst result would be one in which the new product fails and hurts the sales of the existing product.[33]

Multibrands. A company will often introduce additional brands in the same product category. Sometimes the company is trying to establish different features or appeal to different buying motives. Thus, P&G produces nine different brands of detergents. A multibranding strategy also enables the company to lock up more distributor shelf space and to protect its major brand by setting up *flanker brands*. Seiko establishes different brand names for its higher-priced (Seiko Lasalle) and lower-priced watches (Pulsar) to protect its flanks. Sometimes the company inherits different brand names in the process of acquiring competitors. Electrolux, the Swedish multinational, owns a stable of acquired brand names (Frigidaire, Kelvinator, Westinghouse, Zanussi, White, Gibson) for its appliance lines.

A major pitfall in introducing multibrand entries is that each might obtain only a small market share, and none may be particularly profitable. The company will have

From Harley-Davidson Armchairs to Coca-Cola Fishing Lures: The Rise of Corporate Branding

When BMW bought the Rolls-Royce name—and nothing else—for $60 million, it confirmed what savvy investors have always known: A strong brand name is one of the most valuable assets a company has. Now companies are realizing that they shouldn't confine those assets to showrooms, corporate handbooks, stationery, business cards, or the company's core product. Instead, corporations have seized on licensing to push the company name and image. This is why we're suddenly seeing products like Pillsbury doughboy potholders, Coca-Cola Picnic Barbie, and Harley-Davidson armchairs and baby clothes.

In 1997 retail sales from licensing rights in the United States and Canada were $110 billion. Corporate brand licensing claimed 22 percent of that total, the same amount earned from licensing rights to entertainment properties! The practice of corporate brand and trademark licensing is becoming more pervasive because licensing is a low-risk way for companies to increase revenue and raise brand awareness. Certainly the success of Coca-Cola has inspired hundreds of companies to do likewise. Yet, few people know that Coca-Cola did not get into licensing to ramp up its brand awareness, but purely as a defensive manoeuvre. In the early 1980s lawyers advised the company that if it did not get into the T-shirt market, someone else legally could. Coke responded by setting up a licensing program, which started modestly but now consists of a large department overseeing more than 240 licensees and at least 10 000 products. Similarly, after years of having their image "ripped off," the RCMP turned to The Walt Disney Company (Canada) Limited to help it safeguard commercial use of its image. During the five-year term of the program, licensing helped the RCMP generate over $500 000, which it distributed to 85 community policing projects across Canada. When the contract expires in December 1999, the RCMP feels confident that it has learned enough from Disney about licensing to start directly managing the program itself.

Although most companies have long sold promotional merchandise sporting their names and logos to dealers and distributors, full-scale retail merchandising is a real shift. Companies are making this shift not only to build brand awareness in the present but also to ensure it in the future. Caterpillar and John Deere are two companies with narrow markets that are now licensing a wide range of products. Many of these products are geared to young people, who are certainly not the target market for Caterpillar's earth-moving equipment or John Deere's tractors! For instance, Caterpillar has a licensing agreement with Big Smith Brands to make Caterpillar work clothes, and Cat is also teaming up with Mattel to create a line of toys based on its construction equipment. Both Caterpillar and John Deere have cut deals with shoe manufacturers to sell work boots. The "Cat" boot is now Wolverine World's (of Hush Puppies fame) hottest product. David Aaker, author of *Building Strong Brands*, says the new branded offerings will help equipment makers to reach out to younger people. People who appreciate Deere's history "are getting older and older," he says. "They have to get people in their twenties and thirties to understand the tradition."

Sometimes companies get into licensing as a way to extend the brand to a new target market. Although a Harley-Davidson armchair would seem like an unlikely product, it's the motorcycle company's way of reaching out to women, who are only nine percent of its market. It also licenses toys, including a Barbie dressed in a "very feminine outfit" to appeal to future generations of Harley purchasers. The ultimate goal is to sell more bikes to audiences that are not part of the core market.

What's in corporate licensing for the licensees, the manufacturers who pay big bucks for corporate brand names or trademarks? Compared to entertainment properties and celebrities, corporate names are much less risky. What happens to a product brandishing the name of a sports celebrity when that celebrity is busted for drugs? Or what can a manufacturer do with all its Godzilla backpacks after the Godzilla movie flops (as it did)?

Corporations are safer bets. Many have been around for decades, and, besides, they have a surprising appeal for customers. Particularly for baby boomers, nostalgia is the driving force behind the impulse to buy a Coke beach towel. Seth M. Siegel, co-chairman of the Beanstalk Group, which manages licensing for Coca-Cola, Harley-Davidson, and Hormel, says, "We live in a secular society, but people still love to surround themselves with icons that move them."

Sources: Adapted from Constance L. Hays, "No More Brand X: Licensing of Names Adds to Image and Profit," *New York Times*, June 12, 1998, p. D1; with additional information drawn from Royal Canadian Mounted Police New Release 99-09-24, "RCMP to Renew Licensing Agreement with Mounted Police Foundation." (http://www.rcmp-grc.gc.ca.html/nr-99-25.htm). Colleen Hawn, "What's in a Name? Whatever You Make It," *Forbes*, July 27, 1998, pp. 84–88. Carl Quintanilla, "Advertising: Caterpillar, Deere Break Ground in Consumer-Product Territory," *Wall Street Journal*, June 20, 1996, p. B2. Also see David A. Aaaker, *Building Strong Brands* (New York: Free Press, 1995).

dissipated its resources over several brands instead of building a few highly profitable brands. Ideally, a company's brands within a category should cannibalize the competitors' brands and not each other. At the very least, the net profits with multibrands should be larger even if some cannibalism occurs.[34]

New Brands. When a company launches products in a new category, it may find that none of its current brand names are appropriate. If Timex decides to make toothbrushes, it is not likely to call them Timex toothbrushes. Yet establishing a new brand name in the North American marketplace for a mass-consumer-packaged good can cost anywhere from $75 million to $150 million.

Cobrands. A rising phenomenon is the emergence of *cobranding* (also called *dual branding*), in which two or more well-known brands are combined in an offer. Each brand sponsor expects that the other brand name will strengthen preference or purchase intention. In the case of copackaged products, each brand hopes it might be reaching a new audience by associating with the other brand. Amazon.com Inc. and Dell Computer Corporation, for example, recently linked their brands on joint Web sites in the hope of selling more books, videos, music and computers over the Internet. ING Direct and Canadian Tire recently formed an alliance in which they linked their brands to provide in-store banking services at 350 Canadian Tire locations.[35]

Cobranding takes a variety of forms. One is *ingredient cobranding*, when Betty Crocker's brownie mix includes Hershey's chocolate syrup. Another form is *same-company cobranding*, as when General Mills advertises Trix and Yoplait yogurt. Still another form is *joint-venture cobranding*, as in the case of General Electric and Hitachi lightbulbs in Japan and the CIBC Visa Aerogold credit card. Finally, there is *multiple-sponsor cobranding*, as in the case of Taligent, a technological alliance of Apple, IBM, and Motorola.[36]

Many manufacturers make components—motors, computer chips, carpet fibres—that enter into final branded products, and whose individual identity normally gets lost. These manufacturers hope their brand will be featured as part of the final product. Among the few component branders that have succeeded in building a separate identity are Intel, Nutrasweet, and Gortex. Intel's consumer-directed brand campaign convinced many personal computer buyers to buy only computer brands with "Intel Inside." As a result, major PC manufacturers—IBM, Dell, Compaq—purchase their chips from Intel at a premium price rather than buy equivalent chips from an unknown supplier. Searle has convinced many beverage consumers to look for Nutrasweet

An Intel ad for its Pentium II processor.

as an ingredient. Manufacturers of outerwear can charge a higher price if their garments include Gortex. Despite these success stories, most component manufacturers find it hard to convince buyers to insist on a certain component, material, or ingredient in the final product. A consumer is not likely to choose a car because it features Champion spark plugs or Stainmaster upholstery.

BRAND REPOSITIONING

However well a brand is currently positioned, the company may have to reposition it later when facing new competitors or changing customer preferences. 7-Up, for example, successfully repositioned itself from being one of several soft drinks bought primarily by older people who wanted a bland, lemon-flavoured drink, to being the sole "Uncola." Suzuki Canada decided it needed to reposition itself for the new millennium. The company parked its previous slogan, "All you have to do is drive one," and replaced it with the more powerful "Suzuki! Engineered Beyond Belief!" Seven new television spots along with a print campaign will bring home the message that Suzukis are built better than they have to be. Family Channel, the 11-year-old, Toronto-based, commercial-free family entertainment network, also decided to reposition itself in 1999 when research revealed that people thought the channel was a little "too nice," "squeaky clean," and "Pollyannish." As network president Len Cochrane noted, "By re-branding the network, we want Family to become more contemporary and relevant to our viewers with a more universal family appeal."[37]

PACKAGING AND LABELLING

Most physical products have to be packaged and labelled. Some packages—such as the Coke bottle and the L'eggs container—are world famous. Many marketers have called packaging a fifth P, along with price, product, place, and promotion. Most marketers, however, treat packaging and labelling as an element of product strategy.

PACKAGING

We define *packaging* as follows:

- *Packaging* includes the activities of designing and producing the container for a product.

The container is called the *package,* and it might include up to three levels of material. Ralph Lauren's Polo Sport aftershave lotion is in a bottle (*primary package*) that is in a cardboard box (*secondary package*) that is in a corrugated box (*shipping package*) containing six dozen boxes of Polo Sport.

Packaging has become a potent marketing tool. Well-designed packages can create convenience and promotional value. Various factors have contributed to packaging's growing use as a marketing tool:

- *Self-service:* An increasing number of products are sold on a self-service basis. In an average supermarket, which stocks 15 000 items, the typical shopper passes by some 300 items per minute. Given that 53 percent of all purchases are made on impulse, the effective package operates as a "five-second commercial." The package must perform many of the sales tasks: attract attention, describe the product's features, create consumer confidence, and make a favourable overall impression. Retailers are relying on self-service to move even technology-based products. Clearnet, the wireless-phone company, realized that buying such products could be an overwhelming task for many consumers and that packaging could play a key role in simplifying this task. Using pristine graphics on its boxes, a green leaf on a white background, the firm not only differentiated itself from competitors, but it also communicated ease and simplicity to consumers. The package was so successful that it won *Marketing* magazine's 1998 gold award for package design.

- *Consumer affluence:* Rising consumer affluence means consumers are willing to pay a little more for the convenience, appearance, dependability, and prestige of better packages.

- *Company and brand image:* Packages contribute to instant recognition of the company or brand. The Campbell Soup Company estimates that the average shopper sees its familiar red-and-white can 76 times a year, creating the equivalent of $39 million worth of advertising.

- *Innovation opportunity:* Innovative packaging can bring large benefits to consumers and profits to producers. Softsoap cornered the market on pumps for dispensing soap. Toothpaste pump dispensers have captured 12 percent of the toothpaste market because they are more convenient and less messy. Chesebrough-Pond's increased its overall nail-polish sales by 22 percent after introducing its novel Aziza Polishing Pen for fingernails.

Developing an effective package for a new product requires several decisions. The first task is to establish the *packaging concept*: defining what the package should basically *be* or *do* for the particular product. Canadian law stipulates that the container for the product must be constructed, filled, and displayed so that consumers are not misled about either the quality of quantity of the product. Decisions must now be made on additional elements—size, shape, materials, colour, text, and brand mark. Decisions must be made on the amount of text, on cellophane or other transparent films, on a plastic or a laminate tray, and so on. Decisions must be made on "tamperproof" devices. The various packaging elements must be harmonized. The packaging elements must also be harmonized with decisions on pricing, advertising, and other marketing elements.

After the packaging is designed, it must be tested. *Engineering tests* are conducted to ensure that the package stands up under normal conditions; *visual tests*, to ensure that the script is legible and the colours harmonious; *dealer tests*, to ensure that dealers find the packages attractive and easy to handle; and *consumer tests*, to ensure favourable consumer response.

In spite of these precautions, a packaging design occasionally gets through with some basic flaw:

- **Planter Lifesavers Company.** In early 1992 Planter Lifesavers Company introduced a new packaging concept to market its peanuts. It borrowed from the success of vacuum-packed brick-pac coffee and introduced vacuum-packed Planter's fresh roast salted peanuts. The goal was to capitalize on the association between fresh-roasted coffee and fresh-roasted peanuts. Consumers made the connection, all right, but with disastrous results: Soon after the product hit grocery-store shelves, Planter's parent company, Nabisco, began to receive calls from angry supermarket managers wanting to know who was going to pay to clean up their coffee machines. Seems consumers were mistaking the vacuum-packed peanuts for coffee and taking them over to the coffee-grinding machines. The new package had come out during the craze for flavoured coffee. Because peanuts are lumpy, it was hard to read the uneven surface of the package's front panel under supermarket lighting. Needless to say, Planter's scrapped the vacuum pack![38]

Developing effective packaging may cost several hundred thousand dollars and take several months to complete. Companies must pay attention to growing environmental and safety concerns about packaging. Shortages of paper, aluminum, and other materials suggest that marketers should try to reduce packaging. Many packages end up as broken bottles and crumpled cans littering the streets and countryside. All of this packaging creates a major problem in solid waste disposal, requiring huge amounts of labour and energy. Fortunately, many companies have gone "green": S. C. Johnson repackaged Agree Plus shampoo in a stand-up pouch using 80 percent less plastic. P&G eliminated outer cartons from its Secret and Sure deodorants, saving 1.5 million kilograms of paper board per year.

■ **Tetra Pak.** Tetra Pak, a major Swedish multinational, provides an example of the power of innovative packaging and customer thinking. Tetra Pak invented an "aseptic" package that enables milk, fruit juice, and other perishable liquid foods to be distributed without refrigeration. This allows dairies to distribute milk over a wider area without investing in refrigerated trucks and facilities. Supermarkets can carry Tetra Pak packaged products on ordinary shelves, allowing them to save expensive refrigerator space. Tetra's motto is "the package should save more than it cost." Tetra Pak advertises the benefits of its packaging to consumers directly and even initiates recycling programs to save the environment.

LABELLING

Government of Canada
http://strategi.ic.gc.ca/SSG/cp01053e.
html

Sellers must label products. The label may be a simple tag attached to the product or an elaborately designed graphic that is part of the package. In Canada, it is mandatory that labels have three elements: they must identify the product, give the quantity being sold, and state the name and place of business of the producer. There are numerous other regulations affecting labelling practices that vary depending on the type of product being sold. Details can be found on the Government of Canada's Strategis Web Site.

Labels perform several functions. First, the label *identifies* the product or brand—for instance, the name Sunkist stamped on oranges. The label might also *grade* the product; canned peaches are grade labelled A, B, and C. The label might *describe* the product: who made it, where it was made, when it was made, what it contains, how it is to be used, and how to use it safely. Finally, the label might *promote* the product through its attractive graphics. Labels eventually become outmoded and need freshening up. The label on Ivory soap has been redone 18 times since the 1890s, with gradual changes in the size and design of the letters.

There is a long history of legal concerns surrounding labels and packaging. The Canadian public is concerned about false and potentially misleading labelling and packaging such as confusing package sizes and shapes that make price comparisons difficult or health claims on food packages such as the descriptions "light," "high fibre," and "low fat." *The Consumer Packaging and Labelling Act* and *The Weights and Measures Act* are aimed at protecting the public from such abuses. Consumerists have lobbied for additional labelling laws to require *open dating* (to indicate product freshness), *unit pricing* (to facilitate product price comparisons), *grade labelling* (to rate the quality level of certain consumer goods), and *percentage labelling* (to reveal the percentage of each important ingredient). Finally, environmentalists are concerned about the impact of packaging materials on both the stock of non-renewable resources and on the impact of the volume of solid waste on the physical environment. These packaging and labelling issues have mobilized public interest in new legislation, and have motivated enlightened managers to try to employ packaging that is ecological as well as economical.

SUMMARY

1. Product is the first and most important element of the marketing mix. Product strategy calls for making coordinated decisions on product mixes, product lines, brands, and packaging and labelling.

2. In planning its market offering, the marketer needs to think through the five levels of the product. The core benefit is the fundamental benefit or service the customer is really buying. At the second level, the marketer has to turn the core benefit into a basic product. At the third level, the marketer prepares an expected product, a set of attributes that buyers normally expect and agree to when they buy the product. At the fourth level, the marketer prepares an augmented product, one that includes additional services and benefits that distinguish the company's offer from that of competitors. At the fifth and final level, the marketer prepares a potential product, which encompasses all the augmentations and transformations the product might ultimately undergo.

3. Products can be classified in several ways. In terms of durability and reliability, products can be non-durable goods, durable goods, or services. In the consumer-goods category, products are either convenience goods (staples, impulse goods, emergency goods), shopping goods (homogeneous and heterogeneous), specialty goods, or unsought goods. In the industrial-goods category, products fall into one of three categories: materials and parts (raw materials and manufactured materials and parts), capital items (installations and equipment), or supplies and business services (operating supplies, maintenance and repair items, maintenance and repair services, business advisory services).

4. Most companies sell more than one product. A product mix can be classified according to width, length, depth, and consistency. These four dimensions are the tools for developing the company's marketing strategy and deciding which product lines to grow, maintain, harvest, and divest. To analyze a product line and decide how many resources should be invested in that line, product-line managers need to look at sales and profits and market profile.

5. A company can change the product component of its marketing mix by lengthening its product via line stretching (downmarket, upmarket, or both) or line filling, by modernizing its products, by featuring certain products, and by pruning its products to eliminate the least profitable.

6. Branding is a major issue in product strategy. Branding is expensive and time-consuming, and it can make or break a product. The most valuable brands have a brand equity that is considered an important company asset. In thinking about branding strategy, companies must decide whether to brand; whether to produce manufacturer brands, or distributor or private brands; which brand name to use, and whether to use line extensions, brand extensions, multibrands, new brands, or cobrands. The best brand names suggest something about the product's benefits; suggest product qualities; are easy to pronounce, recognize, and remember; are distinctive; and do not carry negative meanings or connotations in other countries or languages.

7. Many physical products must be packaged and labelled. Well-designed packages can create convenience value for customers and promotional value for producers. In effect, they can act as "five-second commercials" for the product. Marketers develop a packaging concept and test it functionally and psychologically to ensure that it achieves its desired objectives and is compatible with public policy and environmental concerns. Physical products also require labelling for identification and possible grading, description, and product promotion. Sellers may be required by law to present certain information on the label to protect and inform consumers.

APPLICATIONS

CHAPTER CONCEPTS

1. Offer a definition of the basic business of each of the following large companies. In other words, what basic needs does each company seek to satisfy? (a) General Motors, (b) Bayer (maker of aspirin), (c) Altimira Mutual Funds, (d) Loblaw, (e) *Canadian Business* (magazine).

2. Most firms prefer to develop a diversified product line to avoid overdependence on a single product. Yet there are certain advantages that accrue to a firm that produces and sells one product. What are some of these advantages?

3. The American Marketing Association established the Edison Award Program in 1986 to recognize excellence in innovation in consumer products. The winners (which are the products themselves) are chosen on the basis of the following criteria:

Marketplace innovativeness—innovative strategy, positioning, advertising, and sales promotion, all of which translate into marketplace success

Profitability and staying power

Technological innovativeness

Market-structure innovativeness—innovation in pioneering a new market or restructuring a present market by creating a new segment or dominating an existing one

Lasting value

Societal impact—the product improves the consumer's lifestyle or increases the consumer's freedom of choice

Some products that have won awards in the past are Kellogg's Healthy Choice cereals, Nabisco's Reduced Fat Oreos, Frito-Lay's Baked Tostitos, and Ferolito's Arizona Iced Tea. Select five products that you believe meet the criteria listed above, and explain why you identified these products as winners.

MARKETING AND ADVERTISING

1. The ad in Figure 1 is for Toyota's Prius model, the world's first hybrid car that runs on gas and electricity. Since it emits 90 percent less carbon monoxide, less hydrocarbons and less nitrogen oxides, it is positioned as being environmentally responsible. What is the core benefit of this product? What are the basic, expected, and augmented products? Analyze this ad, and explain what elements of product and branding strategy are incorporated into the ad's theme and copy.

2. Figure 2 shows a Zippo ad aimed at business markets. Based on this ad and your knowledge of Zippo, discuss the company's product mix. Why would Zippo put its brand name on the three products shown in the ad? How would you categorize the brand strategy represented by this ad? What does this strategy imply about Zippo's perception of its brand equity? Explain your answer.

Figure 1

Figure 2

FOCUS ON TECHNOLOGY

What's in a name? For marketers, brand names are valuable assets that must be selected with care. Some companies hire a specialized marketing research firm to create and test potential brand names, whereas others prefer to handle the process internally. Now "do-it-yourself" marketers can use brand-name-development technology offered by Namestormers.

Namestormers
www.namestormers.com

The company's Web site explains how its NamePro software can be used to generate brand names and offers a free downloadable demonstration. Also on the Web site is an explanation of NameWave, a Web-based service that presents up to 40 brand-name ideas for products in categories selected by the user. What are the advantages of using NamePro or NameWave? What are the disadvantages? If you were responsible for developing a product's brand name, would you choose one of these options? Why or why not?

MARKETING FOR THE 21ST CENTURY

As noted earlier, Pampers is an aggressive brand builder on and off the Internet. In addition to its traditional advertising schedule, Pampers maintains a value-added Web site offering advice and answers to parents' questions about child development and—what else?—toilet training.

Pampers
www.pampers.com

Visit the Pampers site and browse the "What's New" section to see the kind of information parents can find here. Next, go to the "Pampers Diapers" section, and click on the two links that lead to information about having Pampers delivered to your home and buying Pampers in your local area. After you enter your zip code, you will see banner ads for several retailers. Why would these retailers want links to the Pampers Web site? Why would Procter & Gamble highlight these links? How does this site contribute to brand building for all participating retailers as well as for Pampers?

YOU'RE THE MARKETER: SONIC MARKETING PLAN

Decisions about products and branding are critical to the success of any marketing plan. During the planning stages, marketers must consider a variety of issues related to product-mix, product-line length, brand equity, and brand strategies.

At Sonic, you are helping Jane Melody manage product lines and branding for the company's shelf stereos. Look again at the company's current situation, the target market, and the product strategy data already in the marketing plan. Then answer these questions to plan Sonic's product programs (noting the need for additional research where necessary):

- *What is the core benefit of your product? What elements of the potential product should you consider incorporating?*

- *Analyze your current product mix and your current product line. What specific changes do you recommend—and why?*

- *What are the attributes and benefits suggested by the Sonic brand?*

- *What specific line and brand extensions, new brands, or other brand strategies do you recommend for Sonic—and why?*

Consider how your answers to these questions will influence Sonic's marketing efforts. Then, as your instructor directs, summarize your recommendations in a written marketing plan or type them into the Marketing Strategy and Program sections of the Marketing Plan Pro software.

Designing and Managing Services

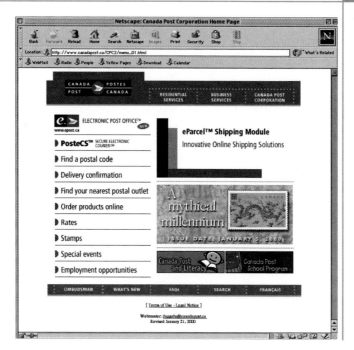

For many years, the term "customer service" seemed to be an oxymoron at Canada's venerable postal service. Plagued by labour disputes and a ballooning operating deficit, the institution just couldn't seem to deliver. Today, however, it has undergone a transformation. Not only did it report $50 million in revenues in 1998–99, but it also developed one of the best reputations of any postal service in the world. It almost flawlessly delivers over nine billion pieces of mail and packages annually. Its mission statement captures its devotion to customer service: *We are in the business to serve all Canadians, businesses and organizations, through the secure delivery of messages, information, and packages to any address in Canada or the world, at a level of quality and value that makes customers want to repeat the experience.* Canada Post was the first postal administration in the world to engage an external auditor to measure its service performance. In 1991, it established a Postal Service Customer Council in each of its postal regions. The Councils provide input on problems and review policies with the aim of continuously improving service.

Canada Post isn't just blowing its own horn when it comes to recognition of its superior level of service. It has achieved an international reputation for providing business solutions to better manage postal services. It has leveraged its experience and established an international consulting subsidiary, Canada Post International Ltd., to sell its expertise. Today, the organization has successfully completed over 80 projects in 35 countries.

Maintaining excellent service at such a large organization is no easy task. The Crown corporation is Canada's thirty-second-largest business and the country's fifth-largest employer. It runs 22 major plants and over 20 000 retail outlets. Its people are critical to its success. It has transformed its former acrimonious culture into an environment defined by fairness, respect, trust, and courtesy. To ensure that its employees have the requisite skills to meet the heavy demands placed on them, Canada Post invests heavily in training. In 1998 alone it spent $56 million in upgrading the skills of its employees.

Canada Post has also leveraged technology to help it improve service. It has established modern call centres accessible by 1-800 numbers. These centres handle over 11 million calls a year and up to 40 000 calls per day. People can use them to help solve problems or obtain information on anything from postal rates to the location of their nearest postal outlet. In addition, Canada Post responds to over 21 500 letters each year. It has developed an easy-to-navigate Web site that gives customers the option of ordering services or finding information on-line. It is in the process of developing a sophisticated bill-payment system with its partner, the Bank of Montreal. Customers will be able to retrieve their bills from a personalized "mailbox" on the Canada Post Web site and pay them through a linked Interac network.

Finally, Canada Post has been highly creative in marketing its specialized services. For example, in an effort to convince mutual fund companies to use more direct mail as part of their spring campaigns, Canada Post sent out a package of information that included a chocolate tool-box and chocolate tools complete with saw, hammer, screwdriver, and pliers under the headline: "Direct Marketing—The Tool You Need to Maximize Your Advertising Investment." Over 40 percent of the companies receiving the information responded—an excellent response rate. Canada Post then follows up on these responses with one-to-one sales presentations. As you can see, today, Canada Post knows how to deliver service and live up to its motto "In Business to Serve"!

Sources: Canada Post Corporation's web site (http://www.canadapost.ca). David Chilton, "Canada Post Increasing Customer Service Efforts," *Strategy: The Canadian Marketing Report*, April 18, 1994, p. 30. Mark De Wolf, "Bill Payment Provides New Vehicle," *Strategy: The Canadian Marketing Report*, January 18, 1999, p. D11. Erica Slomislic, "Special Report: Focus on Financial Services: Canada Post Uses Direct Mail to Sell Mutual Fund Marketers on the Benefits of Direct Mail," *Strategy: The Canadian Marketing Report,* March 12, 1998, DR18.

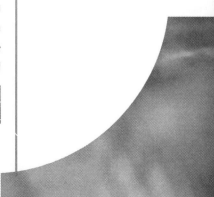

In this chapter, we examine the following questions:

- How are services defined and classified?

- How do services differ from goods?

- How can service firms improve their differentiation, quality, and productivity?

- How can goods-producing companies improve their customer support services?

Philip Kotler believes that every business is a service business: You are not a chemical company. You are a chemical services business. However, marketing theory and practice developed initially in connection with physical products such as toothpaste, cars, and steel. Yet one of the major megatrends of recent years has been the phenomenal growth of services. In 1996 in Canada (the latest year for which Statistics Canada figures are available, services accounted for 64.31 percent of the gross domestic product, compared to 22.75 percent for goods and 6.68 percent for resources). Service occupations will be responsible for all net job growth through the year 2005.[1] These numbers have led to a growing interest in the special problems of marketing services.[2]

THE NATURE OF SERVICES

Service industries are quite varied. The *government sector*, with its courts, employment services, hospitals, loan agencies, military services, police and fire departments, post office, regulatory agencies, and schools, is in the service business. The *private nonprofit sector*, with its museums, charities, places of worship, colleges, foundations, and hospitals, is in the service business. A good part of the *business sector*, with its airlines, banks, hotels, insurance companies, law firms, management consulting firms, medical practices, motion-picture companies, plumbing-repair companies, and real estate firms, is in the service business. Many workers in the *manufacturing sector*, such as computer operators, accountants, and legal staff, are really service providers. In fact, they make up a "service factory" providing services to the "goods factory."

We define a service as follows:

■ A *service* is any act or performance that one party can offer to another that is essentially intangible and does not result in the ownership of anything. Its production may or may not be tied to a physical product.

Services are part of the electronic age. The Canadian Banking Association, for example, estimates that 85 percent of daily transactions are now done electronically, mostly via banking machines and through debit cards, but there is also a dramatic rise in the use of telephone and Internet banking. A recent survey revealed, in fact, that one in five Canadian consumers are no longer interested in visiting their local branch.[3]

Manufacturers and distributors can use a service strategy to differentiate themselves. Acme Construction Supply, for example, has invested more than $189 000 in its Night Owl delivery service: Acme personnel deposit orders into lockboxes at construction sites during the nighttime hours, so materials are available first thing in the morning. Says the company's regional team leader, "People that are very, very price sensitive don't do business here. But people who see the overall value we provide do. And it's very intimidating to our competition. They have to walk around our delivery boxes every day to make their sales calls."[4]

CATEGORIES OF SERVICE MIX

A company's offering to the marketplace often includes some services. The service component can be a minor or a major part of the total offering. Five categories of offerings can be distinguished:

1. *Pure tangible good:* The offering consists primarily of a tangible good such as soap, toothpaste, or salt. No services accompany the product.

2. *Tangible good with accompanying services:* The offering consists of a tangible good accompanied by one or more services. Levitt observes that "the more technologically sophisticated the generic product (e.g., cars and computers), the more dependent are its sales on the quality and availability of its accompanying customer services (e.g., display rooms, delivery, repairs and maintenance, application aids, operator training, installation advice, warranty fulfilment). In this sense, General Motors is probably more service intensive

than manufacturing intensive. Without its services, its sales would shrivel."[5] See the Marketing Insight box, "Selling Services for Profit."

3. *Hybrid:* The offering consists of equal parts of goods and services. For example, people patronize restaurants for both food and service.

4. *Major service with accompanying minor goods and services:* The offering consists of a major service along with additional services or supporting goods. For example, airline passengers buy transportation service. The trip includes some tangibles, such as food and drinks, a ticket stub, and an airline magazine. The service requires a capital-intensive good—an airplane—for its realization, but the primary item is a service.

5. *Pure service:* The offering consists primarily of a service. Examples include baby-sitting, psychotherapy, and massage.

Because of this varying goods-to-service mix, it is difficult to generalize about services without further distinctions. However, some generalizations seem safe:

First, services vary as to whether they are *equipment based* (automated car washes, vending machines) or *people based* (window washing, accounting services). People-based services vary by whether they are provided by unskilled, skilled, or professional workers.

Second, some services require the *client's presence* and some do not. Brain surgery involves the client's presence, but a car repair does not. If the client must be present, the service provider must be considerate of his or her needs. Thus beauty-shop operators will invest in their shop's decor, play background music, and engage in light conversation with the client.

Third, services differ as to whether they meet a *personal need* (personal services) or a *business need* (business services). Physicians will price physical examinations differently for private patients versus employees on a prepaid company health plan. Service providers typically develop different marketing programs for personal and business markets.

Fourth, service providers differ in their *objectives* (profit or non-profit) and *ownership* (private or public). These two characteristics, when crossed, produce four quite different types of organizations. The marketing programs of private schools like Upper Canada College will differ from those of public schools.[6]

CHARACTERISTICS OF SERVICES AND THEIR MARKETING IMPLICATIONS

Services have four major characteristics that greatly affect the design of marketing programs: intangibility, inseparability, variability, and perishability.

Intangibility

Services are intangible. Unlike physical products, they cannot be seen, tasted, felt, heard, or smelled before they are bought. The person getting a face lift cannot see the exact results before the purchase, and the patient in the psychiatrist's office cannot know the exact outcome.

To reduce uncertainty, buyers will look for signs or evidence of the service quality. They will draw inferences about quality from the place, people, equipment, communication material, symbols, and price that they see. Therefore, the service provider's task is to "manage the evidence," to "tangibilize the intangible."[7] Whereas product marketers are challenged to add abstract ideas, service marketers are challenged to add physical evidence and imagery to abstract offers. Consider the following tangible images: "You are in good *hands* with Allstate"; "I've got a piece of the *rock*" (Prudential).

Suppose a bank wants to position itself as the "fast" bank. It could tangibilize this positioning strategy through a number of marketing tools:

1. *Place:* The physical setting must connote quick service. The exterior and interior should have clean lines. The layout of the desks and the traffic flow should be planned carefully. Waiting lines should not get overly long.

Selling Services for Profit

As many companies experience shrinking profit margins on the products they sell, they are trying to make more money on the services they provide. They sometimes charge fees for services that they formerly provided free. In other cases, they are pricing their services higher. Auto dealers today make most of their profit on financing, insurance, and repair services, not on automobiles. Many automakers, including Ford Motor, General Motors, and Honda, are urging dealers to build stand-alone service shops in convenient locations. Dealers are also offering shuttle rides, fax and computer services, and boutiques selling auto-related items. The new service shop in Butler, New Jersey, even has a nail salon.[a]

Here are seven ways manufacturers can create service businesses:

1. Repackaging their product into a system solution: Rather than selling only its products—chemicals, computers, machine tools—the company can embed these products into service programs that meet more of the customers' needs. This type of service has been a large factor driving IBM's turnaround. The computer maker now helps businesses develop, implement, and maintain computer systems that include networks, intranets, and electronic commerce sites. IBM provides the equipment—its own and others'—and then services the system. System solutions now account for 25 percent of IBM's sales.[b]

2. Packaging internal services into saleable external services: Some companies sell an internal competence to other companies. Xerox developed a highly effective internal sales force training program and subsequently decided to launch Xerox Learning Systems to sell its sales training system to other companies. IBM is leveraging its knowledge about computers and selling to other business under its e-commerce banner.

3. Servicing other companies from the company's physical facilities: Companies that manage a physical facility often find they can sell the facility's services to others. Kimberly-Clark operates and maintains its own fleet of corporate aircraft. It has expanded its ability to provide and sell maintenance and overhaul services to other companies operating corporate aircraft.

4. Offering to manage other companies' physical facilities or business processes: At Johnson Controls, a manufacturer of thermostats and energy systems, design engineers who were once confined to their cubicles and harnessed to their computers are now out in their customers' buildings managing the heating and cooling systems they helped to create. Xerox, in part of its transformation from a maker of copiers to "the document company," has not only assumed the copying chores of 4300 large companies but also runs entire mailrooms and ships millions of documents around the world. Xerox Business Services, started in 1992, is the "outsourcing arm of Xerox," and won the Malcolm Baldrige National Quality Award for service in 1997.[c]

5. Selling financial services: Equipment companies often discover that they can profit from financing customers' purchases. General Electric became one of the world's great companies by manufacturing products like refrigerators and lightbulbs. Yet, GE's fastest-growing unit today is GE

(continued)

---

2. *People:* Personnel should be busy. There should be a sufficient number of employees to manage the workload.

3. *Equipment:* Equipment—computers, copying machines, desks—should be and look "state of the art."

4. *Communication material:* Communication materials—text and photos—should suggest efficiency and speed.

5. *Symbols:* The name and symbol should suggest fast service.

6. *Price:* The bank could advertise that it will deposit $5 in the account of any customer who waits in line for more than five minutes.

Service marketers must be able to transform intangible services into concrete benefits. Consider Dun & Bradstreet:

■ **Dun & Bradstreet.** Dun & Bradstreet is a $3 billion firm with an excellent reputation. Its database of 12 million North American companies is so comprehensive that D&B has become something of a central intelligence agency for buyers and sellers. Its 600 field salespeople, for example, help companies determine the creditworthiness of customers. D&B's senior VP of marketing

(continued)

Capital, composed of 28 businesses ranging from credit cards to truck leasing to insurance. Its $56 billion in annual revenues made up about 40 percent of GE's net earnings in 1997, up from 29 percent in 1990. In Germany, electronic giant Siemens earns as much from interest income as from its manufacturing operations. Now the company is setting up its own in-house bank, Siemens Financial Services, to turn a traditional big spender, the old corporate finance division, into a profit centre.[d]

5. Moving into distribution services: Manufacturers can own and operate retailing outlets for their products. Hart Schaffner and Marx is essentially a clothing manufacturer that also operates a series of retail clothing chains. Quaker Oats, the cereal manufacturer, manages several restaurant chains. Many manufacturers also operate factory outlet stores, and some manufacturers have opened their own flagship stores. Sara Lee, for instance, now operates 203 L'eggs/Hanes/Bali/Playtex factory outlet stores, an increase of 53 since 1995. The company also operates 53 Coach stores, 42 Champion stores, 13 Sara Lee stores, and two Hanes Mill Outlet stores. Nike, which used to turn up its nose at the thought of having its goods discounted, now discounts them in the company's own stores. It operates 49 factory outlet stores, as well as 11 NikeTown showcase stores selling at full retail. In Chicago, the Sony Gallery (the first of its kind) is designed to enhance Sony's image. Yet the store carries every consumer electronics product Sony makes.[e]

7. Using the Internet to create new service offerings: Many manufacturers are offering an array of customer services on the Web. Software producer Intuit has created web services (www.quicken.com) that integrate with its desktop programs. Intuit's QuickenMortgage enables Quicken software users to learn about the offerings of and transact with six mortgage lenders. Although all of the services on quicken.com are free so far, the company may add for-profit services, such as Tax Table. Even if services are giveaways, Intuit will reap revenue from advertising and service partners. Trend Micro, a maker of antivirus software, offers customers of its personal product PC-Cillin, a Virus Hospital service for a $30 annual fee. Customers get to send any unknown viruses via e-mail to Trend Micro's virus experts stationed worldwide for a 24-hour turnaround.

[a]Earle Eldridge, "Car Dealers Build Stand-alone Service Centers," *USA Today*, August 21, 1997, pp. B1–B2.

[b]David Einstein, "Bigger and Bluer than Ever/Resurgent IBM Thrives by Meeting Technology Needs for U.S. Business," *San Francisco Chronicle*, November 30, 1998, p. E1.

[c]Del Jones, "Copying Chores Earn Xerox Recognition," *USA Today*, October 16, 1997, p. B4.

[d]Reed Abelson, "Hints of Change at GE Capital as Financial Companies Lose Favor," *New York Times*, October 2, 1998, p. D1; Laura Covill, "Siemens the Financial Engineer," *Euromoney*, August 1998, pp. 65–66.

[e]Richard Halverson, "Bypassing the Marketers in the Middle," *Discount Store News*, May 11, 1998, pp. 70, 108.

Sources: See also Irving D. Canton, "Learning to Love the Service Economy," *Harvard Business Review*, May–June 1984, pp. 89–97; Mack Hanan, *Profits Without Products: How to Transform Your Product Business into a Service* (New York: Amacom, 1992); and Ronald Henkoff, "Service Is Everybody's Business," *Fortune*, June 27, 1994, pp. 48–60.

says, "If we're calling on a bank's credit manager, we'll research the bank's portfolio of customers, and using the information in our database, score them based on their creditworthiness and stability and say, 'You have X% of customers in the high-risk category and X% in low-risk.'"[8]

Dun & Bradstreet
www.dnb.com

Inseparability

Services are typically produced and consumed simultaneously. This is not true of physical goods, which are manufactured, put into inventory, distributed through multiple resellers, and consumed later. If a person renders the service, then the provider is part of the service. Because the client is also present as the service is produced, provider–client interaction is a special feature of services marketing. Both provider and client affect the outcome.

In the case of entertainment and professional services, buyers are very interested in the specific provider. It is not the same concert if Pearl Jam is indisposed and replaced by Celine Dion, or if a legal defence will be supplied by John Nobody because Alan Greenspan is unavailable. When clients have strong provider preferences, price is raised to ration the preferred provider's limited time.

Several strategies exist for getting around this limitation. The service provider can learn to work with larger groups. Psychotherapists have moved from one-on-one therapy to small-group therapy to groups of over 300 people in a large hotel ballroom. The service provider can learn to work faster—the psychotherapist can spend 30 minutes with each patient instead of 50 minutes and can see more patients. The service organization can train more service providers and build up client confidence, as H&R Block has done with its national network of trained tax consultants.

Variability

Because they depend on who provides them and when and where they are provided, services are highly variable. Some doctors have excellent bedside manner; others are less patient with their patients. Some surgeons are very successful in performing a certain operation; others are less successful. Service buyers are aware of this variability and often talk to others before selecting a service provider.

Service firms can take three steps toward quality control. The first is investing in good hiring and training procedures. Recruiting the right service employees and providing them with excellent training is crucial regardless of whether employees are highly skilled professionals or low-skilled workers. Here is an example:

- **ISS International Service System AS.** In an industry marked by low-skilled workers and high staff turnover, ISS, a commercial cleaning service, trains its people relentlessly. Consider the program ISS uses in the division that services small companies. During the first six months on the job, employees are given training in cleaning techniques, such as which chemicals to use on specific stains and surfaces, as well as safety. Then employees move from applied chemistry to applied economics. They learn how to interpret the contracts for each client, and how the client's profitability contributes to ISS. The training makes employees feel they are key to both the client's and the company's profitability.[9]

The second step is standardizing the service-performance process throughout the organization. This is helped by preparing a *service blueprint* that depicts events and processes in a flowchart, with the objective of recognizing potential fail points. Figure 14.1 shows a service blueprint for a nationwide floral-delivery organization.[10] The customer's experience is limited to dialling the phone, making choices, and placing an order. Behind the scenes, the floral organization gathers the flowers, places them in a vase, delivers them, and collects payment. Any one of these activities can be done well or poorly.

The third step is monitoring customer satisfaction through suggestion and complaint systems, customer surveys, and comparison shopping.

Perishability

Services cannot be stored. Some doctors charge patients for missed appointments because the service value existed only at that point. The perishability of services is not a problem when demand is steady. When demand fluctuates, service firms have problems. For example, public-transportation companies have to own much more equipment because of rush-hour demand than if demand were even throughout the day.

Sasser has described several strategies for producing a better match between demand and supply in a service business.[11]

On the demand side:

- *Differential pricing* will shift some demand from peak to off-peak periods. Examples include low early-evening movie prices and weekend discount prices for car rentals.

- *Non-peak demand* can be cultivated. McDonald's opened a breakfast service, and hotels developed minivacation weekends.

- *Complementary services* can be developed during peak time to provide alternatives to waiting customers, such as cocktail lounges in restaurants and automatic-teller machines in banks.

- *Reservation systems* are a way to manage the demand level. Airlines, hotels, and physicians employ them extensively.

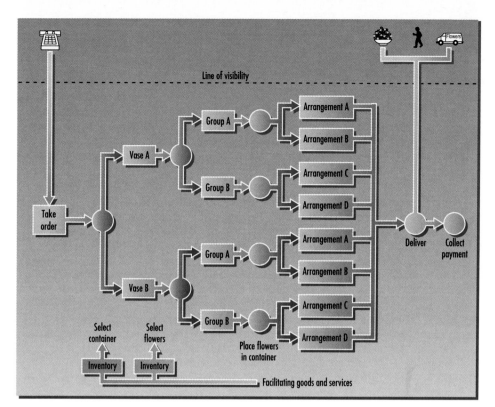

FIGURE 14.1

**A Service-Performance-[...]
Map: Nationwide Floral**

Source: Adapted from G. Lynn Sh[...]
Positioning Through Structura[...]
nal of Marketing, January 198[...]
with permission of the A[...]
Association.

Onta[...]
www[...]

On the supply side:

- *Part-time employees* can be hired to serve peak demand. Universities add part-time teachers when enrolment goes up, and restaurants call in part-time servers when needed.

- *Peak-time efficiency routines* can be introduced. Employees perform only essential tasks during peak periods. Paramedics assist physicians during busy periods.

- *Increased consumer participation* can be encouraged. Consumers fill out their own medical records or bag their own groceries.

- *Shared services* can be developed. Several hospitals can share medical-equipment purchases.

- *Facilities for future expansion* can be developed. An amusement park buys surrounding land for later development.

Club Med has come up with a unique solution to the perishability problem:

- **Club Med.** Founded in 1955, Club Med operates hundreds of Club Med "villages" (resorts) around the world. If the company cannot sell its rooms and air packages, it loses out. Now Club Med uses e-mail to pitch unsold, discounted packages to the 34 000 people in its database. These people are notified early to midweek on rooms and air seats available for travel that weekend. Discounts are typically 30 to 40 percent off the standard package price. An average of 1.2 percent respond to the offers, and Club Med takes in anywhere from $37 500 to $60 000 every month from e-mail sales of "distressed inventory." Before the program, Club Med's only alternative was to rely on travel agents to sell last-minute packages. Club Med's database also includes such information as vacation preferences, preferred sports and activities, preferred time of year for travel, and marital status, as well as geographical data. Although current e-mail offers aren't targeted, the company plans to create one-to-one marketing messages in the future.[12]

Club Med
www.clubn[...]

chapter 14
Designing
and Managing
Services

423

MARKETING STRATEGIES FOR SERVICE FIRMS

Until recently, service firms lagged behind manufacturing firms in their use of marketing. Many service businesses are small (shoe repair, hair salons) and do not use formal management or marketing techniques. There are also professional service businesses (law and accounting firms) that formerly believed it was unprofessional to use marketing. Other service businesses (universities, hospitals) faced so much demand or so little competition until recently that they saw no need for marketing. But this has changed. Consider the case of Ontario Hydro:

■ **Ontario Hydro.** The big power producer is facing a brand-new world, one characterized by deregulation in which it will soon be competing with its customers, Ontario's municipal electric utilities, as well as with new entrants from the United States. With deregulation becoming a reality in 2000, customers will be able to choose their electricity distributor. The stage is set for a battle of epic proportions for the $10-billion Ontario marketplace. Until now, Ontario Hydro hasn't done much to develop relationships with its customers. Many have little awareness of the utility. Thus, it is scrambling to build its brand identify, and it is hiring ad agencies to help it with this task. It is running TV spots touting its high levels of service and it is striving to learn from the experiences of the telephone giants when their industry was deregulated. It has created two separate companies and is developing a strategy of selling electricity along with value-added goods and services. The battle is far from over and it will be an electrifying one to watch.[13]

Traditional four Ps marketing approaches work well for goods, but additional elements require attention in service businesses. Booms and Bitner suggested three additional Ps for service marketing: people, physical evidence, and process.[14] Because most services are provided by *people*, the selection, training, and motivation of employees can make a huge difference in customer satisfaction. Ideally, employees should exhibit competence, a caring attitude, responsiveness, initiative, problem-solving ability, and goodwill. Service companies such as Federal Express and Marriott trust their people enough to empower their front-line personnel to spend up to $150 to resolve a customer problem.

Companies also try to demonstrate their service quality through *physical evidence* and presentation. A hotel will develop a look and observable style of dealing with customers that carries out its intended customer value proposition, whether it is cleanliness, speed, or some other benefit. Finally, service companies can choose among different *processes* to deliver their service. Restaurants have developed such different formats as cafeteria-style, fast-food, buffet, and candlelight service.

Service encounters are affected by several elements (Figure 14.2). Consider a customer visiting a bank to get a loan (service X). The customer sees other customers waiting for this and other services. The customer also sees a physical environment consisting of a building, interior, equipment, and furniture. The customer sees bank personnel and deals with a loan officer. All this is visible to the customer. Not visible is a whole "backroom" production process and organization system that supports the visible business. Thus the service outcome, and whether people will remain loyal to a service provider, is influenced by a host of variables.[15]

In view of this complexity, Gronroos has argued that service marketing requires not only external marketing but also internal and interactive marketing (Figure 14.3).[16] *External marketing* describes the normal work to prepare, price, distribute, and promote the service to customers. *Internal marketing* describes the work to train and motivate employees to serve customers well. Berry has argued that the most important contribution the marketing department can make is to be "exceptionally clever in getting everyone else in the organization to practise marketing."[17]

Interactive marketing describes the employees' skill in serving the client. Because the client judges service not only by its *technical quality* (e.g., Was the surgery successful?)

The Service Business as a System

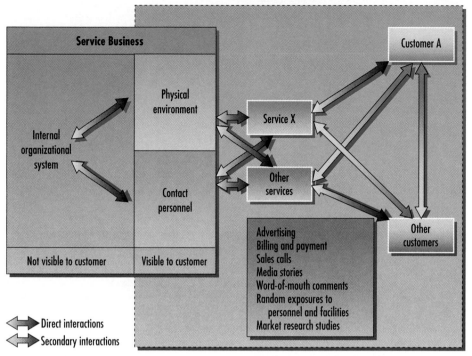

Service Business

| Not visible to customer | Visible to customer |

- Internal organizational system
- Physical environment
- Contact personnel

Service X

Other services

Advertising
Billing and payment
Sales calls
Media stories
Word-of-mouth comments
Random exposures to personnel and facilities
Market research studies

Customer A

Other customers

⬌ Direct interactions
⬌ Secondary interactions

FIGURE 14.2

Elements in a Service Encounter

Source: Slightly modified from P. Eiglier and E. Langeard, "A Conceptual Approach to the Service Offering," in *Proceedings of the EAARM X Annual Conference*, ed. H. Hartvig Larsen and S. Heede (Copenhagen: Copenhagen School of Economics and Business Administration, 1981).

but also by its *functional quality* (e.g., Did the surgeon show concern and inspire confidence?),[18] service providers must deliver "high touch" as well as "high tech."[19] Consider Schwab:

- **Charles Schwab.** Charles Schwab, North America's largest discount brokerage house, uses the Web to create an innovative combination of high-tech and high-touch services. One of the first major brokerage houses to provide on-line trading, Schwab had two million investors in its online trading network in 1998. Yet instead of becoming a no-frills Internet trading operation, Schwab is bringing one of the most comprehensive financial and company information resources on the market, the Analyst's Center, to the Web. It offers account information and proprietary research from retail brokers, among other things. By adding this and other investment tools to its Web site, Schwab

Charles Schwab
www.schwab.com

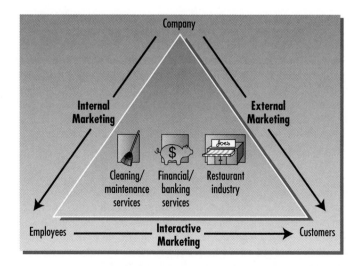

FIGURE 14.3

Three Types of Marketing in Service Industries

FIGURE 14.4

Continuum of Evaluation for Different Types of Products

Source: Valarie A. Zeithaml, "How Consumer Evaluation Processes Differ between Goods and Services," in *Marketing of Services*, ed. James H. Donnelly and William R. George. Reprinted with permission of the American Marketing Association, 1981.

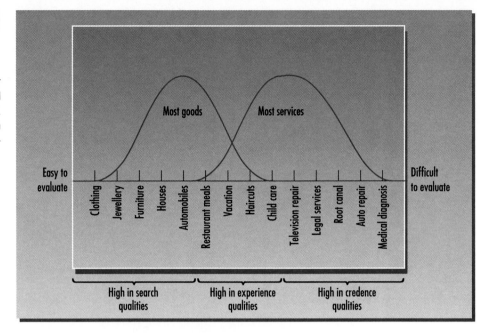

has taken on the role of online investment adviser. But the online trading service has not replaced the personal service offered by Schwab local branches or via the telephone.[20]

For some services, customers cannot judge the technical quality even after they have received the service. Figure 14.4 arrays various products and services according to difficulty of evaluation.[21] At the left are goods high in *search qualities*—that is, characteristics the buyer can evaluate before purchase. In the middle are goods and services high in *experience qualities*—characteristics the buyer can evaluate after purchase. At the right are goods and services high in *credence qualities*—characteristics the buyer normally finds hard to evaluate even after consumption.[22]

Because services are generally high in experience and credence qualities, there is more risk in purchase. This has several consequences. First, service consumers generally rely on word of mouth rather than advertising. Second, they rely heavily on price, personnel, and physical cues to judge quality. Third, they are highly loyal to service providers who satisfy them.

Service companies face three tasks—increasing *competitive differentiation*, *service quality*, and *productivity*. Although these interact, we will examine each separately.

MANAGING DIFFERENTIATION

Service marketers frequently complain about the difficulty of differentiating their services. The deregulation of several major service industries—communications, transportation, energy, banking—precipitated intense price competition. The success of budget-priced airlines, such as Canada 3000, has shown that many flyers care more about travel costs than service. To the extent that customers view a service as fairly homogeneous, they care less about the provider than the price. The alternative to price competition is to develop a differentiated offer, delivery, or image.

Offer

The offer can include innovative features. What the customer expects is called the *primary service package*, and to this can be added *secondary service features*. As the Canadian transportation industry becomes increasingly competitive, many believed train travel would disappear. VIA Rail has responded by increasing services, especially for first-class business travellers—computer plug-ins, a choice of meals, and free alcoholic beverages. It is also tailoring its advertising to different segments of the market. For vacationers, it doesn't offer travel, it offers "experiences."

Many *companies* are using the Web to offer secondary service features that were never possible before:

■ **American Airlines Inc.** As part of their secondary service package, airlines have long offered frequent-flyer programs. Now, American Airlines Inc., Canadian Airlines' partner, has beefed up its frequent-flyer member site using one-to-one marketing software from BroadVision Inc. Members can streamline the booking process by creating a profile of their home airport, usual routes, seating and meal preferences for themselves and their families. With these profiles, American can, say, offer discounts on flights to Disney World for parents whose children's school vacations start in a few weeks.[23]

The major challenge is that most service innovations are easily copied. Still, the company that regularly introduces innovations will gain a succession of temporary advantages over competitors. Through earning a reputation for innovation, it may retain customers who want the best. VanCity Credit Union enjoys the reputation as a leading innovator in the banking industry for such innovations as automatic-teller machines, ethical mutual funds, and broad-spectrum wealth management.

Delivery

A service company can hire and train better people to deliver its service (Home Depot). It can develop a more attractive physical environment in which to deliver the service (Indigo Books and Music stores, Cineplex Odeon movie theatres). Or it can design a superior delivery process (McDonald's).

Progressive Insurance
www.progressive.com

• **Progressive Insurance.** Progressive Insurance stepped into the consumer's shoes and considered how difficult it can be to get an auto accident claim processed and paid by insurance companies. Then, it crafted its service strategy around resolving that difficulty. The company now has a fleet of claims adjusters on the road every day, ready to rush to the scene of any auto accident in their territory. There, the adjusters record all the information they need and often settle claims on the spot.[24]

Image

Service companies can also differentiate their image through symbols and branding. The Bank of Montreal's large capital 'M' is quickly recognized from coast to coast. Several hospitals have attained "megabrand" reputations for being the best in their field, such as the Hospital for Sick Children in Toronto or the Mayo Clinic. American Express is one of several highly branded service companies that have developed a successful international image:

■ **American Express.** For years the charge-card division of American Express positioned itself as the Monarch of Plastic. Ad lines such as "Membership has its privileges" and "American Express, don't leave home without it" cultivated an affluent, upscale market, mainly business professionals who could afford to pay off their Amex bill each month and pay high yearly fees. Worldwide, a record number of 41.5 million people "can't leave home without it." Yet now the company needs to reinvent itself: Credit cards like Visa and Mastercard have eaten into Amex's turf. Customers want value in the form of no-fee affinity credit cards with frequent-flyer miles and other benefits, rather than prestige. In an attempt to fight back, Amex has pushed out an astonishing number of new products, including new credit cards. Amex's new "Blue Card," aimed at upscale 25- to 35-year-olds, won the company's president of international marketing, John Crewe, a listing as one of *Advertising Age*'s "Marketers of the Year" for 1998. The company has retained all the positive things Amex stands for, such as good service, prestige, and value, and made them relevant to the young, hip, affluent consumer.[25]

MANAGING SERVICE QUALITY

A service firm may win by delivering consistently higher-quality service than competitors and exceeding customers' expectations. These expectations are formed by their past experiences, word of mouth, and advertising. After receiving the service, customers compare the *perceived service* with the *expected service*. If the perceived service falls below the expected service, customers lose interest in the provider. If the perceived service meets or exceeds their expectations, they are apt to use the provider again. See the Marketing Memo "Exceeding Customers' Highest Hopes: A Service Marketing Checklist."

Parasuraman, Zeithaml, and Berry formulated a service-quality model that highlights the main requirements for delivering high service quality.[26] The model, shown in Figure 14.5, identifies five gaps that cause unsuccessful delivery:

1. *Gap between consumer expectation and management perception:* Management does not always perceive correctly what customers want. Hospital administrators may think that patients want better food, but patients may be more concerned with nurse responsiveness.

2. *Gap between management perception and service-quality specification:* Management might correctly perceive the customers' wants but not set a specified performance standard. Hospital administrators may tell the nurses to give "fast" service without specifying it quantitatively.

3. *Gap between service-quality specifications and service delivery:* The personnel might be poorly trained, or incapable or unwilling to meet the standard. Or they may be held to conflicting standards, such as taking time to listen to customers and serving them fast.

4. *Gap between service delivery and external communications:* Consumer expectations are affected by statements made by company representatives and ads. If a hospital brochure shows a beautiful room, but the patient arrives and finds the room to be cheap and tacky looking, external communications have distorted the customer's expectations.

5. *Gap between perceived service and expected service:* This gap occurs when the consumer misperceives the service quality. The physician may keep visiting the patient to show care, but the patient may interpret this as an indication that something really is wrong.

The same researchers found five determinants of service quality. These are presented in order of importance.[27]

1. *Reliability:* The ability to perform the promised service dependably and accurately.

2. *Responsiveness:* The willingness to help customers and provide prompt service.

3. *Assurance:* The knowledge and courtesy of employees and their ability to convey trust and confidence.

4. *Empathy:* The provision of caring, individualized attention to customers.

5. *Tangibles:* The appearance of physical facilities, equipment, personnel, and communication materials.

Various studies have shown that excellently managed service companies share the following common practices: a strategic concept, a history of top-management commitment to quality, high standards, systems for monitoring service performance and customer complaints, and an emphasis on employee satisfaction.

Strategic Concept

Top service companies are "customer obsessed." They have a clear sense of their target customers and their needs. They have developed a distinctive strategy for satisfying these needs.

(continued)

5. Do our employees regard service problems as opportunities to impress customers, or as annoyances? Do we prepare and encourage employees to excel in the service recovery process? Do we reward them for providing exceptional recovery service?

6. Do we continuously evaluate and improve our performance against customers' expectations? Do we perform consistently above the adequate service level? Do we capitalize on opportunities to exceed the desired service level?

Source: Excerpted from Leonard L. Berry and A. Parasuraman, *Marketing Services: Competing Through Quality* (New York: Free Press, 1991), pp. 72–73; also see Leonard L. Berry, *On Great Service: A Framework for Action* (New York: Free Press, 1995), and his *Discovering the Soul of Service* (New York: Free Press, 1999).

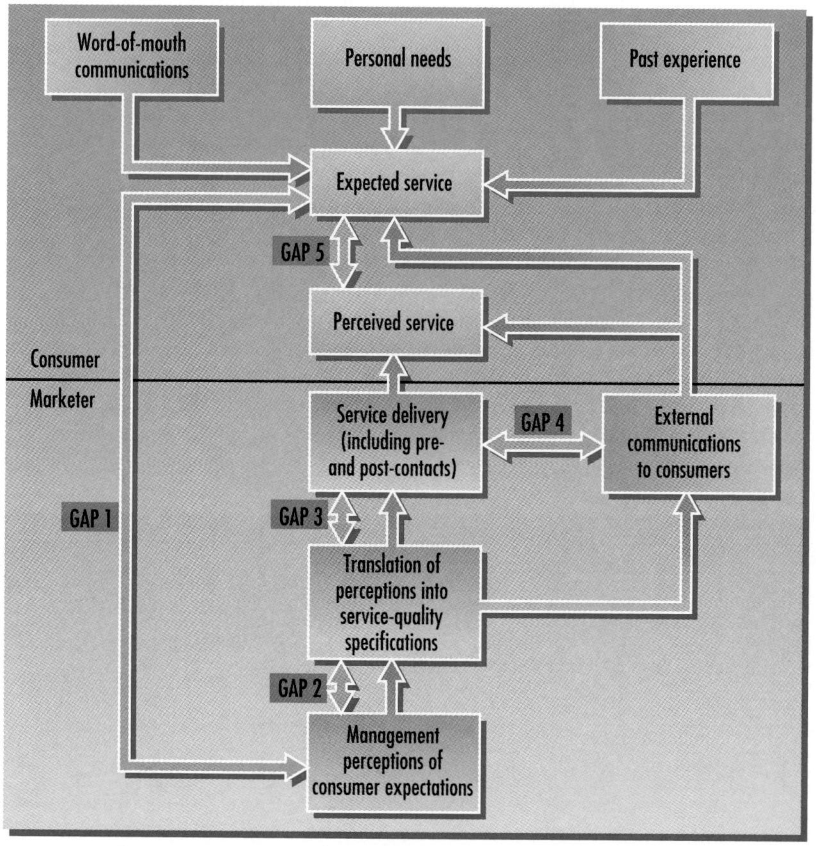

FIGURE 14.5

Service-Quality Model

Source: A. Parasuraman, Valarie A. Zeithaml, and Leonard L. Berry, "A Conceptual Model of Service Quality and Its Implications for Future Research," *Journal of Marketing*, Fall 1985, p. 44. Reprinted with permission of the American Marketing Association. The model is more fully discussed or elaborated in Valarie A. Zeithaml and Mary Jo Bitner, *Services Marketing*, (New York: McGraw Hill, 1996), ch. 2.

Top-Management Commitment

Companies such as Marriott, Disney, and McDonald's have thorough commitments to service quality. Their management looks not only at financial performance on a monthly basis but also at service performance. Ray Kroc of McDonald's insisted on continually measuring each McDonald's outlet on its conformance to QSCV: quality, service, cleanliness, and value. Some companies insert a reminder along with the employees' paycheques: BROUGHT TO YOU BY THE CUSTOMER. Sam Walton of Wal-Mart required the following employee pledge: "I solemnly swear and declare that every customer that comes within 10 feet of me, I will smile, look them in the eye, and greet them, so help me Sam."

High Standards

The best service providers set high service-quality standards. Swissair, for example, aims at having 96 percent or more of its passengers rate its service as good or superior. Citibank aims to answer phone calls within 10 seconds and customer letters within two days. The standards must be set *appropriately* high. A 98 percent accuracy standard may sound good but it would result in Federal Express losing 64 000 packages a day, 10 misspelled words on each page, 400 000 misfilled prescriptions daily, and unsafe drinking water eight days a year. Companies can be distinguished between those offering "merely good" service and those offering "breakthrough" service aiming at 100 percent defect-free service.[28]

Monitoring Systems

Top firms audit service performance, both their own and competitors', on a regular basis. They use a number of measurement devices: comparison shopping, ghost shopping, customer surveys, suggestion and complaint forms, service-audit teams, and letters to the president. General Electric sends out 700 000 response cards a year asking households to rate its service people's performance. Citibank checks continuously on measures of ART (accuracy, responsiveness, and timeliness). Figure 14.6 shows a typical chart to track the bank's speed in answering customer service phone inquiries. It will take action whenever performance falls below the minimum acceptable level. It also raises its performance goals over time.

When designing customer feedback mechanisms such as surveys, marketers need to ask the right questions, as United Parcel Service (UPS) discovered:

UPS
www.ups.com

■ **United Parcel Service.** UPS always assumed that on-time delivery was its customers' paramount concern, and based its definition of quality on the results of time-and-motion studies. To get packages to customers faster, UPS would factor in such details as how long it took elevators to open on certain city apartment blocks and how long it took people to answer their doorbells. Accordingly, UPS' surveys barraged customers with questions about whether they were pleased with delivery time and whether they thought the company could be any speedier. Yet, when the company began asking broader questions regarding how it could improve its service, it discovered that what customers wanted most was more face-to-face contact with drivers. If drivers were less hurried and would answer questions, customers might get practical advice on shipping.[29]

FIGURE 14.6

Tracking Customer Service Performance

part four
Making
Marketing
Decisions

430

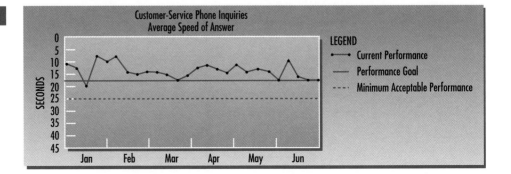

Attribute Number	Attribute Description	Mean Importance Rating[a]	Mean Performance Rating[b]
1	Job done right the first time	3.83	2.63
2	Fast action on complaints	3.63	2.73
3	Prompt warranty work	3.60	3.15
4	Able to do any job needed	3.56	3.00
5	Service available when needed	3.41	3.05
6	Courteous and friendly service	3.41	3.29
7	Car ready when promised	3.38	3.03
8	Perform only necessary work	3.37	3.11
9	Low prices on service	3.29	2.00
10	Clean up after service work	3.27	3.02
11	Convenient to home	2.52	2.25
12	Convenient to work	2.43	2.49
13	Courtesy buses and cars	2.37	2.35
14	Send out maintenance notices	2.05	3.33

[a] Ratings obtained from a four-point scale of "extremely important" (4), "important" (3), "slightly important" (2), and "not important" (1).
[b] Ratings obtained from a four-point scale of "excellent" (4), "good" (3), "fair" (2), and "poor" (1). A "no basis for judgment" category was also provided.

Services can be judged on *customer importance* and *company performance*. *Importance–performance analysis* is used to rate the various elements of the service bundle and identify what actions are required. Table 14.1 shows how customers rated 14 service elements (attributes) of an automobile dealer's service department on importance and performance. For example, "Job done right the first time" (attribute 1) received a mean importance rating of 3.83 and a mean performance rating of 2.63, indicating that customers felt it was highly important but not performed well.

The ratings of the 14 elements are displayed in Figure 14.7 and divided into four sections. Quadrant A shows important service elements that are not being performed at the desired levels; they include elements 1, 2, and 9. The dealer should concentrate on improving the service department's performance on these elements. Quadrant B shows important service elements that are being performed well; the company needs to maintain the high performance. Quadrant C shows minor service elements that are being delivered in a mediocre way but do not need any attention. Quadrant D shows that a minor service element, "Send out maintenance notices," is being performed in an excellent manner. Perhaps the company should spend less on sending out maintenance notices and reallocate the savings toward improving the company's performance on important elements. The analysis can be enhanced by checking on the competitors' performance levels on each element.[30]

Satisfying Customer Complaints

Studies of customer dissatisfaction show that customers are dissatisfied with their purchases about 25 percent of the time but that only about 5 percent complain. The other 95 percent either feel that complaining is not worth the effort, or that they don't know how or to whom to complain.

Of the 5 percent who complain, only about 50 percent report a satisfactory problem resolution. Yet the need to resolve a customer problem in a satisfactory manner is critical. On average, a satisfied customer tells three people about a good product experience, but the average dissatisfied customer gripes to eleven people. If each of them tells still other people, the number of people exposed to bad word of mouth may grow exponentially.

FIGURE 14.7

Importance–Performance
Analysis

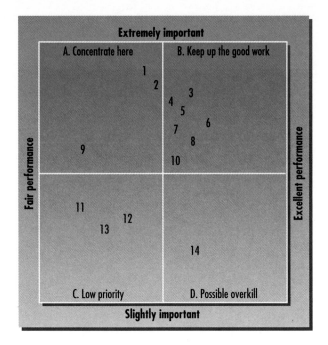

Nonetheless, customers whose complaints are satisfactorily resolved often become more company-loyal than customers who were never dissatisfied. About 34 percent of customers who register major complaints will buy again from the company if their complaint is resolved, and this number rises to 52 percent for minor complaints. If the complaint is resolved quickly, between 52 percent (major complaints) and 95 percent (minor complaints) will buy again from the company.[31]

Tax and Brown have found that companies that encourage disappointed customers to complain—and also empower employees to remedy the situation on the spot—achieve higher revenues and greater profits than companies that don't have a systematic approach for addressing service failures.[32] Tax and Brown found that companies that are effective at resolving complaints:

■ Develop hiring criteria and training programs that take into account employees' service-recovery role.

■ Develop guidelines for service recovery that focus on achieving fairness and customer satisfaction.

■ Remove barriers that make it difficult for customers to complain, while developing effective responses, which may include empowering employees to provide compensation for the failure. Pizza Hut prints its toll-free number on all pizza boxes. When a customer complains, Pizza Hut sends voice mail to the store manager, who must call the customer within 48 hours and resolve the complaint. Sometimes when a Virgin Atlantic Airways flight arrives several hours late at Heathrow Airport in London, CEO Richard Branson may personally come to apologize and distribute tickets for future flights.

■ Maintain customer and product databases that let the company analyze types and sources of complaints and adjust its policies.

Hyatt hotels gets high marks on many of these criteria for developing an effective *goodwill*-recovery program:

■ **Hyatt Hotels.** Hyatt hotels excels in its extraordinary short response time in answering complaints. One business customer, for example, did not like his room. He turned on the television and was greeted by a screen with the Hyatt customer survey. Using the TV remote control, he punched in his evaluations. To his surprise and delight, within five minutes of receiving the electronic communication, the hotel manager called him to say that because the hotel was entirely booked and the room could not be changed, the guest could expect a hospitality gift for his inconvenience. By systematically analyzing customer surveys, Hyatt managers alert employees to problems. Whether it is a vending machine that eats quarters or a stale smell that greets a guest upon first entering a room, Hyatt can quickly channel service requests to thoroughly trained personnel who can resolve them.[33]

Satisfying Both Employees and Customers

Excellently managed service companies believe that employee relations will affect customer relations. Management carries out internal marketing and provides employee support and rewards for good performance. Management regularly audits employee job satisfaction. Karl Albrecht observed that unhappy employees can be "terrorists." Rosenbluth and Peters, in *The Customer Comes Second*, go so far as to say that the company's employees, not the company's customers, have to be made number one if the company hopes to truly satisfy its customers.[34] The Safeway supermarket chain discovered this when it instituted a customer-friendly policy that ended up causing many of its employees to be stressed out.

- **Safeway Stores Inc.** In the 1990s, supermarket chain Safeway instituted Superior Service, an unusually aggressive program to mandate employee friendliness toward customers. Among the rules: Make eye contact with all customers, smile, greet each one, offer samples of products, make suggestions about other possible items to purchase. To ensure compliance, the store employs "mystery shoppers" who secretly grade workers. Those who are graded "poor" are sent to a training program to learn how to be friendlier. Although surveys show that customers are pleased with the program, many employees have admitted being stressed out and several have quit over the plan. "It's so artificial, it's unreal," said one second-generation Safeway employee who quit her job as cashier after 20 years with the chain, partly out of frustration with the Superior Service program. Disgruntled workers complain that they must override their own instincts in favour of the corporate friendliness formula. For instance, employees are required to greet harried customers whose body language tells workers they want to be left alone. The program has set off a spirited debate on the Internet over false versus real friendliness. At one Internet discussion group titled "Forced Smiles at Safeway," opinion ran two-to-one against the program.[35]

An important part of satisfying employees is helping them cope with their lives outside the office. As employees put a higher premium on family time, companies are offering more flexible work schedules. The Royal Bank has been leader in developing family-friendly employment practices as well as supporting research in this area.[36]

MANAGING PRODUCTIVITY

Service firms are under great pressure to keep costs down and increase productivity. There are seven approaches to improving service productivity.

The first is to have service providers work more skilfully. The company can hire and foster more skilful workers through better selection and training.

The second is to increase the quantity of service by surrendering some quality. Many Canadian banks have eliminated some teller positions and have substituted banking machines to increase the number of transactions they can handle.

The third is to "industrialize the service" by adding equipment and standardizing production. Levitt recommended that companies adopt a "manufacturing attitude" toward producing services as represented by McDonald's assembly-line approach to fast-food retailing, culminating in the "technological hamburger."[37] Hyatt is testing self-service machines to facilitate guest check-in and checkout. Southwest and other airlines use ATM-like machines to allow self-service ticket purchasing and boarding passes. Shouldice Hospital located near Toronto, operates only on patients with hernias and has reduced patient stay from the typical seven days to half that time by industrializing the service.[38]

The fourth is to reduce or make obsolete the need for a service by inventing a product solution, the way television substituted for out-of-home entertainment, the wash-and-wear shirt reduced the need for commercial laundries, and certain antibiotics reduced the need for tuberculosis sanitariums.

The fifth is to design a more effective service. How-to-quit-smoking clinics may reduce the need for expensive medical services later on. Hiring paralegal workers reduces the need for more expensive legal professionals.

The sixth is to present customers with incentives to substitute their own labour for company labour. Business firms that are willing to sort their own mail before delivering it to the post office pay lower postal rates. A restaurant that features a self-service salad bar is replacing "serving" work with customer work.

The seventh is to harness the power of technology to give customers access to better service and make service workers more productive. Companies that use their Web sites to empower customers can lessen workloads, capture valuable customer data, and increase the value of their businesses. See the Marketing for the Twenty-First Century box, "The Technologies of Customer Empowerment," for some real-world examples.

Technology has great power to make service workers more productive. For instance:[39]

■ **Cisco Systems.** Cisco makes products that help the Internet function, such as routers, switching devices, relays, and Internet software. Cisco's Knowledge Base of Frequently Asked Questions (FAQs) means a customer can usually get an answer without talking to anyone in the company. Cisco reduced the calls it was receiving by 70 percent or 50 000 calls a month, saving $14 million a month (at $280 a call). Now 700 people answer calls instead of 1000. Each new call and solution goes to a tech writer (Polish & Publish) to be entered into the Knowledge Base, thus reducing the number of future calls.

Companies must avoid pushing productivity so hard that they reduce perceived quality. Some methods lead to too much standardization and rob the customer of customized service; "high touch" is replaced by "high tech." Burger King challenged McDonald's by running a "Have it your way" campaign, where customers could get a "customized" hamburger even though this offer reduced Burger King's productivity somewhat.

MANAGING PRODUCT SUPPORT SERVICES

Thus far we have focused on service industries. No less important are product-based industries that must provide a service bundle. Manufacturers of equipment—small appliances, office machines, tractors, mainframes, airplanes—all must provide *product support services*. In fact, product support service is becoming a major battleground for competitive advantage. Some equipment companies, such as Caterpillar Tractor and John Deere, make over 50 percent of their profits from these services. In the global marketplace, companies that make a good product but provide poor local service support are seriously disadvantaged. When Subaru entered the Australian market, it contracted to use the Australian Volkswagen dealer network to provide parts and service.

Firms that provide high-quality service outperform their less service-oriented competitors. Table 14.2 provides evidence. The Strategic Planning Institute sorted out the top third and the bottom third of 3000 business units according to ratings of "relative perceived service quality." The table shows that the high-service businesses managed to charge more, grow faster, and make more profits on the strength of superior service quality.

The company must define customer needs carefully in designing its service support program. Customers have three specific worries:[40]

The Technologies of Customer Empowerment

Internet-enabled applications don't have to be sophisticated or complex to drive big change in business models. E-mail is proof of that. Real value is added by enabling customers to get information and interact with one another and with your data.

Content Creation

By allowing your customers to create their own content, you increase the value of your business and lessen your workload. Personalized applications let customers increase the worth of the product, also known as value contributions. Shared knowledge bases lead to increased learning and faster cycle times.

Real-world examples: GeoCities gives users a free home page and then—for a fee—lets them upgrade that page or add a small business e-commerce site. Travelocity now lets customers preview vacation locales with navigable QuickTime VR and LivePix destinations on its Web site to create the vacation of their dreams. Ace Hardware's site features a paint calculator that determines how many litres of paint to buy for a given project.

Collaboration

Using collaboration tools, customers can create and learn together. Forums and bulletin boards facilitate community. Conferencing and messaging tools enable globalization of activities. Group games and rating systems can provide information for e-commerce site owners. Polling, surveys, and collaborative filtering facilitate one-to-one marketing.

Real-world examples: E-Trade's game, E-Trade: The Game, lets players experience high-stakes trading and the thrill of competition without risking a dime—while at the same time telegraphing information about product preferences back to the company. Picture Network International's Virtual Lightbox feature lets designers and clients examine images and layouts together before they buy stock photos.

Teaching

Just-in-time learning and point-of-need information distribution pay off for businesses because they improve and support the user's performance. If they are done right, soon users will depend on the service and return.

Real-world examples: Many Canadian universities are getting into distance learning. For example, Athabasca University has created an electronic MBA program that links people from as far afield as Croatia to its campus. Queen's University is another school that demonstrates how far one can go in the direction of improving on, real-world educational experiences with diverse and specific classes, self-paced learning, and an instructor who is only an e-mail away.

Commerce

Online transactions that create friction-free commerce is the goal. If a site can offer a wide selection of merchandise, knowledgeable sales assistance, and no hassles or lines, it will be a desirable alternative to the mall.

Real-world examples: Customdisc.com lets users choose from thousands of songs to create their own audio CDs. The company charges a per-track fee and, in the process, collects information about users' musical tastes.

Control

By harnessing other devices to the Web site, companies can use agents and sensors to manage real-world machinery or processes remotely. Soon everything will be able to talk to everything else—cameras, remote sensors—we'll be able to control them all from the Web.

Real-world examples: Y2KLinks.com uses "Millie," an agent created in Neurostudio, to answer user questions about the year 2000 bug. The Hubble Web site enabled school kids to manipulate the giant telescope from a Web browser.

New Platforms

Soon personal assistants, cell phones, and dashboard computers will have the power and mobility to control all the other applications. New information appliances and smart cards offer great promise for customer-controlled applications.

Real-world examples: Audible.com is introducing a handheld mobile audio reader for its line of audio books. Netscape chief Jim Barksdale predicted that banks would soon be giving away free electronic chequebooks with built-in Web connections in order to move customers to Internet banking.

Source: Adapted from "The Technologies of Customer Empowerment," *New Media*, October 1998, p. 36.

- They worry about reliability and *failure frequency*. A farmer may tolerate a combine that will break down once a year, but not two or three times a year.

- Customers worry about *downtime duration*. The longer the downtime, the higher the cost. The customer counts on the seller's *service dependability*—the seller's ability to fix the machine quickly, or at least provide a loaner.[41]

- Customers worry about *out-of-pocket costs of maintenance and repair*. How much must the customer spend on regular maintenance and repair costs?

TABLE 14.2

	High Third in Service Quality	Low Third in Service Quality	Difference in % Points
Price index relative to competition	7%	−2%	+9%
Change in market share per annum	6	−2	+8
Sales growth per annum	17	8	+9
Return on sales	12	1	+11

Source: Phillip Thompson, Glenn Desourza, and Bradley T. Gale, "The Strategic Management of Service and Quality," *Quality Progress,* June 1985, p. 24.

A buyer takes all these factors into consideration in choosing a vendor. The buyer tries to estimate the *life-cycle cost*, which is the product's purchase cost plus the discounted cost of maintenance and repair less the discounted salvage value. Buyers ask for hard data in choosing among vendors.

The importance of reliability, service dependability, and maintenance vary. A one-computer office will need higher product reliability and faster repair service than an office where other computers are available if one breaks down. An airline needs 100 percent reliability in the air. Where reliability is important, manufacturers or service providers can offer guarantees to promote sales. See the Marketing Insight "Offering Guarantees to Promote Sales."

To provide the best support, a manufacturer must identify the services customers value most and their relative importance. In the case of expensive equipment, such as medical equipment, manufacturers offer *facilitating services* such as installation, staff training, maintenance and repair services, and financing. They may also add *value-augmenting services*. Herman Miller, a major office-furniture company, offers the Herman Miller promise to buyers: (1) five-year product warranties; (2) quality audits after project installation; (3) guaranteed move-in dates; and (4) trade-in allowances on systems products. Chapters.ca bought expensive chairs from Herman Miller for all its employees. To get the service up and running, many employees were working around the clock to provide 24-hour, seven days a week service. Having the best possible chair made their lives more comfortable and productive.

A manufacturer can offer and charge for product support services in different ways. One specialty organic chemical company provides a standard offering plus a basic level of services. If the customer wants additional services, it can pay extra or increase its annual purchases to a higher level, in which case additional services would be included. In a variation on this, Baxter Healthcare offers strategic customers bonus points (called "Baxter dollars") in proportion to how much they buy. They can use the bonus points to trade for different additional services. As another alternative, many companies offer *service contracts* with variable lengths and different deductibles so that customers can choose the service level they want beyond the basic service package.

Companies need to plan product design and service-mix decisions in tandem. Design and quality-assurance managers should be part of the new-product development team. Good product design will reduce the amount of subsequent servicing needed. The Canon home copier uses a disposable toner cartridge that greatly reduces the need for service calls. Kodak and 3M designed equipment allowing the user to "plug in" to a central diagnostic facility that performs tests, locates the trouble, and fixes the equipment over the telephone lines.

POSTSALE SERVICE STRATEGY

Most companies operate customer service departments whose quality varies greatly. At one extreme are departments that simply transfer customer calls to the appropriate person or department for action, with little follow-up. At the other extreme are departments eager to receive customer requests, suggestions, and even complaints and handle them expeditiously.

Offering Guarantees to Promote Sales

All sellers are legally responsible for fulfilling a buyer's normal or reasonable expectations. Warranties are formal statements of expected product performance by the manufacturer. Products under warranty can be returned to the manufacturer or designated repair centre for repair, replacement, or refund. Warranties, whether expressed or implied, are legally enforceable.

Many sellers offer guarantees, general assurances that the product can be returned if its performance is unsatisfactory. (An example would be a "money-back" guarantee.) The customer should find guarantees clearly stated and easy to act upon, and the company's redress should be swift. Otherwise, buyers will be dissatisfied, spread bad word of mouth, and undertake a potential lawsuit. Consider what happened at Domino's Pizza, which underwent phenomenal growth when it guaranteed 30-minute delivery on all telephone orders for its pizzas. A late-arriving pizza would be free (later amended to $3 off the order). But the company had to cancel its guarantee when a U.S. court awarded $117 million to a woman who had been struck by a speeding Domino driver in 1989.

Today many companies promise "general or complete satisfaction" without being more specific. Thus, Procter & Gamble advertises: "If you are not satisfied for any reason, return for replacement, exchange, or refund." Some companies offer an extraordinary promise that sets them apart from their competition and acts as an effective sales tool. For example:

- General Motors' Saturn car division will accept the return of a new car within 30 days if the buyer is not satisfied.

- Hampton Inn motels guarantees a restful night or the customer doesn't have to pay.

- L.L. Bean, the outdoors furnishings company, promises its customers "100 percent satisfaction in every way, forever." If a customer buys a pair of boots and two months later finds that they scuff easily, L.L. Bean will refund the money or replace them with another brand.

- A.T. Cross guarantees its Cross pens and pencils for life. The customer mails the pen to A.T. Cross (mailing envelopes are provided at stores selling Cross writing instruments), and the pen is repaired or replaced at no charge.

- Federal Express won its place in the minds and hearts of mailers by promising next-day delivery "absolutely, positively by 10:30 A.M."

- Oakley Millwork, a supplier of construction industry products, guaranteed that if any item in its catalogue was unavailable for immediate delivery, the customer would get the item free. This customer-pleasing guarantee helped push company sales up 33 percent between 1988 and 1991—a time when housing starts in its area fell 41 percent.

- The School of Business at Queen's University guarantees students in their Science and Technology MBA program a minimum starting salary after they complete the program or they don't have to pay their tuition fees.

- BBBK, a pest extermination company, offers the following guarantee: (1) no payment until all pests are eradicated; (2) if the effort fails, the customer receives a full refund to pay the next exterminator; (3) if guests on the client's premises spot a pest, BBBK will pay for the guest's room and send an apology letter; and (4) if the client's facility is closed down, BBBK will pay all fines, lost profits, and $5000. BBBK is able to charge up to five times more than its competitors, enjoys a high market share, and has paid out only 0.4 percent of sales in guarantees.

Guarantees are most effective in two situations. The first is where the company or the product is not well known. For example, a company might sell a liquid claiming to remove the toughest spots. A "money-back guarantee if not satisfied" would provide buyers with some confidence in purchasing the product. The second situation is where the product's quality is superior to the competition. The company can gain by guaranteeing superior performance knowing that competitors cannot match its guarantee.

Sources: For additional reading, see "More Firms Pledge Guaranteed Service," *Wall Street Journal*, July 17, 1991, pp. B1, B6; and Barbara Ettore, "Phenomenal Promises Mean Business," *Management Review*, March 1994, pp. 18–23. Also see Christopher W. L. Hart, *Extraordinary Guarantees* (New York: Amacom, 1993); and Sridhar Moorthy and Kannan Srinivasan, "Signaling Quality with a Money-Back Guarantee: The Role of Transaction Costs," *Marketing Science* 14, no. 4 (1995): 442–46.

In providing service, most companies progress through a series of stages. Manufacturers usually start out by running their own parts and service department. They want to stay close to the equipment and know its problems. They also find it expensive and time-consuming to train others, and discover that they can make good money running the parts-and-service business. As long as they are the only supplier of the needed parts, they can charge a premium price. In fact, many equipment manufacturers price their equipment low and compensate by charging high prices for parts and service. (This explains why competitors manufacture the same or similar parts and sell them to customers or intermediaries for less. Manufacturers warn customers of the danger of using competitor-made parts, but they are not always convincing.)

Over time, manufacturers switch more maintenance and repair service to authorized distributors and dealers. These intermediaries are closer to customers, operate in more locations, and can offer quicker service. Manufacturers still make a profit on the parts but leave the servicing profit to their intermediaries. Still later, independent service firms emerge. Over 40 percent of auto-service work is now done outside franchised automobile dealerships, by independent garages and chains such as Midas Muffler, Sears, and JCPenney. Independent service organizations handle mainframes, telecommunications equipment, and a variety of other equipment lines. They typically offer a lower price or faster service than the manufacturer or authorized intermediaries.

Ultimately, some large customers take over responsibility for handling their own maintenance and repair. A company with several hundred personal computers, printers, and related equipment might find it cheaper to have its own service personnel on site. These companies typically press the manufacturer for a lower price, because they are providing their own services.

MAJOR TRENDS IN CUSTOMER SERVICE

Lele has noted the following major trends in the customer service area:[42]

1. Equipment manufacturers are building more reliable and more easily fixable equipment. One reason is the shift from electromechanical equipment to electronic equipment, which has fewer breakdowns and is more repairable. Companies are adding modularity and disposability to facilitate self-servicing.

2. Customers are becoming more sophisticated about buying product support services and are pressing for "services unbundling." They want separate prices for each service element and the right to select the elements they want.

3. Customers increasingly dislike having to deal with a multitude of service providers handling different types of equipment. Some third-party service organizations now service a greater range of equipment.[43]

4. *Service contracts* (also called *extended warranties*), in which sellers agree to provide free maintenance and repair services for a specified period of time at a specified contract price, may diminish in importance. Some new-car warranties now cover 160 000 kilometres before servicing. The increase in disposable or never-fail equipment makes customers less inclined to pay from 2 percent to 10 percent of the purchase price every year for a service.

5. Customer service choices are increasing rapidly, and this is holding down prices and profits on service. Equipment manufacturers increasingly have to determine how to make money on their equipment independent of service contracts.

SUMMARY

1. A *service* is any act or performance that one party can offer to another that is essentially intangible and does not result in the ownership of anything. Its production may or may not be tied to a physical product. As North America moves increasingly toward a service economy, marketers have become increasingly interested in the special challenges involved in marketing services.

2. Services are intangible, inseparable, variable, and perishable. Each characteristic poses challenges and requires certain strategies. Marketers must find ways to give tangibility to intangibles; to increase the productivity of service providers; to increase and standardize the quality of the service provided; and to match the supply of services during peak and nonpeak periods with market demand.

3. Service industries lagged behind manufacturing firms in adopting and using marketing concepts and tools, but this situation has now changed. Service marketing strategy calls not only for external marketing but also for internal marketing to motivate employees and interactive marketing to emphasize the importance of both "high tech" and "high touch."

4. The service organization faces three tasks in marketing. (1) It must differentiate its offer, delivery, or image. (2) It must manage service quality in order to meet or exceed customers' expectations. (3) It must manage worker productivity by getting its employees to work more skilfully, increasing the quantity of service by surrendering some quality, industrializing the service, inventing new product solutions, designing more effective services, presenting customers with incentives to substitute their own labour for company labour, or using technology to save time and money.

5. Even product-based companies must provide postpurchase service for their customers. To provide the best support, a manufacturer must identify the services that customers value most and their relative importance. The service mix includes both presale services (facilitating and value-augmenting services) and postsale services (customer service departments, repair and maintenance services).

APPLICATIONS

CHAPTER CONCEPTS

1. A CPA firm has grown from billings of $315 000 to over $5 million since 1987—an annual growth rate of 22 percent. Amazingly, the growth has been accomplished without mergers, acquisitions, or even a large marketing budget. The firm's managing partner, Gary Shamis, admits that the firm's service is excellent but not particularly better than hundreds of good competitors. What, then, is the secret to success for this CPA firm?

The firm uses a multidimensional marketing strategy that began with the drafting of a road map—a list of specific objectives that the firm wanted to achieve. The road map is a working tool that is used and reinforced daily to keep the goals visualized in the minds of the firm's partners and associates. In addition, Shamis believes that clients buy perception and end up with reality. Creating a positive perception requires constant attention and reinforcement. The following marketing tools can help create this perception: (a) publicity, (b) advertising, (c) seminars, (d) printed materials.

For each of these marketing tools, suggest ways that a CPA firm can differentiate its services from those of its competitors, keeping in mind that most CPA firms offer the same types of services. Who should be responsible for implementing the firm's multidimensional success strategy?

2. Identify the core need, service characteristics (quality level, features, styling, brand name, and packaging), and augmented product provided by the customers of the following service organizations: (a) the Canadian Navy, (b) organized religion, (c) a life insurance company.

3. Most new car buyers expect the following scenario: They enter the showroom and are approached immediately by an enthusiastic salesperson who seems to know everything but the answers to their questions. If they ask what the price is, then the salesperson will go in search of someone who can deal. Once it looks like they are about to sign the contract, the salesperson starts selling more options or option packages, rustproofing, extended warranties, and so forth. After the car is delivered and if something goes wrong, it is extremely difficult to get in touch with the salesperson.

Individually or with a group, list some of the underlying reasons for the consumer perception problems facing car dealerships. Then design a new system that would change the dealership culture by introducing the concept of relationship marketing into the process.

1. Figure 1 shows an ad for Ericsson geared for business and consumer audiences. How does the content of this ad reflect Ericsson's application of the three additional Ps for its service business? How does the ad provide evidence of service quality to reduce the uncertainty business customers have about buying an intangible product? What segments of the business and consumer markets does Ericsson seem to be targeting with this ad?

Figure 1

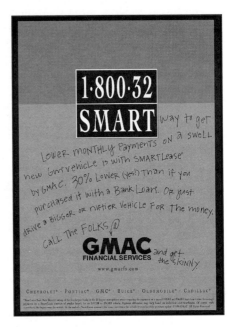

Figure 2

2. The GMAC ad in Figure 2 illustrates one of General Motors' product support services: affordable financing for new car buyers. Is this GMAC service being offered for presale or postsale use? Is the offering bundled or unbundled? Does it represent a facilitating service or a value-augmenting service? Explain your answers.

F O C U S   O N   T E C H N O L O G Y

The Internet is fast becoming part of every marketer's service support strategy. Nearly any product can be differentiated through online service support—even 3M's Post-it notes, those ubiquitous removable notes available in paper and software format. "What did you ever do without them?" asks the Post-it Web site. In case consumers and business users get stuck for an answer, they can surf over to the Post-it site, which offers an ever-changing array of ideas, contests, and good-natured fun.

Stop by the Post-it site and look at the product section, the downloads, and the monthly feature. Why would 3M establish this relatively extensive Web presence for such a well-known product? How do you think Post-it customers are likely to react? What other basic office products for home or commercial use might benefit from similar online service support?

M A R K E T I N G   F O R   T H E   2 1 S T   C E N T U R Y

Lifelong learning is important for career development as well as personal growth. Now computer users who want to empower themselves by learning programming, database techniques, Web site design, and other skills for today's technology can take online classes through ZD University. ZDU is an online service offered by Ziff-Davis, a company that publishes a wide variety of magazines on information technology.

Post-it
www.mmm.com/Post-it

part four
Making
Marketing
Decisions

For a flat monthly or yearly fee, students can sign up for as many ZDU courses as they like, learning at their own pace and on their own schedule.

Browse the ZD University Web site (www.zdu.com/), noting especially the course catalogue, free offers, and ZDU Handbook. How does ZDU manage students' expectations of this online learning service? How does it demonstrate its service quality? Explain how ZDU delivers a winning combination of high tech and high touch to satisfy its students. How will competitors like ZDU affect traditional educators?

ZD University
www.zdu.com/

YOU'RE THE MARKETER:
SONIC MARKETING PLAN

Marketers of any type of good or service need to develop a service strategy when preparing their marketing plans. If their products are intangible, they will want to consider how to manage customers' expectations and satisfaction; if their products are tangible, they will want to create suitable support services.

As Jane Melody's assistant, you are charged with planning product support services for Sonic's shelf stereo products. Start by reviewing the company's current situation and the information you previously entered in your marketing plan. Then respond to the following questions to plan your service strategy (indicating, where necessary, any additional data and research that may be needed):

- *What support services do buyers of shelf stereo products want and need? (As you answer this question, look back at your customer research, Sonic's strengths, and the competitive information you have gathered.)*

- *What postsale service arrangements should Sonic have or improve in order to satisfy customers' complaints?*

- *What kinds of guarantees should Sonic offer to be competitive? To beat the competition?*

- *What type of internal marketing will Sonic need to implement the external marketing of your product service support effectively?*

Consider how your service strategy will help Sonic's overall marketing efforts. Finally, as your instructor directs, summarize your recommendations and plans in a written marketing plan or type them into the Service part of the Marketing Strategy section of the Marketing Plan Pro software.

Designing Pricing Strategies and Programs

Even if you're the most dedicated Honda Civic lover, here's a challenge to your loyalty. The new Sephia from Kia. At thousands less for more power, more space, comparable comforts, outstanding safety and an incredible warranty, the Sephia may very well become your new object of desire. But there's no need to admire it from afar. Heck, press your nose right against the window (we'll clean the smudges later), then jump in and hit the highway. That's exactly what we did on our 200,000 kilometre test drive to prove the Sephia can stand up to everything nature and its birds can throw at it. And we came through with flying colours. (Those darn birds again.) It performed so reliably, we even decided to include Kia Extra Care 24 hour Roadside Assistance for free. So come visit your nearest Kia dealer to see what all the fuss is about. Sure, it's a bit of a detour from the Honda dealer, but so is the price.

Everyone has their price. This could be yours.

Sephia starting at
$12,995

KIA

It's about time everyone had a well-made car.

For the dealer nearest you, call 1 877 KIA-AUTO (542-2886)

PROFILE:

Canadian Marketing Excellence

Philip Kotler admonishes: *You don't sell through price. You sell the price.* This could be the watchword of Kia Canada, a subsidiary of a South Korean company, and the newest entrant into the Canadian automobile marketplace. It has unveiled its 2000 editions of two vehicles, the Sportage, a SUV, and the Sephia. The two vehicles will take on industry giants the likes of Chrysler Neon. What allows it to play in this highly competitive game?

Competitive pricing. With models ranging in price from $15 000 to $19 000, Kia is offering Canadian consumers a low-price alternative in an otherwise high-price industry.

Price competition in the automotive industry is predicted to increase. As manufacturers consolidate their operations around the world, they should realize economies of scale. These economies may result in decreasing car prices.

But will price alone be enough to win over Canadian consumers? Probably not. Although Kia has been selling cars in the United States since 1994, it has no brand equity in Canada. Since buying a car is a high-risk purchase for most consumers, developing the value proposition and the credibility of the brand will also be critical to success. Kia has hired Griffin Bacal Volny as its agency of record to help it in this task. Building brand awareness won't be cheap. Analysts estimate that the advertising budget for the launch will fall between $5 and $10 million. To keep costs down so that it can offer the most competitive prices, Kia may use some of the advertising themes already utilized in the U.S. marketplace.

Brand building is a multi-faceted effort. While television advertising is one of the keys, developing an Internet presence is another essential, if the firm hopes to realize its ambition of reaching the youth market—those people entering the car market for the first time. Kia predicts that its cars will be most attractive to female purchasers and young families.

How is Kia attacking this market? With TV, radio, and print advertising supported by event sponsorship. Consider its two humorous television spots. One shows a Sephia topped by a giant odometer being test-driven across the country by a young family. Not only does the spot demonstrate the car's reliability, but it also appeals to people who want reliability and value with the tag line, "Kia. Because it's about time everyone had a well-made car." It is only then that the odometer clicks over to show the price—$12 995 and the spots make no bones about comparing its price to that of its nearest competitors, Honda Civic and Toyota Corolla. In another spot, two women are portrayed racing for the last parking spot in a crowded shopping-mall lot. Leaping hurdles, the Kia, of course, wins, demonstrating again the value and versatility of the vehicle in a off-beat manner. Yet, advertising alone won't sell the cars. Kia Canada also must establish a dealer network from scratch. It hopes to have 120 dealers revving their engines to sell up to 45 000 vehicles within the next five years. Start your engines….

Sources: Patti Summerfield, "Kia Plays the Value Card in Adapted Creative," *Strategy: The Canadian Marketing Report*. August 16, 1999, p. 6. Lesley Daw, "Korea's Time" *Marketing*, September 13, 1998, pp. 17–18. Patti Summerfield, "Budget Korean Cars Daewoo, Kia to Hit Canadian Streets," *Strategy: The Canadian Marketing Report*. February 15, 1999, p. 4. Patti Summerfield, "Kia Picks Griffin Bacal Volny for Canadian Launch," *Strategy: The Canadian Marketing Report*. March 29, 1999, p. 2.

This chapter examines three questions:

- How should a price be set on a product or service for the first time?

- How should the price be adapted to meet varying circumstances and opportunities?

- When should the company initiate a price change, and how should it respond to a competitor's price change?

Kia
www.kia.com

All profit organizations and many nonprofit organizations set prices on their products or services. Price goes by many names:

> *Price is all around us. You pay rent for your apartment, tuition for your education, and a fee to your physician or dentist. The airline, railway, taxi, and bus companies charge you a fare; the local utilities call their price a rate; and the local bank charges you interest for the money you borrow. The price for driving your car on [Toronto's 407 Highway] is a toll, and the company that insures your car charges you a premium. The guest lecturer charges an honorarium to tell you about a government official who took a bribe to help a shady character steal dues collected by a trade association. Clubs or societies to which you belong may make a special assessment to pay unusual expenses. Your regular lawyer may ask for a retainer to cover her services. The "price" of an executive is a salary, the price of a salesperson may be a commission, and the price of a worker is a wage. Finally, although economists would disagree, many of us feel that income taxes are the price we pay for the privilege of making money.[1]*

Throughout most of history, prices were set by negotiation between buyers and sellers. Setting one price for all buyers is a relatively modern idea that arose with the development of large-scale retailing at the end of the nineteenth century. F.W. Woolworth, Tiffany and Co., John Wanamaker, and others advertised a "strictly one-price policy," because they carried so many items and supervised so many employees.

Now, just 100 years later, the Internet promises to reverse the fixed pricing trend and take us back to an era of negotiated pricing. The Internet, corporate networks, and wireless setups are linking people, machines, and companies around the globe—and connecting sellers and buyers as never before. Web sites like Compare.Net and PriceScan.com allow buyers to compare products and prices quickly and easily. Online auction sites like eBay.com and Onsale.com make it easy for buyers and sellers to negotiate prices on thousands of items—from refurbished computers to antique tin trains. At the same time, new technologies allow sellers to collect detailed data about customers' buying habits, preferences—even spending limits—so they can tailor their products and prices.[2]

Traditionally, price has operated as the major determinant of buyer choice. This is still the case in poorer nations, among poorer groups, and with commodity-type products. Although nonprice factors have become more important in buyer behaviour in recent decades, price still remains one of the most important elements determining company market share and profitability. Consumers and purchasing agents have more access to price information and price discounters. Consumers shop carefully, forcing retailers to lower their prices. Retailers put pressure on manufacturers to lower their prices. The result is a marketplace characterized by heavy discounting and sales promotion. Consider the following cases:[3]

- **Labatt versus Molson.** Canada's two breweries have been in a cut-throat battle for market share. The summer of 1999 witnessed a fierce battle that caused both companies to bleed from the bottom line. Labatt took $4 off the price of a case of 13 of its most popular beers; Molson quickly retaliated. As Michael Palmer, an industry analyst, noted, "It never makes any sense to have a price war, but Labatt believes it has Molson on the run, and it's trying to keep the pressure on." Since the summer months account for up to 75 percent of the $10-billion in annual sales, neither brewer can afford to budge, and in this fight, the consumer ends up the winner.

Mills Corporation
www.millscorp.com

- **Mills Corporation.** America's favourite indoor sport is coming to Canada. Is it Disney World, you might ask? No, it is an immense discount shopping mall. Its counterpart in Florida, Sawgrass Mills, a 1.9-million-square-metre giant located near Fort Lauderdale drew 20 million visitors in 1998 alone, making it the second most popular tourist destination in the state. Today, Mills Corp., along with its Canadian partner, Cambridge Shopping Centers Ltd., are nailing down locations and signing deals with tenants to fill similar malls in Montreal, Toronto, and Vancouver. They plan to open by 2001. The very thought of this huge price-base operation has many Canadian retailers running scared since the mall will bring dozens of U.S. retailers into Canada in one swoop.

Price is the marketing-mix element that produces revenue; the others produce costs. Price is also one of the most flexible elements: It can be changed quickly, unlike product features and channel commitments. At the same time, price competition is the number-one problem facing companies. Yet many companies do not handle pricing well. The most common mistakes are these: Pricing is too cost-oriented; price is not revised often enough to capitalize on market changes; price is set independent of the rest of the marketing mix rather than as an intrinsic element of market-positioning strategy; and price is not varied enough for different product items, market segments, and purchase occasions.

Companies handle pricing in a variety of ways. In small companies, prices are often set by the company's boss. In large companies, pricing is handled by division and product-line managers. Even here, top management sets general pricing objectives and policies and often approves the prices proposed by lower levels of management. In industries where pricing is a key factor (aerospace, railways, oil companies), companies will often establish a pricing department to set or assist others in determining appropriate prices. This department reports to the marketing department, finance department, or top management. Others who exert an influence on pricing include sales managers, production managers, finance managers, and accountants.

SETTING THE PRICE

A firm must set a price for the first time when it develops a new product, when it introduces its regular product into a new distribution channel or geographical area, and when it enters bids on new contract work.

The firm must decide where to position its product on quality and price. In some markets, such as the auto market, as many as eight *price points* can be found

Segment	Example (Automobiles)
Ultimate	Rolls-Royce
Gold Standard	Mercedes-Benz
Luxury	Audi
Special Needs	Volvo
Middle	Buick
Ease/Convenience	Ford Escort
Me Too, but Cheaper	Hyundai
Price Alone	Kia

There can be competition between price–quality segments. Figure 15.1 shows nine price–quality strategies. The diagonal strategies 1, 5, and 9 can all coexist in the same market; that is, one firm offers a high-quality product at a high price, another offers an average-quality product at an average price, and still another offers a low-quality product at a low price. All three competitors can coexist as long as the market consists of three groups of buyers: those who insist on quality, those who insist on price, and those who balance the two considerations.

FIGURE 15.1

Nine Price–Quality Strategies

		Price		
		High	Medium	Low
Product Quality	High	1. Premium strategy	2. High-value strategy	3. Super-value strategy
	Medium	4. Overcharging strategy	5. Medium-value strategy	6. Good-value strategy
	Low	7. Rip-off strategy	8. False economy strategy	9. Economy strategy

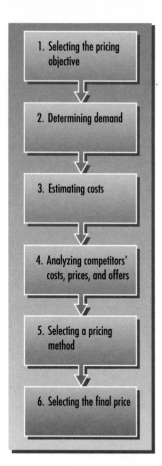

1. Selecting the pricing objective

2. Determining demand

3. Estimating costs

4. Analyzing competitors' costs, prices, and offers

5. Selecting a pricing method

6. Selecting the final price

FIGURE 15.2

Setting Pricing Policy

Intel
www.intel.com

Strategies 2, 3, and 6 are ways to attack the diagonal positions. Strategy 2 says, "Our product has the same high quality as product 1 but we charge less." Strategy 3 says the same thing and offers an even greater saving. If quality-sensitive customers believe these competitors, they will sensibly buy from them and save money (unless firm 1's product has acquired snob appeal).

Positioning strategies 4, 7, and 8 amount to overpricing the product in relation to its quality. The customers will feel "taken" and will probably complain or spread bad word of mouth about the company.

The firm must consider many factors in setting its pricing policy. We will describe a six-step procedure: (1) selecting the pricing objective; (2) determining demand; (3) estimating costs; (4) analyzing competitors' costs, prices, and offers; (5) selecting a pricing method; and (6) selecting the final price (Figure 15.2).

SELECTING THE PRICING OBJECTIVE

The company first decides where it wants to position its market offering. The clearer a firm's objectives, the easier it is to set price. A company can pursue any of five major objectives through pricing: survival, maximum current profit, maximum market share, maximum market skimming, or product-quality leadership.

Companies pursue survival as their major objective if they are plagued with overcapacity, intense competition, or changing consumer wants. Profits are less important than survival. As long as prices cover variable costs and some fixed costs, the company stays in business. However, survival is a short-run objective; in the long run, the firm must learn how to add value or face extinction.

Many companies try to set a price that will maximize current profits. They estimate the demand and costs associated with alternative prices and choose the price that produces maximum current profit, cash flow, or rate of return on investment. This strategy assumes that the firm has knowledge of its demand and cost functions; in reality, these are difficult to estimate. By emphasizing current financial performance, the company may sacrifice long-run performance by ignoring the effects of other marketing-mix variables, competitors' reactions, and legal restraints on price.

Some companies want to maximize their market share. They believe that a higher sales volume will lead to lower unit costs and higher long-run profit. They set the lowest price, assuming the market is price sensitive. Texas Instruments (TI) practises this *market-penetration pricing*. TI will build a large plant, set its price as low as possible, win a large market share, experience falling costs, and cut its price further as costs fall. The following conditions favour setting a low price: (1) The market is highly price sensitive, and a low price stimulates market growth; (2) production and distribution costs fall with accumulated production experience; and (3) a low price discourages actual and potential competition.

Many companies favour setting high prices to "skim" the market. Intel is a prime practitioner of *market-skimming pricing*.

■ **Intel.** One analyst describes Intel's pricing strategy this way: "The chip giant introduces a new, higher-margin microprocessor every 12 months and sends older models down the food chain to feed demand at lower price points." When Intel introduces a new computer chip, it charges as much as $1400 for it, a price that makes it just worthwhile for some segments of the market. These new chips power top-of-the-line PCs and servers purchased by customers who just can't wait. As initial sales slow down, and as competitors threaten to introduce similar chips, Intel lowers the price to draw in the next price-sensitive layer of customers. Prices eventually bottom out close to $280 per chip, making the chip a hot mass-market processor. In this way, Intel skims the maximum amount of revenue from the various segments of the market.[4]

Market skimming makes sense under the following conditions: (1) A sufficient number of buyers have a high current demand; (2) the unit costs of producing a small volume are not so high that they cancel the advantage of charging what the traffic will bear; (3) the high initial price does not attract more competitors to the market; (4) the high price communicates the image of a superior product.

A company might aim to be the product-quality leader in the market. Consider Maytag:

■ **Maytag.** Maytag has long built high-quality washing machines and priced them higher than competitors' products (Maytag used the slogan "Built to last longer," and its ads featured the Maytag repairman asleep at the phone because no one ever calls him for service). Now, in a change of strategy, Maytag still capitalizes on its premium-brand strengths but emphasizes innovative features and benefits. The company is trying to change the purchase cycle from "wear out" to "want in." The objective is to get consumers to buy Maytag appliances with whizbang features at a premium price, even though their old machines are still working. To lure the price-sensitive consumer, Maytag's new ads point out that washers are custodians of what is often a $400 to $500 load of clothes, making them worth the higher price tag. For instance, at $1200 Maytag's new European-style washers sell for double what most other washers cost, yet the company's marketers argue that they use less water and electricity and prolong the life of clothing by being less abrasive.[5]

Maytag
www.maytag.com

Non-profit and public organizations may adopt other pricing objectives. A university aims for *partial cost recovery*, knowing that it must rely on private gifts and public grants to cover the remaining costs. A non-profit hospital may aim for *full cost recovery* in its pricing. A non-profit theatre company may price its productions to fill the maximum number of theatre seats. A social service agency may set a *social price* geared to the varying incomes of clients.

Whatever their specific objective, businesses that use price as a strategic tool will profit more than those who simply let costs or the market determine their pricing. For a further discussion of how businesses accomplish their objectives with pricing, see the Marketing Insight "Power Pricers: How Smart Companies Use Price to Achieve Business Strategies."

DETERMINING DEMAND

Each price will lead to a different level of demand and therefore have a different impact on a company's marketing objectives. The relation between alternative prices and the resulting current demand is captured in a *demand curve* (Figure 15.3[a]). In the normal case, demand and price are inversely related: the higher the price, the lower the demand. In the case of prestige goods, the demand curve sometimes slopes upward. A perfume company raised its price and sold more perfume rather than less! Some consumers take the higher price to signify a better product. However, if too high a price is charged, the level of demand may fall.

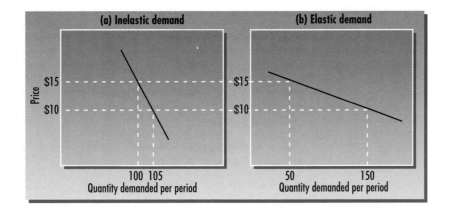

FIGURE 15.3

Inelastic and Elastic Demand

Power Pricers: How Smart Companies Use Price as a Strategic Tool

Executives in general management and across the various functional areas in firms continually complain that pricing is a big headache—and one that is getting worse by the day. Many firms have thrown up their hands with "strategies" like this: "We determine our costs and take our industry's traditional margins," or "The market sets the price, and we have to figure out how to cope with it."

But others have a different attitude: They use price as a key strategic tool. These "power pricers" have discovered the highly leveraged effect of price on the bottom line. Here are some companies whose power-pricing strategies have helped put them ahead of the pack.

■ *Pricing and marketing strategy:* Swatch watch pricing exemplifies the integration of pricing with overall marketing strategy. According to the head of Swatch's design lab, the unchanging $40 for a basic model was to be a "simple price, a clean price. Price has become a mirror for the other attributes we try to communicate. It helps set us apart from the rest of the world. A Swatch is not just affordable, it's approachable. Buying a Swatch is an easy decision to make, an easy decision to live with." The price message at $40 is different from that at $37.50—or the message if there is a $50 list price but the product is usually found on sale at 20 percent off. Like the watch design and advertising, the $40 constant price says, "You can't make a mistake, don't worry, have some fun."

■ *Pricing and the value perspective:* Pharmaceutical company Glaxo introduced its ulcer medication Zantac to attack market incumbent Tagamet. The conventional wisdom was that, as the "second one in," Glaxo should price Zantac 10 percent below Tagamet. However, CEO Paul Girolam knew that Zantac was superior to Tagamet in terms of fewer drug interactions and side effects and more convenient dosing. Adequately communicated to the marketplace, this superiority provided the basis for a price premium. Glaxo introduced Zantac at a significant price premium over Tagamet and still gained the market-leader position.

■ *Customizing price and service based on segment value:* Bugs Burger's Bug Killer price was about five times that of other firms that do battle with rodents on a commercial property. Bugs got his price premium because he focused on a particularly quality-sensitive segment of the market (hotels and restaurants) and gave them what they valued most: guaranteed pest elimination rather than control. The superior value provided to this chosen segment guided his pricing. This enabled him to train and compensate service technicians in a way that motivated them to deliver superior extermination service. Thus the value provided drove the price, which in turn funded the activities necessary to provide the value.

■ *Customizing price based on segment cost and competitive situation:* Fortune has hailed Progressive Insurance as "the prince of smart pricing" in the automobile insurance game. The company collects and analyzes loss data better than anyone else. Its understanding of what it costs to service various types of customers enables it to serve the lucrative high-risk customer no one else wants to insure. Free of competition and armed with a solid understanding of costs, Progressive makes good profits serving this customer base.

Source: Adapted from Robert J. Dolan and Hermann Simon, "Power Pricers," *Across the Board*, May 1997, pp. 18–19.

Price Sensitivity

The demand curve shows the market's probable purchase quantity at alternative prices. It sums the reactions of many individuals who have different price sensitivities. The first step in estimating demand is to understand what affects price sensitivity. Nagle has identified nine factors:

1. *Unique-value effect:* Buyers are less price sensitive when the product is more distinctive.

2. *Substitute-awareness effect:* Buyers are less price sensitive when they are less aware of substitutes.

3. *Difficult-comparison effect:* Buyers are less price sensitive when they cannot easily compare the quality of substitutes.

4. *Total-expenditure effect:* Buyers are less price sensitive the lower the expenditure is as a part of their total income.

5. *End-benefit effect:* Buyers are less price sensitive the smaller the expenditure is to the total cost of the end product.

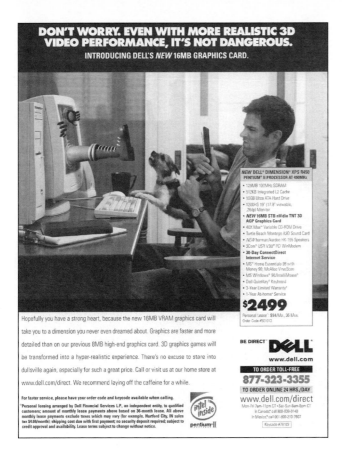

A Dell ad promoting both product characteristics and price.

6. *Shared-cost effect*: Buyers are less price sensitive when part of the cost is borne by another party.

7. *Sunk-investment effect*: Buyers are less price sensitive when the product is used in conjunction with assets previously bought.

8. *Price–quality effect*: Buyers are less price sensitive when the product is assumed to have more quality, prestige, or exclusiveness.

9. *Inventory effect*: Buyers are less price sensitive when they cannot store the product.[6]

A number of forces, such as deregulation and the instant price comparison technology available over the Internet, have turned products into commodities in the eyes of consumers and increased their price sensitivity. Marketers need to work harder than ever to differentiate their offerings when a dozen competitors are selling virtually the same product at a comparable or lower price. More than ever, companies need to understand the price sensitivity of their customers and prospects and the trade-offs people are willing to make between price and product characteristics. In the words of marketing consultant Kevin Clancy, those who target only the price sensitive are "leaving money on the table."[7]

Estimating Demand Curves

Most companies make some attempt to measure their demand curves. They can use different methods.

The first involves statistically analyzing past prices, quantities sold, and other factors to estimate their relationships. The data can be longitudinal (over time) or cross-sectional (different locations at the same time). Building the appropriate model and fitting the data with the proper statistical techniques calls for considerable skill.

The second approach is to conduct price experiments. Bennett and Wilkinson systematically varied the prices of several products sold in a discount store and observed the results.[8] An alternative approach is to charge different prices in similar territories to see how sales are affected.

The third approach is to ask buyers to state how many units they would buy at different proposed prices.[9] But buyers might understate their purchase intentions at higher prices to discourage the company from setting higher prices.

In measuring the price–demand relationship, the market researcher must control for various factors that will influence demand. The competitor's response will make a difference. Also, if the company changes other marketing-mix factors besides its price, the effect of the price change itself will be hard to isolate. Nagle has presented an excellent summary of the various methods for estimating price sensitivity and demand.[10]

Price Elasticity of Demand

Marketers need to know how responsive, or elastic, demand would be to a change in price. Consider the two demand curves in Figure 15.3. With demand curve (a), a price increase from $10 to $15 leads to a relatively small decline in demand from 150 to 133. With demand curve (b), the same price increase leads to a substantial drop in demand from 150 to 50. If demand hardly changes with a small change in price, we say the demand is *inelastic*. If demand changes considerably, demand is *elastic*.

Demand is likely to be less elastic under the following conditions: (1) There are few or no substitutes or competitors; (2) buyers do not readily notice the higher price; (3) buyers are slow to change their buying habits and search for lower prices; (4) buyers think the higher prices are justified by quality differences, normal inflation, and so on. If demand is elastic, sellers will consider lowering the price. A lower price will produce more total revenue. This makes sense as long as the costs of producing and selling more units does not increase disproportionately.[11]

Different price elasticities and the importance of thinking about them can be seen when one considers users of public transit systems. To encourage increased use, many transit authorities, like Ottawa-Carleton, offer riders weekly or monthly passes so that they can avoid having to pay on a per-ride basis. These passes appeal most to daily commuters who receive a significant benefit from the discounted fare. However, since these people are price inelastic, the transit authorities may be leaving "money on the table." In fact, the demand curve of many commuters is perfectly inelastic: No matter what happens to the fare, these people must get to work and get back home. Other commuters have a more elastic demand curve. These are people who live in the city and who might use the subway for other activities if the fare were lowered. Off-peak riders may be the most price elastic of all. This group is made up of seniors and students who might use more public transit services if discount fares were offered.[12]

Price elasticity depends on the magnitude and direction of the contemplated price change. It may be negligible with a small price change and substantial with a large price change. It may differ for a price cut versus a price increase. Finally, long-run price elasticity may differ from short-run elasticity. Buyers may continue to buy from their current supplier after a price increase, because they do not notice the increase, or the increase is small, or they are distracted by other concerns, or they find choosing a new supplier takes time. But they may eventually switch suppliers. Here demand is more elastic in the long run than in the short run. Or the reverse may happen: Buyers drop a supplier after being notified of a price increase but return later. The distinction between short-run and long-run elasticity means that sellers will not know the total effect of a price change until time passes.

ESTIMATING COSTS

Demand sets a ceiling on the price the company can charge for its product. Costs set the floor. The company wants to charge a price that covers its cost of producing, distributing, and selling the product, including a fair return for its effort and risk.

Types of Costs and Levels of Production

A company's costs take two forms, fixed and variable. *Fixed costs* (also known as *overhead*) are costs that do not vary with production or sales revenue. A company must pay bills each month for rent, heat, interest, salaries, and so on, regardless of output.

Variable costs vary directly with the level of production. For example, each hand calculator produced by Texas Instruments involves a cost of plastic, microprocessing chips, packaging, and the like. These costs tend to be constant per unit produced. They are called variable because their total varies with the number of units produced.

Total costs consist of the sum of the fixed and variable costs for any given level of production. *Average cost* is the cost per unit at that level of production; it is equal to total costs divided by production. Management wants to charge a price that will at least cover the total production costs at a given level of production.

To price intelligently, management needs to know how its costs vary with different levels of production.

Take the case in which a company such as TI has built a fixed-size plant to produce 1000 hand calculators a day. The cost per unit is high if few units are produced per day. As production approaches 1000 units per day, average cost falls. The reason is that the fixed costs are spread over more units, with each one bearing a smaller fixed cost. Average cost increases after 1000 units, because the plant becomes inefficient: Workers have to queue for machines, machines break down more often, and workers get in each other's way (Figure 15.4[a]).

If TI believes that it could sell 2000 units per day, it should consider building a larger plant. The plant will use more efficient machinery and work arrangements, and the unit cost of producing 2000 units per day will be less than the unit cost of producing 1000 units per day. This is shown in the long-run average cost curve in Figure 15.4(b). In fact, a 3000-capacity plant would be even more efficient according to Figure 15.4(b). But a 4000-daily production plant would be less efficient because of increasing diseconomies of scale: There are too many workers to manage, and paperwork slows things down. Figure 15.4(b) indicates that a 3000-daily production plant is the optimal size to build, if demand is strong enough to support this level of production.

Accumulated Production

Suppose TI runs a plant that produces 3000 hand calculators per day. As TI gains experience producing hand calculators, its methods improve. Workers learn shortcuts, materials flow more smoothly, procurement costs fall. The result, as Figure 15.5 shows, is that average cost falls with accumulated production experience. Thus the average cost of producing the first 100 000 hand calculators is $10 per calculator. When the company has produced the first 200 000 calculators, the average cost has fallen to $9. After its accumulated production experience doubles again to 400 000, the average cost is $8. This decline in the average cost with accumulated production experience is called the *experience curve* or *learning curve*.

Now suppose three firms compete in this industry, TI, A, and B. TI is the lowest-cost producer at $8, having produced 400 000 units in the past. If all three firms sell the calculator for $10, TI makes $2 profit per unit, A makes $1 per unit, and B breaks even. The smart move for TI would be to lower its price to $9. This will drive B out of the market, and even A will consider leaving. TI will pick up the business that would have gone to B (and possibly A). Furthermore, price-sensitive customers will enter the market at the lower price. As production increases beyond 400 000 units,

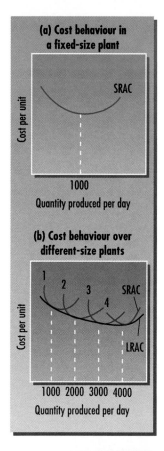

FIGURE 15.4

Cost per Unit at Different Levels of Production per Period

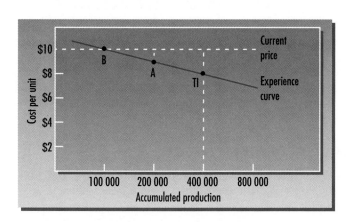

FIGURE 15.5

Cost per Unit as a Function of Accumulated Production: The Experience Curve

chapter 15
Designing
Pricing Strategies
and Programs **451**

TI's costs will drop still further and faster and more than restore its profits, even at a price of $9. TI has used this aggressive pricing strategy repeatedly to gain market share and drive others out of the industry.

Experience-curve pricing nevertheless carries major risks. Aggressive pricing might give the product a cheap image. The strategy also assumes that the competitors are weak and not willing to fight. Finally, the strategy leads the company into building more plants to meet demand while a competitor innovates a lower-cost technology and obtains lower costs than the market leader, who is now stuck with the old technology.

Most experience-curve pricing has focused on manufacturing costs. But all costs, including marketing costs, are subject to learning improvements. If three firms are each investing a large sum of money trying telemarketing, the firm that has used it the longest might achieve the lowest telemarketing costs. This firm can charge a little less for its product and still earn the same return, all other costs being equal.[13]

Differentiated Marketing Offers

Today's companies try to adapt their offers and terms to different buyers. Thus a manufacturer will negotiate different terms with different retail chains. One retailer may want daily delivery (to keep stock lower) while another retailer may accept twice-a-week delivery in order to get a lower price. As a result, the manufacturer's costs will differ with each chain, and its profits will differ. To estimate the real profitability of dealing with different retailers, the manufacturer needs to use *activity-based cost (ABC) accounting* instead of *standard cost accounting*.[14]

ABC accounting tries to identify the real costs associated with serving different customers. Both the variable costs and the overhead costs must be tagged back to each customer. Companies that fail to measure their costs correctly are not measuring their profit correctly. They are likely to misallocate their marketing effort. Identifying the true costs arising in a customer relationship also enables a company to explain its charges better to the customer.

Target Costing

We have seen that costs change with production scale and experience. They can also change as a result of a concentrated effort by the company's designers, engineers, and purchasing agents to reduce them. The Japanese use a method called *target costing*.[15] They use market research to establish a new product's desired functions. Then they determine the price at which the product will sell given its appeal and competitors' prices. They deduct the desired profit margin from this price, and this leaves the target cost they must achieve. They then examine each cost element—design, engineering, manufacturing, sales—and break them down into further components. They consider ways to re-engineer components, eliminate functions, and bring down supplier costs. The objective is to bring the final cost projections into the target cost range. If they can't succeed, they may decide against developing the product because it couldn't sell for the target price and make the target profit. When they can succeed, profits are likely to follow.

ANALYZING COMPETITORS' COSTS, PRICES, AND OFFERS

Within the range of possible prices determined by market demand and company costs, the firm must take the competitors' costs, prices, and possible price reactions into account. If the firm's offer is similar to a major competitor's offer, then the firm will have to price close to the competitor or lose sales. If the firm's offer is inferior, the firm will not be able to charge more than the competitor. If the firm's offer is superior, the firm can charge more than the competitor. The firm must be aware, however, that competitors might change their prices in response.

SELECTING A PRICING METHOD

Given the three Cs—the customers' demand schedule, the cost function, and competitors' prices—the company is now ready to select a price. Figure 15.6 summarizes the three major considerations in price setting. Costs set a floor to the price. Competitors'

FIGURE 15.6

The Three Cs Model for Price Setting

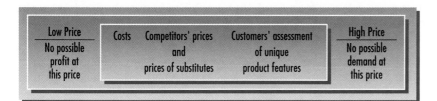

Low Price No possible profit at this price	Costs	Competitors' prices and prices of substitutes	Customers' assessment of unique product features	High Price No possible demand at this price

prices and the price of substitutes provide an orienting point. Customers' assessment of unique product features establishes the ceiling price.

Companies select a pricing method that includes one or more of these three considerations. We will examine six price-setting methods: markup pricing, target-return pricing, perceived-value pricing, value pricing, going-rate pricing, and sealed-bid pricing.

Markup Pricing

The most elementary pricing method is to add a standard markup to the product's cost. Construction companies submit job bids by estimating the total project cost and adding a standard markup for profit. Lawyers and accountants typically price by adding a standard markup on their time and costs. Defence contractors charge their cost plus a standard markup.

Suppose a toaster manufacturer has the following costs and sales expectations:

Variable cost per unit	$ 10
Fixed cost	300,000
Expected unit sales	50,000

The manufacturer's unit cost is given by:

$$\text{Unit cost} = \text{variable cost} + \frac{\text{fixed costs}}{\text{unit sales}} = \$10 + \frac{\$300,000}{50,000} = \$16$$

Now assume the manufacturer wants to earn a 20 percent markup on sales. The manufacturer's markup price is given by:

$$\text{Markup price} = \frac{\text{unit cost}}{(1 - \text{desired return on sales})} = \frac{\$16}{1 - 0.2} = \$20$$

The manufacturer would charge dealers $20 per toaster and make a profit of $4 per unit. The dealers in turn will mark up the toaster. If dealers want to earn 50 percent on their selling price, they will mark up the toaster to $40. This is equivalent to a cost markup of 100 percent.

Markups are generally higher on seasonal items (to cover the risk of not selling), specialty items, slower-moving items, items with high storage and handling costs, and demand-inelastic items, such as prescription drugs. Unfortunately, those least able to pay for prescription drugs are often those most burdened by the markups such as uninsured individuals. In the case of prescription drugs, generic (non-brand-name) drugs command an extraordinarily high markup:

■ **Generic Drugs.** Drugstores and pharmacies are marking up the price of some generics by more than 1000 percent. For example, stores charge an average of $18.08 for a prescription of the generic version of the antipsychotic drug Haldol, 2800 percent more than the $.62 cost the generic manufacturer charges. A prescription for the generic version of Zovirax, an antiviral drug, sells at pharmacies for an average of $61.64, more than eight times the manufacturer's price of $7.22. Not only do pharmacies pocket a handsome profit, but they also look like good guys when they encourage customers to use a generic drug to save money. Indeed, the generic drug is still cheaper than the brand-name counterpart. For their part, pharmacies argue that the high gross margins for generics don't tell the whole story. Just as a patient who visits a doctor and gets handed a Band-Aid is not billed for just the Band-Aid, a pharmacy customer must pay for the pharmacist's time and other expenses of maintaining a pharmacy department.[16]

Does the use of standard markups make logical sense? Generally, no. Any pricing method that ignores current demand, perceived value, and competition is not likely to lead to the optimal price. Markup pricing works only if the marked-up price actually brings in the expected level of sales.

Companies introducing a new product often price it high hoping to recover their costs as rapidly as possible. But a high-markup strategy could be fatal if a competitor is pricing low. This happened to Philips, the Dutch electronics manufacturer, in pricing its videodisc players. Philips wanted to make a profit on each videodisc player. Meanwhile, Japanese competitors priced low and succeeded in building their market share rapidly, which in turn pushed down their costs substantially.

Still, markup pricing remains popular for a number of reasons. First, sellers can determine costs much more easily than they can estimate demand. By tying the price to cost, sellers simplify the pricing task. Second, where all firms in the industry use this pricing method, prices tend to be similar. Price competition is therefore minimized, which would not be the case if firms paid attention to demand variations when they priced. Third, many people feel that cost-plus pricing is fairer to both buyers and sellers. Sellers do not take advantage of buyers when the latter's demand becomes acute, and sellers earn a fair return on investment.

Target-Return Pricing

In *target-return pricing*, the firm determines the price that would yield its target rate of return on investment (ROI). Target pricing is used by General Motors, which prices its automobiles to achieve a 15 to 20 percent ROI. This pricing method is also used by public utilities, which need to make a fair return on their investment.

Suppose the toaster manufacturer has invested $1 million in the business and wants to set price to earn a 20 percent ROI, specifically $200 000. The target-return price is given by the following formula:

$$\text{Target-return price} = \frac{\text{unit cost} + \text{desired return} \times \text{invested capital}}{\text{unit sales}}$$

$$= \$16 + \frac{.20 \times \$1\ 000\ 000}{50\ 000} = \$20$$

The manufacturer will realize this 20 percent ROI provided its costs and estimated sales turn out to be accurate. But what if sales do not reach 50 000 units? The manufacturer can prepare a *break-even chart* to learn what would happen at other sales levels (Figure 15.7). Fixed costs are $300 000 regardless of sales volume. Variable costs, not shown in the figure, rise with volume. Total costs equal the sum of fixed costs and variable costs. The total revenue curve starts at zero and rises with each unit sold.

The total revenue and total cost curves cross at 30 000 units. This is the *break-even volume*. It can be verified by the following formula:

$$\text{Break-even volume} = \frac{\text{fixed cost}}{\text{price} - \text{variable cost}} = \frac{\$300\ 000}{\$20 - \$10} = 30\ 000$$

The manufacturer, of course, is hoping that the market will buy 50 000 units at $20, in which case it earns $200 000 on its $1 million investment. But much depends on price elasticity and competitors' prices. Unfortunately, target-return pricing tends to ignore these considerations. The manufacturer needs to consider different prices and estimate their probable impacts on sales volume and profits. The manufacturer should also search for ways to lower its fixed or variable costs, because lower costs will decrease its required break-even volume.

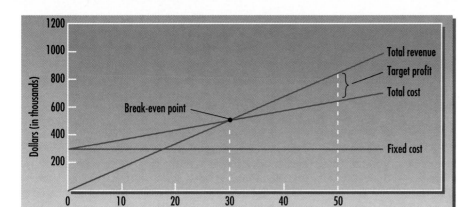

Perceived-Value Pricing

An increasing number of companies base price on the customer's *perceived value*. They see the buyers' perceptions of value, not the seller's cost, as the key to pricing. They use the other marketing-mix elements, such as advertising and sales force, to build up perceived value in buyers' minds.[17]

DuPont is a major practitioner of perceived-value pricing. When DuPont developed its new synthetic fibre for carpets, it demonstrated to carpet manufacturers that they could afford to pay DuPont as much as $3.08 per kilogram for the new fibre and still make their target profit. DuPont calls the $3.08 the *value-in-use price*. But pricing the new material at $3.08 per kilogram would leave the carpet manufacturers indifferent. So it set the price lower than $3.08 to induce carpet manufacturers to adopt the new fibre. DuPont did not use its manufacturing cost to set the price but only to judge whether there was enough profit to proceed in the first place.

DuPont also embeds each chemical into a larger offering so that it is not seen as a commodity but rather as a solution to a customer's problem. Consider the following:

Attribute	Standard Offer	Premium Offer	Added Value
Quality	Impurities less than 10 parts per million	Impurities less than one part per million	$2.80
Delivery	Within two weeks	Within one week	.30
System	Supply chemical only	Supply total system	1.60
Innovation	Little R&D support	High level R&D support	4.00
Retraining	Train initially	Retrain on request	.80
Service	Through home office purchases	Locally available	.50
Price	$230/kilogram	$230/kilogram	$10.00

The chemical is part of a standard offer or a premium offer. The customer who wants the premium offer pays $230 instead of $220 a kilogram. The customer may end up requesting fewer added values. DuPont is willing to *unbundle* the premium offer and charge only for the chosen added values.

Caterpillar also uses perceived value to set prices on its construction equipment. It might price its tractor at $100 000, although a similar competitor's tractor might be priced at $90 000. When a prospective customer asks a Caterpillar dealer why he should pay $10 000 more for the Caterpillar tractor, the dealer answers:

$ 90 000	is the tractor's price if it is only equivalent to the competitor's tractor
$ 7 000	is the price premium for Caterpillar's superior durability
$ 6 000	is the price premium for Caterpillar's superior reliability
$ 5 000	is the price premium for Caterpillar's superior service

$ 2 000	is the price premium for Caterpillar's longer warranty on parts
$110 000	is the normal price to cover Caterpillar's superior value
−$ 10 000	discount
$100 000	final price

The Caterpillar dealer is able to indicate why Caterpillar's tractor delivers more value than the competitor's. Although the customer is asked to pay a $10 000 premium, he is actually getting $20 000 extra value! He chooses the Caterpillar tractor because he is convinced that its lifetime operating costs will be lower.

The key to perceived-value pricing is to determine the market's perception of the offer's value accurately. Sellers with an inflated view of their offer's value will overprice their product. Sellers with an underestimated view will charge less than they could. Market research is needed to establish the market's perception of value as a guide to effective pricing.[18]

Value Pricing

In recent years, several companies have adopted *value pricing,* in which they charge a fairly low price for a high-quality offering. Value pricing says that the price should represent a high-value offer to consumers.

The computer industry has gone from seeking top dollar for computers with the most technology to putting out computers with basic features for lower prices.

Monorail Computer Corporation
www.monorail.com

- ■ **Monorail Computer Corporation.** In 1996, a virtually unknown company, Monorail Computer Corporation, sold computers for as little as $999 in an effort to woo price-sensitive users. Within months, Compaq and Packard Bell NEC followed suit, and the sub-$1000 computer market was born. These companies have pushed retail prices down an average of $400. Now another little-known upstart, Emachines, promises to take value pricing even further. Its E-Tower will sell for less than $500 without a monitor and is designed specifically to appeal to the 55 percent of computerless households with annual incomes of $25 000 to $30 000. Despite its low price tag, however, the E-Tower is loaded with power: a Cyrix microprocessor from National Semiconductor, a two-gigabyte hard drive, 32 megabytes of memory, a CD-ROM drive, and more.[19]

Recently Procter & Gamble created quite a stir by reducing its price on Pampers and Luvs diapers, liquid Tide detergent, and Folger's coffee to value price them. In the past, a brand-loyal family had to pay what amounted to a $1087 premium for a year's worth of P&G products versus private-label or low-priced brands. To offer value prices, P&G underwent a major overhaul. It redesigned the way it develops, manufactures, distributes, prices, markets, and sells products to deliver better value at every point in the supply chain.[20] Value pricing is not a matter of simply setting lower prices on one's products compared to competitors. It is a matter of re-engineering the company's operations to become a low-cost producer without sacrificing quality, and lowering prices significantly to attract a large number of value-conscious customers.

An important type of value pricing is *everyday low pricing (EDLP)*, which occurs at the retail level. A retailer who holds to an EDLP pricing policy charges a constant, everyday low price with no temporary price discounts. These constant prices eliminate week-to-week price uncertainty and can be contrasted to the "high–low" pricing of promotion-oriented competitors. In *high–low pricing*, the retailer charges higher prices on an everyday basis but then runs frequent promotions in which prices are temporarily lowered below the EDLP level.[21]

In recent years, high–low pricing has given way to EDLP at such widely different venues as General Motors' Saturn car dealerships and upscale department stores. Even Eaton's tried it, but with little success. But the leader of EDLP is surely Wal-Mart, which practically defined the term. Except for a few sale items every month, Wal-Mart promises everyday low prices on major brands. "It's not a short-term strategy," says one Wal-Mart executive. "You have to be willing to make a commitment to it, and you have to be able to operate with lower ratios of expense than everybody else."

Retailers adopt EDLP for a number of reasons, the most important of which is that constant sales and promotions are costly and have eroded consumer confidence in the credibility of everyday shelf prices. Consumers also have less time and patience for such time-honoured traditions as watching for supermarket specials and clipping coupons.

Yet, there is no denying that promotions create excitement and draw shoppers. For this reason, EDLP is not a guarantee of success. As supermarkets face heightened competition from their counterparts and from alternative channels, many find that the key to drawing shoppers is using a combination of high–low and everyday low pricing strategies, with increased advertising and promotions.[22]

Going-Rate Pricing

In *going-rate pricing*, the firm bases its price largely on competitors' prices. The firm might charge the same, more, or less than major competitor(s). In oligopolistic industries that sell a commodity such as steel, paper, or fertilizer, firms normally charge the same price. The smaller firms "follow the leader," changing their prices when the market leader's prices change rather than when their own demand or costs change. Some firms may charge a slight premium or slight discount, but they preserve the amount of difference. Thus minor gasoline retailers usually charge a few cents less per litre than the major oil companies, without letting the difference increase or decrease.

Going-rate pricing is quite popular. Where costs are difficult to measure or competitive response is uncertain, firms feel that the going price represents a good solution. It is thought to reflect the industry's collective wisdom as to the price that will yield a fair return and not jeopardize industrial harmony.

Sealed-Bid Pricing

Competitive-oriented pricing is common where firms submit sealed bids for jobs. The firm bases its price on expectations of how competitors will price rather than on a rigid relation to the firm's costs or demand. The firm wants to win the contract, and winning normally requires submitting a lower price bid. At the same time, the firm cannot set its price below cost.

The net effect of these two opposite pulls can be described in terms of the bid's expected profit (Table 15.1). Suppose a bid of $9500 would yield a high chance of getting the contract (say 81 percent) but only a low profit, say $100. The expected profit is calculated by multiplying the company's profit by the probability of winning the bid. Thus the expected profit of this bid is $81. If the firm bid $11 000, its profit would be $1600, but its chance of getting the contract might be reduced, say to 1 percent. The expected profit would thus be only $16. One logical bidding criterion would be to bid the price that would maximize the expected profit. According to Table 15.1, the best bid would be $10 000, for which the expected profit is $216.

Using expected profit for setting price makes sense for the firm that makes many bids. In playing the odds, the firm will achieve maximum profits in the long run. The firm that bids only occasionally or that needs a particular contract badly will not find it advantageous to use the expected-profit criterion. This criterion, for example, does not distinguish between a $1000 profit with a 0.10 probability and a $125 profit with an 0.80 probability. Yet the firm that wants to keep production going would prefer the second contract to the first.

Company's Bid	Company's Profit	Probability of Getting Award with This Bid (Assumed)	Expected Profit
$ 9 500	$ 100	0.81	$ 81
10 000	600	0.36	216
10 500	1,100	0.09	99
11 000	1,600	0.01	16

TABLE 15.1

Effect of Different Bids on Expected Profit

SELECTING THE FINAL PRICE

Pricing methods narrow the range from which the company must select its final price. In selecting that price, the company must consider additional factors, including psychological pricing, the influence of other marketing-mix elements on price, company pricing policies, and the impact of price on other parties.

Psychological Pricing

Many consumers use price as an indicator of quality. When Fleischmann raised the price of its gin from $4.50 to $5.50 a bottle, its liquor sales went up, not down. Image pricing is especially effective with ego-sensitive products such as perfumes and expensive cars. A $100 bottle of perfume might contain $10 worth of scent, but gift givers pay $100 to communicate their high regard for the receiver.

Price and quality perceptions of cars interact.[23] Higher-priced cars are perceived to possess high quality. Higher-quality cars are likewise perceived to be higher priced than they actually are. When alternative information about true quality is available, price becomes a less significant indicator of quality. When this information is not available, price acts as a signal of quality.

When looking at a particular product, buyers carry in their minds a *reference price* formed by noticing current prices, past prices, or the buying context. Sellers often manipulate these reference prices. For example, a seller can situate its product among expensive products to imply that it belongs in the same class. Department stores will display women's apparel in separate departments differentiated by price; dresses found in the more expensive department are assumed to be of better quality. Reference-price thinking is also created by stating a high manufacturer's suggested price, or by indicating that the product was priced much higher originally, or by pointing to a competitor's high price.[24]

Many sellers believe that prices should end in an odd number. Many customers see a stereo amplifier priced at $299 instead of $300 as a price in the $200 range rather than $300 range. Another explanation is that odd endings convey the notion of a discount or bargain. But if a company wants a high-price image instead of a low-price image, it should avoid the odd-ending tactic.

The Influence of Other Marketing-Mix Elements

The final price must take into account the brand's quality and advertising relative to competition. Farris and Reibstein examined the relationships among relative price, relative quality, and relative advertising for 227 consumer businesses and found the following:

- Brands with average relative quality but high relative advertising budgets were able to charge premium prices. Consumers apparently were willing to pay higher prices for known products than for unknown products.

- Brands with high relative quality and high relative advertising obtained the highest prices. Conversely, brands with low quality and low advertising charged the lowest prices.

- The positive relationship between high prices and high advertising held most strongly in the later stages of the product life cycle for market leaders.[25]

Company Pricing Policies

The price must be consistent with company pricing policies. Many companies set up a pricing department to develop policies and establish or approve decisions. The aim is to ensure that the salespeople quote prices that are reasonable to customers and profitable to the company.

Impact of Price on Other Parties

Management must also consider the reactions of other parties to the contemplated price. How will distributors and dealers feel about it? Will the sales force be willing to sell at that price? How will competitors react? Will suppliers raise their prices when they see the company's price? Will the government intervene and prevent this price from being charged?

In the last case, marketers need to know the laws regulating pricing. The Competition Act, Sections 34, 36 and 38, governs pricing policies. For example, one section establishes the rule that sellers must set prices without talking to competitors: *Price-fixing*, also called collusion, is illegal. Consider a recent case:

■ **Jungbunzlauer/Bayer.** Switzerland's Jungbunzlauer International AG and Germany's Bayer AG were recently fined $6.7 million for their roles in an international conspiracy to fix prices of citric acid, a food additive. During the trial, evidence was given that senior representatives of the two companies "engaged in conversations and attended meetings with the representatives of other citric acid producing companies." While most meetings were held outside Canada, at least one took place in Toronto. These meetings led to an unlawful agreement as to the prices and volume at which each company would sell citric acid to customers in Canada.[26]

Other sections of the Competition Act forbid price discrimination. It is illegal for a supplier to discriminate between competitors that purchase like quantities of goods or services. If firms try to import goods into Canada and attempt to sell them below cost, a practice called dumping, Revenue Canada will step in to forbid the practice using the Special Import Measures Act. Other laws seek to protect consumers against deceptive pricing practices. For example, it is illegal for a company to set artificially high "regular" prices, then announce a "sale" at prices close to previous everyday prices. The federal government's Office of Consumer Affairs produces the *Canadian Consumer Handbook* that outlines other concerns and actions consumers can take to have these abuses redressed. People can view this document on-line using the Strategis.ca web site.

ADAPTING THE PRICE

Companies usually do not set a single price but rather a pricing structure that reflects variations in geographical demand and costs, market-segment requirements, purchase timing, order levels, delivery frequency, guarantees, service contracts, and other factors. As a result of discounts, allowances, and promotional support, a company rarely realizes the same profit from each unit of a product that it sells. Here we will examine several price-adaptation strategies: geographical pricing, price discounts and allowances, promotional pricing, discriminatory pricing, and product-mix pricing.

GEOGRAPHICAL PRICING (CASH, COUNTERTRADE, BARTER)

Geographical pricing involves the company in deciding how to price its products to different customers in different locations and countries. For example, should the company charge higher prices to distant customers to cover the higher shipping costs or a lower price to win additional business? Another issue is how to get paid. This issue is critical when buyers lack sufficient hard currency to pay for their purchases. Many buyers want to offer other items in payment, a practice known as *countertrade*. North American companies are often forced to engage in countertrade if they want the business. Countertrade may account for 15 to 25 percent of world trade and takes several forms:[27] barter, compensation deals, buyback agreements, and offset.

■ *Barter:* The direct exchange of goods, with no money and no third party involved. Eminence S.A., one of France's major clothing makers, launched a five-year deal to barter $25 million worth of North American-produced underwear and sportswear to customers in eastern Europe in exchange for a variety of goods and services, including global transportation and advertising space in eastern European magazines.

■ *Compensation deal:* The seller receives some percentage of the payment in cash and the rest in products. A British aircraft manufacturer sold planes to Brazil for 70 percent cash and the rest in coffee.

- *Buyback arrangement*: The seller sells a plant, equipment, or technology to another country and agrees to accept as partial payment products manufactured with the supplied equipment. A North American chemical company built a plant for an Indian company and accepted partial payment in cash and the remainder in chemicals manufactured at the plant.

- *Offset:* The seller receives full payment in cash but agrees to spend a substantial amount of that money in that country within a stated time period. For example, PepsiCo sells its cola syrup to Russia for rubles and agrees to buy Russian vodka at a certain rate for sale in North America.

More complex countertrade deals involve more than two parties. For example, Daimler-Benz agreed to sell 30 trucks to Romania and accept in exchange 150 Romanian-made jeeps, which it sold in Ecuador for bananas, which in turn were sold to a German supermarket chain for deutsche marks. Through this circuitous transaction, Daimler-Benz finally achieved payment in German currency. Deals such as this are carried on by a separate countertrade department within the company. Other companies rely on barter houses and countertrade specialists to assist them.

PRICE DISCOUNTS AND ALLOWANCES

Most companies will adjust their list price and give *discounts* and *allowances* for early payment, volume purchases, and off-season buying (see Table 15.2). Companies must do this carefully or find that their profits are much less than planned.[28]

Jack Trout, author of *Positioning* and several other marketing guidebooks, cautions that some categories tend to self-destruct by always being on sale. Mink coats and mattresses, says Trout, never seem to be sold at anything near list price, and when

TABLE 15.2	
Price Discounts and Allowances	
Cash Discounts:	A *cash discount* is a price reduction to buyers who pay their bills promptly. A typical example is "2/10, net 30," which means that payment is due within 30 days and that the buyer can deduct 2 percent by paying the bill within 10 days. Such discounts are customary in many industries.
Quantity Discounts:	A *quantity discount* is a price reduction to those buyers who buy large volumes. A typical example is "$10 per unit for less than 100 units; $9 per unit for 100 or more units." Quantity discounts must be offered equally to all customers and must not exceed the cost savings to the seller associated with selling large quantities. They can be offered on a noncumulative basis (on each order placed) or a cumulative basis (on the number of units ordered over a given period).
Functional Discounts:	*Functional discounts* (also called *trade discounts*) are offered by a manufacturer to trade-channel members if they will perform certain functions, such as selling, storing, and record keeping. Manufacturers may offer different functional discounts to different trade channels but must offer the same functional discounts within each channel.
Seasonal Discounts:	A *seasonal discount* is a price reduction to buyers who buy merchandise or services out of season. Ski manufacturers will offer seasonal discounts to retailers in the spring and summer to encourage early ordering. Hotels, motels, and airlines will offer seasonal discounts in slow selling periods.
Allowances:	Allowances are extra payments designed to gain reseller participation in special programs. *Trade-in allowances* are price reductions granted for turning in an old item when buying a new one. Trade-in allowances are most common in durable-goods categories. *Promotional allowances* are payments or price reductions to reward dealers for participating in advertising and sales support programs.

automakers get rebate-happy, the market just sits back and waits for a deal. Discount pricing has become the *modus operandi* of a surprising number of companies offering both products and services. Even Pepsi and Coke, two of the most popular brands in the world, engaged in a price war that ultimately tarnished their brand equity. See the Marketing Memo, "Commandments of Discounting," for Jack Trout's discounting directives.

PROMOTIONAL PRICING

Companies can use several pricing techniques to stimulate early purchase.

- *Loss-leader pricing:* Supermarkets and department stores often drop the price on well-known brands to stimulate additional store traffic. The manufacturers of these brands typically disapprove of their products being used as loss leaders because this practice can dilute the brand image and bring complaints from other retailers who charge the list price. Manufacturers have tried to restrain intermediaries from loss-leader pricing through lobbying for retail-price-maintenance laws, but these laws have been revoked.

- *Special-event pricing:* Sellers will establish special prices in certain seasons to draw in more customers. Every August, there are back-to-school sales.

- *Cash rebates:* Auto companies and other consumer-goods companies offer cash rebates to encourage purchase of the manufacturers' products within a specified time period. Rebates can help clear inventories without cutting the stated list price.

- *Low-interest financing:* Instead of cutting its price, the company can offer customers low-interest financing. Automakers have announced three percent financing and in some cases no-interest financing to attract customers.

- *Longer payment terms:* Sellers, especially mortgage banks and auto companies, stretch loans over longer periods and thus lower the monthly payments. Consumers often worry less about the cost (i.e., the interest rate) of a loan and more about whether they can afford the monthly payment.

- *Warranties and service contracts:* Companies can promote sales by adding a free or low-cost warranty or service contract.

- *Psychological discounting:* This strategy involves setting an artificially high price and then offering the product at substantial savings; for example, "Was $359, now $299." Illegitimate discount tactics are fought by Business Bureaus and the Office of Consumer Affairs. However, discounts from normal prices are a legitimate form of promotional pricing.

Promotional-pricing strategies are often a zero-sum game. If they work, competitors copy them and they lose their effectiveness. If they do not work, they waste company money that could have been put into longer-impact marketing tools, such as building up product quality and service or strengthening product image through advertising.

DISCRIMINATORY PRICING

Companies often adjust their basic price to accommodate differences in customers, products, locations, and so on. *Discriminatory pricing* occurs when a company sells a product or service at two or more prices that do not reflect a proportional difference in costs. Discriminatory pricing takes several forms:

- *Customer-segment pricing:* Different customer groups are charged different prices for the same product or service. For example, museums often charge a lower admission fee to students and senior citizens.

- *Product-form pricing:* Different versions of the product are priced differently but not proportionately to their respective costs. Evian prices a 1.5-litre bottle of its mineral water at $2.00. It takes the same water and packages 50 mL in a moisturizer spray for $6.00. Through product-form pricing, Evian manages to charge $4.00 for 50 mL in one form and about $.07 for 50 mL in another.

MARKETING *memo*

Commandments of Discounting

- Thou shalt not offer discounts because everyone else does.
- Thou should be creative with your discounting.
- Thou should use discounts to clear stocks or generate extra business.
- Thou should put time limits on the deal.
- Thou should make sure the ultimate customer gets the deal.
- Thou should discount only to survive in a mature market.
- Thou should stop discounting as soon as you can.

Source: Reprinted from Jack Trout, "Prices: Simple Guidelines to Get Them Right," *Journal of Business Strategy*, November–December 1998, pp. 13–16.

Digital Discrimination: How the Internet Is Revolutionizing Pricing—for Sellers and Buyers

E-commerce is arguably the Web's hottest application. Yet, the Internet is more than simply a new "marketspace." Internet-based technologies are actually changing the rules of the market. Just as the first signs of fixed pricing were found at Aaron Montgomery Ward's mail-order business in the 1870s, a little over a hundred years later the first signs of a return to fluid pricing can be seen on the Internet. Here's a short list of how the Internet allows sellers to discriminate between buyers and allows buyers to discriminate between sellers!

Sellers can . . .

. . . monitor customer behaviour and tailor offers to individuals. Although shopping agent software and price comparison Web sites will tell consumers published prices, they may be missing out on the special deals consumers can get with the help of new technologies. For example, Personify, a San Francisco–based start-up, has software that lets a Web-based merchant identify individual visitors to its Web site. The software studies Web users "clickstream," the way the person navigates through the Web site. Based on that behaviour, the software can instantaneously target shoppers for specific products and prices. If a visitor behaves like a price-sensitive shopper, he or she may be offered a lower price. But buyer beware: Microsoft is exploring software similar to Personify, and Bill Gates predicts that Web sites will soon recognize individual consumers, remember what they paid for items in the past, and charge them a customized price based on that history.

. . . give certain customers access to special prices. Yes, prices are more transparent on the Web, but sellers have found ways to hide special deals. CDnow, an online vendor of music albums, e-mails certain buyers a special Web site address with lower prices. Unless you know the secret address, you pay full price. Microsoft Office has a promotion with iVillage software that offers people who enter iVillage's Web site via Microsoft's site a lower price on add-ons to some Microsoft programs. The computer technology at your local grocer also makes it possible for some customers to get lower prices: Cash registers can print out customized coupons based on the contents of your grocery cart.

. . . change prices on the fly according to changes in demand. Coca-Cola has a bold idea: Why should the price of a can of Coke be the same all the time? Wouldn't people pay more for a cold cola on a sweltering summer day than they would on a cold, rainy one? The beverage giant will begin experimenting with "smart" vending machines that hook up to Coke's internal computer network, letting the company monitor inventory in distant locales—and change prices accordingly. Although consumers might protest if Coke's prices were suddenly raised, it's very possible they can be persuaded to buy a cold pop on a chilly day if the vending machine flashed a special promotion, say 20 cents off. If this concept sounds too fantastic, consider this: Business marketers are already using extranets, private networks that link them with suppliers and customers, to get a precise handle on inventory, costs, and demand at any given moment—and adjust prices instantly.

Both sellers and buyers can . . .

. . . negotiate prices in online auctions and exchanges. Want to sell hundreds of excess and slightly worn widgets? Post a sale on www.eBay.com. Want to purchase vintage baseball cards at a bargain price? Go to Boekhout's Collectibles Mall at www.azww.com. The value of goods and services sold over the Internet using auction technology is predicted to be $193 billion

(continued)

- *Image pricing:* Some companies price the same product at two different levels based on image differences. A perfume manufacturer can put the perfume in one bottle, give it a name and image, and price it at $10 for 10 mL. It can put the same perfume in another bottle with a different name and image and price it at $30 for 10 mL.

- *Location pricing:* The same product is priced differently at different locations even though the cost of offering at each location is the same. A theatre varies its seat prices according to audience preferences for different locations.

- *Time pricing:* Prices are varied by season, day, or hour. Public utilities vary energy rates to commercial users by time of day and weekend versus weekday. A special form of time pricing is *yield pricing*, which is often used by hotels and airlines to ensure high occupancy. To ensure that all its berths are full, for example, a cruise ship may lower the price of the cruise two days before sailing.

For price discrimination to work, certain conditions must exist. First, the market must be segmentable and the segments must show different intensities of demand. Second, members in the lower-price segment must not be able to resell the product to the higher-price segment. Third, competitors must not be able to undersell the firm

(continued)

in the year 2002. That represents 29 percent of all Internet transactions. Of the thousands of Internet auction sites, Onsale and eBay are the largest, and unlike most Internet businesses, are actually turning a profit. More than four million bids have been placed on Onsale since it opened for business in 1995. At eBay, about a million registered users bid on 700 000 items in more than 1000 categories. Suddenly the centuries-old art of haggling is in vogue, and that's because the Internet has made it economical. In the brick-and-mortar world, it costs sellers too much in overhead to negotiate prices with individual buyers. Over the Internet, the cost per transaction drops dramatically so it becomes practical—even profitable—to auction an item for dollars rather than thousands of dollars. The Home Shopping Network can program its computers to accept the 3000 best bids higher than $2.10 for 3000 pieces of costume jewellery. Sellers like auctions because they can get rid of excess inventory. Business marketers, whose transactions account for 68 percent of online auction sales, also use it to offer time-sensitive deals and gauge interest on possible price points for new products. Quite simply, buyers like the bargains they find. After all, eBay began when its owner started searching the Web for vintage Pez containers for his girlfriend.

Buyers can . . .

...get instant price comparisons from thousands of vendors. Price transparency is the buzzword of the Web. No longer do consumers have to expend time and energy to comparison shop. New technologies make it possible to obtain price comparisons with the click of a mouse. Price comparison sites spring up almost daily. Basically these sites rely on huge computer databases of product information. PriceScan lures 9000 visitors a day, most of them corporate buyers. Compare.Net also lets consumers compare prices on thousands of products. Intelligent shopping agents, software shopping robots (called "bots"), take price comparison a step further. Bots like MySimon, Junglee, and Jango seek out products, prices, and reviews from as many as 900 merchants. Vendors are so angered by the use of bots and comparison sites that many have even blocked their Web sites. Yet, a surprising number of retailers are buying up bot companies. Their goal: to develop more sophisticated shopping agents to help them create Internet superstores.

...name their price and have it met. No doubt more Internet start-ups will follow the Priceline business model. Priceline.com allows travellers to name their price for airline tickets booked at the last minute and get a $400 ticket from Halifax to Vancouver as opposed to a $1200 full fare ticket. Using complex software that shops bids to 18 airlines, Priceline brokers around 1000 tickets a day. Founder Jay Walker is taking his style of e-commerce to cars, hotel rooms, and home mortgages. By using services such as Priceline, consumers can fix their own prices. Sellers can use it too: Airlines can fill in demand for empty seats, and hotels will, no doubt, welcome the chance to sell vacant rooms.

Sources: Amy E. Cortese, "Good-Bye to Fixed Pricing?" *Business Week*, May 4, 1998, pp. 71–84; Scott Woolley, "I Got It Cheaper than You," *Forbes*, November 2, 1998, pp. 82–84; Scott Woolley, "Price War!" *Forbes*, December 14, 1998, pp. 182–84; Michael Krauss, "Web Offers Biggest Prize in Product Pricing Game," *Marketing News*, July 6, 1998, p. 8; Julie Pitta, "Competitive Shopping," *Forbes*, February 9, 1998, pp. 92–95; Matthew Nelson, "Going Once, Going Twice ....." *InfoWorld*, November 9, 1998, pp. 1, 64; Leslie Walker, "The Net's Battle of the Bots," *Washington Post*, December 10, 1998, p. B1; Heather Green, "A Cybershopper's Best Friend," *Business Week*, May 4, 1998, p. 84; Rebecca Quick, "Buying the Goods—The Attack of the Robots: Comparison-Shopping Technology is Here—Whether Retailers Like It or Not," *Wall Street Journal*, December 7, 1998, p. R14.

in the higher-price segment. Fourth, the cost of segmenting and policing the market must not exceed the extra revenue derived from price discrimination. Fifth, the practice must not breed customer resentment and ill will. Sixth, the particular form of price discrimination must not be illegal.[29]

As a result of deregulation in several industries, competitors have increased their use of discriminatory pricing. Airlines charge different fares to passengers on the same flight depending on the seating class; the time of day (morning or night coach); the day of the week (workday or weekend); the season; the person's company, past business, or status (youth, military, senior citizen); and so on. Airlines are using yield pricing to capture as much revenue as possible.

Most consumers are probably not even aware of the degree to which they are the targets of discriminatory pricing. For instance, catalogue retailers like Victoria's Secret routinely send out catalogues that sell identical goods except at different prices. Consumers who live in a more free-spending postal code area may see only the higher prices. Office product superstore Staples also sends out office-supply catalogues with different prices.

Computer technology is making it easier for sellers to practise discriminatory pricing. For instance, they can use software that monitors customer's movements over the Web and allows them to customize offers and prices to each customer. New software applications, however, are also allowing buyers to discriminate between sellers by comparing prices instantaneously. For more on this topic, see the Marketing for the 21st Century, "Digital Discrimination: How the Internet is Revolutionizing Pricing—for Sellers and Buyers."

Some forms of price discrimination (in which sellers offer different price terms to different people within the same trade group) are illegal. However, price discrimination is legal if the seller can prove that its costs are different when selling different volumes or different qualities of the same product to different retailers. *Predatory pricing*—selling below cost with the intention of destroying competition—is against the law.

But although predatory pricing is thought to be against the law, courts regard it as a legal fiction: theoretically against the law but almost impossible to prove. A new generation of economists, however, is arguing that it is wrong and illegal, especially where software is concerned. Economist Brian Arthurs holds that once a company gains a decisive lead in an industry, such as computing, where there is a strong tendency for consumers to band around one standard, it is almost impossible for rivals to unseat it (even when the predator raises its prices). The U.S. government's antitrust lawsuit against Microsoft could well bring attention to what many perceive as its predatory pricing tactics, even though the suit focuses on other grievances:

- **Microsoft.** When the software giant targets a market for domination, it frequently wins over customers with an irresistible offer: free products. In 1996, Microsoft started giving away Internet Explorer, its Web browser—and in some cases arguably even "paid" people to use it by offering free software and marketing assistance. The strategy was crucial in wresting market dominance from Netscape Communications Corporation. Netscape constantly revised its pricing structure but "better than free" is not the most appealing sales pitch. Yet it's not the giveaways themselves that cause rivals to label Microsoft as a predator but the company's tendency to raise prices above market levels after it gains the lion's share of the market. The wholesale price it charges PC makers for its Windows operating system (in which is bundled the Internet Explorer) has doubled during the past seven years.[30]

PRODUCT-MIX PRICING

Price-setting logic must be modified when the product is part of a product mix. In this case, the firm searches for a set of prices that maximizes profits on the total mix. Pricing is difficult because the various products have demand and cost interrelationships and are subject to different degrees of competition. We can distinguish six situations involving product-mix pricing: product-line pricing, optional-feature pricing, captive-product pricing, two-part pricing, by-product pricing, and product-bundling pricing.

Product-Line Pricing
Companies normally develop product lines rather than single products and introduce price steps.

- **Intel.** In the fall of 1997, Intel segmented its product line into microprocessors aimed at specific markets, such as cheap PCs, mid-tier "performance" PCs, and powerful corporate servers. This strategy let Intel balance thin profits from products like the Celerons, which sell for as little as $129 and go into low-priced PCs, with cash cows like the Pentium II Xeon workstation and server chips, which cost up to $3000. The company's most profitable chips are the mid-range Pentium IIs, used in 97 percent of all PCs priced over $2225.[31]

In many lines of trade, sellers use well-established price points for the products in their line. A men's clothing store might carry men's suits at three price levels: $200,

$350, and $500. Customers will associate low-, average-, and high-quality suits with the three price points. The seller's task is to establish perceived-quality differences that justify the price differences.

Optional-Feature Pricing

Many companies offer optional products, features, and services along with their main product. The automobile buyer can order electric window controls, defoggers, light dimmers, and an extended warranty. Pricing these options is a sticky problem, because companies must decide which items to include in the standard price and which to offer as options. For many years, auto companies advertised a stripped-down model for $15 000 to pull people into showrooms. The economy model was stripped of so many features that most buyers left the showroom spending $20 000.

Restaurants face a similar pricing problem. Restaurant customers can often order liquor in addition to the meal. Many restaurants price their liquor high and their food low. The food revenue covers costs, and the liquor produces the profit. This explains why servers often press hard to get customers to order drinks. Other restaurants price their liquor low and food high to draw in a drinking crowd.

Captive-Product Pricing

Some products require the use of ancillary, or *captive*, products. Manufacturers of razors and cameras often price them low and set high markups on razor blades and film, respectively.

There is a danger in pricing the captive product too high in the *aftermarket* (the market for ancillary supplies to the main product). Caterpillar, for example, makes high profits in the aftermarket by pricing its parts and service high. This practice has given rise to "pirates," who counterfeit the parts and sell them to "shady tree" mechanics who install them, sometimes without passing on the cost savings to customers. Meanwhile, Caterpillar loses sales.[32]

Two-Part Pricing

Service firms often engage in *two-part pricing,* consisting of a fixed fee plus a variable usage fee. Telephone users pay a minimum monthly fee plus charges for calls beyond a certain area. Amusement parks charge an admission fee plus fees for rides over a certain minimum. The service firm faces a problem similar to captive-product pricing—namely, how much to charge for the basic service and how much for the variable usage. The fixed fee should be low enough to induce purchase of the service; the profit can then be made on the usage fees.

By-product Pricing

The production of certain goods—meats, petroleum products, and other chemicals—often results in by-products. If the by-products have value to a customer group, they should be priced on their value. Any income earned on the by-products will make it easier for the company to charge a lower price on its main product if competition forces it to do so.

Sometimes companies don't realize how valuable their by-products are. Until Zoo-Doo Compost Company came along, many zoos did not realize that one of their by-products—their occupants' manure—could be an excellent source of additional revenue.[33]

Product-Bundling Pricing

Sellers often bundle their products and features at a set price. An auto manufacturer might offer an option package at less than the cost of buying all the options separately. A theatre company will price a season subscription at less than the cost of buying all the performances separately. Because customers may not have planned to buy all the components, the savings on the price bundle must be substantial enough to induce them to buy the bundle.[34]

Some customers will want less than the whole bundle. Suppose a medical equipment supplier's offer includes free delivery and training. A particular customer might ask to forgo the free delivery and training in exchange for a lower price. The customer is asking the seller to "unbundle" or "rebundle" its offer. If a supplier saves $100 by not supplying delivery and reduces the customer's price by $80, the supplier has kept the customer happy while increasing its profit by $20.

INITIATING AND RESPONDING TO PRICE CHANGES

Companies often face situations where they may need to cut or raise prices.

INITIATING PRICE CUTS

Several circumstances might lead a firm to cut its price. One is *excess plant capacity*: The firm needs additional business and cannot generate it through increased sales effort, product improvement, or other measures. It may resort to aggressive pricing. But in initiating a price cut, the company may trigger a price war. Another circumstance is a *declining market share*. General Motors, for example, cut its subcompact car prices by 10 percent on the West Coast when Japanese competition kept making inroads. Companies sometimes initiate price cuts in a *drive to dominate the market through lower costs*. Either the company starts with lower costs than its competitors or it initiates price cuts in the hope of gaining market share and lower costs. But a price-cutting strategy involves possible traps:

- *Low-quality trap:* Consumers will assume that the quality is low.
- *Fragile-market-share trap:* A low price buys market share but not market loyalty. The same customers will shift to any lower-price firm that comes along.
- *Shallow-pockets trap:* The higher-priced competitors may cut their prices and may have longer staying power because of deeper cash reserves.

Companies may have to cut their prices in a period of *economic recession*. During hard times, consumers reduce their spending. Some possible company responses are given in Table 15.3.

TABLE 15.3

Marketing-Mix Alternatives

Strategic Options	Reasoning	Consequences
1. Maintain price and perceived quality. Engage in selective customer pruning.	Firm has higher customer loyalty. It is willing to lose poorer customers to competitors.	Smaller market share. Lowered profitability.
2. Raise price and perceived quality.	Raise price to cover rising costs. Improve quality to justify higher prices.	Smaller market share. Maintained profitability.
3. Maintain price and raise perceived quality.	It is cheaper to maintain price and raise perceived quality.	Smaller market share. Short-term decline in profitability. Long-term increase in profitability.
4. Cut price partly and raise perceived quality.	Must give customers some price reduction but stress higher value of offer.	Maintained market share. Short-term decline in profitability. Long-term maintained profitability.
5. Cut price fully and maintain perceived quality.	Discipline and discourage price competition.	Maintained market share. Short-term decline in profitability.
6. Cut price fully and reduce perceived quality.	Discipline and discourage price competition and maintain profit margin.	Maintained market share. Maintained margin. Reduced long-term profitability.
7. Maintain price and reduce perceived quality.	Cut marketing expense to combat rising costs.	Smaller market share. Maintained margin. Reduced long-term profitability.
8. Introduce an economy model.	Give the market what it wants.	Some cannibalization but higher total volume.

INITIATING PRICE INCREASES

A successful price increase can raise profits considerably. For example, if the company's profit margin is 3 percent of sales, a 1 percent price increase will increase profits by 33 percent if sales volume is unaffected. This situation is illustrated in Table 15.4. The assumption is that a company charged $10 and sold 100 units and had costs of $970, leaving a profit of $30, or 3 percent on sales. By raising its price by 10 cents (1 percent price increase), it boosted its profits by 33 percent, assuming the same sales volume.

A major circumstance provoking price increases is *cost inflation*. Rising costs unmatched by productivity gains squeeze profit margins and lead companies to regular rounds of price increases. Companies often raise their prices by more than the cost increase in anticipation of further inflation or government price controls in a practice called *anticipatory pricing*. Companies hesitate to offer long-term price contracts.

Another factor leading to price increases is *overdemand*. When a company cannot supply all of its customers, it can raise its prices, ration supplies to customers, or both. The price can be increased in the following ways. Each has a different impact on buyers.

- *Delayed quotation pricing:* The company does not set a final price until the product is finished or delivered. Delayed quotation pricing is prevalent in industries with long production lead times, such as industrial construction and heavy equipment.

- *Escalator clauses:* The company requires the customer to pay today's price and all or part of any inflation increase that takes place before delivery. An escalator clause bases price increases on some specified price index. Escalator clauses are found in many contracts involving industrial projects of long duration.

- *Unbundling:* The company maintains its price but removes or prices separately one or more elements that were part of the former offer, such as free delivery or installation. Many restaurants have shifted from total dinner pricing to à la carte pricing. A joke in countries with high inflation is that the current price of a car no longer includes the tires and steering wheel.

- *Reduction of discounts:* The company instructs its sales force not to offer its normal cash and quantity discounts.

A company needs to decide whether to raise its price sharply on a one-time basis or to raise it by small amounts several times. When costs rose for Supercuts stores (a franchised chain of hairdressers), management debated between raising the haircut price immediately from $10 to $12 or raising the price to $11 this year and $12 the following year. Generally, consumers prefer small price increases on a regular basis to sharp price increases.

In passing price increases on to customers, organizations must avoid the image of being a price gouger. Student outcries have been heard across the country as governments have cut back on their support of universities, and universities, in turn, have hiked their tuition fees. Companies and organizations alike need to think of who will bear the brunt of increased prices. Customer memories are long, and they will turn against companies they perceive as price gougers when the market softens. This happened to Kellogg, the breakfast cereal company:

	Before	After
Price	$ 10	$10.10 (a 1 percent price increase)
Units sold	100	100
Revenue	$1000	$ 1010
Costs	–970	–970
Profit	$ 30	$ 40 (a $33\frac{1}{3}$ percent profit increase)

TABLE 15.4

Profits Before and After a Price Increase

■ **Kellogg.** Throughout the 1980s, Kellogg pushed up the prices of its break-fast cereals and its stock price soared. The company justified the price increase by saying that with more and more women working, families would not worry about the rising cost of cereal. Although the strategy worked for quite some time, in the early 1990s people did begin to be concerned about just how much that box of cornflakes was costing, and Kellogg's fortunes began to fade. Kellogg responded by cutting costs and closing plants. The company even lowered cereal prices a bit. But while the move hurt profits, it did not help sales as the company had hoped.[35]

There are some techniques for avoiding this image: One is that a sense of fairness must surround any price increase, and customers must be given advance notice so they can do forward buying or shop around. Sharp price increases need to be explained in understandable terms. Making low-visibility price moves first is also a good technique: Eliminating discounts, increasing minimum order sizes, curtailing production of low-margin products are some examples. And contracts or bids for long-term projects should contain escalator clauses based on such factors as increases in recognized national price indexes.[36]

Companies can also respond to higher costs or overdemand without raising prices. The possibilities include the following:

■ Shrinking the amount of product instead of raising the price. (Hershey Foods maintained its chocolate bar price but trimmed its size. Nestlé maintained its size but raised the price.)

■ Substituting less expensive materials or ingredients. (Many chocolate-bar companies substituted synthetic chocolate for real chocolate to fight the price increases in cocoa.)

■ Reducing or removing product features to reduce cost. (Sears engineered down a number of its appliances so they could be priced competitively with those sold in discount stores.)

■ Removing or reducing product services, such as installation or free delivery.

■ Using less expensive packaging material or larger package sizes.

■ Reducing the number of sizes and models offered.

■ Creating new economy brands. (Jewel food stores introduced 170 generic items selling at 10 percent to 30 percent less than national brands.)

REACTIONS TO PRICE CHANGES

Any price change can provoke a response from customers, competitors, distributors, suppliers, and even government.

Customers' Reactions

Customers often question the motivation behind price changes.[37] A price cut can be interpreted in different ways: The item is about to be replaced by a new model; the item is faulty and is not selling well; the firm is in financial trouble; the price will come down even further; the quality has been reduced.

A price increase, which would normally deter sales, may carry some positive meanings to customers: The item is "hot" and represents an unusually good value.

Customers are most price sensitive to products that cost a lot or are bought frequently. They hardly notice higher prices on low-cost items that they buy infrequently. Some buyers are less concerned with price than with the total costs of obtaining, operating, and servicing the product over its lifetime. A seller can charge more than competitors and still get the business if the customer can be convinced that total lifetime costs are lower.

Competitors' Reactions

A firm contemplating a price change must worry about competitors' reactions. Competitors are most likely to react where the number of firms are few, the product is homogeneous, and buyers are highly informed.

How can a firm anticipate a competitor's reactions? One way is to assume that the competitor reacts in a set way to price changes. The other is to assume that the competitor treats each price change as a fresh challenge and reacts according to self-interest at the time. In this case, the company will have to figure out what lies in the competitor's self-interest. It will need to research the competitor's current financial situation, recent sales, customer loyalty, and corporate objectives. If the competitor has a market-share objective, it is likely to match the price change. If it has a profit-maximization objective, it may react by increasing the advertising budget or improving product quality.

The problem is complicated because the competitor can put different interpretations on a price cut: that the company is trying to steal the market, that the company is doing poorly and trying to boost its sales, or that the company wants the whole industry to reduce prices to stimulate total demand.

RESPONDING TO COMPETITORS' PRICE CHANGES

How should a firm respond to a price cut initiated by a competitor? In markets characterized by high product homogeneity, the firm should search for ways to enhance its augmented product, but if it cannot find any, it will have to meet the price reduction. If the competitor raises its price in a homogeneous product market, the other firms might not match it, unless the price increase will benefit the industry as a whole. By not matching it, the leader will have to rescind the increase.

In nonhomogeneous product markets, a firm has more latitude. The firm needs to consider the following issues: (1) Why did the competitor change the price? Is it to steal the market, to utilize excess capacity, to meet changing cost conditions, or to lead an industrywide price change? (2) Does the competitor plan to make the price change temporary or permanent? (3) What will happen to the company's market share and profits if it does not respond? Are other companies going to respond? (4) What are the competitor's and other firms' responses likely to be to each possible reaction?

Market leaders frequently face aggressive price cutting by smaller firms trying to build market share. Using price, Fuji attacks Kodak, Bic attacks Gillette, and Compaq attacks IBM. Brand leaders also face lower-priced private store brands. The brand leader can respond in several ways:

- *Maintain price:* The leader might maintain its price and profit margin, believing that (1) it would lose too much profit if it reduced its price, (2) it would not lose much market share, and (3) it could regain market share when necessary. The leader believes that it can hold on to good customers and give up the poorer ones. However, the argument against price maintenance is that the attacker gets more confident, the leader's sales force gets demoralized, and the leader loses more share than expected. The leader panics, lowers price to regain share, and finds that regaining its market position is more difficult and costly than expected.

- *Maintain price and add value:* The leader could improve its product, services, and communications. The firm may find it cheaper to maintain price and spend money to improve perceived quality than to cut price and operate at a lower margin.

- *Reduce price:* The leader might drop its price to match the competitor's price. It might do so because (1) its costs fall with volume, (2) it would lose market share because the market is price sensitive, and (3) it would be hard to rebuild market share once it is lost. This action will cut profits in the short run.

- *Increase price and improve quality:* The leader might raise its price and introduce new brands to bracket the attacking brand. Heublein used this strategy when its Smirnoff vodka was attacked by another brand, Wolfschmidt.

- *Launch a low-price fighter line:* Add lower-price items to the line or create a separate lower-price brand. Eastman Kodak introduced a low-priced seasonal film called Funtime. Miller Beer launched a lower-priced beer brand called Red Dog.

The best response varies with situation. The company must consider the product's stage in the life cycle, its importance in the company's portfolio, the competitor's intentions and resources, the market's price and quality sensitivity, the behaviour of costs with volume, and the company's alternative opportunities.

FIGURE 15.8

**Price-Reaction Program for
Meeting a Competitor's Price Cut**

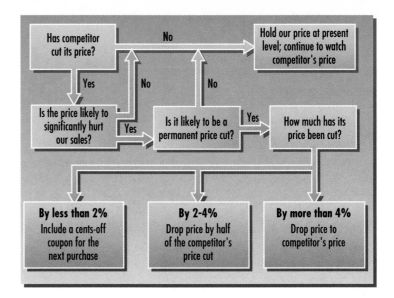

An extended analysis of company alternatives may not be feasible when the attack occurs. The company may have to react decisively within hours or days. It would make better sense for the company to anticipate possible competitors' price changes and to prepare contingent responses. Figure 15.8 shows a *price-reaction program* to be used if a competitor cuts prices. Reaction programs for meeting price changes find their greatest application in industries where price changes occur with some frequency and where it is important to react quickly—for example, in the meatpacking, lumber, and oil industries.

SUMMARY

1. Despite the increased role of nonprice factors in modern marketing, price remains a critical element of the marketing mix. Price is the only one of the four Ps that produces revenue; the other three Ps produce costs.

2. In setting its pricing policy, a company follows a six-step procedure. First, it selects its pricing objective (survival, maximum current profit, maximum market share, maximum market skimming, or product-quality leadership). Second, it estimates the demand curve, the probable quantities that it will sell at each possible price. Third, it estimates how its costs vary at different levels of output, at different levels of accumulated production experience, and for differentiated marketing offers. Fourth, it examines competitors' costs, prices, and offers. Fifth, it selects a pricing method. Finally, it selects the final price, taking into account psychological pricing, the influence of other marketing-mix elements on price, company pricing policies, and the impact of price on other parties.

3. Companies do not usually set a single price, but rather a pricing structure that reflects variations in geographical demand and costs, market-segment requirements, purchase timing, order levels, and other factors. Several price-adaptation strategies are available: (1) geographical pricing; (2) price discounts and allowances; (3) promotional pricing; (4) discriminatory pricing, in which the company sells a product at different prices to different market segments; and (5) product-mix pricing, which includes setting prices for product lines, optional features, captive products, two-part items, by-products, and product bundles.

4. After developing pricing strategies, firms often face situations in which they need to change prices. A price decrease might be brought about by excess plant capacity, declining market share, a desire to dominate the market through lower costs, or economic recession. A price increase might be brought about by cost inflation or overdemand.

5. There are several alternatives to increasing price, including shrinking the amount of product instead of raising the price, substituting less expensive materials or ingredients, and reducing or removing product features.

6. The firm facing a competitor's price change must try to understand the competitor's intent and the likely duration of the change. The firm's strategy often depends on whether it is producing homogeneous or nonhomogeneous products. Market leaders who are attacked by lower-priced competitors can choose to maintain price, raise the perceived quality of their product, reduce price, increase price and improve quality, or launch a low-price fighter line.

APPLICATIONS

CHAPTER CONCEPTS

1. Companies cannot always depend on their customers' recognizing the value of their offer against their competitors' offers. Each company's offer may differ not only in price but also in its impact on the customer's operating cost, working capital cost, ordering cost, setup costs, financing costs, and disposal costs. Sophisticated business-to-business companies use a tool called *economic value to the customer (EVC)* to build up their customer's perceptions of value. EVC is calculated by comparing the product's total costs to the customer against the benefits of the product that the customer is currently using (the *reference product*).

   Figure 1 illustrates how one company determined EVC. Suppose McNally Manufacturing is developing two products, Y and Z, to compete with product X that a customer is currently using.

   New product Y performs the same functions as reference product X, but its start-up costs and postpurchase costs are only $400 (compared to $700 for product X), yielding a $300 savings for the customer. Because the customer's current product X has life-cycle costs of $1000, the economic value that the new product Y offers the customer is $600 ($1000 minus $400). It costs McNally $250 to produce one unit of product Y.

   New product Z has more features or performance characteristics than product X or Y. These extra features of Z's have a perceived incremental value of $300 when compared with the reference product. So, compared to the current product, Z saves $100 in postpurchase costs, resulting in an economic value to the customer of $700. Thus Z provides a higher EVC than Y despite its higher postpurchase costs because it provides additional customer value. It costs McNally $300 to produce one unit of Z.

Figure 1

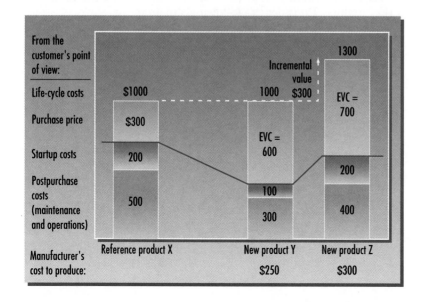

Use Figure 1 to answer the following questions:
   a. What is the highest amount that a firm would be willing to pay for product Y? For product Z?
   b. The firm should set its price at a point between its costs and the EVC that is perceived by the customer. Assume that McNally adopts this practice for products Y and Z, and sets the price of each at $400 and $475, respectively. How much profit will McNally make on each unit of Y and Z sold?
   c. How can McNally Manufacturing use EVC to determine the market segments it should enter with its new products?

2. Three companies A, B, and C produce rapid-relay switches. Industrial buyers are asked to examine and rate the respective companies' offers. To do so, they might use a *diagnostic method*, rating the three offers on a set of attributes. They allocate 100 points to the three companies with regard to each attribute. They also allocate 100 points to reflect the relative importance of the attributes. Suppose the results are as follows:

Importance Weight	Attribute	Products		
		A	B	C
25	Product durability	40	40	20
30	Product reliability	33	33	33
30	Delivery reliability	50	25	25
15	Service quality	45	35	20
100	(Average Perceived Value)	(41.65)	(32.65)	(24.9)

By multiplying the importance weights against each company's ratings, we find that company A's offer is perceived to be above average (at 42), company B's average (at 33), and company's C below average (at 25). (All figures are rounded to the nearest whole number.)

Figure 2 shows the result of company A's lowering its price from $2.55 to $2.00.
   a. Assuming that buyers are willing to pay $2.00 for an average switch (that is, a switch with a perceived value of 33 points), how much could each company charge for its switch?
   b. What strategies might company A follow based on the results graphed in Figure 2? How might company B respond to price changes by company A?

3. Many companies are so ready to grant discounts, allowances, and special terms to their dealers and customers that they fail to realize how little profit may be left when they're done. Consider the following situation:

Figure 2

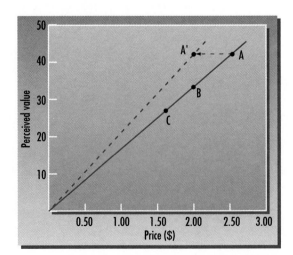

Dealer list price	$6.00
— Order size discount	.10
— Competitive discount	.12
= Invoice price	$5.78
— Payment terms discount	30
— Annual volume discount	.37
— Off-invoice promotions	.35
— Co-op advertising	.20
— Freight	.19
= Pocket price	$4.37

Here the manufacturer quoted a $6.00 list price to a dealer but deducted an order-size discount and a competitive discount, leaving an invoice price of $5.78. However, this number did not represent the manufacturer's pocket price (i.e., what is left in the manufacturer's pocket). Further costs result in the manufacturer's realizing a pocket price of only $4.37. Discuss the financial impact that these price reductions will have on the company's profitability. What percentage of the dealer's list price actually goes into the manufacturer's pocket in this example? What should a company consider before giving discounts?

MARKETING AND ADVERTISING

The Cyrix ad in Figure 3 focuses on the company's lower chip prices, even though no actual chip price is ever mentioned. Because Cyrix is not a personal computer manufacturer and does not sell directly to computer users, why would it publicize its lower chip prices? Which elements of price sensitivity come into play in this Cyrix ad? Do you think demand for computers with lower-priced chips is elastic or inelastic? Why?

E-Trade is an Internet-based securities brokerage firm that offers online stock trading starting at $14.95 per trade, much lower than the prices charged by conventional brokerage firms. The ad in Figure 4 promotes the low price as well as other benefits

Figure 3

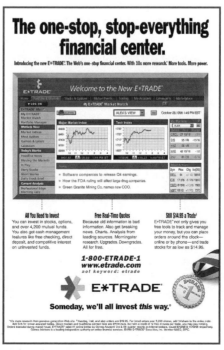

Figure 4

of using E-Trade. Discuss the elasticity of demand in this market and why E-Trade would choose to price its services so low. How would customers and prospects be likely to react to this pricing?

FOCUS ON TECHNOLOGY

For large supermarket and drug chains, managing thousands of prices at dozens or even hundreds of stores was quite a headache before pricing technology came into widespread use. Now retailers routinely input prices from a central point and distribute the information to electronic cash registers throughout the chain. Some software programs go further, preparing files with new unit pricing data that can be printed and posted in each store.

Total Control Information, a software company, makes pricing software specifically for use by large retailers. Read about this program at the company's Web site (www.tcisolutions.com/hqpm.htm). How might this kind of software benefit a supermarket chain that features high–low pricing? How might it benefit a drug chain that uses location pricing?

MARKETING FOR THE 21ST CENTURY

One of the newest twists in pricing strategies is to invite customers to name their price. This is the business model used by Priceline, which launched its Web-based service with a huge media campaign in mid-1998. See how the system works by visiting the Priceline Web site (www.priceline.com). On the left side of the screen, click on "What is priceline.com?" and "How priceline.com works" to find out about the company and the bidding process. Also click to read about future services. What can you say about the price sensitivity of Priceline's customers? What other products might Priceline feature on its Web site? Why?

YOU'RE THE MARKETER: SONIC MARKETING PLAN

Pricing is a critical element in every marketing plan, because it is directly connected to a company's revenue and profit goals. To effectively design and manage pricing strategies, marketers must consider not only their costs but also the perceptions of customers and the reactions of competitors.

As Jane Melody's assistant, you are in charge of pricing Sonic's shelf stereos. Take another look at the company's current situation, especially products, strengths, weaknesses, opportunities, and threats. Also review what you know about target markets and positioning. Then answer the following questions about pricing (indicating where additional research may be needed):

- *What is Sonic's primary pricing objective? Why?*
- *Are Sonic's customers price sensitive? Is demand elastic or inelastic? What are the implications for product pricing?*
- *How can Sonic price its entire product line? How will product pricing work with the other parts of the marketing mix?*
- *What price adaptations (such as discounts, allowances, and promotional pricing) should Sonic consider?*

After you have developed your pricing strategies and programs, summarize your recommendations in a written marketing plan or type them into the Marketing Mix/Pricing section of the Marketing Strategy part of the Marketing Plan Pro software, depending on your instructor's directions.

OVERBRANDING

Ensuring that your company's brand name is well known to the public has been the marketing strategy of the 1990s. But with so many brands pushing for attention, companies now risk turning *off* consumers. It's a fine balancing act in a world over-crowded with brands. Companies follow two basic principles in their branding efforts: they try to create knowledge and awareness of their brand while also attempting to get the brand name to mean something distinct to target consumers.

A brand is a mark and a word that often defines a company's whole identity. Building a successful brand can make you the king of your category. Profits can soar as people become more willing to pay a premium just to wear your logo. Since it costs a lot to build a successful brand, more and more firms are tempted to try and leverage this investment by putting their name on more and more products. This is the tactic of brand extension. However, if one's brand name is on too many products, a firm faces the danger that its core brand will be diluted and it will not continue to have the unique aura it once carried. Even worse, if the brand is extended to too many products, it may turn out that consumers just won't be able to stand the sight of the brand anymore.

Roots is one Canadian firm that has been highly successful at creating a unique brand identity. In fact, for many consumers, when you think Roots, you think Canada. With its sponsorship of the Canadian Olympic team, Roots solidified this position. Today, it is pushing its brand name onto more and more products—beyond leather and clothing—to fragrance, a pet line, and a home collection. The company is trying to be cautious, however, since it realizes that there is the danger of overbranding.

History has shown what can happen when a firm falls victim to this temptation. Consider the case of Nike. It built its reputation by selling shoes designed to enhance athletic performance. It became known as much for its logo, the Swoosh, as it did for its name. It grew to become almost a cult brand and its shoes were a status symbol among youth markets. But the firm went too far. It pasted its logo on so many products that its target market of young people began to turn against it. The phrase "swoosh-stika" became a by-word and more and more people began to question what lay behind the product. The media abounded with stories comparing the amount the firm paid to sponsor elite athletes with what it paid workers in Third World countries to make its products. Consumer protests were even held outside its flagship Nikeworld stores.

Unlike Nike, other firms, such as GreensPlus, a strong niche player in the health market, fear overexpansion and overuse of their brand name. They are worried that if they extend their products and brands into the mainstream marketplace, they will turn off customers and retailers who built the company in the first place.

Questions

1. Outline the arguments for and against brand extensions.
2. Alan Middleton, a professor at York University, contends that the youth market is becoming anti-brand and that this trend will eventually extend to the general population. Do you agree or disagree with this contention?
3. Is Jones Soda a brand? How has its marketing program differed from that of the other companies described in the case?
4. If you were employed as a consultant to GreenPlus, what advice would you give them about how to expand and whether to extend their brand?

Source: Based on "Overbranding," *Venture* 705 (November 24, 1998).

Managing Marketing Channels

CHAPTER

16

PROFILE:

Canadian Marketing Excellence

Robert Glegg, the founder and CEO of Glegg Water Conditioning Inc., a once-unknown company from Guelph, Ontario, has been turning an industry on its ear. First, it developed a new product, the E-CELL, which allows high-tech manufacturing companies and pharmaceutical companies to meet their water-purification needs. Pure water is essential for washing computer chips, manufacturing drugs, and generating steam to run power plants. Until Glegg arrived on the scene, the industry was plagued by poor quality products. Glegg set a new standard with leading-edge technology and high-quality customer service.

But product development and service alone didn't make the industry buzz. Instead, it was Glegg's radical approach to distribution and its new product, E-CELL. The firm didn't have the resources to distribute the product worldwide. The solution: allow his competitors to do it for him. People thought it was madness giving competitors access to his patented product, but it has been madness that has made the cash register ring. Glegg Water Conditioning's rivals can become licensed distributors of the product. Glegg doesn't care what firm customers buy an E-CELL from, as long as they buy it. Getting customer acceptance and a massive installed base is critical since Glegg believed that his E-CELL had the potential to set the technical standard within the industry. And it is.

Has his strategy been successful? Judge for yourself. The firm now boasts over 1000 installations in 30 countries. His client list includes Intel Corp., Shell Group, Dow Chemical Co., Fluor Daniel, Bechtel, IBM, and Exxon Corp. With the backing of GE, growth will continue. Glegg Water Conditioning has been purchased by General Electric, and is now called GE Glegg Water Technologies. Purchase by GE was completed November 18, 1999.

Sources: Cynthia Reynolds, "Pure Madness," *Canadian Business*, April 27, 1999, pp. 50-53. Glegg Water Conditioning, Inc., Web site (http://www.glegg.com).

In this chapter, we address the following questions from the viewpoint of manufacturers:

■ What work is performed by marketing channels?

■ What decisions do companies face in designing, managing, evaluating, and modifying their channels?

■ What trends are taking place in channel dynamics?

■ How can channel conflict be managed?

Glegg Water Conditioning
www.glegg.com

Most producers do not sell their goods directly to the final users. Between them stands a set of intermediaries performing a variety of functions. These intermediaries constitute a marketing channel (also called a trade channel or distribution channel).

Some intermediaries—such as wholesalers and retailers—buy, take title to, and resell the merchandise; they are called *merchants*. Others—brokers, manufacturers' representatives, sales agents—search for customers and may negotiate on the producer's behalf but do not take title to the goods; they are called *agents*. Still others—transportation companies, independent warehouses, banks, advertising agencies—assist in the distribution process but neither take title to goods nor negotiate purchases or sales; they are called *facilitators*.

■ **Marketing channels** are sets of interdependent organizations involved in the process of making a product or service available for use or consumption.[1]

Marketing-channel decisions are among the most critical decisions facing management. The channels chosen intimately affect all the other marketing decisions. The company's pricing depends on whether it uses mass merchandisers or high-quality boutiques. The firm's sales force and advertising decisions depend on how much training and motivation dealers need. In addition, the company's channel decisions involve relatively long-term commitments to other firms. When an automaker signs up independent dealers to sell its automobiles, the automaker cannot buy them out the next day and replace them with company-owned outlets. Corey observed:

> *A distribution system . . . is a key external resource. Normally it takes years to build, and it is not easily changed. It ranks in importance with key internal resources such as manufacturing, research, engineering, and field sales personnel and facilities. It represents a significant corporate commitment to large numbers of independent companies whose business is distribution—and to the particular markets they serve. It represents, as well, a commitment to a set of policies and practices that constitute the basic fabric on which is woven an extensive set of long-term relationships.[2]*

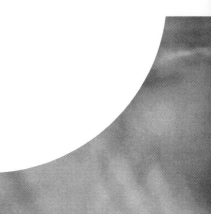

In Chapter 17 we will examine marketing-channel issues from the perspective of retailers, wholesalers, and physical-distribution agencies.

WHAT WORK IS PERFORMED BY MARKETING CHANNELS?

Why would a producer delegate some of the selling job to intermediaries? The delegation means relinquishing some control over how and to whom the products are sold. But producers do gain several advantages by using intermediaries:

- Many producers lack the financial resources to carry out direct marketing. For example, General Motors sells its cars through more than 8100 dealer outlets in North America alone. Even General Motors would be hard pressed to raise the cash to buy out its dealers.

- In some cases direct marketing simply is not feasible. The William Wrigley Jr. Company would not find it practical to establish small retail gum shops throughout the world or to sell gum by mail order. It would have to sell gum along with many other small products and would end up in the drugstore and grocery store business. Wrigley finds it easier to work through the extensive network of privately owned distribution organizations.

- Producers who do establish their own channels can often earn a greater return by increasing their investment in their main business. If a company earns a 20 percent rate of return on manufacturing and only a 10 percent return on retailing, it does not make sense to undertake its own retailing.

Intermediaries normally achieve superior efficiency in making goods widely available and accessible to target markets. Through their contacts, experience, specialization, and scale of operation, intermediaries usually offer the firm more than it can achieve on its own. According to Stern and El-Ansary:

> Intermediaries smooth the flow of goods and services.... This procedure is necessary in order to bridge the discrepancy between the assortment of goods and services generated by the producer and the assortment demanded by the consumer. The discrepancy results from the fact that manufacturers typically produce a large quantity of a limited variety of goods, whereas consumers usually desire only a limited quantity of a wide variety of goods.[3]

Figure 16.1 shows one major source of cost savings effected by using intermediaries. Part (a) shows three producers, each using direct marketing to reach three customers. This system requires nine different contacts. Part (b) shows the three producers working through one distributor, who contacts the three customers. This system requires only six contacts. In this way, intermediaries reduce the number of contacts and the work.

FIGURE 16.1

How a Distributor Effects an Economy of Effort

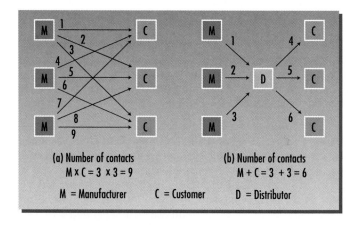

(a) Number of contacts
M × C = 3 × 3 = 9

(b) Number of contacts
M + C = 3 + 3 = 6

M = Manufacturer   C = Customer   D = Distributor

CHANNEL FUNCTIONS AND FLOWS

A marketing channel performs the work of moving goods from producers to consumers. It overcomes the time, place, and possession gaps that separate goods and services from those who need or want them. Members of the marketing channel perform a number of key functions:

- They gather information about potential and current customers, competitors, and other actors and forces in the marketing environment.
- They develop and disseminate persuasive communications to stimulate purchasing.
- They reach agreement on price and other terms so that transfer of ownership or possession can be effected.
- They place orders with manufacturers.
- They acquire the funds to finance inventories at different levels in the marketing channel.
- They assume risks connected with carrying out channel work.
- They provide for the successive storage and movement of physical products.
- They provide for buyers' payment of their bills through banks and other financial institutions.
- They oversee actual transfer of ownership from one organization or person to another.

Some functions (physical, title, promotion) constitute a *forward flow* of activity from the company to the customer; other functions (ordering and payment) constitute a *backward flow* from customers to the company. Still others (information, negotiation, finance, and risk taking) occur in both directions. Five flows are illustrated in Figure 16.2 for the marketing of forklift trucks. If these flows were superimposed in one diagram, the tremendous complexity of even simple marketing channels would be apparent. A manufacturer selling a physical product and services might require three channels: a *sales channel*, a *delivery channel*, and a *service channel*. Thus Dell Computer uses the telephone and the Internet as sales channels, express mail services as the delivery channel, and local repair people as the service channel.

FIGURE 16.2

Five Marketing Flows in the Marketing Channel for Forklift Trucks

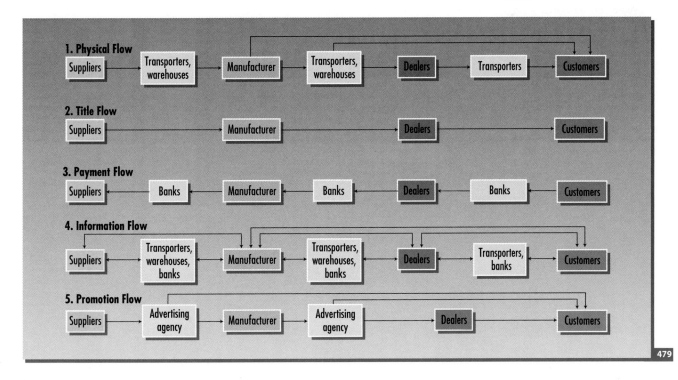

The question is not *whether* various channel functions need to be performed—they must be—but rather *who* is to perform them. All channel functions have three things in common: They use up scarce resources; they can often be performed better through specialization; and they can be shifted among channel members. To the extent that when the manufacturer shifts some functions to intermediaries, the producer's costs and prices are lower, but the intermediary must add a charge to cover its work. If the intermediaries are more efficient than the manufacturer, the prices to consumers should be lower. If consumers perform some functions themselves, they should enjoy lower prices.

Marketing functions, then, are more basic than the institutions that perform them at any given time. Changes in channel institutions largely reflect the discovery of more efficient ways to combine or separate the economic functions that provide assortments of goods to target customers.

CHANNEL LEVELS

The producer and the final customer are part of every channel. We will use the number of intermediary levels to designate the *length* of a channel. Figure 16.3(a) illustrates several consumer-goods marketing channels of different lengths.

A *zero-level channel* (also called a *direct-marketing channel*) consists of a manufacturer selling directly to the final customer. The major examples are door-to-door sales, home parties, mail order, telemarketing, TV selling, Internet selling, and manufacturer-owned stores. Avon sales representatives sell cosmetics door-to-door; Tupperware representatives sell kitchen goods through home parties; Franklin Mint sells collectibles through mail order; Shearson-Lehman brokers use the telephone to prospect for new customers; some exercise equipment manufacturers sell through TV commercials or hour-long "infomercials"; and Singer sells its sewing machines through its own stores.

A *one-level channel* contains one selling intermediary, such as a retailer. A *two-level channel* contains two intermediaries. In consumer markets, these are typically a wholesaler and a retailer. A *three-level channel* contains three intermediaries. In the meat-packing industry, wholesalers sell to jobbers, who sell to small retailers. Longer marketing channels can be found. In Japan, food distribution may involve as many as six levels. From the producer's point of view, obtaining information about end users and exercising control becomes more difficult as the number of channel levels increases.

Avon Canada
www.avon.ca

FIGURE 16.3

Consumer and Industrial Marketing Channels

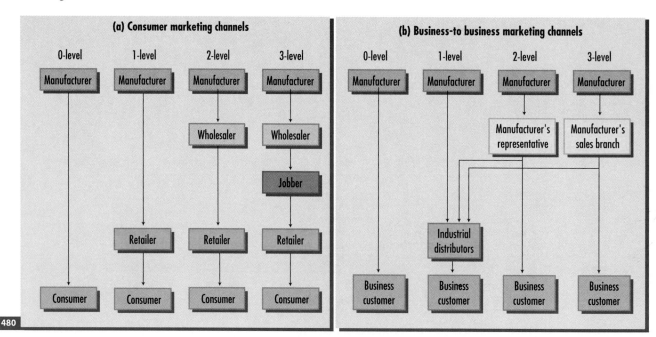

Figure 16.3(b) shows channels commonly used in industrial marketing. An industrial-goods manufacturer can use its sales force to sell directly to industrial customers. Or it can sell to industrial distributors, who sell to the industrial customers. Or it can sell through manufacturer's representatives or its own sales branches directly to industrial customers, or indirectly to industrial customers through industrial distributors. Zero-, one-, and two-level marketing channels are quite common in industrial marketing channels.

Channels normally describe a forward movement of products. One can also talk about *backward channels*. According to Zikmund and Stanton:

> *The recycling of solid wastes is a major ecological goal. Although recycling is technologically feasible, reversing the flow of materials in the channel of distribution—marketing trash through a "backward" channel—presents a challenge. Existing backward channels are primitive, and financial incentives are inadequate. The consumer must be motivated to undergo a role change and become a producer—the initiating force in the reverse distribution process.[4]*

Several intermediaries play a role in backward channels, including manufacturers' redemption centres, community groups, traditional intermediaries such as soft-drink intermediaries, garbage-collection specialists, recycling centres, garbage-recycling brokers, and central-processing warehousing.[5]

SERVICE SECTOR CHANNELS

The concept of marketing channels is not limited to the distribution of physical goods. Producers of services and ideas also face the problem of making their output available and accessible to target populations. Schools develop "educational-dissemination systems" and hospitals develop "health-delivery systems." These institutions must identify out agencies and locations for reaching a population spread out over an area.[6] As Internet technology advances, service industries such as banking, insurance, travel, and stock buying and selling will occur through new channels.

Marketing channels also keep changing in "person" marketing. Before 1940, professional comedians could reach audiences through seven channels: vaudeville houses, special events, nightclubs, radio, movies, carnivals, and theatres. Vaudeville houses have vanished and been replaced by comedy clubs and cable television stations. Politicians also must choose a mix of channels—mass media, rallies, coffee hours, spot TV ads, faxes, Web sites—for delivering their messages to voters.[7]

 # CHANNEL-DESIGN DECISIONS

A new firm typically starts as a local operation selling in a limited market. It usually uses existing intermediaries. The number of intermediaries in any local market is apt to be limited: a few manufacturers' sales agents, a few wholesalers, several established retailers, a few trucking companies, and a few warehouses. Deciding on the best channels might not be a problem. The problem might be to convince the available intermediaries to handle the firm's line.

If the firm is successful, it might branch into new markets. It might have to use different channels in different markets. In smaller markets, the firm might sell directly to retailers; in larger markets, it might sell through distributors. In rural areas, it might work with general-goods merchants; in urban areas, with limited-line merchants. In one part of the country, it might grant exclusive franchises; in another, it might sell through all outlets willing to handle the merchandise. In one country it might use international sales agents; in another, it might partner with a local firm.[8] In short, the channel system evolves in response to local opportunities and conditions.

Designing a channel system calls for analyzing customer needs, establishing channel objectives, and identifying and evaluating the major channel alternatives.

ANALYZING CUSTOMERS' DESIRED SERVICE OUTPUT LEVELS

In designing the marketing channel, the marketer must understand the *service output levels* desired by the target customers. Channels produce five service outputs:

1. *Lot size*: The number of units the channel permits a typical customer to purchase on one occasion. In buying cars for its fleet, Hertz prefers a channel from which it can buy a large lot size; a household wants a channel that permits buying a lot size of one.

2. *Waiting time*: The average time customers of that channel wait for receipt of the goods. Customers normally prefer fast delivery channels.

3. *Spatial convenience*: The degree to which the marketing channel makes it easy for customers to purchase the product. Chevrolet, for example, offers greater spatial convenience than Cadillac, because there are more Chevrolet dealers. Chevrolet's greater market decentralization helps customers save on transportation and search costs in buying and repairing an automobile.

4. *Product variety*: The assortment breadth provided by the marketing channel. Normally customers prefer a greater assortment because more choices increase the chance of finding what they need.

5. *Service backup*: The add-on services (credit, delivery, installation, repairs) provided by the channel. The greater the service backup, the greater the work provided by the channel.[9]

The marketing-channel designer knows that providing greater service outputs means increased channel costs and higher prices for customers. The success of discount stores indicates that many consumers are willing to accept lower-service outputs if they can save money.

ESTABLISHING OBJECTIVES AND CONSTRAINTS

Channel objectives should be stated in terms of targeted service output levels. According to Bucklin, under competitive conditions, channel institutions should arrange their functional tasks to minimize total channel costs with respect to desired levels of service outputs.[10] Usually, several market segments that desire differing service output levels can be identified. Effective planning requires determining which market segments to serve and the best channels to use in each case.

Channel objectives vary with product characteristics. Perishable products require more direct marketing. Bulky products, such as building materials, require channels that minimize the shipping distance and the amount of handling in the movement from producer to consumer. Nonstandardized products, such as custom-built machinery and specialized business forms, are sold directly by company sales representatives. Products requiring installation or maintenance services such as heating and cooling systems are usually sold and maintained by the company or exclusively franchised dealers. High-unit-value products such as generators and turbines are often sold through a company sales force rather than intermediaries.

Channel design must take into account the strengths and weaknesses of different types of intermediaries. For example, manufacturers' reps are able to contact customers at a low cost per customer because the total cost is shared by several clients. But the selling effort per customer is less intense than if company sales reps did the selling. Channel design is also influenced by competitors' channels.

Channel design must adapt to the larger environment. When economic conditions are depressed, producers want to move their goods to market using shorter channels and without nonessential services that add to the final price of the goods. Legal regulations and restrictions also affect channel design. Both Canadian and U.S. laws look unfavourably upon channel arrangements that substantially lessen competition or create a monopoly.

IDENTIFYING MAJOR CHANNEL ALTERNATIVES

After a company has defined its target market and desired positioning, it should identify its channel alternatives. A channel alternative is described by three elements: the types of available business intermediaries, the number of intermediaries needed, and the terms and responsibilities of each channel member.

Types of Intermediaries

The firm needs to identify the types of intermediaries available to carry on its channel work. Here are two examples:

A test-equipment manufacturer developed an audio device for detecting poor mechanical connections in machines with moving parts. Company executives felt this product would sell in all industries where electric, combustion, or steam engines were used, such as aviation, automobiles, railways, food canning, construction, and oil. The sales force was small. The problem was how to reach these diverse industries effectively. The following alternatives were identified:

- *Company sales force:* Expand the company's direct sales force. Assign sales representatives to territories to contact all prospects in the area. Or develop separate sales forces for the different industries.
- *Manufacturers' agency:* Hire manufacturers' agents in different regions or end-use industries to sell the new equipment.
- *Industrial distributors:* Find distributors in the different regions or end-use industries who will buy and carry the device. Give them exclusive distribution, adequate margins, product training, and promotional support.

A consumer electronics company produces cellular car phones. It identified the following channel alternatives:

- *OEM market:* The company could sell its car phones to automobile manufacturers to be installed as original equipment. *OEM* stands for *original equipment manufacture.*
- *Auto-dealer market:* The company could sell its car phones to auto dealers.
- *Retail automotive-equipment dealers:* The company could sell its car phones to retail automotive-equipment dealers through a direct sales force or through distributors.
- *Car phone specialist dealers:* The company could sell its car phones to car phone specialist dealers through a direct sales force or dealers.
- *Mail-order market:* The company could sell its car phones through mail-order catalogues.

Companies should search for innovative marketing channels. The Conn Organ Company merchandises organs through department stores and discount stores, thus drawing more attention than it ever enjoyed in small music stores. The Book-of-the-Month Club merchandises books through the mail. Other sellers have followed with record-of-the-month clubs, candy-of-the-month clubs, flower-of-the-month clubs, fruit-of-the-month clubs, and dozens of others.

Sometimes a company chooses an unconventional channel because of the difficulty or cost of working with the dominant channel. The advantage is that the company will encounter less competition during the initial move into this channel. After trying to sell its inexpensive Timex watches through regular jewellery stores, the U.S. Time Company placed its watches in fast-growing mass-merchandise outlets. Avon chose door-to-door selling because it was not able to break into regular department stores. Rogers Cantel Mobile Communications joined forces with Amway's 100 000 Canadian representatives to increase sales of its wireless telephones.[11]

Rogers Cantel
www.rogers.com

Number of Intermediaries

Companies have to decide on the number of intermediaries to use at each channel level. Three strategies are available: exclusive distribution, selective distribution, and intensive distribution.

Exclusive distribution means severely limiting the number of intermediaries. It is used when the producer wants to maintain control over the service level and service outputs offered by the resellers. Often it involves *exclusive dealing* arrangements, in which the resellers agree not to carry competing brands. By granting exclusive distribution, the producer hopes to obtain more dedicated and knowledgeable selling. It requires greater partnership between seller and reseller and is used in the distribution of new automobiles, some major appliances, and some women's apparel brands.

Selective distribution involves the use of more than a few but less than all of the intermediaries who are willing to carry a particular product. It is used by established companies and by new companies seeking distributors. The company does not have to dissipate its efforts over too many outlets; it enables the producer to gain adequate market coverage with more control and less cost than intensive distribution. Nike, the world's largest athletic shoe maker, is a good example of selective distribution:

Nike
www.nike.com

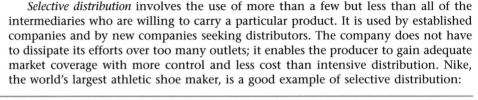

■ **Nike Inc.** Nike sells its athletic shoes and apparel through six different kinds of stores: (1) specialized sports stores, such as golfers' pro shops, where Nike has announced plans for a new line of athletic shoes; (2) general sporting-goods stores, which carry a broad range of styles; (3) department stores, which carry only the newest styles; (4) mass-merchandise stores, which focus on discounted styles; (5) Nike retail stores, including Niketowns in major cities, which feature the complete line, with an emphasis on the newest styles; (6) factory outlet stores, which stock mostly seconds and closeouts. Nike also limits the number of stores in a single geographic area that that can carry its products.[12]

Intensive distribution consists of the manufacturer placing the goods or services in as many outlets as possible. This strategy is generally used for items such as tobacco products, soap, snack foods, and gum, products for which the consumer requires a great deal of location convenience.

Manufacturers are constantly tempted to move from exclusive or selective distribution to more intensive distribution to increase coverage and sales. This strategy may help in the short term but often hurts long-term performance. If Hugo Boss or Alfred Sung expanded from their current high-end retailers to mass merchandisers, they would lose some control over the display arrangements, the accompanying service levels, and the pricing. If these designers allowed their products to be sold at lower-cost retail outlets, these outlets would undercut top-end retailers, resulting in a price war between the various types of distributors. Buyers would attach less prestige to their apparel, and their ability to command premium prices would be reduced.

Terms and Responsibilities of Channel Members

The producer must determine the rights and responsibilities of participating channel members. Each channel member must be treated respectfully and given the opportunity to be profitable.[13] The main elements in the "trade-relations mix" are price policies, conditions of sale, territorial rights, and specific services to be performed by each party.

Price policy calls for the producer to establish a price list and schedule of discounts and allowances that intermediaries see as equitable and sufficient.

Conditions of sale refers to payment terms and producer guarantees. Most producers grant cash discounts to distributors for early payment. Producers might also guarantee distributors against defective merchandise or price declines. A guarantee against price declines gives distributors an incentive to buy larger quantities.

Distributors' territorial rights define the distributors' territories and the terms under which the producer will enfranchise other distributors. Distributors normally expect to receive full credit for all sales in their territory, whether or not they did the selling.

Mutual services and responsibilities are conditions that must be carefully spelled out, especially in franchised and exclusive-agency channels. McDonald's provides franchisees with a building, promotional support, a record-keeping system, training, and general administrative and technical assistance. In turn, franchisees are expected to satisfy company standards regarding physical facilities, cooperate with new promotional programs, furnish requested information, and buy supplies from specified vendors.

EVALUATING THE MAJOR ALTERNATIVES

Each channel alternative needs to be evaluated against *economic*, *control*, and *adaptive* criteria. Consider the following situation:

A Montreal furniture manufacturer wants to sell its line to retailers on the West Coast. The manufacturer is trying to decide between two alternatives:

1. One calls for hiring 10 new sales representatives who would operate out of a sales office in Vancouver. They would receive a base salary plus commissions.

2. The other alternative would use a Vancouver manufacturers' sales agency that has extensive contacts with retailers. The agency has 30 sales representatives, who would receive a commission based on their sales.

Economic Criteria

Each alternative will produce a different level of sales and costs. The first step is to determine whether a company sales force or a sales agency will produce more sales. Most marketing managers believe that a company sales force will sell more. They concentrate on the company's products; they are better trained to sell those products; they are more aggressive because their future depends on the company's success; and they are more successful because many customers prefer to deal directly with the company.

However, the sales agency could conceivably sell more. First, the sales agent has 30 representatives, not just 10. Second, the agency's sales force might be just as aggressive as a direct sales force, depending on the commission level. Third, some customers prefer dealing with agents who represent several manufacturers rather than with salespersons from one company. Fourth, the agency has extensive contacts and marketplace knowledge, whereas a company sales force would need to build these from scratch.

The next step is to estimate the costs of selling different volumes through each channel. The cost schedules are shown in Figure 16.4. The fixed costs of engaging a sales agency are lower than those of establishing a company sales office. But costs rise faster through a sales agency because sales agents receive a larger commission than company salespeople.

The final step is comparing sales and costs. As Figure 16.4 shows, there is one sales level (SB) at which selling costs are the same for the two channels. The sales agency is thus the better channel for any sales volume below SB, and the company sales branch is better at any volume above SB. Given this information, it is not surprising that sales agents tend to be used by smaller firms, or by large firms in their smaller territories where the sales volume is too low to support company salespeople.

Control Criteria

Using a sales agency poses a control problem. A sales agency is an independent firm seeking to maximize its profits. Agents may concentrate on the customers who buy the most, not necessarily of the manufacturer's goods. Furthermore, agents might not master the technical details of the company's product or handle its promotion materials effectively.

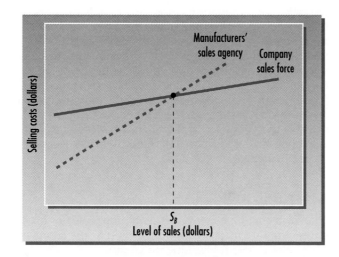

FIGURE 16.4

Break-Even Cost Chart for the Choice between a Company Sales Force and a Manufacturer's Sales Agency

Adaptive Criteria

To develop a channel, members must make some degree of commitment to each other for a specified period of time. Yet these commitments invariably lead to a decrease in the producer's ability to respond to a changing marketplace. In rapidly changing, volatile, or uncertain product markets, the producer needs channel structures and policies that provide high adaptability.

CHANNEL-MANAGEMENT DECISIONS

After a company has chosen a channel alternative, individual intermediaries must be selected, trained, motivated, and evaluated. Channel arrangements must be modified over time.

SELECTING CHANNEL MEMBERS

Producers vary in their ability to attract qualified intermediaries. Toyota was able to attract many new dealers for its new Lexus. However, when Polaroid started, it could not get photographic-equipment stores to carry its new cameras and was forced to use mass-merchandising outlets. Consider what happened at Epson:

Epson
www.epson.com

- **Epson.** Japan's Epson Corporation, a leading manufacturer of computer printers, decided to add computers to its product line. Not happy with its current distributors nor trusting their ability to sell to new types of retail outlets, Epson quietly recruited new distributors. Epson gave Hergenrather, a recruiting company, the following instructions:

- Search for applicants who have two-step distribution experience (factory to distributor to dealer) in either brown goods (TVs) or white goods (refrigerators).
- Applicants have to be CEO types who would be willing and able to set up their own distributorships.
- They will be offered a $120 000 yearly salary plus bonus and $560 000 to help them set up in business; each will add $37 500 of his or her own money, and each will get equity in the business.
- They will handle only Epson products but may stock other companies' software. Each distributor will hire a training manager and run a fully equipped service centre.

The recruiting firm placed want ads in the *Wall Street Journal,* which pulled almost 1700 letters, mostly from unqualified people. Then the firm used the Yellow Pages to get the names of existing distributors and phoned the second-in-command managers. It arranged interviews and, after much work, produced a list of highly qualified individuals. It chose the 12 most qualified candidates.

The final step called for terminating Epson's existing distributors. They were given a 90-day termination notice. Yet in spite of all these steps, Epson never succeeded as a computer manufacturer.[14]

Whether producers find it easy or difficult to recruit intermediaries, they should at least determine what characteristics distinguish the better intermediaries. They will want to evaluate number of years in business, other lines carried, growth and profit record, solvency, cooperativeness, and reputation. If the intermediaries are sales agents, producers will want to evaluate the number and character of other lines carried and the size and quality of the sales force. If the intermediaries are department stores that want exclusive distribution, the producer will want to evaluate locations, future growth potential, and type of clientele.

TRAINING CHANNEL MEMBERS

Companies need to plan and implement careful training programs for their distributors and dealers, because the intermediaries will be viewed as the company by end users. Here are some examples of reseller training programs:

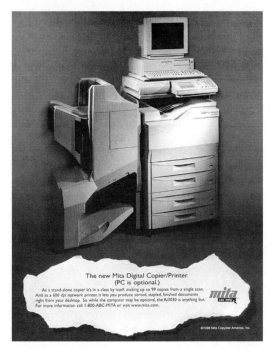

Microsoft requires third-party service engineers to complete a set of courses and take certification exams. Those who pass are formally recognized as *Microsoft Certified Professionals,* and they can use this designation to promote business.

Mita Corporation, producer of photocopying equipment, uses a specially created CD-ROM to train its dealers. A dealer's sales rep walks through all the steps in selling copier equipment, and because the CD-ROM program is interactive, the sales rep can "speak" to a hypothetical customer, make a sales presentation, handle objections, and ask for the sale. The rep's performance is scored and the CD-ROM then offers suggestions for improvement.

Ford Motor Company beams training programs and technical information via its satellite-based *Fordstar Network* to more than 6000 dealer sites. Service engineers at each dealership sit around a conference table and view a monitor on which an instructor explains procedures such as repairing onboard electronics and asks and answers questions.

Ford Motor Company of Canada
www.ford.ca

MOTIVATING CHANNEL MEMBERS

A company needs to view its intermediaries in the same way that it views its end users. The company needs to determine intermediaries' needs and construct a *channel positioning* such that its *channel offering* is tailored to provide superior value to these intermediaries. The company should provide training programs, market research programs, and other *capability-building programs* to improve intermediaries' performance. The company must constantly communicate its view that the intermediaries are partners in the joint effort to satisfy end-using consumers.

■ **Molson Breweries.** The newest senior vice president at Molson's isn't a brewer or even a marketer. He is a logistics expert. As one senior official noted, "It just occurred to me...that we had lots of people who knew about making beer and selling it and marketing it, but we really didn't have a logistics function to speak of." Knowing how to get the product to key customers is getting increasingly important as the firm adds more brands of beer, closes its regional breweries, centralizes its operations, and moves into overseas markets. Moreover, competitive rivalry, whether from Labatt or from small micro-breweries, is increasing. Thus, making channels more efficient to better serve customers is becoming an imperative.[15]

Molson Breweries
www.molson.com

Stimulating channel members to top performance must start with understanding their needs and wants. McVey listed the following propositions to help understand intermediaries:

> [The intermediary often acts] as a purchasing agent for his customers and only secondarily as a selling agent for his suppliers. . . . He is interested in selling any product which these customers desire to buy from him. . . .
>
> The [intermediary] attempts to weld all of his offerings into a family of items which he can sell in combination, as a packaged assortment, to individual customers. His selling efforts are directed primarily at obtaining orders for the assortment, rather than for individual items. . . .
>
> Unless given incentive to do so, [intermediaries] will not maintain separate sales records by brands sold. . . . Information that could be used in product development, pricing, packaging, or promotion planning is buried in nonstandard records of [intermediaries], and sometimes purposely secreted from suppliers.[16]

Producers vary greatly in skill in managing distributors. They can draw on the following types of power to elicit cooperation:

- *Coercive power* occurs when a manufacturer threatens to withdraw a resource or terminate a relationship if intermediaries fail to cooperate. This power can be quite effective if the intermediaries are highly dependent upon the manufacturer. But the exercise of coercive power produces resentment and can lead the intermediaries to organize countervailing power.

- *Reward power* occurs when the manufacturer offers intermediaries an extra benefit for performing specific acts or functions. Reward power typically produces better results than coercive power but can be overrated. The intermediaries are conforming to the manufacturer's wishes not out of conviction but because of an external benefit. They may come to expect a reward every time the manufacturer wants a certain behaviour to occur. If the reward is later withdrawn, the intermediaries feel resentment.

- *Legitimate power* is wielded when the manufacturer requests a behaviour that is warranted under the contract. Thus General Motors may insist that its dealers carry certain inventory levels as part of the franchise agreement. The manufacturer feels it has this right and the intermediaries have this obligation. As long as the intermediaries view the manufacturer as a legitimate leader, legitimate power works.

- *Expert power* can be applied when the manufacturer has special knowledge that the intermediaries value. For example, a manufacturer may have a sophisticated system for sales-lead generation or for distributor sales training. This is an effective form of power, if intermediaries would perform poorly without this help. Once the expertise is passed on to the intermediaries, however, this basis of power weakens. The manufacturer must continue to develop new expertise so that the intermediaries will want to continue cooperating.

- *Referent power* occurs when the manufacturer is so highly respected that intermediaries are proud to be associated. Companies such as IBM, Caterpillar, and Hewlett-Packard have high referent power. Manufacturers will gain cooperation best if they would resort to referent power, expert power, legitimate power, and reward power, in that order, and generally avoid using coercive power.[17]

Intermediaries can aim for a relationship based on cooperation, partnership, or distribution programming.[18] Most producers see the main challenge as gaining intermediaries' *cooperation*. They often use positive motivators, such as higher margins, special deals, premiums, cooperative advertising allowances, display allowances, and sales contests. At times they will apply negative sanctions, such as threatening to reduce margins, slow down delivery, or terminate the relationship. The weakness of this approach is that the producer is using crude stimulus-response thinking.

More sophisticated companies try to forge a long-term *partnership* with distributors. The manufacturer clearly communicates what it wants from its distributors in the way of market coverage, inventory levels, marketing development, account solicitation, technical advice and services, and marketing information. The manufacturer seeks distributor agreement with these policies and may introduce a compensation plan for adhering to the policies. Here are some examples of successful partner-building practices:

- Timken Corporation (roller bearings) has its sales reps make multilevel calls on its distributors.
- DuPont has a distributor marketing steering committee that meets regularly.
- Dayco Corporation (engineered plastics and rubber products) runs an annual week-long retreat with 20 distributors' executives and 20 Dayco executives.
- Vanity Fair, Levi Strauss, and Hanes have formed "quick response" partnerships with discounters and department stores.
- Rust-Oleum introduces a menu of marketing programs each quarter; distributors choose the programs that fit their needs.

The most advanced supply–distributor arrangement is *distribution programming,* which can be defined as building a planned, professionally managed, vertical marketing system that meets the needs of both manufacturer and distributors. The manufacturer establishes a department within the company called *distributor-relations planning.* Its job is to identify distributor needs and build up merchandising programs to help each distributor operate as efficiently as possible. This department and the distributors jointly plan merchandising goals, inventory levels, space and visual merchandising plans, sales-training requirements, and advertising and promotion plans. The aim is to convert the distributors from thinking that they make their money primarily on the buying side (through tough negotiation with the manufacturer) to seeing that they make their money on the selling side (by being part of a sophisticated vertical marketing system). Kraft and Procter & Gamble are two companies with excellent distributor-relations planning.

Too many manufacturers think of their distributors and dealers as customers rather than working partners. Up until now, we have treated manufacturers and distributors as separate organizations. But many manufacturers are distributors of related products made by other manufacturers, and some distributors also own or contract for the manufacture of in-house brands. The Marketing Insight "Jeans by Any Other Name . . . Brand, or Label" illustrates this situation in the jeans industry, but it is common in many others.

EVALUATING CHANNEL MEMBERS

Producers must periodically evaluate intermediaries' performance against such standards as sales-quota attainment, average inventory levels, customer delivery time, treatment of damaged and lost goods, and cooperation in promotional and training programs.

A producer will occasionally discover that it is paying too much to particular intermediaries for what they are actually doing. One manufacturer was compensating a distributor for holding inventories but found that the inventories were actually held in a public warehouse at the manufacturer's expense. Producers should set up functional discounts in which they pay specified amounts for the trade channel's performance of each agreed-upon service. Underperformers need to be counselled, retrained, remotivated, or terminated.

MODIFYING CHANNEL ARRANGEMENTS

A producer must periodically review and modify its channel arrangements. Modification becomes necessary when the distribution channel is not working as planned, consumer buying patterns change, the market expands, new competition arises, innovative distribution channels emerge, and the product moves into later stages in the product life cycle.

No marketing channel will remain effective over the whole product life cycle. Early buyers might be willing to pay for high value-added channels, but later buyers will switch to lower-cost channels. Small office copiers were first sold by manufacturers' direct sales forces, later through office-equipment dealers, still later through mass merchandisers, and now by mail-order firms and Internet marketers.

Jeans by Any Other Name... Brand, or Label

Retailers and manufacturers see the distinctions between types of brands as vital because they have a heavy impact on profits. So they struggle to differentiate brands by image and by distribution channel. Jeans—that staple of the North American wardrobe (a $17 billion annual business)—fall into four classes: national brands, designer labels, private labels, and retail store brands.

National brands are owned by a manufacturer who advertises and sells them nationally. One of the first apparel brands to gain national recognition was Levi Strauss denim jeans in the 1870s. National apparel brands continued to grow in number over the next century, but the 1980s saw a tremendous leap in sales for these brands. Examples of national brand jeans include Levi, still the number-one best-seller, Wrangler and Lee (both products of the VF Corporation), and Guess?. Levi saw great success in the 1980s and 1990s with its non-denim line of casual pants (Dockers) and its line of dress pants (Slates).

Designer labels, a subcategory of national brands, carry the name of a designer and are usually sold at high prices ($150 and up) both nationally and internationally. The apparel industry's current mega-designers—Ralph Lauren, Calvin Klein, Tommy Hilfiger, and Donna Karan—all have their own jeans lines. Even some retired designers, such as Liz Claiborne and Gloria Vanderbilt, have active jeans lines. Calvin Klein is in second place, behind Levi, in national sales. "Calvins" have been market leaders since the famous 1978 ad featuring a teenage Brooke Shields saying: "Do you know what comes between me and my Calvins? Nothing." Some foreign designer labels, such as Hugo Boss, are imported into North America.

A private label is owned by a retailer and found only in its stores. Examples are the 'Our Best' sold by Sobeys, Loblaw's Presidents Choice products, the Kathie Lee Gifford line sold by Wal-Mart, the Truly line sold exclusively at Zellers, and the Canyon River Blues line sold by Sears. A retail store brand is the name of a chain that is used as the exclusive label on most of the items in the store or catalogue. Examples include Roots, Gap, Mark's Work Wearhouse, The Limited, J. Crew, L.L. Bean, and Lands' End. Gap successfully introduced the first complete store-brand jeans line in 1991. Sales of store brands grew 5.8 percent in 1996 and an additional 5 percent in 1997.

Different types of brands have different impacts on profits. Private labels are usually priced well under national brands and far below designer brands. Store-brand prices, on the other hand, are usually close to those of national brands, and above those of private labels. Profit margins, however, are not always in proportion to selling price. The profit margin on store-brand merchandise is typically 5 to 15 percent greater than the profit on national brands.

Sources: "True Blue," *Esquire*, July 1, 1994, p. 102; George White, "Wall Street, California; Fashion Pushes Sales Forward," *Los Angeles Times*, September 8, 1998, p. B1; Sharon Haver, "Shedding Light on Denim's Dark Past," *Rocky Mountain News*, May 28, 1998, p. 6D; Stacy Perman, "Business: Levi's Gets the Blues," *Time*, November 11, 1997, p. 66.

Miland Lele developed the grid in Figure 16.5 to show how marketing channels have changed for PCs and designer apparel at different stages in the product life cycle:

- *Introductory stage*: Radically new products or fashions tend to enter the market through specialist channels (such as hobbyist shops, boutiques) that identify trends and attract early adopters.

- *Rapid growth stage*: As interest grows, higher-volume channels appear (dedicated chains, department stores) that offer services but not as many as the previous channels.

FIGURE 16.5

Channel Value Added and Market Growth Rate

		Value Added by the Channel	
		High	Low
Market Growth Rate	Low	**Introductory** – PCs: hobbyist stores – Designer apparel: boutiques	**Declining** – PCs: mail order – Designer apparel: off-price stores
	High	**Growing** – PCs: specialty retailers – Designer apparel: better department stores	**Mature** – PCs: mass merchandisers – Designer apparel: mass merchandisers

- *Maturity stage*: As growth slows, some competitors move their product into lower-cost channels (mass merchandisers).
- *Decline stage*: As decline begins, even lower-cost channels emerge (mail-order houses, off-price discounters).[19]

In competitive markets with low entry barriers, the optimal channel structure will inevitably change over time. The current structure will necessarily change in the direction of the optimal structure. The change could involve adding or dropping individual channel members, adding or dropping particular market channels, or developing a totally new way to sell goods.

Adding or dropping individual channel members requires an incremental analysis. What would the firm's profits look like with and without this intermediary? An automobile manufacturer's decision to drop a dealer requires subtracting the dealer's sales and estimating the possible sales loss or gain to the manufacturer's other dealers.

Sometimes a producer considers dropping all intermediaries whose sales are below a certain amount. Consider the following:

- **Navistar.** Navistar noted at one time that five percent of its dealers were selling fewer than three or four trucks a year. It cost the company more to service these dealers than their sales were worth. But dropping these dealers could have repercussions on the system as a whole. The unit costs of producing trucks would be higher, because the overhead would be spread over fewer trucks; some employees and equipment would be idled; some business in these markets would go to competitors; and other dealers might become insecure. All these factors would have to be taken into account.

Navistar
www.navistar.com

The most difficult decision involves revising the overall channel strategy.[20] Distribution channels clearly become outmoded with the passage of time. A gap arises between a seller's existing distribution system and the ideal system that would satisfy target customers' needs and desires. Examples abound: Avon's door-to-door system for selling cosmetics had to be modified as more women entered the workforce, and IBM's exclusive reliance on a field sales force had to be modified with the introduction of low-priced personal computers.

Stern and Sturdivant have outlined an excellent framework, called *Customer-Driven Distribution System Design*, for moving a poorly functioning distribution system closer to target customers' ideal system.[21] Essentially, companies have to reduce the gaps between the service outputs that target customers desire, those that the existing channel system delivers, and those that management thinks are feasible within the existing constraints. Six steps are involved:

1. Research target customers' value perceptions, needs, and desires regarding channel service outputs.
2. Examine the performance of the company's and competitors' existing distribution systems in relation to customer desires.
3. Find service output gaps that need corrective action.
4. Identify major constraints that will limit possible corrective actions.
5. Design a "management-bounded" channel solution.
6. Implement the reconfigured distribution system.

CHANNEL DYNAMICS

Distribution channels do not stand still. New wholesaling and retailing institutions emerge, and new channel systems evolve. We will look at the recent growth of vertical, horizontal, and multichannel marketing systems and see how these systems cooperate, conflict, and compete.

VERTICAL MARKETING SYSTEMS

One of the most significant recent channel developments is the rise of vertical marketing systems. A *conventional marketing channel* comprises an independent producer, wholesaler(s), and retailer(s). Each is a separate business seeking to maximize its own profits, even if this goal reduces profit for the system as a whole. No channel member has complete or substantial control over other members.

A *vertical marketing system* (VMS), by contrast, comprises the producer, wholesaler(s), and retailer(s) acting as a unified system. One channel member, the *channel captain,* owns the others or franchises them or has so much power that they all cooperate. The channel captain can be the producer, the wholesaler, or the retailer. VMSs arose as a result of strong channel members' attempts to control channel behaviour and eliminate the conflict that results when independent channel members pursue their own objectives. They achieve economies through size, bargaining power, and elimination of duplicated services. VMSs have become the dominant mode of distribution in the U.S. consumer marketplace, serving between 70 percent and 80 percent of the total market. There are three types of VMS: corporate, administered, and contractual.

Corporate VMS

A *corporate VMS* combines successive stages of production and distribution under single ownership. Vertical integration is favoured by companies that desire a high level of control over their channels. For example, Sears obtains over 50 percent of the goods it sells from companies that it partly or wholly owns. Sherwin-Williams makes paint but also owns and operates 2000 retail outlets.

Administered VMS

An *administered VMS* coordinates successive stages of production and distribution through the size and power of one of the members. Manufacturers of a dominant brand are able to secure strong trade cooperation and support from resellers. Thus Kodak, Gillette, Procter & Gamble, and Campbell Soup are able to command high levels of cooperation from their resellers in connection with displays, shelf space, promotions, and price policies.

Contractual VMS

A *contractual VMS* consists of independent firms at different levels of production and distribution integrating their programs on a contractual basis to obtain more economies or sales impact than they could achieve alone. Johnston and Lawrence call them "value-adding partnerships" (VAPs).[22] Contractual VMSs now constitute one of the most significant developments in the economy. Contractual VMSs are of three types:

1. *Wholesaler-sponsored voluntary chains:* Wholesalers organize voluntary chains of independent retailers to help them compete with large chain organizations. The wholesaler develops a program in which independent retailers standardize their selling practices and achieve buying economies that enable the group to compete effectively with chain organizations.

2. *Retailer cooperatives:* Retailers take the initiative and organize a new business entity to carry on wholesaling and possibly some production. Members concentrate their purchases through the retailer co-op and plan their advertising jointly. Profits are passed back to members in proportion to their purchases. Nonmember retailers can also buy through the co-op but do not share in the profits.

3. *Franchise organizations:* A channel member called a *franchisor* might link several successive stages in the production-distribution process. Franchising has been the fastest-growing retailing development in recent years. Although the basic idea is an old one, some forms of franchising are quite new.

The traditional system is the *manufacturer-sponsored retailer franchise.* Ford, for example, licenses dealers to sell its cars. The dealers are independent businesspeople who agree to meet specified conditions of sales and services. Another is the *manufacturer-sponsored wholesaler franchise.* Coca-Cola, for example, licenses bottlers (wholesalers) in various markets who buy its syrup concentrate and then carbonate, bottle, and sell it to retailers in local markets. A newer system is the *service-firm-sponsored retailer franchise.*

A service firm organizes a whole system for bringing its service efficiently to consumers. Examples are found in the auto rental business (Hertz, Avis), fast-food-service business (McDonald's, Burger King), and motel business (Howard Johnson, Ramada Inn).

The New Competition in Retailing

Many independent retailers that have not joined VMSs have developed specialty stores that serve special market segments. The result is a polarization in retailing between large vertical marketing organizations and independent specialty stores. This development creates a problem for manufacturers. They are strongly tied to independent intermediaries, which they cannot easily give up. But they must eventually realign themselves with the high-growth vertical marketing systems on less attractive terms. Furthermore, vertical marketing systems constantly threaten to bypass large manufacturers and set up their own manufacturing. The new competition in retailing is no longer between independent business units but between whole systems of centrally programmed networks (corporate, administered, and contractual) competing against one another to achieve the best cost economies and customer response. For example, in order to target value-conscious consumers, Gap developed the Old Navy Clothing Company, which was an enormous success. Then to capture a market more upscale than Gap, it bought the Banana Republic chain. Now it has a significant market share at all three price levels.[23]

HORIZONTAL MARKETING SYSTEMS

Another channel development is the horizontal marketing system, in which two or more unrelated companies put together resources or programs to exploit an emerging marketing opportunity. Many supermarket chains have arrangements with local banks to offer in-store banking. Each company lacks the capital, know-how, production, or marketing resources to venture alone, or it is afraid of the risk. The companies might work with each other on a temporary or permanent basis or create a joint venture company. Adler calls this symbiotic marketing.[24] Here are some examples:

- **H&R Block Inc. and GEICO.** H&R Block, the tax preparation chain, entered an agreement with the GEICO insurance companies to provide car insurance information to Block's customers. H&R Block customers now have the opportunity to contact GEICO through a special toll-free number to review their car insurance coverage.

GEICO Direct
www.geico.com

- **Sara Lee Intimates and Wal-Mart.** Sara Lee Intimates and Wal-Mart have had a very successful agreement for 10 years, which has grown their business from an initial $200 million account to a $1.5 billion partnership. Both companies have teams of merchandise, operations, MIS, and marketing executives who are devoted solely to this agreement. They meet regularly to iron out problems and plan joint market-share goals. This requires sharing of marketing information, inventory levels, sales history, price changes, and other "confidential" information.[25]

MULTICHANNEL MARKETING SYSTEMS

In the past, many companies sold to a single market through a single channel. Today, with the proliferation of customer segments and channel possibilities, more companies have adopted multichannel marketing. *Multichannel marketing* occurs when a single firm uses two or more marketing channels to reach one or more customer segments. Here is an example:

- **Steihl.** Steihl Company manufactures three lines of power saws. The first line is targeted to households and small contractors for home repairs; it is sold through *home improvement centres* such as Home Depot. The second line is professional chain saws targeted at larger contractors who specialize in building residential housing; these are sold through *contractor supplies distributors*. The third line is top-end saws that cut concrete and steel girders used by large-scale contractors who build commercial buildings; these are sold exclusively through *specialty cutting-tool distributors*. In each case, the company must differentiate its dealer terms, support programs and incentives, packaging, and prices.

By adding more channels, companies can gain three important benefits. The first is increased market coverage—companies often add a channel to reach a customer segment its current channels can't reach. The second is lower channel cost—companies may add a new channel to lower the cost of selling to an existing customer group (selling by phone rather than personally visiting small customers). The third is more customized selling—companies may add a channel whose selling features fit customer requirements better (adding a technical sales force to sell more complex equipment).

The gains from adding new channels come at a price, however. New channels typically introduce conflict and control problems. Two or more company channels may end up competing for the same customers. The new channels may be more independent and make cooperation more difficult.

Clearly, companies need to think through their channel architecture in advance. Moriarty and Moran propose using the hybrid grid shown in Figure 16.6 to plan the channel architecture.[26] The grid shows several marketing channels (rows) and several demand-generation tasks (columns). The grid can be used to illustrate why using only one marketing channel is not efficient. Consider using only a direct sales force. A salesperson would have to find leads, qualify them, presell, close the sale, provide service, and manage account growth. But it would be more efficient for the company to perform the earlier tasks, leaving the salesperson to invest his or her costly time primarily to close the sale. The company's marketing department would generate leads through telemarketing, direct mail, advertising, and trade shows. The leads would be sorted into hot, warm, and cool by using qualifying techniques such as checking whether a lead wants a sales call and has adequate purchasing power. The department would also run a preselling campaign informing prospects about the company's products through advertising, direct mail, and telemarketing. The salesperson comes to the prospect at a time when the prospect knows about the offering and is ready to talk business. The expensive sales force is used primarily for closing sales and managing the account for further sales. This multichannel architecture optimizes coverage, customization, and control while minimizing cost and conflict.

FIGURE 16.6

The Hybrid Grid

Source: Rowland T. Moriarty and Ursula Moran, "Marketing Hybrid Marketing Systems," *Harvard Business Review*, November–December 1990, p. 150.

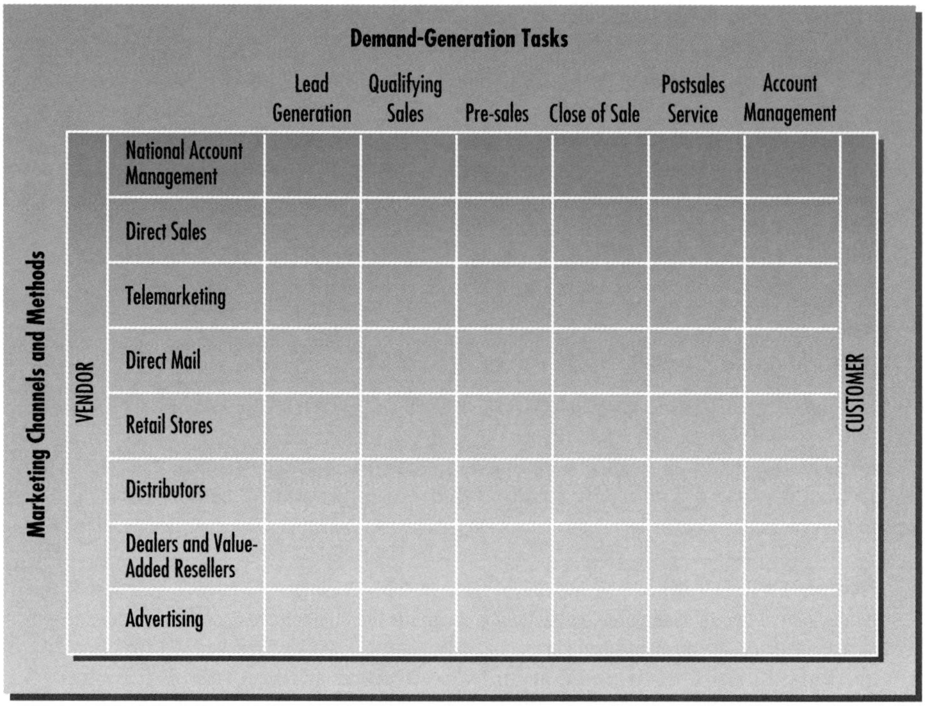

Marketing Channels and Methods	VENDOR	Demand-Generation Tasks						CUSTOMER
		Lead Generation	Qualifying Sales	Pre-sales	Close of Sale	Postsales Service	Account Management	
	National Account Management							
	Direct Sales							
	Telemarketing							
	Direct Mail							
	Retail Stores							
	Distributors							
	Dealers and Value-Added Resellers							
	Advertising							

Companies should use different channels for selling to different-size customers. A company can use its direct sales force to sell to large customers, telemarketing to sell to midsize customers, and distributors to sell to small customers. In this way, the company can serve more customers at an appropriate cost for each. But these gains can be compromised by an increased level of conflict over who has *account ownership*. For example, territory-based sales representatives may want credit for all sales in their territories, regardless of the marketing channel used.

Roles of Individual Firms

Each firm in an industry must define its role in the channel system. McCammon has distinguished five roles:[27]

1. *Insiders* are members of the dominant channel. They enjoy access to preferred sources of supply and high respect in the industry. They want to perpetuate the existing channel arrangements and are the main enforcers of industry codes of conduct.

2. *Strivers* are firms seeking to become insiders. They have less access to preferred sources of supply, which can handicap them in periods of short supply. They adhere to the industry code because of their desire to become insiders.

3. *Complementers* are not part of the dominant channel. They perform functions not normally performed by others in the channel, serve smaller segments of the market, or handle smaller quantities of merchandise. They usually benefit from the present system and respect the industry code of conduct.

4. *Transients* are outside the dominant channel and do not seek membership. They go in and out of the market and move around as opportunities arise. They have short-run expectations and little incentive to adhere to the industry code of conduct.

5. *Outside innovators* are the real challengers and disrupters of the dominant channels. They develop a new system for carrying out the marketing work of the channel; if successful, they force major channel realignments (see the Marketing for the 21st Century box, "How CarMax Is Transforming the Auto Business").

CN wants business to think of it when it comes to distributing their products.

How CarMax Is Transforming the Auto Business

Anyone trying to buy a used car sees it as a dangerous and risky business. From the moment you step on to the used-car lot and meet the used-car salesperson, you are on your guard. The cars may be full of hidden problems, may be overpriced, and may come with little or no warranty. Two companies have emerged to change the face of this industry and its standards. In 1993, Circuit City, a major retailer of electronic products, started Car-Max, the Auto Superstore, to implement a new vision of the used-car business. CarMax now operates 13 stores and is aiming for 90 by 2002.

What is special about CarMax? CarMax locates its superstores, each carrying around 500 used cars, on a large parcel of land on the outskirts of a city near a major highway. Customers enter an attractive display room similar to those found in a new car dealership. Their children can be watched in an attended day-care area complete with toys and games. A sales associate finds out what kind of car customers are seeking and escorts them to a computer kiosk. Using a computer touch screen, the associate retrieves a full listing of the cars in stock that meet the customer's criteria. A colour display of each car can be shown along with the vehicle's features and its fixed selling price. There is no price negotiation and the salesperson, paid a commission on the number of cars sold rather than the value of the cars sold, has no incentive to push the buyer into buying a higher-priced car. In choosing a car, the customer knows that CarMax mechanics carried out a 110-point inspection and made any necessary repairs. Furthermore, the car buyer receives a five-day, money-back guarantee and a 30-day comprehensive warranty. If the buyer wants financing, the CarMax associate can arrange it in 20 minutes. The entire process takes less than an hour.

Why the interest in rationalizing the used-car business? First, new car prices have almost doubled in a decade, causing many buyers to prefer to save by buying a used car, especially given that today's cars are made better and last longer. Second, the substantial growth of car leasing has greatly inflated the supply of used cars. Third, banks are more willing to offer low-cost financing to buyers of used cars, especially when they found that default rates were less for used-car buyers than new car buyers. Finally, dealers have reported earning a higher net profit on used cars, something like $400 compared to the $200 profit on a new car. For all these reasons, CarMax may prefer to call its business "pre-owned cars" or "nearly new cars" rather than "used cars."

CarMax has drawn competitors, among them AutoNation, started by Wayne Huizenga, the founder of Blockbuster Video, in late 1995. It plans on 90 superstores by 2000. Furthermore, AutoNation has formed a chain of new car dealerships carrying multiple brands and now accounts for a one percent share of the $495 billion new-car market. Huizenga is even thinking of offering a house-brand car, tapping into the auto industry's excess capacity, possibly using a South Korean automaker to make AutoNation cars.

Sources: Gabriella Stern, "'Nearly New' Autos for Sale: Dealers Buff Up Their Marketing of Used Cars," *Wall Street Journal*, February 17, 1995, p. B1; Gregory J. Gilligan, "Circuit City's CarMax Superstores Pass $300 Million in Yearly Sales," *Knight-Ridder/Tribune Business News*, April 5, 1997, p. 19.

CONFLICT, COOPERATION, AND COMPETITION

No matter how well channels are designed and managed, there will be some conflict, if for no other reason than the interests of independent business entities don't always coincide. Here we examine three questions: What types of conflict arise in channels? What causes channel conflict? What can be done to resolve conflict situations?

Types of Conflict and Competition

Suppose a manufacturer sets up a vertical channel consisting of wholesalers and retailers. The manufacturer hopes for channel cooperation that will produce greater profits for each channel member. Yet vertical, horizontal, and multichannel conflict can occur. *Vertical channel conflict* means conflict between different levels within the same channel. General Motors came into conflict with its dealers in trying to enforce policies on service, pricing, and advertising. Coca-Cola came into conflict with its bottlers who agreed also to bottle Dr. Pepper. (See the Marketing Insight "Vertical Channel Conflict in the Consumer Packaged-Goods Industry.")

Horizontal channel conflict involves conflict between members at the same level within the channel. Ford car dealers, in one metropolitan area, for example, have complained about other Ford dealers in the same area advertising and pricing too aggressively. Ford Canada has recently started taking a more active role in its dealership network. Rather than the independent dealerships that currently characterize its

Vertical Channel Conflict in the Consumer Packaged-Goods Industry

For many years, large consumer packaged-goods manufacturers enjoyed high market power relative to retailers. Much of this power was based on pull strategies: Manufacturers spent huge amounts on advertising to build brand preference, and as a consequence retailers were obliged to carry their brands. But several developments have been shifting power to the retailers:

1. The growth of giant retailers and their concentrated buying power. (In Switzerland, two retailers—Migros and the Coop—account for 70 percent of all retail food sales.)

2. Retailer development of well-regarded lower-price store brands to compete with manufacturers' brands.

3. The lack of sufficient shelf space to accommodate all the new brands being offered. (The average North American supermarket carries 24 000 items, and manufacturers offer 10 000 new items each year.)

4. Giant retailers' insistence on more trade-promotion money from manufacturers if they want their brands to enter or remain in the store.

5. The reduced funds available to manufacturers to build their brands through advertising, and the erosion of media channels for reaching mass audiences.

6. The retailers' growing marketing and information sophistication (the use of bar codes, scanner data, electronic data interchange, and direct product profitability analyses.)

The growing power of retailers is manifested by their levying of slotting fees upon manufacturers wishing to get new products into the stores; display fees to cover space costs; fines for late deliveries and incomplete orders; and exit fees to cover the cost of returning merchandise to manufacturers.

Manufacturers are discovering that if their brand isn't one of the top two or three national leaders, they might as well drop out. Since the retailer may want to offer no more than four brands within a food category, and supplies two of its own, only the two top national brands will be carried. Minor brands will be driven to produce the store brands.

Manufacturers are trying to figure out how they can regain or hold on to power vis-à-vis retailers. Clearly, manufacturers can't set up their own retail outlets. Nor do manufacturers want to continue to spend so much money on trade promotion. Market-share leaders are resorting to the following strategies to maintain their power:

1. Focus on the brands that have a chance of being number one or two in their category and commit to continuous research to improve quality, features, and packaging.

2. Maintain an active program of line extensions and a careful program of brand extensions. Develop fighter brands to compete with store brands.

3. Spend as much as possible on targeted advertising to build and maintain brand franchise.

4. Treat each major retail chain as a distinct target market, and adjust offers and sales systems to serve each target retailer profitably. Treat them as strategic partners and be ready to customize products, packaging, services, benefits, and electronic linkups.

5. Provide a high level of service quality and new services: on-time, accurate delivery of complete orders; order-cycle time reduction; emergency delivery capability; merchandising advice; inventory management support; simple order processing and billing; and access to real-time information regarding order or shipment status.

6. Consider adopting everyday low pricing as an alternative to trade dealing, which leads to large forecasting errors, forward buying, and geographical diverting of merchandise.

7. Aggressively expand into alternative retail outlets such as warehouse membership clubs, discount merchandisers, convenience stores, and some direct marketing.

Alert manufacturers who want to develop stronger links with their retail customers are implementing a system called efficient consumer response (ECR). Four tools are involved. The first is activity-based cost accounting, which enables the manufacturer to measure and demonstrate the true costs of the resources consumed in meeting a chain's requirements. The second is electronic data interchange (EDI), which improves the manufacturer's ability to manage inventory, shipments, and promotion. The third is a continuous replenishment program (CPR), which enables manufacturers to replenish products on the basis of actual and forecasted store demand. The final tool is flow-through cross-dock replenishment, which allows larger shipments to retailer distribution centres to be reloaded for shipment to individual stores, with little or no storage time lost at the distribution centre. Manufacturers that master ECR will gain an edge over their competitors.

For additional reading, see "Not Everyone Loves a Supermarket Special: P&G Moves to Banish Wildly Fluctuating Prices That Boosts Its Costs," *Business Week*, February 17, 1992, pp. 64–68; Gary Davies, *Trade Marketing Strategies* (London: Paul Chapman, 1993).

business, Ford Canada is establishing Ford Retail Networks. It will own a 40 percent stake in these operations. Ford will use these networks to begin more customer-friendly strategies like single-price selling. It is rumoured that Ford is trying to establish better customer and dealer relationships before Republic Industries Inc., an aggressive U.S. firm, enters the Canadian marketplace and forces a shake-up.[28]

Multichannel conflict exists when the manufacturer has established two or more channels that sell to the same market. When Levi Strauss agreed to distribute its jeans through Sears Canada in addition to its normal specialty-store channel, the specialty stores complained. When several clothing manufacturers—Ralph Lauren and Anne Klein—opened their own stores, the department stores that carried their brands were upset. When Goodyear began selling its popular tire brands through Sears and Wal-Mart it angered its independent dealers. (It eventually placated them by offering exclusive tire models that would not be sold in other retail outlets.) Multichannel conflict is likely to be especially intense when the members of one channel get a lower price (based on larger volume purchases) or work with a lower margin.

Causes of Channel Conflict

It is important to identify the different causes of channel conflict. Some are easy to resolve, others more difficult.

A major cause is *goal incompatibility*. For example, the manufacturer may want to achieve rapid market penetration through a low-price policy. The dealers, in contrast, may prefer to work with high margins and pursue short-run profitability. Sometimes conflict arises from *unclear roles and rights*. IBM sells personal computers to large accounts through its own sales force, and its licensed dealers are also trying to sell to large accounts. Territory boundaries and credit for sales often produce conflict.

By adding new channels, a company faces the possibility of channel conflict. The following three channel conflicts arose at IBM:

1. *Conflict between the national account managers and field sales force*: National account managers rely on field salespeople to make calls at certain national account customers located in the salesperson's territory, sometimes on a moment's notice. Requests from several national account managers to make such calls can seriously disrupt the salesperson's normal call schedule and hurt his or her commissions. Salespeople may not cooperate with national account managers when doing so conflicts with their own interests.

2. *Conflict between the field sales force and the telemarketers*: Salespeople often resent the company's setting up a telemarketing operation to sell to smaller customers. The company tells the salespeople that telemarketers free up their time to sell to larger accounts on which they can earn more commission, but the salespeople still object.

3. *Conflict between the field sales force and the dealers*: Dealers include value-added resellers, who buy computers from IBM and add specialized software needed by the target buyer, and computer retail stores, which are an excellent channel for selling small equipment to walk-in traffic and small business. These dealers frequently can offer specialized software installation and training, better service, and even lower prices than IBM's direct sales force. The direct sales force becomes angry when these dealers pursue large accounts: They want IBM to refuse to sell through dealers who try to sell to large accounts. But IBM would lose a lot of business if it dropped these successful resellers. As an alternative, IBM decided to give partial credit to salespeople for business sold to their accounts by aggressive resellers.

Conflict can also stem from *differences in perception*. The manufacturer may be optimistic about the short-term economic outlook and want dealers to carry higher inventory. Dealers may be pessimistic.

Conflict might arise because of the intermediaries' *great dependence* on the manufacturer. The fortunes of exclusive dealers, such as auto dealers, are intimately affected by the manufacturer's product and pricing decisions. This situation creates a high potential for conflict.

Managing Channel Conflict

Some channel conflict can be constructive and lead to more dynamic adaptation to a changing environment. But too much is dysfunctional. The challenge is not to eliminate conflict but to manage it better. There are several mechanisms for effective conflict management.[29]

An important mechanism is the adoption of *superordinate goals*. Channel members come to an agreement on the fundamental goal they are jointly seeking, whether it is survival, market share, high quality, or customer satisfaction. They usually do this when the channel faces an outside threat, such as a more efficient competing channel, an adverse piece of legislation, or a shift in consumer desires.

A useful step is to *exchange persons* between two or more channel levels. General Motors executives might agree to work for a short time in some dealerships, and some dealership owners might work in GM's dealer policy department. Hopefully, the participants will grow to appreciate the other's point of view.

Cooptation is an effort by one organization to win the support of the leaders of another organization by including them in advisory councils, boards of directors, and the like. As long as the initiating organization treats the leaders seriously and listens to their opinions, cooptation can reduce conflict. But the initiating organization may have to compromise its policies and plans to win their support.

Much can be accomplished by encouraging *joint membership in and between trade associations*. For example, there is good cooperation between the Grocery Manufacturers of America and the Food Marketing Institute, which represents most of the food chains; this cooperation led to the development of the universal product code (UPC). Presumably, the associations can consider issues between food manufacturers and retailers and resolve them in an orderly way.

When conflict is chronic or acute, the parties may have to resort to diplomacy, mediation, or arbitration. *Diplomacy* takes place when each side sends a person or group to meet with its counterpart to resolve the conflict. *Mediation* means resorting to a neutral third party who is skilled in conciliating the two parties' interests. *Arbitration* occurs when the two parties agree to present their arguments to one or more arbitrators and accept the arbitration decision.

LEGAL AND ETHICAL ISSUES IN CHANNEL RELATIONS

For the most part, companies are legally free to develop whatever channel arrangements suit them. In fact, the law seeks to prevent companies from using exclusionary tactics that might keep competitors from using a channel. Here we briefly consider the legality of certain practices, including exclusive dealing, exclusive territories, tying agreements, and dealers' rights.

Exclusive Dealing

Many producers like to develop exclusive channels for their products. A strategy in which the seller allows only certain outlets to carry its products is called *exclusive distribution,* and when the seller requires that these dealers not handle competitors' products, this is called *exclusive dealing*. Both parties benefit from exclusive arrangements: The seller obtains more loyal and dependable outlets, and the dealers obtain a steady source of supply of special products and stronger seller support. Exclusive arrangements are legal as long as they do not substantially lessen competition or tend to create a monopoly and as long as both parties enter into the agreement voluntarily.

Exclusive Territories

Exclusive dealing often includes exclusive territorial agreements. The producer may agree not to sell to other dealers in a given area, or the buyer may agree to sell only in its own territory. The first practice increases dealer enthusiasm and commitment. It is also perfectly legal—a seller has no legal obligation to sell through more outlets than it wishes. The second practice, whereby the producer tries to keep a dealer from selling outside its territory, has become a major legal issue.

Tying Agreements

Producers of a strong brand sometimes sell it to dealers only if they will take some or all of the rest of the line. This practice is called *full-line forcing*. Such tying agreements are not necessarily illegal, but they do violate the law if they tend to lessen competition substantially.

Dealers' Rights

Producers are free to select their dealers, but their right to terminate dealers is somewhat restricted. In general, sellers can drop dealers "for cause." But they cannot drop dealers if, for example, the dealers refuse to cooperate in a doubtful legal arrangement, such as exclusive dealing or tying agreements.

SUMMARY

1. Most producers do not sell their goods directly to final users. Between producers and final users stands one or more marketing channels, a host of marketing intermediaries performing a variety of functions. Marketing-channel decisions are among the most critical decisions facing management. The company's chosen channel(s) intimately affect all other marketing decisions.

2. Companies use intermediaries when they lack the financial resources to carry out direct marketing, when direct marketing is not feasible, and when they can earn more by doing so. The use of intermediaries largely boils down to their superior efficiency in making goods widely available and accessible to target markets. The most important functions performed by intermediaries are information, promotion, negotiation, ordering, financing, risk taking, physical possession, payment, and title.

3. Manufacturers have many alternatives for reaching a market. They can sell direct or use one-, two-, or three-level channels. Deciding which type(s) of channel to use calls for analyzing customer needs, establishing channel objectives, and identifying and evaluating the major alternatives, including the types and numbers of intermediaries involved in the channel. The company must determine whether to distribute its product exclusively, selectively, or intensively, and it must clearly spell out the terms and responsibilities of each channel member.

4. Effective channel management calls for selecting intermediaries and training and motivating them. The goal is to build a long-term partnership that will be profitable for all channel members. Individual members must be periodically evaluated against pre-established standards. Channel arrangements may need to be modified when market conditions change.

5. Marketing channels are characterized by continuous and sometimes dramatic change. Three of the most important trends are the growth of vertical marketing systems, horizontal marketing systems, and multichannel marketing systems.

6. All marketing channels have the potential for conflict and competition resulting from such sources as goal incompatibility, poorly defined roles and rights, perceptual differences, and interdependent relationships. Companies can manage conflict by striving for superordinate goals, exchanging people among two or more channel levels, coopting the support of leaders in different parts of the channel, and encouraging joint membership in and between trade associations.

7. Channel arrangements are up to the company, but there are certain legal and ethical issues to be considered with respect to practices such as exclusive dealing or territories, tying agreements, and dealers' rights.

APPLICATIONS

CHAPTER CONCEPTS

1. "Middlemen are parasites" and "Eliminate the middleman and prices will come down" are charges that have been made for centuries. Assume that marketing intermediaries are legally banned. You now decide that you would like to have a loaf of whole-wheat bread. Beginning with the wheat farmer, explain how the present distribution system works. In other words, how does the wheat get turned into a loaf of bread and into your hands? If this system were eliminated, what would a consumer have to do to get a loaf of bread? How much do you think a loaf of bread would cost?

2. Some marketers advocate that producers move from one channel to another over the product life cycle—direct sales to dealers, to mass merchandisers, to discount warehouse clubs, and the like—if they are to maintain a competitive edge. Design a channel strategy for a cordless power drill as it moves through each stage of the product life cycle.

    a. What should the company's strategic focus be in each stage?

    b. Which channels should be used in each stage?

    c. In which stages of the PLC will margins be the highest?

    d. Which stage(s) should use the most intermediaries, and which stage(s) should use the fewest?

3. Suggest some alternative channels for (a) a small firm that has developed a radically new harvesting machine, (b) a small plastics manufacturer that has developed a picnic pack for keeping bottles and food cold, and (c) a tankless instant water heater. What are the advantages and disadvantages of each channel alternative?

MARKETING AND ADVERTISING

1. The Radio Shack ad shown in Figure 1 pokes fun at the intensive distribution of wireless phone products. Why would makers of cell phones and similar products choose this distribution strategy? What desired service output levels on the part of customers form the foundation for this Radio Shack ad? Explain your answer.

2. Debenhams, a leading U.K. department store, shows off holiday fashions in the ad in Figure 2, which appeared in British women's magazines. Is Debenhams likely to earn higher profits from national brands or store brands? What motivation would Debenhams have for showcasing national brands rather than store brands in its advertising? Why are department stores important channel partners for fashion products?

Figure 1   Figure 2

Web sites that help customers compare prices and services of particular products offered by online retail sites are functioning as complementers, offering comparisons unavailable elsewhere in the channel. But many manufacturers and channel members are concerned about Web sites that facilitate comparison shopping, because these sites tend to focus customers on price rather than on other parts of the marketing mix.

Several comparison shopping Web sites have sprung up for computer hardware and software products, and new sites are coming online to search other product categories, as well. A good example is Acses, a Web site that compares prices and services at 25 Internet book retailers in the United States and Europe. Visit the Acses site and try a search for a particular book. Also read the FAQ to find out more about Acses. Why would consumers visit Acses before visiting well-known online bookstores such as Amazon.com? Why would a book manufacturer or retailer agree to be listed on Acses? What other sites would want to link to the Acses site?

Acses
http://www.acses.com/

CarMax
http://www.carax.com/

MARKETING FOR THE 21ST CENTURY

CarMax, a fast-growing outside innovator that is challenging conventional car dealers, is transforming the way used cars are sold. Point your Internet browser to the CarMax Web site. Click on the photo tour to see the computer kiosks and the interior and exterior of a typical CarMax store. Also click on "vehicle browse" to try out the company's computerized listing of vehicles. How does CarMax satisfy the service output levels desired by consumers who want to buy vehicles for personal use? Explain how CarMax's service output level performance has contributed to its rapid growth and success.

YOU'RE THE MARKETER: SONIC MARKETING PLAN

Marketing channels are an essential ingredient in any manufacturer's marketing plan. By planning the design, management, evaluation, and modification of marketing channels, manufacturers can ensure that their products are available when and where customers want to buy.

You are Jane Melody's assistant at Sonic, and one of your duties is to manage the marketing channels for shelf stereos. Review Sonic's current situation, then respond to the following questions about your marketing channels (indicating any additional research you may need):

- *What is Sonic's evaluation of current channel members?*
- *What channel length is most appropriate for Sonic in its forward movement of new products and its backward movement of defective products?*
- *In determining the number of channel members, should Sonic use exclusive, selective, or intensive distribution? Why?*
- *What levels of service output do Sonic customers desire? How do these levels affect Sonic's channel strategy? How can Sonic support its channel members?*

Think carefully about your answers to these questions and the implications for Sonic's marketing activities. Then, as your instructor directs, enter your comments and recommendations in a written marketing plan or type them into the Marketing Situation and the Marketing Mix/Place sections of the Marketing Plan Pro software.

Managing Retailing, Wholesaling, and Market Logistics

CHAPTER 17

Le plein?

A.L. Van Houtte

Couche-Tard

PROFILE:

Canadian Marketing Excellence

Couche-Tard isn't exactly a household name so you may be surprised to learn that with 1600 outlets it is Canada's largest operator of convenience stores. However, when you hear the names of the company's outlets, you will understand their market reach. They own stores located from Victoria, B.C. to Sept-Iles, Quebec—stores that operate under the Couche-Tard name as well as banners such as Mac's, Becker's, Mike's Mart, and Daisy Mart.

Couche-Tard had humble beginnings. Alain Bouchard founded the company in 1979 when he bought two Provi-Soir depanneurs from Provigo Inc. While growing to be the ninth-largest operator in North America is a feat that is amazing in and of itself, it is even more noteworthy that Bouchard has managed to grow profits by 33 percent at a time when convenience stores' share of food and grocery items fell from 2.1 to 1.7 percent. How has Couche-Tard achieved this remarkable accomplishment? By positioning their stores as destination outlets. Whereas once these stores sold overpriced emergency goods, they now offer a wide range of convenience items that are competitively priced. Many of their well-lit, pleasant shopping environments also feature automated teller machines, fax machines, photocopiers, and stamp machines. Gas bars are located at 435 outlets. As part of its Strategy 2000 concept, Couche-Tard is spending an average of $150 000 per store on new equipment so that it can offer even more high-margin products and services.

Like its larger rivals, Couche-Tard convenience stores have started branding their own food items. They are investing heavily to redesign their stores to match the needs of their local neighbourhoods. Those in upscale areas offer high-margin, mouthwatering fresh-baked goods such as croissants that customers can eat at in-store cafés. Stores located in areas frequented by male, blue-collar workers stock meat-laden Subway-brand sandwiches. Couche-Tard plans to take on Tim Horton's and Dunkin' Donuts in its fight for market share. Not only is the company running a $500 000 radio campaign as part of this fight, but it is also taking a unique approach to advertising. In areas that are saturated by traditional weekly newspaper food flyers, Couche-Tard promotes store specials on postcards sent by mail to customers. They also send out flyers announcing their specials just like the supermarkets, allowing them to significantly increase their profits.

Like many savvy marketers, Couche-Tard knows that employee ability and satisfaction are highly correlated to customer satisfaction. Thus it invests heavily in employee training so that the chain of stores can offer service and merchandising that rivals their larger competitors. After reading the Couche-Tard example, you can see that such firms follow Philip Kotler's advice. "Retailers, wholesalers, and logistical organizations need their own marketing strategies."

Sources: Brian Dunn, "The King of Bread, Butts and Beer," *Marketing*, October 25, 1999, p. 23; Anita Lahey, "Cornered Stores," *Marketing*, August 4, 1997, pp. 10-11; Luis Millan, "King of the Corner Store," *Canadian Business*, September 26, 1997, pp. 101-103.

In the previous chapter, we examined marketing intermediaries from the viewpoint of manufacturers who wanted to build and manage marketing channels. In this chapter, we view these intermediaries—retailers, wholesalers, and logistical organizations—as requiring and forging their own marketing strategies. Some intermediaries dominate the manufacturers who deal with them. Many use strategic planning, advanced information systems, and sophisticated marketing tools. They measure performance more on a return-on-investment basis than on a profit-margin basis. They segment their markets, improve their market targeting and positioning, and aggressively pursue market expansion and diversification strategies.

RETAILING

- Retailing includes all the activities involved in selling goods or services directly to final consumers for personal, non-business use. A *retailer* or *retail store* is any business enterprise whose sales volume comes primarily from retailing.

Any organization selling to final consumers—whether a manufacturer, wholesaler, or retailer—is doing retailing. It does not matter *how* the goods or services are sold (by person, mail, telephone, vending machine, or Internet) or *where* they are sold (in a store, on the street, or in the consumer's home).

TYPES OF RETAILERS

Retail organizations exhibit great variety and new forms keep emerging. There are store retailers, nonstore retailers, and retail organizations.

Consumers today can shop for goods and services in a wide variety of stores. The most important retail-store types are described in Table 17.1. Perhaps the best-known type of retailer is the department store. Japanese department stores such as Takashimaya and Mitsukoshi attract millions of shoppers each year. These stores feature art galleries, cooking classes, and children's playgrounds.

TABLE 17.1

Major Retailer Types

Specialty Store: Narrow product line with a deep assortment, such as apparel stores, sporting-goods stores, furniture stores, florists, and bookstores. A clothing store would be a single-line store; a men's clothing store would be a limited-line store; and a men's custom-shirt store would be a superspecialty store. *Examples:* Harry Rosen, Foot Locker, Mark's Work Warehouse, Moore's The Suit People, Bootlegger, The Body Shop

Department Store: Several product lines—typically clothing, home furnishings, and household goods—with each line operated as a separate department managed by specialist buyers or merchandisers. *Examples:* Sears, The Bay

Supermarket: Relatively large, low-cost, low-margin, high-volume, self-service operation designed to serve total needs for food, laundry, and household maintenance products. Supermarkets earn an operating profit of only about 1 percent on sales and 10 percent on net worth. *Examples:* A&P, Loblaws, Loeb, Provigo, Safeway, Sobeys

Convenience Store: Relatively small store located near residential area, open long hours seven days a week, and carrying a limited line of high-turnover convenience products at slightly higher prices. Many have added takeout sandwiches, coffee, and pastries. *Examples:* 7-Eleven, Beckers

Discount Store: Standard merchandise sold at lower prices with lower margins and higher volumes. True discount stores regularly sell merchandise at lower prices and offer mostly national brands. *Examples:* Wal-Mart, Zellers. Discount retailing has moved into specialty merchandise stores, such as discount sporting-goods stores, electronics stores, and bookstores. *Examples:* No Frills, Food Basics, Future Shop, Play It Again Sports

Off-Price Retailer: Merchandise bought at less than regular wholesale prices and sold at less than retail: often leftover goods, overruns, and irregulars obtained at reduced prices from manufacturers or other retailers. Examples: Penningtons, Winners

 Factory outlets are owned and operated by manufacturers and normally carry the manufacturer's surplus, discontinued, or irregular goods. *Examples:* Mikasa (dinnerware), Dexter (shoes), Highland Queen (mid-priced apparel)

 Independent off-price retailers are owned and run by entrepreneurs or by divisions of larger retail corporations. *Examples:* Bi-Way, The Dollar Store, Bargain Harolds

 Warehouse clubs (or wholesale clubs) sell a limited selection of brand-name grocery items, appliances, clothing, and a hodgepodge of other goods sold at deep discounts to members

(continued)

who pay $25 to $50 annual membership fees. Warehouse clubs serve small businesses and group members from government agencies, nonprofit organizations, and some large corporations. Wholesale clubs operate in huge, low-overhead, warehouselike facilities and offer few frills. They offer rock-bottom prices—typically 20 percent to 40 percent below supermarket and discount-store prices but make no home deliveries and accept no credit cards. *Examples:* Sam's Clubs, Price–Costco, BJ's Wholesale Club

Superstore: Averages 4000 square metres of selling space traditionally aimed at meeting consumers' total needs for routinely purchased food and nonfood items. Usually offer services such as laundry, dry cleaning, shoe repair, check cashing, and bill paying. A new group called "category killers" carry a deep assortment in a particular category and a knowledgeable staff. *Examples:* Chapters, Petsmart, Staples, Home Depot, IKEA

Combination stores are a diversification of the supermarket store into the growing drug-and-prescription field. Combination food and drug stores average 6000 square metres of selling space. *Examples:* Herbie's (groceries, pharmacy)

Hypermarkets range between 9000 and 25 000 square metres and combine supermarket, discount, and warehouse retailing principles. Product assortment goes beyond routinely purchased goods and includes furniture, large and small appliances, clothing items, and many other items. Bulk display and minimum handling by store personnel, with discounts offered to customers who are willing to carry heavy appliances and furniture out of the store. Hypermarkets originated in France. *Examples:* Carrefour and Casino (France); Pyrca, Continente, and Alcampo (Spain); Meijer's (Netherlands)

Catalogue Showroom: Broad selection of high-markup, fast-moving, brand-name goods at discount prices. Customers order goods from a Catalogue in the showroom, then pick these goods up at a merchandise pickup area in the store. Example: Service Merchandise

Sources: For further reading, see Leah Rickard, "Supercenters Entice Shoppers," *Advertising Age,* March 29, 1995, pp. 1–10; Debra Chanil, "Wholesale Clubs: A New Era?" *Discount Merchandiser,* November 1994, pp. 38–51; Julie Nelson Forsyth, "Department Store Industry Restructures for the 90s," *Chain Store Age Executive,* August 1993, pp. 29A–30A; John Milton Fogg, "The Giant Awakens," *Success,* March 1995, p. 51; and J. Douglas Eldridge, "Nonstore Retailing: Planning for a Big Future," *Chain Store Age Executive,* August 1993, pp. 34A–35A.

Retail-store types pass through stages of growth and decline that can be described as the *retail life cycle*.[1] A type emerges, enjoys a period of accelerated growth, reaches maturity, and then declines. Older retail forms took many years to reach maturity; newer retail forms reach maturity much more quickly. Department stores took 80 years to reach maturity, whereas warehouse retail outlets reached maturity in 10 years.

One reason that new store types emerge to challenge old store types is given by the *wheel-of-retailing* hypothesis.[2] Conventional retail-store types typically increase their services and raise their price to cover the cost. These higher costs provide an opportunity for new store forms to emerge offering lower prices and less service.

New store types emerge to meet widely different consumer preferences for service levels and specific services. Retailers can position themselves as offering one of four levels of service:

1. *Self-service:* Self-service is the cornerstone of all discount operations. Many customers are willing to carry out their own locate–compare–select process to save money.

2. *Self-selection:* Customers find their own goods, although they can ask for assistance. Customers complete their transactions by paying a salesperson for the item.

3. *Limited service:* These retailers carry more shopping goods, and customers need more information and assistance. The stores also offer services (such as credit and merchandise-return privileges).

4. *Full service:* Salespeople are ready to assist in every phase of the locate–compare–select process. Customers who like to be waited on prefer this type

of store. The high staffing cost, along with the higher proportion of specialty goods and slower-moving items and the many services, results in high-cost retailing.

By combining these different service levels with different assortment breadths, we can distinguish the four broad positioning strategies available to retailers, as shown in Figure 17.1:

1. *Holt Renfrew:* Stores that feature a broad product assortment and high value added. Stores in this quadrant pay close attention to store design, product quality, service, and image. Their profit margin is high, and if they are fortunate enough to have high volume, they will be very profitable.

2. *Birk's:* Stores that feature a narrow product assortment and high value added. Such stores cultivate an exclusive image and tend to operate on a high margin and low volume.

3. *Sunglass Hut:* Stores that feature a narrow line and low value added. Such stores keep their costs and prices low by designing similar stores and centralizing buying, merchandising, advertising, and distribution.

4. *Zellers:* Stores that feature a broad line and low value added. They focus on keeping prices low so that they have an image of being a place for good buys. They make up for low margin by high volume.

Although the overwhelming majority (97 percent) of goods and services is sold through stores, *nonstore retailing* has been growing much faster than store retailing, amounting to more than 12 percent of all consumer purchases. Some observers predict that as much as half of all general merchandise will be sold through nonstore retailing by the year 2000. Nonstore retailing falls into four major categories: direct selling, direct marketing, automatic vending, and buying services:

1. Direct selling is a $13.5 billion industry, with over 600 companies selling door-to-door or at home sales parties. Well known in one-to-one selling are Avon, Electrolux, Tupperware, and Mary Kay Cosmetics. A salesperson goes to the home of a host who has invited friends, demonstrates the products, and takes orders. Pioneered by Amway, the multi-level (network) marketing sales system consists of companies recruiting independent businesspeople who act as distributors. The distributor's compensation includes a percentage of sales of those the distributor recruits as well as earnings on direct sales to customers.

2. Direct marketing has roots in direct-mail and catalogue marketing (Mountain Equipment Co-op, Canadian Geographic Catalogue, Lands' End, L.L. Bean); it

Mountain Equipment Co-op
www.mec.ca

FIGURE 17.1

Retail Positioning Map

Source: William T. Gregor and Eileen M. Friars, "Money Merchandising: Retail Revolution in Consumer Financial Service" (Cambridge, MA: The MAC Group, 1982).

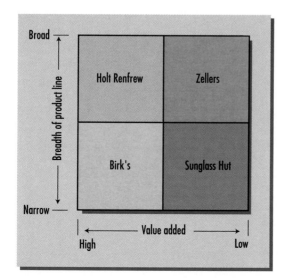

includes telemarketing (1-800-FLOWERS), television direct-response marketing (Home Shopping Network, QVC), and electronic shopping (Chapters.ca, Indigo.ca, Dell.ca).

3. **Automatic vending** is used for a variety of merchandise, including impulse goods such as cigarettes, soft drinks, candy, newspapers, and other products like hosiery, cosmetics, hot food, paperbacks. Vending machines are found in universities, factories, offices, large retail stores, gasoline stations, hotels, restaurants, and many other places. They offer 24-hour selling, self-service, and merchandise that is always fresh.

4. **Buying service** is a storeless retailer serving a specific clientele—usually employees of large organizations—who are entitled to buy from a list of retailers who have agreed to give them discounts in return for membership.

Although many retail stores are independently owned, an increasing number are part of some form of corporate retailing. Corporate retail organizations achieve economies of scale, greater purchasing power, wider brand recognition, and better-trained employees. The major types of corporate retailing—corporate chain stores, voluntary chains, retailer cooperatives, franchises, and merchandising conglomerates—are described in Table 17.2. Franchising is described in detail in the Marketing Insight "Franchise Fever."

MARKETING DECISIONS

Retailers today are anxious to find new marketing strategies to attract and hold customers. In the past they held customers by offering convenient location, special or unique assortments of goods, greater or better services than competitors, and store credit cards. All of this has changed. Today, national brands such as Calvin Klein, Izod, and Levi are found in most department stores, in their own shops, in merchandise outlets, and in off-price discount stores. In their drive for volume, national-brand manufacturers have placed their branded goods everywhere. The result is that retail-store assortments have grown more alike.

TABLE 17.2	
Major Types of Retail Organizations	**Corporate Chain Store:** Two or more outlets commonly owned and controlled, employing central buying and merchandising, and selling similar lines of merchandise. Strongest in department stores, variety stores, food stores, drugstores, shoe stores, and women's clothing stores. Their size allows them to buy in large quantities at lower prices, and they can afford to hire corporate specialists to deal with pricing, promotion, merchandising, inventory control, and sales forecasting. Examples: Black's Photography, HMV, Tip Top Tailors
	Voluntary Chain: A wholesaler-sponsored group of independent retailers engaged in bulk buying and common merchandising. Examples: Independent Grocers Alliance (IGA), True Value Hardware
	Retailer Cooperative: Independent retailers who set up a central buying organization and conduct joint promotion efforts. Examples: Associated Grocers, ACE Hardware
	Consumer Cooperative: A retail firm owned by its customers. In consumer coops residents contribute money to open their own store, vote on its policies, elect a group to manage it, and receive patronage dividends. Examples: Calgary Co-op
	Franchise Organization: Contractual association between a franchiser (manufacturer, wholesaler, service organization) and franchisees (independent businesspeople who buy the right to own and operate one or more units in the franchise system). Franchising has been prominent in dozens of product and service areas. Examples: McDonald's, Subway, Pizza Hut, Jiffy Lube, 7-Eleven
	Merchandising Conglomerate: A free-form corporation that combines several diversified retailing lines and forms under central ownership, along with some integration of distribution and management. Example: Allied Domeq PLC operates Dunkin' Donuts and Baskin-Robbins, plus a number of British retailers and a wine and spirits group

Franchise Fever

Once considered upstarts among independent business owners, franchising generates approximately $90 billion in retail sales annually. According to Francon, Canada's sole franchise research company, Canadians have embraced franchising as a means of self-employment to a far greater extent than the populace of any other country. Over one million Canadians are employed in the franchise industry. This isn't hard to believe in a society where it's nearly impossible to stroll down a city block or drive on a suburban thoroughfare without seeing a franchise outlet such as Tim Horton's, McDonald's, Midas Muffler, or 7-Eleven.

How does a franchising system work? The individual franchisees are a tightly knit group of enterprises whose systematic operations are planned, directed, and controlled by the operation's innovator, called a franchiser. Generally, franchises are distinguished by three characteristics:

1. The franchiser owns a trade or service mark and licenses it to franchisees in return for royalty payments.

2. The franchisee pays for the right to be part of the system. The initial fee is only a small part of the total amount. Start-up costs include rental and lease of equipment and fixtures, and usually a regular license fee. McDonald's franchisees may invest as much as $1 million in initial start-up costs. The franchisee then pays McDonald's a service fee of four percent of sales plus a monthly base rent.

3. The franchiser provides its franchisees with a marketing and operations system for doing business. McDonald's requires franchisees to attend its "Hamburger University" in Oak Brook, Illinois, for three weeks to learn how to manage the business, and the franchisees must adhere to certain procedures in buying materials.

Business format franchising is mutually beneficial to both franchiser and franchisee. Among the benefits reaped by franchisers are the licence to cover a territory, the motivation and hard work of employees who are entrepreneurs rather than "hired hands," the franchisees' familiarity with local communities and conditions, and the enormous purchasing power of the franchisor. Franchisees benefit from buying into a proven business with a well-known and accepted brand name. They find it easier to borrow money from financial institutions, and they receive support in areas ranging from marketing and advertising to site selection and staffing.

The franchise explosion in recent years has increasingly saturated the domestic market. The Canadian Franchise Association works with government to encourage a business climate conducive to the growth of franchising. Its members must abide by the Association's Code of Ethics. It publishes a number of books to help people better understand franchising including the "Investigate Before Investing" information kit, the *Opportunities Canada Franchise and Dealership Guide* that lists over 1500 Canadian franchises, and "Legal Considerations of Franchising in Canada." The Association also hosts seminars, conferences, and trade shows to help practitioners understand the latest trends and developments in franchising.

With the explosive growth of franchising have come a growing number of complaints against parent companies. The most common complaints: franchisers "encroach" on existing franchisees' territory by bringing in another store; higher-than-reported failure rates; and exaggerated claims of support. There are conflicts between the franchisers, who benefit from growth, and the franchisees, who benefit only when they can earn a decent living.

Counterbalancing adversarial franchise arrangements are others committed to franchisee success. M&M Meat Shops, for example, has a targeted support program (TSS) through which it invests in its least profitable franchises to help them improve. Investments can range from $3000 to $20 000, and better still, the franchisees don't have to repay the amount invested.

Some new directions that may deliver both franchiser growth and franchisee earnings are:

■ Strategic alliances with major outside corporations: Fuji arranged with Moto Photo, a one-hour photo developer, to carry its film. Fuji won instant market penetration through Moto Photo's 400 locations, and Moto Photo franchisees enjoyed Fuji's brand-name recognition and advertising reach.

■ Expansion abroad: Fast-food franchises have become very popular throughout the world. Today McDonald's has 10 600 restaurants outside North America, which account for nearly 60 percent of the company's sales and profits. Domino's Pizza, Inc., the world's second-largest pizza chain, has stores in nearly 60 countries. Wendy's International has more than 600 units in foreign countries; it also owns Tim Horton's, Canada's largest donut chain.

■ Nontraditional site locations: Franchises are opening in airports, sports stadiums, university campuses, hospitals, gambling casinos, theme parks, convention halls, and even riverboats.

Sources: Industry Canada Web site, Franchise Associations, http://strategis.ic.gc.ca/SSG/dm01263e.html. John Southerst, "M&M Meat Shops Chain Bolsters Weaker Links," *The Globe and Mail*, March 30, 1999, p. B7. Norman D. Axelrad and Robert E. Weigand, "Franchising—A Marriage of System Members," in *Marketing Managers Handbook*, 3rded., eds. Sidney Levy, George Frerichs, and Howard Gordon (Chicago: Dartnell, 1994), pp. 919–34; Meg Whittemore, "New Directions in Franchising," *Nation's Business*, January 1995, pp. 45–52; "Trouble in Franchise Nation," *Fortune*, March 6, 1995, pp. 115–29; Carol Steinberg, "Millionaire Franchisees," *Success*, March 1995, pp. 65–69; and Deepak Agrawal and Rajiv Lal, "Contractual Agreements in Franchising: An Empirical Investigation," *Journal of Marketing Research*, May 1995, 213–21.

Service differentiation also has eroded. Many department stores have trimmed services, and many discounters have increased services. Customers have become smarter shoppers. They do not want to pay more for identical brands, especially when service differences have diminished. Nor do they need credit from a particular store, because bank credit cards have become almost universal.

In the face of increased competition from discount houses and specialty stores, department stores are waging a comeback war. Once located in the centre of cities, many opened branches in suburban shopping centres, where parking is plentiful and family incomes are higher. Others run more frequent sales, remodel their stores, and experiment with mail order and telemarketing. Facing competition from superstores, supermarkets have opened larger stores, carrying a larger number and variety of items, and upgraded their facilities. Supermarkets have also increased their promotional budgets and moved heavily into private brands to increase profit margins.

We will examine retailers' marketing decisions in the areas of target market, product assortment and procurement, services and store atmosphere, price, promotion, and place.

Target Market

A retailer's most important decision concerns the target market. Until the target market is defined and profiled, the retailer cannot make consistent decisions on product assortment, store decor, advertising messages and media, price, and service levels.

Some retailers have defined their target markets quite well:

- **Canadian Tire.** The day after Eaton's announced its closure and the layoff of 13 000 employees, Canadian Tire said it would create 4000 jobs. The reason: its latest retailing concept, "PartsSource" stores. The company plans to open 200 of these new stores over the next five years. Rather than offering the broad product assortment offered in its traditional outlets, PartsSource will feature just one category—auto parts. But it will stock lots of them, over 20 000 different types in an attempt to attract a specific target market—do-it-yourselfers and professional mechanics. While these two groups don't normally visit stores, Canadian Tire hopes to tap their $4.3 billion worth of business while also deterring the entry of U.S. competitors.[3]

Retailers need to conduct periodic marketing research to ensure that they are reaching and satisfying their target customers. At the same time, a retailer's positioning must be somewhat flexible, especially if it manages outlets in locations with different socioeconomic patterns.

Product Assortment and Procurement

The retailer's *product assortment* must match the target market's shopping expectations. The retailer must decide on product-assortment *breadth* and *depth*. Thus a restaurant can offer a narrow and shallow assortment (small lunch counters), a narrow and deep assortment (delicatessen), a broad and shallow assortment (cafeteria), or a broad and deep assortment (large restaurant). The real challenge begins after defining the store's product assortment. The challenge is to develop a product-differentiation strategy. Here are some possibilities:

- *Feature exclusive national brands that are not available at competing retailers*: Thus Hudson Bay stores might get exclusive rights to carry the dresses of a well-known international designer.

- *Feature mostly private branded merchandise*: Benetton and Gap design most of the clothes carried in their stores. Many supermarket and drug chains carry private branded merchandise.

- *Feature blockbuster distinctive merchandise events*: Pier One will run month-long shows featuring the goods of another country, such as India or China, throughout the store.

- *Feature surprise or ever-changing merchandise*: Benetton changes some portion of its merchandise every month so that customers will want to drop in frequently. Winners offers surprise assortments of distress merchandise (goods that the owner must sell immediately because it needs cash), overstocks, and closeouts.

- *Feature the latest or newest merchandise first*: The Sharper Image leads other retailers in introducing electronic appliances from around the world.

- *Offer merchandise customizing services*: Harrod's of London will make custom-tailored suits, shirts, and ties for customers, in addition to ready-made menswear.

- *Offer a highly targeted assortment*: Lane Bryant carries goods for the larger woman. Brookstone offers unusual tools and gadgets for the person who wants to shop in an "adult toy store."[4]

After deciding on the product-assortment strategy, the retailer must establish procurement sources, policies, and practices. In the corporate headquarters of a supermarket chain, specialist buyers (sometimes called *merchandise managers*) are responsible for developing brand assortments and listening to presentations by salespersons. In some chains, buyers have the authority to accept or reject new items. In other chains, they are limited to screening "obvious rejects" and "obvious accepts"; they bring other items to the buying committee for approval.

Even when an item is accepted by a chain-store buying committee, individual stores in the chain may not carry it. About one-third of the items must be stocked and about two-thirds are stocked at the discretion of each store manager.

Manufacturers face a major challenge trying to get new items onto store shelves. They offer the nation's supermarkets between 150 and 250 new items each week, of which store buyers reject over 70 percent. Manufacturers need to know the acceptance criteria used by buyers, buying committees, and store managers. A.C. Nielsen Company interviewed store managers and found that they are most influenced (in order of importance) by strong evidence of consumer acceptance, a well-designed advertising and sales-promotion plan, and generous financial incentives to the trade.

A.C. Nielsen Company
www.acnielsen.com

Retailers are rapidly improving their skills in demand forecasting, merchandise selection, stock control, space allocation, and display. They are using computers to track inventory, compute economic order quantities, order goods, and analyze dollars spent on vendors and products. Supermarket chains are using scanner data to manage their merchandise mix on a store-by-store basis.

Stores are using *direct product profitability* (DPP) to measure a product's handling costs (receiving, moving to storage, paperwork, selecting, checking, loading, and space cost) from the time it reaches their warehouse until a customer buys it in their retail store. Resellers who have adopted DPP learn to their surprise that the gross margin on a product often has little relation to the direct product profit. Some high-volume products may have such high handling costs that they are less profitable and deserve less shelf space than some low-volume products.

Clearly, vendors are facing increasingly sophisticated buyers. Table 17.3 lists several vendor marketing tools for improving their attractiveness to retailers. Consider how GE initiated better policies to serve its dealers:

TABLE 17.3
Vendor Marketing Tools

1. *Cooperative advertising*: The vendor pays a portion of the retailer's advertising costs for the vendor's product.

2. *Preticketing*: The vendor places a tag on each product listing price, manufacturer, size, identification number, and color; these tags help the retailer reorder merchandise.

3. *Stockless purchasing*: The vendor carries the inventory and delivers goods to the retailer on short notice.

4. *Automatic reordering systems*: The vendor supplies forms and computer links for the automatic reordering of merchandise.

5. *Advertising aids*: Glossy photos and broadcast scripts, for example.

6. *Special prices*: Storewide promotion.

7. *Return and exchange privileges*.

8. *Allowances for merchandise markdowns*.

9. *Sponsorship of in-store demonstrations*.

- **General Electric.** Before the late 1980s, GE operated a traditional system of trying to load its dealers with GE appliances. This approach created problems, especially for smaller independent dealers who could not afford to carry a large stock and who could not meet the price competition of the larger multi-brand dealers. So GE invented an alternative model called the Direct Connect system in which GE dealers carry only display models and rely on a "virtual inventory" to fill orders. Dealers can access GE's order-processing system 24 hours a day, check on model availability, and place orders for next-day delivery. Dealers get GE's best price, GE financing, and no interest charge for the first 90 days. In exchange, dealers must commit to selling nine major GE product categories, generating 50 percent of their sales in GE products, opening their books to GE for review, and paying GE every month through electronic funds transfer. GE dealers' profit margins have skyrocketed, and GE has dealers who are more committed to and dependent on GE. GE now knows the actual sales of its goods at the retail level, which helps it to schedule production more accurately.[5]

Services and Store Atmosphere

Retailers must also decide on the *services mix* to offer customers:

- Prepurchase services include accepting telephone and mail orders, advertising, window and interior display, fitting rooms, shopping hours, fashion shows, trade-ins.
- Postpurchase services include shipping and delivery, gift wrapping, adjustments and returns, alterations and tailoring, installations, engraving.
- Ancillary services include general information, check cashing, parking, restaurants, repairs, interior decorating, credit, rest rooms, baby-attendant service.

The services mix is one of the key tools for differentiating one store from another.

Atmosphere is another element in the store arsenal. Every store has a physical layout that makes it hard or easy to move around. Every store has a "look." The store must embody a planned atmosphere that suits the target market and draws consumers toward purchase. A funeral parlour should be quiet, sombre, and peaceful. A dance club should be bright, loud, and vibrating. Victoria's Secret stores work on the concept of "retail theatre": customers feel they are in a romance novel, with lush music and faint floral scents in the background. Supermarkets have found that varying the tempo of music affects the average time spent in the store and the average expenditures. Some fine department stores vaporize perfume fragrances in certain departments. Restaurants are also presenting "packaged environments":[6]

- **Casual Dining.** Casual dining restaurants, such as Olive Garden, Red Lobster, T.G.I. Friday's, and the Outback Steakhouse, have become a $61 billion North American business, while the much-hyped "theme restaurants" have fallen on hard times. Two prominent theme chains, Fashion Café and Planet Hollywood, are closing outlets. The message seems to be that it takes more than decor to keep people coming back—the food must be good, the prices competitive , and the menu offerings kept updated. Diners also want a casual, family atmosphere.[7]

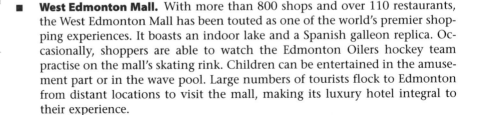

- **West Edmonton Mall.** With more than 800 shops and over 110 restaurants, the West Edmonton Mall has been touted as one of the world's premier shopping experiences. It boasts an indoor lake and a Spanish galleon replica. Occasionally, shoppers are able to watch the Edmonton Oilers hockey team practise on the mall's skating rink. Children can be entertained in the amusement part or in the wave pool. Large numbers of tourists flock to Edmonton from distant locations to visit the mall, making its luxury hotel integral to their experience.

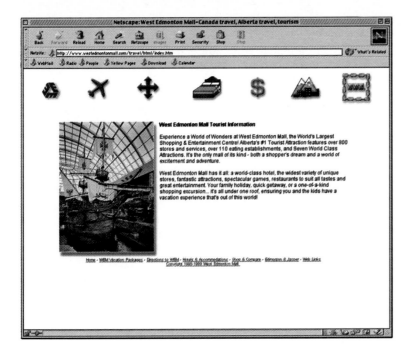

Price Decision

Prices are a key positioning factor and must be decided in relation to the target market, the product-and-service assortment mix, and competition. All retailers would like to achieve high volumes and high gross margins. They would like high *Turns x Earns*, but the two usually do not go together. Most retailers fall into the *high-markup, lower-volume* group (fine specialty stores) or the *low-markup, higher-volume* group (mass merchandisers and discount stores). Within each of these groups are further gradations. Thus Armani's on Bloor Street prices suits starting at $1000. At the other extreme are superdiscounters like Bargain Harolds and The Dollar Store, which sell odd lots and closeouts at prices below those of normal discounters.

Retailers must also pay attention to pricing tactics. Most retailers will put low prices on some items to serve as traffic builders or loss leaders. They will run storewide sales. They will plan markdowns on slower-moving merchandise. For example, shoe retailers expect to sell 50 percent of their shoes at the normal markup, 25 percent at a 40 percent markup, and the remaining 25 percent at cost.

Some retailers have abandoned "sales pricing" in favour of everyday low pricing (EDLP). EDLP could lead to lower advertising costs, greater pricing stability, a stronger image of fairness and reliability, and higher retail profits. General Motors' Saturn division states a low list price for its cars and its dealers don't bargain. Wal-Mart also practises everyday low prices. Feather cites a study showing that supermarket chains practising everyday low pricing are often more profitable than those practising sales pricing.[8]

Promotion Decision

Retailers use a wide range of promotion tools to generate traffic and purchases. They place ads, run special sales, issue money-saving coupons, and run frequent-shopper reward programs, in-store food sampling, and coupons on shelves or at checkout points. Each retailer must use promotion tools that support and reinforce its image positioning. Fine stores will place tasteful full-page ads in magazines such as *Chatelaine*. They will carefully train salespeople to greet customers, interpret their needs, and handle complaints. Off-price retailers will arrange their merchandise to promote the idea of bargains and large savings, while conserving on service and sales assistance.

Place Decision

Retailers are accustomed to saying that the three keys to success are "location, location, and location." Customers generally choose the nearest bank and gas station. Department-store chains, oil companies, and fast-food franchisers exercise great care in selecting locations. The problem breaks down into selecting regions of the country in which to open outlets, then particular cities, and then particular sites. For example, even though Loblaw controls 30 percent of the market in Atlantic Canada, 38 percent of the Ontario market, and 19 percent of the market in Western Canada, it was unable to establish a solid footing in Quebec until recently. In 1998, it acquired Montreal-based Provigo, Quebec's largest food retailer. Now it must decide how to exploit the merger. Not only must it decide what Quebec cities to target for expanded operations, but it must also choose locations within these cities and suburban regions.[9]

Retailers can locate their stores in the central business district, a regional shopping centre, a community shopping centre, a shopping strip, or within a larger store:

- *General business districts*: This is the oldest and most heavily trafficked city area, often known as "downtown." Store and office rents are normally high. Most downtown areas were hit by a flight to the suburbs in the 1960s, resulting in deteriorated retailing facilities. But in the 1990s, a renaissance of interest in downtown apartments, stores, and restaurants began in many cities including Vancouver, Toronto and Winnipeg.

- *Regional shopping centres:* These are large suburban malls containing 40 to 200 stores. They usually draw customers from a 8- to 30-kilometre radius. Typically, malls feature one or two nationally known anchor stores, such as The Bay or Sears, and a great number of smaller stores, many under franchise operation. Malls are attractive because of generous parking, one-stop shopping, restaurants, and recreational facilities. Successful malls charge high rents and may receive a share of stores' sales.

- *Community shopping centres:* These are smaller malls with one anchor store and 20 to 40 smaller stores. A new form of community shopping centre has recently emerged. Large "box" stores, such as Future Shop, Home Depot, and Staples, are clustering their outlets together at one location.

- *Strip malls* (also called *shopping strips*): These contain a cluster of stores, usually housed in one long building, serving a neighbourhood's needs for groceries, hardware, laundry, shoe repair, and dry cleaning. They usually serve people within a five- to ten-minute driving range.

- *A location within a larger store:* Certain well-known retailers—McDonald's, Starbucks, and Tim Horton's—locate new, smaller units as concession space within larger stores or operations, such as airports, schools, or department stores.

In view of the relationship between high traffic and high rents, retailers must decide on the most advantageous locations for their outlets. They can use a variety of methods to assess locations, including traffic counts, surveys of consumer shopping habits, and analysis of competitive locations.[10] Several models for site location have also been formulated.[11]

Retailers can assess a particular store's sales effectiveness by considering four indicators: (1) number of people passing by on an average day; (2) percentage who enter the store; (3) percentage of those entering who buy; and (4) average amount spent per sale.

TRENDS IN RETAILING

At this point, we can summarize the main developments retailers and manufacturers need to take into account as they plan their competitive strategies.

1. New retail forms and combinations continually emerge. Bank branches have opened in supermarkets. For example, Loblaw Companies and the Canadian Imperial Bank of Commerce have recently formed an alliance—President's Choice Financial—that gives CIBC access to a new customer base while Loblaw gains a private-label banking product. A&P countered this move and formed a partnership with Bank of Montreal. Facing increasing pressure from its traditional retail outlets, Cadbury Chocolate is experimenting with its own outlet stores and stand-alone kiosks in Toronto malls. Roots, the icon of the

President's Choice Financial
www.preschoicefinancial.com

part five
Managing
and Delivering
Marketing Programs

great Canadian hinterland, is trying to leverage its brand by launching its first home-furnishings store.[12] Gas stations include food stores that make more profit than the gas operation. Bookstores feature coffee shops. Even old retail forms are reappearing: Many major malls feature pedlars' carts that sell everything from casual wear to antiques. Successful carts average $45 000 a month in sales and can easily top $100 000 in December.

2. New retail forms are facing a shorter life span. They are rapidly copied and quickly lose their novelty.

3. The electronic age has significantly increased the growth of nonstore retailing. Consumers receive sales offers in the mail and over television, computers, and telephones, to which they can immediately respond by calling a toll-free number or via computer.

4. Competition today is increasingly intertype, or between different types of store outlets. Discount stores, catalogue showrooms, and department stores all compete for the same consumers. The competition between chain superstores and smaller independently owned stores has become particularly heated. Because of their bulk buying power, chains get more favourable terms than independents, and the chains' large square footage allows them to put in cafés and bathrooms. In many locations, the arrival of a superstore has forced nearby independents out of business. In the bookselling business, the arrival of a Chapters or Indigo superstore usually puts smaller bookstores out of business. Yet the news is not all bad for smaller companies. Many small independent retailers thrive by knowing their customers better and providing them with more personal service.

5. Today's retailers are moving toward one of two poles, operating either as mass merchandisers or as specialty retailers. Superpower retailers are emerging. Through their superior information systems and buying power, these giant retailers are able to offer strong price savings.[13] These retailers use sophisticated marketing information and logistical systems to deliver good service and immense volumes of product at appealing prices to masses of consumers. In the process, they are crowding out smaller manufacturers, who become dependent on one large retailer and are therefore extremely vulnerable, and smaller retailers, who simply don't have the budget or the buying power to compete. Many retailers are even telling the most powerful manufacturers what to make; how to price and promote; when and how to ship; and even how to reorganize and improve production and management. Manufacturers have little choice: they stand to lose 10 to 30 percent of the market if they refuse.

   Competition from "category killers" is especially deadly. Giant retailers that concentrate on one product category, such as toys (Toys "R" Us), home improvement (Home Depot), office supplies (Staples), grab a lion's share of retailing in the category and force a reduction in the number of manufacturers. As a result of Toys "R" Us controlling 20 percent of toy retailing, six manufacturers now dominate an industry where 10 years ago no manufacturer controlled more than five percent.

6. Department stores such as Sears used to be prized for their one-stop shopping convenience. Gradually, department stores gave way to malls, which feature a few department stores, a wide range of specialty stores, and plenty of parking space. Now supercentres that combine grocery items with a huge selection of nonfood merchandise (Zellers, Wal-Mart) present an alternative format for one-stop shopping.

7. Marketing channels are increasingly becoming professionally managed and programmed. Retail organizations are increasingly designing and launching new store formats targeted to different lifestyle groups. They are not sticking to one format, such as department stores, but are moving into a mix of retail formats. See the Marketing for the 21st Century, "Warner Brothers Studio Stores: Licensed to Make Money."

Warner Brothers Studio Stores: Licensed to Make Money

In transforming film, TV, and music legends into exciting new product lines, Warner Brothers is second only to Disney. From clothing to accessories to animation art to videos to gift items to home furnishings, the Studio Stores are colourful sets crowded with familiar faces: Bugs Bunny and the other Looney Toons characters, Batman, Rugrats, Mattel's Hot Wheels.

A pioneer in the retailing of entertainment-related merchandise, Warner Brothers has 185 Studio Stores in 13 countries around the world. Studio Stores outside the United States have majority-owned and operated partners. Studio Stores are a lesson in how to extend a brand through licensing.

Toys from the Looney Toon Toy Factory are everywhere. Much of the licensed merchandise is either from Giant Merchandising, a WB subsidiary, or from Warner Brothers Consumer Products division, which has more than 3700 active licensees, including DC Comics, Wizard of Oz, Hanna Barbera, and Looney Toons. Prices are mostly mid-level, with a few extremely expensive items for the most ardent collectors. Many items are cleverly packaged, such as the T-shirt that comes wrapped in a film can. Even U.S. postage stamps bearing the likeness of Bugs Bunny have been for sale.

Special events are staged regularly, especially at the flagship store in New York City. David Boreanaz, star of the hit TV show "Buffy the Vampire Slayer," made a personal appearance there, which drew 3000 fans and sold out their stock of Buffy T-shirts in two hours.

The Studio Stores offer a high-energy environment, entertainment for the whole family, and, of course, lots of licensed merchandise to take the fun feeling home. They also serve as ongoing persuasive ads for Warner Brothers movies, TV shows, and music.

Sources: Warner Bros. Web site, "Warner Bros. Studio Store Throws a Bash to Celebrate Marvin the Martian's 50th Year on Earth," *Business Wire*, July 26, 1998; "Warner Bros. Products and ENIC Announce Partnership," *Business Wire*, April 6, 1998; Dan Fost, "That's Entertainment," *Marketing Tools*, June 1, 1998, p. 36.

8. Technology is becoming critical as a competitive tool. Retailers are using computers to produce better forecasts, control inventory costs, order electronically from suppliers, send e-mail between stores, and even sell to customers within stores. They are adopting checkout scanning systems,[14] electronic funds transfer, electronic data interchange,[15] in-store television, and improved merchandise-handling systems.

One innovative scanning system is ShopperTrak, a radar-like system that counts store traffic. When one store used it, it learned there was a shopper surge between the hours of 11 A.M. and 3 P.M. To better handle the shopper flow, the store varied lunch hours for its counter clerks. Pier One Imports uses the same system to test the impact of newspaper ads on store traffic. By combining traffic and sales data, retailers say they can find out how well the store converts browsers into buyers.[16]

9. Retailers with unique formats and strong brand positioning are increasingly moving into other countries.[17] McDonald's, The Limited, Gap, and Toys "R" Us have become globally prominent as a result of their great marketing prowess. While Canadian retailers such as Roots and Harry Rosen are actively pursuing overseas markets to boost profits, it must be noted that North American retailers significantly lag Europe and the Far East when it comes to global expansion. Less than 20 percent of the top North American retailers operate globally, compared to 40 percent of European retailers and 31 percent of Far Eastern retailers. Among foreign-based global retailers are Britain's Marks and Spencer, Italy's Benetton, France's Carrefour hypermarkets, Sweden's IKEA home furnishings stores, and Japan's Yaohan supermarkets.[18]

10. There has been a marked rise in establishments that provide a place for people to congregate, such as coffeehouses, tea shops, juice bars, bookshops, and brew pubs. The Discovery Zone, a chain of children's play spaces, offers indoor spaces where kids can go wild without breaking anything and stressed-out parents can exchange stories. There are also the now-ubiquitous coffeehouses and espresso bars, such as Starbucks, whose numbers have grown from 2500 in 1989 to a forecasted 10 000 by 1999.[19]

■　*Wholesaling* includes all the activities involved in selling goods or services to those who buy for resale or business use. Wholesaling excludes manufacturers and farmers because they are engaged primarily in production, and it excludes retailers.

Wholesalers (also called *distributors*) differ from retailers in a number of ways. First, wholesalers pay less attention to promotion, atmosphere, and location because they are dealing with business customers rather than final consumers. Second, wholesale transactions are usually larger than retail transactions, and wholesalers usually cover a larger trade area than retailers. Third, the government deals with wholesalers and retailers differently regarding legal regulations and taxes.

　Why are wholesalers used at all? Why don't manufacturers sell directly to retailers or final consumers? In general, wholesalers are used when they are more efficient in performing one or more of the following functions:

■　*Selling and promoting*: Wholesalers provide a sales force that helps manufacturers reach many small business customers at a relatively low cost. Wholesalers have more contacts, and often buyers trust wholesalers more than they trust a distant manufacturer.

■　*Buying and assortment building*: Wholesalers are able to select items and build the assortments their customers need, saving the customers considerable work.

■　*Bulk breaking*: Wholesalers achieve savings for their customers through buying in large carload lots and breaking the bulk into smaller units.

■　*Warehousing*: Wholesalers hold inventories, thereby reducing the inventory costs and risks to suppliers and customers.

■　*Transportation*: Wholesalers can often provide quicker delivery to buyers because they are closer to the buyers.

■　*Financing*: Wholesalers finance customers by granting credit, and finance suppliers by ordering early and paying bills on time.

■　*Risk bearing*: Wholesalers absorb some risk by taking title and bearing the cost of theft, damage, spoilage, and obsolescence.

■　*Market information*: Wholesalers supply information to suppliers and customers regarding competitors' activities, new products, price developments, and so on.

■　*Management services and counselling*: Wholesalers often help retailers improve their operations by training sales clerks, helping with store layouts and displays, and setting up accounting and inventory-control systems. They may help industrial customers by offering training and technical services.

THE GROWTH AND TYPES OF WHOLESALING

Wholesaling has grown in North America at a compound rate of 5.8 percent over the past 10 years.[20] A number of factors explain this: the growth of larger factories located some distance from the principal buyers; production in advance of orders rather than in response to specific orders; an increase in the number of levels of intermediate producers and users; and the increasing need for adapting products to the needs of intermediate and final users in terms of quantities, packages, and forms. The major types of wholesalers are described in Table 17.4.

WHOLESALER MARKETING DECISIONS

Wholesaler-distributors have faced mounting pressures in recent years from new sources of competition, demanding customers, new technologies, and more direct-buying programs by large industrial, institutional, and retail buyers. They have had to develop appropriate strategic responses. One major drive has been to increase asset

Merchant Wholesalers: Independently owned businesses that take title to the merchandise they handle. They are called *jobbers, distributors,* or *mill supply houses* and fall into two categories: full service and limited service.

Full-Service Wholesalers: Carry stock, maintain a sales force, offer credit, make deliveries, and provide management assistance. There are two types of full-service wholesalers: (1) *Wholesale merchants* sell primarily to retailers and provide a full range of services. *General-merchandise wholesalers* carry several merchandise lines. *General-line wholesalers* carry one or two lines. *Specialty wholesalers* carry only part of a line. (2) *Industrial distributors* sell to manufacturers rather than to retailers and provide several services—carrying stock, offering credit, and providing delivery.

Limited-Service Wholesalers: Offer fewer services to suppliers and customers. *Cash-and-carry wholesalers* have a limited line of fast-moving goods and sell to small retailers for cash. *Truck wholesalers* primarily sell and deliver a limited line of semiperishable merchandise to supermarkets, small groceries, hospitals, restaurants, factory cafeterias, and hotels. *Drop shippers* operate in bulk industries, such as coal, lumber, and heavy equipment. Upon receiving an order, they select a manufacturer, who ships the merchandise directly to the customer on the agreed-upon terms and time of delivery. The drop shipper assumes title and risk from the time the order is accepted to its delivery to the customer. *Rack jobbers* serve grocery and drug retailers, mostly in nonfood items. They send delivery trucks to stores, and the delivery people set up displays, price the goods, keep them fresh, set up point-of-purchase displays, and keep inventory records. Rack jobbers retain title to the goods and bill retailers only for goods sold to consumers. *Producers' cooperatives* assemble farm produce to sell in local markets. Coop profits are distributed to members at the end of the year. *Mail-order wholesalers* send catalogs to retail, industrial, and institutional customers featuring jewelry, cosmetics, specialty foods, and other small items. Main customers are businesses in small outlying areas. No sales force is maintained. Orders are filled and sent by mail, truck, or other means of transportation.

Brokers and Agents: Do not take title to goods, and perform only a few functions. Main function is to facilitate buying and selling, for which they earn a commission of 2 to 6 percent of the selling price. Generally specialize by product line or customer type.

Brokers: Chief function is bringing buyers and sellers together and assisting in negotiation. They are paid by the party who hired them and do not carry inventory, get involved in financing, or assume risk. The most familiar examples are food brokers, real estate brokers, insurance brokers, and security brokers.

Agents: Represent either buyers or sellers on a more permanent basis. *Manufacturers' agents* represent two or more manufacturers of complementary lines. They enter into a formal written agreement with each manufacturer covering pricing policy, territories, order-handling procedure, delivery service and warranties, and commission rates. Often used in such lines as apparel, furniture, and electrical goods. Most manufacturers' agents are small businesses, with only a few skilled salespeople. *Selling agents* have contractual authority to sell a manufacturer's entire output in such product areas as textiles, industrial machinery and equipment, coal and coke, chemicals, and metals. *Purchasing agents* generally have a long-term relationship with buyers and make purchases for them, often receiving, inspecting, warehousing, and shipping merchandise to buyers. *Commission merchants* take physical possession of products and negotiate sales. They are used most often in agricultural marketing by farmers who do not want to sell their own output and do not belong to producers' cooperatives.

Manufacturers' and Retailers' Branches and Offices: Wholesaling operations conducted by sellers or buyers themselves rather than through independent wholesalers. Separate branches and offices can be dedicated to sales or purchasing. Sales branches and offices are set up by manufacturers to improve inventory control, selling, and promotion. Sales branches carry inventory and are found in such industries as lumber and automotive equipment and parts. *Sales offices* do not carry inventory and are most prominent in dry-goods and notions industries. *Purchasing offices* perform a role similar to that of brokers or agents but are part of the buyer's organization. Many retailers set up purchasing offices in major market centers.

Miscellaneous Wholesalers: A few specialized types of wholesalers are found in certain sectors of the economy. These include agricultural assemblers (which buy the agricultural output of many farms), petroleum bulk plants and terminals (which consolidate the petroleum output of many wells), and auction companies (which auction cars, equipments, and so forth, to dealers and other businesses).

productivity by managing their inventories and receivables better. They also have had to improve their strategic decisions on target markets, product assortment and services, price, promotion, and place.

Target Market
Wholesalers need to define their target markets. They can choose a target group of customers by size (e.g., only large retailers), type of customer (e.g., convenience food stores only), need for service (e.g., customers who need credit), or other criteria. Within the target group, they can identify the most profitable customers and design stronger offers to build better relationships with them. They can propose automatic reordering systems, set up management-training and advisory systems, and even sponsor a voluntary chain. They can discourage less profitable customers by requiring larger orders or adding surcharges to smaller ones.

Product Assortment and Services
The wholesalers' "product" is their assortment. Wholesalers are under great pressure to carry a full line and maintain sufficient stock for immediate delivery. But the costs of carrying huge inventories can kill profits. Wholesalers today are re-examining how many lines to carry and are choosing to carry only the more profitable ones. They are also examining which services count most in building strong customer relationships and which ones should be dropped or charged for. The key is to find a distinct mix of services valued by their customers.

Price Decision
Wholesalers usually mark up the cost of goods by a conventional percentage, say 20 percent, to cover their expenses. Expenses may run 17 percent of the gross margin, leaving a profit margin of approximately three percent. In grocery wholesaling, the average profit margin is often less than two percent. Wholesalers are beginning to experiment with new approaches to pricing. They might cut their margin on some lines in order to win important new customers. They will ask suppliers for a special price break when they can turn it into an opportunity to increase the supplier's sales.

Promotion Decision
Wholesalers rely primarily on their sales force to achieve promotional objectives. Even here, most wholesalers see selling as a single salesperson talking to a single customer instead of a team effort to sell, build, and service major accounts. Wholesalers would benefit from adopting some of the image-making techniques used by retailers. They need to develop an overall promotion strategy involving trade advertising, sales promotion, and publicity. They also need to make greater use of supplier promotion materials and programs.

Place Decision
In the past, wholesalers typically located in low-rent, low-tax areas and put little money into their physical setting and offices. Often the materials-handling systems and order-processing systems lagged the available technologies. Today progressive wholesalers have been improving materials-handling procedures and costs by developing *automated warehouses* and improving their supply capabilities through advanced information systems. Here are two examples:[21]

■ **McKesson.** McKesson, the largest distributor of pharmaceuticals in Canada and the United States, stocks and manages medical supplies and pharmaceuticals for a variety of customers, including hospitals, doctors, nursing homes, and pharmacies. Its retail pharmacy customers include retail chains (such as Rite Aid and CVS), buying groups, and independents. To improve service, it has supplied pharmacies with software applications for ordering. Orders sent in by pharmacists are filled immediately. A human worker in one of McKesson's warehouses fills the order, and the computerized system automatically creates an itemized invoice, seals the box, and conveys it to a shipping dock for overnight delivery. The system also can automatically order replenishment stock from the drug manufacturers.

McKesson
www.mckessonrxsystems.com

Strategies of High-Performance Wholesaler-Distributors

Lusch, Zizzo, and Kenderine studied 136 wholesalers in North America and concluded that the progressive ones are renewing themselves in five ways:

1. Strengthening core operations: Several wholesalers have divested marginal operations and put renewed focus on their core operations. They developed such expertise in distributing their particular product line that manufacturers and retailers couldn't duplicate the efficiency.

2. Expanding into global markets: Wholesalers, especially in the chemical, electronics, and computer fields, have been expanding not only in Canada and Mexico but also in Europe and Asia. Many manufacturers prefer using these wholesaler networks to expand overseas to establishing their own networks.

3. Doing more with less: Wholesalers have been investing heavily in technology, including bar coding and scanning, fully automated warehouses, electronic data interchange, and advanced information technology. This has enabled them to serve manufacturers and retailers who have been unable or unwilling to make investments of their own.

(continued)

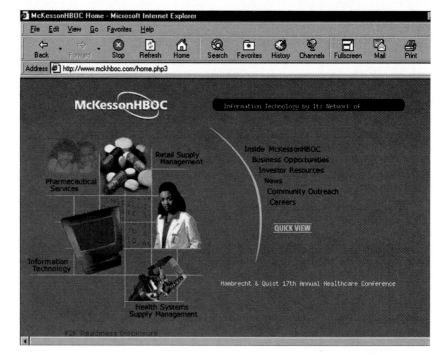

McKesson's Web site home page.

■ **Grainger.** W.W. Grainger, Inc. is one of the largest business-to-business distributors of equipment, components, and supplies in Canada and the United States. It offers over 200 000 products through 520 branches. It has developed and stocked one national, two regional, and six zone distribution centres to guarantee product availability and quick service. The distribution centres are linked by satellite network, which has reduced customer-response time and boosted sales. Grainger also offers a Web site to provide 24-hour-a-day online ordering.

TRENDS IN WHOLESALING

Manufacturers always have the option of bypassing wholesalers or replacing inefficient wholesalers with better ones. Manufacturers' major complaints against wholesalers are as follows: They do not aggressively promote the manufacturer's product line, acting more like order takers; they do not carry enough inventory and therefore fail to fill customers' orders fast enough; they do not supply the manufacturer with up-to-date market, customer, and competitive information; they do not attract high-calibre managers and bring down their own costs; and they charge too much for their services.

It even appeared that wholesalers were headed for a significant decline as large manufacturers and retailers moved aggressively into direct buying programs. Yet savvy wholesalers rallied to the challenge and began to re-engineer their businesses. The most successful wholesaler-distributors adapted their services to meet their suppliers' and target customers' changing needs. They recognized that they had to add value to the channel. They also had to reduce their operating costs by investing in more advanced materials-handling technology and information systems.

Narus and Anderson interviewed leading industrial distributors and identified four ways they strengthened their relationships with manufacturers:

1. They sought a clear agreement with their manufacturers about their expected functions in the marketing channel.

2. They gained insight into the manufacturers' requirements by visiting their plants and attending manufacturer association conventions and trade shows.

3. They fulfilled their commitments to the manufacturer by meeting the volume targets, paying bills promptly, and feeding back customer information to their manufacturers.

4. They identified and offered value-added services to help their suppliers.[22]

As the thriving wholesaling industry moves into the next century, it faces considerable challenges. Many wholesalers are facing increased capital requirements brought about by the increasing need for sophisticated information technology. Rising costs and increased competition are leading to margin compression. The industry remains vulnerable to one of the most enduring trends—fierce resistance to price increases and the winnowing out of suppliers based on cost and quality. Low margins and the need to keep costs in check have led to increasing consolidation in some wholesale industries like the electrical distribution industry.[23] This is accompanied by a trend toward vertical integration, in which manufacturers try to control or own their intermediaries, is still strong. The Marketing Memo, "Strategies of High-Performance Wholesaler-Distributors," outlines some of the strategies used by successful wholesale organizations.

 MARKET LOGISTICS

The process of getting goods to customers has traditionally been called *physical distribution*. Physical distribution starts at the factory. Managers choose a set of warehouses (stocking points) and transportation carriers that will deliver the goods to final destinations in the desired time or at the lowest total cost.

Recently, physical distribution has been expanded into the broader concept of *supply chain management*. Supply chain management starts earlier than physical distribution: attempts to procure the right inputs (raw materials, components, and capital equipment); convert them efficiently into finished products; and dispatch them to the final destinations. An even broader perspective calls for studying how the company's suppliers themselves obtain their inputs all the way back to the raw materials. The supply chain perspective can help a company identify superior suppliers and distributors and help them improve productivity, which ultimately brings down the company's costs.

Unfortunately, the supply chain view sees markets as only destination points. The company would be more effective by considering its target market's requirement first and then designing the supply chain backward from that point. This view is that of *market logistics*.

■ *Market logistics* involves planning, implementing, and controlling the physical flows of materials and final goods from points of origin to points of use to meet customer requirements at a profit.

It leads to an examination of the *demand chain*. Here are some examples of demand chain thinking:

■ A software company normally sees its challenge as producing and packaging software disks and manuals, then shipping them to wholesalers—who ship them to retailers, who sell them to customers. Customers bring the software package to their home or office and download the software onto their hard drive. Market logistics would question this approach. There are two superior delivery systems. The first involves ordering the software to be downloaded onto the customer's hard drive. Alternatively, software could be loaded onto a computer by the computer manufacturer. Both solutions eliminate the need for printing, packaging, shipping, and stocking millions of disks and manuals. The same solutions are available for distributing music, newspapers, video games, films, and other products that deliver voice, text, data, or images.

(continued)

4. Committing to TQM: Instead of just measuring sales and product movement, progressive wholesalers are moving toward managing processes to improve outcomes as perceived by customers. This includes performing quality assessment of their suppliers' products and thereby adding value. As the wholesalers move toward zero-defect customer service, manufacturers and retailers will welcome this trend as contributing to their own capacity to satisfy customers.

5. Marketing support philosophy: Wholesalers are recognizing that their role is not simply to represent the suppliers' interests, or their customers' interests, but to provide marketing support to both, by acting as a valued member of the marketing value chain.

Sources: Robert F. Lusch, Deborah Zizzo, and James M. Kenderdine, "Strategic Renewal in Distribution," *Marketing Management* 2, no. 2 (1993): pp. 20–29. Also see their *Foundations of Wholesaling—A Strategic and Financial Chart Book*, Distribution Research Program (Norman, OK: College of Business Administration, University of Oklahoma, 1996).

■ At one time, German consumers purchased individual bottles of soft drinks. German consumers, however, said they would be willing to buy six bottles at a time in a six-pack. Retailers also favoured this because the bottles could be loaded faster on the shelves, and more bottles would be purchased per occasion. A soft-drink manufacturer proceeded to design the six-packs to fit on store shelves. Then cases and pallets were designed for bringing these six-packs efficiently to the store's receiving rooms. Factory operations were redesigned to produce the new six-packs. The purchasing department let out bids for the new materials. Once the new six-packs hit the market, the manufacturer's market share rose substantially.

■ IKEA, the world's largest furniture retailing chain, is able to sell good-quality furniture at a much lower cost than competitors can. IKEA's cost savings stem from several sources: (1) the company buys such large volumes of furniture that it gets lower prices; (2) the furniture is designed in "knockdown" form and therefore shipped flat at a much lower transportation cost; (3) the customer drives the furniture home, which saves delivery cost; (4) the customer assembles the furniture; and (5) IKEA works on a low markup and high volume, in contrast to many of its competitors. Altogether, IKEA can charge 20 percent less than its competitors for comparable furniture.

The market logistics task calls for *integrated logistics systems* (ILS), involving materials management, material flow systems, and physical distribution, abetted by information technology (IT). Third-party suppliers, such as FedEx Logistics Services or Ryder Integrated Logistics, often participate in designing or managing these systems. Volvo, working with FedEx, set up a warehouse in Memphis with a complete stock of truck parts. A dealer needing a part in an emergency phones a toll-free number, and the part is flown out the same day and delivered that night either at the airport or at the dealer's office or even at the roadside repair site.

Information systems play a critical role in managing market logistics, especially computers, point-of-sale terminals, uniform product codes, satellite tracking, electronic data interchange (EDI), and electronic funds transfer (EFT). These developments have enabled companies to make promises such as "the product will be at dock 25 at 10 A.M. tomorrow," and control this promise through information. Consider the following example:

An ad for Ryder Integrated Logistics, Inc.

- **Wal-Mart.** Wal-Mart was one of the first retailers to make heavy investments in information technology. It equipped its stores with computerized scanning equipment for cash registers. This equipment enabled Wal-Mart to know what customers are buying and therefore to tell manufacturers what to produce and where to ship the goods. Wal-Mart requires its suppliers to ship their goods tagged and hung, so that they can be moved directly into the store's selling space, thus reducing warehousing and data processing costs. As a result, Wal-Mart uses only 10 percent of their space for goods storage, compared to the 25 percent average nonselling space in competitors' stores. Another result of Wal-Mart's computerized ordering system is that Wal-Mart insists on linking its computers directly to its suppliers, bypassing brokers and other intermediaries. Suppliers such as Procter & Gamble, Kraft, and others are given the responsibility of making resupply decisions based on their access to Wal-Mart's information system. To discourage oversupply, Wal-Mart doesn't pay its suppliers until their products are sold.[24]

Market logistics involves several activities. The first is sales forecasting, on the basis of which the company schedules distribution, production, and inventory levels. Production plans indicate the materials the purchasing department must order. These materials arrive through inbound transportation, enter the receiving area, and are stored in raw-material inventory. Raw materials are converted into finished goods. Finished-goods inventory is the link between customer orders and manufacturing activity. Customers' orders draw down the finished-goods inventory level, and manufacturing activity builds it up. Finished goods flow off the assembly line and pass through packaging, in-plant warehousing, shipping-room processing, outbound transportation, field warehousing, and customer delivery and servicing.

Management has become concerned about the total cost of market logistics—the cost to wrap, bundle, load, unload, sort, reload, and transport goods. Logistics can amount to 30 to 40 percent of the product's cost. The grocery industry alone thinks it can decrease its annual operating costs by 10 percent, or $45 billion, by revamping its market logistics. A typical box of breakfast cereal spends 104 days getting from factory to supermarket, chugging through a labyrinth of wholesalers, distributors, brokers, and consolidators.[25] With inefficiencies like these, it's no wonder that experts call market logistics "the last frontier for cost economies." Lower market-logistics costs will permit lower prices, yield higher profit margins, or both. But though the cost of market logistics can be high, a well-planned program can be a potent tool in competitive marketing. Companies can attract additional customers by offering better service, faster cycle time, or lower prices through market-logistics improvements.

What happens if a firm's market logistics are not set up properly? Companies lose customers when they fail to supply goods on time. Kodak launched a national advertising campaign for a new instant camera before it had delivered enough cameras to the stores. Customers found that it was not available and bought Polaroid cameras instead.

MARKET-LOGISTICS OBJECTIVES

Many companies state their market-logistics objective as "getting the right goods to the right places at the right time for the least cost." Unfortunately, this objective provides little practical guidance. No market-logistics system can simultaneously maximize customer service and minimize distribution cost. Maximum customer service implies large inventories, premium transportation, and multiple warehouses, all of which raise market-logistics costs.

A company cannot achieve market-logistics efficiency by asking each market-logistics manager to minimize his or her own logistics costs. Market-logistics costs interact and are often negatively related. For example:

> The traffic manager favours rail shipment over air shipment because rail costs less. However, because the railways are slower, rail shipment ties up working capital longer, delays customer payment, and might cause customers to buy from competitors who offer faster service.

The shipping department uses cheap containers to minimize shipping costs. Cheaper containers lead to a higher rate of damaged goods and customer ill will. The inventory manager favours low inventories. This increases stockouts, back orders, paperwork, special production runs, and high-cost fast-freight shipments.

Given that market-logistics activities involve strong trade-offs, decisions must be made on a total system basis. The starting point is to study what customers require and what competitors are offering. Customers are interested in on-time delivery, supplier willingness to meet emergency needs, careful handling of merchandise, and supplier willingness to take back defective goods and resupply them quickly.

The company must then research the relative importance of these service outputs. For example, service-repair time is very important to buyers of copying equipment. Xerox developed a service-delivery standard that can put a disabled machine anywhere in North America back into operation within three hours after receiving the service request. It then designed a service division of personnel, parts, and locations to deliver on this promise.

The company must also consider competitors' service standards. It will normally want to match or exceed the competitors' service level. But the objective is to maximize profits, not sales. The company must look at the costs of providing higher levels of service. Some companies offer less service and charge a lower price. Other companies offer more service and charge a premium price.

The company ultimately has to establish some promise to the market. Coca-Cola wants to "put Coke within an arm's length of desire." Some companies go even further, defining standards for each service factor.

One appliance manufacturer has established the following service standards: to deliver at least 95 percent of the dealer's orders within seven days of order receipt, to fill the dealer's orders with 99 percent accuracy, to answer dealer inquiries on order status within three hours, and to ensure that damage to merchandise in transit does not exceed one percent.

Given the market-logistics objectives, the company must design a system that will minimize the cost of achieving these objectives. Each possible market-logistics system will lead to the following cost:

$$M = T + FW + VW + S$$

where M = total market-logistics cost of proposed system
   T = total freight cost of proposed system
   FW = total fixed warehouse cost of proposed system
   VW = total variable warehouse costs (including inventory) of proposed system
   S = total cost of lost sales due to average delivery delay under proposed system

Choosing a market-logistics system calls for examining the total cost (M) associated with different proposed systems and selecting the system that minimizes it. If it is hard to measure S, the company should aim to minimize $T+FW+VW$ for a target level of customer service.

MARKET-LOGISTICS DECISIONS

Four major decisions must be made with regard to market logistics: (1) How should orders be handled? (order processing); (2) Where should stocks be located? (warehousing); (3) How much stock should be held? (inventory); and (4) How should goods be shipped? (transportation).

Order Processing

Most companies today are trying to shorten the *order-to-remittance cycle*—that is, the elapsed time between an order's receipt, delivery, and payment. This cycle involves many steps, including order transmission by the salesperson, order entry and customer credit check, inventory and production scheduling, order and invoice shipment, and receipt of payment. The longer this cycle takes, the lower the customer's satisfaction and the lower the company's profits. But companies are making great progress. For example, General Electric operates an information system that checks the customer's credit standing upon receipt of an order, and determines whether and where the items are in stock. The computer issues an order to ship, bills the customer, updates the inventory records, sends a production order for new stock, and relays the message back to the sales representative that the customer's order is on its way—all in less than 15 seconds.

- **Sara Lee.** Sara Lee Branded Apparel, a division of the giant Sara Lee Corporation, says that retail conglomerate, Dayton Hudson's, willingness to share information with its suppliers separates this company from its competitors. Dayton's Global Merchandising System (GMS) is a supply chain system with more than 60 applications, including forecasting, ordering, and trend analysis. A retailer belonging to the Dayton Hudson chain may order a certain number of sweatshirts from Sara Lee Branded Apparel, without specifying more than style. As the delivery date draws near, the retailer analyzes trends for colours and sizes. Based on those forecasts, Sara Lee makes trial lots, and the retailer starts to sell them. If customers buy more navy sweatshirts, the retailer adjusts its order. Result: Both Sara Lee and the retailer have fewer goods in inventory and fewer markdowns.[26]

Sara Lee
www.saralee.com

Warehousing

Every company must store finished goods until they are sold, because production and consumption cycles rarely match. The storage function helps to smooth discrepancies between production and quantities desired by the market. The company must decide on the number of stocking locations. More stocking locations means that goods can be delivered to customers more quickly. But it also means higher warehousing costs.

Some inventory is kept at or near the plant, and the rest is located in warehouses in other locations. The company might own private warehouses and also rent space in public warehouses. *Storage warehouses* store goods for moderate-to-long periods of time. *Distribution warehouses* receive goods from various company plants and suppliers and move them out as soon as possible. For example, after National Semiconductor shut down its six storage warehouses and set up a central distribution warehouse in Singapore, its standard delivery time decreased by 47 percent, its distribution costs fell 2.5 percent, and its sales increased 34 percent.[27]

The older multistoried warehouses with slow elevators and inefficient materials-handling procedures are receiving competition from newer single-storey *automated warehouses* with advanced materials-handling systems under the control of a central computer. The computer reads store orders and directs lift trucks and electric hoists to gather goods according to bar codes, move them to loading docks, and issue invoices. These warehouses have reduced worker injuries, labour costs, pilferage, and breakage and improved inventory control. When the Helene Curtis Company replaced its six antiquated warehouses with a new $32-million facility, it cut its distribution costs by 40 percent.[28]

Inventory

Inventory levels represent a major market-logistics decision. Salespeople would like their companies to carry enough stock to fill all customer orders immediately. However, this is not cost effective. *Inventory cost increases at an increasing rate as the customer service level approaches 100 percent.* Management would need to know by how much sales and profits would increase as a result of carrying larger inventories and promising faster order-fulfilment times, then make a decision.

Inventory decision making involves knowing when to order and how much to order. As inventory draws down, management must know at what stock level to place a new order. This stock level is called the *order (reorder) point*. An order point of 20 means reordering when the stock falls to 20 units. The order point should balance the risks of stockout against the costs of overstock.

The other decision is how much to order. The larger the quantity ordered, the less frequently an order must be placed. The company needs to balance order-processing costs and inventory-carrying costs. *Order-processing* costs for a manufacturer consist of *setup costs* and *running costs* (operating costs when production is running) for the item. If setup costs are low, the manufacturer can produce the item often, and the average cost per item is stable and equal to the running costs. If setup costs are high, however, the manufacturer can reduce the average cost per unit by producing a long run and carrying more inventory.

Order-processing costs must be compared with *inventory-carrying costs*. The larger the average stock carried, the higher the inventory-carrying costs. These carrying costs include storage charges, cost of capital, taxes and insurance, and depreciation and obsolescence. Carrying costs might run as high as 30 percent of inventory value. This means that marketing managers who want their companies to carry larger inventories need to show that the larger inventories would produce incremental gross profit to exceed incremental inventory-carrying costs.

The optimal order quantity can be determined by observing how order-processing costs and inventory-carrying costs sum up at different order levels. Figure 17.2 shows that the order-processing cost per unit decreases with the number of units ordered because the order costs are spread over more units. Inventory-carrying charges per unit increase with the number of units ordered because each unit remains longer in inventory. The two cost curves are summed vertically into a total-cost curve. The lowest point on the total-cost curve is projected down on the horizontal axis to find the optimal order quantity Q^*.[29]

Just-in-time production methods promise to change inventory-planning practices. Just-in-time production consists of arranging for supplies to come into the factory at the rate that they are needed. If the suppliers are dependable, then the manufacturer can carry much lower levels of inventory and still meet customer-order-fulfilment standards. Consider the following example:

Tesco
www.tesco.co.uk

- **Tesco.** Tesco, the large British supermarket chain, has set up an innovative JIT market logistics system. Tesco's management wanted to greatly reduce costly backroom storage space. It accomplished this by arranging twice-a-day delivery of replenishment stock. Ordinarily it would have needed three separate trucks to deliver frozen goods, refrigerated goods, and regular goods on each trip. Instead, it designed new trucks with three compartments to carry the three types of goods.

Transportation

Marketers need to be concerned with transportation decisions. Transportation choices will affect product pricing, on-time delivery performance, and the condition of the goods when they arrive, all of which affects customer satisfaction.

FIGURE 17.2

Determining Optimal Order Quantity

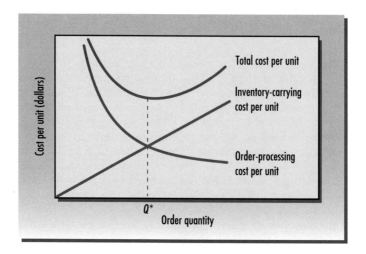

In shipping goods to its warehouses, dealers, and customers, the company can choose among five transportation modes: rail, air, truck, waterway, and pipeline. Shippers consider such criteria as speed, frequency, dependability, capability, availability, traceability, and cost. For speed, air and truck are the prime contenders. If the goal is low cost, then it is water and pipeline.

Shippers are increasingly combining two or more transportation modes, thanks to containerization. *Containerization* consists of putting the goods in boxes or trailers that are easy to transfer between two transportation modes. *Piggyback* describes the use of rail and trucks; *fishyback*, water and trucks; *trainship*, water and rail; and *airtruck*, air and trucks. Each coordinated mode offers specific advantages. For example, piggyback is cheaper than trucking alone, yet provides flexibility and convenience.

In deciding on transportation modes, shippers can choose from private, contract, and common carriers. If the shipper owns its own truck or air fleet, the shipper becomes a *private carrier*. A *contract carrier* is an independent organization selling transportation services to others on a contract basis. A *common carrier* provides services between predetermined points on a scheduled basis and is available to all shippers at standard rates.

ORGANIZATIONAL LESSONS ABOUT MARKET LOGISTICS

Experience with market logistics has taught executives several lessons. The first is that companies should appoint a senior vice president to be the single point of contact for all logistical elements. This executive should be accountable for logistical performance on both cost and customer-satisfaction criteria. The aim is to manage logistics to create high customer satisfaction at a reasonable cost. Here is an example:

■ **Sears.** Sears, Roebuck & Company owns a huge credit company called Sears Credit, which serves over 60 million credit-card holders and accounts for over 50 percent of all merchandise sold in Sears stores. To improve customer service, Sears formed a strategic alliance with Total Systems Services (TSYS), a third-party credit-card processing service. Alan J. Lacy, president of Sears Credit, stressed the ability of TSYS to track delinquent accounts more quickly and effectively, thus improving collections. Lacy is well aware that constant review of logistics—no matter the size of the business—can lead to improved profits.[30]

Market-logistics strategies must be derived from business strategies, rather than solely cost considerations. The logistics system must be information intensive and establish electronic links among all the significant parties. Finally, the company should set its logistics goals to match or exceed competitors' service standards and should involve members of all relevant teams in the planning process.

SUMMARY

1. Retailing includes all the activities involved in selling goods or services directly to final consumers for personal, nonbusiness use. Retailers can be understood in terms of store retailing, nonstore retailing, and retail organizations.

2. Like products, retail-store types pass through stages of growth and decline. As existing stores offer more services to remain competitive, their costs and prices go up, which opens the door to new retail forms that offer a mix of merchandise and services at lower prices. The major types of retail stores are specialty stores; department stores; supermarkets; convenience stores; discount stores; off-price retailers (factory outlets, independent off-price retailers, and warehouse clubs); superstores (combination stores and hypermarkets); and catalogue showrooms.

3. Although the overwhelming majority of goods and services is sold through stores, nonstore retailing has been growing much faster than store retailing. The major types of nonstore retailing are direct selling (one-to-one selling, one-to-many-party selling, and multilevel network marketing); direct marketing; automatic vending; and buying services.

4. Although many retail stores are independently owned, an increasing number are falling under some form of corporate retailing. Retail organizations achieve many economies of scale, such as greater purchasing power, wider brand recognition, and better-trained employees. The major types of corporate retailing are corporate chain stores, voluntary chains, retailer cooperatives, consumer cooperatives, franchise organizations, and merchandising conglomerates.

5. Like all marketers, retailers must prepare marketing plans that include decisions on target markets, product assortment and procurement, services and store atmosphere, price, promotion, and place. These decisions must take into account the major trends in retailing.

6. Wholesaling includes all the activities involved in selling goods or services to those who buy for resale or business use. Manufacturers use wholesalers because wholesalers can perform functions better and more cost effectively than the manufacturer can. These functions include, but are not limited to, selling and promoting, buying and assortment building, bulk breaking, warehousing, transportation, financing, risk bearing, dissemination of market information, and provision of management services and consulting.

7. There are four types of wholesalers: merchant wholesalers (full-service wholesalers like wholesale merchants and industrial distributors, and limited-service wholesalers like cash-and-carry wholesalers, truck wholesalers, drop shippers, rack jobbers, producers' cooperatives, and mail-order wholesalers); brokers and agents (including manufacturers' agents, selling agents, purchasing agents, and commission merchants); manufacturers' and retailers' sales branches, sales offices, and purchasing offices; and miscellaneous wholesalers such as agricultural assemblers and auction companies.

8. Like retailers, wholesalers must decide on target markets, product assortment and services, price, promotion, and place. The most successful wholesalers are those who adapt their services to meet their suppliers' and target customers' needs, recognizing that they exist to add value to the channel.

9. Producers of physical products and services must decide on market logistics—the best way to store and move their goods and services to market destinations. The logistical task is to coordinate the activities of suppliers, purchasing agents, manufacturers, marketers, channel members, and customers. Major gains in logistical efficiency have come from advances in information technology. Though the cost of market logistics can be high, a well-planned market-logistics program can be a potent tool in competitive marketing. The ultimate goal of market logistics is to meet customers' requirements in an efficient and profitable way.

APPLICATIONS

CHAPTER CONCEPTS

1. Identify a major retailer in each of the service level categories that follow and indicate whether its product assortment is deep, broad, or scrambled. Discuss the broad positioning strategy used in each level. *Store Retailers:* Specialty store, department store, mass merchandiser, supermarket, combination store, hypermarket, discount store, catalogue showroom. *Nonstore retailers:* Direct selling, mail-order selling, home shopping, automatic vending, buying service. *Retail Organizations:* Corporate chain, voluntary chain, retailer cooperative, consumer cooperative, franchise organization, merchandising chain.

2. Apply the wheel-of-retailing concept to the brokerage business. How did this industry begin? How has it changed and evolved over the years? Where does the industry stand now?

3. A company's inventory-carrying cost is 30 percent. A marketing manager wants her company to increase its inventory investment from $400 000 to $500 000, believing this would lead to increased sales of $120 000 because of greater customer loyalty and service. The gross profit on sales is 20 percent. Does it pay the company to increase its inventory investment?

M A R K E T I N G   A N D   A D V E R T I S I N G

1. Figure 1 shows an ad by the Canadian Professional Logistics Institute that appeared in a national business publication. Describe the major logistics challenges faced by Clearwater Fine Foods. Describe the major market-logistics decisions that Clearwater must make in order to market lobsters around the world. Why is professional training and support from organizations like the Canadian Professional Logistics Institute important and valuable? Why is logistics becoming an increasingly important issue for many companies like those cited in the ad?

Thanks to logistics, lobsters can fly.

To cities all over the world. Any time of year. And with no genetic engineering required.

"Lobsters are like eggs – an accident waiting to happen," sighs professional logistician Ron Carter of Clearwater Fine Foods in Bedford, Nova Scotia.

As distribution director of the world's largest lobster exporter, Carter knows the tasty crustaceans are worthless unless they arrive fresh and healthy. So the lobsters start their journey relaxing in an Olympic-sized pool, then are transferred to specially designed shelves flushed with seawater. Having a ready supply of premium, hard-shell lobsters in and out of season calls for the kinds of organizational skills only professional logisticians can provide. Which is why Clearwater relies so heavily on people like Ron Carter.

In fact, professional logistics is helping more Canadian companies than ever spread their wings. Many – including Canadian Tire, IBM, Nabisco and Xerox Canada – have joined the Canadian Professional Logistics Institute, the national governing body dedicated to teaching, developing and promoting logistics.

To learn how your business can also profit from logistics and corporate membership in the Logistics Institute, phone or e-mail us today. You never know what may come out of it.

CANADIAN PROFESSIONAL LOGISTICS INSTITUTE
10 King Street East, 4th Floor, Toronto, Ontario M5C 1C3
Tel: (416) 363-3005   Fax: (416) 363-5598
e-mail: loginfo@loginstitute.ca   website: www.loginstitute.ca

Logistics. The driving force of human achievement.

Figure 1

FOCUS ON TECHNOLOGY

Clearance sales are a good way for retailers to mark down excess inventory and sell items quickly to make room for new merchandise. But how do nonstore retailers get the message out to their customers? Catalogue retailer Lands' End promotes its sales in three ways. First, it periodically mails out overstock catalogues loaded with bargains. Second, it posts new sale items twice a week on its Web site, inviting customers to buy with a click of the mouse. Third, it invites customers to subscribe to a weekly Overstocks Newsletter delivered via e-mail.

To see how Lands' End conducts cyberspace clearance sales, visit its Web site. Browse the home page and then click on the overstock section. After looking at the twice-weekly clearance postings, click to read about subscribing to the Overstocks Newsletter. What overall pricing strategy is Lands' End using? Why would the company want to e-mail sale newsletters in addition to posting sale items on its Web site twice a week? Why would customers want to subscribe? Why would the company print an overstocks catalogue in addition to posting sales information on its Web site?

MARKETING FOR THE 21ST CENTURY

Specialty stores selling licensed merchandise are among the brightest stars in the retail universe these days. Consider the Warner Brothers Studio Stores, a chain of 185 outlets operating in Canada, the United States and 11 other countries. You can get a hint of the fun-filled store atmosphere by visiting the chain's Web site, where Bugs Bunny and other licensed characters cavort across pages of licensed merchandise for children, adults, gifts, and the home. How do the license holders benefit from the way the Warner Brothers Studio Stores display and sell their merchandise? How does Warner Brothers benefit from the association with well-known licensed characters?

YOU'RE THE MARKETER: SONIC MARKETING PLAN

Retailers and wholesalers play a critical role in marketing strategy because of their relationships with the final consumer. For this reason, manufacturers need to manage their connections effectively with these intermediaries in the marketing channel.

You are responsible for channel management for Sonic's shelf stereos, including relationships with wholesalers and retailers. Look again at the company's current situation, especially your distribution situation and plans. Then answer these questions about working with wholesalers and retailers:

- *Ideally, what types of retailers should Sonic approach to carry its products? What are the benefits and disadvantages of selling through these retailers?*

- *Of the stores that currently carry Sonic's products, which types of retailers seem to be gaining in popularity—and which are decreasing?*

- *What would Sonic have to do to get its products into retailers on your ideal list? Is this a priority for Sonic?*

- *What role should wholesalers play in Sonic's distribution strategy? Why?*

Now that you have examined Sonic's retail and wholesale opportunities and considered the effect on its marketing plans and goals, summarize your plans and conclusions in a written marketing plan or type them into the Marketing Situation/Channels and Marketing Strategy/Marketing Mix sections of the Marketing Plan Pro software.

Managing Integrated Marketing Communications

PROFILE:

Canadian Marketing Excellence

"Integrated marketing communications is a way of looking at the whole marketing process from the viewpoint of the receiver," says Philip Kotler. Alan Quarry, president of Quarry Integrated Communications, has to agree. "Clients count on us to help build their business, build their brands, build their customer relationships and build their profits.... and we deliver," states Alan Quarry, "head coach" of Quarry Integrated Communications. The firm is based in Waterloo, Ontario, and it also has offices in Toronto and Dallas.

Quarry Integrated Communications focuses on building demand for considered-purchase goods and services in the information technology, financial services, agribusiness, and health care segments. Nortel

Networks, Hewlett-Packard, Royal Bank, Cyanamid Crop Protection, Clarica Life, Hoffmann-la Roche, Elanco Animal Health , FedEx, Merck Frosst, and Sprint Canada are among the clients that work with the Quarry team. They use the full range of integrated services offered by Quarry including strategic communications planning; advertising; public relations; database marketing; graphic design; interactive multimedia; and technical documentation.

Quarry is a highly innovative firm that broke the traditional advertising agency model in the early 1990s and developed a new model for doing business. "The structure of the traditional ad agency seemed dysfunctional and almost anti-client to me," stated Quarry. "All the internal politics and focus on driving mass media spending was not the kind of organization we wanted to be. We couldn't be the type of strategic ally that our clients needed to be successful in the future."

"We believe that mass media advertising is communications 'at' the consumer. Integrated Marketing Communications (IMC) is a conversation 'with' the consumer. There will be a lot less marketing in the future and a lot more 'customerizing' as IMC guru Don Schultz has pointed out. We believe that relationship building dialogue with the customer strengthens and can even improve products and brands."

To solve integrated marketing communications problems, Quarry uses a trademarked four-stage approach called the Demand Builder. It uses the construction process as a metaphor. Demand Builder starts with the Survey Stage, where insights are developed about the customer, the brand, and the category. In the next stage, Architecture, those insights are connected to generate the most powerful strategic idea or connection to the consumer. This is labelled the Keystone. In the Engineering stage, the most effective, relevant communications tools that fit tactics to strategy are carefully selected and integrated. The final stage, Craftsmanship, is where the Quarry team produces work of enduring quality by paying close attention to detail and by emphasizing effective ideas over merely original ones.

To help make this all happen, Quarry Integrated is wired—by the ethernet hubs, Internet routers, T-1 lines, videoconferencing, leading-edge telephony and software that they use to improve communications between Quarry and their clients. This "technology-enhanced communications" approach is another difference between Quarry and many of their competitors. "Lots of ad agencies seem to think of buying technology as being an 'expense ... We think of acquiring the tools we use as an 'investment,'" explained Alan Quarry. "It's a mindset thing. We know that we cannot be a successful, global organization and help our clients build without being tech-savvy."

In an industry characterized by disturbingly high staff-turnover rates, Quarry Integrated has had one of Canada's best track records for continuity. Many believe that Quarry's high retention rate has a lot to do with the environment created at the workplace. It's an environment—without corner offices. In fact, even the president does not have an assigned office. Instead he pushes his mobile work surface around and answers to the nickname "Virtu-Al." It has idea rooms named the Eureka Room and the Kaboom Room. There's a

This chapter examines three major questions:

- How does communication work?

- What are the major steps in developing an integrated marketing communications program?

- Who should be responsible for marketing communications planning?

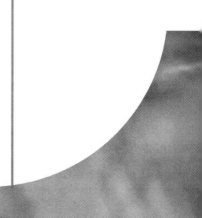

1950s-style diner, called Al's Diner (in honour of Albert Einstein) where the Quarry team and guests meet, work, and access a free supply of fruit, vegetables, and other brain food. It's an environment that offers at least one view of the outside world no matter where you stand. A workplace with the motto *"Think like the customer, Always anticipate, And have fun!"* is posted throughout the offices.

Quarry is also the birthplace of "looping." Looping is an organization structure that focuses all of a company's efforts on the client's needs. Rather than having static units with traditional hierarchies, looping draws together the range of people and skills that can best meet a client's particular requirements. "Looping is a team-based structure which is very organic. It expands and shrinks quickly as needed. It's as much strong communication bonds between individuals who share a common goal—to help the client build their business— as it is a formal organizational process. And I'm happy and proud to say that it works," states Quarry. Many North American agencies have visited Quarry Integrated Communications and have adopted or adapted the looping approach to doing business.

Throughout the Quarry environment you'll find hand-lettered signs:" Our mission is to help our clients build their businesses through integrated communications". Quarry clients throughout North America would agree. Mission accomplished!

Source: Alan Quarry provided the information specifically for publication in *Marketing Management.* In addition to his role as president of Quarry Integrated Communications, he finds time to teaches marketing communications to fourth-year honours business students at Wilfrid Laurier University. He is a strong believer that continuous learning is key to success in the modern economy. "As communicators we can never stop increasing our knowledge about consumer motivation and how effective communications work," states Quarry.

Modern marketing calls for more than developing a good product, pricing it attractively, and making it accessible. Companies must also communicate with present and potential stakeholders, and the general public. Every company is inevitably cast into the role of communicator and promoter. For most companies, the question is not whether to communicate but rather what to say, to whom, and how often.

The *marketing communications mix* consists of five major modes of communication:

1. *Advertising:* Any paid form of nonpersonal presentation and promotion of ideas, goods, or services by an identified sponsor.

2. *Sales promotion:* A variety of short-term incentives to encourage trial or purchase of a product or service.

3. *Public relations and publicity:* A variety of programs designed to promote or protect a company's image or its individual products.

4. *Personal selling:* Face-to-face interaction with one or more prospective purchasers for the purpose of making presentations, answering questions, and procuring orders.

5. *Direct marketing:* Use of mail, telephone, fax, e-mail, or Internet to communicate directly with or solicit a direct response from specific customers and prospects.[1]

The following chapters deal with advertising, sales promotion, and public relations; the sales force and personal selling; and direct and online marketing.

THE COMMUNICATION PROCESS

Today there is a new view of communications as an interactive dialogue between the company and its customers that takes place during the preselling, selling, consuming, and postconsuming stages. Companies must ask not only "How can we reach our customers?" but also "How can our customers reach us?"

Table 18.1 lists numerous communication platforms. Thanks to technological breakthroughs, people can now communicate through traditional media (newspapers, radio, telephone, television), as well as through newer media forms (computers, fax machines, cellular phones, and pagers). By decreasing communication costs, the new technologies have encouraged more companies to move from mass communication to more targeted communication and one-to-one dialogue.

But company communication goes beyond the specific communication platforms listed in Table 18.1. The product's styling and price, the package's shape and colour, the salesperson's manner and dress, the place's decor, the company's stationery—all communicate something to the buyers. Every *brand contact* delivers an impression that can strengthen or weaken a customer's view of the company. The whole marketing mix must be integrated to deliver a consistent message and strategic positioning.

The starting point is an audit of all the potential interactions target customers may have with the product and company. For example, someone interested in purchasing a new computer would talk to others, see television ads, read articles, look for information on the Internet, and observe computers in a store. The marketer needs to assess which experiences and impressions will have the most influence at each stage of the buying process. This understanding will help marketers allocate their communication dollars more efficiently.

To communicate effectively, marketers need to understand the fundamental elements underlying effective communication. Figure 18.1 shows a communication model with nine elements. Two represent the major parties in a communication—*sender* and *receiver*. Two represent the major communication tools—*message* and *media*. Four represent major communication functions—*encoding, decoding, response,* and *feedback*. The last element in the system is *noise* (random and competing messages that may interfere with the intended communication).[2]

TABLE 18.1

Common Communication Platforms

Advertising	Sales Promotion	Public Relations	Personal Selling	Direct Marketing
Print and broadcast ads	Contests, games, sweepstakes, lotteries	Press kits	Sales presentations	Catalogs
Packaging—outer	Premiums and gifts	Speeches	Sales meetings	Mailings
Packaging inserts	Sampling	Seminars	Incentive programs	Telemarketing
Motion pictures	Fairs and trade shows	Annual reports	Samples	Electronic shopping
Brochures and booklets	Exhibits	Charitable donations	Fairs and trade shows	TV shopping
Posters and leaflets	Demonstrations	Sponsorships		Fax mail
Directories	Coupons	Publications		E-mail
Reprints of ads	Rebates	Community relations		Voice mail
Billboards	Low-interest financing	Lobbying		
Display signs	Entertainment	Identity media		
Point-of-purchase displays	Trade-in allowances	Company magazine		
Audiovisual material	Continuity programs	Events		
Symbols and logos	Tie-ins			
Videotapes				

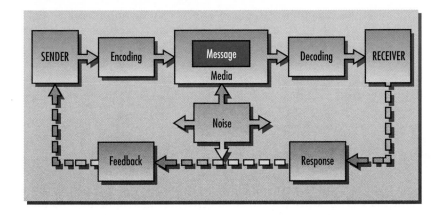

FIGURE 18.1

Elements in the Communication Process

The model underscores the key factors in effective communication. Senders must know what audiences they want to reach and what responses they want to get. They must encode their messages in a way that understands how the target audience usually decodes messages. They must transmit the message through efficient media that reach the target audience and develop feedback channels to monitor the responses.

For a message to be effective, the sender's encoding process must mesh with the receiver's decoding process. The more the sender's field of experience overlaps with that of the receiver, the more effective the message is likely to be. This puts a burden on communicators from one social stratum (such as advertising people) who want to communicate effectively with another stratum (such as factory workers).

The sender's task is to get his or her message through to the receiver. The target audience may not receive the intended message for any of three reasons:

1. *Selective attention:* People are bombarded by 1600 commercial messages a day, of which 80 are consciously noticed and about 12 provoke some reaction. Selective attention explains why ads with bold headlines promising something, such as "How to Make a Million," have a high likelihood of grabbing attention.

2. *Selective distortion:* Receivers will hear what fits into their belief system. As a result, receivers often add things to the message that are not there (*amplification*) and do not notice other things that are there (*levelling*). The communicator's task is to strive for simplicity, clarity, interest, and repetition to get the main points across.

3. *Selective retention:* People will retain in long-term memory only a small fraction of the messages that reach them. If the receiver's initial attitude toward the object is positive and he or she rehearses support arguments, the message is likely to be accepted and have high recall. If the initial attitude is negative and the person rehearses counterarguments, the message is likely to be rejected but to stay in long-term memory. Because much of persuasion requires the receiver's rehearsal of his or her own thoughts, much of what is called persuasion is actually self-persuasion.[3]

The communicator considers audience traits that correlate with persuasibility and uses them to guide message and media development. People of high education or intelligence are thought to be less persuasible, but the evidence is inconclusive. Those who accept external standards to guide their behaviour and who have a weak self-concept appear to be more persuasible, as do persons who have low self-confidence.[4]

Fiske and Hartley have outlined some general factors that influence the effectiveness of a communication:

■ The greater the monopoly of the communication source over the recipient, the greater the recipient's change or effect in favour of the source.

■ Communication effects are greatest where the message is in line with the receiver's existing opinions, beliefs, and dispositions.

- Communication can produce the most effective shifts on unfamiliar, lightly felt, peripheral issues, which do not lie at the centre of the recipient's value system.

- Communication is more likely to be effective where the source is believed to have expertise, high status, objectivity, or likability, but particularly where the source has power and can be identified with.

- The social context, group, or reference group will mediate the communication and influence whether the communication is accepted.[5]

 # DEVELOPING EFFECTIVE COMMUNICATIONS

There are eight steps in developing effective communications. The marketing communicator must (1) identify the target audience, (2) determine the communication objectives, (3) design the message, (4) select the communication channels, (5) establish the total communications budget, (6) decide on the communications mix, (7) measure the communications' results, and (8) manage the integrated marketing communication process.

IDENTIFYING THE TARGET AUDIENCE

The process must start with a clear target audience in mind: potential buyers of the company's products, current users, deciders, or influencers; individuals, groups, particular publics, or the general public. The target audience is a critical influence on the communicator's decisions on what to say, how to say it, when to say it, where to say it, and to whom to say it.

Image Analysis

A major part of audience analysis is assessing the current image of the company, its products, and its competitors.

- *Image* is the set of beliefs, ideas, and impressions a person holds regarding an object. People's attitudes and actions toward an object are highly conditioned by that object's image.

The first step is to measure the target audience's knowledge of the object, using the *familiarity scale:*

Never Heard of	Heard of Only	Know a Little Bit	Know a Fair Amount	Know Very Well

If most respondents circle only the first two categories, the challenge is to build greater awareness.

Respondents who are familiar with the product can be asked how they feel toward it, using the *favourability scale:*

Very Unfavourable	Somewhat Unfavourable	Indifferent	Somewhat Favourable	Very Favourable

If most respondents check the first two categories, then the organization must overcome a negative image problem.

The two scales can be combined to develop insight into the nature of the communication challenge. Suppose area residents are asked about their familiarity with and attitudes toward four local hospitals, A, B, C, and D. Their responses are averaged and shown in Figure 18.2. Hospital A has the most positive image: most people know it and like it. Hospital B is less familiar to most people, but those who know it like it. Hospital C is viewed negatively by those who know it, but (fortunately for the hospital) not too many people know it. Hospital D is seen as a poor hospital, and everyone knows it!

Each hospital faces a different communication task. Hospital A must work at maintaining its good reputation and high awareness. Hospital B must gain the attention of more people. Hospital C must find out why people dislike it and must take steps to improve its quality while keeping a low profile. Hospital D should lower its profile, improve its quality, and then seek public attention.

Each hospital needs to research the specific content of its image. The most popular tool for this research is the *semantic differential*.[6] It involves the following steps:

1. *Developing a set of relevant dimensions:* The researcher asks people to identify the dimensions they would use in thinking about the object: "What things do you think of when you consider a hospital?" If someone suggests "quality of medical care," this dimension would be turned into a five- or seven-point bipolar adjective scale, with "inferior medical care" at one end and "superior medical care" at the other. A set of additional dimensions for a hospital is shown in Figure 18.3.

2. *Reducing the set of relevant dimensions:* The number of dimensions should be kept small to avoid respondent fatigue. There are three types of scales:

   ■ Evaluation scales (good–bad qualities)
   ■ Potency scales (strong–weak qualities)
   ■ Activity scales (active–passive qualities)

   Using these scales as a guide, the researcher can remove scales that fail to provide much information.

3. *Administering the instrument to a sample of respondents:* The respondents are asked to rate one object at a time. The bipolar adjectives should be randomly arranged so that the unfavourable adjectives are not all listed on one side.

4. *Averaging the results:* Figure 18.3 shows the results of averaging the respondents' pictures of hospitals A, B, and C (hospital D is left out). Each hospital's image is represented by a vertical "line of means" that summarizes average perception of that hospital. Hospital A is seen as a large, modern, friendly, and superior hospital. Hospital C, in contrast, is seen as small, dated, impersonal, and inferior.

5. *Checking on the image variance:* Because each image profile is a line of means, it does not reveal how variable the image is. Did everyone see hospital B as shown, or was there considerable variation? In the first case, we would say that the image is highly *specific*; and in the second case, highly *diffused*. Some organizations prefer a diffused image so that different groups will see the organization in different ways.

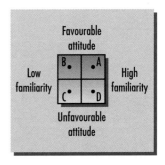

FIGURE 18.2

Familiarity–Favourability Analysis

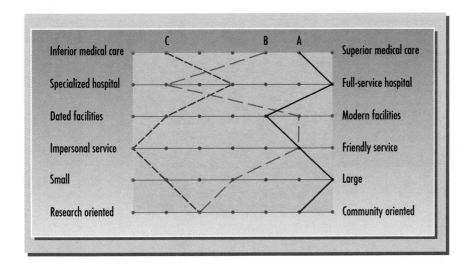

FIGURE 18.3

Images of Three Hospitals (Semantic Differential)

Management should now define a desired image if it differs from the current one. Suppose hospital C would like the public to view more favourably its medical care, facilities, and friendliness. Management must decide which image gaps it wants to close first. Is it more desirable to improve friendliness (through staff training programs) or the quality of its facilities (through renovation)? What would it cost to close a particular gap? How long would it take?

An organization seeking to improve its image must have great patience. Images are "sticky"; they persist long after the organization has changed. Image persistence is explained by the fact that once people have a certain image, they perceive what is consistent with that image. It will take highly disconfirming information to raise doubts and open their minds, especially when people do not have continuous or new firsthand experiences with the changed object. Wolverine World Wide of Rockford, Michigan, discovered this when its Hush Puppies brand of casual shoes lost its fashionable image. Then a fashion designer used Hush Puppies dyed in bright colours. The Hush Puppies image went from stodgy to avant garde. And once the "new" Hush Puppies were in demand, sales went from under 30 000 pairs in 1994 to 1.7 million pairs in 1996.[7]

DETERMINING THE COMMUNICATION OBJECTIVES

Once the target market and its perceptions are identified, the marketing communicator must decide on the desired audience response. The marketer can be seeking a *cognitive, affective,* or *behavioural* response. That is, the marketer might want to put something into the consumer's mind, change an attitude, or get the consumer to act. Even here, there are different models of consumer-response stages. Figure 18.4 summarizes the four best-known *response hierarchy models.*

All these models assume that the buyer passes through a cognitive, affective, and behavioural stage, in that order. This "learn–feel–do" sequence is appropriate when the audience has high involvement with a product category perceived to have high differentiation, as in purchasing an automobile. An alternative sequence, "do–feel–

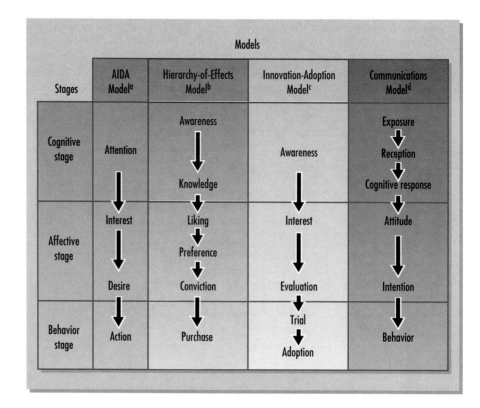

Response Hierarchy Models

Sources: (a) E.K. Strong, *The Psychology of Selling* (New York: McGraw-Hill, 1925), p. 9; (b) Robert J. Lavidge and Gary A. Steiner, "A Model for Predictive Measurements of Advertising Effectiveness," *Journal of Marketing*, October 1961, p. 61; (c) Everett M. Rogers, *Diffusion of Innovation* (New York: Free Press, 1962), pp. 79–86; (d) various sources.

FIGURE 18.4

learn," is relevant when the audience has high involvement but perceives little or no differentiation within the product category, as in purchasing aluminum siding. A third sequence, "learn–do–feel," is relevant when the audience has low involvement and perceives little differentiation within the product category, as in purchasing salt. By choosing the right sequence, the marketer can do a better job of planning communications.[8]

Here we will assume that the buyer has high involvement with the product category and perceives high differentiation within the category. We will illustrate the *hierarchy-of-effects* model (in the second column of Figure 18.4):

- *Awareness:* If most of the target audience is unaware of the object, the communicator's task is to build awareness, perhaps just name recognition, with simple messages repeating the product name. Suppose a small private school in Calgary seeks applicants from Vancouver, but has little name recognition there. Suppose there are 30 000 upscale parents in Vancouver who might potentially be interested in sending their children to the school. The school administration might set the objective of making 70 percent of these parents aware of the school within one year.

- *Knowledge:* The target audience might be aware of the private school's existence but not know much more. The school may want its target audience to know that it is a co-educational school with quality academic programs serving grades 6 through 12. The school thus needs to learn how many people in the target audience have little, some, or much knowledge about the school. If knowledge is weak, the school may decide to select knowledge of its name and teaching programs as its communication objective.

- *Liking:* Once target members know the product, how do they feel about it? If the parents look unfavourably on the school, , the communicator must find out why and then develop a communication campaign to shore up favourable feelings. If the unfavourable view is based on real problems, a communication campaign alone cannot do the job. The school will have to fix its problems and then communicate its renewed quality. Good public relations calls for "good deeds followed by good words."

- *Preference:* The target audience might like the product but not prefer it to others. In this case, the communicator must try to build consumer preference by promoting quality, value, performance, and other features. The communicator can check the campaign's success by measuring audience preference after the campaign.

- *Conviction:* Some of the parents might begin to prefer the school but not yet be convinced because of guilt about sending their children away to school. The communicator's job is to build conviction that doing so will be good for their children. for example, testimonials from satisfied parents might be used.

- *Purchase:* Finally, some members of the target audience might have conviction but not quite get around to taking action. They may wait for more information or plan to act later. The communicator must lead these consumers to take the final step by finding out why the parents are hesitating. If tuition cost is a problem, scholarships might be offered. If unfamiliarity is a problem, parents might be invited to visit the school, look at the facilities, and possibly let the children attend some classes.

DESIGNING THE MESSAGE

Having defined the desired response, the communicator moves to developing an effective message. Ideally, the message should gain *attention*, hold *interest*, arouse *desire*, and elicit *action* (AIDA model—see the first column of Figure 18.4). In practice, few messages take the consumer all the way from awareness through purchase, but the AIDA framework suggests the desirable qualities of any communication.

Formulating the message will require solving four problems: what to say (message content), how to say it logically (message structure), how to say it symbolically (message format), and who should say it (message source).

Message Content

In determining message content, management searches for an *appeal, theme, idea,* or *unique selling proposition.* There are three types of appeals: rational, emotional, and moral.

Rational appeals engage self-interest: They claim the product will produce certain benefits. Examples are messages demonstrating quality, economy, value, or performance. It is widely believed that industrial buyers are most responsive to rational appeals. They are knowledgeable about the product, trained to recognize value, and accountable to others for their choices. Consumers, when they buy certain big-ticket items, also tend to gather information and estimate benefits.

Emotional appeals attempt to stir up negative or positive emotions that will motivate purchase. Marketers search for the right *emotional selling proposition* (ESP). The product may be similar to the competition but have unique associations that can be promoted (examples are Michelin Tires, Harley-Davidson, and Rolex). Communicators also work with negative appeals such as fear, guilt, and shame to get people to do things (brush their teeth, have an annual health checkup) or stop doing things (smoking, alcohol or abuse, overeating). Fear appeals work best when they are not too strong. Research findings indicate that neither extremely strong nor extremely weak fear appeals are as effective as moderate ones. Furthermore, fear appeals work better when source credibility is high and when the communication promises to relieve, in a believable and efficient way, the fear it arouses.[9]

Advertising aimed at women has used fear appeals for generations: fear of not being attractive, fear of being overweight, or fear of being unpopular. However, this is starting to change. In a recent magazine ad for women's sports apparel, Nike showed a Barbie Doll, but stated, "You exercise to feel better about yourself—not to look like some toy." More and more companies like Labatt Breweries and Gatorade are portraying women as they are, not as some unattainable ideal. Kellogg Canada Inc., recently ran new ads for Special K Fibre Cereal that feature real-life Toronto fire fighter, Jacqueline Izzard. The campaign aims to tell women they need to care about their inside as well as their outside if they want to be really, strong, positive women, says company spokeswoman, Christine Lowry. Even cosmetic companies are beginning to use more realism. Cosmetics giant Elizabeth Arden Co., for example, recently introduced its new campaign, "Embrace Yourself." It focuses on older models who look like average people and the advertisements are oriented toward lifestyles rather than appearance. The change came after research revealed that women were turned off by the industry's focus on glamour and unattainable beauty.[10]

Kellogg Canada Inc. has started using real women to promote their Special K Fibre Cereal.

Communicators also use positive emotional appeals such as humour, love, pride, and joy. Evidence has not established that a humorous message is necessarily more effective than a straight version of the same message. Advocates for humorous messages claim that they attract more attention and create more liking and belief in the sponsor. Others maintain that humour can detract from comprehension, wear out its welcome fast, and overshadow the product.[11] Here is an example of successful humour:

- **Joe Boxer.** In 1978, Calvin Klein put male models wearing his new line of white briefs on billboards from coast to coast. Since then this once-staple item has become a fashion-driven one, with many other big name designers putting their names on waistband elastic in search of a piece of this $2.3-billion market. How to stand out in this well-toned crowd is a serious challenge. Joe Boxer chose humour in 1985 and has since turned a $1000 investment into a $100-million line for the whole family. Not only is the product wildly different—the first sale to a major department store was a red plaid number with a detachable raccoon tail—but its advertising and sales promotion also stand out. The wacky Web site (slogan: Wear Clean Underwear) attracts more than one million hits a month. One famous promotion was a deal with Virgin Atlantic Airways, which gave a free round-trip ticket to London on Virgin to those who bought five pairs of Joe Boxers. Stores sold out and five jumbo jets were filled.[12]

Joe Boxer
www.joeboxer.com

Moral appeals are directed to the audience's sense of what is right and proper. They are often used to exhort people to support social causes. An example is the appeal "Silence = Death," which is the slogan of Act-Up, the AIDS Coalition to Unleash Power.

Some advertisers believe messages are most persuasive when they are moderately discrepant with what the audience believes. Messages that state only what the audience already believes at best only reinforce beliefs. If the messages are too discrepant, they will be counterargued and disbelieved.

Companies that sell their products in different countries must be prepared to vary their message. In advertising its hair-care products in different countries, Helene Curtis adjusts its messages. Middle-class British women wash their hair frequently, whereas the opposite is true among Spanish women. Japanese women avoid overwashing their hair for fear of removing protective oils. See the Marketing for the 21st Century "Challenges in Global Advertising and Promotion."

Message Structure

Effectiveness depends on structure as well as content. Hovland's research at Yale has shed much light on message content and its relation to conclusion drawing, one- versus two-sided arguments, and order of presentation.

Some early experiments supported stating conclusions for the audience rather than allowing the audience to reach its own. Subsequent research, however, indicates that the best ads ask questions and allow readers and viewers to form their own conclusions.[13] Conclusion drawing might cause negative reactions if the communicator is seen as untrustworthy, or the issue is seen as too simple or highly personal. Drawing too explicit a conclusion can also limit appeal or acceptance. If Ford had hammered away that the Mustang was for young people, this strong definition might have blocked older age groups from buying it. Some *stimulus ambiguity* can lead to a broader market definition and more spontaneous purchases.

One would think that *one-sided presentations* that praise a product would be more effective than *two-sided arguments* that also mention shortcomings. Yet two-sided messages may be more appropriate, especially when some negative association must be overcome. In this spirit, Heinz ran the message "Heinz Ketchup is slow good" and Listerine ran the message "Listerine tastes bad twice a day."[14] Two-sided messages are more effective with more educated audiences and those who are initially opposed.[15]

Finally, the order in which arguments are presented is important.[16] In the case of a one-sided message, presenting the strongest argument first has the advantage of establishing attention and interest. This is important in newspapers and other media

Challenges in Global Advertising and Promotion

Multinational companies wrestle with a number of challenges in developing global communications programs. First, they must decide whether the product is appropriate for a country. Second, they must make sure that the market segment they address is both legal and customary. Third, they must decide if the style of the ad is acceptable or customary in all the countries involved. Fourth, they must decide whether ads should be created at headquarters or locally.

1. *Product*: Beer, wine, and spirits cannot be advertised or sold in Muslim countries. Tobacco products are subject to strict regulation in many countries; Canada and the United Kingdom now want not only to ban tobacco advertising, but also to outlaw sports sponsorship by tobacco companies. Global harmonization of cosmetic product regulations, known as the Florentine regulations, is being discussed. This will have a significant impact on advertisers, because the regulations affect issues such as product labelling, product safety, animal testing, and updated ingredient listings.

   Avon China Inc. was forced by the Chinese government to stop selling directly to Chinese consumers and to open retail stores, necessitating new advertising and promotion campaigns to reposition the company as a retailer, rather than a direct marketer.

2. Market segment: Coca-Cola has a pool of different commercials for different national market segments. Local and global segments managers decide which commercials work best for which segments. Recently, in a reverse of the usual order, a series of Coca-Cola commercials developed for the Russian market, using a talking bear and a man who transforms into a wolf, was shown in the United States. As Michael O'Neill, president of Coca-Cola's Nordic division, said: "This approach fits perfectly with the global nature of Coca-Cola and offers people a special look into a culture that is different from their own."

   Many U.S. toy makers were surprised to learn that in many countries, Norway and Sweden, for example, no TV ads may be directed at children under 12. Moreover, Sweden is lobbying to extend that ban to all EU member countries. To play it safe, McDonald's advertises itself as a family restaurant in Sweden. In Quebec, advertisers cannot direct messages at children under the age of 13.

3. Style: The style of the ad is also important, because comparative ads, while acceptable and even common in the United States and Canada, are less commonly used in the United Kingdom, unacceptable in Japan, and illegal in India and Brazil. PepsiCo found that its comparative taste test ad in Japan was refused by many TV stations and actually led to a lawsuit. China has restrictive censorship rules for TV and radio advertising; for example, the words "the best" are banned, as are ads that "violate social customs" or present women in "improper ways." Snickers got into trouble in Russia when it ran a ceaseless barrage of poorly dubbed American TV commercials to a people not used to TV advertising. Russian comics then began to take jabs at Snickers, and its brand name became a laughing stock.

4. Local or global: Today, more and more multinational companies are attempting to build a global brand image by using the same advertising in all their markets. FedEx's first global campaign was The Way the World Works. Ericsson, the Swedish telecommunications giant, spent $150 million on a global TV campaign with the tag line "Make yourself heard," which featured 007, James Bond. When Daimler AG and Chrysler merged to become the world's fifth-largest automaker, they ran a three-week ad campaign in more than 100 countries consisting of a 12-page magazine insert, nine newspaper spreads, and a 24-page brochure that was sent to business, government, and union leaders and to the news media. The campaign's tag line was "Expect the extraordinary," and it featured people from both companies working together. But even if a company favours strong corporate standardization, legal restrictions may force adaptations. Coca-Cola's Indian subsidiary was forced to end a promotion that offered prizes such as a trip to Hollywood, because it encouraged customers to buy in order to gamble, in violation of India's established trade practices.

Sources: Brian S. Akre, "Employees and a Pair of Dummies Star in DaimlerChrysler's First Ad Campaign," AP Online, November 15, 1998; Richard C. Morais, "Mobile Mayhem," *Forbes Magazine*, July, 6 1998, p. 138; Patti Bond, "Today's Topic: From Russia with Fizz, Coke Imports Ads," *Atlanta Journal and Constitution*, April 4, 1998, pp. E2; "Working in Harmony," *Soap Perfumery & Cosmetics*, July 1, 1998, p. 27; Rodger Harrabin, "A Commercial Break for Parents," *Independent*, September 8, 1998, p. 19; T. B. Song and Leo Wong, "Getting the Word Out," *The China Business Review*, September 1, 1998; "U.K. Tobacco Ad Ban Will Include Sports Sponsorship," AdAgeInternational.com, May 1997; "Coca-Cola Rapped for Running Competition in India," AdAgeInternational.com, February 1997; "Avon Campaign Repositions Company in China," AdAgeInternational.com, July 1998; Christian Caryl, "We Will Bury You ..... With a Snickers Bar," *U.S. News & World Report*, January 26, 1998, p. 50; Naveen Donthu, "A Cross-Country Investigation of Recall of and Attitude Toward Comparative Advertising," *Journal of Advertising*, 27 (June 22, 1998): 111.

where the audience often does not attend to the whole message. With a captive audience, however, a climactic presentation might be more effective. In the case of a two-sided message, if the audience is initially opposed, the communicator might start with the other side's argument and conclude with his or her strongest argument.[17]

Message Format

The communicator must develop a strong message format. In a print ad, the communicator has to decide on headline, copy, illustration, and colour. If the message is to be carried over the radio, the communicator has to choose words, voice qualities, and vocalizations. The "sound" of an announcer promoting a used automobile has to be different from one promoting a new Cadillac. If the message is to be carried on television or in person, all of these elements plus body language (nonverbal clues) have to be planned. Presenters have to pay attention to facial expressions, gestures, dress, posture, and hairstyle. If the message is carried by the product or its packaging, the communicator must pay attention to colour, texture, scent, size, and shape.

Colour plays a particularly important role in food preferences. When women sampled four cups of coffee that had been taken from brown, blue, red, and yellow containers (all the coffee was identical, although the women did not know this), 75 percent felt that the coffee next to the brown container tasted too strong and nearly 85 percent judged the coffee next to the red container to be the richest.

Message Source

Messages delivered by attractive or popular sources achieve higher attention and recall. This is why advertisers often use celebrities as spokespeople. Celebrities are likely to be effective when they personify a key product attribute. But what is equally important is the spokesperson's credibility. Messages delivered by highly credible sources are more persuasive. Pharmaceutical companies want doctors to testify about product benefits because doctors have high credibility. Anti-drug crusaders will use ex-drug addicts because they have higher credibility for students than teachers do.

What factors underlie source credibility? The three most often identified are expertise, trustworthiness, and likability.[18] *Expertise* is the specialized knowledge the communicator possesses to back the claim. *Trustworthiness* is related to how objective and honest the source is perceived to be. Friends are trusted more than strangers or salespeople, and people who are not paid to endorse a product are viewed as more trustworthy than people who are paid.[19] *Likeability* describes the source's attractiveness. Qualities like candour, humour, and naturalness make a source more likeable. The most highly credible source would be a person who scores high on all three dimensions.

If a person has a positive attitude toward a source and a message, or a negative attitude toward both, a state of *congruity* is said to exist. What happens if the person holds one attitude toward the source and the opposite toward the message? Suppose a homemaker hears a likeable celebrity praise a brand that she dislikes? Osgood and Tannenbaum posit that *attitude change will take place in the direction of increasing the amount of congruity between the two evaluations.*[20] The homemaker will end up respecting the celebrity somewhat less or respecting the brand somewhat more. If she encounters the same celebrity praising other disliked brands, she will eventually develop a negative view of the celebrity and maintain her negative attitudes toward the brands. The *principle of congruity* implies that communicators can use their good image to reduce some negative feelings toward a brand but in the process might lose some esteem with the audience.

SELECTING COMMUNICATION CHANNELS

The communicator must select efficient communication channels to carry the message. For example, pharmaceutical company salespeople can rarely wrest more than 10 minutes' time from a busy physician. Their presentation must be crisp, quick, and convincing. This makes pharmaceutical sales calling extremely expensive. The industry has had to amplify its battery of communication channels. These include placing ads in medical journals, sending direct mail (including audio and videotapes), passing out free samples, and even telemarketing. Pharmaceutical companies sponsor clinical conferences to which they invite and pay for a large number of physicians to spend a weekend listening to leading physicians extol certain drugs in the morning, followed by an afternoon of golf or tennis. Salespeople will arrange evening teleconferences where physicians are invited to discuss a common problem with an expert.

Salespeople also will sponsor small group lunches and dinners. All of these channels are used in the hope of building physician preference for their branded therapeutic agent.

Communication channels are of two types, *personal* and *nonpersonal*. Within each are many subchannels.

Personal Communication Channels

Personal communication channels involve two or more persons communicating directly with each other face to face, person to audience, over the telephone, or through e-mail. Personal communication channels derive their effectiveness through the opportunities for individualizing the presentation and feedback.

A further distinction can be drawn among advocate, expert, and social communication channels. *Advocate channels* consist of company salespeople contacting buyers in the target market. *Expert channels* consist of independent experts making statements to target buyers. *Social channels* consist of neighbours, friends, family members, and associates talking to target buyers. In a study of 7000 consumers in seven European countries, 60 percent said they were influenced to use a new brand by family and friends.[21]

Many companies are becoming acutely aware of the power of "word of mouth." They are seeking ways to stimulate social channels to recommend products and services. Regis McKenna advises a software company launching a new product to promote it initially to the trade press, opinion luminaries, and financial analysts, who can supply favourable word of mouth; then to dealers; and finally to customers.[22] MCI attracted customers with its Friends and Family program, which encourages MCI users to ask friends and family members to use MCI so that both parties will benefit from lower telephone rates. See the Marketing Memo "How to Develop Word-of-Mouth Referral Sources to Build Business."

Personal influence carries especially great weight in two situations. One is with products that are expensive, risky, or purchased infrequently. Here buyers are likely to be strong information seekers. The other situation is where the product suggests something about the user's status or taste. Here buyers will consult others to avoid embarrassment.

Companies can take several steps to stimulate personal influence channels to work on their behalf:

■ *Identify influential individuals and companies and devote extra effort to them:*[23] In industrial selling, the entire industry might follow the market leader in adopting innovations.

■ *Create opinion leaders by supplying certain people with the product on attractive terms:* A new tennis racket might be offered initially to members of high school tennis teams at a special low price. Or Toyota could offer its more satisfied customers a small gift if they are willing to advise prospective buyers.

■ *Work through community influentials such as local disk jockeys, class presidents, and presidents of women's organizations:* When Ford introduced the Thunderbird, it sent invitations to executives offering them a free car to drive for the day. Of the 15 000 who took advantage of the offer, 10 percent indicated that they would become buyers, whereas 84 percent said they would recommend it to a friend.

■ *Use influential or believable people in testimonial advertising:* Quaker Oats pays basketball star Michael Jordan several million dollars to make Gatorade commercials. Jordan is viewed as the world's premiere athlete, so his association with a sports drink is a credible connection, as is his extraordinary ability to connect with consumers, particularly children.

■ *Develop advertising that has high "conversation value":* Ads with high conversation value often have a slogan that becomes part of the national vernacular. In the mid-1980s, Wendy's "Where's the Beef?" campaign (showing an elderly lady named Clara questioning where the hamburger was hidden in all that bread) created high conversation value. Nike's "Just do it" ads have created a popular command for those unable to make up their minds or take some action.

- *Develop word-of-mouth referral channels to build business:* Professionals will often encourage clients to recommend their services. Dentists can ask satisfied patients to recommend friends and acquaintances and subsequently thank them for their recommendations.

- *Establish an electronic forum:* Toyota owners who use an online service line such as America Online can hold online discussions to share experiences.

Nonpersonal Communication Channels

Nonpersonal channels include media, atmospheres, and events.

Media consist of print media (newspapers, magazines, direct mail), broadcast media (radio, television), electronic media (audiotape, videotape, videodisk, CD-ROM, Web page), and display media (billboards, signs, posters). Most nonpersonal messages come through paid media.

Atmospheres are "packaged environments" that create or reinforce the buyer's leanings toward product purchase. Law offices are decorated with Oriental rugs and oak furniture to communicate "stability" and "success."[24] A luxury hotel will use elegant chandeliers, marble columns, and other tangible signs of luxury.

Events are occurrences designed to communicate particular messages to target audiences. Public-relations departments arrange news conferences, grand openings, and sports sponsorships to achieve specific communication effects with a target audience.

Although personal communication is often more effective than mass communication, mass media might be the major means of stimulating personal communication. Mass communications affect personal attitudes and behaviour through a two-step flow-of-communication process. Ideas often flow from radio, television, and print to *opinion leaders* and from these to the less media-involved population groups. This two-step flow has several implications. First, the influence of mass media on public opinion is not as direct, powerful, and automatic as supposed. It is mediated by opinion leaders, people whose opinions are sought or who carry their opinions to others. Second, the two-step flow challenges the notion that consumption styles are primarily influenced by a "trickle-down" or "trickle-up" effect from mass media. People interact primarily within their own social group and acquire ideas from opinion leaders in their group. Third, two-step communication suggests that mass communicators should direct messages specifically to opinion leaders and let them carry the message to others. Pharmaceutical firms should promote new drugs to the most influential physicians first.

Communication researchers are moving toward a social-structure view of interpersonal communication.[25] They see society as consisting of *cliques*, small groups whose members interact frequently. Clique members are similar, and their closeness facilitates effective communication but also insulates the clique from new ideas. The challenge is to create more system openness so that cliques exchange information with others in the society. This openness is helped by people who function as liaisons and bridges. A *liaison* is a person who connects two or more cliques without belonging to either. A *bridge* is a person who belongs to one clique and is linked to a person in another clique.

ESTABLISHING THE TOTAL MARKETING COMMUNICATIONS BUDGET

One of the most difficult marketing decisions is how much to spend on promotion. John Wanamaker, the department-store magnate, said, "I know that half of my advertising is wasted, but I don't know which half."

Industries and companies vary considerably in how much they spend on promotion. Expenditures might amount to 30 to 50 percent of sales in the cosmetics industry and 5 to 10 percent in the industrial-equipment industry. Within a given industry, there are low- and high-spending companies. For example, Nabisco Brands is a high promotion spender in the packaged-goods industry. The low spenders in the same industry are companies like Colonial Cookies, the producers of generic products and house brands for grocery chains like Loblaws. How do companies decide on the

(continued)

2. Solicit testimonials from your customers: Testimonials, once you get them, serve as a silent sales force that you have complete control of. They speak in terms that other customers understand and easily relate to. One strategy to use to get a testimonial is to use a customer-response form that asks for this type of feedback—and permission to quote it.

3. Tell true stories to your customers: Stories are the central vehicle for spreading reputations because they communicate on an emotional level. One proven way to use these stories is in company brochures and newsletters.

4. Educate your best customers: Some companies have found that if they educate their best customers about anything of interest, their loyalty and goodwill are enhanced. You can pick any topic that is relevant to your best customers and become the source of credible, up-to-date information on that topic. One specific new way to educate your customers is to include this information on your company's Web site.

5. Offer fast complaint handling to customers: A speedy response is vital to prevent negative word of mouth from starting, because negative feelings about a product or service may linger for years. When faced with a complaint, the response of every employee must be: "How can I send this person away happy?"

Sources: Scott R. Herriott, "Identifying and Developing Referral Channels," *Management Decision* 30, no. 1 (1992): 4–9; Peter H. Riengen and Jerome B. Kernan, "Analysis of Referral Networks in Marketing: Methods and Illustration," *Journal of Marketing Research*, November 1986, pp. 37–78; Jerry R. Wilson, *Word of Mouth Marketing* (New York: John Wiley, 1991); and Cafferky's Free Word-of-Mouth Marketing Tips, 1999, available at www.geocities.com/wallstreet/cafferkys.

promotion budget? We will describe four common methods: the affordable method, percentage-of-sales method, competitive-parity method, and objective-and-task method.

Affordable Method

Many companies set the promotion budget at what they think the company can afford. One executive said: "Why, it's simple. First, I go upstairs to the controller and ask how much they can afford to give us this year. He says a million and a half. Later, the boss comes to me and asks how much we should spend and I say, 'Oh, about a million and a half.'"[26]

The affordable method of setting budgets completely ignores the role of promotion as an investment and the immediate impact of promotion on sales volume. It leads to an uncertain annual budget, which makes long-range planning difficult.

Percentage-of-Sales Method

Many companies set promotion expenditures at a specified percentage of sales (either current or anticipated) or of the sales price. A railway company executive said: "We set our appropriation for each year on December 1 of the preceding year. On that date we add our passenger revenue for the next month, and then take two percent of the total for our advertising appropriation for the new year."[27] Automobile companies typically budget a fixed percentage for promotion based on the planned car price. Oil companies set the appropriation at a fraction of a cent for each litre of gasoline sold under their own label.

Supporters of the percentage-of-sales method see a number of advantages. First, promotion expenditures will vary with what the company can "afford." This satisfies the financial managers, who believe that expenses should be closely related to the movement of corporate sales over the business cycle. Second, it encourages management to think of the relationship among promotion cost, selling price, and profit per unit. Third, it encourages stability when competing firms spend approximately the same percentage of their sales on promotion.

In spite of these advantages, the percentage-of-sales method has little to justify it. Its reasoning is circular: It views sales as the determiner of promotion rather than as the result. It leads to a budget set by the availability of funds rather than by market opportunities. It discourages experimenting with countercyclical promotion or aggressive spending. Dependence on year-to-year sales fluctuations interferes with long-range planning. There is no logical basis for choosing the specific percentage, except what has been done in the past or what competitors are doing. Finally, it does not encourage building up the promotion budget by determining what each product and territory deserves.

Competitive-Parity Method

Some companies set their promotion budget to achieve share-of-voice parity with competitors. This thinking is illustrated by the executive who asked a trade source, "Do you have any figures that other companies in the builders' specialties field have used that would indicate what proportion of gross sales should be given over to advertising?"[28] This executive believes that by matching competitors, he will maintain his market share.

Two arguments are made in support of the competitive-parity method. One is that competitors' expenditures represent the collective wisdom of the industry. The other is that maintaining competitive parity prevents promotion wars.

Neither argument is valid. There are no grounds for believing that competitors know better what should be spent on promotion. Company reputations, resources, opportunities, and objectives differ so much that promotion budgets are hardly a guide. Furthermore, there is no evidence that budgets based on competitive parity discourage promotional wars.

Objective-and-Task Method

The objective-and-task method calls upon marketers to develop promotion budgets by defining specific objectives, determining the tasks that must be performed to achieve these objectives, and estimating the costs of performing these tasks. The sum of these costs is the proposed promotion budget.

Ule showed how the objective-and-task method could be used to establish an advertising budget. Suppose Helene Curtis wants to launch a new woman's antidandruff shampoo, Clear.[29]

1. *Establish the market-share goal:* The company estimates 50 million potential users and sets a target of attracting eight percent of the market—that is, four million users.

2. *Determine the percentage of the market that should be reached by advertising:* The advertiser hopes to reach 80 percent (40 million prospects) with the advertising message.

3. *Determine the percentage of aware prospects that should be persuaded to try the brand:* The advertiser would be pleased if 25 percent of aware prospects (10 million) tried Clear. This is because it estimates that 40 percent of all triers, or four million people, would become loyal users. This is the market goal.

4. *Determine the number of advertising impressions per 1 percent trial rate:* The advertiser estimates that 40 advertising impressions (exposures) for every one percent of the population would bring about a 25 percent trial rate.

5. *Determine the number of gross rating points that would have to be purchased:* A *gross rating point* is one exposure to one percent of the target population. Because the company wants to achieve 40 exposures to 80 percent of the population, it will want to buy 3200 gross rating points.

6. *Determine the necessary advertising budget on the basis of the average cost of buying a gross rating point:* To expose one percent of the target population to one impression costs an average of $3277. Therefore, 3200 gross rating points would cost $10 486 400 (=$3277 x 3200) in the introductory year.

The objective-and-task method has the advantage of requiring management to spell out its assumptions about the relationship among dollars spent, exposure levels, trial rates, and regular usage.

A major question is how much weight promotion should receive in relation to alternatives such as product improvement, lower prices, or better service. The answer depends on where the company's products are in their life cycles, whether they are commodities or highly differentiable products, whether they are routinely needed or have to be "sold," and other considerations. In theory, the total promotional budget should be established so that the marginal profit from the last promotional dollar just equals the marginal profit from the last dollar in the best nonpromotional use. Implementing this principle, however, is not easy.

DECIDING ON THE MARKETING COMMUNICATIONS MIX

Companies must allocate the promotion budget over the five promotional tools—advertising, sales promotion, public relations and publicity, sales force, and direct marketing. Within the same industry, companies can differ considerably in their allocations. Avon concentrates its promotional funds on personal selling, whereas Revlon spends heavily on advertising. In selling vacuum cleaners, Electrolux spends heavily on a door-to-door sales force, whereas Hoover relies more on advertising.

Companies are always searching for ways to gain efficiency by substituting one promotional tool for another. Many companies have replaced some field sales activity with ads, direct mail, and telemarketing. One auto dealer dismissed his five salespeople and cut his prices, and sales exploded. Companies have also increased their sales-promotion expenditures in relation to advertising. The substitutability among promotional tools explains why marketing functions need to be coordinated. For an account of how companies set their budgets, in practice, see the Marketing Insight "How Do Companies Set and Allocate Their Marketing Communications Budgets?"

How Do Companies Set and Allocate Their Marketing Communications Budgets?

Low and Mohr interviewed managers in consumer-packaged-goods companies on how the marketing communications budget is set and allocated to advertising, sales promotion, and trade promotion. A brand team is formed and, after performing an extensive situation analysis, the team establishes marketing objectives and a broad strategy. After forecasting the brand sales and profits based on the broad strategy, the team develops an initial allocation of the budget to advertising, consumer promotion, and trade promotion. The team relies heavily on the previous year's budget allocation, which may make sense if the environment is stable but not if there is rapid environmental change calling for a fresh set of starting points. The brand plan is presented to senior management, which may require changes. The revised plan is then implemented.

During the year, brand management will adjust allocations in response to competitive and customer developments. Toward the end of the period, brand managers will often replace advertising with more sales promotion if the brand is not meeting its profit objectives.

Low and Mohr also found in their 1998 study that:

- As brands move to the more mature phase of the product life cycle, managers allocate less to advertising and more to promotions.

- When a brand is well differentiated from the competition, managers allocate more to advertising relative to promotions.

- When formal rewards are focused on short-term results, managers allocate less of their budgets to advertising relative to promotions.

- As retailers have more influence, managers allocate less of their budgets to advertising relative to promotions.

- As managers have greater experience with the company, they tend to allocate proportionately more of their budget to advertising relative to consumer and trade promotion.

Sources: See George S. Low and Jakki J. Mohr, *The Advertising Sales Promotion Trade-Off: Theory and Practice* (Cambridge, MA: Marketing Science Institute, Report No. 92-127, October 1992); and their *Brand Managers' Perceptions of the Marketing Communications Budget Allocation Process* (Cambridge, MA: Marketing Science Institute, Report No. 98-105, March 1998). Also see Gabriel J. Beihal and Daniel A. Sheinen, "Managing the Brand in a Corporate Advertising Environment: A Decision-Making Framework for Brand Managers," *Journal of Advertising* 17 (June 22, 1998): 99.

THE PROMOTIONAL TOOLS

Each promotional tool has its own unique characteristics and costs.[30]

Advertising

Because of the many forms and uses of advertising, it is difficult to make all-embracing generalizations.[31] Yet the following qualities can be noted:

- *Public presentation:* Advertising's public nature confers a kind of legitimacy on the product and also suggests a standardized offering. Because many persons receive the same message, buyers know that motives for purchasing the product will be publicly understood.

- *Pervasiveness:* Advertising permits the seller to repeat a message many times. It also allows the buyer to receive and compare the messages of various competitors. Large-scale advertising says something positive about the seller's size, power, and success.

- *Amplified expressiveness:* Advertising provides opportunities for dramatizing the company and its products through the artful use of print, sound, and colour.

- *Impersonality:* The audience does not feel obligated to pay attention or respond to advertising. Advertising is a monologue in front of, not a dialogue with, the audience.

Advertising can be used to build up a long-term image for a product (Coca-Cola ads) or trigger quick sales (a Sears ad for a weekend sale). Advertising can efficiently reach geographically dispersed buyers. Certain forms of advertising (TV advertising) can require a large budget, whereas other forms (newspaper advertising) can be done on a small budget. Advertising might have an effect on sales simply through its presence. Consumers might believe that a heavily advertised brand must offer "good value."

Three relatively new advertising media should be noted. *Advertorials* are print ads that contain editorial content and may be hard to distinguish from a newspaper's or magazine's contents. *Infomercials* are TV commercials that appear to be 30-minute television shows demonstrating or discussing a product. Viewers can phone and order the product and, hence, these infomercials produce directly measurable results. *Banners* are small signs on Web pages advertising an offer or company that can be reached by clicking on the banner.

Sales Promotion

Although sales-promotion tools—coupons, contests, premiums, and the like—are highly diverse, they offer three distinctive benefits:

- *Communication:* They gain attention and usually provide information that may lead the consumer to the product.
- *Incentive:* They incorporate some concession, inducement, or contribution that gives value to the consumer.
- *Invitation:* They include a distinct invitation to engage in the transaction now.

Companies use sales-promotion tools to draw a stronger and quicker buyer response. Sales promotion can be used for short-run effects such as to dramatize product offers and boost sagging sales.

Public Relations and Publicity

The appeal of public relations and publicity is based on three distinctive qualities:

- *High credibility:* News stories and features are more authentic and credible to readers than ads.
- *Ability to catch buyers off guard:* Public relations can reach prospects who prefer to avoid salespeople and advertisements.
- *Dramatization:* Public relations has the potential for dramatizing a company or product.

Marketers tend to underuse public relations; yet a well-thought-out program coordinated with the other promotion-mix elements can be extremely effective.

Personal Selling

Personal selling is the most effective tool at later stages of the buying process, particularly in building up buyer preference, conviction, and action. Personal selling has three distinctive qualities:

- *Personal confrontation:* Personal selling involves an immediate and interactive relationship between two or more persons. Each party is able to observe the other's reactions at close hand.
- *Cultivation:* Personal selling permits all kinds of relationships to spring up, ranging from a matter-of-fact selling relationship to a deep personal friendship. Sales reps will normally have customers' best interests at heart.
- *Response:* Personal selling makes the buyer feel under some obligation for having listened to the sales talk.

Direct Marketing

Although there are many forms of direct marketing—direct mail, telemarketing, Internet marketing—they all share four distinctive characteristics. Direct marketing is:

- *Nonpublic:* The message is normally addressed to a specific person.
- *Customized:* The message can be prepared to appeal to the addressed individual.
- *Up-to-date:* A message can be prepared very quickly.
- *Interactive:* The message can be changed depending on the person's response.

Consumer goods

Sales promotion

Advertising

Personal selling

Public relations

Relative spending

Industrial goods

Personal selling

Sales promotion

Advertising

Public relations

Relative spending

FIGURE 18.5

Relative Spending on Promotional Tools in Consumer versus Business Markets

FACTORS IN SETTING THE MARKETING COMMUNICATIONS MIX

Companies must consider several factors in developing their promotion mix: type of product market, whether to use a push or pull strategy, consumer readiness to make a purchase, stage in the product life cycle, and the company's market rank.

Type of Product Market

Promotional allocations vary between consumer and business markets (see Figure 18.5). Consumer marketers spend on sales promotion, advertising, personal selling, and public relations, in that order. Business marketers spend on personal selling, sales promotion, advertising, and public relations, in that order. In general, personal selling is more heavily used with complex, expensive, and risky goods and in markets with fewer and larger sellers (hence, business markets).

Although advertising is used less than sales calls in business markets, it still plays a significant role. Advertising can perform the following functions in business markets:

- *Awareness building:* Advertising can provide an introduction to the company and its products.

- *Comprehension building:* If the product embodies new features, some explaining can be effectively performed by advertising.

- *Efficient reminding:* If prospects know about the product but are not ready to buy, reminder advertising is more economical than sales calls.

- *Lead generation:* Advertisements offering brochures and carrying the company's phone number are an effective way to generate leads for sales representatives.

- *Legitimization:* Sales representatives can use tear sheets of the company's ads to legitimize their company and products.

- *Reassurance:* Advertising can remind customers how to use the product and reassure them about their purchase.

A number of studies have underscored advertising's important role in business markets. Morrill showed that advertising combined with personal selling increased sales 23 percent over what they had been with no advertising. The total promotional cost as a percentage of sales was reduced by 20 percent.[32] Freeman developed a formal model for dividing promotional funds between advertising and personal selling on the basis of the selling tasks that each performs more economically.[33] Levitt's research also showed the important role advertising can play in business markets. He found:

- A company's reputation improves its sales force's chances of getting a favourable first hearing and an early adoption of the product. Therefore, corporate advertising that can build up the company's reputation will help the sales representatives.

- Sales representatives from well-known companies have an edge if their sales presentations are adequate. But a rep from a lesser-known company who makes a highly effective presentation can overcome the disadvantage.

- Company reputation helps most where the product is complex, the risk is high, and the purchasing agent is less professionally trained.[34]

Lilien researched business marketing practices in a major project called ADVISOR and reported the following:[35]

- The average industrial company set its marketing budget at seven percent of its sales. It spent only 10 percent of its marketing budget on advertising. Companies spent the remainder on sales force, trade shows, sales promotion, and direct mail.

- Industrial companies spent a higher-than-average amount on advertising, where their products had higher quality, uniqueness, or purchase frequency, or where more customer growth was occurring.

- Industrial companies set a higher-than-average marketing budget when their customers were more dispersed or where the customer growth rate was higher.

Personal selling can also make a strong contribution in consumer-goods marketing. Some consumer marketers play down the role of the sales force, using it mainly to collect weekly orders from dealers and to see that sufficient stock is on the shelf. The common feeling is that "salespeople put products on shelves and advertising takes them off." Yet an effectively trained consumer company sales force can make four important contributions:

1. *Increased stock position:* Sales reps can persuade dealers to take more stock and devote more shelf space to the company's brand.

2. *Enthusiasm building:* Sales reps can build dealer enthusiasm by dramatizing planned advertising and sales-promotion backup.

3. *Missionary selling:* Sales reps can sign up more dealers.

4. *Key account management:* Sales reps can take responsibility for growing business with the most important accounts.

Push versus Pull Strategy

The promotional mix is heavily influenced by whether the company chooses a push or pull strategy to create sales. A *push strategy* involves the manufacturer using sales force and trade promotion to induce intermediaries to carry, promote, and sell the product to end users. Push strategy is especially appropriate where there is low brand loyalty in a category, brand choice is made in the store, the product is an impulse item, and product benefits are well understood. A *pull strategy* involves the manufacturer using advertising and consumer promotion to induce consumers to ask intermediaries for the product, thus inducing the intermediaries to order it. Pull strategy is especially appropriate when there is high brand loyalty and high involvement in the category, people perceive differences between brands, and people choose the brand before they go to the store. Companies in the same industry may differ in their emphasis on push or pull. For example, Lever Brothers relies more on push, Procter & Gamble more on pull.

Buyer-Readiness Stage

Promotional tools vary in cost effectiveness at different stages of buyer readiness. Figure 18.6 shows the relative cost effectiveness of four promotional tools. Advertising and publicity play the most important roles in the awareness-building stage. Customer comprehension is primarily affected by advertising and personal selling. Customer conviction is influenced mostly by personal selling. Closing the sale is influenced mostly by personal selling and sales promotion. Reordering is also affected mostly by personal selling and sales promotion, and somewhat by reminder advertising.

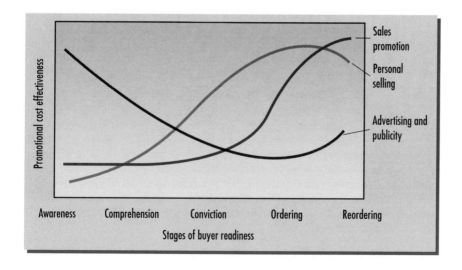

FIGURE 18.6

Cost Effectiveness of Different Promotional Tools at Different Buyer-Readiness Stages

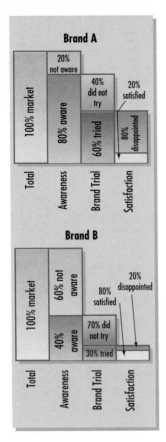

FIGURE 18.7

Current Consumer States for Two Brands

American Association of Advertising Agencies
www.aaaa.org

Product-Life-Cycle Stage

Promotional tools also vary in cost effectiveness at different stages of the product life cycle.

■ In the introduction stage, advertising and publicity have the highest cost effectiveness, followed by personal selling to gain distribution coverage and sales promotion to induce trial.

■ In the growth stage, all the tools can be toned down because demand has its own momentum through word of mouth.

■ In the maturity stage, sales promotion, advertising, and personal selling all grow more important, in that order.

■ In the decline stage, sales promotion continues strong, advertising and publicity are reduced, and salespeople give the product only minimal attention.

Company Market Rank

Market leaders derive more benefit from advertising than sales promotion. Conversely, smaller competitors gain more by using sales promotion in their marketing communications mix.

MEASURING RESULTS

After implementing the promotional plan, the communicator must measure its impact on the target audience. Members of the target audience are asked whether they recognize or recall the message, how many times they saw it, what points they recall, how they felt about the message, and their previous and current attitudes toward the product and company. The communicator should also collect behavioural measures of audience response, such as how many people bought the product, liked it, and talked to others about it.

Figure 18.7 provides an example of good feedback measurement. We find that 80 percent of the consumers in the total market are aware of brand A, 60 percent have tried it, and only 20 percent who have tried it are satisfied. This indicates that the communications program is effective in creating awareness, but the product fails to meet consumer expectations. In contrast, only 40 percent of the consumers in the total market are aware of brand B, and only 30 percent have tried it, but 80 percent of those who have tried it are satisfied. In this case, the communications program needs to be strengthened to take advantage of the brand's power.

 MANAGING AND COORDINATING INTEGRATED MARKETING COMMUNICATIONS

Many companies still rely on one or two communication tools to achieve their communication aims. This practice persists in spite of the fragmenting of mass markets into a multitude of minimarkets, each requiring its own approach; the proliferation of new types of media; and the growing sophistication of consumers. The wide range of communication tools, messages, and audiences makes it imperative that companies move toward *integrated marketing communications* (IMC). As defined by the American Association of Advertising Agencies (four As), IMC is:

> *a concept of marketing communications planning that recognizes the added value of a comprehensive plan that evaluates the strategic roles of a variety of communications disciplines—for example, general advertising, direct response, sales promotion and public relations—and combines these disciplines to provide clarity, consistency, and maximum communications' impact through the seamless integration of discrete messages.*

Here is a creative example of integrated marketing communications:

- **Chapters.ca.** When bookseller Chapters Inc. launched its new Web business aimed at curtailing the inroads made on the Canadian market by Amazon.com, it launched its biggest ever integrated campaign. Spending over $2 million, Chapters brought almost every media into play except television. Aimed at a bright, book-savvy audience, the retailer took a humorous approach to communicate its message about its virtually limitless book selection. One billboard showed a trio of books, *An Unfinished History of the Work, The Neverending Story,* and *Constructing the Quebec Referendum* over the punch line "Books with no ending." Newspaper ads, Web-site banner ads, and the promise of next-day free shipping also helped wean Canadians away from Chapter's American rival.[36]

A study of top management and marketing executives in large consumer companies indicated that over 70 percent favoured the concept of integrated marketing communications. Several large advertising agencies—Ogilvy & Mather, Young & Rubicam, Saatchi & Saatchi—acquired major agencies specializing in sales promotion, public relations, and direct marketing in order to provide one-stop shopping. But to their disappointment, most clients have not bought their integrated marketing communications package, preferring to put together the specialized agencies by themselves.

Why the resistance? Large companies employ several communication specialists to work with their brand managers. Each communication specialist knows little about the other communication tools. Furthermore, the specialists usually have favourite outside agencies and oppose turning their responsibilities over to one superagency. They argue that the company should choose the best specialist agency for each purpose, not second- and third-rate agencies just because they belong to a superagency. They believe that the ad agency will still put most of the advertiser's money into the advertising budget.

Nevertheless, integrated marketing communications does produce stronger message consistency and greater sales impact. It gives someone responsibility—where none existed before—to unify the company's brand images and messages as they come through thousands of company activities. IMC will improve the company's ability to reach the right customers with the right messages at the right time and in the right place.[37]

Advocates of integrated marketing communications describe it as a way of looking at the whole marketing process instead of focusing only on individual parts of it. See the Marketing Memo "Checklist for Integrating Marketing Communications."

SUMMARY

1. Modern marketing calls for more than developing a good product, pricing it attractively, and making it accessible to target customers. Companies must also communicate with present and potential stakeholders, and with the general public. The marketing communications mix consists of five major modes of communication: advertising, sales promotion, public relations and publicity, personal selling, and direct marketing.

2. The communication process consists of nine elements: sender, receiver, message, media, encoding, decoding, response, feedback, and noise. To get their messages through, marketers must encode their messages in a way that takes into account how the target audience usually decodes messages. They must also transmit the message through efficient media that reach the target audience and develop feedback channels to monitor response to the message.

3. Developing effective communications involves eight steps: (a) Identify the target audience, (b) determine the communication objectives, (c) design the message, (d) select the communication channels, (e) establish the total communications budget, (f) decide on the communications mix, (g) measure the communications' results, and (h) manage the integrated marketing communication process.

Checklist for Integrating Marketing Communications

Marketers who have gained the ear of management can take the lead in putting together a proposal for achieving integrated marketing communications. Such proposals often include the following recommendations:

- *Audit the pockets of communications-related spending throughout the organization:* Itemize the budgets and tasks and consolidate these into a single budgeting process. Reassess all communications expenditures by product, promotional tool, stage of the life cycle, and observed effect.

- *Create shared performance measures:* Develop systems to evaluate communications activities. Because IMC attempts to change consumer purchase behaviour, this behaviour must be measured to ultimately demonstrate communications' impact on the bottom line. ROI can be measured either by tracking a company's own communications efforts or through syndicated customer data.

- *Use database development and issues management to understand your stakeholders:* Include customers, employees, investors, vendors, and all other stakeholders at every stage of your communications plan.

- *Identify all contact points for the company and its products:* Use this audit to determine where communications can best be used to reinforce the company's messages. Measure communications' ability to do so at each contact point, whether it be your product packaging, retail display, shareholder meeting or spokesperson, and so on. Work to ensure your communications efforts are occurring when, where, and how your customers want them.

(continued)

- *Analyze trends—internal and external—that can affect your company's ability to do business:* Look for areas where communications can help the most. Determine the strengths and weaknesses of each communications function. Develop a combination of promotional tactics based on these strengths and weaknesses.

- *Create business and communication plans for each local market:* Integrate these into a global communications strategy.

- *Appoint a director responsible for the company's persuasive communications efforts:* This move encourages efficiency by centralizing planning and creating shared performance measures.

- *Create compatible themes, tones, and quality across all communications media:* This consistency achieves greater impact and prevents the unnecessary duplication of work across functions. When creating materials, consider how they can be used for a range of audiences. Make sure each carries your unique primary messages and selling points.

- *Hire only team players:* Employees trained in this new, integrated way of thinking will not be locked into functional silos. Rather, they thrive on group accountability and are open to any new responsibility that enables them to better meet the needs of customers.

- *Link IMC with management processes, such as participatory management:* This produces a fully integrated management effort aimed at meeting corporate goals. An integrated strategy should permit efficiency in each communication function contributing to the success of the corporate mission.

Source: Adapted from Matthew P. Gonring, "Putting Integrated Marketing Communications to Work Today," *Public Relations Quarterly*, Fall 1994, pp. 45–48.

4. In identifying the target audience, the marketer needs to perform familiarity and favourability analyses, then seek to close any gap that exists between current public perception and the image sought. Communications objectives may be cognitive, affective, or behavioural—that is, the company might want to put something into the consumer's mind, change the consumer's attitude, or get the consumer to act. In designing the message, marketers must carefully consider message content, message structure, message format, and message source. Communication channels may be personal (advocate, expert, and social channels) or nonpersonal (media, atmospheres, and events). Although many methods are used to set the promotion budget, the objective-and-task method, which calls upon marketers to develop their budgets by defining their specific objectives, is the most desirable.

5. In deciding on the marketing communications mix, marketers must examine the distinct advantages and costs of each promotional tool. They must also consider the type of product market in which they are selling, whether to use a push or a pull strategy, how ready consumers are to make a purchase, the product's stage in the product life cycle, and the company's market rank. Measuring the marketing communications mix's effectiveness involves asking members of the target audience whether they recognize or recall the message, how many times they saw it, what points they recall, how they felt about the message, and their previous and current attitudes toward the product and company.

6. Managing and coordinating the entire communications process calls for integrated marketing communications (IMC).

APPLICATIONS

CHAPTER CONCEPTS

1. When determining an ad's message content, the communicator must determine what type of message will have the desired effect on the target audience. Bring to class examples of print ads making the following rational or emotional appeals: (a) quality, (b) economy, (c) performance, (d) fear, (e) guilt, (f) humour, (g) pride, (h) sympathy. Explain why you think the advertiser selected this appeal. Do you agree or disagree with the communicator's decision?

2. The major mass media—newspapers, magazines, radio, television, and outdoor media—show striking differences in their capacity for dramatization, credibility, attention getting, and other valued aspects of communication. Describe the special characteristics of each media type, along with its advantages and disadvantages.

3. The Canadian Cancer Society has hired you to develop an integrated marketing communications plan that will inform and persuade people of the risks of skin cancer due to overexposure to the sun. Additionally, the campaign would inform "sunners" how to prevent the disease. In teams of five, develop an integrated marketing communications plan for the Canadian Cancer Society. Use the following grid to help you organize your thoughts.

	Advertising	Public Relations	Sales Promotion	Direct Response
a. Health objective				
b. Target				
c. Purpose				
d. Promise				
e. Support				
f. Personality				
g. Aperture				
h. Consumer contact points				

Definitions:

a. *Health objective:* Goal of the communication in terms of the person's health

b. *Target:* Audience to whom the communication is targeted

c. *Purpose:* A "solution" for helping the target audience meet the health objective

d. *Promise:* What the target audience will receive in return for meeting the health objective

e. *Support:* Sources of credible support for the claims made in the communications

f. *Personality:* The "flavor" of the communication—serious, humorous, and so forth.

g. *Aperture:* Time frame in which to appeal to the target audience

h. *Consumer contact points:* Places at which the target audience can be reached and the forms of media best suited to target audience members

MARKETING AND ADVERTISING

Figure 1, an ad geared toward the business market, describes the Bosch Corporation's century-old tradition of innovation in automotive products and includes a toll-free number for more information. What do you think Bosch wants to accomplish by placing this ad in a national business magazine? As a business marketer, would Bosch be likely to put more of its marketing communications budget toward advertising or toward other modes of communication? Why?

One of our most important developments is turning 100 years old.

One hundred years ago, we built the first reliable ignition system for automobiles. And we've been the spark behind many other automotive innovations ever since. For example, Bosch built the first platinum spark plug in 1985, revolutionizing the industry and inspiring hundreds of imitations. So it's no coincidence that even after 100 years, we're once again re-defining the industry with the revolutionary Bosch Platinum+4. It's the most powerful spark plug you can buy. Four ground electrodes and a pure platinum center electrode combine to deliver improved engine performance. It's the latest development from a company that has a long history of bringing innovation to many aspects of your life.

We bring innovation

BOSCH

Figure 1

FOCUS ON TECHNOLOGY

With integrated marketing communications, every brand contact, regardless of communication channel, plays a strategic role in shaping the customer's view of the company. For this reason, companies with Web sites need to ensure that their online marketing messages are aligned with messages in other media for greater sales impact.

One company that is expert at this is McDonald's. Its television, radio, and print ads have a similar look, and the content is consistent across media. The current advertising theme is also carried through online. Visit the "What's New" area of the company's Web site and note the similarity of the brief online ad to the current advertising campaign. Why would McDonald's create this special ad snippet just for its Web site? Who is the likely target audience? What results might McDonald's expect from this online message?

McDonald's
www.mcdonalds.com/surftheworld/
north/canada/whatsnew/index.html

MARKETING FOR THE 21ST CENTURY

As more marketers take their communications global at the start of the new millennium, they must answer four questions in planning their global advertising and promotion: Are their products suitable for each country? Are their targeted market segments legal and customary? Is their advertising acceptable? Should their ads be created centrally or locally?

Unilever
www.unilever.com/public/unilever/
around/org-arwo.htm

To see how a multinational marketer is addressing these issues, point your Web browser to the "Around the World" section of the Unilever Web site. Click on the arrow near the right side of the screen to keep reading about the company's international focus. Then click on the "brands" link at the top left side of your screen to see a listing of the company's food brands, followed by links to local brand Web sites. Why does Unilever say it is international rather than global? How does this distinction affect its products and its online communications?

YOU'RE THE MARKETER: SONIC MARKETING PLAN

Marketing communications planning is a critical component of every marketing plan, because it drives the way companies connect with their stakeholders, including customers and prospects.

You are responsible for planning integrated marketing communications programs for Sonic's shelf stereos. Take another look at the company's current situation. Also look at the strategies and marketing-mix programs you have planned so far. Then answer these questions about marketing communications for Sonic:

■ *What audience(s) should Sonic be targeting? What communication objectives should it set for each target audience?*

■ *What message design and communication channel (personal or nonpersonal) is most appropriate for each target audience? Why?*

■ *How should Sonic establish its marketing communications budget?*

■ Which promotional tools would be most effective in Sonic's marketing communications mix? Why?

Be sure that your marketing communications plans will support Sonic's overall marketing efforts. Now, as your instructor directs, summarize your ideas in a written marketing plan or type them into the Marketing Mix/Promotion section of the Marketing Plan Pro software.

Managing Advertising,
Sales Promotion,
Public Relations

Handle Without Care

PROFILE:

Canadian
Marketing
Excellence

Unilever Canada's Lever Pond's Division and its agency, Ammirati Puris Lintas, really cleaned up at the October CASSIE awards show. Their "Go ahead. Get dirty." campaign for Sunlight laundry detergent won the Grand Prix and the Gold prize; and their "Young at Heart" advertising for Becel margarine, created by MacLaren McCann Toronto, won a Gold in the category recognizing long-term successful campaigns.

CASSIES is the acronym for "Canadian Advertising Success Stories." The awards were founded in 1993. Prior to their founding, there were virtually no case histories that demonstrated the effectiveness of Canadian advertising. Thus, the intent of the CASSIES was to build a body of knowledge about advertising proven to generate sales, profits, or social objectives. While part of the judging criteria for the CASSIES is the excellence of the creative idea, the awards were designed with the aim of recognizing advertising that absolutely and quantitatively helped a firm or non-profit organization accomplish its objectives. Campaigns submitted for judging must have original Canadian creative, strategies, and executions. Each entrant must demonstrate that advertising has been a major or significant contributor to accomplishing objectives. In the case of business entrants, this means improving sales, share of market, or price levels. If the entrant is a not-for-profit, advocacy, or government organization, it must be demonstrated that the campaign facilitated the attainment of a key objective.

Winning a CASSIE didn't happen overnight. Lever Pond's took a hard look at its Sunlight brand a couple of years ago. At that time it was a weak number-two player with approximately 13 percent of the Canadian marketplace. Tide, the market leader, had a robust 50 percent share. Lever's research discovered that its target consumers, women age 25 to 54 with children, didn't have much faith in the detergent's cleaning ability. Thus, while the starting point for improvement was reformulating the product to improve its cleaning power, Sunlight also had to overcome the mental baggage consumers carried: they regarded Sunlight as a "gentler, softer, not-for-tough-cleaning" brand. Sunlight's solution: get down and get dirty. After extensive qualitative research, the firm and its agency's key insight was that "dirty clothes are bad, but getting them dirty is fun."

The campaign was built around the consumer benefit that people of all ages could go out and enjoy life because they could count on Sunlight to clean their clothes. One of the first ads was titled, "Magnetic Mud." It showed a little boy wearing new clothes being sucked into a mud puddle. Its five-page print ads, which ran among the traditional "beauty ads" in women's magazines such as *Chatelaine, Flare,* and *Elle* showed young women frolicking in the dirt or speckled with mud. Lever supported the campaign with point-of-sale materials such as scratch-and-sniff cards on grocery shelves, and the image of a huge mud puddle set into store floors. Great advertising doesn't come cheaply, however. Lever is reported to have spent $2.8 million on advertising Sunlight in 1998.

Was it worth the expense? Did the campaign clean up more than an award? It was aimed at taking share away from Tide. Lever credits it with accomplishing this task and it can demonstrate that Sunlight increased its sales by 2.5 percent despite a 9.5 percent price increase. Not bad results for glorifying dirt!

Sources: Lara Mills, "Down and Dirty," *Marketing,* April 19, 1999, pp. 12, 16. Lara Mills, "Unilever Cleans Up at CASSIES 99," *Marketing,* November 8, 1999, p. 2. John Gray, "Sunlight Shines at CASSIES," *Strategy: The Canadian Marketing Report,* November 8, 1999, p. 18. Susan Skene, "Why the CASSIES Matter," *Marketing,* May 3, 1999, p. 2. James Dingwall, George Clements, and Alan Middleton, *Canadian Advertising Success Stories, CASSIES 1,* Canadian Congress of Advertising, 1994.

Philip Kotler suggests that the *"best advertising is done by satisfied customers."* In this chapter, we describe the nature and use of three promotional tools—advertising, sales promotion, and public relations. Although their effectiveness is not always easy to gauge, they contribute strongly to marketing performance.

We will consider the following questions:

- What steps are involved in developing an advertising program?

- What explains the growing use of sales promotion, and how are sales-promotion decisions made?

- How can companies exploit the potential of public relations and publicity?

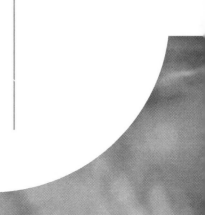

DEVELOPING AND MANAGING AN ADVERTISING PROGRAM

We define advertising as follows:

- *Advertising* is any paid form of nonpersonal presentation and promotion of ideas, goods, or services by an identified sponsor.

Advertisers include not only business firms but also museums, charitable organizations, and government agencies that direct messages to target publics. Ads are a cost-effective way to disseminate messages, whether to build brand preference for Clearnet wireless phones or to educate people to avoid hard drugs.

Organizations handle their advertising in different ways. In small companies, advertising is handled by someone in the sales or marketing department, who works with an advertising agency. A large company will often set up its own advertising department, whose manager reports to the vice president of marketing. The advertising department's job is to propose a budget; develop advertising strategy; approve ads and campaigns; and handle direct-mail advertising, dealer displays, and other forms of advertising. Most companies use an outside agency to help create advertising campaigns and to select and purchase media.

In developing a program, marketing managers must always start by identifying the target market and buyer motives. Then they can make the five major decisions in developing an advertising program, known as the five Ms: *Mission:* What are the advertising objectives? *Money:* How much can be spent? *Message:* What message should be sent? *Media:* What media should be used? *Measurement:* How should the results be evaluated? These decisions are summarized in Figure 19.1 and described in the following sections.

SETTING THE ADVERTISING OBJECTIVES

The advertising objectives must flow from prior decisions on target market, market positioning, and marketing mix.

Many specific communication and sales objectives can be assigned to advertising. Colley lists 52 possible advertising objectives in his *Defining Advertising Goals for Measured Advertising Results.*[1] He outlines a method called DAGMAR (after the book's title) for turning objectives into specific measurable goals. An *advertising goal* (or *objective*) is a specific communication task and achievement level to be accomplished with a specific audience in a specific period of time. Colley provides an example:

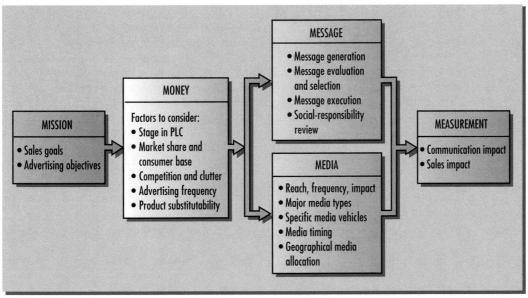

FIGURE 19.1

The Five Ms of Advertising

To increase among 30 million homemakers who own automatic washers the number who identify brand X as a low-sudsing detergent and who are persuaded that it gets clothes cleaner—from 10 percent to 40 percent in one year.

Advertising objectives can be classified according to whether their aim is to inform, persuade, or remind.

- *Informative advertising* figures heavily in the pioneering stage of a product category, where the objective is to build primary demand. Thus the yogurt industry initially had to inform consumers of yogurt's nutritional benefits.

- *Persuasive advertising* becomes important in the competitive stage, where a company's objective is to build selective demand for a particular brand. For example, Chivas Regal attempts to persuade consumers that it delivers more taste and status than other brands of Scotch whiskey. Some persuasive advertising uses *comparative advertising*, which makes an explicit comparison of the attributes of two or more brands.[2] The Burger King Corporation used comparative advertising for its attack on McDonald's (Burger King's burgers are flame-broiled; McDonald's are fried). Schering-Plough claimed that "New OcuClear relieves three times longer than Visine." A company should ensure that it can prove its claim of superiority and cannot be counterattacked in a vulnerable area. Comparative advertising works best when it elicits cognitive and affective motivations simultaneously.[3]

- *Reminder advertising* is important with mature products. Expensive four-colour Coca-Cola ads in magazines are intended to remind people to purchase Coca-Cola. A related form of advertising is *reinforcement advertising*, which seeks to assure current purchasers that they have made the right choice. Automobile ads often depict satisfied customers enjoying special features of their new car.

The advertising objective should emerge from a thorough analysis of the current marketing situation. If the product class is mature, the company is the market leader, and brand usage is low, the proper objective should be to stimulate more usage. If the product class is new, the company is not the market leader, but the brand is superior to the leader, then the proper objective is to convince the market of the brand's superiority.

DECIDING ON THE ADVERTISING BUDGET

How does a company know if it will be spending the right amount? If it spends too little, the effect will be negligible. If it spends too much, then some of the money could have been put to better use. Some critics charge that large consumer-packaged-goods firms tend to overspend on advertising as a form of insurance against not spending enough, and that industrial companies underestimate the power of company and product image building and tend to underspend on advertising.[4]

Advertising has a carryover effect that lasts beyond the current period. Although advertising is treated as a current expense, part of it is really an investment that builds up an intangible asset called *brand equity*. When $5 million is spent on capital equipment, the equipment may be treated as a five-year depreciable asset and only one-fifth of the cost is written off in the first year. When $5 million is spent on advertising to launch a new product, the entire cost must be written off in the first year. This treatment of advertising reduces the company's reported profit and therefore limits the number of new-product launches a company can undertake in any one year.

There are five specific factors to consider when setting the advertising budget:[5]

- *Stage in the product life cycle:* New products typically receive large advertising budgets to build awareness and to gain consumer trial. Established brands usually are supported with lower advertising budgets as a ratio to sales.

- *Market share and consumer base:* High-market-share brands usually require less advertising expenditure as a percentage of sales to maintain their share. To build share by increasing market size requires larger advertising expenditures. On a cost-per-impression basis, it is less expensive to reach consumers of a widely used brand than to reach consumers of low-share brands.

- *Competition and clutter:* In a market with a large number of competitors and high advertising spending, a brand must advertise more heavily to be heard. Even simple clutter from advertisements not directly competitive to the brand creates a need for heavier advertising.

- *Advertising frequency:* The number of repetitions needed to put across the brand's message to consumers has an important impact on the advertising budget.

- *Product substitutability:* Brands in a commodity class (cigarettes, beer, soft drinks) require heavy advertising to establish a differential image. Advertising is also important when a brand can offer unique physical benefits or features.

Marketing scientists have built a number of advertising-expenditure models that take these factors into account. Vidale and Wolfe's model called for a larger advertising budget, the higher the sales-response rate, the higher the sales-decay rate (the rate at which customers forget the advertising and brand), and the higher the untapped sales potential.[6] Unfortunately, this model leaves out other important factors, such as the rate of competitive advertising and the effectiveness of the company's ads.

John Little proposed an adaptive-control method for setting the advertising budget.[7] Suppose the company has set an advertising-expenditure rate based on its most current information. It spends this rate in all markets except in a subset of *2n* markets randomly drawn. In *n* test markets the company spends at a lower rate, and in the other *n* it spends at a higher rate. This procedure will yield information on the average sales created by low, medium, and high rates of advertising that can be used to update the parameters of the sales-response function. The updated function can be used to determine the best advertising-expenditure rate for the next period. If this experiment is conducted each period, advertising expenditures will closely track optimal advertising expenditures.[8]

CHOOSING THE ADVERTISING MESSAGE

Advertising campaigns vary in their creativity. William Bernbach observed: "The facts are not enough. . . . Don't forget that Shakespeare used some pretty hackneyed plots, yet his message came through with great execution." Consider the following example:

Taco Bell
www.tacobell.com

- **Taco Bell.** In 1994, Taco Bell ranked fourth in fast-food chains and its revenues were sagging. Then, in 1997, the chain introduced television spots with a talking chihuahua. The hungry little dog, who became famous for his Spanish-language statement, "Yo Quiero Taco Bell," meaning "I want some Taco Bell," struck a chord with the chain's 18- to 35-year-old customers and spawned an impressive array of chihuahua merchandise such as T-shirts, magnets, hats, and talking dolls—and increased revenues for Taco Bell. The little pooch pushed Taco Bell's sales up 4.3 percent in 1997, and the chain ended the year with $4.5 billion in sales. Taco Bell now spends $300 million a year on advertising and plans a long life for this popular campaign.[9]

Clearly, the creativity factor can be more important than the number of dollars spent. Only after gaining attention can a commercial help to increase brand sales. However, a warning is in order. Creative advertising may not be enough. People must remember the brand and the message the ad conveys.

Advertisers go through four steps to develop a creative strategy: message generation, message evaluation and selection, message execution, and social responsibility review.

Message Generation

The product's "benefit" message should be decided as part of developing the product concept. Yet there is usually latitude for a number of possible messages. Over time, the marketer might want to change the message, especially if consumers seek new or different benefits from the product.

Creative people use several methods to generate possible advertising appeals. Many creative people proceed *inductively* by talking to consumers, dealers, experts, and competitors. Leo Burnett advocates "in-depth interviewing where I come realistically face to face with the people I am trying to sell. I try to get a picture in my mind of the kind of people they are—how they use this product and what it is."[10]

Some creative people use a *deductive* framework for generating advertising messages. Maloney proposed one framework.[11] He saw buyers as expecting one of four types of reward from a product: rational, sensory, social, or ego satisfaction. Buyers might visualize these rewards from results-of-use experience, product-in-use experience, or incidental-to-use experience. Crossing the four types of rewards with the three types of experience generates 12 types of advertising messages. For example, the appeal "gets clothes cleaner" is a rational-reward promise following results-of-use experience. The phrase "real gusto in a great light beer" is a sensory-reward promise connected with product-in-use experience.

How many alternative ad themes should the advertiser create before making a choice? The more ads that are independently created, the higher the probability of finding an excellent one. Yet the more time spent on creating alternative ads, the higher the costs. Under the present commission system, the agency does not like to go to the expense of creating and pretesting many ads. Fortunately, the expense of creating rough ads is rapidly falling due to computers. An ad agency's creative department can compose many alternative ads in a short time by drawing from computer files containing still and video images, type sets, and so on.

Message Evaluation and Selection

A good ad normally focuses on one core selling proposition. Twedt suggested that messages be rated on *desirability, exclusiveness,* and *believability.*[12] For example:

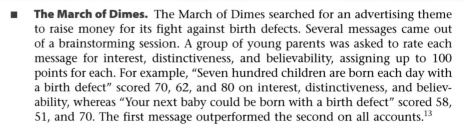

- **The March of Dimes.** The March of Dimes searched for an advertising theme to raise money for its fight against birth defects. Several messages came out of a brainstorming session. A group of young parents was asked to rate each message for interest, distinctiveness, and believability, assigning up to 100 points for each. For example, "Seven hundred children are born each day with a birth defect" scored 70, 62, and 80 on interest, distinctiveness, and believability, whereas "Your next baby could be born with a birth defect" scored 58, 51, and 70. The first message outperformed the second on all accounts.[13]

The advertiser should conduct market research to determine which appeal works best with its target audience.

Message Execution

The message's impact depends not only upon what is said but also on how it is said. Some ads aim for *rational positioning* and others for *emotional positioning*. While many North American ads present an explicit feature or benefit designed to appeal to the rational mind: "gets clothes cleaner"; "Brings relief faster," other use a more emotional appeal. Lipton Canada's Becel margarine, for example, has run a campaign since 1993 that shows older people loving each other and loving life using the theme music "When you are young at heart." Older consumers not only have a strong positive emotional reaction to the ads, but focus groups also show that they find them delightful and a welcome change from segments focused on youth. As the opening case noted, the campaign won a CASSIE award in 1999.

The choice of headlines and copy can make a difference in impact. Lalita Manrai created two ads for the same car. The first ad carried the headline "A New Car"; the second, the headline "Is This Car for You?" The second headline utilized an advertising strategy called *labelling*, in which the consumer is labelled as the type of person who is interested in that type of product. The two ads also differed in that the first ad described the car's features and the second described the car's benefits. In the test, the second ad far outperformed the first in terms of overall product impression, reader interest in buying the product, and likelihood of recommending it to a friend.[14]

Message execution can be decisive for highly similar products, such as detergents, cigarettes, or coffee. Consider the success of Absolut Vodka:

- **Absolut Vodka.** Vodka is generally viewed as a commodity product. Yet the amount of brand preference and loyalty in the vodka market is astonishing.

Most of it is based on selling an image. When the Swedish brand Absolut entered the North American market in 1979, the company sold a disappointing 7000 cases that year. By 1991, sales had soared to over two million cases. Absolut became the largest selling imported vodka with 65 percent of the market. Sales also skyrocketed globally. Its secret weapon: a targeting, packaging, and advertising strategy. Absolut aims for sophisticated, upwardly mobile, affluent drinkers. The vodka is in a distinctive, odd-shaped bottle suggestive of Swedish austerity. The bottle has become an icon and is used as the centrepiece of every ad, accompanied by puns such as "Absolut Magic" or "Absolut Larceny." Well-known artists—including Warhol, Haring, Scharf—designed Absolut ads, and the bottle image always figures in a clever way. Absolut also runs short stories about the brand written by distinguished authors. These ads are designed to appeal to readers of such magazines as *Macleans*, *The New Yorker*, and *Vanity Fair*.[15]

Absolut Vodka
www.absolutvodka.com

In preparing an ad campaign, the advertiser usually prepares a *copy strategy statement* describing the objective, content, support, and tone of the desired ad. Here is the strategy statement for a Pillsbury product called 1869 Brand Biscuits:

■ **Pillsbury.** The advertising *objective* is to convince biscuit users they can buy a canned biscuit that's as good as homemade—Pillsbury's 1869 Brand Biscuits. The *content* consists of emphasizing the following product characteristics: they look like, have the same texture as, and taste like homemade biscuits. *Support* for the "good as homemade" promise will be twofold: (1) 1869 Brand Biscuits are made from a special kind of flour used to make homemade biscuits but never before used in making canned biscuits, and (2) the use of traditional biscuit recipes. The *tone* of the advertising will be a news announcement, tempered by a warm, reflective mood emanating from a look back at traditional baking quality.

Pillsbury
www.pillsbury.com

Creative people must also find a cohesive *style, tone, words*, and *format* for executing the message.

Any message can be presented in a number of execution styles: slice of life, lifestyle, fantasy, mood or image, musical, personality symbol, technical expertise, scientific evidence, and testimonial. The Marketing Insight, "Celebrity Endorsements as a Strategy," focuses on the use of testimonials.

The communicator must choose an appropriate *tone* for the ad. Procter & Gamble is consistently positive in its tone—its ads say something superlatively positive about the product, and humour is almost always avoided so as not to take attention away from the message. In contrast, ads for Staples office-supply superstores focus on a humorous situation rather than on the products themselves.

Memorable and attention-getting *words* must be found. The following themes listed on the left would have had much less impact without the creative phrasing on the right:[16]

Theme	Creative Copy
7-Up is not a cola.	"The Un-Cola."
Let us drive you in our bus instead of driving your car.	"Take the bus, and leave the driving to us."
Shop by turning the pages of the telephone directory.	"Let your fingers do the walking."
We don't rent as many cars, so we have to do more for our customers.	"We try harder."
Red Roof Inns offer inexpensive lodging.	"Sleep cheap at Red Roof Inns."

Creativity is especially required for headlines. There are six basic types of headlines: *news* ("New Boom and More Inflation Ahead . . . and What You Can Do About It"); *question* ("Have You Had It Lately?"); *narrative* ("They Laughed When I Sat Down at the Piano, but Then I Started to Play!"); *command* ("Don't Buy Until You Try All Three"); *1-2-3 ways* ("12 Ways to Save on Your Income Tax"); and *how-what-why* ("Why They Can't Stop Buying").

Celebrity Endorsements as a Strategy

From time immemorial, marketers have used celebrities to endorse their products. A well-chosen celebrity can draw attention to a product or brand, as when Sarah, Duchess of York—better known as Fergie—shows how she's slimmed down thanks to Weight Watchers. Or the celebrity's mystique can transfer to the brand—Bill Cosby entertains a group of kids while eating a bowl of Jell-O.

The choice of the celebrity is critical. The celebrity should have high recognition, high positive affect, and high appropriateness to the product. Bruce Willis has high recognition and high positive affect but might not be appropriate for advertising a World Peace Conference. In 1998, Jerry Seinfeld was the top endorser in terms of the money he earned, a cool $267 million. Oprah Winfrey is the top female. She ranks number four on the list of big money earners and has been able to successfully advertise a large number of products because they have extremely high ratings for well-knownness and likability (known as the *Q factor* in the entertainment industry).

Athletes are a particularly effective group for endorsing athletic products, beverages, and apparel. The premier athlete endorser is Michael Jordan, former star of the Chicago Bulls. By conservative estimates, Jordan earned about $69 million in endorsement money in 1998. Probably best known for his endorsements of Nike's athletic footwear and clothing, Jordan has garnered revenues of $5.2 billion for Nike. Despite his retirement from hockey, Wayne Gretzky continues to score when it comes

to sponsorship contracts. A long line of blue-chip companies such as McDonald's Corp., Tylenol, Hudson Bay Company, Post Cereals, Coca-Cola, and the Campbell Soup Company have paid handsomely for his services.

One of advertisers' main worries is that their celebrity endorsers will become caught in a scandal or embarrassing situation. Ben Johnson became a major embarrassment to his sponsors when he was found to have used drugs to win a Olympic medal. Pepsi dropped Michael Jackson in the wake of child molestation charges. Several sports teams dropped Gary Glitter's arena anthem "Rock and Roll" after he was convicted of possession of child porn. But sponsors such as Roots Canada stuck by Ross Rebagliati despite his testing positive for marijuana.

Insurers are now selling policies to protect advertisers against such risks. One insurance company offers "death, disablement, and disgrace" insurance to cover the failings and foibles of their celebrity endorsers. Alternatively, advertisers can choose to use "spokescharacters." Owens-Corning has used the Pink Panther for nearly 20 years to endorse its insulation products, and Metropolitan Life has used the Peanuts gang to promote its insurance policies. Another way advertisers protect themselves is by using deceased celebrities. Through the wonders of technology, television viewers see screen legends John Wayne pitching Coors beer and Fred Astaire dancing with a Dirt Devil vacuum cleaner. Some celebrities volunteer their endorsements. Canadian swimming gold medallist Mark Tewksbury worked as the spokesperson for the Children's Miracle Network.

Sources: See Irving Rein, Philip Kotler, and Martin Scoller, *The Making and Marketing of Professionals into Celebrities* (Chicago: NTC Business Books, 1997); Gayle MacDonald and Paul Waldie, "In or Out of Hockey, Gretzky Can Score Big," *The Globe and Mail*, April 14, 1999, pp. B1, B6; Roy S. Johnson and Ann Harrington, "The Jordan Effect," *Fortune*, June 22, 1998, pp. 130–38. Milt Freudenheim, "Influencing Doctor's Orders," *New York Times*, November 17, 1998, p. C1.

Format elements such as ad size, colour, and illustration will affect an ad's impact as well as its cost. A minor rearrangement of mechanical elements can improve attention-getting power. Larger-size ads gain more attention, though not necessarily by as much as their difference in cost. Four-colour illustrations increase ad effectiveness and ad cost. By planning the relative dominance of different elements, better delivery can be achieved. New electronic eye movement studies show that consumers can be led through an ad by strategic placement of dominant elements.

A number of researchers into print advertisements report that the *picture, headline*, and *copy* are important, in that order. The reader first notices the picture, and it must be strong enough to draw attention. Then the headline must propel the person to read the copy. The copy itself must be well composed. Even then, a really outstanding ad will be noted by less than 50 percent of the exposed audience. About 30 percent of the exposed audience might recall the headline's main point; about 25 percent might remember the advertiser's name; and less than 10 percent will read most of the body copy. Ordinary ads do not achieve even these results.

An industry study listed the following characteristics for ads that scored above average in recall and recognition: innovation (new product or new uses), "story appeal" (as an attention-getting device), before-and-after illustration, demonstrations, problem solution, and the inclusion of relevant characters that become emblematic of the brand.[17]

In recent years critics have bemoaned the spate of bland ads and slogans and, in particular, the frequent use of the nonreferential "it," as in "Coke is it" and Nike's popular "Just do it"[18] Why do so many ads look or sound alike? Why aren't advertising agencies more creative? Norman W. Brown, former head of the advertising agency of Foote, Cone & Belding, says: "Many ads aren't creative because many companies want comfort, not creativity."

Social Responsibility Review

Advertisers and their agencies must be sure their "creative" advertising doesn't overstep social and legal norms. Most marketers work hard to communicate openly and honestly with consumers. Still, abuses occur, and public policy makers have developed a substantial body of laws and regulations to govern advertising.

Two bodies oversee Canadian advertising practices: the Canadian Radio-Television and Telecommunications Commission (CRTC) and Advertising Standards Canada (formerly the Canadian Advertising Foundation.) The mission of the CRTC is to find a balance between public- and private-sector interests. It governs ownership of broadcasting outlets, licences, and programming content. It handles complaints about programming and advertising. It works closely with Advertising Standards Canada (ASC), which is a national industry association committed to assuring integrity and viability of advertising through industry self-regulation.

Advertising Standards Canada administers the Canadian Code of Advertising Standards, which was first published in 1963. The code has a number of provisions that include dictates that advertisements must not include inaccurate or deceptive claims, that advertisements must not omit relevant information, and that advertising claims must be supportable. The commercial intent of an advertisement must be obvious to the viewer or reader. Furthermore, advertisements must not include deceptive price claims or discounts or unrealistic price comparisons. Advertising to children is subject to a special code (the Broadcast Code for Advertising to Children). It should also be noted that Quebec prohibits advertising to children. The ASC carefully considers and responds to all written consumer complaints submitted to them about advertising that does not comply to the Codes and it also produces *an Advertising Complaints Report*. In addition to the work performed by Canada's two official watchdogs, other groups such as the Media Awareness Network keep their eye on Canadian advertising practices.

Canadian Radio-Television and Telecommunications Commission (CRTC)
www..crtc.gc.ca

Advertising Standards Canada
www.adstandards.com

Media Awareness Network
www.media-awareness.ca

Everyone Has Something To Say About Advertising.
And We Listen.

That's what we're here for. So what do you do if an ad causes you concern? Simple. Let us know. We're Advertising Standards Canada, the industry's self-regulatory body. We administer the Canadian Code of Advertising Standards; a code developed by and for the advertising industry. It sets the standards for responsible advertising in Canada. For more information, call our toll-free line. If you have a concern about an ad, write to us. We guarantee a prompt response.

ADVERTISING STANDARDS
CANADA

You respond to advertising. We respond to you.

350 Bloor Street East, Suite 402, Toronto, Ontario, M4W 1H5 • 1-877-656-8646 • www.adstandards.com

To be socially responsible, advertisers must be careful not to offend ethnic groups, racial minorities, or special-interest groups. Consider the following examples:[19]

- A Nynex spot was criticized by animal-rights activists because it showed a rabbit coloured with a blue dye.

- A commercial for Black Flag insecticide was altered after a veterans' group protested the playing of Taps over dead bugs.

- Ads for Calvin Klein apparel, featuring the waifish model Kate Moss, have come under attack from Boycott Anorexic Marketing.

Some companies have begun to build ad campaigns on a platform of social responsibility:

Ethical Funds
www.ethicalfunds.com

- **Ethical Funds.** When people buy shares in Ethical Funds, they know that fund managers won't invest in corporations involved in the production of military weapons, tobacco, nuclear power, and those with unfair employment practices, poor environmental records, or companies that support reactionary political regimes. A tough-talking advertising campaign for Ethical Funds shows scenes of child labour and people dying from cancer, presumably caused by smoking. The ad asks, "Do you know where your money goes?"

John Linthwaite, president of Vancouver-based Ethical Funds, Inc., says its emphasis is on research. It digs deep to weed out companies that don't meet its ethical standards while ensuring financially sound investments. Ethical Funds has grown from $150 million in assets to more than $3 billion over the last decade.[20]

DECIDING ON MEDIA AND MEASURING EFFECTIVENESS

After choosing the message, the advertiser's next task is to choose media to carry it. The steps here are deciding on desired reach, frequency, and impact; choosing among major media types; selecting specific media vehicles; deciding on media timing; and deciding on geographical media allocation. Then the results of these decisions need to be evaluated.

DECIDING ON REACH, FREQUENCY, AND IMPACT

- *Media selection* involves finding the most cost-effective media to deliver the desired number of exposures to the target audience.

What do we mean by the desired number of exposures? Presumably, the advertiser is seeking a certain response from the target audience—for example, a certain level of product trial. The rate of product trial will depend, among other things, on the level of audience brand awareness. Suppose the rate of product trial increases at a diminishing rate with the level of audience awareness, as shown in Figure 19.2(a). If the advertiser seeks a product trial rate of (say) T^*, it will be necessary to achieve a brand awareness level of A^*.

The next task is to find out how many exposures, E^*, will produce a level of audience awareness of A^*. The effect of exposures on audience awareness depends on the exposures' reach, frequency, and impact:

- *Reach (R):* The number of different persons or households exposed to a particular media schedule at least once during a specified time period.

- *Frequency (F):* The number of times within the specified time period that an average person or household is exposed to the message.

- *Impact (I):* The qualitative value of an exposure through a given medium (thus a food ad in *Good Housekeeping* would have a higher impact than in the *Police Gazette*).

Figure 19.2(b) shows the relationship between audience awareness and reach. Audience awareness will be greater, the higher the exposures' reach, frequency, and

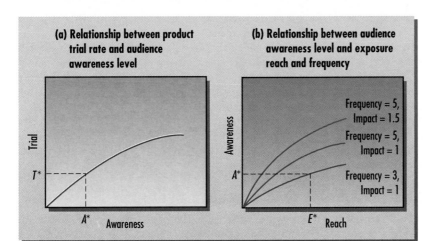

(a) Relationship between product trial rate and audience awareness level

Trial

T^*

A^* Awareness

(b) Relationship between audience awareness level and exposure reach and frequency

Awareness

Frequency = 5, Impact = 1.5

Frequency = 5, Impact = 1

A^*

Frequency = 3, Impact = 1

E^* Reach

impact. The media planner recognizes important trade-offs among reach, frequency, and impact. Suppose the planner has an advertising budget of $1 000 000 and the cost per thousand exposures of average quality is $5. This means the advertiser can buy 200 000 000 exposures ($1 000 000 ÷ [$5/1000]). If the advertiser seeks an average exposure frequency of 10, then the advertiser can reach 20 000 000 people (200 000 000 ÷ 10) with the given budget. But if the advertiser wants higher-quality media costing $10 per thousand exposures, it will be able to reach only 10 000 000 people unless it is willing to lower the desired exposure frequency.

The relationship between reach, frequency, and impact is captured in the following concepts:

■ *Total number of exposures (E):* This is the reach times the average frequency; that is, $E = R \times F$. This measure is referred to as the *gross rating points* (GRP). If a given media schedule reaches 80 percent of the homes with an average exposure frequency of 3, the media schedule is said to have a GRP of 240 (80 × 3). If another media schedule has a GRP of 300, it is said to have more weight, but we cannot tell how this weight breaks down into reach and frequency.

■ *Weighted number of exposures (WE):* This is the reach times average frequency times average impact, that is $WE = R \times F \times I$.

The media planner must determine, with a given budget, the most cost-effective combination of reach, frequency, and impact. Reach is most important when launching new products, flanker brands, extensions of well-known brands, or infrequently purchased brands, or going after an undefined target market. Frequency is most important where there are strong competitors, a complex story to tell, high consumer resistance, or a frequent-purchase cycle.[21]

Many advertisers believe a target audience needs a large number of exposures for the advertising to work. Too few repetitions can be a waste, because they will hardly be noticed. Others doubt the value of high ad frequency. They believe that after people see the same ad a few times, they either act on it, get irritated by it, or stop noticing it. Krugman asserted that three exposures to an advertisement might be enough:

> *The first exposure is by definition unique. As with the initial exposure to anything, a "What is it?" type of cognitive response dominates the reaction. The second exposure to a stimulus . . . produces several effects. One may be the cognitive reaction that characterized the first exposure, if the audience missed much of the message the first time around. . . . More often, an evaluative "What of it?" response replaces the "What is it?" response. . . . The third exposure constitutes a reminder, if a decision to buy based on the evaluations has not been acted on. The third exposure is also the beginning of disengagement and withdrawal of attention from a completed episode.[22]*

Krugman's thesis favouring three exposures must be qualified. He means three actual impressions or *advertising exposures*—the person sees the ad three times. These exposures should not be confused with *vehicle exposures*. If only half the magazine readers look at magazine ads, or if the readers look at ads only every other issue, then the advertising exposure is only half of the vehicle exposures. Most research services estimate vehicle exposures, not ad exposures. A media strategist would have to buy more vehicle exposures than three to achieve Krugman's three "hits."[23] Another factor arguing for repetition is that of forgetting. The job of repetition is partly to put the message back into memory. The higher the forgetting rate associated with a brand, product category, or message, the higher the warranted level of repetition. But repetition is not enough. Ads wear out and viewers tune out. Advertisers should not coast on a tired ad but insist on fresh executions by their advertising agency. For example, Duracell can choose from more than 40 different versions of its basic ad.

CHOOSING AMONG MAJOR MEDIA TYPES

The media planner has to know the capacity of the major media types to deliver reach, frequency, and impact. The major advertising media along with their costs, advantages, and limitations are profiled in Table 19.1.

Media planners make their choice among media categories by considering the following variables:

- *Target-audience media habits:* For example, radio and television are the most effective media for reaching teenagers.
- *Product:* Women's dresses are best shown in colour magazines, and Polaroid cameras are best demonstrated on television. Media types have different potentials for demonstration, visualization, explanation, believability, and colour.

TABLE 19.1

Profiles of Major Media Types

Medium	Advantages	Limitations
Newspapers	Flexibility; timeliness; good local market coverage; broad acceptance; high believability	Short life; poor reproduction quality; small "pass-along" audience
Television	Combines sight, sound, and motion; appealing to the senses; high attention; high reach	High absolute cost; high clutter; fleeting exposure; less audience selectivity
Direct mail	Audience selectivity; flexibility; no ad competition within the same medium; personalization	Relatively high cost; "junk mail" image
Radio	Mass use; high geographic and demographic selectivity; low cost	Audio presentation only; lower attention than television; nonstandardized rate structures; fleeting exposure
Magazines	High geographic and demographic selectivity; credibility and prestige; high-quality reproduction; long life; good pass-along readership	Long ad purchase lead time; some waste circulation; no guarantee of position
Outdoor	Flexibility; high repeat exposure; low cost; low competition	Limited audience selectivity; creative limitations
Yellow Pages	Excellent local coverage; high believability; wide reach; low cost	High competition; long ad purchase lead time; creative limitations
Newsletters	Very high selectivity; full control; interactive opportunities; relative low costs	Costs could run away
Brochures	Flexibility; full control; can dramatize messages	Overproduction could lead to runaway costs
Telephone	Many users; opportunity to give a personal touch	Relative high cost unless volunteers are used
Internet	High selectivity; interactive possibilities; relatively low cost	Relatively new media with a low number of users in some countries

- *Message:* A message announcing a major sale tomorrow will require radio, TV, or newspaper. A message containing a great deal of technical data might require specialized magazines or mailings.

- *Cost:* Television is very expensive, whereas newspaper advertising is relatively inexpensive. What counts is the cost-per-thousand exposures.

Ideas about media impact and cost must be reexamined periodically. For a long time, television was dominant in the media mix. Then researchers began to notice television's reduced effectiveness, which was due to increased commercial clutter (advertisers beamed shorter and more numerous commercials at the audience), increased "zipping and zapping" of commercials, and audience fragmentation due to the growth in cable TV and VCRs. A study of the viewing habits of Canadian consumers, for example, reveals that 19.5 percent view programming on the English national networks, 17.7 view the French networks, another 17.6 percent watch Global and the other independents, 17.4 percent tune into U.S. conventional and superstations, 16.2 percent use Canadian pay and specialty channels, while 6.4 percent subscribe to U.S. pay and specialty channels.[24] Television advertising costs rose faster than other media costs. Several companies found that a combination of print ads and television commercials often were more effective than television commercials alone.

Another reason for review is the continuous emergence of *new media,* such as advertorials and infomercials. Advertorials are print ads that offer editorial content and are difficult to distinguish from newspaper or magazine contents; infomercials are TV commercials that appear to be 30-minute TV shows but are advertisements for products. Advertisers have substantially increased their spending on outdoor media over the last decade. Outdoor advertising provides an excellent way to reach important local consumer segments. Cable television now reaches a majority of North American households and produces billions of dollars in advertising revenue a year. Cable systems make it easier to reach select groups.

Another promising new media site is the store itself. In addition to using older promotional vehicles, such as displays and special price tags, some supermarkets are selling space on their floors for company logos, experimenting with talking shelves, and introducing "videocarts," which contain a computerized screen that carries consumer-benefit information ("cauliflower is rich in vitamin C") and advertiser promotions ("$0.20 off on White Star Tuna this week").

Ads also appear in best-selling paperback books, sports arenas, movie theatres, and movie videotapes. Written material such as annual reports, data sheets, catalogues, and newsletters increasingly carry ads. Many companies that send out monthly bills are including advertising inserts. Some companies mail audiotapes or videotapes that advertise their products to prospects. Here are some other emerging media:

- *Digital magazines (or digizines):* With names like *Trouble & Attitude, Word,* and *Launch,* the latest magazines are not on the newsstand but are available on the Internet. Digizines are much cheaper to start up and operate than are print magazines. Starting a glossy publication for men aged 18 to 34 today would require at least $15 million, whereas digizine start-up costs are $200 000 to $500 000. Still to be worked out, however, is how to price them or earn money through selling advertising.

- *Interactive TV:* Combined computer, telephone, and TV hookups have now made it possible for people to participate in two-way communication with programs or information services via their television sets. Whereas home shopping networks allow customers to call in their orders, *interactive TV* allows consumers to use a computer keyboard to communicate directly with sellers on their TV screen. So far interactive TV technology is only in the testing phase.

- *Fax on demand:* Used most by business marketers, fax-on-demand technology allows businesses to store information in a fax technology program. Customers who need information call a toll-free number, and the fax program automatically faxes the information to them within five minutes. Customers can access the information 24 hours a day, 7 days a week. The service can be set up for as little as $1000, and business marketers feel that the cost savings in postage alone are worth the investment.

The digizine *Word*'s home page: This magazine is available only on the Internet.

Rust and Oliver see proliferation of new media as hastening the death of traditional mass-media advertising as we know it. They see a greater amount of direct producer–consumer interaction, with benefits to both parties. Producers gain more information about their customers and can customize products and messages better; customers gain greater control because they can choose whether to receive an advertising message or not.[25] See the Marketing for the 21st Century "Advertising on the Web: Companies Grab the Brass Ring."

Given the abundant media, the media planner must first decide on how to allocate the budget to the major media types. In launching a new biscuit, Pillsbury might decide to allocate $3 million to daytime network television, $2 million to women's magazines, $1 million to daily newspapers in 20 major markets, and $50 000 to maintaining its home page on the Internet.

SELECTING SPECIFIC VEHICLES

The media planner must search for the most cost-effective media vehicles within each chosen media type. The advertiser who decides to buy 30 seconds of advertising on Canadian network television can pay approximately $45 000 to have a 30-second ad run on CBC's 37 stations. Ads placed on specialty channels may be much cheaper. A 30-second spot on Bravo, the History Channel, or the Life Network may only cost $3000. However, if an advertiser wants to reach the larger North American audience, the firm will have to budget $231 000 for a popular prime-time show such as *Law and Order*, $975 000 for especially popular programs such as *Frasier* and *ER*, or $2 million for an event like the Super Bowl.[26] The planner must rely on media measurement services that provide estimates of audience size, composition, and media cost.

Audience size has several possible measures:

- *Circulation:* The number of physical units carrying the advertising.
- *Audience:* The number of people exposed to the vehicle. (If the vehicle has pass-on readership, then the audience is larger than circulation.)
- *Effective audience:* The number of people with target audience characteristics exposed to the vehicle.
- *Effective ad-exposed audience:* The number of people with target audience characteristics who actually saw the ad.

Media planners calculate the *cost per thousand persons reached* by a vehicle. If a full-page, four-colour ad in *Maclean's* costs $30 563 and *Maclean's* estimated readership is 1 684 052 people (the magazine's circulation is 510 925 and there are 3.3 readers/copy),

Advertising on the Web: Companies Grab the Brass Ring

All signs point to enormous growth in advertising on the Internet. In 1997, Internet advertising revenues in Canada increased by 516 percent over 1996 levels and are forecast to jump to over $56.9 million in 1999 according to the Internet Advertising Bureau of Canada. The financial services sector is the biggest spender, accounting for 20 percent of Internet advertising. Advertising revenues have been growing as a result of more and more people going on-line. The number of Web users has also been expanding: the Statistics Canada 1998 Household Internet Use Survey noted that 35.9 percent of Canadian households are connected—up from 24.6 percent just a year earlier. The survey also revealed that there is a strong correlation between household income and Internet usage. While 50.4 percent of high-income households have people who regularly use the Internet, only 4.1 percent of people from low-income households surf the Net.

Web-based advertising will become an important part of a company's media mix. Numerous companies are committing large advertising budgets to the Internet. Chapters.ca, one of Canada's on-line book retailers, seems to be placing ads everywhere. When you enter a search topic on many of Canada's search engines, a Chapters ad will appear asking you if you are interested in a book on the topic.

Yet many companies are reluctant to commit advertising dollars to the Web. The reason: there is not yet a reliable way to answer two fundamental questions: How many people visit a Web site? and What types of people visit a Web site? With these questions unanswered, it is difficult to compare Internet advertising effectiveness relative to broadcast and print media. This problem is currently being addressed by industry groups such as the Coalition for Advertising Supported Information and Entertainment (CASIE) and the Interactive Advertising Bureau (IAB).

Why is the Internet becoming so attractive to certain advertisers? Some facts about the Web will help to answer this question.

■ Increasingly, consumers would rather visit cyberspace than sit through a sitcom or watch their team lose again. This trend directly challenges companies such as Procter & Gamble, Unilever, Gillette, and many other mass marketers, many of which spend as much as 80 percent of their ad budgets on television.

■ Instead of an ad coming to a consumer, the consumer goes to the ad. Consider a company called Yoyodyne, whose clients include H&R Block, Reader's Digest, and MCI. Yoyodyne designs games and contests (with prizes) that drive traffic to client Web sites. Players must provide an e-mail address and choose Web sites to visit or ads to view, which helps advertisers learn more about them. Yoyodyne, which was recently bought by Yahoo!, signed up a million players in 1997.

■ Powerful search engines will soon allow consumers to search for products and bargains all across the Web. Junglee and C2B technologies are two e-commerce companies that are developing such search engines. Junglee's goal is to enable consumers to comparison shop on a scale never before envisioned; C2B's shopping platform offers Web shoppers information on nearly a million products and connects them with hundreds of merchants. What advertiser wouldn't want to cash in on this bonanza?

■ The Internet allows vendors to build their products on demand, thus keeping inventory to a minimum. Dell Computers gives customers their choice of sound card, videoboard, video monitor, speakers, and memory capacity from a pull-down menu on its Web site. Today Dell is selling $9 million worth of products a day via its Web site and expects that 50 percent of its sales will be Web based by the end of 2000.

■ The Internet is not bound by geography: Amazon.com sells 20 percent of its books to foreign destinations, whereas a physical bookstore serves an area of only a few square kilometres.

But the Web is not simply another medium; it's a profoundly different experience. It is a place to escape the incessant interruptions of everyday life. On-line advertisers used to talk about push—pushing your product through the channel. The Web, however, is not about push; it's about pull. On-line consumers can pull what they want out of cyberspace and leave the rest behind. Web advertisers have to be creative enough to make these consumers want to pull in their messages.

Sources: Statistics Canada, *The Daily*, "Internet Use by Households," July 15, 1999 (http://www.statcan.ca/Daily/English/990715/d990715a.htm). Patti Summerfield, "Internet Ad Revenues Soar: Financial Services Sector Biggest Spender," *Strategy: The Canadian Marketing Report*, May 25, 1998, p. 13. Gary Hamel and Jeff Sampler, "The E-Corporation: More than Just Web-based, It's Building a New Industrial Order," *Fortune*, December 7, 1998, p. 80; Kim Cleland, "Marketers Want Solid Data on Value of Internet Ad Buys," *Advertising Age*, August 3, 1998, p. S18; Xavier Dreze and Fred Zufryden, "Is Internet Advertising Ready for Prime Time?" *Journal of Advertising Research* 38, no. 3 (1998): 7–18.

the cost of exposing the ad to 1000 persons is $18.15. The same ad in *B.C. Outdoor* costs $4084 but since it only reaches 33 402 persons—the cost per thousand is $122.28.[27] The media planner ranks each magazine by cost per thousand and favours magazines with the lowest cost per thousand for reaching target consumers. The magazines themselves often put together a "reader profile" for their advertisers, summarizing the characteristics of the magazine's readers with respect to age, income, residence, marital status, and leisure activities.

Several adjustments have to be applied to the cost-per-thousand measure. First, the measure should be adjusted for *audience quality*. For a baby lotion ad, a magazine read by one million young mothers would have an exposure value of one million; if read by one million old men, it would have almost a zero exposure value. Second, the exposure value should be adjusted for the *audience-attention probability*. Readers of *Vogue* pay more attention to ads than do readers of *Maclean's*. Third, the exposure value should be adjusted for the magazine's *editorial quality* (prestige and believability). Fourth, the exposure value should be adjusted for the magazine's ad placement policies and extra services (such as regional or occupational editions and lead-time requirements).

Media planners are increasingly using more sophisticated measures of effectiveness and employing them in mathematical models to arrive at the best media mix. Many advertising agencies use a computer program to select the initial media and then make further improvements based on subjective factors.[28]

DECIDING ON MEDIA TIMING

In choosing media, the advertiser faces a macroscheduling problem and a microscheduling problem.

The macroscheduling problem involves scheduling the advertising in relation to seasons and the business cycle. Suppose 70 percent of a product's sales occur between June and September. The firm can vary its advertising expenditures to follow the seasonal pattern, to oppose the seasonal pattern, or to be constant throughout the year. Most firms pursue a seasonal policy. Yet consider this example:

> Some years ago, a soft-drink manufacturer put more money into off-season advertising. This resulted in increased nonseasonal consumption of its brand, while not hurting seasonal consumption. Other soft-drink manufacturers started to do the same, with the net result that a more balanced consumption pattern occurred. The previous concentration of advertising had created a self-fulfilling prophecy.

Forrester has proposed using his "industrial dynamics" methodology to test cyclical advertising policies.[29] He believes that advertising has a delayed impact on consumer awareness; awareness has a delayed impact on factory sales; and factory sales have a delayed impact on advertising expenditures. These time-lag relationships can be studied and formulated mathematically into a computer-simulation model. The model can simulate alternative timing strategies to assess varying impacts on company sales, costs, and profits. Rao and Miller also developed a lag (delay) model to relate a brand's share to advertising and promotional expenditures on a market-by-market basis. They tested their model successfully with five Lever brands in 15 districts, relating market share to dollars spent on TV, print, price-off, and trade promotions.[30]

Kuehn developed a model to explore how advertising should be timed for frequently purchased, highly seasonal, low-cost grocery products.[31] He showed that the appropriate timing pattern depends on the degree of advertising carryover and the amount of habitual behaviour in customer brand choice. *Carryover* refers to the rate at which the effect of an advertising expenditure wears out with the passage of time. A carryover of 0.75 per month means that the current effect of a past advertising expenditure is 75 percent of its level in the previous month. *Habitual behaviour* indicates how much brand holdover occurs independent of the level of advertising. High habitual purchasing, say 0.90, means that 90 percent of the buyers repeat their brand choice in the next period.

Kuehn found that when there is no advertising carryover or habitual purchasing, the decision maker is justified in using a percentage-of-sales rule to budget advertising. The optimal timing pattern for advertising expenditures coincides with the expected seasonal pattern of industry sales. But if there is advertising carryover or habitual purchasing, it would be better to time advertising to lead sales. Advertising expenditures should peak before sales peak. Lead time should be greater, the higher the carryover. Furthermore, the advertising expenditures should be steadier, the greater the habitual purchasing.

The microscheduling problem calls for allocating advertising expenditures within a short period to obtain maximum impact.

Suppose the firm decides to buy 30 radio spots in the month of September. Figure 19.3 shows several possible patterns. The left side shows that advertising messages for the month can be concentrated ("burst" advertising), dispersed continuously throughout the month, or dispersed intermittently. The top side shows that the advertising messages can be beamed with a level, rising, falling, or alternating frequency.

The most effective pattern depends upon the communication objectives in relation to the nature of the product, target customers, distribution channels, and other marketing factors. Consider the following cases:

> *A retailer wants to announce a preseason sale of ski equipment. She thinks the target buyers need to hear the message only once or twice. Her objective is to maximize reach, not frequency. She decides to concentrate the messages on sale days at a level rate but to vary the time of day to avoid the same audiences. She uses pattern 1.*
>
> *A muffler manufacturer-distributor wants to keep his name before the public. Yet he does not want his advertising to be too continuous because only three to five percent of the cars on the road need a new muffler at any given time. He chooses intermittent advertising. Furthermore, he recognizes that Fridays are paydays, so he sponsors more messages on Friday. He uses pattern 12.*

The timing pattern should consider three factors. *Buyer turnover* expresses the rate at which new buyers enter the market; the higher this rate, the more continuous the advertising should be. *Purchase frequency* is the number of times during the period that the average buyer buys the product; the higher the purchase frequency, the more continuous the advertising should be. The *forgetting rate* is the rate at which the buyer forgets the brand; the higher the forgetting rate, the more continuous the advertising should be.

In launching a new product, the advertiser must choose among ad continuity, concentration, flighting, and pulsing. *Continuity* is achieved by scheduling exposures evenly throughout a given period. Generally, advertisers use continuous advertising in expanding market situations, with frequently purchased items, and in tightly defined buyer categories. *Concentration* calls for spending all the advertising dollars in a single period. This makes sense for products with one selling season or holiday.

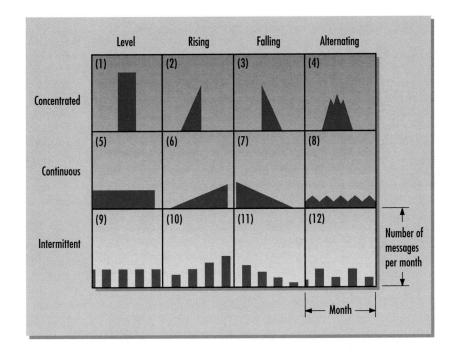

FIGURE 19.3

Classification of Advertising Timing Patterns

Flighting calls for advertising for some period, followed by a hiatus with no advertising, followed by a second period of advertising activity. It is used when funding is limited, the purchase cycle is relatively infrequent, and with seasonal items. *Pulsing* is continuous advertising at low-weight levels reinforced periodically by waves of heavier activity. Pulsing draws upon the strength of continuous advertising and flights to create a compromise scheduling strategy.[32]Those who favour pulsing feel that the audience will learn the message more thoroughly, and money can be saved.

- **Anheuser-Busch.** Anheuser-Busch's research indicated that Budweiser could substantially reduce advertising in a particular market and experience no adverse sales effect for at least 18 months. Then the company could introduce a six-month burst of advertising and restore the previous growth rate. This analysis led Budweiser to adopt a pulsing advertising strategy.

DECIDING ON GEOGRAPHICAL ALLOCATION

A company must decide how to allocate its advertising budget over space as well as over time. The company makes "national buys" when it places ads on national TV networks or in nationally circulated magazines. It makes "spot buys" when it buys TV time in just a few markets or in regional editions of magazines. These markets are called *areas of dominant influence* (ADIs) or *designated marketing areas* (DMAs), and ads reach a market 50 to 80 kilometres from a city centre. The company makes "local buys" when it advertises in local newspapers, radio, or outdoor sites. Consider the following example:

- **Pizza Hut.** Pizza Hut levies a four percent advertising fee on its franchisees. It spends half of its budget on national media and half on regional and local media. Some national advertising is wasted because of low penetration in certain areas. Thus, even though Pizza Hut may have a 30 percent share of the franchised pizza market nationally, this share may vary from 5 percent in some cities to 70 percent in others. The franchisees in the higher market-share cities want much more advertising money spent in their areas. But Pizza Hut doesn't have enough money to cover the whole nation by region. National advertising offers efficiency but fails to address the different local situations effectively.

EVALUATING ADVERTISING EFFECTIVENESS

Good planning and control of advertising depend on measures of advertising effectiveness. Yet the amount of fundamental research on advertising effectiveness is appallingly small. According to Forrester, "probably no more than 1/5 of 1% of total advertising expenditure is used to achieve an enduring understanding of how to spend the other 99.8%."[33]

Most measurement of advertising effectiveness deals with specific ads and campaigns. Most of the money is spent by agencies on pretesting ads, and much less is spent on evaluating their effectiveness. A proposed campaign should be tested in one or a few cities first and its impact evaluated before rolling it out nationally.

Most advertisers try to measure the communication effect of an ad—that is, its potential effect on awareness, knowledge, or preference. They would also like to measure the ad's sales effect.

Communication-Effect Research

Communication-effect research seeks to determine whether an ad is communicating effectively. Called *copy testing*, it can be done before an ad is put into media and after it is printed or broadcast.

There are three major methods of advertising pretesting. The *direct rating method* asks consumers to rate alternative ads. These ratings are used to evaluate an ad's attention, read-through, cognitive, affective, and behaviour strengths (Figure 19.4).

FIGURE 19.4

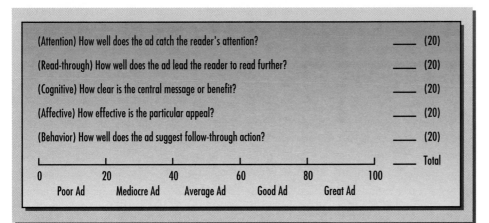

Although an imperfect measure of actual impact, a high rating indicates a potentially more effective ad. *Portfolio tests* ask consumers to view or listen to a portfolio of advertisements, taking as much time as they need. Consumers are then asked to recall all the ads and their content, aided or unaided by the interviewer. Recall level indicates an ad's ability to stand out and to have its message understood and remembered. *Laboratory tests* use equipment to measure physiological reactions—heartbeat, blood pressure, pupil dilation, perspiration—to an ad. These tests measure attention-getting power but reveal nothing about impact on beliefs, attitudes, or intentions. Table 19.2 describes some specific advertising research techniques.

Haley, Stafforoni, and Fox argue that current copy-testing methods have become so familiar and well established that it is easy to overlook their sizeable limitations. These methods tend to be excessively rational and verbal, and to rely primarily on respondents' playback in one form or another. They argue that marketers must take more account of ads' nonverbal elements, which can be very strong influences on behaviour.[34]

TABLE 19.2

For Print Ads. Starch and Gallup & Robinson, Inc. are two widely used print pretesting services. Test ads are placed in magazines, which are then circulated to consumers. These consumers are contacted later and interviewed. Recall and recognition tests are used to determine advertising effectiveness. Starch prepares three readership scores: (1) *noted,* the percentage of readers who recall seeing the ad in the magazine; (2) *seen or associated,* the percentage who correctly identify the product and advertiser with the ad; and (3) *read most,* the percentage who say they read more than half of the written material in the ad. Starch also furnishes data showing the average "read" scores for each product class for the year, and separately for men and women for each magazine, to enable advertisers to compare their ads to competitors' ads.

For Broadcast Ads. *In-home tests:* A videotape is taken into the homes of target consumers, who then view the commercials.

Trailer tests: In a trailer in a shopping center, shoppers are shown the products and given an opportunity to select a series of brands in a simulated shopping situation. Consumers then view a series of commercials and are given coupons to be used in the shopping center. By evaluating redemption, advertisers can estimate the commercials' influence on purchase behavior.

Theatre tests: Consumers are invited to a theater to view a potential new television series along with some commercials. Before the show begins, the consumers indicate their preferred brands in different categories. After the viewing, consumers are again asked to choose their preferred brands in various categories. Preference changes are assumed to measure the commercials' persuasive power.

On-air tests: Tests are conducted on a regular TV channel. Respondents are recruited to watch the program during the test commercial or are selected based on their having viewed the program. They are asked questions about commercial recall.

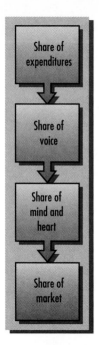

FIGURE 19.5

Formula for Measuring Sales Impact of Advertising

Advertisers are also interested in posttesting the overall communication impact of a completed campaign. If a company hoped to increase brand awareness from 20 percent to 50 percent and succeeded in increasing it to only 30 percent, then the company is not spending enough, its ads are poor, or some other factor has been ignored.

Sales-Effect Research

What sales are generated by an ad that increases brand awareness by 20 percent and brand preference by 10 percent? Advertising's sales effect is generally harder to measure than its communication effect. Sales are influenced by many factors, such as the product's features, price, and availability, as well as competitors' actions. The fewer or more controllable these other factors are, the easier it is to measure effect on sales. The sales impact is easiest to measure in direct-marketing situations and hardest to measure in brand or corporate-image-building advertising.

Companies are generally interested in finding out whether they are overspending or underspending on advertising. One approach to answering this question is to work with the formulation shown in Figure 19.5.

A company's share of advertising expenditures produces a share of voice that earns a share of consumers' minds and hearts and ultimately a share of market. Peckham studied the relationship between share of voice and share of market for several consumer products over a number of years and found a 1-to-1 ratio for established products and a 1.5–2.0 to 1.0 ratio for new products.[35] Using this information, suppose we observed the following data for three well-established firms selling an almost identical product at an identical price:

	(1) Advertising Expenditure	(2) Share of Voice	(3) Share of Market	(4) Advertising Effectiveness (column 3 ÷ column 2)*
A	$2 000 000	57.1	40.0	70
B	1 000 000	28.6	28.6	100
C	500 000	14.3	31.4	220

*Note: An advertising effectiveness rating of 100 means an effective level of advertising expenditure. A rating below 100 means a relatively ineffective advertising level; a level above 100 indicates a very effective advertising level.

Firm A spends $2 million of the industry's total expenditures of $3.5 million, so its share of voice is 57.1 percent. Yet its share of market is only 40 percent. By dividing its share of market by its share of voice, we get an advertising-effectiveness ratio of 70, suggesting that firm A is either overspending or misspending. Firm B is spending 28.6 percent of total advertising expenditures and has a 28.6 market share; the conclusion is that it is spending its money efficiently. Firm C is spending only 14.3 percent of the total and yet achieving a market share of 31.4 percent; the conclusion is that it is spending its money superefficiently and should probably increase its expenditures.

Researchers try to measure the sales impact through analyzing either historical or experimental data. The *historical approach* involves correlating past sales to past advertising expenditures using advanced statistical techniques. Queen's University's Kristin Palda studied the effect of advertising expenditures on the sales of Lydia Pinkham's Vegetable Compound between 1908 and 1960.[36] He calculated the short-term and long-term marginal sales effects of advertising. The marginal advertising dollars increased sales by only $.50 in the short term, suggesting that Pinkham spent too much on advertising. But the long-term marginal sales effect was three times as large. Palda calculated a posttax marginal rate of return on company advertising of 37 percent over the whole period.

Montgomery and Silk estimated the sales effectiveness of three communication tools used in the pharmaceutical industry.[37] A drug company spent 38 percent of its communication budget on direct mail, 32 percent on samples and literature, and 29 percent on journal advertising. Yet the sales-effects research indicated that journal advertising, the least-used communication tool, had the highest long-run effectiveness, followed by samples and literature, and then by direct mail.

Other researchers use an *experimental design* to measure advertising's sales impact. Here is an example:

- **DuPont.** DuPont was one of the first companies to design advertising experiments. DuPont's paint division divided 56 sales territories into high, average, and low market-share territories. DuPont spent the normal amount for advertising in one-third of the group; in another third, two and one-half times the normal amount; and in the remaining third, four times the normal amount. At the end of the experiment, DuPont estimated how much in extra sales was created by higher levels of advertising expenditure. DuPont found that higher advertising expenditure increased sales at a diminishing rate and that the sales increase was weaker in DuPont's high-market-share territories.[38]

DuPont Canada
www.dupont.ca

In allocating an advertising budget geographically, the company should consider area differences in market size, advertising response, media efficiency, competition, and profit margins. Urban developed a media allocation model that uses these geographic variables to allocate the advertising budget. A growing number of companies are striving to measure the sales effect of advertising expenditures instead of settling only for communication-effect measures. Millward Brown International has conducted tracking studies in the United Kingdom for many years to provide information to help advertisers decide whether their advertising is benefiting their brand.[40]

A Summary of Current Research

Professional researchers have drawn some general conclusions that are useful to marketers.[41]

- *The impact of advertising on brand switching:* Tellis analyzed household purchases of 12 key brands of a frequently purchased consumer product and concluded that advertising appears effective in increasing the volume purchased by loyal buyers but less effective in winning new buyers. Advertising appears unlikely to have some cumulative effect that leads to loyalty; rather, features, displays, and especially price have a stronger impact on response than does advertising.[42] These findings did not sit well with the advertising community, and several people attacked Tellis' data and methodology. A set of controlled experiments by the research firm IRI found advertising's impact is grossly underestimated when only a one-year perspective is employed because of lagged effects.

- *The effect of surroundings:* Ads may be more effective when their message is congruent with their surroundings. A "happy" commercial placed within an upbeat television show is more likely to be effective than a downbeat commercial in the same place.[43] In addition, people are more likely to believe a TV or radio ad and to become more positively disposed toward the brand when the ad is placed within a program they like.[44]

- *The effect of positive versus negative messages:* Consumers may sometimes respond more to negative messages than to positive messages. For example, a credit-card company contacted customers who did not use the card for three months. To one group of nonusers it sent a message explaining the benefits of using the card. To another group it sent a message explaining the losses they could suffer by not using the card. The impact of the loss-oriented message was much stronger: the percentage of customers who started to use the card in the loss condition was more than double and the charges of the former customers were more than twice that of the positive message receivers.[45]

SALES PROMOTION

Sales promotion is a key ingredient in marketing campaigns. We define it as follows:

- **Sales promotion** consists of a diverse collection of incentive tools, mostly short term, designed to stimulate quicker or greater purchase of particular products or services by consumers or the trade.[46]

Whereas advertising offers a *reason* to buy, sales promotion offers an *incentive* to buy. Sales promotion includes tools for *consumer promotion* (samples, coupons, cash refund offers, prices off, premiums, prizes, patronage rewards, free trials, warranties, tie-in promotions, cross-promotions, point-of-purchase displays, and demonstrations); *trade promotion* (prices off, advertising and display allowances, and free goods); and *business- and sales force promotion* (trade shows and conventions, contests for sales reps, and specialty advertising).

Sales-promotion tools are used by most organizations, including manufacturers, distributors, retailers, trade associations, and nonprofit organizations. Churches, for example, often sponsor bingo games, theatre parties, testimonial dinners, and raffles.

A decade ago, the advertising-to-sales-promotion ratio was about 60:40. Today, in many consumer-packaged-goods companies, sales promotion accounts for 65 to 75 percent of the combined budget. Sales-promotion expenditures have been increasing as a percentage of budget expenditure annually for the last two decades.

Several factors contribute to the rapid growth of sales promotion, particularly in consumer markets.[47] Internal factors include the following: promotion is now more accepted by top management as an effective sales tool; more product managers are qualified to use sales-promotion tools; and product managers are under greater pressure to increase current sales. External factors include the following: the number of brands has increased; competitors use promotions frequently; many brands are seen as similar; consumers are more price-oriented; the trade has demanded more deals from manufacturers; and advertising efficiency has declined because of rising costs, media clutter, and legal restraints.

The rapid growth of sales-promotion media has created a situation of *promotion clutter* similar to advertising clutter. Consumers might start tuning out, in which case coupons and other promotion media will weaken in their ability to trigger purchase. Manufacturers will have to find ways to rise above the clutter—for instance, by offering larger coupon-redemption values or using more dramatic point-of-purchase displays or demonstrations.

PURPOSE OF SALES PROMOTION

Sales-promotion tools vary in their specific objectives. A free sample stimulates consumer trial, whereas a free management-advisory service aims at cementing a long-term relationship with a retailer.

Sellers use incentive-type promotions to attract new triers, to reward loyal customers, and to increase the repurchase rates of occasional users. New triers are of three types—users of another brand in the same category, users in other categories, and frequent brand switchers. Sales promotions often attract the brand switchers, because users of other brands and categories do not always notice or act on a promotion. Brand switchers are primarily looking for low price, good value, or premiums. Sales promotions are unlikely to turn them into loyal users. Sales promotions used in markets of high brand similarity produce a high sales response in the short run but little permanent gain in market share. In markets of high brand dissimilarity, sales promotions can alter market shares permanently.

Today, many marketing managers first estimate what they need to spend in trade promotion, then what they need to spend in consumer promotion. Whatever is left they will budget for advertising. There is a danger, however, in letting advertising take a back seat to sales promotion because advertising typically acts to build brand loyalty. But the question of whether or not sales promotion weakens brand loyalty is subject to different interpretations. Sales promotion, with its incessant prices off, coupons, deals, premiums, and blaring quality, may devalue the product offering in the buyers' minds. Buyers learn that the list price is largely a fiction. But before jumping to any conclusion, we need to distinguish between *price promotions* and *added-value promotions*. These examples show how certain types of sales promotion can actually enhance brand image:

- Tim Horton's "Roll up the rim to win," promotion, which was launched in 1987 as a means of boosting lagging summer coffee sales, has evolved into a national obsession. In 1999 alone, the chain will give away 13 million food prizes, 5000 TVs, and 15 trucks. But many of the franchisees are more than convinced it is worth the price. Business climbs up to 15 percent during promotion periods.[48]

- Toro, a major manufacturer of lawn mowers and snowblowers, wanted to sell its snowblowers in early September. Knowing that most people would wait to buy until the first snow, Toro offered to include Toro Snow Insurance: the company promised to send a rebate of $50 to each September buyer if it didn't snow before January. This sales promotion did not hurt, and may have helped, Toro's brand image.

- Häagen-Dazs ran a cents-off sales promotion called Sweet Charity where the price savings would be contributed to support public television. This offer enhanced the Häagen-Dazs image by making Häagen-Dazs "a patron of the arts."

- Akai, a Japanese manufacturer of stereo equipment and TV sets, managed to become a TV set market leader in India by running value-added sales promotions. It offered good trade-in value on black-and-white TV sets at the purchase of a new colour TV set. At other times, it would offer a free watch, calculator, or radio, along with the purchase of a new TV set. This steady promotion made Akai a very popular brand in India, and competitors such as Sony were not free to compete in the same way.

Tim Hortons
www.timhortons.com

But usually, when a brand is price promoted too often, the consumer begins to devalue it and buy it mainly when it goes on sale. So there is risk in putting a well-known brand leader on promotion over 30 percent of the time.[49] Dominant brands offer deals less frequently, because most deals only subsidize current users. Brown's study of 2500 instant coffee buyers concluded that:

- Sales promotions yield faster and more measurable responses in sales than advertising does.

- Sales promotions do not tend to yield new, long-term buyers in mature markets because they attract mainly deal-prone consumers who switch among brands as deals become available.

- Loyal brand buyers tend not to change their buying patterns as a result of competitive promotion.

- Advertising appears to be capable of deepening brand loyalty.[50]

There is also evidence that price promotions do not build permanent total category volume.

Small-share competitors find it advantageous to use sales promotion, because they cannot afford to match the market leaders' large advertising budgets. Nor can they obtain shelf space without offering trade allowances or stimulate consumer trial without offering incentives. Price competition is often used by a small brand seeking to enlarge its share, but it is less effective for a category leader whose growth lies in expanding the entire category.[51]

The upshot is that many consumer-packaged-goods companies feel they are forced to use more sales promotion than they wish. Kellogg, Kraft, and other market leaders are trying to return to "pull" marketing by increasing their advertising budgets. They blame the heavy use of sales promotion for decreasing brand loyalty, increasing consumer price sensitivity, brand-quality-image dilution, and a focus on short-run marketing planning.

Farris and Quelch, however, dispute this conclusion.[52] They counter that sales promotion provides a number of benefits that are important to manufacturers as well as consumers. Sales promotions enable manufacturers to adjust to short-term variations in supply and demand. They enable manufacturers to test how high a list price they can charge, because they can always discount it. They induce consumers to try new products instead of never straying from current ones. They lead to more varied retail formats, such as the everyday-low-price store and the promotional-pricing store. They promote greater consumer awareness of prices. They permit manufacturers to sell more

Sales Promotions as Brand Builders

Building brand awareness is a long-term process. What a brand does today predicts what it will do tomorrow. Sales promotions are short term and temporary, whether they are a price reduction, a tie-in with another brand, a coupon, or some other incentive. Here are some tips on how to make a sales promotion an effective brand-building tool.

■ *Make sure the promotion is justified:* A new store opening, a company anniversary, and other kinds of celebrations are all good reasons for running a promotion. They put the brand name in the forefront. Celebrating spring or back-to-school time are not good reasons to run a promotion; they are too generic.

■ *Tie the promotion to a brand's image:* Birth dates and anniversaries are good. For example, Häagen-Dazs could run a promotion on or around July 9 for its Dulce de Leche ice cream to coincide with Argentine National Day. (The flavour and name originated in Argentina.)

■ *Look at every promotion both for the sales job it can do and as a communications tool:* A promotion is one of a brand's many voices; it can help build brand awareness if it says the right things. For example, Bayer aspirin could run a coupon promotion, thus offering a price reduction, and use the promotion to reinforce the name Bayer.

Source: Adapted from Jacques Chevron, "Branding and Promotion: Uneasy Cohabitation," *Brandweek*, September 14, 1998, p. 24.

---

than they would normally sell at the list price. They help the manufacturer adapt programs to different consumer segments. Consumers themselves enjoy some satisfaction from being smart shoppers when they take advantage of price specials.

MAJOR DECISIONS IN SALES PROMOTION

In using sales promotion, a company must establish its objectives, select the tools, develop the program, pretest the program, implement and control it, and evaluate the results.

Establishing Objectives

Sales-promotion objectives are derived from broader promotion objectives, which are derived from more basic marketing objectives developed for the product. The specific objectives for sales promotion vary with the target market. For consumers, objectives include encouraging purchase of larger-size units, building trial among nonusers, and attracting switchers away from competitors' brands. For retailers, objectives include persuading retailers to carry new items and higher levels of inventory, encouraging off-season buying, encouraging stocking of related items, offsetting competitive promotions, building brand loyalty, and gaining entry into new retail outlets. For the sales force, objectives include encouraging support of a new product or model, encouraging more prospecting, and stimulating off-season sales.[53] See the Marketing Memo "Sales Promotions as Brand Builders."

Selecting Consumer-Promotion Tools

The promotion planner should take into account the type of market, sales-promotion objectives, competitive conditions, and each tool's cost effectiveness.

The main consumer-promotion tools are summarized in Table 19.3. We can distinguish between *manufacturer promotions* and *retailer promotions*. The former are illustrated by the auto industry's frequent use of rebates, gifts to motivate test-drives and purchases, and high-value trade-in credit. The latter include price cuts, feature advertising, retailer coupons, and retailer contests or premiums. We can also distinguish between sales-promotion tools that are "consumer-franchise building," which reinforce the consumer's brand understanding, and those that are not. The former impart a selling message along with the deal, as in the case of free samples, coupons when they include a selling message, and premiums when they are related to the product. Sales-promotion tools that are not consumer-franchise building include price-off packs, consumer premiums not related to a product, contests and sweepstakes, consumer refund offers, and trade allowances.

Sales promotion seems most effective when used together with advertising. In one study, a price promotion alone produced only a 15 percent increase in sales volume. When combined with feature advertising, sales volume increased 19 percent; when combined with feature advertising and a point-of-purchase display, sales volume increased 24 percent.[54] Many large companies have a sales-promotion manager whose job is to help brand managers choose the right promotional tool.

Selecting Trade-Promotion Tools

Manufacturers use a number of trade-promotion tools (Table 19.4). Surprisingly, a higher proportion of the promotion pie is devoted to trade-promotion tools (46.9 percent) than to consumer promotion (27.9 percent), with media advertising capturing the remaining 25.2 percent. Manufacturers award money to the trade for four reasons:

1. *To persuade the retailer or wholesaler to carry the brand:* Shelf space is so scarce that manufacturers often have to offer prices off, allowances, buyback guarantees, free goods, or outright payments (called *slotting allowances*) to get on the shelf, and once there, to stay on the shelf.

2. *To persuade the retailer or wholesaler to carry more units than the normal amount:* Manufacturers will offer volume allowances to get the trade to carry more in warehouses and stores. Manufacturers believe the trade will work harder when they are "loaded" with the manufacturer's product.

TABLE 19.3

Major Consumer-Promotion Tools

Samples: Offer of a free amount of a product or service delivered door to door, sent in the mail, picked up in a store, attached to another product, or featured in an advertising offer. Example: Lever Brothers had so much confidence in its new Surf detergent that it distributed free samples to four out of five North American households at a cost of $63 million.

Coupons: Certificates entitling the bearer to a stated saving on the purchase of a specific product: mailed, enclosed in other products or attached to them, or inserted in magazine and newspaper ads. Redemption rate varies with mode of distribution. Coupons can be effective in stimulating sales of a mature brand and inducing early trial of a new brand. The latest data on coupon redemptions suggests Canadian marketers are getting better at targeting consumers. According to a recent study by Markham, Ontario-based coupon-clearing house NCH Promotional Services, Canadian consumers redeemed coupons at roughly the same rate in 1998 as they had for the previous two years, even though overall coupon distribution declined sharply over the same period.

Cash Refund Offers (rebates): Provide a price reduction after purchase rather than at the retail shop: consumer sends a specified "proof of purchase" to the manufacturer who "refunds" part of the purchase price by mail. Example: Toro ran a clever preseason promotion on specific snowblower models, offering a rebate if the snowfall in the buyer's market area was below average.

Price Packs (cents-off deals): Offers to consumers of savings off the regular price of a product, flagged on the label or package. A reduced-price pack is a single package sold at a reduced price (such as two for the price of one). A banded pack is two related products banded together (such as a toothbrush and toothpaste). Example: Air freshener companies sometimes package several types of air fresheners together: for example, a spray mist, carpet deodorizer, and solid air freshener.

Premiums (gifts): Merchandise offered at a relatively low cost or free as an incentive to purchase a particular product. A with-pack premium accompanies the product inside or on the package. The package itself can serve as a premium. A free in-the-mail premium is mailed to consumers who send in a proof of purchase, such as a box top or UPC code. A self-liquidating premium is sold below its normal retail price to consumers who request it. Example: Quaker Oats inserted $7.5 million in gold and silver coins in bags of Ken-L Ration dog food.

Prizes (contests, sweepstakes, games): Prizes are offers of the chance to win cash, trips, or merchandise as a result of purchasing something. A contest calls for consumers to submit an entry to be examined by a panel of judges who will select the best entries. A sweepstake asks consumers to submit their names in a drawing. A game presents consumers with something every time they buy—bingo numbers, missing letters—which might help them win a prize. Example: A British cigarette company included a lottery ticket in each pack, providing the chance to win up to $10 000.

Patronage Awards: Values in cash or in other forms that are proportional to patronage of a certain vendor or group of vendors. Example: Air Canada and Canadian Airlines offer frequent flier plans. Marriott Hotels has adopted an honoured guest plan that awards points for users of its hotels.

Free Trials: Inviting prospective purchasers to try the product without cost in the hope that they will buy the product. Example: Auto dealers encourage free test-drives to stimulate purchase interest; America Online offers free trials of its software.

Product Warranties: Explicit or implicit promises by sellers that the product will perform as specified or that the seller will fix it or refund the customer's money during a specified period. Example: When Chrysler offered a five-year car warranty, substantially longer than GM's or Ford's, customers took notice. Sears' offer of a lifetime warranty on its auto batteries certainly screams quality to the buyers.

Tie-in Promotions: Two or more brands or companies team up on coupons, refunds, and contests to increase pulling power. Multiple sales forces push these promotions to retailers, giving them a better shot at extra display and ad space. Example: MCI has offered 10 minutes of free long-distance service on cans of Crystal Light powdered soft drinks and Taster's Choice coffee, and boxes of Keebler cookies and crackers.

(continued)

| TABLE | 19.3 *(cont.)* |

Major Consumer-Promotion Tools

Cross-Promotions: Using one brand to advertise another noncompeting brand. Example: Nabisco cookies might advertise that they contain Hershey chocolate chips, and the box may even contain a coupon to buy a Hershey product.

Point-of-Purchase (POP) Displays and Demonstrations: POP displays and demonstrations take place at the point of purchase or sale. Many retailers do not like to handle the hundreds of displays, signs, and posters they receive from manufacturers. Manufacturers are creating better POP materials, tying them in with television or print messages, and offering to set them up. Example: The L'Eggs pantyhose display is one of the most creative in the history of POP materials and has been a major factor in the success of this brand.

Sources: For more information, see "Consumer Incentive Strategy Guide," Incentive, May 1995, pp. 58–63; Mark De Wolf, "Coupon Distributors Improving Their Aim," *Strategy: The Canadian Marketing Report,* May 10, 1999, p. D5; William Urseth, "Promos 101," *Incentive,* January 1994, pp. 53–55; William Urseth, "Promos 101, Part II," *Incentive,* February 1994, pp. 43–45; Jonathan Berry, "Wilma! What Happened to the Plain Old Ad?" *Business Week,* June 6, 1994, pp. 54–58; Kapil Bawa, Srini S. Srinivasan, and Rajendra K. Srivastava, "Coupon Attractiveness and Coupon Proneness: A Framework for Modeling Coupon Redemption," *Journal of Marketing Research,* November 1997, pp. 517–25.

3. *To induce retailers to promote the brand by featuring, display, and price reductions:* Manufacturers might seek an end-of-aisle display, increased shelf facings, or price reduction stickers and obtain them by offering the retailers allowances paid on "proof of performance."

4. *To stimulate retailers and their sales clerks to push the product:* Manufacturers compete for retailer sales effort by offering push money, sales aids, recognition programs, premiums, and sales contests.

Manufacturers spend more on trade promotion than they want to spend. The growing power of large retailers has increased their ability to demand trade promotion at the expense of consumer promotion and advertising.[55] These retailers depend on promotion money from the manufacturers. No manufacturer could unilaterally stop offering trade allowances without losing retailer support.

The company's sales force and its brand managers are often at odds over trade promotion. The sales force says that the local retailers will not keep the company's products on the shelf unless they receive more trade-promotion money, whereas the brand managers want to spend the limited funds on consumer promotion and advertising. Because the sales force knows the local market better than do the brand managers sitting at headquarters, companies have given substantial funds to the sales force to handle.

Manufacturers face several challenges in managing trade promotions. First, they often find it difficult to police retailers to ensure that they are doing what they agreed to do. Manufacturers are increasingly insisting on proof of performance before paying

| TABLE | 19.4 |

Major Trade-Promotion Tools

Price-Off: (off-invoice or off-list): A straight discount off the list price on each case purchased during a stated time period. The offer encourages dealers to buy a quantity or carry a new item that they might not ordinarily buy. The dealers can use the buying allowance for immediate profit, advertising, or price reductions.

Allowance: An amount offered in return for the retailer's agreeing to feature the manufacturer's products in some way. An advertising allowance compensates retailers for advertising the manufacturer's product. A display allowance compensates them for carrying a special product display.

Free Goods: Offers of extra cases of merchandise to intermediaries who buy a certain quantity or who feature a certain flavour or size. Manufacturers might offer push money or free specialty advertising items to retailers that carry the company's name.

Source: For more information, see Betsy Spethman, "Trade Promotion Redefined," *Brandweek,* March 13, 1995, pp. 25–32.

any allowances. Second, more retailers are doing *forward buying*—that is, buying a greater quantity during the deal period than they can sell during the deal period. Retailers might respond to a 10 percent off-case allowance by buying a 12-week or longer supply. The manufacturer must schedule more production than planned and bear the costs of extra work shifts and overtime. Third, retailers are doing more *diverting*, buying more cases than needed in a region in which the manufacturer offered a deal and shipping the surplus to their stores to nondeal regions. Manufacturers are trying to handle forward buying and diverting by limiting the amount they will sell at a discount, or producing and delivering less than the full order in an effort to smooth production.[56]

All said, manufacturers feel that trade promotion has become a nightmare. It contains layers of deals, is complex to administer, and often leads to lost revenues. Kevin Price describes trade promotion in the following way:

> *A decade ago, the retailer was a chihuahua nipping at the manufacturer's heels— a nuisance, yes, but only a minor irritant; you fed it and it went away. Today it's a pit bull and it wants to rip your arms and legs off. You'd like to see it roll over, but you're too busy defending yourself to even try. . . . Today management of trade promotions is a president-level issue.*[57]

Selecting Business- and Sales Force Promotion Tools

Companies spend billions of dollars on business- and sales force promotion tools (Table 19.5). These tools are used to gather business leads, impress and reward customers, and motivate the sales force to greater effort. Companies typically develop budgets for each business-promotion tool that remain fairly constant from year to year.

Developing the Program

In planning sales-promotion programs, marketers are increasingly blending several media into a total campaign concept. Kerry E. Smith describes a complete sales-promotion program:

TABLE 19.5

Major Business- and Sales-Force Promotion Tools

Trade Shows and Conventions: Industry associations organize annual trade shows and conventions. Firms selling products and services to the particular industry buy space and set up booths and displays to demonstrate their products. Over 5600 trade shows take place every year, drawing approximately 80 million attendees. Trade show attendance can range from a few thousand people to over 70 000 for large shows held by the restaurant or hotel–motel industries. Participating vendors expect several benefits, including generating new sales leads, maintaining customer contacts, introducing new products, meeting new customers, selling more to present customers, and educating customers with publications, videos, and other audiovisual materials.

Business marketers may spend as much as 35 percent of their annual promotion budget on trade shows. They face a number of decisions, including which trade shows to participate in, how much to spend on each trade show, how to build dramatic exhibits that attract attention, and how to follow up effectively on sales leads.

Sales Contests: A sales contest aims at inducing the sales force or dealers to increase their sales results over a stated period, with prizes going to those who succeed. A majority of companies sponsor annual or more frequent sales contests for their sales force; top performers may receive trips, cash prizes, gifts, or points, which the receiver can turn into a variety of prizes. Incentives work best when they are tied to measurable and achievable sales objectives (such as finding new accounts or reviving old accounts) where employees feel they have an equal chance.

Specialty Advertising: Specialty advertising consists of useful, low-cost items bearing the company's name and address, and sometimes an advertising message that salespeople give to prospects and customers. Common items are ballpoint pens, calendars, and memo pads. One survey indicated that over 86 percent of manufacturers supply their salespeople with specialty items.

A sports trivia game to create pull-through at taverns for a premium beer brand would use TV to reach consumers, direct mail to incentivize distributors, point-of-purchase for retail support, telephones for consumer call-ins, a service bureau for call processing, live operators for data entry, and computer software and hardware to tie it all together. . . . Companies use telepromotions not only to pull product through at retail but also to identify customers, generate leads, build databases and deliver coupons, product samples and rebate offers.[58]

In deciding to use a particular incentive, marketers have several factors to consider. First, they must determine the *size* of the incentive. A certain minimum is necessary if the promotion is to succeed. A higher incentive level will produce more sales response but at a diminishing rate.

Second, the marketing manager must establish *conditions* for participation. Incentives might be offered to everyone or to select groups. A premium might be offered only to those who turn in proof-of-purchase seals or UPC codes. Sweepstakes might not be offered in certain provinces or to families of company personnel or to persons under a certain age.

Third, the marketer must decide on the *duration* of promotion. If the period is too short, many prospects will not be able to take advantage of it. If the promotion runs too long, the deal will lose some of its "act now" force. According to one researcher, the optimal frequency is about three weeks per quarter, and optimal duration is the length of the average purchase cycle.[59] Of course, the optimal promotion cycle varies by product category and even by specific product.

Fourth, the marketer must choose a *distribution vehicle*. A fifteen-cents-off coupon can be distributed in the package, in stores, by mail, or in advertising. Each distribution method involves a different level of reach, cost, and impact.

Fifth, the marketing manager must establish the *timing* of promotion. For example, brand managers develop calendar dates for annual promotions. These dates are used by the production, sales, and distribution departments.

Finally, the marketer must determine the *total sales-promotion budget*. The budget can be built from the ground up, with the marketer choosing the individual promotions and estimating their total cost. The cost of a particular promotion consists of the administrative cost (printing, mailing, and promoting the deal) and the incentive cost (cost of premium or cents-off, including redemption costs), multiplied by the expected number of units that will be sold on the deal. In the case of a coupon deal, the cost would take into account the fact that only a fraction of the consumers will redeem the coupons. For an in-pack premium, the deal cost must include the procurement cost and packaging of the premium, offset by any price increase on the package.

The more common way to develop the budget is to use a conventional percentage of the total promotion budget. For example, toothpaste might get a sales-promotion budget of 30 percent of the total promotion budget, whereas shampoo might get 50 percent. These percentages vary for different brands in different markets and are influenced by stage of the product life cycle and competitive expenditures on promotion.

Pretesting the Program

Although most sales-promotion programs are designed on the basis of experience, pretests should be conducted to determine whether the tools are appropriate, the incentive size optimal, and the presentation method efficient. Strang maintains that promotions usually can be tested quickly and inexpensively and that large companies should test alternative strategies in selected market areas with each national promotion.[60] Consumers can be asked to rate or rank different possible deals, or trial tests can be run in limited geographic areas.

Implementing and Controlling the Program

Marketing managers must prepare implementation and control plans for each individual promotion. Implementation planning must cover lead time and sell-in time. *Lead time* is the time necessary to prepare the program prior to launching it: initial planning, design, and approval of package modifications or material to be mailed or distributed; preparation of advertising and point-of-sale materials; notification of field sales personnel; establishment of allocations for individual distributors; purchasing and printing of special premiums or packaging materials; production of advance inventories in preparation for release at a specific date; and, finally, the distribution to the retailer.[61]

Sell-in time begins with the promotional launch and ends when approximately 95 percent of the deal merchandise is in the hands of consumers.

Evaluating Results

Manufacturers can use three methods to measure sales-promotion effectiveness: sales data, consumer surveys, and experiments.

The first method involves using scanner sales data, which are available from companies such as Information Resources Inc. and Nielsen Media Research. Marketers can analyze the types of people who took advantage of the promotion, what they bought before the promotion, and how consumers behaved later toward the brand and other brands. Suppose a company has a six percent market share in the prepromotion period. The share jumps to 10 percent during the promotion, falls to five percent immediately after the promotion, and rises to seven percent in the postpromotion period. The promotion evidently attracted new triers and also stimulated more purchasing by existing customers. After the promotion, sales fell as consumers worked down their inventories. The long-run rise to seven percent indicates that the company gained some new users.

In general, sales promotions work best when they attract competitors' customers to try a superior product and these customers switch as a result. If the company's product is not superior, the brand's share is likely to return to its prepromotion level. The promotion may have covered its costs, but more likely did not. One study of more than 1000 promotions concluded that only 16 percent paid off.[62]

If more information is needed, *consumer surveys* can be conducted to learn how many recall the promotion, what they thought of it, how many took advantage of it, and how the promotion affected subsequent brand-choice behaviour.[63] Sales promotions can also be evaluated through *experiments* that vary such attributes as incentive value, duration, and distribution media. For example, coupons can be sent to half of the households in a consumer panel. Scanner data can be used to track whether the coupons led more people to buy the product immediately and in the future. This information can then be used to calculate the increase in revenues that stemmed from the promotion.

Beyond the cost of specific promotions, management must recognize additional costs. First, promotions might decrease long-run brand loyalty by making more consumers deal prone rather than advertising prone. Second, promotions can be more expensive than they appear. Some are inevitably distributed to the wrong consumers. Third, there are the costs of special production runs, extra sales force effort, and handling requirements. Finally, certain promotions irritate retailers, who may demand extra trade allowances or refuse to cooperate.[64]

PUBLIC RELATIONS

Not only must the company relate constructively to customers, suppliers, and dealers, but it must also relate to a large number of interested publics. We define a public as follows:

- A *public* is any group that has an actual or potential interest in or impact on a company's ability to achieve its objectives. *Public relations* (PR) involves a variety of programs designed to promote or protect a company's image or its individual products.

A public can facilitate or impede a company's ability to achieve its objectives. PR has often been treated as a marketing stepchild, an afterthought to more serious promotion planning. But the wise company takes concrete steps to manage successful relations with its key publics. Most companies operate a public-relations department.

The PR department monitors the attitudes of the organization's publics and distributes information and communications to build goodwill. When negative publicity happens, the PR department acts as a troubleshooter. The best PR departments spend time counselling top management to adopt positive programs and to eliminate questionable practices so that negative publicity does not arise in the first place. They perform the following five functions:

1. *Press relations:* Presenting news and information about the organization in the most positive light.

2. *Product publicity:* Sponsoring efforts to publicize specific products.

3. *Corporate communication:* Promoting understanding of the organization through internal and external communications.

4. *Lobbying:* Dealing with legislators and government officials to promote or defeat legislation and regulation.

5. *Counselling:* Advising management about public issues and company positions and image. This includes advising in the event of a product mishap.[65]

MARKETING PUBLIC RELATIONS

Marketing managers and PR specialists do not always talk the same language. Marketing managers are much more bottom-line oriented, whereas PR practitioners see their job as preparing and disseminating communications. But these differences are disappearing. Many companies are turning to *marketing public relations* (MPR) to directly support corporate or product promotion and image making. Thus MPR, like financial PR and community PR, serves a special constituency, namely the marketing department.[66]

The old name for MPR was *publicity*, which was seen as the task of securing editorial space—as opposed to paid space—in print and broadcast media to promote or "hype" a product, service, idea, place, person, or organization. But MPR goes beyond simple publicity and plays an important role in the following tasks:

- *Assisting in the launch of new products:* Montreal-based Microcell Solutions, marketers of Fido PCS technology, used an integrated PR campaign under the theme "Fun and Freedom" to increase trial and awareness and to build brand equity. They kicked off the campaign with a media event that involved unleasing the "Fidomobile," a vintage, one-of-a-kind 1942 vehicle pulled by a dozen or more dogs. They held owner-dog lookalike contests and offered free photos to prospective customers and their dogs. People were offered a free phone call anywhere in Canada to demonstrate the capabilities of the phones. They also partnered with *Canine Vision Canada* to reinforce their positioning since both guide dogs and Fido represent freedom to their masters.[67]

- *Assisting in repositioning a mature product:* New York City had extremely bad press in the 1970s until the "I Love New York" campaign began.

- *Building interest in a product category:* Companies and trade associations have used MPR to rebuild interest in declining commodities such as eggs, milk, beef, and potatoes and to expand consumption of such products as tea, pork, and orange juice.

- *Influencing specific target groups:* McDonald's sponsors special neighbourhood events in Latino and African American communities to build goodwill.

- *Defending products that have encountered public problems:* After the January 1999 blizzard ground Pearson International Airport to a halt and left thousands of passengers stranded, Air Canada faced a major image crisis. The airline used broadcast media to publicly apologize for its mishandling of the storm and sent personal letters to its Aeroplan members offering them bonus air miles as an apology.[68]

- *Building the corporate image in a way that reflects favourably on its products:* Iacocca's speeches and his autobiography created a whole new winning image for Chrysler Corporation.

As the power of mass advertising weakens, marketing managers are turning more to MPR. In a survey of 286 U.S. marketing managers, three-quarters reported that their companies used MPR. They found it particularly effective in building awareness and brand knowledge, for both new and established products. MPR is also effective in blanketing local communities and reaching specific ethnic and other groups. In several cases, MPR proved more cost effective than advertising. Nevertheless, it must be planned jointly with advertising. MPR needs a larger budget, and the money might have to come from advertising.[69] In addition, marketing managers need to acquire more skill in using PR resources. Gillette is a trendsetter here: each brand manager is required to have a budget line for MPR and to justify *not* using it.

Clearly, creative public relations can affect public awareness at a fraction of the cost of advertising. The company does not pay for the space or time obtained in the media. It pays only for a staff to develop and circulate the stories and manage certain events. If the company develops an interesting story, it could be picked up by the news media and be worth millions of dollars in equivalent advertising. The Body Shop, for example, has spent very little money on advertising; its success has been almost entirely due to publicity. MPR carries more credibility than advertising. Some experts say that consumers are five times more likely to be influenced by editorial copy than by advertising.

Here is another example of the creative use of MPR:

■ **Microsoft and Windows 95.** Microsoft's campaign launching Windows 95 was an MPR success story. No paid ads for Windows 95 had appeared by August 24, 1995, the launch day. Yet everyone knew about it! The *Wall Street Journal* estimated that 3000 headlines, 6852 stories, and over three million words were dedicated to Windows 95 from July 1 to August 24. Microsoft teams around the world executed attention-grabbing publicity. Microsoft hung a 200-metre Windows 95 banner from Toronto's CN Tower. The Empire State Building in New York was bathed in the red, yellow, and green colours of the Windows 95 logo. Microsoft paid *The London Times* to distribute free its entire daily run of 1.5 million copies to the public. By the end of the first week, North American sales exceeded $150 million, not bad for a $135 product. The lesson is clear: Good advance PR can be much more effective than millions of dollars spent on advertising.

MAJOR DECISIONS IN MARKETING PR

In considering when and how to use MPR, management must establish the marketing objectives, choose the PR messages and vehicles, implement the plan carefully, and evaluate the results. The main tools of MPR are described in Table 19.6.[70]

Establishing the Marketing Objectives
Specific objectives should be set for every MPR campaign. MPR can contribute to the following objectives:

■ *Build awareness:* MPR can place stories in the media to bring attention to a product, service, person, organization, or idea.

■ *Build credibility:* MPR can add credibility by communicating the message in an editorial context.

■ *Stimulate the sales force and dealers:* MPR can help boost sales force and dealer enthusiasm. Stories about a new product before it is launched will help the sales force sell it to retailers.

■ *Hold down promotion costs:* MPR costs less than direct mail and media advertising. The smaller the company's promotion budget, the stronger the case for using PR to gain share of mind.

Whereas PR practitioners will continue to reach their target publics through the mass media, MPR is increasingly borrowing the techniques and technology of direct-response marketing to reach target audience members one to one. PR expert Thomas L. Harris offers suggestions for how PR and direct-response marketing can work together to achieve specific marketing objectives:[71]

Publications: Companies rely extensively on published materials to reach and influence their target markets. These include annual reports, brochures, articles, company newsletters and magazines, and audiovisual materials.

Events: Companies can draw attention to new products or other company activities by arranging special events like news conferences, seminars, outings, exhibits, contests and competitions, anniversaries, and sport and cultural sponsorships that will reach the target publics.

News: One of the major tasks of PR professionals is to find or create favourable news about the company, its products, and its people. News generation requires skill in developing a story concept, researching it, and writing a press release. But the PR person's skill must go beyond preparing news stories. Getting the media to accept press releases and attend press conferences calls for marketing and interpersonal skills.

Speeches: Speeches are another tool for creating product and company publicity. When Bill Gates speaks, people in the computing industry listen. Increasingly, company executives must field questions from the media or give talks at trade associations or sales meetings, and these appearances can build the company's image.

Public-Service Activities: Companies can build goodwill by contributing money and time to good causes. Large companies typically ask executives to support community affairs. In other instances, companies will donate an amount of money to a specified cause. Such cause-related marketing is used by a growing number of companies to build public goodwill.

Identity Media: In a society marked by sensory overload, companies compete for attention. They need a visual identity that the public immediately recognizes. The visual identity is carried by company logos, stationery, brochures, signs, business forms, business cards, buildings, uniforms, and dress codes.

- *Build marketplace excitement before media advertising breaks:* For example, the announcement of a new product offers a unique opportunity for obtaining publicity and for dramatizing the product.

- *Build a core consumer base:* Marketers are increasingly recognizing the value of maintaining consumer loyalty, because it costs far less to keep a consumer than to get a new one.

- *Build a one-to-one relationship with consumers:* Marketers can use telephone hot lines and 800 numbers, plus the Internet, to build and maintain relationships with individual consumers.

- *Turn satisfied customers into advocates:* Customer databases and profiles can yield satisfied customers who can become role models and spokespeople for the product.

- *Influence the influentials:* The influencer may be an authority figure like a teacher, doctor, or pharmacist, but it also can be someone who has a different kind of one-to-one relationship with the consumer, such as a hair stylist or personal trainer.

Choosing Messages and Vehicles

The manager must identify or develop interesting stories to tell about the product. Suppose a relatively unknown university wants more visibility. The MPR practitioner will search for possible stories. Do any faculty members have unusual backgrounds, or are any working on unusual projects? Are any new and unusual courses being taught? Are any interesting events taking place on campus?

If the number of interesting stories is insufficient, the MPR practitioner should propose newsworthy events the university could sponsor. Here the challenge is to create news. PR ideas include hosting major academic conventions, inviting expert or celebrity speakers, and developing news conferences. Each event is an opportunity to develop a multitude of stories directed at different audiences.

Event creation is a particularly important skill in publicising fund-raising drives for nonprofit organizations. Fund-raisers have developed a large repertoire of special events, including anniversary celebrations, art exhibits, auctions, benefit evenings, bingo games, book sales, cake sales, contests, dances, dinners, fairs, fashion shows, parties in unusual places, phonathons, rummage sales, tours, and walkathons. No sooner is one type of event created, such as a walkathon, than competitors spawn new versions, such as readathons, bikeathons, and jogathons.[72]

Both non-profits and for-profit organizations use events to call attention to their products and services. The annual Terry Fox run raises millions of dollars for cancer research. Every summer, Molson runs the Molson Indy through the streets of Toronto, attracting huge crowds. Loto Quebec and Labatt sponsor Montreal's Just for Laughs festival. P&G chose to sponsor a Barry Manilow concert tour under the names of some of its detergent products, because it wanted to attract the middle-aged women who were Barry Manilow fans and who were the target market for the detergents.

The best MPR practitioners are able to find or create stories on behalf of even mundane products such as pork ("the other white meat"), garlic, and potatoes. Here is an example for cat food:

- **9-Lives Cat Food.** One of the top brands of cat food is Star-Kist Foods' 9-Lives. Its brand image revolves around Morris the Cat. The Leo Burnett advertising agency wanted to make Morris more of a living, breathing, real-life feline to whom cat owners and cat lovers could relate. It worked with a public-relations firm that proposed and carried out the following ideas: (1) launch a Morris "look-alike" contest; (2) write a book called *Morris, an Intimate Biography*; (3) establish a coveted award called the Morris, a bronze statuette given to the owners of award-winning cats at local cat shows; (4) sponsor an "Adopt-a-Cat Month," with Morris as the official "spokescat"; and (5) distribute a booklet called "The Morris Method" on cat care. These publicity steps strengthened the brand's market share in the cat-food market.

9-Lives Cat Food
www.9livescat.com

Implementing the Plan

Implementing public relations requires care. Consider placing stories in the media: a great story is easy to place, but most stories are less than great and might not get past busy editors. One of the chief assets of publicists is their personal relationship with media editors. PR people look at media editors as a market to satisfy so that these editors will continue to use their stories.

Evaluating Results

MPR's contribution to the bottom line is difficult to measure, because it is used along with other promotional tools. If it is used before the other tools come into action, its contribution is easier to evaluate. The three most commonly used measures of MPR effectiveness are number of exposures; awareness, comprehension, or attitude change; and contribution to sales and profits.

The easiest measure of MPR effectiveness is the number of *exposures* carried by the media. Publicists supply the client with a clippings book showing all the media that carried news about the product and a summary statement such as the following:

> Media coverage included 3500 column inches of news and photographs in 350 publications with a combined circulation of 79.4 million; 2500 minutes of air time of 290 radio stations and an estimated audience of 65 million; and 660 minutes of air time on 160 television stations with an estimated audience of 91 million. If this time and space had been purchased at advertising rates, it would have amounted to $1 047 000.[73]

The exposure measure is not very satisfying because it contains no indication of how many people actually read, heard, or recalled the message and what they thought afterward. Nor does it contain information on the net audience reached, because publications overlap in readership. Because publicity's goal is reach, not frequency, it would be more useful to know the number of unduplicated exposures.

A better measure is the change in product *awareness, comprehension,* or *attitude* resulting from the MPR campaign (after allowing for the effect of other promotional tools). For example, how many people recall hearing the news item? How many told others about it (a measure of word of mouth)? How many changed their minds after hearing it? In a Potato Board campaign, the board found that the number of people who agreed with the statement "Potatoes are rich in vitamins and minerals" went from 36 percent before the campaign to 67 percent after the campaign, a significant improvement in product comprehension.

Sales-and-profit impact is the most satisfactory measure, if obtainable. For example, 9-Lives sales had increased 43 percent by the end of the Morris the Cat PR campaign. However, advertising and sales promotion had also been stepped up, and their contribution has to be allowed for. Suppose total sales have increased $1 500 000, and management estimates that MPR contributed 15 percent of the total sales increase. Then the return on MPR investment is calculated as follows:

Total sales increase	$1 500 000
Estimated sales increase due to PR (15 percent)	225 000
Contribution margin on product sales (10 percent)	22 500
Total direct cost of MPR program	−10 000
Contribution margin added by PR investment	$ 12 500
Return on MPR investment ($12,500/$10,000)	125%

In the years ahead, we can expect marketing public relations to play a larger role in the company's communication efforts.

SUMMARY

1. *Advertising* is any paid form of nonpersonal presentation and promotion of ideas, goods, or services by an identified sponsor. Advertisers include not only business firms but also charitable, nonprofit, and government agencies that advertise to various publics.

2. Developing an advertising program is a five-step process: (a) set advertising objectives; (b) establish a budget that takes into account stage in product life cycle, market share and consumer base, competition and clutter, advertising frequency, and product substitutability; (c) choose the advertising message, determine how the message will be generated, evaluate alternative messages for desirability, exclusiveness, and believability; and execute the message with the most appropriate style, tone, words, and format and in a socially responsible manner; (d) decide on the media by establishing the ad's desired reach, frequency, and impact and then choosing the media that will deliver the desired results in terms of circulation, audience, effective audience, and effective ad-exposed audience; and (e) evaluate the communication and sales effects of advertising.

3. *Sales promotion* consists of a diverse collection of incentive tools, mostly short term, designed to stimulate quicker or greater purchase of particular products or services by consumers or the trade.

4. Sales promotion includes tools for consumer promotion (samples, coupons, cash refund offers, prices off, premiums, prizes, patronage rewards, free trials, warranties, tie-in promotions, cross-promotions, point-of-purchase displays, and demonstrations); trade promotion (prices off, advertising and display allowances, and free goods); and business- and sales force promotion (trade shows and conventions, contests for sales reps, and specialty advertising).

5. In using sales promotion, a company must establish its objectives, select the tools, develop the program, pretest the program, implement and control it, and evaluate the results. Most people agree that sales promotion works to increase sales and market share in the short run, but does not have much effect in the long run. In addition, marketers face a series of challenges in most forms of sales promotion, especially the high costs of supporting them.

6. A *public* is any group that has an actual or potential interest in or impact on a company's ability to achieve its objectives. *Public relations* (PR) involves a variety of programs designed to promote or protect a company's image or its individual

products. Many companies today use *marketing public relations* (MPR) to support their marketing departments in corporate or product promotion and image making. MPR can affect public awareness at a fraction of the cost of advertising, and is often much more credible. The main tools of PR are publications, events, news, speeches, public-service activities, and identity media.

7. In considering when and how to use MPR, management must establish the marketing objectives, choose the PR messages and vehicles, implement the plan carefully, and evaluate the results. Results are usually evaluated in terms of number of exposures and cost savings; awareness, comprehension, or attitude changes; and sales-and-profit contribution.

APPLICATIONS

CHAPTER CONCEPTS

1. Your company knows that bad publicity could have a lasting negative effect on its future, yet it wants all levels of management to feel comfortable meeting the press with both good news and bad news. Individually or with a group, assist the public-relations staff in developing a 10-point media interview checklist. This checklist will be used by all managers who might possibly be questioned by either the print or electronic media.

Two points to get you started:
- *If a reporter calls, determine the reason for the call and the information sought. If you can't talk at the time or if you need additional information, promise to call the reporter back before his or her deadline. Then make sure you do it.*

- *Don't expect the news story to be exactly the way you would have reported it or written it. Expect some confusion in the facts, but if the mistakes aren't major, don't ask for a correction.*

2. Suppose a brand of aftershave lotion will be marked down $.09 for a limited period. (In other words, the manufacturer will sell the item to retailers or wholesalers for 9 cents less than its normal price.) The item sells regularly for $1.09, of which $.40 represents a contribution to the manufacturers' profits before marketing expenses. The brand manager expects a million bottles to be sold under this deal. The administrative costs of the promotion are estimated at $10 000.

a. Determine the total cost of this promotion.

b. Assume that the company expected to sell 800 000 bottles of the lotion without the promotion. Is the promotion worth undertaking?

3. A dog-food manufacturer is trying to choose between medium A and medium B. Medium A has 10 000 000 readers and charges $20 000 for a full-page ad ($2 per 1,000). Medium B has 15 000 000 readers and charges $25 000 for a full-page ad ($1.67 per 1000). What other information does the dog-food manufacturer need before deciding which is the better medium?

MARKETING AND ADVERTISING

Absolut Vodka's ads always feature its distinctive bottle, as shown in Figure 1. Analyze this ad in terms of message execution, style, and format. What is the most striking part of the ad? Would the ad be as effective if the headline and copy were more prominent than the picture? Why?

The Jell-O sales promotion ad in Figure 2 appeared in women's magazines just before Easter. The "Easter eggs" are actually a new seasonal product, Jell-O* Egg JIGGLERS*. The ad tells consumers how to order the moulds by calling an 800 number or going on the Jell-O Web site. The offer includes faster delivery if ordered by a certain date, a low price per mould, and a token $1 shipping and handling charge.

Figure 1   Figure 2

Absolut, the bottle design, and seal are trademarks owned by V&S Vin & Sprit AB.

What consumer-promotion tool is Jell-O using in this ad? How does Jell-O expect to benefit when consumers take advantage of its offer? Why would a consumer respond to this sales promotion?

FOCUS ON TECHNOLOGY

One of the key concerns marketers have when planning an advertising campaign is how many people they can reach in each medium. But how can marketers gauge ad exposure in cyberspace? One prominent firm working on that issue is Nielsen Media Research—best known for its television ratings—which has teamed up with NetRatings to measure Web and banner traffic by tracking the usage of a representative panel of more than 3500 Internet users.

The technology used by NetRatings and Nielsen examines not only which Web sites and banners are seen by the most people but also how many people have clicked on the banners being measured. Go to the NetRatings Web site (www.netratings.com/), look at its products and services, and check some of the latest reports. What can Net-Rating's measurements tell marketers about Internet advertising in general? About specific sites and banners? Why would a marketer be interested in how many people visit the Yahoo! site?

MARKETING FOR THE 21ST CENTURY

As more advertisers head for the Web to promote their wares, they are seeking assistance from specialized promotion firms such as Yahoo's Yoyodyne, which has designed a variety of games and contests to bring visitors to clients' Web sites. Another on-line sales promotion firm, Sweepstakes Builder, is known for setting up cyberspace sweepstakes promotions. This type of sales promotion helps clients build excitement, boost Web traffic, and bring visitors back to their sites again and again.

Visit the Web site of Sweepstakes Builder and read about its promotions, including the various sweepstakes packages and options. Why do you think advertisers need to use sweepstakes (or other promotions) to support their Web sites? What kinds of objectives would an online advertiser want to set for a sweepstakes promotion developed by Sweepstakes Builder? How should advertisers evaluate the results of such promotions?

Sweepstakes Builder
www.sweepstakesbuilder.com/
home. htm

Advertising, sales promotion, and public relations are among the most visible outcomes of any marketing plan. Marketers plan these programs with special care because of the support they provide for the product, the pricing, and the distribution.

As Jane Melody's assistant, you are responsible for planning the promotion for Sonic's shelf stereo systems. Take a moment to review the company's current situation and the information you have already entered in the marketing plan. Now respond to the following questions to plan your promotion strategy (noting the need for additional data and research where necessary):

- Should you use advertising to promote Sonic's products? If so, what advertising goals will you set, and how will you measure your results?

- What message(s) do you want to communicate to your target audience? What media are most appropriate—and why?

- Should you use consumer or trade promotion or both? Which promotion tools are best suited to Sonic's situation? What do you want to achieve with these promotion tools?

- Should you use public relations to promote Sonic and its products? If so, what are your marketing objectives? What message(s) and vehicle(s) will you use—and why?

Step back and consider how your advertising, sales promotion, and PR plans will affect Sonic's overall marketing efforts. Then, as your instructor directs, summarize your ideas and plans in a written marketing plan or type them into the Marketing Strategy section of the Marketing Plan Pro software.

Managing the Sales Force

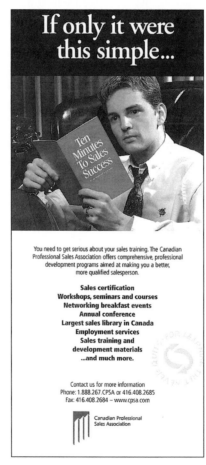

PROFILE:

Canadian Marketing Excellence

The Canadian Professional Sales Association (CPSA) is Canada's largest professional sales organization. The Association offers its membership benefits in terms of savings on travel and insurance. It runs numerous events of interest to sales professionals. For example, its November calendar included seminars entitled "Secrets of Power Negotiating," "Pre-Call Planning Using the Internet," "Effective Business Writing," and "Making Trade Shows Work."

The Association also offers members a number of professional development opportunities through its Sales Institute. The Institute was founded in 1994 with a vision of having the sales profession recognized for the integral role it plays in business development and customer satisfaction. The Institute develops and maintains competency standards for sales professionals. To achieve certification in the program, a candidate must complete 40 hours of sales-related education, successfully complete both written and oral professional exams, as well as meet a two-year practical work experience requirement. In addition, the candidate must agree to abide by the Code of Ethics. It includes provisions requiring sales representatives to maintain honesty and integrity in relationships with customers and colleagues, to accurately represent the products and services of the firms for which the work, to respect competitors, and guard proprietary and confidential information entrusted in them by their companies.

Source: Canadian Professional Sales Association Web site **www.cpsa.com**.

This chapter examines three major questions related to the sales force:

- What decisions do companies face in designing a sales force?

- How do companies recruit, select, train, supervise, motivate, and evaluate a sales force?

- How can salespeople improve their skills in selling, negotiating, and carrying on relationship marketing?

North American firms spend over $230 billion annually on personal selling—more than they spend on any other promotional method. Over 12 million North Americans are employed in sales and related occupations.[1] As competition increases in many markets, selling becomes even more important. When Groupe Boisset of Burgundy, France wanted to introduce new products into the Canadian market, it partnered with Vincor International of Mississauga, Ontario, owner of the Wine Rack retail outlets. Unlike traditional agreements in which the distributor just oversees physical shipment, Vincor took on much wider responsibilities including label design and trade promotions. Vincor will use its 125-member sales force to target restaurants, bars, and liquor stores across the country.[2]

Sales forces are found in nonprofit as well as for-profit organizations. University recruiters are the university's sales force arm. Churches and synagogues use membership committees to attract new members. Agriculture Canada sends specialists to sell farmers on new farming methods. Hospitals and museums use fund-raisers to contact donors and solicit donations.

The term *sales representative* covers a broad range of positions. McMurry distinguished six sales positions, ranging from the least to the most creative types of selling:[3]

1. *Deliverer:* A salesperson whose major task is the delivery of a product (milk, bread, fuel, oil)

2. *Order taker:* A salesperson who acts predominantly as an inside order taker (the salesperson standing behind the counter) or outside order taker (the soap salesperson calling on the supermarket manager)

3. *Missionary:* A salesperson who is not expected or permitted to take an order but whose major task is to build goodwill or to educate the actual or potential user (the medical "detailer" representing an ethical pharmaceutical house)

4. *Technician:* A salesperson with a high level of technical knowledge (the engineering salesperson who is primarily a consultant to the client companies)

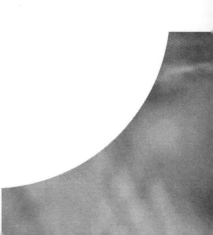

5. *Demand creator:* A salesperson who relies on creative methods for selling tangible products (vacuum cleaners, refrigerators, siding, encyclopedias) or intangibles (insurance, advertising services, or education)

6. *Solution vendor:* A salesperson whose expertise is in the solving of a customer's problem, often with a system of the company's products and services (for example, computer and communications systems)

No one debates the importance of the sales force in the marketing mix. However, companies are sensitive to the high and rising costs (salaries, commissions, bonuses, travel expenses, and benefits) of maintaining a sales force. Because the average cost of a personal sales call ranges from $375 to $750, and closing a sale typically requires four calls, the total cost to close a sale can range from $1500 to $3000.[4] Not surprisingly, companies are seeking to substitute mail- and phone-based selling units to reduce field sales expenses. They also are trying to increase the productivity of the sales force through better selection, training, supervising, motivation, and compensation.

 D ESIGNING THE SALES FORCE

Sales personnel serve as the company's personal link to the customers. The sales representative *is* the company to many of its customers. It is the sales rep who brings back much-needed information about the customer. Therefore, the company carefully needs to consider issues in sales force design—namely, the development of sales force objectives, strategy, structure, size, and compensation. (See Figure 20.1.)

SALES FORCE OBJECTIVES AND STRATEGY

Companies must define the specific objectives they expect their sales force to achieve. The old idea was that the sales force should "sell, sell, and sell." At IBM, salespeople would "push metal" and at Xerox they would "sell boxes." Salespeople had quotas, and the better salespeople met or exceeded their quotas. Later, the idea arose that sales representatives should know how to diagnose a customer's problem and propose a solution. Salespeople do not try to sell a specific product initially. Rather, they show a customer-prospect how their company can help the customer improve its profitability. They seek to join their company with the customer's company as "partners for profit."

Regardless of the selling context, salespeople will have one or more of the following specific tasks to perform:

- *Prospecting:* Searching for prospects, or *leads*
- *Targeting:* Deciding how to allocate their time among prospects and customers
- *Communicating:* Communicating information about the company's products and services
- *Selling:* Approaching, presenting, answering objections, and closing sales
- *Servicing:* Providing various services to the customers—consulting on problems, rendering technical assistance, arranging financing, expediting delivery
- *Information gathering:* Conducting market research and doing intelligence work
- *Allocating:* Deciding which customers will get scarce products during product shortages

Companies need to define the specific objectives they want their sales force to achieve. For example, a company might want its sales representatives to spend 80 percent of their time with current customers and 20 percent with prospects, and 85 percent of their time on established products and 15 percent on new products. If norms are not established, sales representatives might spend most of their time selling established products to current accounts and neglect new products and new prospects.

The sales representative's tasks vary with the state of the economy. During product shortages, sales representatives have no problem selling. Some companies jump to the

FIGURE 20.1

Designing a Sales Force

conclusion that fewer sales representatives are needed during such periods. But this thinking overlooks the salesperson's other roles—allocating the product, counselling unhappy customers, communicating company plans on remedying shortages, and selling company products that are not in short supply.

During periods of product abundance, sales representatives compete vigorously to win customer preference. Companies are increasingly judging their sales reps not only on their sales volume but also on their ability to create customer satisfaction and profit. Here are two examples:

- **Tiffany.** The name *Tiffany* automatically brings to mind expensive jewellery, and this image is cultivated in every aspect of the retailer's marketing. A purchase on the selling floor can be like an investment, so management trains its retail sales staff to be consultants rather than strictly salespeople. Because the consumer is not typically an expert, the salesperson's product knowledge is an important aspect of customer service. Salespeople are trained to offer advice and information about the quality and cut of stones, the suitability of various settings, and the choices available in various price ranges. Even when selling less expensive items, such as a box of stationery or a scarf, the salespeople know that part of the purchase is the experience and prestige of shopping at Tiffany. They also know that a satisfied customer is a potential return customer.

Tiffany
www.tiffany.com

  In addition to its retail sales staff, Tiffany has 155 field reps to serve corporate customers. An initial training program for the corporate sales staff lasts for six to eight weeks, and only when new hires have demonstrated mastery of skills, knowledge, and products are they allowed to deal with customers.[5]

- **Marriott Lodging.** Overnight accommodations can be a large, recurring expense for business travellers, so Marriott courts its major accounts by making their employees' hotel stays cost effective. Compensation for the sales professionals who manage these customers' business is based partly on their role in building long-term customer relationships. The managers of these key accounts have several ways of satisfying their customers beyond offering reduced rates. As Marriott's representative, the key account manager is responsible for solving problems and securing any special services the customer requires. By learning the customer's business, the account manager can assist the customer in planning travel. By working with support from personnel throughout the Marriott organization, the account manager can offer the services of all the Marriott properties.[6]

Companies must deploy sales forces strategically so that they call on the right customers at the right time and in the right way. Sales representatives work with customers in several ways:

- *Sales representative to buyer:* A sales representative discusses issues with a prospect or customer in person or over the phone.
- *Sales representative to buyer group:* A sales representative gets to know as many members of the buyer group as possible.
- *Sales team to buyer group:* A company sales team works closely with the members of the customer's buying group.
- *Conference selling:* The sales representative brings company resource people to discuss a major problem or opportunity.
- *Seminar selling:* A company team conducts an educational seminar for the customer company about state-of-the-art developments.

Today's sales representatives act as "account managers" who arrange fruitful contact between various people in the buying and selling organizations. Cadbury Chocolate Canada significantly improved its relationship with Wal-Mart Canada when it found a account manager who could better understand Wal-Mart's business and help them manage their confectionery category. Sales increasingly calls for teamwork requiring the support of other personnel, such as top management, especially when national accounts or major sales are at stake; technical people, who supply technical information and service to the customer before, during, or after product purchase; customer service representatives, who provide installation, maintenance, and other services; and an office staff, consisting of sales analysts, order expediters, and secretaries. An example of a successful sales team orientation is provided by DuPont. When it heard that corn growers needed a herbicide that could be applied less often, DuPont appointed a team of chemists, sales and marketing executives, and regulatory specialists to solve the problem. They created a product that topped $85 million in sales its first year.[7]

To maintain a market focus, salespeople should know how to analyze sales data, measure market potential, gather market intelligence, and develop marketing strategies and plans. Sales representatives need analytical marketing skills, and these skills become especially important at the higher levels of sales management. Marketers believe that sales forces will be more effective in the long run if they understand marketing as well as selling.

Once the company decides on an approach, it can use either a direct or a contractual sales force. A *direct (company) sales force* consists of full- or part-time paid employees who work exclusively for the company. This sales force includes *inside sales personnel*, who conduct business from the office using the telephone and receive visits from prospective buyers, and *field sales personnel*, who travel and visit customers. A *contractual sales force* consists of manufacturers' reps, sales agents, and brokers, who are paid a commission based on sales.

SALES FORCE STRUCTURE

The sales force strategy has implications for the sales force structure. If the company sells one product line to one end-using industry with customers in many locations, it would use a territorial sales force structure. If the company sells many products to many types of customers, it might need a product or market sales force structure. Table 20.1 summarizes the most common sales force structures, and the Marketing Insight, "Major Account Management—What It Is and How It Works," discusses major account management, a specialized form of sales force structure.

Established companies need to revise their sales force structure as market and economic conditions change. IBM is an excellent example:[8]

■ **IBM.** IBM lost market share in the computing industry for two reasons. First, it failed to see that PCs were the wave of the future. Second, it was burdened by a monolithic marketing and sales organization that had lost touch with its customers. The company's worldwide marketing and sales was organized geographically, with sales reps covering customers in a wide range of industries. IBM reps had gained a reputation for educating their customers about computer technology and solely about IBM products. But gradually the company's "one-size-fits-all presentations" began to turn its increasingly computer-savvy customers off. IBM reps tried to talk GTE out of moving from mainframes to networks of inexpensive computers and pushed its own mainframes instead of listening to GTE's concerns. GTE left IBM and moved to Hewlett-Packard. Ultimately, lost market share and the huge cost of maintaining its sales force made IBM rethink and reorganize its entire sales and marketing operation in the following ways:

■ Between 1990 and 1994, the sales and marketing head count was reduced from 150 000 to 70 000. Furthermore, employees were moved out of their plush offices into no-frills warehouse buildings and also into their homes.

■ Salespeople who formerly reported to regional managers now report to regional executives within specific industries. The company has reorganized vertically along 14 industry-specific lines, such as finance, petroleum, and retail.

TABLE | 20.1

Demand States and Marketing Tasks

Territorial: Each sales representative is assigned an exclusive territory. This sales structure has a number of advantages. First, it results in a clear definition of the salesperson's responsibilities. Second, territorial responsibility increases the rep's incentive to cultivate local business and personal ties. Third, travel expenses are relatively small, because each rep travels within a small area.

Territory size: Territories can be designed to provide either equal sales potential or equal workload. Territories of equal potential provide each sales representative with the same income opportunities and provide the company with a means to evaluate performance. However, because customer density varies by territory, territories with equal potential can vary widely in size. Territories can also be designed to equalize the sales workload so that each sales rep can cover his or her territory adequately.

Territory shape: Territories are formed by combining smaller units, such as counties or states, until they add up to a territory of a given sales potential or workload. Design must take into account the location of natural barriers, the compatibility of adjacent areas, the adequacy of transportation, and so forth. Territory shape can influence the cost and ease of coverage and the sales reps' job satisfaction. Today, companies can use computer programs to design sales territories that optimize such criteria as compactness, equalization of workload or sales potential, and minimal travel time.

Product: The importance of sales reps' knowing their products, together with the development of product divisions and product management, has led many companies to structure their sales forces along product lines. Product specialization is particularly warranted where the products are technically complex, highly unrelated, or very numerous. Kodak uses one sales force for its film products that are intensively distributed, and another sales force to sell complex products that require technical support.

Market: Companies often specialize their sales forces along industry or customer lines. Separate sales forces can be set up for different industries and even different customers. IBM set up a sales office for finance and brokerage customers in New York, another for GM in Detroit, and still another for Ford in nearby Dearborn. The advantage of market specialization is that each sales force can become knowledgeable about specific customer needs. The major disadvantage is that customers are scattered throughout the country, requiring extensive travel.

Complex: When a company sells a wide variety of products to many types of customers over a broad geographical area, it often combines several sales force structures. Sales representatives can be specialized by territory–product, territory–market, product–market, and so on. A sales representative might then report to one or more line and staff managers. Motorola, for example, manages four types of sales forces: (1) a strategic market sales force composed of technical, applications, and quality engineers and service personnel who are assigned to major accounts; (2) a geographic sales force calling on thousands of customers in different territories; (3) a distributor sales force calling on and coaching Motorola distributors; and (4) an inside sales force doing telemarketing and taking orders via phone and fax.

- The sales force retains a mix of industry and product specialists. For instance, if an executive calls on Bank of Montreal in Winnipeg and discovers that the bank needs a software solution, she can call a software specialist in the region to sell the product.

- Sales reps have taken on an active role as consultant rather than mere order taker or product pusher. Their mission is to create customer solutions, even if doing so means recommending a competitor's technology.

- Customers choose how they want to deal with IBM. Some customers want visits from IBM business consultants, product specialists, or systems integrators. Other customers prefer dealing with IBM sales reps over the phone.

SALES FORCE SIZE AND COMPENSATION

Once the company clarifies its strategy and structure, it is ready to consider sales force size. Sales representatives are one of the company's most productive and expensive assets. Increasing their number will increase both sales and costs.

Major Account Management—What It Is and How It Works

Major accounts (also called key accounts, national accounts, global accounts, or house accounts) are typically singled out for special attention. Important customers who have multiple divisions in many locations are offered major account contracts, which provide uniform pricing and coordinated service for all customer divisions. A major account manager (MAM) supervises field sales representatives calling on customer plants within their territories. Large accounts involving collaborative work will be handled by major account programs consisting of cross-functional personnel who handle all aspects of the relationship. The company's largest accounts may get a strategic account management team consisting of cross-functional personnel who are permanently assigned to one customer and who often maintain offices at the customer's facility. For example, P&G stationed a strategic account management team to work with Wal-Mart in its Bentonville, Arkansas, headquarters; P&G and Wal-Mart have already jointly saved $45 billion through supply chain improvements, and profit margins have improved by about 11 percent.

If a company has several such accounts, it is likely to organize a major account management division. The average company manages about 75 key accounts. A company such as Xerox handles about 250 major accounts. In addition to a key account representative, Xerox assigns a "focus executive" to each of these customers. This person maintains a relationship with an executive of the client company so that, in the words of Xerox's director of global account marketing, "There will be better understanding of the big picture, not just the sales picture." In a typical major account management division, the average MAM handles nine accounts. MAMs typically report to the national sales manager who reports to the vice president of marketing and sales, who in turn reports to the CEO.

Major account management is growing for a number of reasons. As buyer concentration increases through mergers and acquisitions, fewer buyers account for a larger share of a company's sales. Thus the largest 20 percent of accounts might account for over 80 percent of a company's sales. Another factor is that many buyers are centralizing their purchases of certain items. This gives them more bargaining power with the sellers. Sellers in turn need to devote more attention to these major buyers. Still another factor is that as products become more complex, more groups in the buyer's organization become involved in the purchase process, and the typical salesperson might not have the skill, authority, or coverage to be effective in selling to the large buyer.

In organizing a major account program, a company faces a number of issues, including how to select major accounts; how to manage them; how to select, manage, and evaluate major

(continued)

Once the company establishes the number of customers it wants to reach, it can use a *workload approach* to establish sales force size. This method consists of the following five steps:

1. Customers are grouped into size classes according to annual sales volume.

2. Desirable call frequencies (number of calls on an account per year) are established for each class.

3. The number of accounts in each size class is multiplied by the corresponding call frequency to arrive at the total workload for the country, in sales calls per year.

4. The average number of calls a sales representative can make per year is determined.

5. The number of sales representatives needed is determined by dividing the total annual calls required by the average annual calls made by a sales representative.

Suppose the company estimates that there are 1000 A accounts and 2000 B accounts in the nation. A accounts require 36 calls a year, and B accounts require 12 calls a year. The company needs a sales force that can make 60 000 sales calls a year. Suppose the average rep can make 1000 calls a year. The company would need 60 full-time sales representatives.

Many companies are shrinking their sales forces because the sales department is one of the costliest to maintain. Consider the case of Coca-Cola Amatil, the Australian Coke franchisee:

(continued)

account managers; how to organize a structure for major account managers; and where to locate major account management in the organization.

In selecting major accounts, companies use a number of criteria. They look for accounts that purchase a high volume (especially of the company's more profitable products), purchase centrally, require a high level of service in several geographic locations, may be price sensitive, and may want a long-term partnering relationship.

The major account managers have a number of duties: acting as a single point of contact; developing and growing customer business; understanding customer decision processes; identifying added-value opportunities; providing competitive intelligence; negotiating sales; and orchestrating customer service. MAMs must be able to mobilize groups within their own organization—salespeople, R&D staff, manufacturing people—to meet customers' needs. MAMs are typically evaluated on their effectiveness in growing their share of the account's business and on their achievement of annual profit and sales volume goals.

Companies often make the mistake of selecting their most productive salespeople as MAMs. But different sets of skills are required for the two jobs. One MAM said, "My position must not be as a salesman, but as a 'marketing consultant' to our customers and a salesman of my company's capabilities as opposed to my company's products."

Major accounts normally receive more favourable pricing based on their purchase volume, but marketers cannot rely exclusively on this incentive to retain customer loyalty. There is always a risk that competitors can match or beat a price or that increased costs may necessitate raising prices. Many major accounts look for added value more than for a price advantage. They appreciate having a single point of dedicated contact; single billing; special warranties; EDI links; priority shipping; early information releases; customized products; and efficient maintenance, repair, and upgrade service. In addition to these practical considerations, there is the value of goodwill. Personal relationships with a MAM, sales reps, and other personnel who value the major account's business and who have a vested and personal interest in the success of that business are compelling reasons for being a loyal customer.

Sources: For further reading, see John F. Martin and Gary S. Tubridy, "Major Account Management," in *AMA Management Handbook*, 3d ed. ed. John J. Hampton (New York: Amacom, 1994), pp. 3-25–3-27; Sanjit Sengupta, Robert E. Krapfel, and Michael A. Pusateri, "The Strategic Sales Force," *Marketing Management*, Summer 1997, pp. 29–34; Robert S. Duboff and Lori Underhill Sherer, "Customized Customer Loyalty," *Marketing Management*, Summer 1997, pp. 21–27; Tricia Campbell, "Getting Top Executives to Sell," *Sales & Marketing Management*, October 1998, p. 39. More information can be obtained from NAMA (National Account Management Association), www.nasm.com.

■ **Coca-Cola Amatil.** Amatil used to maintain an army of reps to call on small milk bar (corner store) accounts. The milk bar reps would often make up to 30 sales calls per day, giving them just enough time to take an order and maybe show one new product. When Amatil looked at the costs of putting these reps in front of milk bar customers—salary, car, phone, office support—it saw a good deal of wasted time and money. Now Amatil contacts these small accounts through telemarketing, and the field reps concentrate on larger accounts. Each milk bar has a day of the week when it will be contacted or when it can phone in. This move has resulted in a much lower cost per order and made small accounts financially feasible.

Coca-Cola Amatil
www.ccamatil.com

To attract top-quality sales reps, the company must develop an attractive compensation package. Sales reps would like income regularity, extra reward for above-average performance, and fair payment for experience and longevity. Management would like to achieve control, economy, and simplicity. Some management objectives will conflict with sales rep objectives. No wonder compensation plans exhibit a tremendous variety from industry to industry and even within the same industry.

Management must determine the level and components of an effective compensation plan. The level must bear some relation to the "going market price" for the profession as a whole as well as the type of sales job and required abilities. For example, the average earnings of a vice-president of marketing in 1998 was $88 000, average salaries of brand managers were $84 000, while senior account executives at advertising agencies had average salaries of just over $60 000. Salaries for marketers, in general, have been rising faster than the inflation rate. Moreover, demand for marketers in Canada is generally growing three times faster than supply.[9] If the market price for salespeople is well defined, the individual firm has little choice but to pay the going rate. However, the market price for salespeople is seldom well defined. Published data on industry sales force compensation levels are infrequent and generally lack sufficient detail.

The company must next determine the four components of sales force compensation—a fixed amount, a variable amount, expense allowances, and benefits. The *fixed amount*, a salary, is intended to satisfy the sales reps' need for income stability. The *variable amount*, which might be commissions, bonus, or profit sharing, is intended to stimulate and reward greater effort. *Expense allowances* enable sales reps to meet the expenses involved in travel, lodging, dining, and entertaining. *Benefits*, such as paid vacations, sickness or accident benefits, pensions, and life insurance, are intended to provide security and job satisfaction. A popular rule favours making about 70 percent of the salesperson's total income fixed and allocating the remaining 30 percent among the other elements. Fixed compensation receives more emphasis in jobs with a high ratio of nonselling to selling duties and in jobs where the selling task is technically complex and involves teamwork. Variable compensation receives more emphasis in jobs where sales are cyclical or depend on individual initiative.

Fixed and variable compensation give rise to three basic types of compensation plans—straight salary, straight commission, and combination salary and commission. Only one-fourth of all firms use either a straight-salary or straight-commission method. Three-quarters use a combination of the two, though the relative proportion of salary versus incentives varies widely.[10]

Straight-salary plans provide sales reps with a secure income, make them more willing to perform nonselling activities, and give them less incentive to overstock customers. From the company's perspective, they provide administrative simplicity and lower turnover. Straight-commission plans attract higher sales performers, provide more motivation, require less supervision, and control selling costs. Combination plans feature the benefits of both plans while reducing their disadvantages.

With compensation plans that combine fixed and variable pay, companies may link the variable portion of a salesperson's pay to a wide variety of strategic goals. Some see a new trend toward de-emphasizing volume measures in favour of factors such as gross profitability, customer satisfaction, and customer retention. For example, IBM now partly rewards salespeople on the basis of customer satisfaction as measured by customer surveys.[11] Here's how Maurice Levy, senior VP of Sales and Marketing at Purolator Courier, motivates his Canadian sales staff:

Purolator
www.purolator.com

■ **Purolator.** The first step in effective sales management is hiring highly motivated, high-performing sales personnel, but then Purolator keeps them going by celebrating sales achievements with an array of sophisticated recognition programs. For example, it has a President's Club that inducts the top 15 percent of the sales force into a Hall of Fame, and then sends them on a trip with their spouse. While rewarding sales increases is important, other incentives focus more on account retention. Maurice Levy notes, "The customer can make a negative buying decision every day, simply by calling someone else. So we have to make sure that our sales incentives focus on both incremental business and customer satisfaction."[12]

MANAGING THE SALES FORCE

Once the company has established objectives, strategy, structure, size, and compensation, it has to move to recruiting, selecting, training, supervising, motivating, and evaluating sales representatives. Various policies and procedures guide these decisions (see Figure 20.2).

RECRUITING AND SELECTING SALES REPRESENTATIVES

At the heart of a successful sales force is the selection of effective representatives. One survey revealed that the top 27 percent of the sales force brought in over 52 percent of the sales. Beyond differences in productivity is the great waste in hiring the wrong people. The average annual turnover rate for all industries is almost 20 percent. When a salesperson quits, the costs of finding and training a new person—plus the cost of lost sales—can run as high as $75 000 to $100 000. A sales force with many new people is less productive.[13]

The financial loss due to turnover is only part of the total cost. If a new representative receives $50 000 a year, another $50 000 goes into fringe benefits, expenses, supervision, office space, supplies, and secretarial assistance. Consequently, the new representative needs to produce sales on which the gross margin at least covers the selling expenses of $100 000. If the gross margin is 10 percent, the new salesperson will have to sell at least $1 000 000 for the company to break even.

Selecting sales reps would be simple if one knew what traits to look for. One good starting point is to ask customers what traits they prefer in salespeople. Most customers say they want the rep to be honest, reliable, knowledgeable, and helpful. The company should look for these traits when selecting candidates.

Another approach is to look for traits common to the most successful salespeople in the company. Charles Garfield, in his study of superachievers, concluded that supersales performers exhibit the following traits: risk taking, powerful sense of mission, problem-solving bent, care for the customer, and careful call planners.[14] Robert McMurry wrote: "It is my conviction that the possessor of an effective sales personality is a habitual 'wooer,' an individual who has a compulsive need to win and hold the affection of others."[15] He listed five additional traits: "A high level of energy, abounding self-confidence, a chronic hunger for money, a well-established habit of industry, and a state of mind that regards each objection, resistance, or obstacle as a challenge."[16] Mayer and Greenberg offered one of the shortest lists of traits. They concluded that the effective salesperson has two basic qualities: *empathy*, the ability to feel as the customer does; and *ego drive*, a strong personal need to make the sale.[17]

After management develops its selection criteria, it must recruit. The human resources department seeks applicants by various means, including soliciting names from current sales representatives, using employment agencies, placing job ads, and contacting college students. Unfortunately, few students decide to go into selling as a career. Reasons include "Selling is a job and not a profession," and "There is insecurity and too much travel." To counter these objections, company recruiters emphasize starting salaries, income opportunities, and the fact that one-fourth of the presidents of large corporations started out in marketing and sales. Selection procedures can vary from a single informal interview to prolonged testing and interviewing, not only of the applicant but of the applicant's spouse.[18] If the spouse is not ready to support the "away from home" lifestyle of the salesperson, the hire will not be a good one.

Many companies give formal tests to sales applicants. Although test scores are only one information element in a set that includes personal characteristics, references, past employment history, and interviewer reactions, they are weighted quite heavily by such companies as IBM, Prudential, Procter & Gamble, and Gillette. Gillette claims that tests have reduced turnover by 42 percent and have correlated well with the subsequent progress of new reps in the sales organization.

TRAINING SALES REPRESENTATIVES

Many companies send their new reps into the field almost immediately, supplied with samples, order books, and a description of the territory. Much of their selling is ineffective. A vice president of a major food company once spent a week watching 50 sales presentations to a busy buyer for a major supermarket chain. Here is what he observed:

> The majority of salesmen were ill prepared, unable to answer basic questions, uncertain as to what they wanted to accomplish during the call. They did not think of the call as a studied professional presentation. They didn't have a real idea of the busy retailer's needs and wants.[19]

Today's customers expect salespeople to have deep product knowledge, to add ideas to improve the customer's operations, and to be efficient and reliable. These demands have required companies to make a much higher investment in sales training.

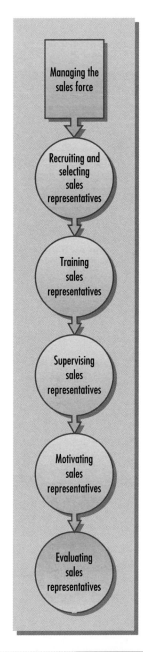

FIGURE 20.2

Managing the Sales Force

Today, new sales reps may spend a few weeks to several months in training. The median training period is 28 weeks in industrial-products companies, 12 in service companies, and 4 in consumer-products companies. Training time varies with the complexity of the selling task and the type of person recruited into the sales organization. At IBM, new reps receive extensive initial training and may spend 15 percent of their time each year in additional training.

Sales training programs have several goals:

- Sales representatives need to know and identify with the company.
- Sales representatives need to know the company's products.
- Sales representatives need to know customers' and competitors' characteristics.
- Sales representatives need to know how to make effective sales presentations.
- Sales representatives need to understand field procedures and responsibilities.

New methods of training are continually emerging, such as role playing, sensitivity training, cassette tapes, videotapes, CD-ROMs, programmed learning, and films on selling. IBM uses a self-study system called Info-Window that combines a personal computer and a laser videodisc. A trainee can practise sales calls with an on-screen actor who portrays a buying executive in a particular industry. The actor-buyer responds differently depending on what the trainee says.

As sales-automation technology has freed reps from the office and put them on the road, it has become more costly to train them by traditional methods. Reps simply are not in the office enough, and they are often overwhelmed with paperwork and information whether in-house or on the road. But technology promises to help reps increase efficiency and productivity. Many companies are now embracing CD-ROM–based interactive training. For instance, reps at Tandem Computers used to complain that they could not keep up with the printed information and training materials the company sent them. Now field reps carry their own miniature training rooms with them—they simply slip a CD-ROM disk into their laptop computers.[20]

SUPERVISING SALES REPRESENTATIVES

New sales representatives are given more than a territory, a compensation package, and training—they are also given supervision. Companies vary in how closely they supervise sales reps. Reps paid mostly on commission generally receive less supervision. Those who are salaried and must cover definite accounts are likely to receive substantial supervision.

Norms for Customer Calls

In the early 1980s, the average salesperson made 5 calls a day; by 1989, 4.2 sales calls a day; and the latest McGraw-Hill survey still shows just over 4.[21] The downward trend is due to the increased use of the phone, fax machines, and e-mail; the increased reliance on automatic ordering systems; and the drop in cold calls owing to better market research information.

How many calls should a company make on a particular account each year? Magee described an experiment where similar accounts were randomly split into three sets.[22] Sales representatives were asked to spend less than five hours a month with accounts in the first set, five to nine hours a month with those in the second set, and more than nine hours a month with those in the third set. The results demonstrated that additional calls produced more sales, leaving only the question of whether the magnitude of the sales increase justified the additional cost. Some later research has suggested that today's sales reps are spending too much time selling to smaller, less profitable accounts when they should be focusing more of their efforts on selling to larger, more profitable accounts.[23]

Norms for Prospect Calls

Companies often specify how much time reps should spend prospecting for new accounts. Spector Freight wants its sales representatives to spend 25 percent of their time prospecting and to stop calling on a prospect after three unsuccessful calls.

Companies set up prospecting standards for a number of reasons. Left to their own devices, many reps will spend most of their time with current customers, who are known quantities. Reps can depend upon them for some business, whereas a prospect might never deliver any business. Some companies rely on a missionary sales force to open new accounts.

Using Sales Time Efficiently

Studies have shown that the best sales reps are those who manage their time effectively.[24] One effective planning tool is configurator software, a program that automates the order-preparation process. Concentra Corporation is a producer of this time-saving product:

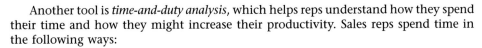

■ **Concentra Corporation.** Configurator software, like a Web site, links the customer to all the resources of the seller, but the software operates through the sales reps. On a sales call, sales reps can present product specifications input by their company's engineers and designers to the technical experts on the customer's staff without having to develop their own technical expertise. Pricing information from the home office can also be accessed. A rep can input information from the client company about such concerns as product customization and scheduling needs. Integrating all this information, the configurator software can virtually write up the order in a matter of minutes. If circumstances require changes in the terms of delivery or payment, for example, the rep can update the agreement quickly and easily. In addition to saving time, configurator software builds goodwill by reducing errors. Everyone involved in the sale—the sales engineers, the rep, and the customer—has the same information at the same time from the same source, so nothing is lost in transmission. Concentra's customers attribute increases in sales and decreases in cancellations to its configurator software programs.[25]

Another tool is *time-and-duty analysis*, which helps reps understand how they spend their time and how they might increase their productivity. Sales reps spend time in the following ways:

■ *Preparation:* Getting information and planning call strategy.

■ *Travel:* In some jobs, travel time amounts to over 50 percent of total time. Travel time can be cut down by using faster means of transportation—but this will increase costs.

■ *Food and breaks:* Some portion of the workday is spent in eating and taking breaks.

■ *Waiting:* Time spent in the buyer's outer office, which is dead time unless the representative uses it to plan or to fill out reports.

■ *Selling:* Time spent with the buyer in person or on the phone.

■ *Administration:* Time spent in report writing and billing, attending sales meetings, and talking to others in the company about production, delivery, billing, sales performance, and other matters.

With so many duties, it is no wonder that actual face-to-face selling time can amount to as little as 25 percent of total working time![26] Companies are constantly seeking ways to improve sales force productivity. Their methods take the form of training sales representatives in the use of "phone power," simplifying record-keeping forms, and using the computer to develop call and routing plans and to supply customer and competitive information.

To reduce time demands on their outside sales force, many companies have increased the size and responsibilities of their inside sales force. In a survey of 135 electronics distributors, Narus and Anderson found that an average of 57 percent of the sales force's members were inside salespeople.[27] As reasons for the growth of the internal sales force, managers cited the escalating cost of outside sales calls and the growing use of computers and innovative telecommunications equipment.

Inside salespeople are of three types. There are *technical support people*, who provide technical information and answers to customers' questions. One encounters them in phoning computer companies and on-line services. There are *sales assistants*, who provide clerical backup for the outside salespersons. They call ahead and confirm appointments, carry out credit checks, follow up on deliveries, and answer customers' questions. There are *telemarketers*, who use the phone to find new leads, qualify them, and sell to them. Telemarketers can call up to 50 customers a day compared to the 4 that an outside salesperson can contact. They can cross-sell the company's other products; upgrade orders; introduce new products; open new accounts and reactivate former accounts; give more attention to neglected accounts; and follow up and qualify direct-mail leads.

The inside sales force frees the outside reps to spend more time selling to major accounts, identifying and converting new major prospects, placing electronic ordering systems in customers' facilities, and obtaining more blanket orders and systems contracts. The inside salespeople spend more time checking inventory, following up orders, and phoning smaller accounts. The outside sales reps are paid largely on an incentive-compensation basis, and the inside reps on a salary or salary plus bonus pay.

Another dramatic breakthrough is the new high-tech equipment—desktop and laptop PCs, videocassette recorders, videodiscs, automatic diallers, e-mail, fax machines, and teleconferencing and videophones. The salesperson has truly gone "electronic." Not only is sales and inventory information transferred much faster, but specific computer-based decision support systems on CDs have also been created for sales managers and sales representatives. For more information on how sales automation is increasing sales productivity, see the Marketing for the 21st Century "Automation for the Personal Touch."

MOTIVATING SALES REPRESENTATIVES

Some sales representatives will put forth their best effort without any special coaching from management. To them, selling is the most fascinating job in the world. They are ambitious and self-starters. But most reps require encouragement and special incentives. This is especially true of field selling:

ACT! is a software program used by many sales reps.

Automation for the Personal Touch

The array of technological resources available to the contemporary sales representative—Web sites, laptop computers, software, printers, modems, fax–copiers, e-mail, cellular phones, and pagers—is giving reps more time for personal interaction with customers. Reps are spending this extra time in a new kind of relationship, which is more productive for both buyer and seller. The old paradigm of the sales presentation in which the rep discerns the customer's needs and then offers the product or service that comes closest to meeting them has been replaced by a new model. In relationship marketing, a rep sells a long-term partnership in which both parties collaborate on identifying needs and developing, maintaining, and updating products and services customized to fulfil them.

One of the most valuable electronic tools for the sales rep is the company Web site, and one of its most useful applications is as a prospecting tool. Company Web sites can help define the firm's relationships with individual accounts and identify those whose business warrants a personal sales call. To make web sites more attractive and more personal, firms like iNago Inc. of Toronto are working to humanize e-commerce by creating "Web People," intellegent, interactive digital agents. These "virtual sales agents" are being programmed to explain the host company's product information with the hope that they will transform a complicated computing experience into a simple conversation.

Even without such "agents," Web sites provide an introduction to self-identified potential customers. Depending on the nature of the business, the initial order may even take place on-line. For more complex transactions, the site provides a way for the buyer to contact the seller—for example, through a link to an e-mail address. The Pall Corporation, a manufacturer of fluid filtration and purification technologies, has all e-mail directed to company headquarters, with leads going directly to the appropriate sales rep. The quality and quantity of leads generated by the Web site have prompted the company to promote its home page on business cards and in advertising.

Not everyone has had such success in using a Web site for sales and sales support. Grainger, an industrial-supply company, had less encouraging results with its initial efforts. Less than one percent of its customers registered to open a Web account, and less than one percent of its revenue for fiscal 1998 came from sales on the Web. Management concluded that its market is simply not among electronic shoppers. Many purchasing agents for its products are janitors or plant managers, who are not yet on-line. So Grainger is taking a slower route to Web commerce, purchasing banners on sites likely to be visited by customers who are connected.

These different experiences illustrate the need for guidelines for companies considering using Web sites for selling purposes. At Texas Instruments, the Web team has developed a set of rules for using this medium effectively, especially in business-to-business selling. TI advocates careful evaluation of the target market's use of the Internet: Are attractive graphics important to potential customers, or are they more concerned about downloading data quickly? Which browsers does the market favour, and is the Web site reachable through them? If the market is international, is the content of the site available in languages other than English? Making a Web site an effective selling tool requires experts in both the medium and the content of the site. The site can attract and keep customers only if the information is kept up-to-date and presented in a way that is easily accessible and appealing to visitors, both technically and in terms of communication style. Selling over the Internet supports relationship marketing by solving problems that do not require live intervention and thus allowing more time to be spent on issues that are best addressed face-to-face.

Sources: Patrick Allossery, "Softening E-commerce with Virtual Sales Agents," *Financial Post*, June 4, 1999, C3. Charles Waltner, "Pall Corp. Wins Business with Info-Driven Web Site," *Net Marketing*, October 1996; Beth Snyder, "Execs: Traditional Sales Still Key," *Net Marketing*, May 1998; John Evan Frok, Grainger's Buy-in Plan," *Business Marketing*, November 1998, pp. 1, 48; Ralph A. Oliva, "Rules of the Road Add to Success," *Marketing Management*, Summer 1997, pp. 43–45.

- The field job is one of frequent frustration. Reps usually work alone, their hours are irregular, and they are often away from home. They confront aggressive, competing sales reps; they have an inferior status relative to the buyer; they often do not have the authority to do what is necessary to win an account; and they sometimes lose large orders they have worked hard to obtain.

- Most people operate below capacity in the absence of special incentives, such as financial gain or social recognition.

- Reps are occasionally preoccupied with personal problems, such as sickness in the family, marital discord, or debt.

The problem of motivating sales representatives has been studied by Churchill, Ford, and Walker.[28] Their basic model says that the higher the salesperson's motivation, the greater his or her effort. Greater effort will lead to greater performance; greater performance will lead to greater rewards; greater rewards will lead to greater satisfaction; and greater satisfaction will reinforce motivation. The model thus implies the following:

- *Sales managers must be able to convince salespeople that they can sell more by working harder or by being trained to work smarter:* But if sales are determined largely by economic conditions or competitive actions, this linkage is undermined.

- *Sales managers must be able to convince salespeople that the rewards for better performance are worth the extra effort:* But if the rewards seem to be set arbitrarily or are too small or of the wrong kind, this linkage is undermined.

The researchers went on to measure the importance of different possible rewards. The reward with the highest value was pay, followed by promotion, personal growth, and sense of accomplishment. The least-valued rewards were liking and respect, security, and recognition. In other words, salespeople are highly motivated by pay and the chance to get ahead and satisfy their intrinsic needs, and less motivated by compliments and security. But the researchers also found that the importance of motivators varied with demographic characteristics:

- Financial rewards were mostly valued by older, longer-tenured people and those who had large families.

- Higher-order rewards (recognition, liking and respect, sense of accomplishment) were more valued by young salespeople who were unmarried or had small families and usually more formal education.

Motivators also vary across countries. Whereas money is the number-one motivator of 37 percent of U.S. salespeople, only 20 percent of salespeople in Canada feel the same way. Salespeople in Australia and New Zealand were the least motivated by a fat paycheque.[29]

Sales Quotas

Many companies set sales quotas prescribing what reps should sell during the year. Quotas can be set on dollar sales, unit volume, margin, selling effort or activity, and product type. Compensation is often tied to degree of quota fulfilment.

Sales quotas are developed from the annual marketing plan. The company first prepares a sales forecast. This forecast becomes the basis for planning production, workforce size, and financial requirements. Management then establishes quotas for regions and territories, which typically add up to more than the sales forecast. Quotas are set higher than the sales forecast to encourage managers and salespeople to perform at their best level. If they fail to make their quotas, the company nevertheless might make its sales forecast.

Each area sales manager divides the area's quota among the area's sales reps. There are three schools of thought on quota setting. The *high-quota school* sets quotas higher than what most sales reps will achieve but that are attainable. Its adherents believe that high quotas spur extra effort. The *modest-quota school* sets quotas that a majority of the sales force can achieve. Its adherents feel that the sales force will accept the quotas as fair, attain them, and gain confidence. The *variable-quota school* thinks that individual differences among sales reps warrant high quotas for some, modest quotas for others.

One general view is that a salesperson's quota should be at least equal to the person's last year's sales plus some fraction of the difference between territory sales potential and last year's sales. The more the salesperson reacts favourably to pressure, the higher the fraction should be.

Supplementary Motivators

Companies use additional motivators to stimulate sales force effort. Periodic *sales meetings* provide a social occasion, a break from routine, a chance to meet and talk with "company brass" and each other, and a chance to air feelings and to identify with a larger group. Sales meetings are an important tool for education, communication, and motivation.

Companies also sponsor *sales contests* to spur the sales force to a special selling effort above what is normally expected. The contest should present a reasonable opportunity for enough salespeople to win. At IBM, about 70 percent of the sales force qualifies for the 100 percent Club. The reward is a three-day trip that includes a recognition dinner and a blue-and-gold pin. The contest period should not be announced in advance. If it is, some salespersons will defer sales and others pad their sales during the period with customer promises to buy that do not materialize after the contest period ends.

Whether a sales contest is focused on selling a specific product or products during a limited time period or is a more general recognition of top revenue earners for the quarter, the reward should be commensurate with the achievement. Reps who are well paid and whose earnings are based in large part on commissions are more likely to be motivated by a trip, a trophy, or merchandise than by a check of equal value. Some companies are reaching for less conventional rewards to motivate their sales personnel and having great success:

- **Creative Staffing.** Ann Machado, founder and owner of Creative Staffing (an employment services firm), rewards both sales and nonsales employees with expensive dinners, parties, chauffeured shopping sprees, flowers, spa sessions, cooking lessons, and extra vacation time. One might think that her company would need an entire department just to develop and deliver rewards, but Machado's secret is letting people pick the reward they want and outline what they'll do to earn it. Then all she has to do is approve it. "Letting people choose their own rewards and goals empowers them," says Machado.[30]

EVALUATING SALES REPRESENTATIVES

We have been describing the *feed-forward* aspects of sales supervision—how management communicates what the sales reps should be doing and motivates them to do it. But good feed-forward requires good *feedback,* which means getting regular information from reps to evaluate performance.

Sources of Information

Management obtains information about its reps in several ways. The most important source is sales reports. Additional information comes through personal observation, customer letters and complaints, customer surveys, and conversations with other sales representatives.

Sales reports are divided between *activity plans* and *write-ups of activity results.* The best example of the former is the *salesperson's work plan,* which sales reps submit a week or month in advance. The plan describes intended calls and routing. This report forces sales reps to plan and schedule their activities, informs management of their whereabouts, and provides a basis for comparing their plans and accomplishments. Sales reps can be evaluated on their ability to "plan their work and work their plan."

Many companies require their representatives to develop an annual *territory marketing plan* in which they outline their program for developing new accounts and increasing business from existing accounts. This type of report casts sales reps into the role of market managers and profit centres. Sales managers study these plans, make suggestions, and use them to develop sales quotas.

Sales reps write up completed activities on *call reports.* Sales representatives also submit expense reports, new-business reports, lost-business reports, and reports on local business and economic conditions.

These reports provide raw data from which sales managers can extract key indicators of sales performance: (1) average number of sales calls per salesperson per day, (2) average sales call time per contact, (3) average revenue per sales call, (4) average cost per sales call, (5) entertainment cost per sales call, (6) percentage of orders per hundred sales calls, (7) number of new customers per period, (8) number of lost customers per period, and (9) sales force cost as a percentage of total sales.

Formal Evaluation

The sales force's reports along with other observations supply the raw materials for evaluation. There are several approaches to conducting evaluations. One type of evaluation compares current performance to past performance. An example is shown in Table 20.2.

The sales manager can learn many things about a rep from this table. Total sales increased every year (line 3). This does not necessarily mean that the person is doing a better job. The product breakdown shows that he has been able to push the sales of product B further than the sales of product A (lines 1 and 2). According to his quotas for the two products (lines 4 and 5), his success in increasing product B sales could be at the expense of product A sales. According to gross profits (lines 6 and 7), the company earns more selling A than B. The rep might be pushing the higher-volume, lower-margin product at the expense of the more profitable product. Although he increased total sales by $1100 between 1998 and 1999 (line 3), the gross profits on total sales actually decreased by $580 (line 8).

Sales expense (line 9) shows a steady increase, although total expense as a percentage of total sales seems to be under control (line 10). The upward trend in total dollar expense does not seem to be explained by any increase in the number of calls (line 11), although it might be related to success in acquiring new customers (line 14). There is a possibility that in prospecting for new customers, this rep is neglecting present customers, as indicated by an upward trend in the annual number of lost customers (line 15).

The last two lines show the level and trend in sales and gross profits per customer. These figures become more meaningful when they are compared with overall company averages. If this rep's average gross profit per customer is lower than the company's average, he could be concentrating on the wrong customers or not spending enough time with each customer. A review of annual number of calls (line 11) shows that he might be making fewer annual calls than the average salesperson. If distances in the territory are similar to other territories, this could mean that he is not putting in a full workday, he is poor at sales planning and routing, or he spends too much time with certain accounts.

TABLE 20.2

Form for Evaluating Sales Representative's Performance

Territory: Midland
Sales Representative: John Smith

	1996	1997	1998	1999
1. Net sales product A	$251 300	$253 200	$270 000	$263 100
2. Net sales product B	423 200	439 200	553 900	561 900
3. Net sales total	674 500	692 400	823 900	825 000
4. Percent of quota product A	95.6	92.0	88.0	84.7
5. Percent of quota product B	120.4	122.3	134.9	130.8
6. Gross profits product A	$50 260	$50 640	$54 000	$52 620
7. Gross profits product B	42 320	43 920	55 390	56 190
8. Gross profits total	92 580	94 560	109 390	108 810
9. Sales expense	$10 200	$11 100	$11 600	$13 200
10. Sales expense to total sales (%)	1.5	1.6	1.4	1.6
11. Number of calls	1 675	1 700	1 680	1 660
12. Cost per call	$6.09	$6.53	$6.90	$7.95
13. Average number of customers	320	24	328	334
14. Number of new customers	13	14	15	20
15. Number of lost customers	8	10	11	14
16. Average sales per customer	$2 108	$2 137	$2 512	$2 470
17. Average gross profit per customer	$289	$292	$334	$326

The rep might be quite effective in producing sales but not rate high with customers. Perhaps he is slightly better than the competitors' salespeople, or his product is better, or he keeps finding new customers to replace others who don't like to deal with him. An increasing number of companies are measuring customer satisfaction not only with their product and customer support service, but also with their salespeople. The customers' opinion of the salesperson, product, and service can be measured by mail questionnaires or telephone calls.

Evaluations can also assess the salesperson's knowledge of the company, products, customers, competitors, territory, and responsibilities. Personality characteristics can be rated, such as general manner, appearance, speech, and temperament. The sales manager can also review any problems in motivation or compliance.[31]

The sales manager can also check that the representative knows and observes the law. For example, it is illegal for salespeople to lie to consumers or mislead them about the advantages of buying a product. In selling to businesses, salespeople may not offer bribes to purchasing agents or others influencing a sale. They may not obtain or use competitors' technical or trade secrets through bribery or industrial espionage. Finally, salespeople must not disparage competitors or competing products by suggesting things that are not true.[32]

PRINCIPLES OF PERSONAL SELLING

Personal selling is an ancient art. It has spawned a large literature and many principles. Effective salespersons have more than instinct; they are trained in methods of analysis and customer management. We will examine three major aspects of personal selling: sales professionalism, negotiation, and relationship marketing.[33] Figure 20.3 shows these aspects in schematic form.

PROFESSIONALISM

Today's companies spend hundreds of millions of dollars each year to train salespeople in the art of selling. Over a million copies of books, cassettes, and videotapes on selling are purchased annually, with such tantalizing titles as *Questions That Make the Sale; Green Light Selling: Your Secret Edge to Winning Sales and Avoiding Dead Ends; You'll Never Get No for an Answer; Secrets of Power Persuasion; What They Don't Teach You in Sales 101; Close! Close! Close! How to Make the Sale; How to Make Money Tomorrow Morning; Samurai Selling;* and *World Class Selling.* One of the most enduring books is Dale Carnegie's *How to Win Friends and Influence People.*

All sales-training approaches try to convert a salesperson from a passive order taker into an active order getter. *Order takers* operate on the assumption that customers know their own needs, resent attempts to influence them, and prefer courteous and self-effacing salespersons. There are two basic approaches in training salespersons to be *order getters,* a sales-oriented approach and a customer-oriented approach. The *sales-oriented approach* trains the person in the stereotyped high-pressure techniques used in encyclopedias or automobiles. This form of selling assumes that customers are not likely to buy except under pressure, that they are influenced by a slick presentation, and that they will not be sorry after signing the order—or, if they are, that it doesn't matter.

The *customer-oriented approach* trains salespeople in customer problem solving. The person learns how to listen and question in order to identify customer needs and come up with sound product solutions. Presentation skills are secondary to customer-need analysis skills. This approach assumes that customers have latent needs that constitute opportunities, that they appreciate constructive suggestions, and that they will be loyal to sales reps who have their long-term interests at heart. The problem solver is a much more congruent concept for the salesperson under the marketing concept than the hard seller or order taker.

No approach works best in all circumstances. Yet most sales-training programs agree on the major steps involved in any effective sales process. These steps are shown in Figure 20.4 and their application to industrial selling is discussed next.[34]

FIGURE 20.3

Managing the Sales Force: Improving Effectiveness

Improving sales force effectiveness

Training in selling techniques and sales professionalism

Negotiation skills

Relationship-building skills

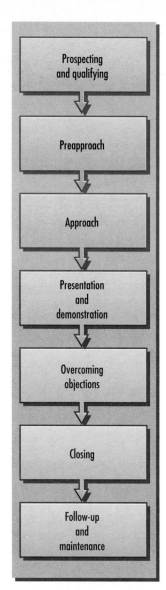

FIGURE 20.4

Major Steps in Effective Selling

Prospecting and qualifying

Preapproach

Approach

Presentation and demonstration

Overcoming objections

Closing

Follow-up and maintenance

Prospecting and Qualifying

The first step in selling is to identify and qualify prospects. Historically, most companies left it to their salespeople to find leads. Now, however, more companies are taking responsibility for finding and qualifying leads so that the salespeople can use their expensive time doing what they can do best: selling. Companies can generate leads in the following ways:

- Examining data sources (newspapers, directories, CD-ROMs) in search of names. Firms can acquire company and industry information from commercial list vendors such as Dun & Bradstreet, R. L. Polk, and TRW.
- Putting up a booth at trade shows to encourage drop-bys.
- Inviting current customers to suggest the names of prospects.
- Cultivating other referral sources, such as suppliers, dealers, noncompeting sales representatives, bankers, and trade association executives.
- Contacting organizations and associations to which prospects belong.
- Engaging in speaking and writing activities that will draw attention.
- Using the telephone, mail, and the Internet to find leads.
- Dropping in unannounced on various offices (*cold canvassing*).

Companies can then qualify the leads by contacting them by mail or phone to assess their level of interest and financial capacity. The leads can be categorized as hot prospects, warm prospects, and cool prospects, with the hot prospects turned over to the field sales force and the warm prospects turned over to the telemarketing unit for follow-up. Even then, it usually takes about four calls on a prospect to consummate a business transaction.

Sometimes companies develop original sales prospecting approaches, as John Deere has done:

- **John Deere.** In 1993 the dwindling demand for farm equipment and the aggressive actions of competitors pushed Deere's managers to create a strategy that involved its hourly assembly workers in finding and approaching prospects. Deere sent some of its more experienced and knowledgeable workers to regional trade exhibits across North America to pitch the company's equipment to dealers and farmers. The workers also made unscheduled visits to local farmers to discuss their special problems. Customers perceived these new "reps" as presenting an honest, grassroots account of what goes into making Deere products. Once the new reps had wooed potential customers with their expertise in advanced manufacturing methods and total quality programs, the company could decide how to introduce sales reps at the optimum time to make further presentations or close the sale.[35]

Preapproach

The salesperson needs to learn as much as possible about the prospect company (what it needs, who is involved in the purchase decision) and its buyers (their personal characteristics and buying styles). The salesperson can consult standard sources (*Who's Who in Canadian Business*, Moody's, Standard & Poor's, Dun & Bradstreet), acquaintances, and others to learn about the company. The salesperson should set call objectives: to qualify the prospect, gather information, make an immediate sale. Another task is to decide on the best *approach*, which might be a personal visit, a phone call, or a letter. The best timing should also be considered because many prospects are busy at certain times. Finally, the salesperson should plan an overall sales strategy for the account.

Approach

The salesperson should know how to greet the buyer to get the relationship off to a good start. The salesperson might consider wearing clothes similar to what buyers wear (for instance, in Calgary, office clothing is more casual than in Montreal); show courtesy and attention to the buyer; and avoid distracting mannerisms, such as staring at the customer. The opening line should be positive; for example, "Mr. Smith, I am Alice Jones from the ABC Company. My company and I appreciate your willingness to see me. I will do my best to make this visit profitable and worthwhile for you and your company." This opening line might be followed by key questions and active listening to understand the buyer's needs.

Presentation and Demonstration

The salesperson now tells the product "story" to the buyer, following the AIDA formula of gaining *attention*, holding *interest*, arousing *desire*, and obtaining *action*. The salesperson uses a *features, advantages, benefits,* and *value* approach (FABV). Features describe physical characteristics of a market offering, such as chip processing speeds or memory capacity. Advantages describe why the features provide an advantage to the customer. Benefits describe the economic, technical, service, and social benefits delivered by the offering. Value describes the summative worth (often in monetary terms) of the offering. Too often, salespeople spend too much time dwelling on product features (a product orientation) and not stressing enough the offering's benefits and value (a customer orientation).

Companies have developed three different styles of sales presentation. The oldest is the *canned approach*, which is a memorized sales talk covering the main points. It is based on stimulus-response thinking; that is, the buyer is passive and can be moved to purchase by the use of the right stimulus words, pictures, terms, and actions. The *formulated approach* is also based on stimulus-response thinking but first identifies the buyer's needs and buying style and then uses a formulated approach to this type of buyer.

The *need-satisfaction approach* starts with a search for the customer's real needs by encouraging the customer to do most of the talking. The salesperson takes on the role of a knowledgeable business consultant hoping to help the customer save money or make more money.

Sales presentations can be improved with demonstration aids such as booklets, flip charts, slides, movies, audio and videocassettes, product samples, and computer-based simulations. Visual aids can show how a product performs and provide other information about it. Booklets and brochures remain useful as "leave behinds" for customer reference. For group presentations, PowerPoint and similar software have replaced the flip chart. These programs enable reps to project professionally prepared visuals on a screen or download them to the laptops of audience members. Johnson & Johnson's Advanced Sterilization Products division uses a visual aid that includes a small video player with five headsets, all easily transported in a briefcase-sized package. Computer animation shows the viewer the inner workings of the Sternad Sterilization System, providing more information in a more engaging way than could be done by displaying the actual machinery—even if the system were portable.[36]

Overcoming Objections

Customers almost always pose objections during the presentation or when asked for the order. *Psychological resistance* includes resistance to interference, preference for established supply sources or brands, apathy, reluctance to giving up something, unpleasant associations created by the sales rep, predetermined ideas, dislike of making decisions, and neurotic attitude toward money. *Logical resistance* might consist of objections to the price, delivery schedule, or certain product or company characteristics. To handle these objections, the salesperson maintains a positive approach, asks the buyer to clarify the objection, questions the buyer in a way that the buyer must answer his or her own objection, denies the validity of the objection, or turns the objection into a reason for buying. Handling and overcoming objections is a part of the broader skills of negotiation.

Closing

Now the salesperson attempts to close the sale. Some salespeople do not reach this stage or do not do it well. They lack confidence or feel uncomfortable about asking for the order or do not recognize the right psychological moment to close the sale.

In a research program known as the Harvard Negotiation Project, Roger Fisher and William Ury arrived at four points for conducting principled negotiations.

1. Separate the people from the problem: Each party must understand the other side's viewpoint and the level of emotion with which they hold it, but the focus should be on the parties' interests rather than their personal differences. Active listening to opposing arguments and addressing the problem in response improve the chance of reaching a satisfactory conclusion.

2. Focus on interests, not positions: The distinction between positions and interests is similar to that between solutions and desired outcome or means and end. By focusing on interests rather than positions, the negotiators are more likely to find a mutually agreeable means of achieving common interests.

3. Invent options for mutual gain: Search for a larger pie rather than arguing over the size of each side's slice. Looking for options that offer mutual gain helps identify shared interests.

4. Insist on objective criteria: Insist that the agreement reflect fair objective criteria independent of either side's position. This approach avoids a situation in which one side must yield to the position of the other. Instead, both sides are yielding to a fair solution based on criteria they both accept.

Source: Adapted from Roger Fisher and William Ury, *Getting to Yes: Negotiating Agreement Without Giving In*, rev. ed. (Boston: Houghton Mifflin, 1992), p. 57.

Salespersons need to know how to recognize closing signs from the buyer, including physical actions, statements or comments, and questions. Salespersons can use one of several closing techniques. They can ask for the order, recapitulate the points of agreement, offer to help the secretary write up the order, ask whether the buyer wants A or B, get the buyer to make minor choices such as the colour or size, or indicate what the buyer will lose if the order is not placed now. The salesperson might offer the buyer specific inducements to close, such as a special price, an extra quantity, or a token gift.

Follow-up and Maintenance

Follow-up and maintenance are necessary if the salesperson wants to ensure customer satisfaction and repeat business. Immediately after closing, the salesperson should cement any necessary details on delivery time, purchase terms, and other matters that are important to the customer. The salesperson should schedule a follow-up call when the initial order is received to make sure there is proper installation, instruction, and servicing. This visit or call will detect any problems, assure the buyer of the salesperson's interest, and reduce any cognitive dissonance that might have arisen. The salesperson should also develop a maintenance and growth plan for the account.

NEGOTIATION

Much business-to-business selling involves negotiating skills. The two parties need to reach agreement on the price and the other terms of sale. Salespersons need to win the order without making deep concessions that will hurt profitability.

Marketing is concerned with exchange activities and the manner in which the terms of exchange are established. In *routinized exchange*, the terms are established by administered programs of pricing and distribution. In *negotiated exchange*, price and other terms are set via bargaining behaviour, in which two or more parties negotiate long-term binding agreements. Although price is the most frequently negotiated issue, other issues include contract completion time; quality of goods and service offered; purchase volume; responsibility for financing, risk taking, promotion, and title; and product safety.

Marketers who find themselves in bargaining situations need certain traits and skills to be effective. The most important are preparation and planning skill, knowledge of subject matter being negotiated, ability to think clearly and rapidly under pressure and uncertainty, ability to express thoughts verbally, listening skill, judgement and general intelligence, integrity, ability to persuade others, and patience.[37]

When to Negotiate

Lee and Dobler have listed the following circumstances where negotiation is an appropriate procedure for concluding a sale:

1. When many factors bear not only on price, but also on quality and service.

2. When business risks cannot be accurately predetermined.

3. When a long period of time is required to produce the items purchased.

4. When production is interrupted frequently because of numerous change orders.[38]

Negotiation is appropriate whenever a *zone of agreement* exists.[39] A zone of agreement exists when there are simultaneously overlapping acceptable outcomes for the parties. This concept is illustrated in Figure 20.5. Suppose two parties are negotiating a price. The seller has a *reservation price*, s, which is the *minimum* he will accept. Any final-contract value, x, that is below s is worse than not reaching an agreement at all. For any $x.s$, the seller receives a surplus. Obviously, the seller desires as large a surplus as possible while maintaining good relations with the buyer. Likewise, the buyer has a reservation price, b, that is the *maximum* he will pay; any x above b is worse than no agreement. For any x,b, the buyer receives a surplus. If the seller's reservation price is below the buyer's—that is, s,b—then a zone of agreement exists, and the final price will be determined through bargaining.

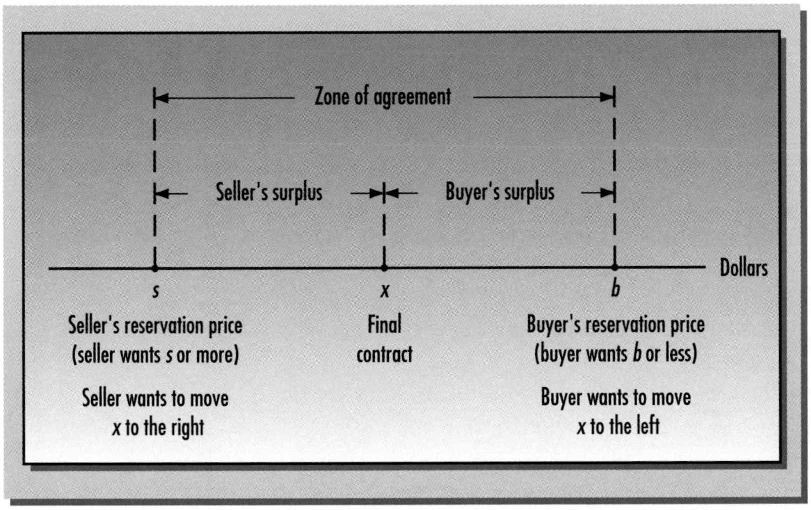

FIGURE 20.5

The Zone of Agreement

Source: Reprinted by permission of the publishers from *The Art and Science of Negotiation,* by Howard Raiffa, Cambridge, MA: The Belknap Press of Harvard University Press, copyright 1982 by the President and Fellows of Harvard College.

There is an obvious advantage in knowing the other party's reservation price and in making one's own reservation price seem higher (for a seller) or lower (for a buyer) than it really is. The openness with which buyers and sellers reveal their reservation prices depends upon the bargainers' personalities, the negotiation circumstances, and expectations about future relations.

Formulating a Negotiation Strategy

Negotiation involves preparing a strategic plan before meeting the other party and making good tactical decisions during the negotiation sessions.

■ A *negotiation strategy* is a commitment to an overall approach that has a good chance of achieving the negotiator's objectives.

Some negotiators pursue a "hard" strategy with opponents, whereas others maintain that a "soft" strategy yields more favourable results. Fisher and Ury propose another strategy, that of "principled negotiation," described in the Marketing Memo "The Principled-Negotiation Approach to Bargaining."

Negotiators use a variety of tactics when bargaining. Bargaining tactics are manoeuvres made at specific points in the bargaining process. Several classic bargaining tactics are listed in Table 20.3. Fisher and Ury have offered tactical advice that is consistent with their strategy of principled negotiation. If the other party is more powerful, the best tactic is to know one's BATNA—Best Alternative to a Negotiated Agreement. By identifying the alternatives if a settlement is not reached, the company sets a standard against which any offer can be measured. Knowing its BATNA protects the company from being pressured into accepting unfavourable terms from a more powerful opponent.

Another set of bargaining tactics are responses intended to deceive, distort, or otherwise influence the bargaining. What tactic should be used when the other side uses a take-it-or-leave-it tactic or seats the other party on the side of the table with the sun in his eyes? A negotiator should recognize the tactic, raise the issue explicitly, and question the tactic's legitimacy and desirability—in other words, negotiate over it. If negotiating fails, the company should resort to its BATNA and terminate the negotiation until the other side ceases to employ these tactics. Meeting such tactics with defending principles is more productive than counterattacking with tricky tactics.

RELATIONSHIP MARKETING

The principles of personal selling and negotiation thus far described are *transaction-oriented* because their purpose is to close a specific sale. But in many cases, the company is not seeking an immediate sale but rather to build a long-term supplier–customer

Acting Crazy	Put on a good show by visibly demonstrating your emotional commitment to your position. This increases your credibility and may give the opponent a justification to settle on your terms.
Big Pot	Leave yourself a lot of room to negotiate. Make high demands at the beginning. After making concessions, you'll still end up with a larger payoff than if you started too low.
Get a Prestigious Ally	The ally can be a person or a project that is prestigious. You try to get the opponent to accept less because the person/object he or she will be involved with is prestigious.
The Well Is Dry	Take a stand and tell the opponent you have no more concessions to make.
Limited Authority	You negotiate in good faith with the opponent, and when you're ready to sign the deal, you say, "I have to check with my boss."
Whipsaw/Auction	You let several competitors know you're negotiating with them at the same time. Schedule competitors' appointments with you for the same time and keep them all waiting to see you.
Divide and Conquer	If you're negotiating with the opponent's team, sell one member of the team on your proposals. That person will help you sell the other members of the team.
Get Lost/Stall for Time	Leave the negotiation completely for a while. Come back when things are getting better and try to renegotiate then. Time period can be long (say you're going out of town) or short (go to the bathroom to think).
Wet Noodle	Give no emotional or verbal response to the opponent. Don't respond to his or her force or pressure. Sit there like a wet noodle and keep a "poker face."
Be Patient	If you can afford to outwait the opponent, you'll probably win big.
Let's Split the Difference	The person who first suggests this has the least to lose.
Trial Balloon	You release your possible/contemplated decision through a so-called reliable source before the decision is actually made. This enables you to test reactions to your decision.
Surprises	Keep the opponent off balance by a drastic, dramatic, sudden shift in your tactics. Never be predictable—keep the opponent from anticipating your moves.

relationship. The company wants to demonstrate that it has the capabilities to serve the account's needs in a superior way. Neil Rackham has developed a method that he calls *SPIN selling* (Situation, Problem, Implication, Need–Payoff). Gone is the script of the slick salesperson, and in its place is the salesperson who knows how to raise good questions and listen and learn. Neil Rackham trains salespeople to raise four types of questions with the prospect:

1. *Situation questions:* These ask about facts or explore the buyer's present situation. For example, "What system are you using to invoice your customers?"

2. *Problem questions:* These deal with problems, difficulties, and dissatisfactions the buyer is experiencing. For example, "What parts of the system create errors?"

3. *Implication questions:* These ask about the consequences or effects of a buyer's problems, difficulties, or dissatisfactions. For example, "How does this problem affect your people's productivity?"

4. *Need–payoff questions:* These ask about the value or usefulness of a proposed solution. For example, "How much would you save if our company could help reduce the errors by 80 percent?"

When—and How—to Use Relationship Marketing

Barbara Jackson argues that relationship marketing is not effective in all situations but is extremely effective in the right situations. She sees transaction marketing as more appropriate with customers who have a short time horizon and low switching costs, such as buyers of commodities. A customer buying steel can buy from one of several steel suppliers and choose the one offering the best terms. The fact that one steel supplier has been particularly attentive or responsive does not automatically earn it the next sale; its terms must be competitive.

In contrast, relationship marketing investments pay off handsomely with customers who have long time horizons and high switching costs, such as buyers of office automation systems. Presumably, the customer for a major system carefully researches the competing suppliers and chooses one from whom it can expect good long-term service and state-of-the-art technology. Both the customer and the supplier invest a lot of money and time in the relationship. The customer would find it costly and risky to switch to another vendor, and the seller would find that losing this customer would be a major loss. Relationship marketing has the greatest payoff with these customers, whom Jackson calls "lost-for-good customers."

In lost-for-good situations, the challenge is different for the in-supplier versus the out-supplier. The in-supplier's strategy is to make switching difficult for the customer. The in-supplier will develop product systems that are incompatible with competitive products and will install proprietary ordering systems that facilitate inventory management and delivery. The out-supplier will design product systems that are compatible with the customer's system, are easy to install and learn, save the customer a lot of money, and promise to improve through time.

Anderson and Narus believe that transaction versus relationship marketing is not so much an issue of the type of industry as of the particular customer's wishes. Some customers value a high service bundle and will stay with that supplier for a long time. Other customers want to cut their costs and will switch suppliers for lower costs. In this case, the company can still retain the customer by agreeing to reduce the price, provided the customer is willing to accept fewer services; or the customer may forgo free delivery or training. This customer would be treated on a transaction basis rather than on a relationship-building basis. As long as the company cuts its own costs by as much or more than its price reduction, the transaction-oriented customer will still be profitable.

Sources: Barbara Bund Jackson, *Winning and Keeping Industrial Customers: The Dynamics of Customer Relationships* (Lexington, MA: D. C. Heath, 1985); and James C. Anderson and James A. Narus, "Partnering as a Focused Market Strategy," *California Management Review*, Spring 1991, pp. 95–113.

Rackham suggests that companies, especially those selling complex products or services, should have their salesperson move from *preliminaries,* to *investigating* the prospect's problems and needs, to *demonstrating* the supplier's superior capabilities, and then *obtaining* a long-term commitment. This approach reflects the growing interest of many companies in moving from pursuing an immediate sale to developing a long-term customer relationship.[40]

More companies today are moving their emphasis from transaction marketing to *relationship marketing.* Today's customers are large and often global. They prefer suppliers who can sell and deliver a coordinated set of products and services to many locations; who can quickly solve problems that arise in different locations; and who can work closely with customer teams to improve products and processes. Unfortunately, most companies are not set up to meet these requirements. Their products are sold by separate sales forces that don't work together easily. The company's technical people may not be willing to spend time to educate a customer.

Companies recognize that sales teamwork will increasingly be the key to winning and maintaining accounts. Yet they recognize that asking people for teamwork doesn't produce it. They need to revise compensation systems to give credit for work on shared accounts. They need to set up better goals and measures for their sales force. They also must emphasize the importance of teamwork in their training programs, while at the same time honouring the importance of individual initiative.[41]

Relationship marketing is based on the premise that important accounts need focused and continuous attention. Salespeople working with key customers must do more than call when they think customers might be ready to place orders. They should call or visit at other times, take customers to dinner, and make useful suggestions about their business. They should monitor key accounts, know their problems, and be ready to serve them in a number of ways.

When a relationship management program is properly implemented, the organization will begin to focus as much on managing its customers as on managing its products. At the same time, companies should realize that while there is a strong and warranted move toward relationship marketing, it is not effective in all situations. Ultimately, companies must judge which segments and which specific customers will respond profitably to relationship management. (For some guidelines, see the Marketing Insight "When—and How—to Use Relationship Marketing.")

SUMMARY

1. Sales personnel serve as a company's link to its customers. The sales rep *is* the company to many of its customers, and it is the rep who brings back to the company much-needed information about the customer.

2. Designing the sales force requires decisions regarding objectives, strategy, structure, size, and compensation. Objectives may include prospecting, targeting, communicating, selling, servicing, information gathering, and allocating. Determining strategy requires choosing the mix of selling approaches that are most effective. Choosing the sales force structure entails dividing territories by geography, product, or market (or some combination of these). Estimating how large the sales force needs to be involves estimating the total workload and how many sales hours (and hence salespeople) will be needed. Compensating the sales force entails determining what types of salaries, commissions, bonuses, expense accounts, and benefits to give, and how much weight customer satisfaction should have in determining total compensation.

3. There are five steps involved in managing the sales force: (a) recruiting and selecting sales representatives; (b) training the representatives in sales techniques and in the company's products, policies, and customer-satisfaction orientation; (c) supervising the sales force, helping reps to use their time efficiently; (d) motivating the sales force, balancing quotas, monetary rewards, and supplementary motivators; (e) evaluating individual and group sales performance.

4. Effective salespeople are trained in the methods of analysis and customer management, as well as the art of sales professionalism. No approach works best in all circumstances, but most trainers agree that selling is a seven-step process: prospecting and qualifying customers, preapproach, approach, presentation and demonstration, overcoming objections, closing, and follow-up and maintenance.

5. Another aspect of selling is negotiation, the art of arriving at transaction terms that satisfy both parties. A third aspect is relationship marketing, which focuses on developing long-term, mutually beneficial relationships between two parties.

APPLICATIONS

CHAPTER CONCEPTS

1. It has been said that there are two parts to every sale—the part performed by the salesperson, and the part performed by his or her organization. What should the company provide for the salesperson to help increase total sales? How does the sales manager's job differ from the sales rep's job?

2. Organizations that achieve good sales and profits year after year—like Dell Computer, Nordstrom, Merck, Four Seasons (hotel chain), Bombardier, Wal-Mart, Air Transat, Hertz, Canadian Tire, Purolator, and DuPont—do so in part because they have good sales management. For example:

   ■ Dell Computer *keeps track of customers through the use of computer technology. Dell offers warranties, upgrades, and lifetime technical support for users. The computers arrive already loaded with an operating system. The company also conducts intense training programs that help the company's marketers sell computers and advanced technology via telemarketing and direct mail.*

- Nordstrom *gives intense, personalized attention to customers and maintains a database on previous purchases so that its sales associates can better assist customers with future purchases. Customers remain very loyal to Nordstrom.*

  Choose any three of the remaining companies and prepare a brief report (three to five pages) on how good sales management contributes to their overall success.

3. For each situation, indicate whether the sales force should be compensated more on a straight-salary plan or more on a commission plan. Explain your rationale for each answer.

  a. Nonselling duties (e.g., providing technical services, giving time to public relations, setting up displays) are most important,

  b. The selling task is complex and involves a sales team, such as in the selling of data processing equipment or heavy machinery.

  c. The key objective is the generation of greater sales volume through new accounts.

  d. The company desires highly entrepreneurial sales reps who will not need much supervision.

  e. Sales show a marked seasonal pattern, with sales very high in some periods and very low in others.

  f. The company's major goal is increased sales coming from one-time transactions.

  g. The company actively seeks long-term relationships with its customers and excellence in customer service.

  h. The selling task is so routine that it amounts to order taking, such as in wholesaling and the selling of staple consumer goods

MARKETING AND ADVERTISING

Investors Group uses print advertisements like the one shown in Figure 1 to appeal to Canadians' needs for financial planning. Using provocative statements and questions, the ads motivate readers to call the toll free number or visit the Web site. Investors Group's network of over 3,800 representatives provides callers with information about their comprehensive range of investment products and financial services. Investors Group serves over one million clients through its dedicated salesforce, working out of 100 Financial Planning Centres across Canada. What kind of training do you think such sales representatives need? How can they qualify prospects? Why are good follow-up and maintenance skills important for these sales representatives?

Figure 1

Figure 2

The Xerox ad shown in Figure 2 is geared toward businesses that produce marketing materials such as brochures in colour. This ad directs interested readers to call a toll-free number and ask for a "Xerox Color Specialist." Which of the six types of sales representatives is this specialist likely to be? Which of the specific sales tasks is this sales rep likely to perform?

FOCUS ON TECHNOLOGY

Automated sales management software helps companies boost the productivity of their sales representatives and better integrate sales activities with overall marketing and corporate strategies. Among the leaders in this technology is Trilogy, whose Selling Chain software includes modules for managing sales compensation, contracts, pricing, proposals, and other aspects of the sales process.

Visit Trilogy's Web site to read about its Selling Chain software www.trilogy.com/ products/selling-chain.asp). Also click on the "SC Commission" button (in the column of products at left) to read about the sales compensation portion of this program, used by sales managers at Hewlett-Packard and many other companies. With this program, what criteria might sales managers want to use to evaluate the performance of their representatives? Why would sales managers want to track the profitability as well as the volume of sales produced by a sales representative?

MARKETING FOR THE 21ST CENTURY

Texas Instruments
www.ti.com/

Many companies are using their Web sites as tools for building long-term relationships between sales representatives and their customers. A case in point is Texas Instruments, which has created a sophisticated Web site to support its sales of multiple product lines, including calculators and semiconductors.

Visit the Texas Instruments Web site. Click on the privacy policy (at bottom of page) to learn why information is collected from visitors. Then return to the home page and click on the TI&ME button (at top right) to see how visitors can customize what they view on this site. What does Texas Instruments do with the information it collects from visitors? Why would a customer want to customize the Web page? Why would Texas Instruments want its customers to set up customized Web pages? What effect is this likely to have on the relationship between customers and their sales representatives?

YOU'RE THE MARKETER:
SONIC MARKETING PLAN

Many marketers—including nonprofit and for-profit organizations—include personal selling in their marketing plans. However, because of the high cost of maintaining a sales force, many marketers are substituting mail and telephone sales for some personal sales calls.

At Sonic, you are helping Jane Melody plan sales strategy for the company's line of shelf stereos. Take a few minutes to review Sonic's current situation and the marketing strategies you have already recommended. Then answer the following questions about Sonic's use of personal selling:

- *Whom should Sonic's sales force be calling on? How can the sales force support Sonic's marketing plan and goals? Would Sonic benefit from major account management?*
- *What sales objectives and quotas should Sonic set for its sales force?*
- What kind of compensation would be most appropriate for the sales force?
- What training should Sonic be providing for new and existing sales representatives?

Once you have answered these questions, consider the implications for Sonic's overall marketing goals and its marketing mix. Depending on your instructor's directions, type your answers and recommendations into a written marketing plan or enter them into the Marketing Strategy/Sales Force section and the Sales Forecast section of the Marketing Plan Pro software.

Managing Direct and On-Line Marketing

PROFILE:

Canadian Marketing Excellence

"More of today's marketing is moving from the marketplace into cyberspace," notes Philip Kotler. This could be the mantra of Alex de Bold, a 26-year-old Ottawa entrepreneur, who has his eye on targeting you, the Canadian university student, with his new web-based business, Professorjones.com. Focusing exclusively on providing textbooks to university students, de Bold based his new business on his own frustrations. He hated standing in long line-ups in campus bookstores. Not only does he offer you on-line ordering and no lines, but he also promises to give you discount prices—not a bad deal! The site is well designed and offers students much more than just on-line purchase convenience. It provides lists of events on various university campuses and career information as well as study aids and on-line student organizers. The site even offers students the ability to set up on-line study group sessions. If students are tired of "hitting the books," they can test their knowledge in an Austin Powers trivia game or see if the stars predict a rosy future for them by visiting the astrology section. Such magic didn't come cheaply, however. The site came with a $1-million price tag. It's a good thing Alex knew something about marketing! He sold the idea to John Kelly, president of JetForm Corp., who financed the venture after Alex impressed him with his vision, passion, and energy.

Sources: http://www.professorjones.com/home. Simon Tuck, "New Web Site Targeted at Students," *Globe and Mail*, September 7, 1999, p. B4. "Web Venture to Peddle Textbooks," *Globe and Mail*, September 7, 1999, p. A5.

In this chapter, we will address the following questions:

- What are the benefits of direct marketing?

- How can companies use integrated direct marketing for competitive advantage?

- How do customer databases support direct marketing?

- What channels do direct marketers use to reach individual prospects and customers?

- What marketing opportunities do on-line channels provide?

- What public and ethical issues do direct and on-line marketing raise?

Today, the explosion of media enables many more companies to sell their products and services directly to customers without intermediaries. The existing media—print and broadcast, catalogues, direct mail, and telephone marketing—have been complemented by fax machines, e-mail, the Internet, and on-line services. Companies are increasingly using all these media to make direct offers to existing customers and to identify new prospects. Direct marketing enables companies to target their offers and to measure their results more accurately.

THE GROWTH AND BENEFITS OF DIRECT MARKETING

The Direct Marketing Association (DMA) defines *direct marketing* as follows:

- **Direct marketing** is an interactive marketing system that uses one or more advertising media to effect a measurable response and/or transaction at any location.

This definition emphasizes a measurable response, typically a customer order. Thus direct marketing is sometimes called direct-order marketing.

Today, many direct marketers see direct marketing as playing a broader role, that of building a long-term relationship with the customer (direct relationship marketing).[1] Direct marketers occasionally send birthday cards, information materials, or small premiums to select members in their customer base. Airlines, hotels, and other businesses build strong customer relationships through frequency award programs and club programs.

Direct Marketing Association
www.the-dma.org

THE GROWTH OF DIRECT MARKETING AND ELECTRONIC BUSINESS

Sales produced through traditional direct-marketing channels (catalogues, direct mail, and telemarketing) have been growing rapidly. Whereas retail sales grow around three percent annually, catalogue and direct-mail sales grew about seven percent in 1997.

These sales include sales to the consumer market (53 percent), business-to-business sales (27 percent), and fund raising by charitable institutions (20 percent). Sales through catalogue and direct mail are estimated at over $475 billion annually. North American per capita annual direct sales are $900.[2]

The extraordinary growth of direct marketing is the result of many factors. Market "demassification" has resulted in an ever-increasing number of market niches with distinct preferences. Higher costs of driving, traffic congestion, parking headaches, lack of time, hassles of shopping with young children, a shortage of retail sales help, and queues at checkout counters all encourage at-home shopping. Consumers appreciate direct marketers' toll-free phone numbers available 24 hours a day, 7 days a week, and their commitment to customer service. The growth of next-day delivery via Federal Express, Purolator, and UPS has made ordering fast and easy. In addition, many chain stores have dropped slower-moving specialty items, creating an opportunity for direct marketers to promote these items directly to interested buyers. The growth of affordable computer power and customer databases has enabled direct marketers to single out the best prospects for any product they wish to sell. Increasingly, business marketers have turned to direct mail and telemarketing in response to the high and increasing costs of reaching business markets through the sales force.

Electronic communication is showing explosive growth. World-wide e-commerce revenues are estimated to have exceeded $20 billion in 1998, a 200 percent increase over 1997. However, the percentage of people on-line varies widely around the world. The United States accounts for a whopping 79.1 percent of all users. Europe is in second place with 8.7 percent of the world's users. Japan is in third place with 4.5 percent. Canada holds fourth place with 3.6 percent. The rest of the world accounts for only 2.3 percent of the users. To serve these users, there are more than 1.5 million Web sites. McKinsey & Company estimates that e-commerce sales could grow to $327 billion by the year 2002.[3]

The creation of the "information superhighway" is revolutionizing commerce. *Electronic business* is the general term for buyers and sellers using electronic means to research, communicate, and potentially transact with one another. *Electronic markets* are sponsored Web sites that (1) describe the products and services offered by sellers and (2) allow buyers to search for information, identify what they need or want, and place orders using a credit card. The product is then delivered physically (to the customer's house or office) or electronically (software can be downloaded to a customer's computer).

THE BENEFITS OF DIRECT MARKETING

Direct marketing benefits customers in many ways. Home shopping is fun, convenient, and hassle-free. It saves time and introduces consumers to a larger selection of merchandise. They can do comparative shopping by browsing through mail catalogues and on-line shopping services. They can order goods for themselves or others. Business customers also benefit by learning about available products and services without tying up time in meeting salespeople.

Sellers also benefit. Direct marketers can buy a mailing list containing the names of almost any group: left-handed people, overweight people, millionaires. They can personalize and customize their messages. According to Pierre Passavant: "We will store hundreds . . . of messages in memory. We will select 10 000 families with 12 or 20 or 50 specific characteristics and send them very individualized laser-printed letters."[4] Direct marketers can build a continuous relationship with each customer. The parents of the newborn baby will receive periodic mailings describing new clothes, toys, and other goods as the child grows. Nestlé's baby food division continuously builds a database of new mothers and mails six personalized packages of gifts and advice at key stages in the baby's life.

Direct marketing can be timed to reach prospects at the right moment, and direct-marketing material receives higher readership because it is sent to more interested prospects. Direct marketing permits the testing of alternative media and messages in search of the most cost-effective approach. Direct marketing also makes the direct marketer's offer and strategy less visible to competitors. Finally, direct marketers can measure responses to their campaigns to decide which have been the most profitable.

THE GROWING USE OF INTEGRATED DIRECT MARKETING

Although direct and on-line marketing are booming, a large number of companies still relegate them to minor roles in their communication–promotion mix. Advertising and sales-promotion departments receive most of the communication dollars and jealously guard their budgets. The sales force may also see direct marketing as a threat when it has to turn over smaller customers and prospects to direct mailers and telemarketers.

However, companies are increasingly recognizing the importance of integrating their marketing communications. Some companies are appointing a chief communications officer (CCO) in addition to a CIO (chief information officer). The CCO supervises specialists in advertising, sales promotion, public relations, and direct–on-line marketing. The aim is to establish the right overall communication budget and the right allocation of funds to each communication tool. This movement has been variously called integrated marketing communications (IMC), integrated direct marketing (IDM), and maximarketing.[5]

How can different communication tools be integrated in campaign planning? Imagine a marketer using a single tool in a "one-shot" effort to reach and sell a prospect. An example of a single-vehicle, single-stage campaign is a one-time mailing offering a cookware item. A single-vehicle, multiple-stage campaign would involve successive mailings to the same prospect. Magazine publishers, for example, send about four renewal notices to a household before giving up. A more powerful approach is the multiple-vehicle, multiple-stage campaign. Consider the following sequence:

News campaign about a new product → Paid ad with a response mechanism → Direct mail → Outbound telemarketing → Face-to-face sales call → Ongoing communication

Compaq
www.compaq.com

For example, Compaq might launch a new laptop computer by first arranging news stories to stir interest. Then Compaq might place full-page ads offering a free booklet on "How to Buy a Computer." Compaq would then mail the booklet to those who responded, along with an offer to sell the new computer at a special discount before it arrives in retail stores. Suppose four percent of those who receive the booklet order the computer. Compaq telemarketers then phone the 96 percent who did not buy to remind them of the offer. Suppose another six percent now order the computer. Those who do not place an order are offered a face-to-face sales call or demonstration in a local retail store. Even if the prospect is not ready to buy, there is ongoing communication.

Ernan Roman says that the use of *response compression*, whereby multiple media are deployed within a tightly defined time frame, increases message reach and impact. The underlying idea is to deploy a sequence of messages with precise timing intervals in the hope of generating incremental sales and profits that exceed the costs involved. Roman cites a Citicorp campaign to market home equity loans. Instead of using only "mail plus an 800 number," Citicorp used "mail plus coupon plus 800 number plus outbound telemarketing plus print advertising." Although the second campaign was more expensive, it resulted in a 15 percent increase in the number of new accounts compared with direct mail alone. Roman concluded:

> *When a mailing piece which might generate a 2% response on its own is supplemented by a toll-free 800-number ordering channel, we regularly see response rise by 50–125%. A skillfully integrated outbound telemarketing effort can add another 500% lift in response. Suddenly our 2% response has grown to 13% or more by adding interactive marketing channels to a "business as usual" mailing. The dollars and cents involved in adding media to the integrated media mix is normally marginal on a cost-per-order basis because of the high level of responses generated. . . . . Adding media to a marketing program will raise total response . . . . because different people are inclined to respond to different stimuli.[6]*

Rapp and Collins' model makes direct-marketing techniques the driving force in the general marketing process.[7] This model recommends the creation of a customer database and advocates making direct marketing a full partner in the marketing

The "Maximarketing" Model for Integrated Marketing

Rapp and Collins' maximarketing model consists of nine steps:

1. Maximized targeting calls upon the marketer to define and identify the best prospects for the offer. The marketer either buys mailing lists or searches the customer database for characteristics that point to high interest, ability to pay, and readiness to buy. "Best customers" include those who buy with some frequency, don't return many orders, don't complain, and pay on time. Mass marketers can go "fishing" for prospects with direct-response advertising in such mass media as television, newspaper supplements, and magazine insert cards.

2. Maximized media lead the direct marketer to examine the exploding variety of media and choose those that allow for convenient two-way communication and measurement of results.

3. Maximized accountability calls for evaluating campaigns on the basis of cost-per-prospect response rather than on the cost-per-thousand exposures.

4. Maximized awareness involves searching for messages that will break through the clutter and reach the prospects' hearts and minds by means of "whole brain" advertising that appeals to a person's rational and emotional sides.

5. Maximized activation means that advertising must trigger purchase or at least advance prospects to a measurably higher stage of buying readiness. Activation devices include statements such as "Send for more information" and "Reply coupon must be returned by September 30."

6. Maximized synergy involves finding ways of doing double duty with the advertising—for instance, combining awareness building with direct response, promoting other distribution channels, and sharing costs with other advertisers.

7. Maximized linkage calls for linking the advertising to the sale by concentrating on the better prospects and spending more of the total budget to convert them.

8. Maximized sales through database building calls on the marketer to continue to market directly to known customers by cross-selling, upgrading, and introducing new products. The marketer keeps enhancing the database with more customer information and ends up with a rich private advertising medium.

9. Maximized distribution involves building additional channels to reach prospects and customers—for instance, when a direct marketer opens retail stores or obtains shelf space in existing retail stores, or when a manufacturer such as General Foods decides to sell a premium brand of coffee directly to the consumer.

Sources: Summarized from Stan Rapp and Thomas L. Collins, Maximarketing (New York: McGraw-Hill, 1987). Also see their Beyond Maximarketing: The New Power of Caring and Daring (New York: McGraw-Hill, 1994), for specific companies and cases of successful maximarketing.

process. Maximarketing consists of a comprehensive set of steps for reaching the prospect, making the sale, and developing the relationship. For more details, see the Marketing Insight "The 'Maximarketing' Model for Integrated Marketing."

Bell Canada, Air Canada, IBM, Ford, and VISA have used integrated direct marketing to build profitable relations with customers over the years. Retailers such as Canadian Tire, Zellers, Mountain Equipment Co-op, Holt Renfrew, and Tilley Endurables regularly send out catalogues to supplement in-store sales. Direct-marketing companies such as L.L. Bean, Eddie Bauer, Franklin Mint, and The Sharper Image made fortunes in the direct-marketing mail-order and phone-order business, then opened retail stores after establishing strong brand names as direct marketers.

 USTOMER DATABASES AND DIRECT MARKETING

Don Peppers and Martha Rogers list the main differences between mass marketing and *one-to-one marketing* (Table 21.1).[8] Companies that know their individual customers can customize their product, offer, message, shipment method, and payment method to maximize customer appeal. Today's companies are building customer databases:

■ A *customer database* is an organized collection of comprehensive data about individual customers or prospects that is current, accessible, and actionable for such marketing purposes as lead generation, lead qualification, sale of a product

	Mass Marketing	One-to-One Marketing
TABLE 21.1	Average customer	Individual customer
	Customer anonymity	Customer profile
Mass Marketing versus One-to-One Marketing	Standard product	Customized market offering
	Mass production	Customized production
	Mass distribution	Individualized distribution
	Mass advertising	Individualized message
	Mass promotion	Individualized incentives
	One-way message	Two-way messages
	Economies of scale	Economies of scope
	Share of market	Share of customer
	All customers	Profitable customers
	Customer attraction	Customer retention

Source: Adapted from Don Peppers and Martha Rogers, *The One-to-One Future* (New York: Doubleday/Currency, 1993). See their Web site: www.1to1.com/articles/subscribe.html.

or service, or maintenance of customer relationships. ***Database marketing*** is the process of building, maintaining, and using customer databases and other databases (products, suppliers, resellers) for the purpose of contacting and transacting.

Many companies confuse a customer mailing list with a customer database. A *customer mailing list* is simply a set of names, addresses, and telephone numbers. A customer database contains much more information. In business marketing, the customer profile contains the products and services the customer has bought; past volumes, prices, and profits; team member names (and their ages, birthdays, hobbies, and favourite foods); status of current contracts; an estimate of the supplier's share of the customer's business; competitive suppliers; assessment of competitive strengths and weaknesses in selling and servicing the account; and relevant buying practices, patterns, and policies. In consumer marketing, the customer database contains demographics (age, income, family members, birthdays), psychographics (activities, interests, and opinions), past purchases, and other relevant information about an individual. For example, the catalogue company Fingerhut possesses some 1400 pieces of information about each of the 30 million households in its massive customer database.

Database marketing is mostly frequently used by business marketers, service retailers (hotels, banks, and airlines), and non-profit organizations (the United Way). It is used less often by packaged-goods retailers (Wal-Mart, Waldenbooks) and consumer-packaged-goods companies, though some (Quaker Oats, Ralston Purina, and Nabisco among them) have been experimenting in this area. A well-developed customer database is a proprietary asset that can give the company a competitive edge.

Armed with the information in its database, a company can achieve much more target market precision than it can with mass marketing, segment marketing, or niche marketing. The company can identify small groups of customers who receive fine-tuned marketing offers and communications. Lands' End, for example, has tons of information about its customers and their past purchases: This is called a *data warehouse*. Lands' End engaged IBM to use a set of techniques called *data mining* to cluster its customers into segments. IBM identified 5200 different *market cells*. One market cell consisted of 850 customers who had purchased a blue shirt and red tie. This alerted Lands' End to the possible interest of these customers in buying a dark blue jacket, at which point it sent them a special offer. Lands' End would expect a higher response rate to this offer than if it made it to one million customers independently of past purchase patterns.

United Way of Canada
www.uwc-cc.ca

According to Donnelley Marketing Inc.'s annual survey of promotional practices, 56 percent of manufacturers and retailers currently have or are building a database, an additional 10 percent plan to do so, and 85 percent believe they'll need database marketing to be competitive in the next millennium.[9]

Companies use their databases in four ways:

1. *To identify prospects:* Many companies generate sales leads by advertising their product or offer. The ads generally contain a response feature, such as a business reply card or toll-free phone number. The database is built from these responses. The company sorts through the database to identify the best prospects, then contacts them by mail, phone, or personal call in an attempt to convert them into customers. Here's how Scudder, the giant mutual fund company, used direct marketing to enter the Canadian marketplace.

Scudder Funds of Canada
www.scudder.ca

- **Scudder.** Scudder Funds of Canada knew it faced a major challenge when it first entered the booming Canadian marketplace in 1995. There were over 1000 funds already in place and although Scudder was a well-known entity in the United States, it wasn't even a blip on Canadian's radar screens. Since it was a no-load fund, it could not entice brokers with fat commissions to push its funds. Nor, as a Canadian start-up, could it pitch people based on its performance history. So Scudder decided to go after savvy, mature investors using an integrated campaign. It built awareness with TV and print advertising that incorporated a direct response mechanism, a 1-800 number. A sophisticated call tracking system told Scudder which ad had generated a call. From the pool of prospects generated by the advertising along with lists of people who subscribed to financial publications such as the *Globe and Mail* and the *Financial Post,* Scudder developed a mailing list. The mailings provided straightforward information on the company, its products, and investing in general. The response rate was 3.5 percent, but this resulted in over $12 million in sales. Today, despite increasing competition, Scudder continues to grow at rates in excess of 300 percent and it now holds over $600 million in assets.[10]

2. *To decide which customers should receive a particular offer:* Companies set up criteria describing the ideal target customer for an offer. Then they search their customer databases for those most closely resembling the ideal type. Companies such as The Limited, Federal Express, and VanCity Credit Union are now creating vast data warehouses that allow them to pinpoint which customers are profitable and which are not. They manipulate the data to compare the complex mix of marketing and servicing costs that go into retaining each individual customer versus the revenues he or she is likely to bring in. By noting response rates, the company can improve its target precision over time. Following a sale, it can set up an automatic sequence of activities: One week later, send a thank-you note; five weeks later, send a new offer; ten weeks later (if customer has not responded), phone the customer and offer a special discount.

3. *To deepen customer loyalty:* Companies can build interest and enthusiasm by remembering customer preferences; by sending appropriate gifts, discount coupons, and interesting reading material. Here is an example:

- **Mars.** Mars is a market leader not only in candy but also in pet food. In Germany, Mars has compiled the names of virtually every cat-owning German family by contacting veterinarians and also advertising a free booklet titled "How to Take Care of Your Cat." Those who requested the booklet filled out a questionnaire. As a result, Mars knows the cat's name, age, and birthday. Mars now sends a birthday card to each cat in Germany each year, along with a new cat-food sample or money-saving coupons for Mars brands. Do the cat owners appreciate this? You bet!

4. *To reactivate customer purchases:* Companies can install automatic mailing programs (*automatic marketing*) that send out birthday or anniversary cards, Christmas shopping reminders, or off-season promotions. The database can help the company make attractive or timely offers.

Database marketing requires a large investment. Companies must invest in computer hardware, database software, analytical programs, communication links, and skilled personnel. The database system must be user friendly and available to key marketing groups. A well-managed database hopefully will lead to sales gains that cover more than its costs. Royal Caribbean uses its database to offer spur-of-the-moment cruise packages to fill all the berths on its ships. Fewer unbooked rooms mean maximized profits for the cruise line.

But many things can go wrong if database marketing is not done carefully. At CNA Insurance, five programmers worked for nine months loading five years of claims data into a computer, only to discover that the data had been miscoded. Even if coded correctly, the data must be updated continuously because people move, drop out, or change their interests.

Customer privacy is another important concern for database marketers. A recent Canadian Direct Marketing Association Usage Survey showed that 63 percent of responding companies (all direct marketers in consumer, business-to-business or non-profit sectors) did not make their customer lists available for rental or exchange purposes. For instance, American Express, long regarded as a leader on privacy issues, does not sell information on specific customer transactions. However, Amex found itself the target of consumer outrage when it announced a partnership with KnowledgeBase Marketing Inc., which would have made data on people available to any merchant who accepts AmEx cards. Amex killed the partnership. America Online, also targeted by privacy advocates, junked a plan to sell subscribers' telephone numbers.[11]

Canadian Direct Marketing Association
www.cdma.org

MAJOR CHANNELS FOR DIRECT MARKETING

Direct marketers can use a number of channels for reaching prospects and customers. These include face-to-face selling, direct mail, catalogue marketing, telemarketing, TV and other direct-response media, kiosk marketing, and on-line channels.

FACE-TO-FACE SELLING

The original and oldest form of direct marketing is the field sales call. Today most industrial companies rely heavily on a professional sales force to locate prospects, develop them into customers, and grow the business. Or they hire manufacturers' representatives and agents to carry out the direct-selling task. In addition, many consumer companies use a direct-selling force: insurance agents, stockbrokers, and distributors working for direct-sales organizations such as Avon, Amway, Mary Kay, and Tupperware.

DIRECT MAIL

Direct-mail marketing involves sending an offer, announcement, reminder, or other item to a person at a particular address. Using highly selective mailing lists, direct marketers send out millions of mail pieces each year—letters, flyers, foldouts, and other "salespeople with wings." Some direct marketers mail audiotapes, videotapes, CDs, and computer diskettes to prospects and customers. The company that produces the Nordic Track Cardiovascular Exerciser advertises a free videotape showing the equipment's uses and health advantages. Ford sends a computer diskette called "Disk Drive Test Drive" to consumers responding to its ads in computer publications. The diskette's menu provides technical specifications and attractive graphics about Ford cars, and answers frequently asked questions. Apple Canada used direct mail in late 1999 to increase awareness and adoption of its new iMac computer. Targeting "experienced Mac users," Apple offered prospects a free, limited-edition iMac watch for test-driving an iMac and providing feedback.

Direct mail is a popular medium because it permits target market selectivity, can be personalized, is flexible, and allows early testing and response measurement. Although the cost per thousand people reached is higher than with mass media, the people reached are much better prospects.

Until recently, mail was paper-based. Canada Post has an extensive program that helps business use direct mail effectively. For-profit mail carriers such as Federal Express, Purolator, DHL, or Airborne Express also offer such services. Recently, three new forms of mail delivery appeared:

1. *Fax mail:* Fax machines enable one party to send a paper-based message to another party over telephone lines. Today's computers can also serve as fax machines. Fax mail can be sent and received almost instantaneously. Marketers have begun to send fax mail announcing offers, sales, and events to prospects and customers. Fax numbers of companies and individuals are now available through published directories.

2. *E-mail:* E-mail (short for *electronic mail*) allows users to send a message or file from one computer directly to another. The message arrives almost instantly but is stored until the receiving person turns on the computer. Marketers are beginning to send sales announcements, offers, and other messages to e-mail addresses—sometimes to a few individuals, sometimes to large groups.

3. *Voice mail:* Voice mail is a system for receiving and storing oral messages at a telephone address. Telephone companies sell this service as a substitute for answering machines. Some marketers have set up programs that will dial a large number of telephone numbers and leave the selling message in the recipients' voice mailboxes.

In constructing an effective direct-mail campaign, direct marketers must decide on their objectives, target markets and prospects, offer elements, means of testing the campaign, and measures of campaign success.

Objectives

Most direct marketers aim to receive an order from prospects. Some people judge a campaign's success by the response rate. An order-response rate of two percent is normally considered good, although this number varies with product category and price. Others assess the effectiveness of the campaign based on the number of prospects who turn into customers and actually place orders for the product or service.

Direct mail has other objectives as well, such as producing prospect leads, strengthening customer relationships, and informing and educating customers for later offers.

Target Markets and Prospects

Direct marketers need to identify the characteristics of prospects and customers who are most able, willing, and ready to buy. Bob Stone recommends applying the R-F-M formula (*recency, frequency, monetary amount*) for rating and selecting customers: The best customer targets are those who bought most recently, who buy frequently, and who spend the most. Points are established for varying R-F-M levels, and each customer is scored. The higher the score, the more attractive the customer.[12]

Prospects can also be identified on the basis of such variables as age, sex, income, education, and previous mail-order purchases. Occasions provide a good departure point for segmentation. New parents will be in the market for baby clothes and baby toys; university students will buy computers and small television sets; newlyweds will be looking for housing, furniture, appliances, and bank loans. Another useful segmentation variable is consumer lifestyle groups, such as computer buffs, cooking buffs, and outdoor buffs. For business markets, Dun & Bradstreet runs an information service that provides a wealth of data.

In business-to-business direct marketing, the "prospect" is often not an individual but a group of people or a committee that includes both decision makers and multiple decision influencers. See the Marketing Memo, "When Your Customer Is a Committee . . .," for tips on crafting a direct-mail campaign aimed at business buyers.

Once the target market is defined, the direct marketer needs to obtain specific names. Here is where mailing-list acquisition and mailing-list–database building come into play. The company's best prospects are customers who have bought its products in the past. Additional names can be obtained by advertising some free offer. The direct marketer can also buy lists of names from list brokers. But these lists often have problems, including name duplication, incomplete data, and obsolete addresses. The better lists include overlays of demographic and psychographic information. Direct marketers typically buy and test a sample before buying further names from the same list.

Offer Elements

Nash sees the offer strategy as consisting of five elements—the product, the offer, the medium, the distribution method, and the creative strategy.[13] Fortunately, all of these elements can be tested.

In addition to these elements, the direct-mail marketer must decide on five components of the mailing itself: the outside envelope, sales letter, circular, reply form, and reply envelope. Here are some findings:

■ The outside envelope will be more effective if it contains an illustration, preferably in colour, or a catchy reason to open the envelope, such as the announcement of a contest, premium, or benefit. Envelopes are more effective when they contain a colourful commemorative stamp, when the address is hand-typed or handwritten, and when the envelope differs in size or shape from standard envelopes. *Harper's* magazine is well known for using provocative teasers on its envelopes: "Inside: the government's secret plan to nationalize your bank. Christian singles dating questionnaire. The world according to Oliver North. How Wall Street plans to profit from AIDS." Other envelopes employ "fascinations," as they were called by the late Mel Martin, a copywriter for Boardroom Inc. Catchy headlines like these worked year after year after year on envelopes for Boardroom Inc.'s promotions: "What Credit Card Companies Don't Tell You" or "What Never to Eat on an Airplane."[14]

■ The sales letter should use a personal salutation and start with a headline in bold type. The letter should be printed on good-quality paper and be brief. A computer-typed letter usually outperforms a printed letter, and the presence of a pithy postscript increases the response rate, as does the signature of someone whose title is important.

■ In most cases, a colourful circular accompanying the letter will increase the response rate by more than its cost.

■ Better results are obtained when the reply form features a toll-free number and contains a perforated receipt stub and guarantee of satisfaction.

■ The inclusion of a postage-free reply envelope will dramatically increase the response rate.

Testing Elements

One of the great advantages of direct marketing is the ability to test, under real marketplace conditions, the efficacy of different elements of an offer strategy, such as product features, copy, prices, media, or mailing lists.

Direct marketers must remember that response rates typically understate a campaign's long-term impact. Suppose only two percent of the recipients who receive a direct-mail piece advertising Samsonite luggage place an order. A much larger percentage became aware of the product (direct mail has high readership), and some percentage may have formed an intention to buy at a later date (either by mail or at a retail outlet). Furthermore, some of them may mention Samsonite luggage to others as a result of the direct-mail piece. To derive a more comprehensive estimate of the promotion's impact, some companies are measuring direct marketing's impact on awareness, intention to buy, and word of mouth.

Measuring Campaign Success: Lifetime Value

By adding up the planned campaign costs, the direct marketer can determine in advance the needed break-even response rate. This rate must be net of returned merchandise and bad debts. Returned merchandise can kill an otherwise effective campaign. The direct marketer needs to analyze the main causes of returned merchandise (late shipment, defective merchandise, damage in transit, not as advertised, incorrect order fulfilment).

By carefully analyzing past campaigns, direct marketers can steadily improve their performance. Even when a specific campaign fails to break even, it can still be profitable. Consider the following situation:

> *Suppose a membership organization spends $10 000 on a new-member campaign and attracts 100 new members, each paying annual dues of $70. It appears that the campaign has lost $3000 ($10 000–$7000). But if 80 percent of the new members renew their membership in the second year, the organization gets another $5600 without any effort. It has now received $12 600 ($7000 + $5600) for its investment of $10 000. To determine the long-term break-even rate, one needs to know the percentage who renew each year and for how many years they renew.*

This example illustrates the concept of *customer lifetime value*, which we first examined in Chapter 2.[15] A customer's ultimate value is not revealed by a purchase response to a particular mailing. Rather, the customer's lifetime value is the expected profit made on all future purchases net of customer acquisition and maintenance costs. For an average customer, one would calculate the average customer longevity, average customer annual expenditure, and average gross margin, minus the average cost of customer acquisition and maintenance (properly discounted for the opportunity cost of money). Data Consult claims it is able to estimate the expected lifetime value of a customer from as few as three or four transactions. This information enables marketers to adjust the nature and frequency of communications.

After assessing customer lifetime value, the company can focus its communication efforts on the more attractive customers. These efforts include sending communications that do not "sell" anything but rather maintain interest in the company and its products. Such communications may include free newsletters, booklets, and brochures, all of which build a stronger customer relationship.

CATALOGUE MARKETING

Catalogue marketing occurs when companies mail one or more product catalogues to selected addressees. They may send *full-line merchandise* catalogues, *specialty consumer* catalogues, and *business* catalogues, usually in print form but also sometimes as CDs, videos, or on-line. Sears sends out general merchandise catalogues. Holt Renfrew, Tilley Endurables, and Mountain Equipment Co-op send specialty clothing catalogues to the their respective target markets. Through its catalogues, Avon sells cosmetics and IKEA sells furniture. Thousands of small businesses, such as Hampstead House Books of Thornhill, Ontario, issue specialty catalogues. Large businesses such as Grainger, Merck, and others send catalogues to business prospects and customers.

Catalogues are a huge business—the $130 billion North American catalogue industry has jumped eight percent annually from 1993 to 1998. Although no one knows exactly how many new consumer catalogues were introduced each year, industry executives estimate that 200 to 300 were introduced between 1996 and 1998. The Direct Marketing Association estimates there are currently up to 10 000 mail-order catalogues of all kinds. Someone who frequently buys from catalogues can easily receive 70 catalogues in a single week over the holiday season. The success of a catalogue business depends on the company's ability to manage its customer lists so carefully that there is little duplication or bad debts, to control its inventory carefully, to offer quality merchandise so that returns are low, and to project a distinctive image. Some companies distinguish their catalogues by sending swatches of materials, operating a special hotline to answer questions, sending gifts to their best customers, and donating a percentage of the profits to good causes.

The weak dollar has given the Canadian catalogue industry a boost as people become increasingly reluctant to order from American firms. While Canadians spend 50 percent less per capita than their American counterparts on catalogue shopping, we still represent a $2.2-billion market. The latest Canadian trend is the development of "magalogues"—catalogues that resemble magazines with their glossy paper, high

(continued)

- Tell your customer-by-committee that you're communicating with others in the organization.

- Make your decision influencers feel important. They can be your biggest advocates.

- When communicating with different audiences, make sure you anticipate— and address—their individual buying objectives and objections.

- When your database or mailing lists can't help you reach all the key people, ask for help. Ask the individual you're addressing to pass along your information to the right person or people. You may even want to include a separate envelope with a routing slip and sales message tailored to the audience that will receive it.

- When doing a lead-generation mailing, make sure to ask for the names and titles of those who might be interested and involved in the buying decision. Enter this into your database and make sure you're communicating with these people in some fashion.

- Even though it may seem like a lot of work (and expense) to write different versions of the same letter and create different offers, there's a big payoff. For instance, whereas the final decision maker may be interested in having a payback calculated, others are more likely to be interested in day-to-day benefits such as safety, convenience, and time savings. Tailor your offer to your targets.

Source: Adapted from Pat Friesen, "When Your Customer Is a Committee ...," Target Marketing, August 1998, p. 40.

quality photography, and editorial material in addition to advertising. Developed by innovative retailers such as Land Rover, Holt Renfrew, and Loblaw Cos. Ltd., they are used to help retailers carve out distinct identities and build closer bonds with consumers. Harry Rosen Menswear not only sends its publication, *Harry*, to its best customers, it also makes it available on newsstands for a price of $6. Sales revenues help offset the cost of production.[16]

Global consumers in Asia and Europe are catching on to the catalogue craze. In the 1990s, U.S. catalogue companies such as L.L. Bean, Lands' End, and Patagonia began setting up operations in Japan—and with great success. In just a few years foreign catalogues—mostly from the United States and a few from Europe—have won five percent of the $20 billion Japanese mail-order catalogue market. A full 90 percent of L.L. Bean's international sales come from Japan. One reason international companies have flourished in Japan is that they offer high-quality merchandise aimed at specific groups. For decades Japanese consumers shunned Japanese catalogues because they were a hodgepodge of everything from cheap dresses and necklaces to diapers and dog foods. International catalogues also often contain two other items unusual in Japan: a lifetime, no-questions-asked guarantee and pictures of top models.

Cataloguers have also received a big boost from the Internet—about three-quarters of catalogue companies present merchandise and take orders over the Internet. The Land's End Web site, which debuted in 1995, now receives 180 000 e-mail queries a year, surpassing the print-mail response.[17] Of course, by putting their entire catalogues on the Internet, catalogue companies have better access to global consumers than ever before. They also save considerable printing and mailing costs and also offer some unique services. Although Eddie Bauer's on-line catalogue hasn't yet supplanted its paper one, the on-line version gives customers a chance to "try on" the clothing!

- **Eddie Bauer Inc.** In its latest attempt to build its brand over the Internet, casual apparel maker Eddie Bauer is letting customers enter a "virtual dressing room." Although visitors to Eddie bauer.com will find the same khaki, denim, and knit basics found in the retailer's catalogues and in its stores, the site is more than just an electronic sales flyer. If customers want to see how that holiday sweater will look with khakis or to try a sports jacket with the plaid

Eddie Bauer's Internet home page: Customers can "try on" clothes in a virtual dressing room.

pants, they can just click and drag the items to see how they look together. Because half the consumers who visit the Web site have never shopped at Eddie Bauer before, their experience on-line is an important first contact with the company. The virtual dressing room as well as other special services ensure that the first contact is a memorable one.[18]

TELEMARKETING

Telemarketing describes the use of telephone operators to attract new customers, to contact existing customers to ascertain satisfaction levels, or to take orders. In the case of routinely taking orders, it is called *telesales*. Many customers routinely order goods and services by telephone. The telephone recently spawned *home banking*. First Direct, set up in 1989 by Britain's Midland Bank, operates entirely by telephone (subsequently adding fax and Internet channels as well) and has no branches or physical presence. With 850 000 customers and adding 12 500 new ones each month, Midland represents the future for the financial industry.[19] Even medical services are being offered over phone lines. In return for a monthly fee, firms such as Toronto's MedAction offer subscribers "telephone triage"—health information provided by registered nurses over the phone. [20]

Telemarketing has become a major direct-marketing tool. In 1998, telemarketers sold $723 billion worth of products and services to consumers and businesses. The average household receives 19 telemarketing calls each year and makes 16 calls to place orders.

Some telemarketing systems are fully automated. Automatic-dialling and recorded-message players (ADRMPs) can dial numbers, play a voice-activated advertising message, and take orders from interested customers on an answering-machine device or by forwarding the call to an operator.

Telemarketing is increasingly used in business as well as consumer marketing. Raleigh Bicycles uses telemarketing to reduce the amount of personal selling needed for contacting its dealers. In the first year, sales-force travel costs were reduced by 50 percent and sales in a single quarter went up 34 percent. Telemarketing, as it improves with the use of videophones, will increasingly replace, though never eliminate, more expensive field sales calls. An increasing number of salespeople have made five- and six-figure sales without ever meeting the customer face-to-face. As salespeople and buyers become more comfortable with e-commerce, sales travel costs will go down.

Effective telemarketing depends on choosing the right telemarketers, training them well, and providing performance incentives. Telemarketers should have pleasant voices and project enthusiasm. Women are more effective than men for selling many products. Telemarketers should initially train with a script and then move toward more improvisation. The telemarketer needs to know how to end the conversation if the prospect seems to be a poor one. The call should be made at the right time, which is late morning and afternoon to reach business prospects, and evening hours between 7 and 9 P.M. to reach households. The telemarketing supervisor can build enthusiasm by offering prizes to the first one who gets an order or to the top performer. Given privacy issues and the higher cost per contact, precise list selection is critical.

OTHER MEDIA FOR DIRECT-RESPONSE MARKETING

Direct marketers use all the major media to make direct offers to potential buyers. Newspapers and magazines carry abundant print ads offering books, articles of clothing, appliances, vacations, and other goods and services that individuals can order by dialling a toll-free number. Radio ads present offers to listeners 24 hours a day. Television is used by direct marketers in three ways to promote direct sales:

1. *Direct-response advertising:* A classic example is Dial Media's ads for Ginsu knives, which ran for seven years and sold almost three million sets of knives worth over $60 million in sales. Some companies prepare 30- and 60-minute *infomercials*, which resemble documentaries (on quitting smoking, curing baldness, or losing weight), carry testimony from satisfied users of the

product or service, and include a toll-free number for ordering or getting further information. Chrysler developed "Chrysler Showcase," a 30-minute infomercial touting Chrysler's brand heritage and the exterior design, performance, handling, and premium features in the new Chrysler 300M, LHS, and Concorde. It aired on national cable networks as well as United Airlines SkyTV. Infomercials are more profitable than most people realize and are used to good effect to sell high-ticket items. They share the product's story and benefits with millions of additional prospects at a cost per lead or cost per order that usually matches or beats direct mail or print ads. In 1998, an estimated $1.5 billion in sales was generated by infomercials. They have generated up to $120 million in sales in just one year—two to five times that amount if the product is also available in retail stores.[21]

2. *At-home shopping channels:* Some television channels are dedicated to selling goods and services. U.S. based Home Shopping Network (HSN), which broadcasts 24 hours a day, and Canada's Rogers Media-owned company, The Shopping Channel (TSC), consist of the program's hosts offering bargain prices on such products as jewellery, lamps, collectible dolls, and power tools. Viewers call in their orders on a toll-free number and receive delivery within 48 hours. TSC's sales topped $115 million in 1998. To celebrate its twelfth birthday, TSC began offering its wares over the Internet (www.tsc.ca). Called TSC On-Line, the initiative is part of a broader plan to expand outside the confines of the tube. Although it drew a television audience of approximately 1.8 million viewers per week (32 percent of all households in English Canada with cable access), TSC hopes to expand sales. In addition to its new web site, TSC offers a new quarterly catalogue, TSC In-Print, and has opened a 5 000-square-metre retail outlet, The Shopping Channel OffAir.[22]

3. *Videotext and interactive TV:* Here the consumer's TV set is linked with a seller's catalogue by cable or telephone lines. Consumers can place orders via a special keyboard device connected to the system. Much research is now going on to combine TV, telephones, and computers into interactive TV.

KIOSK MARKETING

Some companies have designed "customer-order-placing machines" called *kiosks* (in contrast to vending machines, which dispense actual products) and placed them in stores, airports, and other locations. Burnaby's B.C.'s Infotouch Technologies Corp. is a firm that produces software that runs these machines for a number of clients worldwide. It develops customized kiosks for banks, insurance companies, tourist attractions, and government agencies. While the 30-employee firm generated $2 million in sales in 1999, it hopes to take an even bigger bite of the $320 million North American market. [23]

E LECTRONIC COMMERCE

The most recent channels for direct marketing are electronic channels. The term *electronic commerce* (e-commerce) is defined by Anthony Wensley, a professor at the University of Toronto, as using the Internet and the Web to radically transform the way businesses add value. E-commerce describes a wide variety of electronic platforms, such as the sending of purchase orders to suppliers via electronic data interchange (EDI); the use of fax and e-mail to conduct transactions; the use of ATMs, EFTPOS, and smart cards to facilitate payment and obtain digital cash; and the use of the Internet and on-line services. All of these involve doing business in a "marketspace" as compared to a physical "marketplace" [24]

Underlying electronic business are two phenomena: *digitalization* and *connectivity.* Digitalization consists of converting text, data, sound, and image into a stream of "bits" that can be dispatched at incredible speed from one location to another. Connectivity involves building networks and expresses the fact that much of the world's business is carried over networks connecting people and companies. These networks are called *intranets* when they connect people within a company; *extranets* when they connect a company with its suppliers and customers; and the Internet when they connect users to an amazingly large "information highway."

A recent Angus Reid survey revealed that the most popular purchases made by Canadian consumers over the Internet thus far have been software (30 percent), books (19 percent), CDs (8 percent), Internet services and memberships (4 percent), videos (4 percent), computer accessories (4 percent), concert and movie tickets (3 percent), computer hardware (3 percent), and clothing (3 percent).[25] There is also growing e-commerce in airline tickets, food, flowers, wine, clothing, and electronics.

Business transactions over the Internet are at a much higher volume and cover a great variety of goods and services. Business-to-business e-commerce transactions far outstrip business-to-consumer sales. Estimates of the size of this market vary widely. Forrester Research Inc. predicts that e-commerce will grow to $490 billion by the year 2002. The Gartner Group suggests that North American e-commerce will be worth more than $1390 billion by 2002. No matter which figure you believe, there is considerable growth in the amount of Internet financial transacting (stock trading, home banking, insurance sales).[26] Here we will focus on e-commerce channels, of which there are two types:

1. *Commercial channels:* Various companies have set up on-line information and marketing services that can be accessed by those who have signed up for the service and pay a monthly fee. The best-known on-line service provider and the Goliath of the on-line services industry is America Online with an estimated 14 million subscribers. Microsoft network (MSN) and Prodigy are trailing far behind AOL with 2.45 million and one million subscribers, respectively.[27] These channels provide information (news, libraries, education, travel, sports, reference), entertainment (fun and games), shopping services, dialogue opportunities (bulletin boards, forums, chat rooms), and e-mail.

2. *The Internet:* The Internet is a global web of computer networks that has made instantaneous and decentralized global communication possible. Internet usage has surged with the recent development of the user-friendly World Wide Web and Web browser software such as Netscape Navigator and Microsoft Internet Explorer. Users can surf the Internet and experience fully integrated text, graphics, images, and sound. Users can send e-mail, exchange views, shop for products, and access news, recipes, art, and business information. The Internet itself is free, though individual users need to pay an Internet service provider to be hooked up to it.

Angus Reid
www.angusreid.com

THE ON-LINE CONSUMER

As a whole, the Internet population is younger, more affluent, better educated, and more male than the general population. Internet usage also varies by province. While the 1998 average for regular Internet usage was 35.9 percent, Albertans lead the pack with 45.1 percent of households reporting regular use of the Internet. British Columbia has the next highest usage rates (42 percent), followed by Ontario (39 percent), and Nova Scotia (37.9 percent). Quebec trails with only 26.2 percent of adults regularly using the Internet. A shortage of French-language sites may partially explain Quebec's lower usage rates.[28]But as more people find their way onto the Internet, the cyberspace population is becoming more mainstream and diverse. Younger users are more likely to use the Internet for entertainment and socializing. Yet 45 percent of users are age 40 or older and use the Internet for investment and more serious matters. Internet users in general place greater value on information and tend to respond negatively to messages aimed only at selling. They decide what marketing information they will receive about which products and services and under what conditions. In on-line marketing, the consumer, not the marketer, gives permission and controls the interaction.

Internet "search engines," such as Yahoo!, Infoseek, Canoe and Excite, give consumers access to varied information sources, making them better informed and more discerning shoppers. Buyers have gained the following capabilities in the new information-rich regime:

1. They can get objective information for multiple brands, including costs, prices, features, and quality, without relying on the manufacturer or retailers.

2. They can initiate requests for advertising and information from manufacturers.

3. They can design the offerings they want.

4. They can use software agents to search for and invite offers from multiple sellers.

These new buyer capabilities mean that the exchange process in the age of information has become customer initiated and customer controlled. Marketers and their representatives are held at bay until customers invite them to participate in the exchange. Even after marketers enter the exchange process, customers define the rules of engagement, and insulate themselves with the help of agents and intermediaries. Customers define what information they need, what offerings they are interested in, and what prices they are willing to pay. In many ways, this customer-initiated and customer-controlled marketing completely reverses time-honoured marketing practices.

Consider how people can now use the Internet to buy automobiles or get home mortgage loans:

Automobile Protection Association
www.apa.ca

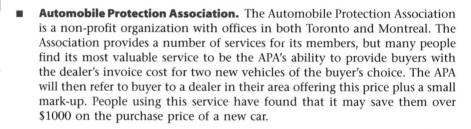

■ **Automobile Protection Association.** The Automobile Protection Association is a non-profit organization with offices in both Toronto and Montreal. The Association provides a number of services for its members, but many people find its most valuable service to be the APA's ability to provide buyers with the dealer's invoice cost for two new vehicles of the buyer's choice. The APA will then refer to buyer to a dealer in their area offering this price plus a small mark-up. People using this service have found that it may save them over $1000 on the purchase price of a new car.

i/money
www.imoney.com/mortgages

Canada Mortgage
www.CanMortgage.com

■ **Mortgage Rates.** Prospective home buyers can research home mortgage rates and interest rate trends, use financial tools to analyze loans, and sign up for an e-mail service that keeps them informed of trends in loan rates. They can apply on-line for a home mortgage from a variety of home mortgage providers and obtain responses within one business day. See the information provided on the Web pages posted by i/money or Canada Mortgage to get a sense of the services they provide.

ON-LINE MARKETING: ADVANTAGES AND DISADVANTAGES

Why have on-line services become so popular? They provide three major benefits to potential buyers:[29]

1. *Convenience:* Customers can order products 24 hours a day wherever they are. They don't have to sit in traffic, find a parking space, and walk through countless aisles to find and examine goods.

2. *Information:* Customers can find reams of comparative information about companies, products, competitors, and prices without leaving their office or home.

3. *Fewer hassles:* Customers don't have to face salespeople or open themselves up to persuasion and emotional factors; they also don't have to wait in line.

On-line services also provide a number of benefits to marketers:

- *Quick adjustments to market conditions:* Companies can quickly add products to their offering and change prices and descriptions.

- *Lower costs:* On-line marketers avoid the expense of maintaining a store and the costs of rent, insurance, and utilities. They can produce digital catalogues for much less than the cost of printing and mailing paper catalogues.

- *Relationship building:* On-line marketers can dialogue with consumers and learn from them. Marketers can download useful reports or a free demo of their software or a free sample of their newsletter.

- *Audience sizing:* Marketers can learn how many people visited their on-line site and how many stopped at particular places on the site. This information can help improve offers and ads.

Clearly, marketers are adding on-line channels to find, reach, communicate, and sell. On-line marketing has at least five great advantages. First, both small and large firms can afford it. Second, there is no real limit on advertising space, in contrast to print and broadcast media. Third, information access and retrieval are fast, compared to overnight mail and even fax. Fourth, the site can be visited by anyone anyplace in the world, at any time. Fifth, shopping can be done privately and swiftly.

However, on-line marketing is not for every company nor for every product. The Internet is useful for products and services where the shopper seeks greater ordering convenience (e.g., books and music) or lower cost (e.g., stock trading or news reading). The Internet is also useful where buyers need information about feature and value differences (e.g., automobiles or computers). The Internet is less useful for products that must be touched or examined in advance. But even this has exceptions. Who would have thought that people would order expensive computers from Dell or Gateway without seeing and trying them in advance! People regularly order flowers and wine on-line, sight unseen. Consider the following:

- **Calyx & Corolla (C&C).** C&C is a direct floral retailer started by a visionary entrepreneur, Ruth M. Owades. Customers can order fresh flowers and bouquets from a four-colour catalogue by phoning 1-800-877-0998 or by placing an order on the C&C Web site, which also shows floral bouquets. The order goes immediately to one of 25 growers in the C&C network, who picks and packages the flowers and ships the order via Federal Express. When the flowers arrive, they are fresher and last about 10 days longer than flowers ordered from store-based retailers. Owades credits her success to a sophisticated information system and her strong alliances with FedEx and the growers.

Calyx & Corolla
www.calyxandcorolla.com

Calyx & Corolla's home page also includes the FedEx logo: FedEx is C&C's shipper.

- **Virtual Vineyards.** Virtual Vineyards is the brainchild of master sommelier Peter Granoff and Silicon Valley engineer Robert Olson. The idea behind the site is to make it easy to locate and purchase hard-to-find wine, food, and gifts from artisan producers. Virtual Vineyards features over 300 wines from 100 California and European wineries, and about 200 food and gift items from 70 producers. It makes the often-intimidating topic of wine congenial for those who might be afraid to ask what "carbonic maceration" means. Virtual Vineyards hosts a monthly wine club. It features Q&A columns with the "Cork Dorks" and the "Food Dude," wine and food pairing suggestions, and "Peter's Tasting Chart"—a visual picture of the taste characteristics of each wine. The newest offering is an on-line self-paced wine appreciation course offered through DigitalThink, a publisher of Web-based training courses. Students, of course, must supply their own wine![30]

CONDUCTING ON-LINE MARKETING

Marketers can do on-line marketing by creating an electronic presence on the Internet; placing ads on-line; participating in forums, newsgroups, bulletin boards, and Web communities; and using e-mail and Webcasting.

Electronic Presence

Thousands of businesses have established a presence on the Internet. Many of these Web sites offer users a wide variety of services.

A company can establish an electronic presence on the Web in two ways: It can buy space on a commercial on-line service or it can open its own Web site. Buying a location on a commercial service involves renting storage space on the on-line service's computer or establishing a link from the company's own computer to the on-line service's shopping mall. For example, JCPenney has links to America Online, Compu-Serve, and Prodigy. The on-line services typically design the storefront for which the company pays the on-line service an annual fee plus a small percentage of the company's on-line sales.

Alternatively, tens of thousands of companies have created their own Web sites, typically aided by a professional Web design agency. These sites take two basic forms:

1. *Corporate Web site:* A company offers basic information about its history, mission and philosophy, products and services, and locations. It might also offer current events, financial performance data, and job opportunities. These sites are set up to answer customer questions by e-mail, build closer customer relationships, and generate excitement about the company. They are designed to handle interactive communication *initiated by the consumer.* Ironically, a recent study has revealed that the fast-moving Silicon Valley firms, which pushed the Internet revolution, fall down in providing basic corporate information. The Shelly Taylor and Associates study of 50 corporate Web sites at technology companies including Cisco, Yahoo!, and Excite found that many sites made it hard for customers, investors, and prospective employees to contact them and gather information. Most do better for job seekers, yet almost half of the firms surveyed did not allow job seekers to submit applications electronically, and 84 percent did not give the date a job was posted. The lesson for marketers: Pay attention to the basics, such as providing names, phone numbers and dates, and making it easy for customers to purchase products on-line.[31]

2. *Marketing Web site:* This kind of Web site is designed to bring prospects and customers closer to a purchase or other marketing outcome. The site might include a catalogue, shopping tips, and promotional features such as coupons, sales events, or contests. In order to attract visitors, the company promotes its Web site in print and broadcast advertising, and through *banner* ads that pop up on other Web sites.

A key challenge is designing a Web site that is attractive on first view and interesting enough to encourage repeat visits. Early Web sites were mainly text based. They have increasingly been replaced by graphically sophisticated Web sites that provide text, sound, and animation (see, for example, www.gap.com or www.1800 flowers.com). To encourage revisits, companies run fresh news and feature stories, contests, and special offers. Canadian businesses have been criticized for their somewhat slow movement onto the Web and many Canadian consumers complain about the lack of Canadian sites. However, this is starting to change. Consider some examples of well-designed Canadian sites:[32]

- **Videoflicks.** The site for this Toronto-based company has grown into a million-dollar business and has been named by TopTenLinks.com, an independent survey firm, as one of the top five video merchants on the Web. The site is easy to search by movie title or actor. What sets it apart is customer service, says owner Kavanagh. "All the staff are movie buffs—all the way from people taking the orders to the shippers."

Videoflicks
www.videoflicks.com

Garden Crazy
www.gardencrazy.com

- **GardenCrazy.** Billed as Canada's first site devoted exclusively to gardening, this Saint-Timothé, Quebec company provides an on-line catalogue of over 8000 plants. The site also includes a weekly advice column, contexts, and links to other sites of interest to gardening enthusiasts. It was recently recognized by pollster Angus Reid as one of Canada's top Web sites.

Business marketing is actually the driving force behind the e-commerce juggernaut. At least 50 large enterprises, including Chevron, Ford Motor Company, General Electric, and Merck, have invested millions in Web procurement systems to automate corporate purchasing. The result: Invoices that used to cost $100 to process now cost as little as $20. General Electric is now requiring all its partners to join its Web procurement network—the Trading Process Network (TPN)—in an initiative that could save GE as much as $200 million per year by 2003. If companies are buying on the Internet, then you can be sure the companies selling over the Internet are raking in the profits. Cisco, Dell, Ingram Micro, and Intel have multibillion-dollar sales on their Web sites and are paving the way for a future in which almost all intercompany business is conducted over the Internet. The Web has also proved to be the perfect medium for business cyberbazaars, those sites where business buyers and sellers transact business across geographic boundaries. Here's one example:

- **Medical EquipNet.** In 1996 Cynthia Schuster launched the Medical EquipNet to serve as a clearinghouse for companies, doctors' offices, and hospitals in the market to buy and sell used or refurbished medical equipment. Because this secondary market is transaction-oriented and geographically scattered, the site opens up another cost-effective sales channel. Those who use the site to sell their wares are seeing a significant increase in profits. For instance, by 1998, Pyramid Medical Inc., in Los Alemedos, California, had sold an estimated $1.5 million of product using Medical EquipNet.[33]

Not only must companies make sure their Web sites are well designed and informative, but they must also ensure that they are not unwittingly stranding surfers—and potential customers—in cyberspace. Most marketers plaster the same URL (Web site address) on all their promotional literature. Yet, if someone is drawn to the site in search of specific product information, he usually has to wade through items like the company's philosophy, its history, or the résumés of the chief executives. Or, in order to get to the product she seeks, a customer may have to go through so many pages that she loses interest and exits. This problem has led many companies to develop "microsites"—small, specialized Web sites for specific occasions or products. The big motion-picture studios created separate sites for new films rather than sending people to the studios' main Web sites. Now other companies are using microsites for the following situations: new-product launches, promotional campaigns, contests, recruiting, crisis communication, specific product information for those who click on a banner ad, and media relations. Companies should consider developing a microsite for any situation in which specific, detailed information needs to be made available quickly and easily.[34]

Advertising On-line

Companies can place on-line ads in three ways. They can place classified ads in special sections offered by the major commercial on-line services. Ads can also be placed in certain Internet newsgroups that are set up for commercial purposes. Finally, the company can pay for *on-line ads* that pop up while subscribers are surfing on-line services or Web sites. These include banner ads, pop-up windows, "tickers" (banners that move across the screen), and "roadblocks" (full-screen ads that users must click through to get to other screens).

Web advertising is showing double-digit growth. The on-line ad outlay in 1998 was estimated at $3 billion. Costs are reasonable compared with those of other advertising media. For example, Web advertising on ESPNet SportsZone, which attracts more than 500 000 Web surfers and 20 million "hits" per week, costs about $450 000 per year. To sell on-line advertising, Yahoo! employs 100 cyberspace salespeople who demonstrate how on-line ads can reach people with certain interests or living in specific postal code areas.

Still, surfers ignore most banner ads. One measure is the "click-through rate" showing how many computer users point their mouse at an ad and ask for more information. When rates get to be less than one percent, advertisers worry that they have chosen the wrong site. Advertisers are clamouring for better measures of advertising impact. Web advertising is still playing only a minor role in the promotion mixes of most advertisers.[35]

Forums, Newsgroups, Bulletin Boards, and Web Communities

Companies may decide to participate in or sponsor Internet forums, newsgroups, and bulletin boards that appeal to special interest groups. *Forums* are discussion groups located on commercial on-line services. A forum may operate a library, a "chat room" for real-time message exchanges, and even a classified ad directory. America Online boasts some 14 000 chat rooms. It recently introduced "buddy lists," which alert members when friends are on-line, allowing them to exchange instant messages.

Newsgroups are the Internet version of forums. However, these groups are limited to people posting and reading messages on a specified topic. Internet users can participate in newsgroups without subscribing. Thousands of newsgroups deal with every imaginable topic: healthy eating, caring for your Bonsai tree, exchanging views about the latest soap-opera happenings.

Bulletin board systems (BBSs) are specialized on-line services that centre on a specific topic or group. Over 60 000 BBSs deal with topics such as vacations, health, computer games, and real estate. Marketers can participate in newsgroups and BBSs but must avoid introducing a commercial tone into these groups.

Web communities are commercially sponsored Web sites where members congregate on-line and exchange views on issues of common interest. One such community is Agriculture Online where farmers and others can find commodity prices, recent farm news, and chat rooms of all types. The site is attracting as many as five million hits per month. Parent Soup is an on-line community of more than 200 000 parents who spend time on-line gathering information, chatting with other parents, and linking with related sites.

On-line buyers increasingly create product information, not just consume it. They join Internet interest groups to share product-related information, with the result that "word of Web" is joining "word of mouth" as an important buying influence.

E-mail and Webcasting

Companies can also sign on with any of a number of Webcasting services such as Pointcast and Ifusion, which automatically download customized information to recipients' PCs. For a monthly fee, subscribers can specify the channels and topics—news, company information, entertainment—they want to receive. Then they can sit back while the Webcaster automatically delivers information of interest to their

ESPNet SportsZone
www.espnetsportszone.com

Agriculture Online
www.agriculture.com

Parent Soup
www.parentsoup.com

screens. Called "push" programming, on-line marketers see this as an opportunity to deliver information and ads to subscribers without the subscriber having to make a request. Webcasters must be careful, however, not to overload subscribers with "junk e-mail."[36]

A company can encourage prospects and customers to send questions, suggestions, and even complaints to the company via e-mail. Customer service reps can quickly respond to these messages. The company may also develop Internet-based electronic mailing lists. Using the lists, on-line marketers can send out customer newsletters, special product or promotion offers based on purchasing histories, reminders of service requirements or warranty renewals, or announcements of special events.

However, in using e-mail as a direct-marketing vehicle, companies must be extra careful not to develop a reputation as a "spammer." *Spam* is the term for unsolicited e-mail. Consumers accustomed to receiving junk mail in their real mailboxes are often enraged to find unsolicited marketing pitches in their e-mail boxes. There's a lot of spam out there. Of the 500 000 or so messages sent on an average day within Usenet groups, about 300 000 are spam. The problem has become so critical that both AOL and CompuServe were involved in suits with one of the more notorious originators of spam, Cyber Promotions, which has sent bulk e-mail for a variety of organizations. As a result, several U.S. states, as well as the federal government, have proposed legislation to limit or prohibit spam broadcasting. Yet despite the possibility of being perceived as a spammer, some marketers are racing to take advantage of the potential of e-mail marketing. They're savvy about doing it, too.[37] See the Marketing for the 21st Century box "'Click Here If You Want to Hear Our Promotional Pitch': Rewriting the Rules of D-mail with E-mail."

THE PROMISE AND CHALLENGES OF ON-LINE MARKETING

According to its most ardent apostles, on-line marketing will bring profound changes to various sectors of the economy. Consumers' ability to order direct will seriously hurt certain groups, particularly travel agents, stockbrokers, insurance salespeople, car dealers, and bookstore owners. These intermediaries will be *disintermediated* by on-line services.[38] At the same time, some *reintermediation* will take place in the form of new on-line intermediaries, called *infomediaries,* who help consumers shop more easily and obtain lower prices. Here are two examples:[39]

- **BuyBuddy Inc.** This Toronto-based online shopping assistant offers consumers around the world an easy and intuitive way to buy technology-based products such as computers or software on the Web. The consumer-focused

Intelligent shopping agents are helping consumers save money on-line.

Pointcast
www.pointcast.com

Ifusion
www.ifusion.com

BuyBuddy Inc.
www.buybuddy.com

"Click Here if You Want to Hear Our Promotional Pitch": Rewriting the Rules of D-mail with E-mail

Companies that send marketing pitches via e-mail walk a fine and dangerous line. One false move—such as sending an e-mail to a customer who didn't request one—can ruin a company's reputation overnight. Yet, if a company does an e-mail campaign right, it can not only build customer relationships but also reap additional profits, all for a fraction of the cost of a "d-mail," or direct-mail, campaign.

More and more companies are beginning to walk that fine line because e-mail marketing offers several tangible benefits. The Internet gives marketers immediate access to millions of prospects and customers. Studies show that 80 percent of Internet users respond to e-mail within 36 hours, in contrast with the two percent response rate of the average direct mail campaign. Also, compared to other forms of on-line marketing, e-mail is a hands-down winner. Consider the "click-through" rate. A click-through occurs whenever a user follows links—whether they are provided through a site's ad banners or e-mail—to a company's home page or sales site. Click-through rates for ad banners have dropped to less than one percent whereas click-through rates for e-mail are running around 80 percent. Then there's cost. Paper, printing, and postage are expensive and getting more so every year. Microsoft spent approximately $70 million a year on paper-driven campaigns.

Now, the software giant sends out 20 million pieces of e-mail every month at a significant savings over the cost of paper-based campaigns.

There is a catch, though. In order to achieve a stellar click-through or get recipients to respond quickly—or at all—marketers must follow the cardinal rule of e-mail marketing: Get the consumer's permission. In fact, Seth Godin, a pioneer of direct marketing on the Web and CEO of Yoyodyne Inc. (recently acquired by Yahoo!), has even come up with the term "permission-based marketing" to define the new e-mail marketing model. According to Godin, consumers are weary of unwanted marketing pitches. Permission-based marketing provides the perfect remedy by using the interactivity of the Internet to let consumers have a say in what is sent to them. Godin compares permission-based marketing to dating; if a company conducts itself well in its first contact with consumers, it will build up the trust that encourages them to open up to subsequent offers.

One company that has been successful in using permission-based marketing in its e-mail campaigns is Iomega Corporation, which markets peripheral computer storage devices such as the popular Zip drive. Iomega runs several e-mail campaigns and always starts with its registered-customer-installed base. From this select list, it mails only to those who have given Iomega permission to send them e-mail. By targeting customers who actively agree to receive e-mail, companies can avoid being blackballed on the Internet and increase their chances of getting a positive response or sale.

(continued)

---

business model educates the prospective buyer on the product area, conducts a needs assessment by asking a few simple questions, and offers the best price and an unbiased comparison of online vendors selling the product. If the product is too expensive for the customer, he or she can choose to be notified via e-mail when the cost falls to a predetermined price. The partners plan to extend the service to books and videos in 2000.

■ **Online Film Services Inc.** Taking on the role of a Hollywood casting agent, Vancouver-based Online Film Services allows casting directors to look at thousands of actors' photos and résumés over a secure network.

Ardent fans of on-line marketing also see it as changing world commerce. The on-line marketer can reach a global market. Today Amazon sells over 20 percent of its books to foreign purchasers. Quelch and Klein believe that the Internet will lead to the more rapid internationalization of small- to medium-size enterprises (SMEs).[40] The advantages of scale economies will be reduced, global advertising costs will be less, and smaller enterprises offering specialized products will be able to reach a much larger world market.

At the same time, less ardent Web commentators cite a number of challenges that on-line marketers face:

■ *Limited consumer exposure and buying:* Web users are doing more surfing than buying. Only an estimated 18 percent of surfers actually use the Web regularly for shopping

Online Film Services Inc.
www.castingworkbook.com

Amazon
www.amazon.com

Whereas consumers who are peeved at receiving lots of junk mail simply toss it in the garbage, angry consumers can strike back on-line. With just a quick e-mail to friends, all those on their listserve, or other Web sites—or by setting up their own anti-company Web site—an irate consumer can give offending companies a bad reputation almost instantaneously. For this reason, companies that use e-mail marketing pitches effectively not only go to those who "opt-in" but offer recipients the chance to "opt-out" at every turn. At Iomega, for instance, every single e-mail, even those sent to people on record as consenting to additional mailings, provides customers with an opt-out.

Yet asking permission and providing an opt-out escape is only one facet of crafting a successful e-mail marketing campaign: You must have something of value to offer. Here are some other important guidelines followed by pioneering e-mail marketers.

- *Give the customer a reason to respond:* Yoyodyne Inc. offers surfers powerful incentives for reading e-mail pitches and on-line ads. The innovative direct-marketing firm uses e-mail trivia games, scavenger hunts, and instant-win sweepstakes to lure customers. So far more than a million Internet surfers have agreed to wade through product information from companies such as Sprint, Reader's Digest, and Major League Baseball in order to vie for prizes like a trip to the Caribbean or a bag of gold.

- *Personalize the content of your e-mails:* The Web allows companies to personalize e-mails based on past purchases or interactions, and customers are more receptive to personalized pitches. Cyberbookstore Amazon.com has gained a loyal following by sending willing customers recommendations based on past purchases. IBM's "Focusing on You News Digest" is distributed directly to customers' office e-mail, delivering to them only "the news they choose." Customers who agree to receive the newsletter select from topics listed on an interest profile.

- *Offer something the customer couldn't get via direct mail:* Direct-mail campaigns take a lot of time to plan, carry out, and mail. Because e-mail campaigns can be carried out more quickly, they can offer time-sensitive information. Travelocity, a travel site on the Web, sends frequent e-mails called Fare Watchers pitching last-minute cheap airfares. Club Med uses e-mail to pitch unsold, discounted vacation packages to the 34 000 people in its database.

If marketers play by all of these "rules," they stand to turn e-mail into one of the hottest new marketing mediums.

Sources: Nicole Harris, "Spam That You Might Not Delete," *Business Week*, June 15, 1998, pp. 115–18; Matt Barthel, "Marketer: Banks Miss Web's Real Strength—Relationships," *American Banker*, October 21, 1998, p. 19; Jay Winchester, "Point, Click, Sell," *Sales & Marketing Management*, November 1998, pp. 100–101; Michelle L. Smith "One to One: Put the Customer in the Information Driver Seat and Build Better Relationships," *Direct Marketing*, January 1998, pp. 37–39; Roberta Fusaro, "More Sites Use E-mail for Marketing," *Computerworld*, October 19, 1998, pp. 51–54; Mary Kuntz, "Point, Click—And Here's the Pitch," *Business Week*, February 9, 1998, pp. ENT8–ENT10.

or to obtain commercial services such as travel information. The major on-line buyers today are businesses rather than individual consumers.

- *Skewed user demographics and psychographics:* On-line users are more upscale and technically oriented than the general population, making them ideal for computers, electronics, and financial services but less so for mainstream products.

- *Chaos and clutter:* The Internet offers millions of Web sites and a staggering volume of information. Navigating the Web can be frustrating. Many sites go unnoticed and even visited sites must capture visitors' attention within eight seconds or lose them to another site.

- *Security:* Consumers worry that unscrupulous interlopers will intercept their credit-card numbers. Companies worry that others will invade their computer systems for espionage or sabotage purposes. The Internet is becoming more secure, but there is a continuous race between the pace of new security measures and new code-breaking measures.

- *Ethical concerns:* Consumers worry about privacy: Companies might make unauthorized use of their names and other information, such as selling it to others. In 1997 the U.S. Federal Trade Commission said an investigation of 674 commercial Web sites revealed that 92 percent collected personal information, but only 14 percent disclosed what they did with it. Since then, threats of government intervention have spurred an increasing number of Web merchants to post privacy policies. The Canadian government has been more proactive with regard to regulation. It passed Bill C-6, its policy on regulation of Internet privacy. This Bill was a milestone in that it represented a consensus-based approach among business, government, and consumers. The Bill deals with the issues of on-line data collection, the use of those data, the disclosure of such information, and the protection of consumer privacy.

Another privacy concern is the prevalent use of "cookies" by on-line marketers. Cookies are text files that sit on a user's computer in order to identify that person when he or she revisits Web sites. Although cookies spare users the hassle of having to identify themselves and type in their password every time they visit a Web site, they also monitor a user's every move. A cookie can tell Web merchants how long customers linger at different products. The Web merchant can then follow Web window shoppers and use the information to target promotions at them on return visits.[41] There is also the ethical concern that the Internet helps upscale consumers shop more efficiently while leaving poorer consumers who have less access to the Internet to pay higher prices.

■ *Consumer backlash.* Just as the Web has shifted power to consumers by giving them more product information than ever before, it has given them a more potent, effective means of expressing disgruntlement or even outrage. Rogue Web pages, often launched by irate consumers or former employees, have taken on a range of big-name companies, such as BMW, Apple Computers, United Airlines, and Burger King. Pages such as "Down with Snapple" or "Wal-Mart Sucks" are seen by millions. The information in them may be valid, but they can also spread unfounded rumours. Whereas some companies, particularly large, powerful corporations, shrug off these pages, others are concerned enough to hire firms to monitor activity at these sites.[42]

PUBLIC AND ETHICAL ISSUES IN DIRECT MARKETING

Direct marketers and their customers usually enjoy mutually rewarding relationships. Occasionally, however, a darker side emerges:

■ *Irritation:* Many people find the increasing number of hard-sell direct-marketing solicitations to be a nuisance. They dislike direct-response TV commercials that are too loud, too long, and too insistent. Especially bothersome are dinnertime or late-night phone calls, poorly trained callers, and computerized calls placed by an auto-dial recorded-message player.

■ *Unfairness:* Some direct marketers take advantage of impulsive or less sophisticated buyers. TV shopping shows and infomercials may be the worst culprits. They feature smooth-talking hosts, elaborately staged demonstrations, claims of drastic price reductions, "while they last" time limitations, and unexcelled ease of purchase to capture buyers who have low sales resistance.

■ *Deception and fraud:* Some direct marketers design mailers and write copy intended to mislead buyers. They may exaggerate product size, performance claims, or the "retail price." Political fundraisers sometimes use gimmicks such as "lookalike" envelopes that resemble official documents, simulated newspaper clippings, and fake honours and awards. Some nonprofit organizations pretend to be conducting research surveys when they are actually asking leading questions to identify donors. Canada's Direct Marketing Association investigates written complaints received from consumers; however, often by the time the buyers realize they have been bilked and alert the authorities, the thieves have fled to another location.

■ *Invasion of privacy:* It seems that almost every time consumers order products by mail or telephone, enter a sweepstakes, apply for a credit card, or take out a magazine subscription, their names, addresses, and purchasing behaviour may be added to several company databases. Critics worry that marketers may know *too* much about consumers' lives, and that they may use this knowledge to take unfair advantage.

Should AT&T be allowed to sell marketers the names of consumers who frequently call catalogue companies' 800 numbers? Is it right for credit bureaus to compile and sell lists of people who have recently applied for credit cards? Is it right for states to sell the names and addresses of driver's license holders, along with height, weight, and gender information, allowing apparel retailers to target people with special clothing offers?

People in the direct-marketing industry are attempting to address these issues. They know that, left untended, such problems will lead to increasingly negative consumer attitudes, lower response rates, and calls for greater provincial and federal regulation. In the final analysis, most direct marketers want the same thing that consumers want: honest and well-designed marketing offers targeted only to those consumers who appreciate hearing about the offer.

SUMMARY

1. *Direct marketing* is an interactive marketing system that uses one or more advertising media to effect a measurable response or transaction at any location. Direct marketing is now widely used in consumer markets, business-to-business markets, and markets for charitable contributions.

2. One of the most valuable direct-marketing tools is the *customer database*, an organized collection of comprehensive data about individual prospects or customers. Companies use their databases to identify prospects, decide which customers should receive a particular offer, deepen customer loyalty, and reactivate customer purchases.

3. Direct marketers use a wide variety of channels to reach prospects and customers. The oldest form of direct marketing is the sales call. Direct-mail marketing involves sending an offer, announcement, reminder, or other item to a person at a particular address. Catalogue marketing and telemarketing are popular forms of direct marketing. Growing in importance are television direct-response marketing and infomercials, as well as online marketing, home shopping channels, and videotext and interactive TV marketing. Other forms of media, such as magazines, newspapers, and radio, are also used in direct marketing.

4. To be successful, direct marketers must plan campaigns carefully. They must decide on objectives, target markets and prospects precisely, design the offer's elements, test the campaign, and establish measures to determine the campaign's success.

5. There are two types of on-line marketing channels: commercial on-line services and the Internet. On-line advertising offers convenience to buyers and lower costs to sellers. Companies can choose to go on-line by creating electronic storefronts; placing ads on-line; participating in forums, newsgroups, bulletin boards, and Web communities; and using e-mail and Webcasting.

6. Although some companies still relegate direct and on-line marketing to a subsidiary role in the marketing–communications mix, many companies have begun practising *integrated marketing communications*, also called *integrated direct marketing* (IDM). IDM programs, which focus on a multimedia approach to advertising, are generally much more effective than single communications programs.

7. Direct marketers and their customers usually enjoy mutually rewarding relationships. However, marketers must avoid campaigns that irritate consumers, are perceived as unfair, are deceptive or fraudulent, or invade customers' privacy.

APPLICATIONS

CHAPTER CONCEPTS

1. Don E. Schultz, an expert on integrated marketing from Northwestern University, says that he receives calls from marketing practitioners who say, "We heard you speak (or read your book, or talked to some of your clients, or something else), and

we're ready to get into integrated marketing communications. We know a database is the heart of the process you are developing." They go on to say what their product is and ask, "How big should the computer be, and what type of software should we buy?" Why are these the wrong questions to ask for companies just beginning to use database marketing? What questions should they ask first? What precautions should a company take once its database is up and running?

2. Describe the marketing objectives and target markets of the following organizations. What benefits might each organization receive from marketing on the Internet? (a) Sears, (b) Harry Rosen, (c) the United Nations World Food Program, (d) Ticketmaster, (e) Hallmark, (f) TD Bank, (g) Air Canada.

3. Retail catalogues were one of the first forms of direct marketing as we know it today. Some retail stores are now using catalogues, delivered through the mail, with newspapers, or on the Internet, to increase in-store sales. Why would retail stores decide to issue catalogues? Why might an established retail store decide to use direct and on-line marketing for the first time?

MARKETING AND ADVERTISING

Many nonprofit organizations, such as the Earthjustice Legal Defense Fund, use direct-response advertising to solicit contributions. The magazine ad in Figure 1 asks consumers to call a toll-free number or visit a Web site and pledge a contribution to support lawyers fighting for endangered species. The ad talks about the urgency of the problem and explains that these lawyers have already saved hundreds of endangered species, but they need help to save more. Says the ad: "You don't have to be a lawyer . . . to get involved." What offer is Earthjustice making to consumers? What benefits will consumers gain from responding to this offer? What is Earthjustice likely to do with the names of people who respond to this ad? Why?

United Nations World Food Program
www.thehungersite.com

Figure 1

FOCUS ON TECHNOLOGY

Data mining is a sophisticated computerized analysis used by marketers to identify meaningful patterns in a data warehouse of customer purchasing information. With data mining, marketers can determine which customers are the best to target for a particular offer. They can also figure out which customers are their most profitable and then design special retention programs to reinforce those customers' loyalty.

What kinds of ethical and public concerns are raised by the increased use of data warehouses and data mining? Should consumers be allowed to opt out of some company data warehouses? Should companies be required to notify consumers when their names and other personal information are added to certain data warehouses? Do you think government regulation is needed to control the collection and use of personal details in data warehouses? Defend your answer.

MARKETING FOR THE 21ST CENTURY

As more companies get involved in e-commerce, they must beware of irritating consumers by sending unwanted e-mail to promote their products. Netiquette, the unwritten rules that guide Internet etiquette, suggests that marketers ask customers for permission to e-mail marketing pitches—and tell recipients how to stop the flow of e-mail promotions at any time.

Iomega
www.iomega.com

To see permission-based marketing in action, visit the Web site of Iomega, which makes the Zip drive and other computer storage devices. The company constantly runs contests to encourage people to register at its site. Click to enter any contest, then read the entire entry form. You will notice that Iomega asks permission to e-mail you marketing material and to give your name to other marketers. Iomega also asks other questions, such as which of its products you own. Why would Iomega ask about your ownership of its products? Why would the company want to share your name with other marketers? What would you gain by granting permission for Iomega to give your name to others?

YOU'RE THE MARKETER: SONIC MARKETING PLAN

As e-commerce continues to grow, more marketers are including on-line as well as direct and on-line marketing in their marketing plans. Even manufacturers who sell their goods through wholesalers and retailers can use direct and on-line marketing as part of multiple-vehicle, multiple-stage campaigns to boost the effectiveness of their marketing communications.

You are Jane Melody's assistant at Sonic, where you are developing and coordinating marketing programs for the company's shelf stereo systems. Look again at Sonic's current situation, its goals, and its strategies. Also review the other marketing-mix programs you have already planned. Then answer the following questions about creating direct and on-line marketing for Sonic:

- *If Sonic lacks a good database, what does it need to know about its customers (the consumer market) and its distributors (the business market)? How can it gather this information?*

- *How can Sonic use direct or on-line marketing to support consumer promotions and communications? To support trade promotions and communications?*

- *Which messages and channels would be most appropriate for reaching consumers who buy Sonic products? For reaching retailers who buy Sonic products? What programs would you recommend, and when should these be scheduled?*

- *How can Sonic use its Web site to communicate with both consumers and retailers?*

Consider how the on-line and direct-marketing programs you are recommending will mesh with Sonic's other programs and support Sonic's goals and strategies. As your instructor directs, summarize your recommendations in a written marketing plan, or type them into the Marketing Mix section and the Programs and Tactics section of the Marketing Plan Pro software.

Managing the Total Marketing Effort

PROFILE:

Canadian Marketing Excellence

Phillip Kotler recently noted that, "The marketing organization will have to redefine its role from managing customer interactions to integrating all the company's customer-facing processes." Perhaps Kellogg Canada understands this dictate better than most other Canadian firms. *Marketing Magazine* certainly thought so when it elected Kellogg as its 1998 Marketer of the Year. They praised Kellogg for its "landmark advertising, category creation and [its] single-minded quest for consumer intimacy."

How does a company long focused on products in a mature category become customer intimate? Kellogg Canada is credited with developing an oranizational culture that values provocative thinking rather than sticking with "tried and true" practices. Rough cuts of the now-famous "Designer" campaign for Special K, in which a fat man is shown coming down a runway in women's clothing, were so innovative that Kellogg's CEO confessed they made his hands sweat. The solid Marketing and Corporate Affairs team that developed the "Look Good on Your Own Terms" campaign was taking a major risk in moving away from the traditional "diet" product positioning of the brand. But the advertising was breakthrough and spoke to women in a manner never seen before in the stodgy cereal category.

Kellogg Canada is part of a global company committed to market leadership whose mission is to build long-term growth in volume and profit by providing nutritious food products of superior value. Its marketing strategy is built around a strategy of differentiation through quality. The high standards that distinguish its products also distinguish its marketing practices. Kellogg uses a product management organizational structure. Product managers are responsible for building brand equity and each product's advertising. Marketers are also responsible for the initiation of new product development. For example, they were part of the Kellogg Canada team that launched Vector, a "flaked meal replacement in a bowl," the long-awaited entry into the sports nutrition market. They must also keep their fingers on the pulse of the public. Utilizing state-of-the-art research monitors, they work to better understand consumers and build relationships with them. This is partially accomplished through its award-winning advertising.

Kellogg has also leveraged its Web sites to help it interact with consumers. It presents recipes and a Kids Party Planner on their Rice Krispies site. When Kellogg and its agency partners, Leo Burnett and J. Walter Thompson, developed the micro-site for Special K, they worked to get consumer feedback on what they wanted the Web site to be. Today, the site not only allows women to view its women-empowering advertising, but it also provides women with valuable nutritional information, and offers them the opportunity to communicate directly with Kellogg's. The site has received thousands of visitors.

Kellogg also believes that integrity, ethical practices, and social responsibility are the cornerstones of its business. It not only engages in fair and honest practices, it works to show respect for each employee as well as its consumers, customers, suppliers, shareholders, and communities in which it operates. This is more than lip service at Kellogg. Their philanthropic support is rooted in the Working Together to Help Kids Grow pledge. The company demonstrates this commitment through various charitable partnerships, including the Kids Help Phone (over six million boxes of Kellogg products display the 1-800 phone number), Invest in Kids, Children's Wish, and the new Children's Own Museum in Toronto.

Have all these efforts paid off for Kellogg? Judge for yourself. Despite the fact that private-label cereals have attempted to eat away at Kellogg's share, it still has seven of the top ten brands in Canada's $750 million ready-to-eat cereal market. Don't you think this is pretty firm evidence that Kellogg's move to thinking of itself as a "consumer engagement" company is working?

In this chapter, we will answer the following questions:

- What are the trends in company organization?

- How are marketing and sales organized in companies?

- What is the marketing department's relation to other departments in the company?

- What steps can a company take to build a stronger customer-focused culture?

- How can a company improve its marketing-implementation skills?

- What tools are available to help companies audit and improve their marketing activities?

Sources: Helga Breir ,"Interactive Agencies: Leo Burnett," *Strategy: The Canadian Marketing Report*, October 12, 1998, p. 16. Lara Mills, "Snap, Crackle, Pop," *Marketing*, December 22/29, 1997, pp. 1, 6-7. Kellogg Company Web page (www.kelloggs.com). Fred Jaques, Presentation to Marketing Ethics Comm 338, Queen's University, Fall 1996. Lara Mills ,"Kellogg Stresses 'True Innovation,'" *Marketing*, February 8, 1999, p. 9. "For the Record: Ikea, Kellogg Sponsor Kids' Museum," *Strategy: The Canadian Marketing Report*, October 12, 1998, p. 10. Lara Mills, "Truly New Products," October 18, 1999, p. 2.

We now turn from the strategic and tactical management of marketing to its administration. Our goal is to examine how firms organize, implement, evaluate, and control their marketing activities.

RENDS IN COMPANY ORGANIZATION

Companies often need to restructure their business and marketing practices in response to significant changes in the business environment, such as globalization, deregulation, computer and telecommunications advances, and market fragmentation. The main responses of business firms to a rapidly changing environment have included these:

- *Re-engineering:* Appointing teams to manage customer-value building processes and trying to break down department walls between functions.

- *Outsourcing:* A greater willingness to buy more goods and services from outside vendors when they can be obtained cheaper and better this way.

- *Benchmarking:* Studying "best practice companies" to improve the company's performance.

- *Supplier partnering:* Increased partnering with fewer but larger value-adding suppliers.

- *Customer partnering:* Working more closely with customers to add value to their operations.

- *Merging:* Acquiring or merging with firms in the same industry to gain economies of scale and scope.

- *Globalizing:* Increased effort to both "think global" and "act local."

- *Flattening:* Reducing the number of organizational levels to get closer to the customer.

- *Focusing:* Determining the most profitable businesses and customers and focusing on them.

- *Empowering:* Encouraging and empowering personnel to produce more ideas and take more initiative.

All these trends will undoubtedly have an impact on marketing organization and practices.

The role of marketing in the organization must also change. Traditionally, marketers have played the role of intermediaries, charged with understanding customer needs and transmitting the voice of the customer to various functional areas in the organization, who then acted upon these needs. Underlying this conception of the marketing function was the assumption that customers were hard to reach and could not interact directly with other functional areas. But in a networked enterprise, every functional area can interact with customers, especially electronically. Marketing no longer has sole ownership of customer interactions; rather, marketing needs to integrate all the customer-facing processes so that customers see a single face and hear a single voice when they interact with the firm.

Another way to look at these changes in marketing organization and role is through the analogy of sports: See the Marketing Insight "Sports Analogies for the Marketing Organization."

ARKETING ORGANIZATION

Over the years, marketing has grown from a simple sales department into a complex group of activities. We will examine how marketing departments have evolved in companies, how they are organized, and how they interact with other company departments.

Sports Analogies for the Marketing Organization

Much has been made about the value of teamwork in accomplishing a company's marketing goals. Michael Hammer, management consultant, uses a football analogy to point out the value of a relatively flat organization. Each of the offensive and defensive players has a particular job, but it is executed by cooperating with teammates. A coach oversees the process of carrying out the team's game plan, assisted by offensive and defensive coaches. In addition, personal coaches give players individual guidance. To respond to changing circumstances, each player must be responsive to several coaches. Sometimes personal initiative is required. Similarly, the manager in a business coaches team members to do their jobs. Managers are not necessarily more capable of performing these tasks than employees, but they are in a position to coordinate the parts of the process and, when necessary, offer individual encouragement and guidance. Like the football team, the effective organization must not have too many layers of management. Otherwise top managers are too far removed from the work processes to offer any supervision.

Strategy consultant Adrian J. Slywotzky has a different set of sport analogies. He sees football as descriptive of business in the 1960s and 1970s: The pace of football is fast during plays, but quiet during the considerable downtime between plays. Similarly, large firms that made successful plays could take time to catch their corporate breath before the next play. Slywotzky sees the quicker pace of the 1980s in terms of basketball. Speed in getting new products to market became a more important consideration, especially for producers of new electronic equipment. Then came the 1990s, with their chess-like mind games. Each move is strategic, but even more important than the next move is a mastery of patterns of moves. Knowing the possibilities for changing the position of each piece and having alternative series of moves can enable the player to adjust to changing situations. Today, like the well-rounded athlete who learns the rules and strategies of each new game and practices new skills, a serious player in the business field develops the moves and muscle to be a winner.

Sources: Michael Hammer, "Beyond the End of Management," in Rethinking the Future, ed. Rowan Gibson (London: Nicholas Brealey, 1996), pp. 94–105; Adrian Slywotsky, Value Migration: How to Think Several Moves Ahead of the Competition (Boston: Harvard Business School Press, 1996), pp. 7–8, 18–19.

THE EVOLUTION OF THE MARKETING DEPARTMENT

Marketing departments have evolved through six stages. Companies can be found in each stage.

Stage 1: Simple Sales Department

Small companies typically appoint a sales vice president, who manages a sales force and also does some selling. When the company needs marketing research or advertising, the sales vice president hires help from the outside (Figure 22.1[a]).

Stage 2: Sales Department with Ancillary Marketing Functions

As the company expands, it needs to add or enlarge certain functions. For example, an East Coast firm that plans to open in the West will need to conduct marketing research to learn about customer needs and market potential. It will have to advertise its name and products in the area. The sales vice president will hire a marketing research manager and an advertising manager to handle these activities. He or she might hire a marketing director to manage these and other marketing functions (Figure 22.1[b]).

Stage 3: Separate Marketing Department

The continued growth of the company will warrant additional investment in marketing research, new-product development, advertising and sales promotion, and customer service. Yet the sales vice president normally focuses time and resources on the sales force. Eventually the CEO will see the advantage of establishing a separate marketing department headed by a marketing vice president, who reports, along with the sales vice president, to the president or executive vice president (Figure 22.1[c]). At this stage, sales and marketing are separate functions that are expected to work closely together.

This arrangement permits the CEO to obtain a more balanced view of company opportunities and problems. Suppose sales start slipping. The sales vice president might

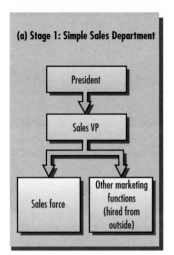

(a) Stage 1: Simple Sales Department

President

Sales VP

Sales force | Other marketing functions (hired from outside)

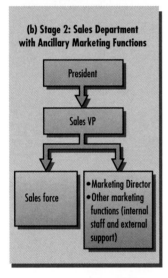

(b) Stage 2: Sales Department with Ancillary Marketing Functions

President

Sales VP

Sales force | • Marketing Director • Other marketing functions (internal staff and external support)

F I G U R E   22.1

Stages in the Evolution of the Marketing Department

recommend hiring more salespeople, raising sales compensation, running a sales contest, providing more sales training, or cutting the price so the product will be easier to sell. The marketing vice president will want to analyze the forces affecting the marketplace. Is the company going after the right segments and customers? Do the target customers have a changing view of the company's and competitors' products? Are changes in product features, styling, packaging, services, distribution, or promotion warranted?

Stage 4: Modern Marketing Department

Although the sales and marketing vice presidents should work together, their relationship is often strained and marked by distrust. The sales vice president resents efforts to make the sales force less important in the marketing mix, and the marketing vice president seeks a larger budget for non-sales force activities.

The marketing manager's task is to identify opportunities and prepare marketing strategies and programs. Salespeople are responsible for implementing these programs. Marketers rely on marketing research, try to identify and understand market segments, spend time in planning, think long term, and aim to produce profits and gains in market share. Salespeople, in contrast, rely on street experience, try to understand each individual buyer, spend time in face-to-face selling, think short term, and try to meet their sales quotas.

If there is too much friction between sales and marketing, the company president might place marketing activities back under the sales vice president, instruct the executive vice president to handle conflicts, or place the marketing vice president in charge of everything, including the sales force. This last solution is the basis of the modern marketing department, a department headed by a marketing and sales executive vice president with managers reporting from every marketing function, including sales management (Figure 22.1[d]).

Stage 5: Effective Marketing Company

A company can have an excellent marketing department and yet fail at marketing. Much depends on how the other departments view customers. If they point to the marketing department and say, "They do the marketing," the company has not implemented effective marketing. Only when all employees realize that their jobs are created by customers does the company become an effective marketer.[1]

Stage 6: Process- and Outcome-Based Company

Many companies are now refocusing their structure on key processes rather than departments. Departmental organization is increasingly viewed as a barrier to the smooth performance of fundamental business processes such as new-product development, customer acquisition and retention, order fulfilment, and customer service. In the interest of achieving customer-related process outcomes, companies are now appointing process leaders who manage cross-disciplinary teams. Marketing and salespeople are consequently spending an increasing percentage of their time as process team members. As a result, marketing personnel may have a solid-line responsibility to their teams and a dotted-line responsibility to the marketing department. Each team sends periodic evaluations of the marketing member's performance to the marketing department. The marketing department is also responsible for training its marketing personnel, assigning them to new teams, and evaluating their overall performance (Figure 22.1[e]).

ORGANIZING THE MARKETING DEPARTMENT

Modern marketing departments take numerous forms. The marketing department may be organized by function, geographic area, products, or customer markets.

Functional Organization

The most common form of marketing organization consists of functional specialists reporting to a marketing vice president, who coordinates their activities. Figure 22.2 shows five specialists. Additional specialists might include a customer-service manager, a marketing-planning manager, and a market-logistics manager.

It is quite a challenge to develop smooth working relations within the marketing department. Cespedes has urged companies to improve the critical interfaces among field sales, customer service, and product management groups, because they collectively have a major impact on customer satisfaction. He has proposed several ways to form tighter links among these three key marketing groups.[2]

The main advantage of a functional marketing organization is its administrative simplicity. However, this form loses effectiveness as products and markets increase. First, a functional organization often leads to inadequate planning for specific products and markets. Products that are not favoured by anyone are neglected. Second, each functional group competes with the other functions for budget and status. The marketing vice president constantly must weigh the claims of competing functional specialists and faces a difficult coordination problem.

Geographic Organization

A company selling in a national market often organizes its sales force (and sometimes other functions, including marketing) along geographic lines. The national sales manager may supervise four regional sales managers, who each supervise six zone managers, who in turn supervise eight district sales managers, who supervise ten salespeople.

Several companies are now adding area market specialists (regional or local marketing managers) to support the sales efforts in high-volume, distinctive markets. One such market might be Toronto where 32 percent of the households are visible minorities. The two largest groups are Chinese Canadians (335 185) and Canadians from Southeast Asia (329 840). Compare this the make-up of the Winnipeg population. Here only 10 percent of the population is a visible minority and most of these people originate from Arab countries. The Toronto specialist would know the city's customer and trade makeup, help marketing managers at headquarters adjust their marketing mix for Toronto and its diverse population, and prepare local annual and long-range plans for selling all the company's products.

Several factors have fuelled the move toward regionalization and localization. The North American mass market has slowly subdivided into a profusion of minimarkets along demographic lines: baby boomers, senior citizens, Chinese Canadians, single mothers—the list goes on.[3] Improved information and marketing research technologies have also spurred regionalization. Data from retail-store scanners allow instant tracking of product sales, helping companies pinpoint local problems and opportunities. Retailers themselves strongly prefer local programs aimed at consumers in their cities and neighbourhoods. To keep retailers happy, manufacturers now create more local marketing plans. Quebec has many distinct needs and tastes, and many firms design unique strategies to reach consumers in this province.

- ■ **Molson.** In 1999, Molson launched a new product, its first alcoholic lemonade in both Ontario and Quebec, but it developed unique marketing strategies for each province. The product bore the brand name Arctic in Ontario and Tornade in Quebec. Market conditions in the two provinces are totally different, warranting different strategies, explains Sylvie Levesque, brand manager, Molson Breweries, Ontario Division. In Ontario, the new brand must face off against an entrenched competitor, "Mike's Hard Lemonade," but in Quebec, the competitive battle for the category is just beginning. Labatt also just introduced a product, a lemon malt called Boomerang.[4]

Some firms, like Campbell Soup, adapt their products to meet variations in international tastes. A kitchen opened in Hong Kong in 1991 develops recipes for the Asian market, and soups marketed in Latin America feature spicy flavours. Packaging and advertising are also geared to regional and national differences. For example, cans are avoided in Japan, where many shoppers carry their groceries on foot. In Mexico, large cans are popular because families tend to be large. In Poland, where consumption of soup is high and most of it is homemade, Campbell Soup appeals to working mothers by offering eight varieties of condensed tripe soup that can be prepared quickly and easily.[5]

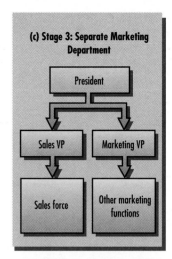

(c) Stage 3: Separate Marketing Department

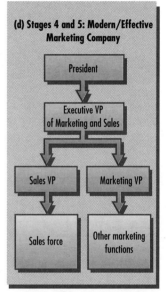

(d) Stages 4 and 5: Modern/Effective Marketing Company

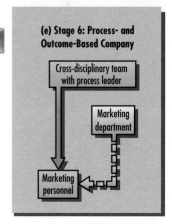

(e) Stage 6: Process- and Outcome-Based Company

F I G U R E 22.1 (cont.)

FIGURE 22.2

Functional Organization

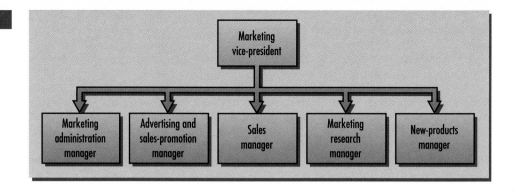

Regionalization may be accompanied by a move toward branchising. Branchising means empowering the company's districts or local offices to operate more like franchises. IBM told its branch managers to "make it your business." The branches resemble profit centres and local managers have more strategy latitude and incentive.

Regionalization is also being adopted by multinationals operating across the globe. Quaker Oats has set up a European headquarters in Brussels, and British Petroleum has chosen Singapore for managing its operations in Asia and the Middle East.[6]

Product- or Brand-Management Organization

Companies producing a variety of products and brands often establish a product (or brand-) management organization. The product-management organization does not replace the functional management organization but rather serves as another layer of management. A product manager supervises product category managers, who in turn supervise specific product and brand managers. A product-management organization makes sense if the company's products are quite different, or if the sheer number of products is beyond the ability of a functional marketing organization to handle. Kraft uses a product-management organization in its Post Division. Separate product category managers are in charge of cereals, pet food, and beverages. Within the cereal product group, there are separate subcategory managers for nutritional cereals, children's pre-sweetened cereals, family cereals, and miscellaneous cereals.

Product and brand managers have these tasks:

- Developing a long-range and competitive strategy for the product
- Preparing an annual marketing plan and sales forecast
- Working with advertising and merchandising agencies to develop copy, programs, and campaigns
- Stimulating support of the product among the sales force and distributors
- Gathering continuous intelligence on the product's performance, customer and dealer attitudes, and new problems and opportunities
- Initiating product improvements to meet changing market needs

These tasks are common to both consumer- and industrial-product managers. However, consumer-product managers typically manage fewer products and spend more time on advertising and sales promotion. They are often younger and MBA-educated. Industrial-product managers spend more time with customers and laboratory and engineering personnel, think more about the technical aspects of their product and possible design improvements, and work more closely with the sales force and key buyers.

The product-management organization introduces several advantages. The product manager can concentrate on developing a cost-effective marketing mix for the product. The product manager can react more quickly to problems in the marketplace than a committee of functional specialists can. The company's smaller brands are less neglected, because they have a product advocate. Product management also is an excellent training ground for young executives, because it involves them in almost every area of company operations (Figure 22.3).

FIGURE 22.3

The Product Manager's Interactions

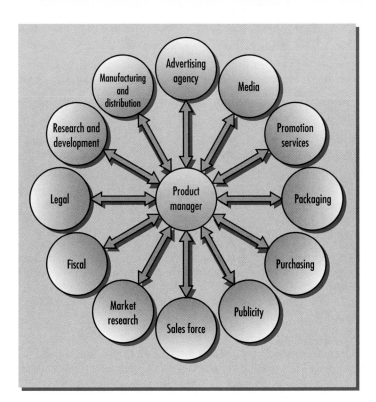

But a product-management organization has some disadvantages. First, product management creates some conflict and frustration. Typically, product managers are not given enough authority to carry out their responsibilities effectively. They have to rely on persuasion to get the cooperation of advertising, sales, manufacturing, and other departments. They are told they are "minipresidents" but are often treated as low-level coordinators. They are burdened with a great amount of paperwork. They often have to go over the heads of others to get something done.

Second, product managers become experts in their product but rarely achieve functional expertise. They vacillate between posing as experts and being cowed by real experts. This is unfortunate when the product depends on a specific type of expertise, such as advertising.

Third, the product management system often turns out to be costly. One person is appointed to manage each major product. Soon product managers are appointed to manage even minor products. Each product manager, usually overworked, pleads for an associate brand manager. Later, both overworked, they persuade management to give them an assistant brand manager. With all these people, payroll costs climb. In the meantime, the company continues to increase its functional specialists in copy, packaging, media, sales promotion, market surveys, and statistical analysis. The company is soon saddled with a large and costly structure.

Fourth, brand managers normally manage a brand for only a short time. Either they move up in a few years to another brand, or they transfer to another company. Short-term involvement with the brand leads to short-term marketing planning and plays havoc with building the brand's long-term strengths.

Fifth, the fragmentation of markets makes it harder to develop a national strategy from headquarters. Brand managers must please more regional-based trade groups and rely more on the local sales force.

Pearson and Wilson have suggested five steps to make the product management system work better:[7]

1. Clearly delineate the limits of the product manager's role and responsibility.

2. Build a strategy-development-and-review process to provide a framework for the product manager's operations.

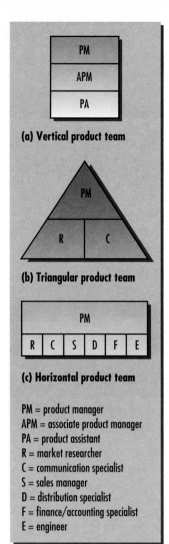

(a) Vertical product team

(b) Triangular product team

(c) Horizontal product team

PM = product manager
APM = associate product manager
PA = product assistant
R = market researcher
C = communication specialist
S = sales manager
D = distribution specialist
F = finance/accounting specialist
E = engineer

FIGURE 22.4

Three Types of Product Teams

3. Take into account areas of potential conflict between product managers and functional specialists when defining their respective roles.

4. Set up a formal process that forces to the top all conflict-of-interest situations between product management and functional line management.

5. Establish a system for measuring results consistent with the product manager's responsibilities.

A second alternative is to switch from product managers to product teams. There are three types of product-team structures in product management (Figure 22.4):

1. Vertical product team: Product manager, associate product manager, and product assistant (Figure 22.4[a]). The product manager is the leader and deals with other managers to gain their cooperation. The associate product manager assists in these tasks and also does some paperwork. The product assistant carries out most of the paperwork and routine analysis.

2. Triangular product team: Product manager and two specialized product assistants, one who takes care of marketing research and the other, marketing communications (Figure 22.4[b]). The Hallmark Company uses a "marketing team" consisting of a market manager (the leader), a marketing manager, and a distribution manager.

3. Horizontal product team: Product manager and several specialists from marketing and other functions (Figure 22.4[c]). 3M has teams consisting of a team leader and representatives from sales, marketing, laboratory, engineering, accounting, and marketing research. Dow Corning sets up teams of five to eight people; each team manages a specific product, market, and process.

A third alternative is to eliminate product manager positions for minor products and assign two or more products to each remaining manager. This is feasible where two or more products appeal to a similar set of needs. A cosmetics company does not need separate product managers for each product because cosmetics serve one major need—beauty. A toiletries company needs different managers for headache remedies, toothpaste, soap, and shampoo, because these products differ in use and appeal.

A fourth alternative is to introduce category management, in which a company focuses on product categories to manage its brands. Here is an example:

- **Kraft.** Kraft has changed from a classic brand-management structure, in which each brand competed for organizational resources and market share, to a category-based structure in which category business directors (or "product integrators") lead cross-functional teams composed of representatives from marketing, R&D, consumer promotion, and finance. The category business directors have both broad responsibility and bottom-line accountability. No longer viewed solely as marketers, they are as responsible for identifying opportunities to improve the efficiency of the supply chain as they are for developing the next advertisement. Kraft's category teams work in conjunction with process teams dedicated to each product category and with customer teams dedicated to each major customer (Figure 22.5).[8]

Category management is not a panacea. It is still a product-driven system. Colgate recently moved from brand management (Colgate toothpaste) to category management (toothpaste category) to a new stage called "customer-need management" (mouth care). This last step finally focuses the organization on a basic customer need.[9]

Market-Management Organization

Many companies sell their products to a diverse set of markets. Canon sells its fax machines to consumer, business, and government markets. Dofasco sells its steel to the railway, construction, and public-utility industries. When customers fall into different user groups with distinct buying preferences and practices, a market management organization is desirable. A markets manager supervises several market managers

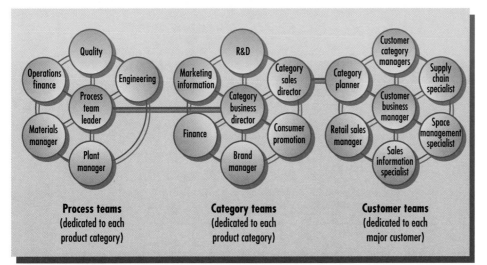

FIGURE 22.5

Managing Through Teams at Kraft

Source: Michael George, Anthony Freeling, and David Court, "Reinventing the Marketing Organization," *The McKinsey Quarterly* no. 4, (1994): 43–62.

Process teams
(dedicated to each product category)

Category teams
(dedicated to each product category)

Customer teams
(dedicated to each major customer)

(also called market-development managers, market specialists, or industry specialists). The market managers draw upon functional services as needed. Market managers of important markets might even have functional specialists reporting to them.

Market managers are staff (not line) people, with duties similar to those of product managers. Market managers develop long-range and annual plans for their markets. They must analyze where their market is going and what new products their company should offer to this market. Performance is judged by their market's growth and profitability. This system carries many of the same advantages and disadvantages of product management systems. Its strongest advantage is that the marketing activity is organized to meet the needs of distinct customer groups rather than focused on marketing functions, regions, or products per se.

Many companies are reorganizing along market lines and becoming market-centred organizations. Xerox has converted from geographic selling to selling by industry, as has IBM, which recently reorganized its 235 000 employees into 14 customer-focused divisions. Hewlett-Packard has set up a structure in which salespeople concentrate on businesses within individual industries.

Several studies have confirmed the value of market-centred organization. Slater and Narver created a measure of market orientation and then analyzed its effect on business profitability. They found a substantial positive effect of market orientation on both commodity and noncommodity businesses.[10]

Product-Management/Market-Management Organization

Companies that produce many products flowing into many markets tend to adopt a matrix organization. Consider DuPont.

- **DuPont.** DuPont was a pioneer in developing the matrix structure (Figure 22.6). Its textile fibres department consists of separate product managers for rayon, acetate, nylon, orlon, and dacron; and separate market managers for menswear, women's wear, home furnishings, and industrial markets. The product managers plan the sales and profits of their respective fibres. Their aim is to expand the use of their fibre. They ask market managers to estimate how much of their fibre they can sell in each market at a proposed price. The market managers, however, are more interested in meeting their market's needs than pushing a particular fibre. In preparing their market plans, they ask each product manager about the fibre's planned prices and availabilities. The final sales forecasts of the market managers and the product managers should add to the same grand total.

Companies like DuPont can go one step further and view their market managers as the main marketers, and their product managers as suppliers. The menswear market

FIGURE 22.6

Product-/Market-Management Matrix System

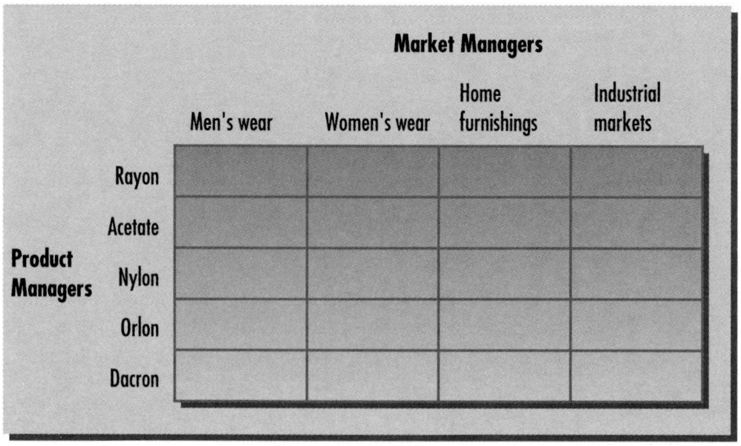

manager, for example, would be empowered to buy textile fibres from DuPont's product managers or, if DuPont's price is too high, from outside suppliers. This system would force DuPont product managers to become more efficient. If a DuPont product manager cannot match the "arm's length pricing" levels of competitive suppliers, then perhaps DuPont should not continue to produce that fibre.

A matrix organization would seem desirable in a multiproduct, multimarket company. The rub is that this system is costly and often creates conflicts. There is the cost of supporting all the managers. There are also questions about where authority and responsibility should reside. Here are two of many dilemmas:

1. How should the sales force be organized? Should there be separate sales forces for rayon, nylon, and the other fibres? Or should the sales forces be organized according to menswear, women's wear, and other markets? Or should the sales force not be specialized? (The marketing concept favours organizing the sales force by markets, not product.)

2. Who should set the prices for a particular product or market? Should the nylon product manager have final authority for setting nylon prices in all markets? What happens if the menswear market manager feels that nylon will lose out in this market unless special price concessions are made? (Product managers nevertheless should retain the ultimate authority over pricing, in the author's opinion.)

By the early 1980s a number of companies had abandoned matrix management. But matrix management has resurfaced and is flourishing today in the form of "business teams" staffed with full-time specialists reporting to one team boss. The major difference is that companies today provide the right context in which a matrix can thrive—an emphasis on flat, lean team organizations focused around business processes that cut horizontally across functions.[11]

Corporate–Divisional Organization

As multiproduct–multimarket companies grow, they often convert their larger product or market groups into separate divisions. The divisions set up their own departments and services. This raises the question of what marketing services and activities should be retained at corporate headquarters.

Divisionalized companies have reached different answers to this question:

- *No corporate marketing:* Some companies lack a corporate marketing staff. They don't see any useful function for marketing at the corporate level. Each division has its own marketing department.

- *Moderate corporate marketing:* Some companies have a small corporate marketing staff that performs a few functions, primarily (1) assisting top management with overall opportunity evaluation, (2) providing divisions with consulting assistance on request, (3) helping divisions that have little or no marketing, and (4) promoting the marketing concept throughout the company.

- *Strong corporate marketing:* Some companies have a corporate marketing staff that, in addition to the preceding activities, also provides various marketing services to the divisions, such as specialized advertising services, sales-promotion services, marketing research services, sales-administration services, and miscellaneous services.

Do companies tend to favour one of these models? The answer is no. Some companies have recently installed a corporate marketing staff for the first time; others have expanded their corporate marketing department; others have reduced its size and scope; and still others have eliminated it altogether.

The potential contribution of a corporate marketing staff varies in different stages of the company's evolution. Most companies begin with weak marketing in their divisions and often establish a corporate staff to bring stronger marketing into the divisions through training and other services. Some members of the corporate marketing staff might be transferred to head divisional marketing departments. As the divisions become strong in their marketing, corporate marketing has less to offer them. Some companies then decide corporate marketing has done its job and proceed to eliminate the department.[12]

MARKETING RELATIONS WITH OTHER DEPARTMENTS

In principle, all business functions should interact harmoniously to pursue the firm's overall objectives. In practice, however, interdepartmental relations are often characterized by deep rivalries and distrust. Some interdepartmental conflict stems from differences of opinion as to what is in the company's best interests, some from real trade-offs between departmental well-being and company well-being, and some from unfortunate stereotypes and prejudices.

In the typical organization, each business function has a potential impact on customer satisfaction. Under the marketing concept, all departments need to "think customer" and work together to satisfy customer needs and expectations. The marketing department must drive this point home. The marketing vice president has two tasks: (1) to coordinate the company's internal marketing activities and (2) to coordinate marketing with finance, operations, and other company functions to serve the customer.

Yet there is little agreement on how much influence and authority marketing should have over other departments. Typically, the marketing vice president must work through persuasion rather than authority. Other departments often resist bending their efforts to meet the customers' interests. Inevitably, departments define company problems and goals from their viewpoint. As a result, conflicts of interest are unavoidable. We will briefly examine the typical concerns of each department.

R&D

The company's drive for successful new products is often thwarted by weak working relations between R&D and marketing. In many ways, these groups have different cultures.[13] R&D is staffed with scientists and technicians who pride themselves on scientific curiosity and detachment, like to work on challenging technical problems without much concern for immediate sales payoffs, and prefer to work without much supervision or accountability. The marketing–sales department is staffed with business-oriented people who pride themselves on a practical understanding of the marketplace, like to see many new products with promotable sales features, and feel compelled to pay attention to product cost. Marketers see the R&D people as maximizing technical qualities rather than designing for customer requirements. R&D people see marketers as gimmick-oriented hucksters who are more interested in sales than in the product's technical features.

A balanced company is one in which R&D and marketing share responsibility for successful market-oriented innovation. The R&D staff must take responsibility not only for innovation but also for a successful product launch. The marketing staff must take responsibility not only for new sales features but also for correctly identifying customer needs and preferences.

Gupta, Raj, and Wilemon concluded that a balanced R&D–marketing coordination is strongly correlated with innovation success.[14] R&D–marketing cooperation can be facilitated in several ways:[15]

- Sponsor joint seminars to build understanding and respect for each other's goals, working styles, and problems.

- Assign each new project to functional teams including an R&D person and a marketing person, who work together through the project's life. R&D and marketing jointly establish the development goals and marketing plan.

- Encourage R&D participation into the selling period, including involvement in preparing technical manuals, participating in trade shows, carrying out postintroduction marketing research with customers, and even doing some selling.

- Work out conflicts by going to higher management, following a clear procedure. In one company, R&D and marketing both report to the same vice president.

Merck is a company that recognizes the strong connection between marketing and R&D:

Merck
www.merck.com

- **Merck.** The description on its Web site reveals the close relationship of Merck's departments: "Merck is a worldwide research-intensive company that discovers and develops, manufactures and markets human and animal health products and services." The research focus at Merck is on the development of prescription drugs—Merck is the world's largest seller of these products—and much of its marketing effort involves dissemination of medical and pharmaceutical information. Publications include The Merck Index, a single-volume technical encyclopedia; *The Merck Manual*, said to be the world's most widely used medical text; *The Merck Manual of Medical Information—Home Edition*, a plain-English version of *The Merck Manual*; and *The Merck Veterinary Manual*. In addition, articles placed in professional journals provide publicity about Merck's research activities. Like its competitors, Merck provides advertising brochures and videotapes to doctors and other health professionals, informing them about the benefits of its drugs. Merck advertises selectively to consumers, because they do not ordinarily choose their prescription drugs. Maxalt, a treatment for migraine headaches, is not marketed directly to consumers. However, men who seek a treatment for baldness are encouraged, in frequent TV commercials, to ask their doctors about Propecia.[16]

Engineering

Engineering is responsible for finding practical ways to design new products and new production processes. Engineers are interested in achieving technical quality, cost economy, and manufacturing simplicity. They come into conflict with marketing executives when the latter want several models produced, often with product features requiring custom rather than standard components. Engineers see marketers as wanting "bells and whistles" on the products rather than intrinsic quality. They often think of marketing people as inept technically, as continually changing priorities, and as not fully credible or trustworthy. These problems are less pronounced in companies where marketing executives have engineering backgrounds and can communicate effectively with engineers.[17]

Purchasing

Purchasing executives are responsible for obtaining materials and components in the right quantities and quality at the lowest possible cost. They see marketing executives pushing for several models in a product line, which requires purchasing small quantities of many items rather than large quantities of a few items. They think that marketing insists on too high a quality of ordered materials and components. They also dislike marketing's forecasting inaccuracy, which causes them to place rush orders at unfavourable prices or to carry excessive inventories.

Manufacturing

Manufacturing people are responsible for the smooth running of the factory to produce the right products in the right quantities at the right time for the right cost. They have spent their lives in the factory, with its attendant problems of machine breakdowns, inventory stockouts, and labour disputes. They see marketers as having little understanding of factory economics or politics. Marketers complain about insufficient capacity, delays in production, poor quality control, and poor customer service. Yet marketers often turn in inaccurate sales forecasts, recommend features that are difficult to manufacture, and promise more factory service than is reasonable.

Marketers do not see the factory's problems, but rather the problems of their customers, who need the goods quickly, who receive defective merchandise, and who cannot get factory service. The problem is not only poor communication but an actual conflict of interest.

Companies settle these conflicts in different ways. In manufacturing-driven companies, everything is done to ensure smooth production and low costs. The company prefers simple products, narrow product lines, and high-volume production. Sales campaigns calling for a hasty production buildup are kept to a minimum. Customers on back order have to wait.

In marketing-driven companies, the company goes out of its way to satisfy customers. In one large toiletries company, marketing personnel call the shots and manufacturing people have to fall in line, regardless of overtime costs or short runs. The result is high and fluctuating manufacturing costs, as well as variable product quality.

Companies need to develop a balanced orientation in which manufacturing and marketing jointly determine what is in the company's best interests. Solutions include joint seminars to understand each other's viewpoints, joint committees and liaison personnel, personnel exchange programs, and analytical methods to determine the most profitable course of action.[18]

Company profitability depends on achieving effective working relations. Marketers need to understand the marketing potentials of new manufacturing strategies—the flexible factory, automation and robotization, just-in-time production, and total quality management. Manufacturing strategy depends upon whether the company wants to win through low cost, high quality, high variety, or fast service. Manufacturing is also a marketing tool insofar as potential customers may want to visit the factory to assess how well it is managed.

Operations

The term *manufacturing* is used for industries making physical products. The term *operations* is used for industries that create and provide services. In the case of a hotel, for example, the operations department includes front-desk people, doormen, and waiters and waitresses. Because marketing makes promises about service levels, it is extremely important that marketing and operations work well together. If operations personnel lack a customer orientation and motivation, negative word of mouth will eventually destroy the business. Operations staff members may be inclined to focus on their convenience and give ordinary service, whereas marketers want the staff to focus on customer convenience and provide extraordinary service. Marketing people must fully understand the capabilities and mind-set of those delivering the service and continuously try to improve attitudes and capabilities.

Finance

Financial executives pride themselves on being able to evaluate the profit implications of different business actions. Marketing executives ask for substantial budgets for advertising, sales promotions, and sales force, without being able to prove how much revenue these expenditures will produce. Financial executives suspect that the forecasts are self-serving. They think marketing people do not spend enough time relating expenditures to results. They think marketers are too quick to slash prices to win orders, instead of pricing to make a profit. They claim that marketers "know the value of everything and the cost of nothing."

But marketing executives often see financial people as "knowing the cost of everything and the value of nothing." They see finance as controlling the purse strings too tightly and refusing to invest in long-term market development. They think financial people see all marketing expenditures as expenses rather than investments and are overly conservative and risk averse, causing many opportunities to be lost. The solution lies in giving marketing people more financial training and giving financial people more marketing training. Financial executives need to adapt their financial tools and theories to support strategic marketing.

Accounting

Accountants see marketing people as lax in providing sales reports on time. They dislike the special deals salespeople make with customers because these require special accounting procedures. Marketers dislike the way accountants allocate fixed-cost burdens to different products in the line. Brand managers may feel that their brand is more profitable than it looks, the problem being that it is assigned too high an overhead burden. They would also like accounting to prepare special reports on sales and profitability by segments, important customers, individual products, channels, territories, order sizes, and so on.

Credit

Credit officers evaluate potential customers' credit standing and deny or limit credit to the more doubtful ones. They think marketers will sell to anyone, including those from whom payment is doubtful. Marketers, in contrast, often feel that credit standards are too high. They think that "zero bad debts" really means the company lost a lot of sales and profits. They feel they work too hard to find customers to hear that they are not good enough to sell to.

STRATEGIES FOR BUILDING A COMPANYWIDE MARKETING ORIENTATION

Many companies are beginning to realize that they are not really market and customer driven—they are product or sales driven. These companies—such as Baxter, General Motors, Shell, and Nortel —are attempting to reorganize themselves into true market-driven companies. The task is not easy. It won't happen as a result of the CEO making speeches and urging every employee to "think customer." The change will require a change in job and department definitions, responsibilities, incentives, and relationships. The Marketing Memo, "Audit: Characteristics of Company Departments That Are Truly Customer Driven," shows an audit instrument that can be used to evaluate which company departments are truly customer driven.

What steps can a CEO take to create a market- and customer-focused company?

1. *Convince the senior management team of the need to become customer focused:* The CEO personally exemplifies strong customer commitment and rewards those in the organization who do likewise.

2. *Appoint a senior marketing officer and a marketing task force:* The task force should include the CEO; the vice presidents of sales, R&D, purchasing, manufacturing, finance, and human resources; and other key individuals.

3. *Get outside help and guidance:* Consulting firms have considerable experience in helping companies move toward a marketing orientation.

4. *Change the company's reward measurement and system:* As long as purchasing and manufacturing are rewarded for keeping costs low, they will resist accepting some costs required to serve customers better. As long as finance focuses on short-term profit, it will oppose major investments designed to build satisfied, loyal customers.

5. *Hire strong marketing talent:* The company needs a strong marketing vice president who not only manages the marketing department but also gains respect from and influence with the other vice presidents. A multidivisional company would benefit from establishing a strong corporate marketing department.

6. *Develop strong in-house marketing training programs:* The company should design well-crafted marketing training programs for corporate management,

Audit: Characteristics of Company Departments That Are Truly Customer Driven

R&D
- ___ They spend time meeting customers and listening to their problems.
- ___ They welcome the involvement of marketing, manufacturing, and other departments on each new project.
- ___ They benchmark competitors' products and seek "best of class" solutions.
- ___ They solicit customer reactions and suggestions as the project progresses.
- ___ They continuously improve and refine the product on the basis of market feedback.

Purchasing
- ___ They proactively search for the best suppliers rather than choose only from those who solicit their business.
- ___ They build long-term relations with fewer but more reliable high-quality suppliers.
- ___ They don't compromise quality for price savings.

Manufacturing
- ___ They invite customers to visit and tour their plants.
- ___ They visit customer factories to see how customers use the company's products.
- ___ They willingly work overtime when it is important to meet promised delivery schedules.
- ___ They continuously search for ways to produce goods faster or at lower costs.
- ___ They continuously improve product quality, aiming for zero defects.
- ___ They meet customer requirements for "customization" where this can be done profitably.

Marketing
- ___ They study customer needs and wants in well-defined market segments.
- ___ They allocate marketing effort in relation to the long-run profit potential of the targeted segments.
- ___ They develop winning offerings for each target segment.
- ___ They measure company image and customer satisfaction on a continuous basis.
- ___ They continuously gather and evaluate ideas for new products, product improvements, and services to meet customers' needs.
- ___ They influence all company departments and employees to be customer centered in their thinking and practice.

Sales
- ___ They have specialized knowledge of the customer's industry.
- ___ They strive to give the customer "the best solution."
- ___ They make only promises that they can keep.
- ___ They feed back customers' needs and ideas to those in charge of product development.
- ___ They serve the same customers for a long period of time.

Logistics
- ___ They set a high standard for service delivery time and they meet this standard consistently.
- ___ They operate a knowledgeable and friendly customer service department that can answer questions, handle complaints, and resolve problems in a satisfactory and timely manner.

Accounting
- ___ They prepare periodic "profitability" reports by product, market segment, geographic areas (regions, sales territories), order sizes, and individual customers.
- ___ They prepare invoices tailored to customer needs and answer customer queries courteously and quickly.

Finance
- ___ They understand and support marketing expenditures (e.g., image advertising) that represent marketing investments that produce long-term customer preference and loyalty.
- ___ They tailor the financial package to the customers' financial requirements.
- ___ They make quick decisions on customer creditworthiness.

Public Relations
- ___ They disseminate favorable news about the company and they "damage control" unfavorable news.
- ___ They act as an internal customer and public advocate for better company policies and practices.

Other Customer Contact Personnel
- ___ They are competent, courteous, cheerful, credible, reliable, and responsive.

divisional general managers, marketing and sales personnel, manufacturing personnel, R&D personnel, and others. GE, Motorola, and Arthur Andersen run these programs.

7. *Install a modern marketing planning system:* The planning format will require managers to think about the market environment, opportunities, competitive trends, and other forces. These managers then prepare strategies and sales and profit forecasts for specific products and segments and are accountable for performance.

8. *Establish an annual marketing excellence recognition program:* Business units that believe they have developed exemplary marketing plans should submit a

description of their plans and results. The winning teams would be rewarded at a special ceremony. The plans would be disseminated to the other business units as "models of marketing thinking." Such programs are carried on by Arthur Andersen, Becton-Dickinson, and DuPont.

9. *Consider reorganizing from a product-centred to a market-centred company:* Becoming market centred means setting up an organization that will focus on the needs of specific markets and coordinate the planning and providing of the company products needed by each segment and major customer.

10. *Shift from a department focus to a process–outcome focus:* After defining the fundamental business processes that determine its success, the company should appoint process leaders and cross-disciplinary teams to reengineer and implement these processes.

DuPont successfully made the transition from an inward-looking to an outward-looking orientation. Under CEO Richard Heckert's leadership, DuPont undertook a number of initiatives to build a "marketing community." Several divisions were reorganized along market lines. The company held a series of marketing management training seminars, which were ultimately attended by 300 senior people, 2000 middle managers, and 14 000 employees. It established a corporate marketing excellence recognition program and honoured 32 employees from around the world who had developed innovative marketing strategies and service improvements.[19] It takes a great amount of planning and patience to get managers to accept the fact that customers are the foundation of the company's business and its future. But it can be done.

 # MARKETING IMPLEMENTATION

We now turn to the question of how marketing managers can effectively implement marketing plans. We define marketing implementation as follows:[20]

■ **Marketing implementation** is the process that turns marketing plans into action assignments and ensures that such assignments are executed in a manner that accomplishes the plan's stated objectives.

A brilliant strategic marketing plan counts for little if it is not implemented properly. Consider the following example:

> *A chemical company learned that customers were not getting good service from any of the competitors. The company decided to make customer service its strategic thrust. When this strategy failed, a postmortem revealed a number of implementation failures. The customer service department continued to be held in low regard by top management; it was understaffed; and it was used as a dumping ground for weak managers. Furthermore, the company's reward system continued to focus on cost containment and current profitability. The company had failed to make the changes required to carry out its strategy.*

Whereas strategy addresses the what and why of marketing activities, implementation addresses the who, where, when, and how. Strategy and implementation are closely related in that one layer of strategy implies certain tactical implementation assignments at a lower level. For example, top management's strategic decision to "harvest" a product must be translated into specific actions and assignments.

Bonoma identified four sets of skills for implementing marketing programs:

1. *Diagnostic skills:* When marketing programs do not fulfil expectations, was the low sales rate the result of poor strategy or poor implementation? If implementation, what went wrong?

2. *Identification of company level:* Implementation problems can occur at three levels: the marketing function, the marketing program, and the marketing policy level.

3. *Implementation skills:* To implement programs successfully, marketers need other skills: allocating skills for budgeting resources, organizing skills to develop an effective organization, and interaction skills to motivate others to get things done.

4. *Evaluation skills:* Marketers also need monitoring skills to evaluate the results of marketing actions.[21]

The skills needed to implement a marketing plan for nonprofit organizations are the same as those needed for commercial enterprises, as the Alvin Ailey Dance Theater discovered.

■ **Alvin Ailey.** Like many nonprofit cultural organizations, the company founded by Alvin Ailey in 1958 always seemed to be operating in the red, despite its ability to attract full houses. The costs of mounting a production are, by their nature, greater than the income that can be generated by ticket sales alone, and Ailey had neither a talent for nor a personal interest in the fund-raising aspects of directing the company. Judith Jamison, the principal dancer who succeeded Ailey as director at his death in 1989, has managed to turn the financial picture around. Her success can be attributed in large part to her skill at motivating others to carry out a marketing effort. A 1993 National Arts Stabilization grant provided matching funds when the company halved its deficit within a year. An executive director and support staff whose marketing and management expertise matched the company's artistic professionalism have managed to keep the company in the black since then. Two groups of experienced marketers are implementing the plan. One is the board of directors, many of whose members are executives of major financial corporations or their spouses. The other group has been recruited from businesses that are using their association with the Ailey company for their own marketing purposes. For example, Healthsouth Corporation provides free physical therapy to the dancers and benefits from the association in marketing its chain of sports medicine clinics. Jaguar, the official car of Alvin Ailey, has made a large donation in exchange for this designation and the right to use Alvin Ailey in advertising and for access to its mailing list. With an audience that is almost half African American and 43 percent of which is between the ages of 19 and 39, Ailey is providing access to an important market for its corporate partners and earning their enthusiastic support.[22]

Alvin Ailey American Dance Theatre
www.alvinailey.org

EVALUATION AND CONTROL

To deal with the many surprises that occur during the implementation of marketing plans, the marketing department continuously has to monitor and control marketing activities. In spite of this need, many companies have inadequate control procedures. This conclusion was reached in a study of 75 companies of varying sizes in different industries. The main findings were these:

■ Smaller companies do a poorer job of setting clear objectives and establishing systems to measure performance.

■ Less than half of the companies studied knew their individual products' profitability. About one-third of the companies had no regular review procedures for identifying and deleting weak products.

■ Almost half of the companies fail to compare their prices with those of the competition, to analyze their warehousing and distribution costs, to analyze the causes of returned merchandise, to conduct formal evaluations of advertising effectiveness, and to review their sales force's call reports.

■ Many companies take four to eight weeks to develop control reports, which are occasionally inaccurate.

Table 22.1 lists four types of marketing control needed by companies: annual-plan control, profitability control, efficiency control, and strategic control.

ANNUAL-PLAN CONTROL

The purpose of annual-plan control is to ensure that the company achieves the sales, profits, and other goals established in its annual plan. The heart of annual-plan control is management by objectives. Four steps are involved (Figure 22.7). First, management sets monthly or quarterly goals. Second, management monitors its performance in the marketplace. Third, management determines the causes of serious performance deviations. Fourth, management takes corrective action to close the gaps between goals and performance.

This control model applies to all levels of the organization. Top management sets sales and profit goals for the year that are elaborated into specific goals for each lower level of management. Each product manager is committed to attaining specified levels of sales and costs; each regional and district sales manager and each sales representative is also committed to specific goals. Each period, top management reviews and interprets the results.

Managers use five tools to check on plan performance: sales analysis, market-share analysis, marketing expense-to-sales analysis, financial analysis, and market-based scorecard analysis.

Sales Analysis

Sales analysis consists of measuring and evaluating actual sales in relation to sales goals. Two specific tools are used in sales analysis.

Sales-variance analysis measures the relative contribution of different factors to a gap in sales performance. Suppose the annual plan called for selling 4000 widgets in the first quarter at $1 per widget, for total revenue of $4000. At quarter's end, only 3000 widgets were sold at $.80 per widget, for total revenue of $2400. The sales performance

TABLE 22.1

Types of Marketing Control

Type of Control	Prime Responsibility	Purpose of Control	Approaches
I. Annual-plan control	Top management Middle management	To examine whether the planned results are being achieved	■ Sales analysis ■ Market-share analysis ■ Marketing expense–to–sales analysis ■ Financial analysis ■ Market-based scorecard analysis
II. Profitability control	Marketing controller	To examine where the company is making and losing money	Profitability by: ■ product ■ territory ■ customer ■ segment ■ trade channel ■ order size
III. Efficiency control	Line and staff management Marketing controller	To evaluate and improve the spending efficiency and impact of marketing expenditures	Efficiency of: ■ sales force ■ advertising ■ sales promotion ■ distribution
IV. Strategic control	Top management Marketing auditor	To examine whether the company is pursuing its best opportunities in markets, products, and channels	■ Marketing-effectiveness review ■ Marketing audit ■ Marketing excellence review ■ Company ethical and social responsibility review

variance is $1600, or 40 percent of expected sales. How much of this underperformance is due to the price decline and how much to the volume decline? The following calculation answers this question:

Variance due to price decline = ($1.00 − $.80)(3000) = $ 600   37.5%

Variance due to volume decline = ($1.00)(4000 − 3000) = $1000   62.5%

                                                    $1600   100.0%

Almost two-thirds of the variance is due to failure to achieve the volume target. The company should look closely at why it failed to achieve expected sales volume.

Microsales analysis looks at specific products, territories, and so forth that failed to produce expected sales. Suppose the company sells in three territories and expected sales were 1500 units, 500 units, and 2000 units, respectively. The actual sales volume was 1400 units, 525 units, and 1075 units, respectively. Thus territory 1 showed a 7 percent shortfall in terms of expected sales; territory 2, a 5 percent improvement over expectations; and territory 3, a 46 percent shortfall! Territory 3 is causing most of the trouble. The sales vice president can check into territory 3 to see what explains the poor performance: Territory 3's sales representative is loafing or has a personal problem; a major competitor has entered this territory; or business is in a recession in this territory.

Market-Share Analysis

Company sales do not reveal how well the company is performing relative to competitors. For this purpose, management needs to track its market share. Market share can be measured in three ways: Overall market share is the company's sales expressed as a percentage of total market sales. Served market share is its sales expressed as a percentage of the total sales to its served market. Its served market is all the buyers who are able and willing to buy its product. Served market share is always larger than overall market share. A company could capture 100 percent of its served market and yet have a relatively small share of the total market. Relative market share can be expressed as market share in relation to its largest competitor. A relative market share over 100 percent indicates a market leader. A relative market share of exactly 100 percent means that the company is tied for the lead. A rise in relative market share means a company is gaining on its leading competitor.

Conclusions from market-share analysis, however, are subject to certain qualifications:

- *The assumption that outside forces affect all companies in the same way is often not true:* The early reports on the harmful consequences of cigarette smoking caused total cigarette sales to falter, but not equally for all companies.

- *The assumption that a company's performance should be judged against the average performance of all companies is not always valid:* A company's performance should be judged against the performance of its closest competitors.

- *If a new firm enters the industry, then every existing firm's market share might fall:* A decline in market share might not mean that the company is performing any worse than other companies. Share loss depends on the degree to which the new firm hits the company's specific markets.

- *Sometimes a market-share decline is deliberately engineered to improve profits:* For example, management might drop unprofitable customers or products to improve its profits.

- *Market share can fluctuate for many minor reasons:* For example, market share can be affected by whether a large sale occurs on the last day of the month or at the beginning of the next month. Not all shifts in market share have marketing significance.[23]

Managers must carefully interpret market-share movements by product line, customer type, region, and other breakdowns. A useful way to analyze market-share movements is in terms of four components:

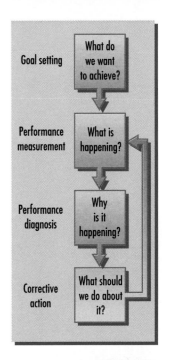

FIGURE 22.7

The Control Process

Overall market share	=	Customer penetration	×	Customer loyalty	×	Customer selectivity	×	Price selectivity

where:

- *Customer penetration* is the percentage of all customers who buy from the company.

- *Customer loyalty* is the purchases from the company by its customers expressed as a percentage of their total purchases from all suppliers of the same products.

- *Customer selectivity* is the size of the average customer purchase from the company expressed as a percentage of the size of the average customer purchase from an average company.

- *Price selectivity* is the average price charged by the company expressed as a percentage of the average price charged by all companies.

Now suppose the company's dollar market share falls during the period. The overall market-share equation provides four possible explanations: The company lost some of its customers (lower customer penetration); existing customers are buying less from the company (lower customer loyalty); the company's remaining customers are smaller in size (lower customer selectivity); or the company's price has slipped relative to competition (lower price selectivity).

Marketing Expense-to-Sales Analysis

Annual-plan control requires ensuring that the company is not overspending to achieve sales goals. The key ratio to watch is marketing expense–to–sales. In one company, this ratio was 30 percent and consisted of five component expense-to-sales ratios: sales force–to–sales (15 percent); advertising-to-sales (5 percent); sales promotion–to–sales (6 percent); marketing research–to–sales (1 percent); and sales administration–to–sales (3 percent).

Management needs to monitor these ratios, which will normally exhibit small fluctuations that can be ignored. Fluctuations outside the normal range are a cause for concern. The period-to-period fluctuations in each ratio can be tracked on a control chart (Figure 22.8). This chart shows that the advertising expense–to–sales ratio normally fluctuates between 8 percent and 12 percent, say 99 out of 100 times. In the fifteenth period, however, the ratio exceeded the upper control limit. One of two hypotheses can explain this occurrence: (1) The company still has good expense control, and this situation represents a rare chance event. (2) The company has lost control over this expense and should find the cause. If no investigation is made to determine whether the environment has changed, the risk is that some real change might have occurred, and the company will fall behind. If the environment is investigated, the risk is that the investigation will uncover nothing and be a waste of time and effort.

FIGURE 22.8

The Control-Chart Model

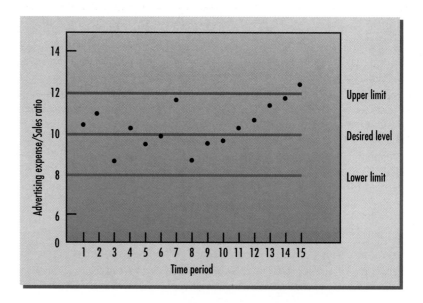

The behaviour of successive observations even within the upper and lower control limits should be watched. Note in Figure 22.8 that the level of the expense-to-sales ratio rose steadily from the ninth period onward. The probability of encountering six successive increases in what should be independent events is only 1 in 64.[24] This unusual pattern should have led to an investigation sometime before the fifteenth observation.

Financial Analysis

The expense-to-sales ratios should be analyzed in an overall financial framework to determine how and where the company is making its money. Marketers are increasingly using financial analysis to find profitable strategies beyond sales building.

Management uses financial analysis to identify the factors that affect the company's rate of return on net worth[25] The main factors are shown in Figure 22.9, along with illustrative numbers for a large chain-store retailer. The retailer is earning a 12.5 percent return on net worth. The return on net worth is the product of two ratios, the company's return on assets and its financial leverage. To improve its return on net worth, the company must increase the ratio of its net profits to its assets or increase the ratio of its assets to its net worth. The company should analyze the composition of its assets (i.e., cash, accounts receivable, inventory, and plant and equipment) and see if it can improve its asset management.

The return on assets is the product of two ratios, the profit margin and the asset turnover. The profit margin in Figure 22.9 seems low, whereas the asset turnover is more normal for retailing. The marketing executive can seek to improve performance in two ways: (1) Increase the profit margin by increasing sales or cutting costs; and (2) increase the asset turnover by increasing sales or reducing the assets (e.g., inventory, receivables) that are held against a given level of sales.[26]

Market-Based Scorecard Analysis

Most company measurement systems amount to preparing a financial-performance scorecard at the expense of more qualitative measures. Companies would do well to prepare two market-based scorecards that reflect performance and provide possible early warning signals.

A *customer-performance scorecard* records how well the company is doing year after year on such customer-based measures as:

- New customers
- Dissatisfied customers
- Lost customers
- Target market awareness
- Target market preference
- Relative product quality
- Relative service quality

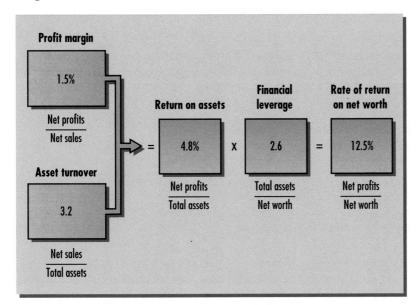

FIGURE 22.9

Financial Model of Return on Net Worth

Norms should be set for each measure, and management should take action when results get out of bounds.

The second measure is called a stakeholder-performance scorecard. Companies need to track the satisfaction of various constituencies who have a critical interest in and impact on the company's performance: employees, suppliers, banks, distributors, retailers, stockholders. Again, norms should be set for each group and management should take action when one or more groups register increased levels of dissatisfaction.[27] Consider Hewlett-Packard's program:

- **Hewlett-Packard.** Each division of Hewlett-Packard evaluates its performance on a customer-based scorecard that monitors 18 to 20 "business fundamentals." Some, such as customer satisfaction and on-time delivery, are rated for all divisions; other indicators are tracked according to the nature of the division's business. The company is thus able to gauge the effects of its marketing strategies on sales and profits and to identify areas where improvements in performance can lead to improved quantitative results.

Focusing on customer-based criteria for evaluating the company's success was what led to the development of HP's global account management (GAM) program in the 1990s. As the largest international corporations redirected their purchases of computer-related products and services from the most powerful hardware to the most productive software, and then to the quest for electronic solutions to problems affecting their global business, HP responded by becoming a partner and adviser in problem solving. The GAM system develops a relationship between HP's top managers and the client corporation. A senior sales executive is assigned as global account manager, providing on-site service at the corporate headquarters of the global account. The customer's chief information officer provides a broad overview of the company's needs, and the global account manager helps to develop solutions.[28]

PROFITABILITY CONTROL

Here are some disconcerting findings from a bank profitability study:

> We have found that anywhere from 20 to 40 percent of an individual institution's products are unprofitable, and up to 60 percent of their accounts generate losses.
> Our research has shown that, in most firms, more than half of all customer relationships are not profitable, and 30 to 40 percent are only marginally so. It is frequently a mere 10 to 15 percent of a firm's relationships that generate the bulk of its profits.
> Our profitability research into the branch system of a regional bank produced some surprising results . . . 30 percent of the bank's branches were unprofitable.[29]

Clearly, companies need to measure the profitability of their products, territories, customer groups, segments, trade channels, and order sizes. This information will help management determine whether any products or marketing activities should be expanded, reduced, or eliminated.

Marketing-Profitability Analysis

We will illustrate the steps in marketing-profitability analysis with the following example:

> The marketing vice president of a lawnmower company wants to determine the profitability of selling its lawnmower through three types of retail channels: hardware stores, garden supply shops, and department stores. The company's profit-and-loss statement is shown in Table 22.2.

Step 1: Identifying Functional Expenses Assume that the expenses listed in Table 22.2 are incurred to sell the product, advertise it, pack and deliver it, and bill and collect for it. The first task is to measure how much of each expense was incurred in each activity.

			TABLE	22.2
Sales		$60 000		
Cost of goods sold		39 000	**A Simplified Profit-and-Loss**	
Gross margin		$21 000	**Statement**	
Expenses				
Salaries	$9 300			
Rent	3 000			
Supplies	3 500			
		15 800		
Net profit		$ 5 200		

Suppose that most salary expense went to sales representatives and the rest went to an advertising manager, packing and delivery help, and an office accountant. Let the breakdown of the $9300 be $5100, $1200, $1400, and $1600, respectively. Table 22.3 shows the allocation of the salary expense to these four activities.

Table 22.3 also shows the rent account of $3000 allocated to the four activities. Because the sales reps work away from the office, none of the building's rent expense is assigned to selling. Most of the expenses for floor space and rented equipment are for packing and delivery. The supplies account covers promotional materials, packing materials, fuel purchases for delivery, and home office stationery. The $3500 in this account is reassigned to the functional uses made of the supplies.

Step 2: Assigning Functional Expenses to Marketing Entities The next task is to measure how much functional expense was associated with selling through each type of channel. Consider the selling effort. The selling effort is indicated by the number of sales made in each channel. This number is found in the selling column of Table 22.4. Altogether, 275 sales calls were made during the period. Because the total selling expense amounted to $5500 (see Table 22.3), the selling expense per call averaged $20.

Advertising expense can be allocated according to the number of ads addressed to the different channels. Because there were 100 ads altogether, the average ad cost $31.

The packing and delivery expense is allocated according to the number of orders placed by each type of channel. This same basis was used for allocating billing and collection expense.

Step 3: Preparing a Profit-and-Loss Statement for Each Marketing Entity A profit-and-loss statement can now be prepared for each type of channel (Table 22.5). Because hardware stores accounted for half of total sales ($30 000 out of $60 000), this channel is charged with half the cost of goods sold ($19 500 out of $39 000). This leaves a gross margin from hardware stores of $10 500. From this must be deducted the proportions of the functional expenses hardware stores consumed. According to Table 22.4, hardware stores received 200 out of 275 total sales calls. At an imputed value of $20 a call, hardware stores have to be charged with a $4000 selling expense. Table 22.4 also shows that hardware stores were the target of 50 ads. At $31 an ad, the hardware stores are charged with $1,550 of advertising. The same reasoning applies in computing the share of the other functional expenses to charge to hardware stores. The result is that hardware stores gave rise to $10 050 of the total expenses. Subtracting this from the gross margin, the profit of selling through hardware stores is only $450.

This analysis is repeated for the other channels. The company is losing money in selling through garden-supply shops and makes virtually all of its profits through

Natural Accounts	Total	Selling	Advertising	Packing and Delivery	Billing and Collecting
Salaries	$ 9 300	$5 100	$1 200	$1 400	$1 600
Rent	3 000	—	400	2 000	600
Supplies	3 500	400	1 500	1 400	200
	$15 800	$5 500	$3 100	$4 800	$2 400

TABLE 22.3

Mapping Natural Expenses into Functional Expenses

TABLE 22.4

Bases for Allocating Functional Expenses to Channels

Channel Type	Selling	Advertising	Packing and Delivery	Billing and Collecting
Hardware	200	50	50	50
Garden supply	65	20	21	21
Department stores	10	30	9	9
	275	100	80	80
Functional expense	$5 500	$3 100	$4 800	$2 400
÷ No. of Units	275	100	80	80
Equals	$ 20	$ 31	$ 60	$ 30

department stores. Notice that gross sales is not a reliable indicator of the net profits for each channel.

Determining Corrective Action

It would be naive to conclude that the company should drop garden-supply shops and possibly hardware stores so that it can concentrate on department stores. The following questions need to be answered first:

■ To what extent do buyers buy on the basis of type of retail outlet versus brand?

■ What are the trends with respect to the importance of these three channels?

■ How good are the company marketing strategies directed at the three channels?

On the basis of the answers, marketing management can evaluate five alternatives:

■ Establish a special charge for handling smaller orders.

■ Give more promotional aid to garden-supply shops and hardware stores.

■ Reduce the number of sales calls and the amount of advertising going to garden-supply shops and hardware stores.

■ Do not abandon any channel as a whole but only the weakest retail units in each channel.

■ Do nothing.

In general, marketing-profitability analysis indicates the relative profitability of different channels, products, territories, or other marketing entities. It does not prove that the best course of action is to drop the unprofitable marketing entities, nor does it capture the likely profit improvement if these marginal marketing entities are dropped.

Direct versus Full Costing

Like all information tools, marketing-profitability analysis can lead or mislead marketing executives, depending on the degree of their understanding of its methods and

TABLE 22.5

Profit-and-Loss Statements for Channels

	Hardware	Garden Supply	Dept. Stores	Whole Company
Sales	$30 000	$10 000	$20 000	$60 000
Cost of goods sold	19 500	6 500	13 000	39 000
Gross margin	$10 500	$ 3 500	$ 7 000	$21 000
Expenses				
Selling ($20 per call)	$ 4 000	$ 1 300	$ 200	$ 5 500
Advertising ($31 per advertisement)	1 550	620	930	3 100
Packing and delivery ($60 per order)	3 000	1 260	540	4 800
Billing ($30 per order)	1 500	630	270	2 400
Total Expenses	$10 050	$ 3 810	$ 1 940	$15 800
Net profit or loss	$ 450	$ (310)	$ 5 060	$ 5 200

limitations. The lawnmower company showed some arbitrariness in its choice of bases for allocating the functional expenses to its marketing entities. "Number of sales calls" was used to allocate selling expenses, when in principle "number of sales working-hours" is a more accurate indicator of cost. The former base was used because it involves less record keeping and computation.

Far more serious is another judgmental element affecting profitability analysis. The issue is whether to allocate full costs or only direct and traceable costs in evaluating a marketing entity's performance. The lawnmower company sidestepped this problem by assuming only simple costs that fit in with marketing activities. But the question cannot be avoided in real-world analyses of profitability. Three types of costs must be distinguished:

1. *Direct costs:* These are costs that can be assigned directly to the proper marketing entities. Sales commissions are a direct cost in a profitability analysis of sales territories, sales representatives, or customers. Advertising expenditures are a direct cost in a profitability analysis of products to the extent that each advertisement promotes only one product. Other direct costs for specific purposes are sales force salaries and travelling expenses.

2. *Traceable common costs:* These are costs that can be assigned only indirectly, but on a plausible basis, to the marketing entities. In the example, rent was analyzed in this way.

3. *Nontraceable common costs:* These are costs whose allocation to the marketing entities is highly arbitrary. To allocate "corporate image" expenditures equally to all products would be arbitrary, because all products do not benefit equally. To allocate them proportionately to the sales of the various products would be arbitrary because relative product sales reflect many factors besides corporate image making. Other examples are top management salaries, taxes, interest, and other overhead.

No one disputes including direct costs in marketing cost analysis. There is a small amount of controversy about including traceable common costs, which lump together costs that would change with the scale of marketing activity and costs that would not change. If the lawnmower company drops garden-supply shops, it will probably continue to pay the same rent. In this event, its profits would not rise immediately by the amount of the present loss in selling to garden-supply shops ($310).

The major controversy concerns whether the nontraceable common costs should be allocated to the marketing entities. Such allocation is called the full-cost approach, and its advocates argue that all costs must ultimately be imputed in order to determine true profitability. But this argument confuses the use of accounting for financial reporting with its use for managerial decision making. Full costing has three major weaknesses:

1. The relative profitability of different marketing entities can shift radically when one arbitrary way to allocate nontraceable common costs is replaced by another.

2. The arbitrariness demoralizes managers, who feel that their performance is judged adversely.

3. The inclusion of nontraceable common costs could weaken efforts at real cost control. Operating management is most effective in controlling direct costs and traceable common costs. Arbitrary assignments of nontraceable common costs can lead them to spend their time fighting arbitrary cost allocations rather than managing controllable costs well.

Companies are showing a growing interest in using marketing-profitability analysis or its broader version, activity-based cost accounting (ABC), to quantify the true profitability of different activities. According to Cooper and Kaplan, ABC "can give managers a clear picture of how products, brands, customers, facilities, regions, or distribution channels both generate revenues and consume resources."[30] To improve profitability, managers can then examine ways to reduce the resources required to perform various activities, or make the resources more productive or acquire them at a lower cost. Alternatively, management may raise prices on products that consume heavy amounts of support resources. The contribution of ABC is to refocus management's attention away from using only labour or material standard costs to allocate full cost, and toward capturing the actual costs of supporting individual products, customers, and other entities.

EFFICIENCY CONTROL

Suppose a profitability analysis reveals that the company is earning poor profits in certain products, territories, or markets. Are there more efficient ways to manage the sales force, advertising, sales promotion, and distribution in connection with these marketing entities?

Some companies have established a marketing controller position to improve marketing efficiency. Marketing controllers work out of the controller's office but specialize in the marketing side of the business. At companies such as General Foods, DuPont, and Johnson & Johnson, they perform a sophisticated financial analysis of marketing expenditures and results. They examine adherence to profit plans, help prepare brand managers' budgets, measure the efficiency of promotions, analyze media production costs, evaluate customer and geographic profitability, and educate marketing personnel on the financial implications of marketing decisions.[31]

Sales Force Efficiency

Sales managers need to monitor the following key indicators of efficiency in their territory:

- Average number of calls per salesperson per day
- Average sales call time per contact
- Average revenue per sales call
- Average cost per sales call
- Entertainment cost per sales call
- Percentage of orders per 100 sales calls
- Number of new customers per period
- Number of lost customers per period
- Sales force cost as a percentage of total sales

When a company starts investigating sales force efficiency, it often finds areas for improvement. General Electric reduced the size of one of its divisional sales forces after discovering that its salespeople were calling on customers too often. When a large airline found that its salespeople were both selling and servicing, they transferred the servicing function to lower-paid clerks. Another company conducted time-and-duty studies and found ways to reduce the ratio of idle-to-productive time.

Advertising Efficiency

Many managers believe it is almost impossible to measure what they are getting for their advertising dollars. But they should try to keep track of at least the following statistics:

- Advertising cost per thousand target buyers reached by media vehicle
- Percentage of audience who noted, saw or associated, and read most of each print ad
- Consumer opinions on the ad's content and effectiveness
- Before and after measures of attitude toward the product
- Number of inquiries stimulated by the ad
- Cost per inquiry

Management can take a number of steps to improve advertising efficiency, including doing a better job of positioning the product, defining objectives, pretesting messages, using computer technology to guide the selection of media, looking for better media buys, and doing posttesting.

Sales-Promotion Efficiency

Sales promotion includes dozens of devices for stimulating buyer interest and product trial. To improve sales-promotion efficiency, management should record the costs and sales impact of each promotion. Management should watch the following statistics:

- Percentage of sales sold on deal
- Display costs per sales dollar
- Percentage of coupons redeemed
- Number of inquiries resulting from a demonstration

A sales-promotion manager can analyze the results of different sales promotions and advise product managers on the most cost-effective promotions to use.

Distribution Efficiency

Management needs to search for distribution economies in inventory control, warehouse locations, and transportation modes. One problem is that distribution efficiency declines when the company experiences strong sales increases. Peter Senge describes a situation in which a strong sales surge causes the company to fall behind in meeting delivery dates (Figure 22.10).[32] This leads customers to bad-mouth the company and eventually sales fall. Management responds by increasing sales force incentives to secure more orders. The sales force succeeds but once again the company slips in meeting delivery dates. Management needs to identify the real bottleneck and invest in more production and distribution capacity.

STRATEGIC CONTROL

From time to time, companies need to undertake a critical review of overall marketing goals and effectiveness. Each company should periodically reassess its strategic approach to the marketplace with marketing-effectiveness reviews and marketing audits. Companies can also perform marketing excellence reviews and ethical–social responsibility reviews.

The Marketing-Effectiveness Review

Here is an actual situation.

> The president of a major industrial-equipment company reviewed the annual business plans of various divisions and found several lacking in marketing substance. He called in the corporate vice president of marketing and said:
>
> *I am not happy with the quality of marketing in our divisions. It is very uneven. I want you to find out which of our divisions are strong, average, and weak in marketing. I want to know if they understand and are practising customer-oriented marketing. I want a marketing score for each division. For each deficient division, I want a plan for improving marketing effectiveness over the next several years. I want evidence next year that each deficient division is improving its capabilities.*
>
> The corporate marketing vice president agreed. His first inclination was to base the evaluation on each division's performance in sales growth, market share, and profitability. His thinking was that high-performing divisions had good marketing leadership and poor-performing divisions had poor marketing leadership.

But good results could be due to a division's being in the right place at the right time. Another division might have poor results in spite of excellent marketing planning.

A company's or division's marketing effectiveness is reflected in the degree to which it exhibits the five major attributes of a marketing orientation: customer philosophy, integrated marketing organization, adequate marketing information, strategic orientation, and operational efficiency (see the Marketing Memo "Marketing Effectiveness Review Instrument"). Most companies and divisions receive scores in the fair-to-good range.[33]

F I G U R E 22.10

Dynamic Interactions Between Sales Orders and Distribution Efficiency

Source: Adapted from Peter M. Senge, *The Fifth Discipline.* © 1990 by Peter M. Senge. Used by permission of Doubleday, a division of Bantam Doubleday Dell Publishing Group, Inc.

Marketing Effectiveness Review Instrument

(Check One Answer to Each Question)

Customer Philosophy

A. *Does management recognize the importance of designing the company to serve the needs and wants of chosen markets?*

0___Management primarily thinks in terms of selling current and new products to whoever will buy them.

1___Management thinks in terms of serving a wide range of markets and needs with equal effectiveness.

2___Management thinks in terms of serving the needs and wants of well-defined markets and market segments chosen for their long-run growth and profit potential for the company.

B. *Does management develop different offerings and marketing plans for different segments of the market?*

0___No.　　1___Somewhat.　　2___To a large extent

C. *Does management take a whole marketing system view (suppliers, channels, competitors, customers, environment) in planning its business?*

0___No. Management concentrates on selling and servicing its immediate customers.

1___Somewhat. Management takes a long view of its channels although the bulk of its effort goes to selling and servicing the immediate customers.

2___Yes. Management takes a whole marketing systems view, recognizing the threats and opportunities created for the company by changes in any part of the system.

Integrated Marketing Organization

D. *Is there high-level marketing integration and control of the major marketing functions?*

0___No. Sales and other marketing functions are not integrated at the top and there is some unproductive conflict.

1___Somewhat. There is formal integration and control of the major marketing functions but less than satisfactory coordination and cooperation.

2___Yes. The major marketing functions are effectively integrated.

E. *Does marketing management work well with management in research, manufacturing, purchasing, logistics, and finance?*

0___No. There are complaints that marketing is unreasonable in the demands and costs it places on other departments.

1___Somewhat. The relations are amicable although each department pretty much acts to serve its own interests.

2___Yes. The departments cooperate effectively and resolve issues in the best interest of the company as a whole.

F. *How well organized is the new-product development process?*

0___The system is ill defined and poorly handled.

1___The system formally exists but lacks sophistication.

2___The system is well structured and operates on teamwork principles.

Adequate Marketing Information

G. *When were the latest marketing research studies of customers, buying influences, channels, and competitors conducted?*

0___Several years ago.　　1___A few years ago.　　2___Recently.

H. *How well does management know the sales potential and profitability of different market segments, customers, territories, products, channels, and order sizes?*

0___Not at all.　　1___Somewhat.　　2___Very well.

I. *What effort is expended to measure and improve the cost effectiveness of different marketing expenditures?*

0___Little or no effort.　　1___Some effort.　　2___Substantial effort.

Strategic Orientation

J. *What is the extent of formal marketing planning?*

0___Management conducts little or no formal marketing planning.

1___Management develops an annual marketing plan.

2___Management develops a detailed annual marketing plan and a strategic long-range plan that is updated annually.

K. *How impressive is the current marketing strategy?*

0___The current strategy is not clear.

1___The current strategy is clear and represents a continuation of traditional strategy.

2___The current strategy is clear, innovative, data based, and well reasoned.

L. *What is the extent of contingency thinking and planning?*

0___Management does little or no contingency thinking.

1___Management does some contingency thinking but little formal contingency planning.

2___Management formally identifies the most important contingencies and develops contingency plans.

(continued)

The Marketing Audit

Companies that discover weaknesses should undertake a thorough study known as a marketing audit.[34]

■ A **marketing audit** is a comprehensive, systematic, independent, and periodic examination of a company's—or business unit's—marketing environment, objectives, strategies, and activities with a view to determining problem areas and opportunities and recommending a plan of action to improve the company's marketing performance.

Let us examine the marketing audit's four characteristics:

1. *Comprehensive*: The marketing audit covers all the major marketing activities of a business, not just a few trouble spots. It would be called a functional audit if it covered only the sales force, pricing, or some other marketing activity. Although functional audits are useful, they sometimes mislead management. Excessive sales force turnover, for example, could be a symptom not of poor sales force training or compensation but of weak company products and promotion. A comprehensive marketing audit usually is more effective in locating the real source of marketing problems.

2. *Systematic*: The marketing audit is an orderly examination of the organization's macro- and micromarketing environment, marketing objectives and strategies, marketing systems, and specific activities. The audit indicates the most needed improvements, which are then incorporated into a corrective action plan involving both short-run and long-run steps to improve overall marketing effectiveness.

3. *Independent:* A marketing audit can be conducted in six ways: self-audit, audit from across, audit from above, company auditing office, company task force audit, and outsider audit. Self-audits, in which managers use a checklist to rate their own operations, lack objectivity and independence.[35] The 3M Company has made good use of a corporate auditing office, which provides marketing audit services to divisions on request.[36] Generally speaking, however, the best audits come from outside consultants who have the necessary

objectivity, broad experience in a number of industries, some familiarity with the industry being audited, and the undivided time and attention to give to the audit.

4. *Periodic:* Typically, marketing audits are initiated only after sales have turned down, sales force morale has fallen, and other problems have occurred. Companies are thrown into a crisis partly because they failed to review their marketing operations during good times. A periodic marketing audit can benefit companies in good health as well as those in trouble.

A marketing audit starts with a meeting between the company officer(s) and the marketing auditor(s) to work out an agreement on the audit's objectives, coverage, depth, data sources, report format, and time frame. A detailed plan as to who is to be interviewed, the questions to be asked, the time and place of contact, and so on is prepared so that auditing time and cost are kept to a minimum. The cardinal rule in marketing auditing is: Don't rely solely on company managers for data and opinion. Customers, dealers, and other outside groups must also be interviewed. Many companies do not really know how their customers and dealers see them, nor do they fully understand customer needs and value judgements.

The marketing audit examines six major components of the company's marketing situation. The major questions are listed in Table 22.6.

The Marketing Excellence Review

Companies can use another instrument to rate their performance in relation to the best practices of high-performing businesses. The three columns in Table 22.7 distinguish among poor, good, and excellent business and marketing practices. Management can place a check on each line as to its perception of where the business stands. The resulting profile exposes the business's weaknesses and strengths, highlighting where the company might move to become a truly outstanding player in the marketplace.

The Ethical and Social Responsibility Review

Companies need to evaluate whether they are truly practising ethical and socially responsible marketing. Business success and continually satisfying the customer and other stakeholders are intimately tied to adoption and implementation of high standards of business and marketing conduct. The most admired companies in the world abide by a code of serving people's interests, not only their own. See the Marketing for the 21st Century "Marketing Fair Labour Practices."

Business practices are often under attack because business situations routinely pose tough ethical dilemmas. One can go back to Howard Bowen's classic questions about the responsibilities of businesspeople:

> *Should he conduct selling in ways that intrude on the privacy of people, for example, by door-to-door selling . . . ? Should he use methods involving ballyhoo, chances, prizes, hawking, and other tactics which are at least of doubtful good taste? Should he employ "high pressure" tactics in persuading people to buy? Should he try to hasten the obsolescence of goods by bringing out an endless succession of new models and new styles? Should he appeal to and attempt to strengthen the motives of materialism, invidious consumption, and "keeping up with the Joneses"?[37]*

Clearly the company's bottom line cannot be the sole measure of corporate performance: Ethical issues must be dealt with in many aspects of its business. There are selling issues such as bribery or stealing trade secrets; advertising issues such as false and deceptive advertising; channel issues such as exclusive dealing and tying agreements; product issues such as quality and safety, warranties, and patent protection; packaging issues such as accurate labelling and use of scarce resources; price issues such as price-fixing, discrimination, and resale price maintenance; and competitive issues such as barriers to entry and predatory competition.

Raising the level of socially responsible marketing calls for a three-pronged attack. First, society must use the law to define, as clearly as possible, those practices that are illegal, antisocial, or anticompetitive. Second, companies must adopt and disseminate

TABLE 22.6

Components of a Marketing Audit

Part I. Marketing Environment Audit
Macroenvironment

Demographic:	What major demographic developments and trends pose opportunities or threats? What actions has the company taken in response?
Economic	What major developments in income, prices, savings, and credit will affect the company? What actions has the company been taking in response?
Environmental	What is the outlook for the cost and availability of natural resources and energy needed by the company? What about the company's role in pollution and conservation? What steps has the company taken?
Technological	What are the major changes in product and process technology? What is the company's position in these technologies?
Political	What changes in laws and regulations might affect marketing strategy and tactics? What is happening in these areas that affects marketing strategy?
Cultural	What is the public's attitude toward business and toward the company's products? What changes in customer lifestyles and values might affect the company?

Task Environment

Markets	What is happening to market size, growth, geographical distribution, and profits? What are the major market segments?
Customers	What are customers' needs and buying processes? How do customers and prospects rate the company and its competitors on reputation, product quality, service, sales force, and price? How do different customer segments make their buying decisions?
Competitors	Who are the major competitors? What are their objectives, strategies, strengths, weaknesses, sizes, and market shares? What trends will affect competition and substitutes for the company's products?
Distribution and Dealers	What are the main trade channels for bringing products to customers? What are the efficiency levels and growth potentials of the different channels?
Suppliers	What is the outlook for the availability of key resources? What are trends among suppliers?
Facilitators and Marketing Firms	What is the outlook for transportation services, warehousing facilities, and financial resources? How effective are the company's advertising agencies and marketing research firms?
Publics	Which publics represent particular opportunities or problems? What steps has the company taken to deal effectively with each public?

Part II. Marketing Strategy Audit

Business Mission	Is the business mission clearly stated in market-oriented terms? Is it feasible?
Marketing Objectives and Goals	Are the company and marketing objectives and goals stated clearly enough to guide marketing planning and performance measurement? Are the marketing objectives appropriate?
Strategy	Has management articulated a clear marketing strategy for achieving its objectives? Is the strategy convincing? Is the strategy appropriate to the stage of the product life cycle, competitors' strategies, and the state of the economy? Is the company using the best basis for market segmentation? Does it have clear criteria for rating segments and choosing the best ones? Has it developed accurate profiles of each target segment? Has the company developed an effective positioning and marketing mix for each target segment? Are marketing resources allocated optimally to the major elements of the marketing mix?

Part III. Marketing Organization Audit

Formal Structure	Does the marketing vice president have adequate authority and responsibility for company activities that affect customer satisfaction? Are the marketing activities optimally structured along functional, product, segment, end-user, and geographical lines?

(continued)

(continued)

Functional Efficiency	Are there good communication and working relations between marketing and sales? Is the product management system working effectively? Are product managers able to plan profits or only sales volume? Are there any groups in marketing that need more training, motivation, supervision, or evaluation?
Interface Efficiency	Are there any problems between marketing and manufacturing, R&D, purchasing, finance, accounting, or legal that need attention?

Part IV. Marketing Systems Audit

Marketing Information System	Is the marketing intelligence system producing accurate, sufficient, and timely information? Are company decision makers asking for enough marketing research, and are they using the results? Is the company employing the best methods for market measurement and sales forecasting?
Marketing Planning Systems	Is the marketing planning system well conceived and effectively used? Do marketers have decision support systems available? Does the planning system result in acceptable sales targets and quotas?
Marketing Control System	Are the control procedures adequate to ensure that the annual-plan objectives are being achieved? Does management periodically analyze the profitability of products, markets, territories, and channels of distribution? Are marketing costs and productivity periodically examined?
New-Product Development	Is the company well organized to gather, generate, and screen new-product ideas? Does the company do adequate research and analysis before investing in new ideas? Does the company carry out adequate product and market testing?

Part V. Marketing Productivity Audit

Profitability Analysis	What is the profitability of the company's different products, markets, territories, and channels of distribution? Should the company enter, expand, contract, or withdraw from any business segments?
Cost-Effectiveness Analysis	Do any marketing activities seem to have excessive costs? Can cost-reducing steps be taken?

Part VI. Marketing Function Audit

Products	What are the company's product-line objectives? Is the current product line meeting the objectives? Should the product line be stretched or contracted? Which products should be phased out? Added? What are the buyers' knowledge and attitudes toward the company's and competitors' product quality, features, styling, brand names, and so on? What areas of product and brand strategy need improvement?
Price	What are the company's pricing objectives, policies, strategies, and procedures? To what extent are prices set on cost, demand, and competitive criteria? Do the customers see the company's prices as being in line with the value of its offer? What does management know about the price elasticity of demand, experience curve effects, and competitors' prices and pricing policies? To what extent are price policies compatible with the needs of distributors and dealers, suppliers, and government regulation?
Distribution	What are the company's distribution objectives and strategies? Is there adequate market coverage and service? How effective are distributors, dealers, manufacturers' representatives, brokers, agents, and others? Should the company consider changing its distribution channels?
Advertising, Sales Promotion,	What are the company's advertising objectives? Is the right amount being spent on advertising? What do customers and the public think about the advertising? Are the media well chosen? Is the internal advertising staff adequate? Is the sales promotion budget adequate? Is there effective and sufficient use of sales promotion tools such as samples, coupons, displays, and sales contests? Is the company making enough use of direct, on-line, and data base marketing?
Sales Force	What are the sales force's objectives? Is the sales force large enough to accomplish the company's objectives? Is the sales force organized along the lines? Are there enough sales managers to guide the field sales representatives? Does the sales force show high morale, ability, and effort? Are procedures adequate for setting quotas and evaluating performance? How does the company sales force compare to competitors' sales forces?

Poor	Good	Excellent
Product driven	Market driven	Market driving
Mass-market–oriented	Segment-oriented	Niche-oriented and customer-oriented
Product offer	Augmented product offer	Customer solutions offer
Average product quality	Better than average	Legendary
Average service quality	Better than average	Legendary
End-product–oriented	Core-product–oriented	Core-competency–oriented
Function-oriented	Process-oriented	Outcome-oriented
Reacting to competitors	Benchmarking competitors	Leapfrogging competitors
Supplier exploitation	Supplier preference	Supplier partnership
Dealer exploitation	Dealer support	Dealer partnership
Price driven	Quality driven	Value driven
Average speed	Better than average	Legendary
Hierarchy	Network	Teamwork
Vertically integrated	Flattened organization	Strategic alliances
Stockholder driven	Stakeholder driven	Societally driven

The Marketing Excellence Review: Best Practices

a written code of ethics, build a company tradition of ethical behaviour, and hold their people fully responsible for observing ethical and legal guidelines. Third, individual marketers must practise a "social conscience" in their specific dealings with customers and various stakeholders.

The new millennium holds a wealth of opportunities for companies. Technological advances in solar energy, on-line computer networks, cable and satellite television, genetic engineering, and telecommunications promise to change the world as we know it. At the same time, forces in the socioeconomic, cultural, and natural environments will impose new limits on marketing and business practice. Companies that are able to innovate new solutions and values in a socially responsible way are the most likely to succeed. Consider Working Assets:

■ **Working Assets.** Working Assets long-distance telephone service competes with AT&T, MCI, and Sprint in the same way the major carriers compete with each other: low rates, clear transmissions over fibre optic lines, efficient operators, and convenient calling cards. But it adds a unique appeal to its selected market niche. The customers addressed in the advertising line "We make your voice heard" are people who identify themselves as supporters of progressive causes. On its monthly bills, the company provides information about two current issues along with the names and phone numbers of influential people the customer is invited to call free of charge. For a fee, the customer may have a prepared letter sent to these leaders on his or her behalf. Customers are also invited to vote for the nonprofit organizations that receive one percent of their monthly charges. Appealing to this target market's interest in preserving the environment, Working Assets uses recycled paper and soy-based ink, and it plants 17 trees for every ton of paper it consumes. In all its business practices, the company has a consistent program of corporate citizenship that matches the ethics of its market. For those who need further inducement, Working Assets offers of a year's worth of monthly coupons for a free container of frozen desserts from Ben and Jerry's, another corporate supporter of progressive causes. Working Assets' corporate idealism has had a favourable effect on the practical side of its business. For five successive years, Working Assets has been recognized by Inc. in its list of the fastest growing companies and has been featured in *Fortune*, *Newsweek*, the *New York Times*, and the *Washington Post*.

Working Assets
www.wald.com

Marketing Fair Labour Practices

Globalization is a fact of life in the apparel industry, from manufacturing to marketing of clothing, accessories, and footwear in all price ranges. Labels bearing the names of North American-owned companies may also indicate that the items are produced in other countries, often less developed nations of Latin America and the Pacific Rim. A series of news reports in the mid-1990s brought to public attention the fact that many of these products were made by underpaid, overworked, and sometimes underage employees of sweatshops. Unfavourable stories about the Asian factories that made Nike athletic shoes were so much in the news that the company formed an independent commission to inspect them. Many skeptical consumers remained suspicious about the findings of the investigation. In letters to the editors of their hometown newspapers, they objected to paying high prices so that millionaire athletes could become even richer from advertising endorsements while the factory workers earned less than a living wage. A clothing line produced in Honduras brought similar negative attention to TV talk-show hostess Kathie Lee Gifford.

In August 1996, representatives of 18 organizations, including fashion producers and retailers, unions, and human rights groups, came together in the White House Apparel Industry Partnership to establish voluntary standards for working conditions in factories that produced goods for the U.S. apparel industry. They agreed on a number of provisions, including a ban on hiring forced labour or children under the age of 14, a minimum wage at least in compliance with the laws of the host country,

a maximum 60-hour work week with at least one day off, protection from harassment and abuse, and recognition of workers' right to form unions and bargain collectively. A monitoring group composed of representatives of the producers, unions, and human rights organizations was to ensure compliance, and businesses that met the standards would be entitled to carry a "no sweat" label.

In 1998, a task force of the partnership unveiled a plan to establish the Fair Labor Association as the oversight agency. But by the end of the year, the agreement had lost significant support. Some members of the partnership complained that they were left out of the negotiations detailing the standards and procedures for monitoring compliance. UNITE, the apparel workers' union, withdrew from the partnership in protest. Meanwhile, the American Apparel Manufacturers Association, impatient with the progress of the White House partnership, developed its own program called Responsible Apparel Production (RAP), with similar standards and its own certification agency. A pilot program began with 30 factories in the United States, Asia, and Latin America, and factories of both AAMA members and nonmembers were invited to inquire about becoming certified.

Although UNITE and its allies fear that the manufacturers will make only superficial improvements and that certification or a no sweat label will be a misrepresentation, the disagreements between the two sides reveal their common convictions: Labour must be recognized as an important stakeholder in every employer's business. Fair labour practices are a critical marketing issue as well as a matter of corporate ethics.

Sources: Vanessa Groce, "Chronicle," *Earnshaw's Infants', Toddlers', and Girls' and Boys' Wear Review*, October 1996, p. 36; Steven Greenhouse, "Voluntary Rules on Apparel Labor Prove Hard to Set," *New York Times*, February 1, 1997, pp. A1, A7; "No Sweat? Sweatshop Code is just first step to end worker abuse," *Solidarity*, June–July, 1997, p. 9. See also the Web sites of UNITE, Corporate Watch, and the American Apparel Manufacturers Association.

SUMMARY

1. The modern marketing department evolved through six stages. In the first stage, companies start out with simply a sales department. In the second stage, they add ancillary marketing functions, such as advertising and marketing research. In the third stage, a separate marketing department is created to handle the increased number of ancillary marketing functions. In the fourth stage, both sales and marketing report to a sales and marketing vice president. In the fifth stage, all of a company's employees are market and customer centred. In the sixth stage, marketing personnel work mainly on cross-disciplinary teams.

2. Modern marketing departments can be organized in a number of ways. Some companies are organized by functional specialization; others focus on geography and regionalization. Still others emphasize product and brand-management or market-segment management. Some companies establish a matrix organization consisting of both product and market managers. Some companies have strong corporate marketing, others have limited corporate marketing, and still others place marketing only in the divisions.

3. Effective modern marketing organizations are marked by a strong cooperation and customer focus among the company's departments: marketing, R&D, engineering, purchasing, manufacturing, operations, finance, accounting, and credit.

4. A brilliant strategic marketing plan counts for little if it is not implemented properly. Implementing marketing plans calls for skills in recognizing and diagnosing a problem, assessing the company level where the problem exists, implementation skills, and skills in evaluating the implementation results.

5. The marketing department has to monitor and control marketing activities continuously. The purpose of annual-plan control is to ensure that the company achieves the sales, profits, and other goals established in its annual plan. The main tools of annual-plan control are sales analysis, market-share analysis, marketing expense—to-sales analysis, financial analysis, and market-based scorecard analysis.

6. Profitability control seeks to measure and control the profitability of various products, territories, customer groups, trade channels, and order sizes. An important part of controlling for profitability is assigning costs and generating profit-and-loss statements.

7. Efficiency control focuses on finding ways to increase the efficiency of the sales force, advertising, sales promotion, and distribution.

8. Strategic control entails a periodic reassessment of the company and its strategic approach to the marketplace, using the tools of the marketing-effectiveness review and the marketing audit. Companies should also undertake ethical–social responsibility reviews.

APPLICATIONS

CHAPTER CONCEPTS

1. Rewrite the questions in the Components of a Marketing Audit (Table 22.6) in such a way that they reflect the individual problems and terminology associated with your industry. Be as specific and as detailed as you can when writing the questions. If you are not presently employed, rewrite the questions for either a company you have worked for or one for which you would like to work in the future.

2. A large manufacturer of industrial equipment has a salesperson assigned to each major city. Regional sales managers supervise the sales representatives in several cities. The chief marketing officer wants to evaluate the profit contribution of the different cities. How might each of the following costs be allocated to each of the cities: (a) the aggregate costs of sending bills to customers; (b) district sales manager's expenses; (c) national magazine advertising; and (d) marketing research?

3. NAPLCO (North American Phillips Lighting Corporation) wanted to put Norelco bulbs on supermarket shelves as a third national brand (GE had 60 percent of the market and Westinghouse had 20 percent of the market). Lightbulb purchases had been slowly declining over the last five years. Lightbulbs were the grocer's most profitable store item per linear metre of goods stocked. NAPLCO concluded that the strong Norelco name, proven capability at making quality lightbulbs, and profits for supermarkets would make this project very successful. After conducting consumer research, it created a new and clever gravity-fed display and novel transparent and protective package for the bulbs themselves. The display held 12 of the most popular lightbulb types. (Most supermarkets carried 50 types of lightbulbs, and double that number constituted a full line.) Norelco decided not to do any consumer advertising, but to rely more heavily on push money. It also decided to use a broker rather than hire its own sales force. After two and a half years, gross sales of Norelco's bulbs were $1.1 million against a projected $7.5 million. Why do you think the project failed from an implementation standpoint?

When ConAgra introduced the new Healthy Choice Savory Selections packaged cold cuts shown in the ad in Figure 1, it had to coordinate the work of the marketing department with the work of the purchasing, manufacturing, finance, accounting, and credit departments. Outline how marketing would interact with each of these other departments in the course of developing and launching the three new flavours.

Figure 1

Larger and multinational companies have a particularly difficult time grappling with the complexities of coordinating and controlling marketing activities across departmental and national borders—let alone time zones. Now technology is available to help everyone involved in the planning process juggle roles and responsibilities, avoiding overlap and smoothing the way for more effective implementation and control.

To see a sample screen from this software, visit the Web site of Copernicus, a marketing-strategy consulting firm. The Copernicus software, customized for each company, shows who is responsible for which activities. It also includes the company's mission, vision, and goals, as well as the marketing objectives and a full set of budgets, forecasts, and schedules. This technology runs on the company's intranet, so it is accessible to everyone who participates in marketing planning. Why are budgets and schedules important for marketing control? Why do managers need to see the company goals and marketing objectives as they create each year's marketing plan?

Copernicus
www.copernicusmarketing.com/
market/docs/planners.htm

part five
Managing
and Delivering
Marketing Programs

With globalization spreading throughout the apparel industry, fair labour practices have become a high-profile marketing issue—and a matter of corporate ethics—for North American companies. Recent news reports have covered the plight of underpaid, overworked, and sometimes underage employees in factories across Latin America and the Pacific Rim.

Search for the latest news on this key issue using your favourite search engine (such as Metafind.com). There are also sites that focus on this issue. For example, go to Child Labour Links of Child Labour Resolutions . Also check the U.S. Department of Labor's Bureau of International Labor Affairs Web site for more information. Have any U.S. companies with international factories been charged with unfair labour practices lately? How are these companies responding to the charges? Labour issues are regulated by provincial governments in Canada. Are these governments doing anything about these problems?

Child Labour Links
www.tuac.ca/pubs.traventf/links.htm

Child Labour Resolutions
www.islandnet.com/~bloomer/child.htm

U.S. Department of Labor's Bureau of International Labor Affairs
www.dol.gov/dol/ilab/

YOU'RE THE MARKETER: SONIC MARKETING PLAN

No marketing plan is complete without provisions for organizing, implementing, evaluating, and controlling the total marketing effort. In addition to measuring progress toward financial targets and other objectives, marketers need to plan how they will audit and improve their marketing activities.

You are Jane Melody's assistant at Sonic. Your role is to recommend how Sonic can manage the marketing of its shelf stereos. Review the company's current situation. Also look at the goals, strategies, and programs you have developed for Sonic's marketing plan. Now answer these questions about managing the company's marketing activities:

- What is the most appropriate organization for Sonic's marketing and sales departments?

- What can Sonic do to create a more market- and customer-focused organization?

- What control measures should Sonic incorporate into its marketing plan?

- What can Sonic do to evaluate its marketing and its level of ethical and socially responsible marketing?

After you have answered these questions, either summarize your recommendations in a written marketing plan or type them into the Controls section of the Marketing Plan Pro software, depending on your instructor's directions.

SELLING ON-LINE—RETAILERS' RISKY VENTURE?

A new phenomenon took place in 1999: many of Canada's big retail chains went on-line for the first time. These companies were responding to the fact that increasing numbers of Canadians were logging onto the World Wide Web at unprecedented rates. They wanted Canadian on-line shopping alternatives since the low Canadian dollar made shopping at U.S.-based sites prohibitively expensive. However, on-line shopping has not always been a happy experience for on-line retailers or on-line shoppers alike. While some believe that there is a lot of money to be made "e-tailing," others are more skeptical.

First there is the cost of going on-line. Larry Stevenson, president of Chapters.ca, explains that it took $22 million just to launch their division. They hired a staff on 130, and had to develop their credit-card capability and security features as well as the site itself. Even though the site has been an award-winner, Chapters found that having a site alone wasn't a sufficient condition for doing business. The company still needed customer support services, which could be accessed through a 1-800 number and supported by a call centre. Chapters also had to build a distribution facility from the ground up, and it had to have the latest in technology since they were quickly handling over 1000 orders a day. The highly automated warehouse came with a $10 million price tag. Next, they had to spend heavily on advertising and marketing. Even though Chapters had a strong brand and retail presence before going on-line, lots of work had to be done to acquaint potential consumers with their new on-line capabilities. These costs haven't deterred Stevenson, however. Even though he can't see profits on the immediate horizon, he believes that the model of success is one of getting in early and going big if one wants to win in the on-line retailing game.

Jeffery Wortsman of Danier, the Canadian leather-goods merchandiser, has taken quite a different approach and is a much more cautious entrant. Danier waited two years before taking the plunge.

First, the company waited for technology prices to go down. Even then, working with consultants from IBM's e-business division, they were faced with options that would cost $250 000 to $450 000 just to start the on-line business. To cover these costs, the firm would have to do $1 to $1.2 million in sales to break even. For Danier, this meant setting a sales target of one percent of their total sales. Wortsman is like many other Canadian retailers who believe they don't have much choice about having an on-line presence since consumers are starting to change their shopping habits. Even with such a conservative sales estimate, some analysts, like Jim Carroll, author of many Internet texts including the *Canadian Internet Handbook*, believe that Danier and other on-line retailers are spending too much for what they can expect to get back. Excessive media hype of the Internet has led many retailers to inflate their expectations.

Being a successful on-line merchant takes much more than just a Web site, however. One has only to examine the Christmas 1999 nightmare experienced by Patriot Computers of Markham, Ontario. Patriot advertised heavily before the Christmas season, placing banner ads on television channel guides telling consumers they could buy their children Barbie or Hot Wheels personal computers for $0.99 a day. The company was flooded with orders. They had to post a flashing message on their Web site stating that they might be unable to guarantee Christmas deliveryÑnot what parents with children clamouring for their promised PC wanted to hear come Christmas morning!

Thus, while on-line sales amount to $282 million for the gift-giving season, some fear consumers won't come back to sites where service hasn't been satisfactory. Poor customer service, out-of-stock merchandise, suppliers unable to meet demand, botched orders, and late deliveries have plagued many operators. While some retailers have been nimble and able to surf the e-tailing wave, others have wiped out.

Questions

1. In addition to Web-site development, what other aspects of consumer behaviour and the marketing mix must on-line retailers consider?

2. Compare and contrast the sites of a number of on-line merchants (if you are not an experienced on-line shopper, visit any of the sites mentioned in this case or try wwwtoadhalltoys.com (a Winnipeg toy retailer), www.Sears.ca, www.indigo.ca, www.samcd.com, or www.HMV.com. Explain what you like and dislike about the various sites. What features make the site sticky (i.e., make you stay and browse and finally make a purchase) versus what things make you abandon the site quickly?

3. Jeff Wortsman of Danier noted that many firms are developing multi-channel strategies. Danier, for example, relies on retail outlets, its web site and catalogues to generate sales. Why are more and more firms using multiple channels? What are the challenges associated with this strategy?

Sources: Based on "E-commerce," *Venture* 723 (October 5, 1999); Marina Strauss, "It's an E-Christmas as Shoppers Flock On-line," *Globe and Mail*, December 18, 1999, pp. A1, A7. Keith McArthur, "Shopping on the Internet Takes Crowds Out of Christmas, *Globe and Mail*, December 18, 1999, p. A7. Nick Jones, Jones Consulting Inc., Presentation at Queen's University, "E-Commerce: It's More Than Just a Website," September 1999.

MODROBES: FROM UNIVERSITY CASE COMPETITION TO THE REAL WORLD FIRM

Some people have "entrepreneur" written all over them. One of those people is Steve "Sal" Debus, or, Saldebus, a young man who describes himself as an artist, not just a clothing designer and merchandiser. He began his career at age 10 designing shoes for his favourite brand names—NIKE, BROOKS, and CONVERSE. Although he never actually received a royalty for his "new, funky" shoe pictures, he kept the vision alive and was determined to create his own style.

His first winning idea came about as the result of the sore butt he got while writing four-hour political science exams while attending Brock University. "Exam pants" were born—a lightweight, extremely comfortable utility pant. Similar to the pants worn by operating-room physicians, the main stylistic difference in Exam Pants was the quilted foam padding sewn into the rear end of the pant, easy-access side pockets, a widened leg, and a secret pocket. "Hey, they were so damn comfortable I wore them every day for a month," exclaimed Sal. However, the pants had one limitation. Since Sal wasn't too enthused with his new nickname—"Fat ass"—he went on to design a slightly different pant.

Today, Debus is the founder and president of Toronto-based Modrobes Saldebus Lounge Clothing Inc., a firm he established in 1996. His line of comfortable, easy-care, casual clothing has been a hit with young people. At first, with little money for distribution, he went from campus to campus selling Exam Pants off folding tables. Nonetheless, his sales pitch grabbed a lot of attention. He promised prospective buyers that if his pants weren't the most comfortable piece of clothing they had ever owned, he would refund their money. Who could resist such an offer? His first-year sales were $70 000. Today they top $3 million. While Sal could leave the selling to someone else—his pants now are available in over 350 stores—he still regularly hits the road in order to keep in touch with the ever-changing youth market. In the summer of 1999, for example, he and his team went off to Rome, NY to the Woodstock music festival, his first foray into the U.S. market.

Keeping in touch is important because Sal has lofty dreams for his young company. He sees it as a rival for the big players like Levi. He believes he can make inroads against the jeans companies since denim is not a good fit for modern style. People aren't working in factories but behind computers where there is a need for something more comfortable and lighter weight, Sal believes. Before reaching this lofty goal, however, he must overcome some significant hurdles in his path. None of these seem to worry Sal, who has his own style of taking on these challenges.

Questions

1. What strategy does Modrobes employ?

2. Steve does a lot of marketing at events. How should he measure success for these efforts?

3. What does Steve "Sal" Debus see as the biggest threat to his company? How is he attempting to overcome this threat?

4. What actions does he have to take if he is to grow his company into a credible threat to firms like Levi?

Sources: Based on "ModRobes," *Venture* 724 (October 12, 1999); ModRobes Web site http://www.modrobes.com. Astrid Van Den Broek, "Targeting Yourself," *Marketing*, August 2, 1999, p. 9.

Order of Cases	Relevant Chapters
A. Riverside Credit Union	4, 6, 9
B. Ralph the Optician	8, 10, 15, 17
C. Rocky Mountain House	2, 3, 5, 8, 9, 15, 17, 19
D. Restaurant Le Petit Prince	14, 18, 19
E. Assiniboine Credit Union	14, 15, 18
F. Denormalization of Tobacco in Canada	6, 9, 18
G. Kingston Symphony	2, 3, 6, 9, 13, 14, 19, 22

CASE STUDIES

A. RIVERSIDE CREDIT UNION

Frank Timmerman, vice president of marketing at Riverside Credit Union, sat at his desk with a smile on his face. After months of effort, he felt that now he really had a handle on Riverside Credit Union's membership. He had been in charge of the initiative to segment the membership base to determine how various members contributed to the profitability of the credit union. He also wanted to know which members to focus on in terms of building their business to ensure future profitability. Timmerman also believed that gaining a better understanding of the various segment profiles would help his credit union better target appropriate financial products to members.

Background

Riverside Credit Union is a well-established credit union with just over 100 000 retail members and a small but rapidly growing business membership of about 10 000 members. Credit unions are similar to banks in many respects, but they also differ in several key ways. Like banks, credit unions offer many financial services—everything from savings and chequing accounts to investment advice. However, unlike banks, credit unions don't have customers—they have members. The members are the actual owners of the credit union. Furthermore, credit unions have a strong sense of social responsibility, in addition to financial responsibility.

Riverside Credit Union, for example, describes itself as a democratic, ethical, and innovative provider of financial services to its members. It is committed to conducting business in a way that strengthens not only its own long-term success but also contributes to the social, economic, and environmental well-being of the community in which it operates.

Riverside Credit Union has been quite successful and has assets under administration of almost $2.5 billion. Much of its success is due to its excellent member service culture, the regular introduction of new competitive products, and an aggressive pricing policy that ensures that members always receive some of the best rates available. Riverside Credit Union also has a good distribution network with which to serve its members. It has 15 branches, 30 automated teller machines, PC banking, a call centre that is mostly dedicated to servicing members, and an interactive voice-response, phone-banking system. Riverside also has a number of mortgage development managers. During the past two years, the branch sales force had been realigned to focus more on relationship selling. The sales force has placed the greatest emphasis on members with high deposit balances.

Riverside Credit Union is located in a large urban area that, until recently, has grown faster than the rest of the country. During the last year or so, however, the economy has been slowing, resulting in greater competition between financial institutions. There is also more competition from category killers that are focusing on specific product areas such as credit cards and mortgages. The Internet has facilitated this type of banking as well as business conducted by other "direct" financial institutions that are aggressively competing for savings and investment accounts, with rates approaching term-deposit levels. Continuing pressure on margin has made it impossible for Riverside Credit Union to maintain its aggressive pricing policy and as such it has experienced some erosion of its core business.

Riverside Credit Union has long prided itself on its strong product marketing group. Timmerman was a member of this group. One of the tools that has been invaluable to the marketing group has been the Member Database Information System (MDIS). This database captured all of the product information (except the off-balance mutual fund business). Timmerman knew that although there had been a lot of member analysis and research, most of it revolved around specific products. Little was known about the full value or nature of the relationships Riverside Credit Union had with its membership.

Thus, under Timmerman's leadership, a new project was launched so that the marketing department could deepen its understanding of the membership. Timmerman believed that it was critical that Riverside Credit Union be able to anticipate its members needs and manage to build long-term relationships with the members. The information currently available in the database wasn't up to this task. Therefore, a detailed segmentation analysis was conducted of the entire retail membership. The marketing team hired an expert in segmentation to assist with the work. When the project started, no one knew exactly what the results would show.

Segmentation Approach

Timmerman believed that getting this type of information was a pressing need given the growing competition in his marketplace. Since he had only a short time frame within which to complete the initial study, he decided to only use the data currently available in the MDIS for the analysis. Any external data he might want, or external research he might conduct later, could be added later once he had a firmer understanding of the various member segments. Timmerman and the team believed that information such as share of wallet would be too difficult to get for the entire membership or would be too inaccurate to be useful.

Timmerman and his team decided there were three things they most needed to know about the membership: (1) profitability of the relationships, (2) behaviour of the members with respect to their usage of various Riverside Credit Union products and services, and (3) future potential. Details on each of these dimensions and the data that were used in the analysis are outlined below:

Profitability was examined by summing the margin, fee, and service charge revenue for each member and then subtracting the expenses. With the assistance of accounting, the total cost for each transaction type was identified and then it was divided by the total number of transactions to generate a per-transaction cost. With input from sales and branch operations, set-up and maintenance costs were also determined. Expenses were subtracted from revenues to calculate profitability for each member. Even though there were a few missing numbers, the team agreed that the calculation would represent the relative profitability of one member versus another. Profitability would be examined by value and by decile to understand the dynamics of the membership.

Member behaviour or the type of financial relationship the person had with Riverside Credit Union was the next variable analyzed. To understand this, Riverside compiled all of the data it had for each member for the past year. This included transactional data, member age, their account information, information on what channel they used, length of their membership, and so on. A clustering technique was used to group members so that those who demonstrated similar "behaviour" were grouped together while keeping the groups as distinct as possible from the other groups.

Potential—Predictive models were developed for the core products offered by Riverside Credit Union (RRSPs, mortgages, term deposits, loans, credit cards, lines of credit, and so on). These models were created using statistical techniques (such as regression). The models were formulated using data from members who had previously purchased the product. The model can then be used to predict future sales of that product. Riverside Credit Union had used predictive models successfully in the past to target product campaigns and it was fairly comfortable with their use. Each member would be scored for each product. This information was then added to the analysis.

Segmentation Results

Profitability: Table One summarizes the annual member profitability analysis.

Behaviour Segments: Seven different member segments emerged from the analysis. They are described below in Table 2 in order of average profitability. Each segment profile also includes a description of average funds under administration (FUA) and average products per member.

Frank conducted some further analysis that quickly showed that although segments 6 and 7 had the lowest average profit and did cost Riverside Credit Union money to serve, most of the members who had negative profitability were in segment 4 (30 percent of segment 4 generated approximately 60 percent of the total negative profit). The segment 4 members did a lot of transactions across all channels, but they did not have high enough balances or revenue to offset the transaction costs.

TABLE 1

Profit Tier	No of Members	Percentage	Cum %	Avg Annual Profit
Top 10%	300	.3	.3	$9000
10 to 20	1000	1.0	1.3	$2700
20 to 30	1300	1.3	2.6	$2077
30 to 40	1900	1.9	4.5	$1421
40 to 50	2300	2.3	6.8	$1174
50 to 60	3000	3.0	9.8	$ 900
60 to 70	4000	4.0	13.8	$ 675
70 to 80	6000	6.0	19.8	$ 450
80 to 90	8000	8.0	27.8	$ 338
90 to 100	35 000	35.0	62.8	$ 77
Zero Profit	19 200	19.2	82.0	$ 0
Negative profit	18 000	18.0	100.0	($100)
Total	100 000			

Potential: All of the behaviour segments had some members that had higher predictive scores for some products. When the overall scores were combined to give an indication of relative potential Frank was able to create an index for each segment. Under the indexing system, a score of 100 is average, anything over 100 means higher than average potential. Table 3 outlines the segment indexes.

The segmentation analysis provided tremendous insight to the marketing department, not only about the current status of the membership but also about the future potential of the individual segments. With more knowledge about which members were profitable, the team was able to develop member-focused strategies geared to

TABLE 2

Segment	# Members	Avg Profit	Avg FUA	Products/Member
1	12 000	$900	$150 000	4.5
	Complex relationship, with multiple products, mortgage holders, with RRSPs, high lending, utilize all channels with high transaction levels.			
2	8000	$600	$51 000	3.5
	High-balance non- RRSP savers, average transaction levels, traditional channel usage (phone, branch, ATM) slightly older, low lending.			
3	13 000	$310	$27 000	2.3
	Older, average transactions, average balances, low lending, ATM and branch transactors.			
4	25 000	$225	$22 000	3.2
	High lending, high transactions, all channels, similar to segment 1 except low mortgage usage, high credit card penetration			
5	15 000	$135	$10 000	2.2
	Savers (RRSP and other), average balances low transactions, limited channels.			
6	7000	$20	$3100	.3
	Younger, savers with lower balances and average transactions.			
7	23 000	$17	$1100	1.1
	Single product accounts, inactive, low transactions, low balances.			

TABLE 3

Segment	Potential Index	High Potential Products
1	125	Mortgage, RRSP, LOC, Credit Card
2	150	Terms, RRSP
3	140	RRSP, Term
4	200	RRSP, Mortgage, Credit Card, Loans
5	100	RRSP, Mortgage, Credit Card
6	55	Term
7	40	Low on most, some Credit Card

either help Riverside Credit Union retain the member or grow the relationship through targeted cross-selling programs. The marketing department used the information to help restructure their department. Frank was convinced that it would help in the transition from being product focused to becoming more member focused.

Questions

1. What observations would you make about the various members and how they contribute to the profitability of the organization?

2. What challenges will Frank have in convincing people at the branches to utilize the new segmentation scheme?

3. What strategies can Riverside Credit Union develop that exploit its new understanding of the membership? In other words, given the different types of behaviour and the different types of relationships the members have with Riverside, what kinds of programs and marketing tactics would you consider for each segment?

4. Which segments would you target for growth, and what products/services would you think about promoting?

5. Which segments would you most want to protect from the inroads of competition? What would you do to help ensure the loyalty of members within this (these) segments?

6. If you were in Frank's job as vice president, marketing in Riverside's head office, how would you share this information with members of the branch sales teams to help them focus on the "right" members?

7. How would you use the information to make pricing decisions for products and service charges?

Source: Jeff Schulz, vice president of marketing at VanCity Credit Union and Peggy Cunningham, Queen's University, wrote this case for *Marketing Management*, January 2000. The case was prepared for use in class discussions and is not intended to illustrate the effective or ineffective handling of a management situation. Some data have been disguised to protect confidentiality. No portion of this case may be reproduced by any means without prior written permission.

B. RALPH THE OPTICIAN

The new glasses that you selected yesterday are ready. Try them on and I will make the final adjustments. Now look at yourself in the mirror—these new glasses help convey your image of successful, good taste.

Maurice, now that I looked after you as my customer, I want to become your client. I need some advice about a threat that my business is facing. If you have some time, we could have a coffee in my office and I will tell you about my dilemma.

I agreed. Ralph poured two cups of freshly brewed Blue Mountain coffee and closed the door so that we would not be disturbed.

Maurice, I have been an optician for almost 30 years and over time, with hard work I have built a successful business and now earn a good income. I take pride in the fact that over the years I was able to successfully adjust to the major changes in my business. For example, there have been technical changes such as the introduction of contact lenses, shatterproof lenses, and graduated bifocals. My staff and I periodically attend seminars and courses so that we are knowledgeable about the latest innovations.

Other kinds of changes have been more difficult for me. Over time major optical firms such as LensCrafters and Sears started to operate in Canada. These chains tend to place great emphasis on heavy promotion and low price. In addition, LensCrafters offers the added convenience that your new lenses will be ready in about an hour.

In fact, the share of the market held by independent opticians such as me is declining as the price-sensitive segment of the market grows. Despite reduced market share, however, my sales are growing because the market is now growing quickly thanks to aging baby boomers. As people age, usually starting in their forties, they tend to need reading glasses or glasses for distance. Even people who wear contact lens often require reading glasses for close work. There is also evidence that as some people age, they are less likely to wear contacts for long periods.

What did I do to protect my business against my large, price-oriented competitors?

First, I upgraded the type of frames that I carry. Instead of carrying a large selection of low-and medium-priced frames by unknown manufacturers, we have upgraded and now place the emphasis on well-known, quality designs such as Fendi, Gucci, Hugo Boss, Alfred Sung, and Givenchy. It is not uncommon for a person to pay $300 to $450 for a new pair of glasses at my store. This is very different from the chains, where I think the average price would probably be $100 to $150 a pair.

Second, my staff and I are very careful to give customers as much time as needed to find the proper frames, to fully answer questions, and to explain any technical differences between the options. We never rush a decision. In fact, many of our customers have been dealing with us for years and if possible we try to greet them by name and acknowledge the fact that we recognize and appreciate their ongoing business. Based on statistics, the average pair of glasses lasts two years. However, some of my customers are fashion-conscious and buy new frames more often.

Third, I implemented a print and radio advertising program. Although my budget is modest compared to the major chains, I make an impact by concentrating my promotion in periodic short bursts when I feature a special item or a sale.

Although all opticians sell products that enhance sight, my product is different in that I not only help clients see better but also look better, and convey the image that he or she wants. A frame makes a statement on your face, and the statement changes from style to style. To support the fashion orientation of my business, I purchased a camera and television device that allows the customer to more objectively see how he or she looks in the frame. In addition, I subscribe to magazines such as *Vogue* and *Elle* to see what frames are being shown to the fashion leaders.

Everybody who sells glasses is basically in competition with everybody else. However, some of us are licensed as opticians and others are optometrists. Opticians specialize in selling glasses; optometrists are permitted to sell glasses but they are also trained to diagnose eye disease and prescribe corrective lenses. Ophthalmologists, on the other hand, are medical doctors who specialize in eye diseases. They prescribe corrective lenses, but most do not sell glasses or contact lenses.

Because I don't prescribe lenses, it is important to be located close to ophthalmologists' offices and to hospitals with eye clinics, so that it is convenient for clients to enter my store after they receive a new vision prescription. As you know, my location is excellent in that I am close to a large number of busy ophthalmologists and two major hospitals.

The aggressive chains sell their products on different variations of price. For example, Price Club charges substantially less than you might expect to pay for contact lenses and bifocals. Their prices on frames also tend to be good value. However, because Price Club does volume business, their customer service is not as good as mine. In addition, their selection of frames is oriented to more popular price points and although the frames tend to be reasonably fashionable, they are designed for the mass market. As a result, they do not sell the same frames that I do. Price Club does not advertise or run promotions. Their promotion is mainly through word-of-mouth advertising and a large membership who appreciate the Price Club philosophy of low mark-up and low or no-frills service.

Another pricing technique used by some competitors is the famous two-for-one sale. Some of these two-for-one sales offer really good value to the shopper. Because of the high mark-up on frames and glasses, the retailer can actually make some money on a true two-for-one sale. However, some two-for-one sales are designed to offer you a deal on part of the purchase, but you must pay full price on the rest. For example, the sale may be two-for-one for the lenses, but you pay full price for the frames (or vice versa). Sometimes, any additional features that you select, such as scratchproof or ultraviolet coating, are charged at full price for both pairs.

Because of the multitude of brand names and styles, it is very difficult for most of us to know what is a fair price for a pair of frames and lenses. Because we lack the expertise, we have to take the seller's word for quality and price. The sale boils down to which seller(s) does the buyer trust.

Maurice, I apologize for being so long-winded to get to my problem. I read in yesterday's newspaper that Price Club, an aggressive discounter of vision products, is planning to open a new outlet about eight kilometres from my store. I need to know what kinds of changes I should make to my operation (I think you call it a marketing mix) so that I will not lose a lot of business to my new competitor.

About three months ago, I participated in an omnibus marketing research study and asked people why they prefer to do business with a specific source of eyewear. This is a sample of the type of responses given (see appendix).

APPENDIX

Respondent Quotations—Omnibus Study

Ralph's

I spend thousands of dollars each season on designer clothes. Why should I risk hurting my appearance by wearing inexpensive glasses or glasses that are not in fashion?

I want distinctive frames. I do not want to see many people wearing the same style of frames.

The first thing that people notice is your face. If I have to wear glasses, they should help to convey a very positive first impression of who I am.

I trust Ralph and his staff. The frames and the lenses that they have recommended have always been excellent.

I like their service, never rushed, always helpful. One thing that I especially like in today's impersonal world, they greet me by name.

A friend told me how satisfied she was with Ralph's selection of frames and his service. She was right. In the last six years, I bought five pairs of glasses from Ralph's.

Price Club

My insurance company allows me to spend up to $100 for a pair of glasses. I try to find a deal so that I do not have to pay anything out of my pocket.

I usually wear contacts. I need an inexpensive pair of glasses for the occasional time when I can't wear my contact lenses.

I am on a tight budget; if I can save money and still get a quality product, I am especially happy.

I have been shopping at Price Club for many years. I trust their pricing. In addition, I like being able to shop for eyewear at the same time I shop for other things.

When I go to another optician, a member of the staff wants to help me select my frames and gives me an opinion of how he or she thinks I look in the frames. I prefer to browse and make up my own mind as to how I look. At Price Club, there is no pressure to buy.

Glasses are glasses.

The author acknowledges the cooperation and assistance of Denise Villeneuve and Greta Auerbach.

C. ROCKY MOUNTAIN HOUSE CO-OP*

Frank Gallagher, general manager of Rocky Mountain House Co-op (RMHC), was sitting in his office reviewing the performance of his organization when Milt Zirk, petroleum manager of the company, hurried into the room. "Frank, I'm afraid I've got some bad news," exclaimed Milt. "The word is out that United Farmers of Alberta (UFA) is planning to open a new petroleum outlet in Rocky Mountain House. The petroleum end of our business has been going fairly well for us over the past couple of years. This could really mess things up! You know they are very aggressive marketers, and because they are a co-op like us, they could really eat into our market share. Frank, I'm worried! We're going to have to make sure we're ready for them. We've got to develop a plan to minimize their impact on our sales and profits."

Rocky Mountain House Co-op

Rocky Mountain House Co-op is a retail outlet located in Rocky Mountain House, Alberta, approximately 80 kilometres west of Red Deer, on Highway 11. Rocky Mountain House is a community of approximately 6000 people with both an agricultural and commercial economic base. The area is characterized by mixed farming, with most farms being relatively small and having at least some livestock. Industry in the area includes general business, trucking, construction, oil exploration, and logging.

The trading area served by RMHC is much larger than Rocky Mountain House itself and contains the following communities: Alder Flats, Alhambra, Caroline, Condor, Leslieville, Nordegg, Rocky Mountain House, and Stauffer. The trading area has an approximate population of 16 000 people and a radius of 50 kilometres, although the trading area on the west extends nearly 100 kilometres to the Rocky Mountains.

RMHC is a co-operative-type business. Co-operatives are like regular businesses except they are owned by their users who purchase shares in the business. Instead of earning "profits," co-operatives earn "savings" that can be returned to members through "patronage dividends." RMHC is owned by 7332 active members. For the most part, these "owners" are people in the trading area who have become members by purchasing shares in the organization. Each share is valued at $1.00 and a minimum of five shares must be purchased to become a member. The main reason for being a member is to share in the savings of the business through patronage dividends. Patronage dividends are based on the amount of business a member does each year and have amounted to about five percent of purchases at RMHC over the past several years. In addition, members have a voice in the affairs of the co-op through their right to elect a board of directors to represent their views.

RMHC is involved in a number of retail businesses that they classify under three divisions: home centre, shopping centre, and petroleum. The home centre consists of building materials, hardware, animal health products, livestock feed, livestock equipment, and twine; the shopping centre consists of food, hardware, clothing and a cafeteria; and the petroleum division consists of bulk fuels, propane, oil/lubes, cardlock, and a gas bar. Despite the fact that Rocky Mountain House is in a significant grain-producing area of the province, RMHC has elected so far not to sell crop supplies. Sales, cost of goods sold, and gross margins for each division for 1995 are shown in Exhibit 1. Exhibit 2 shows the operating statement of RMHC for the same year.

EXHIBIT 1

Product Line Breakdown

	Home Centre	Shopping Centre	Petroleum
Sales	$4 620 000	$11 044 000	$2 550000
Less: Cost of Goods Sold	$3 536 000	$8 418 000	$2 294 000
Gross Margin	$1 084 000	$2 626 000	$256 000
Less: Operating Expenses	$931 000	$2 106 000	$189 000
Contribution	$153 000	$520 000	$67 000

In 1995, RMHC received patronage dividends of $683 000 from Federated Co-operatives Limited in Saskatoon, the large wholesaling co-operative owned by several hundred local co-ops like RMHC across Western Canada. Like most other local co-ops, RMHC used Federated Co-op as their main source of supply for all products they sold. The patronage dividend they received from Federated was based on a percentage of purchases. In the same year, RMHC allocated $614 000 in patronage dividends to local owners. This, together with current savings, left RMHC with retained savings of slightly more than $1 million. This represented funds the organization could use for future expansion.

Petroleum Division

The petroleum division of RMHC has always been a tough business. Margins in the petroleum division are much lower than in other area of the company, largely due to intense competition and the commodity-type products being sold. In the Rocky Mountain House trading area alone there are six major oil companies competing for a total fuel market of approximately 26.9 million litres. Exhibit 3 lists the major petroleum companies with facilities in Rocky Mountain House and their approximate fuel sales.

Most of the 26.9 million litres of petroleum sold in the Rocky Mountain House trading area went to commercial accounts. Commercial accounts purchased 18.3 million litres in 1995 compared to 6.1 million litres to farm accounts and 2.5 million liters to consumers. Although precise market shares were not known, Milt estimated that Co-op and Esso were the major petroleum suppliers in the area, followed by Shell, Petro-Canada, Turbo, and Husky. Exhibit 4 shows approximate market shares for each company by type of account.

RMHC currently sells four product lines in petroleum: bulk fuels, propane, oil/lubes, and gas bar (self-service pumps at the shopping centre). Sales, cost of goods sold, and gross margins for these products in 1995 are shown in Exhibit 5. Exhibit 6 shows the petroleum department expenses for the same year.

EXHIBIT 2

Operating Statement

Sales	$18 214 000
Less: Cost of Goods Sold	$14 248 000
Gross Margin	$3 966 000
Less: Operating Expenses	$3 226 000
Contribution	$740 000
Less: Indirect Interest Expense	($96 000)
Less: General Overhead	$432 000
Savings	$404 000
Patronage Dividends from Federated Co-ops	$683 000
Retained Savings	$1 087 000

EXHIBIT 3

Competitive Petroleum Suppliers

	Estimated Litres
Co-op	5 900 000
Esso	7 500 000
Shell	4 000 000
Petro Canada	3 500 000
Turbo	3 500 000
Husky	2 500 000
Total	26 900 000

	Farm	Commercial	Consumer	Total
Co-op	34%	17%	30%	23%
Esso	31%	27%	27%	28%
Shell	13%	15%	16%	15%
Petro-Canada	6%	17%	4%	13%
Turbo	12%	13%	13%	13%
Husky	4%	11%	10%	9%
	100%	100%	100%	100%

EXHIBIT 4

Approximate Market Shares by Type of Account

	Fuels	Propane	Oil/lubes	Gas Bar	Total
Sales	$2 016 000	$41 000	$126 000	$367 000	$2 550 000
Cost of Goods	$1 829 000	$34 000	$106 000	$325 000	$2 294 000
Gross Margin	$187 000	$7 000	$20 000	$42 000	$256 000

EXHIBIT 5

Financial Summary for Petroleum Products

Depreciation	$5 600
Utilities	$500
Insurance	$4 900
Repairs & Maintenance	$9 000
Taxes & Licences	$4 600
Total Standby Costs	$24 600
Employee Benefits	$18 000
Staff Discounts	$1 600
Training	$1 800
Salaries & Wages	$99 000
Uniforms	$1 500
Total Staff Costs	$121 900
Advertising & Promotion	$5 600
Delivery Trucks	$29 000
Other Expenses	$7 900
Total Operating Costs	$189 000
Contribution	$67 000

EXHIBIT 6

Petroleum Department Expenses

Like most petroleum suppliers in the area, RMHC sells five types of petroleum products: premium gasoline, regular gasoline, clear diesel, marked gasoline, and marked diesel. Exhibit 7 shows 1995 sales of the five products in each of the major markets while Exhibit 8 shows current pricing for each product in each major market. Marked gasoline and marked diesel is dyed purple to distinguish it from clear product. This is done to identify the product as tax-exempt because it is used for off-road purposes and not subject to normal fuel taxes. At the moment, this means marked fuels sell for approximately $0.09 per litre less than clear fuels that are intended for on-road use and subject to a road tax. The prices established by RMHC are very similar to other petroleum suppliers in the area. Only Turbo and Husky sell petroleum at lower prices than other companies in the area and, in both cases, the differences are very small.

Margins on petroleum products do not vary by type of product, but do vary by type of customer. Current margins in the farm market are $0.049 per litre; in the commercial market are $0.034 per litre; and in the consumer market are $0.063 per litre.

In the petroleum end of the business, RMHC deals with three main types of customers: farms accounts, commercial accounts, and consumers.

At the moment, RMHC has about 350 farm accounts, which purchase 2 086 000 million litres of fuel. Although the average farm account purchases about 6000 litres of fuel each year, some purchase much larger amounts and many purchase much smaller amounts. The largest RMHC farm account purchases nearly 20 000 litres of fuel a year. Farms in the RMHC trading area are somewhat smaller than typical Alberta farms. A very high proportion of these farms have livestock as their principal operation.

Commercial accounts represent the major proportion of RMHC petroleum business. At the moment, RMHC has 175 commercial accounts, which together purchase approximately 3 113 000 litres of fuel and range in size from 5000 litres per year to as much as 300 000 litres per year. The average commercial account buys 18 000 litres. Exhibit 9 provides a breakdown of commercial accounts into various types of businesses.

EXHIBIT 7		Farm	Commercial	Consumer	Total
Petroleum Sales by Market	Premium Gasoline			16 500	16 500
	Regular Gasoline	200 000	1 173 000	666 500	2 039 500
	Clear Diesel		1 154 000	63 000	1 217 000
	Marked Gasoline	949 000	50 000		999 000
	Marked Diesel	937 000	736 000		1 673 000
	Total	2 086 000	3 113 000	746 000	5 945 000

EXHIBIT 8		Farm	Commercial	Consumer
Petroleum Prices by Market	Premium Gasoline			$0.540
	Regular Gasoline	$0.495	$0.480	$0.500
	Clear Diesel		$0.390	$0.420
	Marked Gasoline	$0.403	$0.390	
	Marked Diesel	$0..300	$0.300	

EXHIBIT 9

Type of Account	Percent
General Business	29%
Loggers	11%
Truckers	18%
Construction	17%
Oil Company Contractors	22%
Institutional	3%

The final category of customer is individual consumers, which currently purchase 746 000 litres of fuel. About 80 percent of consumer sales are through the gas bar at the shopping centre and the remaining 20 percent through the cardlock system described opposite.

Although all three type of accounts (farm, commercial, and consumer) can use the cardlock system, it is particularly popular among commercial accounts. The cardlock system allows approved buyers 24-hour access to bulk fuels at the main RMHC petroleum outlet. To obtain fuel, the buyer inserts a card into a metering device, which then pumps the requested amount of a certain type of fuel into the user's tank. The user's name and the amount of the purchase are recorded electronically for future billing. Use of this system is growing very rapidly among farm and commercial accounts because of convenience and cost savings. The price of fuel purchased through the cardlock is generally $0.008 per litre less than bulk delivery. Although RMHC has a good, very clean cardlock operation, there are two problems that make it less than ideal. One problem is the fact that currently it does not sell marked gasoline and does not have the capability of adding this product into the existing system. This undoubtedly prevents some potential customers from using the RMHC cardlock. Another issue with the cardlock is that access to the facility is slightly more difficult than some customers would like.

At the moment, the marketing program used by RMHC is fairly similar to that used by other petroleum suppliers in the area. In 1995, less than $6000 per year was being spent on advertising petroleum products. Most of this was for ads place in local newspapers highlighting special deals on oils and lubricants (see Appendix A for a sample ad). In addition to advertising, a substantial amount of selling is done by Milt on the farm, at the offices of commercial accounts and on the phone. Milt maintains contact at least four times a year with most customers, and more often with larger customers. Some very large customers are contacted on a weekly basis. In addition, he spends a considerable amount of time calling on prospective customers. Milt's philosophy is that regular contact with prospects will put him in contention for their business if there is ever a reason for a customer to switch. History shows this to be a good strategy as RMHC has picked up a number of new customers each year when they became dissatisfied with their present supplier. Customer loyalty in petroleum, however, is very high. Milt figures that less than 10 percent of customers change suppliers each year. Milt also follows the practice of driving the delivery truck himself on occasion so he can have more contact with customers.

Frank and Milt have long believed that the success of RMHC in the petroleum business was due to a number of factors:

■ The company provides excellent service. All RMHC employees are top-notch individuals committed to providing good service. In addition, the company prides itself on clean, modern facilities and prompt attention to detail. Any customer who needs fuel can expect to receive it the same day an order is placed. RMHC currently spends more than its competitors on staff training.

■ Co-op products are quality products produced under strict quality-control measures.

- Patronage refunds provide customers with "cash back" at the end of the year based on their volume of business. For many customers this is a real incentive to do business with a co-op.

- The company has an excellent highway location in Rocky Mountain House. This provides excellent visibility in the community.

- RMHC offers a wide range of products, making "one-stop shopping" possible for customers.

United Farmers of Alberta

United Farmers of Alberta (UFA), like RMHC, is a member-owned co-operative. UFA has approximately 30 outlets in Alberta in which they sell petroleum and a complete line of farm supplies. In addition, they operate approximately 90 outlets in which only petroleum products are sold through bulk plants, cardlocks, and gas bars. UFA has shown considerable growth in recent years through very aggressive marketing. This growth has come both from an increase in the number of retail distribution points and an increase in the volume sold through existing outlets.

Recently, UFA was granted a development permit to build a farm-supply facility in Rocky Mountain House. The permit allows UFA to construct a facility that contains a 800-square metre building, bulk petroleum plant, gas bar, cardlock, and a farm-supply distribution facility. It is expected that UFA will sell a complete line of both crop and livestock farm supplies through this facility. It is also expected that UFA will construct a cardlock facility that is larger than any other in the area and will sell a compete line of fuels.

The entry of UFA into this market has the potential of causing significant problems for RMHC for a number of reasons:

- UFA is a co-op like RMHC and therefore very similar in structure and philosophy. As a result, they might be considered a good alternative for many current RMHC customers.

- The fact that they are building a complete farm-supply outlet might be attractive to many current RMHC customers who would like to purchase crop supplies where they buy petroleum.

- UFA's facility will be much newer than that of RMHC. This is of particular concern for the cardlock.

- UFA currently has a number of commercial accounts on the fringes of the RMHC trading area. This gives them a foothold into the market.

- UFA has demonstrated a willingness in similar situations to enter new markets in a very aggressive manner. Often this entails aggressive pricing, introductory advertising in local media, a direct mail campaign targeted to larger potential customers, and special introductory deals.

- UFA traditionally supports its marketing efforts with a high level of excellent service. This includes the availability of skilled technical experts who can answer questions and help customers make informed buying decisions, attention to detail in all aspects of the business, and frequent sales calls (either by phone or in person) with key customers.

Decision

Although initially Frank was not overly concerned about the situation, as he considered it in more detail, he began to worry about the potential effects it might have. RMHC had worked hard over the last 10 years to build a strong customer base and some of this investment in time and marketing dollars appeared to be at risk. To determine the seriousness of the situation and to develop some plans to counteract it, Frank called a meeting with Milt for early next week.

The meeting began by Frank raising the issue of what impacts the entry of UFA might have on RMHC. After some discussion, they agreed that if RMHC did nothing to soften the impact, it was conceivable they could lose a significant portion of both their farm and commercial business, especially the larger accounts that were more price sensitive. Although it was hard to come up with specific numbers, they felt that up to a quarter of their present volume might be at risk. What was even more alarming was the fact that RMHC had three very large commercial customers who each purchased 300 000 litres of fuel a year. Losing these people alone would result in a very large sales decline. Although these large commercial accounts had been with RMHC for a number of years, and Milt provided a high level of personal service through almost weekly contact, it was conceivable they could switch allegiance if they perceived greater value in another supplier.

Given the seriousness of the situation, they then began to discuss alternative courses of action they might pursue to counteract the problem. A number of possibilities were identified and briefly discussed.

1. The first idea that came to mind was to pursue a pre-emptive pricing strategy. Under this strategy, RMHC would begin immediately cutting prices and margins to existing customers. The idea behind this strategy, of course, was to solidify business relationships with customers to the point that it would make it very difficult for UFA to woo customers away from RMHC.

2. A second strategy they discussed was to match UFA's promotional programs dollar for dollar and engage in a substantial amount of local advertising and direct marketing themselves. Although neither Frank nor Milt had a precise idea of what UFA would spend entering the Rocky Mountain House market, they felt $30 000 was not an unrealistic amount. They considered stressing two main points in the promotion: their excellent staff and their outstanding record of providing patronage dividends. Frank envisioned ads and direct mail pieces with picture and human interest stories about the staff as well as charts showing the steady growth in patronage dividends over the past few years.

3. Another idea they considered was to develop a program in which the rate of patronage dividends would vary by department. Under such a scheme it would be possible for the petroleum division, for example, to announce a patronage dividend of eight percent, where some other division's dividend might decline to three percent. They felt this might be particularly effective in the short run to meet a competitive challenge.

4. Yet another alternative they were considering was to get into the fertilizer and ag-chemical business. On the assumption that some RMHC customers might be attracted to UFA because they had a complete line of crop and livestock supplies, this might provide existing customers with enough reason to stay with RMHC. It would, however, be a major investment for RMHC in a business they knew little about. Frank estimated it would require an investment of approximately $600 000 in facilities and working capital. In addition, two new full-time people would be required to run the business and work with farm customers. An additional five seasonal employees would be needed for a couple of months each year to help during peak sales seasons. Total additional labour costs would amount to approximately $150 000 plus another $50 000 in administrative costs. Margins on fertilizer were typically in the 15 to 20 percent range on product that sold for an average price of $250 per ton. Although an average farmer in the Rocky Mountain House trading area currently used only 25 to 30 tons of fertilizer a year, use appeared to be growing fairly rapidly as more farmers started using fertilizer and those already using fertilizer were increasing application rates. Ag chemicals were not widely used in the Rocky Mountain House trading area, so this would be considered a break-even business that simply provided a complementary service to farmers who purchased fertilizer. Presently there are three fertilizer suppliers serving the 1200 farmers in the Rocky Mountain House trading area. One of these suppliers is a large independent farm supply outlet specializing in crop inputs while the other two are smaller operations, one of which is the local Esso dealer.

5. The final alternative Frank identified was to move up construction of a new bulk petroleum facility. The current facility was old and starting to show its age. Of particular concern was the fact that the cardlock system had reached its capacity and could not add a tank and pumping system for marked gasoline. Frank knew that the new UFA facility would be "state of the art" and have ample capacity for the present and for future expansion. Although Frank hoped to get another five years out of the present facility, he felt one option was to invest immediately in new facilities so they would be ready at least by the time the UFA facility was built. A new facility that would include a new bulk plant, an expanded sales area and a new and expanded cardlock would cost $300 000 to construct.

Frank and Milt concluded the meeting wondering what to do. They agreed to consider the options more fully and do some real thinking about the consequences of each option and then meet again in a week to make a decision.

D. RESTAURANT LE PETIT PRINCE

It was a very hot, sunny Tuesday July afternoon. Ginette and I were sitting at a table on the terrace of Restaurant Le Petit Prince, situated in the village of Morin-Heights in the lower Laurentians.

"Maurice, I wanted to meet with you to see if you have some advice for us. Our restaurant is successful and we refuse reservations on many Saturday evenings, especially during the peak seasons, because we are fully booked. However, during the rest of the week, and in the off seasons we run way below capacity. In fact, we found that we were better off closing on Mondays and Tuesdays.

"Before we continue, may I offer you something to drink? Perhaps a glass of wine, a beer or a cup of coffee?"

"Thank you. I wouldn't mind a coffee with milk."

"You have been a patron at this restaurant for a long time Maurice, but there is some background information that you may not know that may help you to better understand the restaurant's present situation.

"First, I should tell you that although I work full time at the restaurant, and I enjoy the work and I especially like talking to our patrons, I do not have a restaurant background. My husband, Gaétan, is the one who is knowledgeable about restaurants and worked hard to realize his dream to own his own restaurant that was known for its service, quality of food, and fair prices.

"As a summer job, Gaétan worked in the restaurant at the Hotel Chateau Montebello, a well-known CP Hotel located between Montreal and Ottawa. He liked his work, was good at it, and his capabilities were quickly recognized by hotel management. Over a period of time, he worked himself up from bus boy to maitre d'. He then spent four years as general manager of the restaurant of the Chateau Champlain, a prestigious CP Hotel in Montreal.

"As I mentioned earlier, Gaétan had a dream that he wanted to become a reality. In 1992, we purchased Beatles, a restaurant located at this site. Beatles was a chicken-and-ribs-type restaurant, serving $7.95 meals, and did a significant happy-hour business. When we bought Beatles, the owners were serving 80 to 100 meals per week, with most of the business being done on weekends.

"Beatles was the code name for the previous owner's battalion in World War II. It was not a good name for a fine French restaurant, however, so we decided to run a competition for a new, more suitable name. We put up notices and gave customers ballots to complete. We chose this approach because it indicated to our clientele that a new name was coming, and not another change in management, and that we valued their input. In fact, we received 200 to 300 different suggestions. We also used the transition period to introduce the French-cuisine menu that we wanted to offer. At the end of the first year, we announced the rebirth of the restaurant as Restaurant Le Petit Prince. Beatles, the noisy bar restaurant, was history.

"We work very hard to develop a good rapport with our guests. We make it a policy to remember every regular's name. We find the time at some point in the evening to talk to our guests, even if it is for just a minute or two. We have a nice relationship with our clientele."

"Yes," I interrupted, "I was very pleased when you not only remembered my name, but where I live, and how long ago it was since the last time we ate at Le Petit Prince.

"My wife and I did go to Beatles once before you purchased the restaurant and, of course we have become regulars at Le Petit Prince. We know how different Petit Prince is from Beatles. Ginette, are most of your guests from the Morin-Heights area?"

"It is interesting that you asked that question. When we took over Beatles, it was a local restaurant; more than 80 percent of its customers came from Morin-Heights. Now the distribution of our guests is very different.

"In fact, it is not uncommon for people to drive about an hour from Montreal to dine at Le Petit Prince on a Saturday evening.

"Not only do our guests come from a wider area, but they are also older than the previous Beatles customer and they spend considerably more—the average bill runs about $35 per person, excluding taxes and gratuities.

	Percent of Total	Travel Time (minutes)
Morin-Heights	10	5-10
Saint-Adolphe-d'Howard	20	10-15
Saint-Sauveur	20	10-15
Lachute	20	25-30
Saint-Agathe-des-Monts	10	30-35
Others	20	———

In a typical resort area there are pronounced fluctuations in demand for recreation services. Weekends and holidays are much busier than weekdays. We also have the major summer and winter seasons. The spring is quiet and, except for a few weekends when the foliage is at its peak, the fall is not busy.

We tend to draw most of our clientele from weekenders (people who rent for a season or who own property in the area) and full-time residents. Although we get a few tourists, they do not generate a great deal of revenue. Since we make a point of getting to know our regulars by name, and occasional visitors by face, we have noticed that we tend to have different clientele during the summer and winter seasons.

After seven years of hard work, we are pleased that on average we now serve a little more than 200 meals per week."

"Excuse me for interrupting," I said, Abut what is the capacity of the restaurant?"

"As you know, we have two dining rooms. Downstairs we can seat about 50 people and the upstairs room accommodates 40 guests. We can serve approximately 90 guests at a time, based on one seating per evening. Most of our guests reserve for about 7:00 to 7:30 in the evening. Therefore, we turn our tables over only once during the evening. We prefer that they enjoy their evening with us. Some restaurants give their guests a choice of two seating times. As a result, if there is demand, they can turn their tables twice each evening. But Gaétan and I do not want to rush our guests.

As I said a few minutes ago, many Saturday evenings, especially during the ski season or the summer vacation period, we sell out. In December, January, and February, we tend to average about 250 meals per week, while in the slow season of March, April, and May, we drop to 150 customers per week.

If we can build our non-peak business, instead of just earning a living, we would have a financially successful operation."

After Ginette refilled my coffee cup, I asked her how she and Gaétan promoted Le Petit Prince—what they have done and what they are contemplating doing to increase their off-peak business?

"Maurice, let me answer your questions in the order that you asked them.

First, when we took over the restaurant, we placed advertisements in the local newspapers. When people came to Le Petit Prince, we asked them how they heard about us. Nobody mentioned the ads. Almost everyone said that the restaurant was recommended to them by people who have been here. Therefore we stopped placing ads and yet our business continues to grow. The only promotion, of a sort, that we do is to donate $25 gift certificates to worthwhile local charities and public-service organizations."

"The size of your two dining rooms are suitable for meetings and parties. Have you approached these organizations to hold their meetings/events at your restaurant during the week?"

"No, we have not. The only promotion for meetings and parties appears on the back of our business cards. It says that we are available Monday and Tuesdays to host private parties. This is only partially correct. Depending on the season, and the number of people invited, we would consider hosting a private party any evening except Saturday. Over the last year we had three or four wedding parties and a similar number of other private parties at Le Petit Prince.

We also tried joint promotions with the ski hills—Ski Saint-Sauveur and Ski Morin-Heights. On weeknights, if people brought in their ski passes from one of these hills, they would receive a 10 percent reduction on their food bill. But this promotion increased our already-low weekday volume by only five percent. There are probably two key reasons for this lack of success: first, the weekday business at the ski hills, as is ours, is much lower than the weekend levels. Second, skiing for most families, is a very expensive activity and does not leave a lot of money in the family budget for a nice dinner, especially if you are also paying for a hotel room.

We looked at becoming associated with one or more of the popular coupon books. Typically with this concept, the client orders two main courses and receives the least expensive one free. If you order a table d'hote meal (a complete meal), a 25 percent discount is offered on up to four meals ordered at one time. This concept is very popular and generates business, including some first-time customers. However, these coupons are valid every evening, and we do not want to generate more Saturday volume, especially at discount prices.

For a variety of reasons, including maintaining the image and reputation that we have worked hard to build, we eliminated ideas such as ladies' nights or men's evenings, and happy hours."

"Does that mean that you are not doing anything to build your off-peak sales?" I asked.

"No, we have tried two different approaches that involve our product and we are thinking of trying a third strategy and we are willing to consider other options..

About two years ago, we introduced an all-you-can-eat leg-of-lamb special for $16.95 plus taxes. We told our regular clientele about it by printing a small flyer that was placed on the tables when we presented the bills. After a slow start, this special, which is only offered on Thursdays, started to generate increased sales. It has now become profitable to open on Thursday evenings. In fact, until recently, more than 75 percent of the Thursday meals served were the lamb special. Now, over time, as the volume continues to grow, there has been a shift to less than 25 percent of the guests order the lamb and the rest of the business comes from our regular-priced meals and the alcohol that is ordered.

The second promotion failed despite the fact that it made perfect sense to us. A church is located across the street from our restaurant and every Sunday, on average, 150 worshipers leave the church and pass by our restaurant. As a result, we decided to open for Sunday lunch. We averaged five to eight meals for Sunday lunch, which did not even cover labour costs, let alone food costs. At the end of the season, we dropped the idea of Sunday lunch."

"You know," I said, "Most of the medium- and higher-priced restaurants in Saint-Sauveur do not open for lunch. These restaurants are considered by their clientele as an evening's entertainment. During the day, there is too much competition for one's time in terms of leisure activities, such as skiing, water sports, or other outdoor activities. Although there may be many people in the area on the weekends, lunch is usually a matter of convenience, not a major activity.

Ginette, I apologize for interrupting you. What was the new strategy that you were thinking of implementing?"

"Maurice, although we have concentrated on building off-peak business, we are open to ideas to shift the excess Saturday evening business to other evenings, probably Friday or Sunday. For example, a new strategy under consideration is the expansion of our Thursday leg-of-lamb special. On Sunday evenings, we are contemplating offering a roast beef special for $18.95. This should attract some of the weekenders before they head home to the city.

It was suggested by someone that we raise our prices by $2.00 a meal and offer more specials on the other evenings. This might encourage price-sensitive people to shift from Saturday to the lower-cost evenings. However, I am uncertain as to whether this would work or not and whether there is a danger of pricing my restaurant out of the market for the excellent Saturday evening business that we now have.

Another suggestion was to provide our regular Saturday evening clients with a coupon, not valid on Saturday evenings, for 15 percent off their next visit. However, I am concerned about offering discount coupons because they reduce our mark-up. In the restaurant business the cost of food is usually 28 to 32 percent. The more expensive the restaurant, the lower the percentage cost of food. At Le Petit Prince, we work on a food and alcohol cost of 30 percent. That leaves 70 percent to cover all other costs and to produce a profit. Our overhead costs, which include salaries, business and property taxes, heat, repairs, and depreciation are $236 000 per year, so we can't afford to make any price errors.

In addition, when I discussed coupons with several other restaurant owners, they told me that, based on their experiences, about 20 percent of my regular clients would use a coupon. And I would get their business at full mark-up if I didn't offer the discount coupon. If we cut prices by 15 percent, it comes out of our mark-up. Depending on how much additional volume we do, it may or may not pay to offer the discount.

A third suggestion was to offer early-bird specials, say for arrival before 6:00 p.m. This will allow us to offer a second sitting at about 8:30 p.m. This concept is very popular in the United States and is also used by some restaurants in St. Sauveur.

Maurice, do you have any suggestions on how we might manage the demand so that we do not have to turn away business on Saturday, while we run significantly below capacity on other evenings?"

Appendix A

Morin Heights, a small community in the Laurentian foothills, is located about 70 kilometres from Montreal. If traffic is not congested, it takes about 60 minutes from the beginning of the Laurentian autoroute in Montreal to Morin Heights.

However, the exit of the autoroute for Morin Heights is at St. Sauveur, a major resort centre; which has many motels, hotels, and bed and breakfasts, and three major ski hills. A check of the yellow pages telephone book identified 57 restaurants in Saint-Sauveur, ranging from low-priced fast food to expensive gourmet restaurants. Included in the mix are an assortment of ethnic restaurants, steak houses, several French-cuisine restaurants, and a few bring-your-own-wine restaurants (which are unique to Quebec).

In addition to people who either regularly or occasionally weekend in Saint-Sauveur, many people drive up to spend the day or just the evening.

Morin Heights is very different. Although it does have a good ski hill, there are a few bed and breakfasts but no major hotels or motels and the area does not attract many day tourists. There are nine restaurants in Morin Heights, none of which competes in price and type of food with Le Petit Prince. However, six to eight minutes away by car people have access to the 57 restaurants of Saint-Sauveur.

Appendix B

Selected comments from the Guest Book

- "A real find—excellent service, good food at a fair price."
- "It is great to find a restaurant that does not rush you through your meal so that another group of people can be served that evening."
- "Unless I reserve early in the week for Saturday evening, I often find it difficult to get a reservation."
- "Saturday evening is our usual main night out during the week. This time, on an impulse, we came to Petit Prince without reservations on a Friday. It is a great way to separate us from the stresses of the city so that we are more fully able to relax during the weekend."
- "It was well worth the hour drive in each direction to spend a Saturday evening at Le Petit Prince."
- "Your leg of lamb special is great. I order it almost every time. My wife usually orders a regular table d'hote—we are both happy."
- "My husband and I prefer to frequent Le Petit Prince on either a Friday or Sunday evening. The restaurant is less crowded."
- "My mouth waters for the turnip-maple syrup soup and the chicken supreme with apricot sauce, and the service is superb and never rushed."

E. ASSINIBOINE CREDIT UNION'S 1999 MORTGAGE CAMPAIGN

Carolyn Rogers, vice president of sales, sat at her desk wondering what had gone wrong. It was time to think about the 1999 annual Residential Mortgage Campaign and Carolyn didn't want a repeat of last year's results. The mortgage market had always been relatively competitive but in recent years the competition seemed to intensify. All financial institutions, including credit unions, had identified residential mortgages as a core piece of business. They were viewed as the key to an overall financial relationship with a consumer—if you have someone's mortgage, your chances of getting the rest of their business improved as well. This thinking led to aggressive price discounting and marketing efforts on the part of all competitors.

Assiniboine Credit Union thus did its share of aggressive price discounting and flashy advertising as part of the 1998 Mortgage Campaign. They placed ads in newspapers that read, "Losing interest in renting? You can get up to $2500 cash back on your new mortgage," and their Web site asked, "Need more room? Up to 1.25% off your new mortgage!" They placed inserts in members' statements and placed ads on buses. Examples of this material can be found in Appendix A.

During that campaign, and in recent months, branches were applying an average rate discount of 0.75 percent. Carolyn shook her head as she reviewed the figures outlining the results. While the strategy had resulted in significant growth, the profitability of Assiniboine's mortgage portfolio had not kept pace. In fact, after some more detailed analysis, Carolyn discovered that the overall profitability had declined by almost four percent even though the size of the portfolio had increased by five percent. Something had to change for the new campaign!

Background

Assiniboine Credit Union was founded in 1943 with just over $100 in assets as a credit union designed to serve employees of Winnipeg Electric Company. Today, the Assiniboine Credit Union has eight branches and over 42 000 members. It also has a business loan centre, community loan centre, dealer finance department, and its own financial planning and investment arm, Assiniboine Financial Group. It has $500 million in assets under management. Despite the growth it has experienced during its 56-year history, Assinboine still sticks to core principles: "offering banking the way it should be...strong, reliable and member-driven." Assiniboine doesn't measure success by size alone. Guided by principles of social justice, it takes what its board of directors calls a "values-added" approach to doing business. This approach is centred on the belief that a financial institution has an obligation to give back to the community from which it profits. Like the banks with which it competes, the credit union offers a full range of financial products and services, but it also prides itself on following policies that are fair and just and that contribute to building strong, self-reliant communities.

Changing Times

In recent years, credit unions in general, and Assiniboine Credit Union in particular, had undergone significant shifts in their thinking about how they should be run. Recently, there had been a move to give branch managers more authority to make pricing decisions. However, Carolyn was beginning to wonder if they should have developed some more definite policies about responsibility for profitability at the same time.

Carolyn had tried talking to the managers at the various branches. But they were quick to defend their aggressive pricing. They indicated that the discounts were standard in the marketplace and noted that, in most cases, they were only matching what the competition was offering. Carolyn, always the cynic, conducted her own survey of the competition to test this theory. She found that while it was true about discounts being offered, the competition went one step further. They almost always tied the price discounts to an analysis of the consumer's overall financial relationship with the institution. Some discounts were only given on the condition that the mortgagee also brought additional business to the bank or credit union. While Carolyn's branch managers assured her this was the case at all Assiniboine branches, Carolyn had her doubts that this was taking place.

Next Steps

Sitting at her desk, Carolyn began reading some material on relationship pricing. She thought her competitors seemed to have the key to price discounting. Discounts should only be given to customers with whom the institution had a strong relationship that it wanted to retain or to those people who offered a lot of future profit potential as their business with the branch grew. Carolyn was increasingly convinced that this would be the key to her profitability dilemma. Rather than just offering customers a discount, she also wondered whether they might like a new feature. Perhaps some members would like a cash-back bonus instead of a rate discount, or in combination with a rate discount. Carolyn hoped that many members would choose this option because it was a cheaper feature for the credit union to offer than the rate discount.

When designing the 1999 Mortgage Campaign, Carolyn wanted to keep it simple and she didn't think her external communications would have to be that different from the advertising she had used previously. The real challenge, she believed, would be to get the branch managers on side. Requiring them to link discounts to the member's overall relationship or to new business and then track that business would be new for most managers. She was sure the idea would meet with some resistance. While account managers within the branches were quick to discount a mortgage just to get the business, Carolyn believed that often they didn't analyze whether that decision was a profitable one. Moreover, the idea of actually letting a mortgage go to the competition if analysis showed it might not be profitable would also be new and counterintuitive concept for many people on the sales team.

Carolyn had to stop thinking about this and get moving putting the new campaign together. Where should she start was the question of the day. Grabbing her third cup of coffee of the morning, she knew she had to make a decision now.

Questions

1. Should Carolyn concentrate on the external advertising and promotional campaign or should she focus on internal communications? Why?

2. How can Carolyn help branch managers and account managers better understand the concept of relationship pricing?

3. What tools would you use to communicate with branch managers?

Source: Carolyn Rogers, vice president of sales, Assiniboine Credit Union. and Peggy Cunningham, Queen's University wrote this case for *Marketing Management*, January 2000. The case was prepared for use in class discussions and is not intended to illustrate the effective or ineffective handling of a management situation. Some data have been disguised to protect confidentiality. No portion of this case may be reproduced by any means without prior permission.

APPENDIX

EXHIBIT 1

Website

EXHIBIT 2

Bus Ad

You can **Get** up to
$2500
cash back

or 1.25% off your
new mortgage rate!

ASSINIBOINE
CREDIT UNION

EXHIBIT 3

Statement Insert

Need
more
room?

You can **Get** up to
$2500
cash back
on your new mortgage!

Or get up to 1.25% off your interest rate!
Increase your buying power even more with
a pre-approved mortgage that's guaranteed
for 90 days! Ask us for details.

ASSINIBOINE
CREDIT UNION

Banking the way it should be.

EXHIBIT 4

Print Ad

Need
more
room?

You can **Get** up to
$2500
cash back on your new mortgage!

Or get up to 1.25% off your interest rate! Increase
your buying power even more with a pre-approved mortgage!
Call your nearest branch for details.

ASSINIBOINE
CREDIT UNION

Banking the way it should be.

F. DENORMALIZATION OF TOBACCO IN CANADA[1]

Introduction
In Canada each year there are more than 40 000 smoking-related deaths. According to the 1996 census, approximately 23 percent of Canadian adults smoke. Health Canada, a department of the Canadian federal government, has been charged with the responsibility of reducing the smoking rate in Canada, in order to reduce the illness and premature death associated with smoking. In early 1999, the Minister of Health promised to allocate $50 million over the next five years to develop a tobacco denormalization program to tackle this problem.

Background
Health Canada has sponsored several anti-smoking programs in the past. However, these social marketing programs have generally been hampered by relatively low levels of funding, never exceeding $2 million per year. Given the billions of dollars raised each year in Canada through tobacco taxes, this level of funding for anti-tobacco programs is extremely small. However, tobacco tax revenues go into the federal and provincial governments' general revenue, and there is no mechanism for earmarking or allocating part of these funds for tobacco prevention. Some argue that these funds are needed to pay for the additional health care costs that smokers cost the Canadian health care system.

Because Health Canada has not had much money for running these social marketing campaigns, it has had to make tough decisions in the past about which market segment to target. Traditionally, the youth segment was targeted. One rationale for this choice of target group was that a small amount of money would have a bigger impact against this fairly narrow target group. It also seemed easier and far more effective to try to prevent young people from starting to smoke, whereas it would be extremely difficult to convince older smokers to quit once they were already addicted to nicotine.

Campaign Themes
In the past, Health Canada has held the belief that fear appeals don't work, particularly for a teenage target market. Therefore, instead of trying to scare teens into not smoking, Health Canada's campaigns have focused on encouraging positive lifestyles. For example, one campaign that ran from 1978–84 used the slogan, "A broken cigarette is a little freedom gained," and featured scenarios with older and younger brothers and sisters enjoying fresh air and outdoor activities in pristine surroundings. Another campaign running from 1985–90 used the slogan, "Break free—for a new generation of non-smokers," and attempted to make non-smoking seem "cool" by linking it with rock-video-style commercials featuring Canadian pop groups. Both campaigns encouraged youth to adopt positive lifestyles and avoid the smoking habit.

Attacking Tobacco Marketing Through Legislation
Given that Health Canada has had so little money to allocate to smoking prevention campaigns in the past, one solution has been to use legislation to reduce smoking incidence. Legislation has been used to attack the tobacco industry's ability to market their product, by attacking their 4 Ps (product, price, place, and promotion). The following chart illustrates the types of legislation that currently exist, as well as some of the other types of legislation that could potentially be enacted in the future.

Denormalization of Tobacco
Tougher legislation and renewed anti-smoking social marketing campaign efforts are two key parts to a successful tobacco denormalization campaign. Recently several U.S. states, particularly California, Florida, and Massachusetts, have run high-profile anti-tobacco campaigns that have had a significant impact on reducing smoking incidence. Some of these campaigns have been funded out of money gained through taking tobacco companies to court to regain health care costs expended on smokers. A major settlement between the tobacco companies and the attorneys general of all 50 U.S.

[1] This case was prepared by Anne M. Lavack, Ph.D., Associate Professor, University of Winnipeg. The case is intended to be used for purposes of discussion and learning, and is not intended to illustrate either a "right" or "wrong" solution.

Type of Marketing Strategy being limited	Existing Legislation	Ideas for Possible Future Legislation
Legislation governing Environmental-Tobacco Smoke (ETS)—"Place"	Limit where smoking may take place: ■ workplaces ■ public indoor spaces ■ restaurants ■ queues (line-ups)	Limit where smoking may take place: ■ bars ■ public outdoor spaces ■ areas where children are present (e.g., cars)
Marketing Legislation—"Place"	■ licensing of tobacco sellers	■ limit number of outlets selling tobacco ■ limit tobacco sales to special outlets such as liquor stores
Marketing Legislation—"Product"	■ warning labels on 25% of the package ■ list tar and nicotine content	■ increase size of warning labels to 50% of package ■ add graphics to warning labels (e.g., skull & crossbones) ■ plain (white) label packaging for all brands ■ list all ingredients on the package ■ list all smoke by-products on the package ■ impose maximum tar and nicotine limits
Marketing Legislation—"Promotion"	■ limit tobacco advertising to adult magazines and newspapers only ■ limit tobacco sponsorship to on-site promotion only ■ limit point-of-purchase advertising (regulate size of signs, etc.)	■ eliminate tobacco advertising ■ eliminate tobacco sponsorship ■ eliminate point-of-purchase advertising
Legislation to Increase Taxes—"Price"	■ increase tobacco taxes to make tobacco less affordable, thereby reducing consumption (but in line with U.S. prices so that it doesn't provoke smuggling)	■ increase tobacco taxes to make tobacco even less affordable, thereby reducing consumption even more (but there is a risk of provoking smuggling if prices go too high)

states in 1999 means that each U.S. state will have a 25-year stream of income as a result of having sued the major tobacco companies. Many U.S. states are now using these funds to pay for anti-tobacco campaigns. Some states, such as Massachusetts, are actually spending as much as $5 per citizen annually on their new anti-tobacco campaigns.

Problem

The Canadian government would like to get involved in running a high-profile tobacco denormalization campaign to help reduce the incidence of smoking in Canada. As a consultant to the Ministry of Health, what recommendations would you have for such a campaign, particularly regarding:

1. the amount of money to spend

2. what target groups the campaign should be directed at

3. what types of messages to feature

4. what issues to focus on

5. what times of year to run the campaign.

As well, what recommendations would you have regarding:

6. types of new legislation regarding tobacco advertising, marketing, or sponsorship

7. types of new legislation regarding smoking restrictions.

G. KINGSTON SYMPHONY ASSOCIATION

As Katherine Carleton sifted through the overflowing files in the crowded Brock Street office, she sighed in frustration. As general manager for the Kingston Symphony Association (KSA) for the past 18 months, she was only just starting to acknowledge to herself the contradictions of KSA's situation. On one hand, the rising costs of putting on the various programs of the Symphony, plus cutbacks from government, were hindering the success and future growth of the Symphony. On the positive side, community support for the association could not be ignored. Moreover, musicians involved with the KSA were genuinely committed to the organization's success, even to the point of volunteering their services. Clearly, there was tremendous potential for success; just as clearly, the four people who had preceded her in the general manager's job in the past seven years, had achieved only mixed results. Katherine knew that there must be a way to overcome the year-to-year conflict between rising costs and maintaining the Symphony's role as a high-quality cultural organization in the community.

History of Kingston Symphony Association

The founder of the Queen's music department, composer Graham George, established the Kingston Symphony Association in 1952. It has since grown to include the Kingston Symphony, Kingston Choral Society (established in 1953), Kingston Symphony Chamber Players, Kingston Youth Orchestra (established in 1968), Kingston Junior Strings, the Kingston Community Strings, and KSA Volunteer Committee.

Today, the KSA provides professional musicians with the opportunity to work as performers, leaders, and teachers in a way that affects concert-goers, fellow musicians, music students, school children, and members of the community at large.

Profile of Kingston Area

The Greater Kingston Area, located in eastern Ontario, Canada, has a population of approximately 130 000. It is surrounded by several smaller communities. Kingston is also within two to three hours travel time from the large urban populations of Toronto, Ottawa, and Montreal. VIA Rail and Air Canada service the community. The downtown area is located just minutes from Highway 410. Kingston is also within close proximity to the state of New York (which is important since about one-sixth of all visitors to the Kingston region are American).

In addition to the events organized by the Symphony, a number of other organizations from the Kingston community host a variety of fine arts and cultural events. While there is activity year-round, there is a particular emphasis on the summer tourism season. The summer season highlights a variety of arts and craft shows, musical events, theatre productions, exhibitions highlighting local talent and cultural heritage events, and many athletic competitions including CORK (Canadian Olympic training Regatta, Kingston). In the fall, several art tours are offered and throughout the fall and winter season, a number of concerts are held at Queen's University. A 1998 tourism study on the Kingston area showed that over two million people visited Kingston in 1996, with just under a million coming for a same-day visit, and another 1.2 million staying overnight. Over half of Kingston's visitors stated that they came to the city for pleasure. More importantly, visitors account for $170 million in tourism spending annually in the Kingston area.

The population of the Kingston area fluctuates highly during the year with the influx of students in September for programs at Queen's University, Royal Military College, and St. Lawrence College. Queen's University is the home of a music department that also coordinates its own student symphony.

KSA Organizational Structure
Administration
The KSA general office is located in downtown Kingston. It houses the general manager, Katherine Carleton, and assistant manager Andrea Haughton. The rest of

Lauren Dmytrenko developed this case under the supervision of Dr. Peggy Cunningham. It is not meant to represent effective or ineffective managerial decisions. The authors wish to thank Katherine Carlton for sharing her insights and challenges with us. Copyright Queen's University School of Business, 1999. Used with permission.

the administrative staff work on a part-time basis and do not spend significant amounts of time in the office. These positions include the personnel manager, operations manager, orchestral librarian, publicist, administrative assistant, and volunteer coordinator.

Katherine Carleton, the fifth general manager to hold the office since 1992, has been working for the KSA for 18 months. There have been three different assistant managers during her tenure. These two positions are the only two full-time, permanent positions in the office. While some dedicated volunteers have mitigated this high turnover rate, its impact on the KSA's long-term success cannot be ignored.

When thinking about the future of the Symphony, Katherine admits that it is easier to stick to what has been done traditionally. She also realizes, however, the opportunity for change and innovation. She is willing to take on the challenge.

Board of Directors

In common with most non-profit organizations, the KSA board of directors is accountable for the work of the KSA. The board of directors is composed of dedicated volunteers from the community, many of whom are employed in the financial and legal industry, or are retired. In addition to using the services of many of these professionals, the board of directors is also essential to the volunteer, fundraising, and sponsorship efforts of the KSA. It was the board's connections, for example, that helped develop major sponsorships of KSA events, such as the Kingston Whig-Standard's Beat Beethoven Run. However, along with the talents of the board of directors come hectic schedules. The challenge has been to keep committees active and individual directors focused on their volunteer duties for the KSA. Furthermore, Katherine feels that there is a need to develop the skills possessed by the board of directors so that best use is made of their talents and their energy is directed at more tangible projects.

The board of directors is structured into a number of committees on which the various members serve. These include outreach, special events, planning and resources, nominating executive, development, and personnel. There is currently no set group that advises the business manager on the marketing and promotion activities of the KSA; however, such a committee may be developed in the upcoming year.

KSA Volunteer Committee

For a symphony of its size, the KSA has an extraordinary large group of committed community volunteers. It currently has 200 of these individuals. The KSA volunteer committee operates year-round and organizes major fundraising events such as the annual fall book fair, the nearly-new sale, and the weekly bingo event. The committee's mandate is to link the community with the orchestra, both financially and socially. The group coordinates all volunteer ushers for KSA events, and dedicates a portion of its fundraising efforts towards awards for young musical talent in the Kingston area. A tri-annual newsletter, *Symphonic Notes*, keeps volunteer committee members, who pay a $15 annual membership fee, updated on the successes of events and future planning efforts.

Despite the financial troubles of the KSA in past years, the volunteer committee has been a dependable and generous supporter of the Symphony and its activities. The committee raised $50 000 ($20 000 above what was projected) in the 1998–99 Season. Of this amount, $46 000 was given directly to the KSA. The remaining funds went toward providing a series of in-school concerts for younger children ($2000) and a KSA Endowment Fund ($2000).

Many committee members are retired individuals who are able to dedicate a lot of time to committee events. They thrive on the feeling that they belong to something important. Events such as the annual book fair require a full-year commitment from the volunteer convenor and because of the workload, few individuals are willing to take on the job for more than one year at a time. Many events have seen the same two or three individuals rotate responsibility over the years. Marshalling new volunteers is becoming increasingly difficult, with the general shift in the population towards dual-career families who have limited free time. People have found that large events such as the book fair are impossible for a person to coordinate if they already hold a full-time job.

The Musicians

The KSA's appeal to the community is reflected in the composition of its musicians. Players as young as age 10 participate in the Junior Strings, while individuals in their late seventies are members of the Choral Society. However, the spirit remains the same no matter one's age. One musician was quoted as saying that the Kingston Symphony gave him an opportunity "to play challenging music and develop his skills outside of the school setting, while also meeting other talented musicians and friends from the Kingston area."

Glen Fast has been the Kingston Symphony's music director for eight years and is under contract until 2003. His popularity in the music community has led to numerous guest performances for the National Arts Centre Orchestra, Calgary Philharmonic, and Winnipeg Symphony. He was formerly music director of Victoria Symphony's Summer Festival and assistant conductor of the Vancouver Symphony. Glen has provided a stable vision for the Symphony in the past and the Symphony has steadily improved under his leadership. Katherine describes him as "open but cautious" in venturing far from the current program set-up. Glen's salary is based on a fee per concert, with more funding allocated to shaping new programs rather than repeat programs. His salary averages $40 000 per year.

The Kingston Symphony is the flagship program of the KSA. Over 50 musicians participate in the season programs, including nine principal musicians with contracts specifying annual compensation ranging from $11 000 to $24 000 per year. The remainder of the KSA players are paid on a fee-for-service basis; their annual income from the Kingston Symphony averages $1500 per person. When principal players cannot take part for some reason, additional musicians are "on call" and play on a more informal basis. However, though principal players have the flexibility to decline playing, most make a concerted effort to take part due to their love for the music and the "family" feeling the Symphony generates.

The musicians involved with KSA take great pride in their talent and work. They are admitted to the orchestra following a competitive audition, and work primarily in the September to April period. Rehearsals and concerts take place on evenings and weekends. Qualified younger musicians take part out of high school or from the music department at Queen's. However, the relationship with the Queen's music department can be delicate, as most of the students are required to take part in the university-based symphony. Many of the faculty members, including the Queen's Conductor, play on a regular basis with the Kingston Symphony, however.

Other KSA programs operate under a separate budget from the KSA, with conductors receiving minimal compensation for their work. The Kingston Choral Society is composed of 90 singers, who rehearse weekly and have four performances per year. The 45-member youth orchestra offers high school students a unique opportunity to hone their talent. Professional coaching from the Kingston Symphony musicians will soon be offered, thanks to funding from the Community Foundation of Greater Kingston. The Junior Strings offers younger musicians a strong training ground to further advance their music and gain performance experience. The Community Strings, also known as TGIF within the KSA, consists of adults, many of whom are seniors who simply love to play. Many of these other KSA groups take part in individual fundraising. They present their own concerts and other activities.

Symphony Events

Regular Season Programs

KSA's regular season runs from September to April and consists of two major series: Masterworks and Friday Night Live.

The Masterworks series is performed on Sunday afternoons at either the Grand Theatre or Grant Hall (Queen's campus). This series typically involves larger orchestras and the repertoire is delicately balanced between standard and ground-breaking material. Masterworks soloists are typically Canadian. They may be either established or rising performers. Past soloists have included the Kingston Symphony's core musicians, Rivka Golani, Lakshmi Ranganathan, and others. The audience for the Masterworks Series comprises season-ticket holders (50 percent of capacity) and single-ticket buyers (25 to 40 percent), whose numbers and demographic profile vary depending on program, venue, time of year, and the attractiveness of the programming.

The Friday Night Live series began in 1992–93 as an ensemble development exercise involving a smaller, classical-sized orchestra. Soloists in this program are often local (though this will change slightly in the 1999–00 season) and include Kingston Symphony principal players. Katherine's visual inspection of the audience indicates to her that this audience is younger, and somewhat less musically sophisticated than the Masterworks audience; however, their enthusiasm for the music is evident.

The Symphony has lacked success running "pops"-style concerts, and Katherine wonders whether the Symphony simply diluted its audience of supporters by offering them more product, rather than increasing the number of supporters by providing greater variety. She also notes that adding concerts increases financial risk, while there also exists the possibility that the musicians would not be as committed to a repertoire of this nature if they didn't find it challenging.

To encourage patrons to attend a Symphony performance, the KSA offers a volunteer driver service for people who are concerned about parking and walking to the concert hall. There is also a childcare program for the Sunday afternoon concerts, and volunteer ushers are responsible for calling taxis prior to the show ending to assist with traffic congestion.

Educational Programs

Grade 4 students have had the pleasure of participating in the KSA's educational programs for seven years. As a joint venture between the KSA, Queen's School of Music, Limestone District School Board, and the Algonquin and Lakeshore Roman Catholic School Board, the Kingston Symphony provides the orchestra (with funding solicited from corporate sponsors) for six concerts for grade 4 students. The school boards provide facilities, busing, funds for service costs, and the talents of two lead teachers who assist Glen Fast in developing the programs. In addition, under the guidance of Dr. Roberta Lamb, Queen's music students develop and present 12 in-class lessons to grade 4 students in the area.

The KSA Outreach Coordinator recently revived the school concert program in which the Symphony's professional core visits schools in an area extending from Belleville to Brockville. The performances blend music and biography.

Summer Events

Two KSA summer events have had huge success in attracting large crowds, including many families who do not attend Symphony events during the regular season. The night at Fort Henry that includes a lively rendition of Tchaikovsky's 1812 Overture (with live cannons and fireworks) takes place mid-July over two nights. Sales from this event reached $27 000 in 1998. The biggest risk of this event is the unpredictable weather. Losses can be significant if it rains.

For the last two years, the Symphony has also given a free performance on Canada Day in front of City Hall. The Symphony uses this opportunity to venture away from some of the traditional classical music pieces to include theme songs from popular movies and television shows such as *Star Wars* and *The Muppet Show*. As this is a free event, attendance is high (even if a thunderstorm is threatening overheard as seen in July 1999). It is generally considered to be successful—but Katherine wonders how to leverage this success into increased ticket sales—and indeed, how to track if this is happening.

This is not a new question for the KSA. But summer programming carries an element of risk: a Gilbert and Sullivan operetta production in the summer of 1997 resulted in a loss due to cost over-runs, optimistic revenue projections, and inclement weather. As well, staff were pushed to the edge: the summer period typically dedicated to preparation for the coming season was instead devoted to the staged production. Key tasks went undone and both full-time staff members resigned at the end of the summer.

Katherine recognizes that the development of a more comprehensive summer season during peak tourist season presents a huge opportunity for the KSA. But staff turnover and tight finances present equal challenges. There is very limited tolerance for risk and every staff change means a few steps backward during the learning curve. To add to the challenge, the KSA has a long planning horizon. It must schedule all summer programs in December of the previous year.

Audience Profile

Masterworks subscribers have been described as loyal, long term, and musically sophisticated symphony patrons. They are typically between the ages of 40 and 60, homeowners, educated (hold a university degree or equivalent), and possibly come from double-income households ($50 000+). Katherine senses that Queen's University represents an untapped market of sophisticated consumers. Many faculty and staff are prepared to travel to Ottawa or Toronto to get their classical music "fix" in preference to attending Kingston Symphony events.

Single-ticket buyers include a substantial student audience and people interested in a particular program due to repertoire and/or guest performers. However, the KSA has conducted no market research to determine the specific audience composition of single-ticket buyers. Thus, they have little guidance on whom to target with new program development and ticket information. What is obvious, though, is that the audience core is aging, and new ideas are needed to attract a new core of Symphony goers.

Financing and Fundraising

Five and a half years ago, the KSA had an accumulated deficit of $133 117 on total revenues of $434 995. Although the past five years have been marked by an overall diminution of government support, the Kingston Symphony has succeeded in allocating more money on programming and community outreach, while reducing the deficit by over $100 000. Much of this success is related to substantially increased fundraising activity, with smaller but equally significant growth in ticket sales. (See Exhibit A for 1998–1999 Finances Report.)

Ticket Sales

Ticket sales can be segmented into three groups: season subscriptions, singles, and special event tickets (i.e., Fort Henry performance). The KSA has seen a shift in the past few years to higher single-ticket purchases over subscription purchases. This has been exemplary of the changing lifestyle shift of Symphony attendees. People seem reluctant to commit to certain Symphony dates a year in advance, as their lifestyles become busier. Most individuals are happy to purchase a week before, or even the night of a performance.

In the 1997–98 season, the concept of "student rush" tickets was introduced. With little promotion of the deal for local students, only 97 rush tickets were sold. However, after visits with the Queen's music department students, sales rose dramatically to 900 sold in the 1998–99 season. The KSA is looking to reach beyond music students to other faculties within the university; however, the Symphony has not typically budgeted to do extensive media advertising on campus, reasoning that the costs would outweigh the benefits.

The change in ticket purchasing habits has meant the KSA endures more stress when it comes closer to performance time. Katherine wonders if steps can be taken to convert single-ticket buyers into subscribers, to reduce this stress. At the same time, she intuits that some people are prepared to pay a premium for the convenience of last-minute decision making. (See Exhibit B for 1998–99 Season Attendance Figures.)

Katherine recognizes that she has many empty seats at each symphony concert, and that both finances and the players' morale would be helped by filling those seats. She wonders how to ensure that potential audiences for the hardcore classics the Symphony presently presents are reached. She also concedes that some change to the current product mix might be necessary.

The Symphony's biggest cost each year is its payments to players for participation in rehearsals and concerts, followed by administration, concert production costs (included venue rental for rehearsals and concerts, totalling $18 000 in 1998–99), and marketing. Katherine concluded that it would only make sense to try to bring more money from the Symphony's core activity—the concerts. She must determine the viability of all the programs to maximize the revenue they will bring in and then balance the shortfall with a comprehensive program of fundraising from other sources.

Annual Fund and Endowment Campaign

The KSA coordinates three major campaigns for charitable donations from individuals, in September (for renewals), February (Spring fundraising), and a catch-up period before the end of the fiscal year.

KSA's private donations have made up about eight percent of annual revenues in the past three years. Donor categories (Conductor's Circle Member—$1000+, Patron—$500–$999, Benefactor—$300–$499, Friend—$150–$299, Supporter—$75–$149, and Other—up to $75) are assigned on the basis of the total gift, and each level offers specific benefits to the donor including receptions, VIP seating at Symphony events, and a vote at the annual general meeting.

The KSA is enrolled in the Ontario Arts Endowment Fund Program, an Ontario Government initiative that matches, dollar for dollar, any endowment contributions the Symphony raises. The KSA can have up to $94 774 matched by the end of the 1999–2000 season, for a potential fund of almost $190 000. The KSA will have access to the income from this fund in perpetuity. The present balance of the KSA fund is $80 000, including matched contributions.

Grants

The KSA currently receives just over $100 000 in grants from the Canada Arts Council, the Ontario Arts Council, City of Kingston, and the school boards (to facilitate the grade 4 program). Few other opportunities exist to apply for other grants and the current ones have been diminishing as all arts programs go through significant cutbacks from government.

Weekly Bingo

Each second Wednesday, the KSA hosts bingo at the Community Spirit Bingo Hall in Kingston. This fundraising effort requires considerable human resources since 15 volunteers are needed each bingo day to help out. Musicians, volunteer committee members, administrative staff, and members of the board of directors have volunteered for bingo. Though Wednesday mornings and afternoons are not the most popular time for bingo, the funds from the bingo are distributed per the amount of time the organization spends running it, thus meaning the KSA reaps the benefits of some of the busier bingos run on the weekend. Katherine worries that, while bingo provides significant funds each year (over $38 000 in 1998–99), it may not be the best use of the volunteers' talents and time. However, for the time being, the bingo appears to be a guaranteed source of funds for the KSA and there appears to be no threat of losing this fundraising opportunity.

Annual Golf Tournament

Each year the KSA hosts a golf tournament at the Garrison Golf Club, involving approximately 120 golfers. The 1998B99 Season tournament raised $6797 for the KSA; however, this was about $700 less than what was expected.

Beat Beethoven

Beat Beethoven, a fairly new venture of the KSA, has been extremely successful. Athletes have one hour to finish a run during which time the Kingston Symphony plays a Beethoven symphony that has been timed to finish on the hour. The event has been successful in attracting participation by both competitive and recreational athletes of all ages. Besides the runners themselves, many people gather in the park to listen to the Symphony, and volunteers pass out promotional materials for the Symphony. Annual proceeds from Beat Beethoven are in the $8000–$11 000 area, with almost 1000 people actively participating in June 1999.

Nevada

The Symphony raises approximately $4000 per year from its Nevada site in downtown Kingston. This passive form of fundraising provides limited funds; however, it requires limited efforts from the KSA staff and volunteers.

Vehicle Lotteries

For the past five years, the Symphony has been involved in vehicle lotteries, doing two per year on average. The most successful of these have been lotteries for Harley-Davidson motorcycles. The Symphony raises roughly $25 000 per Harley lottery, and has a loyal database of over 1400 names of Harley ticket buyers. The lotteries are operated in-house by Symphony staff with minimal requirement for volunteer involvement. A positive aspect of the lotteries is their demonstrated capacity to bring the Symphony money from other sources than the traditional and often-tapped

Symphony patron; however, they do take up a high proportion of office time and energy while they are running. Katherine has come to value the financial contribution the lotteries make to the Symphony bottom line, while questioning whether they can be better managed. How can she and her staff keep the money coming while they keep the music and audiences growing?

KSA's Promotional Efforts

Publications

The KSA produces a number of publications to promote the KSA events. A small handbook (25 000 printed at a cost of $5000 plus $800 for design) is sent out to all former subscription purchasers and donors in early March, followed by a second wave mailed to single-ticket buyers from the previous year. With this also follows a small pamphlet (500 produced) outlining the KSA's Annual Fund and Endowment Campaign. To date, no detailed conversion rates exist about the success of these publications.

Once the season has started, a concert program is distributed at KSA events, highlighting in more detail the events, the people behind the scenes, and the support of numerous community sponsors (through ads). The cost for the concert program is approximately $6000 for 9000 two-colour programs, with advertising amounting to $21 000 (which helps to cover the costs of other publications).

In addition to the annual mailouts, brochures are distributed by hand at other venues in the Kingston area that would attract potential Symphony customers ("classical intuitive hangouts"), such as Chapters & Indigo bookstores, public libraries, upscale restaurants, and the Grand Theatre. Postcards and posters are also used marginally, and have been successful in promoting events.

Local Media

The KSA receives significant coverage through the local daily newspaper, the Kingston Whig-Standard, and also spends roughly $9000 per year advertising in this paper. The paper reviews events and features upcoming attractions. Little has been done in conjunction with the Queen's Journal. (See Exhibit C for Queen's Journal Rates.) The KSA also advertises in a biweekly free newspaper, spending roughly $1500 per year on this. The KSA's publicist ensures that coverage of Symphony events appears in local magazines, through public service announcements and press releases. Local television, both regular and cable, are also occasionally able to feature the symphony on news shows. A recent shift in format for local radio stations has caused Katherine to question the value of continuing to advertise on radio. With an increased emphasis on the youth market, the stations have de-emphasized interviews and talk features, places where the Symphony could ensure that its paid advertising was amplified through free coverage. The university radio station is the only local broadcaster playing any classical music locally, but its audience numbers are low.

A Web site (http://novatech.on.ca/kingston_symphony/benefit.html) was designed by a volunteer (in exchange for a concert subscription) in 1998. It has not been updated since the 1998 season began, and is not easy to find. The Symphony currently does not have its own e-mail address. Other Kingston-area Web sites such as www.whatsonkingston.com, www.1000-islands.net and the Kingston Economic Development Corporation Web site www.kingstonarea.on.ca all have links to local tourist attractions and events; however, no Symphony events are currently described on these sites. To attain a domain name such as www.kingstonsymphony.ca would cost the KSA $80.25 with no renewal fee. Internet Kingston offers web-hosting packages at $214 annually for five megabytes of space. However, the KSA would still require an individual to update the KSA page as needed. They are unsure about whether they should employ a "web-master" or look for a volunteer who would monitor the site and help ensure interactivity such as responses to e-mail queries. The KSA does recognize the potential for a more comprehensive Web site; however, their current staffing constraints have prevented them from utilizing the Internet more effectively.

Looking to the Future

Katherine Carleton knows that future success rests on successfully executing a careful balancing act. Traditionally, the KSA has served the needs of its players as much as it has fulfilled the need for community-based cultural entertainment. She must respect the desires of these diverse stakeholders when thinking about new marketing initiatives to attract new audiences or financial resources. Furthermore, she must be careful not to alienate her traditional loyal audiences or core of devoted volunteers in her search for new business. She must keep in mind the susceptibility of the Symphony to financial risk. Thus, any experimental initiatives have to maximize the benefits while minimizing these downside risks. Finally, she needs to ensure that the choices she makes are sustainable in terms of staff and volunteer workload.

Glancing at the upcoming season's budget (see Exhibit D) and attempting to organize herself before the new season begins, Katherine knows that any major program changes must be decided upon before the new holiday season. She must act now in order to be able, physically and financially, to organize the KSA efforts. She wonders what information the KSA should obtain to make better programming and marketing decisions. Are there community partnerships that the KSA should be exploring? And finally, what else can the KSA do to grow and attract new audience members without sacrificing any of the great qualities the Symphony already has? While finding answers to these questions is critical, Katherine wonders if she has taken on too daunting a task.

KSA 12-Month Finances
(June 1, 1998 to May 31, 1999)

REVENUE			
Earned	**Original Budget**	**to May 31, 1999**	**Projected**
Subscriptions	$73 000	$73 967	$73 967
Singles	87 000	70 868	70 868
1812 Tickets	20 000	27 397	27 397
Program Advertising	10 000	14 676	14 676
Performance Fees	-	3 213	3 213
Other Income	-	87	87
Total Earned	190 000	190 208	190 208
Donations			
Sponsorship	64 625	60 125	61 125
Individuals	54 000	51 175	51 175
Foundations	8 750	12 750	12 750
Volunteer Committee	30 000	46 000	46 000
Choral Society	3 000	3 000	3 000
Total Donations	160 375	173 050	174 050
Grants			
Canada Council	17 750	21 125	21 125
Ontario Arts Council	65 000	65 000	65 000
City of Kingston	20 000	11 250	11 250
School Boards	4 000	5 300	5 300
Advance Lottery Funding	-	2 703	9 703
Total Grants	106 750	105 378	112 378
Special Projects			
Golf Tournament	7 500	6 797	6 797
Beat Beethoven	8 500	8 640	8 640
Bingo	20 000	32 650	36 250
Nevada	2 500	4 259	4 259
Lotteries	45 000	37 858	37 858
Gala	30 000	27 453	27 453
Total Special Projects	113 500	117 657	121 257
TOTAL REVENUE	**$570 625**	**$586 293**	**$597 893**

EXPENSES

Artistic	Original Budget	to May 31, 1999	Projected
Subscriptions	$73 000	$73 967	$73 967
Music Director	$38 900	$40 691	$40 691
Membership Fees	800	1 069	1 069
Guest Conductors	2 500	2 500	2 500
Youth Orchestra	4 667	4 000	4 333
Choral Society asst/piano	4 760	5 979	5 979
Guest Soloists	58 000	58 450	58 450
Principals	112 000	113 057	113 057
General Orchestra	76 155	73 524	73 524
Import Players	14 740	7 463	7 463
Union Dues, Orchestra	700	437	700
Composer's Fees (fdtns)	0	10 000	10 000
Total Artistic	313 222	317 170	317 766
Production			
Orchestra and Import Travel	9 220	11 496	11 496
Guest Soloist Travel Etc.	3 000	3 400	3 400
Music Rental	3 000	1 909	1 909
Music Purchase	2 000	784	784
Librarian	3 504	2 797	3 796
Operations Manager	6 000	6 000	6 000
Personnel Manager	5 100	5 104	5 104
Outreach/Vol. Coordinator	6 504	6 212	6 212
Equipment rent/purchase/maintenance	250	2 009	2 009
Hall Rental	18 000	15 880	15 880
IATSE	4 200	1 512	1 512
Non-union Stage Crew	4 600	4 541	4 541
Beat Beethoven	750	612	612
1812 and July 1st	28 100	29 812	29 812
Truck Rental/Movers	5 500	3 515	3 515
Production Miscellaneous	2 000	1 322	1 322
Fees and Licences	2 382	2 904	2 904
Box Office Management	6 000	4 155	4 155
Total Production	110 110	103 964	104 963
Promotion and Fundraising			
Media Advertising	$15 000	$13 291	$13 291
Subscription Costs	7 500	7 207	7 207
Posters/Flyers	3 000	3 060	3 060
Brochures/artwork/photos	2 000	271	271
Concert Programs	6 500	11 176	11 176
Mailing/Distribution	3 000	2 165	2 165
Receptions	2 200	1 510	1 510
Donor Recognition	2 000	3 468	3 468
Miscellaneous	-	140	140
Total Promotion and Fundraising	41 200	42 288	42 288
Administration			
Salary (General Manager)	40 000	40 000	40 000
Salary (Assistant G.M.)	23 000	24 557	25 000
Other Admin. Staff	6 000	11 873	11 873
Employee Benefits	4 400	5 294	5 294
Office Rent	6 720	6 720	6 720

Administration (cont'd)	Original Budget	to May 31, 1999	Projected
Office Supplies	4 000	4 014	4 014
Computer Supplies	700	627	627
Equipment Purchase	1 500	162	162
Equipment Lease/Supplies	4 700	3 468	4 000
Equipment Servicing	500	150	150
Telephone	4 400	4 318	4 318
Courier	2 700	2 330	2 330
Insurance	4 100	3 646	3 646
Postage/Mailing	2 400	2 584	2 584
Bank Charges	3 000	4 967	4 967
Administrative Misc.	4 200	2 412	2 412
Audit/Legal	2 500	3 041	3 041
Total Administration	114 820	120 163	121 138
TOTAL REVENUES	$570 625	$586 293	$597 893
TOTAL EXPENSES	$579 352	$583 585	$586 085
SURPLUS/(DEFICIT)	($8 727)	$2 708	$11 808
Accumulated Deficit from Previous Years	($28 009)	($28 009)	($28 009)
PROJECTED SURPLUS/(DEFICIT)	($36 736)	($25 301)	($19 441)

Concert Date	# of Audience Members
July 10 & 11	2408*
Masterworks Series 1, October 4	607
Friday Night Live Series 1, October 23	660
Masterworks Series 2, November 15	693
Choral Series 1, November 18	277
Choral Series 2, December 15 & 16	1158
Friday Night Live Series 2, January 15	655
Masterworks Extra, January 29	453
Choral Series 3, January 31	708
Choral Series 3, February 1	486
Masterworks Series 4, February 21	551
Friday Night Live Series 3, March 5	688
Friday Night Live Series 5, March 28	655
Friday Night Live Extra, March 29	459
Friday Night Live Series 4, April 16	693
Friday Night Live Series 6, April 25	644

*Fort Henry Concert - includes 898 tickets sold by Grand Theatre, plus tickets sold through Fort Henry, the Symphony Office, and at the door on the night of the concerts.

EXHIBIT C

Queen's Journal Advertising Rates

Size	Dimensions	Campus Rate (AMS affiliated organizations)	Local Rate (Kingston Area)
Full Page	10" × 15"	$367.50	$682.50
Half Page	10" × 7.5"	183.75	341.25
Quarter Page	5" × 7.5"	91.88	170.63
Sixth Page	5" × 5.6"	61.25	127.40
Eighth Page	4" × 4.7"	45.94	85.54
Coupon	4" × 3"	29.40	54.60
Business Card	4" × 2.5"	24.50	45.50
Earlug (Front Page)	—	70.00	40.00
Earlug (Inside Section)	—	35.00	35.00

Colour Rates (Subject to Availability):

Description	Size	Campus Rate (AMS affiliated organizations)	Local Rate (Kingston Area)
Full Colour	Full page	$350.00	$350.00
Full Colour	Half page	350.00	350.00
One Extra Colour	Any Ad	90.00	120.00
One Extra Colour	Earlug	12.00	12.00

Additional Items

Inserts (minimum 1000)	$120.00
Choice of Positioning	Additional 10%
Typesetting	Min. $10.00

1999/2000 Budget Projections

Earned Revenue		
Single Tickets	$110 000	
Subscriptions	75 000	
Fees & Guarantees	3 500	
Program Advertising	12 000	
Endowment Income	2 700	
Total Earned Revenue		$203 200
Private Sector Revenue		
Individual Donations	55 000	
Corporate Donations	5 000	
Corporation Sponsors	60 000	
Foundations	23 900	
Volunteer Committee	40 000	
Choral Society	3 000	
Total Private Sector		186 900
Special Projects		
Beat Beethoven	12 000	
Golf Tournament	9 000	
Lotteries	47 500	
Gala	25 000	
Bingo	30 000	
Nevada	3 500	
Total Special Events		127 000
Grants		
Canada Council	30 000	
Ontario Arts Council	70 000	
City of Kingston	11 250	
School Boards	4 000	
Total Grants		115 250
TOTAL REVENUE		$632 350

Artistic

Music Director	$40 000	
Guest Conductor	1 800	
Youth Orchestra	5 000	
KCS Costs	5 000	
Soloists	56 050	(includes NACO)
Principals	112 032	
General Orchestra	101 835	
Imports	18 680	
Travel	11 840	
Total Artistic		$352 237

Production

Music Rental/Purchase	7 000	
Librarian	3 600	
Operations Manager	8 000	
Personnel Manager	5 100	
Outreach Coordinator	6 500	
Equipment	14 400	(includes new chair purchase—
Hall Rental	18 000	Trillium Foundation)
IATSE	4 200	
Non-union Crew	4 600	
Beat Beethoven	612	
Trucks/cartage	6 000	
Fees and Licences	2 700	
Box Office	6 000	
Fort Henry Special Costs	11 000	
Miscellaneous	2 000	
Total Production		$99 712
TOTAL PRODUCTION AND ARTISTIC EXPENSES		$451 949

Promotion

Media Advertising	$15 000	
Subscription Brochure & Distribution	7 400	
Posters/Flyers/Postcards	4 500	
Photography	500	
Concert Programs	7 500	
Direct Mail/Poster Distribution	1 000	
Receptions	2 200	
Signs & Banners	1 400	
Miscellaneous	1 000	
Total Promotion		$40 500

Fundraising

Brochure	500	
Mailing	920	
Donor & Sponsor Benefits	1 500	
Miscellaneous	500	
Total Fundraising		3 420

Administration

General Manager	40 000
Assistant Manager	25 000
Administrative Assistant	13 000
Benefits	8 000
Rent	6 720
Supplies	4 000
Computer (including Y2K expense)	6 600
Equipment Purchase	1 500

Leasing	5 000	
Servicing	200	
Phone	4 000	
Courier	3 000	
Insurance	1 700	
Postage	3 000	
Bank Charges	3 000	
Audit & Legal Expenses	4 000	
Miscellaneous	2 500	
Total Administration		131 220
TOTAL PROMOTION, FUNDRAISING & ADMINISTRATION EXPENSES		$175 140

NOTES

Chapter 1

1. Sam Hill and Glenn Rifkin, *Radical Marketing* (New York: Harper Business, 1999).

2. Jay Conrad Levinson and Seth Grodin, *The Guerrilla Marketing Handbook* (Boston: Houghton Mifflin, 1994).

3. "Gross Domestic Product at Factor Cost, Primary Industries," Statistics Canada Table, http://www.statcan.ca/english/Pgdb/Economy/Primary/prim03.htm.

4. See Philip Kotler, "Dream Vacations: The Booming Market for Designed Experiences," *The Futurist*, October 1984, pp. 7–13, and B. Joseph Pine II and James Gilmore, "Welcome to the Experience Economy," *Harvard Business Review*, July-August 1998, pp. 97–105.

5. See Irving J. Reinj, Philip Kotler, and Martin Stoller, *High Visibility* (Chicago: NTC Publishers, 1998).

6. See Philip Kotler, Irving J. Rein, and Donald Haider, *Marketing Places: Attracting Investment, Industry, and Tourism to Cities, States, and Nations* (New York: The Free Press, 1993).

7. See Carl Shapiro and Hal R. Varian, "Versioning: The Smart Way to Sell Information," *Harvard Business Review*, November-December 1998, pp. 106–14.

8. Peter Drucker, *Management: Tasks, Responsibilities, Practices* (New York: Harper & row, 1973), pp. 64–65.

9. *Dictionary of Marketing Terms*, 2nd ed., Peter D. Bennett (Chicago: American Marketing Association, 1995).

10. See Jeffrey Rayport and John Sviokla, "Managing in the Marketspace," *Harvard Business Review*, November-December 1994, pp. 141–50. Also see their "Exploring the Virtual Value Chain," *Harvard Business Review*, November-December 1995, pp. 75–85.

11. From a lecture by Mohan Sawhney, faculty member at Kellogg Graduate School of Management, Northwestern University, June 4, 1998.

12. See Regis McKenna, *Relationship Marketing* (Reading MA: Addison-Wesley, 1991); Martin Christopher, Adrian Payne, and David Ballantyne, *Relationship Marketing: Bringing Quality, Customer Service, and Marketing Together* (Oxford, England: Butterworth-Heinemann, 1991), and Jagdish N. Sheth and Atul Parvatiyar, eds., Relationship Marketing: Theory, Methods, and Applications, 1994 Research Conference Proceedings, Center for Relationship Marketing, Roberto C. Goizueta Business School, Emory University, Atlanta, GA.

13. See James C. Anderson, Hakan Hakansson, and Jan Johanson, "Dyadic Business Relationships Within a Business Network Context," *Journal of Marketing*, October 15, 1994, pp. 1–15. "Sector Competitiveness Framework Series: Primary Steel Highlights," http://www.strategic.ic.gc.ca/SSG/mm01072e.html.

14. See Neil H. Borden, "The Concept of the Marketing Mix," *Journal of Advertising Research*, 4 (June), pp. 2–7. For another framework, see George S. Day, "The Capabilities of Marketing-Driven Organizations," Journal of Marketing, 58, no. 4 (October 1994): 37–52.

15. E. Jerome McCarthy, *Basic Marketing: A Managerial Approach*, 12th ed. (Homewood IL: Irwin, 1996). Two alternative classifications are worth noting. Frey proposed that all marketing-decision variables could be categorized into two factors: the offering (product, packaging, brand, price and service) and methods and tools (distribution channels, personal selling, advertising, sales promotion, and publicity). See Albert W. Frey, *Advertising*, 3rd ed. (New York: Ronald Press, 1961),p. 30. Lazer and Kelly proposed a three-factor classification: goods and service mix, distribution mix, and communications mix. See William Lazer and Eugene J. Kelly, *Managerial Marketing: Perspectives and Viewpoints*, rev. ed. (Homewood, IL: Irwin, 1962), p. 413.

16. Robert Lauterborn, "New Marketing Litany: 4P's Passe; C-Words Take Over," *Advertising Age*, October 1, 1990, p. 26. Also see Frederick E. Wester Jr., Defining the New Marketing Concept," *Marketing Management* 2, no. 4 (1994), 22–31; and Frederick E. Webster Jr., "Executing the New Marketing Concept," *Marketing Management* 3, no. 1 (1994): 8–16. See also Ajay Menon and Anil Menon, "Enviropreneurial Marketing Strategy: The Emergence of Corporate Environmentalism as Marketing Strategy," *Journal of Marketing* 61, no. 1 (January 1997): 51–67.

17. Kathleen Dechant and Barbara Altman, "Environmental Leadership: From Compliance to Competitive Advantage," *Academy of Management Executive*, vol. 8, no. 3, 1994, pp. 7–19. Also see Gregory R. Elliott, "The Marketing Concept—Necessary, but Sufficient? An Environmental View," *European Journal of Marketing* 24, no. 8 (1990): 20–30.

18. Stanley Hollander, Question posed in his doctoral seminar at Michigan State University in 1994. Dr. Hollander was asking his students to explore the reasons why a stage-wise view of the evolution of marketing had persisted despite research that demonstrated the inaccuracy of this view.

19. Paul C. Judge, "Are Tech Buyers Different?" *Business Week*, January 26, 1998, pp. 64–65, 68. B. G. Yovovich, "Webbed Feat," *Marketing News*, January 19, 1998, pp. 1, 18.

20. See Theodore Levitt's classic article, "Marketing Myopia," *Harvard Business Review*, July-August 1960, pp. 45–56.

21. See Bruce I. Newman, *The Marketing of the President* (Thousand Oaks, CA: Sage Publications, 1993).

22. See Karl Albrecht and Ron Zemke, *Service America!* (Homewood, IL: Dow-Jones-Irwin, 1985), pp. 6–7.

23. See John B. McKitterick, "What Is the Marketing Management Concept?" *The Frontiers of Marketing Thought and Action* (Chicago: American Marketing Association, 1957), pp. 71–82; Fred J. Borch, "The Marketing Philosophy as a Way of Business Life," *The Marketing Concept: Its Meaning to Management*, Marketing series, No. 99 (New York: American Management Association, 1957), pp. 3–5; and Robert J. Keith,

"The Marketing Revolution," *Journal of Marketing*, January 1960, pp. 35–38.

24. Theodore Levitt, "Marketing Myopia," *Harvard Business Review*, July-August 1960, p. 50.

25. Gary Hamel and C.K. Prahalad, *Competing for the Future* (Boston: Harvard Business School Press, 1994.)

26. Akio Morita, *Made in Japan* (New York: Dutton, 1986), Chapter 1.

27. See Patricia Sellers, "Getting Customers to Love You," *Fortune*, March 13, 1989, pp. 38–49.

28. Suzanne L. MacLachlan, "Son Now Beats Perdue Drumstick," *Christian Science Monitor*, March 9, 1995, p. 9; Sharon Nelton, "Crowing over Leadership Succession," *Nations' Business*, May 1995, p. 52.

29. See Bro Uttal, "Selling Is No Longer Mickey Mouse at AT&T," *Fortune*, July 17, 1978, pp. 98–104.

30. See Thomas V. Bonoma and Bruce H. Clark, *Marketing Performance Assessment* (Boston: Harvard Business School Press, 1988).

31. Richard Barnet, *Global Dreams: Imperial Corporations and the New World Order* (New York: Simon & Schuster, 1994), pp. 170–171; Michael R. Czinkota, Ilka A. Ronkainen, and John J. Tarrant, *The Global Marketing Imperative* (Chicago: NTC Business Books, 1995), p. 249.

32. James Pollock, "The Green Devolution," *Marketing*, April 15, 1996, p. 9.

33. See Hamish Pringle and Marjorie Thompson, *Brand Soul: How Cause-Related Marekting Builds Brands* (New York: John Wiley & Sons, 1999). Also see Marilyn Collins, "Global Corporate Philanthropy—Marketing Beyond the Call of Duty?", *European Journal of Marketing* , 27, No. 2, 1993, pp. 46–58.

34. John Gray, "Web Ad Prices Dropping While Overall Spending Rises," *Strategy, The Canadian Marketing Report*, March 15, 1999, p. 3. "Feds Accept Banner Ads," *Strategy, The Canadian Marketing Report*, September 28, 1998, p. 12. "Banner Ads as Effective as TV: Study," and "More Canadians Surfing the Web," *Strategy, The Canadian Marketing Report*, March 1, 1999, p. 16.

Chapter 2

1. Mac Attacks," *USA Today*, March 23, 1998, 01B.

2. See, for example, "Value Marketing: Quality, Service, and Fair Pricing Are the Keys to Selling in the '90s," *Business Week*, November 11, 1991, pp. 132–40.

3. See Irwin P. Levin and Richard D. Johnson, "Estimating Price-Quality Tradeoffs Using Comparative Judgments," *Journal of Consumer Research*, June 11, 1984, pp. 593–600.

4. Lexus Canada's Web Site (http://www.lexuscanada.com); Sinclair Stewart, "Putting The Customer First," *Strategy: The Canadian Marketing Report*, November 9, 1998, P DR2. David Todd, "Special Report: Top Database Marketers: Top In Automotive: Lexus Builds Luxury Car Connection," *Strategy: The Canadian Marketing Report*, July 21, 1997, P. DR13.

5. Thomas A. Stewart, "A Satisfied Customer Isn't Enough," *Fortune,* July 21, 1997, pp. 112–113.

6. Michael J. Lanning, *Delivering Profitable Value* (Oxford, U.K.: Capstone, 1998). Simon Knox and Stan Maklan, *Competing on Value: Bridging the Gap Between Brand and Customer Value* (London, Eng.: Financial Times, 1998).

7. See Tamara J. Erickson and C. Everett Shorey, "Business Strategy: New Thinking for the '90s," *Prism*, Fourth Quarter 1992, pp. 19–35.

8. See Robert Kaplan, *The Balanced Scorecard: Translating Strategy Into Action* (Boston: Harvard Business School Press, 1996), as a tool for monitoring stakeholder satisfaction.

9. See Jon R. Katzenbach and Douglas K. Smith, *The Wisdom of Teams: Creating the High-Performance Organization* (Boston: Harvard Business School Press, 1993) and Michael Hammer and James Champy, *Reengineering the Corporation* (New York: HarperBusiness, 1993).

10. T. Michael Nevens, Gregory L. Summe, and Bro Uttal, "Commercializing Technology: What the Best Companies Do," *Harvard Business Review*, May-June 1990, p. 162.

11. David Bosworth, "Case Study: Tourism Suppliers Lure Brits West," *Strategy: The Canadian Marketing Report*, 13 April 1998, p. D.10; Canadian Tourism Commission's Web Site: http://www.canadatourism.com.

12. George S. Day, "The Capabilities of Market-Driven Organizations," *Journal of Marketing,* October 1994, p. 38

13. "Business: Microsoft's Contradiction," *The Economist*, January 31, 1998, pp. 65–67. Andrew J. Glass, "Microsoft Pushes Forward, Playing to Win the Market; Passion for Technology: Hard Driving Culture Said to Have Led Company into Antitrust Trouble," *Atlanta Constitution,* June 24, 1998, D; 12; 12.

14. Daniel Howe, "A Note to Daimler-Chrysler: It's Not a Small World After All," *Detroit News*, May 19, 1998, B4. Bill Vlasic, "The First Global Car Colossus," *Business Week,* May 18, 1998, pp. 40–43. Pamela Harper, "Business Cultures at War," *Electronic News*, August 3, 1998, pp. 50, 55.

15. James C. Collins and Jerry I. Porras, *Built to Last: Successful Habits of Visionary Companies* (New York: HarperBusiness, 1994).

16. F. G. Rodgers and Robert L. Shook, *The IBM Way: Insights into the World's Most Successful Marketing Organization* (New York: Harper & Row, 1986).

17. Gary Hamel, "Strategy as Revolution," *Harvard Business Review*, July–August 1996, pp. 69–82.

18. See Paul J. H. Shoemaker, "Scenario Plannning: A Tool for Strategic Thinking," *Sloan Management Review*, Winter 1995, pp. 25–40.

19. Michael E. Porter, *Competitive Advantage: Creating and Sustaining Superior Performance* (New York: Free Press, 1985).20. Michael Hammer and James Champy, Reengineering the Corporation (New York: HarperBusiness, 1993).

21. See George Stalk, "Competing on Capability: The New Rules of Corporate Strategy," *Harvard Business Review*, March-April 1992, pp. 57–69; and Benson P. Shapiro, V. Kasturi Rangan, and John J. Sviokla, "Staple Yourself to an Order," *Harvard Business Review*, July-August 1992, pp. 113–22.

22. Mark Evans, "Rogers Cantel Going Door-to-Door with Amway," *Globe and Mail*, February 2, 1999, B1, B17.

Myron Magnet, "The New Golden Rule of Business," *Fortune*, November 28, 1994, pp. 60–64.23.

23. See Jeffrey Gitomer, *Customer Satisfaction is Worthless: Customer Loyalty is Priceless: How to Make Customers Love You, Keep Them Coming Back and Tell Everyone They Know* (Austin, TX: Bard Press, l998).

24. See Frederick F. Reichheld, "Learning from Customer Defections," *Harvard Business Review,* March-April 1996, pp. 56–69.

25. Frederick F. Reichheld, "Learning from Customer Defections," *Harvard Business Review*, March-April 1996, pp. 56–69.

26. Frederick F. Reichheld, "Learning from Customer Defections," *Harvard Business Review*, March-April 1996, pp. 56–69.

27. See *Technical Assistance Research Programs (TARP)*, U.S. Office of Consumer Affairs Study on Complaint Handling in America, 1986.

28. Karl Albrecht and Ron Zemke, *Service America!* (Homewood Il: Dow-Jones Irwin, l985), pp. 6–7.

29. Courtesy L.L. Bean, Freeport, Maine.

30. Courtesy L.L. Bean, Freeport, Maine.

31. See Frederick F. Reichheld, *The Loyalty Effect* (Boston: Harvard Business School Press, 1996).

32. Ian H. Gorrdon, *Relationship Marketing* (Toronto: John Wiley & sons Canada, Ltd., 1998), p. 9. Patti Summerfield, "Special Report: Pharmaceutical/ Health and Beauty," *Strategy: The Canadian Marketing Report*, June 22, 1998, p. 17.33.

33. David Bosworth, "Air Canada Spreads Its Relationship Marketing Wings," *Strategy: The Canadian Marketing Report*, June 22, 1998, p. D2.34.

34. Jill Whysel, "The Web Offers a Way to 'Sell' Complex Financial Products Without a Sales Pitch," *Marketing*, March 15, 1999, p. 22.

35. Leonard L. Berry and A. Parasuraman, *Marketing Services: Competing Through Quality* (New York: Free Press, 1991), pp. 136–142. See also Richard Cross and Janet Smith, *Customer Bonding: Pathways to Lasting Customer Loyalty* (Lincolnwood, IL: NTC Business Books, 1995).

36. Constance L. Hays, "What Companies Need to Know Is in the Pizza Dough," *New York Times,* July 26, l998, 3, 1:1.

37. James H. Donnelly, Jr., Leonard L. Berry, and Thomas W. Thompson, *Marketing Financial Services—A Strategic Vision* (Homewood, IL: Dow Jones-Irwin, 1985), p. 113.

38. Quoted in Don Peppers and Martha Rogers, *The One to One Future: Building Relationships One Customer at a Time* (New York): Currency Doubleday, 1993), p. 108.

39. Carl Sewell and Paul Brown, *Customers for Life* (New York: Pocket Books, 1990), p. 162.

40. William A. Sherden, *Market Ownership: The Art & Science of Becoming #1* (New York: AMACOM, 1994), p. 77.

41. Robert J. Bowman, "Good Things, Smaller Packages," *World Trade*, Vol. 6, No. 9, October 1993, pp. 106–110.

42. Michael J. Lanning and Lynn W. Phillips, "Strategy Shifts Up a Gear," *Marketing*, October 1991, p. 9.

43. Lynn O'Rourke Hayes, "Quality is Worth 11,000 in the Bank," *Restaurant Hospitality*, March 1993, p. 68.

44. See Thomas M. Petro, "Profitability: The Fifth 'P' of Marketing," *Bank Marketing*, September 1990, pp. 48–52; and Petro, "Who Are Your Best Customers?" *Bank Marketing*, October 1990, pp. 48–52.

45. "Quality: The U.S. Drives to Catch Up," *Business Week*, November 1982, pp. 66–80, here p. 68. For a recent assessment of progress, see "Quality Programs Show Shoddy Results," *The Wall Street Journal*, May 14, 1992, Section B, p. 1.

46. See "Quality in Europe," *Work Study*, January/February 1993, p. 30; Ronald Henkoff, "The Hot New Seal of Quality," *Fortune*, June 28, 1993, pp. 116–120; Amy Zukerman, "One Size Doesn't Fit All," *Industry Week*, January 9, 1995, pp. 37–40, and "The Sleeper Issue of the '90s," *Industry Week*, August 15, 1994, pp. 99–100, 108.

47. Robert D. Buzzell and Bradley T. Gale, *The PIMS Principles: Linking Strategy to Performance* (New York: Free Press, 1987), Chapter 6. PIMS stands for Profit Impact of Market Strategy.

48. See "The Gurus of Quality: American Companies Are Heading the Quality Gospel Preached by Deming, Juran, Crosby, and Taguchi," *Traffic Management*, July 1990, pp. 35–39.

49. See Cyndee Miller, "U.S. Firms Lag in Meeting Global Quality Standards," *Marketing News*, February 15, 1993.

50. J. Daniel Beckham, "Expect the Unexpected in Health Care Marketing Future," *The Academy Bulletin*, July 1992, p. 3.

Chapter 3

1. Steve Harrell, in a speech at the plenary session of the American Marketing Association's Educators' Meeting, Chicago, August 5, 1980.

2. See "The New Breed of Strategic Planning," *Business Week*, September 7, 1984, pp. 62–68.

3. See Drucker, *Management: Tasks, Responsibilities and Practices* (New York: Harper & Row, 1973), Chapter 7.

4. Donald P. Robin and R. Eric Reidenbach, "Social Responsibility, Ethics, and Marketing Strategy: Closing the Gap Between Concept and Application," *Journal of Marketing*, January 1987, pp. 44–58.

5. Eric Gilboord, "Make Mission Statement Point of Focus for Firm," *Globe and Mail*, March 30, 1999, p. B7.

6. ServiceMaster's mission and objectives taken from their web site (http://www.svm.com).

7. Nortel Network's mission statement taken from their web site (http://www.nortelnetworks.com/corporate)

8. See Noranda Inc.'s 1998 Annual Report, "Focused on Profitable Growth," p. 3.

9. See "The Hollow Corporation," *Business Week*, March 3, 1986, pp. 57–59. Also see William H. Davidow and Michael S. Malone, *The Virtual Corporation* (New York: Harper Business, 1992).

10. For more discussion, see Laura Nash, "Mission Statements—Mirrors and Windows," *Harvard Business Review*, March-April 1988, pp. 155–56.

11. Theodore Levitt, "Marketing Myopia," *Harvard Business Review*, July-August 1960, pp. 45–56.

12. Derek Abell, *Defining the Business: The Starting Point of Strategic Planning* (Englewood Cliffs, NJ: Prentice-Hall, 1980), Chapter 3.

13. See Roger A. Kerin, Vijay Mahajan, and P. Rajan Varadarajan, *Contemporary Perspectives on Strategic Planning* (Boston: Allyn & Bacon, 1990).

14. A hard decision must be made between harvesting and divesting a business. Harvesting a business will strip it of its log-run value, in which case it will be difficult to find a buyer. Divesting, on the other hand, is facilitated by maintaining a business in a fit condition in order to attract a buyer.

15. See Peter Patel and Michael Younger, "A Frame of Reference for Strategy Development," *Long Range Planning*, April 1978, pp. 6–12, and S. J. Q. Robinson, et al., "The Directional Policy Matrix—Tool for Strategic Planning," *Long Range Planning*, June 1978, pp. 8–15.

16. For a contrary view, however, see J. Scott Armstrong and Roderick J. Brodie, "Effects of Portfolio Planning Methods on Decision Making: Experimental Results," *International Journal of Research in Marketing* (1994), pp. 73–84.

17. The same matrix can be expanded into nine cells by adding modified products and modified markets. See S. J. Johnson and Conrad Jones, "How to Organize for New Products," *Harvard Business Review*, May-June 1957, pp. 49–62.

18. George Stalk, Philip Evans, and Lawrence E. Shulman, "Competing Capabilities: The New Rules of Corporate Strategy," *Harvard Business Review*, March-April 1992, pp. 57–69.

19. See Michael E. Porter, *Competitive Strategy: Techniques for Analyzing Industries and Competitors* (New York: Free Press, 1980), Chapter 2.

20. Michael E. Porter, "What is Strategy?" *Harvard Business Review,* November-December 1996, pp. 61–78.

21. Martin du Bois and Douglas Lavin, "American Express, Vias Form Smart-Card Unit," *Wall Street Journal,* July 30, 1998, B, 6:3.

22. For readings on strategic alliances, see Peter Lorange and Johan Roos, *Strategic Alliances: Formation, Implementation and Evolution* (Cambridge, MA: Blackwell, 1992), and Jordan D. Lewis, *Partnerships for Profit: Structuring and Managing Strategic Alliances* (New York: Free Press, 1990).

23. Konrad Yakabuski, "Seagram Does Net Deal with BMG," *Globe and Mail,* April 8, 1999, pp. B1, B4.

24. "E-Commerce," *Globe and Mail,* April 9, 1999, p. B6.

25. Roberta Maynard, "Striking the Right Match," *Nation's Business,* May 1996, p. 18.

26. See Robin Cooper and Robert S. Kaplan, "Profit Priorities from Activity-Based Costing," *Harvard Business Review*, May-June 1991, pp. 130–35.

27. See Thomas J. Peters and Robert H. Waterman, Jr., *In Search of Excellence: Lessons from America's Best-Run Companies* (New York: Harper & Row, 1982), pp. 9–12. The same framework is used in Richard Tanner Pascale and Anthony G. Athos, *The Art of Japanese Management: Applications for American Executives* (New York: Simon & Schuster, 1981).

28. See Terrence E. Deal and Allan A. Kennedy, *Corporate Cultures: The Rites and Rituals of Corporate Life* (Reading, MA: Addison-Wesley, 1982); "Corporate Culture," *Business Week*, October 27, 1980, pp. 148–160; Stanley M. Davis, *Managing Corporate Culture* (Cambridge, MA: Ballinger, 1984), and John P. Kotter and James L. Heskett, *Corporate Culture and Performance* (New York: Free Press, 1992).

29. Wendy Zellner, "Can EDS Shed Its Skin?" *Business Week*, November 15, 1993, pp. 56–57.

30. Michael J. Lanning and Edward G. Michaels, "A Business Is a Value Delivery System," McKinsey Staff Paper, No. 41, June 1988 (McKinsey & Co., Inc.).

31. E. Jerome McCarthy, *Basic Marketing: A Managerial Approach*, 12th ed. (Homewood, IL: Irwin, 1996). Two alternative classifications are worth noting. Frey proposed that all marketing-decision variables could be categorized into two factors: the *offering* (product, packaging, brand, price and service) and *methods and tools* (distribution channels, personal selling, advertising, sales promotion, and publicity). See Albert W. Frey, *Advertising*, 3d ed. (New York: Ronald Press, 1961), p. 30. Lazer and Kelly proposed a three-factor classification: *goods and service mix, distribution mix*, and *communications mix*. See William Lazer and Eugene J. Kelly, *Managerial Marketing: Perspectives and Viewpoints*, rev. ed. (Homewood, IL: Irwin, 1962), p. 413.

32. Robert Lauterborn, "New Marketing Litany: 4 P's Passe; C-Words Take Over," *Advertising Age*, October 1, 1990, p. 26.

Chapter 4

1. See James C. Anderson and James A. Narus, *Business Market Management: Understanding, Creating and Delivering Value* (Upper Saddle River, N.J.: Prentice-Hall, 1998), pp.

2. John Koten, "You Aren't Paranoid If You Feel Someone Eyes You Constantly," *The Wall Street Journal*, March 29, 1985, pp. 1, 22; "Offbeat Marketing," *Sales & Marketing Management*, January 1990, p. 35; and Erik Larson, "Attention Shoppers: Don't Look Now But You Are Being Tailed," *Smithsonian Magazine*, January 1993, pp. 70–79.

3. From *Consumer Europe 1993*, a publication of Euromonitor, pnc. London: Tel +4471 251 8021; U.S. offices: (312) 541–8024.

4. Donna DeEulio, "Should Catalogers Travel the EDI Highway?," *Catalog Age*, Vol. 11, No. 2, February 1994, p. 99.

5. David Chilton, "Special Report: Technology for Marketers: Laptop has simplified the work of the salesforce," *Strategy: The Canadian Marketing Report*, January 6, 1997, p. 20. "Special Report: Technology & Communications Tools for Marketers: Salesforce Automation Requires Careful Planning," *Strategy: The Canadian Marketing Report*, September 15, 1997, p. 25.

6. David Chilton, "Special Report: Technology for Marketers: Laptop has simplified the work of the salesforce," *Strategy: The Canadian Marketing Report*, January 6, 1997, p. 20. "Special Report: Technology & Communications Tools for Marketers: Salesforce Automation Requires Careful Planning," *Strategy: The Canadian Marketing Report*, September 15, 1997, p. 25.

7. Kevin Helliker, "Smile: That Cranky Shopper May Be a Store Spy," *The Wall Street Journal,* November 30, 1994, B, 1:3, 6:6.

8. Kevin Marron, "Competitive Intelligence Pros Refine Snooping to New Level," and "Even Want Ads Yield Nuggets of Information," *Globe and Mail*, August 19, 1997, p. C3. Web site of the Society of Competitive Intelligence Professionals, http://www.scip.org.

9. Kevin Marron, "Competitive Intelligence Pros Refine Snooping to New Level," and "Even Want Ads Yield Nuggets of Information," *Globe and Mail*, August 19, 1997, p. C3. Web site of the Society of Competitive Intelligence Professionals, http://www.scip.org.

10. Kevin Marron, "Competitive Intelligence Pros Refine Snooping to New Level," and "Even Want Ads Yield Nuggets of Information," *Globe and Mail*, August 19, 1997, p. C3. Web site of the Society of Competitive Intelligence Professionals, http://www.scip.org.

11. Don Peppers, "How You Can Help Them," *Fast Company*, October-November 1997, pp. 128–36.

12. See *1994 Survey of Market Research*, eds. Thomas Kinnear and Ann Root (Chicago: American Marketing Association, 1994).

13. See William R. BonDurant, "Research: The 'HP Way'," *Marketing Research*, June 1992, pp. 28–33.

14. For a discussion of the decision-theory approach to the value of research, see Donald R. Lehmann, *Market Research and Analysis*, 3rd ed. (Homewood, IL: Irwin, 1989), Chapter 2.

15. For an excellent annotated reference to major secondary sources of business and marketing data, see Gilbert A. Churchill, Jr., *Marketing Research: Methodological Foundations*, 6th ed. (Fort Worth, TX: Dryden, 1994.

16. Thomas L. Greenbaum, *The Handbook for Focus Group Research* (New York: Lexington Books, 1993).

17. Sarah Schafer, "Communications: Getting a Line on Customers," *Inc. Tech*, 1996, p. 102; see also Alexia Parks, "On-line Focus Groups Reshape Market Research Industry," Marketing News, May 12, l997, p. 28.

18. Dean Takahashi, "Design Ethnographers Sweat Tiny Details," *Globe and Mail*, October 27, 1998, B20. Zena Olijnyk, "Mayta Learns in Real Homes," *Financial Post*, May 31, 1999, p. C3.

19. Roger D. Blackwell, James S. Hensel, Michael B. Phillips, and Brian Sternthal, *Laboratory Equipment for Marketing Research* (Dubuque, IA: Kendall/ Hunt Publishing Co., 1970); and Wally Wood, "The Race to Replace Memory," *Marketing and Media Decisions*, July 1986, pp. 166–67.

20. Chris Serb, "If You Liked the Food, Press 1," *Hospitals and Health Networks*, April 5,1997, p. 99.

21. G. K. Sharman, "Sessions Challenge Status Quo," *Marketing News*, November 10, l997, p. 18. Anonymous, "Prepaid Phone Cards Are Revolutionizing Market Research Techniques," *Direct Marketing* , March l998, p. 12.

22. Selwyn Feinstein, "Computers Replacing Interviewers for Personnel and Marketing Tasks," *The Wall Street Journal*, October 9, 1986, p. 35.

23. For further reading, see Joanne Lipman, "Single-Source Ad Research Heralds Detailed Look at Household Habits," *The Wall Street Journal*, February 16, 1988, p. 39; Joe Schwartz, "Back to the Source," *American Demographics*, January 1989, pp. 22–26; and Magid H. Abraham and Leonard M. Lodish, "Getting the Most Out of Advertising and Promotions," *Harvard Business Review*, May-June 1990, pp. 50–60.

24. John D.C. Little, "Decision Support Systems for Marketing Managers," *Journal of Marketing*, Summer 1979, p. 11.

25. Gary L. Lilien and Arvind Rangaswamy, *Marketing Engineering: Computer-Assisted Marketing Analysis and Planning* (Reading, MA: Addison Wesley, 1998).

26. John D.C. Little, "BRANDAID: A Marketing Mix Model, Part I: Structure; Part II: Implementation," *Operations Research*, Vol. 23, 1975, pp. 628–73.

27. Leonard M. Lodish, "CALLPLAN: An Interactive Salesman's Call Planning System," *Management Science*, December 1971, pp. 25–40.

28. David B. Montgomery, Alvin J. Silk, and C.E. Zaragoza, "A Multiple-Product Sales-Force Allocation Model," *Management Science*, December 1971, pp. 3–24.

29. S.W. Hess and S.A. Samuels, "Experiences with a Sales Districting Model: Criteria and Implementation," *Management Science*, December 1971, pp. 41–54.

30. John D.C. Little and Leonard M. Lodish, "A Media Planning Calculus," *Operations Research*, January/February 1969, pp. 1–35.

31. Magid M. Abraham and Leonard M. Lodish, "PROMOTER: An Automated Promotion Evaluation System," *Marketing Science*, Spring 1987, pp. 101–23.

32. Raymond R. Burke, Arvind Rangaswamy, Jerry Wind, and Jehoshua Eliashberg, "A Knowledge-Based System for Advertising Design," *Marketing Science*, Vol. 9, No. 3, 1990, pp. 212–29.

33. John D.C. Little, "Cover Story: An Expert System to Find the News in Scanner Data," Sloan School, MIT Working Paper, 1988.

34. Wendy Stueck, "Royal Roads' Boot Camp for Business," *The Globe and Mail*, January 21, 1999, p. B12.

35. Jill Vardy, "Corel Turns Focus on Internet Graphic Arts," *Financial Post*, April 30, 1999, p. C3

36. For further discussion, see Gary L. Lilien, Philip Kotler, and K. Sridhar Moorthy, *Marketing Models* (Englewood Cliffs, NJ: Prentice Hall, 1992).

37. See Russell L. Ackoff, *A Concept of Corporate Planning* (New York: Wiley-Interscience, 1970), pp. 36–37.

38. For suggested strategies related to the market area's *BDI* standing, see Don E. Schultz, Dennis Martin, and William P. Brown, *Strategic Advertising Campaigns* (Chicago: Crain Books, 1984), p. 338.

39. Patrick Brethour, "$2 Coin Proves To Be Hot Issue," *Globe and Mail*, June 3, 1996, p. B8.

40. Jeff Harrington, "Juiced-up Orange Juice? Yuck, Buyers Say: Today AcuPoll Releases 10 Best and Six Worst New Products of '97," *Detroit News*, December 7, l997, D3.

41. See Jacob Gonik, "Tie Salesmen's Bonuses to Their Forecasts," *Harvard Business Review*, May-June 1978, pp. 116–23.

42. See Norman Dalkey and Olaf Helmer, "An Experimental Application of the Delphi Method to the Use of Experts," *Management Science*, April 1963, pp. 458–67. Also see Roger J. Best, "An Experiment in Delphi Estimation in Marketing Decision Making," *Journal of Marketing Research*, November 1974, pp. 447–52.

Chapter 5

1. Dana Canedy, "Mattel Looks at Life Beyond Barbie," *Financial Post*, April 7, 1999, p. C13. Gene Del Vecchio, "Keeping It Timeless, Trendy," *Advertising Age*, March 23, 1998, p. 24.

2. John Heinzl, "Food Makers Do the Mashed Potato," *Globe and Mail*, November 4, 1998, p. B29.

3. Gerald Celente, *Trend Tracking* (New York: Warner Books, 1991).

4. See Faith Popcorn, *The Popcorn Report* (New York: Harper Business, 1992).

5. John Kettle wrote this material specifically for *Marketing Management*, May 14, 1999.

6. John Naisbitt and Patricia Aburdene, *Megatrends 2000* (New York: Avon Books, 1990).

7. Pam Weisz, "Border Crossings: Brands Unify Image to Counter Cult of Culture," *Brandweek*, October 31, 1994, pp. 24–28.

8. Much of the statistical data in this chapter is drawn from the *World Almanac and Book of Facts*, 1994 and the *Statistical Abstract of the United States*, 1994 (Washington, DC: U.S. Bureau of the Census, 1995)..

9. Donella H. Meadows, Dennis L. Meadows, Jorgen Randers, and William W. Behrens III, *The Limits to Growth* (New York: New American Library, 1972), p. 41.

10. Philip Kotler and Eduardo Roberto, *Social Marketing: Strategies for Changing Public Attitudes* (New York: Free Press, 1989).

11. "Kettle's Future," *Globe and Mail,* January 21, 1999, p. B12.

12. Sally D. Goll, "Marketing: China's (Only) Children Get the Royal Treatment," *Wall Street Journal*, February 8, 1995, B, 1:3.

13. John Kettle, "Canada Shows Its Age," Kettle's Future, *Globe and Mail*, January 17, 1997, p. B11. Jim McElgunn, "Foot Puts the Boot to Current 'Life-Cycle' Trends," *Marketing*, June 15, 1992, p. 1; Daniel Stoffman, "Completely Predictable People," *Globe and Mail Report on Business Magazine*, November 1990, pp. 78–84; "Boomers Slowing Pace of Leisure," *Toronto Star*, June 20, 1993, G3.

14. Astrid Van Den Broek, "Brand Makeovers," *Marketing*, April 26, 1999, p. 21.

15. Bill Stoneman, "Beyond Rocking the Ages: An Interview with J. Walker Smith," *American Demographics*, May 1998, pp. 45–49. Margot Hornblower, "Great X," *Time*, June 9, 1997, pp. 58–59. Bruce Horowitz, "Gen X in a Class by Itself," *USA Today*, September 23, 1996, p. B1.

16. Jaine Lopiano-Misdom and Joanne de Luca, "Street Scene," *Across the Board*, March 1998, p. 14.

17. David Leonhardt, "Hey Kids, Buy This," *Business Week*, June 30, 1997, pp. 62–67. Lisa Krakowka, "In the Net," *American Demographics*, August 1998, p. 56.

18. Bill Stoneman, "Beyond Rocking the Ages: An Interview with J. Walker Smith," *American Demographics*, May 1998, pp. 45–49. Margot Hornblower, "Great X," *Time*, June 9, 1997, pp. 58–59. Bruce Horowitz, "Gen X in a Class by Itself," *USA Today*, September 23, 1996, p. B1.18.

19. Bobby Siu, "Ethnic Marketing: Demographic Wave Well Worth Riding," *Strategy: The Canadian Marketing Report*, July 6, 1998, p. 15.

20. Bobby Siu, "Ethnic Marketing: Demographic Wave Well Worth Riding," *Strategy: The Canadian Marketing Report*, July 6, 1998, p. 15. David Todd, "Special Report: Multicultural Marketing: Nike Takes It to the Streets," *Strategy: The Canadian Marketing Report*, August 17, 1998, p. 26.

21. Bobby Siu, "Ethnic Marketing: Demographic Wave Well Worth Riding," *Strategy: The Canadian Marketing Report*, July 6, 1998, p. 15. David Todd, "Special Report: Multicultural Marketing: Nike Takes It to the Streets," *Strategy: The Canadian Marketing Report*, August 17, 1998, p. 26.

22. Susanne Hiller, "Cohabitation on the Rise from Coast to Coast," *National Post*, April 24, 1999, p. B2.

23. Laura Koss-Feder, "Out and About," *Marketing News*, May 25, 1998, pp. 1, 20.

24. Dana Canedy, "As the Purchasing Power of Women Rises, Marketers Start to Pay More Attention to Them," *New York Times*, July 2, 1998, p. 6.

25. Bruce Little, "We're a Nation on the Move," *Globe and Mail*, April 19, 1999, p. A2. Mark MacKinnon, "A Little Country, A Little High Tech," *Globe and Mail*, March 8, 1999, pp. B1, B5.

26. John Kettle, "Who Will Buy What as the Years Go By," *Globe and Mail, February 4, 1999, p. B10*. Bruce Little, "Eateries Lose Appeal, But Gambling on Rise," *Globe and Mail, October 19, 1998, p. A8*. Jim McElgunn and Joanne Van der Burgt, "A Marketing Profile of gamblers," *Marketing, October 21, 1998, p. 28*.

27. David Leonhardt, "Two-Tier Marketing," *Business Week, March 17, 1997*, pp. 82–90. Mark MacKinnon, "The Myth of the Rich American," *Globe and Mail, December 31, 1999*, pp. B1, B7.

28. David Thomas, "Consumers Are Spending Faster Than They Earn," *Financial Post*, November 3, 1998, p. C6.

29. Keith McArthur, "Canadians Put Environment First," *Globe and Mail*, June 23, 1997, p. A4.

30. "Are There High-tech Industries or Only High-tech Firms?" *StatsCan Daily,* December 10, 1998.

31. Francoise L. Simon, "Marketing Green Products in the Triad," *The Columbia Journal of World Business*, Fall & Winter 1992, pp. 268–85; and Jacquelyn A. Ottman, *Green Marketing: Responding to Environmental Consumer Demands* (Lincolnwood, IL: NTC Business Books, 1993).

32. Mark MacKinon, "Foreign Ownership is on the Rise," *Globe and Mail*, February 1, 1999, pp. B1, B7. Barrie McKenna, "Canada's Ranking Slips in Ability to Innovate," *Globe and Mail*, March 21, 1999, p. B3. "White House to Name 22 Technologies It Says Are

Crucial to Prosperity, Security," *The Wall Street Journal*, April 26, 1991, p. 2.

33. See "R&D Scoreboard: On A Clear Day You Can See Progress," *Business Week*, June 29, 1992, pp. 104–25.

34. See Dorothy Cohen, *Legal Issues on Marketing Decision Making* (Cincinnati: South-Western, 1995).

35. Rajiv Chandrasekaran, "AOL Settles Marketing Complaints," *The Washington Post*, May 29, 1998, F01.

36. Arnold Mitchell of the Stanford Research Institute, private publication.

37. Lautens, "Other Canadian Values," *Toronto Star*, 1990 (see http://courses/bus.ualberta.ca/consumer-behavior/lectures/Culture/sld011.htm). Suzanne Peters, *1995 Exploring Canadian Values – Synthesis Report*, Ottawa: Canadian Policy Research Network. Stuart H. Surlin and Barry Berlin, "TV, Values, and Culture in U.S.-Canadian Borderland Cities: A Shared Perspective, *Canadian Journal of Communications*, (http://www.cjc.ca/BackIssues/16.3/surlin.html

38. Glenn Collins, "From Taco Bell, a Healthier Option," *The New York Times*, February 9, 1995, D, 4:3.

Chapter 6

1. Joshua Macht, "The New Market Research," *Inc.*, July 1998, pp. 87–94.

2. See Fundamental Canadian Values (http://www.interlog.com/~vcc) and Leon G. Schiffman and Leslie Lazar Kanuk, *Consumer Behaviour*, 6th ed. (Upper Saddle River, NJ: Prentice Hall, 1997).

3. Shawna Steinberg, "Oh, Canada in the Spotlight," *Marketing*, November 2, 1998, pp. 10–11.

4. Eve Lazarus, "Native Hospitality," *Marketing*, May 10, 1999, pp. 12–15.

5. Leon G. Schiffman and Leslie Lazar Kanuk, *Consumer Behaviour*, 6th ed. (Upper Saddle River, NJ: Prentice Hall, 1997).

6. Courteny Kane, "Advertising: TBWA/Chiat Day Brings 'Street Culture' to a Campaign for Levi Strauss Silver Tab Clothing," *New York Times*, August 14, l998, D, 8:3.

7. See Rosann L. Spiro, "Persuasion in Family Decision Making," *Journal of Consumer Research*, March 1983, pp.

393–402; Lawrence H. Wortzel, "Marital Roles and Typologies as Predictors of Purchase Decision Making for Everyday Household Products: Suggestions for Research," in *Advances in Consumer Research*, Vol. 7, ed. Jerry C. Olson (1989), pp. 212–15; David J. Burns, "Husband-Wife Innovative Consumer Decision Making: Exploring the Effect of Family Power," *Psychology & Marketing*, May/June 1992, pp. 175–189; Robert Boutilier, "Pulling the Family's Strings, " *American Demographics*, August 1993, pp. 44–48. For cross-cultural comparisons of husband/wife buying roles, see John B. Ford, Michael S. LaTour, and Tony L. Henthorne, "Perception of Marital Roles in Purchase-Decision Processes: A Cross-Cultural Study," *Journal of the Academy of Marketing Science*, Spring 1995, pp. 120–131.

8. George Moschis, "The Role of Family Communication in Consumer Socialization of Children and Adolescents," *Journal of Consumer Research*, March 1985, pp. 898–913.

9. John Steere, "How Asian-Americans Make Purchase Decisions," *Marketing News*, March 13, 1995, p. 9.

10. Lyle V. Harris, "Men Rule the Aisles," *Globe and Mail*, May 6, 1999, p. C5.

11. Tom Peters, "Opportunity Knocks," *Forbes*, June 2, 1997, p. 132.

12. Alan Alder, "Purchasing Power Women's Buying Muscle Shops Up in Car Design, Marketing," *Chicago Tribune*, September 29, 1996, p. 21A.

13. James U. McNeal, "Tapping the Three Kids' Markets," *American Demographics*, April 1998, pp. 37–41.

14. David Leonhardt, "Hey Kid, Buy This," *Business Week*, June 30, 1997, pp. 62–67.

15. Rob Yoegel, "Reaching Youth on the Web," *Target Marketing*, November 1997, pp.38–41.

16. See Lawrence Lepisto, "A Life Span Perspective of Consumer Behaviour," in *Advances in Consumer Research*, ed. Elizabeth Hirshman and Morris Holbrook, Vol. 12 (Provo, UT: Association for Consumer Research, 1985), p. 47. Also see Gail Sheehy, *New Passages: Mapping Your Life Across Time* (New York: Random House, 1995).

17. Arnold Mitchell, *The Nine American Lifestyles* (New York: Warner Books), pp. viii-x, 25–31; Personal communication from the VALS tm Program, Business Intelligence Center, SRI Consulsting, Menlo Park, CA, February 1, 1996.

18. Stuart Elliott, "Sampling Tastes of a Changing Russia," *The New York Times*, April 1, 1992, pp. D:1, 19.

19. See Harold H. Kassarjian and Mary Jane Sheffet, "Personality and Consumer Behaviour: An Update," in *Perspectives in Consumer Behaviour*, ed. Harold H. Kassarjian and Thomas S. Robertson (Glenview, IL: Scott, Foresman, 1981), pp. 160–80.

20. See M. Joseph Sirgy, "Self-Concept in Consumer Behaviour: A Critical Review," *Journal of Consumer Research*, December 1982, pp. 287–300.

21. See Thomas J. Reynolds and Jonathan Gutman, "Laddering Theory, Method, Analysis, and Interpretation," *Journal of Advertising Research*, February-March 1988, pp. 11–34.

22. See Jan Callebaut, et al., *The Naked Consumer: The Secret of Motivational Research in Global Marketing* (Antwerp, Belgium: Censydiam Institute, 1994).

23. Abraham Maslow, *Motivation and Personality* (New York: Harper & Row, 1954), pp. 80–106.

24. See Frederick Herzberg, *Work and the Nature of Man* (Cleveland: William Collins, 1966); and Henk Thierry and Agnes M. Koopman-Iwerna, "Motivation and Satisfaction," in *Handbook of Work and Organizational Psychology*, ed. P. J. Drenth (New York: John Wiley, 1984), pp. 141–42.

25. Bernard Berelson and Gary A. Steiner, *Human Behaviour: An Inventory of Scientific Findings* (New York: Harcourt Brace Jovanovich, 1964), p. 88.

26. See Alice M. Tybout, Bobby J. Calder, and Brian Sternthal, "Using Information Processing Theory to Design Marketing Strategies," *Journal of Marketing Research*, February 1981, pp. 73–79.

27. Wai-Sum Siu and Carmen Hau-Ming Chan, "Country-of-origin Effects on Product Evaluation: The Case of Chinese Consumers in Hong Kong," *Journal of International Marketing and Marketing Research*, October 1997, pp. 115–122.

28. Anonymous, "International: Old Wine in New Bottles," *The Economist*, February 21, 1998, p. 45.

29. Johnny K. Johansson, "Determinants and Effects of the Use of 'Made In' Labels," *International Marketing Review* (UK), Vol. 6, Iss. 1, 1989, pp. 47–58; Warren J. Bilkey and Erik Nes, "Country-of-Origin Effects on Product Evaluations," *Journal of International Business Studies*, Spring-Summer 1982, pp. 89–99; and P. J. Cattin et al., "A Cross-Cultural Study of 'Made-In' Concepts," *Journal of International Business Studies*, Winter 1982, pp. 131–41.

30. See David Krech, Richard S. Crutchfield, and Egerton L. Ballachey, *Individual in Society* (New York: McGraw-Hill, 1962), Chap. 2.

31. Patti Summerfield, "Dairy Farmers Go for MoOOre with Teen-targeted Campaign," *Strategy: The Canadian Marketing Report*, September 15, 1997, p. 8. David Todd, "Quebec Milk Producers Play on Emotional Ties," *Strategy: The Canadian Marketing Report*, March 1, 1999, p. 31.

32. See Henry Assael, *Consumer Behaviour and Marketing Action* (Boston: Kent, 1987), Chap. 4.

33. Herbert E. Krugman, "The Impact of Television Advertising: Learning without Involvement," *Public Opinion Quarterly*, Fall 1965, pp. 349–56.

34. Marketing scholars have developed several models of the consumer buying process. See John A. Howard and Jagdish N. Sheth, *The Theory of Buyer Behaviour* (New York: Wiley, 1969); and James F. Engel, Roger D. Blackwell, and Paul W. Miniard, *Consumer Behaviour*, 8th ed. (Fort Worth, TX: Dryden, 1994).

35. See William P. Putsis, Jr. and Narasimhan Srinivasan, "Buying or Just Browsing? The Duration of Purchase Deliberation," *Journal of Marketing Research*, August 1994, pp. 393–402.

36. See Chem L. Narayana and Rom J. Markin, "Consumer Behaviour and Product Performance: An Alternative Conceptualization," *Journal of Marketing*, October 1975, pp. 1–6.

37. See Paul E. Green and Yoram Wind, *Multiattribute Decisions in Marketing: A Measurement Approach* (Hinsdale, IL: Dryden Press, 1973), Chap. 2; Leigh McAlister, "Choosing Multiple Items from a Product Class," *Journal of Consumer Research*, December 1979, pp. 213–24.

38. This expectancy-value model was developed by Martin Fishbein in "Attitudes and Prediction of Behaviour," in *Readings in Attitude Theory and Measurement*, ed. Martin Fishbein (New York: John Wiley, 1967), pp. 477–92. For a critical review, see Paul W. Miniard and Joel B. Cohen, "An Examination of the Fishbein-Ajzen Behavioural-Intentions Model's Concepts and Measures,"*Journal of Experimental Social Psychology*, May 1981, pp. 309–39.
    Other models of consumer evaluation include: the *ideal-brand model*, which assumes that a consumer compares actual brands to her ideal brand and chooses the brand that comes closest to her ideal brand; the *conjunctive model*, which assumes that a consumer sets minimum acceptable levels on all the attributes and considers only the brands that meet all the minimum requirements; and the *disjunctive model*, which assumes that a consumer sets minimum acceptable levels on only a few attributes and eliminates those brands falling short. For a discussion of these and other models, see Green and Wind, *Multiattribute Decisions in Marketing*.

39. See Harper W. Boyd, Jr., Michael L. Ray, and Edward C. Strong, "An Attitudinal Framework for Advertising Strategy," *Journal of Marketing*, April 1972, pp. 27–33.

40. See Jagdish N. Sheth, "An Investigation of Relationships among Evaluative Beliefs, Affect, Behavioural Intention, and Behaviour," in *Consumer Behaviour: Theory and Application*, eds. John U. Farley, John A. Howard, and L. Winston Ring (Boston: Allyn & Bacon, 1974), pp. 89–114.

41. Martin Fishbein, "Attitudes and Prediction of Behaviour," in *Readings in Attitude Theory and Measurement*, ed. Martin Fishbein (New York: John Wiley, 1967), pp. 477–92. 42.

42. See Raymond A. Bauer, "Consumer Behaviour as Risk Taking," in *Risk Taking and Information Handling in Consumer Behaviour*, ed. Donald F. Cox (Boston: Division of Research, Harvard Business School, 1967); and James W. Taylor, "The Role of Risk in Consumer Behaviour," *Journal of Marketing*, April 1974, pp. 54–60.

43. See Priscilla A. La Barbera and David Mazursky, "A Longitudinal Assessment of Consumer Satisfaction/Dissatisfaction: The Dynamic Aspect of the Cognitive Process," *Journal of Marketing Research*, November 1983, pp. 393–404.

44. See Ralph L. Day, "Modeling Choices among Alternative Responses to Dissatisfaction," in *Advances in Consumer Research*, Vol. 11 (1984), pp. 496–99. Also, see Philip Kotler and Murali K. Mantrala, "Flawed Products: Consumer Responses and Marketer Strategies," *Journal of Consumer Marketing*, Summer 1985, pp. 27–36.

45. See Barry L. Bayus, "Word of Mouth: The Indirect Effects of Marketing Efforts," *Journal of Advertising Research*, June/July 1985, pp. 31–39.

46. See Albert O. Hirschman, *Exit, Voice, and Loyalty* (Cambridge, MA: Harvard University Press, 1970).

47. See Mary C. Gilly and Richard W. Hansen, "Consumer Complaint Handling as a Strategic Marketing Tool," *Journal of Consumer Marketing*, Fall 1985, pp. 5–16.

48. See James H. Donnelly, Jr. and John M. Ivancevich, "Post-Purchase Reinforcement and Back-Out Behaviour," *Journal of Marketing Research*, August 1970, pp. 399–400.

49. Pam Weisz, "Avon's Skin-So-Soft Bugs Out," *Brandweek*, June 6, 1994, p. 4.

Chapter 7

1. Frederick E. Webster, Jr., and Yoram Wind, *Organizational Buying Behaviour* (Englewood Cliffs, NJ: Prentice Hall, 1972), p. 2.

2. John H. Sheridan, "An Alliance Built on Trust," *Industry Week*, March 17, 1997, pp. 66–70.

3. Jill Vardy, "Compaq Profit Won't Even Come Close to Forecasts," *Financial Post*, April 10, 1999, pp. D1, D2.

4. Shawn Tully, "How Cisco Mastered the Net," *Fortune*, August 17, 1998, pp. 107–210. "Tourism Commission Launches Industry Website," *Ad-News On-Line Daily*, May 17, 1999, p. 1.

5. Minda Zetlin, "It's All the Same to Me," *Sales & Marketing Management,* February 1994, pp. 71–75.

6. Robert Hiebeler, Thomas B. Kelly, and Charles Ketteman, *Best Practices: Building Your Business with Customer-focused Solutions* (New York: Arthur Andersen/Simon & Schuster, 1998), pp. 122–124.

7. Michael Collins, "Breaking into the Big Leagues," *American Demographics,* January 1996, p. 24.

8. Anonymous, "Women and Minorities Account for a Growing Share of Purchase Decisionmakers," *The American Salesman,* September 1996, p.8.

9. Patrick J. Robinson, Charles W. Faris, and Yoram Wind, *Industrial Buying and Creative Marketing* (Boston: Allyn & Bacon, 1967).

10. See Daniel H. McQuiston, "Novelty, Complexity, and Importance as Causal Determinants of Industrial Buyer Behaviour," *Journal of Marketing,* April 1989, pp. 66–79, and Peter Doyle, Arch G. Woodside, and Paul Mitchell, "Organizational Buying in New Task and Rebuy Situations," *Industrial Marketing Management,* February 1979, pp. 7–11.

11. Urban B. Ozanne and Gilbert A. Churchill, Jr., "Five Dimensions of the Industrial Adoption Process," *Journal of Marketing Research,* 1971, pp. 322–28.

12. Greg Crone, "Paving the Drive to Privatization," *Financial Post,* April 24, 1999, p. D10.

13. See Donald W. Jackson, Jr., Janet E. Keith, and Richard K. Burdick, "Purchasing Agents' Perceptions of Industrial Buying Center Influence: A Situational Approach," *Journal of Marketing,* Fall 1984, pp. 75–83.

14. Frederick E. Webster, Jr., and Yoram Wind, *Organizational Buying Behaviour* (Englewood Cliffs, NJ: Prentice Hall, 1972), p. 6.

15. Frederick E. Webster, Jr., and Yoram Wind, *Organizational Buying Behaviour* (Englewood Cliffs, NJ: Prentice Hall, 1972), p. 78–80.

16. See " 'I Think You Have a Great Product, But It's Not My Decision,' " *American Salesman,* April 1994, pp. 11–13.

17. See " 'I Think You Have a Great Product, But It's Not My Decision,' " *American Salesman,* April 1994, pp. 11–13.

18. Frederick E. Webster, Jr., and Yoram Wind, *Organizational Buying Behaviour* (Englewood Cliffs, NJ: Prentice Hall, 1972), pp. 33–37.

19. Terrence Belford, "Shake, Rattle and Recycle," Special Report: Business and the Environment, *Financial Post,* October 24–26, 1998, p. R13.

20. Sara Lorge, "Purchasing Power," *Sales and Marketing Management,* June 1998, pp. 43–46.

21. Tim Minahan, "OEM Buying Survey—Part 2: Buyers Get New Roles But Keep Old Tasks," *Purchasing,* July 16, 1998, pp. 208–209.

22. Shawn Tully, "Purchasing's New Muscle," *Fortune,* February 20, 1995; Mark Fitzgerald, "Decentralizing Control of Purchasing," *Editor and Publisher,* June 18, 1994, pp. 8, 10.

23. [Korean] Anonymous, "Tips, Tricks and Pitfalls to Avoid When Doing Business in the Tough But Lucrative Korean Market," *Business America,* June 1997, p. 7. [Latin America] Dana May Casperson, "Minding Your Manners in Latin America," *Sales and Marketing Management,* March 1998, p. 96. [Mexico] Valerie Frazee, "Getting Started in Mexico," *Workforce,* January 1997, pp. 16–17. [France] [Japan] [Germany] Teresa C. Morrison, Wayne A. Conaway, and Joseph J. Douress, *Dun & Bradstreet's Guide to Doing Business Around the World* (New York: Prentice Hall, 1997).

24. James C. Anderson and James A. Narus, *Business Market Management: Understanding, Creating and Delivering Value* (Upper Saddle River, NJ: Prentice Hall, l998).

25. See Robert E. Wayland and Paul M. Cole, *Customer Connections: New Strategies for Growth* (Boston: Harvard Business School Press, 1997), pp. 161–68.

26. Patrick J. Robinson, Charles W. Faris, and Yoram Wind, *Industrial Buying and Creative Marketing* (Boston: Allyn & Bacon, 1967).

27. John H. Sheridan, "Buying Globally Made Easier," *Industry Week,* February 2, 1998, pp. 63–64.

28. See "Xerox Multinational Supplier Quality Survey," *Purchasing,* January 12, 1995, p. 112.

29. See Donald R. Lehmann and John O'Shaughnessy, "Differences in Attribute Importance for Different Industrial Products," *Journal of Marketing,* April 1974, pp. 36–42.

30. Tim Minahan, "OEM Buying Survey—Part 2: Buyers Get New Roles But Keep Old Tasks," *Purchasing,* July 16, 1998, pp. 208–209.

31. Rick Mullin, "Taking Customer Relations to the Next Level," *The Journal of Business Strategy,* Jan/Feb 1997, pp. 22–26.

32. Chad Kaydo, "Good Service Travels Fast," *Sales & Marketing Management,* May 1998, pp. 22–24.

33. Kitty Vineyard, "Trends. . . in Single Sourcing," *Electrical Apparatus,* November 1996, p. 12.

34. Robert Hiebeler, Thomas B. Kelly, and Charles Ketteman, *Best Practices; Building Your Business with Customer-Focused Solutions* (New York: Arthur Andersen/Simon & Schuster,1998), pp. 124–126.

35. Julie Bort, "Selling High Technology to Uncle Sam." Larry Light and Lisa Sanders, "Uncle Sam's PC Shopping Binge," *Business Week,* October 28, 1996, p. 8.

Chapter 8

1. Michael E. Porter, *Competitive Strategy* (New York: Free Press, 1980), pp. 22–23.

2. See Al Ries and Jack Trout, *Marketing Warfare* (New York: McGraw-Hill, 1986).

3. See Leonard M. Fuld, *The New Competitor Intelligence: The Complete Resource for Finding, Analyzing, and Using Information About Your Competitors* (New York: Wiley, 1995); John A. Czepiel, *Competitive Marketing Strategy* (Englewood Cliffs, NJ: Prentice Hall, 1992).

4. See Hans Katayama, "Fated to Feud: Sony versus Matsushita," *Business Tokyo,* November 1991, pp. 28–32.

5. Michael Krantz, "Click Till You Drop," *Time,* July 20, 1998, pp. 34–39. Michael Krauss, "The Web Is Taking Your Customers for Itself," *Marketing News,* June 8, 1998, p. 8.

6. See Kathryn Rudie Harrigan, "The Effect of Exit Barriers upon Strategic Flexibility," *Strategic Management Journal* 1 (1980), pp. 165–76.

7. See Michael E. Porter, *Competitive Advantage* (New York: Free Press, 1985), pp. 225, 485.

8. Porter, *Competitive Strategy*, Chap. 13.

9. Porter, *Competitive Strategy*, Chap. 7.

10. "The Hardest Sell," *Newsweek*, March 30, 1992, p. 41.

11. William E. Rothschild, *How to Gain (and Maintain) the Competitive Advantage* (New York: McGraw-Hill, 1989), Chap. 5.

12. See Robert V. L. Wright, *A System for Managing Diversity* (Cambridge, MA: Arthur D. Little, December 1974).

13. The following has been drawn from various Bruce Henderson writings, including "The Unanswered Questions, The Unsolved Problems" (paper delivered in a speech at Northwestern University in 1986); *Henderson on Corporate Strategy* (New York: Mentor, 1982); and "Understanding the Forces of Strategic and Natural Competition," *Journal of Business Strategy*, Winter 1981, pp. 11–15.

14. For more discussion, see Leonard M. Fuld, *Monitoring the Competition* (New York: Wiley, 1988).

15. Anonymous, "Spy/Counterspy," *Context*, Summer 1998, pp. 20–21.

16. Steven Flax, "How to Snoop on Your Competitors," *Fortune*, May 14, 1984, pp. 29–33.

17. Porter, *Competitive Advantage*, pp. 226–27.

18. Porter, *Competitive Advantage*, Chap. 6.

19. Paul Lukas, "First: Read Column, Rinse, Repeat," *Fortune*, August 3, 1998, p. 50.

20. See Carla Rapoport, "You Can Make Money in Japan," *Fortune*, February 12, 1990, pp. 85–92; Keith H. Hammonds, "A Moment Kodak Wants to Capture," *Business Week*, August 27, 1990, pp. 52–53; Alison Fahey, "Polaroid, Kodak, Fuji Get Clicking," *Advertising Age*, May 20, 1991, p. 18; and Peter Nulty, "The New Look of Photography," *Fortune*, July 1, 1991, pp. 36–41.

21. Erika Rasmusson, "The Jackpot," *Sales & Marketing Management*, June 1998, pp. 35–41.

22. Deborah Stokes, "Consumers Love 'Churn'," *Financial Post*, March 1, 1999, p. C13.

23. The intensified competition that has taken place worldwide in recent years has sparked management interest in models of military warfare, particularly as described in the writings of Sun-Tsu, Mushashi, von Clausewitz, and Liddell-Hart. Sun Tsu, *The Art of War* (London: Oxford University Press, 1963); Miyamoto Mushashi, *A Book of Five Rings* (Woodstock, NY: Overlook Press, 1974); Carl von Clausewitz, *On War* (London: Routledge & Kegan Paul, 1908); and B. H. Liddell-Hart, *Strategy* (New York: Praeger, 1967).

24. These six defence strategies, as well as the five attack strategies, are taken from Philip Kotler and Ravi Singh, "Marketing Warfare in the 1980s," *Journal of Business Strategy*, Winter 1981, pp. 30–41. For additional reading, see Gerald A. Michaelson, *Winning the Marketing War: A Field Manual for Business Leaders* (Lanham, MD: Abt Books, 1987); Al Ries and Jack Trout, *Marketing Warfare* (New York: McGraw-Hill, 1986); Jay Conrad Levinson, *Guerrilla Marketing* (Boston, MA: Houghton-Mifflin Co., 1984); and Barrie G. James, *Business Wargames* (Harmondsworth, England: Penguin Books, 1984).

25. Seanna Broder, "Reheating Starbucks," *Business Week*, September 28, 1998, p. A1.

26. See Michael E. Porter, *Competitive Strategy* (New York: Free Press, 1980), Chap. 4.

27. Richard Thomkins, "Wal-Mart Invades Food Chain Turf," *St. Louis Post-Dispatch*, October 7, 1998, p. C1.

28. *Relative market share* is the business' market share in its served market relative to the combined market share of its three leading competitors, expressed as a percentage. For example, if this business has 30 percent of the market and its three largest competitors have 20 percent, 10 percent, and 10 percent: 30/(20 + 10 + 10) ' 75 percent % relative market share.

29. Sidney Schoeffler, Robert D. Buzzell, and Donald F. Heany, "Impact of Strategic Planning on Profit Performance," *Harvard Business Review*, March-April 1974, pp. 137–45; and Robert D. Buzzell, Bradley T. Gale, and Ralph G. M. Sultan, "Market Share—A Key to Profitability," *Harvard Business Review*, January-February 1975, pp. 97–106.

30. See Buzzell et al., "Market Share," pp. 97, 100. The results held up in more recent PIMS studies, where the database now includes 2600 business units in a wide range of industries. See Robert D. Buzzell and Bradley T. Gale, *The PIMS Principles: Linking Strategy to Performance* (New York: Free Press, 1987).

31. Richard G. Hamermesh, M. J. Anderson, Jr., and J. E. Harris, "Strategies for Low Market Share Businesses," *Harvard Business Review*, May-June 1978, pp. 95–102.

32. Carolyn Y. Woo and Arnold C. Cooper, "The Surprising Case for Low Market Share," *Harvard Business Review*, November-December 1982, pp. 106–13; also see their "Market-Share Leadership—Not Always So Good," *Harvard Business Review*, January-February 1984, pp. 2–4.

33. This curve assumes that pre-tax return on sales is highly correlated with profitability and that company revenue is a surrogate for market share. Michael Porter, in his *Competitive Strategy*, p. 43, shows a similar **V**-shaped curve.

34. Patricia Sellers, "McDonald's Starts Over," *Fortune*, June 22, 1998, pp. 34–35. David Leonhardt, "McDonalds Can It Regain Its Golden Touch?" *Business Week*, March 9, 1998, pp. 70–77.

35. Steve Hamm, "Microsoft's Future," *Business Week*, January 19, 1998, pp. 58–68.

36. Philip Kotler and Paul N. Bloom, "Strategies for High Market-Share Companies," *Harvard Business Review*, November-December 1975, pp. 63–72. Also see Michael E. Porter, *Competitive Advantage* (New York: Free Press, 1985), pp. 221–26.

37. Robert D. Buzzell and Frederick D. Wiersema, "Successful Share-Building Strategies," *Harvard Business Review*, January-February, 1981, pp. 135–44.

38. Ronald Henkoff, "P&G: New & Improved," *Fortune,* October 14, 1996, pp. 151–160.

39. Zachary Schiller, "Ed Artzt's Elbow Grease has P&G Shining," *Business Week,* October 10, 1994, pp. 84–85.

40. Sarah Lorge, "Top of the Charts: Procter & Gamble," *Sales & Marketing Management,* July 1998, p. 50. Jane Hodges, "P & G Tries to Push Online Advertising," *Fortune,* September 28, 1998, p. 280.

41. See Robert J. Dolan, "Models of Competition: A Review of Theory and Empirical Evidence," in *Review of Marketing,* ed. Ben M. Enis and Kenneth J. Roering (Chicago: American Marketing Association, 1981), pp. 224–34.

42. Kevin Maney, "Sun Rises on Java's Promise CEO MCNealy Sets Sights on Microsoft," *USA Today,* July 14, 1997, p. B, 1:3. Robert D. Hof, "A Java in Every Pot?; Sun Aims to Make it the Language of all Smart Appliances," *Business Week,* July 27, 1998, p. 71.

43. Holman W. Jenkins, Jr., "Business World: On a Happier Note, Orange Juice," *Wall Street Journal,* September 23, 1998, p. A, 23.

44. Dennis Slocum, "Aggressive ING Rings Up Growing Sales in Canada," *Globe and Mail,* December 2, 1997, p. B9.

45. Peter Fitzpatrick, "Canadian Considers No-frills Flying," *Financial Post,* April 12, 1999, p. C3. Mathew Ingram, "WestJet on the Right Flight Path," *Globe and Mail,* September 8, 1998, p. B2. Frankie Thornhill, "Why the Dog Cried," *Marketing,* October 27, 1997, pp. 26–27.

46. Theodore Levitt, "Innovative Imitation," *Harvard Business Review,* September–October 1966, pp. 63 ff. Also see Steven P. Schnaars, *Managing Imitation Strategies: How Later Entrants Seize Markets from Pioneers* (New York: Free Press, 1994).

47. Stuart F. Brown, "The Company that Out-Harleys Harley," *Fortune,* September 28, 1998, pp. 56–57.

48. Allen J. McGrath, "Growth Strategies with a '90s Twist," *Across the Board,* March 1995, pp. 43–46.

49. David Berman, "Mr. Chips, You Make Good Small Talk," *Canadian Business,* December 24, 1998, pp. 94–97.

50. Donald K. Clifford and Richard E. Cavanaugh, *The Winning Performance: How America's High- and Midsize Growth Companies Succeed* (New York: Bantam Books, 1985).

51. Jim Kirk, "Company Finds itself, Finds Success Alberto-Culver Adopts Strategy of Knowing Its Strengths and Promoting Small Brands, Rather Than Tackling Giants," *Chicago Tribune,* January 22, 1998, Business Section, p. 1.

52. Reported in E. R. Linneman and L. J. Stanton, *Making Niche Marketing Work* (New York: McGraw-Hill, 1991).

53. See Bro Uttal, "Pitching Computers to Small Businesses," *Fortune,* April 1, 1985, pp. 95–104; also see Stuart Gannes, "The Riches in Market Niches," *Fortune,* April 27, 1987, pp. 227–30.

Chapter 9

1. Regis McKenna, "Real-Time Marketing," *Harvard Business Review,* July-August 1995, pp. 87–95, p. 87.

2. See James C. Anderson and James A. Narus, "Capturing the Value of Supplementary Services," *Harvard Business Review,* January-February 1995, pp. 75–83.

3. "Royal Bank and SNFB Charge It with McGill Alumni Visa," *Adnews On-Line Daily,* July 8, 1999, p. 1.

4. See Tevfik Dalgic and Maarten Leeuw, "Niche Marketing Revisited: Concept, Applications, and Some European Cases," *European Journal of Marketing,* 28, no. 4 (1994), 39–55.

5. Robert E. Linneman and John L. Stanton, Jr., *Making Niche Marketing Work: How to Grow Bigger by Acting Smaller* (New York: McGraw-Hill, 1991).

6. Robert Blattberg and John Deighton "Interactive Marketing: Exploiting the Age of Addressability" *Sloan Management Review,* 33, no. 1 (1991), 5–14.

7. David Akin, "Web Retailing Gains Market Muscle as Concerns Fade," *Financial Post,* December 26, 1998, p. D4. Paul Davidson, "Entrepreneurs Reap Riches from Net Niches," *USA Today,* April 20, 1998, p. B3. Wendy Stueck, "Founder Sows eSeeds for Online Sales," *Globe and Mail,* March 22, 1999, p. B8.

8. See Don Peppers and Martha Rogers, *The One to One Future: Building Relationships One Customer at a Time* (New York: Currency/Doubleday, 1993).

9. B. Joseph Pine II, *Mass Customization* (Boston: Harvard Business School Press, 1993); and B. Joseph Pine II, Don Peppers, and Martha Rogers, "Do You Want to Keep Your Customers Forever?" *Harvard Business Review,* March-April 1995, pp. 103–14.

10. "Creating Greater Customer Value May Require a Lot of Changes," *Organizational Dynamics,* Summer 1998, p. 26.

11. Susan Moffat, "Japan's New Personalized Production," *Fortune,* October 22, 1990, pp. 132–35.

12. Alan R. Andreasen and Russell W. Belk, "Predictors of Attendance at the Performing Arts," *Journal of Consumer Research,* September 1980, pp. 112–20.

13. Catherine Arns, "PC Makers Head for 'SoHo,'" *Business Week,* September 28, 1992, pp. 125–126; Gerry Khermouch, "The Marketers Take Over," *Brandweek,* September 27, 1993, pp. 29–35.

14. For a market-structure study of the hierarchy of attributes in the coffee market, see Dipak Jain, Frank M. Bass, and Yu-Min Chen, "Estimation of Latent Class Models with Heterogeneous Choice Probabilities: An Application to Market Structuring," *Journal of Marketing Research,* February 1990, pp. 94–101.

15. "Your Office Magazine Launching as Votre Bureau," *AdNew On-line Daily,* June 17, 1999, p. 2. "Hallmark Salutes Quebec, Looks to Mark Millennium," *AdNew On-line Daily,* June 18, 1999, p. 2. Kate Kane, "It's a Small World," *Working Woman,* October 1997, p. 22.

16. "Zellers Delivering New Baby Catalogue," *AdNews On-line Daily,* June 16, 1999, p. 2.

17. Leah Rickard, "Gerber Trots Out New Ads Backing Toddler Food Line," *Advertising Age,* April 11, 1994, pp. 1, 48.

18. "Sega to Target Adults with Brand Extensions," *Marketing Week,* March 12, 1998, p. 9.

19. Emily Nelson, "Marketing and Media: Kodak Focuses on Putting Kids Behind Instead of Just in Front of a Camera,"

Wall Street Journal, May 6, 1997, p. B8. Emily Neslon, "Want to Improve Your Photos? Experts Say, First Bring Camera," *Wall Street Journal*, October 3, 1996, p. B1.

20. *American Demographics*, August 1986.

21. Lisa Napoli, "A Focus on Women at iVillage.com," *New York Times*, August 3, 1998, D6:3.

22. Douglas Todd, "Poorer Canadian Families Give the Biggest Donations," *National Post,* January 22, 1999, p. A9.

23. Doug Saunders, "Wine's in, Midway's Out at Traditional Fairs," *Globe and Mail*, August 16, 1996, p. A1.

24. Patrick Allossery, "Generation X the Right Target for Volkswagen," *The Financial Post*, February 8, 1999, p. C4. For more on generations, see Michael R. Solomon, Judith L. Zaichkowsky, and Rosemary Polegato, *Consumer Behaviour*, Canadian ed. (Scarborough, ON: Prentice Hall, 1999), Chapter 15, and Frank Feather, *The Future Consumer* (Toronto: Warwick Publishing Co., 1994), pp. 69–75.

25. Geoffrey Meredith and Charles Schewe, "The Power of Cohorts," *American Demographics*, December 1994, pp. 22–29.

26. "Harvey's Gearing Up for Summer of Love Campaign," *AdNews On-Line Daily,* July 7, 1999, p. 1.

27. Andrew E. Serwer, "42,496 Secrets Bared," *Fortune*, January 24, 1994, pp. 13–14; Kenneth Labich, "Class in America," *Fortune*, February 7, 1994, pp. 114–126.

28. Cindy Wolff, "A Little Fifi Chic," *National Post*, December 22, 1998, p. B1.

29. Jenny Lee, "Mock-Meat Is Nothing to Sneer At," *Financial Post*, March 15, 1999, p. C3.

30. Junu Bryan Kim, "Taking Comfort in Country: After Decade of '80s Excess, Marketers Tap Easy Lifestyle as Part of Ad Messages," *Advertising Age*, January 11, 1993, p. S1–S4.

31. Jeff Gremillion, "Can Smaller Niches Bring Riches?" *Mediaweek,* October 20, 1997, pp. 50–51.

32. This classification was adapted from George H. Brown, "Brand Loyalty—Fact or Fiction?" *Advertising Age*, June 1952–January 1953, a series.

33. Other leading suppliers of geodemographic data are ClusterPlus (by Donnelly Marketing Information Services) and Acord (C.A.C.I., Inc.).

34. Christina Del Valle, "They Know Where You Live—and How You Buy," *Business Week*, February 7, 1994, p. 89.

35. See Michael J. Weiss, *The Clustering of America* (New York: Harper & Row, 1988).

36. See Norton Paley, "Cut Out for Success," *Sales & Marketing Management*, April 1994, pp. 43–44.

37. Michele Marchetti, "Dell Computer," *Sales & Marketing Management*, October 1997, pp. 50–53.

38. Geoffrey Brewer, "Lou Gerstner Has His Hands Full," *Sales & Marketing Management*," May 1998, pp. 36–41.

39. Thomas S. Robertson and Howard Barich, "A Successful Approach to Segmenting Industrial Markets," *Planning Forum*, November-December 1992, pp.5–11.

40. V. Kasturi Rangan, Rowland T. Moriarty, and Gordon S. Swartz, "Segmenting Customers in Mature Industrial Markets," *Journal of Marketing*, October 1992, pp. 72–82.

41. For another interesting approach to segmenting the business market, see John Berrigan and Carl Finkbeiner, *Segmentation Marketing: New Methods for Capturing Business* (New York: HarperBusiness, 1992).

42. Wendy Brandes, "Advertising: Black-Oriented Radio Tunes Into Narrower Segments," *The Wall Street Journal*, February 13, 1995, B, 5:1.

43. Wendell R. Smith, "Product Differentiation and Market Segmentation as Alternative Marketing Strategies," *Journal of Marketing*, July 1956, p. 4.

44. See Bart Macchiette and Roy Abhijit, "Sensitive Groups and Social Issues," *Journal of Consumer Marketing*, Vol. 11, No. 4, 1994, pp. 55–64.

45. Mark De Wolfe, "Industry Amends Rules for Marketing to Kids," *Strategy: The Canadian Marketing Report*, March 15, 1999, p. D2. Charlotte Parsons, "Women Pay More for Identical Items," *Globe and Mail*, August 3, 1993, p. A1, A2. Marina Strauss, "Labatt targeted Youth, Consultant Says," *Globe and Mail*, July 21, 1995, p. B3.

46. See "Selling Sin to Blacks," *Fortune*, October 21, 1991, p. 100; Martha T. Moore, "Putting on a Fresh Face," *USA Today*, January 3, 1992, pp. B1, B2; Dorothy J. Gaiter, "Black-Owned Firms Are Catching an Afrocentric Wave," *The Wall Street Journal*, January 8, 1992, p. B2; and Maria Mallory, "Waking Up to a Major Market," *Business Week*, March 23, 1992, pp. 70–73.

47. See Philip Kotler, "Megamarketing," *Harvard Business Review*, March-April 1986, pp. 117–24.

Chapter 10

1. Edwin T. Crego, Jr., and Peter D. Schiffrin, *Customer Centered Reengineering* (Homewood, IL: Irwin, 1995).

2. Some of these bases are discussed in David A. Garvin, "Competing on the Eight Dimensions of Quality," *Harvard Business Review*, November-December 1987, pp. 101–9.

3. Web site and Elizabeth Church, "Chocolate Maker Resists Asian Flu," *Globe and Mail*, February 2, 1999, p. B13.

4. See Bernd Schmitt and Alex Simonson, *Marketing Aesthetics: The Strategic Management of Brand, Identity, and Image* (New York: Free Press, 1997).

5. Gerry Khermouch, "'Zona Sets Collectible Max-packs," *Brandweek*, April 20, 1998, p. 16.

6. See Philip Kotler, "Design: A Powerful but Neglected Strategic Tool," *Journal of Business Strategy*, Fall 1984, pp. 16–21. Also see Christopher Lorenz, *The Design Dimension* (New York: Basil Blackwell Inc., 1986).

7. Paul Brent, "Want an iMac? Join the Waiting List," *Financial Post*, March 3, 1999, pp. C1, C2. "Hot R.I.P: The Floppy Disk," *Rolling Stone*, August 20, 1998, p. 86. Owen Edwards, "Beauty and the Box," *Forbes*, October 5, 1998, p. 131.

8. "Consumers Roll Out the Welcome Mat for Electronic Services," *Globe and Mail*, April 29, 1999, p. R6.

9. For further reading, George Stalk, Jr., and Thomas M. Hout, *Competing Against Time* (New York: Free Press, 1990); Joseph D. Blackburn, *Time-Based Competition* (Homewood, IL: Irwin, 1991); Christopher Meyer, *Fast Cycle Time* (New York: Free Press,

1993); and "The Computer Liked Us," *U.S. News & World Report*, August 14, 1995, pp. 71–72.

10. Ian C. MacMillan and Rita Gunther McGrath, "Discovering New Points of Differentiation," *Harvard Business Review*, July-August 1997, pp. 133–145.

11. Adapted from Tom Peters's description in *Thriving on Chaos* (New York: Knopf, 1987), pp. 56–57.

12. Ian C. MacMillan and Rita Gunther McGrath, "Discovering New Points of Differentiation," *Harvard Business Review*, July-August 1997, pp. 133–145.

13. See "Club for the Smart," *Marketing News*, May 23, 1994, p. 1.

14. Ian C. MacMillan and Rita Gunther McGrath, "Discovering New Points of Differentiation," *Harvard Business Review*, July-August 1997, pp. 133–145.

15. See "The 25 Best Sales Forces," *Sales and Marketing Management*, July l998, pp. 32–50.

16. For a similar list, see Leonard L. Berry and A. Parasuraman, *Marketing Services: Competing Through Quality* (New York: Free Press, 1991), p. 16.

17. Susan Greco, "Inside-Out Marketing," *Inc.*, January 1998, pp. 51–59.

18. Erin Davies, "Selling Sex and Cat Food," *Fortune,* June 9, 1997, p. 36.

19. Heather Schoffield, "Tequila's Sun Rises for Upscale Consumers," *Globe and Mail*, April 28, 1999, p. B27.

20. Patrick Allossery, "Customers Know Your Brand Best," *Financial Post*, April 23, 1999, p. C3.

21. "Four Reasons Nike's Not Cool," *Fortune*, March 30, 1998, pp. 26–27.

22. See "Swatch: Ambitious," *The Economist*, April 18, 1992, pp. 74–75. See also http://www.swatch.com/.

23. Theodore Levitt, "Marketing Success through Differentiation—of Anything," *Harvard Business Review*, January–February, 1980.

24. Gregory S. Carpenter, Rashi Glazer, and Kent Nakamoto, "Meaningful Brands From Meaningless Differentiation: The Dependence on Irrelevant Attributes," *Journal of Marketing Research*, August 1994, pp. 339–350.

25. Paul Brent, "It's Not a Bike, It's a Brand," *Financial Post,* January 16, 1999, pp. D1, D3.

26. Al Ries and Jack Trout, *Positioning: The Battle for Your Mind* (New York: Warner Books, 1982).

27. Rosser Reeves, *Reality in Advertising* (New York: Knopf, 1960).

28. See Al Ries and Jack Trout, *Positioning: The Battle for Your Mind* (New York: Warner Books, 1982).

29. Rene Y. Darmon, "Multiple Joint Space for Improved Advertising Strategy," *Canadian Marketer*, 10, no. 1 (1979), 10–14; Richard M. Johnson, "Market Segmentation: A Strategic Management Tool," *Journal of Marketing Research*, Vol. 9, February 1971, pp. 12–18.

30. See Yoram J. Wind, *Product Policy: Concepts, Methods and Strategy* (Reading, MA: Addison-Wesley, 1982), pp. 79–81; and David Aaker and J. Gary Shansby, "Positioning Your Product," *Business Horizons*, May–June 1982, pp. 56–62.

31. Some authors distinguished additional stages. Wasson suggested a stage of competitive turbulence between growth and maturity. See Chester R. Wasson, *Dynamic Competitive Strategy and Product Life Cycles* (Austin, TX: Austin Press, 1978). *Maturity* describes a stage of sales growth slowdown and *saturation*, a stage of flat sales after sales have peaked.

32. John E. Swan and David R. Rink, "Fitting Market Strategy to Varying Product Life Cycles," *Business Horizons*, January–February 1982, pp. 72–76; and Gerald J. Tellis and C. Merle Crawford, "An Evolutionary Approach to Product Growth Theory," *Journal of Marketing*, Fall 1981, pp. 125–34.

33. See William E. Cox, Jr., "Product Life Cycles as Marketing Models," *Journal of Business*, October 1967, pp. 375–84.

34. See Jordan P. Yale, "The Strategy of Nylon's Growth," *Modern Textiles Magazine,* February 1964, pp. 32 ff. Also see Theodore Levitt, "Exploit the Product Life Cycle," *Harvard Business Review,* November–December 1965, pp. 81–94.

35. Chester R. Wasson, "How Predictable Are Fashion and Other Product Life Cycles?" *Journal of Marketing*, July 1968, pp. 36–43.

36. Chester R. Wasson, "How Predictable Are Fashion and Other Product Life Cycles?" *Journal of Marketing*, July 1968, pp. 36–43.

37. William H. Reynolds, "Cars and Clothing: Understanding Fashion Trends," *Journal of Marketing*, July 1968, pp. 44–49.

38. Patrick Butters, "What Biggest Selling Adult Game Still Cranks Out Vexing Questions," *Insight on the News*, January 26, 1998, p. 39.

39. Robert D. Buzzell, "Competitive Behavior and Product Life Cycles," in *New Ideas for Successful Marketing*, eds. John S. Wright and Jack Goldstucker (Chicago: American Marketing Association, 1956), p. 51.

40. Kathryn Leger, "Quebec Cookie Maker Takes on Kellogg," *Financial Post*, April 3, 1999, p. C8.

41. William T. Robinson and Claes Fornell, "Sources of Market Pioneer Advantages in Consumer Goods Industries," *Journal of Marketing Research*, August 1985, pp. 305–17.

42. Glen L. Urban, et al., "Market Share Rewards to Pioneering Brands: An Empirical Analysis and Strategic Implications," *Management Science*, June 1986, pp. 645–59.

43. Gregory S. Carpenter and Kent Nakomoto, "Consumer Preference Formation and Pioneering Advantage," *Journal of Marketing Research*, August 1989, pp. 285–98.

44. Frank R. Kardes, Gurumurthy Kalyanaram, Murali Chankdrashekaran, and Ronald J. Dornoff, "Brand Retrieval, Consideration Set Composition, Consumer Choice, and the Pioneering Advantage," *Journal of Consumer Research*, June 1993, pp. 62–75. See also Frank H. Alpert and Michael A. Kamins, "Pioneer Brand Advantage and Consumer Behavior: A Conceptual Framework and Propositional Inventory," *Journal of the Academy of Marketing Science*, Summer 1994, pp. 244–253.

45. Steven P. Schnaars, *Managing Imitation Strategies* (New York: Free Press, 1994).

46. Peter N. Golder and Gerald J. Tellis, "Pioneer Advantage: Marketing Logic or Marketing Legend?" *Journal of Marketing Research*, May 1992, pp. 34–46.

47. Thomas S. Robertson and Hubert Gatignon, "How Innovators Thwart New Entrants into their Market,"

Planning Review, September–October 1991, pp. 4–11, 48.

48. John B. Frey, "Pricing Over the Competitive Cycle," speech presented at the 1982 Marketing Conference, Conference Board, New York.

49. Linda Himelstein, "Yahoo! The Company, The Strategy, The Stock," *Business Week*, September 7, 1998, pp. 66–76.

50. See Joulee Andrew and Daniel C. Smith, "In Search of the Marketing Imagination: Factors Affecting the Creativity of Marketing Programs for Mature Products," *Journal of Marketing Research*, May 1996, pp. 174–87; William Boulding, Eunkyu Lee, and Richard Staelin, "Mastering the Mix: Do Advertising, Promotion, and Sales Force Activities Lead to Differentiation?" *Journal of Marketing Research*, May 1994, pp. 159–72.

51. John Bigness, "New twists Revive Past Product Hits," *Houston Chronicle*, October 11, 1998, p.8. Denise Gellene, "An Old Dog's New Tricks: Hush Puppies' Return in the '90s Is No Small Feet," *The Los Angeles Times*, August 30, 1997, p. D1.

52. Elizabeth Church, "Chocolate Maker Resists Asian Flu," *Globe and Mail*, February 2, 1999, p. B13.

53. Brian Wansink and Michael L. Ray, "Advertising Strategies to Increase Usage Frequency," *Journal of Marketing*, January 1996, pp. 36–46.

54. Sinclair Stewart, "Service the New Watchword, Say Dailies," *Strategy: The Canadian Marketing Report,* October 26, 1998, p. 29. Patti Summerfield, "Media Agencies Welcoming Post," *Strategy: The Canadian Marketing Report,* October 26, 1998, p. 12.

55. Vanessa O'Connell, "Food: After Years of Trial and Error, A Pickle Slice That Stays Put," *Wall Street Journal*, October 6, 1998, p. B1; Anonymous, "Vlasic's Hamburger-Size Pickles," *Wall Street Journal*, October 5, 1998, p. A26.

56. Donald W. Hendon, Classic Failures in Product Marketing (New York: Quorum Books, 1989), p. 29.

57. Allen J. McGrath, "Growth Strategies with a '90s Twist," *Across the Board*, March 1995, pp. 43–46.

58. R. S. Alexander, "The Death and Burial of 'Sick Products,' " *Journal of Marketing*, April 1964, p. 1.

59. See Philip Kotler, "Phasing Out Weak Products," *Harvard Business Review*, March–April 1965, pp. 107–18; Richard T. Hise, A. Parasuraman, and R. Viswanathan, "Product Elimination: The Neglected Management Responsibility," *Journal of Business Strategy*, Spring 1984, pp. 56–63; and George J. Avlonitis, "Product Elimination Decision Making: Does Formality Matter," *Journal of Marketing*, Winter 1985, pp. 41–52.

60. See Kathryn Rudie Harrigan, "The Effect of Exit Barriers upon Strategic Flexibility," *Strategic Management Journal*, 1 (1980), pp. 165–76.

61. Kathryn Rudie Harrigan, "Strategies for Declining Industries," *Journal of Business Strategy*, Fall 1980, p. 27.

62. See Philip Kotler, "Harvesting Strategies for Weak Products," *Business Horizons*, August 1978, pp. 15–22; and Laurence P. Feldman and Albert L. Page, "Harvesting: The Misunderstood Market Exit Strategy," *Journal of Business Strategy*, Spring 1985, pp. 79–85.

63. John Grossmann, "A Follow-Up on Four Fabled Frenzies," *Inc.*, October 1994, pp. 66–67; Conrad Berenson and Iris Mohr-Jackson, "Product Rejuvenation: A Less Risky alternative to Product Innovation," *Business Horizons*, November-December 1994, pp. 51–56.

64. Nariman K. Dhalla and Sonia Yuspeh, "Forget the Product Life Cycle Concept!" *Harvard Business Review*, January–February 1976, pp. 102–12, here p. 105.

65. Alec Ross, "Sea Kayak Sales Make Waves," *The Financial Post*, May 3, 1999, p. C3.

66. Marnik G., Dekimpe and Dominique M. Hanssens, "Empirical Generalizations About Market Evolution and Stationarity," *Marketing Science*, 14. No. 3, Pt. 1 (1995, pp. G109–21.

Chapter 11

1. *New Products Management for the 1980s* (New York: Booz, Allen & Hamilton, 1982).

2. Derek DeCloet, "Way, Way Too Cool," *Canadian Business*, August 27, 1999, p. 30. Brian Hutchinson, "See Spot Fly," *Canadian Business*, July 1996, pp. 91–94.

3. Christopher Power, "Flops," *Business Week,* August 16, 1993, pp. 76–82. 3. Erika Rasmussen, "Staying Power," *Sales & Marketing Management,* August 1998, pp. 44–46.

4. Thomas Keane, "The Fate of New Products," *Marketing*, May 17, 1999, p. 21.

5. Robert G. Cooper and Elko J. Kleinschmidt, *New Products: The Key Factors in Success* (Chicago: American Marketing Association, 1990). David Steinhart, "Wheelchair Design Wins Entrepreneurial Award," *Financial Post*, March 23, 1999, C4.

6. Modesto A. Madique and Billie Jo Zirger, "A Study of Success and Failure in Product Innovation: The Case of the U.S. Electronics Industry," *IEEE Transactions on Engineering Management*, November 1984, pp. 192–203.

7. Michelle Conlin, "Too Much Doodle?" *Forbes,* October 19, 1998, pp. 54–55; Tim Stevens, "Idea Dollars," *Industry Week,* February 16, 1998, pp. 47–49. http://www.newswire.ca/releases/March 1998/11/c2359.html. http://www.newswire.ca/releases/December 1997/11/c5504.html.

8. See David S. Hopkins, *Options in New-Product Organization* (New York: Conference Board, 1974); Doug Ayers, Robert Dahlstrom, and Steven J. Skinner, "An Exploratory Investigation of Organizational Antecedents to New Product Success," *Journal of Marketing Research*, February 1997, pp. 107–16.

9. See Robert G. Cooper, "Stage-Gate Systems: A New Tool for Managing New Products," *Business Horizons*, May–June 1990, pp. 44–54. See also his "The New Prod System: The Industry Experience," *Journal of Product Innovation Management* 9 (1992): 113–27.

10. Robert Cooper, *Product Leadership: Creating and Launching Superior New Products* (New York: Perseus Books, 1998).

11. Eric von Hippel, "Lead Users: A Source of Novel Product Concepts," *Management Science*, July 1986, pp. 791–805. Also see his *The Sources of Innovation* (New York: Oxford University Press,

1988); and "Learning from Lead Users," in *Marketing in an Electronic Age*, ed. Robert D. Buzzell (Cambridge, MA: Harvard Business School Press, 1985), pp. 308–17.

12. Constance Gustke, "Built to Last," *Sales & Marketing Management,* August 1997, pp. 78–83.

13. Mark Hanan, "Corporate Growth through Venture Management," *Harvard Business Review*, January–February 1969, p. 44. See also Carol J. Loomis, "Dinosaurs?" *Fortune*, May 3, 1993, pp. 36–42.

14. "The Ultimate Widget: 3–D 'Printing' May Revolutionize Product Design and Manufacturing," *U.S. News & World Report*, July 20, 1992, p. 55.

15. Tom Dellacave Jr., "Curing Market Research Headaches," *Sales & Marketing Management,* July 1996, pp. 84–85.

16. Dan Deitz, "Customer-Driven Engineering," *Mechanical Engineering,* May 1996, p. 68.

17. The full-profile example was taken from Paul E. Green and Yoram Wind, "New Ways to Measure Consumers' Judgments," *Harvard Business Review* (July–August 1975), pp. 107–17. Copyright 8 1975 by the President and Fellows of Harvard College; all rights reserved. Also see Paul E. Green and V. Srinivasan, "Conjoint Analysis in Marketing: New Developments with Implications for Research and Practice," *Journal of Marketing*, October 1990, pp. 3–19; Jonathan Weiner, "Forecasting Demand: Consumer Electronics Marketer Uses a Conjoint Approach to Configure Its New Product and Set the Right Price," *Marketing Research: A Magazine of Management & Applications*, Summer 1994, pp. 6–11; Dick R. Wittnick, Marco Vriens, and Wim Burhenne, "Commercial Uses of Conjoint Analysis in Europe: Results and Critical Reflections," *International Journal of Research in Marketing*, January 1994, pp. 41–52.

18. See Robert Blattberg and John Golanty, "Tracker: An Early Test Market Forecasting and Diagnostic Model for New Product Planning," *Journal of Marketing Research*, May 1978, pp. 192–202; Glen L. Urban, Bruce D. Weinberg, and John R. Hauser, "Premarket Forecasting of Really New Products," *Journal of Marketing*, January 1996, pp. 47–60; Peter

19. See Roger A. Kerin, Michael G. Harvey, and James T. Rothe, "Cannibalism and New Product Development," *Business Horizons*, October 1978, pp. 25–31.

20. The present value (V) of a future sum (I) to be received t years from today and discounted at the interest rate (r) is given by $V5I_t/(11r)^t$. Thus $\$4,761,000/(1.15)^5 = \$2,346,000$.

21. See David B. Hertz, "Risk Analysis in Capital Investment," *Harvard Business Review*, January–February 1964, pp. 96–106.

22. See John Hauser, "House of Quality," *Harvard Business Review*, May–June 1988, pp. 63–73. Customer-driven Engineering Is Also Called "Quality Function Deployment." See Lawrence R. Guinta and Nancy C. Praizler, *The QFD Book: The Team Approach to Solving Problems and Satisfying Customers through Quality Function Deployment* (New York: AMACOM, 1993); V. Srinivasan, William S. Lovejoy, and David Beach, "Integrated Product Design for Marketability and Manufacturing," *Journal of Marketing Research,* February 1997, pp. 154–63.

23. Marco Iansiti and Alan MacCormack, "Developing Products on Internet Time," *Harvard Business Review,* September–October 1997, pp. 108–17; Srikant Datar, C. Clark Jordan, and Kannan Srinivasan, "Advantages of Time Based New Product Development in a Fast-Cycle Industry," *Journal of Marketing Research,* February 1997, pp. 36–49; Christopher D. Ittner and David F. Larcker, "Product Development Cycle Time and Organizational Performance," *Journal of Marketing Research,* February 1997, pp. 13–23.

24. Tom Peters, *The Circle of Innovation,* (New York: Alfred A. Knopf, 1997), p. 96.

25. Tom Peters, *The Circle of Innovation,* (New York: Alfred A. Knopf, 1997), p. 99.

26. Faye Rice, "Secrets of Product Testing," *Fortune*, November 28, 1994, pp. 172–74; Lawrence Ingrassia, "Taming the Monster: How Big Companies Can

Change: Keeping Sharp: Gillette Holds Its Edge by Endlessly Searching for a Better Shave," *Wall Street Journal*, December 10, 1992, p. A1.

27. Gerry Khermouch, "Plate Tectonics," *Brandweek,* February 12, 1996, p. 1.

28. Audrey Choi and Gabriella Stern, "The Lessons of R?gen: Electric Cars are Slow, Temperamental and Exasperating," *Wall Street Journal*, March 30, 1995, p. B1.

29. Patti Summerfield, "Olestra Fat-free Cooking Oil Still Under Review in Canada," *Strategy: The Canadian Marketing Report*, March 30, 1998, p. 3. John Schwartz, "After 2 Years of Market Tests, Olestra Products Going National; Consumer Advocates Still Concerned About Health Risks," *Washington Post,* February 11, 1998, p. A3.

30. Christopher Power, "Will It Sell in Podunk? Hard to Say," *Business Week*, August 10, 1992, pp. 46–47.

31. See Kevin J. Clancy, Robert S. Shulman, and Marianne Wolf, *Simulated Test Marketing: Technology for Launching Successful New Products* (New York: Lexington Books, 1994); and V. Mahajan and Jerry Wind, "New Product Models: Practice, Shortcomings, and Desired Improvements," *Journal of Product Innovation Management* 9 (1992): 128–39; Glen L. Urban, John R. Hauser, and Roberta A. Chicos, "Information Acceleration: Validation and Lessons from the Field," *Journal of Marketing Research,* February 1997, pp. 143–53.

32. Christopher Power, "Will It Sell in Podunk? Hard to Say," *Business Week*, August 10, 1992, pp. 46–47.

33. Robert McMath, "To Test or Not to Test. . .," *American Demographics*, June 1998, p. 64.

34. "Asia Show—Developing new links," *The Financial Post,* September 10, 1997, p. NAE 1. "Trade Fairs: The Launching Pad to Export Markets," *Canadian Business*, January 1994, Advertising Supplement.

35. Paul Kedrosky, "The Blair Witch Accountants," *National Post*, August 21, 1999, p. C11.

36. For further discussion, see Robert J. Thomas, "Timing—The Key to Market Entry," *Journal of Consumer Marketing,*

Summer 1985, pp. 77–87; Thomas S. Robertson, Jehoshua Eliashberg, and Talia Rymon, "New Product Announcement Signals and Incumbent Reactions," *Journal of Marketing,* July 1995, pp. 1–15; Frank H. Alpert and Michael A. Kamins, "Pioneer Brand Advantages and Consumer Behavior: A Conceptual Framework and Propositional Inventory," *Journal of the Academy of Marketing Science,* Summer 1994, pp. 244–36.

37. John Gray, "U.S. Optical Company Eyes Vancouver Market," *Strategy: The Canadian Marketing Report,* February 15, 1999, p. 8.

38. Robert G. Cooper and Elko J. Kleinschmidt, *New Products: The Key Factors in Success* (Chicago: American Marketing Association, 1990), pp. 35–38.

39. Erika Rasmusson, "Staying Power," *Sales & Marketing Management,* August 1998, pp. 44–46.

40. Quentin Hardy, "Iridium's Orbit to Sell a World Phone, Play to Executive Fears of Being out of Touch: Satellite Consortium Chooses That Pitch for Bid to Build a Global Brand Overnight," *Wall Street Journal,* June 4, 1998 p. A1; Sally Beatty, "Iridium Is Betting Satellite Phone Will Hook Restless Professionals," *Wall Street Journal,* June 22, 1998, p. B6.

41. Philip Kotler and Gerald Zaltman, "Targeting Prospects for a New Product," *Journal of Advertising Research,* February 1976, pp. 7–20.

42. Jim Carlton, "From Apple, a New Marketing Blitz," *Wall Street Journal,* August 14, 1998, p. B1.

43. For details, see Keith G. Lockyer, *Critical Path Analysis and Other Project Network Techniques* (London: Pitman, 1984). Also see Arvind Rangaswamy and Gary L. Lilien, "Software Tools for New Product Development," *Journal of Marketing Research,* February 1997, pp. 177–84.

44. The following discussion leans heavily on Everett M. Rogers, *Diffusion of Innovations* (New York: Free Press, 1962). Also see his third edition, published in 1983.

45. Gillian Newson and Eric Brown, "CD-ROM: What Went Wrong?" *NewMedia,* August 1998, pp. 32–38.

46. Rogers, *Diffusion of Innovations,* p. 192. Also see S. Ram and Hyung-Shik Jung, "Innovativeness in Product Usage: A Comparison of Early Adopters and Early Majority," *Psychology and Marketing,* January–February 1994, pp. 57–68.

47. Eve Lazarus, "New Product Ideas Keep Flowing from B.C. Dairy," *Marketing,* December 21/28, 1998, p. 10.

48. See Hubert Gatignon and Thomas S. Robertson, "A Propositional Inventory for New Diffusion Research," *Journal of Consumer Research,* March 1985, pp. 849–67; Vijay Mahajan, Eitan Muller, and Frank M. Bass, "Diffusion of New Products: Empirical Generalizations and Managerial Uses," *Marketing Science,* 14, no. 3, part 2 (1995); G79–G89; Fareena Sultan, John U. Farley, and Donald R. Lehmann, "Reflection on 'A Meta-Analysis of Applications of Diffusion Models,'" *Journal of Marketing Research,* May 1996, pp. 247–49; Minhi Hahn, Sehoon Park, and Andris A. Zoltners, "Analysis of New Product Diffusion Using a Four-segment Trial-repeat Model," *Marketing Science,* 13, no. 3 (1994), 224–47.

49. Joshua Levine, "TV in the Classroom," *Forbes,* January 27, 1997, p. 98.

Chapter 12

1. Jason Meyers, "Canadian Economy: First the Flu, Now a Hangover," Canadian Economic Outlook Supplement to *Canadian Business Magazine,* February 12, 1999. "Celebrating Excellence in Exporting," Information Supplement, *Canadian Business Magazine,* February 12, 1999. John Alden, "What in the World Drives UPS?" *International Business,* April 1998, pp. 6–71.

2. For more on shifting borders, see Terry Clark, "National Boundaries, Border Zones, and Marketing Strategy: A Conceptual Framework and Theoretical Model of Secondary Boundary Effects," *Journal of Marketing,* July 1994, pp. 67–80.

3. Michael E. Porter, *Competitive Strategy* (New York: Free Press, 1980), p. 275.

4. Marc Gunther, "They All Want to Be Like Mike," *Fortune,* July 21 1997, pp. 51–53.

5. Joann S. Lublin, "Too Much, Too Fast," *Wall Street Journal,* September 26, 1996, p. R8.

6. Yumiro Ono, "On a Mission: Amway Grows Abroad, Sending 'Ambassadors' to Spread the Word," *Wall Street Journal,* May 14, 1997, p. A1.

7. Igal Ayal and Jehiel Zif, "Market Expansion Strategies in Multinational Marketing," *Journal of Marketing,* Spring 1979, pp. 84–94.

8. See Kenichi Ohmae, *Triad Power* (New York: Free Press, 1985); and Philip Kotler and Nikhilesh Dholakia, "Ending Global Stagnation: Linking the Fortunes of the Industrial and Developing Countries," *Business in the Contemporary World,* Spring 1989, pp. 86–97.

9. John Heilemann, "All Europeans Are Not Alike," *The New Yorker,* April 28–May 5, 1997, pp. 174–81.

10. Jason Meyers, "Canadian Economy: First the Flu, Now a Hangover," Canadian Economic Outlook Supplement to *Canadian Business Magazine,* February 12, 1999. Emeric Lepoutre, "Europe's Challenge to the US in South America's Biggest Market: The Economic Power of the Mercosur Common Market Is Indisputable," *Christian Science Monitor,* April 8, 1997, p. 19; Ian Katz, "Is Europe Elbowing the U.S. Out of South America?" *Business Week,* August 4, 1997, p. 56. "Canada-Chile Free Trade," http://www.appletonlaw.com/internat_bux_sol/canada-chile.html.

11. Paul Brent, "It's Tough to Make It South of the Border," *Financial Post,* March 10, 1999, C6. Zena Olijnyk, "Plan to Quit U.S. Lifts Future Shop Stock 24%," *Financial Post,* March 10, 1999, C6.

12. Charlene Marmer Solomon, "Don't Get Burned by Hot New Markets," *Workforce,* January 1998, pp. 12–22.

13. Russ Banham, "Not-So-Clear Choices," *International Business,* November–December 1997, pp. 23–25.

14. Russ Banham, "Not-So-Clear Choices," *International Business,* November–December 1997, pp. 23–25.

15. "In Brief: e-Trade Licensing Deal Gives It an Israeli Link," *American Banker,* May 11, 1998.

16. Cynthia Kemper, "KFC Tradition Sold Japan on Chicken," *Denver Post*, June 7, 1998, p. J4.

17. John Gray, "TD Waterhouse Thinks Global, Shops Local," *Strategy: The Canadian Marketing Report*, July 19, 1999, p. 6. Laura Mazur and Annik Hogg, *The Marketing Challenge* (Wokingham, England: Addison-Wesley, 1993), pp. 42–44; Jan Willem Karel, "Brand Strategy Positions Products Worldwide," *Journal of Business Strategy* 12, no. 3 (May–June 1991): 16–19.

18. Paula Dwyer, "Tearing Up Today's Organization Chart," *Business Week*, November 18, 1994, pp. 80–90.

19. Russ Banham, "Not-So-Clear Choices," *International Business*, November–December 1997, pp. 23–25.

20. See Jan Johanson and Finn Wiedersheim-Paul, "The Internationalization of the Firm," *Journal of Management Studies*, October 1975, pp. 305–22.

21. See Stan Reid, "The Decision Maker and Export Entry and Expansion," *Journal of International Business Studies*, Fall 1981, pp. 101–12; Igal Ayal, "Industry Export Performance: Assessment and Prediction," *Journal of Marketing*, Summer 1982, pp. 54–61; and Somkid Jatusripitak, *The Exporting Behavior of Manufacturing Firms* (Ann Arbor, MI: University of Michigan Press, 1986).

22. Warren J. Keegan, *Multinational Marketing Management*, 5th ed. (Upper Saddle River, NJ: Prentice Hall, 1995), pp. 378–81.

23. J. S. Perry Hobson, "*Feng Shui*: Its Impacts on the Asian Hospitality Industry," *International Journal of Contemporary Hospitality Management* 6, no. 6 (1994): 21–26; Bernd H. Schmitt and Yigang Pan, "In Asia, the Supernatural Means Sales," *New York Times*, February 19, 1995, pp. 3, 11.

24. "What Makes a Company Great?" *Fortune*, October 26, 1998, pp. 218–26.

25. David Leonhardt, "It Was a Hit in Buenos Aires— So Why Not Boise?" *Business Week*, September 7, 1998, pp. 56–58.

26. "The Growth of Global Retailers," *The Journal of Business Strategy*, May–June 1998, p. 14.

27. Ben Dolven, "Find the Niche," *Far Eastern Economic Review*, March 26, 1998, pp. 58–59.

28. Richard P. Carpenter and the Globe Staff, "What They Meant to Say Was . . .," *Boston Globe*, August 2, 1998, p. M6.

29. Carlos Briceno, "Labatt Believes Going 'Glocal' Will Melt the Ice for Carlsberg," *Beverage World*, September 30–October 31, 1988, p. 17.

30. Maricris G. Briones, "The Euro Starts Here," *Marketing News*, July 20, 1998, pp. 1, 39.

31. Elliott Masie, "Global Pricing in an Internet World," *Computer Reseller News*, May 11, 1998, pp. 55, 58.

32. Ram Charan, "The Rules Have Changed," *Fortune*, March 16, 1998, pp. 159–62.

33. Paula Dwyer, "Tearing Up Today's Organization Chart," *Business Week*, November 18, 1994, pp. 80–90.

34. See Christopher A. Bartlett and Sumantra Ghoshal, *Managing Across Borders* (Cambridge, MA: Harvard Business School Press, 1989).

35. Martha M. Hamilton, "Going Global: A World of Difference; Daimler-Chrysler Joins Growing List of Titans That Must Find New Ways to Compete," *Washington Post*, May 10, 1998, p. H1; Jeremy Main, "Globe-zilla," *Working Woman*, October 1998, p. 9; Charles Fleming and Leslie Lopez, "The Corporate Challenge—No Boundaries: BB's Dramatic Plan to Recast Its Business Structure Along Global Lines: It May Not Be Easy—or Wise," *Wall Street Journal*, September 28, 1998, p. R16.

Chapter 13

1. T. L. Stanley, "Brand Builders: Bio-Genetics at A&E," *Brandweek*, April 6, 1998, pp. 22–23.

2. This discussion is adapted from Theodore Levitt, "Marketing Success through Differentiation—of Anything," *Harvard Business Review*, January–February 1980, pp. 83–91. The first level, core benefit, has been added to Levitt's discussion.

3. See Harper W. Boyd Jr. and Sidney Levy, "New Dimensions in Consumer Analysis," *Harvard Business Review*, November–December 1963, pp. 129–40.

4. Theodore Levitt, *The Marketing Mode* (New York: McGraw-Hill, 1969), p. 2.

5. For some definitions, see *Dictionary of Marketing Terms*, ed. Peter D. Bennett (Chicago: American Marketing Association, 1995). Also see Patrick E. Murphy and Ben M. Enis, "Classifying Products Strategically," *Journal of Marketing*, July 1986, pp. 24–42.

6. This illustration is found in Benson P. Shapiro, *Industrial Product Policy: Managing the Existing Product Line* (Cambridge, MA: Marketing Science Institute, September 1977), pp. 3–5, 98–101.

7. See David A. Aaker, "Should You Take Your Brand to Where the Action Is?" *Harvard Business Review*, September–October 1997, pp. 135–43.

8. See Steuart Henderson Britt, "How Weber's Law Can Be Applied to Marketing," *Business Horizons*, February 1975, pp. 21–29.

9. Jeannette Hanna and Christopher Walmsley, "New Approaches to Brand Appeal," *The Financial Post Magazine*, CEO Annual 1998, pp. 146–150.

10. See Jean-Noel Kapferer, *Strategic Brand Management: New Approaches to Creating and Evaluating Brand Equity* (London: Kogan Page, 1992), pp. 38 ff; Jennifer L. Aaker, "Dimensions of Brand Personality," *Journal of Marketing Research*, August 1997, pp. 347–56.

11. Rod McQueen, "The Fall of Eaton's: Who's to Blame," *The Financial Post*, August 21, 1999, pp. D1, D8.

12. David A. Aaker, *Building Strong Brands* (New York: Free Press, 1995). Also see Kevin Lane Keller, *Strategic Brand Management: Building, Measuring, and Managing Brand Equity* (Upper Saddle River, NJ: Prentice Hall, 1998).

13. David A. Aaker, *Building Strong Brands* (New York: Free Press, 1995). Also see Kevin Lane Keller, *Strategic Brand Management: Building, Measuring, and Managing Brand Equity* (Upper Saddle River, NJ: Prentice Hall, 1998). Also see Jeannette Hanna and Christopher Walmsley, "New Approaches to Brand Appeal," *The Financial Post Magazine*, CEO Annual 1998, pp. 146–150, Patrick Barwise et al., *Accounting for Brands* (London: Institute of Chartered Accountants in England and Wales, 1990); and Peter H. Farquhar, Julia Y. Han, and Yuji Ijiri, "Brands on

the Balance Sheet," *Marketing Management*, Winter 1992, pp. 16–22. Brand equity should reflect not only the capitalized value of the incremental profits from the current use of the brand name but also the value of its potential extensions to other products.

14. Kurt Badenhausen with Joyce Artinian and Christopher Nikolov, "Most Valuable Brands," *Financial World*, September–October 1997, pp. 62–63.

15. Evan Schwartz, "The Brand Man," *Context*, Summer 1998, pp. 54–58.

16. Margaret Webb Pressler, "The Power of Branding," *Washington Post*, July 27, 1997, p. H1.

17. Scott Davis and Darrell Douglass, "Holistic Approach to Brand Equity Management," *Marketing News*, January 16, 1995, pp. 4–5.

18. Carol Howes and Peter Fitzpatrick, Canadian Airlines to Adopt a Retro Look," *The Financial Post*, January 13, 1998, p. C1, C4. Oliver Bertin, "Canadian Airlines Changes Name, Uniforms, Logo," *Globe and Mail*, January 13, 1998, B7.

19. For further reading, see Brian F. Harris and Roger A. Strang, "Marketing Strategies in the Age of Generics," *Journal of Marketing*, Fall 1985, pp. 70–81.

20. "President's Choice Continues Brisk Pace," *Frozen Food Age*, March 1998, pp. 17–18; Warren Thayer, "Loblaw's Exec Predicts: Private Label to Surge," *Frozen Food Age*, May 1996, p. 1.

21. Jo Marney, "The Health of Brands," *Marketing*, July 21/28, 1997, p. 24. Helena Katz, "The Sweet Taste of House Brands," *Marketing*, November 2, 1998, p. 10. Fawzia Sheikh, "Zellers Aims for $200M in Truly Sales, *Marketing*, March 8, 1999, p. 2. Wendy Cuthbert, "Shoppers Drug Mart Boosts Status with Addition of Quo," *Strategy: The Canadian Marketing Report*, July 15, 1999, p. 30.

22. Quoted in "Trade Promotion: Much Ado About Nothing," *Promo*, October 1991, p. 37.

23. See Paul S. Richardson, Alan S. Dick, and Arun K. Jain, "Extrinsic and Intrinsic Cue Effects on Perceptions of Store Brand Quality," *Journal of Marketing*, October 1994, pp. 28–36.

24. Patricia Nakache, "Secrets of the New Brand Builders," *Fortune*, June 22, 1998, pp. 167–70.

25. See Kim Robertson, "Strategically Desirable Brand Name Characteristics," *Journal of Consumer Marketing*, Fall 1989, pp. 61–70.

26. John Burgess, "$60,000 for One Good Word; Firms May Pay Through the Nose for a Name," *Washington Post*, October 21, 1996, p. F19.

27. Zena Olijnyk, "Martha Proves To Be a Powerhouse at Zellers," *The Financial Post*, November 6, 1998, B25.

28. See Steven M. Shugan, "Branded Variants," *1989 AMA Educators' Proceedings* (Chicago: American Marketing Association, 1989), pp. 33–38.

29. Robert McMath, "Product Proliferation," *Adweek (Eastern Ed.) Superbrands 1995 Supplement,* 1995, pp. 34–40; John A. Quelch and David Kenny, "Extend Profits, Not Product Lines," *Harvard Business Review*, September–October 1994, pp. 153–60; and Bruce G. S. Hardle, Leonard M. Lodish, James V. Kilmer, David R. Beatty, et al., "The Logic of Product-Line Extensions," *Harvard Business Review*, November–December 1994, pp. 53–62.

30. Al Ries and Jack Trout, *Positioning: The Battle for Your Mind* (New York: Mc-Graw-Hill, 1981).

31. From Srinivas K. Reddy, Susan L. Holak, and Subodh Bhat, "To Extend or Not to Extend: Success Determinants of Line Extensions," *Journal of Marketing Research*, May 1994, pp. 243–62. See also Morris A. Cohen, Jehoshua Eliashberg, and Teck H. Ho, "An Anatomy of a Decision-Support System for Developing and Launching Line Extensions," *Journal of Marketing Research,* February 1997, pp. 117–29; V. Padmanabhan, Surendra Rajiv, and Kannan Srinivasan, "New Products, Upgrades, and New Releases: A Rationale for Sequential Product Introduction," *Journal of Marketing Research*, November 1997, pp. 456–72.

32. Julia Flynn, "Then Came Branson," *Business Week*, October 26, 1998, pp. 116–20.

33. Barbara Loken and Deborah Roedder John, "Diluting Brand Beliefs: When Do Brand Extensions Have a Negative Impact?" *Journal of Marketing,* July 1993, pp. 71–84; Deborah Roedder John, Barbara Loken, and Christopher Joiner, "The Negative Impact of Extensions: Can Flagship Products Be Diluted," *Journal of Marketing*, January 1998, pp. 19–32; Susan M. Broniarcyzk and Joseph W. Alba, "The Importance of the Brand in Brand Extension," *Journal of Marketing Research,* May 1994, pp. 214–28 (this entire issue of *JMR* is devoted to brands and brand equity).

34. See Mark B. Taylor, "Cannibalism in Multibrand Firms," *Journal of Business Strategy*, Spring 1986, pp. 69–75.

35. Simon Avery, "Dell, Amazon Strike Co-marketing Deal," *Financial Post*, March 11, 1999, p. C10. "ING Direct and Canadian Tire Banking on It," *Adnews On-Line*, September 27, 1999, p. 1.

36. Bernard L. Simonin and Julie A. Ruth, "Is a Company Known by the Company It Keeps? Assessing the Spillover Effects of Brand Alliances on Consumer Brand Attitudes," *Journal of Marketing Research,* February 1998, pp. 30–42.

37. "Family Channel Updates On-Air Look and Attitude," *Adnews On-Line Daily*, September 23, 1999, p. 1. "Suzuki Canada Engineered Beyond Belief," *Adnews On-Line Daily*, October 1, 1999, p. 1.

38. Robert M. McNath, "Chock Full of (Pea)nuts," *American Demographics*, April 1997, p. 60.

Chapter 14

1. Ronald Henkoff, "Service Is Everybody's Business," *Fortune*, June 27, 1994, pp. 48–60.

2. See G. Lynn Shostack, "Breaking Free from Product Marketing," *Journal of Marketing*, April 1977, pp. 73–80; Leonard L. Berry, "Services Marketing Is Different," *Business*, May–June 1980, pp. 24–30; Eric Langeard, John E. G. Bateson, Christopher H. Lovelock, and Pierre Eiglier, *Services Marketing: New Insights from Consumers and Managers* (Cambridge, MA: Marketing Science Institute, 1981); Karl Albrecht and Ron Zemke, *Service America! Doing Business in the New Economy* (Homewood, IL: Dow Jones–Irwin, 1986); Karl Albrecht, *At America's Service* (Homewood, IL: Dow Jones—

Irwin, 1988); and Benjamin Scheider and David E. Bowen, *Winning the Service Game* (Boston: Harvard Business School Press, 1995).

3. "Consumers Roll Out the Welcome Mat for Electronic Services," *Globe and Mail Advertising Supplement*, April 29, 1999, p. R6.

4. John R. Johnson, "Service at a Price," *Industrial Distribution*, May 1998, pp. 91–94.

5. Theodore Levitt, "Production-Line Approach to Service," *Harvard Business Review*, September–October 1972, pp. 41–42.

6. Further classifications of services are described in Christopher H. Lovelock, *Services Marketing*, 3d ed. (Upper Saddle River, NJ: Prentice Hall, 1996). Also see John E. Bateson, *Managing Services Marketing: Text and Readings*, 3d ed. (Hinsdale, IL: Dryden, 1995).

7. See Theodore Levitt, "Marketing Intangible Products and Product Intangibles," *Harvard Business Review*, May–June 1981, pp. 94–102; and Berry, "Services Marketing Is Different."

8. Geoffrey Brewer, "Selling an Intangible," *Sales & Marketing Management*, January 1998, pp. 52–58.

9. "Business: Service with a Smile," *The Economist*, April 25, 1998, pp. 63–64.

10. See G. Lynn Shostack, "Service Positioning Through Structural Change," *Journal of Marketing*, January 1987, pp. 34–43.

11. See W. Earl Sasser, "Match Supply and Demand in Service Industries," *Harvard Business Review*, November-December 1976, pp. 133–40.

12. Carol Krol, "Case Study: Club Med Uses E-mail to Pitch Unsold, Discounted Packages," *Advertising Age*, December 14, 1998, p. 40.

13. Sonja Rasula, "Miller Readies for Deregulation," *Marketing*, March 29, 1999, p. 2. Sinclar Stewart, "Ontario Hydro Prepares for Pitch," *Strategy: The Canadian Marketing Report*, July 19, 1999, p. 4. Patti Summerfield, "Hydro Ramps Up for Deregulation," *Strategy: The Canadian Marketing Report*, p. 1.

14. See B. H. Booms and M. J. Bitner, "Marketing Strategies and Organizational Structures for Service Firms," in *Marketing of Services*, eds. J. Donnelly and W. R. George (Chicago: American Marketing Association, 1981), pp. 47–51.

15. Keaveney has identified more than 800 critical behaviours of service firms that cause customers to switch services. These behaviours fit into eight categories ranging from price, inconvenience, and core service failure to service encounter failure, failed employee response to service failures, and ethical problems. See Susan M. Keaveney, "Customer Switching Behavior in Service Industries: An Exploratory Study," *Journal of Marketing*, April 1995, pp. 71–82. See also Michael D. Hartline and O. C. Ferrell, "The Management of Customer-Contact Service Employees: An Empirical Investigation," *Journal of Marketing*, October 1996, pp. 52–70; Lois A. Mohr, Mary Jo Bitner, and Bernard H. Booms, "Critical Service Encounters: The Employee's Viewpoint," *Journal of Marketing,* October 1994, pp. 95–106; Linda L. Price, Eric J. Arnould, and Patrick Tierney, "Going to Extremes: Managing Service Encounters and Assessing Provider Performance," *Journal of Marketing*, April 1995, pp. 83–97.

16. Christian Gronroos, "A Service Quality Model and Its Marketing Implications," *European Journal of Marketing* 18, no. 4 (1984); 36–44. Gronroos' model is one of the most thoughtful contributions to service-marketing strategy.

17. Leonard Berry, "Big Ideas in Services Marketing," *Journal of Consumer Marketing*, Spring 1986, pp. 47–51. See also Walter E. Greene, Gary D. Walls, and Larry J. Schrest, "Internal Marketing: The Key to External Marketing Success," *Journal of Services Marketing* 8, no. 4 (1994): 5–13; John R. Hauser, Duncan I. Simester, and Birger Wernerfelt, "Internal Customers and Internal Suppliers," *Journal of Marketing Research,* August 1996, pp. 268–80.

18. Christian Gronroos, "A Service Quality Model and Its Marketing Implications," *European Journal of Marketing* 18, no. 4 (1984); 36–44.

19. See Philip Kotler and Paul N. Bloom, *Marketing Professional Services* (Upper Saddle River, NJ: Prentice Hall, 1984).

20. Laurie J. Flynn, "Eating Your Young," *Context*, Summer 1998, pp. 45–47; see also Mark Schwanhausser, "Schwab Evolves in the Web Era," *Chicago Tribune*, October 12, 1998, Business Section, p. 10; and John Evan Frook, "Web Proves It's Good for Business," *Internet Week*, December 21, 1998, p. 15.

21. See Valarie A. Zeithaml, "How Consumer Evaluation Processes Differ between Goods and Services," in Donnelly and George, eds., *Marketing of Services*, pp. 186–90.

22. Amy Ostrom and Dawn Iacobucci, "Consumer Trade-offs and the Evaluation of Services," *Journal of Marketing*, January 1995, pp. 17–28.

23. Robert D. Hof, "Now It's Your Web," *Business Week*, October 5, 1998, pp. 164–76.

24. Ian C. MacMillan and Rita Gunther McGrath, "Discovering New Points of Differentiation," *Harvard Business Review*, July–August 1997, pp. 133–45.

25. Suzanne Bidlake, "John Crewe, American Express Blue Card," *Advertising Age International,* December 14, 1998, p. 10; Sue Beenstock, "Blue Blooded," *Marketing*, June 4, 1998, p. 14; Pamela Sherrid, "A New Class Act at AMEX," *U.S. News & World Report,* June 23, 1997, pp. 39–40.

26. A. Parasuraman, Valarie A. Zeithaml, and Leonard L. Berry, "A Conceptual Model of Service Quality and Its Implications for Future Research," *Journal of Marketing*, Fall 1985, pp. 41–50. See also Susan J. Devlin and H. K. Dong, "Service Quality from the Customers' Perspective," *Marketing Research: A Magazine of Management & Applications*, Winter 1994, pp. 4–13; William Boulding, Ajay Kalra, and Richard Staelin, "A Dynamic Process Model of Service Quality: From Expectations to Behavioral Intentions," *Journal of Marketing Research*, February 1993, pp. 7–27.

27. Leonard L. Berry and A. Parasuraman, *Marketing Services: Competing Through Quality* (New York: Free Press, 1991), p. 16.

28. See James L. Heskett, W. Earl Sasser Jr., and Christopher W. L. Hart, *Service Breakthroughs* (New York: Free Press, 1990).

29. David Greising, "Quality: How to Make It Pay," *Business Week*, August 8, 1994, pp. 54–59.

30. John A. Martilla and John C. James, "Importance-Performance Analysis," *Journal of Marketing*, January 1977, pp. 77–79.

31. See John Goodman, Technical Assistance Research Program (TARP), U.S. Office of Consumer Affairs Study on Complaint Handling in America, 1986; Albrecht and Zemke, *Service America!*; Berry and Parasuraman, *Marketing Services*; Roland T. Rust, Bala Subramanian, and Mark Wells, "Making Complaints a Management Tool," *Marketing Management* 1, no. 3 (1992): 41–45; Stephen S. Tax, Stephen W. Brown, and Murali Chandrashekaran, "Customer Evaluations of Service Complaint Experiences: Implications for Relationship Marketing," *Journal of Marketing*, April 1998, pp. 60–76.

32. Stephen S. Tax and Stephen W. Brown, "Recovering and Learning from Service Failure," *Sloan Management Review*, Fall 1998, pp. 75–88.

33. Robert Hiebeler, Thomas B. Kelly, and Charles Ketteman, *Best Practices: Building Your Business with Customer-Focused Solutions* (New York: Arthur Andersen/Simon & Schuster, 1997), pp. 184–185.

34. See Hal F. Rosenbluth and Diane McFerrin Peters, *The Customer Comes Second* (New York: William Morrow, 1992).

35. Kirstin Downey Grimsley, "Service with a Forced Smile; Safeway's Courtesy Campaign Also Elicits Some Frowns," *Washington Post*, October 18, 1998, p. A1.

36. See Royal Bank Web site, www.royalbank.ca.

37. Theodore Levitt, "Production-Line Approach to Service," *Harvard Business Review*, September–October 1972, pp. 41–52; also see his "Industrialization of Service," *Harvard Business Review*, September–October 1976, pp. 63–74.

38. See William H. Davidow and Bro Uttal, *Total Customer Service: The Ultimate Weapon* (New York: Harper & Row, 1989).

39. Nilly Landau, "Are You Being Served?" *International Business*, March 1995, pp. 38–40.

40. See Milind M. Lele and Uday S. Karmarkar, "Good Product Support Is Smart Marketing," *Harvard Business*

Review, November–December 1983, pp. 124–32.

41. For recent research on the effects of delays in service on service evaluations, see Shirley Taylor, "Waiting for Service: The Relationship Between Delays and Evaluations of Service," *Journal of Marketing*, April 1994, pp. 56–69; Michael K. Hui and David K. Tse, "What to Tell Consumers in Waits of Different Lengths: An Integrative Model of Service Evaluation," *Journal of Marketing*, April 1996, pp. 81–90.

42. Milind M. Lele, "How Service Needs Influence Product Strategy," *Sloan Management Review*, Fall 1986, pp. 63–70.

43. However, see Ellen Day and Richard J. Fox, "Extended Warranties, Service Contracts, and Maintenance Agreement—A Marketing Opportunity?" *Journal of Consumer Marketing*, Fall 1985, pp. 77–86.

Chapter 15

1. David J. Schwartz, *Marketing Today: A Basic Approach*, 3d ed. (New York: Harcourt Brace Jovanovich, 1981), p. 271.

2. Amy E. Cortese, "Good-Bye to Fixed Pricing?" *Business Week*, May 4, 1998, pp. 71–84.

3. Gayle MacDonald, "Cheers, Beer Drinkers! Labatt, Molson Crack Open a Price War," *Globe and Mail*, July 15, 1999, pp. B1, B6. Sean Silcoff, "Retail that Rocks," *Canadian Business*, November 27, 1998, pp. 48–58.

4. Andy Reinhardt, "Pentium: The Next Generation," *Business Week*, May 12, 1997, pp. 42–43; David Kirkpatrick, "Intel's Amazing Profit Machine," *Fortune*, February 17, 1997, pp. 60–72.

5. Steve Gelsi, "Spin-Cycle Doctor," *Brandweek*, March 10, 1997, pp. 38–40; Tim Stevens, "From Reliable to 'Wow,'" *Industry Week*, June 22, 1998, pp. 22–26.

6. Thomas T. Nagle and Reed K. Holden, *The Strategy and Tactics of Pricing*, 2d ed. (Upper Saddle River, NJ: Prentice Hall, 1995), ch. 4. This is an excellent reference book for making pricing decisions.

7. Kevin J. Clancy, "At What Profit Price?" *Brandweek*, June 23, 1997, pp. 24–28.

8. See Sidney Bennett and J. B. Wilkinson, "Price-Quantity Relationships and Price Elasticity Under In-Store Experimentation," *Journal of Business Research*, January 1974, pp. 30–34.

9. John R. Nevin, "Laboratory Experiments for Estimating Consumer Demand—A Validation Study," *Journal of Marketing Research*, August 1974, pp. 261–68; and Jonathan Weiner, "Forecasting Demand: Consumer Electronics Marketer Uses a Conjoint Approach to Configure Its New Product and Set the Right Price," *Marketing Research: A Magazine of Management & Applications*, Summer 1994, pp. 6–11.

10. Thomas T. Nagle and Reed K. Holden, *The Strategy and Tactics of Pricing*, 2d ed. (Upper Saddle River, NJ: Prentice Hall, 1995), ch. 13.

11. For summary of elasticity studies, see Dominique M. Hanssens, Leonard J. Parsons, and Randall L. Schultz, *Market Response Models: Econometric and Time Series Analysis* (Boston: Kluwer Academic Publishers, 1990), pp. 187–91.

12. Gene Epstein, "Economic Beat: Stretching Things," *Barron's*, December 15, 1997, p. 65.

13. See William W. Alberts, "The Experience Curve Doctrine Reconsidered," *Journal of Marketing*, July 1989, pp. 36–49.

14. See Robin Cooper and Robert S. Kaplan, "Profit Priorities from Activity-Based Costing," *Harvard Business Review*, May–June 1991, pp. 130–35. For more on ABC, see ch. 24.

15. See "Japan's Smart Secret Weapon," *Fortune*, August 12, 1991, p. 75.

16. Elyse Tanouye, "Drugs: Steep Markups on Generics Top Branded Drugs," *Wall Street Journal*, December 31, 1998, p. B1.

17. Tung-Zong Chang and Albert R. Wildt, "Price, Product Information, and Purchase Intention: An Empirical Study," *Journal of the Academy of Marketing Science*, Winter 1994, pp. 16–27. See also G. Dean Kortge and Patrick A. Okonkwo, "Perceived Value Approach to Pricing," *Industrial Marketing Management*, May 1993, pp. 133–40.

18. For an empirical study of nine methods used by companies to assess customer value, see James C. Anderson,

Dipak C. Jain, and Pradeep K. Chintagunta, "Customer Value Assessment in Business Markets: A State-of-Practice Study," *Journal of Business-to-Business Marketing* 1, no. 1 (1993): 3–29.

19. Roger Crockett, "PC Makers Race to the Bottom," *Business Week*, October 12, 1998, p. 48.

20. Bill Saporito, "Behind the Tumult at P&G," *Fortune*, March 7, 1994, pp. 74–82.

21. Stephen J. Hoch, Xavier Dreze, and Mary J. Purk, "EDLP, Hi-Lo, and Margin Arithmetic," *Journal of Marketing*, October 1994, pp. 16–27; Rajiv Lal and R. Rao, "Supermarket Competition: The Case of Everyday Low Pricing," *Marketing Science* 16, no. 1 (1997); 60–80.

22. Becky Bull, "No Consensus on Pricing," *Progressive Grocer*, November 1998, pp. 87–90.

23. Gary M. Erickson and Johny K. Johansson, "The Role of Price in Multi-Attribute Product-Evaluations," *Journal of Consumer Research*, September 1985, pp. 195–99.

24. K. N. Rajendran and Gerard J. Tellis, "Contextual and Temporal Components of Reference Price," *Journal of Marketing*, January 1994, pp. 22–34.

25. Paul W. Farris and David J. Reibstein, "How Prices, Expenditures, and Profits Are Linked," *Harvard Business Review*, November–December 1979, pp. 173–84. See also Makoto Abe, "Price and Advertising Strategy of a National Brand Against Its Private-Label Clone: A Signaling Game Approach," *Journal of Business Research*, July 1995, pp. 241–50.

26. Thomas Claridge, "Food Additive Firms Fined for Price Fixing," *Globe and Mail*, October 22, 1998, p. B7.

27. See Michael Rowe, *Countertrade* (London: Euromoney Books, 1989); P. N. Agarwala, *Countertrade: A Global Perspective* (New Delhi: Vikas Publishing House, 1991); and Christopher M. Korth, ed., *International Countertrade* (New York: Quorum Books, 1987).

28. See Michael V. Marn and Robert L. Rosiello, "Managing Price, Gaining Profit," *Harvard Business Review*, September–October 1992, pp. 84–94. See also Gerard J. Tellis, "Tackling the

Retailer Decision Maze: Which Brands to Discount, How Much, When, and Why?" *Marketing Science* 14, no. 3, pt. 2 (1995); 271–99.

29. For more information on specific types of price discrimination that are illegal, see Henry Cheesman, *Contemporary Business Law* (Upper Saddle River, NJ: Prentice Hall, 1995).

30. Mike France, "Does Predatory Pricing Make Microsoft a Predator?" *Business Week*, November 23, 1998, pp. 130–32. See also Joseph P. Guiltinan and Gregory T. Gundlack, "Aggressive and Predatory Pricing: A Framework for Analysis," *Journal of Advertising*, July 1996, pp. 87–102.

31. Andy Reinhardt, "Who Says Intel's Chips Are Down?" *Business Week*, December 7, 1998, pp. 103–4.

32. See Robert E. Weigand, "Buy In-Follow On Strategies for Profit," *Sloan Management Review*, Spring 1991, pp. 29–37.

33. Susan Krafft, "Love, Love Me Doo," *American Demographics*, June 1994, pp. 15–16.

34. See Gerald J. Tellis, "Beyond the Many Faces of Price: An Integration of Pricing Strategies," *Journal of Marketing*, October 1986, p. 155. This excellent article also analyzes and illustrates other pricing strategies.

35. "Costly Cornflakes," *New York Times*, January 12, 1999, p. A1.

36. Eric Mitchell, "How Not to Raise Prices," *Small Business Reports*, November 1990, pp. 64–67.

37. For excellent review, see Kent B. Monroe, "Buyers' Subjective Perceptions of Price," *Journal o f Marketing Research*, February 1973, pp. 70–80.

Chapter 16

1. Louis W. Stern and Adel I. El-Ansary, *Marketing Channels*, 5th ed. (Upper Saddle River, NJ: Prentice Hall, 1996).

2. E. Raymond Corey, *Industrial Marketing: Cases and Concepts*, 4th ed. (Upper Saddle River, NJ: Prentice Hall, 1991), ch. 5.

3. Louis W. Stern and Adel I. El-Ansary, *Marketing Channels*, 5th ed. (Upper Saddle River, NJ: Prentice Hall, 1996), pp. 5–6.

4. William G. Zikmund and William J. Stanton, "Recycling Solid Wastes: A Channels-of-Distribution Problem," *Journal of Marketing*, July 1971, p. 34.

5. For additional information on backward channels, see Marianne Jahre, "Household Waste Collection as a Reverse Channel—A Theoretical Perspective," *International Journal of Physical Distribution and Logistics* 25, no. 2 (1995): 39–55; and Terrance L. Pohlen and M. Theodore Farris II, "Reverse Logistics in Plastics Recycling," *International Journal of Physical Distribution and Logistics* 22, no. 7 (1992): 35–37.

6. Ronald Abler, John S. Adams, and Peter Gould, *Spatial Organizations: The Geographer's View of the World* (Upper Saddle River, NJ: Prentice Hall, 1971), pp. 531–32.

7. See Irving Rein, Philip Kotler, and Martin Stoller, *High Visibility* (New York: Dodd, Mead, 1987).

8. For a technical discussion of how service-oriented firms choose to enter international markets, see M. Krishna Erramilli, "Service Firms' International Entry-Mode Approach: A Modified Transaction-Cost Analysis Approach," *Journal of Marketing*, July 1993, pp. 19–38.

9. Louis P. Bucklin, *Competition and Evolution in the Distributive Trades* (Upper Saddle River, NJ: Prentice Hall, 1972). Also see Stern and El-Ansary, *Marketing Channels*.

10. Louis P. Bucklin, *A Theory of Distribution Channel Structure* (Berkeley: Institute of Business and Economic Research, University of California, 1966).

11. Mark Evans, "Rogers Cantel Going Door-to-Door with Amway," *Globe and Mail*, February 2, 1999, p. B1, B17.

12. Will Anderson, "Vendor Irate at Jersey Decision," *Atlanta Journal and Constitution*, October 17, 1996, p. R1; William McCall, "Nike Posts $72M Loss," The Associated Press, December 12, 1998; Philana Patterson, "Athletic Shoe Industry Hurt When Buyers Drag Feet," *Star Tribune*, December 26, 1997, p. 7B.

13. For more on relationship marketing and the governance of marketing channels, see Jan B. Heide, "Interorganizational Governance in Market-

ing Channels," *Journal of Marketing*, January 1994, pp. 71–85.

14. Arthur Bragg, "Undercover Recruiting: Epson America's Sly Distributor Switch," *Sales and Marketing Management*, March 11, 1985, pp. 45–49.

15. Casey Mahood, "Molson Looks to Logistics Leader," *Globe and Mail*, January 22, 1999, p. B25.

16. Philip McVey, "Are Channels of Distribution What the Textbooks Say?" *Journal of Marketing*, January 1960, pp. 61–64.

17. These bases of power were identified in John R. P. French and Bertram Raven, "The Bases of Social Power," in *Studies in Social Power*, ed. Dorwin Cartwright (Ann Arbor, MI: University of Michigan Press, 1959), pp. 150–67.

18. See Bert Rosenbloom, *Marketing Channels: A Management View*, 5th ed. (Hinsdale, IL: Dryden, 1995).

19. Miland M. Lele, *Creating Strategic Leverage* (New York: John Wiley, 1992), pp. 249–51. This fact struck the manufacturer of the MicroFridge, a combination minirefrigerator and microwave oven.

20. For an excellent report on this issue, see Howard Sutton, *Rethinking the Company's Selling and Distribution Channels*, research report no. 885, Conference Board, 1986, 26 pp.

21. Louis W. Stern and Adel I. El-Ansary, *Marketing Channels*, 5th ed. (Upper Saddle River, NJ: Prentice Hall, 1996), p. 189.

22. Russell Johnston and Paul R. Lawrence, "Beyond Vertical Integration—The Rise of the Value-Adding Partnership," *Harvard Business Review*, July–August 1988, pp. 94–101. See also Judy A. Siguaw, Penny M. Simpson, and Thomas L. Baker, "Effects of Supplier Market Orientation on Distributor Market Orientation and the Channel Relationship: The Distribution Perspective," *Journal of Marketing*, July 1998, pp. 99–111; Narakesari Narayandas and Manohar U. Kalwani, "Long-Term Manufacturer—Supplier Relationships: Do They Pay Off for Supplier Firms?" *Journal of Marketing*, January 1995, pp. 1–16.

23. David A. Aaker, "Should You Take Your Brand to Where the Action Is?" *Harvard Business Review*, September 1, 1997, p. 135.

24. Lee Adler, "Symbiotic Marketing," *Harvard Business Review*, November–December 1966, pp. 59–71; and P. "Rajan" Varadarajan and Daniel Rajaratnam, "Symbiotic Marketing Revisited," *Journal of Marketing*, January 1986, pp. 7–17.

25. Robin Lewis, "Partner or Perish," *WWD Infotracs: Strategic Alliances*, February 24, 1997, p. 4.

26. See Rowland T. Moriarty and Ursula Moran, "Marketing Hybrid Marketing Systems," *Harvard Business Review*, November–December 1990, pp. 146–55. Also see Gordon S. Swartz and Rowland T. Moriarty, "Marketing Automation Meets the Capital Budgeting Wall," *Marketing Management* 1, no. 3 (1992).

27. Bert C. McCammon Jr., "Alternative Explanations of Institutional Change and Channel Evolution," in *Toward Scientific Marketing*, ed. Stephen A. Greyser (Chicago: American Marketing Association, 1963), pp. 477–90.

28. Greg Keenan, "Ford Targets Bigger Stake in Dealerships," *Globe and Mail*, November 18, 1998, p. B1.

29. This section draws on Louis W. Stern and Adel I. El-Ansary, *Marketing Channels*, 5th ed. (Upper Saddle River, NJ: Prentice Hall, 1996), ch. 6.

Chapter 17

1. William R. Davidson, Albert D. Bates, and Stephen J. Bass, "Retail Life Cycle," *Harvard Business Review* (November–December 1976), pp. 89–96.

2. Stanley C. Hollander, "The Wheel of Retailing," *Journal of Marketing*, July 1960, pp. 37–42.

3. Sean Silcoff, "Winners Take Everything," *Canadian Business*, September 24, 1999, pp. 46–50.

4. Laurence H. Wortzel, "Retailing Strategies for Today's Marketplace," *Journal of Business Strategy*, Spring 1987, pp. 45–56.

5. See Michael Treacy and Fred Wiersema, "Customer Intimacy and Other Discipline Values," *Harvard Business Review*, January–February 1993, pp. 84–93.

6. For more discussion, see Philip Kotler, "Atmospherics as a Marketing Tool," *Journal of Retailing*, Winter 1973–1974, pp. 48–64; and Mary Jo Bitner, "Servicescapes: The Impact of Physical Surroundings on Customers and Employees," *Journal of Marketing*, April 1992, pp. 57–71. Also see B. Joseph Pine II and James H. Gilmore, *The Experience Economy* (Boston: Harvard Business School Press, 1999).

7. Shannon Stevens, "The Return of Red Lobster," *American Demographics*, October 1998; Chelsea J. Carter, "Theme Restaurants Face Trouble," Associated Press, December 17, 1998.

8. Frank Feather, *The Future Consumer* (Toronto: Warwick Publishing, 1994), p. 171. Also see Stephen J. Hoch, Xavier Dreeze, and Mary E. Purk, "EDLP, Hi-Lo, and Margin Arithmetic," *Journal of Marketing*, October 1994, pp. 1–15.

9.. "Loblaw's and Provigo to Merge in $2 Billion deal," *Canoe Money* (http://www.canoe.ca/MergerManie/oct30_lablaws.html), October 30, 1998.

10. R. L. Davies and D. S. Rogers, eds., *Store Location and Store Assessment Research* (New York: John Wiley, 1984).

11. See Sara L. McLafferty, *Location Strategies for Retail and Service Firms* (Lexington, MA: Lexington Books, 1987).

12. David Bosworth, "Bank of Montreal, A&P Team for In-store Banking," *Strategy: The Canadian Marketing Report*, June 22, 1998, p. 2. Zena Olijnyk, "Canada is in their Roots, *Financial Post*, November 11, 1998, p. C4. Erica Zlomislic, "Loblaw Taps CIBC for President's Choice Financial," ," *Strategy: The Canadian Marketing Report*, February 16, 1998, p. 2.

13. Jay L. Johnson, "Supercenters: An Evolving Saga," *Discount Merchandiser*, April 1995, pp. 26–30.

14. See Catherine Yang, "Maybe They Should Call Them 'Scammers,'" *Business Week*, January 16, 1995, pp. 32–33; Ronald C. Goodstein, "UPC Scanner Pricing Systems: Are They Accurate?" *Journal of Marketing*, April 1994, pp. 20–30.

15. For a listing of the key factors involved in success with an EDI system, see R. P. Vlosky, D. T. Wilson, and P. M. Smith, "Electronic Data Interchange

Implementation Strategies: A Case Study," *Journal of Business & Industrial Marketing* 9, no. 4 (1994): 5–18.

16. "Business Bulletin: Shopper Scanner," *Wall Street Journal*, February 18, 1995, p. A1.

17. For further discussion of retail trends, see Louis W. Stern and Adel I. El-Ansary, *Marketing Channels*, 5th ed. (Upper Saddle River, NJ: Prentice Hall, 1996).

18. Shelley Donald Coolidge, "Facing Saturated Home Markets, Retailers Look to Rest of World," *Christian Science Monitor*, February 14, 1994, p. 7; Carla Rapoport with Justin Martin, "Retailers Go Global," *Fortune*, February 20, 1995, pp. 102–8.

19. Gherry Khermouch, "Third Places," *Brandweek*, March 13, 1995, pp. 36–40.

20. See Bert McCammon, Robert F. Lusch, Deborah S. Coykendall, and James M. Kenderdine, *Wholesaling in Transition* (Norman: University of Oklahoma, College of Business Administration, 1989).

21. Hoover's Company Profiles, 1999, and company Web sites.

22. James A. Narus and James C. Anderson, "Contributing as a Distributor to Partnerships with Manufacturers," *Business Horizons*, September–October 1987. Also see James D. Hlavecek and Tommy J. McCuistion, "Industrial Distributors—When, Who, and How," *Harvard Business Review*, March–April 1983, pp. 96–101.

23. Douglas Chandler, " A Conversation on Consolidation," *Electrical Wholesaling*, January 1999, http://www.ewweb.com/articles/0199ew01.htm.

24. Rita Koselka, "Distribution Revolution," *Forbes,* May 25, 1992, pp. 54–62.

25. Ronald Henkoff, "Delivering the Goods," *Fortune*, November 28, 1994, pp. 64–78.

26. Tom Stein and Jeff Sweat, "Killer Supply Chains—Six Companies Are Using Supply Chains to Transform the Way They Do Business," *Information Week*, November 11, 1998, p. 36.

27. Ronald Henkoff, "Delivering the Goods," *Fortune*, November 28, 1994, pp. 64–78. 29.

28. Rita Koselka, "Distribution Revolution," *Forbes,* May 25, 1992, pp. 54–62.

29. The optimal order quantity is given by the formula $Q^{*'}2DS/IC$, where D'annual demand, S'cost to place one order, and I'annual carrying cost per unit. Known as the economic-order quantity formula, it assumes a constant ordering cost, a constant cost of carrying an additional unit in inventory, a known demand, and no quantity discounts. For further reading on this subject, see Richard J. Tersine, *Principles of Inventory and Materials Management*, 4th ed. (Upper Saddle River, NJ: Prentice Hall, 1994).

30. Sears Press Release, "Sears Announces Strategic Alliance with Total Systems, Inc." May 14, 1998.

Chapter 18

1. The definitions are adapted from Peter D. Bennett, ed., *Dictionary of Marketing Terms* (Chicago: American Marketing Association, 1995).

2. For an alternate communication model developed specifically for advertising communications, see Barbara B. Stern, "A Revised Communication Model for Advertising: Multiple Dimensions of the Source, the Message, and the Recipient," *Journal of Advertising*, June 1994, pp. 5–15.

3. See Brian Sternthal and C. Samuel Craig, *Consumer Behavior: An Information Processing Perspective* (Upper Saddle River, NJ: Prentice Hall, 1982), pp. 97–102.

4. However, research by Cox and Bauer showed a curvilinear relation between self-confidence and persuasibility, with those moderate in self-confidence being the most persuasible. Donald F. Cox and Raymond A. Bauer, "Self-Confidence and Persuasibility in Women," *Public Opinion Quarterly*, Fall 1964, pp. 453–66; and Raymond L. Horton, "Some Relationships between Personality and Consumer Decision-Making," *Journal of Marketing Research*, May 1979, pp. 233–46.

5. See John Fiske and John Hartley, *Reading Television* (London: Methuen, 1980), p. 79. For the effects of expertise on persuasion, see also Elizabeth J. Wilson and Daniel L. Sherrell, "Source Effects in Communication and Persuasion Research: A Meta-Analysis of Effect Size," *Journal of the Academy of Marketing Science*, Spring 1993, pp. 101–12.

6. The semantic differential was developed by C. E. Osgood, C. J. Suci, and P. H. Tannenbaum, *The Measurement of Meaning* (Urbana: University of Illinois Press, 1957).

7. John Bigness, "Back to Brand New Life," *Chicago Tribune*, October 4, 1998; Chris Reidy, "Putting on the Dog to be Arnold's Job," *Boston Globe*, August 28, 1998.

8. See Michael L. Ray, *Advertising and Communications Management* (Upper Saddle River, NJ: Prentice Hall, 1982).

9. See Michael R. Solomon, Judith L. Zaichkowsky, and Rosemary Polegato, *Consumer Behaviour*, Canadian Edition (Scarborough, ON: Prentice Hall Canada, 1999), p.280, n. 77, n. 78 for references to research articles on fear appeals.

10. Paul Brent, "New Kellogg Ads Carry a Weightier Message," *National Post*, April 19, 1999, C4. Charlie Gillis, "Advertising's Quiet Revolution," *National Post*, July 21, 1999, p. A3

11. Kevin Goldman, "Advertising: Knock, Knock. Who's There? The Same Old Funny Ad Again," *Wall Street Journal*, November 2, 1993, p. B10. See also Marc G. Weinberger, Harlan Spotts, Leland Campbell, and Amy L. Parsons, "The Use and Effect of Humor in Different Advertising Media," *Journal of Advertising Research*, May–June 1995, pp. 44–55.

12. William Kissel, "The Bottom Line," *Los Angeles Times*, July 9, 1998, p. 1; Joe Boxer Web site; David B. Wolfe, "Boomer Humor," *American Demographics*, July 1998.

13. See James F. Engel, Roger D. Blackwell, and Paul W. Minard, *Consumer Behavior*, 8th ed. (Fort Worth, TX: Dryden, 1994).

14. See Ayn E. Crowley and Wayne D. Hoyer, "An Integrative Framework for Understanding Two-Sided Persuasion," *Journal of Consumer Research*, March 1994, pp. 561–74.

15. See C. I. Hovland, A. A. Lumsdaine, and F. D. Sheffield, *Experiments on Mass Communication*, vol. 3 (Princeton, NJ: Princeton University Press, 1948), ch. 8; and Crowley and Hoyer, "An Integrative Framework for Understanding Two-sided Persuasion." For an alternative viewpoint, see George E. Belch, "The Effects of Message Modality on One- and Two-Sided Advertising Messages," in *Advances in Consumer Research*, eds. Richard P. Bagozzi and Alice M. Tybout (Ann Arbor, MI: Association for Consumer Research, 1983), pp. 21–26.

16. Curtis P. Haugtvedt and Duane T. Wegener, "Message Order Effects in Persuasion: An Attitude Strength Perspective," *Journal of Consumer Research*, June 1994, pp. 205–18; H. Rao Unnava, Robert E. Burnkrant, and Sunil Erevelles, "Effects of Presentation Order and Communication Modality on Recall and Attitude," *Journal of Consumer Research*, December 1994, pp. 481–90.

17. Brian Sternthal and C. Samuel Craig, *Consumer Behavior: An Information Processing Perspective* (Upper Saddle River, NJ: Prentice Hall, 1982), pp. 282–84.

18. Herbert C. Kelman and Carl I. Hovland, "Reinstatement of the Communication in Delayed Measurement of Opinion Change," *Journal of Abnormal and Social Psychology* 48 (1953): 327–35.

19. David J. Moore, John C. Mowen, and Richard Reardon, "Multiple Sources in Advertising Appeals: When Product Endorsers Are Paid by the Advertising Sponsor," *Journal of the Academy of Marketing Science*, Summer 1994, pp. 234–43.

20. C. E. Osgood and P. H. Tannenbaum, "The Principles of Congruity in the Prediction of Attitude Change," *Psychological Review* 62 (1955): 42–55.

21. Michael Kiely, "Word-of-Mouth Marketing," *Marketing*, September 1993, p. 6.

22. See Regis McKenna, *The Regis Touch* (Reading, MA: Addison-Wesley, 1985); and Regis McKenna, *Relationship Marketing* (Reading, MA: Addison-Wesley, 1991).

23. Michael Cafferky has identified four kinds of people companies try to reach to stimulate word-of-mouth referrals: opinion leaders, marketing mavens, influentials, and product enthusiasts. *Opinion leaders* are people who are widely respected within defined social groups, such as fashion leaders. They have a large relevant social network, high source credibility, and a high propensity to talk. *Marketing mavens* are people who spend a lot of time learning the best buys (values) in the marketplace. *Influentials* are people who are socially and politically active; they try to know what is going on and influence the course of events. *Product enthusiasts* are people who are known experts in a product category, such as art connoisseurs, audiophiles, and computer wizards. See *Let Your Customers Do the Talking* (Chicago: Dearborn Financial Publishing, 1995), pp. 30–33.

24. See Philip Kotler, "Atmospherics as a Marketing Tool," *Journal of Retailing*, Winter 1973–1974, pp. 48–64.

25. See Everett M. Rogers, *Diffusion of Innovations*, 4th ed. (New York: Free Press, 1995).

26. Quoted in Daniel Seligman, "How Much for Advertising?" *Fortune*, December 1956, p. 123. For a good discussion of setting promotion budgets, see Michael L. Rothschild, *Advertising* (Lexington, MA: D. C. Heath, 1987), ch. 20.

27. Albert Wesley Frey, How Many Dollars for Advertising? (New York: Ronald Press, 1955), p. 65.

28. Albert Wesley Frey, *How Many Dollars for Advertising?* (New York: Ronald Press, 1955), p. 49.

29. Adapted from G. Maxwell Ule, "A Media Plan for 'Sputnik' Cigarettes," *How to Plan Media Strategy* (American Association of Advertising Agencies, 1957 Regional Convention), pp. 41–52.

30. Sidney J. Levy, *Promotional Behavior* (Glenview, IL: Scott, Foresman, 1971), ch. 4.

31. Relatively little research has been done on the effectiveness of business-to-business advertising. For a survey, see Wesley J. Johnson, "The Importance of Advertising and the Relative Lack of Research," *Journal of Business & Industrial Marketing*, 9, no. 2 (1994): 3–4.

32. *How Advertising Works in Today's Marketplace: The Morrill Study* (New York: McGraw-Hill, 1971), p. 4.

33. Cyril Freeman, "How to Evaluate Advertising's Contribution," *Harvard Business Review*, July–August 1962, pp. 137–48.

34. Theodore Levitt, *Industrial Purchasing Behavior: A Study in Communication Effects* (Boston: Division of Research, Harvard Business School, 1965).

35. See Gary L. Lilien and John D. C. Little, "The ADVISOR Project: A Study of Industrial Marketing Budgets," *Sloan Management Review*, Spring 1976, pp. 17–31; and Gary L. Lilien, "ADVISOR 2: Modeling the Marketing Mix Decision for Industrial Products," *Management Science*, February 1979, pp. 191–204.

36. Paul Brent, "Chapters Ads Promote New Web Site," *National Post*, April 26, 1999, p. C4.

37. See Don E. Shultz, Stanley I. Tannenbaum, and Robert F. Lauterborn, *Integrated Marketing Communications: Putting It Together and Making It Work* (Lincoln-wood, IL: NTC Business Books, 1992); and Ernan Roman, *Integrated Direct Marketing: The Cutting-Edge Strategy for Synchronizing Advertising, Direct Mail, Telemarketing, and Field Sales* (Lincoln-wood, IL: NTC Business Books, 1995).

Chapter 19

1. *Defining Advertising Goals for Measured Advertising Results* (New York: Association of National Advertisers, 1961).

2. See William L. Wilkie and Paul W. Farris, "Comparison Advertising: Problem and Potential," *Journal of Marketing*, October 1975, pp. 7–15.

3. See Randall L. Rose, Paul W. Miniard, Michael J. Barone, Kenneth C. Manning, and Brian D. Till, "When Persuasion Goes Undetected: The Case of Comparative Advertising," *Journal of Marketing Research*, August 1993, pp. 315–30; Sanjay Putrevu and Kenneth R. Lord, "Comparative and Noncomparative Advertising: Attitudinal Effects under Cognitive and Affective Involvement Conditions," *Journal of Advertising*, June 1994, pp. 77–91; Dhruv Grewal, Sukumar Kavanoor, and James Barnes, "Comparative Versus Noncomparative Advertising: A Meta-Analysis," *Journal of Marketing*, October 1997, pp. 1–15; Dhruv Grewal, Kent B. Monroe, and P. Krishnan,

"The Effects of Price-Comparison Advertising on Buyers' Perceptions of Acquisition Value, Transaction Value, and Behavioral Intentions," *Journal of Marketing,* April 1998, pp. 46–59.

4. For a good discussion, see David A. Aaker and James M. Carman, "Are You Overadvertising?" *Journal of Advertising Research*, August–September 1982, pp. 57–70.

5. See Donald E. Schultz, Dennis Martin, and William P. Brown, *Strategic Advertising Campaigns* (Chicago: Crain Books, 1984), pp. 192–97.

6. M. L. Vidale and H. R. Wolfe, "An Operations-Research Study of Sales Response to Advertising," *Operations Research*, June 1957, pp. 370–81.

7. John D. C. Little, "A Model of Adaptive Control of Promotional Spending," *Operations Research*, November 1966, pp. 1075–97.

8. For additional models for setting the advertising budget, see Gary L. Lilien, Philip Kotler, and K. Sridhar Moorthy, *Marketing Models* (Upper Saddle River, NJ: Prentice Hall, 1992), ch. 6.

9. "The Best Awards: Retail/Fast-Food," *Advertising Age*, May 18, 1998, p S8; Karen Benezra, "Taco Bell Pooch Walks the Merch Path," *Brandweek*, June 8, 1998, p. 46; Bob Garfield, "Perspicacious Pooch Scores for Taco Bell," *Advertising Age,* March 9, 1998, p. 53.

10. See "Keep Listening to That Wee, Small Voice," in *Communications of an Advertising Man* (Chicago: Leo Burnett Co., 1961), p. 61.

11. John C. Maloney, "Marketing Decisions and Attitude Research," in *Effective Marketing Coordination*, ed. George L. Baker Jr. (Chicago: American Marketing Association, 1961), pp. 595–618.

12. Dik Warren Twedt, "How to Plan New Products, Improve Old Ones, and Create Better Advertising," *Journal of Marketing*, January 1969, pp. 53–57.

13. See William A. Mindak and H. Malcolm Bybee, "Marketing Application to Fund Raising," *Journal of Marketing*, July 1971, pp. 13–18.

14. Lalita Manrai, "Effect of Labeling Strategy in Advertising: Self-Referencing versus Psychological Reactance" (Ph.D. dissertation, Northwestern University, 1987).

15. James B. Amdorfer, "Absolut Ads Sans Bottle Offer a Short-Story Series," *Advertising Age,* January 12, 1998, p. 8.

16. L. Greenland, "Is This the Era of Positioning?" *Advertising Age*, May 29, 1972.

17. David Ogilvy and Joel Raphaelson, "Research on Advertising Techniques That Work—And Don't Work," *Harvard Business Review*, July–August 1982, pp. 14–18.

18. Joanne Lipman, "It's It and That's a Shame: Why Are Some Slogans Losers?" *Wall Street Journal*, July 16, 1993, p. A4; Paul Farhi, "The Wrong One Baby, Uh-Uh: Has Madison Avenue Lost It?" *Washington Post*, February 28, 1993, p. C5.

19. Kevin Goldman, "Advertising: From Witches to Anorexics: Critical Eyes Scrutinize Ads for Political Correctness," *Wall Street Journal*, May 19, 1994, p. B1.

20. Adapted from Sandra Cordon, "Where High Road Meets Bottom Line: Ethical Mutual Funds Avoid Companies Deemed Socially Irresponsible," *The London Free Press,* October 9, 1998, p. D3.

21. Donald E. Schultz, Dennis Martin, and William P. Brown, *Strategic Advertising Campaigns* (Chicago: Crain Books, 1984), p. 340.

22. See Herbert E. Krugman, "What Makes Advertising Effective?" *Harvard Business Review*, March–April 1975, p. 98.

23. See Peggy J. Kreshel, Kent M. Lancaster, and Margaret A. Toomey, "Advertising Media Planning: How Leading Advertising Agencies Estimate Effective Reach and Frequency" (Urbana: University of Illinois, Department of Advertising, paper no. 20, January 1985). Also see Jack Z. Sissors and Lincoln Bumba, *Advertising Media Planning*, 3d ed. (Lincolnwood, IL: NTC Business Books, 1988), ch. 9.

24. Canadian Media Directors' Council, "1999–2000 Media Digest," p. 16.

25. Roland T. Rust and Richard W. Oliver, "Notes and Comments: The Death of Advertising," Journal of Advertising, December 1994, pp. 71–77.

26. Canadian Media Directors' Council, "1999–2000 Media Digest," p. 22. Gene Accas, "Prime Prices Fall with Shares," *Broadcasting & Cable*, September 28,

1998, p. 36; "Hilfilger Hikes Ads to New Level: First Designer to Go Super Bowl Route," *Daily News Record* 28, no. 7 (January 16, 1998): 2.

27. Canadian Media Directors' Council, "1999–2000 Media Digest," p. 40.

28. See Roland T. Rust, *Advertising Media Models: A Practical Guide* (Lexington, MA: Lexington Books, 1986).

29. See Jay W. Forrester, "Advertising: A Problem in Industrial Dynamics," *Harvard Business Review*, March–April 1959, pp. 100–10.

30. See Amber G. Rao and Peter B. Miller, "Advertising/Sales Response Functions," *Journal of Advertising Research*, April 1975, pp. 7–15.

31. See Alfred A. Kuehn, "How Advertising Performance Depends on Other Marketing Factors," *Journal of Advertising Research*, March 1962, pp. 2–10.

32. See also Hani I. Mesak, "An Aggregate Advertising Pulsing Model with Wearout Effects," *Marketing Science*, Summer 1992, pp. 310–26; and Fred M. Feinberg, "Pulsing Policies for Aggregate Advertising Models," *Marketing Science*, Summer 1992, pp. 221–34.

33. Jay W. Forrester, "Advertising: A Problem in Industrial Dynamics," *Harvard Business Review*, March–April 1959, p. 102.

34. Russell I. Haley, James Staffaroni, and Arthur Fox, "The Missing Measures of Copy Testing," *Journal of Advertising Research*, May–June 1994, pp. 46–56. (Also see this May–June 1994 issue of the *Journal of Advertising Research* for more articles on copy testing.)

35. See J. O. Peckham, *The Wheel of Marketing* (Scarsdale, NY: privately printed, 1975), pp. 73–77.

36. Kristian S. Palda, *The Measurement of Cumulative Advertising Effect* (Upper Saddle River, NJ: Prentice Hall, 1964), p. 87.

37. David B. Montgomery and Alvin J. Silk, "Estimating Dynamic Effects of Market Communications Expenditures," *Management Science*, June 1972, pp. 485–501.

38. See Robert D. Buzzell, "E. I. Du Pont de Nemours & Co.: Measurement of Effects of Advertising," in his *Mathematical Models and Marketing Management* (Boston: Division of Research, Graduate School of Business Administration,

Harvard University, 1964), pp. 157–79.

39. See Glen L. Urban, "Allocating Ad Budgets Geographically," *Journal of Advertising Research*, December 1975, pp. 7–16.

40. See Nigel Hollis, "The Link Between TV Ad Awareness and Sales: New Evidence from Sales Response Modelling," *Journal of the Market Research Society*, January 1994, pp. 41–55.

41. In addition to the sources cited below, see David Walker and Tony M. Dubitsky, "Why Liking Matters," *Journal of Advertising Research*, May–June 1994, pp. 9–18; Abhilasha Mehta, "How Advertising Response Modeling (ARM) Can Increase Ad Effectiveness," *Journal of Advertising Research*, May–June 1994, pp. 62–74; Karin Holstius, "Sales Response to Advertising," *International Journal of Advertising* 9, no. 1, (1990): 38–56; John Deighton, Caroline Henderson, and Scott Neslin, "The Effects of Advertising on Brand Switching and Repeat Purchasing," *Journal of Marketing Research*, February 1994, pp. 28–43; Anil Kaul and Dick R. Wittink, "Empirical Generalizations About the Impact of Advertising on Price Sensitivity and Price," *Marketing Science* 14, no. 3, pt. 1, (1995): G151–60; and Ajay Kalra and Ronald C. Goodstein, "The Impact of Advertising Positioning Strategies on Consumer Price Sensitivity," *Journal of Marketing Research*, May 1998, pp. 210–24.

42. Gerald J. Tellis, "Advertising Exposure, Loyalty, and Brand Purchase: A Two-Stage Model of Choice," *Journal of Marketing Research*, May 1988, pp. 134–44. Also see "It's Official: Some Ads Work," *The Economist*, April 1, 1995, p. 52; Dwight R. Riskey, "How TV Advertising Works: An Industry Response," *Journal of Marketing Research*, May 1997, pp. 292–93.

43. See Michael A. Kamins, Lawrence J. Marks, and Deborah Skinner, "Television Commercial Evaluation in the Context of Program Induced Mood: Congruency versus Consistency Effects," *Journal of Advertising*, June 1991, pp. 1–14.

44. See Kenneth R. Lord and Robert E. Burnkrant, "Attention versus Distraction: The Interactive Effect of Program Involvement and Attentional Devices on Commercial Processing," *Journal of Advertising*, March 1993, pp. 47–60; Kenneth R. Lord, Myung-Soo Lee, and Paul L. Sauer, "Program Context Antecedents of Attitude Toward Radio Commercials," *Journal of the Academy of Marketing Science*, Winter 1994, pp. 3–15.

45. See Yoav Ganzach and Nili Karashi, "Message Framing and Buying Behavior: A Field Experiment," *Journal of Business Research*, January 1995, pp. 11–17.

46. From Robert C. Blattberg and Scott A. Neslin, *Sales Promotion: Concepts, Methods, and Strategies* (Upper Saddle River, NJ: Prentice Hall, 1990). This text provides the most comprehensive and analytical treatment of sales promotion to date.

47. Roger A. Strang, "Sales Promotion—Fast Growth, Faulty Management," *Harvard Business Review*, July–August 1976, pp. 116–19.

48. John Heinzl, "Tim Hortons Rrrolls Up a Winner," *Globe and Mail*, March 24, 1999, p. B29.

49. For a good summary of the research on whether promotion erodes the consumer franchise of leading brands, see Blattberg and Neslin, *Sales Promotion*.

50. Robert George Brown, "Sales Response to Promotions and Advertising," *Journal of Advertising Research*, August 1974, pp. 36–37. Also see Carl F .Mela, Sunil Gupta, and Donald R. Lehmann, "The Long-Term Impact of Promotion and Advertising on Consumer Brand Choice," *Journal of Marketing Research*, May 1997, pp. 248–61; Purushottam Papatla and Lakshman Krishmamurti, "Measuring the Dynamic Effects of Promotions on Brand Choice," *Journal of Marketing Research*, February 1996, pp. 20–35.

51. F. Kent Mitchel, "Advertising/Promotion Budgets: How Did We Get Here, and What Do We Do Now?" *Journal of Consumer Marketing*, Fall 1985, pp. 405–47.

52. See Paul W. Farris and John A. Quelch, "In Defense of Price Promotion," *Sloan Management Review*, Fall 1987, pp. 63–69.

53. For a model for setting sales promotions objectives, see David B. Jones, "Setting Promotional Goals: A Communications Relationship Model," *Journal of Consumer Marketing* 11, no. 1 (1994): 38–49.

54. See John C. Totten and Martin P. Block, *Analyzing Sales Promotion: Text and Cases*, 2d ed. (Chicago: Dartnell, 1994), pp. 69–70.

55. See Paul W. Farris and Kusum L. Ailawadi, "Retail Power: Monster or Mouse?" *Journal of Retailing*, Winter 1992, pp. 351–69.

56. See "Retailers Buy Far in Advance to Exploit Trade Promotions," *Wall Street Journal*, October 9, 1986, p. 35; Rajiv Lal, J. Little, and J. M. Vilas-Boas, "A Theory of Forward Buying, Merchandising, and Trade Deals," *Marketing Science* 15, no. 1 (1996), 21–37.

57. "Trade Promotion: Much Ado About Something," *PROMO*, October 1991, pp. 15, 37, 40.

58. Quoted from Kerry E. Smith, "Media Fusion," *PROMO*, May 1992, p. 29.

59. Arthur Stern, "Measuring the Effectiveness of Package Goods Promotion Strategies" (paper presented to the Association of National Advertisers, Glen Cove, NY, February 1978).

60. Roger A. Strang, "Sales Promotion—Fast Growth, Faulty Management," *Harvard Business Review*, July–August 1976, p. 120.

61. Kurt H. Schaffir and H. George Trenten, *Marketing Information Systems* (New York: Amacom, 1973), p. 81.

62. See Magid M. Abraham and Leonard M. Lodish, "Getting the Most Out of Advertising and Promotion," *Harvard Business Review*, May–June 1990, pp. 50–60.

63. See Joe A. Dodson, Alice M. Tybout, and Brian Sternthal, "Impact of Deals and Deal Retraction on Brand Switching," *Journal of Marketing Research*, February 1978, pp. 72–81.

64. Books on sales promotion include Totten and Block, *Analyzing Sales Promotion: Text and Cases*; Don E. Schultz, William A. Robinson, and Lisa A. Petrison, *Sales Promotion Essentials*, 2d ed. (Lincolnwood, IL: NTC Business Books, 1994); John Wilmshurst, *Below-the-Line Promotion* (Oxford, England: Butterworth/Heinemann, 1993); and Robert C. Blattberg and Scott A. Neslin, *Sales Promotion: Concepts, Methods, and Strategies* (Upper Saddle River, NJ: Prentice Hall, 1990). For an expert

systems approach to sales promotion, see John W. Keon and Judy Bayer, "An Expert Approach to Sales Promotion Management," *Journal of Advertising Research*, June–July 1986, pp. 19–26.

65. Adapted from Scott M. Cutlip, Allen H. Center, and Glen M. Broom, *Effective Public Relations*, 8th ed. (Upper Saddle River, NJ: Prentice Hall, 1997).

66. For an excellent account, see Thomas L. Harris, *The Marketer's Guide to Public Relations* (New York: John Wiley, 1991). Also see *Value-Added Public Relations* (Chicago: NTC Business Books, 1998).

67. Danielle D'Agostino, "Teaching Brands New Tricks," *Marketing*, February 22, 1999, p. 28.

68. Liza Finlay, "Snowed Under," *Marketing*, February 22, 1999, p. 4.

69. Tom Duncan, *A Study of How Manufacturers and Service Companies Perceive and Use Marketing Public Relations* (Muncie, IN: Ball State University, December 1985). For more on how to contrast the effectiveness of advertising with the effectiveness of PR, see Kenneth R. Lord and Sanjay Putrevu, "Advertising and Publicity: An Information Processing Perspective," *Journal of Economic Psychology*, March 1993, pp. 57–84.

70. For further reading on cause-related marketing, see P. Rajan Varadarajan and Anil Menon, "Cause-Related Marketing: A Co-Alignment of Marketing Strategy and Corporate Philanthropy," *Journal of Marketing*, July 1988, pp. 58–74.

71. Material adapted from Thomas L. Harris, "PR Gets Personal," *Direct Marketing*, April 1994, pp. 29–32.

72. See Dwight W. Catherwood and Richard L. Van Kirk, *The Complete Guide to Special Event Management* (New York: John Wiley, 1992).

73. Arthur M. Merims, "Marketing's Stepchild: Product Publicity," *Harvard Business Review*, November–December 1972, pp. 111–12. Also see Katerine D. Paine, "There Is a Method for Measuring PR," *Marketing News*, November 6, 1987, p. 5.

Chapter 20

1. See Rolph Anderson, *Essentials of Personal Selling: The New Professionalism* (Upper Saddle River, NJ: Prentice Hall, 1995); and Douglas J. Dalrymple, *Sales Management: Concepts and Cases*, 5th ed. (New York: John Wiley, 1994).

2. Erica Zlomislic, "Distribution Deal Uncorked: Vincor Flexes Sales Muscle for New French Joint-venture Partner," *Strategy: The Canadian Marketing Report*, May 11, 1998, p. 1.

3. Adapted from Robert N. McMurry, "The Mystique of Super-Salesmanship," *Harvard Business Review*, March–April 1961, p. 114. Also see William C. Moncrief III, "Selling Activity and Sales Position Taxonomies for Industrial Salesforces," *Journal of Marketing Research*, August 1986, pp. 261–70.

4. For estimates of the cost of sales calls, see *Sales Force Compensation* (Chicago: Dartnell's 27th Survey, 1992), and *Sales & Marketing Management*'s 1993 sales manager's budget planner (June 28, 1993), pp. 3–75.

5. Sarah Lorge, "A Priceless Brand," *Sales & Marketing Management*, October 1998, pp. 102–10.

6. Sanjit Sengupta, Robert E. Krapfel, and Michael A. Pusateri, "The Strategic Sales Force," *Marketing Management*, Summer 1997, p. 33.

7. Christopher Power, "Smart Selling: How Companies Are Winning Over Today's Tougher Customer," *Business Week*, August 3, 1992, pp. 46–48.

8. Ira Sager, "The Few, the True, the Blue," *Business Week*, May 30, 1994, pp. 124–26; Geoffrey Brewer, "IBM Gets User-Friendly," *Sales & Marketing Management*, July 1994, p. 13.

9. "Dun & Bradstreet/Marketing Salary Survey 1999," *Marketing*, September 27, 1999, pp. 24–26. Muriel Draaisma, "The Booming Marketing Job Market," *Marketing*, September 27, 1999, pp. 20–21.

10. Luis R. Gomez-Mejia, David B. Balkin, and Robert L. Cardy, *Managing Human Resources* (Upper Saddle River, NJ: Prentice Hall, 1995), pp. 416–18.

11. "What Salespeople Are Paid," *Sales & Marketing Management*, February 1995, pp. 30–31; Power, "Smart Selling," pp. 46–48; William Keenan Jr., ed., *The Sales & Marketing Management Guide to Sales Compensation Planning: Commissions, Bonuses & Beyond* (Chicago: Probus Publishing, 1994).

12. Mark De Wolf, "Special Report: Motivating the Salesforce: What really motivates the salesperson today?" *Strategy: The Canadian Marketing Report*, August 18, 1997, p. 19.

13. George H. Lucas Jr., A. Parasuraman, Robert A. Davis, and Ben M. Enis, "An Empirical Study of Sales Force Turnover," *Journal of Marketing*, July 1987, pp. 34–59.

14. See Charles Garfield, *Peak Performers: The New Heroes of American Business* (New York: Avon Books, 1986); "What Makes a Supersalesperson?" *Sales & Marketing Management*, August 23, 1984, p. 86; "What Makes a Top Performer?" *Sales & Marketing Management*, May 1989; and Timothy J. Trow, "The Secret of a Good Hire: Profiling," *Sales & Marketing Management*, May 1990, pp. 44–55.

15. Robert N. McMurry, "The Mystique of Super-Salesmanship," *Harvard Business Review*, March–April 1961, p. 114. Also see William C. Moncrief III, "Selling Activity and Sales Position Taxonomies for Industrial Salesforces," *Journal of Marketing Research*, August 1986, p. 117.

16. Robert N. McMurry, "The Mystique of Super-Salesmanship," *Harvard Business Review*, March–April 1961, p. 114. Also see William C. Moncrief III, "Selling Activity and Sales Position Taxonomies for Industrial Salesforces," *Journal of Marketing Research*, August 1986, p. 118.

17. David Mayer and Herbert M. Greenberg, "What Makes a Good Salesman?" *Harvard Business Review*, July–August 1964, pp. 119–25.

18. James M. Comer and Alan J. Dubinsky, *Managing the Successful Sales Force* (Lexington, MA: Lexington Books, 1985), pp. 5–25.

19. From an address given by Donald R. Keough at the 27th Annual Conference of the Super-Market Institute, Chicago, April 26–29, 1964. Also see Judy Siguaw, Gene Brown, and Robert Widing II, "The Influence of the Market Orientation of the Firm on Sales Force Behavior and Attitudes," *Journal of Marketing Research*, February 1994, pp. 106–16.

20. Robert L. Lindstrom, "Training Hits the Road," *Sales & Marketing Management*, June 1995, pp. 10–14.

21. *Sales Force Compensation* (Chicago: Dartnell's 25th Survey, 1989), p. 13.

22. See John F. Magee, "Determining the Optimum Allocation of Expenditures for Promotional Effort with Operations Research Methods," in *The Frontiers of Marketing Thought and Science*, ed. Frank M. Bass (Chicago: American Marketing Association, 1958), pp. 140–56.

23. Michael R. W. Bommer, Brian F. O'Neil, and Beheruz N. Sethna, "A Methodology for Optimizing Selling Time of Salespersons," *Journal of Marketing Theory and Practice*, Spring 1994, pp. 61–75.

24. See Thomas Blackshear and Richard E. Plank, "The Impact of Adaptive Selling on Sales Effectiveness Within the Pharmaceutical Industry," *Journal of Marketing Theory and Practice*, Summer 1994, pp. 106–25.

25. "Automation Nation," *Marketing Tools*, April 1997; Scott Hample, "Made to Order," *Marketing Tools*, August 1997.

26. "Are Salespeople Gaining More Selling Time?" *Sales & Marketing Management*, July 1986, p. 29.

27. James A. Narus and James C. Anderson, "Industrial Distributor Selling: The Roles of Outside and Inside Sales," *Industrial Marketing Management* 15 (1986): 55–62.

28. See Gilbert A. Churchill, Jr., Neil M. Ford, and Orville C. Walker Jr., *Sales Force Management: Planning, Implementation and Control*, 4th ed. (Homewood, IL: Irwin, 1993). Also see Jhinuk Chowdhury, "The Motivational Impact of Sales Quotas on Effort," *Journal of Marketing Research*, February 1993, pp. 28–41; Murali K. Mantrala, Prabhakant Sinha, and Andris A. Zoltners, "Structuring a Multiproduct Sales Quota-Bonus Plan for a Heterogeneous Sales Force: A Practical Model-Based Approach," *Marketing Science* 13, no. 2 (1994): 121–44; Wujin Chu, Eitan Gerstner, and James D. Hess, "Costs and Benefits of Hard-Sell," *Journal of Marketing Research*, February 1995, pp. 97–102.

29. "What Motivates U.S. Salespeople?" *American Salesman*, February 1994, pp. 25, 30.

30. "A Gift for Rewards," *Sales & Marketing Management*, March 1995, pp. 35–36.

31. See Philip M. Posdakoff and Scott B. MacKenzie, "Organizational Citizenship Behaviors and Sales Unit Effectiveness," *Journal of Marketing Research*, August 1994, pp. 351–63.

32. For further reading, see Dorothy Cohen, *Legal Issues in Marketing Decision Making* (Cincinnati, OH: South-Western, 1995).

33. For an excellent summary of the skills needed today by sales representatives and sales managers, see Rolph Anderson and Bert Rosenbloom, "The World Class Sales Manager: Adapting to Global Megatrends," *Journal of Global Marketing* 5, no. 4 (1992): 11–22.

34. Some of the following discussion is based on W. J. E. Crissy, William H. Cunningham, and Isabella C. M. Cunningham, *Selling: The Personal Force in Marketing* (New York: John Wiley, 1977), pp. 119–29.

35. Norton Paley, "Cultivating Customers," *Sales & Marketing Management*, September 1994, pp. 31–32.

36. "Notebook: Briefcase Full of Views: Johnson and Johnson Uses Virtual Reality to Give Prospects an Inside Look at Its Products," *Marketing Tools*, April 1997.

37. For additional reading, see Howard Raiffa, *The Art and Science of Negotiation* (Cambridge, MA: Harvard University Press, 1982); Max H. Bazerman and Margaret A. Neale, *Negotiating Rationally* (New York: Free Press, 1992); James C. Freund, *Smart Negotiating* (New York: Simon & Schuster, 1992); Frank L. Acuff, *How to Negotiate Anything with Anyone Anywhere Around the World* (New York: American Management Association, 1993); and Jehoshua Eliashberg, Gary L. Lilien, and Nam Kim, "Searching for Generalizations in Business Marketing Negotiations," *Marketing Science* 14, no. 3, pt. 1 (1995): G47–G60.

38. See Donald W. Dobler, *Purchasing and Materials Management*, 5th ed. (New York: McGraw-Hill, 1990).

39. This discussion of zone of agreement is fully developed in Raiffa, *Art and Science of Negotiation*.

40. Neil Rackham, *SPIN Selling* (New York: McGraw-Hill, 1988). Also see his *The SPIN Selling Fieldbook* (New York: McGraw-Hill, 1996); and his latest book, coauthored with John De Vincentis

Rethinking the Sales Force New York: McGraw-Hill, 1996.

41. See Frank V. Cespedes, Stephen X. Doyle, and Robert J. Freedman, "Teamwork for Today's Selling," *Harvard Business Review*, March–April 1989, pp. 44–54, 58. Also see Cespedes, *Concurrent Marketing: Integrating Product, Sales, and Service* (Boston: Harvard Business School Press, 1995).

Chapter 21

1. The terms *direct-order marketing* and *direct relationship marketing* were suggested as subsets of direct marketing by Stan Rapp and Tom Collins in *The Great Marketing Turnaround* (Upper Saddle River, NJ: Prentice Hall, 1990).

2. Figures are for 1997 and supplied by National Mail Order Association, tel: 612–788–1673.

3. Cynthia Reynolds, "E-Commerce: Hype, Hype Hooray!," *Supplement to Canadian Business*, February 12, 1999. For an update on the most recent statistics, go to www.commerce.net/nielsen/.

4. Pierre A. Passavant, "Where Is Direct Marketing Headed in the 1990s?" an address in Philadelphia, May 4, 1989.

5. Don E. Schultz, Stanley I. Tannenbaum, and Robert F. Lauterborn, *Integrated Marketing Communications* (Lincolnwood, IL: NTC Business Books, 1993);; Stan Rapp and Thomas L. Collins, *Maximarketing* (New York: McGraw-Hill, 1987), and *Beyond Maximarketing: The New Power of Caring and Daring* (New York: McGraw-Hill, 1994).

6. Ernan Roman, *Integrated Direct Marketing: The Cutting Edge Strategy for Synchronizing Advertising, Direct Mail, Telemarketing, and Field Sales* (Lincolnwood, IL: NTC Business Books, 1995), p. 3.

7. Stan Rapp and Thomas L. Collins, *Maximarketing* (New York: McGraw-Hill, 1987).

8. See Don Peppers and Martha Rogers, *The One-to-One Future* (New York: Doubleday/Currency, 1993).

9. Jonathan Berry, "A Potent New Tool for Selling: Database Marketing," *Business Week*, September 5, 1994, pp. 56–62; Vincent Alonzo, "'Til Death Do

Us Part," *Incentive*, April 1994, pp. 37–41.

10. Deborah Stokes, "How a Company with Zero Profile in Canada Cracked this Market," *Marketing*, October 5, 1998, p. 16.

11. David Foley, "Speaking Directly: More Companies Taking Their Lists Private," *Strategy: The Canadian Marketing Report*, August 4, 1997, p. 15. Bruce Horovitz, "AmEx kills database deal after privacy outrage," *USA Today*, July 15, 1998, p. B1.

12. Bob Stone, *Successful Direct Marketing Methods*, 6th ed. (Lincolnwood, IL: NTC Business Books, 1996). Also see David Shepard Associates, *The New Direct Marketing*, 2nd ed. (Chicago: Irwin, 1995); and Amiya K. Basu, Atasi Basu, and Rajeev Batra, "Modeling the Response Pattern to Direct Marketing Campaigns," *Journal of Marketing Research*, May 1995, pp. 204–12.

13. Edward L. Nash, *Direct Marketing: Strategy, Planning, Execution*, 3d ed. (New York: McGraw-Hill, 1995).

14. Rachel McLaughlin, "Get the Envelope Opened!" *Target Marketing*, September 1998, pp. 37–39.

15. Also see Richard J. Courtheoux, "Calculating the Lifetime Value of a Customer," in Roman, *Integrated Direct Marketing*, pp. 198–202. Also see Rob Jackson and Paul Wang, *Strategic Database Marketing* (Lincolnwood, IL: NTC Business Books, 1994), pp. 188–201.

16. Margaret Nearing, "A Comfy Place to Shop," *Marketing*, December 7, 1998, p. 19. Zena Olijnyk, "Retailers Turn to 'Magalogues,'" *Financial Post*, January 20, 1999, p. C8.

17. Bruce Horovitz, "Catalog Craze Delivers Holiday Deals," *USA Today*, December 1, 1998, p. 3B.

18. De'Ann Weimer, "Can I Try (Click) That Blouse (Drag) in Blue?" *Business Week*, November 9, 1998, p. 86.

19. See David Woodruff, "Twilight of the Teller?" *Business Week*, European Edition, July 20, 1998, pp. 16–17.

20. David Berman, "Dial M for migraine," *Canadian Business*, August 28, 1998, pp. 29–32.

21. "Infomercial Offers Multiple Uses," *Direct Marketing*, September 1998, p. 11; Tim Hawthorne, "When and Why to Consider Infomercials," *Target Marketing*, February 1998, pp. 52–53.

22. Theresa Dillon, "TSC Takes on New Frontiers: The Shopping Channel Spins Off Catalogue, Web Presence," *Strategy: The Canadian Marketing Report*, June 7, 1999, p. D1.

23. Wendy Stueck, "Infotouch Presses Interactive Kiosk Business," *Globe and Mail*, June 4, 1999, p. B7.

24. See Anthony Wensley, "B2B Traffic on the Rise," *Financial Post*, September 22, 1999, p. E2; Jeffrey F. Rayport and John J. Sviokla, "Managing in the Marketspace," *Harvard Business Review*, November–December, 1994, pp. 75–85. Also see their "Exploiting the Virtual Value Chain," *Harvard Business Review*, November–December 1995, pp. 141–50.

25. "Shoppers Turning to Cyberspace," *Globe and Mail Special Interest Report E-Commerce*, March 30, 1999, pp. C1, C15.

26. Forrester Research, Inc. has presented some of the following estimates for the year 2002: durable goods, $99 billion; wholesaling of office supplies, electronics goods, and scientific equipment, $89 billion; travel, $7.4 billion; consumer purchases of computer hardware and software, $3.8 billion; and books, music, and entertainment, $3.8 billion. See H. Green and S. Browder, "Cyberspace Winners: How They Did It," *Business Week*, June 22, 1998, pp. 82–85.

27. "Making "OL A-O.K.," *Business Week*, January 11, 1999, p. 65; MSN and Prodigy statistics from Jupiter Communications survey, February 1998.

28. Tyler Hamilton, "Alberta No. 1 Province On-line in Canada," *Globe and Mail*, July 16, 1999, p. B7.

29. See Daniel S. Janal, *Online Marketing Handbook 1998 Edition: How to Promote, Advertise and Sell Your Products and Services on the Internet* (New York: John Wiley, 1998).

30. Gerald D. Boyd, "Cyberspace Caters to Wine Buffs," *San Francisco Chronicle*, May 8, 1998, p. 4.

31. Don Clark, "Study Finds Many Tech Firms' Web Sites Lack Basic Information for Customers," *Wall Street Journal*, August 19, 1998, p. B5.

32. Mark Evans, "Canadians Cast Net on Rough Seas," *Globe and Mail*, July 15, 1999, pp. 1–2.

33. Melanie Berger, "It's Your Move," *Sales & Marketing Management*, March 1998, pp. 44–53.

34. Greg Hansen, "Smaller May Be Better for Web Marketing," *Marketing News*, January 19, 1998, pp. 10, 13. For an excellent discussion of ways to attract viewers to Web sites, see Richard T. Watson, Sigmund Akselsen, and Leyland F. Pitt, "Attractors: Building Mountains in the Flat Landscape of the World Wide Web," *California Management Review*, Winter 1998, pp. 36–56.

35. See George Anders, "Internet Advertising, Just Like Its Medium, Is Pushing Boundaries," *Wall Street Journal*, November 30, 1998, p. 1.

36. See Mary J. Cronin, "Using the Web to Push Key Data to Decision Makers," *Fortune*, September 29, 1997, p. 254.

37. Jay Winchester, "Point, Click, Sell," *Sales & Marketing Management*, November 1998, pp. 100–101.

38. See Joseph Alba, John Lynch, Barton Weitz, Chris Janiszewski, Richard Lutz, Alan Sawyer, and Stacy Wood, "Interactive Home Shopping: Consumer, Retailer, and Manufacturer Incentives to Participate in Electronic Marketplaces," *Journal of Marketing*, July 1997, pp. 38–53.

39. Mark Evans, "Canadians Cast Net on Rough Seas," *Globe and Mail*, July 15, 1999, pp. 1–2.

40. J. A. Quelch and L. R. Klein, "The Internet and International Marketing," *Sloan Management Review*, Spring 1996, pp. 60–75.

41. Nick Wingfield, "Making the Sale— A Marketer's Dream: The Internet Promises to Give Companies a Wealth of Invaluable Data About Their Customers. So, Why Hasn't It?" *Wall Street Journal*, December 7, 1998, p. R20.

42. Stephanie Armour, "Companies Grapple with Gripes Posted on Web," *USA Today*, September 16, 1998, p. 5B.

Chapter 22

1. See Frederick E. Webster Jr., "The Changing Role of Marketing in the Corporation," *Journal of Marketing*, October 1992, pp. 1–17. Also see Ravi

S. Achrol, "Evolution of the Marketing Organization: New Forms for Turbulent Environment," *Journal of Marketing*, October 1991, pp. 77–93; and John P. Workman Jr., Christian Homburg, and Kjell Gruner, "Marketing Organization: An Integrative Framework of Dimensions and Determinants," *Journal of Marketing*, July 1998, pp. 21–41.

2. See Frank V. Cespedes, *Concurrent Marketing: Integrating Product, Sales, and Service* (Boston: Harvard Business School Press, 1995), and *Managing Marketing Linkages: Text, Cases, and Readings* (Upper Saddle River, NJ: Prentice Hall, 1996).

3. Robert E. Lineman and John L. Stanton Jr., "A Game Plan for Regional Marketing," *Journal of Business Strategy,* November–December 1992, pp. 19–25.

4. Natalie Bahadur, "Molson Rolls Out Alcoholic Lemonade: Uses Separate Strategies for Quebec, Ontario Markets," *Strategy: The Canadian Marketing Report*, January 4, 1999, p. 5.

5. Scott Hume, "Execs Favor Regional Approach," *Advertising Age*, November 2, 1987, p. 36; "National Firms Find that Selling to Local Tastes Is Costly, Complex," *Wall Street Journal,* February 9, 1987, P. B1; Paul A. Herbig, *Handbook of Cross-Cultural Marketing* (New York: International Business Press, 1998), pp. 45–46.

6. ". . . and Other Ways to Peel the Onion," *The Economist*, January 7, 1995, pp. 52–53.

7. Andrall E. Pearson and Thomas W. Wilson Jr., *Making Your Organization Work* (New York: Association of National Advertisers, 1967), pp. 8–13.

8. Michael George, Anthony Freeling, and David Court, "Reinventing the Marketing Organization," *The McKinsey Quarterly* no. 4 (1994): 43–62.

9. For further reading, see Robert Dewar and Don Schultz, "The Product Manager, an Idea Whose Time Has Gone," *Marketing Communications*, May 1989, pp. 28–35; "The Marketing Revolution at Procter & Gamble," *Business Week*, July 25, 1988, pp. 72–76; Kevin T. Higgins, "Category Management: New Tools Changing Life for Manufacturers, Retailers," *Marketing News*, September 25, 1989, pp. 2, 19; George S. Low and

Ronald A. Fullerton, "Brands, Brand Management, and the Brand Manager System: A Critical-Historical Evaluation," *Journal of Marketing Research*, May 1994, pp. 173–90; and Michael J. Zenor, "The Profit Benefits of Category Management," *Journal of Marketing Research,* May 1994, pp. 202–13.

10. Stanley F. Slater and John C. Narver, "Market Orientation, Customer Value, and Superior Performance," *Business Horizons*, March–April 1994, pp. 22–28. See also Frederick E. Webster, *Market-Driven Management: Using the New Marketing Concept to Create a Customer-Oriented Company* (New York: John Wiley, 1994); John C. Narver and Stanley F. Slater, "The Effect of a Market Orientation on Business Profitability," *Journal of Marketing*, October 1990, pp. 20–35; Bernard Jaworski and Ajay K. Kohli, "Market Orientation: Antecedents and Consequences," *Journal of Marketing*, July 1993, pp. 53–70; and Rohit Deshpandé and John U. Farley, "Measuring Market Orientation," *Journal of Market-Focused Management* 2 (1998): 213–32.

11. Richard E. Anderson, "Matrix Redux," *Business Horizons*, November–December 1994, pp. 6–10.

12. For further reading on marketing organization, see Nigel Piercy, *Marketing Organization: An Analysis of Information Processing, Power and Politics* (London: George Allen & Unwin, 1985); Robert W. Ruekert, Orville C. Walker, and Kenneth J. Roering, "The Organization of Marketing Activities: A Contingency Theory of Structure and Performance," *Journal of Marketing*, Winter 1985, pp. 13–25; Tyzoon T. Tyebjee, Albert V. Bruno, and Shelby H. McIntyre, "Growing Ventures Can Anticipate Marketing Stages," *Harvard Business Review*, January–February 1983, pp. 2–4; and Andrew Pollack, "Revamping Said to be Set at Microsoft," *New York Times*, February 9, 1999, C1.

13. Gary L. Frankwick, Beth A. Walker, and James C. Ward, "Belief Structures in Conflict: Mapping a Strategic Marketing Decision," *Journal of Business Research*, October–November 1994, pp. 183–95.

14. Askok K. Gupta, S. P. Raj, and David Wilemon, "A Model for Studying R&D–Marketing Interface in the

Product Innovation Process," *Journal of Marketing*, April 1986, pp. 7–17.

15. See William E. Souder, *Managing New Product Innovations* (Lexington, MA: D. C. Heath, 1987), ch. 10 and 11; and William L. Shanklin and John K. Ryans Jr., "Organizing for High-Tech Marketing," *Harvard Business Review*, November– December 1984, pp. 164–71; and Robert J. Fisher, Elliot Maltz, and Bernard J. Jaworski, "Enhancing Communication Between Marketing and Engineering: The Moderating Role of Relative Functional Identification," *Journal of Marketing*, July 1997, pp. 54–70.

16. David J. Morrow, "Struggling to Spell R-E-L-I-E-F," *New York Times*, December 29, 1998, pp. C1, C18; "JAMA Study Shows Merck-Medco's Partners for Healthy Aging Program Significantly Reduces the Use of Potentially Harmful Medication by Seniors," *Business Wire*, October 12, 1998.

17. See Robert J. Fisher, Elliot Maltz, and Bernard J. Jaworski, "Enchancing Communication Between Marketing and Engineering," *Journal of Engineering*, July 1997, pp. 54–70.

18. See Benson P. Shapiro, "Can Marketing and Manufacturing Coexist?" *Harvard Business Review*, September–October 1977, pp. 104–14. Also see Robert W. Ruekert and Orville C. Walker Jr., "Marketing's Interaction with Other Functional Units: A Conceptual Framework and Empirical Evidence," *Journal of Marketing*, January 1987, pp. 1–19.

19. Edward E. Messikomer, "DuPont's 'Marketing Community,'" *Business Marketing*, October 1987, pp. 90–94. For an excellent account of how to convert a company into a market-driven organization, see George Day, *The Market-Driven Organization: Aligning Culture, Capabilities and Configuration to the Market* (New York: Free Press, 1999).

20. For more on developing and implementing marketing plans, see H. W. Goetsch, *Developing, Implementing & Managing an Effective Marketing Plan* (Chicago: American Marketing Association; Lincolnwood, IL: NTC Business Books, 1993).

21. Thomas V. Bonoma, *The Marketing Edge: Making Strategies Work* (New

York: Free Press, 1985). Much of this section is based on Bonoma's work.

22. Emily Denitto, "New Steps Bring Alvin Ailey into the Business of Art," *Crain's New York Business*, December 7, 1998, pp. 4, 33.

23. See Alfred R. Oxenfeldt, "How to Use Market-Share Measurement," *Harvard Business Review*, January–February 1969, pp. 59–68.

24. There is a one-half chance that a successive observation will be higher or lower. Therefore, the probability of finding six successively higher values is given by $(\frac{1}{2})^6 = \frac{1}{64}$.

25. Alternatively, companies need to focus on factors affecting shareholder value. The goal of marketing planning is to increase shareholder value, which is the present value of the future income stream created by the company's present actions. Rate-of-return analysis usually focuses on only one year's results. See Alfred Rapport, *Creating Shareholder Value*, rev. ed. (New York: Free Press, 1997).

26. For additional reading on financial analysis, see Peter L. Mullins, *Measuring Customer and Product Line Profitability* (Washington, DC: Distribution Research and Education Foundation, 1984).

27. See Robert S. Kaplan and David P. Norton, *The Balanced Scorecard* (Boston: Harvard Business School Press, 1996).

28. Richard Whiteley and Diane Hessan, *Customer Centered Growth* (Reading MA: Addison Wesley, 1996), pp. 87–90; and Adrian J. Slywotzky, *Value Migration: How to Think Several Moves Ahead of the Competition* (Boston: Harvard University Press, 1996), pp. 231–35.

29. The MAC Group, Distribution: *A Competitive Weapon* (Cambridge, MA: MAC Group, 1985), p. 20.

30. See Robin Cooper and Robert S. Kaplan, "Profit Priorities from Activity-Based Costing," *Harvard Business Review*, May–June 1991, pp. 130–35.

31. Sam R. Goodman, *Increasing Corporate Profitability* (New York: Ronald Press, 1982), ch. 1. Also see Bernard J. Jaworski, Vlasis Stathakopoulos, and H. Shanker Krishnan, "Control Combinations in Marketing: Conceptual Framework and Empirical Evidence," *Journal of Marketing*, January 1993, pp. 57–69.

32. See Peter M. Senge, *The Fifth Discipline: The Art and Practice of the Learning Organization* (New York: Doubleday Currency, 1990), ch. 7.

33. For further discussion of this instrument, see Philip Kotler, "From Sales Obsession to Marketing Effectiveness," *Harvard Business Review*, November–December 1977, pp. 67–75.

34. See Philip Kotler, William Gregor, and William Rodgers, "The Marketing Audit Comes of Age," *Sloan Management Review*, Winter 1989, pp. 49–62. For an interesting alternative approach, see the *Copernican Decision Navigator*, available from Copernican at (617) 630–8705.

35. Useful checklists for a marketing self-audit can be found in Aubrey Wilson, *Aubrey Wilson's Marketing Audit Checklists* (London: McGraw-Hill, 1982); and Mike Wilson, *The Management of Marketing* (Westmead, England: Gower Publishing, 1980). A marketing audit software program is described in Ben M. Enis and Stephen J. Garfein, "The Computer-Driven Marketing Audit," *Journal of Management Inquiry*, December 1992, pp. 306–18.

36. Philip Kotler, William Gregor, and William Rodgers, "The Marketing Audit Comes of Age," *Sloan Management Review*, Winter 1989, pp. 49–62.

37. Howard R. Bowen, *Social Responsibilities of the Businessman* (New York: Harper & Row, 1953), p. 215. Also N. Craig Smith and Elizabeth Cooper-Martin, "Ethics and Target Marketing: The Role of Product Harm and Consumer Vulnerability," *Journal of Marketing*, July 1997, pp. 1–20.

1.1	Courtesy of Sony Music Canada	10.3	Heart & Stroke Foundation of Canada
1.2	Courtesy City of Toronto Works & Emergency Services Department, Spring 1999 advertising campaign	10.4	(Logos) Courtesy of Bombardier Inc. Courtesy of Nortel Networks
1.3	Mount Saint Vincent University	10.5	Courtesy of Holmes & Lee
1.6	Courtesy of Chapters	11.1	Joseph Marranca Photography
2.1	Courtesy of Saturn & Cossette Communications Marketing	11.2	3M Corporation
2.2	Courtesy of Lexus/Toyota Canada	12.1	Produit De Piscines Vogue/Vogue Pool Products
3.1	Courtesy of Gap Adventures Ltd. Great Adventure People	12.3	Courtesy of Oracle
3.2	Courtesy of Proton World International	13.1	Campbell Soup Co. Ltd.
4.1	Rocky Mountaineer Railtours/Bryant, Fulton & Shee	13.4	Courtesy of Toyota Canada Inc.
5.1	Courtesy of Calgary Stampeeders	14.1	Courtesy of Canada Post Corporation
6.1	Courtesy of Ch!ckaboom	14.2	Via Rail Canada Inc.
6.2A	Courtesy of Kraft Canada Inc.	14.3	Courtesy of Ericsson
6.3	Grouse Mountain Resorts Inc.	15.1	Courtesy of Kia and Griffin Bacal Volny
6.4	Image Dynamics Corp.	16.1	GE Glegg Water Technologies
6.5	Quebec Dairy Board	16.3	Courtesy of Canadian National
7.1	Courtesy of STSsystems/The STS Group	17.1	Alimentation Couche-Tard
7.2	Courtesy of IBM Canada Ltd.	17.2	West Edmonton Mall
7.3	Export Development Corporation	17.5	"Reprinted with permission of the Canadian Professional Logistics Institute".
7.4	Aramark/Formerly Versa Services	18.1	© 1998 Quarry Integrated Communications Inc.
8.1	Courtesy of Canadair		
8.2	© 1999 Globe Information Services	18.2	Kellogg Canada Inc.
8.3	Courtesy of Procter & Gamble Inc.	19.1	© 1999 Lever Pond's. Used with Permission. All rights Reserved.
8.4	Courtesy of Westjet		
8.5	Ad reproduced by kind permission of Canada Post	19.2	Courtesy of Advertising Standards Canada
9.1	Courtesy of DuPont Canada	20.1	Canadian Professional Sales Association
9.2	Brunico Communications Inc.	20.3	Courtesy of Investors Group
9.3	Volkswagen & Arnold Communications, Inc.	21.1	Canadian Press CNW
10.1	Photo courtesy of Air Canada	21.4	Buy Buddy.com
10.2	Courtesy of Apple Canada/TRWA/SHIAT/DAY Advertising	22.1	Kellogg Canada Inc.

COMPANY/BRAND INDEX

SUBJECT INDEX

Guerrilla marketing research, 228–29
Guppies, 240

Harvesting, 311
Headlines, types of, 563
Heuristics, 123
High-performance businesses, nature of, 42–47
  organization, 45–47
  processes, 44–45
  resources, 45
  stakeholders, 44
Harvesting, as business strategy, 73
Herzberg's theory of motivation, 177
Hierarchy-of-effects model of communications, 539
  awareness, 539
  conviction, 539
  knowledge, 539
  liking, 539
  preference, 539
  purchase, 539
High-low pricing, 456
Holding, as business strategy
Home improvement centres, 493
Horizontal diversification strategy, 79
Horizontal integration, 78
Horizontal marketing systems, 493
Household patterns, 148
Humanistic marketing, 26
Hybrid Grid, 494

Idea committee, 330–31
Idea manager, 330
Ideas
  DROP-error, 331
  GO-error, 331
  marketing, 5
    for new products, 330
  screening, 330–31
Identity media, 588
Image analysis, 536–38
  familiarity scale, 536
  image defined, 536
  semantic differential, 537
Image differentiation, 292
  atmosphere, 293
  events, 293
  media, 293
  symbols, 293
Image pricing, 462
Immigrants, 174
Importance-performance analysis, 431
Impulse goods, 389
Incentives, for answering survey, 119
Income
  distribution, 150
  segmentation, 263–64
Index of Consumer Confidence, 133
Individualization, 28
Industrial goods classification, 390–91
  capital items, 390
  materials and parts, 390
  supplies and business services, 391

Industry
  classification of, 222
  classification for differentiation, 284–85
  competitive equilibrium, 226
  competitive structure, 222
  cost structures, 223
  defined, 221
  degree of globalization, 223
  degree of vertical integration, 223
  entry, mobility and exit barriers, 222–23
Industry competition, 15
Industrial economies, 150
Industrializing economies, 150
Industry scope, 69
Infomercial, 569
Information. See also Data; Marketing intelligence system
  active search for, 183
  analyzing, 120
  collecting for marketing research, 119–20
  gathering, see Marketing information systems; Sales information systems
  international, on-line, 112
  marketing, 5
Ingredient cobranding, 409
Innovation, managing, see New product development
Inseparability of services, 421–22
Institutional market, 210
Intangibility of services, 419–21
Integrative growth, 78
Integrated logistics systems, 522
Integrated marketing, 23
  direct marketing, 624–215
  maximarketing model, 625
Integrated marketing communications, 29, 532
  defined, 552
  managing and coordinating, 552–53
Intensive distribution, 484
Intensive growth, 77–78
Interactive phone surveys, 119
Interactive TV, 569, 634
Intercept interviews, 119
Intermediaries, see also Marketing channels
  cooperation, ways of gaining, 488
  number of, 483–84
    as source of new product ideas, 330
  types of, 483
  understanding, 488
Internal environment analysis, 81
Internal records system, 105–106
  order-to-payment
  sales information systems, 105–106 cycle, 105
Internet
  advertising, 404–405, 571
  branding on, 404–405
  business-to-business transactions, 635
  catalogue shopping, 632
  competition from 219–21
    and competitive intelligence gathering, 228–29

consumers, 635–36
  effect on pricing, 444
  ethics for targeting kids, 172
  focus groups on-line, 114
  interviews, 119
  marketing on, 636–44
    and marketing research, 109, 111, 112
  most popular purchases on, 635
  purchasing, 200, 201
  revolutionizing pricing, 462
  search engines, 636
  secondary service features, offering, 427
  Web sites, see Web sites
Interviews
  in-depth, 176
  types, for market research, 119
Intranets, 201, 635
Intrepreneurial marketing, 3
Introduction stage, product life cycle
  Competitive cycle, 305–306
  marketing strategies, 303–307
  pioneer advantage, 304–305
  rapid penetration, 304
  rapid skimming, 304
  slow penetration, 304
  slow skimming, 304
Inventor, 305
Inventory management, 48, 525–27
  just-in-time production methods, 526
Irregular, 7
ISO 9000, 61

Joint-venture cobranding, 409
Just-in-time production, 202, 203, 526

Keiretsu, 201
Kiosk marketing, 634

Labelling, 412
  as advertising strategy, 562
Laddering, 176
Last customer analysis, 42
Latent demand, 7
Lead generation, 50, 550
Lead qualification, 50
Learning
  as factor in buying behaviour, 178
  defined, 178
  discrimination vs. generalizing, 178
  drives and cues, 178
Learning, curve, 451
Legitimate power, 488
Liaison, 545
Licensing products, 408
Lifestyle
  and buying behaviour, 172–75
  defined, 172
  segmentation, 173–75, 265
Limited-service wholesalers, 518
Lobbying, 156
Location pricing, 462
Logistics alliances, 85
Longer payment terms, 461
Long-term contracts, 200
Looping, 533
Loss-leader pricing, 461

Low-interest financing, 461
Loyal status, 267–68

Macroenvironments, 89
  analyzing needs in, 141–44
  demographic environment, 145–49
  economic environment, 150
  identifying and responding to major forces in, 144–56
  natural environment, 151–53
  political-legal environment, 155–56
  technological, 153–55
Mail questionnaire, 119
Makers, 173
Malcolm Baldrige National Quality Award, 60
Manage by objectives, 82–83
Manufacturer-sponsored retailer franchise, 492
Manufacturer-sponsored wholesaler franchise, 492
Manufacturers' and retailers' branches and offices, 518
Manufacturing sector, 418
Market
  business vs. consumer, 194–96
  defined, 9
  for market demand forecasts, 124–25
  target, 20
Market-based scorecard analysis, 669–70
Market-Buildup method, 129
Market cells, 626
Market-challenger strategies, 239–42
  blitz, 241
  bypass attack, 241
  choose specific attack strategy, 242–43
  choose general attack strategy, 240–43
  define the strategic objective and opponents, 239–40
  encirclement strategy, 241
  flank attack, 240–41
  frontal attack, 240
  guerrilla warfare, 242
  technical leapfrogging, 241
Market demand
  area market potential, 129
  available market, 124
  composite of sales force opinions, 132–33
  current, estimating, 128–31
  defined, 126
  expert opinions, 133
  industry sales and market shares, 130–31
  institutional, 210
  market-test method, 133
  measures of, 124
  past-sales analysis, 133
  penetrated market, 125
  potential market, 124
  primary, 127
  qualified available market, 125
  selective, 127
  served market, 125
  survey of buyers' intentions, 132
  target market, 125
  total market potential, 128

Transaction, 12
Transfer, 12
Trend(s)
  analyzing in
    macroenvironment, 141–44
  defined, 141
Tweens, 162–63, 166
Two-factor theory, 177
Two-part pricing, 465
Tying agreements, 499–500

Unanticipated situational factors, 186
Unbundling, 467
Underpositioning, 297
Unique selling proposition, 41
Unique selling proposition, 297
Unit pricing, 412
Unwholesome demand, 7
Usage rates, 266
User status, 266–67

Value
  customer, defined, 36–38
  defined, 11–12
  gap, 41

Value-adding partnerships
  (VAPs), 492
Value chain, 47–49
Value-delivery network, 49–50
Value-delivery process, 87
Value-delivery sequence, 88–89
Value delivery system, 41
Value-in-use price, 455
Value proposition, 41
Value/price ratios, 38
Value pricing, 456–57
Values
  corporate culture, 47
  segmentation by, 265
Values and Lifestyles (VALS)
  framework, 172
Variable costs, 451
Vertical integration, 223
Vertical marketing systems,
  491–93
  administered, 492
  contractual, 492
  corporate, 492
Vertical scope, 69
Videocarts, 569
Video lottery terminals, 149

Videotext TV, 634
Virtual companies, 28
Virtual reality, 154
Visionary companies, 47
Volume industry, 285

Wants, defined, 11
Warehouses, 525
Warranties, 461, 581
Webcasting, 640–41
Web sites
  advertising on, 640
  company, 607
  corporate, 638
  designing, 638–39
  marketing, 638–39
  microsites, 639–40
  Webcasting, 640–41
  Web communities, 640
Wholesaler(s)
  functions, 517
  marketing decisions, 517,
    519–20
  place decision, 519
  price decision, 519

product assortment and
  services, 519
promotion decision, 519
Wholesaler-sponsored voluntary
  chains, 492
Wholesaling, 517–21
  defined, 517
  growth and types of, 517, 518
  target market, 519
Wizards, 174
Word-of-mouth referrals, 544–45
World Wide Web, *see also* E-
  commerce; Internet
  company Web sites, 607
  advertising on, 571

Yankelovich Monitor, 158
Yield pricing, 462

Zero customer feedback time, 88
Zero defects, 89
Zero product-improvement time,
  88
Zero purchasing time, 88
Zero setup time, 89